Theology and poetry in the middle english lyric:

A Study of Sacred History and Aesthetic Form

BY SARAH APPLETON WEBER

Theology and poetry in the middle english lyric

A Study of Sacred History and Aesthetic Form

OHIO STATE UNIVERSITY PRESS

Library of Congress Catalogue Card Number: 68–18940

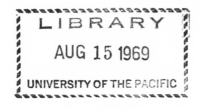

To Matthew Howard
and Bernadine Whitmer

preface

This is a study of the ways in which medieval Christian theology determined the aesthetic characteristics of the Middle English religious lyric. Such a study has yet to be made before there is any full understanding of the lyrics. It is also a theoretical study of the relationship of beauty and poetry to theology. I would like to show, as it has been demonstrated for art, music, and drama,[1] in what a profound way medieval theology shaped the purpose of these poems and the sensibility of the audience; how theology provided the poetry with certain unique forms and established a certain kind of relationship between the poet and his audience.

Although in recent years the works of several major authors have been reappraised in light of their theological context,[2] among the critics of the Middle English religious lyric there has generally been a desire to avoid consideration of theology, which they find to be either "on the fringes of criticism"[3] or hostile to poetry.[4] To my knowledge two important studies outside the field of Middle English have sought through theology to reveal the purpose and aesthetic quality of a medieval religious poem. The first of these is Étienne Gilson's explication of "Iesu dulcis memoria."[5] Using the conception of love in St. Bernard's sermon on the Canticle of Canticles, he shows that the poem defines the mystical coming of the presence of God into the soul and the soul's aspiration to heaven of which this was only a fleeting foretaste. The second is by Walter Ong, S.J., who uses the theology of St. Thomas Aquinas to explain the texture of the poetry in the hymns of

Thomas and Adam of St. Victor. In his analysis of the relationship between wit and mystery in Latin hymnody, Father Ong states a thesis which I believe also holds true for many of the Middle English religious lyrics as they are related to the theological formulation of sacred history by the liturgy of the medieval Church: "Here Christian teaching does more than merely supply the matter for poetry, and more than merely suggest an 'architechtonic' framework for literature. . . . Rather, at the point to which the trail of wit leads, the very texture of poetry itself—the element which makes literature literature—is seen to come into functional contact with the heart of Christian doctrine, the mysteries distinctive of Christianity as these lie in their own distinctive way within the human mind." [6]

The liturgy of the medieval Church was medieval man's living contact with theology.[7] Medieval music and the new forms of drama evolved from the liturgy,[8] and along side the classical and didactic tradition of poetry maintained by the early religious poets an entirely new poetry also developed.[9] As the research indicates in Carleton Brown's anthologies, *English Lyrics of the XIIIth Century* and *Religious Lyrics of the XIVth Century,* a great many of the Middle English religious lyrics are simply translations from Latin hymns and sequences used in the Roman rite which existed in England from the time of the Benedictine monastic foundations.[10] But the liturgy was also the source and texture from which many original English lyrics developed. The valuable comprehensive work of Dr. Natalie White shows that the organization, the phrasing, the images, the metrical forms—in short, the rhetorical fabric of these English lyrics, developed from the liturgy.[11] Among the poems are those based upon Latin meditations, especially the homilies of the early Church Fathers and the sermons of St. Bernard of Clairvaux that were assimilated into the liturgy by the lessons of the Office, homilies which themselves were ordered according to the themes and forms of the liturgy.[12] Besides the official liturgy of the Church, the devotional practices of the English clergy and people, originating in Latin and also using the forms of the liturgy, were the basis of many types of lyrics. For example, there are the metrical meditations of the Hours of the Cross and the Compassion of Mary, which were attached to the canonical Hours of the Divine Office.[13] There are special prayers on the five wounds of Christ and many poems on the joys of Mary (see below, Part III).

The liturgy was fundamentally a sacred history which shaped the history of man from his birth to his death to the plan of redemption. It was itself an event with two modes, an objective mode, the perpeptual re-enactment of the history of God's redemption of man; and a subjective mode, the response of the soul in his journey to God. The liturgy shaped the seasons of the year, the days, the hours, and the beginning and end of the actions of men. And the method of the liturgy's formulation of the history of redemption provided certain dynamic forms and principles of proportion for the lyrics which evolved from it.

The following pages which consider a number of the lyrics that developed from the liturgy are not a historical study of sources, but primarily a structural study of the lyrics' order and proportion whose method grows by analogy to the medieval liturgy's dynamic and architectural structuring of the universe. A glance at the Table of Contents will show its general outlines.

Since the liturgy is a history, I have restricted the selection of lyrics to be analyzed to those which tell its main events, and I have excluded lyrics which are formed primarily by the inner experience of the speaker, such as those of the school of Richard Rolle. To show the fundamental principle that an understanding of the over-all coherence of the plan of sacred history and of the relationship between events is necessary to the understanding of each one of the events, I have grouped the poems to be discussed in the same order as the sequence of events in the liturgy.

The life, the dynamic tension of the liturgy, lies in its purpose of reuniting man to God. Although theology contains and speaks of the Divine, the medieval theologian saw that it is fundamentally limited and shaped to the human point of view. This limit is felt by the soul who ascends to God, as a darkness, or by the soul who contemplates God descending to man by the human incarnation of His Son, as a source of joy. According to medieval Christian theology, Mary is the central human being through whom Christ entered history and through whom now in the present, as she is in heaven united to Christ, man himself will be led to Christ. To show that the medieval Church conceived the events of sacred history to be focused within man and fitted to the exigency of man's capacity,[14] I have chosen to consider those poems which use Mary as the medium through whom the events of sacred history are seen and to whom the poet appeals to be united to Christ.

I hope to show by my classification that to divorce the lyrics from the objective aspect of theology, the events of sacred history, is to lose the means of understanding the principle of order behind the poetry[15] and also to lose the unique Christian concept the poet has, as part of the Church, of the identity of his situation with his listeners'. To contradict the idea that medieval Christian dogma was basically static and to indicate that there were innumerable varieties of ways in which the poet might conceive these events within their over-all relationship to the whole plan of sacred history, I have chosen several poems on each event. In each part of the study, by discussing the limitations of the evaluations various critics of the lyrics have made, I will attempt to indicate the central importance of theology to the purpose, form and structure of these lyrics.

Using Mary as the medium through whom the events take place and are experienced will provide a figure by which the subjective dimension of the human experience of joy and sorrow can be studied as it is affected by the incarnation, death and resurrection of Mary's Son. These poems will serve to define how medieval theology modified the concept of human emotion by its Christian definition of the ultimate objects of fear and desire and how the modern reader must adjust his view of subjective experience to comprehend fully the poem's effect.

Thus the study develops in three parts by a series of corresponding meditations. Part I is on the annunciation and birth of Christ; Part II is on Christ's crucifixion and Mary's sorrow; Part III is on Mary's joy in heaven as it defines the joy of mankind. Within each part there is (1) a poem which introduces the new subject matter and new forms, (2) then two shorter poems which clarify principles of criticism, and (3) a final poem which develops the subject matter and illustrates the variety of treatments possible for one event. The theological subject is always presented preceding the poetry. The whole study, therefore, is introduced by a description of the way in which the liturgy reformulates sacred history; then each part, except for Part I which is prepared for by the material of the Introduction, is introduced by an explanation of the event which provides its subject and proportion; and within each part also the theological subject of each poem is presented before the analysis of its form.

Once the full context of the poems has been given, with its possibilities both for beauty and for monotony, it will be possible to set up some standard by which to divide the good lyrics from the bad, and in Part III, "The Figure of Delight," I will show why some lyrics which may be theologically valid are at the same time not good poetry, and why, on the other hand, some theology which does not use poetic form arouses the same delight as good poetry does. In the concluding section of the study, I will draw together some of the general aesthetic characteristics of the Middle English lyric which are the result of the fundamental orientation of the poetry in medieval Christian theology.

acknowledgments

I am most deeply indebted to Professor Morton W. Bloomfield for his invaluable encouragement and guidance in the undertaking of this study and to him personally for his profound example of humanity and scholarship. In coming to the subject of medieval theology and poetry and in developing the particular method of approach, I am fundamentally indebted as well to the years of association and to discussions with Professor Anthony Nemetz, William F. Lynch, S.J., Professor Elizabeth Sewell, the late Matthew Howard, and also with Professors Robert M. Estrich and Francis Lee Utley. I am grateful furthermore to my husband who has tirelessly given of his energy and critical judgment during the long preparation of the text, and to the late Professor Lois T. Hartley who helped in many ways to bring the book to completion. I would like to thank particularly Newland F. Smith, III, for making available to me the material on the Sarum liturgy from the Seabury-Western Library; John Plummer and the staff of the Pierpont Morgan Library for generously giving me access to material and manuscripts, as well as for their patient assistance in obtaining photographic reproductions; the Committee on Aid to Faculty Research and Publication of Smith College for a grant for manuscript preparation; and Walter Muir Whitehill and the Board of Control of the John Anson Kittredge Educational Fund for making it possible to have the illustrations placed to support the structural principle of the book.

Acknowledgments are gratefully extended to the following for their kind permission to quote from their works: to the Clarendon Press, Oxford, for permission to quote the two sequences from *The Sarum Missal: Edited from Three Early Manuscripts,* edited by J. Wickham Legg (1916), and for permission to quote from Carleton Brown's three editions of Middle English lyrics, Nos. 22, 31, 41, 44, 45, 47, 49 from *English Lyrics of the XIIIth Century* (1932); Nos. 26, 56, 60, 64, 132 from *Religious Lyrics of the XIVth Century* (2d ed. rev.; 1957); and No. 81 from *Religious Lyrics of the XVth Century* (1939); to Methuen & Company, Ltd. for permission to quote from George Kane, *Middle English Literature* (1951); and to B. Herder Book Co. for permission to quote from Erwin Esser Nemmers' translation of St. Bonaventure's *Breviloquium* (1946). Finally, I would like to acknowledge the following for their generous permission to reproduce material from their collections: The Pierpont Morgan Library for permission to reproduce fols. 23 and 142 from the Tiptoft Missal, M. 107; All Souls College, Oxford, for permission to reproduce fols. 3, 4 and 5 of the Amesbury Psalter, MS 6; the Trustees of the British Museum for permission to reproduce fol. 124 of the Psalter of Robert de Lisle, Arundel MS 83; and the Österreichische Nationalbibliothek, Vienna, for permission to reproduce fol. 1vo of Cod. 1179.

S. A. W.

contents

INTRODUCTION: The Theology of Sacred History: The Liturgy of the Medieval Church 1
Sacred History 3
The Beginning and End of History 4
The Center of History 5
Three Reformulations of Sacred History by the Liturgy of the Church 7
The Seasonal Cycle 9
The Hours of the Day 10
The Ladder 15

PART I: The Annunciation and Birth of Christ 27
"Gabriel, fram Evene-King" 32
The Inner Form 32
The External Form 40
The "Maiden Makeles" 47
"Nu Þis Fules Singet hand Maket Hure Blisse" 48
"I Syng of a Myden Þat Is Makeles" 55
"Als I Lay vp-on a Nith" 69
The Setting 74
The Foretelling 75
The Structure 81

PART II: The Crucifixion 87
"Þe Milde Lomb Isprad o Rode" 94
The Transformation of Suffering by Love 95
The Transfiguration of Disorder by Beauty 103
Mary's Sorrow 110
"Wy Haue ȝe No Reuthe on My Child?" 111
"Suete Sone, Reu on Me, & Brest Out of Þi Bondis" 117
"Stond Wel, Moder, vnder Rode" 125
The Dialogue 126
The Intelligible Cross 133
The Dialogue Form 136

PART III: The Joy of Mary 147
The Names of Joy: "Glade Us Maiden, Moder Milde" 156
The Vision of Joy: "Leuedy, for þare Blisse/ þat Þu Heddest at þe Frume" 167
The Figure of Delight 175

CONCLUSION 193
The Poem: The Sacred History 197
The Poet and His Audience: The Church 204
Poetry and the Eternal Art: A Note on the Work of St. Bonaventure 209

APPENDIXES 213
"Ave mundi spes Maria" 215
"Stabat iuxta Christi crucem" 217
"Heyl be þou, marie, milde quene of heuene!" 220

Notes to the Text and Appendixes 223
Abbreviations in the Notes 225
Notes to Illustrations 261
Selected Bibliography 269
Index 279

illustrations

1. God the Creator of Heaven and Earth. Moralized Bible, Österreichische Nationalbibliothek Cod. 1179, fol. 1vo. / *Frontispiece*

2. The Mass, Elevation of the Host. Tiptoft Missal, New York, Pierpont Morgan Library M. 107, fol. 142. / *facing page 7*

3. The Annunciation. Psalter of Amesbury Abbey, Oxford, All Souls College MS 6, fol. 3. / *facing page 28*

4. The Birth of Christ and the Tree of Jesse. Tiptoft Missal, New York, Pierpont Morgan Library M. 107, fol. 23. / *facing page 47*

5. The Birth of Christ and the First Events of His Childhood. Psalter of Robert de Lisle, British Museum, Arundel MS 83, fol. 124. / *facing page 61*

6. The Crucifixion. Psalter of Amesbury Abbey, Oxford, All Souls College MS 6, fol. 5. / *facing page 88*

7. The Virgin and the Child Enthroned. Psalter of Amesbury Abbey, Oxford, All Souls College MS 6, fol. 4. / *facing page 148*

introduction

The Theology of Sacred History:

The Liturgy of the Medieval Church

SACRED HISTORY

IN ORDER TO UNDERSTAND THE RELATIONSHIP BETWEEN THE LITURGY AND the medieval religious lyric, it is necessary to study the liturgy not as a collection of prayers or formulas, but as both a history and a method of formulating history. There is a profound analogy to be developed between the medieval theologian's understanding of the events of creation and the universe as the language of God—theology its grammar—and the modern linguist's approach to semantics through structure—through phonemic, morphemic and syntactic analysis:[1] for the medieval liturgy might be seen as the meta-language of creation.

History can be explained simply as a chronicle of events, a succession of dates, and time may be given only a descriptive ordering value. Or the principle the historian uses to formulate history may be a logical one, and time may be conceived in terms of cause and effect. The medieval liturgy, however, was formulated as a sacred history: that is, the principle of explanation was God, Who is beyond time, in His relationship to man, who is in time. For the medieval soul God was both the ground of value—i.e., the origin, end, and center of time—and the means of understanding it. (See Figure 1 and descriptive note.) It is necessary to outline the nature of this view of history before the full dimensions of the liturgy itself can be made clear.

The Beginning and End of History

For the medieval theologian the principle of sacred history was living, dynamic, since it was not only the basis of interpreting past events, but it also gave the meaning of the present and the direction of the future. According to sacred history, events literally begin at the beginning with God and end at the end in God. God is their foundation and their purpose. In its sequence, this sacred history begins with the creation of the world for God's glory, the disobedience of man through pride, and man's fall. It tells of God's remedy for this, a second creation, more wonderful than the first: the coming of God Himself into the world through Christ, the Second Person of the Holy Trinity, Who redeems man through His incarnation, death, and resurrection. It tells how Christ, after ascending to His Father, sends the Holy Spirit, the Advocate, to establish the Church and to perpetuate it with His gifts of grace and with the sacraments, by which men are taught, sustained, and united to Christ until the consummation of all things at the end of time. The end of time will occur with Christ's second coming in majesty, with the resurrection of the dead, and the final judgment where man is fixed in the pains of hell or the eternal joy of paradise. Sacred history encompasses all time, and each event is given significance by its context in the total plan. Sacred history gives meaning to individual action as well, so that every thing done, every act, offers information and has value by its context in sacred history.

This order, with God as the beginning and end and with history conceived of as stages in the creation of a new reality, is fundamentally Hebraic and is the principle of order of the accounts in Holy Scripture.[2] From the time of the early Church, Holy Scripture was the foundation of commentary and theological refinement, and the order of events in Scripture became the structural basis for some of the later more general theological works.[3] The same principle of order was used in the early technique of catechesis put forward by St. Augustine and implied by St. Gregory of Nyssa. Histories of the world were organized according to the stages of sacred history. This order is at the heart of Augustine's *City of God,* for example, which is two contrasted stories, the origin and the final end of the City of God and the City of Earth.[4]

Many Middle English works are ordered by sacred history, among them works of instruction such as *Cursor Mundi,* which divides history into seven ages from the creation and fall to the end of the world.[5] Sacred history is also the principle by which the three dramatic cycles of Chester, York, and Wakefield are ordered. One purpose of this study will be to show how each of the Middle English lyrics that meditates on an event is conceived in the context of the beginning and the end of sacred history and that the total plan of sacred history is incorporated as a structural principle of the poem.

The Center of History

God is not only the beginning and the end of history; the second dynamic principle of sacred history is that God is the center. God the Father through the Holy Spirit sends His Son into history, and Christ, being both God and man, becomes the means whereby man is united to God and raised up to Him.

The central events of sacred history, to which all events point, in which all events culminate, are the Incarnation, the moment God enters the world by taking on man's human nature through Mary; Christ's passion and death, the moment He atones for man's sin; Christ's resurrection from the dead, showing His godhood and thus giving the guarantee of man's hope for his own future resurrection; and, nine days after Christ's ascension, Pentecost, when through the coming of the Holy Spirit Christ establishes His Church which will be for man the means of union with God through grace and knowledge until the end of time. Thus the Church provides the central focus of present history. It is the present moment's unity with God through Christ, and it is the particular point of view from which the Christian soul interprets all things, from which he relates himself in an historical present to a past, to the present, to the future. It is this central focus of history in the present time, on Christ within the Church, which establishes the basic proportion of value, the divine *ratio,* among events lived in the context of sacred history.

A perception of this divine *ratio* or proportion among events informed the method by which the exegete interpreted Holy Scripture, and it is the principle by which the liturgy reformulates sacred history. Based on the precedent of Christ in the Gospel, Who applied the words of the psalms and prophets to His own coming, and on the practice of the authors of the New Testament themselves, especially on St. Paul, the exegete divided Holy Scripture into the Old and the New Testament. The incarnation and death of Christ, Who is Himself the New Testament, was seen to fulfill the events and prophecies of the Old by which His coming and death were prefigured. Thus at the same time as they were historical realities, the events, historical personages and sayings of the Old Testament were applied to the actions and words of Christ in the New and were seen to have allegorical value relative to the value of Christ.[6]

Although with the Acts of the Apostles, the Epistles and the Apocalypse, Holy Scripture as such is complete, the Old Testament and the New are not as yet completely fulfilled. Scripture is assumed into the living Church which perpetuates in the present all things in Christ until His second coming.[7] The liturgy is the re-enactment of sacred history in the present. It reformulates Holy Scripture perpetually according to the divine *ratio* of events.[8] Through its sacraments it is the present means for the Christian soul of achieving the purpose of his life, the union with God in heaven.[9]

We shall see that this proportioning of events is also the principle of structuring in the religious lyrics, that it defines the role of the poet and his relationship to his audience, as well as defining the character of the audience itself, and that it also determines the power and beauty of the poem. A description of the ways in which the liturgy reformulates sacred history will provide the method and context for studying the poems.

nrm supplices rogamus
mus uti accepta heas
hec dona. hec munu

Three Reformulations of Sacred History by the Liturgy of the Church

THE LITURGY, WHICH WAS THE FORM OF THE SACRIFICE AND PRAYER AND sacraments of the medieval Church, is more than a symbolic form of worship. It is the reformation, reformulation and reconsecration of all things in Christ. It extends from Him as the center to all time and action. Articulating for the Church the events of sacred history until the end of time, it is the present interpreting the past; and at the same time this present is the means to and a foreshadowing of the beatific vision.

The center of the liturgy is the Mass, or the sacrament of the Eucharist.[10] The Mass is the perpetual re-enactment of the sacrifice of the New Testament in which the sacrifice of the cross is made present through Christ. Christ is the sacrificing priest and also the sacrificial victim, and the priest at the altar is His visible representative and His living instrument. Through him Christ offers Himself to the Father in sacrifice and gives Himself to the faithful as food. (See Figure 2 and descriptive note.) The central part, or Canon, of the Mass has three sections [11]: (1) the oblation of the gifts; (2) the sacrifice itself, consisting of the consecration of the bread and wine into the Body and Blood of Christ and the offering of Christ to the Father, which extends to the Pater Noster; and (3) the communion in which the Body and Blood of Christ are consumed.[12]

Fig. 2.—The Mass, Elevation of the Host. Illuminated "T" of the first words of the Canon "Te igitur . . . ," New York, Pierpont Morgan Library M. 107, fol. 142. The illumination shows the Mass as the perpetuation in present time of the redemptive death of Christ on the cross. For more extended discussion, refer to the Notes to Illustrations.

The Mass is the perpetual objective focus around which the rest of the liturgy of the Church is centered, uniting the sacrifice of Christ to each soul. Deep from within this center radiate the other sacraments, which are the unchanging rituals that mark the stages of the individual's worldly life with the stages of the coming of grace into the soul: baptism at birth, the cleansing of the soul from the original sin inherited at conception from Adam; penance, the cleansing of the soul from individual sins; confirmation, the strengthening in maturity by the spiritual gifts of the Holy Spirit; extreme unction at death, the anointing of the senses and the viaticum; and the sacraments of the state of life—marriage and holy orders. Every aspect of the individual's life is brought by the liturgy into direct relationship with the life of Christ, and the Mass and the other sacraments—the act of redemption and its application to individual souls—are the perpetual powers by which man is reformed into the likeness of Christ.

Besides the central sacrifice and communion of the Mass which never vary, the liturgy of the Church is composed of parts which vary, yet which bear a fixed relationship to each other and to the Canon. The liturgy reformulates sacred history according to three main proportions. Around the sacrifice and communion of the Mass gather the parts of the Mass called the Proper which vary according to the time and the occasion of the year. This is the seasonal cycle, in which the liturgy adapts the seasons of the year to the stages in the history of the redemption of man by God, so that through each year the Christian soul relives Christ's coming, His passion and death, His resurrection, and the founding of the Church.

Through the Divine Office the liturgy reformulates sacred history in a second way. The Office organizes the psalms and lessons of Holy Scripture, the homilies and prayers of the Church into a series of eight "hours" which correspond to the stages of the rising and the setting of the sun, so that the Christian soul can unite his prayer with the Church throughout each day. The Hours are made up of an unvarying sequence of readings, but also a variable proper part which, in relation to the Proper of the Mass, is adapted to the liturgical cycle of the seasons.

The third way in which the liturgy reformulates sacred history is by the fact that the parts into which it arranges these other varying forms are themselves ordered in a fixed relationship to each other. This order has levels of value, a scale of being, with Christ present in the sacrifice of the Mass as its focus and as the meaning of all the other parts. This third proportioning is the composition of meaning itself within the liturgy and, as we shall see below, within the individual lyrics.

The Seasonal Cycle

First of all, the Proper of the Mass and the Office re-enact sacred history as it is related in Scripture and formulated in the present by the Church, by fitting it to the natural or temporal cycle of birth and death in the year. The seasons of the year are divided by the Church according to the stages of the redemption: in autumn, Advent, the season preparing for the coming of Christ, His birth in the world and also for His second coming at the end of time; in late winter and early spring, Lent, the long season of penance preparing for the passion and death of Christ, which culminates in the spring in Easter, the glorious season of Christ's resurrection, His forty days on earth before His ascension to the Father, and the nine days of waiting for the Holy Spirit; and finally, in summer, the season of Pentecost, which celebrates the mysteries of the Church, such as the Holy Trinity (the First Sunday after Pentecost) and Corpus Christi (Thursday after Trinity Sunday),[13] and which foreshadows in its liturgy the heavenly Jerusalem.

Besides celebrating the events of the redemption according to the seasons of the year, there is a second yearly cycle within the Mass and Office. The Proper of the Saints, organized according to a fixed calendar of the individual days and months of the year rather than the seasons, commemorates the lives of individuals as they have revealed or imitated Christ throughout the history of the Church and thus incorporates into the liturgical year the events coming after the death of Christ and after Pentecost.[14] The liturgy chosen to commemorate the saints was categorized into several common forms which reflected the traditional distinctions made between individual states of life within the Church. The Common of the Saints in the thirteenth century Sarum Missal contains a Common for apostles, martyrs, bishops, confessors, doctors, abbots, and virgins.[15] Individual Propers were also composed for special saints, as for the Feast of St. Thomas of Canterbury.[16] Individual events in a saint's life were occasionally commemorated, as, for example, on January 25, the Conversion of St. Paul.[17] Of the saints, Mary alone was venerated on each of the most important occasions of her life.

As well as the commemoration of the saints throughout the year, there were also Votive Masses, Masses said so that the needs and desires of the people coming at any time or occasion of the year could be articulated within the Church. There were special Masses for the pope, for the whole Church, for the bishop and other clergy, for the king; Masses for oneself, for a friend, for penitents, against the temptations of the flesh and evil thoughts; Masses for invoking the graces of the Holy Spirit, for the gift of tears, a Mass "pro quacunque tribulacione," Masses for calm winds, against invaders and plagues, for sailors, for those in chains, for the infirm, and a Mass even for the mortality of man.[18] By means of these Masses every moment and desire of a man's life, or of a congregation's life, was articulated and consecrated by the liturgy of the Church.

The Hours of the Day

The second way sacred history was formed to the life of the soul by the medieval liturgy was by the singing of the hours of the day:

> The prophet saith: *Seven times a day have I given praise to thee.* We shall observe this sacred number of seven, if we fulfill the duties of our service in the Hours of Lauds, Prime, Terce, Sext, None, Vespers, and Compline; for it was of these Day Hours that he said: *Seven times a day have I given praise to thee.* But of the Night Office the same prophet saith: *At midnight I rose to give praise to thee.* At these times, therefore, let us render praise to our Creator *for the judgements of his justice:* that is, at Lauds, Prime, Terce, Sext, None, Vespers, and Compline; and let us rise in the night to praise him.[19]

These are the words of St. Benedict in Chapter XVI of the Holy Rule he composed for his monks, in the section where he tells "How the Work of God Is to Be Performed in the Day-Time."[20] Although St. Benedict (d. 543) did not institute any of these Offices, through his order of monks they were diffused throughout Christendom.[21] The Divine Office was said by both the secular and the religious clergy, and it reached the lay people through the public recitation of Matins, Vespers and Compline in the great cathedral churches and also in manuals of devotion, such as the *Horae,* or Prymers, by means of which the Little Office of the Blessed Virgin was said.[22]

The eight Hours of the Divine Office enclose the course of the natural day in prayer and they reformulate sacred history through using Scripture in such a way as to relate each day to the seasonal cycle of the year and to interpret the passage of a day in the life of the individual soul. According to the length and complexity of their contents, the Hours can be grouped into three main types.[23] Matins, said early in the morning, is the longest and most central Hour.[24] Lauds, said at dawn, and Vespers, said late in the afternoon, form a second shorter type, and Prime, Terce, Sext, None and Compline which do not vary as much as the other three Hours make up the third, simpler type of Office.[25] At Matins the readings from Scripture, the homilies, antiphons, and responses develop most profoundly the theme of the day in the cycle of the year.

The norm established by St. Benedict was for the readings of Matins to cover the whole of Scripture during the year, together with commentaries from the Fathers on the selections read.[26] The order in which the Old Testament readings were arranged was adapted to correspond with the cycle of the Church year which followed the history of the coming of Christ, and these readings maintained the allegorical relationship between the events and figures of the Old Testament and the incarnation of Christ. In Advent Isaiah's prophecy of the coming Messiah was read. The story of creation was read on Septuagesima Sunday, and Genesis and Exodus read from then until Passion Sunday to prepare for the new creation accomplished by Christ's crucifixion and resurrection.[27] Jeremiah was read in Passiontide;[28] then in the midsummer season of the Holy Spirit, the Book of Kings, followed by Ecclesiasticus, Job, Tobias, Judith, Machabees and Ezechiel.[29] On Sundays and feast days the last lesson at Matins was the selection from the Gospel which was to be read at the Mass of that day, and it was preceded by a reading of one of the Fathers' commentaries on it.

Just as the readings of Matins originally were intended to comprehend all of Holy Scripture during the liturgical year, so, St. Benedict explains, the Hours were composed to provide for the saying of the one hundred and fifty psalms of the Psalter once a week.[30] The psalms said were not varied according to the season, although on Sundays and special feast days, the Office contained the more joyful psalms. But within the Hours of the Office, the hymns, the antiphons, the invitatory and responses, and the readings, all varied, reflecting the aspect of sacred history commemorated in that particular season of the year.

It is the shorter Hours said throughout the day which relate the stages of life of the individual soul to the rhythm of the day. The hymns with which each Hour opens reflect the leading thought of the hour, expressing a correspondence between the time of day, the needs of the soul and the coming of Christ into the world. At Prime, the sun dawns, the Church rises to meet Christ the spiritual sun. The "Jam lucis orto sidere"[31] asks that God may keep our acts from harm, that we guard our tongues, hearts, and carnal desires, and that finally when daylight has gone we may sing His glory. The hymn for Terce invokes the Holy Spirit to take possession of our hearts and enkindle them with the fire of divine love. Sext, said in the heat of the day, compares the heat of the sun to the passions and asks that noxious heat be extinguished. None, addressing God Who remains immovable through the gradation of the light of the day, asks for a death in the light of eternal glory. Finally, Compline, said at the ending of the day, asks for protection from nightly fantasies, from the devil, and from bodily pollution.

Just as the Mass had a Proper for the individual saints' feasts, so individual Offices were composed for the celebration of saints' feasts. The Sarum Breviary provides for a Common of the Saints which corresponds to that of the Mass, a Common for apostles, evangelists, martyrs, confessors, and virgins. Some of the Offices of the saints were composed in poetical form, using rhyme and meter. The Franciscans adopted this practice and set out whole Offices in the same rhythmical and metrical pattern. The composition of Offices in poetical form occurred in England as well as on the Continent. Around the beginning of the thirteenth century, for example, Julian Spires (d. 1250) wrote Offices of St. Francis and St. Anthony. The Archbishop of Canterbury, John of Peckham (ca. 1297), composed an Office of the Holy Trinity imitating Julian's Office of St. Francis.[32]

Thus the Hours of the Divine Office unite the progress of the activities of the day and the passage of the Christian soul through life to sacred history which the liturgy orders in the great seasonal cycle of the year. We shall see that this seasonal cycle itself is formulated by another movement of hierarchical relationship effected by the fixed order of the liturgy as it culminates in the present prayer of the Church when the Church offers Christ in the sacrifice of the Mass.

Mary

Because of Mary's unique relationship to Christ as His mother and therefore the doorway through which Christ came to earth and the gate through which man will reach heaven, the liturgy of the Church formulated Mary's part in sacred history, honoring and invoking her beside her Son as the means of reaching Him. The important stages in her life were commemorated as they related to the life of Christ. Honoring Mary's own birth as the preparation of Christ's coming, on December eighth the liturgy celebrated the Feast of Mary's Conception and on September eighth the Feast of her Nativity.[33] Commemorating her central role as the virgin mother of Christ, on March twenty-fifth the Church celebrated the Feast of the Annunciation, and through the Christmas season the liturgy referred often to her motherhood.[34] On February second, also, came the Feast of the Purification, when the candles were blessed for the year and the readings commemorated the presentation of Christ in the Temple. It is the account of the presentation by Luke which foreshadows Mary's suffering at her Son's crucifixion and death, for Luke tells how Simeon prophesied that Mary's heart would be pierced by a sword (Luke 2:34–35), a prophecy that we shall see in the lyrics is fundamental to the definition of Mary's sorrow.[35] And finally, on August fifteenth, the liturgy celebrated Mary's assumption into heaven, the event which came as the consequence of her being the mother of God.[36] In the Middle English Marian lyrics the themes and content of the liturgy of Mary's feasts are used by the poet to name and define her beauty as he seeks her intercession, and it is Mary's position in the present as Queen of Heaven and Mother of Mercy that establishes the fundamental proportion and context of the poems.

As well as being honored in these individual feasts, Mary was especially commemorated on Saturdays. In the Lady Chapel, a side chapel built in cathedral and collegiate churches in Mary's honor, her Mass would be said if there were no major feast taking precedence.[37] Reflecting the changing focus of the liturgy throughout the seasons of the year, the Proper of these Saturday Masses changed three times: for the season of Advent, for the season from Christmas to the Purification, for the season from the Purification to Advent again (with changes in this season in the Gospel reading of Eastertide).[38] The principle of variation was, as in the Matins readings, to make a correspondence between the season and the stages in the redemption of man by Christ. That from Advent to Christmas, the season which prepares for Christ's coming, used the Mass of the Annunciation; that from Christmas to the Purification, the season which celebrates the appearance of the Messiah, used the themes of Christmas; and that from the Purification to Advent, the spring and summer seasons which celebrate the founding of the

Church, used the theme of Mary as mother in heaven, where, analogous to the Church, she draws men to Christ.

Just as the form of the seasonal cycle of the Mass celebrated Mary, so the Church consecrated the hours of the day to her. In the tenth century the custom grew up of saying a daily Office devoted solely to the Blessed Virgin, which along with the Office of the Dead began to be said in addition to the Divine Office. The order of this Office, referred to as the *Horae,* or Hours of the Virgin, and later in English as the Prymer, was the same as for the Divine Office, but there was no variation by day or season.[39] Since the *Horae* did not vary with the cycle of the Church year and did not change with the days of the week, they offered a fixed form of perpetual praise of Mary, defining her virgin birth, celebrating her union in heaven with Christ. A form of poetry used for devotion attached itself to these Hours which reflected the sequence of the canonical Hours of the day in the Divine Office. The sequence of the Hours of the day was ordered to correspond with the events of the life of Christ, and more frequently in a series of metrical meditations called Hours of the Cross or of the Passion, they were made to correspond with the stages of His passion. Corresponding to the Hours of the Passion, the *Horae* sometimes included the Hours of Mary's Compassion.

The devotion in the *Horae* of the Hours of the Passion and the Hours of Mary's Compassion produced many Middle English versions.[40] The method by which the devotion was organized illustrates for us a fundamental principle of form behind the lyrics we shall study which springs from the *ratio* Christ establishes between events, that there is a symmetrical correspondence between events and inner experiences as they are defined by the stages of sacred history. Always the governing focus of the correspondence to which the others point and by which they are defined is Christ.

The principle is clearly illustrated by the Hours of the Cross and the Compassion as they are composed in the Sarum *Horae.*[41] At Prime, Christ is accused before Pilate and bound (Mary sees Him flagellated and spat upon, and twists her hands). At Terce, the Jews condemn Him, crown Him with thorns and lead Him to Golgotha (Mary sorrows about His crowning, His shoulders suffering under the cross). At Sext, Christ is nailed to the cross, hung between the two thieves, and is given gall to drink (Mary, seeing her Child lifted on the cross, between thieves, and given gall to drink, cries out). At None, Christ dies, the soldier pierces His side, the earth trembles, the sun is hidden (Mary, weeping, sees Him expire, give His spirit to the Father crying out *Eloi,* and, seeing His side pierced, she falls transfixed by sorrow).

At Vespers, Christ is taken down from the cross (Mary holds and kisses Him). At Compline, Christ, anointed with spices, is placed in the sepulchre. In Him, the poet says, is the hope of the future life (Mary mourns in confusion, not desiring to leave but to die with Him there, until at last by His resurrection her Son is exalted). The Hours correspond to the stages in the passion. Mary is the counterpart of Christ's suffering, expressing, as well as her own, the inner sorrow of those who love Him.

In the Sarum *Horae* there is yet another poetic meditation appended to the Passion of Christ and the Compassion of Mary which illustrates through Mary the double potentiality each hour of the day has for sorrow and for joy. Added at a date possibly later than Hours of the Passion and Compassion, before each Hour, beginning with Matins, there is a woodcut with a quatrain of verse under it depicting the sources of Mary's joy and sorrow as mother of Christ. The woodcut pictures an event in her life; the quatrain of English verse explains its meaning. These are, at Lauds, the visitation; at Prime, Christ's nativity; at Terce, the angel's annunciation to the shepherds; at Sext, the epiphany of Christ to the Three Kings; at None, Christ's circumcision; at Vespers, the flight of the Holy Family into Egypt; and, finally, at Compline, the assumption, reception, and coronation of Mary in heaven.

The liturgy of Mary is the reflection of the life of Christ and points to Christ as its source and end and its center. Her place closest to Christ, and her life in the most perfect image of His, is praised, meditated on and invoked. Her life is celebrated through the course of the year, in the seasonal cycle, and the hours of each day are consecrated to her in the *Horae,* in which the life of Christ is seen through the present joy of Mary, who by her assumption is the promise of man's final joy.

The Ladder

We have mentioned that the Mass is the focal point of the liturgy, the central re-enactment of sacred history offered perpetually by Christ through the priest and the body of worshippers, to be done until the end of time. The third reformulation of sacred history is by order of the fixed parts of the liturgy as they relate to Christ. Whereas through the changing seasonal cycle and the movement of the Hours, the focus of the liturgy on sacred history varies, through the fixed sequence of parts, these variations move in a fixed order of value, much as in early polyphony the variation in melody moved from point to point of a stable harmony.[42] The parts of the Mass are ordered as they relate more or less closely to Christ, or to use the inverse image, as they radiate out from the center which is Christ. This fixed hierarchical relationship establishes the second dynamic relationship between the soul and Christ, that of closer and closer union.

To illustrate this third reformulation of sacred history by the medieval Church, and to show how it is the foundation of meaning in sacred history, I will describe, using the Sarum Missal, how the hierarchical order in which the variable parts of the Proper of the Mass of the Annunciation are arranged affects the way these parts are interpreted. These variable parts are of three kinds: readings—the Gospel and the Lesson; shorter passages from Scripture and tradition—the Gradual, Tract, Offertory and Communion Verses; and three prayers, the Collect, Secret and Postcommunion. Having defined the principle of the ladder of value, we can then begin the study of the poems themselves as theology shaped them.[43]

The Gospel

The Proper of the Mass, the texts of the Mass varying according to the feast of the day, focuses on a short reading from one of the four Gospels which states the event or the theme of the event in sacred history being commemorated. The reading for the Feast of the Annunciation is Luke 1:26–38:

> And in the sixth month, the angel Gabriel was sent from God into a city of Galilee, called Nazareth. To a virgin espoused to a man whose name was Joseph, of the house of David: and the virgin's name was Mary. And the angel being come in, said unto her: Hail, full of grace, the Lord is with thee: blessed art thou among women. Who having heard, was troubled at his saying and thought with herself what manner of salutation this should be. And the angel said to her: Fear not, Mary, for thou hast found grace with God. Behold thou shalt conceive in thy womb and shalt bring forth a son: and thou shalt call his name Jesus. He shall be great and shall be called the Son of the Most High. And the Lord God shall give unto him the throne of David his father: and he shall reign in the house of Jacob forever. And of

> his kingdom there shall be no end. And Mary said to the angel: How shall this be done, because I know not man? And the angel answering, said to her: The Holy Ghost shall come upon thee and the power of the Most High shall overshadow thee. And therefore also the Holy [one] which shall be born of thee shall be called the Son of God. And behold thy cousin Elizabeth, she also hath conceived a son in her old age: and this is the sixth month with her that is called barren. Because no word shall be impossible with God. And Mary said: Behold the handmaid of the Lord: be it done to me according to thy word. And the angel departed from her.[44]

This passage from Luke as it is selected by the liturgy is the unit chosen for the commentary by the homilists[45] and on which the Middle English poets base their account of the annunciation. Generally the sermon of the Mass, which in the Sarum Missal comes after the Credo, would be based upon the passage in the Gospel reading, and several of the lessons read at Matins would be homilies of the Fathers on this same text. It is through the incorporation of the commentary on Scripture of the early Fathers into the Office that the Church preserved her traditional interpretation of Scripture and from which the Church formulated new commentary. And it is these sermons and homilies which develop the Gospel reading in its context of sacred history.

The Lesson

Preceding the Gospel and preparing for it is the Epistle or Lesson which is taken from a part of Scripture other than the Gospels, sometimes a selection from the Old Testament, or from the Acts of the Apostles, or an Epistle of Paul, James, Peter or John.[46] By coming before the Gospel reading and being used as a preparation for it, the Lesson is given direct application to the event or words related in the Gospel. It is set in an allegorical relationship to the Gospel, in terms of which its full meaning is made clear. The Lesson for the Feast of the Annunciation is Isaiah 7:10–15:

> And the Lord spoke again to Achaz, saying: Ask thee a sign of the Lord thy God, either unto the depth of hell, or unto the

> height above. And Achaz said: I will not ask, and I will not tempt the Lord. And he said: Hear ye therefore, O house of David: Is it a small thing for you to be grievous to men, that you are grievous to my God also? Therefore the Lord himself shall give you a sign. Behold a virgin shall conceive and bear a son: and his name shall be called Emmanuel. He shall eat butter and honey, that he may know to refuse the evil, and to choose the good.

The method of the liturgy and the method of Scripture and scriptural commentators is the same in applying this prophecy to the words of the angel and the event of the annunciation. Already in his wording of the Vulgate translation of the passage from Isaiah, "ecce virgo concipiet, et pariet filium, et vocabitur nomen ejus Emmanuel," St. Jerome made the relationship between the two explicit, "ecce concipies in utero et paries filium, et vocabis nomen ejus Jesum."[47]

In the readings of Matins for the Feast of the Annunciation in the York Breviary, in his homily on the Gospel, St. Ambrose uses this same method of juxtaposing events of the Old to the New Testament to describe the significance of the annunciation. Using Genesis 3:13–16, which describes the penalty given to the serpent and to woman for her disobedience, and by developing the correspondences and symmetries in sacred history, the Matins lesson formulates the doctrine of Mary's virginal conception and parturition. First of all, St. Ambrose conceives of Mary as the second Eve, expressing the traditional interpretation of God's curse to the serpent as a prophecy applying to the Virgin Mary: "I will put enmities between thee and the woman, and thy seed and her seed: she shall crush thy head, and thou shalt lie in wait for her heel." And he contrasts Mary to Eve whom God punished by the curse: "I will multiply thy sorrows, and thy conceptions. In sorrow shalt thou bring forth children." Mary is the second Eve, but where Eve disobeyed, Mary is obedient to God's word, and where Eve brought sorrow and will bear children in sorrow, Mary brings joy and bears her Child in joy. She bears Christ, but remains a virgin:

> Precisum est in ea illud eve infelicitatis elogium: in tristitia paries filio. [*sic*] quia ista in leticia dominum parturivit. Virgo quippe genuit: quia virgo concepit. Inviolata peperit: quia in conceptu

> libido non fuit. Extitit enim sine corruptione gravida: et in partu virgo puerpera.[48]

Using this same method of juxtaposition of the Old Testament to the New, the medieval theologian saw Mary not only as the second Eve, but as the fulfillment of many other events and figures: the valiant woman (Prov. 31:10–31), the burning bush of Moses (Exod. 3:2–3), the flowering of the rod of Aaron (Num. 17:8), the rod of the root of Jesse (Isa. 11:1–2, Rom. 15:12), the fleece of Gideon (Judg. 6:36–40); he saw her as Judith, as Rachel, as the sling of David, as the closed gate (Ezek. 44:2).[49] Many of these relationships were made by the liturgy on the feasts of Mary as it applied passages to Mary from Ecclesiasticus, the Psalms, the Canticles. This method of conceiving events and people and phrases of the Old Testament as figures of Mary is fundamental to the poetry evolving from the liturgy, and it is fundamental to the Middle English religious lyrics.[50] We shall see that even when actual biblical figures are not used, the poet will develop his definition of different aspects of Mary in each poem by juxtaposing one event or concept to another in a way analogous to the methods of the liturgy and the homilists. And as in the liturgy, the juxtaposition will be made always in relation to Christ as the center of value.

Passages from Scripture and Tradition

Leading up to the Lesson, joining the Lesson to the Gospel reading, introducing the offering of the bread and the wine in the Mass, and occurring at the time of communion are shorter passages taken from Scripture and tradition, the Introit, the Gradual and Tract, the Offertory and the Communion Verses. These were taken from the psalms, the prophets, the Gospel, homilies and poetic tradition.[51] By their position in the Mass, they, like the Lesson, were interpreted in relation to the central events celebrated by the feast and recounted in the Gospel. On the Feast of the Annunciation, the Introit of the Mass, which is said after the preparatory psalm and the confession, consists of another prophecy of Isaiah (Isa. 45:8).[52]

> Drop down, ye heavens, from above, and let the skies pour down righteousness: let the earth open, and bring forth a saviour.

> *Ps.* And let righteousness spring up together: I the Lord have created it.[53]

By the Introit those present are prepared for the theme of the Lesson and the Gospel, and at the same time invoke God to fulfill the prophecy contained in it.

Between the reading of the Lesson and the Gospel, the Gradual is sung by the choir and said privately by the priest as the subdeacon prepares the bread and wine. The Gradual for the Annunciation again illustrates the way in which the liturgy selects and rearranges Scripture giving it new meaning as the passage is set in relationship to the event being celebrated. Here the Gradual (and the Tract which follows) focuses on the holiness of Mary as the medium through whom Christ came. The Gradual applies to the theme several verses of Psalm 44, and it introduces the salutation of the angel (Luke 1:28), anticipating the account in the reading of the Gospel that will follow:

> Lift up your heads, O ye gates, and be ye lift up, ye everlasting doors: and the king of glory shall come in.
>
> *V.* Who shall ascend into the hill of the Lord? or who shall rise up in his holy place? even he that hath clean hands and a pure heart.
>
> Alleluya. *V.* Hail, Mary, full of grace, the Lord is with thee: blessed art thou among women.

In the context of Mary's feast the verses of Psalm 44 are applied so that they refer to the special purity and grace of Mary which made her a fitting place for the Lord to dwell. The order of verses is changed from that in the psalm, so that the theme of the entry of the Lord comes before the description of the holiness of Mary, revealing by its position that the Lord is the source of her holiness. The description of Mary's holiness in the first verse provides the transition to the *Alleluia* and New Testament verse, where Mary is named and honored by the salutation given to her by the angel at the annunciation.[54]

In the Sarum liturgy a sequence usually follows the Gradual on feast days. It is through the sequences that poetry is directly incorporated into the texture of the Mass. The sequence is a rhythmic or metrical structure of words and music which evolved from the practice of troping or farsing ("filling") the long melisma of the *Alleluia* sung in the Eastern season.[55] As with liturgical drama, its early forms can be traced back to the ninth century and the monastery of St. Gall.[56] By the twelfth century sequences had become very popular throughout Europe. The *Laetebundus* melody, for example, had at least a hundred imitations. Adam of St. Victor (d. 1192), who used metrical rhyming verse pairs with a changed melody for each pair, gave the sequence its highest development.[57] Many Middle English lyrics developed from liturgical sequences, and we shall see examples of this in four of the poems to be discussed below.

The sequence used on the Feast of the Annunciation, "Ave mundi spes Maria," develops from the verse of the Gradual, "Hail, Mary, full of grace, the Lord is with thee: blessed art thou among women," and it is a series of modifications, much like farsings, of the angel's greeting (see Appendix I).[58] It uses many of the modes of formulation in the liturgy which we shall see are used in the English lyrics: the traditional figures for Mary—the burning bush, the rose, the rod of Jesse, the lily of chastity; the application of the liturgy to the individual soul; and the three focuses of liturgical time.

Because the Annunciation falls during Lent, it has a Tract, which is said privately by the celebrant and ministers while the sequence is being sung:[59]

> Hail, Mary, full of grace, the Lord is with thee.
> *V*. Blessed art thou among women, and blessed is the fruit of thy womb.
> *V*. The Holy Ghost shall come upon thee, and the power of the Highest shall overshadow thee.
> *V*. Therefore, also that holy thing that shall be born of thee shall be called the Son of God.

The emphasis of the Tract is that Mary will bear God. The verses, taken again from the Gospel to follow, repeat the last verse of the Gradual and combine it with a second salutation, Elizabeth's greeting to Mary inspired by the Holy Spirit at Mary's visit to her (Luke 1:42). Preceding the angel's words of prophecy that Mary shall bear God, they remind those present of the prophecy's fulfillment. The two verses which follow are the angel's reply to Mary's question, "How shall this be done, because I know not man?" They explain how the prophecy of Isaiah is to be brought about; the Father is to be God, the Son is to be God. Thus prepared for both by prophecy and a description of the holiness of the mother and the nature of the Child, the Gospel is read.

After the Gospel reading comes the Credo. Following the Credo and the sermon comes the Offertory as the priest offers the bread and wine which are to be consecrated. The Offertory Verse repeats the combined salutation of the angel and Elizabeth, here as the expression of praise. After the consecration, oblation and communion, the Communion Verse is said. The Communion Verse repeats the essential element of the Lesson, the sign given in Isaiah's prophecy: "Behold, a virgin shall conceive, and bear a son: and shall call his name Emmanuel."

Prayers

A third type of formulation in the Proper remains to be mentioned that is also a structural principle of the Middle English lyric. At three moments the liturgy formulates special prayers for the feast and the intention of the Mass, channelling the prayers of the present congregation. These are the Collect, the Secret, and the Postcommunion prayers. The Collect follows the Gloria and precedes the Lesson. As Jungmann points out, the Collect is based on the Roman oration, which in its simplest type is the barest petition, a request. While the Secret and Postcommunion are close to this simple form, for the Feast of the Annunciation, as for the other major feast days, the Collect is an amplified petition:

> O God, who wast pleased that thy Word should take flesh in the womb of the blessed virgin Mary, through the message of an angel; grant unto us thy suppliants, that as we believe her to be truly the mother of God, so we may be aided by her intercession before thee. Through [our Lord Jesus Christ thy Son, who liveth and reigneth with thee in the unity of the Holy Ghost, God, world without end].

The Collect makes visible the outlines of the universe in which the prayer of the Church is conceived: "It arises in the communion of holy Church and ascends through Christ to God on high."[60] In all Collects of the Roman liturgy the address is to God the Father rather than to Christ, Who generally is not mentioned except in the closing formula. This focus on God the Father reflects the end and object of the Church's prayer in the Mass. The fact that Christ is mentioned in the concluding formula reflects the Church's conception of the universe in terms of sacred history, as the congregation asks for the gifts *through* Christ. The Church offers the petition to God *"through the mediation* of Christ, who (as St. Paul says) 'lives on still to make intercession on our behalf' (Heb. 7:25)."[61]

Besides being the address to God the Father through the mediation of Christ, there is another aspect of the Collect which is also, as we shall see, central to the lyrics. The prayer is worded in the plural, "we." In this "we" it is the Church that prays, the petitioners and recipients of God's gifts. Jungmann explains:

> The Church is included here not only conceptually, but actually. In liturgical prayer there is—there must be—in fullest reality a communion in which all those participate who join with the priest as he performs the service, all those who are represented expressly by the greeting and its answer and by the comprehensive *Oremus*. Even in a small group of faithful, with the priest standing at the altar at their head, not only is there present a number of Christians, but the Church itself is there in its hierarchic structure—God's people of the New Covenant in the order and arrangement given them by Christ.[62]

This is the identity of the "us" which so often forms the point of view in the Middle English lyric.

In the Collect for the Annunciation, the fact that the Church celebrates Mary's feast is reflected in the relative clause, which mentions the annunciation, and in the petition, which contains a profession of faith that Mary is truly the mother of God. Most Middle English religious lyrics are ultimately addresses to Christ as man's redeemer. The lyrics which focus on Mary will all have a double mediation. The address to Christ comes through a prayer to Mary. The ultimate purpose of the poet and his audience is that of the Church, to be united through Christ to God the Father in heaven.

The Secret is the last variable part before the Canon of the Mass, and on the Feast of the Annunciation it anticipates the coming mystery.[63]

> Strengthen, we beseech thee, O Lord, our minds in the mysteries of the true faith; that we who stedfastly confess him who was conceived of a virgin to be very God and very man, may by the power of the same saving incarnation be found worthy to attain unto everlasting happiness. Through etc.

The Postcommunion prayer applies the graces of the Mass to the congregation.

> We beseech thee, O Lord, to pour thy grace into our hearts, that as we have known the incarnation of thy Son Christ by the message of an angel, so by his cross and passion we may be brought unto the glory of his resurrection. Through etc.

The prayers of the feast have a three-fold perspective: on the two central events of the Incarnation, the coming and the death and the resurrection of Christ, as these are defined by the third, the particular theme of the feast—the words of the angel to Mary and her role as the virgin mother of Christ. Just as the lessons and verses are related ultimately to the Gospel in which the central event of the feast is told, so in the prayers the Church applies the theme of the whole Mass to the souls of the faithful who petition God, by Mary's intercession, through Christ.

The position in the movement of the Mass of these variable parts, the Introit, Collect, Lesson, Gradual, Sequence, Tract, Gospel reading, Offertory, Secret, Communion and Postcommunion, never varies. They remain in their position relative to the unchanging parts—the entry psalm, the Kyrie and Gloria, the prayers of preparation which lead to the Credo—like the frame of a ladder through which the succession of feasts moves, each new theme being reformulated as the ladder juxtaposes new units of words.

Besides the fixed hierarchy of the variable parts of the Mass there is also the analogous fixed order of the material in the Hours of the Divine Office and the devotion of the Little Hours in the English Prymer, with the psalms, the readings, the many antiphons, verses and responses, all applying events, images, phrases in Scripture to the themes of Mary's feasts. In the Prymer, for example, are gathered some of the most beautiful antiphons, which develop the Old Testament types of Mary as they celebrate her virgin motherhood: for Prime, "O þou wondurful chaunge! þe makere of mankynde, takynge a bodi wiþ a soule, of a maide vouchide saaf be bore, & so, forþ goynge man, wiþ-outen seed, ȝaf to us his god-hede"; for Terce, "Whanne he was born wondurfulliche of a maide, þanne was fulfillid holi writ. þou cam doun as reyn in-to a flees, for to make saaf mankynde: þee we preisen, oure god"; for Sext, "Bi þe buysch þat moises siȝ vnbrent, we knowen þat þi preisable maidenhede is kept. modir of god, preie for us"; for None, "The rote of iesse haþ burioned; a sterre is risun of iacob; a maide haþ borun oure saueour. þee we preisen, oure god"; for Evensong, or Vespers, "Aftir þi child-berynge, þou leftist maide wiþ-outen wem. modir of god, preie for us"; for Compline, "Hail, quene of heuenes, modir of þe king of aungelis! O marie, flour of virgines, as þe rose or þe lilie, make preiers to þi sone, for þe helþe of alle cristen men." [64]

The third reformulation of sacred history by the liturgy, then, is through the fixed hierarchical order of the parts of the Mass and the Office. The form of the liturgy is itself an interpretation of Scripture and sacred history. The form generates a meaning ordered to lead closer and closer to Christ. This form is both a sequence in time and a hierarchy of reality. As sequence and hierarchy it is analogous to the principle of sacred history which it formulates, which recounts the coming of God into history and the drawing of man into God through Christ. It is also, considered in the subjective mode, analogous to the movement through grades of perception of the soul in its ascent into Christ.

By these formulations the materials of Scripture and the meditations of the Church are reordered and juxtaposed with a triple focus. At the center of the Proper is the Gospel reading, the first focus, in the light of which the Lesson, the psalms and verses are defined and expressed, and around which the Office is built. The Gospel itself and its galaxy of reflections in the Proper is defined in relationship to a deeper focus, to the present sacrifice of the Mass to which it points. The feast of the occasion and the desires of the people present are, in a third focus, united to the present sacrifice through the Collects and other prayers. In the medieval liturgy the Mass stands in direct relationship to God, being Christ's offering to the Father, and the means by which the past, assimilated to the present, points to the future union in the ultimate focus of the beatific vision.

part one

The Annunciation and Birth of Christ

Fig. 3.—The Annunciation. First of four miniatures preceding the Amesbury Abbey Psalter, Oxford, All Souls College MS 6, fol. 3 (see Figs. 6 and 7). For more extended discussion, refer to the Notes to Illustrations.

AVE MARIA·GRACIA PLENA

Gabriel, fram evene-king
sent to þe maide swete,
broute þire blisful tiding
And faire he gan hire greten:
"heil be þu ful of grace a-rith!
for godes sone, þis euene lith,
for mannes louen
wile man bicomen,
and taken
fles of þe maiden brith,
manken fre for to maken
of senne and deules mith."

Mildeliche im gan andsweren
þe milde maiden þanne:
"Wichewise sold ichs beren
child with-huten manne?"
þangle seide, "ne dred te nout;
þurw þoligast sal ben iwrout
þis ilche þing,
war-of tiding
ichs bringe,
al manken wrth ibout

þur þi swete chiltinge,
and hut of pine ibrout."

Wan þe maiden understud
and þangles wordes herde,
mildeliche with milde mud
to þangle hie andswerde:
"hur lordes þeumaiden iwis
ics am, þat her a-bouen is.
anenttis me,
fulfurthed be
þi sawe;
þat ics, sithen his wil is,
maiden, withhuten lawe
of moder, haue þe blis."

Þangle wente a-wei mid þan,
al hut of hire sithte;
hire wombe arise gan
þurw þoligastes mithe.
in hire was crist biloken anon,
Suth god, soth man ine fleas and bon,
and of hir fleas
iboren was
at time.
War-þurw us kam god won,
he bout us hut of pine
and let im for us slon.

Maiden, moder makeles,
of milche ful ibunden,
bid for hus im þat þe ches
at wam þu grace funde,
þat he forgiue hus senne and wrake,
and clene of euri gelt us make,
and eune blis,
wan hure time is

to steruen,
hus giue, for þine sake
him so her for to seruen
þat he us to him take.

"Gabriel, fram Evene-King"

TO BEGIN TO SHOW HOW FUNDAMENTAL THE KNOWLEDGE OF THE THEOlogical form behind the poem is to achieving the full reading of a medieval religious lyric, I would like to take the English version of "Angelus ad virginem," the song sung by Nicholas in Chaucer's *Miller's Tale,* and set it back into its context as a liturgical sequence commemorating the coming of Christ.[1] The sequence is an appeal to Mary by virtue of the beauty of her virgin motherhood, and it was with humorous irony that Chaucer put its words into the lecherous clerk's mouth.

The Inner Form

Mother and Maid

As part of the Mass the Latin sequence was composed to be sung after the Lesson containing Isaiah's prophecy that a virgin should conceive (Isa. 7:10–15) and before the Gospel reading telling of the annunciation by the angel and Mary's acceptance (Luke 1:26–38), and it opens with almost the same words as the Gospel, "Missus est angelus Gabriel a Deo . . . ad virginem." The author of the English version has used the Gospel account and through praising Mary's part in Christ's coming, he gives the Gospel its full context in sacred history. The manner in which the author has modified his account from that in the Gospel reveals the central focus of the sequence.

The first three stanzas tell of the angel's coming to Mary. (See Figure 3.)

In the Gospel the focus is on the angel's annunciation of the moment of the coming of the Messiah. Immediately after the angel's salutation, Mary is troubled in her heart about the import of the angel's greeting. The angel, who reads her unspoken thoughts, tells her to fear not. With his next announcement, of the coming of Israel's King, he mentions Mary's motherhood, telling her that she will bear Jesus, Who will be called the Son of God and Who will reign forever. Whereas the Gospel account begins with the angel's greeting and Mary's being troubled by what the salutation means, the English poem combines the angel's greeting with his announcement that she will conceive the King and begins by focusing on Mary's virgin motherhood: "heil be þu ful of grace a-rith!/ for godes sone . . . wile man bicomen,/ and taken/ fles of þe maiden brith."[2] Because of His love, the angel continues, through the "maide swete" God will become man and will free man from sin and punishment. Mary is not disturbed, as she is in the Gospel, by the nature of the greeting, but by the fact that, vowed to virginity, she will conceive a child, and stanza two is devoted to Mary's questioning of the angel and to his explanation. How can this birth take place without her having known man, she asks. The angel replies, through the power of the Holy Spirit. All men will be redeemed by her childbearing, he continues, his words "swete chiltinge" suggesting both that Mary will remain a virgin at her Child's conception and bring forth her Child without pain.[3]

In stanza three, speaking of Mary again as "maiden," the poet gives Mary's acceptance. The first part (lines 29–33) paraphrases Mary's words of consent in the Gospel, "anenttis me,/ fulfurthed be/ þi sawe." The last three lines expand her reply, again shifting the words of the Gospel to emphasize the idea of her virgin motherhood, as if she herself had fully formulated the doctrine at that moment: "þat ics, sithen his wil is,/ maiden, withhuten lawe/ of moder, haue þe blis"—that I according to His will shall have the bliss of maidenhood without the law of motherhood. This "law" refers to the punishment given by God to Eve for her sin: that she shall bring forth her children in pain and sorrow. Mary, the second Eve, contrasted to Eve by her obedience and humility, will bring forth the Son of God in joy.[4]

In the fourth stanza, the poet tells of Christ's actual growth in Mary's womb, repeating the idea that Christ's flesh was her flesh, echoing the idea spoken in the Gradual of the spring and summer Masses of Mary: "O virgin mother of God, he whom the whole world cannot contain hid himself in thy womb, and was made man."[5] He tells that in time Christ was born for man's salvation.

Stanza five is the climax of the appeal to Mary in virtue of her virgin motherhood. "Maiden, moder makeles," Mary is addressed by a title that recurs often in Middle English. The word "makeles" had two denotations: the first, to be without an equal, matchless, peerless; and the second, a later use of the word, to be mateless. When applied to Mary, "makeles" has the same special connotations as the Latin *singularis*. Of all creatures, Mary is unique because she is the only woman to be both maid and mother. This matchlessness is the special sign of her closeness to God and also of the fact that her Son is divine.[6] The address in this last stanza to Mary as "maiden, moder makeles" comes at the fitting moment, after the poet has defined her matchless quality, and it is with this title that the poet appeals to her mercy (lines 53–60).

Yet the event has been set also in a wider context. Mary has been conceived of always as the medium through whom God came, who opened heaven to man. The Feast of the Annunciation is Mary's feast, yet only because it celebrates her important role in sacred history before Christ Himself became manifest. At the same time as he has modified the account of the annunciation from that given in the Gospel into a full definition of the virgin motherhood, the poet has used the virgin motherhood he defines as a figure through which to show the importance of the annunciation in sacred history.[7]

The Context of Sacred History

First of all, the concept of sacred history is important to the wider purpose and structure of the poem. Each of the first three stanzas which are given to recounting the Gospel event of the angel's coming and Mary's reply is placed by the poet explicitly in the context of the total plan of salvation. In stanza one, the angel is said to come from God with, in line three, "blisful" tiding. Seen in its context in sacred history, "blisful" suggests more than one joyful occasion. From Mary's perspective at the moment of the annunciation, "blisful" can refer to the joy of Christ's birth which will follow. From the full perspective of the soul living in the present age of the Church, who looks back on the annunciation, "blisful" refers to the bliss of heaven, which Christ's birth and death have opened for man. This is the point of view of the poet and the audience for whom he writes. The last three lines of stanza one make this full meaning of the bliss the angel announces explicit by recounting Christ's coming as part of the total plan of sacred history: This Son of God will come to set man free from sin and the power of the devil.

As in stanza one, in each of the next two stanzas the poet devotes the last three lines to giving the event its significance in the total plan of sacred history. In the second stanza, the angel repeats his explanation of the purpose of the Incarnation, but in a different manner from the first. The angel does not say that man will be bought by Mary's Child Himself, but, focusing on Mary's virgin motherhood, which we saw was the special focus of the poem, he says that man will be bought through Mary's sweet bearing of the Child. In other words, by means of the painless giving birth by a virgin mother man will be brought from pain. The concept of being brought from pain has the same references in time as the concept of "blis." There is a reflection backward and forward in sacred history of the figure of pain. If we think of past history, pain refers to the pain which has come as a penalty of the Fall; of the present, pain refers to the pain of this life; of the future, pain refers to the pain of an eternal hell. From the point of view of the events related in the poem, latent in this figure of pain is the pain that will follow from Christ's birth, the pain He will take on Himself in His passion and death and which will be the means whereby man will be released from pain. Christ's pain will be mentioned in stanza four.

The last three lines of the third stanza contain Mary's consent to God's will and the explicit theological formulation of Mary's painless giving birth, the "swete chiltinge" which was only suggested in the second stanza. They bring to a climax the focus of the poem on Mary. Seen from the perspective of the moment of the annunciation, this birth will be a source of "blis" to Mary by being painless. From the point of view of man in present time seeing the whole of God's plan, the "blis" of the painless birth will be the mark of her special grace with God. With these last three lines the poet has now completely formulated the meaning of Mary's virginal conception and giving birth to Christ.[8]

The first three stanzas together told of the event of the annunciation, giving in the last three lines of each stanza its significance through Mary in the context of sacred history. The last two stanzas, four and five, by making the implications explicit fulfill the first three.

Þangle wente a-wei mid þan,
  al hut of hire sithte;
hire wombe arise gan

þurw þoligastes mithe.
in hire was crist biloken anon,
Suth god, soth man ine fleas and bon,
and of hir fleas
iboren was
at time.
War-þurw us kam god won,
he bout us hut of pine
and let im for us slon.

In the fourth stanza, to define fully the reason for joy, the poet tells of the events in sacred history which have occurred as a consequence of the annunciation. Through the power of the Holy Spirit (as the angel had said) Christ, true God and true man, was conceived, swelled in Mary's womb, and was born. The last three lines here in stanza four speak of Christ in Whom sacred history centers, saying that through His conception and birth the rest of the events of the redemption were able to be fulfilled. Christ died, was resurrected and opened heaven ("god won") to man.

In this stanza Mary's painless conception and giving birth to Christ have yet another application, which is made clear by these last three lines. The angel had told Mary in stanza one that man would be bought through her virginal conception, that he would be freed from sin and the power of the devil. In stanza two the concept of painless birth was suggested and applied to the first stanza. The redemption of man through Mary's "swete chiltinge" was expressed by the figure of release from pain. We find here in stanza four that the fulfillment of the angel's promise is told in respect to a third pain. Through the crucifixion of Christ, His pain and death, man is bought and given heaven. The crucifixion is more explicitly treated in the Latin version of the sequence from the Arundel MS, where the last three lines read:

affigens humero
    crucem qui dedit ictum
soli mortifero.[9]

Tracing the central emphasis of the poem as it has been developed, we see the following applications of the figure of pain and joy. Stanza one: through Christ's birth from the virgin man will be bought. Stanza two: the painless "chiltinge," a sign that the Child is God, will release man from the pain of hell. Stanza three: a childbearing which is exempt from motherhood's law of giving birth in pain—that is, the "blis" of Mary's virginal childbearing—prefigures man's birth into joy and bliss. In the fourth stanza, the angel's promise given in stanza one, that man will be bought, is explicitly fulfilled. As in stanza two, sorrow and joy are seen under the figure of pain and release. Mary's actual giving birth in joy is juxtaposed to a second birth. Through the pain of Christ's passion man is released from his pain into the joyful hope of heaven.

Thus in "Gabriel, fram evene-king" the event of Christ's virginal conception and birth has been used as a principle of form. The poet has selected the figure of pain changing to joy and used it to make a symmetrical correspondence between the events he relates. And this poem provides our first example of a Middle English poet's use of certain principles of proportion and symmetry in sacred history which, as was shown in the Introduction, are present in the liturgy.

To recall briefly what we saw defined by the readings of the Mass of the Annunciation and the homily of St. Ambrose, the proportion and symmetry between the events of sacred history are based on the doctrine that the first creation, which fell, has been recreated by Christ Who is the New Adam.[10] There are three principles of proportion between the first creation and its re-creation. First, the events of the new creation, the Incarnation and Redemption, have occurred in a fitting correspondence to the events of the first. They have been applied like poultices to heal the wounds of the old, or like lights to transfigure them, in a way which does not destroy but is appropriate to them. Second, not only does the new creation assume and transform the old, but because Christ, through the Incarnation, is their redeemer, or re-creator, all events which lead to Christ's coming find their end and significance in Him.[11] The focus in Christ establishes the third principle of proportion. Because their significance can be fully defined only in terms of the events of the new creation, the events which lead to the coming of Christ have their full meaning and value only as they prefigure the new. As we have seen in regard to both Scripture and liturgy, the Old Testament events are significant not only in themselves but as types of the events to come in the New.

The symmetrical proportioning of the events of the old and the new creation has been used by the Middle English poet as a structural principle of the poem we are studying. In the first three stanzas the poet uses the event of Mary's painless childbearing, her virgin motherhood, as a figure through which to formulate the truth of the second event, man's spiritual redemption from the pain of sin and death. In the fourth stanza in a second juxtaposition of events, the birth of Christ, which for Mary was painless, is contrasted to the spiritual rebirth of man through the pain and death of Christ at His crucifixion. This pain of Christ reflects a further correspondence, going back to the Fall. Mary bore Christ "withhuten lawe/ of moder." But in her compassion at Christ's death, Mary suffered the pains from which she was exempt in Christ's birth. Thus, through her pain during man's spiritual delivery, she becomes the spiritual mother of mankind. In Part II we shall see the significance of this concept developed fully in the poems on Mary's suffering at the crucifixion of Christ:

Nu is time þat þu ȝielde
kende þat þu im withelde
  þo þi child was of þe born;
Nu he hoschet wit goulinge
þat þu im in þi chiltinge
  al withelde þar biforn.

Nu þu fondest, moder milde,
wat wyman drith with hir childe,
  þei þu clene maiden be;
Nu þe's ȝiolden arde and dere
þe þine werof þu were
  ine ti chiltuing quite and fre.[12]

The Final Purpose, or the Full Form

The fifth stanza makes the ultimate purpose of the poem explicit. It is the culmination of the third movement in the poem and subsumes the other two. The first focus was on Mary's virgin motherhood. The poem is a sequence in her honor, telling of her as the medium through which Christ came. This focus culminates in stanza three. The second focus was the relationship of Mary's virginal conception and "chiltinge" to the redemptive plan of history. In stanza four the angel's promise is fulfilled. The sweet birth with the corresponding painful death of Christ has released man from pain and opened heaven to him. Now, in the fifth stanza, these two movements are drawn into a third focus, which is the present moment in sacred history. This is the full context in which the poem has been conceived. In terms of sacred history, the present moment, as we have seen, refers to the time of the Church, which stands after the Incarnation and Crucifixion, after Christ's ascension, and looks with hope towards Christ's second coming in glory. In terms of the poem, the present moment is also the time of the actual participation in the poem by the speaker or singer and his audience, and it is for those living in this moment that the poet shapes his poem into a prayer to Mary.

Maiden, moder makeles,
of milche ful ibunden,
bid for hus im þat þe ches
at wam þu grace funde,
þat he forgiue hus senne and wrake,
and clene of euri gelt us make,
and eune blis,
wan hure time is
to steruen,
hus giue, for þine sake
him so her for to seruen
þat he us to him take.

Mary's title "Maiden, moder makeles" has been prepared by the account in the earlier stanzas. But now it is joined with a second title she has received by the fact of Christ's death for mankind, Mary "of milche ful ibunden," full ready with mercy. "Bid for hus," the poet petitions Mary in virtue of the events that have been related, that we who are living in the hope established by the angel's coming, by Mary's acceptance, and by the birth and death of Christ, may, for Mary's sake, have the joy of heaven.

By the petition in stanza five the initial words (stanza one) of the angel's salutation are given their full meaning. The poet asks Mary by virtue of the fact that Christ chose her (line 51), "Gabriel, fram evene-king/ sent to þe maide swete," and he asks her because she found grace with Him (line 52). Corresponding to the title with which the angel greeted Mary, "Heil be þu ful of grace a-rith!" (line 5), the title "of milche ful ibunden" serves as its ultimate interpretation: Mary was full of grace, of God's favor; in time she became full of Christ, for "in hire was crist biloken" (line 41); and now, finding grace with Christ, Mary is a source of grace for man. Implicit in this final petition is Mary's position as Queen of Heaven, in the perpetual present that will last until the end of time and transcends time. She, being the medium of Christ's coming and redeeming, can ask that He forgive us our sins and free us from His vengeance, and that when we shall die, He give us the "blis" of heaven. This is the full meaning of the "blisful tiding" (line 3) brought by the angel.

But the last three lines develop the petition to enter bliss in another way, making it more exact. Bliss is spoken of as Christ Himself. Not only the future, but the course of man's life is assumed into Him, bringing the subject of the poem to the full circle characteristic of sacred history: God is the beginning—the angel is sent by God; Christ, God and man, is the middle or center—He is conceived and born into the world. He suffers and dies, and then raises Himself and ascends to the Father. There He reigns as heaven's King and man's hope and final end.

The way the whole poem moves to a petition and the way the petition is formed in terms of sacred history is analogous to the Mass liturgy. Just as the Mass is the re-enactment of the crucifixion to unite the present congregation to God, so the poem which relates the event of the annunciation to the crucifixion of Christ is made by the poet into a prayer in order to apply the events to himself and his listeners for their "god won." In the Collect for the Feast of the Annunciation the address to God is amplified by a relative clause which incorporates the significance of the feast day, beginning "O God, who wast pleased that thy Word should take flesh in the womb of the blessed virgin Mary, through the message of an angel. . . ."[13] In the poem the petition has two relative clauses, "þat þe ches/ at wam þu grace funde," but they refer not directly to the subject of the feast, the fact that God took flesh, but to the central fact by which the poem was formed; that is, to Mary's own special relationship with God, her virgin motherhood.

The External Form

Up to this point in our explication of the poem, we have seen that the poet adapts the theological concepts of Mary's virgin motherhood and of sacred history in a manner analogous to their formulation by the liturgy, and it is the study of these theological ocncepts that has revealed both the over-all form and the purpose of the poem. We have noticed also that sacred history is both the subject matter of the poem and the method by which meaning itself evolves. The poem tells of the past time when Christ entered history, how He redeemed man. This coming is applied through Mary to the present moment in hope of the future bliss of heaven.

The external form mirrors this movement. The whole consists of (1) the first three stanzas, presenting the annunciation of Christ's coming, its implications, and Mary's consent; (2) the last two, presenting the fulfillment of the promises, as stanza four recounts the actual coming of Christ and the redemption of all men, and as stanza five, in virtue of the first three stanzas, petitions for the future fulfillment of those in the present. The overall structure is a theme—the birth of Christ through Mary—and its fulfillment.

The structure of the individual stanzas mirrors the structure of the whole. The first three stanzas provide a clear example of the form. Each stanza consists of an opening statement presented in a quatrain, then a couplet which introduces the main theme of the stanza, and finally an elaboration of the theme which extends to the last three lines. The last three lines relate the theme explicitly to the full context of sacred history. A study of the structure of the melody to which the poem was set supports the conception of the form we have reached through analysis of the meaning. The music would strongly affect how the parts of the sequence would be felt and understood by both the singer and the listener.

The music [14] is based on a single melody which is developed in two ways, and each section of the melody, the theme and its two developments, is repeated.[15] The first unit of melody, the statement of the theme, corresponds in the stanza of the poem to lines one to four—the basic melody with lines one and two, the repetition with lines three and four.

Gabriel, fram evene-king
  sent to þe maide swete,
broute þire blisful tiding
  And faire he gan hire greten

Thus the opening quatrain of each stanza, with its abab rhyme (except the first, which has an imperfect b rhyme) corresponds to the first unit of the melody which states the theme. In each of the first three stanzas of the poem this quatrain tells the action. The rest of the stanza, lines five through twelve, in the same way as the music, develops the opening melody.

In the music, lines five through twelve are two developments of the melody each based on a melodic inversion of it; that is, the higher tones are substituted for the lower ones—the melody is turned inside out. The first musical inversion (lines 5–6) is shorter than the original melody. Line six is the repetition of line five. In the stanza, this first short development of the melody corresponds to a rhymed couplet which introduces the central theological idea which the rest of the stanza develops.

heil be þu ful of grace a-rith!
for godes sone, þis euene lith [16]

The couplet provides the third rhyme of the poem, which is repeated later in the last three lines of the stanza (10–12).

The second melodic inversion corresponds in the poem's stanza to lines seven through ten, its repetition to lines eleven and twelve. Lines seven through ten introduce the fourth and fifth rhymes, with line ten repeating the rhyme of the couplet:

for mannes louen
wile man bicomen,
and taken
fles of þe maiden brith,
manken fre for to maken
of senne and deules mith.

But the repetition of the second development of the melody is irregular. One melodic phrase has been omitted. The fact is reflected in the poem's stanza, where the last two lines, lines eleven and twelve, do not correspond in length exactly to lines seven through ten. According to the structure of the melody, line eleven in the stanza corresponds to the phrases developed in lines seven through nine. Nothing in either the original Latin or the English line eleven indicates the melodic parallel. Lines ten and twelve, which rhyme, are musically identical. The effect of the omitted melodic phrase is to make the repetition of the second development flow as a further development and to make the musical setting of lines seven through twelve sound more like an evolving unit. Finally, the rhyme scheme, which has supported both the melodic and stanzaic structure of lines one through six, in the last four lines works against both the music and the syntax to bind them into a unit whose rhyme ties them to the couplet.[17]

It is important to realize that the music these words were written for is not in a metrical phrasing of notes. The music was adapted to the clear articulation of Latin words. It does not follow a rhythm of regular measure, but flows in groups of neums, or clusters of notes which are determined by syllabic shift and accent of the words they are set to, the clusters being made up of units of one, two or three notes.

The formal relationship between the sections of the melody would have affected the listeners' understanding of the relationship of the parts of the stanza. In music a sense of form comes from a relationship between levels of pitch and extension of phrases in time. Although the music of "Gabriel, fram evene-king" develops one basic melody, each of the two developments of it contrasts and is set in a symmetrical relationship of height and length to the other. The first statement of the melody provides the mean. The first section of the melodic inversion (lines 7–10) ascends to the highest point of the music in a succession of phrases climaxing at line nine, which is the shortest line of the stanza and the one which precedes the final group of three lines that relate the whole of the first part to sacred history. It then drops abruptly an octave below its last phrase to the lowest position. The shortened repetition retains and echoes the climax and the drop. This means that the tenth and twelfth lines are the lowest, contrasting radically in pitch to the ninth and eleventh which lead to them. The correspondence between lines ten and twelve makes the last three lines into a concluding unit. Approximating in length the opening statement of the melody, the last three lines bring the final repetition back into relationship with the opening.

The music, then, is one theme that unfolds by two developments of its inversion. It reaches a climax at line nine and resolves in the last three lines by the symmetry of the contrasting low lines ten and twelve, which in the stanza rhyme with the couplet (lines 5–6) of the first development. The form of the music, statement (lines 1–4), development (lines 5–12), with a conclusion (lines 10–12), is reflected in the stanza form. Not only do the music and the stanza form correspond to each other, but they correspond to the development of meaning within stanzas one through three, in which lines one through four describe the action and the succeeding lines develop its significance, first through a statement of the theological truth (the couplet) and then its expansion (lines 7–9), and finally through showing its relationship to sacred history (lines 10–12).

However, after stanza three, this correspondence shifts when the poet begins to set the event of the annunciation that the whole poem celebrates in its full and present context of sacred history. If we stand back for a moment from the individual stanzas, we can see that there is a parallel between the development in one stanza and the development in the whole poem. Just as in each stanza lines five through twelve develop the event told in the opening quatrain, so stanzas four through five are the development of the event of the annunciation related in stanzas one through three. Just as lines ten through twelve relate the first part of the stanza to sacred history, so the last two stanzas relate the whole event to sacred history. Stanza four modifies this development of meaning by narrating the fulfillment of the event told in stanzas one through three. The fact that each stanza is sung to the same music suggests to the listener that the development in stanza four is an application to the old, and in stanza five suggests it again, as the poet applies the whole sequence of events to the present moment.

By first studying the three movements of the whole poem—the focus on Mary's maiden motherhood, the context of sacred history, the movement towards petition—and by describing the stanza form through using the structure of the music, we have found that the poet develops his theme by a series of juxtaposed statements which are proportionately related. The structural principle of the poem seems to be developed by an ordered series of correspondences, the later ones fulfilling the earlier.[18]

We noted above that the events of sacred history have a proportion and symmetry. The coming of Christ into history is a re-creation by which the events of the first creation are sanctified and fulfilled. We saw, by juxtaposing the events told in one stanza of the poem to those of another in the same way as the succeeding events are juxtaposed in sacred history, that the corresponding parts of the succeeding stanzas in the poem could be seen to fulfill the preceding ones. Thus, the painless birth was seen as a figure, but also as an effective cause, of man's delivery from death—all men, and particularly those still journeying to future joy. The painless childbearing was seen to gain its effect for man by Christ Himself taking on the pain through His passion and death to secure man's rebirth into grace.

Now that the units which compose each stanza have been singled out and confirmed by a study of the music, we can see an analogous symmetry and proportion present in the poem's external structure. As the whole poem develops from the Annunciation to the petition in present time, each part of the individual stanza can be seen to be related to the corresponding section of the preceding stanzas. Thus, if we juxtapose the opening quatrains, we find they present the simple narrative sequence of the poem: (1) Gabriel descends and greets Mary; (2) Mary questions how she can bear a child without having known man; (3) when she has understood, she answers Gabriel; (4) then, after the angel leaves, the Child swells in Mary's womb; (5) the poet addresses Mary: Maiden and mother, pray for us to Him Who chose you and with Whom you found grace.

If we juxtapose the couplets, we find the theological statement of truth developing the narrative quatrain: (1) the angel hails Mary and announces God's Son;[19] (2) in stanza two he tells her the coming of God's Son will be accomplished by the Holy Ghost; (3) in stanza three Mary begins the response of obedience upon which the salvation of all depends; (4) in stanza four the poet tells how it was Christ, true God and true man, of flesh and bone, Who was "biloken" in Mary; and, finally, (5) in stanza five he forms the petition of what man desires, the forgiveness of his sins.

It is wrenching the context, however, to consider the couplet separately, for in each stanza it initiates the lines which follow. In the first three stanzas which tell of the annunciation, lines seven through ten complete the development of the theological idea begun in lines five and six, as (1) in stanza one the angel continues to explain that God's Son Whom he announces will take flesh of Mary; (2) in stanza two he finishes explaining that the events he bears tidings of will be accomplished through the Holy Ghost; and (3) in stanza three Mary completes her response to the angel and declares herself obedient to his words. But just as in the whole poem stanzas four and five act to fulfill the event recounted in stanzas one through three, so within the development of these two stanzas themselves, lines seven through ten act to fulfill what was presented by lines one through six, as (4) stanza four recounts that which follows from Mary holding Christ within her, the event of His birth; and (5) stanza five formulates that which man desires as a consequence of the forgiveness asked for in the couplet, the fact of future entrance into "eune blis."

Finally, if we juxtapose the last lines of each stanza, which we have already seen to establish the principle of proportion for the whole poem in relation to sacred history, we find the development of the event's deepest significance for man as (1) in stanza one the angel explains that God will take flesh of the sinless maiden to free man from sin; (2) in stanza two he says that through her painless childbearing man will be bought from pain; and as (3) in stanza three, which formulates God's plan of the Incarnation in relation to the central figure of Mary's painless giving birth, Mary accepts God's plan that she be mother and maiden, exempt from the penalty of Eve. In the last two stanzas, which reflect the modification in the development of the whole poem, lines ten through twelve apply the painless birth of Christ to the poet and his audience to establish the final point of view in sacred history, as (4) in stanza four these lines recount Christ's crucifixion, which accomplished the liberation of all mankind from pain and which makes possible the petition formed in (5) stanza five where the last three lines recall the deepest meaning of man's rebirth from pain: So let us serve Christ here on earth, the poet prays, that when we die, Christ will "us to him take." And the poem ends suggesting the fact that rebirth into bliss is rebirth into union with Christ Himself.

The "Maiden Makeles"

A COMMON CRITICISM OF THE MEDIEVAL RELIGIOUS LYRIC IS ILLUSTRATED by George Kane's statement that, although by itself one of these poems may seem good, when studied with specimens of its own kind, the religious lyric seems to recede into a common sameness of theme and effect. This is in the first place, Kane says, because the number of themes is limited. Then, the variations of these are minute, and the degrees of "poetic transport" are not great. The limited number of themes and the few signs of developing technique except as it reflects the progress in the secular lyrics, confirm "a suggestion there implicit of the static nature of this particular combination of medium and subject which the few exceptions fail to dismiss." [1]

In answer to this common criticism of the medieval religious lyric, and as a bare suggestion of the variety possible in the treatment of one dogmatic theme, I would like to discuss two other poems which treat the conception and birth of Christ. These are the thirteenth century "Exemplum de beata virgine & gaudiis eius," which begins "Nu þis fules singet hand maket hure blisse," [2] and the late fourteenth century poem which is based on it, "I syng of a myden þat is makeles." [3]

FIG. 4.—The Birth of Christ and the Tree of Jesse. Illuminated "P" of the Introit, Third Mass on Christmas Day, New York, Pierpont Morgan Library M. 107, fol. 23. Christ's birth is presented in the context of Christ's kingship. The folio shows a triple focus: on the present feast of Christmas, as it is the fulfillment of the past, and also the means of union with Christ and His mother who reign in heaven. For more extended discussion, refer to the Notes to the Illustrations.

"Nu Þis Fules Singet hand Maket Hure Blisse"

Leo Spitzer refers to the first of these two poems on the "maiden makeles" as "quite mediocre." Using the words of W. W. Greg who pointed out their relationship, he says: "The 'not very remarkable' thirteenth-century version is a quite traditional poem about the Annunciation, including a mention of the tree of Jesse, a transcription of the *Ave Maria* and a prayer at the end."[4] In this brief description of the poem, Spitzer simply lists three traditional theological subjects, implying by this listing that the poet has related them in a similar mechanical way. I believe that Spitzer's opinion that this poem is an ununified collection of traditional concepts comes from a misunderstanding of the purpose of the poem, which in turn arises from a misunderstanding of the theological subject behind it. My intention in explicating this poem will be not to decide whether or not it is a "remarkable poem," but to show that a unified purpose and structure can be found by studying its theological subject matter, and also to provide a background for a discussion of its later offspring, "I syng of a myden þat is makeles."

Exemplum de beata virgine & gaudiis eius

Nu þis fules singet hand maket hure blisse
and þat gres up þringet and leued þe ris;
of on ic wille singen þat is makeles,
þe king of halle kinges to moder he hire ches.

Heo his wit-uten sunne and wit-uten hore,
I-cumen of kinges cunne of gesses more;
þe louerd of monkinne of hire was yboren
to bringen us hut of Sunne, elles wue weren for-lore.

Gabriel hire grette and saide hire, "aue!
Marie ful of grace, vre louer be uit þe,
þe frut of þire wombe ibleset mot id be.
þu sal go wit chide, for sout ic suget þe."

and þare gretinke þat angle hauede ibrout,
he gon to bi-þenchen and meinde hire þout;

he saide to þen angle, "hu may tiden þis?
of monnes y-mone nout y nout iuis."

Mayden heo was uid childe & Maiden her biforen,
& maiden ar sot-hent hire chid was iboren;
Maiden and moder nas neuer non wimon boten he—
wel mitte he berigge of godes sune be.

I-blessed beo þat suete chid & þe moder ec,
& þe suete broste þat hire sone sec;
I-hered ibe þe time þat such chid uas iboren,
þat lesed al of pine þat arre was for-lore.

Even though one section includes part of the Gospel on the annunciation, it is imprecise to say that this is a poem about the annunciation. Because our last poem developed the events in the Gospel account, it could be also designated as a poem on the annunciation, yet it was, more specifically, a poem invoking and defining Mary as the medium of God's coming and therefore the medium of man's deliverance from pain and of man's entry into heaven. The defining of the tree of Jesse and what Spitzer calls the *Ave Maria* are two aspects of the unified conception of the poem, which describes Mary not as the medium of our salvation, but as unique because she is the mother of God. The purpose of the poet's address to her is not petition as in the previous poem, but praise.

The poem moves in three stages. The first, stanzas one and two, defines the setting and the subject of praise, the "makeles" one chosen by the King to be His mother, and it proposes the first paradox, that a child might choose his own mother. The second, stanzas three and four, tells of the annunciation and proposes the second paradox, that a virgin might conceive without man, and asks how this might be. And the third, the last two stanzas, shows that what lies behind the paradoxes is cause for giving praise to God.

The opening stanza of the poem might be said to be merely a friar's adaptation of a conventional beginning of a secular love song, used perhaps to capture the audience's attention, or perhaps to identify a secular melody to which the poem might be set.[5] Yet the opening serves a purpose more integral to the poem. By classifying Mary conventionally, with all other women who come to mind to be praised in the spring season of love, it establishes the way her identity will be handled. The subject of the poem will be one that is matchless, a woman unequaled by all other women. Neither the mother nor her Child will be directly identified, and the unique fact that her King and Child is God will be withheld until line twenty. By speaking of Mary and her Child as comparable to all mankind, the poet can heighten the effect of the paradoxes in the conception and birth of God and heighten, in turn, the listeners' feeling of wonder.

But we cannot expect that the audience was unaware that Mary was the subject of the poem. In fact, in stanza one it can be seen that the poet already plays on his listeners' knowledge of the full identity of Mary and Christ by implying the present situation of events in sacred history, and we shall see in the last stanza that the event of Christ's birth is the basis of praise. Christ would be recognized by the title, "king of halle kinges," as He is now, in glory with the Father.[6] And Christ would be recognized in the paradoxes. This King chose the "makeles" one not only, as the love lyric context would suggest to the listener, to be His spouse, but to be His mother. What child has chosen his mother? What mother is at the same time a spouse? Mary herself would be recognized as the mother of the King of Kings, and also as she is in present time, after her bodily assumption, the Queen of Heaven.[7] It is from this perspective in the present time of sacred history that the poet takes his listeners back into past time to recall the nature of this mother's matchlessness.

> Heo his wit-uten sunne and wit-uten hore,
> I-cumen of kinges cunne of gesses more;
> þe louerd of monkinne of hire was yboren
> to bringen us hut of Sunne, elles wue weren for-lore.

The "on . . . þat is makeles" is a fit choice for a king. She is sinless and without stain.[8] Not only is she sinless, but she comes of a kingly line. With the mention of Jesse's root, again the poet calls on his listeners' knowledge of Mary's place in sacred history. In the lessons and antiphons of Christmas and Advent and in the Masses celebrating the nativity of Mary, the liturgy applies to Mary's giving birth to Christ Isaiah's prophecy of the Messiah:

> And there shall come forth a rod out of the root of Jesse: and a flower shall rise up out of the root (Isa. 11:1).[9]

Developing the implication of the last line in stanza one, the last two lines of stanza two give the central reason why the King of Kings chose this mother. Mary's beauty is seen to be the result of God's design in sacred history to redeem man. The "louerd of monkinne"—now named from the point of view of His humanity—was born of her, the sinless one, to bring man out of sin; otherwise man had been lost. Having given the purpose of the King's entry into time, the poet then tells of the moment itself when the King's choice of the matchless one to be His mother was announced to her:

Gabriel hire grette and saide hire, "aue!
Marie ful of grace, vre louer be uit þe,
þe frut of þire wombe ibleset mot id be.
þu sal go wit chide, for sout ic suget þe."

Using the Gospel account of the annunciation, the poet modifies it for the purposes of his poem. As in "Gabriel, fram evene-king," the angel combines his salutation to Mary with his announcement of the birth. But in this poem, "þe frut of þire wombe ibleset mot id be" is substituted for the Gospel lesson's "blessed art thou among women." This is the blessing given to Mary, after her conception of Christ, by Elizabeth, the mother of John the Baptist (Luke 1:39–47), which in Mary's feasts the liturgy traditionally couples with the angel's salutation.[10] By substituting for the angel's blessing of Mary herself the blessing of the fruit of her womb, the poet puts greater emphasis on Mary's coming motherhood to heighten the paradox of Mary's virginity, which will be presented for the first time in the next stanza. The poet also, as he does throughout the poem, omits the Gospel's identification of the matchless one's Child with the Messiah.

The fourth stanza establishes Mary's virginity. As in "Gabriel, fram evene-king," Mary searches her thought, not troubled by the greeting as in the Gospel account, but about the impossibility of her conceiving without having known man. Yet after her question, "hu may tiden þis?/ of monnes y-mone nout y nout iuis," the account breaks off. By withholding the angel's answer, the poet gives emphasis to Mary's question.

Stanzas five and six, the third section, reach a climax of paradox, give the solution to it, and complete the purpose of praise.

Mayden heo was uid childe & Maiden her biforen,
& maiden ar sot-hent hire chid was iboren;

Maiden and moder nas neuer non wimon boten he—
wel mitte he berigge of godes sune be.

This mother remained a maid after she had conceived, as well as before, and a maid after her Child was born. No other woman has been maiden and mother but she. Well might she be the bearer of God's Son. The last line of stanza five suggests a double truth. Since her fitness has been the theme of the poem, line twenty seems at first glance to mean that this unique fact makes her a fitting mother of the Son of God. But seen as the resolution of the two paradoxes, that a child chooses his mother, that a mother remains a virgin, her matchlessness serves also as a sign that the Child she bore is God. God only could choose His mother. God only could cause a virgin to conceive without her knowing man, and God only could be born without disturbing her virginity. Her Son then must be God.

I-blessed beo þat suete chid & þe moder ec,
& þe suete broste þat hire sone sec;
I-hered ibe þe time þat such chid uas iboren,
þat lesed al of pine þat arre was for-lore.

In this last stanza, the poet fulfills the purpose of praising the matchless mother, and applies to Mary the words of a third blessing given to her during the Gospel account of Christ's ministry and traditionally applied to her by the liturgy which celebrates her queenship of heaven.[11] Then in the second two lines of the stanza, the praise reaches beyond Mary to the full meaning in sacred history of her motherhood. Referring back to line eight where the purpose of the King's birth was given, the last two lines speak of the purpose as fulfilled. Christ has been born, man redeemed. The praise extends beyond the mother and Child to the moment itself when such a Child was born, Who loosed all, who before were lost, from pain.

The indirect mode used to refer to Mary in the opening stanza is retained significantly in the last. In the same way as Mary was called "on . . . þat is makeles," the three elements praised in this stanza are identified solely in terms of their relation to the event of the coming of the unique Child. The Child is praised first as "þat . . . chid"; the mother as the mother of that Child, "þe moder ec." Time itself is praised only because of its relationship to the birth of that unique Child, "I-hered ibe þe time þat such chid uas iboren." Finally, in the last two lines, even the Child Himself, identified in stanza five as "godes sune," is made relative to the purpose of His birth, as He is named "such chid." And the whole chain of praise, of the mother, the time, the Child, is made to spring from gratitude for the redemption of mankind.

The rhyme "iboren" and "for-lore[n]" is repeated at three important points in the poem, possibly to emphasize the final focus I have suggested. It occurs at the end of the first section, lines seven and eight, with the mention of the purpose of the birth, which sets the King of Kings and His mother in the context of sacred history. In lines seventeen and eighteen the rhyme is repeated. These are the lines in which the poem's paradoxes culminate, as the poet presents Mary's virgin motherhood. And, finally, the rhymes are repeated in the last stanza, where the verb form, modified from emphasizing a general purpose, "to bringen us hut of Sunne," presents the fact as fulfilled, "þat lesed al of pine."

The heading of this poem, "Exemplum de beata virgine & gaudiis eius," indicates the poem may have been used in a sermon, as does the fact that the poem is found in a miscellany of English, French and Latin works, compiled probably by Dominican preaching friars in the second half of the thirteenth century.[12] The joys on which the poem is based are the first two of five joys traditionally celebrated in medieval England (see Part III). Mary's joys—the annunciation, the birth of Christ, the resurrection and ascension, and Mary's own assumption—reflect the steps of man's redemption, and Mary's final joy of being bodily in heaven is the promise of man's final joy.

For the particular combination of images used to describe Mary in this poem, two sources can be seen. One is the concept of the tree of Jesse as formulated by the medieval artist, and the other, as was mentioned above, is the liturgy's celebration of Mary in her present joy as Queen of Heaven. The concept of the tree of Jesse began to have a traditional artistic form in the late eleventh and early twelfth century. In stained glass windows and in illuminated manuscripts depicting the tree, the artist would show at the bottom of the representation Jesse lying asleep, and springing up from him, a tree on which the prophets and kings were arranged. (See Figure 4.) At the top would be Christ in majesty, the flower of the tree. Mary would be below Him as the stem of the flower. Later, beginning with the thirteenth century and the upsurge in devotion to Mary, the tree was often conceived with Mary enthroned and the Christ Child in her lap.[13] Occasionally, grouped at the bottom of the representation, would be some of the events in the life of Mary, such as the annunciation and birth of Christ, the presentation in the Temple.[14] Many of the elements in the artistic conception of the tree of Jesse are in this poem—the representation of Christ as the King of Kings, of Mary as Queen and mother of Christ, the mysteries of Christ's birth.

Some of the concepts in the poem can be found also in the daily Masses and Offices devoted to Mary in the spring and summer season. The Mass used from the Purification on February second to the beginning of Advent, with the exception of Easter week, celebrates Mary's timeless aspect, as she is in present time, Queen of Heaven, with the angel's prophecy of her blessedness now fulfilled. The Introit of the Mass is "Hail, holy mother, who didst bring forth in childbirth the king who ruleth over heaven and earth for ever and ever. *Ps.* Blessed art thou among women, and blessed is the fruit of thy womb."[15] The Gospel lesson is Luke 11:27–28, the source of lines twenty-one and two of this poem, which tells about the woman crying out from the crowd to bless the mother of Christ.[16]

I would like briefly to refer back to Spitzer's summary of "Nu þis fules singet hand maket hure blisse" as a "traditional poem about the Annunciation, including a mention of the tree of Jesse, a transcription of the *Ave Maria* and a prayer at the end." My purpose is not to put an undue amount of weight on a description which Spitzer obviously sketched in to provide the basis of his detailed study of the poem derived from it, but to find fault with what seems to be the attitude of Spitzer, and of Kane also, that when certain "traditional" themes or forms appear they must necessarily each be about a limited subject or have a certain static relationship to each other.

"Nu þis fules singet hand maket hure blisse" is, in fact, not a poem on the annunciation, but a poem in praise of Mary as mother and virgin because she is a sign of the redemption of man. Her qualities are conceived in their timeless aspect, as she is now, the Queen of Heaven. The poem defines her matchlessness by recalling the past events of her life which have made her unique, and from the definition of her beauty rises the praise in the last stanza. There is no "transcription of the *Ave Maria,"* but the angel's salutation combined with Elizabeth's greeting is introduced into the narrative of the annunciation as part of the definition of Mary's virgin motherhood. The angel's salutation is later developed by the third salutation in stanza five from Luke 10. All three salutations, as they do in the liturgy, emphasize the theme of her blessedness. How the poet modifies the account from that in the Gospel further illustrates that the subject of the poem is not directly the annunciation, but Mary's special quality of virgin motherhood. The poet's reference to Mary springing from the root of Jesse is an integral part of his demonstration that she is fit to be the mother of the King, and at the same time it introduces the human lineage of her Son, Who, until the end of the poem, is presented explicitly only in His human nature. And finally, the "prayer at the end" grows from the purpose of praise which was announced at the beginning and which was carefully prepared for by means of the entire poem.

"I Syng of a Myden Þat Is Makeles"

"I syng of a myden þat is makeles" is the counterpart of the poem which is its source. This poem also praises Mary for her unique quality of being virgin and mother. In the same way as in "Nu þis fules singet," Christ is presented as the King of Kings and Mary is called "makeles";[17] Mary's identity is withheld until the end, and the revelation that she is "godes moder" gives the purpose and direction of the poem. However, in this poem, instead of being introduced in general terms as the "on . . . þat is makeles," Mary is spoken of immediately, in line one, as the "myden þat is makeles." Eliminating other aspects of Mary's beauty, the poet focuses solely on the quality of Mary's virgin motherhood. It is this great concentration and the poet's use of imagery that has made this poem, contrary to its source, appeal unanimously to the readers of our time.[18]

I syng of a myden   þat is makeles,
kyng of alle kynges   to here sone che ches.

he cam also stylle   þer his moder was
as dew in aprylle,   þat fallyt on þe gras.

he cam also stylle   to his moderes bowr
as dew in aprille,   þat fallyt on þe flour.

he cam also stylle   þer his moder lay
as dew in aprille,   þat fallyt on þe spray.

moder & mayden   was neuer non but che—
wel may swych a lady   godes moder be.

The first poem begins with the King of Kings choosing the maiden to be His mother and tells of the angel's announcement and Mary's question. However, omitting any account of the annunciation, this shorter poem begins (lines 1–2) with the fact of Mary's acceptance of the King of Kings to be her son. This beginning has the effect of transferring the sovereign choice which in the last poem was the King's to Mary in this poem, and Mary's choice initiates the movement of the poem. The rest of the poem develops the result of her choice, describing the quality of the King's response to it. He came to her as still as the dew in April, so still that while she became His mother, she remained a virgin. No other woman has had this unique prerogative. Well may such a lady be the mother of God.

What has been modified or omitted from the earlier version is a result of this poem's concentration on the single event in sacred history, the actual coming of the King. Omitted is direct reference to Mary's quality of sinlessness, to her descent from the tribe of Jesse, to the fact that the King's coming was to release man from sin and punishment. Instead, the poet develops the manner of the King's conception and birth, and by using several comparisons suggests the qualities of the "myden" through whom He was born. The context of sacred history is present by implication only, as the comparisons the poet chooses have their associations in liturgical and exegetical tradition.

> But is there any creature—except perhaps her who alone merited to have in herself this most blessed experience—is there, I ask, any creature capable of comprehending with his intellect or of discerning by his reason how the inaccessible Splendour of the Godhead poured Itself into the Virgin's womb, and how of that small portion of her body which It animated and united hypostatically to Itself, It made a shadow, as it were, for her whole being, in order that she might be able to endure the approach and the presence of such intolerable brightness? [19]

Among the possible denotations of the adverb "stylle" in Middle English, three are useful to us here. The most evident meaning is that He came without noise or commotion, quietly, silently.[20] "Stylle" might even connote a sense of motionlessness, to suggest that the King disturbed or changed nothing in the maiden with His coming. "Stylle" could also mean "secretly." If we think of the homilist and of St. Bernard's words above, this could suggest that He came mysteriously in a manner hidden to human reason; or if we think of the secular love song context, it could suggest that He came secretly, as a lover would steal to his lady's bower.[21] In the fourteenth and fifteenth centuries "still" (from Latin *destillare*) was used as a verb, meaning to trickle down or fall in minute drops, so that in these lines which compare His coming to the falling of dew, "stylle" by a play on words could reinforce the comparison.

"He cam also stylle . . . as dew in aprylle," the secular love setting of spring in "Nu þis fules singet" is adapted in this poem to suggest fertility,[22] the freshness of April rain that brings growth. But more fundamental are the associations with liturgical tradition, which, especially in Advent and on the Feast of the Annunciation, applies to the conception and birth of the Messiah the Old Testament figures of falling dew. Such is the passage from Isaiah, which contains all the connotations of fertility present in the poem and which was used as the Introit for the Feast of the Annunciation: "Drop down, ye heavens, from above, and let the skies pour down righteousness: let the earth open, and bring forth a saviour" (Isa. 45:8).[23] A second figure of falling dew was applied by the Office during Advent and on the Annunciation to the conception and birth of Christ. This is the figure from Judges 6:34–40 of the dew falling on Gideon's fleece, which was used also in the Prymer's antiphon for Prime: "Whanne he was born wundurfulliche of a maide, þanne was fulfillid holi writ. þou cam doun as reyn in-to a flees, for to make saaf mankynde."[24] In the selection of antiphons and especially in the sequences, these two figures were associated by the liturgy with the flowering of the rod of Jesse.[25]

But this poem is very unlike "Nu þis fules singet" in the way it uses traditional sources. Here the traditional attributes of Mary are not presented by narration, but by suggestion and association only, and the poem develops, as a modern poem might, by a series of accumulating associations. The simile of falling dew is repeated, with an incremental effect, three times,[26] and each time the poet develops the simile so that it reveals an aspect of the delicacy and beauty of her to whom Christ came.

First, with each repetition of "he cam also stylle," the poet indicates the nature of the place to which the King came. In line three it is presented as unspecified and without connotations: He came so quietly "þer his moder was." But in line five, the place is made more concrete: He came "to his moderes bowr," as a lover to her secret place. "Bowr" in its general sense denoted an inner room, a chamber or bedroom, and was especially applied to a lady's private apartment. It was also used figuratively to refer to Mary's womb or body.[27] This suggestion that Christ came as a lover would stir associations of the liturgy used during the summer months for Mary's feasts, where images from the Canticle of Canticles were applied to her—Mary was "my sister, my spouse," "a garden enclosed."[28]

In the third repetition, line seven, the King is seen to come closer to Mary's person, to "þer his moder lay." Being used to the many representations of the nativity in painting after the Council of Trent, one is apt to overlook that the thirteenth and fourteenth century manuscript illumination and sculpture of the nativity represented Mary as reclining. We see this, for example, in the nativity scene from the Tiptoft Missal (Figure 4). In the early fourteenth century East Anglian Psalter of Robert de Lisle (Figure 5), Mary is represented at the bottom of the illumination resting on a couch. Joseph sits beside her. Above her the Christ Child is lying on a box-like, altar-like cradle. Mary looks down and away from the Child. Above Christ are the ox and the ass and above them the star. Joseph, the Christ Child and the others look to the star. Another example of Mary reclining at the birth of Christ is included in a series of scenes around the tree of Jesse from the Gorleston Psalter, which is also early fourteenth century East Anglian.[29]

The place the King came to is developed more profoundly by the second part of the simile, the figure used for the place upon which the dew falls. Each figure seems to refer to Mary herself, so that in the three repetitions she is compared to the "gras," the "flour," and then the "spray." Besides its connotations in nature of fertility and delicacy, "gras" also has traditional liturgical associations with the Feast of the Annunciation, where it is used in a Vespers antiphon: "Orietur sicut sol Salvator mundi: et descendet in uterum virginis sicut ymber super gramen."[30] As well as the many applications of "flour" to Mary in art, from the great rose windows of the cathedrals to the lily of virginity traditionally present in illuminations and paintings of the annunciation "flour" suggests again the liturgy's use of the Canticle of Canticles in relation to Mary: "I am the flower of the field, and the lily of the valleys. As a lily among thorns, so is my love among the daughters."[31] In Middle English the word "spray" meant the small slender twigs of trees or shrubs and more particularly, in the early fifteenth century, a single twig. Because the poem is based on "Nu þis fules singet," and because of the liturgical association of Mary's descent from "gesses more" with her maiden motherhood, the readers of this poem have in general interpreted "spray" to refer to the blooming rod of Jesse.[32]

Thus in this accumulation of associations about the place to which the "kyng of alle kynges" came it is possible to see simultaneously in the King's coming both the coming of Christ to Mary in His conception by the Holy Spirit and the coming of Christ into the world at His birth. The poem can be read to describe either event. If we think of the poem so that the falling dew refers to the coming of the Holy Spirit, in the threefold repetition we see Him approach closer and closer to the mother—to the place, to her bower, to herself. Just as tradition sees in the fleece of Gideon a type of Mary's virginity, so the growing things on which the dew falls, "þe gras," "þe flour," "þe spray," can be seen to develop the same traditional application to Mary. On the other hand, if we read the series of developing figures as referring to the painless giving birth to Christ, we see Christ transforming the nature of His presence as He comes, from being the King, to being the Child of the maiden, Who comes to the place beside her, "þer his moder lay." The figures of the grass, the flower, the spray still suggest His conception and emphasize the delicacy and beauty of Mary, which remain inviolate.

In their analyses of "I syng of a myden þat is makeles," both Spitzer and Kane suggest that there is an inherent opposition between poetry and dogma. They believe this particular poem succeeds because it has moved beyond dogma to poetry, or, in Spitzer's words, beyond "the burden of Biblical lore. . . . We may conclude then that the simile of the dew, even though inspired by dogmatic literature, has been relived by this extraordinary poet who was able to give the pristine beauty of nature to a venerable scriptural concept."[33] Kane defines the opposition in terms of a contrast he finds between religious emotion or theology and the imagination. In the body of the poem (lines 3–8):

> Not the intellect but the imagination is invoked, required to comprehend the magnitude of the contrast between the greatness of the "kyng of alle kynges" and the silence of his arrival in "his moderes bowr" . . . A great restraint is imposed in this part of the poem; there are no superlatives, no expressions of the poet's own emotion, no intrusions of his personality. The emphatic statement is reserved for the last stanza, which returns to the theme of the first, the maiden's matchlessness and the reason for it. Out of this assertion the plain words of that last stanza, tremendous in their implications, create a climax that is intensified not only by the theology of the doctrine and the faith that enlivens it, but also by the emotions, aesthetic and personal,

> which the imaginative portion of the poem have excited. . . . *The Maiden Makeles* is, in my opinion, an instance of the ideal religious lyric, that farthest removed from the expression of homily or doctrine or devotion with tags and tricks of poetry attached to it.[34]

It seems to me that by assuming the distinction between the opening and closing sections of the poem and the central section to be that of intellect and imagination, Kane separates the poem into three "themes," whereas the poem is actually a unified conception explaining why the maiden is "makeles." The imagination is used in all three sections. In the first, it is used to consider the quality of the maid and her choice, and the power and implications of the King of Kings Whom the listener identifies as a figure for Christ in majesty as contrasted to Christ the son of one of His creatures. In the second, the listener considers a fact which is the result and purpose of the rest and yet which is itself a sign of the literal identity of the King and the maiden. To discover this is all a use of the imagination, which associates the figures with the truth being related in the poem. The main difference between the opening and closing sections and the central part of the poem is that by the poet's repeating yet varying a series of figures, in the central part of the poem the delight the listeners' senses feel in their proportion and variety is perhaps more intense. Yet to isolate this section from the total context would be to cut the delight off from its total reflection of the beauty of the mystery of the virgin birth, which gives the section its meaning and larger purpose.

The modern critics' habit of contrasting intellect and imagination and of considering content and form as separable aspects of a poem is not adequate for approaching the Middle English religious lyric, for the proportions and effect of these poems issue directly *from* their subject matter. This point will be more fully illustrated by the following studies. Formulating a criterion by which a lyric can be considered good or bad must wait until Part III, after a fuller consideration of the poetry has given a fuller experience with the subject matter and proportions of the poems.

Gloria in Excelsis Deo

Lullay, lullay, la lullay, Mi dere moder, lullay

[I]

Als i lay vp-on a nith
Alone in my longging,
Me þouthe i sau a wonder sith,
A maiden child rokking.

[II]

Þe maiden wolde with-outen song
Hire child o slepe bringge;
Þe child þouthte sche dede him wrong,
& bad his moder sengge.

FIG. 5.—The Birth of Christ and the First Events of His Childhood. Miniature from the Psalter of Robert de Lisle, British Museum, Arundel MS 83, fol. 124. Composed of six corresponding yet contrasting scenes, the folio illustrates an iconic and symmetrical proportioning of narrative similar to that of "Als i lay vp-on a nith." For more extended discussion, refer to the Notes to Illustrations.

[III]

"Sing nov, moder," seide þat child,
"Wat me sal be-falle
Here after wan i cum to eld—
So don modres alle.

[IV]

Ich a moder treuly
Þat kan hire credel kepe
Is wone to lullen louely
& singgen hire child o slepe.

[V]

Suete moder, fair & fre,
Siþen þat it is so,
I preye þe þat þu lulle me
& sing sum-wat þer-to."

[VI]

"Suete sone," seyde sche,
"Wer-offe suld i singge?
Wist i neuere ȝet more of þe
But gabrieles gretingge.

[VII]

He grette me godli on is kne
& seide, 'heil! marie.
Ful of grace, god is with þe;
Beren þu salt Messye.'

[VIII]

I wondrede michil in my þouth,
for man wold i rith none.
'Marie,' he seide, 'drede þe nouth;
Lat god of heuene alone.

[IX]

Þe holi gost sal don al þis.'
He seyde with-outen wone
Þat i sulde beren mannis blis,
Þe my suete sone.

[X]

He seide, 'þu salt beren a king
In king dauit-is see,
In al Iacobs woniing
Þer king suld he be.'

[XI]

He seyde þat elizabetʒ,
Þat baraine was be-fore,
A child conceyued hatʒ—
'To me leue þu þe more.'

[XII]

I ansuerede bleþely,
For his word me paiʒede:
'Lo! godis seruant her am i!
Be et as þu me seyde.'

[XIII]

Þer, als he seide, i þe bare
On midwenter nith,
In maydened with-outen kare,
Be grace of god almith.

[XIV]

Þe sepperdis þat wakkeden in þe wolde
Herden a wonder mirthe
Of angles þer, as þei tolde,
In time of þi birthe.

[XV]

Suete sone, sikirly
no more kan i say;
& if i koude fawen wold i,
To don al at þi pay."

[XVI]

"Moder," seide þat suete þing,
"To singen I sal þe lere
Wat me fallet to suffring,
& don wil i am here.

[XVII]

Wanne þe seuene daiȝes ben don,
Rith as habraham wasce,
Kot sal i ben with a ston
In a wol tendre place.

[XVIII]

Wanne þe tuelue dayȝes ben do,
Be leding of a stere
Þre kingges me sul seke þo
With gold, ensens, & mirre.

[XIX]

Þe fourti day, to fille þe lawe,
We solen to temple i-fere;
Þer simeon sal þe sey a sawe
Þat changen sal þi chere.

[XX]

Wan i am tuelue ȝer of elde,
Ioseph & þu, murningge,
Solen me finden, moder milde,
In þe temple techingge.

[XXI]

Til i be þretti at þe leste
I sal neuere fro þe suerue,
But ay, moder, ben at þin heste,
Ioseph & þe to serue.

[XXII]

Wan þe þretti ȝer ben spent,
I mot be-ginne to fille
Wer-fore i am hidre sent,
Þoru my fadres wille.

[XXIII]

Ion baptist of merite most
Sal baptize me be name;
Þan my fader & þe holi gost
Solen witnessen wat i ame.

[XXIV]

I sal ben tempted of satan,
Þat fawen is to fonde,
Þe same wise þat was Adam,
but i sal betre with-stonde.

[XXV]

Disciples i sal gadere
& senden hem for to preche,
Þe lawes of my fader,
In al þis werld to teche.

[XXVI]

I sal ben so simple
& to men so conning
Þat most partiȝe of þe puple
Sal wiln maken me king."

[XXVII]

"Suete sone," þan seyde sche,
"No sorwe sulde me dere,
Miht i ȝet þat day se
A king þat þu were."

[XXVIII]

"Do wey, moder," seide þat suete,
"Þerfor kam i nouth,
But for to ben pore & bales bete,
Þat man was inne brouth.

[XXIX]

Þerfore wan to & þretti ʒer ben don
& a litel more,
Moder, þu salt maken michil mon
& seen me deyʒe sore.

[XXX]

Þe sarpe swerde of simeon
Perse sal þin herte,
For my care of michil won
Sore þe sal smerte.

[XXXI]

Samfuly for i sal deyʒe,
Hangende on þe rode,
For mannis ransoun sal i payʒe
Myn owen herte blode."

[XXXII]

"Allas! sone," seyde þat may,
"Siþen þat it is so,
Worto sal i biden þat day
To beren þe to þis wo?"

[XXXIII]

"Moder," he seide, "tak et lithte,
For liuen i sal a-ȝeyne,
& in þi kinde þoru my mith,
for elles i wrouthte in weyne.

[XXXIV]

To my fader I sal wende
In myn manhed to heuene;
Þe holigost i sal þe sende
With hise sondes seuene.

[XXXV]

I sal þe taken wan time is
to me at þe laste,
to ben with me moder in blis—
Al þis þan haue i caste.

[XXXVI]

Al þis werld demen i sal,
at þe dom risingge,
Suete moder, here is al
Þat i wile nou singge."

[XXXVII]

Serteynly, þis sithte i say,
Þis song i herde singge,
Als i lay þis ȝolis-day
Alone in my longingge.

"ALS I LAY VP-ON A NITH"

> Thus the whole world is described in a most orderly sequence by Scripture as proceeding from beginning to end, in accordance with the peculiar beauty of its well-designed song. One can view, following the sequence of time, the variety, multiplicity and symmetry, order, rectitude and beauty of the many judgments proceeding from the wisdom of God governing the world. As no one can see the beauty of a song unless his view extends over the whole verse, so no one sees the beauty of the order and governance of the universe unless he beholds the whole of it. Because no man is so long-lived that he can see the whole of it with the eyes of the flesh and because no man can foresee the future by himself, the Holy Ghost has provided man with Holy Scripture, the length of which is measured by the extent of the universe.[1]

WE HAVE SEEN THAT SACRED HISTORY, DEFINED BY THEOLOGY AND BASED ON Scripture, is the account of two creations, the creation of the world and of Adam and Eve, and Adam's rejection of God and fall from grace; the re-creation, or reformation, of all things by Christ, as history prepared for and witnessed the birth, life, death and resurrection of its Redeemer. We have seen, because the second creation is the reformation of the first, that the events of sacred history bear a symmetrical relationship to each other, as events of the second creation are applied to and transfigure the events of the old. Christ in becoming man is the second Adam, Mary the second Eve. We have seen, finally, that besides the symmetrical proportioning, there is a hierarchical value among events in relation to the Incarnation. As history approaches closer and closer to the appearance of Christ, it grows closer to its fulfillment, its reunion with God.

In reading "Gabriel, fram evene-king" which celebrates a single one of the events in sacred history, we found these same proportions. The event of the annunciation was told in such a way that it reflected, through the figure of the maiden mother, the total course of sacred history, from the fall of man, to Christ's resurrection and ascension, and, finally, to man's own future entry into heaven. And we found that the meaning of the poem depended partly upon the relationship between events as arranged proportionally to each other by the sequence of stanzas: the painless birth, applied to man's release through the pain of Christ's death, gave man rebirth from the pain of Adam's sin.

But the definition of the beauty of sacred history is incomplete unless it includes the achievement of its purpose, the restoration of man's delight. In "Gabriel, fram evene-king," the petition in the last stanza reflected this purpose. As man, living now, joined to Christ in the Church, the poet and his audience looked back from the present and, in virtue of both past and present, expressed hope for a future which had been foretold and prefigured, but which still awaited consummation.

From this point of view in the present, looking back with the poet and his audience, we are able to see the beauty of the plan of sacred history. We see not only the ordered relationships of the sequence of its events, but its end, the ultimate transformation of pain to joy. The beauty of this transformation reflects the goodness and wisdom of the Creator and is the basis of praise.

The next poem to be discussed organizes the events of sacred history in terms of their end in joy. For mankind seen in the light of sacred history, the experiences of joy and sorrow have very specific definition. Sorrow as defined by theology is the loss of God and the physical and spiritual pain resulting from it. Man's joy is his union with God in the beatific vision of heaven. The fulness of joy, or delight, is relative to the degree of closeness of man's union with God.

The sin of Adam and Eve was the beginning of all man's sorrow. It caused an infinite gulf between God and man. Only the infinite God could join the gap. In His incarnation, Christ, both God and man, took on Himself all the suffering caused by sin. Christ's crucifixion and death released man from the bondage to sin through Adam and reunited man to God. Thus the annunciation of Christ's coming is called the beginning of joy. But the reunion is as yet unconsummated. After Christ rose from the dead, the choice between separation from God and eternal suffering or union with God and eternal joy has been given to the power of the individual's free will, as each soul works out his salvation. Because the value of the suffering of Christ is infinite, man has as many possibilities to reject sorrow and accept joy as the moments he has to live and to decide.

Sorrow, then, after the Incarnation, when it is formulated by theology, has two possible definitions. It may be the absolute sorrow that comes from the loss of eternal joy because of sin. This is the sorrow expressed in the Middle English poems of penitence. Or, on the other hand, it may be a relative sorrow, which, springing from a limited view of suffering, makes the suffering appear to be absolute. The restricted view cuts the sufferer off from awareness that the final experience of history is transfiguring joy. This restricted view is natural to humanity. It can be widened only by the point of view of Divinity.

We have seen that Mary is the medium for the coming of God into history, and that being the one through whom heaven was reopened, she replaces Eve through whom heaven was lost. Just as Christ takes on the pains of man to give him rebirth, so Mary, spiritually suffering Christ's pains, becomes the spiritual mother of man. In "Gabriel, fram evene-king," Mary, having been assumed into heaven, was appealed to as she is now, from the point of view of present time. Being the creature closest to God, she was seen as man's intercessor as well as the sign of his joy. Yet even in heaven her spiritual motherhood, since man still suffers, can still cause her sorrow. It is sorrow because of her bond with man that, for example, is the subject of the fourteenth century "Quia amore langueo":

> I byd, I byde in grete longyng,
> I loue, I loke when man woll craue,
> I pleyne for pyte of peynyng [2]

However, just as every man during this life has imperfect vision, so Mary, the human mother of God, was subject during her life on earth to seeing what happened under its limited aspect of joy or sorrow. As a human mother, Mary's sorrow was greatest for her Son. We shall see, in Part II, that the poet uses Mary's limited human view as the source of drama in the poems on the compassion of Mary. In these poems, the poet will focus on the pains of Christ and exclude the implications of the future joyful outcome of the crucifixion, until the suffering portrayed reaches a great degree of intensity. In this way his poem can reflect the immensity of the consequences of sin which caused such pain, and through this knowledge it can turn man's heart towards Christ.

Yet Mary's experience of the events during her life was not defined solely by the limitation of her own viewpoint. The matter is more complex. Her experience of joy and sorrow was fundamentally related to the fact that the events of sacred history themselves have the double potentiality of joy and sorrow depending upon how wide the context is in which they are presented. Thus, in the lyrics about Mary, each of the events of her life with her Son may be presented either in the light of joy or in the light of sorrow. The events are joyful when they look towards her Son's final glory, which is the source of her own and of mankind's joy, or they are sorrowful when they look towards her Son's passion. Shown by the poet in its joyful aspect, Christ's birth will be described as the coming of the Messiah: seen in its mortal poverty and humility, it will be shown to foreshadow His crucifixion.

The fact that the outcome of sacred history is ultimately joyful always has the power to transfigure sorrow to joy. In the poems on Mary's compassion at the crucifixion, for example, the poet will often transfigure the present sorrow by introducing into his poem Christ's resurrection, ascension and Mary's assumption. It is especially the dialogues between Christ and Mary, or Christ and man, or Mary and man, that are structured by this metamorphosis of sorrow to joy. The dialogues of the mother of God with her Son are dialogues between the limited view of humanity and the omniscience of God. We shall see that it is theology's formulation of the plan of sacred history that provides the poet with the Divine perspective.

The next poem to be discussed is a dialogue between the Blessed Virgin and her Child from the preaching book compiled in 1372 by Friar John of Grimestone.[3] The manuscript is an extensive and varied collection of Latin theological materials arranged by subject, with Latin and English poetry interspersed. There are short verses, moral lyrics, paraphrases and songs. Among the selection of poems from it in Carleton Brown's *Religious Lyrics of the Fourteenth Century* are dialogues and laments spoken by Christ and Mary.

The group of poems about the nativity and the group about the passion can illustrate for us the double potentiality the events have for sorrow or joy. Of those on the nativity, one (Brown, No. 57) is simply a song in praise of

Christ's birth, which relates how the words of the angel to Mary, the words of the prophets, the angels' song, the visit of the Magi, all manifested that the Child was God; but then, in contrast, how cruelly He was put to death for man's sake. Another (No. 58) has Joseph speak, "a man of þe elde lawe," who testifies to Mary's virginal conception and giving birth. The poem contrasts Christ's poverty at His birth to the kingly nature of His Father in heaven. There are three poems about the poverty of Christ in His cradle. One (No. 59) is a lament by man because he is the cause of Christ's suffering. One (No. 65), prompted by the idea of the Christ Child weeping in the cradle, rues the suffering Christ will have and, in order to appeal to man to repent, describes His passion. In the last one (No. 75), first Christ, shivering with cold, tells man to learn to love as He loves, and then Mary addressing Christ, laments that she cannot help Him now or at His passion.

For the most part these poems see Christ's birth as it foreshadows His passion. They dwell on Christ's suffering to stir as sense of sorrow and repentence in the listener. The innocent child embodies Christ's innocence. By juxtaposing His passion to His nativity, relating the passion to an innocent child, a poet could dramatically illustrate the injustice of Christ's suffering.

"Als i lay vp-on a nith" (No. 56) uses all the principles I have mentioned. The dramatic basis of the poem is the limitation of Mary's point of view as she hears of her Son's life and death. The poet uses the second joy of Mary, the event of Christ's nativity, as it contains the potentiality for both joy and sorrow, and he organizes the events of the Incarnation as each reveals the glory or the suffering of Christ.

The Child tells His own story. Throughout the tale because her perspective is limited, Mary repeatedly mistakes the significance of an event. Each sorrow and each joy she hears of only foreshadows a later moment, which she will suffer or rejoice in, with increasing intensity, until she finally comprehends the joyful outcome of events. Through the course of the telling, her initial limited understanding is transformed by the Child, until she can recognize the full implications of what His godhood means for herself and for man.

The listeners' view is limited rhetorically by the poem to that of Mary. Although, like Christ in the poem and like the author, the audience has a knowledge of the whole, through watching the events of Christ's life unfold as they are presented to Mary, they see the plan in a new, limited way, as she saw it for the first time. Yet the fact that the listeners remain simultaneously aware of the total plan of sacred history adds an ironic dimension to the poem. As Christ first asks Mary to recount to Him His future, they immediately anticipate the pain that will be caused her if this seemingly happy request is fulfilled, and they sympathize with the sorrow that Mary, who is now unaware, will feel. They wonder at the motives with which the Christ Child asks to know, since the knowledge will make His mother suffer. At the same time, they see the irony of the Child's own situation, that He asks to hear, a future not of joy, as one would hope for a child, but a future of crucifixion and death. If the listener projects his thoughts beyond, however, he will also think of the ultimately joyous outcome, when Christ will return in glory.

The Setting

Als i lay vp-on a nith
Alone in my longging,
Me þouthe i sau a wonder sith,
A maiden child rokking.

The poem is set in a vision framework, to translate the listeners to another time and place, to a "maiden" rocking a child.[4] The paradox of mother and maid is not emphasized, but is one of the accepted mysteries of the vision. The presence of a maiden rocking her child leads the listener to expect her to sing a lullaby. Paradoxically, however, the maid has desired to make her Child sleep without a song. Then, incongruously to the expectations formed by the setting, it is the Child who speaks from His cradle. He will sing His own lullaby. The incongruity of the Infant speaking is an incongruity potential to every act of Christ because of the fact that He is God and both the source and the object of all human action. As God, He conceives Himself through Mary. Here as God He will tell His own story, and as God He will transform His own sorrow to joy.

Voicing the listeners' expectation of hearing a lullaby, the Child says that since mothers are wont to tell their children what will happen to them, and that since every good mother sings her child to sleep, so also should His mother sing Him to sleep with the same tale. Replying that she knows only what the events leading up to the present moment of His birth foretell, His mother begins to sing of those. The listeners' perspective is narrowed to hers, to her joy as it must have been at Christ's birth with the words of Gabriel in her heart and the angel's prophecy of the Messiah confirmed by the fact of her painless giving birth to the Child.

The Foretelling

Mary's Tale: The Proposal; The Acceptance and Birth

He grette me godli on is kne
& seide, "Heil! marie.
Ful of grace, god is with þe;
Beren þu salt Messye."

The poet begins the story of the Child's life by having Mary tell what the angel said to her. The Gospel account of the annunciation is used, but in contrast to the first two poems discussed, it is used to emphasize the prophetic aspect of the angel's words to Mary. You shall bear the Messiah, the Savior of mankind.

I wondrede michil in my þouth,
for man wold i rith none.
"Marie," he seide, "drede þe nouth;
Lat god of heuene alone.

Þe holi gost sal don al þis."
He seyde with-outen wone
Þat i sulde beren mannis blis,
Þe my suete sone.

As in "Gabriel, fram evene-king," the angel's salutation contains both the greeting and the prophecy of Mary's motherhood and Mary is puzzled about how she, a virgin, shall conceive. By emphasizing that it is the God of heaven alone, the Holy Ghost, by Whom she shall conceive, the angel reassures her. She shall give birth "with-outen wone," outside the law of women; that is, without pain.[5]

In lines 35–36 which follow this phrase, because of her limited understanding, Mary makes her first error of interpretation. Not yet knowing the full meaning of the angel's prophecy as history will fulfill it, she identifies "mannis blis" with the immediate joy of "þe my suete sone," the Infant lying before her. It will not be until her Child tells her of His resurrection and final heavenly glorification that she will fully comprehend "mannis blis."

> He seide, "þu salt beren a king
> In king dauit-is see,
> In al Iacobs woniing
> Þer king suld he be."

In contrast to the other poems, here, where the significant events in the life of Christ will be related one by one, the poet has the angel develop the messianic significance of Mary's Child. His words prophesy Christ's kingship: You shall bear a king for David's throne—David's see—Who shall be king over all the house of Jacob.[6] The angel then gives the sign to Mary, also in the Gospel account, which will provide her with proof of his words: If barren Elizabeth can conceive, so must you believe what I say is true. And, in Stanza XII, Mary tells how, believing and pleased, she accepted.

In the next four stanzas, Mary recounts to her Son how the angel's prophecy was fulfilled. As the angel had said, Mary bore her Child without pain. Not only this, but at the time of His birth the Shepherds heard the angels rejoicing that He was the Messiah. These two facts testify to the truth of the angel's words, and in joy Mary finishes her account of her conception and giving birth. Now she can tell her Child no more. But in the same way as she had not fully comprehended "mannis blis" in the preceding stanzas, so here, she mistakes Christ's birth itself for the full accomplishment of the joy she will comprehend only in Stanzas XXXIV–XXXVI.

> "Moder," seide þat suete þing,
> "To singen I sal þe lere
> Wat me fallet to suffring,
> & don wil i am here.

Christ from the cradle then begins to instruct His mother. As the Son of God Who already has the view of His whole life, what He says establishes the tension in the poem between Mary's joy and her sorrow. Immediately He contradicts her joyous view by speaking of the events of His life as "What it befalls Me to suffer and do while I am here." Although in its relationship to the phrase "& don," "to suffring" suggests the meaning, what He will undergo or experience, the verb carries with it in Middle English all the connotations of injury, punishment and death, especially when it is applied to Christ. The poet uses it here in direct contrast to Mary's joy and to introduce the idea of pain. Pain is the theme of the events the Child tells next: those which foreshadow His crucifixion.

Christ's Tale: Childhood

The next five stanzas tell of four events of Christ's childhood. Each stanza is introduced with a measure of time, and each stanza has a twofold purpose. The first is to present an element of suffering which foreshadows His passion and reflects also Mary's coming sorrow. The second is to use each event to point to the Child as the Messiah, either as He fulfills the law or as He is singled out as the Son of God.[7] When the seven days "ben don," the Child begins, He will suffer pain as He fulfills the law of Abraham by being circumcised, cut in a "wol tendre place." When twelve days have passed, He continues, the three kings, led by a star, will seek Him with their gifts of gold, frankincense, and myrrh.[8] Implicit is the homilist's interpretation of their visit as the testimony of the gentiles that the Child is King, Priest and Messiah.[9] After forty days, again in order to fulfill the law, the Child says, He will be presented in the Temple. Simeon will recognize Him as the Glory he has waited in old age to see, and he will prophesy. The Child does not say explicitly that Simeon's prophecy will be of a sword of sorrow that will pierce Mary's heart (Luke 2:34–35), but suggests it by contrasting the sword's effect of sorrow to Mary's present joy: Simeon's "sawe . . . changen sal þi chere."

The final event the Child foretells will happen when He is twelve years old and teaches the elders in the Temple. The Gospel account (Luke 2:41–52) relates this story from Mary and Joseph's view, how, losing their Child after spending the Passover in Jerusalem, they return and search for Him for three days. When they find Him teaching in the Temple, Mary rebukes Him: "Son, why hast thou done so to us? Behold thy father and I have sought thee sorrowing." But He replies to them: "How is it that you sought me? Did you not know that I must be about my father's business?"

(See lines 48–49.) His reply asserts His primary purpose on earth, to do the will of His Father.

The Gospel account ends: "And he went down with them and came to Nazareth and was subject to them. And his mother kept all these words in her heart. And Jesus advanced in wisdom and age and grace with God and men" (Luke 2:51–52). In paraphrasing it, the account in the poem transforms what in the Gospel is a summary of Christ's childhood years into a prophecy which summarizes the rest of His childhood: saying that until Christ is "þretti at þe leste" (Luke 3:23), He will be obedient to His mother and Joseph. As well as being a prediction, Christ's words in the poem have the effect of a reply and reassurance for Mary's rebuke. It is as if He intends to assuage Mary's sorrow, the sorrow of both the Mary He will hurt at that future time and the Mary to whom He now talks from the cradle, whom He is causing by his tale to suffer everything in anticipation of the events.

Christ's Tale: The Divine Mission Begins

The next five stanzas, as complement to His human childhood, recount the divine mission of Christ's manhood, as He begins to fulfill His purpose, to redeem man. Lines eighty-five through eighty-eight fulfill the previous quatrain and act as a transition. Then the four aspects of His mission are described which lead towards the fulfilling of the prophecy that He is the Messiah. The first event the Child tells of shows He is the Son of God. He will be baptized by His forerunner John, and the form of a dove will appear and the Voice will testify, "Thou art my beloved Son. In thee I am well pleased" (Luke 3:21–22). The next event He recounts is how He will withstand the Devil. As Adam was, so Christ will be tempted by Satan, but unlike Adam, Christ will resist the temptation (Luke 4:1–13). And next, the Child relates how He will establish His Church, gathering disciples to teach His Father's law over the whole world. And then, finally, He tells how His simplicity and knowledge will attract the people, so that most of them will desire to make Him King.

Mary's Response of Joy, the Contradiction

At this point Mary bursts out in joy. Yet again she has mistaken a limited joy for full joy, and ignoring the prediction of sorrow present earlier in her

Son's description of His childhood, she says, Sweet Son, no sorrow should ever injure me if I could see that day on which You would be King. The poem arrives at the climax of the opposition between sorrow and joy. To Mary the kingship her Son foretells seems truly to fulfill what the angel of the annunciation had prophesied, and she rejoices. But her joy would have intense ironic overtones for the audience of the poem; for, being ignorant of the rest of His story, Mary does not realize what is entailed before her desire for her Son's future glory can be fulfilled. Before Christ finally ascends into His true kingship of heaven, He must undergo all the sorrow His humanity will suffer on earth.

Although, in Stanza XXVI, the Child had seemed to predict His kingship, His words to Mary had been carefully qualified: the "most partiȝe" of the people, but not all, "sal wiln," shall desire to, but not actually make Him king. In Stanza XXVIII Christ reproves Mary for her false assumption, and the next three stanzas (lines 113–124) plunge her into sorrow. In words which echo His correction, in Stanza XVI, of Mary's joy at His birth, Christ contradicts her statement that no sorrow would ever injure her: "Do wey, moder," he says, it was not for this I came, but to be poor and to amend man's sorrow. Therefore, when two or more years of My mission have been accomplished, contrary to what you have said, you will mourn much and see Me die a cruel death.

The Child foretells His death in terms of the suffering Mary will experience. Taking up Simeon's words that Mary "changen sal þi chere," He explains first that the change she will experience will be from joy to sadness. The figure of the sword piercing her heart, present in Luke's account but which the Child had omitted from His own, is here introduced and interpreted in relation to His passion. The sword to pierce Mary's heart will be the abundant compassion she will suffer at His own great pain, for, the Child starkly reveals, He will hang shamefully on the cross:

> Samfuly for i sal deyȝe,
> Hangende on þe rode,
> For mannis ransoun sal i payȝe
> Myn owen herte blode.

For the ransoming of man I shall pay the blood of My own heart. This is not a figurative statement, because Mary will witness her Son's heart pierced by a lance. Out of this blood and water, the Church would spring.[10] Mary could not have imagined that from the birth she gave to her Child "with-outen wone" would come this "care of michil won," the rebirth of man in exchange for the blood of her Son's heart.

Now is the moment of Mary's greatest sorrow, the deepest contradiction of the joy she felt at her Son's birth. Mary's view takes her no further. She is fixed to the moment of her Son's death. Alas, she says, Why shall I endure that day, to bear Thee for that woe? The context of their dialogue seems ultimately tragic.

Mary's Response of Sorrow, the Transformation

"Allas! sone," seyde þat may,
"Siþen þat it is so,
 Worto sal i biden þat day
 To beren þe to þis wo?"

But Mary is again mistaken. Just as, in the previous section, her joy at Christ's earthly kingship had the implications of not being final, so here, her sorrow at the crucifixion contains implications of its outcome in joy. Mary has focused on His suffering only, but the Child had suggested that the giving of His heart's blood for man's ransom from pain was part of a higher purpose.

"Moder," he seide, "tak et lithte,
 For liuen i sal a-ȝeyne,
 & in þi kinde þoru my mith,
 for elles i wrouthte in weyne.

Christ replies to her outburst, and asserts the power of His godhood over the suffering of His humanity: Mother, bear this lightly, for I shall live again and in your nature through my power. His words foretell His resurrection as a renewal of His birth in human nature, and He replies to Mary's despairing question from the preceding stanza, Why did I bear You if it is to such a death?, by affirming: Or else I have wrought in vain.

The point of Mary's greatest suffering is when Christ suffers most and when He seems least powerful, when He seems, in fact, to die. But this is also the moment when the Child asserts His godhood most fully. With His assertion He transforms the moment. The last section moves from passion to action, as the Child goes on to tell how He shall return to His Father in His human nature, to heaven. He shall send the Holy Ghost with His seven gifts. And when Mary's time comes to die, He shall take Mary with Him to be a mother in heaven. All this He has planned. With these words, the angel's prophecy at the annunciation is fulfilled joyously and completely.

We have reached the moment in the events of sacred history from which the poet himself speaks and in which his audience hears the poem. Just as the Child tells Mary what will happen after her own death, so, in the last stanza, He foretells the last judgment, when He will come again as King and Judge and in virtue of His resurrection all men will rise from the dead. Here the Child stops speaking. The poet takes his listeners out of the context of his dream vision, into the reality of the occasion on which the vision took place, as in the last verse he specifies the context of the first:

> Serteynly, þis sithte i say,
> Þis song i herde singge,
> Als i lay þis ȝolis-day
> Alone in my longingge.

The time is the festival of Christmas. The fact that the listeners now celebrate the event of the nativity testifies that the birth of the Child has in fact occurred, that the story foretold has happened, that the Child was God; that sorrow, solitude and longing have been turned into joy, that the Child and His mother are now in heaven together in joy. The listeners can rejoice in hope for themselves and praise the mother and the Child as they have revealed the beauty of God's plan.

The Structure

From this summary of the poem, it is possible, as did the poet and his audience, to look back on the story told by the mother and Child and to see in it a certain order and beauty of proportion. So regular do the proportions appear to be that they enable us to divide the poem into exact units, which may well reflect the units of melody to which the song was set. If we omit the opening and closing frame quatrains, leaving them to be a special introduction and an echoing conclusion, the poem falls naturally into seven groups of five stanzas.[11] These units of five quatrains, in turn, can be seen to be ordered by their subject matter into, first, a unit of five stanzas which gives the setting and, then, three groups of ten stanzas each which recount the life of Christ. This grouping by subject matter has been represented above by the headings given to the poem's analysis. Correspondences between the organization of the different stages of the telling and the repetition of certain patterns of phrasing support the proportions in the poem made apparent by the subject matter.

The introductory five quatrains (II–VI) provide the lullaby setting and prepare for Mary's singing of the annunciation and birth of her Son. In the first group of ten stanzas (VII–XVI), Mary tells her part of the tale. In the first unit of five within this group (VII–XI) she relates the proposal, the angel's greeting and prophecy of the Messiah; and in the second unit (XII–XVI) she relates the fulfillment of the proposal, her acceptance and the consequent birth of Christ. She ends her tale in a spirit of joy. "He grette me godli on is kne" in the first unit is responded to by "I ansuerede bleþely" in the second. And corresponding to the last of the introductory stanzas (VI), this first group of ten quatrains ends with a quatrain (XVI) that leads into the next part, as Christ says He will tell of what in His life He will suffer and do. Christ's tale occupies the second and third group of ten stanzas.

The second group (XVII–XXVI) divides also into two units of five quatrains each. The first five (XVII–XXI) tell of Christ's childhood, ending with His promise of obedience to Mary and Joseph until "i be þretti at þe leste." Each stanza of the five tells of one event. Each opens with a phrase indicating an interval of time: "Wanne þe seuene daiȝes ben don," "Wanne þe tuelue dayȝes ben do," "Þe fourti day, to fille þe lawe," "Wan i am tuelue ȝer of elde," "Til i be þretti at þe leste." Complementary to the first, the second unit of five stanzas (XXII–XXVI), beginning "Wan þe þretti ȝer ben spent," tells of Christ's manhood. As the stanzas recount the acts of His divine mission, they develop the promise of His childhood and bring Christ's tale to the moment when the people desire to make Him king. At this point, Mary interrupts her Child's story with her second expression of joy. In the same way as in this group's first unit of five, in the second unit each stanza tells of one event, and each stanza repeats a phrase, "I sal."

The last group of ten stanzas (XXVII–XXXVI) shows Christ's contradiction of Mary's joy and her sorrow at its extreme; then it counterbalances her sorrow with Christ's account of the ultimately joyful outcome of events. In the first unit of five (XXVII–XXXI) the sorrow is told. "Do wey moder,"

Christ contradicts Mary's "Suete sone," and then He tells how she will suffer at His crucifixion. His explanation of why she will suffer begins with a phrase which echoes the phrase introducing each of the events of His mission, "Þerfore wan to & þretti ȝer ben don," and reinforces the idea in the preceding stanza that the Child's suffering is the true way in which His mission will be fulfilled. In the first stanza of the second and final unit of five (XXXII–XXXVI), Mary cries out in despair that she ever gave birth; whereupon Christ counters with a prediction of His resurrection and of man's glory (XXXIII–XXXVI). The despairing " 'Allas! sone,' seyde þat may" is countered by " 'Moder,' he seide." Christ's foretelling of the glorious events of His life continues to recall the manner in which He recounted His mission. After Christ foretells ultimate joy, the poem concludes with the frame quatrain (XXXVII), which makes explicit the setting of the vision on "ȝolis-day."

With a cursory reading, one might classify "Als i lay vp-on a nith" as an example of the religious lyrics which, in Kane's terms, would seem to recede into a common background of indistinguishable accounts of the life of Christ.[12] However, it can be seen from the summary of the poem and of its proportions that through the dialogue of God with man, the poet is reflecting in his poem the beauty of the transformation in history of man's pain into joy, the beauty of the Incarnation.

There are two principles of proportion by which the poet organizes this transformation. As in the case of "Gabriel, fram evene-king," both are also principles of proportion in the events of sacred history. The first is that the poet presents the Incarnation in the form of the fulfillment of truth. The poem develops as the recounting of a series of three prophecies and fulfillments: the annunciation of "mannis blis," fulfilled by the birth of Christ and ultimately by His resurrection and ascension to glory; the prophecy of Simeon, fulfilled by the crucifixion; and the angel's prophecy of Christ's kingship, first falsely seeming to be fulfilled by the Child's account of Palm Sunday and then truly fulfilled by the Child's foretelling of His return in glory at the last judgment.

The first principle of proportion, the fulfillment of truth, works in relation to the second, the dramatic fulfillment of desire. The movement of the poem is not controlled, as it was in "Gabriel, fram evene-king" by the objective sequence of events in history, but by the minds conceiving it. There is first of all the point of view of Mary; the principle revealing the symmetry of events is the reflection of joy and sorrow in Mary's heart, in a progression which reveals more and more the full implications of the manhood and godhood of her Child, as her pain and joy grow more intense. Although the movement of the poem is controlled by the perspective of Mary, the perspective of the listeners from the first transcends what she knows. They see the events more from the point of view of the Child, Who has knowledge of the whole.

The poem begins in the spirit of Mary's joy at Christ's birth. This incomplete joy is countered by Christ's story of the pain present in the events of His childhood, but reestablished by the foretelling of His mission, which ends with the telling of a second, but also incomplete joy, His Palm Sunday kingship. To Mary's second mistaken rejoicing, Christ replies in a way that plunges her into deepest sorrow; only again to raise her, with the account of His resurrection, ascension and of her own assumption, to a comprehension of fullest joy. Thus the poem moves from joy to joy, in three stages: first, from an initial limited joy; then, counter to suggested sorrow, to a second deeper but misconceived joy; then finally, counter to the experience of most intense sorrow, to the comprehension of ultimate joy.

Given these two principles of structure in the poem, if in our mind's eye—in the same way as we juxtaposed the individual stanzas of "Gabriel, fram evene-king"—we exclude the introductory five quatrains and place the three groups of ten stanzas which recount the life of Christ side by side, we can see that the development of the narrative is symmetrically proportioned according to the units of five stanzas. Within each group of ten stanzas, the first and second units of five contrast, yet complement each other. Thus the first five quatrains in each group develop Mary's experience of sorrow, while they also prefigure or prepare for the second unit of five stanzas; the second five quatrains, while fulfilling the events related in the first unit, contrary to the first develop Mary's experience of joy. The principle of structure corresponds to that found in the Psalter of Robert de Lisle. (See Figure 5 and its descriptive note.)

We can see the proportion established in the first group of ten stanzas (VII–XVI). The first unit of five presents the story of the annunciation of Christ's birth. The annunciation contains the prophecy of joy in the words "mannis blis." Yet latent in the prophecy is sorrow. The words "with-outen wone" refer back in sacred history to the penalty of Eve and refer forward to the pains Mary will suffer at the rebirth of man. In the second unit of five, the story of the actual birth of Christ fulfills the event that was promised in the first unit, and Mary is joyful.

In the second group of ten stanzas, the first unit of five presents the story of the events of Christ's childhood. While confirming His messiahship by the circumcision, epiphany, presentation, and then the finding in the Temple, the stanzas specifically develop what the Child will suffer: the wound, when He is cut; death, in the gift of myrrh; crucifixion, in the prophecy of Simeon; and finally, separation from His parents, in the search of Mary and Joseph for their Son at Passover. The second unit of five, correspondingly, fulfills the promise of the Child's divinity and kingship by the story of the events of His manhood, and Mary experiences great joy.

In the third group of ten, the first unit of five, which is the description of the crucifixion, fulfills the promise of suffering both implicit in the first unit in the story of Christ's birth and explicit in the first unit of the second group in the story of Christ's childhood. The description of her Child's crucifixion causes Mary's most intense experience of sorrow. The second unit of five fulfills ultimately the angel's prophecy in the first group of ten of "mannis blis" and completes the account in the second group of ten of Christ's mission, by manifesting His victory as God over sin and death. At the same time it counters the crucifixion by foretelling the events to follow it and provides the full cause for Mary's joy.[13]

Not only does the poet proportion the vision narrative of the life of Christ according to these two principles, but he sets the whole dream vision in relation to his audience by means of them. The introductory five quatrains place the dialogue at the time of Christ's nativity. By the two frame quatrains' setting of the poem itself at the time of the celebration of Christmas in the Church year, an analogy is established between the situation of the poet and his audience and the situation of the Christ Child and Mary.

Thus the poem can be seen, more deeply, to act as a prophecy and fulfillment of truth in relation to the audience. Just as for Mary the birth of her Child is the fulfillment of the words of the angel at the annunciation, so for the audience the fact that it is "ȝolis-day" gives testimony that the Child speaking in the poem has in fact been born. As the Child foretells the rest of His life to Mary in terms of the fulfillment of what was prophesied in order that He may teach her the ultimately joyful outcome of events, so through Mary the audience recalls the outcome of events they know have already actually come to pass, and they are reminded that, indeed, except for the last judgment, all the Child has foretold has come to pass.

Because of its setting, the whole poem can also be seen to act as the dramatic fulfillment of desire in relationship to the audience. That the deeper purpose of the poet is focused beyond Mary and on the audience's desire for joy is revealed by his handling of the last two stanzas. The dialogue of the poem is left incomplete. Omitting Mary's response, the poet concludes the poem with the Child's account of final joy. It is for the listener to apply the significance of Christ's tale, beyond its consequences for Mary, to himself. The frame quatrains make this application clear. The opening quatrain introduces the dialogue as a dream vision witnessed by a solitary speaker who lay one night alone in his "longging." The concluding quatrain, affirming the vision was true, reveals that it took place on Christmas Day. The setting on "ȝolis-day" is a testimony to the listener that the ultimate transformation of his own solitary longing into joy has in fact been made possible.

There is, finally, a further general comparison to be made between the movement of sorrow to joy in the poem and the point of view of the audience established by the poem's setting at Christmastide. There is an analogy between Christ's view in the poem of the progression of the events in His life and the perspective in time of the liturgy of the Church as it looks forward from the Christmas season. After the joyous celebration of Christmas will come the penitential season of Lent, culminating on Palm Sunday, when Christ's entry into Jerusalem will be celebrated, and in Holy Week, when the passion and death of Christ will be relived by the Church. The sorrowing at the passion on Good Friday will be succeeded by the rejoicing at the resurrection on Easter. This in turn will be succeeded by the joyous time of Ascension and Pentecost, and the triumphant summer season of feasts, which includes the celebration of Mary's assumption, and whose liturgy prefigures the joy of the Heavenly Jerusalem, to be established by the second coming of Christ and the resurrection and final judgment of mankind.

part two

The Crucifixion

Fig. 6.—The Crucifixion. The third of four miniatures preceding the Amesbury Abbey Psalter, Oxford, All Souls College MS 6, fol. 5. The crucifixion is presented as the moment of man's redemption, and like "Þe milde Lomb isprad o rode," it illustrates an artistic transformation of the event of pain and disorder into an event of divine significance and beauty. For more extended discussion, refer to the Notes to Illustrations.

IHC NAZARENUS
REX IUDEORUM

Tunc terra tremuit et sol sua luminaria clausit. Moerebantque poli, moerebant sydera cuncta. Omne suum iubar amisit luna dolendo recessitque omnes ab alto aethere fulgor. Finduntur duri lapides, scinduntur fastigia templi. Petrae durissimae scissae sunt et momenta aperta. Surrexerunt multi apertis tumulis fatentes voce magna Christum esse Deum. Cogitare nunc libet quantus dolor tunc infuit matri, cum sic dolebant, quae insensibilia erant.[1]

IN PART I WE CONSIDERED THE PLAN OF REDEMPTION FROM THE PERSPECTIVE of Christ's joyous birth. All salvation depended upon Mary's acceptance of the words of the angel. When Mary agreed to God's will, as she became the medium through whom Christ assumed the nature of man, she also became the medium of man's joy. At the moment of Christ's birth all creation rejoiced.

Opposed to that moment of Christ's coming in sacred history is the moment of His death, the time of Mary's deepest sorrow, when "the veil of the temple was rent in two from the top even to the bottom: and the earth quaked and the rocks were rent" (Matt. 27:51). Yet, what seems to be the moment of man's complete rejection of God and the complete denial of Christ's power accomplishes man's redemption. At this moment the greatest sorrow begins to be transformed to joy. Mary through her suffering at Christ's death becomes the mother of mankind, Mother of Mercy. These are the mysteries that occupy the poets who write about the crucifixion and death of Christ.

The sin of Adam, because it was an offense against God Who is infinite, had infinite consequences. Christ's passion and death, because God Himself assumed man's sin, had infinite merit, which is offered inexhaustibly for the salvation of every man who has sinned. The dimensions of the loss caused by the fall of man are fully defined by the intensity of the suffering Christ underwent at His death. In the present age of the Church each man has been bound to Christ by the grace flowing from the crucifixion, by his baptism. Thus for him to contemplate the crucifixion is an experience of both joy and sorrow. He experiences joy because he knows Christ was crucified for the redemption of his own sins and for the restoration of his joy; yet he suffers sorrow as he beholds the great pain Christ suffered, because he realizes that he in fact has caused Christ's suffering by his own rejection of Him. But this great suffering he beholds also manifests the great love Christ has for him, and, recognizing this, the soul feels doubly joyful. Yet because the great love Christ has for him, in turn, stirs him to love Christ more, even more deeply does the soul sorrow at Christ's pain. Full sorrow for the Christian soul is not in realization, but in action, requiring the amendment of his life.

As counterparts to the lyrics on the joyous annunciation and birth of Christ, I would like to discuss four lyrics on Christ's crucifixion and death, in which Mary is used as the medium through whom the poet formulates the significance of the event. By analyzing these poems, I would like to illustrate further in what way a consideration of the theological dimension of the Middle English religious lyric is necessary for the full understanding of both its purpose and its structure and also to illustrate how the structural principle of each poem varies as the poet considers the different events of sacred history.

The poems are "Þe milde Lomb isprad o rode," a thirteenth century sequence from the same manuscript as "Gabriel, fram evene-king," two short fourteenth century lyrics from Friar Grimestone's preaching book which re-create what Mary must have said under the cross, and a thirteenth century dialogue which presents the words that Mary and Christ might have exchanged during the crucifixion. All four of these poems derive from a common tradition springing from two dialogues, the *Beatae Mariae et Anselmi de passione Domini,* attributed to St. Anselm of Canterbury [2] and the *Lamentatio St. Bernardi de compassione Mariae,* attributed to St. Bernard of Clairvaux.[3] The St. Anselm dialogue is a brief retelling of the whole passion, from the arrest of Christ in the Garden of Gethsemane to His entombment. St. Anselm asks a simple question about what happened, and Mary describes the events, mostly in the words of the four Gospels and in the same phrases from the psalms that are used in the Passiontide liturgy to formulate the feelings of Christ.

It is the dialogue between St. Bernard and Mary, however, that provides the full background for the poems. In this dialogue, St. Bernard asks Mary to tell the sorrow she suffered at her Son's death in order that his own heart be moved to share the full extent of her sorrow. By means of St. Bernard's questions and Mary's replies, the earlier events of the passion are briefly told. Most of the dialogue relates what Mary felt and said as Christ hung on the cross. In a series of rhythmical laments Mary appeals to her Son and to the Jews to let her die with her Son. Christ, in turn, appeals to His mother, whose unassuageable grief wounds Him the most severely of all His wounds. But so long as Mary sees her Son suffer, her grief cannot be lessened. Finally, after consoling Mary by explaining that He must suffer and die to fulfill His Father's will to save mankind, and after giving her over to the care of St. John, Christ dies. Even after His death, as Christ is taken down from the cross and placed in the tomb, His mother continues to mourn. The dialogue between St. Bernard and Mary was influential on Middle English poetry other than the poems we shall discuss. There are several metrical versions,[4] and certain other lyrics printed by Brown seem to have been influenced by it.[5] I will include various selections from the dialogue as its subject matter contains parallels to each of the poems.[6]

Þe milde Lomb isprad o rode,
heng bihornen al oblode,
for hure gelte, for hure gode—
    for he ne gelte neure nout.
Feawe of hise im warn biliued,
Dred hem hadde im al bireued
Wan he seyen here heued
    to so scanful deth ibrout.

Þis moder, þar im stud bisiden,
ne leth no ter other vnbiden,
wan hoe sei hire child bitiden
    swics pine and deien gelteles.
Saint Iohan, þat was im dere,
on other alue im stud ek fere,
and biheld with murne chere
    is maister þat im Louede and ches.

Sore and arde he was iswungen,
feth and andes þurew istungen,
Ac mes of alle is othre wunden
    im dede is modres sorwe wo.
In al his pine, in al his wrake,
þat he drei for mannes sake

he sei is moder serwen maken—
    wol reufuliche he spac hire to.

He seide, "wiman lou! me here,
þi child þat þu to manne bere.
With-uten sor and wep þu were
    þo ics was of þe iborn.
Ac nu þu must þi pine dreien,
wan þu sicst me with þin eyen
pine þole o rode, and deien
    to helen man þat was forlorn."

Seint Iohan þe wangeliste
hir understud þurw hese of criste;
fair he kept hire and bi-wiste,
    and serwed hire fram and to fot.
Reuful is þe meneginge
of þis deth and tis departinge,
þar-in is blis meind with wepinge,
    for þar-þurw us kam alle bot.

He þat starf in hure kende,
Leue us so ben þar-of mende
þat he giue us atten ende
    þat he hauet us to ibout.
Milsful moder, maiden clene,
mak þi milce up-on hus sene,
and brinc hus þurw þi suete bene
    to þe blis þat faillet nout.

"Þe Milde Lomb Isprad o Rode"

"Þe Milde Lomb Isprad o Rode" defines simultaneously two aspects of the reformation of sacred history by Christ for the salvation of man.[7] First, it defines the enormity of the offense of man's sin by showing the intensity of its consequences—the degree of the suffering caused to Christ—while it defines the infinite value of the Victim atoning for the offense of man. Second, by showing the intensity of the suffering Christ accepted, it reveals the extent of Christ's love for man.

Describing the crucifixion from the point of view of the poet and his audience, that of man in the present moment of sacred history as he is himself in transition from sorrow to joy, the meditation contains both the aspects of sorrow and joy. The crucifixion is violation and ugliness, yet Christ, transcending this, is love and beauty. The means in the poem by which the poet shows Christ's suffering is the very means by which the poet also reveals the transformation of the suffering. Further, the poem is itself given power to transform the lives of its hearers in virtue of this same Person the poet is recalling, when at the end the meditation becomes an efficacious prayer for final joy.

Since the crucifixion has its double power, the transformation of suffering by love and the transfiguration of ugliness by beauty, we shall analyze the poem from these two points of view, always as the poem reflects back to the double perspective of sorrow mingled with joy from which the poet and his audience meditate.

The Transformation of Suffering by Love

There are three movements in this poem: stanzas one and two, which describe the setting and the significance of the suffering of Christ; stanzas three and four, which show the intensity of Christ's suffering through His compassion for Mary's suffering on His behalf; and stanzas five and six, which apply the meditation to those present who "ben þar-of mende." The whole poem is constructed in terms of the audience's awareness: their awareness of Who the Victim is, of what the context of the event in sacred history is; the special awareness the friends of Christ have of these facts.

In the first two stanzas, there are two components to the suffering shown, the physical pain inflicted on Christ's body and the interior suffering caused to Christ or suffered by others. In the first four lines of the first stanza, the poet describes Christ on the cross; in the next four, he describes the flight of the disciples and the unfaithfulness of those closest to Him, except for the few who believed in Him.

> Þe milde Lomb isprad o rode,
> heng bihornen al oblode,
> for hure gelte, for hure gode—
>   for he ne gelte neure nout.
> Feawe of hise im warn biliued,
> Dred hem hadde im al bireued
> Wan he seyen here heued
>   to so scanful deth ibrout.

In the opening lines, Christ is presented to the listeners from a double point of view: not simply as He would appear to the outward eye, which is how the unfaithful disciples saw Him, but as He would appear to the faithful, with the insight given to them by their own context in the present moment of sacred history. Man has rejected God, but his rejection has been turned by God into saving sacrifice. Using the Church's application to Christ of Isaiah's prophecy (Isa. 53), the poet presents Christ through the figure of the Lamb.[8] The Lamb expresses the inner nature and significance of the Victim, Christ's meekness, His innocence, His value as a sacrifice for man, "for hure gelte." Spread on the cross as if it were an altar, the Lamb suggests, more profoundly, the Paschal Lamb, sacrificed for the salvation of man, Whose sacrifice is renewed at each Mass until the end of time.[9]

While the opening lines reveal the inner significance of the Victim, the third and fourth define mankind's relationship to Him. "For hure gelte, for hure gode," describes the two fundamental relationships in sacred history that man has to God. The Lamb hangs because of man's guilt; that is, He hangs because of Adam's sin and because of all men's sins after Adam's sin, and He hangs because of this greatest sin, man's crucifixion of Him. And the Lamb hangs also on behalf of man, for his good; that is, He hangs so that through His suffering man will be reunited with God, ultimately in heaven. With the pronoun "hure" in line three, the poet applies this guilt and good not to the generality of "all men," but directly to his present audience, to "us." With "for he ne gelte neure nout" in line four, the poet affirms, in contrast to "us," Christ's innocence. Implied by this fact that Christ suffers although innocent is His choice to suffer as a free gift.[10]

The next four lines complete the description of Christ's abjection and sorrow. These lines indicate indirectly the ignominy and ugliness of the sacrifice, while they also revealed the significance in sacred history of His death. Fear had taken Christ's disciples when they saw their "heued" brought to such a shameful death. Christ was so shrouded by the ugliness of sin that the disciples were blinded to His godhood, and so they fled.[11] By referring to Christ as the "heued" of the disciples, the poet reveals a second aspect of Christ's saving sacrifice. The Victim is the source of unity, for in Him are all things, "And he is before all: and by him all things consist. And he is the head of the body, the church." The figure of the "heued" is the familiar one applied to Christ by St. Paul (Col. 1:14–22).[12] The flight of the disciples is the fulfillment of Christ's prophecy at the Last Supper: "All of you shall be scandalized in me this night. For it is written: *I will strike the shepherd: and the sheep of the flock shall be dispersed*" (Matt. 26:31).

In addition to establishing that Christ is the source of unity, the desertion by the group of disciples defines the personal dimension of Christ's sorrow. Besides suffering although innocent, besides being racked with pain, Christ suffers humanly, from desertion by His most loved friends. They have not struck Him or nailed Him, but they have abandoned Him. Implied by their fear is disbelief in the power of His godhood. By fleeing, the disciples provide the audience with the example of man's deepest rejection of Christ.

Yet in contrast to the disciples, some remained faithful. In stanza two it is shown that Christ's mother and John have not rejected Him. The disciples and Mary and John are those who know Christ most closely. By retaining their vision of Who the dying One is through their love for Him, Mary and John provide the example of those who feel compassion for His suffering.

Þis moder, þar im stud bisiden,
ne leth no ter other vnbiden,
wan hoe sei hire child bitiden
    swics pine and deien gelteles.
Saint Iohan, þat was im dere,
on other alue im stud ek fere,
and biheld with murne chere
    is maister þat im Louede and ches.

Stanza two defines the intensity of Mary and John's compassion by showing the inner source and outward effect of their sorrow. The first four lines describe Mary's compassion, the second John's. The primary cause of Mary's sorrow is her motherhood. "Þis moder" beholds the suffering of "hire child." She sees on the cross not only a man, but a man who is her child, with all the past associations, with all his early helplessness and innocence. The second cause of Mary's suffering is her perception of "swics pine," the increasing intensity of the pain of Christ's suffering, and the third is her knowledge that He is "gelteles," that He suffers unjustly. Whereas Mary's sorrow is that of a mother for her son, John's sorrow is that of a man for a lord who is the source of all his "gode," not material good, but the spiritual good of love. Following the liturgical and artistic tradition that St. John was the most beloved disciple of Christ,[13] the poet identifies John as the one "þat was im dere." This Master "þat im Louede and ches," Who had singled out and cherished him, John sees dying a shameful death.

Suffering because of sin is the source both of Christ's pain and of Mary and John's compassion. Christ's physical attitude and condition are the effects of man's sin. His wounds manifest the disorder of sin. The bodies of Mary and John do not cause them pain as Christ's body causes Him, but their bodies are used to express their inner pain, their compassion. They reflect Christ's suffering like a living mirror. Just as, in stanza one, Christ's suffering was introduced first by His physical position "isprad o rode" and then by the fact He was "bihornen al ablode," so, in stanza two, Mary's compassion is introduced first by her physical position beside her Son and then by the fact of her attitude of weeping, she "ne leth no ter other vnbiden." St. John, "þat was im dere," is also shown in this double way, first as placed on the other side of Christ, and then as beholding his master "with murne chere," mournful aspect or countenance.

The next two stanzas use Christ's physical pain and inner compassion to convey the intensity of His suffering as evidence of the capacity of His love, and they show how His love transcends all pain. In these stanzas the poet multiplies sorrow upon sorrow to an increasing intensity which Christ absorbs in Himself, as His mercy, the expression of His love, transforms the demands of justice, that man be separated from God by his sin, into the joy of union. This transformation begins to be presented in stanza three:

> Sore and arde he was iswungen,
> feth and andes þurew istungen,
> Ac mes of alle is othre wunden
>   im dede is modres sorwe wo.
> In al his pine, in al his wrake,
> þat he drei for mannes sake
> he sei is moder serwen maken—
>   wol reufuliche he spac hire to.

In the first two lines, the poet conveys the intensity of Christ's physical suffering by adding details. By describing Christ's body swinging, he suggests the pain of the "sore" and the "arde" pressure of weight on His "feth and andes þurew istungen." He then, in the next two lines, adds the greatest wound of all Christ's wounds, His mother's grief. In the first two stanzas, the outer or physical aspect was defined as expressive of the inner source of suffering. Here in this stanza, the intensity of Christ's physical suffering is shown in order to emphasize by contrast His deepest suffering, the inner pain caused by Mary's compassion for Him.

This inner pain manifests more fully the degree of the intensity of Christ's love. To define this love is the purpose of the next four lines, the climax of intensity. The poet speaks of the pain that Christ suffered for man comprehensively as "al his pine," "al his wrake," as if the pain were so intense that nothing was any longer distinguishable except pain itself, like a light so bright that it blinds, or a sound so loud that it deafens—and the organ of perception is shattered and destroyed, as Christ's body was shattered and destroyed. Yet through this most intense destructive sorrow, Christ discerns His mother sorrowing, and sorrow transcends itself to absorb yet more sorrow: "wol reufuliche he spac hire to." "Wol reufuliche" expresses the full extent of His sorrow, as impelled by her suffering, Christ speaks out:

> . . . wiman lou! me here,
> þi child þat þu to manne bere.
> With-uten sor and wep þu were
>   þo ics was of þe iborn.
> Ac nu þu must þi pine dreien,
> wan þu sicst me with þin eyen
> pine þole o rode, and deien
>   to helen man þat was forlorn.

What Christ does is to name the very thing that is the cause of Mary's most intense sorrow. Behold Me here, your Child Whom you bore to be man. It is as if by articulating the cause of her suffering, Christ desired to intensify her sorrow. Yet, rather, will He define the full significance of Mary's pain in order to transform it by her awareness and acceptance. To her grief now at His crucifixion He contrasts the fact of her painless giving birth to Him: You were without sorrow and weeping when I was born of you. By reminding her that she gave birth without suffering, He recalls to her the ultimate source and meaning of His birth. The painless childbearing was the sign that her Child was God and a sign of God's infinite respect for the desires and capacity of His creature; and the birth of her Child manifested man's salvation. That moment was full of joy—the antithesis of this present moment of crucifixion, when the enormity of sin rends the Creator with suffering, violates His nature as man, and rejects His power as God.

"Ac nu þu must þi pine dreien." Christ does not speak in order to lessen Mary's pain, but says, Now at this moment you must suffer your pain when you see Me suffer on the cross and die to heal man who was lost. The second four lines balance by contrast against the first, making a transition from the moment of Christ's birth to the present moment. Implied in these four lines is a kind of justice of sacred history. All women suffer in childbirth. Mary's painless childbearing was the unique exception. But if Mary is truly a mother, she also must suffer. Her suffering, however, has been transposed from the moment of giving birth to her Son to the moment of her Son's death. Because Christ dies "to helen man þat was forlorn"—for the spiritual rebirth of man—through her pain at Christ's death, Mary co-operates with Christ to become the spiritual mother of man.

Yet in contrast to two poems on the passion to be discussed below,[14] although this traditional idea of the justice of Mary's suffering in her spiritual motherhood is implicit, in this poem Christ's words do not express it directly. Instead, the poet recasts the traditional application, so that he may develop it in the context of the third and fourth stanzas, which tell of Christ's compassion for His mother's suffering. These words which command Mary to bear her suffering have burst forth from Christ at the moment when He experiences the greatest sorrow for His mother. Now she must suffer, He explains to her, as He must suffer, to heal man who was lost. As He chose Mary to be the instrument of His birth, now, in asking Mary to bear her suffering, which is "mes of alle is othre wunden" (line 19), Christ chooses her to be the greatest instrument of His pain.

It is to this degree of suffering that the poem has been mounting. Step by step the intensity of the sorrow has been defined, revealing the enormity of man's sin which Christ took on Himself. The suffering was defined first, in stanza one, as it deformed Christ, and then, in stanza two, as its effects on Christ caused suffering to those who loved Him. The suffering of Mary, the one closest to Him, was in turn shown, in stanzas three and four, to cause Christ's most intense sorrow. But by defining the intensity of Christ's suffering and the implied enormity of sin which caused it, the poet has been demonstrating the immensity of Christ's love. The sorrow He asks Mary to bear, who is the instrument of His most excruciating pain, will also be the instrument by which He expresses perpetually His deepest love for man.

The listener, who is bound personally to the crucifixion by his baptism and by his unity with the Church, thus finds himself loved to an inconceivable degree. He is one who has sinned, who, like the unfaithful disciples, without vision that the Sufferer is God or that he himself is the reason for His suffering, flees the ugliness and terror of the crucifixion. He has caused Christ's crucifixion, and thus has caused Mary's sorrow which, in turn, causes Christ's greatest suffering. The more intensely aware of the meaning and extent of the suffering he becomes, the more he despises himself and realizes that in all justice God should take vengeance on him, yet the more aware he becomes of Christ's transforming love for him. This is the source of his hope, and all he finds he can do is to cry out for mercy. It is to this point of awareness in the meditation that the poem has moved.

The last two stanzas apply the meditation to the listener by recalling him to the context of the present moment from which the crucifixion has been seen. The poet does this by virtue of the love demonstrated in the poem, and asks for mercy—to be brought to bliss, the "gode" introduced at the beginning of the poem. First, the poet relates the events immediately after Christ's death, and then he makes the transition to the present moment in sacred history.

> Seint Iohan þe wangeliste
> hir understud þurw hese of criste;
> fair he kept hire and bi-wiste,
> and serwed hire fram and to fot.

The first four lines of the fifth stanza temper Mary's suffering. At the command of Christ, St. John the Evangelist received Mary, and he protected her and served her in every way. Here the poet shows that Christ's particular love for Mary extends to her after His death through the disciple closest to Him. Like the author of the *Lamentatio St. Bernardi,* the poet has varied his account from its source in the Gospel of St. John in order to emphasize Christ's love for Mary.[15] Concluding the account of the effect of the crucifixion on Mary and John, these four lines also lead the narrative in time to the present moment from which the poet has conceived his meditation on the suffering and love of Christ.

> Reuful is þe meneginge
> of þis deth and tis departinge,
> þar-in is blis meind with wepinge,
> for þar-þurw us kam alle bot.

The last four lines of the stanza are the heart of the poem, bringing the event from the past to bear on the present in such a way that the event has power to transform its hearers. Its function is analogous to that of the last two stanzas of the sequence from the same manuscript, "Gabriel, fram evene-king."[16] "Reuful is þe meneginge/ of þis deth and tis departinge"—Full of sorrow is the recalling of this death and departing. The word "reuful" has been given its full connotations by the first three stanzas in which Christ and Mary's suffering have been defined, so that the listener has realized his double position, both as one who causes the suffering and as one full of compassion for the Lamb Who suffered "for hure gelte." The last two lines of the stanza express the double response of the listener's soul to this position, as through realization of the intensity of Christ's suffering he accepts his guilt, and through recognizing the intensity of God's love for man, he affirms his hope: Therein is bliss mingled with weeping, "for þar-þurw us kam alle bot," for by means of His death all profit came to us. The use of the past tense in line forty reflects the fact that the purpose of the suffering, "for hure gode,"—the purpose with which Christ consoled Mary—has been achieved. Implied in this one line are the other events of the redemption which define the poet and his listeners' present relationship to the crucifixion: Christ's resurrection, ascension, and the founding of the Church which is the means to future joy. And the poet forms the last stanza as the complete acceptance of the consequences of the earlier part of the poem.

> He þat starf in hure kende,
> Leue us so ben þar-of mende
> þat he giue us atten ende
>   þat he hauet us to ibout.
> Milsful moder, maiden clene,
> mak þi milce up-on hus sene,
> and brinc hus þurw þi suete bene
>   to þe blis þat faillet nout.

The last stanza is made up of two petitions, one to Christ, one to Mary. Each is conceived from the poet and his audience's perspective of the present moment in relationship to the meditation on the past event. The first petition is made indirectly, worded as an instruction for "us," those now present for whom redemption has been defined: Let us be so mindful of Him Who died in our nature that He give us at the end what He has bought for us. The suffering itself is referred to indirectly by the comparison to a purchase, and the circumlocution and indirectness seem to reflect the awareness that man is responsible for the incredible suffering, as if man's awareness of the greatness of the offense makes it impossible for him to approach Christ directly. Implied also in the fact of the great suffering is the great joy of heaven. Yet this joy, like the guilt—of such immensity that the poet does not dare to name it—is defined only indirectly as "þat he hauet us to ibout," what Christ has bought for us. Nor is Christ Himself named, but defined in terms of how He was presented in the poem, as He Who died in our nature, the power and means of our redemption.[17] The power called upon by the poet in this petition grows directly out of the fact that the poem is a meditation. He asks that the response of Christ be a response to the intensity with which the poet and his audience recall Christ.

Direct petition is made only when the poet turns to Mary, the instrument through whom Christ took our nature, and through whose suffering Christ expressed His greatest love. The fact that the poet appeals to Mary directly is a consequence of her position in heaven in the present time of sacred history, where she is now the spiritual mother of man. But it is also a reflection of what the poet had revealed in his poem. For by asking Mary's mercy the poet fulfills the implications in the command of Christ to Mary that she suffer for mankind. It is as if here the poet says, Your Son asked you to suffer for us, and this request caused Him His greatest suffering; now be merciful to us, as He said. Mary is not named, but given her titles "milsful moder, maiden clene," recalling the paradox of virgin motherhood which is the sign that her Child was God and joining this to her quality of mercy. Her mercy, in virtue of Christ's mercy, is called upon: Merciful mother, spotless maiden, make manifest that mercy, through which you bore your suffering and which is our means to reunion with God, and bring us through thy sweet prayer to never ending happiness. The whole meditation on the crucifixion, then, has been transformed, through present petition, to achieve the final resolution of all sorrow: joy that never ends.

The Transfiguration of Disorder by Beauty

The second aspect of the sequence I would like to discuss is its beauty. Although the crucifixion is an event of disorder and destruction, through the dimension of theology the poet reveals the deeper beauty and power of the Divine: the means by which the poet describes the suffering and violation of Christ have a proportion and beauty which reflect the power of Christ's transformation of suffering by His love. There are three aspects of this beauty, which correspond to the three movements in the poem as described above. These aspects are order and proportion, intensity of perception, and power to achieve the fullest delight. The beauty exists always proportionate to the audience, to man in his present perspective of sorrow mingled with joy.[18]

In stanzas one and two, which we saw above described the setting and significance of the suffering of Christ, the poet has transformed the disorder and destruction of the crucifixion by presenting it in an objective and proportioned way, a process that can be compared to the artist's presentation of the crucifixion in Figure 6 (descriptive note). First of all, the two figures by which the poet has chosen to reveal the inner nature of Christ establish Him in His position as the center of sacred history. By the figure of the Lamb the Victim is manifested as the Messiah, the event of His crucifixion as the sacrifice which redeems all men; while by the figure of the "heued" the Victim is revealed as the ground of mankind's unity in God. Then also, the event of destruction and disorder is presented by the poet in such a way as to reveal, with an almost geometrical proportioning, the Victim as the central power of the poem and Mary and John as the instruments through which His love will be demonstrated. In stanza one, the first four lines present the crucified Christ, His bodily suffering; the second four lines, the bereaved Christ, His inner suffering. Then, complementing and contrasting stanza one, stanza two describes the compassion of Mary and John, the first four lines presenting the grief of Christ's mother, the second four lines, the grief of His disciple John.

In stanzas one and two, the suffering of Christ and the compassion of Mary and John are further made to correspond and thus to reinforce each other by the poet's selection of the elements of description. Each person is introduced by the epithet which defines the cause of suffering: Christ, Who suffers for man's redemption is named "þe milde Lomb"; Mary who suffers for her Son is named "þis moder"; John who suffers for his Lord is named "Saint Iohan, þat was im dere." The epithet is followed by a phrase giving the bodily position and situation of each: Christ is "isprad o rode," Mary "im stud bisiden," and John "on other alue im stud ek fere,/ and biheld." And, lastly, the effect of their suffering is described: the "milde Lomb" is bathed with blood, Mary weeps, John has "murne chere." Taken together, the opening two stanzas are held in symmetry, creating the impression of a still tableau.

Also in the first two stanzas, the painful details of the suffering itself are minimized by use of language whose stylization and abstractness convey rather the inner significance of the suffering than the immediate fact of physical violation and destruction. In stanza one, the poet's depiction of the crucified Christ through the figures of the Lamb and the Head conveys rather than the torment of an individual man, the eternal significance of the Victim. Only two physical details of Christ's suffering are given. The Lamb is "isprad o rode," as a sacrificial animal would be spread upon an altar. There is no mention in this stanza of the use of nails, of the pressure of His weight hanging on them. The second detail refers to the Lamb as "bihornen al oblode." "Bihornen" with its connotations of a covering quality and profusion, rather than suggesting the severity of Christ's wounds suggests the generosity of Christ's love and the sacramental power of His blood—a ritual spilling, rather than the literal horror of the body's rupture and pouring out of life blood.[19]

The compassion of Mary and John is also presented in such a manner that rhetorical stylization minimizes the harsh evidence of their suffering. The poet uses synecdochic figures. Mary's tears are described to show their abundance, signifying rather than conveying the intensity of her inner suffering, as she "ne leth no ter other vnbiden," allowed no tear to await the other. John's grief is indicated by one generalized detail, the mournful countenance caused by the loss of his Lord. The description, in lines five through eight, of the fleeing of the disciples also is stylized to indicate the inner significance of their desertion. The poet presents first a summary statement, "Feawe of hise im warn biliued," which anticipates, by contrast to the next stanza, the presence of Mary and John. Then in figurative language he gives the explanation of why few believed: first by personification—dread had deprived Him of His disciples; then by metonymy—when they saw "here heued" brought to such a shameful death. Thus, formal ordering of the scene and the use of stylized figures for description of physical details are both means by which the poet reveals concealed behind the ugliness of suffering the inner value of the crucifixion, the power which gives the crucifixion its value "for hure gode."

There is yet another formal proportion of relationship between the opening two stanzas, which reflects through and is modified by the whole poem: that of the implied relationship of the unfaithful disciples to the faithful Mary and John and of both of these to the listener.[20] As we saw above, the first four lines of stanza one center on Christ's suffering caused by His painful crucifixion, the second four on His suffering caused by the disciples' desertion, save a "feawe." We saw how stanza two complements stanza one as a mirror image of it. But the second stanza is set in relation to the first in a way that significantly contrasts it. The last four lines of stanza one about the unfaithful disciples are contrasted by the whole of stanza two which tells of those who are faithful. Whereas the unfaithful disciples fled at Christ's suffering and thus caused Him more suffering, Mary and John remained. With their compassion they complement Christ's passion. We remarked how for the listener, as he beholds the crucifixion, the unfaithful disciples and the faithful Mary and John embody the two causes of man's sorrow: sorrow at having offended God, compassion for the suffering God underwent for his sake.

But in the light of stanzas three and four, the relationship between the unfaithful disciples and the faithful Mary and John is modified by yet another application of their compassion to the suffering of Christ. In stanza two, Mary and John are united to Christ by their compassion; however, in stanzas three and four the poet shows us that this compassion is an additional wound to Christ. Because Christ loves Mary, her compassion becomes "mes of alle is othre wunden," and it is assumed by Him so that it increases His own suffering. In retrospect we can see that, paradoxically, Mary's relation to Christ is in fact comparable to the unfaithful disciples' relation to Him—she causes a pain to Christ, found to be even more severe than the pain they caused. Thus as well as through the action related in the poem, by means of the formal proportioning itself the poet manifests how Christ assumes all sorrow to Himself, and by the very proportioning of the poem the ground of awareness is being prepared so that at the end of the poem the listener, who has found in himself both the unfaithful disciples and the compassionate Mary and John, will accept the love Christ offers to him by asking that it be given.

In stanzas three and four, which we saw above showed the intensity of Christ's suffering through His compassion for Mary's suffering on His behalf, the second mode of beauty can be seen. Taking the scene he had composed objectively in stanzas one and two, the poet translates it into an event experienced from a single point of view, that of Christ, reproportioning the crucifixion according to the elements of the human perspective of suffering and love. By giving the crucifixion Christ's order of value, the poet can reveal the full intensity of Christ's suffering. By revealing this intensity, the poet can, in turn, heighten the listeners' perception of Christ's pain, and correspondingly, according to the purpose of his poem, heighten their perception of Christ's love. Christ's deepest suffering is interior, and it is defined in these stanzas by the fullest expression of His love, when Christ asks Mary to bear her suffering—the greatest cause of His own suffering—for the love of man.

There are four ways the poet conveys the intensity of experience: by accumulation of separate pains, by adding a pain to an already full pain, by contrasting to this pain the most intense memory of delight, and finally by

Christ and Mary voluntarily consenting to suffer this pain without end. The first two ways by which the poet conveys the intensity are seen in stanza three, which shows the intensity of pain Mary's suffering causes Christ, and the second two in the fourth stanza, where Christ asks Mary to support this pain for the love of mankind.

In stanza three the poet defines the intensity of Christ's suffering in two ways and juxtaposes the second to the first. He defines the intensity of Christ's suffering by accumulating pain and by paradoxically adding one more pain to a pain already entire. In the opening four lines (17–20), the poet develops two sources of physical pain, to emphasize the pain of crucifixion. Christ was swung sorely and hard. We are given a feeling of shifting that suggests the heaviness of His body's pull. Then the poet mentions the nails in His hands and His feet, and our perception of the pain is intensified as we realize this swinging heaviness is pulling on the pierced feet and hands. But "mes of alle is othre wunden," the poet says, adding the third and greatest suffering, His mother's sorrow caused Him woe. In the second four lines of the stanza (21–24), he restates the pain her suffering causes Christ by defining it a second way, in terms of Christ's sensitivity of perception. His most sensitive organ of perception is not bodily. It is His love, and it is by His love He perceives Mary's pain, which adds to His already all inclusive suffering a pain transcending pain, brought by a perception transcending perception.

Stanza four is the climax of the expression of the intensity of Christ's suffering as it defines Mary's suffering. Christ cries out from His love, which made him perceive through all His blinding pain Mary's pain, to comfort Mary. But the comfort is by knowledge, not by release. He defines for Mary the source of her pain and its full intensity, and then prolongs it, doing both by relating her pain to the purpose of His suffering and death. In the first four lines (25–28) by recalling Mary's painless giving birth, Christ defines the deepest source of Mary's pain. First, by recalling His relationship to Mary as her son, the source of her greatest happiness, He names also the source of her greatest suffering. Second, by contrasting to Mary's present sorrow the joy of His painless birth into the world, He heightens the present sorrow, which is to end in His painful death. The last four lines of stanza four (29–32) prolong the suffering He has defined as Christ commands Mary to bear her suffering, which is His deepest suffering, for the love of mankind. Focused now on Mary's choice to obey or disobey, the expression of the most intense degree of suffering has been reached. The stanzas which follow define it as the most intense degree of love, as Christ dies and the poet appeals to Mary, through her mercy to intercede for us.

In stanzas three and four, the poet has taken the elements of stanzas one and two and used the power of Christ's love to define the depth of suffering. In the imagination's eye nothing in the tableau the poet originally presented has moved. Christ hangs above, Mary and John stand below. The development has been, rather, in the point of view, which was changed to that of Christ. The poet has defined the interior dimension of Christ's suffering caused by Mary's pain, which, in turn, causes Christ to cry out and explain to Mary that they both suffer for love of mankind. It is in virtue of the power of love shown in the first four stanzas that the rest of the poem is formed.

The third mode of beauty used by the poet is the transformation of the recollection of the crucifixion into a source of power in order to attain for his audience its consequence, eternal delight. This he achieves in the last two stanzas, which, as we saw above, apply the meditation to those in the present time of sacred history who "ben þar-of mende." The purpose of the "meneginge" given in stanzas one through four was not merely to stir sorrow for sin and compassion for the Sufferer and for His mother. It was to recall also that the crucifixion is the event through which all profit, all "gode," has actually come to the poet and to his audience. And in the last two stanzas the poet translates the past event into its literal relationship with his present audience so that he can make it a means to procure what "He þat starf in hure kende . . . hauet us to ibout." To unite his listener "to þe blis þat faillet nout," he reproportions the meditation a third time, and expresses, in virtue of what has been remembered, the poet and the listeners' present desire.

He does this in two stages, the application of the memory to the present moment and the making of a prayer. Stanza five, by telling what happened after Christ's death, recalls the listeners to the fact that Christ's death has occurred, and that their lives have now the possibility of redemption. The fact is incorporated by implication only, as the first four lines of stanza five (33–36) describe how after Christ's death John cared for Mary. In the mind's eye, the tableau of the opening stanza has been modified. The head figure is gone from the cross; the two figures on either side beneath have joined. The dominant fact in these lines remains Christ's love for Mary as seen in the loving protection of her by John. In the second four lines (37–40), the poet makes the event's relationship to the listeners, which has been implied throughout the earlier part of the poem, explicit. Christ died in our nature.

The memory of His death leaves us full of sadness. Yet bliss is mingled with this weeping, for through His death came to us "alle bot," all profit.

In the last stanza, the meditation is transformed into a prayer for final joy. The nature of the power of the prayer is defined in the first four lines (41–44). The poet exhorts the listeners to keep Christ so deeply in their hearts that He will give them the joy He bought. In defining the value of remembering Christ, the poet's words reveal the central, and until now only implicit, proportion in the poem: the relationship of Christ's experience of suffering to the experience of those who meditate upon it. Let us be so intensely aware of Christ that at the end (at our death, at the last judgment) He will give us the bliss He has bought for us. As we observed above, although these lines are an exhortation to the listeners to be mindful of Christ, they can be seen actually to be an indirect prayer to Christ for His own response—the indirectness seeming to reflect man's sense of nothingness in the face of the crime he has committed and his sense of the power of God's love for him shown in the suffering of the crucifixion.[21]

For the audience, the value of the "meneginge" to achieve the response of Christ and that "blis þat faillet nout" (line 48) will correspond proportionately to the intensity of the power with which they recollect the crucifixion, not seeing in it simply the central fact of salvation, but seeing in it, more deeply, the revelation of the person of Christ. With a purpose analogous to that found in "Gabriel, fram evene-king," it is in order to intensify the response of his audience to Christ Himself that the poet has carefully shaped the recollection. In so far as the listeners respond to Him "þat starf in hure kende," Who in our nature gave Himself to death, Christ will respond to them and give that Joy that never fails, that Joy which is Christ Himself. Yet the poet does not let the power to reach the response of Christ rest finally with the audience alone, or even with the poem by means of which he has shaped the audience's response. The last four lines are a direct appeal to Mary. As she is the instrument Christ uses to redeem man and as she is the medium the poet has used to show both the degree of Christ's suffering and the degree of His love for man, so through the final prayer, Mary is called upon to be what Christ asked her to be, the medium of man's joy.

Mary's Sorrow

SINCE PERHAPS THE ADVENT OF THE RENAISSANCE SONNET, IT HAS BEEN THE accepted manner of lyric poetry for a poet to focus on the intensity of a moment of experience, or on a wider experience as if it were only one moment, or for a poet to make his poem the intense expression of a single personal voice. It has also been a fundamental conception of criticism that to be effective as poetry a lyric must convey intensity of emotion.[1] That theology by nature has an adverse effect on a poem's power to achieve this emotional intensity has been the particular expectation of our modern sensibility that has limited our appreciation of the Middle English religious lyric, which depends upon theology for its subject matter and many of its aesthetic qualities. The conclusions of George Kane in *Middle English Literature* illustrate how this point of view can affect our evaluation of the lyrics.

In his chapter on the religious lyric Kane devotes a major section to what he calls the meditative lyric; that is, poetry which involves "the intent contemplation of a religious subject for the purpose of inducing a devout state of mind." For Kane, poetry "connected with this contemplative activity is by its nature more happily circumstanced than that which is concerned with the simple formal expression of worship," or simple devotional poetry, because contemplation and meditation are activities of the imagination.[2] In evaluating and classifying the meditative lyrics according to their effectiveness as poetry, Kane separates the emotional effect that an individual poem might have on the listener from its theological dimension and holds that the greatest effectiveness is achieved by the most intense expression of "human" experience, in such a way that "specifically religious treatment" is excluded.[3]

To clarify the relationship in the religious lyrics of the emotional intensity of a poem to its theological dimension, I would like to discuss two short poems which restrict the point of view from which the crucifixion is seen entirely to Mary's experience of sorrow. Each poem is composed so that the listener identifies with Mary's perspective, and her suffering is used to make the listener's meditation on the crucifixion more intense. Focusing on a moment of time as though the full meaning of the crucifixion is contained entirely in the agony of the present, each lyric excludes an explicit setting of the event in its total context of sacred history.

The two poems are from the Friar Grimestone preaching book, the same manuscript in which "Als i lay vp-on a nith" is found. As the lullaby did, so these envision through the eyes of Mary, and thus through the love of a mother for her child, what happens to Christ. But in these two poems her Son does not speak. Only Mary cries out. The first poem is an appeal by Mary to those who have put Christ on the cross, in which the listener's perspective is restricted entirely to the suffering caused Mary by her human bond with her Son. The second poem is an appeal by Mary to her Son, in which the listener contemplates what Mary must have suffered from the realization that her Son Who was dying was God and had all power to release Himself and comfort His mother. Both poems are evaluated by Kane for their effectiveness in inducing meditation. In the following two studies, I would like to indicate what kind of importance the theological dimension has in a religious lyric that excludes any explicit setting of the crucifixion in the context of sacred history, and, further, to show that the presence of the theological dimension is not necessarily restrictive, but can in fact deepen the effectiveness of a poem.

"Wy Haue ȝe No Reuthe on My Child?"

Fili, dulcor unice, singulare gaudium, vita animae meae et omne solatium, fac ut ego ipsa nunc tecum moriar, quae te ad mortem genui, sine matre noli mori! O fili, recognosce miseram et exaudi precem meam! Decet enim filium exaudire matrem desolatam. Exaudi me obsecro, in tuo me suscipe patibulo, ut qui una carne viuunt, et uno amore se diligunt, una morte pereant! O Judaei impii, o Judaei miseri, nolite mihi parcere! Ex quo natum meum crucifixistis, et me crucifigite, aut alia quacunque morte saeua me perimite, dummodo cum meo filio simul moriar! Male solus moritur. Orbas orbem radio, me Judaea filio, gaudio et dulcore. Vita mea moritur, et salus perimitur, atque de terra tollitur tota spes mea. Cur ergo viuit mater post filium in dolore? Tollite, suspendite matrem cum pignore! [4]

In this first lyric which Brown entitles "The Blessed Virgin's Appeal to the Jews," [5] in contrast to "Þe milde Lomb isprad o rode" the divine perspective has been darkened from the poem. The wider purpose, man's redemption, is excluded. Mary speaks solely as the mother of her Son and is made the intercessor not for mankind, but for Christ. Whereas in "Þe milde Lomb isprad o rode" the intensity of Christ's suffering was shown to define the intensity of Christ's love, in this poem where Mary is the central figure, the intensity of Mary's love for her Son is shown in order to define the intensity of Mary's suffering. The intensity of her love is expressed in her desire to be united to her Son; the intensity of her suffering is the direct result of her being separated from Him. Christ's silence in the poem increases the sense of Mary's helpless distance from the Center of her love. The poem develops according to the two poles of intensity: the intensity of suffering defined by the intensity of love.

Wy haue ȝe no reuthe on my child?
Haue reuthe on me ful of murning,
Taket doun on rode my derworþi child,
Or prek me on rode with my derling.

More pine ne may me ben don
Þan laten me liuen in sorwe & schame;
Als loue me bindet to my sone,
so lat vs deyȝen boþen i-same.[6]

The poem opens with Mary's crying out in recognition that her Son's torturers have no mercy for Him: Why have you no pity on my Child? Have pity on me, full of mourning. She makes herself the medium of Christ's expression, presenting her suffering, which is caused by His suffering, as the evidence to bend His torturers' hearts. Then she offers two ways in which the torturers may show pity. They may take her Child down from the cross, or they may join her to Him on the cross. By requesting His descent to her or her being joined to Him, Mary's words reveal to the listeners her situation of separation. The alternatives she gives also express to them the fact of her love. In the first alternative she desires to relieve her Son of pain; the first failing, she desires, in the second, to be joined to His pain.

While the first stanza presents the bodily setting of suffering and love—Christ hangs on the cross, Mary stands below—the second stanza develops the inner meaning. The first two lines express Mary's greatest inner pain: No greater pain could be caused me than (while He is dead) to let me live on in sorrow and shame. This inner pain she desires to resolve, in the last two lines, by an expression of greatest love: As love binds me to my Son, so let us die both together.

The poet has organized the poem in a series of oppositions. Each opposition expresses both a desire for union because of Mary's love and an increase of the sorrow that Mary is trying to prevent. The external structure of the first stanza embodies their separation, as its focus alternates twice in balanced pairs of lines from Christ to Mary (lines 1–2), from Christ to Mary (lines 3–4): Have pity on Him or have pity on me; take Him down or raise me up. But what Mary desires expresses indirectly also their union and love. Pity for her will be pity for Him. If he is lowered, they will be together; if she is raised, they will be together. The second stanza expresses the separation and union as two ways of resolving the situation, in the first two lines, separation; in the second two, union. Whereas the first stanza was made up of four lines of syntactically independent clauses, the second stanza is made up of opposing two line syntactic units: "More pine ne may me ben don/ Þan laten me liuen in sorwe & schame" and "Als loue me bindet to my sone,/ so lat vs deyȝen boþen i-same."

Mary's address in the poem is literally to the Jews. Her appeal rises out of her moment of most intense suffering as mother of her Son. Yet even in a poem so clearly and simply restricted to the mother's suffering at the moment of her Son's crucifixion, we can see implicit for its audience a wider context and purpose. According to Brown, immediately above the poem in the manuscript the following saying appears, which suggests the English lyric was directly inspired by the *Lamentatio St. Bernardi:* "Quare ut ait B. in persona uirginis ad Iudeos. Si non placet compati filio compatimini matri."[7] Upon comparison certain similarities between the two works are apparent. As in the *Lamentatio,* in this poem the passion is seen from the point of view of the mother of Christ, and as in the *Lamentatio,* Mary's closeness to Christ, her knowledge of Him as His mother, is the source of her great suffering. The two works have essentially the same purpose. The *Lamentatio* opens with an introductory section in which St. Bernard beseeches Mary in heaven to relate her sorrow during the crucifixion of her Son, so that he too may share in her compassion and receive the gift of tears. The same motive is evident in the saying that introduces the English poem, and the intensity of Mary's appeal to the Jews in the poem would draw deeply also on the listeners' compassion for Mary. For the listener, being made aware of Mary's grief might suggest further not only that he, like St. Bernard, sympathize with Mary, but also that he, like the Jews, have pity on Mary's Son—that he cease from sin because it is his sins that have nailed her Son to the cross.

Kane professes that to give a subject "religious" treatment the poet must attempt to induce "religious emotion" by explicit means. The increase in effectiveness of the meditative lyric is, he holds, on the contrary precisely in proportion as the artistic considerations are not subordinated to the religious ones, but are made foremost. There must be a creative transformation of the religious subject into poetry by the process of selection, rejection, arrangement. It is because it succeeds in this that Kane places "The Blessed Virgin's Appeal to the Jews" highest in the group of meditative lyrics.[8] It is illuminating to compare the principles of effectiveness Kane defines as he describes this poem to the practice of the author of the *Lamentatio,* for they radically contrast those embodied by the Latin work. The contrast will show more precisely how different from the medieval is the modern understanding of the power the theological dimension has to heighten the intensity of emotion.

The excellence of "The Blessed Virgin's Appeal to the Jews," Kane explains, is due to the poet's concentrating on the most striking feature of the situation, which is "Mary's emotion as a human mother face to face with her suffering Son." The listeners can take Mary into their hearts because she speaks with the voice of any disconsolate mother to her Son's torturers:

> No detailed description of the crucifixion, and no suggestion of the enormity of the sacrifice made there, could convey Mary's grief as completely as this desperate plea. Moreover, no specifically religious treatment exists with such a powerful effect of inducing first sympathy and then devotion in the reader. He knows the identity of "my derling," and will the more readily make the transference from the particular instance to the general

> plan which necessitated the suffering and occasioned the unhappiness because, as this imaginative experience is presented, it could be the grief of all mothers.[9]

The modern reader of a religious lyric rarely grasps in what way the contrary principle can be true for a medieval author. It is not the typical, but the individual and particular associations that Mary and Christ have, as it is in all human relationships, that are seen to cause and to convey intensity of suffering. Further, the fact that Mary is not any mother, her Son not any child, but that she is the mother of God and that she shared the uniquely profound experiences of His life and death is what reveals their suffering to be far greater than any other human being's suffering. In his method of presenting Mary's compassion the author of the *Lamentatio* illustrates these latter principles clearly. It is first of all by recalling the events of Mary and Christ's life together that the *Lamentatio* begins to attempt to comprehend what Mary suffered during Christ's passion. These individual events establish that in the same way as Mary was closest to Christ throughout His life, so she was foremost in grief at His suffering and death. As the dialogue opens, the author has St. Bernard say:

> Ipsa enim portauit regem gloriae, illum omni petenti datura. Ipsa genuit eum, lactauit eum, die octaua circuncidit, et quadragesima praesentauit in templo, duos tuttures vel duos pullos columbarum pro eo offerens in holocaustum. Fugiens ab Herode ipsum portauit in Aegyptum, lactans eum et nutriens, curam illius habens, sequens eum fere quocunque pergebat. Credo etiam firmiter quod ipsa mater Jesu erat inter illas faeminas quae ipsum sequebantur ministrantes ei. Nullus debet inde admirari si sequebatur eum, cum ipse esset totus eius dulcor, solatium, desiderium et solamen. Hanc etiam arbitror fuisse inter illas dolentes atque gementes, quae lamentabantur flentes dominum.[10]

Although they are facts of the history of God made man, they can, to support Kane's view, be seen to be restricted to the human facts of her Son's incarnation. However, reading on in the dialogue, we find that the author builds on the intensity which he has conveyed through the human facts by using also the miraculous or divine aspects of the life of Mary's Son. It is through these aspects particularly that he conveys how Mary's grief at her

Son's crucifixion surpasses any other grief immeasurably. The power of the supernatural fact to convey this can be seen, for example, early in the dialogue, in the way in which the author uses Mary's present glorious queenship of heaven. "O that you had shown me your tears of joy on that day when you entered into the eternal joy with your Son," St. Bernard says to Mary, "so I might have known the degree of bitter pain you suffered to see Him die":

> Vtinam dolor iste sic quotidie inhaereret visceribus meis, sicut inhaesit tunc tuis! Vtinam die qua assumpta fuisti in coelum ut in aeternum gauderes cum filio tuo, mihi indicasses lachrymas tuas, ut per illas cognoscerem quantum tibi amaritudinis fuit, cum Jesum dilectum tibi, heu, heu et parum dilectum mihi, clauis in ligno confixum, capite inclinato suum sanctissimum exhalare videres spiritum! . . . Quare ego miser non ploro, cum abiectio plebis factus est filius Dei patris? Veruntamen tu, domina, gaude gaudio magno valde ab ipso nunc glorificata in coelis, quae in mente tantis clauis amarissimis fuisti confixa tuae piissimae mortis! [11]

"Truly, you, Lady, now glorified in heaven, rejoice with very great joy from Him, you, most devoted one, who were transfixed in your heart by such bitter nails." It is the supernatural magnitude of Mary's glory now which to St. Bernard can reveal the true magnitude of her compassion then. Again, for example, towards the end of the dialogue the author has St. Bernard convey the extent of sorrow just after Christ gives up His spirit, by describing the grief of the angels. In terms which to the modern reader might seem to be rhetorical hyperbole, but which to the Christian soul telling of the death of the Son of God could have the value of fact, St. Bernard says: "O who among the Angels and Archangels, contrary to their nature, did not weep, when the author of nature, the immortal God and man, died."

> O quis tunc Angelorum Archangelorumque etiam contra naturam suam non fleret, ubi auctor naturae, Deus immortalis, homo, mortuus jacebat? Videbant Christi corpus sic male tractatum ab impiis, sic laceratum a pessimis, jacere exanime suo sanguine cruentatum. Videbant etiam illam piissimam, illam sanctissimam ac beatissimam virginem, matrem eius, tantis cru-

> ciari singultibus, tam amaris repleri doloribus, tam abundantibus lachrymis madidari, sic amarissime flere, quod nullo modo poterat suas lachrymas refrenare. Et quis poterat tunc a lachrymis se abstinere? Fiebat proinde maeror et luctus ab Angelis ibidem praesentibus, qualis decebat spiritus almos: imo mirarer, si omnes Angeli in illa beatudine ubi flere est impossibile non fleuissent. Credo propter quod et loquor, quia dolebant, si dolere valebant. Sicut enim fuit possible Deum per assumptum hominem mori, ita forte possibile Angelos bonos dolere de morte Domini Dei sui.

"Rather I would be amazed if all the Angels in their beatitude, where it is impossible to weep, did not weep. Therefore I believe and say that, having the power to weep, they wept. For if it was possible for God through assuming the nature of man to die, it is truly possible for the good Angels upon the death of their Lord God to weep." [12]

It is difficult for the modern reader to grasp how the theological as well as the human dimension can be fertile ground for the imagination. The next poem will illustrate this point further. It is a poem in which the point of view of the telling is also restricted to that of Mary, but one which uses its listeners' knowledge of theology to achieve its full effect. "Suete sone, reu on me, & brest out of þi bondis," or as it is entitled by Brown, "Lamentacio dolorosa," is Mary's appeal to her Son, Who, besides the Jews, is the second possible source of release from suffering.[13] She appeals to her Son because she knows He is God and has the power to release them. The poem is also classed by Kane as a meditative lyric, but he considers it inferior to "The Blessed Virgin's Appeal to the Jews," and he gives only a summary description of it. The poem will provide for us a good example of how knowledge of a theological concept can explain seemingly unrelated aspects of a poem as well as reveal its power.

"Suete Sone, Reu on Me, & Brest Out of Þi Bondis"

Suete sone, reu on me, & brest out of þi bondis;
For nou me þinket þat i se, þoru boþen þin hondes,
Nailes dreuen in-to þe tre, so reufuliche þu honges.
Nu is betre þat i fle & lete alle þese londis.

Suete sone, þi faire face droppet al on blode,
& þi bodi dounward is bounden to þe rode;
Hou may þi modris herte þolen so suete a fode,
Þat blissed was of alle born & best of alle gode!

Suete sone, reu on me & bring me out of þis liue,
for me þinket þat i se þi detȝ, it neyhit suiþe;
Þi feet ben nailed to þe tre—nou may i no more þriue,
For al þis werd with-outen þe ne sal me maken bliþe.[14]

On first reading, the poem seems to be a simple appeal by Mary to Christ, as His mother, to release her from her suffering. The first stanza gives the appeal, the reason for it, and the effect on Mary of Christ's suffering. The second stanza seems to enlarge on the details of Christ's suffering to emphasize Mary's suffering. The last repeats the appeal most intensely at the moment of Christ's death. This is indeed the basic movement of the poem, but to understand the full dimensions of Mary's appeal to her Son and to explain certain phrases more fully, a modern reader needs to be aware of the meaning of Christ's divine identity.

If he reads the poem as if Mary saw Christ solely as her human child suffering, he would understand Mary's appeal to be one with no possibility of fulfillment, a fruitless one. The poem would seem therefore to have simply the sentimental value of expressing a mother's inability to accept the extreme pain and ignominy of her son's situation. The purpose of the poem, as in the last poem, would seem to be solely to effect compassion in the poet's audience. But when the reader recognizes that the conception of the poem depends fundamentally on the idea that Mary's dying son is God, he sees the essential question expressed by her appeal and, also, God's unspoken answer. If this man is God, the all powerful, He can burst His bonds. Why, then, doesn't He? Mary, who loves Him most and knows Him most fully, because she is most fully aware of the significance of the situation can ask this question most forcibly. Christ's silent death, through wounding the one closest to Him, is thus recognized to be Christ's willing choice because of His love for man.

When the reader looks at the poem with this question in mind, he sees that it progresses by two deep movements. The first movement is Mary's gradual inner realization as she sees Christ crucified that her Son, Who is

God, is dying. The clauses "for nou me þinket þat i se" (line 2), "for me þinket þat i se" (line 10), phrased in an indefinite way, express two aspects of the incomprehensibility to Mary of her Son's death: first, the incongruity of the fact that God, Who is Life itself, should suffer and die; and at the same time, the mother's inability to absorb the full reality of her son's suffering, "Hou may þi modris herte þolen . . . ?" (line 7). The poem shows Mary's gradual recognition of her Child's death as she tells bit by bit how He suffers.

The second movement of the poem is the manifestation of the intensity and value of what is happening to Mary's Child so as to fully define the causes of Mary's pain. First, the progress of His suffering is shown until He reaches the point of death. At the same time in the poem, the value of the One dying is gradually manifested—from Mary's opening statement that He is her son, through her description that He is "best of alle gode," to her final desire to be taken from this life because without Him life itself has no value. The value of Christ is revealed in order to reveal fully the value of Mary's loss and thus to show the full depth of her sorrow.

In the opening two lines Mary's appeal to her Son indicates both her desire to see Him released from suffering and her knowledge that He has the power to release Himself: Sweet Son, have pity on me and burst out of your bonds! It is as if we hear echoed in Mary's appeal the blasphemous taunt in the Gospel called up to Christ as He hung on the cross: "Vah, thou that destroyest the temple of God and in three days dost rebuild it: save thy own self. If thou be the Son of God, come down from the cross."[15] Paradoxically conceived by His mother, the words sound to the audience not as a denial of His godhood, but as an affirmation spoken in faith of it. Mary knows that her Son has the power. Why does He not, then, release Himself?

In lines three and four, Mary gives the reason for her appeal, "for nou me þinket" expressing the incomprehensibility of the fact of which she is gradually becoming aware. For now it seems to me, she says, that I see, through both Your hands, nails driven into the tree, so sorrowfully do You hang. The phrase "nailes dreuen" being suspended in the sentence, as if Mary cannot admit the sight, the syntactical structure acts to emphasize the cruelty of the nails, as does the contrast of her Son's pierced hands to the pierced inanimate wood of the tree behind them. Added at the end, the clause "so reufuliche þu honges" can modify the words on the effect of the nails or those on the cause of Mary's realization. Mary's next consideration—Now it is wiser that I flee and abandon these parts—echoes a second time the account of the passion in the Gospels, reflecting back to the way Christ was abandoned by His disciples in the Garden of Gethsemane.[16] Or perhaps this line is a momentary suggestion that if Mary finds her Son is truly powerless, she will despair of life itself, a suggestion looking forward to the desire she will state fully in stanza three, that if her Son dies, she desires to die as well.

The second stanza enlarges on the details of her Son's suffering. In lines five and six, Mary describes Christ's face covered with blood, His body bound down on the cross. The fairness of Christ's face is contrasted to the violation of it by His wounds and His power to move to the fact that He is bound down. Lines seven and eight of the stanza, by showing the value of the One suffering, both increase the sense of the injustice of the situation and intensify the evil of the torture. In these lines Mary frames her experience into a question which is the expression of her dilemma through the whole poem, "Hou may þi modris herte þolen . . ." How can Your mother's heart endure? I know my Son is not simply blessed and good, but most blessed "of alle born & best of alle gode!" How can I support this sorrow, to see so sweet a Child, One Who is not only my son, but Power and Goodness itself, bound and destroyed?

In the last stanza, Mary perceives that Christ is dying: For it seems to me, she says, that I see your death, it is nearing quickly. Before in stanzas one and two, she suffered for His suffering as her son, for His being bound down and wounded as God; now she suffers the actual loss of both her son and God. But as it seems most strongly to be denied by His death, in this last stanza Mary gives her Son's eternal value its strongest affirmation. Looking closely at Mary's last appeal, we see that even at His death she calls upon His supreme power: Sweet Son, have pity on me and bring me out of this life. From the beginning of the poem, through Mary's vision the poet has posed to his audience the incongruity that God could die, and through Mary's appeal to her Son he has shown the value and meaning of this death. Now in the last stanza, as Mary sees Christ's death to be imminent, the paradox shifts, from the incongruity that God Who has power over death could die, to the incongruity that God Who in fact is dying would choose to do so. By the vision that Mary retains of her Son's divinity, Mary reveals God's love for man and man's blind rejection of God that caused the manifestation of His love.

In his summary description of "Lamentacio dolorosa," Kane describes it as a poem "in which Mary prays to her Son either to break out of his bonds or let her die." He criticizes it for being unnecessarily explicit, although, he finds, it is good enough to illustrate the superiority of the method which concentrates on Mary's "bewildered grief" and leaves "to the reader some effort of understanding." "The Blessed Virgin's Appeal to the Jews," however, is the best of this kind of meditative poem.[17] Although Kane's summary is brief, it does show us that to exclude the theological dimension of a poem is misleading, and it reflects the inaccessibility of some of the lyrics to such an approach.

By describing Mary's last appeal as an alternative to the first appeal she makes, Kane ignores the almost ballad-like progression of Mary's inner perception as she recognizes the inconceivable, that God is dying. Rather than being too explicit, each detail given of the crucifixion in this poem heightens the inner fact Mary is realizing. To her Son's omnipotence, Mary's sight opposes His hands held by nails to a tree. To His value as the most blessed of all born and best of all good, her eyes oppose His face covered with blood, His body bound to a shameful cross. And as she realizes His death, her eyes seem to sink down to His feet nailed to the tree. Far from being the weaker of the poems, "Lamentacio dolorosa" suggests even deeper dimensions to the death of Mary's Son than "The Blessed Virgin's Appeal to the Jews."

Mary's affirmation of God's power in the last stanza suggests that for Mary and for man, the loss of her Son will not only be the loss of a son to death which has power over man, but the loss of God Who has power over death from the world, that with her Son's death, the world's death will occur. The fact is implied by Mary's final words in the poem: Now may I live no longer, for even the entire world without you shall never make me happy. As the Son of God leaves the world, virtually all good, all life itself withdraws. Mary's final words embody for the poem's audience the dichotomy of man's situation in present life, which is both a life lived in Christ and a life lived in "the world." In Mary can be seen the Christian who prays against the temptation of the world. Rather than being separated from God, he will choose death. More deeply, Mary's appeal expresses the positive desire of the contemplative soul, whose affections are so centered on Christ that he feels to live his present transitory life is only a suffering and separation from Christ, Whom alone he loves, and Whom he can see now only "through a glass in a dark manner: but then face to face" (I Cor. 13:12).[18]

"Stond wel, moder, vnder rode,
bihold þi child wyth glade mode,
blyþe moder mittu ben."
"Svne, quu may bliþe stonden?
hi se þin feet, hi se þin honden,
nayled to þe harde tre."

"Moder, do wey þi wepinge;
hi þole þis ded for mannes thinge—
for owen gilte þoli non."
"Svne, hi fele þe dede stunde,
þe swerd is at min herte grunde,
þat me byhytte symeon."

"Moder, reu vpon þi bern!
þu wasse awey þo blodi teren,
it don me werse þan mi ded."
"Sune, hu mitti teres wernen?
hy se þo blodi flodes hernen
huth of þin herte to min fet."

"Moder, nu y may þe seyn,
bettere is þat ic one deye
þan al man-kyn to helle go."

"Sune, y se þi bodi swngen,
þi brest, þin hond, þi fot þur-stungen—
no selli þou me be wo."

"Moder, if y dar þe tellen,
yif y ne deye þu gost to helle;
hi þole þis ded for þine sake."
"Sune, þu best me so minde,
with me nout; it is mi kinde
þat y for þe sorye make."

"Moder, merci! let me deyen,
for adam ut of helle beyn,
and al mankin þat is for-loren."
"Sune, wat sal me to rede?
þi pine pined me to dede,
let me deyn þe bi-foren."

"Moder, mitarst þu mith leren
wat pine þolen þat childre beren
wat sorwe hauen þat child for-gon."
"Sune, y wot y kan þe tellen,
bute it be þe pine of helle
more sorwe ne woth y non."

"Moder, reu of moder kare!
nu þu wost of moder fare,
þou þu be clene mayden man."
"Sune, help alle at nede,
alle þo þat to me greden—
mayden, wyf and fol wyman."

"Moder, y may no lenger duellen,
þe time is cumen y fare to helle,
þe þridde day y rise upon."
"Sune, y wyle wi'the funden,
y deye ywis of þine wnden,
so reuful ded was neuere non."

When he ros þan fel þi sorwe,
þe blisse sprong þe þridde morewe,
wen bliþe moder were þu þo.
Moder, for þat ilke blisse,
bisech vre god, vre sinnes lesse,
þu be hure chel ayen hure fo.

Blisced be þu, quen of heuene,
bring us ut of helle leuene
þurth þi dere sunes mith.
Moder, for þat hithe blode
þat he sadde vpon þe rode,
led us in-to heuene lith. Amen.

"Stond Wel, Moder, vnder Rode"

BEFORE SPEAKING OF THE SHORT MEDITATIVE POEMS ABOVE, KANE EVALUATES the religious poet's use of the dialogue as one of the less successful means of treating the crucifixion.

> It tends to diffuseness and clumsy handling or else, by the obviousness of its standard answers to the customary rhetorical questions of her lamentations, distracts attention from what seems the most striking feature of the situation, namely Mary's emotion as a human mother face to face with her suffering Son. The dialogue treatment is the easy way of showing how an incarnate God and His mother are victims of the conflict between divine and human purposes. By dialogue the reasons for this conflict can be not only made explicit but also developed beyond any possibility of misconception, or else Christ can offer consolation to His Mother within which doctrinal instruction for the hearers is contained. Poetry, however, does not necessarily thrive on the obvious. . . .[1]

Among the dialogues he refers to, Kane includes the thirteenth century sequence "Stond wel, moder, vnder rode."[2] I would like to discuss this dialogue as the final example of a poem on the crucifixion. Here, not only does Christ speak, not only does Mary lament or appeal, but there is an exchange between the two. Thus the poem forms a complement to the three others we have considered, as well as illustrating yet another way the crucifixion was conceived by the medieval poet. It will give us another opportunity to study the relationship of theology to these lyrics and to see further results of this method of approach.

The Dialogue

> Iste erat dolor meus maximus quia videbam me deseri ab eo quem genueram, nec supererat alius, quia mihi erat unicus. Vox mea fere perierat omnis, sed dabam gemitus suspiriaque doloris. Volebam loqui, sed dolor verba rumpebat. . . . Videbam morientem quem diligebat anima mea et tota liquefiebam prae doloris angustia. Aspiciebat et ipse benignissimo vulto me, matrem plorantem, et verbis paucis voluit me consolari, sed ego nullo modo consolari potui.[3]

The dialogue of "Stond wel, moder, vnder rode" can be seen to be the counterpart of that in "Als i lay vp-on a nith," set at the moment that is the negation of the moment of the dialogue between the mother and the Child in His cradle. Whereas "Als i lay vp-on a nith" opened in the spirit of Mary's joy at Christ's birth, "Stond wel" opens at the moment of Mary's deepest sorrow at Christ's death. As He does in the former poem, Christ instructs Mary about the meaning of an event of His life and the dialogue opposes the omniscience of her Son's divinity to the limited vision of Mary's humanity. But in "Stond wel" Christ is not presented to be as aloof and relentless as in "Als i lay vp-on a nith" where in foretelling His suffering He showed no sorrow for causing His mother's pain or fear for Himself. Here, His mother's suffering causes His own greatest sorrow and His humanity seems to suffer and struggle in the same way as Mary's does. In this poem, as in the other, the poet has used the figure of joy and sorrow to structure the poem, but the joy and sorrow, from the beginning of the poem to the end, is conceived not as it is reflected in the vision and heart of Mary, but from the perspective of the cosmic view of theology looking back on the crucifixion as it is ultimately the source of all man's joy.

As did "Als i lay," "Stond wel" begins with an ironic contrast between the situation and the command of Mary's Son. It begins at the moment when

Mary's Child, suffering on the cross, is about to die. Yet, paradoxically, He commands Mary to rejoice:

> "Stond wel, moder, vnder rode,
> bihold þi child wyth glade mode,
> blyþe moder mittu ben."
> "Svne, quu may bliþe stonden?
> hi se þin feet, hi se þin honden,
> nayled to þe harde tre."

Christ commands Mary to be happy beneath the cross. Mary cannot understand Christ's request for her to stop sorrowing. In reply she simply presents what she sees, that her Son suffers. In the same way as in "Als i lay vp-on a nith" Mary's words expressed the natural joy of a mother at her child's birth, Mary's reply here expresses the natural agony of a mother at the suffering of her son.

This first stanza establishes the opposition fundamental to the poem. In the same way as in the lullaby, the opposition reflects the gulf between the divine and human perspectives of sorrow and joy, which for Mary will become more incomprehensible as Christ's death approaches. In "Stond wel, moder, vnder rode," however, the divine view will not gradually widen the capacity of Mary's understanding, but at each exchange between Mary and her Son, His suffering will remain in her heart as an absolute. The first nine stanzas follow a consistent pattern, opposing in the first three lines the words of Christ to, in the second three lines, the reply of Mary. In each stanza Christ's words begin with "Moder," Mary's reply with "Sune."

> "Moder, do wey þi wepinge;
> hi þole þis ded for mannes thinge—
> for owen gilte þoli non."
> "Svne, hi fele þe dede stunde,
> þe swerd is at min herte grunde,
> þat me byhytte symeon."

For the second time Christ commands Mary to cease weeping and proposes to her the significance of His suffering. It is not My guilt I suffer for, but the guilt of man. Mary, however, replies in deeper sorrow, for she senses her Son's death is near. Now, at the moment of her most profound suffering, she realizes what the prophecy of Simeon meant: the sword Simeon had said would be ground in her heart is the wound she feels at the death of her Son.[4]

The next stanza reaches the first climax of the suffering their love for each other causes and a sudden reversal. In response to Mary's sorrow, suddenly overcome by compassion for His mother's suffering and as if His human nature could not endure the sorrow of His human mother, Christ cries out for her to have mercy on Him. He appeals to Mary just as she herself had appealed to Him, and His cry is caused, as hers was, by what He sees.

> "Moder, reu vpon þi bern!
> þu wasse awey þo blodi teren,
> it don me werse þan mi ded."
> "Sune, hu mitti teres wernen?
> hy se þo blodi flodes hernen
> huth of þin herte to min fet."

To the tears of blood her Son sees her weep Mary simply opposes again what she beholds, the blood running out of her Son's heart down to her feet. Her suffering is His suffering. Her comprehension extends no further. The intensity of the suffering of each is reflected through the speech of the other, as through Christ we see Mary's pain for her Son is so great that her tears are blood, through Mary Christ is so deeply wounded in His heart that the blood flows down to Mary.[5]

Christ then reasons with Mary a second time, wrestling to put her absolute grief in relation to His eternal plan. He presents the same reason He gave in stanza two, now formulated in a new way, opposing their sorrow to the eternal sorrow of man.

> "Moder, nu y may þe seyn,
> bettere is þat ic one deye
> þan al man-kyn to helle go."
> "Sune, y se þi bodi swngen,
> þi brest, þin hond, þi fot þur-stungen—
> no selli þou me be wo."

To emphasize to Mary the value of what He is doing, He weighs His own death, that of one man, against the fact that all mankind will go to hell if He does not die. By comparing death and hell He has defined the stakes for which He suffers. Hell is man's separation from God, his eternal loss, but Christ's single death will outweigh this loss. Although Christ has here clearly defined the divine significance and power of His crucifixion, Mary simply repeats what she has said before, enumerating the points of Christ's suffering she can see, the physical agony and coming death of her Son. How can you make me happy through woe? she asks.

In a third way, a way which replies directly to her question and, brutally, would seem to demand from Mary a deeper response of pain, Christ then explains His suffering and death.

"Moder, if y dar þe tellen,
yif y ne deye þu gost to helle;
hi þole þis ded for þine sake."
"Sune, þu best me so minde,
with me nout; it is mi kinde
þat y for þe sorye make."

I suffer for man's guilt, one man dying rather than all; and—if I can dare to say so to you—I suffer this for you, for if I do not die, you yourself will go to hell. The dilemma is analogous to the dilemma proposed by "Þe milde Lomb isprad o rode,"[6] where the one who loves Christ most causes Him His greatest pain and is classed with fallen mankind as an instrument of His crucifixion. Again Mary is powerless to stop grieving. As in the first part of the stanza Christ revealed that she was the source of His suffering, so in the second three lines Mary replies by presenting the fact that her motherhood is the deepest source of her compassion: Son, you are so much in my mind. Do not blame me. It is my nature that I sorrow for you.

A fourth time Christ cries out beseeching Mary, this time in words which a sinner might use to appeal to Mary for aid.

"Moder, merci! let me deyen,
for adam ut of helle beyn,
and al mankin þat is for-loren."
"Sune, wat sal me to rede?
þi pine pined me to dede,
let me deyn þe bi-foren."

Just as the suffering Christ had, paradoxically, told Mary to be happy, so now He cries out, God, paradoxically entreating one of His creatures to let Him die. Mother, mercy! Let Me die so that I can buy Adam out of hell and all mankind which is lost. Just as the angel of the annunciation sought Mary's consent that she be the mother of Christ, so here the poet has Christ plead with Mary that she accept His death to become the mother of mankind. Replying, Mary accepts His death, but she then offers her death for His death, turning His appeal into an appeal of her own. What shall I say to this? Your pain has pained me to death. Let me die before you. For Mary, pain remains an absolute fact. The next two stanzas focus on her pain, developing the parallel between Mary's painless giving birth to Christ and her suffering at the crucifixion, in yet another way from the poems mentioned earlier, as an element of persuasion.[7] Christ uses it to gain Mary's consent that she become the mother of mankind.

> "Moder, mitarst þu mith leren
> wat pine þolen þat childre beren
> wat sorwe hauen þat child for-gon."
> "Sune, y wot y kan þe tellen,
> bute it be þe pine of helle
> more sorwe ne woth y non."

Using the sorrow Mary suffers now to make Mary one with the sorrow of every mother, Christ says, Now for the first time you can learn what pain they suffer who bear children, what sorrow they suffer who lose their children. And as if Mary's heart is opened by the intensity of her own pain of motherhood, Mary's mode of reply changes. No longer opposing her pain to the requests of her Son as an absolute, she sets it in relation to the greatest pain possible for mankind, the very pain from which Christ is buying man through His suffering and death. Son, I know I can tell you, she replies, that except it be the pain of hell I know of no greater sorrow.

It is after Christ has reasoned with Mary step by step to explain that He is dying to redeem mankind and Mary herself, and after Mary has made the fullest expression of her sorrow and seen it in relation to the greatest sorrow man can suffer, that Christ cries out a fifth time from the cross and asks Mary to pity mankind.

> "Moder, reu of moder kare!
> nu þu wost of moder fare,
> þou þu be clene mayden man."

"Sune, help alle at nede,
alle þo þat to me greden—
mayden, wyf and fol wyman."

Mother, have pity on mothers' sorrow. Now you know the lot a mother suffers, although you are a maiden. Opened to the sorrow of mankind by her sorrow at the death of her own son, Mary becomes the intercessor for mankind, and in the second three lines instead of opposing to Christ's words her own sorrow, Mary fulfills the request of her Son and makes her first intercessory prayer. Both the death of Christ which follows and her prayer will become the basis for the final petition by the poet in the last stanza. Son, she prays, help all in need, all those who cry to me—maiden, or wife, or unchaste woman.

As if the moment could come only with Mary's consent and after her words of petition for mankind, Christ now announces His death.

"Moder, y may no lenger duellen,
þe time is cumen y fare to helle,
þe þridde day y rise upon."
"Sune, y wyle wi'the funden,
y deye ywis of þine wnden,
so reuful ded was neuere non."

With the announcing of His death and His descent into hell, Christ foretells His resurrection, but in this poem only time, not the power of words, can release Mary from sorrow. It will be only when the events themselves transform sorrow to joy through Christ's actual rising from the dead that Mary's heart will change and she be able to obey Christ's opening command to be joyful. To Christ's prophecy Mary opposes her desire to go with her Son and the fact that she herself is dying of His wounds.

The first three lines of the next stanza narrate that what Christ foretold in fact came true. But the death and descent into hell are omitted to present the outcome of events in terms of Mary's joy.

When he ros þan fel þi sorwe,
þe blisse sprong þe þridde morewe,
wen bliþe moder wer þu þo.

Moder, for þat ilke blisse,
bisech vre god, vre sinnes lesse,
þu be hure chel ayen hure fo.

When He rose, the poet says, then your sorrow fell. "Blisse" sprang up on the third morning, and then were you the happy mother your Son had commanded you to be. With this stanza there is an abrupt change in the manner of the poem. There is a transition from past time to the present, and as the poet forms a petition to Mary in virtue of that same "blisse" that is hers, the point of view has shifted from that of Christ and Mary at the moment of Christ's death to that of the poet and his audience in present time. Although the dialogue has ceased, the stanza retains its proportioning into two parts. While the first three lines narrate Christ's rising and the springing up of Mary's joy, the second three, customarily devoted to Mary's reply of sorrow, present the petition of those "at nede" (line 46). Now Mary is in joy above while the poet and his audience stand below on earth, from the position that had been hers seeking her intercession. But the poet's words echo the words with which Christ addressed Mary, and appropriately so, for in fact man in the present is the spiritual child of Mary. "Moder," the poet addresses her, Beseech our God to loose our sins. Be our shield against the devil ("hure fo").

Then in the last stanza, the poet develops the full significance of the appeal for those for whom he composes his poem. He makes the prayer into a power to preserve from hell and to lead to final joy.

Blisced be þu, quen of heuene,
bring us ut of helle leuene
þurth þi dere sunes mith.
Moder, for þat hithe blode
þat he sadde vpon þe rode,
led us in-to heuene lith. Amen.

In the first three lines he asks Mary as Queen of Heaven to bring "us" through her Son's power out of hell's flames. The limits of sorrow and joy having been demonstrated by the debate between Christ and Mary and by the narration of the facts of Christ's death and resurrection, the soul now knows what to seek, and the poet concludes with his most powerful claim. Again addressing Mary as "moder," and setting in opposition to the figure of hell's flames the figure, in the last line, of "heuene lith," the poet beseeches Mary: For that precious blood that He shed upon the cross—that very blood that caused your bloody tears and salvation for man—lead us finally into the light of heaven, the light in which you now rejoice as blessed while we stand here below seeking the light.

The Intelligible Cross

> Hence Scripture treats of the whole universe as regards height and depth, first and last, and as regards an intermediate course under the form of a certain intelligible cross in terms of which the whole mechanism of the universe has to be described and in a certain way seen by the light of the mind.[8]

"Stond wel, moder, vnder rode," like "Als i lay vp-on a nith," is about the transformation of sorrow to joy. It tells of how Mary's sorrow at Christ's death was turned to joy by His resurrection, and it explains that Christ's suffering reflected in Mary's compassion is the means of transformation of man's eternal sorrow to eternal joy. "Als i lay vp-on a nith" had its dynamic center in the transformation of Mary's incompletely realized joy to joy fully realized through Christ's explaining to her the implications of His birth. In Christ's birth was implied His suffering and death. The structure of "Als i lay" was determined by the stages of Mary's reactions of joy and sorrow as Christ foretold the joys and sorrows of His life, and the poem ended when the Child told of the final mystery, the resurrection and last judgment when He will come again in glory. By his knowledge of the full plan of history, the listener knew more than Mary whose limited vision determined the structure of the poem. His fuller knowledge gave him an ironic view of what Mary saw, until through her knowledge of the story of her Son's life as it unfolded, her vision corresponded in scope with the listener's.

Although in "Stond wel, moder, vnder rode" the structure is also governed by the concepts of joy and sorrow, the principle of development differs fundamentally from "Als i lay." In the first place, the poem is not a gradual transformation of Mary's limited understanding of sorrow and joy through her imagined experience of a series of events. The poet, rather, chooses three moments of time and at each moment sets joy in opposition to sorrow. The first is the moment of psychological definition just before Mary's sorrow and Christ's suffering reach their greatest intensity, the moment of Christ's death. The second is the moment of the resurrection, the past event in sacred history which transforms Christ's death to life and Mary's sorrow to joy. The third is the poet and his audience's time of present transition, as they seek by virtue of Christ's death and resurrection to experience eternal joy.

The first moment is contained in the section of dialogue between Christ and Mary (lines 1–54). It is introduced as a joyous moment by Christ, Who opposes to Mary's human vision of sorrow at her Son's death the fact that by His death He will transform cosmic sorrow, the sorrow of all mankind. The dialogue develops this fundamental opposition of divine joy to human sorrow, as first Christ explains the divine reason for His death and then Mary counters by giving her own vision, limited to her "kinde," of the suffering of Her Son. Each repeats the vision again, and then again, and each time the intensity of opposition builds (lines 7–30), until out of desire to release man from sorrow and yet in an agony of compassion for His mother, Christ cries out to His mother to let Him die, whereupon she replies with her request to die first (lines 31–36). Together the two voices define the whole dimension of the passion, Christ giving the supernatural value, Mary offering the human—as if the suffering of Christ's spirit were presented in the first four lines and the suffering of His flesh, through Mary's vision, were given in the second four.

The second moment is the moment of the event which transforms Christ's death to life, Mary's sorrow to joy (lines 55–57). The divine command in the dialogue to be joyful is made fully comprehensible to Mary by the power of an event in history, which is the dimension that creates her experience. When Christ rose, then Mary's sorrow fell, the poet says. But indirectly this moment introduces a second opposition which arises out of the event. This is the separation of Mary from her Son that occurs with His ascension, for Mary's joy can be full only when she is reunited to her Son in heaven. Her assumption into heaven is implied in the transition between the second and third moments of the poem, as line fifty-eight, "Moder, for þat ilke blisse," establishes that now in the present Mary experiences joy in heaven.

The third moment, expressed in lines fifty-eight through sixty-six, is that defined by the poet and his audience's petition in present time. Mary has become a means to joy for man, as man raises his petition to her. A significant proportion is established by the third moment. Mary's position now corresponds to the position which in the dialogue Christ had in relation to Mary. As Mary had stood below Christ at the crucifixion, so man stands below Mary, on earth and still in sorrow. Just as in the poem the resurrection transformed Mary's sorrow to joy, so analogously the poem has reformed man's knowledge of human sorrow and suffering to an understanding of cosmic sorrow and cosmic joy, so that in the last lines man sees his alternative: to have the flames of hell or the light of joy in heaven.

The opposition of supernatural joy to the sorrow of hell, of the eternal vision of this cosmic joy to the limited vision of human joy and suffering, and the transformation of both these kinds of sorrow to joy provides the structural movement of the poem. The structure of the poem embodies the transformation of sorrow to joy in two proportions: there is the opposition of high to low and there is the horizontal movement of sequence of events, the transformation of the past and present to future. These two proportions correspond to the dimension of awareness and the dimension of time.

The dimension of awareness is developed first by the dialogue section. It is a vertical dialogue of things above with things below, which in terms of the poem opposes three levels of significance or application. The first is the literal. Christ hangs on the cross above Mary. Mary weeps below. Christ commands Mary to be glad. This is the level at which Mary comprehends Christ's suffering. Revealed by Christ's command to Mary is the inner level, the level of the abyss between man and God, the separation of the divine point of view from the human and of the purpose of the Son of God from the understanding of His human mother. Revealed also by Christ's words is yet a third level of opposition, the deeper source of the second. At the time of the dialogue mankind lies imprisoned in hell. God is above in heaven. It is Christ's death in time that will join the two—as it will resolve each of the oppositions. By suspending the horizontal movement of time with the dialogue between Christ and Mary the poet intensifies the oppositions. The ninth stanza (lines 49–54), where Christ announces that His time has come and Mary says she desires to go with Him, acts in the poem as a prophecy which foretells the movement to come in the tenth stanza.

Then in the tenth stanza by the narration of events the poet develops the horizontal movement of time, and we see the three levels of vertical opposition simultaneously transformed. Omitting Christ's descent into hell which He had also prophesied, the poet focuses instead on the third day, the day of Christ's resurrection from the dead (lines 55–57), for this is the event which transforms the literal opposition between Mary's sorrow and Christ's joy. As Christ bodily rises, Mary's sorrow falls. She becomes joyful, to fulfill the original request of Christ with which the poem opened. Then in the petition of the last nine lines, with Christ's ascension and the assumption of Mary implied, the transformation of the second and third oppositions is revealed. In present time Christ is literally above in heaven, with Mary united to Him. For Mary the abyss of understanding has been closed and her view has become Christ's view. But the final petition reveals also that in the present moment of time there is a separation between Mary and mankind, because for mankind the horizontal time has only incompletely resolved the oppositions. Until his own resurrection and judgment day mankind will remain in an incomplete relationship to joy. But by the power of Christ's death and resurrection which accomplished Mary's joy, he has the power to obtain the joyful end of his own destiny, and Mary's presence in heaven is both a sign and the means of man's own entry into final joy. In the horizontal movement of time, through prayer and good actions he can be drawn up from the depth of a potentially eternal hell into the height of the eternal light of heaven. It has been the purpose of the poem, having in the first section defined its nature, having in the second worked its transformation, and now having in the third applied its power by prayer, to make the outlines of this cross and the source of its power intelligible.

The Dialogue Form

In his survey of the contents of the St. John's College manuscript, M. R. James describes the incomplete version of this dialogue, which corresponds to the Royal version we are using, as a song both in Latin and in English.[9] However, a reference to James' description of the Latin text upon which the dialogue is based, shows that the opening lines are the following:

Stabat iuxta Christi crucem
stabat uite uidens ducem
nitens uale facere.

And a reading of the Latin sequence which James quotes shows that it does not correspond exactly with "Stond wel, moder, vnder rode," although both poems have the same stanzaic form. "Stabat iuxta Christi crucem" is not a dialogue between Christ and Mary, but a narrative of the sufferings of Christ just before His death from the point of view of Mary's compassion. Yet the basic structure of the English poem is analogous to the structure of the Latin sequence, and it appears that the dialogue is an adaptation of it.[10] The narrative sequence referred to by James exists in two Middle English versions printed in Brown's anthology of thirteenth century English lyrics. Only the latter part remains of the first version, and the second is a complete translation of the sequence.

Of the two English narrative versions, the incomplete one is closer to the Latin original.[11] On the other hand, "Stond wel, moder, vnder rode" and the complete English narrative version, "Iesu cristes milde moder," share elements neither in the Latin nor in the incomplete English version.[12] Because the complete English version retains the narrative method of its Latin source and yet in some respects its contents are closer to "Stond wel, moder, vnder rode," it provides us with an excellent basis for comparing the narrative and dialogue treatments of the sequence. By showing the similarities of "Stond wel, moder, vnder rode" to "Iesu cristes milde moder" and at the same time by pointing out in what way the English poem is modified from the Latin, I can indicate what particular purpose is achieved through the use of dialogue and offer an evaluation of George Kane's judgment about the effectiveness of the dialogue form.

Both "Iesu cristes milde moder" and "Stond wel, moder, vnder rode" begin with a section which meditates on the suffering of Christ through the compassion of Mary. Then both poets apply to the moment of Mary's most intense suffering the contrast of the moment of her painless giving birth and show that her suffering binds her to the nature of womankind. Next, both poems make a transition through sacred history to the present and end with a prayer made in virtue of the events the poets have told before. The most striking difference between the two poems is that the poet of "Stond wel" has changed the point of view from that of a compassionate observer, who through eleven stanzas speaks of what Mary must have experienced and then petitions Mary, into the nine stanzas of dialogue which interchange the points of view of both Christ and Mary. Only in the final two stanzas does he use the view of the speaker of the narrative version.

Iesu cristes milde moder
stud, biheld hire sone o rode
    þat he was ipined on; [3]
þe sone heng, þe moder stud
and biheld hire childes blud,
    wu it of hise wundes ran. [6]

Þo he starf þat king is of lif,
dreriere nas neuerre no wif
þan þu were, leuedi, þo;
þe brithe day went in-to nith,
þo ihesu crist þin herte lith
was iqueint with pine and wo.

Þi lif drei ful harde stundes
þo þu seye hise bludi wundes,
and his bodi o rode don.
Hise wundes sore and smerte
stungen þureu and þurw þi herte,
as te bihichte simeon.

Nu his heued with blud bi-sprunken,
nu his side with spere istungen,
þu bihelde, leuedi fre.
Nu his hondes sprad o rode,
nu hise fet washen wit blode
an i-naillet to þe tre.

Nu his bodi with scurges beten,
and his blud so wide hut-leten
maden þe þin herte sor.
War-so þu castest thin eyen,
pine strong þu soie im dreien—
ne mithte noman þolie mor.

Nu is time þat þu ʒielde
kende þat þu im withelde
þo þi child was of þe born;
Nu he hoschet wit goulinge
þat þu im in þi chiltinge
al withelde þar biforn.

Nu þu fondest, moder milde,
wat wyman drith with hir childe,
þei þu clene maiden be;

Nu þe's ȝiolden arde and dere
þe pine werof þu were
    ine ti chiltuing quite and fre.

Sone after the nith of sorwen
sprong þe lith of edi morwen;
    ine þin herte, suete may,
þi sorwen wende al to blisse,
þo þi sone al mid-iwisse
    aros hup-on þe tridde day.

Welle wat þu were blithe,
þo aros fram deth to liue,
    þur þe hole ston he glod;
Al so he was of þe boren,
bothen after and biforen,
    hol bilof þi maidenhod.

Neue blisse he us broute,
þat mankin so dere boute
    and for us ȝaf is dere lif.
Glade and blithe þu us make
for þi suete sones sake,
    edi maiden, blisful wif.

Quen of euene, for þi blisse
lithe al hure sorinesse,
    and went hur yuel al in-to gud.
Bring hus, moder, to þi sone,
mak hus eure with im wone,
    þat hus boute wit his blud. Amen.

"Iesu cristes milde moder" begins with five stanzas of meditation on Christ's suffering on the cross as it affects Mary. The first three stanzas set the scene. The poet opens his meditation by saying, Mary stood while Christ hung. Then, addressing Mary, the speaker says, No one was ever sadder than you. The day turned to night when the Light of your heart was quenched.

As you saw the wounds of your Son, your life suffered the wound Simeon foretold. After these three introductory stanzas, in stanzas four and five the poet describes Christ's bloody wounds, beginning at His head and moving to His limbs, then to His body, saying that wherever Mary cast her eyes she could see only her Son's pain. The first five stanzas of the narrative version correspond to stanzas one through six of the dialogue version, where by opposing Mary's suffering to Christ's exhortations that she be "bliþe," the poet of "Stond wel" gradually increases the sense of intensity of Mary's suffering. Stanza six of the dialogue reaches a climax as both Christ and Mary cry out to die.

In stanzas six and seven of the narrative version the poet develops the traditional correspondence between Mary's suffering and her painless giving birth. He uses it to suggest the accumulation of pain, saying, Now nature exacts with usury what it withheld at the birth of your Son—as if not only is Mary's present suffering just, but that justice exacts over and beyond for the time she had not suffered. In the dialogue it is stanzas seven and eight which develop the parallel, not, however, to suggest the justice of Mary's pain, but to relate her pain to God's mercy, as she agrees to become the intercessor for mankind.

In stanzas eight and nine of the narrative version, as in the dialogue the poet uses the transition of sacred history, her Son's resurrection, to change Mary's sorrow to joy. In recounting the resurrection, however, he develops a third correspondence to Mary's painless childbearing. Christ's body rose through solid stone ("þur þe hole ston"), just as when He was born of Mary He left her maidenhood whole before and after His birth.[13] In "Stond wel" this third correspondence has been omitted. In its place the poet puts the stanza of dialogue where Christ foretells His resurrection and Mary asks to go with Him, and the event in time, which in "Iesu cristes milde moder" is given two stanzas, he condenses into three lines.

Finally, in stanzas ten and eleven of the narrative version, the poet applies the joy to man and appeals to Mary to make all man's sorrow into bliss. This corresponds in the dialogue version to the second half of stanza ten and the whole of the concluding stanza eleven. The dialogue section of "Stond wel, moder, vnder rode" has extended through stanza nine. Now the last two stanzas of the poem use the same point of view as the whole of the narrative version, and its final stanza contains the same elements as the final stanza of the narrative version.

In the narrative version of the sequence, the divine point of view is not developed fully throughout the poem. It is only given briefly at the end, at the point after Christ's suffering as seen through Mary's compassion has been related, after the speaker has pointed out the parallels to the virgin birth, and after he has related the resurrection and made the third parallel to Christ's rising through solid stone. It comes, in the last two stanzas, as the introduction to his prayer:

> Neue blisse he us broute,
> þat mankin so dere boute
> and for us ȝaf is dere lif.

In his notes on "Stond wel, moder, vnder rode," Brown indicates that its ultimate source is the dialogue of St. Anselm or St. Bernard.[14] This source, or a similar source, has provided the poet of the dialogue with the divine point of view from which Christ speaks to console or debate with Mary. There are many points of similarity between Christ's thoughts in the *Lamentatio St. Bernardi* and what He says to Mary in "Stond wel, moder, vnder rode." In the *Lamentatio,* after Mary has expressed the depth of her sorrow, her Son replies at length, gently reminding Mary first of the purpose for which He took her flesh and became her Son, which is now the most intense source of her sorrow. How else can He fulfill His purpose, He reminds her. Then, as He does in line fifty-one of "Stond wel, moder, vnder rode," He prophesies that He will rise again on the third day after His death, appearing to both His disciples and to Mary. Put away your sorrow, He tells her, for then He will go to the glory of His Father. By His one death all mankind will be saved. In what way can what pleases the Father displease you? Do not weep, I will not leave you, He consoles her. You will be with Me for all time. You know well whence I proceed, whence I come. Why are you sad if I ascend to the place from which I have come? [15] Yet although Christ's thoughts in "Stond wel, moder, vnder rode" seem to be based on those of Christ in the dialogue of the *Lamentatio,* as in his adaptation of the narrative sequence, the changes the poet has made in the material he uses reflect the particular purpose of his poem.

In the first place, in "Stond wel, moder, vnder rode" the poet opens the dialogue with Christ telling Mary to be glad, before He has recalled to her the reasons that should make her glad, so that His command to His mother who sees Him hanging on the cross seems incongruous and paradoxical, and Mary can reply only by opposing to His command the evidence of suffering before her. Second, the poet sustains this opposition between Christ and Mary's view by withholding until the very end of the dialogue the mention by Christ of His own happy outcome, that He will rise again. We see that by his use of both the narrative source and the *Lamentatio* the poet has recast the theme of Christ's crucifixion, Mary's compassion and Christ's compassion for Mary, into a debate of cosmic joy with human sorrow.

Returning to Kane's evaluation of the dialogue form's effectiveness in treating the crucifixion, it seems to me that the dialogue form of the sequence we have examined provides dimensions to the religious lyric which are not easily conveyed by a narrative form. The deepest dimension provided is the expression of the Christian quality of the divine perspective. The dialogue form is the embodiment in its most perfect expression of the medieval theology of the Incarnation, where God manifests Himself and His love for man through Himself becoming incarnate and assuming human nature. In understanding the dialogue to be merely the easiest means of doctrinal instruction Kane shows the common point of view of critics who classify medieval Christian theology without considering its subject matter, and who equate it with a kind of dispassionate and static body of knowledge which is opposed to what can be humanly experienced and felt. By pointing out two essential differences between the English narrative form of the sequence "Iesu cristes milde moder" and the dialogue form of "Stond wel, moder, vnder rode," I would like to illustrate two points about this poet's use of the dialogue form which show the insufficiency of Kane's view.

In the first place, rather than the poet using the dialogue treatment of "Stond wel, moder, vnder rode" to show how "an incarnate God and His mother are victims of the conflict between divine and human purposes," as Kane suggests, the poet shows rather how the divine purpose transforms the suffering of Mary into the greatest manifestation of God's love for man. And second, the dialogue form of the sequence, rather than being used to give "doctrinal instruction," is used to convey to man a much more intimate and personal view of sacred history than the narrative form.

The first point can be illustrated by the contrast we noted between how the poets of the two forms relate Mary's human suffering to the significance of sacred history. In the narrative version and in the Latin original, the poet has used the correspondences between events to point out two symmetrical relationships in the plan of sacred history. (1) When Christ took His mother's flesh, Mary did not suffer pain. But Christ's suffering and death which caused man's spiritual rebirth, caused Mary's spiritual suffering. (2)

Christ's resurrection in His glorified flesh was as miraculous as His birth, for just as Mary remained a virgin, so Christ passed with His body through the stone of His tomb leaving it whole. His resurrection was given as a sign, just as His birth from a virgin was a sign, of His divinity. The poet of the dialogue, however, has modified this parallel to make Mary's suffering show God's accessibility to man. Omitting the second parallel in the narrative version, of Christ's virgin birth to His rising through a stone, he has focused on the first parallel which defines Mary's human motherhood. He has used the relationship of Mary's intense suffering at the crucifixion as it contrasts to her painless giving birth and made it the basis by which Christ unites Mary to the suffering of mankind, to become the spiritual mother of those for whose ultimate joy her Son is dying. Mary's second motherhood through her sorrow—the intensity of which the poet has defined through the dialogue by opposing it to joy—is made a power by which mankind can appeal to Mary to intercede for them, as, in fact, the poet does appeal at the close of the poem.

The unique power of the dialogue form can be seen in "Stond wel, moder, vnder rode" in how the poet conveys through sacred history the feeling of God for man. The dialogue and the narrative versions develop their subject matter in essentially the same proportions. They both begin with a meditation on Christ's suffering through the compassion of Mary, then explain her suffering in relation to her painless giving birth, and then tell of the resurrection of Christ which is the source of man's spiritual rebirth. But the poet of the dialogue has presented the crucifixion, not, as the poet of the narrative does, to point out the intensity of Christ's pain as Mary saw it in the evidence of His physical suffering, but to express the inner conflict of love between the human and the divine. He has drawn the divine or inner meaning of Mary's suffering at Christ's pain back from where it began to be developed in stanzas six and seven of the narrative version into the opening section of the dialogue and formed it into a loving voice which explains to Mary the inner meaning of what she sees with her eyes. In each exchange of the dialogue the divine purpose of love for man is opposed to Mary's particular human love for her Son, which she expresses simply through describing what she sees. Yet the divine point of view does not deny the pain Mary feels because of her human motherhood of Him, rather, as in "Þe milde Lomb isprad o rode," her human love adds to the suffering of divine love, and Christ transforms her love for Him with His own love for her, into love for man. The difference between the way the narrative and the dialogue treat this inner dimension can be clearly illustrated by the way the poets convey the compassion of Mary.

The poet of the narrative version focuses on the moment of Christ's approaching death, suspending the movement of time before Christ's death and resurrection in a present moment made up of detail upon detail of suffering. As time is held still, these details accumulate:

> Nu his heued with blud bi-sprunken,
> nu his side with spere istungen,
> þu bihelde, leuedi fre.
> Nu his hondes sprad o rode,
> nu hise fet washen wit blode
> an i-naillet to þe tre.

This intense suffering of Christ which the poet conveys through repetition he applies to Mary as she is impressed with each detail:

> Nu his bodi with scurges beten,
> and his blud so wide hut-leten
> maden þe þin herte sor.
> War-so þu castest thin eyen,
> pine strong þu soie im dreien—
> ne mithte noman þolie mor.

The poet continues to intensify the present concentration of the moment by repeating "nu" throughout his theological explanation of Mary's suffering: "Nu is time þat þu ȝielde . . . Nu he hoschet wit goulinge . . . Nu þu fondest . . . Nu þe's ȝiolden arde and dere/ þe pine werof þu were/ ine ti chiltuing quite and fre" (lines 31–42).

The poet of the dialogue, on the other hand, suspends the movement of time, not by an accumulating intensity of details, but by the desire of Christ and Mary, expressed in the love they reveal for each other. Throughout the first eight stanzas Christ pleads with Mary to accept her suffering on His behalf, while Mary opposes His plea by pointing out the severity of His suffering which causes her own. The intensity built up is the inner intensity of two wills rather than of accumulating physical details. It is an intensity of love which then is transferred by both Christ and Mary to man, as at Christ's request Mary makes her first intercessory prayer on man's behalf.

In the narrative version of the sequence the succession of events in time, suspended by the speaker's concentration on the most intense moment of suffering during the crucifixion, is suspended further until after he develops the parallels in sacred history. In the dialogue, the succession of events is shown to depend upon the will of Christ and to reflect His central quality, love of mankind. Thus Christ first foretells what will happen after His death, in order to console Mary. And instead of giving divine reasons—I suffer to buy Adam, and even you, from hell—He offers her the promise of the joy of His own humanity which will rise from the dead. The events which follow, told by a speaker whose view is analogous to that used in the whole narrative version, confirm Christ's words, and as well as bringing Mary joy they are a consolation to the listener to whom the events apply.

In the narrative version of the sequence the events move with a relentless quality of impersonal and symmetrical form by which Christ and Mary suffer as one part of the total design of God's justice and mercy. The impersonal form allows mankind (the listener) to stand back and recognize the meaning of the design. In the dialogue version, however, the form expresses Christ's will as it is touched by compassion for His mother, the compassion which through Mary's consent He turns to compassion for mankind. And mankind is engaged and caught up as the object of the love expressed in the debate of the poem.

part three

The Joy of Mary

Fig. 7.—The Virgin and Child Enthroned. Second of four miniatures preceding the Amesbury Abbey Psalter, Oxford, All Souls College MS 6, fol. 4. The miniature illustrates the relationship of mankind in present time to Mary, and to Christ seen through Mary, in the joy of heaven. For more extended discussion, refer to the Notes to Illustrations.

We ought at all times to praise and honour Mary, and with all devotion to meditate on her sweetness; but to-day, on the feast of her Assumption, we should especially rejoice with her, for to-day was her joy made full. Great was her joy when the angel saluted her. Great was her joy when she experienced the coming of the Holy Ghost, and that wonderful union took place within her womb between the Son of God and her flesh, so that He who was the Son of God became her Son also. Great was her joy when she held that Son within her arms, kissed Him, ministered unto Him; and when she heard His discourses, and beheld His miracles. And because she had been greatly saddened in His passion, she had marvellous joy in His resurrection, and still more in His ascension. But all these joys were surpassed by the joy which she received to-day.[1]

WE HAVE STUDIED POEMS IN WHICH, THROUGH THE MEDIUM OF MARY, THE medieval religious poet conceived two of the focal points of sacred history, the birth of Christ and His death and resurrection. We have seen how in the joy Mary felt at Christ's birth were the seeds of her sorrow at His suffering and death, and how the sorrow was transfigured by Christ's resurrection into a final joy which her first joy had foreshadowed. The last event of Mary's life on earth to be celebrated in the yearly cycle of the liturgy was the assumption, the event which brought Mary into the joy of heaven. The other joyful events of her life, the annunciation, Christ's birth, His resurrection after His death, and His ascension, were seen in relation to this final destiny of Mary. It is on the occasion of this feast that St. Aelred, with his words above, urges his congregation especially to rejoice.[2]

Christ came through Mary. Through Christ's passion and death which redeemed man and in virtue of her motherhood of Christ and her spiritual suffering at His death, Mary became the spiritual mother of mankind. Yet at the same time Mary was herself a human being whose joy, like all man's, was to be defined by the degree of closeness of her union with God. Because through the Incarnation Christ took Mary's flesh and she became His mother, Mary shared a closer bond with Him than any other creature.[3] All her beauty and joy as described by the medieval poet came from this relationship. Her maiden motherhood, the source of her title "maiden makeles," was the effect and the sign of her special union. Of Mary's spiritual suffering during Christ's passion, the deepest was caused by being separated from her Son at His death. At His resurrection her joy was restored to an even stronger degree than her first joy experienced at His birth. At His ascension into glory, while Mary remained on earth physically separated from Christ, as man remains now, she was spiritually joined to Christ by the memories of their life, and she lived in loving expectation of her own entry into heaven.[4] At her death, through her assumption by Christ into heaven, she was reunited bodily and spiritually into the full glory of her Son. This union in present time with Christ in majesty is the basis of her title, Queen of Heaven.

A sermon on Mary's five joys to be found in John Mirk's *Festial* describes the meaning of this joyful queenship:

> The v. joye was yn hur assumpcyon, when scho segh hur swete sonne come wyth gret multitude of angelys and sayntys, and fache hur ynto Heuen, and crowned hur qwene of Heuen, and emperess of hell, and lady of all þe world. Syþen all þat ben yn Heuen, schull do hur reuerens and worschyp; and þos þat ben yn hell, schall be buxom to hur byddyng; and þos þat byn yn erthe, schall do hur seruyce and gretying.[5]

A sermon in the *Festial* for the Feast of the Assumption presents the perfection of her queenship in detail:

> And soo crist set hur þer by hym yn his trone, and crowned hur qwene of Heuen, and emperice of hell, and lady of al þe worlde, and hath a hygh ioy passyng all þe sayntys. And as þe sonne leghtenyth al þe day, ryght soo scho lyghtenyth al þe cowrt of Heuen. And al þat byn yn Heuyn byn buxom to hur and redy at hur commaundement, and don hur worschyp in honowre, as þay owyn forto do to hor Lordis modyr and hor qwene; and ys þer of on wyll and one loue wyth þe holy Trinyte þat grauntyth hur what þat euer scho askyth, and at hur prayer rewardyth all hur seruantes. And þus scho sittyþe yn Heuen next to þe Trinite, wyth body gloryfyet, and ys yn full certeyne þat þes ioyes schuld dure for euermor. Þus was þis assumpcyon don ioyfully.
>
> Hit was don alsoo holy, þat is, yn body and yn soule puttyng away the comyn condicion of monkynd, þat ys, forto dey; and so þe body turnyd ynto corupcyon and stynkyng careyne. But for encheson þat Crist toke flesch and blode of oure ladyys body, and so were on flesch and on body, þerfor scho was outtakyn of þat condicion, and was fat ynto Heuen yn body and yn soule.[6]

Mary, the first human being after Christ to have entered heaven, is both the pledge and type of man's own future resurrection and glory. As she was the gate through which God came to earth, so now after her assumption, because of her closeness to God, Mary becomes the gate through which humanity will be reunited to God. As Queen of Heaven she becomes intercessor for man. Her role is the full fruit of the pain she suffered at the crucifixion which made her the mother of man, and it provides the basis of the title given her by the medieval poet: "milsful moder," or Mother of Mercy.[7]

In the religious lyrics we have considered it is Mary's assumption that has defined the present relationship of the poet and his audience to her. The direct appeal to Mary in the petition of the poems has been made with the recognition that she is now Queen of Heaven. When we come to the many English poems which celebrate the five joys of Mary, we find this state of Mary in heaven is the subject. These poems have a double movement which is established by the context of the poet and his audience in sacred history: they look back upon the joyful events in Mary's life from the present perspective of Mary as Queen of Heaven; while at the same time, by enumerating the joys of her life on earth, they define the aspects of Mary's heavenly joy. Mary's heavenly joy is the fulfillment of her earthly joys and the definition of man's future joy.

The devotion of the five joys of Mary—the annunciation and the birth of Christ, His resurrection, His ascension, and Mary's assumption into heaven —was popular in England by the time the first poems appeared in the English tongue after the Conquest, and it continued to be so through the fifteenth century. In his *Auteurs spirituels et textes dévots du moyen âge latin,* Dom A. Wilmart gives evidence that although the number of Mary's joys celebrated varied widely, in England the tradition of five was the most common.[8] *The Index of Middle English Verse* lists nineteen extant poems on the subject from this period.[9] Developing from popular devotional life rather than from the official liturgy of the Church, the joys of Mary are to be found in various places and take different forms. The devotion was often included in the *Horae* or Prymers. In the *Horae Eboracenses,* for example, the Latin book of the Hours of the Virgin Mary according to the use of York, we find after Compline two hymns, each followed by a verse and response and a prayer on the theme of the hymn.[10] The first, "Gavde virgo, mater Christi," according to the heading above it, "De gaudijs beate Marie virginis corporalibus," is about the five joys Mary experienced during her life on earth. Corresponding to the devotion of Mary's earthly joys, the second hymn, "Gavde flore virginali," is about "Alia gaudia beatissime Marie virginis spiritualia." The seven heavenly joys it celebrates are the same as those above in the *Festial* sermon.[11] There are also many examples of the five joys depicted in the illuminations of the Psalters and the *Horae* of the period.[12]

As early as the twelfth century there were legends of special graces granted and miracles performed by Mary for those who honored her five joys.[13] A correspondence between the five joys and the five wounds of Christ was often made. In *Our Lady's Dowry,* T. E. Bridgett gives a picturesque example of this from two wills. One provided that at the Mass and Dirge there be five men dressed in black, standing for the five wounds of Christ, and five women in white, signifying Mary's five joys; and the other, that at every holy day during divine services five candles be burned on the deadman's grave for Christ's wounds and five for Mary's joys.[14] Besides corresponding in number to Christ's wounds, Mary's five joys were seen to correspond to the five letters of her name. We find an example of this in the thirteenth century *Ancrene Riwle,* where a devotion of the five joys follows a similarly organized devotion of the cross. The devotion of the joys is a combination of meditation, recitation of psalms, and a litany-like petition. It consists first of a prayer meditation on the joy, next an antiphon of part of the angelic salutation, "Ave Maria gratia plena dominus tecum," which is followed in turn by a canticle or psalm. The first joy's canticle is the *Magnificat,* the rest of the joys having psalms whose first letters, with that of the *Magnificat,* spell in order *M-A-R-I-A.* Finally, after each psalm the whole Ave Maria is to be repeated five times. Concluding his description, the author of the devotion points out, "The psalms are chosen so that their first letters are those of Our Lady's name, as you may notice, and the prayer about her five greatest joys runs in fives. If you count the greetings in the antiphons, you will find five in each." [15]

The origin of the devotion is obscure. The earliest known example in the English tongue is the description given in the *Riwle.* In his Appendix to M. B. Salu's translation of the *Riwle,* Dom Gerard Sitwell traces the concept behind the devotion to the eleventh century antiphon: "Gaude Dei genetrix, virgo immaculata: gaude quod gaudium ab angelo suscepisti: gaude quod genuisti eterni luminis claritatem, gaude mater, gaude sancte Dei genetrix. Virgo tu sola innupta. Te laudet omnis filii creatura genetricem lucis: sis pro nobis pia interventrix." [16] He indicates this antiphon was connected to the five joys in twelfth century anecdotes about the beneficial results of the devotion. Dom Wilmart suggests the same source,[17] while Natalie White proposes an antiphon used in almost every feast of Mary: "Gaude Maria virgo: cunctas hereses sola interemisti in universo mundo." [18] The earliest example of the poetic development of the devotion seems to be the eleventh century Latin hymn, "Gavde virgo, mater Christi," which was included in the York *Horae.* This is the source of the first Middle English poems we shall consider on Mary's joy.

Glade us maiden, moder milde,
þurru þin herre þu were wid childe—
Gabriel he seide it þe—
Glade us, ful of gode þine,
þam þu bere buten pine
wid þe, lilie of chastete.

Glade us of iesu þi sone
þat þolede deit for monis loue;
þat dehit was, quiic up aros.
Glade us maiden, crist up stey
& in heuene þe i-sey;
He bar him seluen into is clos.

Glade us marie, to Ioye ibrout,—
Muche wrchipe crist hau þe i-worut—
in heuene brit in þi paleis;
Þer þat frut of þire wombe
Be i-yefin us forto fonden
in Ioye þat is endeles.

Gavde virgo, mater Christi,
que per aurem concepisti
Gabriele nuncio.

Gaude quia Deo plena,
peperisti sine pena
cum pudoris lilio.

Gaude quia tui nati,
quem dolebas mortem pati,
fulget resurrectio.

Gaude Christo ascendente,
quod in celum, te vidente,
motu fertur proprio.

Gaude quod post ipsum scandis,
et est honor tibi grandis
in celi palatio.

Vbi fructus ventris tui
per te detur nobis frui:
in perenni gaudio.

The Names of Joy: "Glade Us Maiden, Moder Milde"

THE OTHER POEMS WE HAVE STUDIED HAVE BEEN FORMULATED FROM THE PERspective of sacred history; that is, they have been a meditation on a past event —the annunciation or the death of Christ—as seen from the point of view of the present in which the poem was conceived. The meditation was then applied to the present as a way of future fulfillment. This was evident especially in "Gabriel, fram evene-king," "Þe milde Lomb isprad o rode," and "Stond wel, moder, vnder rode." In "Wy haue ȝe no reuthe on my child?" and "Suete sone, reu on me," the context of the present was not explicitly mentioned in the poem, yet the full meaning and the structure became clear only in relationship to the present as it was defined by sacred history. Using his present knowledge of the meaning of the crucifixion and his own union with it, the listener responded to the meditation as if it were a definition of the present. Those who wound Christ, the poet implied, are those who sin; those who have compassion on Him are those who turn to Him with love and refrain from sin.

When we consider the poems which have as their subject Mary's joy, we find, however, that the fundamental principle of proportion and perspective is modified. The nature of the relationship which the poet and his audience have to Mary in the present becomes the source of movement in the poem. This relationship is defined by sacred history. The explicit point of view of a poem on the joys is the present time. The dynamic basis of movement in the poem is the difference between the quality of the present in which mankind is and the quality of the present in which Mary is. There is a double discrepancy between the two presents, one of grace and, paradoxically, one of time. Both the poet and his audience and Mary occupy the same temporal place in the sequence of events of sacred history, but in terms of state man is separated from Mary in the same way he is separated from heaven. Theology defines the distance. Two facts, both of history, separate man from heaven. The first is that man is in a state of sin and imperfection which only time and grace have the power to remedy. His state is partly a consequence of the second and original cause of separation, the fall of man through the sin of Adam and the fact that the redemption of man still awaits its consummation in the future second coming of Christ. The future event will eternally fix man's relationship to heaven, when time will take the form of the eternal separation from or eternal union with God. Thus man in the present time lives in relation to heaven, much as Mary lived after Christ's ascension, in a tension of love and hope. Mary, because of her sinlessness and because at her death she was assumed by Christ into heaven, is in a state which corresponds to the state man desires to be in. The first human to enter heaven bodily after Christ, besides being man's intercessor, she is the means of defining man's future joy.

In "Glade us maiden, moder milde" the poet addresses Mary as she is now, having been assumed into heaven, from his own present imperfect state of sadness and joy. He speaks to her across the gap, not of space, but of state and time. By recalling and defining the five joys which led Mary into the joy of heaven, it is his purpose to secure for himself and for his audience the perfection of the joy of Mary, and the poet's words themselves, by reaching across the gap to Mary, become a means to joy. To describe the separate causes of Mary's joy on earth, the poet uses the sequence of time, those past events of Mary's life which have led to her present joy in heaven. To describe her state in heaven, the poet uses the figure of place. The poet and his audience are "here" on earth; Mary rejoices "there" in heaven.

Because Mary's joyful state in heaven is her full union with Christ, the aspect of joy in each event recalled consists of an aspect of her union with Christ. First, at His conception and His birth, there is Mary's joy in her maiden motherhood of Christ; then at His resurrection, there is her joy in the redemption of man and in Christ's own release from pain; and at His ascension, her joy in seeing Him enter glory; finally, at her assumption, there is Mary's ultimate joy in her own union with Christ in heaven. Because the poet defines the past joys of Mary's life in light of Mary's eternal present in heaven in order to address her, his words transform the events into timeless names of Mary. Furthermore, the poet distinguishes the individual joys from each other and orders them proportionately, a fact which will become clearer as we consider how the method of the Middle English poet differs from that used by the poet of his Latin source.

The thirteenth century "Glade us maiden, moder milde"[19] is a close translation of the eleventh century hymn "Gavde virgo, mater Christi," the first known example of the devotion of Mary's five joys. According to Brown, in the manuscript the Latin text alternates stanza by stanza with the English verses. Although Brown says that the rhyme scheme of the English follows that of the Latin original, when we compare Brown's edition to the York Latin version of the poem, we see a significant difference.[20] The Latin poem is in six three-line stanzas, and the whole of the Latin develops as a single unit. This development is reflected in the fact that throughout the poem the third line of each of the six stanzas is identically rhymed (aab, ccb, ddb, etc.). On the other hand, the English poet has grouped his stanzas into three units of six lines, each unit rhyming aabccb. This difference in the stanza grouping of the English version is one of several variations made by the English poet which establish the particular proportions of his poem. So that we can see more clearly the purpose of the English version, I have included the York Latin text for comparison.[21]

"Glade us maiden, moder milde," the poet begins with the exhortation that introduces each of the joys, addressing Mary as she is in her present joy in heaven. "Gavde virgo, mater Christi," the Latin begins. Already in the first line two important variations from the Latin version can be seen. The English poet has shifted the command which in the Latin tells Mary herself to rejoice, to apply to "us," explicitly incorporating the joy of mankind into the poem. The English verb suggests two meanings. Let us rejoice, the command may mean, referring to the joy man feels contemplating the significance of the virgin motherhood of Mary. Or, Mary, make us glad, it may mean, the poet having in mind the petition and purpose of his poem to secure for man "Ioye þat is endeles."[22] For the Latin poem's "Christi" the poet has substituted "milde," minimizing the presence of Christ in the first stanza to focus entirely on Mary, and he has added to the title presenting the paradox of her maiden motherhood, a title suggesting her motherhood of man.

With line two the poet introduces a second paradox, "þurru þin herre þu were wid childe," corresponding in the Latin to "que per aurem concepisti." The poet has drawn a phrase from the liturgy, which as well as suggesting

Christ's nature as the Word, emphasizes by its paradoxical meaning the fact of Mary's virginity. (See Figure 3.)[23] By words and phrasing the English conveys a physical concreteness to the expression of the mystery of Christ's conception, as after stating that Mary became with child through her ear, in a separate clause the poet adds, "Gabriel he seide it þe," suggesting that the angel's words themselves were the cause of her conceiving. In the Latin stanza the conception which preserved Mary's virginity is described more with the play of wit than the physical literalness. We shall see later that the English poet deliberately uses this characteristic of concreteness to establish certain correspondences between the events he describes.

"Glade us, ful of gode þine," in the beginning of his second address, the poet echoes the angel's salutation to Mary as "full of grace." Substituting for the abstract word "grace" the proper name "gode," he introduces the theme of the second joy and proposes yet a third paradox to explain the first two. The child conceived was God. Mary, bodily carrying God, was literally "full of God." Being full of God is the basis of her second joy: first, that she should bear God in such an intimate way; second, in lines five and six, that in giving birth to God, Who was bodily present, she should suffer no pain.[24] The insertion of the editorial comma by Brown makes interpretation of "wid þe, lilie of chastete" difficult. The comma causes "lilie of chastete" to appear to be another title for Mary, corresponding to "moder milde." But the Latin helps us to clarify the poet's intention here: "peperisti sine pena/ cum pudoris lilio." You gave birth without pain, like the lily of chastity. "Wid þe" can mean "like," so that "lilie of chastete" is not used as another epithet for Mary, but as a figure for comparison.[25] The phrase means, Mary bore God without pain, in a birth that preserved her virginity; she is in this like the lily of chastity.

The fact that the poem is oriented in present time and condition and is an appeal to Mary is reflected in the language with which the poet has described these first two events which caused Mary's joy. Rather than recounting the joys by means of transitive verbs as happenings occurring by cause and effect, by casting them into descriptive phrases the poet has presented the events as if they were the attributes of Mary. In lines one through three the means and the effect of the angel's annunciation, "þurru þin herre þu were wid childe," are given as the cause, and the actual cause is appended as a qualifying thought, "Gabriel he seide it þe," so that the means and the effect are included not as part of the event, but as they show why the poet names Mary maiden and mother. In a similar way, in lines four through six the action of the event is linked to the descriptive phrase "ful of gode þine" by a relative pronoun "þam," which introduces in a descriptive clause, "þu bere buten pine," followed in turn, in the sixth line, by another descriptive clause comparing the event to the quality of the lily. By minimizing the action of an event in order to define a state or quality of Mary, the poet achieves his double purpose, both to define Mary's joys and at the same time by virtue of them to name Mary in present time.

The next stanza, repeating the appeal that Mary make us glad, contrasts to the first stanza in which the poet of the English version has made the motherhood of Mary the focus. It presents her next two joys by centering on Christ as His godhood is shown, first, after His death, in His resurrection, and then in His ascension into glory.

> Glade us of iesu þi sone
> þat þolede deit for monis loue;
> þat dehit was, quiic up aros.

Make us glad in Jesus thy Son; or possibly, let us rejoice in Jesus thy Son. In the third joy, as in the first two, the poet formulates the events into a way of naming. Speaking of Jesus as Mary's Son, he identifies Him further by two relative clauses, the tense holding the action of the events into a past time as facts which the poet uses to show why we should rejoice and why Mary should give us joy in regard to her Son Who is the source of all our joy.

The differences between the Latin and the English versions of the poem in the lines on the resurrection and ascension are marked. The Latin poet began his poem by naming Mary "mater Christi," using the part of her Son's name that identifies Him as the Messiah, whereas the poet of the English version told of His conception and birth entirely withholding the name of Mary's Son in order to focus on the "maiden moder" through whom Christ came. Here, the Latin poet has obscured the name of Mary's Son to emphasize Mary's suffering. Referring to Him indirectly, through the suffering of Mary, "quia tui nati,/ quem dolebas mortem pati," he contrasts to the suffering the bursting forth of His resurrection, "fulget resurrectio." The English poet, on the other hand, as he tells of how Mary's Son is crucified and rises, names Him for the first time. He does not use the name "Christ," but the personal name "iesu," which emphasizes the human bond between Mary and Christ and the humanity "þat þolede deit for monis loue." The English poet stresses the cosmic meaning of the event, that Jesus suffered death because of His love for mankind. And by his abrupt contrasting of life to death, "þat dehit was, quiic up aros," he emphasizes the power which Christ will fully reveal in the next joy, His ascension, where for the first time the poet will name Him "crist."

Glade us maiden, crist up stey
& in heuene þe i-sey;
He bar him seluen into is clos.

"Make us glad, maiden," the poet repeats the address of the opening stanza as he reaches the central point in his poem and prepares to present the upward motion of Mary's own assumption. The account of the fourth joy, when "crist up stey," was prepared for by the third joy, when Christ "quiic up aros." It is the basis for the fifth joy, when Mary will be brought to joy, and for mankind's appeal in the last three lines for "Ioye þat is endeles." As he tells how Christ in entering heaven prepared a place for Mary and for mankind, for the first time the English poet presents the joy as an action. In a series of three clauses with three active verbs and one implied active verb, he says, Christ ascended, you saw Him (go into) heaven, He bore Himself into His "clos."

It is at this point in the Latin and the English that both poets name Christ. "Gaude Christo ascendente,/ quod in celum, te vidente,/ motu fertur proprio." Rejoice in Christ ascending, Who as you watched was carried into heaven by His own power. Make us glad, maiden, the English poet says, Christ ascended and you saw Him go into heaven. By His own power He bore Himself into His enclosure. Stressing the tangible place Christ entered, the English poet prepares for his description, in the next stanza, of Mary herself in her bright palace in heaven.[26]

Glade us marie, to Ioye ibrout,—
Muche wrchipe crist hau þe i-worut—
in heuene brit in þi paleis;
Þer þat frut of þire wombe
Be i-yefin us forto fonden
in Ioye þat is endeles.

"Give us joy Mary, brought to joy." The poet begins the last stanza by repeating the appeal a fifth time to introduce Mary's fifth joy. With the final joy he addresses Mary for the first time by her proper name, as if her name could be uttered only after the events which define her nature have been told. The poet returns to the mode of the first two joys. Again making an event into an attribute by which to identify Mary, he tells the fifth joy with an infinitive phrase, describing Mary as she is in the present as a result of her assumption. The assumption forms the final component of her name.

After addressing Mary as she now is in heaven, the poet bridges the time from that historically past moment of the assumption to the historically present moment in which he has named the joys. Brown's punctuation with dashes in line fourteen emphasizes the double possibility of temporal application. By the joys in the past and through all time "muche wrchipe crist haue þe i-worut." Now that the poet has oriented Mary's joy in literal time, in line fifteen he specifies Mary's perpetual state of joy, her condition, in terms of a place in heaven. This place was prepared for in the three lines on the ascension. Mary has now been placed in that same "clos" into which Christ bore Himself. In the English version the poet has given a further concreteness to Mary's palace. First, by placing her in heaven "brit," then by distinguishing her own palace from the rest of heaven, he has given a separate identity to Mary's joy within the joy of Christ. No such specific development of place is suggested by the Latin version, where the synthetic grammatical relationships of "in celi palatio" suggest rather the general quality of heaven, its richness, brightness and glory.

Omitting the appeal "Glade us," the last three lines put instead of a sixth joy of Mary the possible joy of mankind. They define the poet and his audience's present relationship to Mary's final joy, which they have not experienced, through the use of the figure "þat frut of þire wombe." This figure of fruit, used as well by the Latin poet and often found in the liturgy, is presented in sharp contrast to the categories of time and space by which the poet has organized his poem.[27] It is a mystical figure expressing the unitive experience of God: "Þer," in that palace, give us the fruit of thy womb to taste, to try, to experience in endless joy. Christ is the source, the experience of Him the fruit or state itself of joy, "Ioye þat is endeles." But at the same time as the poet reveals a glimpse of heavenly delight, with these last three lines he has defined mankind's distance from joy. "Þer," in that place, distinguishes by space the place where the joy will be experienced from the place where man is now. "Þat frut . . . be i-yefin us forto fonden," by verb tense and time and by the very fact that Christ is presented in a figure of which Mary is the basis and medium, the poet shows man's distance in time and vision from the future endless enjoyment. This distance is what, through naming and securing Mary's intercession, the poet seeks to close with his words.

Looking back at the structure of the whole poem from the perspective of this final petition to Mary in virtue of the five joys by which the poet has named her, a certain proportionate correspondence between the parts of the poem can be seen which explains the modifications the poet of the English version has made from his Latin source. The two joys of the last stanza of the English poem, with their account of Mary's entry into the palace of heaven and the petition to Mary that there in heaven the fruit of her womb be given us to experience in endless joy, correspond to the two joys of the opening stanzas, where the coming of Christ is seen through her motherhood. The opening stanza and the closing stanza are focused on Mary's motherhood, the last fulfilling the first, but in an imperfect way. The two joys of the central stanza tell of the manifestation of God as man, and the events of the resurrection and ascension of Christ are the power in history by which the present moment and the hope of the future have been made possible. Now, by virtue of the events of the two central joys—the resurrection and the ascension—as she was the mother of Christ, so Mary has become the mother of man's future joy. Man's joy will be the experience of the beatific vision. Now in his position on earth his joy is hidden from him, but both by virtue of the Incarnation and through Mary who was the medium of Christ's taking flesh, and who is now in fact in heaven, man asks to be granted joy.

The whole poem is an address to Mary with the end of joy in view. The way in which the poet transforms events to names reflects the proportions the poet has established. Mary's names are aspects of the state of joy. The fact that the ascension is recounted not as a name, but as an event, expresses the element of time and the power which have established the poem's proportion. Because of the ascension of Christ into heaven, Mary could be assumed to Him. Now in present time man stands below; Mary is above. Now again Mary is the medium of birth, but this time of man's entrance into heaven, and now again as during Mary's pregnancy, the glory of Christ is hidden from man in the present moment as man hopes for but does not fully experience joy.[28] (See Figure 7 and descriptive note.)

The English poet's choice of stanzaic form corresponds to this same proportion of Christ being hidden, then revealed, then hidden again, as the poet couples the annunciation with Christ's birth, the resurrection with His ascension, and Mary's assumption with mankind's final prayer.[29] And the poet's withholding of the messianic name of Mary's Son until the events of the resurrection and ascension and the hiding of His identity again in the last three lines are further components of this same proportion. The succession of titles for Mary, "maiden, moder," "ful of gode," "maiden" again, and finally her full naming, "marie," in the last stanza show the shift of focus through the poem until the poet formulates his final petition in virtue of what he has already said.

As part of this double correspondence between parts of the poem—the first two joys on Mary's motherhood of God corresponding to the last two on her motherhood of man, and the central two joys which manifest Christ to the endless joy of Mary revealed, yet concealed, in the figure of the fruit of her womb—there is another structural quality of the English version which distinguishes it from the Latin. Because the poet has fixed the events as timeless names, and because he embodies the quality of Mary's joy in a figure of space, the effect of the poem on the mind's eye is pictorial. Like illuminated figures or figures in stained glass, each naming of Mary presents an image of the joy, and we can compare the poet's presentation of the joys to their illuminations.[30] In the lines on the annunciation and birth we see Mary and the angel, his words of salutation, the dove descending to the Virgin's ear, the lily. In the resurrection we see Christ bursting from His tomb, and in the ascension we see Him disappear with only His feet left below the clouds of heaven which enclose Him, while Mary and the disciples stand below gazing up. We then see Mary enthroned in a palace in heaven. But the final figure of Christ, which shows His present hidden relationship to man, is not given in visual concepts. In the figure of man's future fullness of joy, Christ is presented to the blind senses as what man can touch and taste and consume.

Leuedy, for þare blisse
þat þu heddest at þe frume,
Þo þu wistest myd-iwisse
þat ihesus wolde beo þi sune,—
Þe hwile we beoþ on lyue þisse
sunnen to don is vre wune—
Help vs nv þat we ne mysse
of þat lif þat is to cume.

Moder, bliþe were þu þo
hwanne þu iseye heouen-king
Of þe ibore wiþ-vte wo
þat scop þe and alle þing.
Beo vre scheld from vre ivo
& yef vs þine blessyng;
And bi-wyte vs euer-mo
from alle-kunnes suneging.

Leuedi, al myd rihte
þu were gled and bliþe
Þo crist þureh his myhte
aros from deþe to lyue,

Þat alle þing con dihte
  and wes i-boren of wyue.
He make vs clene and bryhte
  for his wundes fyue.

From þe Munt of olyuete
  þo þi sone to heouene steyh,
Þu hit by-heolde myd eye swete,
  for he wes þin heorte neyh.
Þer he haueþ imaked þi sete
  in o stude þat is ful heyh,
Þer þe schulen engles grete,
  for þu ert boþe hende and sleyh.

Þe king þat wes of þe ibore,
  to heouene he þe vette
To þare blisse þat wes for-lore,
  & bi hym-seolue sette,
Vor he hedde þe icore.
  wel veyre he þe grette;
Blyþe were þu þer-vore,
  þo engles þe imette.

Moder of Milce & mayde hende,
  ich þe bidde as i con;
Ne let þu noht þe world vs blende
  þat is ful of vre i-von,
Ac help vs at vre lyues ende,
  þu þat bere god and mon,
And vs alle to heouene sende
  hwenne we schulle þis lif for-gon.

Ihesus, for þire moder bene
  þat is so veyr and so bryht
Al so wis, so heo is quene
  of heouene and eorþe—& þet is ryht,—
Of vre sunnes make vs clene
  & yef vs þat eche lyht,
And to heouene vs alle i-mene,
  louerd, þu bryng, for wel þu Miht.

The Vision of Joy: "Leuedy, for Þare Blisse/ Þat Þu Heddest at Þe Frume"

It seems strange indeed that after what has been shown of God's closeness to our souls there are so few concerned about perceiving the First Principle within themselves. Distracted by many cares, the human mind does not enter into itself through the memory; beclouded by sense images, it does not come back to itself through the intelligence; and drawn away by the concupiscences, it does not return to itself through the desire for interior sweetness and spiritual joy. Therefore, completely immersed in things of sense, the soul cannot re-enter into itself as the image of God.

And just as, when one has fallen, he must lie where he is unless another is at hand to raise him up, so our soul could not be perfectly lifted up out of these things of sense to see itself and the eternal Truth in itself had not Truth, taking human form in Christ, become a ladder restoring the first ladder that had been broken in Adam.[1]

"Leuedy, for Þare Blisse/ Þat Þu Heddest at Þe Frume"[2] is a prayer for wisdom in its most precise theological sense, a prayer to see God and not to be blinded by the world. The purpose of the poem is, by defining in so far as possible the joy man will experience in heaven, to appeal to its power. The poet addresses Mary in her state, now, in heaven, and against her joy he juxtaposes man's own present with its sorrow. As in the poems on the crucifixion, this sorrow has its theological dimensions: it springs from man's limited view of suffering or his separation from God by sin. In this poem the poet seeks to transform both man's limited vision to light and his state of separation to union with God by defining step by step the events of Mary's increasing awareness of joy and closeness to her Son.

With the opening of his poem, the poet does not address Mary as Maiden Mother or Queen of Heaven, but simply as "Leuedy."[3] He speaks to her as one with courtly power, in recognition that she is the mother of God, and he appeals to her by virtue of her joy at this. In contrast to "Glade us maiden, moder milde," the event of the first joy is not made into a name for Mary. Rather, it is described as the state of awareness Mary had which came from her realization—"þu wistest myd-iwisse"—that her son would be Jesus. The qualifying phrase "at þe frume" recognizes that the first joy, the annunciation, was the beginning of Mary's present joy in heaven and also the beginning for man of the ultimate joy which he will experience in his final union with Christ.[4]

To this beginning joy of Mary's life on earth the poet opposes the present sorrow of himself and his listeners. While in this life, he says, it is our custom perpetually to sin. Yet this perpetual kind of sin, as life itself, has really only an apparent perpetuality, for it will reach an end at the end of each man's life, when man will be eternally separated from or eternally united to God. Just as Mary's joy is a foreshadowing of man's perpetual joy, so man's perpetual sinning in this life is the reflection of the perpetual sorrow man may enter in the next. It is against this sorrow and in the awareness of Mary's perpetual joy and her first joy that the poet appeals to Mary. Help us now so that we do not miss that life of joy which is to come. Implied in the term "þat lif" is the possibility also of being cut off from life, for to miss that life, eternal joy, would be to come to hell, which is not life, but eternal death.

Mother, the poet addresses Mary the second time, in stanza two, describing the joy she had in her motherhood, you were happy when you saw the King of Heaven born of you without pain. Now in the poem, with "þu iseye" we recognize that Christ has become bodily manifest to the world. But "þu iseye" has a double sense, the outer one referring to the joy of Mary at seeing her Child after His birth, and the inner one referring to the mystery of Mary's giving birth without pain. Giving birth to her Child without pain affirmed her knowledge that this was God Whom she had borne, King of Heaven "þat scop þe and alle þing." With this last phrase the poet echoes the words so frequently used in the summer liturgy to honor Mary's motherhood: "Hail, holy mother, who didst bring forth in childbirth the king who ruleth over heaven and earth for ever and ever"; and also "Blessed and to be venerated art thou, O virgin Mary, who without touch of shame wast found mother of the Saviour. *V.* O virgin mother of God, he whom the whole world cannot contain enclosed himself in thy womb, and was made man."[5] Not only did Mary bear the Child without pain, but the Child she held within her was He Whom the whole world cannot contain: He to Whom you gave birth is He Who made you and every created thing. Thus the poet spells out the full implications of the Child she contemplated then, the knowledge which was the basis of her second joy.

That the appeal of the second half of the stanza is by virtue of this second joy is implicit. As he would appeal to a mother, the poet appeals to Mary to protect us during the interval of this life, that she be our shield from our foe. And, he asks her, give us your "blessyng"; that is, give us the joy that you had—literally, give us God Himself. The same paradox stated in relation to the joy, that Mary bore her Creator, is implied also in the petition. By virtue of the fact that Mary bore the King of Heaven and Creator of all things, now we may ask for Him as our own. The last two lines of the stanza develop the request for protection, extending it to cover every moment of time, every kind of defection from life, "alle-kunnes suneging": Protect us forever from every kind of sinning (or from all mankind's sinning).

Again, in stanza three, the poet addresses Mary as "Leuedi," as he speaks of the joy she experienced when Christ rose from the dead: With good reason were you glad and joyful when Christ through His own power rose from death to life. Mary was right not only to rejoice at the fact that Christ rose from the dead, but that He did it through His own power. According to Brown's edition, the petition in this stanza comprises only the last two lines, and lines twenty-one and twenty-two develop the meaning of Mary's joy. Christ's resurrection is seen to be a second birth which the poet presents in light of the first as another action by the Creator. It was fitting that He "þat scop þe and alle þing," He "þat alle þing con dihte," Who ordained all things, "and wes i-boren of wyue," Whom Mary had seen born from her, should rise. And just as the last stanza contained the paradox that God Who made all things should be born of a woman, so this presents the paradox that a man born of woman should raise himself from the dead.[6] The fact that a man should rise from the dead prepares the ground for the rest of the joyful events and the final petition of the poem.

In this stanza of joy at the resurrection, the poet recalls in his petition the efficacy of the passion, the necessary condition of the resurrection, as he prays: Let Him make us clean and bright by His five wounds. With its indefinite verb tense, the appeal seems to cover an indefinite time, reaching even into the next life where man will be in the purity and light of eternal joy. But because the poem is a prayer for vision, the petition by the virtue of Christ's five wounds may have a special significance. The *Ancrene Riwle,* for example, applies Christ's five wounds to cleanse the five senses: "Ah, Jesus, grant me Thy mercy; Jesus, hung on the cross for my sins, by those five wounds from which Thou didst there bleed, heal my soul, bleeding from all the sins with which it has been wounded through my five senses. Grant this in remembrance of Thy wounds, dear Lord." [7] The poet here may mean, let the five wounds of Christ purify the five senses that we may be bright and clear and thus see God. Perhaps, too, the poet had in mind the numerical correspondence of the wounds to the five joys which he is using to come to eternal light.

From þe Munt of olyuete
þo þi sone to heouene steyh,
Þu hit by-heolde myd eye swete,
for he wes þin heorte neyh.

When your Son ascended from Mount Olivet to heaven, the poet continues, you beheld His ascension with sweet eye, because He was near your heart. With the fourth joy the poet tells of the climax of Mary's spiritual joy. Her spiritual joy is signified by the joy of her "eye" which is the window of her soul. Beholding Christ's ascension, her eye was "swete." She was gladdened because her Son, near to her heart, went into the glory of His godhood from which He had so mysteriously descended by being born and by dying. Her joy was a spiritual joy, for He was bodily apart from her whose flesh He was, not with her as He had been on earth. Now He has been manifested in His full power, but His power has literally separated Him from Mary.[8]

Just as Christ's resurrection has prepared the ground for man's reunion with God, so this joy prepares for Mary's ultimate joy, and in the structure of the poem there is a modification. In the first three stanzas, complementary to Mary's vision of joy, the poet had juxtaposed man's petition from his present state of sorrow. But in this stanza and the next there is no direct appeal by man. Instead the poet shuts out the perspective of present time and restricts the view to the past. The next four lines are a prophecy:

> Þer he haueþ imaked þi sete
> in o stude þat is ful heyh,
> Þer þe schulen engles grete,
> for þu ert boþe hende and sleyh.

In his imagination the speaker has projected himself into the past moment after Christ has ascended and left Mary on earth. As did the poet of "Als i lay vp-on a nith" who imagined what Mary knew at Christ's birth, he enters the limitations of what Mary must have understood at the moment of the ascension, as she felt joyous for Christ's joy, but sad to be separated from Him. And in place of his petition, the poet speaks to Mary, almost as though to console her for her loss of Christ: There, he says, He has made your seat, in a place that is very high; there angels shall greet you, for you are both "hende and sleyh." [9] Because of her beauty and grace Christ will send for her. She will be assumed into heaven. The poet again describes Mary in courtly terms, as he would speak of a noble lady, as he will speak of her when she is Queen of Heaven (line 41).

By dwelling on the moment of Christ's ascension the poet has effected a pause in the narrative of the five joys. He has emphasized the event in the past when the situation of Mary was most like the present situation of the poet and his audience who now appeal to her. In the place of man's appeal the poet has prophesied Mary's assumption. By prophesying her desire's fulfillment, the poet has uttered the desire of Mary's heart. The language of the foretelling appears as the grammatical inverse of man's appeal in the other stanzas, and the declarative statement could be rephrased into man's supplication to Christ for his own experience of eternal joy: There make our place in heaven. There let us see the court of heaven and Your glory. By virtue of Your five wounds, make us bright that "we ne mysse/ of þat lif þat is to cume" (line 8).

By the fifth joy the prophecy of the fourth is fulfilled: The King Who was born of you fetched you into heaven, to that bliss that was lost, and set you beside Himself. In "Glade us maiden, moder milde" the fact that man had lost his joy was explained at the same time as the poet told of Christ's death which brought back man's joy, in order to show the purpose of His death.

Here, in line thirty-five, man's lost joy is mentioned in order to define the significance of the joy of heaven into which Mary is assumed. At the same time it defines why, in the first stanza, the poet had described the first joy of Mary as "þare blisse/ þat þu heddest at þe frume." The first joy of Mary by virtue of the Incarnation and its consequences literally *was* the beginning again of the joy that had been forfeited by man.

Not only does it define the first joy accurately, but the mention of lost joy defines the meaning of joy itself. Just as the source of sorrow is separation from God, so the source of joy is union with God. Up to this event in the poem the poet has described three aspects of Mary's union, first the nature of the One to Whom Mary will be united, second the completeness of her experience of union, and third the movement of uniting. Throughout the joys of the poem the godhood of Christ, first mysteriously hidden during His birth in the flesh through a woman, yet signified by the fact that the birth was painless and that Mary remained a virgin, has been manifested until in His full glory He ascends to heaven. Mary's experience of joy has increased as Christ's godhood became more manifest, and as He ascended it became most deep. Yet her experience of joy could not be full until she was with Him in body as well as spirit. The means of Mary's final union has been the movement of the events of sacred history which join man to God, the birth, death, and resurrection of Christ, His ascension, and in this stanza, Mary's assumption.

This stanza, then, embodies what Mary's full joy means. Christ has fetched her into heaven. Whereas at the ascension Christ was called Mary's "sone" to heighten the sense of their human separation, now in heaven, to reflect His glory, Christ is called King—yet linked still to His mother and manhood by the relative clause "þat wes of þe ibore," echoing line eleven. The King fetched her to heaven, to the joy that had been lost, and placed her beside Him. For, the poet explains, to express Christ's love for Mary by showing Christ desired her, "he hedde þe icore," He had chosen her. How fairly He greeted her! And "Blyþe were þu þer-vore," the poet claims, echoing the opening of stanza two which described Mary's joy in beholding God both physically and spiritually at His birth.

Now, having prepared both the full definition of Mary's joy and the full definition of man's desire by showing his present state and indicating his joys in the future, the poet concludes his poem on the five joys with an appeal to Mary and an appeal to Christ, in the present, the direct appeal that he had omitted from his description of the ascension and assumption. The poet asks, as he had prepared his audience to ask by the last four lines of the ascension stanza, for what he and his listeners desire.

> Moder of Milce & mayde hende,
> ich þe bidde as i con;
> Ne let þu noht þe world vs blende
> þat is ful of vre i-von,
> Ac help vs at vre lyues ende,
> þu þat bere god and mon,
> And vs alle to heouene sende
> hwenne we schulle þis lif for-gon.

Mother of Mercy and courteous maid, the poet addresses her, referring both to her maiden motherhood and to her heavenly beauty (line 32): I pray to you as I know how. Do not let the world blind us, the world that is full of our foes. In so far as I can see, I pray that we may see. How fittingly the poet's prayer for vision comes, defining those foes from which he had appealed in stanza two (line 13) that we be shielded. And as he had asked for Mary's blessing then (line 14), now he asks with the implications of the blessing having been made clear: Do not let us be blinded, but help us at our lives' end, you who have borne God and man. Mary's title Mother of Mercy is used in its full sense to mean Mary the mother of Christ Who is our mercy, Who has been fully manifested as both God and man to restore our joy. The last two lines complete the meaning of the help the poet requests at "vre lyues ende": When we shall lose this life, send us all to heaven.

Now in relation to Christ the poet and his audience stand exactly as Mary had stood in the fourth stanza, looking up after Christ Who has ascended into heaven. The second part of the final petition addresses Christ:

> Ihesus, for þire moder bene
> þat is so veyr and so bryht
> Al so wis, so heo is quene
> of heouene and eorþe—& þet is ryht,—
> Of vre sunnes make vs clene
> & yef vs þat eche lyht,
> And to heouene vs alle i-mene,
> louerd, þu bryng, for wel þu Miht.

Jesus, for Your mother's prayer who is so fair and so bright—the poet appeals to Christ through a power of Mary which comes from Christ; that is, through her beauty, which is the radiance of her joyous state. Just as wise she is as she is queen of heaven and of earth—and that is right—the poet continues to describe Mary in terms of her glory. "Wis" is a fitting adjective for Mary in the context of the poem, for the poet has shown that of all creatures she is wisest;[10] that is, in the words of Bonaventure with which we opened this section, Mary has been most perfectly "lifted up" to see herself and the "eternal Truth in itself." Her position as Queen of Heaven is both the source and the fruit of her wisdom.[11] "Wis" is in keeping also with Mary's traditional definition in the liturgy, which applies to her passages from Ecclesiasticus in which Wisdom speaks.[12] For man, folly, which is the sin opposing wisdom, consists in his "plunging his sense into earthly things, whereby his sense is rendered incapable of perceiving Divine things."[13] It was just this sin from which in the previous stanza the poet appealed to Mary to defend himself and his audience, "Ne let þu noht þe world vs blende" (line 43).

In this final petition to Christ the poet has rephrased his appeal, summarizing the petitions of the whole poem into one by using the two fundamental sources of man's distance from joy, his sin—his state—and his distance in time. For the sake of Your mother's prayer, who is beautiful and wise, and thus with right the queen of heaven and earth, he prays, cleanse our sins so that we may have light, so that like Mary we may experience Your joy. And, as You brought Mary into bliss, bring us too in time all to heaven, "for wel þu Miht." As You are God "þat scop . . . alle þing" (line 12), Who "aros from deþe to lyue" (line 20), and "þat alle þing con dihte" (line 21), and by virtue of the fact that You fetched Mary "to þare blisse þat wes for-lore" (line 35), well do You have that power to bring us to heaven if You choose. Mary's full vision and power and Christ's glory and power have been fully defined and invoked to be in turn the power by which man may cross that gap between himself and the sovereign Good.

The Figure of Delight

> Not yet, then, have I told or conceived, O Lord, how greatly Your blessed shall rejoice. They will rejoice according as they will love, and they will love according as they will know. How far will they know You, Lord, and how much will they love You? Truly eye has not seen nor ear heard, nor has it entered into the heart of man in this life how much they will know You and love You in that life.[1]

ST. BONAVENTURE COMPOSED HIS "BREVILOQUIUM" TO SHOW HOW THEOLOGY discourses about God, that "the truth of Holy Scripture is by God, from God, in accord with God, and because of God, so that this science may deservedly appear to be a single and orderly science and not undeservedly be named theology."[2] After, in the manner of theology, he has described "first, the Trinity of God; second, the creation of the world; third, the corruption of sin; fourth, the incarnation of the Word; fifth, the grace of the Holy Ghost; sixth, the sacramental remedy; and seventh, the state of the final judgment," and after he has defined the glories of paradise, he ends his whole endeavor of formulating the truth of Scripture with St. Anselm's description of the joy of heaven.

To describe heaven Anselm uses all the categories by which language can raise the mind to describe the good of heaven. To teach his reader the idea of the good, he describes all goods man may desire, and shows that all these goods shall be enjoyed: "Why do you wander abroad, little man, in search of the goods of soul and body? Love the one good in which are all goods, and it is enough. Seek the simple good which is all good, and it is enough. What do you love, my flesh? What do you seek, my soul? There is whatever you love, whatever you seek." Beauty, swiftness, life, satisfaction of hunger and thirst; melody, pure pleasure, wisdom, power, security: "But what a joy and how great it is, where is there a good of such a kind or so great? Heart of man, needy heart, heart acquainted with sorrows, overwhelmed with sorrows, how greatly would you rejoice if you abounded in all these things? Ask your inner self whether it could contain its joy over so great a blessedness for itself."

To teach his reader to contemplate the extent of man's joy, he makes him aware how the heart will overflow with joy and its joy be multiplied in so much and to the degree that anyone else whom his heart loves possesses the same blessedness: "Thus in that perfect love of innumerable blessed angels and sainted men where none will love another less than himself, everyone will rejoice for each of the others as for himself." Then upon this he multiplies the fact that each man will love God beyond comparison and more than himself and all the others with himself: "If they will so love God with all their heart and all their mind and all their soul, still all their heart and all their mind and all their soul will not suffice for the worthiness of this love. Surely they will so rejoice with all their heart and all their mind and all their soul that all their heart and all their mind and all their soul will not suffice for the fullness of their joy."

But here Anselm breaks off his description as the joy exceeds the capacity of his heart and his words, and he turns with the boldness of perfect love of God to ask, as God bids him to ask, to enter into that joy. Approaching the center of the joy opened to man through the redemption, man can no longer speak. As Bonaventure says, having reached the seventh stage of his journey of the mind to God, "De excessu mentali et mystico, in quo requies datur intellectui, affectu totaliter in Deum per excessum transeunte":

> If you wish to know how these things may come about, ask grace, not learning; desire, not the understanding; the groaning of prayer, not diligence in reading; the Bridegroom, not the teacher; God, not man; darkness, not clarity; not light, but the fire that wholly inflames and carries one into God through transporting unctions and consuming affections. God Himself is this fire, and *His furnace is in Jerusalem;* and it is Christ who

enkindles it in the white flame of His most burning Passion. This fire he alone truly perceives who says: *My soul chooseth hanging, and my bones, death.* He who loves this death can see God, for it is absolutely true that *Man shall not see me and live.*

Let us, then, die and enter into this darkness. Let us silence all our care, our desires, and our imaginings. With Christ crucified, let us pass *out of this world to the Father,* so that, when the Father is shown to us, we may say with Philip: *It is enough for us.* Let us hear with Paul: *My grace is sufficient for thee,* and rejoice with David, saying: *My flesh and my heart have fainted away: thou art the God of my heart, and the God that is my portion forever. Blessed be the Lord forever, and let all the people say: so be it, so be it.* Amen.[3]

The Middle English lyrics which we have discussed are fundamentally prayer. Their aim has been ultimate union with God. Yet there is an essential poverty at the center of man's prayer to God. The theologians are unanimous in identifying it, from the time of Paul: "We see now through a glass in a dark manner: but then face to face. Now I know in part: but then I shall know even as I am known" (1 Cor. 13:12). There is a fundamental discrepancy between the world and God no matter how profoundly man searches for God's image in it.[4] The poverty of creation as it confronts God is expressed in different ways. By the mystics it is called darkness.[5] By theologians it is put forth in the fundamental teaching that the world is created for the glorification of God, that nothing is to be loved in itself, but to be used to love God; that all things are signs.[6] At its most creative, the fundamental poverty in the prayer of the world, as in the life of St. Francis, allows the "freedom of the sons of God" and creates a deeper beauty. At its least creative, it produces monotony and ugliness.

Taken as a group, the medieval religious lyrics reflect the essential disproportion between the experience of delight and both the capacity of man's desire for delight and the unknown possibilities of delight. This poverty of experience is a result both of man's faulty desire, his sin and defection, or his condition; and of the gap between the present moment in sacred history and what is yet to come to pass—the event of the second coming of Christ Who will judge the living and the dead and establish whether a man, depending upon the quality of his desire, shall dwell in eternal sorrow or eternal joy. In spite of the fact of a falling short of the full experience of delight, a fall which reflects the fall of Adam from original joy, the Christian soul can name the delight he most deeply desires. Although neither has he experienced it directly nor does he yet know even the full extent of his desire for it, through the power of grace and with the perspective of theology he can call upon it. Recognizing this gap between the experience of delight and the desire for it which theology defines and the life of the Church bridges, will help us understand why so many of the medieval religious lyrics are unpoetic and flat. The flat lyrics are those which, seeking delight, use both the traditional formulations of theology and the traditional forms of poetry in a way that is not itself a source of delight to the beholder.

For the medieval theologian, the basis of beauty was proportionality, to be found in the ordered unity and diversity of God's creation. The proportions of beauty were reflected in the science of numbers—arithmetic and geometry (time and space)—from which were derived music, the plastic arts and architecture, and poetry.[7] The divine proportioning of creation and history was revealed by God through Christ, the New Testament, and established in its perpetual forms—its order and hierarchy—in the living liturgy of the Church. Each of the lyrics we have considered so far has been constructed in some manner proportionate to the event of sacred history it celebrates (the figure of virgin motherhood for the sequence on the annunciation, the cross for that on the crucifixion) or to the sorrow or joy it effects in mankind (to Mary's experience in "Als i lay," to Christ's in "Þe milde Lomb"). The structural proportions of sacred history transcend the individual arts, finding their definition in the proportions of the creative action of God, which is revealed in His Word, the expression of His thought, or Christ.

Rather than evaluating the religious lyrics as they do or do not effect intensity of the audience's emotion, which has been the tendency of most of the modern critics, I would like to set up a structural criterion and contrast the religious lyrics which are ordered in a unity proportioned by their subject matter to those which are ordered by the poverty of disproportionate dead forms. To illustrate the differences between religious poems which seem flat and unproportioned and the proportioned religious lyrics, and also to show their relationship to the proportioning of sacred history, I would like to compare the form of "Leuedy, for þare blisse" with that of two other works which use the five joys of Mary. The first is a prayer which is not in poetic form, but which uses sacred history to define the third joy of Mary in a way that figures the delight to be experienced in the proportions of the prayer itself; this is the prayer of the third joy in the *Ancrene Riwle*. The second is a prayer on the five joys which is in poetic form and which uses sacred history, but which does not figure delight in the prayer itself. "Leuedy, for þare blisse" will provide an example of a prayer in poetic form, which uses sacred history, and which at the same time in itself figures forth delight.

> O Lady, St Mary, because of the great joy that thou hadst when thou sawest thy dear and precious Son, after His grievous death, risen to joyful life, His Body sevenfold brighter than the sun, grant me to die with Him and to rise in Him, to die to the world and to live spiritually, to share His sufferings as a companion, on earth, that I may be His companion in happiness, in heaven. Because of the great joy that thou hadst, O Lady, in his blessed resurrection, after thy great sorrow, lead me, after the sorrow in which I live here, to thy happiness.[8]

The purpose of this prayer from the *Riwle* is single: that because of Mary's joy in the resurrection, the soul who prays be united to her Son Who is God. The kind of union is established by sacred history, which defines both where man is in the present and who he is in relation to God. Ultimately the desire of the prayer reaches from the relation with God at this present moment to union with God in body and soul through Christ in heaven. Heaven is embodied by the figure of Mary's happiness, for she is in heaven now. What makes us feel the beauty of the prayer is that the author structures the expression of this specific desire in several ways which are proportioned to each other.

The author structures the prayer by three aspects of sacred history, describing (1) Mary's joy, as it is caused by (2) Christ's resurrection, and (3) man's present desire to be led to future heavenly joy by the power of Mary's joy. First, Mary's joy is defined by her seeing her "dear and precious Son, after His grievous death, risen to joyful life." We recall that in the crucifixion poems Mary's deepest sorrow was caused both by her motherhood, which established the "dearness" of her Son to her, and by the fact that He Who died was God Himself, the "best of alle gode,"[9] which established the "preciousness" of her Son to her. His death, which by the crucifixion poems has been shown to encompass all sin and sorrow, is spoken of less fully here because the author concentrates on the second aspect of the prayer, Christ's joyful rising. The joy of the event is revealed by the brightness of Christ's body, "sevenfold brighter than the sun." Using the third aspect of sacred history's definition of desire, the power of the event in relation to man, the author then forms his prayer in correspondence with the resurrection as he has defined it and in virtue of Mary's joy: As Christ died and rose again, so let me die and live.

But man is different in state and nature from Christ, and the author describes the Christian soul's dying and rising in a mode proper to man who is still in this imperfect life. The author draws two analogies of dying and rising as figures of Christ's dying and rising. The first analogy is in the prayer's asking, Grant that I die and rise with Christ by dying to the world (which is what separates me from Christ in heaven) and living spiritually (which is the life that joins me to Christ until the day of my resurrection). The second is expressed in the next clause, that I die and rise with Christ by sharing His suffering as a companion on earth so that I may be—or my suffering through His merit will merit for me to be—His companion in happiness in heaven. The distinctions are theological. Earth is opposed to heaven. Man's suffering is defined as dying to the world while in the world and his suffering is opposed to the happiness of heaven.[10] The prayer then summarizes the three aspects in relation to Mary's fifth and final joy, as it looks forward to the last of the five prayers: Because of your great joy following upon your great sorrow at Christ's crucifixion, lead me from the sorrow I suffer on earth to your great joy now in Heaven.

In all, there have been five different analogies drawn in the prayer, Mary's sorrow becoming joy, Christ rising from death, the Christian soul rising to live spiritually, the soul rising to heaven as Christ's companion, and finally the soul rising to the final joy Mary now has in heaven. The basis of the different analogies is the distinction in nature and state between Christ, Mary and the soul. These distinctions are formulated in terms of time, now and then; in terms of space, earth and heaven; and, because the focus of these differences is man, in terms of his nature of body and spirit, each with its distinct aspect of suffering or sorrow and of joy. These different analogies are fundamentally a result of the way theological distinctions between sorrow and joy, body and spirit are proportioned by the event in sacred history which is the subject of the prayer.

At the same time, the five different analogies are unified in the prayer as a whole. This becomes evident when we consider the structure of the prayer as a work in itself. By "structure" here I mean simply the principle by which the author has ordered the expression of his purpose in the medium through which he speaks, the figures of thought, the configuration of sentences, the sounds.

Each part of the prayer is built on the figure of rising, rising from depth to height, sorrow to joy, body to spirit, this world to the next, and the reader feels increasing delight as he sees the harmony of these figures together. First, encompassing the whole prayer, is Mary's joy in her Son. Then comes the first figure, her Son rising from death to life with His glory, the source of Mary's joy, shining back to her joy. Then comes the second figure, the Christian soul's death told in three modifications of dying and rising, the first to die with Him and rise in Him (now the soul in grace is in Christ; later the soul in glory will be in Christ); second, to die to the world and to live spiritually; and, third, to share His sufferings on earth as a companion, so that the soul may be His companion in heaven. Finally, there is the great concluding summary motion which specifies Mary's joy then, at the time of her third joy, so that the soul may experience now the happiness she had then —a figure, based on the theological definition of time as sacred history, which applies the whole prayer to the expression of the soul's desire. The rhythm of the phrases adds yet another reflection of the proportion in the prayer.

Because the focus on the event in sacred history is the determining factor—in this prayer it has been the resurrection—the principle of similarity between the analogies used by the theologian will change as the character of the event chosen changes. This can be illustrated by contrasting the above prayer to the one in the *Ancrene Riwle* on the first joy:

> O Lady, St Mary, because of the great joy that thou hadst within thee when Jesus, God, God's Son, after the angel's greeting, took flesh and blood in thee, and of thee, receive my greeting with the same *Ave,* and make me account every outward joy but little. But give me interior comfort, and let me have the joys of heaven through thy merits. And as surely as there was never any sin in that flesh that He took from thee nor in thine own, as we believe, after that taking flesh, whatever there may have been before, cleanse my soul of fleshly sins.[11]

The unifying event in this prayer is the moment *after* the annunciation, the moment of the conception of Christ *within* Mary, as He takes her flesh. Thus in the first part, Mary's joy is described to be within, an inner joy (Christ is within her). Christ is defined both as He was inside Mary, after the angel's greeting, and also as He is God and God's Son. The prayer then defines the joy of the Christian soul in terms of Mary's joy. The greeting that came to Mary is applied to the soul (that he be filled with joy), so that as Mary had

Christ inside her, so may he seek interior comfort (the soul is at war now with concupiscence) only in order that he may have the joys of Heaven through Mary's merits. The second part of the prayer develops, again through theology, how Christ is of Mary's flesh and what the quality of Mary's flesh is, in order to secure the same quality for the Christian soul.

In each of the five prayers on the joys in the *Riwle* the event determines the figure by which the theological concepts are organized. The Christian soul remains the constant element of focus since always there is the correspondence between himself and the aspect of joy in the event, and the whole series is unified by the fact that these joys are all Mary's joys, seen in the light of her final joy.

The fourteenth century "Heyl be þou, marie, milde quene of heuene" will provide an example of a poem which I think is typical of the religious verses we would hesitate to call poetry.[12] Although the language is in poetic form, this prayer lacks the proportioned development of its parts. The poem is a fourteen stanza version of the devotion to Mary's five joys. It is much longer than the six stanzas of "Glade us maiden, moder milde" because to the traditional joys the poet has added an introductory stanza and three concluding stanzas, as well as three stanzas on the passion followed by a stanza of summary petition. Each stanza is followed by the angelic salutation in Latin.[13]

The poem falls into sections: the first, three stanzas including a stanza of introduction, contains the first two joys; the second, of five stanzas, names the third joy of the resurrection, for three stanzas dwells on its complement the passion, and ends with a summary supplication. The third section, of three stanzas, includes the ascension, Mary's assumption and a supplication to Mary in heaven. These last three stanzas ask Mary in three different ways to help the speaker out of sin and to hear his prayer so that he may go to heaven. A study of the first three stanzas will be enough to point out characteristics of this type of poem, since the remaining ones only bear out the principles embodied by the first three.

> Heyl be þou, marie, milde quene of heuene!
> Blessed be þi name & god it is to neuene.
> To þe i mene mi mone, i preie þou her mi steuene,
> Ne let me neuere deie in none of þe sennes seuene.

There are three theological aspects to the petition, which reflect the purpose of the poem, (1) a naming of the power the speaker appeals to, (2) a securing of the energy or the means the speaker desires—the supplication—and (3) the defining of the desired effect of the prayer. As the prayer begins, Mary is named with the words of the angelic salutation, "Heyl be þou, marie," as if the speaker were using the power of the Ave Maria to reach Mary. Then she is addressed by a second title in virtue of the fact she is now in heaven, "milde quene of heuene." As if explaining why the poet has named her twice, and again using part of the Ave Maria to do so, the speaker declares, "Blessed be þi name." Then to be sure there is no ambiguity, he says the same thing in yet a more precise way, "& god it is to neuene." This triple naming suggests that the speaker believes there is power in a name, in a word itself, by its mere enunciation. Mary's name is a special name, and in itself it will bring good.

In the third line the speaker tells his purpose, To you, Mary, I utter sadly my lament. To be more explicit about his purpose he says it a second time, I pray you hear my voice. Then in the last line he makes his request, explaining the effect he desires to achieve by his prayer, Let me never die in any of the seven sins. By specifying "neuere" (and emphasizing it by two negatives), he makes his desire cover all time. It covers both the time of this life and aspires to affect the state of the next: in this life never let me commit a deadly sin; in regard to the next, do not let me leave this life when I am in the state of one of the seven sins. As if to seal his request, to the stanza he adds the angelic salutation in Latin.

> Heil, seinte marie, quene cortas & hende!
> For þe ioye þat þou haddest wan crist þe aungel sende;
> & seide þat þe holi gost scholde in þi bodi wende,
> Þou bring me out of sinne & schuld me fram þe fende.

The speaker identifies the first joy. Again he names Mary by echoing the angelic salutation. Again he addresses her as she is now, Queen of Heaven, "cortas & hende." Now he names her joy, the aspect of her power he is calling upon, For the joy you had when Christ sent the angel and said the Holy Ghost should come into your body. The bare theological facts are given. "Wan crist þe aungel sende" recalls the other poems where the annunciation and birth of Christ have been presented in their profound contrast to Christ's power as King of Heaven. Here, however, no figure of kingship is given. Christ is named directly, and just as directly the means of His coming is named, as the speaker says, "Þe holi gost scholde in þi bodi wende." To this account which defines the means of power he wishes to secure, the speaker adds his petition: Bring me out of sin (that I am in now), and shield me from the fiend (whom I shall meet in the future). He speaks to secure his present joy and to preserve it into the future. In this stanza, as in the last, each of the three aspects—the naming, the specifying of the power he desires to use, and finally his petition—is said in two ways. Again the stanza is followed by the Ave.

> Ioyful was þin herte with-outen eni drede
> Wan ihesu crist was of þe boren fayrest of alle þede,
> & þou mayde bi-fore & after as we in bok rede;
> Lefdi for þat ioie þou helpe me at nede.

The third stanza is much like the second, except that the order of the naming is varied. The speaker begins by naming first, not Mary, but the joy he uses as the power to gain his desires. Your heart was joyful, without any fear, when Christ was born, the fairest of all men, and you remained a maid before and after. He adds the tag, "as we in bok rede," which, besides completing the line (although it actually disrupts the rhythm), suggests he is adding to his prayer not only the power of precision, but also that of the authority of the written word. "Lefdi," he names her, introducing the name he will use for the next five stanzas, "for þat ioie"—his explicit specifying of the power acts as a repetition—"helpe me at nede." The condition *when,* as it did above, covers all time, both now when I am in need, and whenever I am in need. The Ave follows.

The qualities of the poem are clear. Each stanza contains a triple naming: of Mary upon whom the fulfillment of the speaker's desire depends; of the power by virtue of which she has her power (ultimately Christ) and with which the speaker appeals to her; and finally a naming of the effect the speaker desires.[14] There are three important conditions to obtain the power, which depend ultimately on the willingness and the accessibility of the power to which the appeal is made. The effectiveness of the speaker's prayer depends first upon his knowledge of the power and of its extent. This is the function of theology here, to establish the correctness of the naming. The theology correct, the first condition is fulfilled. There remains then the power of the appeal itself as a condition of the prayer's success, and this will depend upon the second and third conditions, the accuracy of the triple naming and the intensity with which the soul appeals. In this poem, the intensity of the petition is not based on an intensity of faith, but rather on argument by insistence.

Already in the first three stanzas we have seen these conditions working. Both clarity and intensity are sought through repetition. On the one hand, each stanza has named Mary, the means of power and the effect desired, and each one has named her not only once, but twice, so that each line seems to fall into two halves.[15] Repetition comes also from the fact that each stanza is made an individual block unit of power, sealed, so to speak, by the Ave which follows it, as if not only the events called upon had power, but the fact of naming and the words themselves have power. Then, too, there are the elements of repetition such as the monorhyming of the stanza, which uniformly breaks into four lines, each with two units; the repetition of words from one stanza to the next, such as in the name "Ladi," or the use of "for þe" to introduce the joy; and finally the repetition after each stanza of the Ave. The fact that the Ave is in Latin is an added means of power, as it calls upon the power of traditional phrasing of the salutation in Scripture and in the liturgy, and thus by implication calls on its power in sacred history as the salutation by which all joy came to mankind.

The fundamental source of the poem's poverty of expression is that the elements developed—the naming of Mary, the naming of the joy or power, and the naming of the desired effect—lack any principle of unity or limit proportionate to the subject. The poem develops by what seems to be all-inclusive enumeration, which could stretch to infinity in any direction. The naming of Mary is repetition which is designed to include all namings of her. Mary is addressed "marie" or "ladi" and given her traditional epithets, full of grace, holy, good, lady of counsel, flower of all. But the naming is done for its own power, with no such specific application to the joy mentioned as the naming had above in "Glade us maiden, moder milde."

In regard to the joys by whose power the poet hopes to secure his request, the poet does not relate one joy to the other in any way, but selects only the aspects of each event which make it easy to identify. The principle by which the poet chooses what factors to include is traditional association, which he does not modify into any relationship proportionate to the unity of his poem. The clearest evidence of this is the way the poet includes the prayer of Christ's five wounds. In the two other poems on the five joys discussed above, each poet referred to the passion as it helped to define the resurrection in the context of his purpose for that poem. Here, however, the passion is given three whole stanzas and is used as a source of power independently. The section is included as a separate devotion which is to add to the power of the speaker's total appeal.

Finally, the third aspect, the effect the poet desires from his prayer, is stated in the same unproportioned way. The poet tries to extend the effectiveness to all occasions: he extends it to the time while he lives, and to the time when he dies, and to the rest of time, forever; he states it negatively—help me out of sin, and positively—bring me everlasting joy; and he states it figuratively—bring me to that high King, to that eternal light. But again he has not defined these appeals in a proportioned relationship to his particular prayer at this particular moment in this particular state.

Quantity, repetition, comprehensiveness are the principles by which the poet selects, and each principle works autonomously. The unity they give to the poem is exterior, independent of any unified configuration of structure, and what we have is a series of petitions unified solely because they are in the same stanza form, organized only in so far as they follow the sequence traditional to the devotion of the five joys and as they articulate the three aspects of the prayer necessary to achieve its purpose.

As a final indication of what sense of unity the poet (or scribe) of this poem had, in the three stanzas which follow the last of the joys, we see that he has given the poem three conclusions. And in the last stanza he has repeated the first. Turning the first stanza inside out, giving it a new end rhyme (but keeping the original rhyme as an inner rhyme), he has repeated the same phrases, the same thoughts, as if to be sure his request were understood by reminding Mary of how it began.[16]

To contrast a theological poem which has proportion to this theological prayer which is in the stanzaic form of poetry but which does not have proportion, let us turn back briefly to describe the structure of "Leuedy, for þare blisse/ þat þu heddest at þe frume." The purposes of the two poems are essentially the same: to enter eternal joy by Mary's five joys. In the fourteenth century poem the speaker has sought to secure his end by directly invoking the power or means without considering his prayer as an object of delight in itself. However, the poet of "Leuedy, for þare blisse" conceives what it is he desires by unifying his poem into a proportioned figure of his prayer to be wise. The fourteenth century poet has used exterior principles of form to organize his poem—similarities of sentence structure, rhyme, stanza, and refrain, organized by the numerical sequence of five—whereas these exterior elements of structure are used by the poet of "Leuedy, for þare blisse" in a proportion reflecting the nature itself of his desire.

In "Leuedy, for þare blisse" we find the same three theologically defined aspects as in the prayer from the *Ancrene Riwle:* Mary who experiences joy; Christ Who is the joy itself; and the Christian soul who, in virtue of Christ's redemption of man, through the analogy of man's joy with Mary's desires to enter eternal joy. But they are focused in a new proportion. The purpose of the poem is by contemplating Mary's joys to ask for final joy with Mary in heaven. The poem is a movement in time to make the poet and his audience aware of joy, and because it is founded in the imperfect light and darkness of man's present vision, it unfolds into a double awareness—an increasing awareness of joy and a corresponding recognition of darkness, the gap, or lack of joy.

The double vision of the poem is reflected on several levels. The first is manifested in the telling of Mary's first three joys in the first three stanzas. Each account of joy is complemented by a petition which expresses man's separation from and desire for joy: Mary's joy fills the first part of the stanza, man's petition the second.[17] The first joy speaks of Mary's joy because of her inner knowledge of Christ (He was in her body, He was God). The second speaks of her knowledge of Christ by her senses (her joyful giving birth to Him without pain) and again, her inner knowledge of the joyful fact of His Godhood revealed by this. The third speaks of her inner joy at her sight of His rising to life. The statement of each one of these joys is complemented by a petition. The first is: Now while we are here (separated in space from the "there" that is heaven), we sin (the separation in state from God Who is the source of joy); help us not to miss that life that is to come. The second is: Be our shield from our foe (stand between us and death "now"); give us thy blessing (both "now" and "then"); and protect us forevermore (stand between us and death always, that we may live forever) from all kinds of sinning (on every occasion). And the third is: That Christ make us clean (forgive our sins) and bright (pure so that we may see). These three joys, as in the last poem we discussed, are each introduced by an address which names Mary, "Leuedy," "Moder," "Leuedi."

The second reflection of the double vision is in the symmetrical proportioning of the account of the events of sacred history, where Mary's individual joys are seen as partial in relationship to her present joy in heaven, and her present joy in heaven, in so far as man can know it, is the power by which he aspires to his own final joy. The fourth stanza which tells of the ascension, the moment when Christ, Who is the source of Mary's joy, is above in heaven while Mary remains below, relates the event in sacred history by which the transformation to joy is worked. As in the *Ancrene Riwle* prayer the resurrection prefigures and is the promise of man's resurrection, so in this poem the ascension, Christ's entry into glory, prefigures and is made the basis of Mary's assumption into heaven. The assumption in turn prefigures and is the promise for the present audience of future joy with Christ in heaven. The moment of the fourth stanza, after Christ's ascension and before Mary's assumption, is the time in Mary's life when her state—joyful for Christ's joy, sorrowful for her separation from Him—prefigures man's own present state in which he makes his prayer. And in this stanza on the ascension, the lines of petition are replaced by a prophecy which looks forward in the poem to the definition of the third proportioned figure of the double vision in the last two stanzas; that is, the petition of the poet below to Mary above, as she is now Queen of Heaven. This last proportioned figure will express the present perpetual relationship of man to joy until his death.

By fulfilling the prediction in the last part of the fourth stanza, as it tells how Mary was assumed bodily into heaven, the fifth stanza completes Mary's joy, while it also defines her separation from man. With this joy the poet defines heaven. First he tells how Mary was assumed by Christ. "Þe king þat wes of þe ibore,/ to heouene he þe vette." (There is implicit in the referring back to the second and third joys, to Christ's birth and His resurrection, another corresponding figure: the King Who descended, temporarily separated from His glory, now has arisen.) Next the poet defines heaven by what man has been and will be in relation to Christ. Christ fetched Mary "to þare blisse þat wes for-lore,/ & bi hym-seolue sette."

The first three stanzas each contained a joy and a prayer, the fourth told of Christ's joy and of Mary's future joy (her prayer), the fifth told of Mary's full joy. Now, corresponding to the petition in the latter part of the first three stanzas, the sixth and the seventh complement the joys in the fourth and the fifth by expanding the petition of man by defining man's distance from joy.

The fact that the poem ends with a prayer to Christ following the prayer to Mary completes its structural symmetry. Mary's joy is the basis of the poet's prayer. Yet Christ Himself, being that Joy, is the source of power, for it was in virtue of His resurrection and ascension that Mary was assumed into heaven, and just as Christ "fetched" Mary into heaven, as the poet foretold He would, now the poet says, So let Him bring us to heaven all together, "for wel þu Miht."

To summarize: The poem recounts and embodies a movement into joy through the power of Christ, a movement which both articulates and provides the power of man's prayer. The central figure according to which the stanzas are built is double. It is the moment of Christ's ascension, when Mary is beholding Him with "eye swete": as it foreshadows the present moment when the audience, after learning of her joy, stands and beholds Mary's joy with vision. This double figure is composed of a joy and an unrealized promise of joy. The first three stanzas, with their first lines of the joy and their last of the petition, prefigure this proportion in the poem in a double way. They reflect the fact that at the time when the poem is composed, Mary has already been assumed and the poet and his listener are looking up at her in petition: at the same time these stanzas move back in the past to tell of Mary's own relation to God, which is the source of her joy, and to prepare for the account of the ascension, which will define man's position now in relationship to Christ and prepare for hers. The ascension figure is defined then in stanza four and fulfilled by the rest of the poem, in which after her assumption, Mary becomes the medium through which man defines the joy he desires and Christ becomes the clear basis of power. But in relation to man the fulfillment of the ascension figure by the last stanza is qualified. His joy is less fulfilled than Mary's present joy which is used to express the fulfillment. Mary's joy as a result of Christ's resurrection, ascension, and her own assumption defines for man the exact condition of his present moment. It defines the power by which he will reach joy, and at the same time as it defines his lack of joy, it brings him to the joy it has prepared. The last stanzas accomplish, too, the formal fulfillment of the poem, as the poet achieves his purpose: by virtue of Mary's five joys he raises an efficacious prayer to her expressing man's desire to enter the final joy Mary has entered.

Whereas the fourteenth century poem was seen to be unified by a numerical series and by a similarity of parts achieved through repetition—organized by the exterior shells of form—we see here that the internal proportions of the thirteenth century poem are further reflected by its stanzaic structure. The shell, or in this case body, of the form—the arrangement of words throughout the whole—has a proportion itself which again reflects the purpose of the whole. The choice of the stanzaic form, a series of octaves, is suited to the deeper form, the double complement of petition and joy. In stanzas one, two, and four the second quatrain is the exact complement of the first quatrain in the octave, as it poses a petition arising out of the definition of joy and man's distance from joy.

In the case of stanza three, the principle of complementary proportion in stanzas one, two and four argues for a revision of Brown's punctuation, which interprets the petition to comprise the last two lines only. It is possible that the poet meant to break this stanza in the middle as well:

Leuedi, al myd rihte
  þu were gled and bliþe
Þo crist þureh his myhte
  aros from deþe to lyue.
Þat alle þing con dihte
  and wes i-boren of wyue,
He make vs clene and bryhte
  for his wundes fyue.

The petition would then begin at line twenty-one, and the poet would be repeating the fact from stanza two that Mary's Child was the creator of all things in order to name Christ. With the revised punctuation, the stanza would paraphrase: Lady, with good reason were you glad and joyful when Christ through His own power rose from death to life. [Let Him] Who created all things and was born of womankind by virtue of His five wounds make us clean and bright. Yet in any event, stanza three differs significantly from stanzas one and two in the fact that these lines are a petition not to Mary but to Christ. Coming at this point in the sequence of joys, the petition to Christ reflects the manifestation of His power in the resurrection, and it prefigures and prepares for the final prayer of the poem in stanza seven, where the poet addresses Christ directly.

In stanzas four and five the complementary four lines of the octave are not petitions by man. They focus instead on Mary: in stanza four they present the poet's prophecy of her future joy; in stanza five they describe Mary's joy fulfilled as she enters heaven. The sixth stanza also shows this same complementary structure. It has a first quatrain of negative statement, I pray to you as I know how, do not let the world blind us; the second of a positive statement, help us at our lives' end and send us to heaven. And, finally, in the last stanza we see the effect of the transformation of the whole poem, as in the first four lines where Mary's joy has been presented, the poet appeals to Christ through Mary's beauty in heaven; and in the last four lines, which have reflected man's distance from joy in past stanzas, the poet expresses the desire that Christ cleanse us from sin and, the complement to cleansing, that He bring us to light, bring us to heaven.

To figure delight, a work must have first of all a principle of unity so that its parts have a proportionate relationship among themselves, beyond any coherence they may have by principles exterior to the unity of the poem, such as the numerical order of five joys, the acrostic order of *M-A-R-I-A,* or a set stanzaic form. In the poems we have considered, especially "Gabriel, fram evene-king," "Als i lay vp-on a nith" and "Stond wel, moder, vnder rode," in the prayer from the *Ancrene Riwle,* and in this last poem, the delight the listener takes in the poem comes from the fact that the poem embodies itself in a reflexive way. Its subject and purpose, its structure and use of stanzaic form all bear a proportionate relationship to each other, unified yet disparate in their reflection. Through this proportioning the listener feels some sense of the poem as an entity in itself. Thus he is affected by it as a unified experience which is part of his general experience, but which, not being identical with it, captures his attention and in so far as it speaks to his desire, its beauty of proportion causes delight. It will be the purpose of the following section to show that, as with the other elements of the poetry we have discussed, in the medieval religious lyric this delight has its specific theological dimension.

conclusion

FOR THE MEDIEVAL CHRISTIAN REALITY WAS FORMULATED BY THE THEOLOGY of the Church, whose center was the liturgy. It was the liturgy which constantly brought sacred history to bear according to the "exigency of human capacity" on the life of the Christian soul.[1] Generalizing from the lyrics we have studied, it is clear that medieval Christian theology informed the reality of the Middle English poet to such a profound extent that it determined his concept of a poem, the purpose of each of his poems, and the structure he used in formulating his poem.

There are several consequences of this for the reader of the Middle English lyrics. In the first place, the religious lyric cannot be fully understood or evaluated as a work of a purely "poetic imagination" which acts independently from the subject matter it considers, because, as we have seen, there is no discontinuity in the lyrics between subject matter and the form and structure of the poems. The purpose, the subject matter, the form and structure of the medieval religious lyric can be discovered only through a knowledge of medieval Christian theology which had a unique subject matter and a unique mode of knowing.

In the second place, theology is not a mode of knowledge which is necessarily opposed to poetry. The "dogma" used by the poets is not a static body of knowledge as it is conceived to have been by such modern critics as Spitzer and Kane. Dogma was formulated and perpetuated by the Church, not principally in the scholastic writings, but in the dynamic forms of the liturgy—the Mass, the sacraments, the Divine Office—which were the points of union between the soul and God during this life. Rather than giving a static quality to the lyrics, theology provided the poet with innumerable forms and variations of form through which the poet and his audience sought to be united to God.[2]

We have seen, for example, that although one poem may be on the same subject of sacred history as another, the focus of each poem and the unifying principle of formal proportion of structure may vary widely from poem to poem. The contrast between the accounts of the annunciation in the Gospel, in the two poems on the "maiden makeles," and in "Gabriel, fram evene-king" illustrates this point, as do the four very different poems discussed in Part II which focus on the same moment of the crucifixion, the moment just before Christ's death, "Þe milde Lomb isprad o rode," the two poems on Mary's sorrow, and "Stond wel, moder, vnder rode."

Not only is medieval theology not opposed to poetry, but it has provided the poets with new ways of formulating reality. Looking at the objective aspect of the Middle English lyric—that is, how the poet presented the actions of God in history—we see how the poet reformulated sacred history in his poem in a way analogous to its reformulation within the liturgy. Looking at the subjective aspect of the lyrics—that is, the response of the Christian soul to God—we see how the poet sought, united with his audience, through his poem to be reformed and joined to God. In the following two sections I will describe some of the forms theology provided for the Middle English lyric, first in their objective aspect of sacred history and then in their subjective aspect of the individual's experience of God. In a final section I will suggest the direction future study might take in developing an aesthetic theory appropriate to the medieval religious lyric.

The Poem: The Sacred History

IN EACH OF THE LYRICS THERE HAS BEEN A SIMILAR POINT OF VIEW IN TIME. The past, present, and future are oriented to the present moment. The present moment is defined by the liturgy of the Church as the perspective from which the events of sacred history are reformulated again and again. The liturgy's orientation in the present is a reflection of the fundamental fact of Christian theology that the plan of redemption is centered on man, and that it is focused on each man as he lives in the present in relation to Christ as He manifests Himself in the present. None of the events of sacred history is told independently of its relationship to the present. In the poems which formulate a past event, the past is used in the present as a power by which to secure the promise of the future:

> Reuful is þe meneginge
> of þis deth and tis departinge,
> þar-in is blis meind with wepinge,
>   for þar-þurw us kam alle bot.

There is no attempt to recreate the past for its own sake, because in sacred history no event has occurred only for its own sake. Each event is part of the total plan which has its beginning in creation by God, its end in union with God, and its center in Christ Who, coming into history, is the means of man's union with God:

"Suete sone," þan seyde sche,
"No sorwe sulde me dere,
 Miht i ȝet þat day se
 A king þat þu were."

"Do wey, moder," seide þat suete,
"Þerfor kam i nouth,
 But for to ben pore & bales bete,
 Þat man was inne brouth.

 Þerfore wan to & þretti ȝer ben don
 & a litel more,
 Moder, þu salt maken michil mon
 & seen me deyȝe sore."

In the poems each event in sacred history is used both as a figure and a power. In the same way as the exegetes saw an event of the Old Testament to be fulfilled by an event of the New, the event the poem formulates is both fulfilled by a future event and prefigures the events yet to come. This relationship between events in sacred history is shown explicitly by the poems which end with a petition. The poet uses a figure formulated from his point of view in the present by which to organize the past and to secure for both himself and his audience the hope for the future. In "Gabriel, fram evene-king," it was the figure of Mary's virginal conception and painless childbearing as it delivers mankind in the present from pain to joy; in "Þe milde Lomb isprad o rode," the figure of the love that transforms suffering; in "Stond wel, moder, vnder rode," the intelligible cross; in "Glade us maiden, moder milde," the five aspects of Mary's joy as Queen of Heaven; and, finally, in "Leuedy, for þare blisse," the figure of vision transforming blindness, as mankind on earth appeals to Mary in heaven.

The nature of these figures is one of the most important illustrations of how the forms in the Middle English religious lyric reflect a specifically Christian theology.[3] Each of these figures which provide the basic proportion in the lyrics is taken from the subject matter of sacred history, the redemption of man by Christ, as theology formulated it. The figures are unique to Christian theology. "Gabriel, fram evene-king" uses the paradox of Mary's virgin motherhood. "Þe milde Lomb" is based upon the doctrine that God's infinite love for man is expressed through the sacrifice of His Son and the affliction of His human mother. "Stond wel, moder" uses the power of the cross as it penetrates and reforms history. "Leuedy, for þare blisse" uses the moment between Christ's ascension and Mary's assumption to define the present position of man on earth in relation to his future joy in heaven.

In the poems which have no explicit prayer of petition at the end, such as "Als i lay vp-on a nith," "Wy haue ȝe no reuthe on my child?" and "Suete sone, reu on me & brest out of þi bondis," the application of the past event in the poem to the listener is implied by the listener's own context in sacred history. It is because the listener is himself living sacred history that he relates himself to the scene as the poet shapes it for his meditation. We saw that the listener's understanding of his context is used by the poet as he structures his poem. In "Als i lay vp-on a nith," for example, the poet used the discrepancy between the listener's present knowledge of the final outcome of sacred history and Mary's ignorance of it at the time of Christ's birth to create a dimension of irony in his poem, and in the last stanza it was by referring to the listener's present celebration of Christmas that the poet transformed the Child's tale into a testimony of truth. In "Lamentacio dolorosa" it was only by recognizing the use the poet made of the listener's part in sacred history that the full meaning of the poem became clear. Contrary to Kane's reading of Mary's appeal as a simple alternative offered to her Son to burst His bonds or to let her die, we came to see that the poem was a carefully developed ballad-like progression of Mary's inner awareness that her Son, Who was God, was dying.

It is the intensity of the meditation in the poems without a petition that determines its value as prayer. The intensity of joy or sorrow with which the listener contemplates the event directly affects the power of the meditation to secure the listener's final joy. The poet of "Þe milde Lomb" said this explicitly in his prayer to Christ:

> He þat starf in hure kende,
> Leue us so ben þar-of mende
> þat he giue us atten ende
>   þat he hauet us to ibout.

We have found in the lyrics we have studied that medieval theology's perception of the symmetry and proportion of sacred history is what fundamentally determines how the poets conceive the theological figures by which they establish the basic proportions of their poems. The redemption of man, the incarnation, death and resurrection of Christ, is a reformation of the events of the first creation—the creation, temptation and fall of man, and his expulsion from paradise. Christ is the second Adam; the cross the second tree; Mary is the second Eve.

This symmetry of sacred history is repeated in turn in the life of each man, who is related to the events of the first creation and to those of the second, since he is bound by nature to Adam and bound by nature and grace to Christ. Thus his life becomes an imitation of Christ and an overcoming of the sins of Adam. As Christ died and rose, so man crucifies the Adam in himself that he may rise, or from another view, in his baptism dies to sin and enters the life of grace. Through the liturgy of the Church and the sacraments, the correspondences within sacred history and within the life of a man are joined.

A knowledge of the concept of symmetry is fundamental to understanding the thirteenth and fourteenth century Christian's way of ordering and associating events of sacred history. We have seen, for example, how it lies behind the development of the devotion to the joys of Mary and how it is present in the devotions of the *Ancrene Riwle,* where the five wounds of Christ are applied to the five senses of man and where Mary's five corporal joys are organized by the five letters of her name.[4] We have seen that it is the principle by which such poems as the Hours of the Cross and the corresponding Hours of Mary's Compassion developed from the Hours of the Office.[5] The concept of the symmetry of sacred history is strikingly present in the methods of illumination of the Psalters and the *Horae,* as the Psalter of Robert de Lisle illustrates (Figure 5). One of the most interesting examples is found in a thirteenth century York Psalter edited by Eric G. Millar, where, in the illuminations showing the relationship between the life of Christ and that of David, not only are moments of their life made to correspond, but the figures themselves are selected and placed in a mirror-like relationship to each other.[6]

The most fully developed example of the symmetry of sacred history in the poems we have analyzed is that provided by Mary's manner of giving birth. Mary, the second Eve, is the mother of Christ Who was born without pain. Mary's painless giving birth to Christ corresponds by contrast to the law of "kende," the pain womankind suffers in giving birth to her children as a penalty for the original sin of Eve. This painful giving birth of man corresponds in turn to the painful death of Christ which atoned for all sin and by which man was loosed from pain. Mary's painless giving birth to Christ corresponds to and prefigures the spiritual rebirth of man. Mary's suffering at Christ's painful death makes her the mother of man for whom she suffers birth pangs. Finally, the painless birth of Christ was compared to Christ's rising from the tomb. Christ's rising is the sign and promise of man's final release from pain, for at the end of the world man, too, will be resurrected, and there will be a final dying and rising when he is judged.[7] We have seen how, as well as being a principle of proportion between the events of sacred history, this method of applying one event to another is a principle of the structural organization of the lyrics.

For example, in "Gabriel, fram evene-king" when one stanza was juxtaposed to another, we found that the organization within each stanza corresponded: first the event was introduced, then its significance, and then its relationship to sacred history was made. We found that the order of each stanza also corresponded to the order of the development of the poem as a whole, as the first three stanzas told of the event of the annunciation, the fourth told of its fulfillment and made the transition to the fifth stanza, which set the whole poem in its context of the present moment. In "Als i lay vp-on a nith" we saw, when the poem was divided into three groupings of ten stanzas according to Mary's experience of sorrow or joy, that there was a double principle of correspondence, one determined by the alternation of joyful with sorrowful events and one determined by the prophecy of the events and their fulfillment. The symmetrical correspondence between events in sacred history was seen also in "Leuedy, for þare blisse," where Mary's joys were ordered to correspond to the present position of man in relationship to Mary: as man stands on earth below, looking up to Mary who is in heaven, and prays for heavenly joy. The correspondence between the relationship to Christ of Mary and John, the unfaithful disciples, and the listener in "Þe milde Lomb isprad o rode" and that between the three moments of suspended time in "Stond wel, moder, vnder rode" provided other examples.

A second aspect of the symmetrical relationships which medieval theology perceived between events of sacred history is that of the ladder of value, where things or events have more value the closer they are to Christ. The ladder of value arises from the principle in sacred history of the fulfillment of all things by Christ. We saw how the event of Christ's coming is prepared for in creation and how Christ's life, because it is the new creation, as well as having direct points of correspondence to the first creation and fall, fulfills the promises of His coming, so that the Old Testament events become figures for and testimonies to the events of His life in the New. Thus the early events of sacred history are fulfilled by the last events, and all relationships are defined by man's present closeness to or distance from Christ. This hierarchy of value was shown above as it exists in the fixed order of parts in the Mass and Office.[8] In the poems, the principle corresponds both to an increase of awareness of Christ and to the passage of time into Christ, the two central facts of the life of the Christian soul.

For example, in "Als i lay vp-on a nith" and the poems on the joys, we saw how the experience of the joy of Mary at her motherhood of Christ was only completed through time, by her assumption into heaven where she is now most closely united to Christ. In "Als i lay" the principle of the fulfillment of events by later events in sacred history as they draw closer to Christ was used by the poet as a dramatic device in the poem: Mary was constantly deceived, mistaking the incomplete joys in Christ's life for His full joy, which only events would define for her. And it could be seen also in the temporal series of prophecies and fulfillments upon which the poet constructed the poem. "Stond wel, moder, vnder rode," with its series of dyings and risings centering in the death and resurrection of Christ, was another example of this, as the final implication of the figure, the second coming of Christ and the last judgment, was yet to be fulfilled.

This same concept of fulfillment of all things in Christ works analogously as a structural principle in the lyrics. The completion of the poet's purpose in the poem stands in the same relationship to the events or parts of his poem as Christ does to the events of sacred history. The significance of the beginning of a poem is only fulfilled at the end and in virtue of the end, just as in sacred history we have seen that the significance of events becomes clearer and clearer through the life of Christ as through His resurrection, the joyful implications of His birth are made clear. Just as in sacred history the end is yet to be fulfilled by Christ's second coming and the last judgment, so the poet uses his poem as a means to obtain the union with Christ which for himself and his audience is still incomplete.

This concept of fulfillment used as a structural principle of the lyrics is especially clear when we consider how the poet develops the meaning of his names for Mary. As we saw in the unpoetic fourteenth century poem on the five joys, theology gives Mary many names: Maiden and Mother, Queen of Heaven, Lady, Mother of Mercy. Each one of these descriptive titles is given to Mary by virtue of her relationship to Christ. Her relationship to Christ is established by the events of her life with Him in time: Maiden and Mother,

her motherhood of Christ; Queen of Heaven and Lady, her assumption by Christ into heaven; and Mother of Mercy, her compassion which has made her the mother of mankind. The poet uses these names, which, when applied to Mary now in her position closest to Christ and highest of creatures, define the source of power by which she intercedes for mankind.

The evolution of the significance of Mary's names within a single poem can be seen best in the poems which praise her or petition her. In these poems, at the same time as the events of sacred history are related, they become the way by which the meaning of her name is gradually revealed. We saw how the full meaning of Maiden and Mother was defined in "Gabriel, fram evene-king." First, through the words exchanged by Mary and the angel at the annunciation, the poet presented the virginal conception and childbearing. Having made the concept clear, in stanza four by telling of the actual birth, death and resurrection of Christ, he showed its consequences for the redemption of man. Only with the meaning of Mary's maiden motherhood fully defined by these events, did the poet then raise to Mary his petition using that name with its full power, "maiden, moder makeles."

We saw this principle of defining a name of Mary by events was the purpose also of the poets of both "Nu þis fules singet" and "I syng of a myden þat is makeles," who by telling of the event of her virgin motherhood defined Mary as the "maiden makeles." "Glade us maiden, moder milde" is an example of a poem which defines Mary in terms of her queenship in heaven, as each event was related in order to describe an aspect of her joy, until finally in the last stanza, with the sum total of the aspects of her joy complete, the poet called her by her personal name "Mary." It is as if the whole poem were for the purpose of defining what her name means.

But very seldom do these thirteenth and fourteenth century poems use her personal name. By identifying Mary through the events that mark her relationship to Christ, Who is the center of sacred history and the means and object of man's redemption, Mary's descriptive titles name her deeper or more literal identity and are an explicit recognition that Christ is the source of her value, glory, and power.

THE POET AND HIS AUDIENCE: THE CHURCH

ONE OF THE MOST INTERESTING EFFECTS OF THEOLOGY ON THE MIDDLE English lyric is on the poet's concept of his relationship with his audience. This effect is shown by the poet's constant use of the word and concept "us" in the poems studied above. This "us" unites the poet to his listener in a common endeavor:

Maiden, moder makeles,
  of milche ful ibunden,
bid for hus im þat þe ches
  at wam þu grace funde,
    þat he forgiue hus senne and wrake,
    and clene of euri gelt us make,
    and eune blis,
    wan hure time is
    to steruen,
    hus giue, for þine sake
    him so her for to seruen
    þat he us to him take.

Milsful moder, maiden clene,
mak þi milce up-on hus sene,
and brinc hus þurw þi suete bene
  to þe blis þat faillet nout.

Glade us marie, to Ioye ibrout,—
 Muche wrchipe crist hau þe i-worut—
  in heuene brit in þi paleis;
Þer þat frut of þire wombe
Be i-yefin us forto fonden
  in Ioye þat is endeles.

The use of "us" is the result of the fact that the poet defines himself and his audience as medieval theology defines the relationship of man to man within the Church. The "us" as we have seen the context of the poems define it is established by the poet and his listener's own relationship to the events of sacred history, in a way analogous to the origin of Mary's names. The "us" signifies those who have been created by God and redeemed by Christ, set in relationship to Him in present time through the grace and sacraments of the Church. Just as Mary is identified by the coming of Christ in sacred history, as Mother and Maid, Queen of Heaven and Mother of Mercy, so through his context in sacred history each man shares a common identity: as Adam fell, we fell; as Christ took man's nature, so He joined Himself to us; as He died, so we must die to the world; and as He was resurrected, so we must be reborn in Him. The center of man's definition is the present, in his state of sorrow mingled with joy, and in virtue of the past, through Christ he will enter eternal joy. It is this identity of man in relationship to Christ as it is defined by theology that binds the poet to the audience he addresses, so that the poet is himself included in the "us" which is expressed in the petition of the poems and by which both the poet and his audience are bound to the very heart of the poem's subject.

It is this "us" for whose love "Godes sone . . . wile man bicomen" and who will "þur þi swete chiltinge . . . hut of pine" be brought (Gabriel, fram evene-king). It is this "us" for whom Christ says to Mary "hi þole þis ded" (Stond wel, moder, vnder rode), "þole o rode, and deien/ to helen man þat was forlorn" (Þe milde Lomb isprad o rode). And it is this "us" for whom Mary is given her special honor as Queen of Heaven:

Why was I crouned and made a quene?
Why was I called of mercy the welle?
Why shuld an erþly woman bene
So hygh in heuen a-boue aungelle?
For þe, mankynde, þe truþe I telle.[9]

In the Middle English religious lyrics we have studied, the first person plural pronoun has rarely been used in the nominative case. As in the poems man is related to the events of sacred history, he becomes the object of the acts of Christ, through Whom, by Whom, and in Whom man is. The basic relationship of man to God defined by these lyrics is that of God, the source of power, to man, the object of the power. Sacred history expresses what God has done for man, and the man who defines himself in relation to God will open himself to be reformed by God. This relationship to events of sacred history is what defines the subjective element in the lyrics. Man is fundamentally oriented by Christian theology to what is beyond himself.

Through sacred history man understands his desires. Through the perspective of sacred history sorrow and joy take on eternal dimensions and are defined in relationship to the soul's union or separation from God. As we saw in Part II, the deepest sorrow for the Christian soul is experienced because of separation from God by sin and because of his compassion for the suffering caused to God Himself by man's sin. As we saw in Part III with the poems on Mary's joys, the fullest joy is experienced as a result of union with God. This is because God Himself is the source of all joy. The relative power of sorrow and joy in a man's life is defined only by the sequence of events of sacred history, which through Christ, if man is willing, ultimately transforms all sorrow to joy.

This essentially optimistic view of the meaning of life is a result of the two events which opposed sorrow and joy and in which joy triumphed, the death and the resurrection of Christ. Christ's death contains the ultimate sorrow. He transforms this sorrow which is the result of all man's sorrow, by His resurrection, to ultimate joy. In each poem the state of joy and sorrow is formulated in relation to man's experience in the present and in the light of Christ's redemptive act. Man sees his life in the present, defined by Christ's death and resurrection, as yet unfulfilled, and he struggles to apply the merits of Christ's suffering to transform his own present sorrow into everlasting joy. Thus in the present he lives both sorrowing and rejoicing. Full and eternal joy will be defined only by the fulfilling of history by the last judgment of man and the fixing of his eternal separation or union with God.

The definition of Mary's joy and sorrow in the poems we have studied provides the clearest example of this. We have seen sacred history's transforming of sorrow to joy to be the organizing principle of "Als i lay vp-on a nith," "Þe milde Lomb," and "Stond wel, moder, vnder rode," and of the poems on the joys of Mary. Ultimately each of these poems revealed its orientation in the present mixed state of man as we saw man's desire formulated in the petitions of the poems. The petitions were formulated in virtue of the events which contain the promise of joy and which are defined by Christ Who is the transforming power. In the poems we have studied, Mary has been the means of defining the fullest human dimensions of sorrow and joy, the means of expressing the sorrow and joy of both her Son and herself, and of man. In virtue of her final joy which is the fruit of the redemption, she is both the sign of man's joy and his advocate for joy.

This definition of the soul's desires by theology affects the Middle English poet's purpose in composing his poem: the Middle English poet does not desire only to speak to his listener, but to refashion him. The poem must not only be suited to reach the audience to whom he speaks, but through his poem the poet tries as well to form his audience to the One to Whom they speak together. We saw, for example, in "Þe milde Lomb" and "Stond wel, moder, vnder rode" how the poet sought to move his listener to live so intensely what Christ and Mary suffered that the intensity of the response would have the power to bring his audience to joy. This purpose was seen most clearly in the lyrics which personify Christ and Mary, such as the two above and the shorter two lyrics of Mary's sorrow, her appeal to the Jews and her appeal to her Son. Here, through having the listener identify with the feelings of Christ and Mary (defined in *both* their theological and human dimensions), the poet sought to move the listener by compassion to change his life.

In the poems we have studied on the events of sacred history the point of view has been "I" only in the two lyrics and in the dialogues which personify Mary and Christ. However, in the many lyrics which are composed from the point of view of the first person singular and which we have not considered, the purpose of the poet is the same: the speaker seeks always to redefine himself in relationship to Christ Who is within yet beyond him. This can be seen, for example, in the lyrics of penitence, or the religious love lyrics, or the lyrics of the school of Richard Rolle which seek explicitly to reform the mind and affections by the passion of Christ.[10]

Yet in four of the poems we have studied, the "I" pronoun has appeared where it was not used in the personification of Mary or Christ and where it referred to a person distinct from the "us" we have seen to be the object of the actions of Christ. In these instances it was used to identify the poet or speaker in his relationship as poet to the audience or to Mary. Just as the "us" in the poems receives its definition in relation to the events of the redemption, so this "I" receives its definition specifically in relation to the purpose of the poem in which it appears.[11]

This use of "I" occurs in a line from each of the "maiden makeles" poems: "Of on ic wille singen þat is makeles" and "I syng of a myden þat is makeles." In each case the "I" refers to the singer of the poem. The purpose of the poem is to praise the singularity of the virgin mother, and the poet identifies himself with all poets so that he can set his praise of Mary up against all the poets' praises of other women and prove her matchlessness.

Als i lay vp-on a nith
Alone in my longging,
Me þouthe i sau a wonder sith,
A maiden child rokking.

. . . .

Serteynly, þis sithte i say,
Þis song i herde singge,
Als i lay þis ȝolis-day
Alone in my longingge.

In these frame quatrains of "Als i lay vp-on a nith," the "I" refers to the seer of the vision, and the poet uses the "I" to add a testimony of truth. In the first quatrain "I" acts as a witness who, "alone" and in "longging," can be identified with anyone who might hear the poem. In the last quatrain the speaker is used to set the song in present time, "þis ȝolis-day," the fact of Christmas giving proof that the event seen in the vision has occurred.

Finally, in "Leuedy, for þare blisse" the two stanza invocation to Mary and to Christ at the end of the poem contains the clause, "Ich þe bidde as i con." Here the "I" refers again to the poet, who offers a prayer to Mary for his audience. By means of his poem he has established the limits of man's vision of joy in order to pray for the light of heaven. In the same way, by means of the identity he gives himself in the petition he establishes the limits of his knowledge of prayer in order to secure Mary's sympathy and aid. His limitation represents that of all mankind for whom he prays.

Poetry and the Eternal Art
A Note on the Work of St. Bonaventure

JUST AS THE POEM TAKES ON THE FORMS THROUGH WHICH THEOLOGY CONsiders sacred history and just as the poet, united to his audience through the Church, seeks to refashion both himself and his audience through the sacred history he relates, so the object of poetry itself is transformed by theology. Poetry, when it comes into relationship with medieval theology, is not an autonomous art, but is assumed as part of the endeavor of the Christian soul into being a means by which he may reach eternal delight. An aesthetic theory appropriate to the nature of the medieval religious lyric, including the religious lyrics composed in the ancient classical tradition, can be formed only when beauty is defined in its relationship to the Eternal Art.[12] If this is not attempted, then the aesthetic proportions will always remain hidden, as they have been, in what seems to the modern reader to be the non-poetic activities of the commentator and theologian. The possibilities can only be adumbrated here by using the work of one medieval theologian to suggest the direction such a study might take.

The theology of St. Bonaventure provides an excellent example of how an aesthetic theory appropriate to the medieval religious lyric might be defined, for his theology is a definition of the Eternal Art.[13] According to Bonaventure the end of the Eternal Art in its relationship to man is delight, or union with God in the beatific vision. In discoursing about the Eternal Art, Bonaventure works in a way that corresponds to the aesthetician who discourses about the art of poetry. At the same time, in discoursing about the

Eternal Art, Bonaventure works in a way analogous to the poet, because, like the poet's poem, his theological work provides a figure which is proportionate to the delight he defines and which is the means by which he moves the mind and affections of his reader to God.

Bonaventure's *Breviloquium* is a summa of sacred history in the objective mode of theology. In it the theologian defines the breadth, length, height and depth of Holy Scripture, that through this knowledge his reader may "arrive at the fullness of knowledge and plenitude of love for the Most Blessed Trinity whence the desires of all holy men tend and in whom is found the end and complement of all truth and goodness." As he defines the dimensions of Holy Scripture, Bonaventure orders his discourse according to the beauty of the plan of sacred history, to consider first the Holy Trinity, then the creation, fall, redemption, sanctification and last judgment of man; thus the structure of the work is proportionate to the subject matter of the work, in the same way as we have seen the structure of the religious lyric to be proportionate to its subject.[14]

An example of the subjective mode of theology can be seen in Bonaventure's *Itinerarium mentis in Deum,* where he formulates by a hierarchy of value the seven stages of the soul's contemplation of God.[15] The first three ways of perceiving God are in the mirror of creation: (1) considering creatures *outside* of man as the vestiges of God; (2) considering God *within* creatures in the way the world enters man's soul; and (3) seeing the image of God in man's natural powers, his memory, intellect and elective faculty. After these first three steps of the journey of the mind to God, Bonaventure introduces sacred history, and in the fourth he describes how man's ability to see God through His image imprinted on our natural powers was dimmed by original sin. Man's soul could not be perfectly lifted up had not Christ become a ladder restoring the first ladder that had been broken by Adam. In the last three steps Bonaventure describes the restoration of the soul's spiritual senses through the theological virtues of faith, hope, and charity, by which the soul may mount up to contemplate the unity and trinity of God. The proportion basic to Bonaventure's discourse is that of man as he beholds and is lifted up to God, a proportion similar to that which we found in "Leuedy, for þare blisse/ þat þu heddest at þe frume." Bonaventure's work, organized into six corresponding ascending parts and a seventh that speaks of how the mind must pass over not only the visible world, but even beyond itself into God, is the proportioned figure of the ascent of the mind to God.[16] The proportion basic to the *Itinerarium* is analogous to the proportionate relationship of the poem to its audience. And like the poet, the theologian

Bonaventure is both the forming agent of his work and united to the audience whom he seeks to refashion through it.

In the *Breviloquium* the categories Bonaventure uses to discourse about theology are those which consider the Eternal Art as a source of delight, and he summarizes theology (the work of the Eternal Art) in terms of three proportionate correspondences which he explains in his *Itinerarium mentis in Deum* are necessary for a work to cause its beholder delight. These principles given in the *Itinerarium,* which I will describe briefly, are strikingly analogous to the general principles of form in the religious lyric as I have shown them above, and it is in the *Itinerarium*'s definition of Beauty as it leads to Eternal Delight that we can find the outlines of a theory which might provide the basis for an aesthetic theory of the medieval religious lyric.[17]

The definition is put forth in Chapter II of the *Itinerarium,* which concerns the second stage of the journey of the mind to God, "The Consideration of God in His Footsteps in this Visible World." Bonaventure uses man's apprehension of created beauty as the foundation for his theory of beauty in the Eternal Art. (1) The first proportion causing delight is that of formal beauty, a proportionate correspondence between the original and the similitude which emanates from it. In the Eternal Art, Christ is the image of the Father, Who generates Him. (Christ is beauty—*speciositas.*) What we have called the figure of the poem, the proportion of a poem to its theological subject—the coming of the Son of God into history and His redemption of man—can be seen to be defined by this first proportion. (2) The second proportion is that of the fitness of the similitude generated to the one who beholds it. In the Eternal Art, Christ becomes man in order to refashion man to share the life of God. (Christ is sweetness—*suavitas.*) We saw this sweetness of Christ embodied in the "stylle" falling of the dew on the flower in "I syng of a myden þat is makeles." It was embodied also by the Child's tale widening Mary's comprehension of sorrow and joy in "Als i lay vp-on a nith" and by the other poems in Friar Grimestone's preaching book which meditate on Christ's love for man through His suffering the mortality and frailty of His humanity. The religious lyric itself, as it is shaped for and reshapes its audience, demonstrates this proportion. (3) The third proportionate correspondence is a proportion of power, the capacity of the similitude generated to satisfy the needs of its beholder. Christ satisfies man's deepest need, for in Him man experiences Eternal Delight. (Christ is nourishment—*salubritas.*) The representation of Christ as the fruit of Mary's womb expresses this proportion. The proportion was reflected in the petitions of the poems and their power as prayer to achieve for the poet and his audience "eune blis," "Ioye þat is endeles," the final union with Christ in heaven. And it was reflected in the apprehension of the poem itself in so far as the poem was a figure of delight.

Finally, the work of St. Bonaventure can provide us not only with a theoretical framework, but with a specific illustration of how poetry relates to the Eternal Art. In his meditation *Lignum vitae* he composes a poem through which to meditate on the Tree of Life.[18] The work begins with a Prologue in which the author explains the purpose of the meditation and which also includes an explanation of a visual diagram of the Tree of Life that accompanies the meditation. The Prologue is then followed by the poem, which Bonaventure uses as his table of contents. Using the "wood of the Holy Gospels," the poem describes the mysteries of the origin, passion and glorification of Christ through the figure of the Tree of Life with its twelve fruits, which are aspects of the virtue of Christ. It moves from the past to the present and figures the future, concluding with a prayer for the seven gifts of the Holy Spirit. The meditation itself then follows. This consists of a line by line interpretation of the poem.[19] The principle of *Lignum vitae* suggests our modern method of textual explication, only the poem is conceived to have a far different function;[20] and Bonaventure's conception of poetry will serve to recall again the general points about the relationship of theology to poetry drawn from the preceding study of the Middle English religious lyric.

In his Prologue, describing the purpose of his meditation and his reason for using poetry, Bonaventure says that he works so that man will not be forgetful of the Lord's passion, nor ungrateful. He intends through his meditation to awaken the affections and the senses to God: to vivify the memory, to sharpen and form the intellect, and so to fill the will with love that the soul can truly say the words of the bride in the Canticle: "Fasciculus myrrhae dilectus meus mihi, inter ubera mea commorabitur." For the modern exegete the goal of his work is to discover the meaning of the poem. For the theologian of the Eternal Art the goal is beyond the work. The poem and the meditation are a means to bring the soul to God. For St. Bonaventure the endeavor of poetry and theology is single. His poem is incorporated into and becomes the form and the source of the theology with which he explicates and meditates on the Tree of Life. And his poem is used as the proportionate figure of the subject, analogous in sacred history to the created universe reformed by Christ, through which the affections and the mind are raised to God.

Appendixes

I

SEQUENCE, FEAST OF THE ANNUNCIATION

THIRTEENTH CENTURY SARUM MISSAL[1]

Ave mundi spes Maria aue mitis aue pia aue plena gracia.
Aue uirgo singularis que per rubrum designaris non passum incendia.

Aue rosa speciosa aue iesse uirgula.
Cuius fructus nostri luctus relaxabat uincula.

Aue carens simili mundo diu flebili reparasti gaudium.
Aue cuius uiscera contra mortis federa ediderunt filium.

Aue uirginum lucerna per quam fulsit lux superna hiis quos umbra tenuit.
Aue uirgo de qua nasci et de cuius lacte pasci rex celorum uoluit.

Aue gemma celi luminarium.
Aue sancti spiritus sacrarium.

O quam mirabilis et quam laudabilis hec est uirginitas.
In qua per spiritum facta paraclitum fulsit fecunditas.

O, quam sancta quam serena quam benigna quam amena esse uirgo creditur
Per quam seruitus finitur porta celi aperitur et libertas redditur.

O castitatis lilium tuum precare filium qui salus est humilium.
Ne nos pro nostro uicio in flebili iudicio subiciat supplicio. 16

Set nos tua sancta prece mundet a peccatis fece.
Collocet in lucis domo amen dicat omnis homo.

II

SEQUENCE, PASCHALTIDE

THIRTEENTH CENTURY SARUM MISSAL[2]

Stabat iuxta Christi crucem
stabat uidens mundi ducem
uite ualefacere.
Stabat uirgo necnon mater
et quid sit euentus ater
nouo nouit funere.

Stabat uirgo spectans crucem.
et utramque pati lucem
set plus suam doluit.
Illa stabat hic pendebat
et que foris hic ferebat
intus hec sustinuit.

Intus cruci conclauatur
intus suo iugulatur
mater agni gladio.
Intus martyr consecratur.
intus tota concrematur
amoris incendio.

Modo manus modo latus
modo ferro perforatus
oculis resumitur.
Modo capud spinis sutum
cuius orbis totus nutum
et sentit et sequitur.

Os uerendum litum sputis
et flagellis rupta cutis
et tot riui sanguinis
Probra risus et que restant
orbitati tela prestant
et dolori uirginis.

Tempus nacta trux natura
nunc reposcit sua iura
nunc dolores acuit.
Nunc extorquet cum usura
gemitus quos paritura
natura detinuit.

Hec nunc parit nunc scit uere
quam maternum sit dolere
quam amarum parere.
Nunc se dolor orbitati
dilatus in partu nati
presentat in funere.

Nunc scit mater uim meroris
seruat tamen hec pudoris
uirginalis graciam.
Nam pudicos gestus foris
non deflorat uis doloris
intus urens anxiam.

Triduanus ergo fletus
leta demum est deletus
surgentis uictoria.

Leta lucet spes dolenti
nato namque resurgenti
conresurgunt gaudia.

Christi nouus hic natalis
formam partus uirginalis
clauso seruat tumulo.
Hinc processit hinc surrexit
hinc et inde christus exit
intacto signaculo.

Eya mater eya leta
fletus tui nox expleta
lucessit in gaudium.
Nostre quoque letum mane
nocti plusquam triduane
tuum redde filium. amen.

III

AN ORISON OF THE FIVE JOYS[3]

Heyl be þou, marie, milde quene of heuene!
Blessed be þi name & god it is to neuene.
To þe i mene mi mone, i preie þou her mi steuene,
Ne let me neuere deie in none of þe sennes seuene.
Aue maria gracia plena dominus tecum.

Heil, seinte marie, quene cortas & hende!
For þe ioye þat þou haddest wan crist þe aungel sende;
& seide þat þe holi gost scholde in þi bodi wende,
Þou bring me out of sinne & schuld me fram þe fende.
Aue maria gracia plena dominus tecum.

Ioyful was þin herte with-outen eni drede
Wan ihesu crist was of þe boren fayrest of alle þede,
& þou mayde bi-fore & after as we in bok rede;
Lefdi for þat ioie þou helpe me at nede.
Aue maria gracia plena dominus tecum.

Ladi, ful of grace, gladful was þi chere
Wan ihesu crist fram deþ aros þat was þe lef & dere;
Ladi, for þe loue of him þat lay þin herte nere,
Help me out of senne þer wile þat i am here.
Aue maria gracia plena dominus tecum.

Ladi, ful of myȝte, mek & milde of mode,
For þe loue of swete ihesu þat don was on þe rode,
& for his woundes fiue þat runnen alle a-blode,
Þou help me out of senne, ladi fayr & gode.
Aue maria gracia plena dominus tecum.

Ladi, seinte marie, fair & goud & swete,
For þe loue of þe teres þat þi-self lete
Wan þou seye ihesu crist nayled hond & fete,
Þou ȝeue me grace in herte my sennes for to bete.
Aue maria gracia plena dominus tecum.

In counsayl þou art best, & trewe in alle nede,
to sinful men wel prest & redi in goud dede.
Ladi, for þe loue of him þou seye on rode blede,
Þou help me now & euere & saue me at þe nede.
Aue maria gracia plena dominus tecum.

Ladi, flour of alle, so rose in erber red,
To þe i crie & calle, to þe i make my bed;
Þou be in stude & stalle þer i draue to ded;
Let me neuere falle in hondes of þe qued.
Aue maria gracia plena dominus tecum.

Marie, for þat swete ioie þat þou were þan inne
Wan þou seie ihesu crist, flour of al mankinne,
Steye vp to heuene þer ioye is euere inne,
Of bale be þou mi bote & bring me out of sinne.
Aue maria gracia plena dominus tecum.

Marie, for þat swete ioye wan þou fram erþe was tan,
In-to þe blisse of heuene with aungeles mani an,
& i-set bi swete ihesu in fel & flecsch & ban,
Þou bringe me to ioyes þat neuere schal be gon.
Aue maria gracia plena dominus tecum.

Marie, ful in grace, þat sittest in trone,
now i þe biseche þou graunte me mi bone:
Ihesu to loue & drede, my lif t'amende sone,
& bringe me to þat heye kyng þat weldeþ sune & mone.
Aue maria gracia plena dominus tecum.

For þi ioies fiue, ladi fair & bryȝt,
& for þi mayden-hede & þi moche myȝt,
Þou helpe me to come in-to þa iche lyȝt.
Þer ioye is with-oute ende & day viþote nyȝt.
Aue maria gracia plena dominus tecum.

Ladi, seynte marie, ȝif þat þi wille were,
As þou art ful of ioye & i am ful of care,
Þou help me out of sinne & lat me falle namare,
& ȝeue me grace in erþe my sinnes to reve sare.
Aue maria gracia plena dominus tecum.

Ladi, quene of heuene, þou here me wit wille;
Y praye þov her mi steuene & let my soule neuere spille
In non of þe sinnes seuene þorw no fendes wille:
Nou bring my saule to heuene, þer-in a place to fille.
Aue maria gracia plena dominus tecum.

Notes to the Text and Appendixes

ABBREVIATIONS IN THE NOTES

Brown, *XIII*	*English Lyrics of the XIIIth Century,* ed. Carlton Brown. Oxford, 1932.
Brown, *XV*	*Religious Lyrics of the XVth Century,* ed. Carlton Brown. Oxford, 1939.
Brown, *XIV*	*Religious Lyrics of the XIVth Century,* ed. Carlton Brown, rev. G. V. Smithers. 2d ed. Oxford, 1957.
EETS, E.S.	Early English Text Society. Extra Series.
EETS, O.S.	Early English Text Society. Original Series.
Legg	*The Sarum Missal: Edited From Three Early Manuscripts,* ed. J. Wickham Legg. Oxford, 1916.
MED	*Middle English Dictionary,* ed. Hans Kurath and Sherman M. Kuhn. Ann Arbor, Michigan, and London, 1952——.
OED	*The Oxford English Dictionary.* 12 vols. and supplement. Oxford, 1933.
PL	Patrologiae Cursus Completus. Series Latina, ed. J.-Paul Migne. 221 vols. Paris, 1844–64.
S.M.	*The Sarum Missal in English.* Translated by Frederick E. Warren. 2 vols. London, 1911.
S.B.	Sarum Breviary, for *Breviarium ad usum insignis ecclesiae Sarum,* ed. Francis Proctor and Christopher Wordsworth. 3 vols. Cambridge, 1882, 1879, 1886.
Y.B.	York Breviary, for *Breviarium ad usum insignis ecclesie* [*sic.*] *Eboracensis,* ed. Stephan W. Lawley. Surtees Society, Vols. LXXI, LXXV. Durham and London, 1880 for 1871, 1883 for 1882.

PREFACE

1. See the work of Emile Mâle, esp. *L'art religieux du XIIIe siècle en France* (8 éd.; Paris, 1948); Otto Pächt, *The Rise of Pictorial Narrative in Twelfth-Century England* (Oxford, 1962); Otto Pächt, C. R. Dodwell and Francis Wormold, *The St. Albans Psalter (Albani Psalter)* (London, 1960), pp. 47 ff.; Harry Bober, "In Principio. Creation Before Time," in *Essays in Honor of Erwin Panofsky,* ed. Millard Meiss (2 vols.; New York, 1961), I, 13–28, and II, 5–8; Otto von Simson, *The Gothic Cathedral* (New York, 1956); Erwin Panofsky, *Gothic Architecture and Scholasticism* (New York, 1957); Adolf Katzenellenbogen, *The Sculptural Programs of Chartres Cathedral: Christ. Mary. Ecclesia* (Baltimore, 1959). See also Manfred Bukofzer, "Speculative Thinking in Mediaeval Music," *Speculum,* XVII (April, 1942), 165–80, and "*Caput:* A Liturgico-Musical Study," *Studies in Medieval and Renaissance Music* (New York, 1950). For a recent and very full study of the Holy Week services and medieval drama, see O. B. Hardison, Jr., *Christian Rite and Christian Drama in the Middle Ages* (Baltimore, 1965); also, Mary D. Anderson, *Drama and Imagery in English Medieval Churches* (Cambridge, 1963 [1964]); Eleanor A. Prosser, *Drama and Religion in the English Mystery Plays: A Re-evaluation* (Stanford, 1961), and among the articles, especially Mary H. Marshall, "Aesthetic Values of the Liturgical Drama," *English Institute Essays 1950* (New York, 1951), 89–115, and Rosemary Woolf, "The Effect of Typology on the English Mediaeval Plays of Abraham and Isaac," *Speculum,* XXXII (October, 1957), 805–25. See also below, note 8.

2. See Durant W. Robertson, Jr., and Bernard F. Huppe, *Piers Plowman and Scriptural Tradition* (Princeton, 1951); Morton W. Bloomfield, *Piers Plowman as a Fourteenth-century Apocalypse* (New Brunswick, New Jersey, 1961); and Robertson and Huppe, *Fruyt and Chaf: Studies in Chaucer's Allegories* (Princeton, 1963); Robertson, *A Preface to Chaucer: Studies in Medieval Perspectives* (Princeton, 1962); Robert M. Jordan, *Chaucer and the Shape of Creation: The Aesthetic Possibilities of Inorganic Structure* (Cambridge, Mass., 1967).

3. Arthur K. Moore, *The Secular Lyric in Middle English* (Lexington, 1951), p. vii. See also John Speirs, *Medieval English Poetry: The Non-Chaucerian Tradition* (London, 1957), p. 47.

4. See Frank A. Patterson, *The Middle English Penitential Lyric* (New York, 1911), who conceives of theology as "the cold, intellectual tenets of scholasticism" against which arose the tradition of mysticism from which, he claims, the lyrics sprang (p. 4);

also, George Kane, *Middle English Literature* (London, 1951), who says that the religious subject "as a whole had a restrictive effect" upon its poets (pp. 178–79). Stephen Manning, *Wisdom and Number* (Lincoln, 1962), vii-xi, has well summarized the traditional tendency of critics to find little of interest in the theological quality of the lyrics; however, his book offers a general rhetorical orientation for the Middle English religious lyric rather than a theological one. Rosemary Woolf, *The English Religious Lyric in the Middle Ages* (Oxford, 1968), which surveys the different kinds of religious lyrics and their spiritual background from the thirteenth to the fifteenth century, was published while my study was at the printer. Although our two studies are complementary, they approach the subject in a fundamentally different way. See especially pp. 9–11; chap. iv, pp. 116–26, 134 ff.

5. "Sur le *Iesu dulcis memoria," Speculum,* III (July, 1928), 322–34.

6. "Wit and Mystery: A Revaluation in Mediaeval Latin Hymnody," *Speculum,* XXII (July, 1947), 312.

7. The religious would be in daily contact with the Mass and the Divine Office. Lanfranc's *Regularis concordia* exhorted their daily reception of the Eucharist, and all the religious said some form of the Divine Office. See David Knowles, *The Monastic Order in England* (2d ed.; Cambridge, 1963), p. 469, and below, pp. 10 ff. Regarding lay participation, see *The Lay Folks' Mass Book,* ed. Thomas F. Simmons, EETS, O.S., No. 71 (London, 1879), pp. 128–47, 596–97, and John Lydgate's poem, "The Interpretation and Virtues of the Mass," *The Minor Poems of John Lydgate,* ed. Henry N. MacCracken, Part I, EETS, E.S., No. 107 (London, 1911 for 1910), pp. 84–115. Both urge frequent attendance at Mass as an efficacious substitute for the sacraments of penance and communion. For evidence of frequent lay participation, see Walter J. Ong, S.J., "A Liturgical Movement in the Middle Ages," *American Ecclesiastical Review,* CXIV (February, 1946), 104–13, and Natalie E. White, "The English Liturgical Refrain Lyric Before 1450, with Special Reference to the Fourteenth Century" (Ph.D. dissertation, Stanford University, 1945), pp. 35–41. See also *The Lay Folks' Catechism,* ed. Simmons and Henry E. Nolloth, EETS, O.S., No. 118 (London, 1901), *passim.*

8. See especially Frank Ll. Harrison, *Music in Medieval Britain* (London, 1958); Edmund K. Chambers, *The Mediaeval Stage* (2 vols.; Oxford, 1903), Vol. II; Karl Young, *The Drama of the Medieval Church* (2 vols.; Oxford, 1933); Hardin Craig, *English Religious Drama of the Middle Ages* (Oxford, 1955); and Hardison, *Christian Rite and Christian Drama.*

9. See Herbert Musurillo, S.J., *Symbolism and the Christian Imagination* (Baltimore, 1962), chaps. vii, viii; Ernst Curtius, *European Literature and the Latin Middle Ages,* trans. Willard Trask (New York, 1953), pp. 150–51, 458–62.

10. For examples of translations, see Brown, *XIII,* Nos. 4, 22, 42, 44, 47; Brown, *XIV,* the translations of Friar William Herebert, Nos. 12–15, 17–22, 24–25; and also Nos. 37, 38, 40, 41, 44, 45. For a detailed discussion of the development of the Roman rite, see Joseph A. Jungmann, S.J., *The Mass of the Roman Rite: Its Origins and Development (missarum sollemnia)* (2 vols.; New York, 1951), I, 49–127, and for its prevalence under Norman influence in the collegiate churches of York and Salisbury and in the colleges and grammar schools, see Harrison, chap. i.

11. In Natalie White's "The English Liturgical Refrain Lyric," the concept of refrain lyric includes every kind of repetition based upon a liturgical form, from trope, sequence, versus, Office hymn, salutation, litany, meditation, to the sermon form which she finds to be the basis of the Vernon poems. See also Stuart H. L. Degginger, "The Earliest Middle English Lyrics: 1150–1325, an Investigation of the Influence of Latin,

Provençal, and French" (Ph.D. dissertation, Columbia University, 1954). This comprehensive study of the sources of the Middle English religious lyrics' stanzaic forms covers the period from the Godric Songs to the poems of William of Shoreham and concludes that the influence of religious Latin poetry, both liturgical and non-liturgical, was paramount (pp. 190 ff.). For a thorough description of the types and origin of Latin liturgical poetry, see Ruth E. Messenger, *The Medieval Latin Hymn* (Washington, D.C., 1953).

12. See, for example, Brown, *XIII,* Nos. 23, 28, 29, 33–37, 45, 49, 56, 70; Brown, *XIV,* Nos. 1–5, 60, 64, 128.

13. See, for example, Brown, *XIV,* Nos. 34, 55; *The Prymer or Lay Folks' Prayer Book,* ed. Henry Littlehales, Part I, EETS, O.S., No. 105 (London, 1895), and *Horae Eboracenses,* ed. Christopher Wordsworth, Surtees Society, Vol. CXXXII (Durham and London, 1920 for 1919), where the poetic meditations follow each hour; also *Cursor Mundi,* ed. Richard Morris, Part V, EETS, O.S., No. 68 (London, 1878), lines 25487–618; *The Poems of William of Shoreham,* ed. Matthias Konrath, EETS, E.S., No. 86 (London, 1902), pp. 79–85, and *The Lay Folks' Mass Book,* pp. 82–87. See below, Introduction, pp. 14 ff.

14. The phrase is borrowed from Bonaventure, *Breviloquium,* Prologue, par. 3 (trans. Erwin E. Nemmers [St. Louis, 1946]), whose work has profound relevance for the study of theology and poetry. See below, Conclusion, pp. 209 ff. The concept is fundamental to his definition and description of Holy Scripture, which describes "the contents of the whole universe" and which human capacity can grasp because man has born in him a "certain most noble mirror in which the universality of earthly things is reflected naturally and even supernaturally." Sacred history's proportioning to man's capacity is a principle also of the lyrics.

15. Following the sequence of the liturgy will at the same time provide a cumulative introduction to the subject matter of the lyrics. Both Patterson (*The Penitential Lyric,* Introduction) and Kane (*Middle English Literature,* pp. 108–10) have chosen a subjective classification by which to consider the Middle English religious lyric. Patterson, believing mysticism is the dominating influence on the poetry, has divided the lyrics by what he calls the inner factor of unity of emotion, according to the different states of mystical progress: purification, illumination, and contemplation. However, his classification fails to distinguish differences between the poems of focus and structure. Kane classifies the lyrics by the religious function the poet desires his poem to perform for the reader, a moralizing or a devotional one. Yet also by taking away the objective aspect of theology, Kane severs the devotional state of the affections from their object which is defined by sacred history and thus makes the poems seem to be autonomous dull exercises needing the reader's separate act of "creative" and "poetic" imagination to make them into poetry. For further discussion, see below, pp. 47 ff., 59 ff., 110 ff., 120 ff., 136 ff.

INTRODUCTION

1. See especially Noam Chomsky, *Syntactic Structures* and *Current Issues in Linguistic Theory* (The Hague, 1957, 1964); and also Kenneth Pike, *Language in Relation to a Unified Theory of the Structure of Human Behavior* (3 vols.; Glendale, California,

1954–1960), who applies structural linguistic analysis analogically to non-verbal behavior, and see below, note 42.

2. See Claude Tresmontant, *Essai sur la pensée hébraïque* (Paris, 1953), especially pp. 216 ff. The books of the Old Testament were arranged in liturgical order as they were read through the year at the great Jewish feasts, a principle found also in the Gospel of Matthew who sought to provide for the synagog worship of Christians commentaries about Christ to correspond with the Jewish readings and to fulfill them. See Louis Bouyer, *Life and Liturgy* (London, 1956), pp. 110 ff.

3. Before the development of the method of disputation in the first half of the twelfth century, the teaching of theology was indistinguishable from that of Scripture; theology *was* the study and exegesis of Scripture. The two methods are described in detail by Henri de Lubac, S.J., who shows the profound consequences for theology of the contrast between the biblical method and the rationalistic method of Dominican and Franciscan scholastics. *Exégèse médiévale: les quatre sens de l'Écriture* (4 vols.; Paris, 1959, 1961, 1964), Vols. I and II, especially chap. i, sec. 5. See also David Knowles, *The Monastic Order in England* (2d ed.; Cambridge, 1963), pp. 515–16, and Beryl Smalley, *The Study of the Bible in the Middle Ages* (2d ed.; Oxford, 1952), *passim.* On the consequences for the theology of the Eucharist and the Church, see also Henri de Lubac, *Corpus Mysticum: l'Eucharistie et l'Église au moyen âge, étude historique* (Paris, 1944), Part I, chap. ii; Part II, chap. x.

4. In early catechesis theology was summed up by a narrative called the *historia,* from the Fall to the Last Things, and interspersed with *theoria,* symbolic explanations of different stages of the story to explain the meaning to the catechist. See Herbert Musurillo, S.J., "Symbolism and Kerygmatic Theology," *Thought,* XXXVI (Spring, 1961), 59 ff. See also Ernst Curtius' description of the medieval concept of universal history, *European Literature and the Latin Middle Ages,* trans. Willard Trask (New York, 1953), pp. 450 ff.

5. For the table of contents see Part V, EETS, O.S., No. 68 (London, 1878), pp. 1–6. The first age is from the creation to the offspring of Cain; the second, Noah to Babylon; the third, Abraham to the coming of David; the fourth, David to the building of the Temple of Solomon; the fifth, prophecies, the conception and birth of Christ; the sixth, the baptism of Christ, His ministry, passion and death, the coming of the Holy Spirit, the Apostles, Mary's assumption, the finding of the Holy Cross; the seventh, Antichrist, the Judgment, Hell, Heaven and the end of the world.

6. For a succinct summary of the development of biblical typology and a gathering of types, see Johan Chydenius, *The Typological Problem in Dante: A Study in the History of Medieval Ideas,* Societas scientiarum Fennica, commentationes humanarum litterarum, Vol. XXV, No. 1 (Helsingfors, 1958). See also Erich Auerbach, "Figura," in *Scenes from the Drama of European Literature* (New York, 1959), 11–76, and below, note 8.

7. The distinction between Scripture and tradition was not clearly made until the Reformation, to counter the Protestant emphasis on ancient tradition. Henri de Lubac, *Exégèse médiévale,* I, 44–56. See above, note 6.

8. This principle of the divine *ratio* has been described and analyzed from many points of view and is central to any understanding of the relationship of medieval theology to literary form. It is fundamental to both Scriptural exegesis and the forms of the liturgy. See below, pp. 15 ff. The most profound analysis is the monumental study by Henri de Lubac, S.J., *Exégèse médiévale: les quatre sens de l'Écriture.* Many studies have discussed its significance for literature. See Durant W. Robertson, Jr., and Bernard

F. Huppe, *Piers Plowman and Scriptural Tradition* (Princeton, 1951); Morton W. Bloomfield, "Symbolism in Medieval Literature," *Modern Philology,* LVI (November, 1958), 73–81; Huppe, *Doctrine and Poetry: Augustine's Influence on Old English Poetry* (New York, 1959); the three "Essays on Patristic Exegesis in the Criticism of Medieval Literature" in *Critical Approaches to Medieval Literature: Selected Papers from the English Institute 1958-1959,* ed. Dorothy Bethurum (New York, 1960); Robertson, *A Preface to Chaucer: Studies in Medieval Perspectives* (Princeton, 1962), pp. 6 ff., 52 ff., 286 ff.; Robert M. Jordan, *Chaucer and the Shape of Creation: The Aesthetic Possibilities of Inorganic Structure* (Cambridge, Mass., 1967). See also Émile Mâle, *L'art religieux de XIIIe siècle en France* (8 éd.; Paris, 1948), Book IV, chap. i. Especially useful is Erich Auerbach's essay "Figura," which traces the history of the concept as it combines Greek and Hebraic methods and was adopted by the early Church Fathers, and then uses it to interpret the *Commedia.* Auerbach points out that the doctrine of fourfold meaning was given by Augustine a realistic historical and concrete character, "for three of the four meanings became concrete, historical, and interrelated, while only one remains purely ethical and allegorical" (p. 42). The approach to meaning through *history* is fundamentally the method of my study which moves one step behind the particular applications made by the exegetes and shows how the liturgy formulated and established the proportions of the events of sacred history. On the common activity of the liturgy and of exegesis, see Henri de Lubac, *Exégèse médiévale,* I, 155 ff.

9. In the work of the Fathers and scholastic theologians *sacramentum* had a wider meaning and was used interchangeably with *mysterium* to refer to the actions by which God communicates Himself to man. Thus the sacraments were defined in their relation to the Old and the New Testaments, which were seen, by actual origin of their names, as two instruments of salvation, two legislations, two institutions which are both, although differently, sacramental institutions. Henri de Lubac, *Corpus Mysticum,* pp. 74–76. See for example, Innocent III's introduction to his *Mysteriorum Evangelicae Legis et sacramenti Eucharistiae,* PL, Vol. CCXVII, esp. cols. 763–73, and chap. i, Book IV of G. Durandus' *Rationale divinorum officiorum,* ed. Jean Beleth (Naples, 1859). For medieval commentary on the Mass as the fulfillment of Old Testament types, see Joseph A. Jungmann, S.J., *The Mass of the Roman Rite: Its Origins and Development* (*missarum sollemnia*) (2 vols.; New York, 1951), I, 109 ff. See also Jean Daniélou, S.J., *The Bible and the Liturgy* (Notre Dame, Indiana, 1956) for the definition of the sacraments by catechesis and commentary of the early Church as they "carry on in our midst the *mirabilia,* the great works of God in the Old Testament and the New" (p. 5).

10. As representative of the Mass in the medieval English Church I have chosen the use of Sarum, which differed only in particulars from the uses of York and Durham. For the texts of the liturgy of thirteenth century Sarum and earlier I will refer to *The Sarum Missal,* ed. J. Wickham Legg (Oxford, 1916), and for a translation of the Mass and for the liturgy of fifteenth century Sarum I will use *The Sarum Missal in English,* trans. Frederick E. Warren (London, 1911). A thorough history of the development and particulars of the Sarum ritual is given by Legg in *The Sarum Missal,* pp. v-xvii, and by Walter H. Frere in *The Use of Sarum* (2 vols.; Cambridge, 1898–1901), II, xii ff. See also *The Sarum Missal Done into English,* trans. A. Harford Pearson (2d ed. rev.; London, 1884), where Pearson gives valuable information on the rubrics and a history of the forms of the High and Low Mass from the eleventh to the sixteenth century, pp. xxxvii-lxix. *History of the Holy Eucharist in Great Britain* (2 vols.; London, 1881) by T. E. Bridgett provides an excellent introduction to the writings of English theologians on the Eucharist and to the spirit of the liturgy from the earliest times of the Church in England to the Reformation. A useful source for the types of books in which the texts

of the liturgy were kept during the Middle Ages is Christopher Wordsworth and Henry Littlehales, *The Old Service-Books of the English Church* (London, 1904). See also J. Wickham Legg, *Tracts on the Mass,* Henry Bradshaw Society, Vol. XXVII (London, 1904), and William Maskell, *The Ancient Liturgy of the Church of England According to the Uses of Sarum, York, Hereford and Bangor and the Roman Liturgy Arranged in Parallel Columns* (Oxford, 1882), which uses fifteenth century MSS. For two works specifically on lay participation, see *The Lay Folks' Catechism, or the English and Latin Versions of Archbishop Thoresby's Instruction for the People,* ed. Thomas F. Simmons and Henry E. Nolloth, EETS, O.S., No. 118 (London, 1901), and *The Lay Folks' Mass Book or the Manner of Hearing Mass with Rubrics and Devotions for the People,* ed. Thomas F. Simmons, EETS, O.S., No. 71 (London, 1879).

11. In the Gregorian Sacramentary the Canon was understood to begin with the prayer, "Te igitur clementissime pater." The conception of the place of ending varied. Jungmann, II, 103 ff. See Legg, pp. 221–29; *S.M.,* I, 42–56. For the significant structure of the Tiptoft Missal (Figure 2), see descriptive note. For the various methods of considering the Mass in the history of the commentary on the Roman rite, see Jungmann, especially I, 86–91, 109–17, and for a popular treatise on the necessary understanding and fitting behavior of the layman during the central part of the Mass, see *The Lay Folks' Mass Book,* lines 247 ff., and pp. 128–47.

12. There is no provision in the Sarum rubrics for the congregation's communion, and according to Jungmann during this period lay people communicated rarely (II, 361 ff.). However, this did not mean that the layman did not participate in the Mass. See Walter J. Ong, S.J., "A Liturgical Movement in the Middle Ages," *American Ecclesiastical Review,* CXIV (February, 1946), 109 ff., and above, Preface, note 7.

13. For Trinity Sunday, see Legg, pp. 170–73. There is no Mass of Corpus Christi in Legg. The observance of the feast was instituted by the Bishop of Liège in 1264 and a few years later extended to the whole Church. See Herbert Musurillo, S.J., *Symbolism and the Christian Imagination* (Baltimore, 1962), pp. 161 ff. According to Frere, *The Use of Sarum,* II, xvii ff., the festival seems to have been deferred in Salisbury until about 1312–19. For its institution elsewhere in England, see Frere, also *S.M.,* II, 630.

14. The saints' feasts were listed in the *Calendarium* (see Legg, pp. xxi-xxxii), and the lives of the saints read during the Divine Office were collected in the *Martyrologium* and *Legenda.* See *The Old Service Books,* pp. 133–51.

15. Legg, pp. 354–83.

16. Legg, p. 33.

17. Legg, p. 243.

18. Legg, pp. 392–412.

19. *The Rule of St. Benedict in Latin and English,* ed. and trans. Justin McCann, O.S.B. (London, 1952), p. 61. The saying of the Divine Office was the central occupation of the monastic communities. See for example, David Knowles, *The Monastic Order in England,* pp. 538–60.

20. Referring to the words of Psalm 118: 164, 62, Benedict divides the Office into seven day Hours and an eighth night Hour. The Hour of early morning, which is now called Lauds, was originally called Matins, or the Morning Office, and the Night Office, which now is called Matins, was originally called Nocturns whereas now the term "nocturns" is used rather to refer to the several divisions within the Night Office. For a listing of Middle English versions of the Rule and an edition of three fifteenth century texts, see *Three Middle-English Versions of the Rule of St. Benet and Two Contempo-*

rary Rituals for the Ordination of Nuns, ed. Ernst A. Kock, EETS, O.S., No. 120 (London, 1902).

21. Benedict's Rule is the first complete detailed description of the Office of the western Church. In 528 the Emperor Justinian had decreed that the clergy throughout the empire should recite the night, morning and evening Offices. In the early Middle Ages in monastic communities, the Psalter, the Bible and the homilies of the Fathers used for the readings, and an Antiphonary and Responsale were found with their musical setting in separate texts. These were combined, the readings shortened, into a single book for the convenience of the officials of the Roman Curia, called *Breviarium secundum consuetudinem Romanae Curiae.* As the Franciscans began to use it on their missionary journeys, it became the predominant form of the Office of the secular clergy. For a brief history, see Pius Parsch, *The Breviary Explained* (St. Louis, 1952), pp. 10 ff. See also David Knowles, *The Monastic Order in England,* chap. i, and *The Religious Orders in England* (Cambridge, 1950), pp. 173 ff., p. 318. For a detailed discussion of choir service books and a history of the customs of Sarum, see Frere, *The Use of Sarum,* I, xi-xii, and for the Offices themselves, see II, *Ordinale Sarum.* See also *The Old Service-Books,* pp. 26–35.

22. Matins, Mass and Vespers were said daily in the churches. The whole population attended on Sundays and feast days, probably Matins and Vespers as well as the Mass. Natalie E. White, "The English Liturgical Refrain Lyric Before 1450, with Special Reference to the Fourteenth Century" (Ph.D. dissertation, Stanford University, 1945), pp. 35–41. The liturgy, Dr. White holds, was the life of the people, and the lay people of the medieval Church understood the liturgy in a personal way. She uses information from William Maskell, *Monumenta ritualia ecclesiae Anglicanae* (Oxford, 1882); Cardinal Gasquet, *Parish Life in Medieval England* (New York, 1906); and Edward L. Cutts, *Parish Priests and Their People in the Middle Ages in England* (London, 1898). See also Ong, *American Ecclesiastical Review,* CXIV, 104–13.

23. For the readings, antiphons, responses and hymns of the Divine Office as said at Sarum, I will refer to the *Breviarium ad usum insignis ecclesiae Sarum,* ed. Francis Proctor and Christopher Wordsworth (3 vols.; Cambridge, 1882, 1879, 1886). The outlines of the Office can be found on the First Sunday of Advent, in the fourteenth century *Ordinale Sarum,* pp. 208–33, where Frere prints material omitted from S.B.

24. For Benedict's description of the Divine Office, see the Rule, chaps. viii-xix. Matins begins with an opening verse with the invitatory, interlaced with Psalm 94, and a hymn. This is followed by a series of three nocturns, each made up of (1) the recitation of six psalms preceded and followed by antiphons, and (2) lessons taken from the Old and New Testaments, from the lives of the saints and the homilies of the Fathers of the Church. These lessons begin with a blessing from the Abbot and end with a response and a verse which interlace and repeat. On Sundays and feast days are added three canticles. The Gospel of the day with its commentary, and the *Te Deum,* Nicetas' rhythmical prose hymn of praise to the Holy Trinity, would conclude Matins. Throughout the year according to the solemnity of the feast and the spirit of the season, the number of nocturns increases or decreases and the hymns change or are omitted.

25. Vespers actually anticipates Matins, introducing the theme of the next day's feast, and each of the greater feasts has a Proper for the first and for a second Vespers said on the feast. Lauds and Vespers have four psalms, and having four or more antiphons which are proper to the individual feasts, they reiterate during the day the themes of Matins and Mass. Lauds is more complex than Vespers, for each day includes besides the psalms a canticle from the Old Testament followed by the *Laudate* psalms 148, 149 and

150. Both Lauds and Vespers end with a chapter (short lesson), hymn and New Testament canticle (Lauds, the *Benedictus;* Vespers, the *Magnificat*) and additional prayers. The simpler Hours begin with a hymn, have only one proper antiphon to introduce their three psalms, and end with a short chapter and prayers. From the second through the sixth day of the week the psalms of Prime, Terce, Sext and None do not vary. The evening hour, Compline, begins with a short lesson and the *Confiteor,* has no antiphons, and remains the same for every day of the week.

26. The Rule, chap. ix. For the Roman Curia Breviary, the lessons were shortened. See Parsch, pp. 88 ff. for a description of the lessons. See also *The Old Service-Books,* pp. 129–45.

27. See *Ordinale Sarum* for Advent, pp. 8–9; for Septuagesima, pp. 53 ff.

28. *Ordinale Sarum,* p. 63.

29. *Ordinale Sarum,* pp. 90 ff. Until the season of Pentecost the spirit of the liturgy "is correlated with the story of Christ's life. . . . In the time after Pentecost, in presenting the kingdom of Christ, the liturgy employs a prototype, taken from the annals of the Old Testament theocracy. As unfolded in the liturgy, the historical account of the *civitas Dei* is accordingly a prophetic vision, fulfilled in the course of the ages by the Church of Christ," Parsch, p. 92, quoting Herwegen, *Alter Quellen neuer Kraft.*

30. The Rule, chaps. xvii-xviii. In addition to the recitation of the Hours of the Office, through the Middle Ages and especially in the monasteries the devotional practice grew of reciting daily the seven Penitential Psalms, the fifteen Gradual Psalms as well as Matins, Lauds and Vespers of All Saints and of the Dead. See *The Prymer,* Part II, EETS, O.S., No. 109 (London, 1897), pp. xxii-xxiii; also *The Monastic Order in England,* pp. 540 ff.

31. S.B., Vol. II, col. 37. For Terce, see "Nunc sancte nobis Spiritus," col. 57; Sext, "Rector potens verax Deus," col. 61; None, "Rerum Deus tenax vigor," col. 65; and Compline, "Te lucis ante terminum," col. 224. See *Ordinale Sarum,* pp. 4, 12, 15.

32. Peter Wagner, *Introduction to the Gregorian Melodies,* trans. Agnes Orme and E. G. Wyatt (2d ed.; London, 1901), Part I, pp. 260–71. See also, *Analecta hymnica medii aevi,* ed. Guido M. Dreves, S.J., Vols. V, XIII, XVIII, XXIV-XXVII, XLVa.

33. In the Proper of the thirteenth century Crawford Missal as edited by Legg in *The Sarum Missal,* the Conception is not indicated on December 8, but is combined on September 8 with the Nativity, *In natiuitate et concepcione sancte Marie,* and in the Calendar on December 8 is entered, "Concepcio sancte mariae. ix lec. Sarum nichil." The Calendar of Paris, Arsenal MS 135 (about 1300), however, lists the feast (Legg, p. 510). Legg gives no information about the early fourteenth century Morris and Bologna Missals. Preconquest liturgical texts show the Feast of the Conception was being celebrated in England from about 1030. Although under Lanfranc's Statutes the feast was excluded from the calendar, it was reintroduced by Anselm the younger from about 1121 and was defended strongly against Bernard's attack in 1140 by the English. *The Monastic Order in England,* pp. 510 ff. See the full discussion by T. R. Bridgett in *Our Lady's Dowry* (London, 1875), pp. 25 ff., 231–34, and *The Dogma of the Immaculate Conception: History and Significance,* ed. E. D. O'Connor, C.S.C. (South Bend, Indiana, 1958), chaps. iv, v.

34. Legg, pp. 259–60, 27 ff., and see below, Part I, "Gabriel fram Evene-King," note 3. The Feast of the Visitation, first celebrated by the Franciscans, was instituted only in 1389 by Urban VI, the date of July 2 fixed in 1441. However, the account of Mary's visit

to Elizabeth (Luke 1:39–47) was read at Mass and Matins on Saturday the Fourth Week of Advent (Legg, p. 20; S.B., Vol. I, col. xxii), and Elizabeth's greeting to Mary combined with the angel's salutation was incorporated into the liturgy. See below, Part I, "Nu Þis Fules Singet hand Maket Hure Blisse," note 10. On the incorporation of the feast, see *Our Lady's Dowry,* p. 235, and *The Old English Service-Books,* pp. 190–93.

35. Legg, pp. 246–50. The Gospel selection read at Mass was Luke 2:22–32, which ends before the prophecy. The theme of Mary's sorrow was developed in the lessons of Matins (see the commentary on Luke by Ambrose, S.B., Vol. III, cols. 137–39) and in sermons and meditations on the passion. See below, Part II.

36. For the Propers of the vigil, the feast, and the octave, see Legg, pp. 307–9, and for a discussion of the meaning of the feast, see below, Part III, *passim.* The Assumption was reckoned by Lanfranc as among the five principal festivals of the year. *Our Lady's Dowry,* p. 228, also chap. vi.

37. The Saturday Mass of Mary was introduced by Alcuin in the ninth century with the six other Votive Masses, one for each day in the week (Jungmann, I, 220 ff.), and from 1225 a Votive Mass of Mary was said daily in the Salisbury Lady Chapel (Frank Ll. Harrison, *Music in Medieval Britain* [London, 1958], pp. 77–78). See *S.M.,* II, 74, which points out the significance traditionally attributed to having the Saturday Mass.

38. Legg, pp. 387–91. *Music in Medieval Britain,* pp. 79 ff.

39. The Hours varied little, also, from region to region. By the twelfth century the Hours had been so generally adopted by the secular clergy that saying them became an obligation of custom. At Salisbury they were said daily by 1230. Perhaps as early as 1323, and certainly by the later part of the fourteenth century, the saying of the *Horae* in English became a popular lay devotion. The English *Horae,* or Prymers, were the means by which many of the phrases and concepts of the liturgy were repeated outside of the Churches. For the origin and background, see Edmund Bishop, *The Prymer,* Part II, EETS, O.S., No. 109, xi-xxxviii; William Maskell, *Monumenta ritualia ecclesiae Anglicanae, The Occasional Offices of the Church of England According to the Ancient Use of Salisbury, The Prymer in English, and Other Prayers and Forms, with Dissertations and Notes* (2d ed., 3 vols.; London, 1882), III, i-lxvii; and Christopher Wordsworth, *Horae Eboracenses, The Prymer or Hours of the Blessed Virgin Mary, According to the Use of the Illustrious Church of York,* Surtees Society, Vol. CXXXII (Durham and London, 1920 for 1919), pp. xiii-xlvii.

40. See above, Preface, note 13, and Brown, *XIV,* Nos. 34, 55; *XV,* Nos. 93, 94. *The Index of Middle English Verse,* ed. Carleton Brown and Rossell Hope Robbins (New York, 1943) lists 16 versions of the Hours of the Passion. Many of these are translations or versions of the eight stanza Latin poem, "Patris sapientia veritas divina" of the *Horae,* attributed to various authors in the fourteenth century (Wordsworth, *Horae Eboracenses,* p. xxiv). However, the example from *Cursor Mundi* is strikingly different. Each Hour is structured by several levels of correspondence: of a moment of the passion with a moment of the birth or the resurrection of Christ, of these with the falling into sin and cleansing of the soul as they lead, in turn, to the resurrection at the last judgment and to heavenly joy (EETS, O.S., No. 68, lines 25487–618). On the origin of the devotion, see especially Wordsworth, *Horae Eboracenses,* pp. xxiii-xxv, xxxii.

41. See the Hours as separately printed by Maskell in his introduction to *Monumenta ritualia,* III, ix-x, and by Wordsworth in his notes to *Horae Eboracenses,* after each Hour, pp. 47 ff. Of interest also is Maskell's listing of the reasons traditionally given for the division of the day into seven Hours, p. viii.

42. In his "Speculative Thinking in Mediaeval Music," *Speculum,* XVII (April, 1942), 165–80, Manfred Bukofzer demonstrates a significant analogy between the method of composition of music in the Middle Ages, and of poetry and philosophy as well, and the medieval theologian's method of glossing Scripture, where his additions were "generally in the nature of commentaries upon the original, and if these commentaries were themselves subjected to interpolation, the additions became comments on the commentary" (p. 172). His interesting plate of a MS which demonstrates the glossing technique provides us with a graphic embodiment of the ladder relationship of the readings of the Mass. There is also a profound analogy to be made between this structuring by the liturgy and Noam Chomsky's "transformation machine," a kernel of theoretical structural sequences from which other grammatical sentences can be derived, *Syntactic Structures, passim.* The medieval mind would move one level deeper in the analogy, from the exterior structure manifested, to the meta-language itself, the Person of the Word through Whom the language of creation comes into being and is understood.

43. With certain exceptions (to be noted), Warren's translation of the Proper parts of the Mass of the Annunciation will be used for the following description of the ladder of value. *S.M.,* II, 319–22.

44. Vulgate, trans. Douay-Rheims (London, 1914). Warren does not include an English translation of the Gospel readings and the Lessons. Although the Missal readings were not based on a standard text of the Latin Bible, because my object is to show principles by which meaning is established and not to analyze sources, I will supplement the texts of Legg and Warren with the above English translation of the Vulgate.

45. The liturgical unit was the basis, for example, of Bernard of Clairvaux' four sermons on the glories of the Virgin Mary (*Super missus est*). This unit was defined by the liturgy before the chapter divisions of Scripture had been uniformly established in hermeneutical practice and provides another example of how the liturgy formulated the medieval concept of sacred history in relation to Holy Scripture. See Beryl Smalley, *The Study of the Bible in the Middle Ages,* pp. 221–24; Jungmann, I, 459.

46. See *S.M.,* II, 591–613, Scriptural Index. For the basis and development of the choice of readings, see Jungmann, I, 393 ff. and 419.

47. See also Matt. 1:22–33. Regarding the choice of Old Testament passages for prophetic value and as illustration of the New Testament, see Jungmann, I, 396–99. See also Innocent III, who compares the Lesson's relationship to the Gospel reading to John being sent before Christ: "Epistola vero vox legis est, suam imperfectionem Joannis testimonio profitentis, et ad perfectionem evangelicam transmittentes," PL, Vol. CCXVII, col. 816; also Aquinas, *Summa theol.,* III, Q 83, Art. 4; Durandus, Book IV, chap. xvi, sec. 3; and in English, Lydgate, "The Interpretation and Virtues of the Mass," in *The Minor Poems of John Lydgate,* ed. Henry N. MacCracken, EETS, E.S., No. 107 (London, 1911), lines 216–40, 257–64.

48. *Breviarium ad usum insignis ecclesie Eboracensis,* ed. Stephan W. Lawley, Surtees Society, Vols. LXXI, LXXV (2 vols.; Durham, London, and Edinburgh, 1880 for 1871, 1883 for 1882), Vol. II, col. 237. The same correspondence between Mary and Eve can be found in the second stanza of the hymn for Vespers on the feast, "Ave maris stella": "Sumens illud Ave/ Gabrielis ore, funda nos in pace,/ mutans nomen Evae," S.B., Vol. III, col. 233. The parallel is used as a structural proportion in the lyrics.

49. See especially Bernard's second sermon, *Super missus est.* For an English translation, see *St. Bernard's Sermons for the Seasons and Principal Festivals of the*

Year, trans. Mt. Melleray (3 vols.; Westminster, Md., 1950), I, 68 ff. See also Honorius of Autun, *Speculum Ecclesiae,* PL, Vol. CLXII, cols. 904 ff.

50. See especially the sequences for Mary's feasts, Legg, pp. 522–23; *The Liturgical Poetry of Adam of St. Victor,* trans. Digby S. Wrangham (3 vols.; London, 1881), II, Nos. 8, 73, 74; III, No. 89; and in Middle English, see William of Shoreham, Brown, *XIV,* No. 32.

51. The Introit, for example, for the Saturday Mass of Mary to be said from the Purification to Advent is by Sedulius, *S.M.,* II, 95. See Jungmann on the origin and relation of these passages to feasts of the day, I, 421 ff., esp. 434.

52. Although in the Sarum Missal "Introit" referred to the entrance of the clergy and "Officium" or "Office" to the chant, to avoid confusing this "Office" with the Office of the Hours of the Day, I will use the term "Introit" to refer to the text chanted. Harrison, *Music in Medieval Britain,* p. 60; *S.M.,* I, 23.

53. Warren's translation (*S.M.,* II, 319) has lost some of the connotations of the Latin: "Rorate celi desuper et nubes pluant iustum aperiatur terra et germinet saluatorem. *Ps.* Et iusticia oriatur simul ego dominus creaui eum" (Legg, p. 259).

54. The process of rearranging texts and omitting parts to give the word of God to the people is called *centonization,* or "patchwork," Jungmann, I, 403.

55. Tropes were additions to the texts of the liturgy: either words added which dissolved a melisma (an extended melody sung on one syllable) into a syllabic melody, or both words and music which extended older chants, or combinations of both methods. See Gustave Reese, *Music in the Middle Ages* (New York, 1940), pp. 186–89. The final vowel, called the *jubilus,* was prolonged, and melodic strophes were developed for the sake of the choir's taking a breath. Each strophe was repeated. Words could be added, perhaps to guide the singer in remembering the music, and the strophes fell into parallel lines. A collection of melodies grew, with or without words, under parts of the melody, which usually modulated to the dominant halfway through.

56. For a history and description of the Latin sequence, see Ruth Ellis Messenger, *The Medieval Latin Hymn* (Washington, D.C., 1953), especially chap. iii. Around 1100 there were about 54 sequences in use in the Sarum Rite, and in the later liturgy as many as 101. In the reform of the Mass books under Pius V (1570) only four were retained, Jungmann, I, 437. For those in Legg, see pp. 461–96. For other Latin sequences, see Guido M. Dreves, S.J., *Analecta hymnica medii aevi,* where Jungmann estimates 5,000 are collected. Troping or farsing of certain other parts of the Mass was a widespread practice. Legg includes 19 farsings of the Kyrie (pp. 1–6, 538–40), 15 of the Sanctus (pp. 540–43) and 17 of the Agnus Dei (pp. 544–47). The later Sarum Missal has a farsed Lesson from Isaiah 11:2, 6, 7 on Christmas Day (*S.M.,* I, 96–97) and mentions in the rubrics farsings for the Gloria appropriate to the feasts of Mary (*S.M.,* I, 25–26). See Reese, pp. 190 ff., also Natalie White, "The English Liturgical Refrain Lyric," pp. 71 ff., and Harrison, *Music in Medieval Britain,* pp. 64–76.

57. For an edition of both the Latin texts and an English translation, see *The Liturgical Poetry of Adam of St. Victor,* trans. Digby S. Wrangham (3 vols.; London, 1881).

58. For a discussion of the sources and development of this type of poem, see Natalie White, "The English Liturgical Refrain Lyric," pp. 116–95. Warren's translation of the sequence (*S.M.,* II, 320–21) deprives it of power. Appendix I gives the Latin text found in Legg, p. 480.

59. Harrison, *Music in Medieval Britain,* p. 63; *S.M.,* II, 321.

60. *The Mass of the Roman Rite,* I, 379. The following description is based on Jungmann, pp. 359–90.

61. Jungmann, I, 382.

62. Jungmann, I, 383–84.

63. Part of the Preface also varies according to the season and the day, but to a lesser extent than the texts of the Proper, and the variations are to be found in a separate section of the Missal with the corresponding variations to be made in the *Communicantes* prayer of the Canon. See Legg, pp. 211–15; *S.M.,* I, 34–41.

64. *The Prymer,* Part I, pp. 18, 21, 24, 27, 29, 35. For differences between antiphons used by the rites of York, Durham and Sarum, see *Horae Eboracenses,* p. xxviii.

PART I

"Gabriel, fram Evene-King"

1. Only the opening words appear, *Canterbury Tales,* I (A), line 3216. The English version exists only in Arundel MS 248, leaf 154, and is presented here from Brown, XIII, No. 44. The MS contains as well the Latin sequence and musical setting. For the Latin and English with a facsimile of the music, see Frederick J. Furnivall, Chaucer Society, 1st Ser., No. 73 (London, 1885), Appendix II, pp. 695–96. See also Guido M. Dreves, S.J., *Analecta hymnica medii aevi,* Vol. VIII (Leipzig, 1890), No. 51, "De annunciatione B.M.V."

2. The association of Mary's fear with her conception is made by the juxtaposition of the responses and verses to the readings of Matins; for example, S.B., Vol. III, col. 237; Y.B., Vol. II, col. 237. Homilies on Luke 1:26–38 traditionally maintained the Gospel's distinction between Mary's being troubled at the salutation and her simply questioning at the announcement of the virginal conception and birth. See, for example, Bede, S.B., Vol. I, col. lxxiv, and Vol. III, col. 235; see also Bernard's third sermon on the glories of the Virgin Mother (*Super missus est*) in *St. Bernard's Sermons for the Seasons and Principal Festivals of the Year,* trans. Mt. Melleray (3 vols.; Westminster, Md., 1950), I, 104–5.

3. The theme that Mary's childbearing was painless is developed especially in the Christmas liturgy. See Legg, p. 389 and *S.M.,* II, 84. See also the homilies for Advent and Christmas, of Origin, S.B., Vol. I, col. clviii; Augustine, S.B., Vol. I, cols. civ-cvii, and Bernard, Fourth Sermon for Christmas Eve, *Sermons,* I, 346–48. See Vespers antiphon, *The Prymer,* ed. Henry Littlehales, Part I, EETS, O.S., No. 105 (London, 1895), p. 29.

4. The tradition of Mary as the second Eve has its roots especially in the Vulgate translation of Gen. 3:15–16, where God proclaims enmity between the seed of woman and the serpent and that Eve shall bring forth her children in sorrow. The parallel between Eve and Mary is developed fully in the homily of Ambrose on the Annunciation, Y.B., Vol. II, cols. 236–39. See above, Introduction, pp. 18 ff. The poets' application of the contrast between the law of motherhood and Mary's painless childbearing to Mary's becoming the mother of man through the compassion she suffered at the death of her Son will be developed below, especially in Part II.

5. Gradual, Masses of Mary from Purification to Advent, *S.M.,* II, 95; "Uirgo dei genetrix quem totus non capit orbis in tua se clausit uiscera factus homo," Legg, p. 390. The same verse was used later on the Visitation, *S.M.,* II, 390, and is the basis later also for the third lesson of Matins in *The Prymer,* p. 6.

6. The *OED* lists as the earlier meaning of the word "peerless," derived from "make," an (or one's) equal, peer, match. The first citation given for its later denotation of "mateless" is 1425. For examples of *singularis,* see Legg, first sequence for the Purification, lines 23–24, p. 466, and sequence in commemoration of the BVM, lines 13, 21, p. 493; *The Liturgical Poetry of Adam of St. Victor,* ed. and trans. Digby S. Wrangham (3 vols.; London, 1881), Vol. I, No. 3, lines 59–61; Vol. II, No. 66, lines 1–4, No. 73, lines 29–30, 43–45, 63–66, and Vol. III, No. 90, lines 65–68. For the restricted application to Mary of *specialis* or *specialiter* when her uniqueness is to be distinguished from the singularity of every man in relation to the Church, see Henri de Lubac, S.J., *Méditation sur l'Église* (3ᵉ éd.; Paris, 1954), pp. 301 ff. For fuller discussion of "makeles," see below, "I Syng of a Myden Þat Is Makeles," note 17.

7. The meaning of "figure" used in this study in regard to the Middle English lyric will be made clearer below as it is illustrated by the poems in later chapters. It has been chosen in order to point out the analogy between a structural principle of the lyrics and the liturgy and homilists' method of formulating the proportions of sacred history. (See above, Introduction, pp. 5 ff., 10 ff., and 17 ff.) For an especially useful analysis of the term, see Erich Auerbach's comprehensive essay, "Figura," in *Scenes from the Drama of European Literature: Six Essays* (New York, 1959), pp. 11–76.

8. The Latin version of the sequence, Arundel MS 248, leaf 154, differs considerably from the simpler English version, containing more abstract, even witty, theological language and manipulation of syntax. In contrast to the English poem, the ideas of virginal conception and parturition are introduced in stanza 1 ("concipies,/ & paries/ intacta"). The actions and concepts are presented as logical paradoxes. The grammatical constructions flow tensely against the stanzaic form, as, in contrast to the more rigid conformity of thought to stanzaic structure in the English version, the thought moves without break from the opening to the closing lines of each stanza.

9. Furnivall, Chaucer Society, p. 696, lines 46–48. The variation from the Latin by the English poet emphasizes Christ's death as being man's rebirth into hope.

10. See Jean Daniélou, S.J., *The Bible and the Liturgy* (Notre Dame, Indiana, 1956), pp. 5, 21, 53. For a development of the parallel in a Middle English work of instruction, see from the Vernon MS, "A Treatise of the Manner and Mede of the Mass," as printed in *The Lay Folks' Mass Book,* ed. Thomas F. Simmons, EETS, O.S., No. 71 (London, 1879), especially pp. 483–508. For a short description of sacred history in these terms, see Bonaventure's *Breviloquium,* trans. Erwin E. Nemmers (St. Louis, 1946), and below, Conclusion. In various ways the proportions of the poems to be discussed below embody the principles of the symmetry of sacred history.

11. "Jésus-Christ fait donc l'unité de l'Écriture parce qu'il en est la fin et la plénitude. Tout y a rapport à Lui. Il en est, finalement, le seul Object. . . ." Henri de Lubac, S.J., *Exégèse médiévale: Les quatre sens de l'Écriture* (4 vols.; Paris, 1959, 1961, 1964), I, 322. The conception is fully developed by medieval theologians in relation to the unity of the Old and the New Testaments. See *Exégèse médiévale,* "L'Acte du Christ," I, 318, *passim.*

12. Brown, *XIII,* No. 47, "Our Lady Sorrows for Her Son," lines 31–42, also from Arundel MS 248.

13. *S.M.,* II, 319.

14. For the facsimile of the monodic setting, see Furnivall, Chaucer Society, plate facing p. 695.

15. Repetition of each melodic unit with a variation in the words is the characteristic structural development of the sequence which was originally sung by two groups in alternation. See above, Introduction, pp. 20 ff., also Gustave Reese, *Music in the Middle Ages* (New York, 1940), pp. 187–89, and Frank Ll. Harrison, *Music in Medieval Britain* (London, 1958), pp. 64–70.

16. The syntactic unit begun in the couplet of stanza 1 extends through line 9, and the generally offered translation of "þis euene lith" is, in apposition to "godes sone," "this light of heaven." See, e.g., Brown, *XIII,* glossary, "liht," R. T. Davies, *Medieval English Lyrics: A Critical Anthology* (Evanston, 1964), p. 100. However, one can argue, on the strength of the couplet rhyme and the melodic unit and by analogy to the handling of the couplet in stanzas 3–5, that the phrase means, God's Son "will descend this evening." "Lith" according to the *OED* had a tradition of use in relation to the Incarnation, and the unetymological *e* of "euen" (*MED*) could be taken as a dative in adverbial use, in which case lines 5–9 would read: "Hail be thou, truly full of grace, for the Son of God this evening will descend,/ for love of man/ will become man,/ and take/ flesh of thee, maiden bright."

17. The effect suggests that of the Latin poem, which in its handling of the syntax and greater complexity of thought has a greater unity and suspense. The clearer, more consistent divisions within the stanza of the English poem allow the symmetry of proportion in development, to be described below, pp. 44 ff.

18. The principle of development is analogous to the medieval conception of *proportio* fundamental to many kinds of structure. For a discussion of this idea and sources, see below, Part III, "The Figure of Delight," note 7.

19. See note 16.

THE "MAIDEN MAKELES"

1. *Middle English Literature* (London, 1951), pp. 177–78.

2. Brown, *XIII,* No. 31, from Trinity College Cambridge MS 323.

3. Brown, *XV,* No. 81, from Sloane MS 2593.

4. "*Explication de Texte* Applied to Three Great Middle English Poems," *Archivum Linguisticum,* III (1951), 159. See W. W. Greg, *Modern Philology,* VII (October, 1909), 165–67. See also Kane's evaluation: "I would not have this lyric thought too bad; it has the charm of the archaic, but its author is over-explicit and will not assume knowledge or readiness to cooperate in the reader. His elaborate demonstrations of the obvious detract from the quality of the poem. Moreover, his attitude to the subject is mainly religious, and little affected by the operation of the creative imagination," *Middle English Literature,* p. 162.

5. See below, p. 53 and note 12.

6. The kingship of Christ is a theme especially of Advent and Christmas, when the Church relives the coming of Christ in the Incarnation and anticipates His second coming as Judge and King from His place in glory. See especially Isa. 1–10; the homilies of Gregory on Luke 21 (S.B., Vol. 1, cols. lxxxvii ff.) and Matt. 11 (S.B., Vol. 1, cols.

cvii ff.); the Christmas liturgy, S.B., Vol. I, cols. clv-clvi, *S.M.,* I, 100; and Bede, S.B., Vol. III, cols. 237 ff. See also Figure 4 and its descriptive note. In a sermon for the Second Sunday of Advent, Acquinas compares the second coming of Christ to Proverbs 19:12, "As the roaring of a lion, so also is the anger of a king: and his cheerfulness as the dew upon the grass," saying that the anger of God in His second coming will be like the roaring of the lion, but His mildness now is like the gentleness of falling dew. See Jean Leclercq, O.S.B., *L'idée de la royauté du Christ au moyen âge* (Paris, 1959), p. 104.

7. The themes are liturgical. See Introit, Mass of the B.V.M., Purification to Advent: "Hail, holy mother, who didst bring forth in childbirth the king who ruleth over heaven and earth for ever and ever," *S.M.,* II, 95. Mary is celebrated as both mother and spouse of God through the application to her of passages from Canticles and Ecclesiasticus in the antiphons of Vespers and Matins for the Assumption, S.B., Vol. III, cols. 685 ff., 687 ff., and in the Lessons of the Mass, Legg, p. 308, *S.M.,* II, 465. For a full discussion of Mary's queenship of heaven, see below, Part III, "The Joy of Mary."

8. For the development of the dogma of the Immaculate Conception, see above, Introduction, note 33.

9. See, e.g., S.B., Vol. I, cols. viii, xxxiv, xxxvii, clv. See also, S.B., Vol. III, cols. 235, 238, and homily attributed to Fulbert, col. 774; Gradual, Mass of Mary's Nativity: "The nativity of the glorious virgin Mary, sprung from the seed of Abraham, of the tribe of Judah, from the famous root of David," *S.M.,* II, 491, also Legg, p. 319; Gradual, Mass of B.V.M., Saturday after Easter, Legg, p. 390, *S.M.,* II, 97; and antiphon for None, *The Prymer,* ed. Henry Littlehales, Part I, EETS, O.S., No. 105 (London, 1895), p. 24. Matt. 1:1–16, the generation of Christ from David, is read at Matins, Christmas Day, S.B., Vol. I, col. clxxxvi, and on Octave of the Nativity of Mary, Legg, p. 319, *S.M.,* II, 493. See also *The Liturgical Poetry of Adam of St. Victor,* ed. and trans. Digby S. Wrangham (3 vols.; London, 1881), Vol. I, Nos. 2, 5; Vol. III, Nos. 90, 96.

10. Legg, pp. 259, 388; *S.M.,* II, 95, 321, 391, 462; S.B., Vol. III, col. 236; *The Prymer,* p. 4.

11. "Blessed is the womb that bore thee and the paps that gave thee suck" (Luke 11:27). See below pp. 53 ff. and note 15.

12. See Brown, *XIII,* xx-xxii.

13. Louis Réau, *Iconographie de l'art chrétien* (6 vols.; Paris, 1955–1959), Vol. IV, pp. 129–40. For a detailed discussion of the tree of Jesse in medieval commentary, drama and illuminations up to the twelfth century, see Arthur Watson, *The Early Iconography of the Tree of Jesse* (London, 1934).

14. For examples, see Eric G. Millar, *English Illuminated Manuscripts of the XIVth and XVth Centuries* (Paris, 1928), especially pl. 15.

15. *S.M.,* II, 95; Legg, p. 389.

16. Legg, p. 391; *S.M.,* II, 98.

17. The primary meaning in this poem, in "Gabriel, fram evene-king," and in "Nu þis fules singet" is "without an equal, matchless." See above pp. 34 and p. 34, note 6. See also the careful distinction made as the maiden in *Pearl* (ed. E. V. Gordon [Oxford, 1953]) plays on the words "makeles" and "maskelles," lines 721–88. Addressing Mary (line 435) and referring to Christ (line 757) as "makeles," she refuses for herself the title "makeles quene," classing herself as one of "a hondred and forty fowre þowsande flot" who are "maskelles," "unblemyst" (lines 781–86). See, however, Stephen Manning,

Wisdom and Number (Lincoln, 1962), pp. 160–61, and note 23, pp. 168–69, who gives primary importance to its later denotation of "mateless."

18. See W. W. Greg, pp. 165–67; Kane, p. 165; John Speirs, *Medieval English Poetry: The Non-Chaucerian Tradition* (London, 1957), pp. 67–69; Barbara C. Raw, "'As dew in Aprille,'" *Modern Language Review,* LV (July, 1960), 411–14; Stephen Manning, pp. 158 ff., J. Copley, "I Syng of a Myden," *Notes and Queries,* IX (April, 1962), 134–37; and R. T. Davies, *Medieval English Lyrics: A Critical Anthology* (Evanston, 1964), pp. 18–19.

19. From Bernard's fourth sermon on the glories of the Virgin Mother in *St. Bernard's Sermons for the Seasons and Principal Festivals of the Year,* trans. Mt. Melleray (3 vols.; Westminster, Md., 1950), I, 118.

20. See *OED,* "still," adv.

21. The few examples given by *OED* of this meaning are from the thirteenth and fourteenth centuries, e.g., *King Horn* (Camb. MS, line 287), "Þu schalt wiþ me to bure gon,/ To speke wiþ Rymenhilde stille."

22. See John Speirs, *Medieval English Poetry,* p. 68, for an exaggerated development of the natural and pagan imagery in this poem. According to R. T. Davies, April may suggest the month which begins the new age of man's redemption, *Medieval English Lyrics,* pp. 18, 335.

23. *S.M.,* II, 139; Legg, p. 259. For text and discussion of the Mass, see Introduction, "The Ladder," pp. 15–25. See also verse and response for Vespers, S.B., Vol. II, col. 234; antiphon for Matins, S.B., Vol. III, col. 235; and in Advent, antiphon for Lauds, S.B., Vol. I, col. cxviii.

24. *The Prymer,* p. 21; S.B., Vol. I, cols. cvii, ccxcii. Judges 6:34–40 tells how Gideon twice asked God for a sign that the Israelites would overcome the enemy. Twice he put a fleece on the threshing floor. The first morning he found that miraculously God had cast dew on the fleece while the ground remained dry. The second morning the fleece remained dry while the ground was found wet with dew. The sign of the fleece was applied to the fact that Mary bore Christ while remaining a virgin. Associated often with this story from Judges was Ps. 71:6, "Descendet sicut pluvia in vellus." See F. J. E. Raby, *A History of Christian-Latin Poetry from the Beginnings to the Close of the Middle Ages* (Oxford, 1927), pp. 371 ff. The figure was common in the hymns to Mary, e.g., Adam of St. Victor, *Liturgical Poetry,* Vol. II, No. 66; Vol. III, No. 95.

25. See the second and third antiphons and the first nocturn of Matins, Feast of the Annunciation, Y.B., Vol. II, col. 236, *passim;* S.B., Vol. III, col. 235, *passim.* The association of these figures with the conception and birth of Christ is made especially by the sequences and hymns. See Visitation, Y.B., Vol. II, Appendix II, col. 739, and Adam of St. Victor, Vol. I, No. 4; Vol. III, No. 96.

26. Stephen Manning, *Wisdom and Number,* pp. 158–67, points out the numerical symbolism of the poem's structure, the five stanzas suggesting Mary's five joys, the five letters in her name *Maria,* and finds in the threefold occurrence of the dew image a sign of the Holy Trinity's operation in the incarnation.

27. "Bour," according to *MED,* n. 2 (b), referred often to a lady's bed chamber where a lover came; in the *Ormulum* the word was used of Mary's chamber at the annunciation. For examples of its figurative application to Mary's womb, see 3 (a).

28. Cant. 4:12, from the Lesson of the Octave of the Assumption, *S.M.,* II, 465. See also John Mirk, "Crist sayde to hur: 'Com, my swete, com my flour, com my culuer,

myn owne boure, com my modyr, now wyth me; for Heuyn qwene I make þe!' " *Mirk's Festial: A Collection of Homilies, by Johannes Mirkus (John Mirk)*, ed. Theodor Erbe, EETS, E.S., No. 96 (London, 1905), p. 224. See above, note 7.

29. Millar, *MSS of the XIVth and XVth Centuries,* pl. 15.

30. S.B., Vol. III, col. 233. See also the Vespers antiphon of the Second Sunday in Advent, after the chapter, "In die illa erit germen Domini in magnificentia et gloria; et fructus terrae sublimis: et exultatio his qui salvati fuerint de Israel" (Isa. 4:2), and the verse, "Rorate caeli . . . ," S.B., Vol. I, col. lxxxi. This antiphon and the following passage from the Canticle of Moses (Deut. 32), sung regularly at Saturday Lauds, bear a close relationship to the image of the poem: "Concrescat ut pluvia doctrina mea: fluat ut ros eloquium meum. Quasi imber super herbam, et quasi stillae super gramina: quia nomen Domini invocabo." S.B., Vol. II, cols. 187–88.

31. Lesson for Octave of the Assumption, *S.M.,* II, 465, and for the Visitation, *S.M.,* II, 389—quoted from Douay-Rheims Bible, Cant. 2:1–2. Legg indicates other passages from the Canticles. See also S.B., Vol. III, cols. 47, 391–92, 413, 785. Flowers are applied to Mary especially in the sequences, e.g., Annunciation, *S.M.,* II, 320–21 (see below, Appendix I), and the many sequences for the Assumption, *S.M.,* II, 466 ff., Adam of St. Victor, Vol. II, No. 73.

32. For liturgical sources see above, note 9; also Raw, pp. 412–13; Manning, p. 165; Davies, p. 18. The poet, too, may here have had in mind the Old Testament figure of the burning bush which Yahweh caused to be a sign for Moses: "Bi þe buysch þat moises siȝ vnbrent, we knowen þat þi preisable maidenhede is kept. modir of god, preie for us!" (antiphon for Sext, *The Prymer,* p. 24) a figure frequently used with that of the flowering rod and the fleece in sequences. See Advent, Mass of Mary, *S.M.,* II, 78 ff.; and Adam of St. Victor, Nativity, Vol. II, No. 74.

33. *Archivum Linguisticum,* III, 158–59.

34. *Middle English Literature,* pp. 164–65.

"Als I Lay vp-on a Nith"

1. Bonaventure, *Breviloquium,* trans. Erwin E. Nemmers (St. Louis, 1946), Prologue, sec. 2, 4.

2. Brown, *XIV,* No. 132, lines 17–19.

3. Brown, *XIV,* No. 56, from Edinburgh Advocates Library MS 18. 7. 21.

4. Besides relating the poem to the genre of vision poetry, the setting is typical also of the formal opening identified by Edmund K. Chambers as the *chanson d'aventure,* which begins with a narrative preface in which the poet pretends he witnesses the action he reports. Chambers and Frank Sidgwick, *Early English Lyrics, Amorous, Divine, Moral & Trivial* (London, 1907), p. 266. For fuller discussion, see Helen E. Sandison, *The "Chanson d'aventure" in Middle English* (Bryn Mawr, 1913). The function of the setting for this poem will be discussed below.

5. Although *OED* lists "withouten wone" as an idiom meaning "without delay" (citing a single example) and in his edition Richard L. Greene glosses the phrase with the same meaning (*The Early English Carols* [Oxford, 1935], p. 383), the context of the phrase in this poem is the mystery of the virgin birth, and I prefer Brown's gloss of "wone" with its primary denotation as "custom" or "accustomed." Taken as a whole,

Mary's statement means that the angel prophesied she should bear man's bliss without womankind's penalty of pain (see above, "Gabriel, fram Evene-King," notes 3 and 4) and implicitly makes the relationship between her painless giving birth and the redemption of man. This translation is borne out in line 51, by the actual birth "in maydened with-outen kare."

6. The word "see" with its connotations of ecclesiastical power, although seeming to be anomalous, perhaps is used to suggest by contrast the falsity of Mary's later assumption that her Son will be an earthly king, whereas the words mean He is to be a king in the context of a spiritual kingdom or priesthood.

7. The four events are those celebrated by the Christmas and Epiphany season liturgy: the Circumcision on January 1, the Octave of Christmas, Legg, pp. 35–36; the Epiphany on January 6, Legg, pp. 37–39; the Purification on February 2, Legg, pp. 246–50; the finding of Jesus in the Temple is not a festival, but the account in Luke is the Gospel reading for the First Sunday after Epiphany, Legg, p. 41. See below, pp. 85 ff.

8. "Tria sunt munera preciosa que optulerunt magi domino in die ista et habent in se diuina misteria. In auro ut ostendatur regis potencia. In thure sacerdotem magnum considera. Et in mirra dominicam sepulturam." Response on Epiphany, Legg, p. 37, and S.B., Vol. I, col. cccxxiv. This was the traditional homiletic application. See, e.g., "In epiphania Domini," *Old English Homilies of the Twelfth Century,* ed. Richard Morris, EETS, O.S., No. 53 (London, 1873), p. 45; *Cursor Mundi,* Part II, EETS, O.S., No. 59 (London, 1875), lines 11492–506; and A. Harford Pearson, *The Sarum Missal Done into English* (2d ed. rev.; London, 1884), p. 38. See also Figure 5.

9. Besides the manifestation of Christ to the gentile Kings, two other events are classed as epiphanies: the baptism of Christ by John (Stanza XXIII), which is commemorated in the Gospel for the Octave of the Epiphany (Legg, p. 39), and Christ's changing of the water into wine at the wedding at Cana, commemorated in the Gospel for the Second Sunday after Epiphany (Legg, p. 42). The three epiphanies are the subject of the hymn "Hostis Herodes impie," sung at Vespers from the Epiphany through the Octave. Text, S.B., Vol. I, col. cccxix. See also *St. Bernard's Sermons for the Seasons and Principal Festivals of the Year,* trans. Mt. Melleray (3 vols.; Westminster, Md., 1950), II, 1–14.

10. John 19:31–37 and I John 5:6–8. See below, p. 128, and Figures 2 and 6.

11. Greene, *Early English Carols,* p. cxxv, classifies this poem as a "Lullay Carol" in the Anglo-Irish Franciscan tradition, although in its narrative and dramatic qualities it seems to have ballad-like characteristics. It is difficult to believe that the refrain was repeated after each of the 37 stanzas as would be characteristic of a carol (see Greene, pp. cxxxii ff.). The story might have been sung consecutively, breaking according to the tale into the regular units of five stanzas, each followed by the "lullay" refrain.

12. George Kane, *Middle English Literature* (London, 1951), pp. 178 ff. See this attitude, for example in R. T. Davies' anthology, *Medieval English Lyrics* (Evanston, 1964). No. 38 is an abridged edition of "Als i lay vp-on a nith," in which the angel's prophecy and sign that the Child is to be the Messiah (Stanzas IX–XI) are omitted as well as the entire tale told by Christ up through His passion (Stanzas XVII–XXI). The implication is that since these parts of the tale are the standard story of the life of Christ, for the understanding of the poem they need not be repeated.

13. So regularly measured are the stages of the telling in each of the five units, that one is tempted to look for further correspondences between them. Putting the units of

five side by side one can see, for example, (1) in the first part of each unit the developing figure of birth and baptism: annunciation and birth of Christ, circumcision (traditional Old Testament type of baptism) and resurrection (fulfillment of Christ's birth, traditional figure for man's rebirth in baptism); (2) in the second part of each unit, Christ's Divinity: His conception by the Holy Spirit, His painless birth, His epiphany to the Magi, the overthrow of Satan, His purpose to liberate man, His ascension into the glory of His godhood; (3) in the third part, the Church: the presentation in the Temple, the sending of the disciples, the sending of the Holy Spirit; (4) in the last part, the development of the poem's narrative.

PART II

"Þe Milde Lomb Isprad o Rode"

1. From *Lamentatio St. Bernardi de compassione Mariae,* a sermon attributed to Bernard of Clairvaux, as printed from the Antwerp ed. (1616), cols. 156 ff., in G. Kribel, "Studien zu Richard Rolle de Hampole II," *Englische Studien,* VIII (1885), 98.

2. PL, Vol. CLIX, cols. 271–90. For a general description of Mary's laments in Middle English poetry up to the fifteenth century, see George C. Taylor, "The English 'Planctus Mariae,'" *Modern Philology,* IV (April, 1907), 605–37.

3. My references to sources differ from those given by Brown. For the source of the two thirteenth century poems and the fourteenth century "Wy haue ȝe no reuthe on my child?" Brown refers to the Migne edition of the Bernard dialogue, *Liber de passione Christi et doloribus et planctibus matris ejus,* PL, Vol. CLXXXII, cols. 1133–42. See Brown, *XIII,* pp. 200–201, 204, and *XIV,* p. 265. However, the Kribel version will be the source used for this study, because it is fuller, provides more parallels to the English poems, and uses the fulfillment of Simeon's prophecy in a way identical to Brown, *XIII,* No. 47, lines 31–36. According to Brown, who refers to the words immediately above the poem in the MS, the fourteenth century "Suete sone, reu on me & brest out of þi bondis" is based on a meditation ascribed to Bede. See Brown, *XIV,* p. 266, note on No. 64. However, we shall see below its close relationship to the *Lamentatio* attributed to Bernard.

4. See, e.g., the two versions also published by G. Kribel, pp. 67–114, also *Cursor Mundi,* ed. Richard Morris, Part V, EETS, O.S., No. 68 (London, 1878), lines 23945–4730, and *Yorkshire Writers: Richard Rolle of Hampole and His Followers,* ed. Carl Horstman (2 vols.; London, 1895–96), II (1895), 274–82.

5. Brown, *XIV,* Nos. 67, 128.

6. For a full definition of the theological concepts relevant to the following poems, see the sermon on Christ's passion, *St. Bernard's Sermons for the Seasons and Principal Festivals of the Year,* trans. Mt. Melleray (3 vols.; Westminster, Md., 1950), II, 135–53.

7. Brown, *XIII,* No. 45, from Arundel MS 248.

8. This is the manner also in which Mary portrays Christ in *Lamentatio St. Bernardi:* "Et ipse me videns fuit in cruce eleuatus et ligno durissimis clauis affixus. Stabam et ego videns eum, et ipse videns me plus dolebat de me quam de se. Ipse vero tanquam agnus coram tondente se vocem non dabat, nec aperiebat os suum. Aspiciebam

ego infaelix et misera Deum meum et filium meum in cruce pendentem et morte turpissima morientem. Tantoque dolore et tristitia vexabar in mente quod non posset explicari sermone. . . ." Kribel, p. 90. See also below, note 11.

9. The Paschal Lamb as a figure for Christ is defined most fully by the liturgy of Passiontide and Easter. The Eucharist was instituted in the framework of the Feast of Passover (Exod. 12). See especially Maunday Thursday readings commemorating the institution of the Eucharist, the Good Friday readings of Exod. 12:1–11 and of the Passion according to John 18, 19:1–37 (Legg, pp. 102 ff. and pp. 109 ff.; *S.M.*, I, 236 and 251 ff.), and the Easter Preface (Legg, p. 213, *S.M.*, I, 36). In the Canon of the Mass the figure is used after the fraction of the Host, when the words of John the Baptist (John 1:29) are applied in the Agnus Dei (see Figure 2 and descriptive note). For a presentation of the Lamb suggestive of this poem, see stanzas 6 and 7 of Venantius Fortunatus' hymn, "Pange lingua gloriosi," sung during the Adoration of the Cross on Good Friday (Legg, pp. 113–14; *S.M.*, I, 259–61, also S.B., Vol. I, col. dccxxix). For commentary, see Innocent III, PL, Vol. CCXVII, col. 853; Aquinas, *Summa theol.*, III, Ques. 73, art. 6. The ultimate revelation of Christ through the figure of the Lamb is in the Apocalypse, especially chaps. 5, 14, 19, 22.

10. "Christ's afflictions ought to be of such a kind that He could suffer nothing without His consent. This is so not only because of the blessedness and omnipotent divinity united in Him by which He was able to repel all, but also because of His most perfect innocence which in the order of natural justice is not allowed to suffer anything unwillingly." Bonaventure, *Breviloquium*, trans. Erwin E. Nemmers (St. Louis, 1946), Part IV, chap. iii, sec. 4. "He was offered because it was his own will, and he opened not his mouth" (Isa. 53:7). See also Bernard, *Sermons*, II, 137–38, and "He alone had power to lay down his life: no man could take it away from Him: He offered it of His own will," pp. 138–39.

11. This carries out the suggestion from Isaiah 53:2–3 of the suffering servant: "There is no beauty in him, nor comeliness: and we have seen him, and there was no sightliness, that we should be desirous of him: Despised and the most abject of men, a man of sorrows and acquainted with infirmity: and his look was as it were hidden and despised. Whereupon we esteemed him not." Mary develops the theme also in the *Lamentatio St. Bernardi:* "Erat enim aspectu dulcis, colloquio suauis et omni conuersatione benignissimus. Manabat namque sanguis eius ex quatuor partibus rigantibus undis, ligno manibus pedibusque confixis. De vultu illius pulchritudo effluxerat omnis, et qui erat prae filiis hominum speciosa forma, videbatur omnium indecorus. Videbam quod complebatur illud propheticum in eo: Vidimus eum et non erat ei species neque decor. Vultum enim illius iniquorum Judaeorum foedaverat liuor." Kribel, pp. 90–91.

12. For the evolution of the concept "corpus mysticum," the mystical body, as it first referred to the sacramental Body of Christ and later, through scholastic defense of the Eucharist and especially at the time of Boniface VIII, came to be distinguished from the "Real Presence" of Christ in the Eucharist and to refer to the body *"ecclésial"* of the Church, see Henri de Lubac, S.J., *Corpus Mysticum: l'Eucharistie et l'Église au moyen âge, étude historique* (Paris, 1944).

13. The tradition begins with the Gospel of John himself. See John 13:23, 19:25–27 and John 21:19–24 which was read at Mass and Matins on December 27, John's feast day (Legg, p. 31; *S.M.*, I, 109; S.B., Vol. I, col. ccxxiii). The theme is developed in the antiphons and responses of his feast, first nocturn (S.B., Vol. I, cols. ccxv ff.), along with the theme of John resting his head on Christ's breast at the Last Supper (John 13:23), of John's virginity, and of Christ's commending Mary to John's care. See also Y.B., Vol.

I, cols. 103 ff. According to Bede, John was worthy of this title because of his special chastity: "Diligebat autem eum Jesus: quia specialis praerogativa castitatis ampliori dilectione eum fecerat dignum." His chastity also made him a fitting servant of Christ's mother (S.B., Vol. I, col. ccxxiv; Y.B., Vol. I, col. 109). Bede's statement and the themes of Matins are the basis of the sequence for John's feast day (Legg, pp. 463–64; *S.M.*, I, 109). See also the Apostrophe to St. John following the English metrical version of the *Lamentatio* in *Cursor Mundi,* lines 24659–730.

14. Brown, *XIII,* Nos. 47, 49, see below, pp. 130–31, 142–45. In the *Lamentatio* the prophecy's fulfillment is used not to show the justice of Mary's suffering, but to convey its intensity: "Nec lingua poterit loqui nec mens cogitare valebit, quanto dolore afficiebantur pia viscera Mariae. Nunc soluis virgo cum usura quod in partu non habuisti a natura. Dolorem pariendo filium non sensisti, quem millies replicatum filio moriente passa fuisti. Juxta crucem stabat emortua mater, quae ipsum ex spiritu sancto concepit." Kribel, pp. 98–99 (the reference is missing from Migne, *Liber de passione Christi*). In chap. xii of the Anselm dialogue the virtue of faith is stressed, as it is Mary's faith in her Son's godhood that causes the sword to pierce her soul: "Tunc matri potuit dicere: *Audi filia, et vide* (Ps. 44:11), audi voces blasphemantium filium tuum, et vide dolorem meum. Scis enim quod de Spiritu sancto concepisti me, et quod virgo genuisti me, et qualiter aluisti me. Unde ex quo isti non credunt in me, tu tamen crede in me, et compatere. Tunc iterum gladius Simeonis animam pertransivit." PL, Vol. CLIX, col. 284.

15. The Gospel simply states: "When Jesus therefore had seen his mother and the disciple standing whom he loved, he saith to his mother: Woman behold thy son. After that, he saith to the disciple: Behold thy mother. And from that hour the disciple took her to his own." John 19:26–27. These verses are included in the Gospel read for the Mass of Mary during Paschaltide, Legg, p. 391; *S.M.*, II, 98. The *Lamentatio* has: "Et quo ego vado, tu non potes venire modo, venies autem postea. Interim Joannes, qui est nepos tuus, reputabitur tibi filius, curam habebit tui et erit solatium fidelissimum tibi. Inde dominus intuitus Joannem ait: Ecce mater tua! El seruies, curam illius habebis eam tibi commendo, suscipe matrem tuam, imo magis suscipe matrem meam!" Kribel, pp. 96–97. See also above, note 13.

16. The past event of sacred history, the focus of the first part of the poem, is applied to the present moment as defined by the point of view of the Church, as in virtue of the past event, the poet formulates man's present petition for future joy. The reformulation is analogous to the form of the Collect of the Mass, above, Introduction, pp. 22 ff.

17. The indirect naming follows the same principle as seen in "Nu þis fules singet," Part I, p. 52–53. The One spoken of is identified by His unique and special act for mankind. The significance of this identifying of Christ, Mary and mankind by virtue of their relationship to the events of sacred history is developed below, pp. 163 ff., 204 ff.

18. These three aspects of beauty correspond generally to those systematically described by Edgar de Bruyne, *Études d'esthétique médiévale* (3 vols.; Brugge, 1946), especially to Hugh of St. Victor's definition of beauty (II, 203, *passim*). They are fully defined also by Bonaventure, *Itinerarium mentis in Deum,* chap. ii (see the trans. by Philotheus Boehner, O.F.M. [St. Bonaventure, New York, 1956]). The third aspect, the power to achieve delight, is the key proportion for the definition of beauty in terms of theology and will be discussed more fully in Part III, "The Figure of Delight," and in the Conclusion.

19. These connotations are borne out by commentary. See, e.g., Bede who, commenting on John the Baptist's "Behold the Lamb of God . . ." (John 1:29), explains how

Christ washed us from sin in His blood: not only did He do so when His blood was given for us on the cross or when by means of His passion we are washed by the waters of baptism, but truly He washes our sins in His blood, "cum ejusdem beatae passionis ad altare memoria replicatur, cum panis et vini creatura in sacramentum carnis et sanguinis ejus ineffabili Spiritus sanctificatione transfertur." PL, Vol. XCIV, col. 75.

20. Although having a different significance for each poem by virtue of the differing subjects of each, this proportioning of the components of a stanza to the components of the following stanzas is analogous to the proportioning of stanzas in "Gabriel, fram evene-king" and "Als i lay vp-on a nith." See above, pp. 44 ff., 81 ff.

21. It is interesting to note the poet's exhortation in relation to Jungmann's comment that in Eucharistic piety from the end of the twelfth century the idea of spiritual communion replaced that of sacramental reception of Christ: "With an appeal to the Augustinian *Crede et manducasti,* this form of piety, when one turned with loving faith to Christ, contemplated His Passion with profoundest love, devoutly assisted at Holy Mass or looked up at the Sacred Host, was explained as a work scarcely less valuable than sacramental Communion itself." *The Mass of the Roman Rite: Its Origins and Development* (*missarum sollemnia*) (2 vols.; New York, 1951), II, 364.

Mary's Sorrow

1. For a longstanding definition of lyric, see Francis Turner Palgrave: "Lyrical has been here held essentially to imply that each Poem shall turn on some single thought, feeling, or situation. In accordance with this, narrative, descriptive, and didactic poems, —unless accompanied by rapidity of movement, brevity, and the coloring of human passion,—have been excluded." *The Golden Treasury of the Best Songs and Lyrical Poems in the English Language,* edited and revised by C. Day Lewis (London, 1954), p. 21. For a view more influential on the present generation of critics, see Cleanth Brooks and Robert Penn Warren, *Understanding Poetry: An Anthology for College Students* (2d ed.; New York, 1953), especially "The Dramatic Aspect of Poetry," p. lix, and how poetry tends towards concentration for an effect of greater intensity, p. 71. See also 3d ed., 1960, pp. xiii–xiv. In *A Preface to Chaucer: Studies in Medieval Perspectives* (Princeton, 1962), Durant W. Robertson, Jr., points out the incorrectness particularly of reading medieval love poetry with the romantic idea that poetry is to arouse and express emotions, pp. 14–17. He also discusses the non-dramatic quality of medieval poetry, pp. 37–51. In *Wisdom and Number* (Lincoln, 1962), Preface and Chapter I, Stephen Manning warns about reading Middle English lyrics with such concepts as those of Palgrave or Brooks and Warren, putting the lyrics in the broader classification of songs. But his approach through the categories of rhetoric does not seem to me to account adequately for the essential unity of form with its theological content.

2. *Middle English Literature* (London, 1951), p. 129. See the following pages in Kane for a discussion of the meditative lyric.

3. *Middle English Literature,* pp. 148–49.

4. *Lamentatio St. Bernardi de compassione Mariae,* ed. G. Kribel, *Englische Studien,* VIII (1885), 92–93.

5. Brown, *XIV,* No. 60.

6. The transcription of these two poems omits Brown's indications of emendations of the texts.

7. " 'Why,' as Bernard said, in the character of Mary, to the Jews, 'if it does not

please you to pity the Son do you not pity the mother!' " Brown, *XIV,* p. 265, note on No. 60.

8. *Middle English Literature,* pp. 148–49.

9. *Middle English Literature,* p. 149.

10. Kribel, pp. 85–86.

11. Kribel, p. 87.

12. Kribel, pp. 109–10.

13. Brown, *XIV,* No. 64.

14. Noting that immediately above this poem is written in the MS, "Beda. Audi cum Maria quae dixit," Brown points out a general similarity between the poem and *De meditatione passionis Christi per septem diei horas libellus* (PL, Vol. XCIV, cols. 561–68) sometimes ascribed to Bede. Brown, *XIV,* p. 266. The passage Brown quotes is Mary's prayer, first to her Son to remember her and all His servants and then to God the Father to accept her Son. Brown himself indicates the parallel is not verbal, and it seems to me the mode of Mary's lamentation is closer to the spirit of the following section of the *Lamentatio St. Bernardi* than to the passages ascribed to Bede: "O fili carissime, o benignissime nate, misereri matri tuae et suscipe preces eius! Desine nunc mihi esse durus, qui cunctis semper fuisti benignus! Suscipe matrem tuam in cruce ut vivam tecum post mortem semper! Nihil mihi dulcius est quam te amplexato, in cruce tecum mori; et nil certe amarius quam viuere post tuam mortem. O vere Dei nate, tu mihi pater, tu mihi mater, tu mihi filius, tu mihi sponsus, tu mihi anima eras. Nunc, orbor patre, viduor sponso, desolor filio, omnia perdo. . . . Fili dulcissime, omnia tibi possibilia sunt, sed etsi non vis ut moriar tecum, mihi saltem relinque aliquod benignum consilium!" Kribel, 93–94.

15. Matt. 27:40. See also Mark 25:29–32 and Luke 23:35–43. It is precisely this context which is given in the Anselm dialogue when Christ explains to Mary that now is the moment that the sword foretold by Simeon pierces her soul. It is in contrast to those who challenged Christ to come down from the cross and they would believe, that Mary stands beneath the cross and suffers. PL, Vol. CLIX, cols. 283–84.

16. Matt. 26:56. See also Mark 14:50.

17. *Middle English Literature,* p. 148.

18. Mary will take this same position again after Christ's ascension. In the poems on Mary's joys the situation of man in present time in relation to heavenly joy is included explicitly in the poems, as, after Mary's assumption, man raises his prayer to her. See below, pp. 149 ff., 162–64, 187 ff.

"Stond Wel, Moder, vnder Rode"

1. George Kane, *Middle English Literature* (London, 1951), p. 148.

2. Brown, *XIII,* No. 49. My transcription of this poem omits indications of Brown's emendations. In his notes to the poem, Brown lists four known texts, one incomplete: Digby MS 86 (Brown's A text), British Museum Royal MS 12 E. I (Brown's B text), Harley MS 2253, and St. John's College Cambridge MS E. 8. Of the several editions of Harley 2253, the text I have referred to in comparing the versions is that included in Bruce Dickins and R. M. Wilson, *Early Middle English Texts* (New York, 1951), pp. 129–30. Both the Royal and the incomplete St. John's College texts are accompanied by music. Of the three complete versions I use the Royal (Brown's B text). This choice is

in agreement with Brown (p. 205); that is, although it is a later text than Digby, it appears to be the more authentic of the two. As Brown says, lines 37–39 of Digby seem to miss the purpose of the poem and lines 43–44 to be a perversion of the same lines in Royal. On the other hand, in Harley 2253 the stanza which is in Royal as stanza six is used as stanza three. I find Royal preferable to Harley because in this stanza the two appeals, of Christ to Mary to let Him die and of Mary to Christ that He let her die before Him, come as a climax reached just before Christ uses Mary's suffering to make her mother of mankind.

3. *Lamentatio St. Bernardi de compassione Mariae,* ed. G. Kribel, *Englische Studien,* VIII (1885), 91.

4. "Nam gladius mortis Christi animas utrorumque transibat. Transibat saeuus, saeuus perimebat utrunque. Quo magis amabat, saevior fiebat in matre. Vulnera Christi morientis erant vulnera matris dolentis." Kribel, p. 97.

5. This motif of Mary's tears of blood is neither in the Latin *Lamentatio* nor in the *Cursor Mundi* version of it, but is in the English metrical versions of the school of Richard Rolle. See the versions printed by Kribel, lines 81–96, and that in *Yorkshire Writers: Richard Rolle of Hampole and His Followers,* ed. Carl Horstmann (2 vols.; London, 1895–1896), II, 274–82, lines 49–64. Compare this theme to the stanzas in "Als i lay vp-on a nith," lines 117–24, where to the sword piercing Mary's heart Christ opposes His own heart's blood to be shed for the redemption of man. See above, pp. 79–80.

6. See also *Lamentatio St. Bernardi,* Kribel, p. 90.

7. See above, "Þe Milde Lomb Isprad o Rode," pp. 99–100 and note 14; see below, pp. 142–45.

8. Bonaventure, *Breviloquium,* trans. Erwin E. Nemmers (St. Louis, 1946), Prologue, sec. 6, 4, develops both this statement and his definition of theology from Eph. 3:14–19. A considerable symbolic tradition, following from the earlier Fathers, especially Augustine, was based on Paul's description of these four dimensions of the charity of God and the idea of the universe as an intelligible cross. For a gathering of commentaries, see Anton E. Schönbach, *Altdeutsche Predigten* (2 vols.; Graz, 1886–1888), II (1888), 177–89; see also Jacob Gretser, *Opera omnia* (17 vols.; Ratisbon, 1734–41), Vols. I–III. A celebrated example of the tradition is Rabanus Maurus, *De laudibus sanctae crucis,* PL, Vol. CVII, cols. 133–294, in which the mysteries of the Christian faith are figured in poetry whose words are emblematically diagrammed in the form of the cross and then explicated. For a re-evaluation of the poem, and a comparison of it to the vision of Teilhard de Chardin, see Henri de Lubac, S.J., *Exégèse médiévale: les quatre sens de l'Ecriture* (4 vols.; Paris, 1959, 1961, 1964), I, 161 ff. In "Stond wel, moder, vnder rode" man's life in present time is proportioned to the cross. See below, pp. 135 ff.

9. Montague Rhodes James, *A Descriptive Catalogue of the MSS in the Library of St. John's College Cambridge* (Cambridge, 1913), No. 111, p. 145. See also Brown, *XIII,* pp. 203–4.

10. A version of the sequence is printed in Guido M. Dreves, *Analecta hymnica medii aevi,* Vol. VIII (Leipzig, 1890), No. 58, and with slight variations another is found in the Paris, Arsenal MS 135 of the Sarum Missal, printed in Legg, p. 530. For the version from the Sarum Missal, see below, Appendix II. For an edition of the music, see John Stainer, *Early Bodleian Music: Sacred & Secular Songs, Together with Other MS Compositions in the Bodleian Library, Oxford, Ranging from about* A.D. *1185 to about* A.D. *1505* (2 vols.; London, 1901), II, 8–9. Contrasting to the music of "Gabriel, fram evene-king," this music develops in a continuous progression, with the second

three lines of the two parts of the stanzas an approximate repetition of the first, corresponding to the movement of thought in the series of more and more intense oppositions which are resolved finally in the last three stanzas by the succession of events.

11. Brown, *XIII,* No. 4, from Tanner MS 169 *. After the section relating Mary's present grief to her painless child-bearing, both the incomplete English version and the Latin sequence have an additional stanza summarizing Mary's sorrow (Brown, No. 4, lines 19–24, "Stabat iuxta Christi crucem," lines 43–48). In the final prayer both the incomplete English version and the Latin sequence address Mary as mother (the English has both mother and maid, "Milde moder, maiden oa"). See also Arthur S. Napier, *History of the Holy Rood-tree . . . with Notes on the Orthography of the Ormulum and A Middle English Compassio Marie,* EETS, O.S., No. 103 (London, 1894), pp. 75–86. Napier points out the similarity of "Iesu cristes milde moder" to the Latin sequence.

12. Brown, *XIII,* No. 47, from the same Arundel MS 248 as "Gabriel, fram evene-king" and "Þe milde Lomb isprad o rode." Both the complete English narrative and the English dialogue versions omit the stanza summarizing Mary's sorrow and add a stanza before the last one so that the last two stanzas are very similar. The next to the last stanzas of both begin by referring to the bliss Christ brought by His resurrection and then invoking Mary to make "us" happy as well. The last stanzas begin in both with an address to Mary, Queen of Heaven, and then ask her, for the blood Christ shed, to bring us to heaven.

13. The correspondence is made in the Latin and the incomplete English version, the English adding a fourth correspondence, "For, so gleam glidis þurt þe glas" (line 33).

14. *XIII,* p. 204.

15. "O mater mollis ad fluendum, mollis ad dolendum, tu scis quia ad hoc veni et ad hoc de te carnem assumpsi ut per crucis patibulum saluarem genus humanum. Quomodo ergo implebuntur scripturae? sic enim oportet me pati pro salute generis humani. Die namque tertia resurgam, tibi et discipulis meis patenter apparens; desine flere et dolorem depone, quia ad patrem vado et ad gloriam paternae maiestatis percipiendam ascendo! Congratulare mihi, quia nunc inueni ovem errantem quam tam longo tempore perdideram. Moritur unus ut totus inde reuiuiscat mundus. Vnius ob meritum cuncti periere minores, et nunc saluantur unius ob meritum. Quod placet Deo patri, quomodo displicet tibi? Mater dulcissima, calicem quem dedit mihi pater, non vis ut bibam illum? Noli flere mulier, noli flere mater speciosissima! non te desero, non te derelinquo. Tecum sum et tecum ero omni tempore saeculi. Secundum carnem subjaceo imperio mortis, secundem diuinitatem sum et ero semper immortalis et impassibilis. Bene scis unde processi et unde veni. Quare ergo tristaris, si illuc ascendo unde descendi? Tempus est ut reuertar ad eum qui me misit." Kribel, pp. 95–96.

PART III

The Names of Joy

1. Aelred of Rievaulx, "In Assumptione B. Mariae," PL, Vol. CXCV, col. 309, trans. T. E. Bridgett, *Our Lady's Dowry* (London, 1875), pp. 107–8.

2. To see again the variety of ways in which an author can use the events of sacred

history, contrast these words of Aelred, which seek to expand man's comprehension of the meaning of Mary's joy by multiplying joy upon joy, to those, quoted above, pp. 115 ff., by the author of the *Lamentatio St. Bernardi,* who uses the quality of Mary's present great joy in heaven to indicate by contrast the intense degree to which she must have suffered at the crucifixion. See also how Aelred develops Mary's joy by contrasting to each earthly joy a heavenly counterpart, cols. 309–10, and compare Aelred to Anselm, quoted below, pp. 175 ff., on heavenly joy.

3. " . . . Ita non est ei tantum creatura, ancilla, amica, filia, sed etiam mater," Aelred, col. 309.

4. See Aelred, cols. 310, 313–14. Aelred affirms the possibility of Mary's bodily assumption, but leaves the question open as he applies to Mary's state phrases from Canticles and Paul's description of Christ's revelation to him: "But one thing I dare most surely affirm, that to-day the Blessed Virgin—'whether in the body or out of the body I know not, God knoweth'—ascended into heaven. . . ." Bridgett's translation, p. 109. See also the letter ascribed to Jerome read at Matins on the Assumption, S.B., Vol. III, cols. 687 ff.

5. "De Anunciacione dominica sermo breuis," *Mirk's Festial: A Collection of Homilies by Johannes Mirkus (John Mirk),* ed. Theodor Erbe, Part I, EETS, E.S., No. 96 (London, 1905), pp. 109–10.

6. "De Assumpcione Beate Marie Uirginis . . . ," *Mirk's Festial,* Part I, pp. 224–25.

7. "Þe milde Lomb isprad o rode," line 45. See also "Gabriel, fram evene-king," line 50. This title of Mary is behind the words with which in "Stond wel, moder, vnder rode" Christ cries out to Mary, "Moder, merci! let me deyen" (line 31), so that He may buy Adam out of hell and Mary may become full of pity for mankind.

8. Paris, 1932. For the variety of numbers, see Wilmart, pp. 327 ff. and p. 328, note 1. For evidence of the popularity of the five joys, see also Brown, *XIII,* p. 179, note on No. 18, and J. Vincent Crowne, "Middle English Poems on the Joys and on the Compassion of the Blessed Virgin Mary," *Catholic University Bulletin,* VIII (July, 1902), 304–16. There was a strong devotion to Mary's seven celestial joys, which according to tradition were shown by Mary to Thomas à Becket because he had repeated her five earthly joys so faithfully. See *Mirk's Festial,* p. 232; *Horae Eboracenses,* ed. Christopher Wordsworth, Surtees Society, Vol. CXXXII (Durham and London, 1920 for 1919), p. 64, note 4; Bridgett, *Our Lady's Dowry,* pp. 65–66; and Wilmart, p. 329. For additional texts of English poems on the seven joys, consult *Index of Middle English Verse,* ed. Carleton Brown and Rossell Hope Robbins (New York, 1943), Nos. 462, 465, 896, 1025, 1033. The *Supplement to the Index of Middle English Verse,* ed. Rossell Hope Robbins and John Cutler (Lexington, 1965), lists none. See Brown, *XV,* 304, note to No. 33. Finally, there was also wide devotion to Mary's fifteen earthly and heavenly joys. See, for example, Wilmart, pp. 339–58, and two poems by Lydgate in *The Minor Poems of John Lydgate,* ed. Henry N. MacCracken, EETS, E.S., No. 107 (London, 1911 for 1910), pp. 260–79.

9. The *Supplement* records only an additional fragment on Mary's five joys.

10. *Horae Eboracenses,* pp. 63–64.

11. The seven heavenly joys are Mary's matchlessness, the brightness of her glory, the honor she receives from all beings, the willingness of her Son to grant her request, her place next to the Holy Trinity, her rewarding of those who serve her, and, finally, the fact that her joy is endless. *Horae Eboracenses,* pp. 64–66; *Mirk's Festial,* pp. 232–33.

12. For example, the initials of the verse beginning each Hour in the fourteenth

century *Horae* for Humphrey de Bohun (Bodleian MS Auct. D. 4.4) depict the joys of Mary and include the crucifixion and resurrection. *The Bohun MSS,* ed. Montague R. James, Roxburghe Club, No. 200 (Oxford, 1936), pls. 31–35. The fourteenth century *Horae* for Joan II of Navarre begins each Hour with a joy. *Thirty-Two Miniatures from the Book of Hours of Joan II, Queen of Navarre,* ed. Henry Y. Thompson, Roxburghe Club, No. 137 (London, 1899), Part II, pls. 14–19 (the reproduction is not comprehensive). Also there are evidences of the joys in association with the tree of Jesse. For example, in the fourteenth century Gorleston Psalter, below in the illumination, woven into the design of the tree, is the series of five of Mary's joys during Christ's childhood. Eric G. Millar, *English Illuminated MSS of the XIVth and XVth Centuries* (Paris, 1928), pl. 15. For other examples of joys in the Psalters, see Millar, pls. 8 and 35. The most clear example of the concept is in the fourteenth century Peterborough Psalter (Cambridge Corpus Christi College MS 53), where before each psalm are two pages of joys, a joy to each page, followed by two pages of figures, an Old Testament Prophet and a New Testament Apostle. The sequence of joys is the annunciation, nativity, resurrection, ascension, and the coronation of the Virgin. Mary's joys are followed by Christ's passion. *A Peterborough Psalter and Bestiary of the Fourteenth Century,* ed. Montague R. James, Roxburghe Club, No. 178 (Oxford, 1921), pls. 2–3, 6–7, 10. This same pattern is followed by other artists. See Millar, pls. 28–29, 37–39.

13. Wilmart, pp. 331 ff.

14. Bridgett, p. 67. For other examples of the joys and a discussion of their origin and popularity, see pp. 65–73. On their application to Christ's wounds, see also Wilmart, pp. 331–32.

15. *The Ancrene Riwle* (*The Corpus MS: "Ancrene Wisse"*), trans. M. B. Salu (London, 1955), pp. 17–18. This edition is a modern English rendering of the Cambridge Corpus Christi College MS 402.

16. *Ancrene Riwle,* p. 195.

17. "Gaude dei genitrix uirgo inmaculata./ Gaude que gaudium ab angelo suscepisti./ Gaude que genuisti aeterni luminis claritatem./ Gaude mater./ Gaude sancta dei genitrix uirgo./ Tu sola mater innupta./ Te laudat omnis factura domini [genitricem lucis]./ Pro nobis supplica./ [Sis pro nobis, quesumus, perpetua interuentrix]." Wilmart, p. 331.

18. "The English Liturgical Refrain Lyric before 1450" (Ph.D. dissertation, Stanford University, 1945), p. 60. In a footnote Dr. White says it was used at Matins for the Fourth Week of Advent and that it appeared also in the liturgy of the Assumption and Purification. She gives no evidence for the direct connection of this antiphon with the joys. See S.B., Vol. II, col. 286; S.B., Vol. III, col. 143; Y.B., Vol. I, col. 690; Y.B., Vol. II, col. 501.

19. Brown, *XIII,* No. 22. The poem is from the same Trinity College Cambridge MS 323 as "Nu þis fules singet hand maket hure blisse." For a description of the MS, see Brown, *XIII,* pp. xx–xxi.

20. According to Brown, *XIII,* p. 181, the English poem is a literal rendering of "Gavde virgo, mater Christi," which he says is to be found in Guido M. Dreves, S.J., *Analecta hymnica medii aevi,* Vol. XXXI, No. 172. However, the English differs considerably from the *Analecta hymnica* version, which is an expanded six six-line stanza version, the first three lines of each stanza taken together corresponding to the stanzas of the English poem. The above York version represents the Latin equivalent of the English poem and will be used as the basis of comparison. The York Latin stanzas

and the English version seem to represent the core of the devotion to which various elements could be added, such as commentary on the meaning of each joy, as in the case of the expanded *Analecta hymnica* version; or such as an Ave after each stanza, as the note to "Gavde virgo, mater Christi" indicates (p. 63). The two poems on the five joys to be discussed below reflect these methods of expansion. For another expanded version in English see that in *The Minor Poems of the Vernon MS,* ed. Carl Horstmann, Part I, EETS, O.S., No. 98 (London, 1892), pp. 25–26. For Latin hymns on the joys, see esp. *Analecta hymnica,* Vol. XXXI, Nos. 86–91, 170–95.

21. *Horae Eboracenses,* pp. 63–64. The poem is followed, to complete the devotion, by a verse, response and prayer:

> *V.* Benedicta es a Filio tuo, domina.
>
> *R.* Quia per te fructum vite communicauimus.
>
> Oremus.
>
> Deus, qui beatissimam virginem Mariam in conceptu et partu [dilecti Filii tui] virginitate seruata duplici gaudio letificasti: quique eius gaudia Filio tuo resurgente et ad celos ascendente multiplicasti: presta, quesumus, vt ad illud ineffabile gaudium, quo assumpta tecum gaudet in celis, eius meritus et intercessione valeamus peruenire. Per [eundem] Christum Dominum nostrum.

22. The Latin *gaude,* the imperative of *gaudeo,* is intransitive and means "rejoice," as in line 1, "Rejoice, virgin, mother of Christ." "Gladen" according to *MED* had both an intransitive and transitive use. The transitive use was frequent, meaning, to make joyful, fill with joy or bliss.

23. "*R.* Suscipe verbum virgo Maria quod tibi a Domino per angelum transmissum est: concipies per aurem Deum paries et hominem. Ut benedicta dicaris inter omnes mulieres. *V.* Paries quidem filium: sed virginitatis non patieris detrimentum: efficieris gravida et eris mater semper intacta. Ut benedicta dicaris." Matins for the Annunciation, S.B., Vol. III, cols. 236–37. See also Matins for Christmas Day, S.B., Vol. I, col. clxxvi.

24. Brown glosses "gode" as the dative of "god" meaning "good." Yet because the Latin says "quia Deo plena" and the second joy celebrates Mary's painless giving birth not to an abstraction, "good," but to God incarnate in the flesh, "gode" appears to be the dative of "god," meaning "God."

25. See *OED,* "with" 15, "In the same way as; as—does or did, is or was, etc.; like." This poem provides an example of the use earlier than those cited (by Richard Rolle, Langland). The epithet "castitatis lilium," closer to the English poet's rendering here, is applied to Mary in the sequence used for the Annunciation (see Appendix I, line 39), and used also on the second day during the Octave of the Assumption. Legg, p. 479.

26. The use in this poem of the word "clos" is the only example cited by the *MED* of the word used to signify heaven. The other examples indicate the word was normally used to denote a tangible dwelling of some sort on earth. The absence of other examples reinforces my opinion that the author appropriates the word to stress the concept of space. Conceiving of Christ's "clos" with physical concreteness is a particularly English characteristic in illumination. For examples of the ascension, see Millar, *English Illuminated MSS from the Xth to the XIIIth Century* (Paris, 1926), pls. 61, 98; *MSS of*

the XIVth and XVth Centuries, pls. 25, 28, 35. A particularly interesting example is found in the Tiptoft Missal, Pierpont Morgan Library M. 107, fol. 163vo. Below the clouds which cut off the top of the ascending Christ, Christ's feet are visible on either side of the trailing hem of His garment, and His right hand is lowered below the clouds in the sign of divinity. On earth, with the disciples grouped in two clusters behind them, kneel Mary and Peter facing each other. Christ's ascent has left a gap in the center of the group, bridged only by the praying hands of Mary. In the Pentecost illumination, fol. 168vo, the gap is filled entirely by the figure of Mary around whom the disciples cluster as the dove of the Holy Spirit descends on her. See also Meyer Schapiro, "The Image of the Disappearing Christ: The Ascension in English Art Around the Year 1000," *Gazette des beaux-arts,* 6th Ser., Vol. XXIII (1943), 134–52. For a possible relationship to English drama, see Mary D. Anderson, *Drama and Imagery in English Medieval Churches* (Cambridge, 1963), Part III.

27. It is the figure used by Elizabeth as she salutes Mary at the visitation, "Blessed art thou among women and blessed is the fruit of thy womb," joined often by the liturgy with the angel's salutation at the annunciation. Legg, pp. 259, 388; *S.M.,* II, 95, 321, 391, 462; S.B., Vol. III, col. 236. The same figure concludes the antiphon "Salve regina": "Et Jesum, benedictum fructum ventris tui,/ Nobis post hoc exilium ostende," *Horae Eboracenses,* p. 62. And it is developed also on the Assumption by Bede, who interprets the birth of Christ as a fulfillment of the psalm verse: "Etenim Dominus dabit benignitatem: et terra nostra dabit fructum suum," S.B., Vol. III, cols. 693–94.

28. This is the position characteristic of man until Christ comes again. See the readings, verses and prayers of the Ascension liturgy, which use Acts 1:10–11. Legg, pp. 154–58; *S.M.,* I, 328–34. The Introit, for example, is: "Why stand ye gazing up into heaven? alleluya. He shall so come in like manner as ye have seen him go into heaven, alleluya, alleluya, alleluya. *Ps.* And while they looked steadfastly toward heaven, as he went up, behold, two men stood by them in white apparel, which also said: Ye men of Galilee . . ." etc. *S.M.,* I, 329. For the representation in illuminations, see above, note 26.

29. The same coupling of joys is found in the prayer following the York "Gavde virgo, mater Christi."

30. See for comparison, Tiptoft Missal, Pierpont Morgan Library M. 107, fol. 163vo, fol. 231vo, and fol. 253vo. See also, Millar, *MSS from the Xth to the XIIIth Century,* pl. 83, and *MSS of the XIVth and XVth Centuries,* pls. 8, 15, 22–25, 28, 29, 37, 38.

The Vision of Joy

1. *St. Bonaventure's "Itinerarium mentis in Deum,"* trans. Philotheus Boehner, O.F.M. (St. Bonaventure, New York, 1956), chap. iv, secs. 1–2.

2. Brown, *XIII,* No. 41, from Jesus College Oxford MS 29.

3. The title "leuedy" is used in poems which emphasize Mary's position as Queen of Heaven, and it is when the religious poet addresses her in heaven that he often adapts secular courtly love lyric terms. The contrast between the religious and courtly poems is fundamentally the difference between what is the object of the poet's desire rather than between the expressions of it. In this poem the fundamental prayer is that man both recognize and obtain the real object of his desire as theology defines it, the joy of heaven. In the famous poem from this same MS, "Friar Thomas de Hales' Love Ron"

(Brown, *XIII,* No. 43), the difference between the earthly and heavenly objects of love provides the structural and dynamic basis of the poem. See also below, note 9.

4. "Frume" according to *MED* is derived from the OE "fruma" and can mean both first in time (*MED* cites this line as an example) and at the beginning or at the start. Thus it can refer both to the first of the five joys and to the beginning of the heavenly joy once lost by Adam (line 35).

5. Introit and Gradual of the Vigil of the Assumption, Legg, 307; *S.M.,* II, 462, 463; also Gradual for the Mass of Mary from the Purification to Advent, *S.M.,* II, 95; and in *The Prymer,* third lesson for Matins, antiphon for Lauds and Prime, chapter for Lauds and Vespers.

6. For an alternative reading of this stanza, see below, "The Figure of Delight," pp. 189–90.

7. *The Ancrene Riwle* (*The Corpus MS: "Ancrene Wisse"*), trans. M. B. Salu (London, 1955), p. 11.

8. See above, p. 150 and note 4. For another example of the distinction between Mary's bodily and spiritual joy, see the prayer of the fourth joy in the *Riwle,* where it is the basis for the application of the prayer to the human soul: "O Lady, St Mary, because of the great joy that thou hadst when thou sawest thy fair and blessed Son, whom the Jews had thought to shut away in the tomb, rising on Ascension Thursday, in such glory and power, to His happiness in His heavenly kingdom, grant that I may, with Him, cast all the world underfoot and rise now in heart, at my death in spirit and at the day of judgement all bodily, to the joys of heaven" (p. 16).

9. These terms, meaning "courteous," "kind," "graceful," were often applied to both Christ and Mary. See Brown, *XIII,* No. 55, "Iblessed beo þu, lauedi so feir and so hende" (line 25); for other thirteenth century examples, see Nos. 60, 61, 65. No. 43, "Friar Thomas de Hales' Love Ron," defines Christ by comparing Him to an earthly king. See above, note 3.

10. Among the corrections he suggests of Carleton Brown's *English Lyrics of the XIIIth Century,* Kemp Malone would, it seems to me incorrectly for the reasons above, emend "wis" (line 51) to "iwis." "Notes on Middle English Lyrics," *Journal of English Literary History,* II (April, 1935), 60.

11. See the relevant definition of folly and wisdom in John Conley's "Pearl and a Lost Tradition," *Journal of English and Germanic Philology,* LIV (1955), 332–47. Folly, he quotes Aquinas, "denotes the dulness of sense in judging, and chiefly as regards the highest cause, which is the last and the sovereign good," p. 344, and for a full discussion see pp. 344–47. There are, in fact, similarities between the concerns of these two poems. The dramatic center of each is the distance between the object of desire and the one who desires, as they move through a prompting to vision, to a knowledge of heavenly bliss. In the case of *Pearl* the prompting is done by the maiden who makes possible the speaker's inner journey to the heavenly Jerusalem. In "Leuedy, for þare blisse" the prompting is done by a series of joys which are defined in terms of Mary's vision of God and which lead, through the events of sacred history, into heaven, increasing the poet's and the audience's knowledge of the nature of happiness. Like the speaker in *Pearl,* the poet in this poem reaches a gap he cannot cross. For the speaker in *Pearl* it is a river which separates him from the maiden. For the poet and his audience in "Leuedy, for þare blisse" it is the gap between their experience and the experience they desire of God, the gap of time and state, to be resolved only "hwenne we schulle þis lif for-gon" (line 48).

12. Ecclus. 24 is applied to Mary on the Feast of her Nativity (Legg, 319) and her

Conception (*S.M.*, II, 256), and also for the Vigil and Feast of the Assumption (Legg, 307, 308; *S.M.*, II, 463, 465).

13. Conley, p. 344.

The Figure of Delight

1. Anselm, quoted by Bonaventure in *Breviloquium,* trans. Erwin E. Nemmers (St. Louis, 1947), Part VII, chap. vii, sec. 9.

2. *Breviloquium,* Prologue, sec. 6, 6. The following quote is taken from Part I, chap. i, 1, and the quotes from Anselm are from Part VII, chap. vii, secs. 7–8.

3. *St. Bonaventure's "Itinerarium mentis in Deum,"* trans. Philotheus Boehner, O.F.M. (St. Bonaventure, New York, 1956), chap. vii, sec. 6.

4. A classic example of this is Augustine's *De Trinitate,* Book XV, chaps. xxiii–xxiv, where, after defining the Holy Trinity, then seeking It in all created things, even in the deepest soul of man, Augustine reveals the discrepancy between his words and the reality, which man will contemplate only in eternity. PL, Vol. XLII, cols. 1090–91.

5. See above, Bonaventure. The dedication of the life of St. Francis to poverty, to the infancy and suffering of Christ, expresses this spirituality. The classic expression of the darkness is the *Cloud of Unknowing.* See EETS, O.S., Nos. 218 (London, 1944), 231 (London, 1955 for 1949).

6. Again see Augustine, his *De doctrina Christiana,* Book I, chaps. xxiii–xxvii. PL, Vol. XXXIV, cols. 27–30.

7. In seeking for the aesthetic foundation of liturgical poetry, the theory of musical and numerical proportions is of much more value than theories of rhetoric deriving from classical precedent. See Ernst R. Curtius, *European Literature and the Latin Middle Ages,* trans. Willard Trask (New York, 1953), chaps. viii and xii. The principle of music was a movement of numbers from unity to diversity in a series of proportionate ratios. The entire universe was described in terms of the proportion of numbers, for which the Holy Trinity was the divine pattern. The mathematical conception was the basis of the discussions of music by Augustine and Boethius who influenced the later theorists. See Augustine, *De musica,* Book I, PL, Vol. XXXII, cols. 1081–100. For a general survey of this concept and the various definitions of proportion in number, see Edgar de Bruyne, *Etudes d'esthétique médiévale* (3 vols.; Brugge, 1946), especially "L'harmonie universelle," I, 9–26, on Boethius, also 306–16, 323 ff., 367 ff.; II, on Hugo of St. Victor, 205 ff., 216; and III, on Grosseteste, 126 ff., and Bonaventure, 189–226. For modern studies, see Leo Spitzer, "Classical and Christian Ideas of World Harmony: Prolegomena to an Interpretation of the Word 'Stimmung,'" *Traditio,* II (1944), 409–69 and III (1945), 307–64. Otto von Simson, *The Gothic Cathedral* (New York, 1956). Harry Bober, "In Principio. Creation Before Time," *Essays in Honor of Erwin Panofsky,* ed. Millard Meiss (2 vols.; New York, 1961), I, 13–28 and II, 5–8. Durant W. Robertson, Jr., *A Preface to Chaucer: Studies in Medieval Perspectives* (Princeton, 1962), pp. 114 ff. Robert M. Jordan, *Chaucer and the Shape of Creation: The Aesthetic Possibilities of Inorganic Structure* (Cambridge, Mass., 1967), chap. ii.

8. *The Ancrene Riwle* (*The Corpus MS: "Ancrene Wisse"*), trans. M. B. Salu (London, 1955), p. 16.

9. See "Suete sone, reu on me & brest out of þi bondis," Brown, *XIV,* No. 64, line 8.

10. Notice how because the author shifts the object of man's desire from being Christ to being the world, sorrow has an inverse definition: to "suffer" is to detach

oneself from the object of love which is not God Himself. When the object is Christ, to "suffer" is to be separated from Him.

11. *Ancrene Riwle,* p. 15. "Whatever there may have been before" is interpreted by the editor to refer to the twelfth century controversy about the Immaculate Conception of Mary. See above, Introduction, note 33.

12. Brown, *XIV,* No. 26, from St. John's College Cambridge MS 256. For full text, see Appendix III.

13. It was common in the devotion to pause after each joy and say other prayers. See, for example, the instructions to the anchoresses in the *Riwle,* where each prayer, as above, is followed by the "Ave Maria Dominus tecum," then further an antiphon, a psalm, and five Aves. See also above, "The Names of Joy," note 20, as well as "Mary moder, wel þe bee" in the *Minor Poems of the Vernon MS,* ed. Carl Horstmann, Part I, EETS, O.S., No. 98 (London, 1892), pp. 25–26, and the fifteenth century "Gawde, to whom gabryell was sent" in *Anglia,* XXVI (1903), 257–58.

14. The poet names Mary in stanza four: Lady, full of grace (the second element of the Ave); in five: Lady, full of might, meek and mild in aspect; in six: Lady, holy Mary, fair and good and sweet; in seven: Lady, best in counsel, true in need, prompt and quick with good deeds for sinful man; in eight (the climax): Lady, flower of all, as a red rose in a garden; then in nine: echoing the beginning, Mary; in ten: again Mary; in eleven: Mary, full of grace who sits on a throne; in twelve: Lady fair and bright; in thirteen: Lady, holy Mary; and finally, in fourteen: Lady, Queen of Heaven. He defines the power in virtue of which he appeals in stanza four: for the joy you felt when Christ rose, for the love of Him Who lay close to your heart; in five: for the love of Jesus sweet Who was killed on the cross, for His five wounds that ran blood; in six: for the love of the tears you shed when you saw Christ nailed hand and foot; in seven: for the love of Him Whom you saw bleed on the cross; in eight: (because) to thee I cry and call, to thee I make my prayer; in nine: for that sweet joy you were in when you saw Christ ascend to heaven wherein is everlasting joy; in ten: for that sweet joy when you were taken from earth by angels into the bliss of heaven and set by sweet Jesus in flesh and bone; in eleven: (because) I pray you, grant my prayer; in twelve: for thy five joys, for thy maidenhood, and thy great power; in thirteen: if it were thy will, as thou art full of joy and I am full of care; and finally in fourteen: hear me with will, I pray you hear my voice. And as the third element, the poet specifies the effect he desires in stanza four: help me out of sin while I am here; in five: help me out of sin; in six: give me grace in my heart to amend my sins; in seven: help me now and forever, save me in necessity; in eight: be in the place where I draw to death, never let me fall into the hands of the evil one; in nine: be my remedy for pain, bring me out of sin; in ten: bring me to joys that will last forever; in eleven (the most precise prayer): grant that I may fear and love Christ, that I amend my life soon, bring me to that high King Who wields sun and moon; in twelve: help me to come into that eternal light where joy is without end day and night; in thirteen: help me out of sin and let me fall no more, give me grace on earth sorely to rue my sins; and, finally, in fourteen: let my soul never spill in any of the seven sins through any fiend's will, and bring my soul to heaven to fill a place there.

15. Occasional inner rhyme emphasizes their binary nature, as, for example, the rhyme of "heuene," "steuene," "seuene" and again "heuene" in the last stanza (see discussion below).

16. In two of the four versions of the poem this stanza is lacking. See Brown, *XIV,* p. 254.

17. The complementary structure reflects also the traditional practice of adding to the core of each joy commentary or an additional prayer, such as the angelic salutation in "Heyl be þou, marie, milde quene of heuene." See also above, "The Names of Joy," note 20, for a development of this idea and examples.

CONCLUSION

1. Bonaventure, *Breviloquium,* trans. Erwin E. Nemmers (St. Louis, 1946), Prologue, 3. See Preface, note 14, and below.

2. See above, especially Part I, "The 'Maiden Makeles,'" Part II, "Mary's Sorrow," and "The Dialogue Form."

3. For a discussion of the nature of these figures, see above, especially Part III, "The Figure of Delight," and also Part II, pp. 142 ff.

4. See above, Part III, p. 152.

5. See Introduction, pp. 14–15.

6. *A Thirteenth Century York Psalter: A Manuscript Written and Illuminated in the Diocese of York about A.D. 1250,* Roxburghe Club, No. 216 (Oxford, 1952). See pls. 3, 5, 6, and for other examples of this type of correspondence, especially pls. 8, 10.

7. See above, pp. 18 ff., and also "Gabriel, from Evene-King," pp. 33, 34 ff.; "Þe Milde Lomb Isprad o Rode," pp. 99–100 and note 14; "Stond Wel, Moder, vnder Rode," pp. 129–31, 142–45.

8. See above, Introduction, "The Ladder," pp. 15 ff., and also below, descriptive note to Figure 2. For a discussion of the general medieval tendency to think in symmetrical patterns, characteristically arranged with reference to an abstract hierarchy, see Durant W. Robertson, Jr., *A Preface to Chaucer: Studies in Medieval Perspectives* (Princeton, 1962), pp. 6 ff.

9. Brown, *XIV,* No. 132, lines 81–85.

10. Brown, *XIII,* Nos. 2, 5, 32, 64, 65, 84, and 3, 34, 50, 63, 78; Brown, *XIV,* Nos. 80, 83–85.

11. On this subject, see Leo Spitzer, "Note on the Poetic and the Empirical 'I' in Medieval Authors," *Traditio,* IV (1946), 414–22. For analogous examples, see above, "Nu Þis Fules Singet hand Maket Hure Blisse." pp. 52–53, and "Þe Milde Lomb Isprad o Rode," pp. 102–3 and note 17.

12. For a full survey of the development and modification of classical aesthetics and the rhetoric of the schools, see Edgar de Bruyne, *Études d'esthétique médiévale* (3 vols.; Brugge, 1946). The Church's principle of adapting pagan elements, as Gregory the Great urged his missionaries to do, penetrated almost every area, from the allegorization of Virgil and the classics to the transformation of Greek science and math in the schemata used to illustrate text books and to illuminate Scripture. Although the lyrics we have been discussing had their origin in the liturgy, the poetry which continued to use classical forms shared their purpose and use in a way fundamentally defined by Christian theology. For two relevant studies, see Peter D. Scott, "Alcuin as Poet: Rhetoric and Belief in His Latin Verse," *University of Toronto Quarterly,* XXXIII (April, 1964), 233–57, and Philip W. Damon, "Style and Meaning in the Mediaeval Latin Nature Lyric," *Speculum,* XXVIII (July, 1953), 516–20. The idea is shown clearly

in relation to MS illumination by Harry Bober, "In Principio. Creation Before Time," *Essays in Honor of Erwin Panofsky,* ed. Millard Meiss (2 vols.; New York, 1961), I, 13–28; II, 5–8.

13. For a full development of this idea, see Sister Emma Jane Marie Spargo, *The Category of the Aesthetic in the Philosophy of St. Bonaventure* (St. Bonaventure, New York, 1953).

14. *Breviloquium,* Prologue, 5 and *passim.* Also, see above, "The Figure of Delight," pp. 175 ff. My quoting has, for the sake of brevity, eliminated the central fact, that Bonaventure has stated the purpose of his work by means of an invocation to Christ, the knowledge and love of Whom is the basis of knowledge of Scripture.

15. *St. Bonaventure's "Itinerarium mentis in Deum,"* trans. Philotheus Boehner, O.F.M. (St. Bonaventure, New York, 1956).

16. See above, "The Vision of Joy," pp. 167 ff.; "The Figure of Delight," pp. 176 ff.

17. For a full discussion of Bonaventure's aesthetic theory, see Edgar de Bruyne, III, 191 ff. In defining the medieval theory of beauty, Robertson focuses on the first proportion *speciositas,* thus losing its relationship to *suavitas* and *salubritas.* These two proportions he considers in the separate contexts of figurative expression and the use of beauty. See *A Preface to Chaucer,* pp. 114 ff. In his chapter "Elements of Medieval Aesthetic Theory," Robert M. Jordan also concentrates on the nature of formal beauty. See *Chaucer and the Shape of Creation: The Aesthetic Possibilities of Inorganic Structure* (Cambridge, Mass., 1967), pp. 10–43.

18. *Opera omnia* (10 vols.; Ad Claras Aquas [Quaracchi], 1882–1902), Vol. VIII, Opusculum III, pp. 68–86.

19. The tradition corresponds to the methods of exegesis. The tradition, followed by Dante in the *Vita nuova,* goes back to the early Middle Ages and Prosper, Aldhelm, Bede, Alcuin, Sedelius Scottus and Gauthier de Spire. The *Carmen Paschale* of Sedelius, for example, is doubled by an *Opus Paschale.* See also Rabanus Maurus, who, using Sedelius as his authority, follows the same principle in *De laudibus sanctae crucis* (PL, Vol. CVII, cols. 133–294). For details and the relationship to exegesis, see Henri de Lubac, S.J., *Exégèse médiévale: les quatre sens de l'Écriture* (4 vols.; Paris, 1959, 1961, 1964), I, 164, note 6.

20. I refer here to the tradition influential in American criticism defined by Brooks and Warren, used by the New Critics, and the method normally taught to students of literature. In their "Letter to the Teacher (1938)," Brooks and Warren took their stand against the different substitutes for study of the poem: (1) Paraphrase of logical and narrative content; (2) Study of biographical and historical materials; (3) Inspirational and didactic interpretation. "The poem in itself, if literature is to be studied as literature, remains finally the object for study." *Understanding Poetry: An Anthology for College Students* (rev. ed.; New York, 1953), p. xi.

APPENDIXES

1. Legg, p. 480.
2. Legg, p. 530.
3. Brown, *XIV,* No. 26.

Notes to Illustrations

FIGURE 1 (FRONTISPIECE)

God the Creator of Heaven and Earth. Full folio miniature preceding Genesis of a Moralized Bible written for St. Louis (d. 1270). Vienna, Österreichische Nationalbibliothek Cod. 1179, fol. 1vo.

God is shown creating and encompassing the universe. Seated on a throne and surrounded by a four-lobed aureole which is borne by angels, the Creator holds the universe in His lap. His head bends meditatively, and with the geometer's tool in His right hand He designs His creation. Above the square frame (out of the picture) an inscription appears comparing Him to the potter: "Hic orbis figulus disponit singula solus." See Alexandre de Laborde, *La Bible moralisée illustrée* (5 vols.; Paris, 1911–1927), Vol. IV, pl. 672; Vol. V, pp. 86–93.

The miniature precedes a narration of sacred history from Genesis through Job, in which the scene of an event of the Old Testament is coupled with an illustration of its allegorical interpretation in light of the New. Each scene is accompanied by a paraphrase of the Vulgate. Job is followed by a moralized Apocalypse of St. John.

The figure of the Creator is the same as that of Christ in the New Testament scenes, as is the case also in the Moralised Bible, Oxford, Bodleian MS 270 b. For Christ's role in the creation of the world as defined in Hebrews 1:1–3 and medieval commentary upon the text, see R. E. Kaske, "The Character 'Figura' in *Le Mystère d'Adam,*" *Mediaeval Studies in Honor of Urban Tigner Holmes, Jr.,* ed. John Mahoney and John E. Keller (Chapel Hill, 1965), pp. 103–10. On the subject of the Creator being represented as Christ on Chartres, see Sister Emma Jane Marie Spargo, *The Category of the Aesthetic in the Philosophy of St. Bonaventure* (St. Bonaventure, New York, 1953), pp. 22 ff.

FIGURE 2

The Mass, Elevation of the Host. Illuminated "T" of the first words of the Canon "Te igitur . . . ," from the Sarum Missal ascribed to Ely Cathedral, commissioned by

Hawyse Tiptoft and her husband John Clavering, ca. 1315. New York, Pierpont Morgan Library M. 107, fol. 142 (see Fig. 4).

The priest is raising the Host over the altar while a deacon raises the veiled paten. Springing from out of the Tau which forms two arches over the priest and deacons is the cross on which the dead Christ hangs, the sacramental blood flowing down its stem from Christ's side, hands, and feet. Mary stands on Christ's right, the gesture of her arms expressing her grief and suggesting an attitude of prayer. The disciple John stands on Christ's left, holding the Scriptures and seeming by his attitude to be both listening and pointing towards Christ. John Clavering kneels to the left of the Tau. Out of the photograph are three other figures. On the left border just below John Clavering kneels his wife, Hawyse Tiptoft. On the right border of the folio, in larger size, are John the Evangelist and below him John the Baptist. They gaze on the Host, holding emblems to signify that Christ is the Lamb of God (John 1:29; Apoc., chaps. 5, 14, 19, 22).

The Tiptoft Missal is of particular interest, for its organization strikingly exemplifies how the liturgy reformulates sacred history, according to the divine *ratio,* to center on the actions of the Church in present time. The Ordinary (fols. 138–49), which contains the Canon of the Mass, has been placed, so that it interrupts the Proper of the Seasons, just after the texts recounting the passion. Here, it stands in its position of theological significance as the re-enactment of the passion in the present. The illumination of the elevation of the Host serves in the Missal as the principal image of the crucifixion. Continuing by analogy to the events of the redemption, the Ordinary of the Mass is then followed by the Easter Mass of the resurrection, and the proper texts for the Easter season. See Legg, pp. xx and 227 note 3, and also Legg's *Tracts on the Mass,* Henry Bradshaw Society, Vol. XXVII (London, 1904), p. xi. The two other illuminations in the Ordinary develop aspects of the Mass: one, preceding the collection of Preface texts, depicts the blessing of the chalice (fol. 139); and the other, illuminating the "Per omnia saecula saeculorum" formula preceding every Preface, portrays the sacrifice of Isaac (fol. 141vo), an event traditionally interpreted to prefigure Christ's sacrifice on the cross.

The principle, furthermore, by which certain feasts in the Proper have been singled out to receive large letter illuminations reflects a consistent focus on the theme of the Church, with Mary as the main figure. These are the Annunciation (fol. 231vo), Christmas (fol. 23), the Presentation (fol. 226vo), the Ascension (fol. 163vo), Pentecost (fol. 168vo), and the Assumption (fol. 253vo). Each illumination depicts the event being celebrated, and it is composed in relationship to the others as the event prefigures or develops the foundation of the Church.

Finally, the Introit for Trinity Sunday (fol. 176) has an especially beautiful illumination of the perpetuation of Christ's redemptive sacrifice in present time. Within the "B" of "Benedicta" the Father sits enthroned, holding in His outstretched arms the cross on which Christ hangs. The Father gazes out at the observer. Christ's eyes are open also, signifying His eternal life. His hands, in counter direction to those of the Father, are open wide as if to manifest Himself or to uplift the observer. In the form of a dove, His wings spread out also along the arms of the cross, the Spirit issues from the Son to the Father, representing the perpetual renewal of Christ's oblation of Himself to the Father for mankind.

Also contained in the Tiptoft Missal are four illuminations of saints and one of the dedication of a Church. See fols. 179, 180, 181, 216, and 218.

FIGURE 3

The Annunciation. First of four miniatures preceding a Psalter written for a nun of Amesbury Abbey, Wilts, ca. 1250. Possibly from a Salisbury atelier. Oxford, All Souls College MS 6, fol. 3 (see Figs. 6 and 7).

The approaching angel remains separated from the Virgin by the central column of the two arches, his right hand raised in proclamation. The salutation, inscribed on the scroll opening from his left hand, penetrates down into the Virgin's space. At the same time, from the center of the arch above her, a dove bearing the nimbus of divinity descends to the Virgin's ear, signifying Mary's virginal conception of Christ by the Holy Spirit. In her left hand the Virgin holds the Scriptures foretelling the coming of the Messiah.

The miniatures of the Amesbury Psalter are designed in a proportionate relation to each other. A scene of Mary and Christ on earth is contrasted and alternated by a scene of Mary and Christ in glory, so that the sequence presented is: the Annunciation, fol. 3 (Fig. 3), contrasted by the Virgin and Child Enthroned, fol. 4 (Fig. 7); the Crucifixion, fol. 5 (Fig. 6), contrasted by Christ in Majesty, fol. 6.

See below, pp. 58–59, and Eric G. Millar, *English Illuminated MSS from the Xth to the XIIIth Century* (Paris, 1926), pp. 96–97, pls. 81–83.

FIGURE 4

The Birth of Christ and the Tree of Jesse. Illuminated "P" from first words of the Introit, "Puer natus est . . . ," Third Mass on Christmas Day. Tiptoft Missal, New York, Pierpont Morgan Library M. 107, fol. 23 (see Fig. 2 and descriptive note).

The visual center, contained in the letter "P," depicts the theme of the present feast, the celebration of the birth and humanity of Christ Who is God. The reclining Mary receives the Child from a midwife, while at the foot of her couch Joseph meditates. The "P" springs as the central branch from the tree of Jesse, which, setting Christ's birth in the context of the past, reveals Christ's kingly lineage in the Old Testament. At the bottom of the page Jesse reclines, meditating. The two side branches which embrace the page support the Old Testament kings and prophets who preceded and pointed to Christ. At the branches' summit, ruling over the page, is Christ as He is in present time, Redeemer and King of Heaven, bearing the wounds of His humanity and crucifixion: on Christ's right an angel bears the crown of thorns, on His left one bears the cross. Enthroned below at the base of the tree of Jesse, in a position that corresponds to Christ's above, Mary reigns as she is in present time, Queen by virtue of her motherhood of Christ. See also below, pp. 53–54, 58.

FIGURE 5

The Birth of Christ and the First Events of His Childhood. From the Psalter of Robert, Baron de Lisle, given to his daughter Audere in 1339. Probably from a court atelier at Westminster. British Museum, Arundel MS 83, fol. 124.

The events, the nativity, the annunciation to the shepherds, the circumcision, the adoration of the Magi, the presentation in the Temple, and the flight into Egypt, are ordered from left to right by sequence of time into three groups of two panels; the corners of all the frames, knotted together by flowers, unify the events into a whole. Counter to the sequence of narrative, the scenes are also ordered into two groups of three panels by the contrast in color between the square settings, panels 1, 4 and 5, panels 2, 3 and 6. The scenes are ordered in yet a third proportion by theme. Those on the left, from top to bottom, depict the events that concern Christ in the Temple, those on the right depict the events that reveal Christ to the world.

The thematic proportioning is evident from the correspondences in design and meaning. The panels on the left show a similar grouping of figures in the two lower Temple scenes; there are parallels between the priest (in 3) and Simeon (in 5) in type, gesture and garment; a repetition of the lamp and altar motifs; and a repetition in Mary's gesture of offering her Child. The elements in the nativity scene can be seen to foreshadow the Temple scenes, as the figure of Joseph is developed by the figures of the priest and Simeon; the traditional iconographic parallel is made between the box-like manger and the two altars, and the motif of the star is repeated in the lamps. Finally, the cloth which covers Mary's couch in the nativity appears in the circumcision covering the altar; while in the presentation the altar is bare and a veil of respect, suggesting the veil used by a priest to handle the sacred vessels, covers the hands of Simeon. The panels on the right develop a consistent theme, beginning with the incursion of the angel who announces the Christ Child, moving through the manifestation of the Child to the Magi, and ending with the collapse of a devil before the Child as He departs into exile. The figure of the old man—the shepherd, the king, Joseph—dominates each of the compositions, and the motif of a figure upon a base is repeated in the young piping shepherd, in the mother and Child enthroned, and in the idol falling from its pedestal.

In panels 3 through 6 there is an interplay between the Child's humanity and His divinity. In the circumcision scene the Child is naked, His nimbus bears no rays, and He draws back with a gesture of pain. By contrast, in the presentation He is robed, crowned by a rayed nimbus, and, holding His mother's veil, He reaches towards Simeon's welcoming veiled hands. In the adoration of the Magi, dressed in a full-sleeved garment, crowned by a rayed nimbus and standing on His mother's lap (with Mary herself shown as a crowned queen), He blesses the king and takes the gift of gold which signifies His kingship. In the flight into Egypt, the Child again is robed and bears a rayed nimbus as Mary carries Him into exile, led by Joseph. Turned entirely back towards the shelter of His mother, the Child reaches to her to be nourished.

See below, pp. 81 ff., also Eric G. Millar, *English Illuminated MSS of the XIVth and XVth Centuries* (Paris, 1928), pls. 7–13, and Lucy Freeman Sandler, *The Psalter of Robert de Lisle* (3 vols.; Ph.D dissertation, New York University Institute of Fine Arts, 1964).

FIGURE 6

The Crucifixion. Third of four miniatures preceding a Psalter written for a nun of Amesbury Abbey, Wilts, ca. 1250. Possibly from a Salisbury atelier. Oxford, All Souls College MS 6, fol. 5 (see Figs. 3 and 7).

Although the artist has chosen different iconographic elements to reveal the death of Christ as the moment of mankind's redemption, certain aspects of the portrayal can be compared to stanzas one and two of "Þe milde Lomb isprad o rode" (see above, pp. 103 ff.). The harsh violence of the event is minimized and its significance is revealed both by the elements and the artist's handling of the composition. The scene is proportioned geometrically into four sections by the cross, which, rising out of the hill, is backed by a plain crosspiece set into the rectangular border of the miniature. Christ hangs in the center, dead, His body bowed to the right, the blood flowing from His right side and from the wounds of His head, hands and feet. Symmetrically, under the arms of the cross, Mary stands on Christ's right and John stands on His left, both bowed meditatively by grief. On either side above the arms of the cross are the darkened sun and moon. Slanting over the top of the cross is the placard reading "Jesus of Nazareth, King of the Jews" (John 19:19). But the symmetrical, still-seeming figures also reveal life. Christ's head bears the rayed nimbus of divinity, His garment is richly decorated, the knotted end blows, His blood pours abundantly. The cross itself bears stumps of branches to signify that it is in fact the Tree of Life, and its placard, tilting precariously, joins the cross with heaven above. The garments and limbs of Mary and John are caught in motion, and all the figures break out beyond their borders.

The fact that the moment of crucifixion is the moment of redemption is embodied here in the actions of the figures represented in the framing borders. At the four corners in circular medallions incensing angels kneel, perpetually adoring the Divine Redeemer. Into the center of each of the frame's sides, four other arch-like medallions are woven. In the medallion above Christ, between two other adoring angels, is God the Father. Crowned by a rayed nimbus and gazing out of the frame at the observer, He holds the Spirit to His breast, Who in the form of a dove appears to have just ascended to Him from His Son (see the Tiptoft Missal, fol. 176). In the corresponding medallion below Christ, thrusting up into the hill of the cross, is Adam who rises out of his grave with two other souls, having been redeemed by Christ's blood which is flowing down from the cross upon them. On the right side of the frame, towards which Christ leans, and just beyond Mary (who is herself a figure of the Church), the triumphing Church is represented. She bears her standard of victory and holds the sacramental chalice of Christ's blood. On the left, beside John (who is traditionally a figure of the Synagog), the Synagog swoons, her standard breaking, her vessel turned down and spilling out its contents.

FIGURE 7

The Virgin and Child Enthroned. Second of four miniatures preceding the Psalter written for a nun of Amesbury Abbey, Wilts, ca. 1250. Oxford, All Souls College MS 6, fol. 4 (see Figs. 3, 6).

The enthroned Virgin and Child are seated in the center of the frame, within an arch suggestive of a church or the heavenly Jerusalem. According to the promise of power to those who trust in the Lord (Compline Psalm 90, verse 13), the Virgin treads underfoot the lion and the dragon. With the head and body of a boy or young man and crowned by the rayed nimbus of divinity, the Child relaxes on His mother's knee and is nourished by her. The Virgin bends over Him, supporting Him with her left hand and with her right offering Him her breast; yet it is the Child Who lifts and guides His mother's hand.

Within the arch kneels the figure of a praying nun. Her prayer, issuing from her hands on a scroll, repeats the angel's salutation at the annunciation (see Fig. 3), adding the incomplete syllables "bene" of "blessed." As the angel's words descended from heaven to earth then, so the nun's words ascend from earth to Mary in heaven. But in the context of present time, this salutation sounds as a prayer confirming Mary's blessedness and an invocation of Mary's power in virtue of her closeness to her Son. Above the arch, penetrating down through it with their censors, are two adoring angels. All eyes, even those of the infernal lion and dragon, contemplate the mother and Child, while the Virgin contemplates the Child. With the eternal gaze of God, the eyes of the Child stare out of the miniature at the observer, drawing the observer's eyes to Himself, and through His hand, to His mother's breast, to her inclining head, which bends down over her Child, leading the observer's gaze back to the eyes of the Child.

Selected Bibliography

Adam of Saint Victor. *The Liturgical Poetry of Adam of Saint Victor, from the Text of Gautier.* Translated by Digby S. Wrangham. 3 vols. London: Kegan Paul, Trench, & Co., 1881.

The Ancrene Riwle (*The Corpus MS: "Ancrene Wisse"*). Translated into Modern English by M. B. Salu, with an Introduction by Dom Gerard Sitwell, O.S.B., and a Preface by J. R. R. Tolkien. ("The Orchard Books.") London: Burns & Oates, 1955.

Anderson, Mary D. *Drama and Imagery in English Medieval Churches.* Cambridge: Cambridge University Press, 1963 [1964].

Anselm of Canterbury, Saint (Attributed). *Beatae Mariae et Anselmi de passione Domini.* Patrologiae cursus completus. Series Latina, ed. J.-P. Migne. Vol. CLIX. Paris, 1854. Cols. 271–90.

Auerbach, Erich. "Figura," in *Scenes from the Drama of European Literature: Six Essays.* New York: Meridian Books, 1959. Pp. 11–76.

Augustine, Aurelius, Saint. *De doctrina Christiana.* Patrologiae cursus completus. Series Latina, ed. J.-P. Migne. Vol. XXXIV. Paris, 1887. Cols. 15–122.

———. *De musica.* Patrologiae cursus completus. Series Latina, ed. J.-P. Migne. Vol. XXXII. Paris, 1877. Cols. 1081–194.

———. *De Trinitate.* Patrologiae cursus completus. Series Latina, ed. J.-P. Migne. Vol. XLII. Paris, 1886. Cols. 819–1098.

Bede, Venerable. *De meditatione passione Christi per septem diei horas libellus.* Patrologiae cursus completus. Series Latina, ed. J.-P. Migne. Vol. XCIV. Paris, 1862. Cols. 561–68.

Bernard of Clairvaux, Saint (Attributed). *Liber de passione Christi et doloribus et planctibus matris ejus.* Patrologiae cursus completus. Series Latina, ed. J.-P. Migne. Vol. CLXXXII. Paris, 1879. Cols. 1133–42.

———. *St. Bernard's Sermons for the Seasons & Principal Festivals of the Year.* Translated from the Original Latin by a Priest of Mount Melleray. 3 vols. Westminster, Md.: The Newman Press, 1950.

BETHURUM, DOROTHY (ed.). *Critical Approaches to Medieval Literature: Selected Papers from the English Institute 1958–1959.* New York: Columbia University Press, 1960.

BLOOMFIELD, MORTON W. "Symbolism in Medieval Literature," *Modern Philology,* LVI (November, 1958), 73–81.

BOBER, HARRY. "In Principio. Creation Before Time," in *Essays in Honor of Erwin Panofsky,* ed. MILLARD MEISS. ("De artibus opuscula," Vol. XL.) 2 vols. New York: New York University Institute of Fine Arts, 1961. I, 13–28; II, 5–8.

The Bohun Manuscripts. A Group of Five Manuscripts Executed in England about 1370 for Members of the Bohun Family. Described by MONTAGUE RHODES JAMES, with an Introductory Note by ERIC G. MILLAR. Roxburghe Club, No. 200. Oxford: Printed for the Club by Oxford University Press, 1936.

BONAVENTURE, SAINT. *Breviloquium.* Translated by ERWIN E. NEMMERS. St. Louis: B. Herder Book Co., 1946.

———. *Lignum vitae. Opera omnia,* ed. Studio et Cura PP. Collegii a S. Bonaventura. 10 vols. Ad Claras Aquas (Quaracchi): Ex typogr. Collegii S. Bonaventurae, 1882–1902. Vol. VIII, Opusculum III, pp. 68–86.

———. *Saint Bonaventure's "Itinerarium mentis in Deum."* With an Introduction, Translation and Commentary by PHILOTHEUS BOEHNER, O.F.M. ("Works of Saint Bonaventure," Vol. II.) Saint Bonaventure, New York: The Franciscan Institute, 1956.

Breviarium ad usum insignis ecclesie Eboracensis, ed. STEPHAN W. LAWLEY. Surtees Society, Vols. LXXI, LXXV. Durham, London and Edinburgh: Andrews & Co., Whittaker & Co., Bernard Quaritch and Blackwood & Sons, 1880 for 1871, 1883 for 1882.

Breviarium ad usum insignis ecclesiae Sarum, ed. FRANCIS PROCTER and CHRISTOPHER WORDSWORTH. 3 vols. Cambridge: Cambridge University Press, 1882, 1879, 1886.

BRIDGETT, T. E. *History of the Holy Eucharist in Great Britain.* 2 vols. London: C. Kegan Paul & Co., 1881.

———. *Our Lady's Dowry: Or How England Gained and Lost That Title.* London: Burns & Oates, 1875.

BROWN, CARLETON (ed.). *English Lyrics of the XIIIth Century.* Oxford: Clarendon Press, 1932.

———. *A Register of Middle English Religious and Didactic Verse.* 2 vols. Oxford: Printed for the Bibliographical Society at the University Press, 1916–20.

———. *Religious Lyrics of the XVth Century.* Oxford: Clarendon Press, 1939.

———. *Religious Lyrics of the XIVth Century.* 2d ed., rev. G. V. Smithers. Oxford: Clarendon Press, 1957.

BROWN, CARLETON, and ROBBINS, ROSSELL HOPE. *The Index of Middle English Verse.* New York: Printed for the Index Society by Columbia University Press, 1943.

BRUYNE, EDGAR DE. *L'esthétique du moyen âge.* ("Essais philosophiques," No. 3.) Louvain: Editions de l'Institut Supérieur de Philosophie, 1947.

———. *Études d'esthétique médiévale.* ("Rijksuniversiteit te Gent[:] werken uitgegeven door de Faculteit van de Wijsbegeerte en letteren," Nos. 97, 98, 99.) Brugge, 1946.

BUKOFZER, MANFRED. "Speculative Thinking in Mediaeval Music," *Speculum,* XVII (April, 1942), 165–80.

Bukofzer, Manfred. *Studies in Medieval and Renaissance Music.* New York: W. W. Norton & Co., Inc., 1950.

Chambers, Edmund K. *The Mediaeval Stage.* 2 vols. London: Oxford University Press, 1903.

Chambers, Edmund K., and Sidgwick, Frank. *Early English Lyrics: Amorous, Divine, Moral & Trivial.* London: A. H. Bullen, 1907.

Chomsky, Noam. *Current Issues in Linguistic Theory.* ("Janua Linguarum studia memoriae Nicolai van Wijk dedicata," ed. Cornelis H. Van Schooneveld, Stanford University, Series Minor, No. 38.) London, The Hague, Paris: Mouton & Co., 1964.

———. *Syntactic Structures.* ("Janua Linguarum studia memoriae Nicolai van Wijk dedicata," ed. Cornelis H. Van Schooneveld, Stanford University, No. 4.) The Hague: Mouton & Co., 1957.

Chydenius, Johan. *The Typological Problem in Dante: A Study in the History of Medieval Ideas.* ("Societas scientiarum Fennica, Commentationes humanarum litterarum," Vol. XXV, No. 1.) Helsingfors, 1958.

Craig, Hardin. *English Religious Drama of the Middle Ages.* Oxford: Clarendon Press, 1955.

Crowne, J. Vincent. "Middle English Poems on the Joys and on the Compassion of the Blessed Virgin Mary," *The Catholic University Bulletin,* VIII (July, 1902), 304–16.

Cursor Mundi (The Cursur o the World). A Northumbrian Poem of the XIVth Century in Four Versions, Two of Them Midland . . . , ed. Richard Morris. Part V. Early English Text Society, Original Series, No. 68. London: Printed for the Society by K. Paul, Trench, Trübner & Co., 1878.

Curtius, Ernst Robert. *European Literature and the Latin Middle Ages.* Translated by Willard R. Trask. ("Bollingen Series," Vol. XXXVI.) New York: Pantheon Books, 1953.

Daniélou, Jean, S.J. *The Bible and the Liturgy.* ("University of Notre Dame Liturgical Studies," Vol. III.) Notre Dame, Indiana: University of Notre Dame Press, 1956.

Davies, Reginald Thorne (ed.). *Medieval English Lyrics: A Critical Anthology.* Evanston: Northwestern University Press, 1964.

Degginger, Stuart H. L. "The Earliest Middle English Lyrics: 1150–1325. An Investigation of the Influence of Latin, Provençal, and French." Unpublished Ph.D. dissertation, Columbia University, 1954.

Dreves, Guido M., S.J., and Blume, Clemens, S.J. (eds.). *Analecta hymnica medii aevi.* 55 vols. Leipzig: O. R. Reisland, 1886–1922.

Durandus, Gulielmus. *Rationale divinorum officiorum.* Accedit aliud divinorum officiorum rationale a Joanne Beletho. Neapoli: Apud Josephum Dura, 1859.

Frere, Walter Howard (ed.). *The Use of Sarum.* The Original Texts Edited from the Manuscripts with an Introduction and Index. 2 vols. Cambridge: Cambridge University Press, 1898, 1901.

Gilson, Étienne. "Sur le *Iesu dulcis memoria," Speculum,* III (July, 1928), 322–34.

Greene, Richard Leighton (ed.). *The Early English Carols.* Oxford: Clarendon Press, 1935.

———. *A Selection of English Carols.* Oxford: Clarendon Press, 1962.

Hardison, O. B., Jr. *Christian Rite and Christian Drama in the Middle Ages. Essays in the Origin and Early History of Modern Drama.* Baltimore: The Johns Hopkins Press, 1965.

HARRISON, FRANK LL. *Music in Medieval Britain.* ("Studies in the History of Music," ed. EGON WELLESZ.) London: Routledge and Kegan Paul, 1958.

Horae Eboracenses. The Prymer or Hours of the Blessed Virgin Mary, According to the Use of the Illustrious Church of York. With Other Devotions as They Were Used by the Lay-Folk in the Northern Province in the XVth and XVIth Centuries, ed. CHRISTOPHER WORDSWORTH. Surtees Society, Vol. CXXXII. Durham and London: Andrews & Co. and Bernard Quaritch, 1920 for 1919.

HORSTMANN, CARL (ed.). *Yorkshire Writers: Richard Rolle of Hampole, an English Father of the Church, and His Followers.* 2 vols. London and New York: S. Sonnenschein & Co. and Macmillan & Co., 1895–96.

HUPPE, BERNARD F. *Doctrine and Poetry: Augustine's Influence on Old English Poetry.* Albany: State University of New York, 1959.

INNOCENT III, POPE. *Mysteriorum Evengelicae Legis et sacramenti Eucharistiae.* Patrologiae cursus completus. Series Latina, ed. J.-P. MIGNE. Vol. CCXVII. Paris, 1890. Cols. 763–916.

JORDAN, ROBERT M. *Chaucer and the Shape of Creation: The Aesthetic Possibilities of Inorganic Structure.* Cambridge: Harvard University Press, 1967.

JUNGMANN, JOSEPH A., S.J. *The Mass of the Roman Rite: Its Origins and Development* (*missarum sollemnia*). 2 vols. New York: Benziger, 1951.

KANE, GEORGE. *Middle English Literature: A Critical Study of the Romances, the Religious Lyrics, "Piers Plowman."* London: Methuen & Co., Ltd., 1951.

KNOWLES, DAVID. *The Monastic Order in England: A History of Its Development from the Times of St. Dunstan to the Fourth Lateran Council 940–1216.* 2d ed. Cambridge: Cambridge University Press, 1963.

———. *The Religious Houses of Medieval England.* London: Sheed & Ward, 1940.

———. *The Religious Orders in England.* Cambridge: Cambridge University Press, 1950.

KRIBEL, G., "Studien zu Richard Rolle de Hampole II: *Lamentatio St. Bernardi de compassione Mariae,*" *Englische Studien,* VIII (1885), 67–114.

The Lay Folks' Catechism, or the English and Latin Versions of Archbishop Thoresby's Instruction for the People. Together with a "Wycliffite Adaption" of the same and the Corresponding Canons of the Council of Lambeth, ed. THOMAS FREDERICK SIMMONS and HENRY EDWARD NOLLOTH. Early English Text Society, Original Series, No. 118. London: Printed for the Society by K. Paul, Trench, Trübner & Co., 1901.

The Lay Folks' Mass Book, or the Manner of Hearing Mass, with Rubrics and Devotions for the People, in Four Texts, and Offices in English, According to the Use of York, from Manuscripts of the Xth to the XVth Century, ed. THOMAS FREDERICK SIMMONS. Early English Text Society, Original Series, No. 71. London: Printed for the Society by N. Trübner & Co., 1879.

LEGG, J. WICKHAM (ed.). *The Sarum Missal. Edited from Three Early Manuscripts.* Oxford: Clarendon Press, 1916.

———. *Tracts on the Mass.* Henry Bradshaw Society, Vol. XXVII. London: Printed for the Society by Harrison and Sons, 1904.

LUBAC, HENRI DE, S.J. *Corpus Mysticum: l'Eucharistie et l'Église au moyen âge, étude historique.* ("Théologie: études publiées sous la direction de la Faculté de Théologie S.J. de Lyon-Fourvière," No. 3.) Paris: Aubier, 1944.

———. *Exégèse médiévale: les quatre sens de l'Écriture.* 4 vols. ("Théologie: études publiées sous la direction de la Faculté de Théologie S.J. de Lyon-Fourvière," Nos. 41, 42, 59.) Paris: Aubier, 1959, 1961, 1964.

LYDGATE, JOHN. "The Interpretation and Virtues of the Mass," in *The Minor Poems of John Lydgate,* ed. HENRY NOBLE MACCRACKEN. Early English Text Society, Extra Series, No. 107. London: Printed for the Society by K. Paul, Trench, Trübner & Co., 1911 for 1910. Pp. 87–115.

MÂLE, ÉMILE. *L'art religieux du XIIIe siècle en France, étude sur l'iconographie du moyen âge et sur ses sources d'inspiration.* 8e éd. Paris: A. Colin, 1948.

MALONE, KEMP. "Notes on Middle English Lyrics," *English Literary History,* II (April, 1935), 58–65.

MANNING, STEPHEN. *Wisdom and Number: Toward a Critical Appraisal of the Middle English Religious Lyric.* Lincoln: University of Nebraska Press, 1962.

MARSHALL, MARY H. "Aesthetic Values of the Liturgical Drama," in *English Institute Essays 1950.* New York: Columbia University Press, 1951. Pp. 89–115.

MASKELL, WILLIAM (ed.). *The Ancient Liturgy of the Church of England According to the Uses of Sarum, York, Hereford and Bangor and the Roman Liturgy Arranged in Parallel Columns, with Preface and Notes.* 3d ed. Oxford: Clarendon Press, 1882.

———. *Monumenta ritualia ecclesiae Anglicanae. The Occasional Offices of the Church of England According to the Use of Salisbury, the Prymer in English, and Other Prayers and Forms, with Dissertations and Notes.* 2d ed. 3 vols. Oxford: Clarendon Press, 1882.

MESSENGER, RUTH ELLIS. *The Medieval Latin Hymn.* Washington, D.C.: Capital Press, 1953.

MILLAR, ERIC G. *English Illuminated Manuscripts from the Xth to the XIIIth Century.* Paris and Brussels: Les éditions G. Van Oest, 1926.

———. *English Illuminated Manuscripts of the XIVth and XVth Centuries.* Paris and Brussels: Les éditions G. Van Oest, 1928.

Mirk's Festial. A Collection of Homilies by Johannes Mirkus (John Mirk), ed. THEODOR ERBE. Part I. Early English Text Society, Extra Series, No. 96. London: Printed for the Society by K. Paul, Trench, Trübner & Co., Ltd. 1905.

MUSURILLO, HERBERT A., S.J. *Symbolism and the Christian Imagination.* Baltimore: Helicon Press, 1962.

NEMETZ, ANTHONY. "Literalness and the *Sensus Literalis,*" *Speculum,* XXXIV (January, 1959), 76–89.

Old English Homilies of the Twelfth Century, from the Unique MS B. 14. 52 in the Library of Trinity College Cambridge, ed. RICHARD MORRIS. Early English Text Society, Original Series, No. 53. London: Printed for the Society by N. Trübner & Co., 1873.

ONG, WALTER J., S.J. "A Liturgical Movement in the Middle Ages," *The American Ecclesiastical Review,* CXIV (February, 1946), 104–13.

———. "Wit and Mystery. A Revaluation in Mediaeval Latin Hymnody," *Speculum,* XXII (July, 1947), 310–41.

PÄCHT, OTTO. *The Rise of Pictorial Narrative in Twelfth-Century England.* Oxford: Clarendon Press, 1962.

PÄCHT, OTTO, DODWELL, C. R., and WORMOLD, FRANCIS. *The Saint Albans Psalter* (*Albani Psalter*). London: The Warbug Institute, 1960.

PANOFSKY, ERWIN. *Gothic Architecture and Scholasticism.* New York: Meridian Books, 1957.

PARSCH, PIUS. *The Breviary Explained.* St. Louis: B. Herder Book Co., 1952.

PATTERSON, FRANK ALLEN. *The Middle English Penitential Lyric: A Study and Collection of Early Religious Verse.* ("Columbia University Studies in English," No. 35.) New York: Columbia University Press, 1911.

A Peterborough Psalter and Bestiary of the Fourteenth Century. Described by MONTAGUE RHODES JAMES. Roxburghe Club, No. 178. Oxford: Printed for the Club by Oxford University Press, 1921.

PIKE, KENNETH L. *Language in Relation to a Unified Theory of the Structure of Human Behavior.* 3 vols. Glendale, California: Summer Institute of Linguistics, 1954, 1955, 1960.

PROSSER, ELEANOR A. *Drama and Religion in the English Mystery Plays: A Re-evaluation.* ("Stanford Studies in Language and Literature," Vol. XXIII.) Stanford: Stanford University Press, 1961.

The Prymer or Lay Folks' Prayer Book (*With Several Facsimiles*), ed. HENRY LITTLEHALES. Early English Text Society, Original Series, Nos. 105, 109. London: Printed for the Society by K. Paul, Trench, Trübner & Co., Ltd., 1895, 1897.

RABANUS MAURUS. *De laudibus sanctae crucis.* Patrologiae cursus completus. Series Latina, ed. J.-P. MIGNE. Vol. CVII. Paris, 1864. Cols. 133–294.

RABY, FREDERICK J. E. *A History of Christian-Latin Poetry from the Beginnings to the Close of the Middle Ages.* Oxford: Clarendon Press, 1927.

RÉAU, LOUIS. *Iconographie de l'art chrétien.* 6 vols. Paris: Presses universitaires de France, 1955–59.

REESE, GUSTAVE. *Music in the Middle Ages.* New York: W. W. Norton & Co., 1940.

ROBBINS, ROSSELL HOPE. "The Authors of the Middle English Religious Lyrics," *Journal of English and Germanic Philology,* XXXIX (1940), 230–38.

———. "The Burden in Carols," *Modern Language Notes,* LVII (January, 1942), 16–22.

———. "The Earliest Carols and the Franciscans," *Modern Language Notes,* LIII (April, 1938), 239–45.

———. "Friar Herebert and the Carol," *Anglia,* LXXV (1957), 194–98.

ROBBINS, ROSSELL HOPE, and CUTLER, JOHN L. *Supplement to the Index of Middle English Verse [by] Carleton Brown and Rossell Hope Robbins.* Lexington: University of Kentucky Press, 1965.

ROBERTSON, DURANT W., JR. *A Preface to Chaucer: Studies in Medieval Perspectives.* Princeton: Princeton University Press, 1962.

ROBERTSON, DURANT W., JR., and HUPPE, BERNARD F. *Piers Plowman and Scriptural Tradition.* ("Princeton Studies in English," No. 31.) Princeton: Princeton University Press, 1951.

The Rule of Saint Benedict in Latin and English. Edited and translated by JUSTIN MCCANN, O.S.B. ("The Orchard Books.") London: Burns Oates, 1952.

SANDISON, HELEN E. *The "Chanson d'aventure" in Middle English.* ("Bryn Mawr College Monographs," Vol. XII.) Bryn Mawr: Bryn Mawr College, 1913.

The Sarum Missal Done Into English. Translated by A. HARFORD PEARSON. 2d ed. London: The Church Printing Co., 1884.

The Sarum Missal in English. Translated by FREDERICK E. WARREN. ("The Library of Liturgiology & Ecclesiology for English Readers," ed. VERNON STALEY, Vols. VIII, IX.) 2 vols. London: Alexander Moring, Ltd., 1911.

SCHAPIRO, MEYER. "The Image of the Disappearing Christ: The Ascension in English Art Around the Year 1000," *Gazette des beaux-arts,* 6th Ser., XXIII (1943), 134–52.

SIMSON, OTTO VON. *The Gothic Cathedral: Origins of Gothic Architecture and the Medieval Concept of Order. With an Appendix on the Proportions of the South Tower of Chartres Cathedral by Ernst Levy.* ("Bollingen Series," Vol. XLVIII.) New York: Pantheon Books, 1956.

SMALLEY, BERYL. *The Study of the Bible in the Middle Ages.* 2d ed. Oxford: Basil Blackwell, 1952.

SPARGO, EMMA JANE MARIE, SISTER. *The Category of the Aesthetic in the Philosophy of Saint Bonaventure.* ("Philosophy Series," ed. ALLAN B. WOLTER, O.F.M., No. 11.) Saint Bonaventure, New York: The Franciscan Institute, 1953.

SPEIRS, JOHN. *Medieval English Poetry: The Non-Chaucerian Tradition.* London: Faber and Faber, 1957.

SPITZER, LEO. "Classical and Christian Ideas of World Harmony: Prolegomena to an Interpretation of the Word 'Stimmung,'" *Traditio,* II (1944), 409–64; III (1945), 307–64.

———. "*Explication de Texte* Applied to Three Great Middle English Poems," *Archivum Linguisticum,* III (1951), 1–22, 137–65.

———. "Note on the Poetic and Empirical 'I' in Medieval Authors," *Traditio,* IV (1946), 414–22.

STAINER, JOHN, SIR (ed.). *Early Bodleian Music: Sacred and Secular Songs. Together with Other Manuscript Compositions in the Bodleian Library, Oxford, Ranging from about A.D. 1185 to about A.D. 1505.* With an Introduction by E. W. B. NICHOLSON and Transcriptions into Modern Musical Notation by J. F. R. STAINER and C. STAINER. 2 vols. London: Novello and Co., Ltd., 1901.

TAYLOR, GEORGE C. "The English 'Planctus Mariae,'" *Modern Philology,* IV (April, 1907), 605–37.

———. "The Relation of the English Corpus Christi Play to the Middle English Religious Lyric," *Modern Philology,* V (July, 1907), 1–38.

A Thirteenth Century York Psalter. A Manuscript Written and Illuminated in the Diocese of York about A.D. 1250. Described by ERIC GEORGE MILLAR. Roxburghe Club, No. 216. Oxford: Printed for the Club by Oxford University Press, 1952.

Thirty-Two Miniatures from the Book of Hours of Joan II, Queen of Navarre. A Manuscript of the Fourteenth Century. Presented by HENRY YATES THOMPSON. Roxburghe Club, No. 137. London: Printed for the Club by The Chiswick Press, 1899.

Three Middle-English Versions of the Rule of St. Benet and Two Contemporary Rituals for the Ordination of Nuns, ed. ERNST A. KOCK. Early English Text Society, Original Series, No. 120. London: Printed for the Society by K. Paul, Trench, Trübner & Co., Ltd., 1902.

Tresmontant, Claude. *Essai sur la pensée hébraïque.* ("Lectio divina," No. 12.) Paris: Éditions du Cerf, 1953.

Wagner, Peter. *Introduction to the Gregorian Melodies: A Handbook of Plainsong. Part I, Origin and Development of the Forms of the Liturgical Chant up to the End of the Middle Ages.* Translated by Agnes Orme and E. G. P. Wyatt. 2d ed. London: Plainsong & Mediaeval Music Society, 1901.

Watson, Arthur. *The Early Iconography of the Tree of Jesse.* London: Oxford University Press, 1934.

Wehrle, William O. *The Macaronic Hymn Tradition in Medieval English Literature.* Washington, D.C.: The Catholic University of America, 1933.

White, Natalie E. "The English Liturgical Refrain Lyric Before 1450, with Special Reference to the Fourteenth Century." Unpublished Ph.D. dissertation, Stanford University, 1945.

William of Shoreham. *The Poems of William of Shoreham,* ed. Matthias Konrath. Early English Text Society, Extra Series, No. 86. London: Printed for the Society by K. Paul, Trench, Trübner & Co., Ltd., 1902.

Wilmart André, O.S.B. *Auteurs spirituels et textes dévots du moyen âge latin, études d'histoire littéraire.* Paris: Bloud et Gay, 1932.

Woolf, Rosemary. "The Effect of Typology on the English Mediaeval Plays of Abraham and Isaac," *Speculum,* XXXII (October, 1957), 805–25.

———. *The English Religious Lyric in the Middle Ages.* Oxford: Clarendon Press, 1968.

Wordsworth, Christopher, and Littlehales, Henry. *The Old Service-Books of the English Church.* ("The Antiquary's Books," ed. J. Charles Cox.) London: Methuen & Co., 1904.

Young, Karl. *The Drama of the Medieval Church.* 2 vols. Oxford: Clarendon Press, 1933.

Index

Adam, 130, 177–78, 205, 267; Christ as second, 37, 200; sin of (original sin), 8, 70–71, 90, 96, 157, 200, 210
Adam of St. Victor, vii–viii, 21
Adoration of the Magi, 15, 73, 77, 85, 265–66
Advent, season of, 9, 11, 13; and lyric, 50, 57. *See also* Coming of Christ
Aelred of Rievaulx, 149, 150, 150 n. 2
Aesthetic theory, 178 n. 7, 209, 211–12. *See also* Beauty; Delight; Proportionate correspondences; Religious lyric
Allegorical interpretation of Scripture, 5–6, 11, 37, 178, 198, 201–2, 263; in literature, 6 n. 8; in Matins readings, 11, 11 n. 29, 17; and order of proper texts of Mass, 17–22, 24–25. *See also* Divine *ratio;* Exegesis; Juxtaposition; Ladder; Moralised Bibles; Symmetry of sacred history
"Als i lay vp-on a nith," 61–68 (text), 69–86, 111, 126–27, 133, 171, 178, 191, 198, 199, 201, 202, 206, 208, 211
Ambrose, method of commentary, 18, 37. *See also* Fathers of the Church
Amesbury Psalter, proportion in, 264–65, 266–67
Ancrene Riwle, 152, 170, 200; prayer on five joys in, 152–53, 179–82, 187–191 *passim*
Angels, grief of, 116–17
Angel's salutation, 13 n. 34, 20, 21, 22, 51, 54, 153, 181; in lyric, 33, 39–40, 48, 49, 51, 54, 159, 182–86 *passim;* MS illumination of, 164, 265, 267. *See also* Elizabeth, blessing of given to Mary
"Angelus ad virginem," 32, 35 n. 8, 36, 43 n. 17. *See also* "Gabriel, fram evene-king"
Annunciation, event of: as first joy in lyrics on five joys, 152, 168, 183, 187; and joy, 71, 150, 168; MS illumination of, 53–54, 58, 164, 264–65; in other lyrics, 32–46 *passim,* 48, 49, 51, 54, 82, 83, 84, 163, 178; poet's modification of Gospel account of, 32–34, 49, 51, 54, 56, 75, 76, 196 (*see also* Angel's salutation). *See also* Annunciation, Feast of; Annunciation, Mass of
Annunciation, Feast of, 13, 23; and lyrics, 34, 57, 58; Matins readings for, 11, 18–19, 37
Annunciation, Mass of, 13, 16–25, 32, 37; Collect of, 22–24, 40; Communion Verse of, 22; Gospel reading of, 16–17 (*see also* Annunciation, event of); Gradual of, 20–21, Introit of, 19–20;

Annunciation, Mass of—*Continued*
Lesson of, 17–19, 22, 32; Offertory Verse of, 22; Postcommunion of, 23–24; Secret of, 23; Sequence of, 21, 215–16; Tract of, 20, 21
Annunciation to the Shepherds, 15, 76, 265–66
Anselm of Canterbury, 90, 175–76; dialogue of, *see Beatae Mariae et Anselmi de passione Domini*
Ascension, event of, 4, 5, 9, 102, 150, 152; as fourth joy in lyrics on five joys, 157, 160–62, 170–71, 172–73, 182, 187–89, 199; MS illumination of, *see* Disappearing Christ; and Mary as figure of poet and audience, 171, 188–89; in other lyrics, 72, 81, 83, 86, 134, 136
Assumption, event of, 15, 50, 149–51; as fifth joy in lyrics on five joys, 152, 157, 161–62, 163–64, 171–72, 180, 182, 188, 190; Mary as figure of future joy of poet and audience, 15, 151, 188; in other lyrics, 72, 81, 134, 136, 151. *See also* Assumption, Feast of; Mary, as Queen of Heaven
Assumption, Feast of, 13, 86, 149, 150
Audience: knowledge of context in sacred history used by poet, 49–50, 60, 113–14, 117–19, 135–36, 151–52, 156–57, 187–90 *passim,* 199, 202 (*see also* Point of view); lyric proportioned to, 41, 43, 60, 85–86, 94–95, 103, 105–6, 108–9, 187–91, 207, 210–11, 212 (*see also* Beauty; Delight; Religious lyric, focus of on man); reformed by lyric, 73, 81, 94, 108–9, 135, 175–76, 196, 199, 207, 210–12; relation to subject of lyric, 50, 60, 85–86, 90, 96–97, 100–2, 105–9 *passim,* 111, 114–15, 121, 134–36, 143–45, 151–52, 156–57, 162–63, 171, 188–89, 197, 198, 199, 205, 207, 212; unity with poet, *see* Church. *See also* Crucifixion; Desire; Poet; Point of view
Augustine, 4, 177 n. 4 and 6; *City of God,* 4. *See also* Fathers of the Church
Ave Maria. *See* Angel's salutation
"Ave mundi spes Maria," sequence of Mass of Annunciation, 21, 58 n. 31, 215–16 (text)

Baptism, 8, 90, 100, 200. *See also* Sacraments
Baptism of Christ, 78
Beatae Mariae et Anselmi de passione Domini, 90–91, 100 n. 14, 119 n. 15, 141
Beatific vision, 7, 25, 70, 163, 209. *See also* Joy, of heaven; Delight
Beauty, 70, 83, 94, 103–9, 177, 266–67; Bonaventure's theory of and religious lyric, 211–12; and Eternal Art, 209. *See also* Christ; Delight; Proportionality; Symmetry of sacred history
Bernard of Clairvaux, vii, viii, 56, 90. *See also Lamentatio St. Bernardi*
Bible. *See* Holy Scripture; Moralised Bibles
Birth of Christ, 9, 15, 150; as it foreshadows crucifixion in lyrics, 72–73, 77, 79–80, 81–86 *passim* (*see also* Painless childbearing, Law of motherhood); MS illumination of, 53–54, 58, 164, 265, 265–66; as second joy in lyrics on five joys, 152, 157, 159–60, 163–64, 168–69, 182, 184, 187; use of event in other lyrics, 34–40 *passim,* 50–54, 56–59. *See also* Christmas, Feast of
Blessed Virgin's Appeal to the Jews. *See* "Wy haue ȝe no reuthe on my child?"
Bliss. *See* Joy
Blood of Christ, 79–80, 105, 128, 133, 264, 266, 267
Bonaventure: *Breviloquium,* 69, 96 n. 10, 133, 175–76, 210–11; conception of poetry, 212; definition of beauty, 211–12; "exigency of human capacity," ix n. 14, 195; *Itinerarium mentis in Deum,* 167, 176–77, 210–12; *Lignum vitae,* 212; method of theology, 209–12
Bridgett, T. E., 152
Bukofzer, Manfred, 16 n. 42
Burning bush, figure of, 19, 21, 58 n. 32

Canon of the Mass. *See* Mass

Canonical Hours. *See* Divine Office

Canticle of Canticles (Song of Solomon), vii, 19, 58, 212

Canticles (of Divine Office), 11 n. 24 and 25, 153

Catechesis, order of, 4

Chanson d'aventure, 74 n. 4. *See also* Vision setting of "Als i lay vp-on a nith"

Chester plays, order of, 5

Chomsky, Noam, 16 n. 42

Christ: as beauty, 94, 211–12; and creation, 169, 263; as Child, 49–55, 59, 72–86, 97, 265–66, 267; divinity of, 4, 5, 40, 50, 52, 72, 78, 80–81, 85, 96, 111, 115–17, 118, 120, 121, 142–45, 160, 163, 170, 172, 181, 266 (*see also* Point of view); as Fruit of Mary's womb, 164, 211–12; as Head, 96, 104; human nature of, 5, 33, 51, 55, 60, 83–84, 106–7, 115, 126, 128, 160, 163, 168, 172, 181, 207, 211, 266; as King of Heaven, 23, 40, 49–60 *passim,* 136, 168–69, 172, 174, 188, 265; as Ladder, 210; as Lamb, 95–96, 104, 264; life of, 8, 14–15, 72–86, 126, 200, 201–2, 211, 265–66; love of, 95, 100, 102, 106–8, 118, 120, 144–45 (*see also* Compassion of Mary); as New Testament, 5–6; power of, 111, 117, 120, 132, 161, 169–70, 174, 188–89, 207; as second Adam, *see* Adam; union with, 4, 5, 6, 8, 40, 46, 168, 179–80, 200, 202, 211–12 (*see also* God, Joy); as Word, 159, 178, 211

Christmas, Feast of, 13, 50, 81, 83, 85–86. *See also* Birth of Christ; Vision setting of "Als i lay vp-on a nith"

Church: founding of, 4–5, 8, 78–79, 102 (*see also* Pentecost); MS illumination of, 264, 266; Mary as figure of, 13–14, 264; as perspective of sacred history in present time, 4–6, 9, 34, 39, 86, 90, 177–78, 197–208 *passim,* 264 (*see also* Time, liturgical); structure of prayer of, 22–25; as unity of poet, audience, and mankind, ix, 6, 23, 204–6, 210–11. *See also* Point of view, of "us"

Circumcision, 15, 77, 85; MS illumination of, 265–66

Classical tradition of poetry, religious lyrics in, viii, 209 n. 12. *See also* Lyric

Collect, of the Mass, 16, 22–24, 25

Coming of Christ, 4, 8, 89, 201–2, 205; in Divine Office, 11–12; and figure of falling dew, 57–59, 211; in lyrics, 34, 37, 56–60, 72, 163. *See also* Advent; Incarnation

Common of the Saints in Sarum liturgy, 9, 12

Communion, of Body and Blood of Christ in Mass, 7, 19, 22; spiritual, and "þe milde Lomb," 109 n. 21

Communion Verse, of the Mass, 16, 19, 22, 24

Compassion of Mary, 13–15, 38, 71–72, 78–85 *passim,* 89, 96–109 *passim,* 110–21, 126–31, 132–45 *passim,* 150, 160; and Christ's love for mankind, 100, 104, 106–9, 142, 143, 198–99; and divinity of Mary's Son, 111, 114–17, 118–21, 125, 142–45; and law of motherhood, 33, 38, 75, 79–80, 84, 99–100, 130–31, 137, 140, 143, 200–1 (*see also* Mary, motherhood of mankind); MS illumination of, 264, 266–67; and Mary's human bond with her Son, 97, 111, 112, 113–17, 118, 127–36 *passim,* 143; as mirror of Christ's suffering, 15, 97, 105–6, 112, 133; poet's presentation of, 71–72, 105, 109, 120, 143–45; as wound of Christ, *see* Suffering of Christ on the cross. *See also* Hours of the Compassion of Mary; John; Simeon, sword of

Compline, 10, 11 n. 25, 12; hymn for, 12; Prymer antiphon for, 25; in Sarum *Horae* metrical devotions, 15. *See also* Divine Office

Conception of Mary, Feast of, 13. *See also* Immaculate Conception

Corpus Christi, Feast of, 9

Correspondences. *See* Proportionate correspondences

Creation (created world): divine

Creation—*Continued*
proportioning of, 178; as language of God, 3, 16 n. 42, 210; poem as, 212; poverty of, 177
Creation (event of), 3, 4–5, 37, 197, 200, 201; and new creation, 4, 11, 37, 200, 201–2 (*see also* Incarnation, Redemption)
Criticism of lyric. *See* Religious lyric
Cross: as altar, 95; as figure of proportion in lyric, 136, 178, 198, 199; the "intelligible cross," 133 n. 8, 133–36, 198. *See also* Tree of Life
Crucifixion of Christ, 11, 40, 70, 79, 82, 83, 87–145 *passim*, 160–61, 178; audience's relation to, 90, 94–97, 100–3, 105–6, 108–9; Christ's choice to die, 96, 118, 128–30; death of Christ, 4, 8, 89, 96, 99, 107–17 *passim*, 118–21, 126, 128–33, 136, 144, 179, 200–1, 206; disciples' desertion of Christ, 95, 96–97, 100, 105–6; foreshadowing of, 72, 77, 83, 85; and joy, 71–73, 99, 126–33 *passim* (*see also* Resurrection of Christ); MS illumination of, 265, 266–67; Mary given into care of John, 97 n. 13, 101; poet's presentation of, 94 *passim*, 103–8, 136–45; as sacrifice, 7, 94, 95, 96, 104, 198–99 (*see also* Mass). *See also* Compassion of Mary; John; Passion of Christ; Suffering of Christ on the cross
Crucifixion of Man, 180–81, 200
Cursor Mundi, 4–5, 14 n. 40

Delight, heavenly: and Eternal Art, 209–12; experience of, 70, 175–78; lyric as figure of, 60, 108–9, 162, 178–91, 209–12; as a proportion of beauty, 103, 108, 211–12. *See also* Desire; Joy
Descent into hell, 131
Desire: of audience, 85, 108, 172–74, 191; and beauty, 211–12; of mankind, x, 171, 172, 177–78, 180 n. 10, 206–7; and proportion of lyric, 83, 121, 144, 171, 174 n. 11, 183, 185, 186, 207; and proportion of prayer on third joy in *Ancrene Riwle*, 179–81. *See also* Delight, heavenly; Prayer; Subjective mode
Devotion: manuals of, 10; poetry of, 14, 110; practices of in Church, viii, 152–53
Dialogue form in lyric, 72, 83, 85, 86, 125, 126–31 *passim*, 133–36, 136–45
Didactic tradition of poetry, viii. *See also* Lyric
Disappearing Christ, image of, 164, 164 n. 30. *See also* Ascension, event of
Divine Office, viii, 8, 10–12, 195; fixed sequence of parts in, 8, 11, 24–25, 202 (*see also* Ladder); Hours of, 8, 10–12, 14; readings of, viii, 11 (*see also* Allegorical interpretation of Scripture); variable proper parts of, 8, 11. *See also* *Horae;* Prymer
Divine *ratio*, among events, 4–6, 69–70, 178; and exegesis, 5; and form of liturgy, 5, 6 n. 8, 264; and form of lyric, 6, 14. *See also* Ladder; Tiptoft Missal
Drama, medieval religious, vii, viii, 5, 21

Easter, 8, 9, 13, 86
Elizabeth: blessing of given to Mary, 13 n. 34, 21, 51, 54, 162 n. 27 (*see also* Fruit of Mary's womb); conception of John a sign to Mary, 76
Emotion. *See* Religious lyric, theology and intensity of emotion in
Epiphany. *See* Adoration of the Magi
Epistle. *See* Lesson, of the Mass
Eternal Art. *See* Aesthetic theory
Eucharist. *See* Communion; Mass; Sacraments
Eve, Mary as second, 19 n. 48, 33, 18, 71, 200. *See also* Law of motherhood
Exegesis, method of: and divisions of Scripture, 5–6, 17; and explication of poetry, 6 n. 8, 209, 212; and liturgy, 11, 17; and theology, 4, 4 n. 3. *See also* Allegorical interpretation of Scripture
Exemplum de beata virgine & gaudiis eius. *See* "Nu þis fules singet hand maket hure blisse"

"Exigency of human capacity." *See* Bonaventure; Sacred history, focus of in man
Explication, modern method of. *See* Exegesis

Falling dew, figure of, 50 n. 6, 56–60, 211
Fall of man, 4–5, 35, 38, 90, 157
Fathers of the Church, commentary of, viii, 11, 17. *See also* Ambrose; Juxtaposition
Figure, 19, 21, 34 n. 7, 37–38, 45–46, 57–59, 60, 136, 140, 143, 158–59, 162–64, 171, 178, 179, 180–81, 187, 188–89, 198–99, 202, 210, 211, 212. *See also* Allegorical interpretation of Scripture; Christ; Delight; Mary; Proportionate correspondences
Finding of Jesus in the Temple, 77–78, 85
Five Joys. *See* Joys of Mary
Five wounds of Christ, viii, 152, 170, 185, 200
Flight into Egypt, 15, 265–66
Francis of Assisi, 177; poetical office of, 12
Fruit of Mary's womb, figure of, 162–64, 211. *See also* Elizabeth, blessing of given to Mary

"Gabriel, fram evene-king," 29–31 (text), 32–46, 49, 51, 70, 71, 75, 83, 84, 90, 101, 156, 178, 191, 196, 198–99, 201, 203, 204, 205
"Gaude Dei genetrix, virgo immaculata," 153
"Gavde flore virginali," 152
"Gaude Maria virgo: cunctas hereses sola interemisti in universo mundo," 153
"Gavde virgo, mater Christi," 152, 153, 155 (text), 155–64 *passim. See also* "Glade us maiden, moder milde"
Gideon's fleece, figure of, 19, 57, 59
Gilson, Étienne, vii
"Glade us maiden, moder milde," 154 (text), 156–64, 168, 171, 182, 185, 198, 203, 205. *See also* "Gavde virgo, mater Christi"
God: and the proportion of sacred history, viii–ix, 3–5, 40, 70, 178, 196; union with, ix, 5, 6, 70, 96, 98, 121, 157, 162, 167, 168, 172, 177, 197, 206, 209. *See also* Objective mode; Point of view, of divinity; Subjective mode
Gorleston Psalter, 58
Gospel reading, of the Mass, 11, 16–17, 18–25 *passim. See also* Allegorical interpretation of Scripture
Grace, 4, 5, 23, 90, 152, 157, 178, 205
Gradual, of the Mass, 16, 19, 20, 24
Greene, Richard, 82 n. 11
Gregory of Nyssa, catechesis of, 4

Heaven: good of, 174–75; as light, 132–33, 135–36, 168; as place, 161–64; as Mary's happiness, 179, 180–81, 188 (*see also* Mary, joy of). *See also* Delight; Joy
Heavenly Jerusalem, 9, 86
Hell, 4, 35, 128–133 *passim,* 135, 136, 168. *See also* Sorrow
"Heyl be þou marie, milde quene of heuene!" 178–79, 182–86, 189, 220–22 (text)
Holy Scripture: focus of in man, ix n. 14, 210; glossing of and lyric, 16 n. 42; Hebraic order of accounts in, 4; reformulation of by liturgy, 6, 7–25 *passim* (*see also* Allegorical interpretation of Scripture); and theology, 4, 4 n. 3, 175, 210 (*see also* Tradition). *See also* Exegesis
Holy Spirit, 4, 5, 9, 33, 59, 164; seven gifts of, 8, 212
Homily, form of and liturgy, viii, 8, 17, 19
Horae (Hours of the Virgin), 10, 14–15, 152, 200. *See also Horae Eboracenses;* Prymer; Hours of the Passion; Sarum *Horae*

Horae Eboracenses, 152–53
Hours of the Office. *See* Divine Office
Hours of Mary's Compassion, viii, 14–15, 200. *See also* Hours of the Passion
Hours of the Passion (or Cross), viii, 14–15, 200. *See also* Hours of Mary's Compassion
Hymns, vii–viii, 21 n. 56; of Divine Office, 11–12. *See also* Sequence

"I," use of, in lyrics. *See* Point of view
"Iesu cristes milde moder," 38, 136, 137–39 (text), 139–45. *See also* "Stabat iuxta Christi crucem"
"Iesu dulcis memoria," vii
Immaculate Conception, 13 n. 33, 50, 181 n. 11
"In a tabernacle of a toure," 71, 205
Incarnation of Christ, ix, x, 4, 5–6, 11, 24, 37, 69–73, 115, 163, 172; beauty of, 83, 211; and dialogue form, 142. *See also* Coming of Christ; Paradoxes of the Incarnation in lyric; Redemption
Introit, of the Mass, 19 n. 52, 19–20, 24
Irony in lyric, 73–74, 77, 126–27, 199
Isaiah, prophecy of, 11, 17–22 *passim,* 32, 50, 57, 95, 96 n. 11
"I syng of a myden þat is makeles," 47, 48, 55 (text), 55–60, 196, 203, 208

"Jam lucis orto sidere," 12
James, Montague, 136
Jesse: rod of, 19, 21, 50, 54, 57, 58; tree of, 48, 49, 53–54, 58, 152 n. 12, 265
John: as beloved disciple, 101; compassion of, 96, 97–98, 104, 105–6, 108, 264, 266–67; Mary in the care of, 91, 101, 108
John of Grimestone's preaching book, 72–73, 90, 111, 211
John of Peckham, poetical office by, 12
Jordan, Robert, 211 n. 17
Joy, ix, x, 18, 34, 36, 70–71, 89, 90, 136, 157–64 *passim,* 172, 177–78, 180, 187, 189, 206–7; Christ is, 40, 109, 162, 164, 187; of heaven, 4, 34, 40, 71, 83, 100–103, 108–9, 132, 134, 143, 157, 161–63, 168, 170–74 *passim,* 175–77, 205, 211–12 (*see also* Delight, Heaven); Mary as medium of, 5, 18, 109, 134–35, 157–64 *passim,* 189, 207; and sorrow of events and context of sacred history, 15, 34, 71–86, 94, 109, 126–27, 132, 133–35, 142, 178, 206–7 (*see also* Sorrow); transformation of sorrow to joy by sacred history, 71–72, 73, 81–86, 89, 126, 131, 133–36, 206. *See also* Joys of Mary; Mary, joy of; Painless childbearing; Resurrection of Christ
Joys of Mary: earthly and heavenly joys, 151–52; five joys, 53, 151–53, 156–57, 158 n. 21, 158–91, 200, 206. *See also* Mary, joy of
Jungmann, Joseph, 22, 23
Juxtaposition, method of, 18–19, 20, 24, 33 n. 2, 37–38, 44–46, 84, 201. *See also* Allegorical interpretation of Scripture; Proportionate correspondences

Kane, George, vii n. 4, ix n. 15, 47, 48 n. 4, 59, 60, 110–11, 114–15, 117, 120–21, 125, 137, 142, 195, 199

Ladder (order of parts of Mass and Office), 8–9, 15–25, 201–3; and lyric, 8–9, 203; and names for Mary, 202–3. *See also* Christ; Allegorical interpretation of Scripture; Mass
Lamb, figure of, 95–96, 104, 264
"Lamentacio dolorosa." *See* "Suete sone, reu on me, & brest out of þi bondis"
Lamentatio St. Bernardi de compassione Mariae, 89, 90–91, 96 n. 11, 100 n. 14, 101, 111–12, 113–17, 118 n. 14, 126, 128 n. 4, 141, 142
Last judgment, 4, 81–86 *passim,* 109, 136, 177, 201, 206
Lauds, 10, 11 n. 25; in Sarum *Horae* metrical devotions, 15. *See also* Divine Office
Law of motherhood (Gen. 3: 16). *See*

Compassion of Mary; Painless childbearing
Laymen, devotional practices of, viii, 14 n. 39. *See also* Liturgy, participation in
Lesson, of the Mass, 16, 17–19, 20–25 *passim. See also* Allegorical interpretation of Scripture
"Leuedy, for þare blisse," 165–66 (text), 167–74, 178, 179, 186–91, 198, 199, 201, 208, 210
Lily of chastity, figure of, 21, 58, 159, 164
Linguistic analysis, 3, 16 n. 42
Listener. *See* Audience
Liturgy, viii–ix, 3, 4 n. 2, 5–25, 37, 178, 195–208 *passim;* participation in by clergy and laymen, viii n. 7, 7 n. 12, 10, 10 n. 22, 14 n. 39, 109 n. 21. *See also* Church; Mary; Religious lyric; Sacred history; Time
Love lyric: religious, 207; secular, 49, 50, 57, 168 n. 3, 171 n. 9. *See also* Lyric
"Lullay, lullay, la lullay, mi dere moder, lullay." *See* "Als i lay vp-on a nith"
Lyric, 110, 110 n. 1. *See also* Classical tradition of poetry; Didactic tradition of poetry; Love lyric; Penitential lyric; Religious lyric; Richard Rolle, lyrics of the school of; Secular lyric

"makeles," 34, 34 n. 6, 55. *See also* Virgin motherhood of Mary
Manning, Stephen, vii n. 4, 110 n. 1
Mary: beauty of, 51, 54–55, 57–59, 60, 150, 171, 173, 174; descent from the root of Jesse, 50, 53, 56, 58; enthroned, 53, 164, 267; figures of, 19, 21, 24–25, 53–54, 58, 59, 185 (*see also* Figure); as figure of humanity, x, 72, 86, 111, 113–17, 121, 136, 151, 157, 168, 171, 173, 188–89, 207; as intercessor, 13, 40, 109, 112 (for Christ), 131, 140, 144, 151, 162–63, 169, 173, 174 (*see also* Prayer); joy of, 15, 53, 71–72, 74, 75–85 *passim,* 107, 127–36 *passim,* 149–52, 156–57, 162–74 *passim,* 202, 206 (*see also* Joy, Joys of Mary); as Lady, 56, 57, 168, 169, 171, 173, 184, 185, 187, 202–3; Laments of, 90 n. 2; liturgy of, 9, 12–25, 34, 37, 54, 57, 58, 86, 149, 150, 169; as "maiden makeles," *see* Virgin motherhood of Mary; as mother of God, 23, 33, 35, 49–60 *passim,* 103, 130, 159, 164, 169, 187; as mother of mankind, 38, 52, 71, 89, 99–100, 103, 106–8, 130–31, 143, 150, 158, 163–64, 201, 203 (*see also* Compassion of Mary, Law of motherhood); as Mother of Mercy, 13, 39, 89, 103, 108, 151, 173, 202–3, 205; in present time as Queen of Heaven, ix, 13–14, 40, 50, 53–54, 81, 103, 116, 132–33, 134, 136, 150–52, 156–57, 160–64 *passim,* 170–74 *passim,* 183, 188, 198, 202–3, 205, 265, 266; without sin, 50, 51, 56, 157 (*see also* Immaculate Conception); sorrow of, *see* Compassion of Mary; titles of, *see* Naming, of Mary; union of with Christ, 14, 112–13, 120, 134, 150, 157, 160, 172, 203; wisdom of, 174. *See also* Eve; Painless childbearing; Point of view
Mass, 7–9, 15–25, 195; canon of, 7, 8, 23; Christ as focus and meaning of, 7, 8, 16, 19, 22–24, 25, 264 (*see also* Crucifixion, as sacrifice); congregation's prayer in, 10, 22–25; fixed sequence of parts as interpretation of texts in, 15–25, 202, 264 (*see also* Allegorical interpretation of Scripture); and lyric, 8–9, 16 n. 42, 19, 20–21, 23, 32, 40, 95–96, 109 n. 21 (*see also* Sequence; Religious lyric, relation of to liturgy); MS illumination of, 264; Proper of, 8, 16–25 (*see also* Annunciation, Mass of)
Masses of Mary. *See* Saturday Masses of Mary
Matins, 10, 11 n. 24; readings of from Scripture and Fathers of the Church, 11, 17
Mirk, John, *Festial,* 150–51, 152
Moralised Bibles, and allegorical interpretation, 263

Music: of individual lyrics, 41–44, 49, 81; medieval, vii, viii, 15–16, 16 n. 42, 178 n. 7

Naming, 102 n. 17, 157–58, 182–86, 202–3, 205; of Christ, 51, 52–53, 60, 102, 109, 160–61, 164, 172; of Mary, 34, 39, 49–50, 52, 55, 60, 103, 132, 150, 151, 152, 157–64 *passim,* 182–86, 191, 200, 202–3. *See also* Christ; Mary

Narrative form in lyric, 81–86, 136–45, 265–66

Nativity of Christ. *See* Birth of Christ; Christmas, Feast of

Nativity of Mary, Feast of, 13, 50

New Testament. *See* Christ; Holy Scripture

None, 10, 11 n. 25; hymn for, 12; Prymer antiphon for, 24–25; in Sarum *Horae* metrical devotions, 14–15. *See also* Divine Office

"Nu þis fules singet hand maket hure blisse," 47–48, 48–49 (text), 49–55, 56, 57, 58, 196, 203, 208

Objective mode, viii–ix, 25, 83–84, 196, 197–203, 210

Offertory Verse, of the Mass, 16, 19, 24

Office. *See* Divine Office

Offices: of the Dead, 11 n. 30, 14; of the Holy Trinity, 12; poetical, 12; of the Saints, 11 n. 30, 12; of the Virgin Mary, *see Horae,* Prymer

Old Testament. *See* Holy Scripture

Ong, Walter, vii–viii. *See also* Liturgy, participation in

Painless childbearing, 18, 33, 34–40, 59, 75, 99, 107, 130, 137, 140, 142–43, 159, 168–69, 172, 198, 200–1. *See also* Compassion of Mary, and law of motherhood; Redemption; Virgin motherhood

Palgrave, Francis, 110 n. 1

Paradoxes of the Incarnation in lyric, 49–52, 74, 120, 127, 129–30, 141, 158, 159, 169. *See also* Point of view, of divinity

Passion of Christ, 5, 8, 9, 72–73, 90, 134, 170, 182, 185–86, 212. *See also* Crucifixion; Hours of the Passion; Suffering of Christ on the Cross

Patterson, Frank, vii n. 4, ix n. 15

Paul: Epistles of, 5–6, 23, 96, 121, 177; Feast of the Conversion of, 9

Pearl, 55 n. 17, 174 n. 11

Penitential lyric, 71, 207. *See also* Lyric

Pentecost: event of, 5; season of, 9, 11, 81, 86. *See also* Church; Holy Spirit

Petition. *See* Prayer

Poet: identity of situation of with audience, ix, 6, 204–5, 210–11 (*see also* Church, Point of view); purpose of, 23, 49, 55, 85, 109, 157, 196, 202, 207, 211–12; as speaker in lyric, 86, 171, 205, 207–8; and theologian, 210. *See also* Audience

Point of view, use of in lyric: of audience, 34–35, 73–75, 79, 81, 83–86, 94, 95–100 *passim,* 101–3, 103–9 *passim,* 111, 132; of divinity, 71–72, 73–86 *passim,* 106–8, 111, 112, 126–33 *passim,* 134–35, 137, 140–41, 142–43; of "I," 206, 207–8 (*see also* Poet, as speaker); of Mary, ix, 34–35, 71–72, 73–81 *passim,* 83–84, 96–97, 111–13, 114–20 *passim,* 121, 126–33 *passim,* 134–36, 137–45 *passim,* 171, 199; of "us," 23, 96, 102, 158, 204–5, 207–8 (*see also* Church)

Postcommunion prayer, of the Mass, 16, 22, 24

Prayer, 8, 22–23, 177; discussion of in individual lyrics, 39–40, 55, 70, 102–3, 108–9, 131–33, 134–35, 140–41, 162–64, 167–72 *passim,* 172–74, 187–91 *passim;* general characteristics of in lyric, 23, 151, 177–86, 197–99, 205, 207, 211–12 (as a proportion of beauty); of the Mass, 22–25. *See also Ancrene Riwle;* Church; Point of view, of "us";

Religious lyric, focus of in man in present time
Presentation of Christ in the Temple, 13, 53–54, 77, 85; MS illumination of, 265–66. *See also* Purification, Feast of; Simeon, sword of
Prime, 10, 11 n. 25, 12; hymn for, 12; Prymer antiphon for, 24; in Sarum *Horae* metrical devotions, 14–15. *See also* Divine Office
Proper of the Mass. *See* Mass
Proper of the Saints. *See* Common of the Saints
Prophets, 5–6, 19, 53, 265. *See also* Isaiah
Proportionality, 44 n. 18, 178. *See also* Beauty; Proportionate correspondences
Proportionate correspondences: of beauty, 211–12; in liturgy, 11–12, 13, 14–15, 18, 19 n. 48, 152–53, 200; in lyrics, 37–38, 44–46, 81–86, 103–6, 134–36, 140, 142–43, 145, 156–57, 163–64, 170–71, 173, 177–86 *passim,* 187–91, 199–203; in MS illumination, 200, 265, 265–66. *See also* Aesthetic theory; Figure; Symmetry of sacred history
Prymer, 10, 14, 24–25, 57, 152. *See also* *Horae;* Mary, figures of
Psalms, 5, 8, 11, 19, 24, 25, 153
Psalter of Robert de Lisle, 58, 84, 200, 265–66
Purification, Feast of, 13. *See also* Presentation of Christ in the Temple

Queen of Heaven. *See* Mary, in present time
"Quia amore langueo." *See* "In a tabernacle of a toure"

Redemption of man, viii, ix, 8, 9, 13, 33–46 *passim,* 51, 52, 53, 70–71, 79–80, 89, 90, 94–103 *passim,* 157, 176, 197, 198, 200–1, 206, 211. *See also* Painless childbearing
Religious lyric: aesthetic theory of, *see* Aesthetic theory, Beauty, Delight; classification of, ix n. 15; comparison of to a theological work, 209–12; correspondences in, *see* Proportionate correspondences; criticism of and theology, vii, ix, 40–41, 110–11, 117–21, 195, 209-12 *passim;* evaluation of, x, 55, 110–11, 117–21, 175–91, 195; focus of on man in present time, 39–40, 44, 50, 94–96, 100–3, 108–9, 111, 121, 132, 133–36, 137, 156–57, 159, 162–63, 168, 171, 177–78, 188–89, 197–99, 201, 205, 206–7 (*see also* Church, Sacred history, "Exigency of human capacity"); modern assumption of opposition between theology and poetry in, vii n. 4, 47–48, 59–60, 110–11, 114–15, 117, 120–21, 142–45, 195–96; objective aspect of, ix, 196 (*see also* Objective mode); power of to achieve delight, 6, 94, 102–3, 157, 163, 174, 184–85, 189, 190–91, 197, 198, 202, 212; proportions in and events of sacred history, *see* Figure, Proportionate correspondences; purpose of, *see* Aesthetic theory, Delight, Desire, Poet; relation of to liturgy, viii–ix, 3, 6, 8–9, 13, 19, 21, 37–38, 40–41, 56–59 *passim,* 77, 81, 85–86, 95–96, 105, 109 n. 21, 151–53, 162, 164, 174, 195–96, 197–208 *passim* (*see also* Mass, Prayer); structure of and plan of sacred history, 4–6, 13, 14–15, 34–38, 40–41, 43–46, 69–70, 81–86, 132–36, 145, 177–78, 181–82, 188–91, 196, 197–203 (*see also* Divine *ratio;* Proportionate correspondences; Sacred history, context of events in plan of); subjective aspect of, ix n. 15, x, 83, 196, 201, 204–8 (*see also* Subjective mode); theology and intensity of emotion in, x, 109, 110–17, 118, 120–21, 142, 178, 198, 207, 212; variety in subject and treatment of, ix–x, 47–48, 54–56, 83, 125–26, 142, 150 n. 2, 196. *See also* Audience; Lyric; Mass; Poet; Point of view
Resurrection of Christ, 4, 5, 11, 102, 134–36 *passim,* 140, 143; as figure of proportion, 180–81, 202; foretold by Christ at crucifixion, 80, 83, 131, 135, 140, 141, 142; MS illumination of,

Resurrection of Christ—*Continued*
164; and resurrection of man, 5, 188, 201; as third joy in lyrics on five joys, 150, 152, 157, 160–61, 163–64, 169–70, 179–81, 182, 187; and transformation of sorrow to joy, x, 72, 131–32, 133–36, 206 (*see also* Joy)

Resurrection of man, 4, 5, 86, 136, 151, 152, 188, 200

Robertson, Durant, 110 n. 1, 202 n. 8, 211 n. 17

Rolle, Richard, lyrics of the school of, ix, 207

Roman rite, viii

Rule of St. Benedict, 10–11

Sacraments, 4, 6, 7, 8, 95–96, 105, 195, 200, 205

Sacred history: Christ as center of events of, 5–6, 36, 37, 40, 104, 197 (*see also* Divine *ratio,* Ladder, Symmetry of sacred history); context of events in plan of, ix, 4, 17, 32, 34–40 *passim,* 44, 56, 111, 197, 199 (*see also* Audience, knowledge of context in sacred history); focus of in man, ix, 142–45 (*see also* Dialogue form), 195, 197; formulation of by liturgy (interpretation of), viii, 3, 5–25; perspective in present time, *see* Church, Time, Mary, Religious lyric; sequence of events in, viii–ix, 4–5, 25, 83, 197, 206, 210 (*see also* Symmetry of sacred history); and structure of prayer on five joys in *Ancrene Riwle,* 179–82; use of events of in lyrics, ix, 5, 6, 34–41, 45–46, 56, 94, 103–4, 157–64 *passim,* 171, 178–79, 181, 187–89, 196, 198, 203, 206 (*see also* Figure; Religious lyric, variety in subject and treatment of; Proportionate correspondences)

St. Gall, monastery of, 21

Saints. *See* Common of the Saints; Office of the Saints

Salutation of the angel. *See* Angel's salutation

Salvation. *See* Redemption

Sarum *Horae,* 14–15, 200

Sarum, liturgy of, 7 n. 10, 9, 11 n. 23, 12, 14–15, 16, 20. *See also* Liturgy; Sarum *Horae*

Saturday Masses of Mary, 13–14, 54, 169

Scripture. *See* Holy Scripture

Seasonal Cycle, ix, 8–9, 11–25 *passim;* and "Als i lay vp-on a nith," 86

Second coming of Christ, 4, 5, 6, 86, 157, 177

Secret, of the Mass, 16, 22, 23, 24

Secular lyrics, 47, 49, 50, 57. *See also* Lyric

Sequence, of the Mass, viii, 20–21, 24, 32, 38, 41 n. 15, 57, 90, 125, 136–37, 215–16

Sermon, of the Mass, 17, 22. *See also* Fathers of the Church; Homily

Sext, 10, 11 n. 25, 12; hymn for, 12; Prymer antiphon for, 24; in Sarum *Horae* metrical devotions, 14–15. *See also* Divine Office

Simeon, sword of, 13, 77, 78–79, 83, 85, 90 n. 3, 119 n. 15, 127–28, 140. *See also* Presentation of Christ in the Temple; Compassion of Mary

Sin, 5, 8, 89–90, 177–78; in lyrics, 33, 72, 94, 96, 97, 99, 100, 109, 114, 128–29, 157, 168, 169, 174, 183, 206. *See also* Adam, sin of (original sin); Hell; Sorrow; Suffering of Christ on the Cross

Sitwell, Gerard, 153

Sorrow, x, 18, 70–71, 90, 101, 103, 116–17, 128, 131, 134–35, 168, 172, 177, 180, 198, 206; and man's limited view of suffering, 71–73, 74–86 *passim,* 116–17, 126–36 *passim,* 168 (*see also* Subjective mode). *See also* Angels, grief of; Compassion of Mary; Crucifixion, audience's relation to; Joy, and sorrow of events, transformation of sorrow to joy; Sin; Suffering of Christ on the Cross

Speaker. *See* Poet

Speirs, John, 57 n. 22

Spires, Julian, poetical office by, 12
Spitzer, Leo, 48, 49, 54, 59, 195
"Stabat iuxta Christi crucem," 136–37, 217–19 (text). *See also* "Iesu cristes milde moder"
"Stond wel, moder, vnder rode," 122–24 (text), 125–45, 156, 178, 191, 196, 198, 199, 201, 202, 205, 206–7
Subjective mode, ix, ix n. 15, 16, 25, 70–72, 83–84, 196, 205–8, 210
"Suete sone, reu on me, & brest out of þi bondis," 110, 117, 117–18 (text), 118–21, 156, 196, 199, 207
Suffering of Christ on the cross, 71, 90–100, 103–8, 118–21 *passim,* 126–31 *passim,* 137, 139–140, 143–45, 157, 206; caused by man's sin, 70, 73, 90, 94, 97, 101, 102, 109, 129; intensity of, 94, 98–100, 103, 106–8, 112, 119, 120, 144; Mary's compassion as most severe wound, 91, 98–100, 106–8, 126, 128, 129, 133, 142; revealing Christ's love, *see* Christ, love of. *See also* Cross; Crucifixion; Hours of the Passion; Sorrow
Symmetry of sacred history, 14–15, 18, 37–38, 69–70, 178, 199–203. *See also* Allegorical interpretation of Scripture; Creation; Divine *ratio;* Figure; Proportionate correspondences; Sacred history

"Te lucis ante terminum," 12
Temptation in the desert, 78
Terce, 10, 11 n. 25, 12; hymn for, 12; Prymer antiphon for, 24; in Sarum *Horae* metrical devotions, 14–15. *See also* Divine Office
"Þe milde Lomb isprad o rode," 90, 91, 92–93 (text), 94–109, 112, 129, 143, 156, 178, 196, 197, 198–99, 201, 204, 205, 206, 207, 266–67
Theological virtues, 210
Theology, vii–viii, ix–x, 3, 4, 157, 175–78, 179–91 *passim,* 195–212. *See also* Holy Scripture; Liturgy; Sacred history; Religious lyric
Thomas Aquinas, vii–viii, 174 n. 11
Thomas à Becket: Feast of, 9; and seven heavenly joys, 152 n. 8
Time, 3–5, 8, 178, 181; liturgical, 5–6, 7, 21, 25, 156–57, 197, 212, 265; used in lyrics, 51, 52, 77, 81, 85, 111, 133–36, 144–45, 156–57, 162–63, 171, 174, 183, 184, 186, 187, 189, 201–202. *See also* Church, as perspective of sacred history in present time; Mary, in present time; Religious lyric, focus of on man in present time
Tiptoft Missal, 7 n. 11, 58, 161 n. 26, 263–64, 265
Tract, of the Mass, 16, 19, 21, 24
Tradition, 6 n. 7, 17, 19, 56–57, 185
Tree of Jesse. *See* Jesse
Tree of Life, 212, 266–67. *See also* Bonaventure; Aesthetic theory
Trinity, 4, 9, 12, 210, 264
Trinity Sunday, 9, 264
Troping, 20–21, 21 n. 56
Typology. *See* Allegorical interpretation of Scripture; Figure; Mary, figures of

"Us," use of in lyrics. *See* Point of view

Vespers, 10, 11 n. 25; Prymer antiphon for, 25; in Sarum *Horae* metrical devotions, 15. *See also* Divine Office
Virgin motherhood of Mary, 18, 24, 32–34, 35–40 *passim,* 51–52, 54, 55–60 *passim,* 74, 103, 131, 140, 143, 150, 157–58, 159, 164, 172, 173, 178, 198, 202–3, 205; and the "maiden makeles," 34, 39, 48, 49–54 *passim,* 55, 56, 60, 150, 203; virginal conception, 17–18, 33, 35, 36, 49, 56, 58–59, 157, 158–59, 181, 198, 265; virginal parturition, 17–18, 33, 35, 36, 56, 58–59, 159 (*see also* Painless childbearing). *See also* Mary
Vision, of joy, 162–64, 167–74, 208; as figure in lyric, 187–90, 198
Vision setting of "Als i lay vp-on a nith," 74, 81, 82, 83, 85–86, 208. *See also Chanson d'aventure*

Visitation, event of, 15. *See also* Elizabeth
Visitation, Feast of, 13 n. 34
Votive Masses, 10

Wakefield plays, order of, 5
White, Natalie, viii, 153. *See also* Liturgy, participation in
Wilmart, André, 152, 153
Wisdom, theological definition of, and "Leuedy, for þare blisse," 167, 174
Wit, vii–viii, 159
Woolf, Rosemary, vii n. 4
World, 4–5, 121, 167, 173, 174, 177. *See also* Creation (created world)
Wounds of Christ. *See* Circumcision; Five wounds of Christ; Suffering of Christ on the cross
"Wy haue ȝe no reuthe on my child?" 111–12, 112 (text), 112–17, 121, 156, 196, 207

York *Horae. See Horae Eboracenses*
York plays, order of, 5

Seeking a Premier Economy

The Economic Effects of British Economic Reforms, 1980–2000

National Bureau
of Economic Research
Comparative Labor Markets Series

Seeking a Premier Economy
The Economic Effects of British Economic Reforms, 1980–2000

Edited by

David Card, Richard Blundell, and Richard B. Freeman

The University of Chicago Press

Chicago and London

David Card is the Class of 1950 Professor of Economics at the University of California–Berkeley and a research associate of the National Bureau of Economic Research (NBER). Richard Blundell is the Leverhulme Research Professor at University College London, director of the Economic and Social Research Council Centre for the Microeconomic Analysis of Public Policy, Institute for Fiscal Studies, and research director at the Institute for Fiscal Studies. Richard B. Freeman is the Herbert Ascherman Professor of Economics at Harvard University, program director of the NBER labor studies program, and senior research fellow at the Centre for Economic Performance of the London School of Economics.

The University of Chicago Press, Chicago 60637
The University of Chicago Press, Ltd., London

Printed in the United States of America
13 12 11 10 09 08 07 06 05 04 1 2 3 4 5
ISBN: 0-226-09284-4 (cloth)

Library of Congress Cataloging-in-Publication Data

Seeking a premier economy : the economic effects of British economic reforms, 1980–2000 / edited by David Card, Richard Blundell, and Richard B. Freeman.
p. cm. — (National Bureau of Economic Research comparative labor markets series)
"The papers were presented at a preliminary conference and a final conference at the Centre for Economic Performance, London, UK"—Ack.
Includes bibliographical references and index.
ISBN 0-226-09284-4 (cloth : acid-free paper)
1. Great Britain—Economic policy—1997—Congresses.
2. Great Britain—Economic policy—1979–1997—Congresses.
3. Great Britain—Economic conditions—1997—Congresses.
4. Great Britain—Economic conditions—1979–1997—Congresses.
I. Title: Economic effects of British economic reforms, 1980–2000.
II. Card, David E. (David Edward), 1956– III. Blundell, Richard.
IV. Freeman, Richard B. (Richard Barry), 1948– V. London School of Economics and Political Science. Centre for Economic Performance. VI. Series.

HC256.7.S44 2004
330.941′0858—dc22 2003066282

♾ The paper used in this publication meets the minimum requirements of the American National Standard for Information Sciences—Permanence of Paper for Printed Library Materials, ANSI Z39.48-1992.

Relation of the Directors to the Work and Publications of the National Bureau of Economic Research

1. The object of the NBER is to ascertain and present to the economics profession, and to the public more generally, important economic facts and their interpretation in a scientific manner without policy recommendations. The Board of Directors is charged with the responsibility of ensuring that the work of the NBER is carried on in strict conformity with this object.

2. The President shall establish an internal review process to ensure that book manuscripts proposed for publication DO NOT contain policy recommendations. This shall apply both to the proceedings of conferences and to manuscripts by a single author or by one or more coauthors but shall not apply to authors of comments at NBER conferences who are not NBER affiliates.

3. No book manuscript reporting research shall be published by the NBER until the President has sent to each member of the Board a notice that a manuscript is recommended for publication and that in the President's opinion it is suitable for publication in accordance with the above principles of the NBER. Such notification will include a table of contents and an abstract or summary of the manuscript's content, a list of contributors if applicable, and a response form for use by Directors who desire a copy of the manuscript for review. Each manuscript shall contain a summary drawing attention to the nature and treatment of the problem studied and the main conclusions reached.

4. No volume shall be published until forty-five days have elapsed from the above notification of intention to publish it. During this period a copy shall be sent to any Director requesting it, and if any Director objects to publication on the grounds that the manuscript contains policy recommendations, the objection will be presented to the author(s) or editor(s). In case of dispute, all members of the Board shall be notified, and the President shall appoint an ad hoc committee of the Board to decide the matter; thirty days additional shall be granted for this purpose.

5. The President shall present annually to the Board a report describing the internal manuscript review process, any objections made by Directors before publication or by anyone after publication, any disputes about such matters, and how they were handled.

6. Publications of the NBER issued for informational purposes concerning the work of the Bureau, or issued to inform the public of the activities at the Bureau, including but not limited to the NBER Digest and Reporter, shall be consistent with the object stated in paragraph 1. They shall contain a specific disclaimer noting that they have not passed through the review procedures required in this resolution. The Executive Committee of the Board is charged with the review of all such publications from time to time.

7. NBER working papers and manuscripts distributed on the Bureau's web site are not deemed to be publications for the purpose of this resolution, but they shall be consistent with the object stated in paragraph 1. Working papers shall contain a specific disclaimer noting that they have not passed through the review procedures required in this resolution. The NBER's web site shall contain a similar disclaimer. The President shall establish an internal review process to ensure that the working papers and the web site do not contain policy recommendations, and shall report annually to the Board on this process and any concerns raised in connection with it.

8. Unless otherwise determined by the Board or exempted by the terms of paragraphs 6 and 7, a copy of this resolution shall be printed in each NBER publication as described in paragraph 2 above.

Contents

Acknowledgments ix

Introduction 1
David Card, Richard Blundell, and Richard B. Freeman

1. **What Have Two Decades of British Economic Reform Delivered?** 9
David Card and Richard B. Freeman

2. **Seeking a Premier-League Economy: The Role of Privatization** 63
Richard Green and Jonathan Haskel

3. **Shared Modes of Compensation and Firm Performance: U.K. Evidence** 109
Martin J. Conyon and Richard B. Freeman

4. **Characteristics of Foreign-Owned Firms in British Manufacturing** 147
Rachel Griffith and Helen Simpson

5. **The Surprising Retreat of Union Britain** 181
John Pencavel

6. **Pension Reform and Economic Performance in Britain in the 1980s and 1990s** 233
Richard Disney, Carl Emmerson, and Sarah Smith

7. **Labor Market Reforms and Changes in Wage Inequality in the United Kingdom and the United States** 275
Amanda Gosling and Thomas Lemieux

8. **Whither Poverty in Great Britain and the United States? The Determinants of Changing Poverty and Whether Work Will Work** 313
Richard Dickens and David T. Ellwood

9. **Mobility and Joblessness** 371
Paul Gregg, Stephen Machin, and Alan Manning

10. **Has "In-Work" Benefit Reform Helped the Labor Market?** 411
Richard Blundell and Hilary Hoynes

11. **Active Labor Market Policies and the British New Deal for the Young Unemployed in Context** 461
John Van Reenen

Contributors 497
Author Index 499
Subject Index 505

Acknowledgments

The contributions in this volume are the result of a major research project on the economy of the United Kingdom organized jointly by the National Bureau of Economic Research (NBER) and the Centre for Economic Performance (CEP) of the London School of Economics and the Economic and Social Research Council Centre for the Microeconomic Analysis of Public Policy at the Institute for Fiscal Studies (IFS). The motivation for the project was the continuing effort of U.K. governments, from the Conservatives in the 1980s through Labour in the 1990s, to improve economic efficiency in the country by developing more market-friendly policies and economic institutions. The project benefited greatly from discussions with numerous government, union, business, and academic experts and leaders in the United Kingdom, many of whom were involved with developing and introducing these policies.

The papers were presented at a preliminary conference and a final conference at the Centre for Economic Performance, London, United Kingdom. We thank the many conference participants, particularly the discussants, for their many valuable comments. The volume would not have been possible without the valuable assistance of the staff at NBER and the CEP. We are particularly grateful to Jennifer Amadeo-Holl of the NBER.

The research for this volume was done by economists from the CEP, the IFS, and the NBER. The IFS is an independent research institute dedicated to providing rigorous analysis of economic policy and of the functioning of the U.K. economy. It disseminates that research widely through publications, the media, and regular meetings with all levels of government. The CEP is an interdisciplinary research center at the London School of Economics. In 2003 it won the Queen's Prize as the outstanding science center in the United Kingdom. The major portion of the funding for this project came from the CEP as part of its ongoing efforts to analyze the U.K. economy and assess private and public policies to improve U.K. economic performance.

Introduction

David Card, Richard Blundell, and Richard B. Freeman

In the 1980s and 1990s, successive U.K. governments enacted a series of economic reforms designed to establish a more market-oriented economy. The goal was to arrest the long-term economic decline in the United Kingdom relative to other advanced countries and to establish a premier-league economy that would improve living standards for all citizens.[1] At the beginning of the period, the United Kingdom was a highly regulated economy with large nationalized industries, an extensive welfare state, and exceptionally obstreperous labor-management relations. By the end of the period, the United Kingdom was one of the least regulated and nationalized economies in the Organization for Economic Cooperation and Development (OECD), with a welfare system that was increasingly based on in-work benefits, rather than benefits to persons out of work, and a trade union movement that was concerned with the "value added" that unions can bring to the economy more than other union movements in the advanced world. Indexes of economic freedom that measure the market friendliness of economic policies and institutions show that the United Kingdom had moved from the middle of the pack of OECD countries to a lead position, close to that of the United States. Nearly all groups and po-

David Card is the Class of 1950 Professor of Economics at the University of California–Berkeley and a research associate of the National Bureau of Economic Research (NBER). Richard Blundell is the Leverhulme Research Professor at University College London, director of the Economic and Social Research Council Centre for the Microeconomic Analysis of Public Policy, Institute for Fiscal Studies, and research director at the Institute for Fiscal Studies. Richard B. Freeman is the Herbert Ascherman Professor of Economics at Harvard University, program director of the NBER labor studies program, and senior research fellow at the Centre for Economic Performance of the London School of Economics.

1. "Premiere league" refers to the top athletic league in football or soccer in the United Kingdom.

litical parties in the United Kingdom had come to accept many of the initially controversial changes that constituted the "Thatcher Revolution," albeit with different emphases and concerns over how best to assure that the market reforms benefitted society as a whole.

The extent and breadth of the changes in its economic policies and institutions that the United Kingdom introduced from 1980 to 2000 are breathtaking. Among the many changes that occurred were the following:

- Privatization of most of the nationalized industries and of many governmental functions that had never before been performed by private groups
- Development of new in-work benefits and a reduction in the incentives for persons to be out of work, accompanied by other more active labor market policies
- Revised labor laws that limited union powers and increased the potential for members to affect key decisions, leading to substantial changes in union attitudes and policies in the 1980s and the introduction of new modes for union recognition in the 2000s
- Changes in the structure and financing of the educational system, covering students from age four through the university level, with the development of a national curriculum and a more centralized education system
- Development of new modes of financing pensions that shifted the burden of funding from the state to individuals through company pension plans or private plans
- The enacting of tax laws that encouraged employee share ownership
- Increased housing ownership by the sale of council flats to residents
- Elimination of restrictions on capital flows
- Restructuring of the National Health Insurance medical system
- Elimination of wage council's modes of setting minimum wages and eventual introduction of a national minimum wage
- Regular publication of league tables in the public sector to measure the effectiveness of individual hospitals and schools

During the reform period, the secular decline of the United Kingdom in productivity and gross domestic product (GDP) per capita relative to other advanced countries—including such major European Union (EU) competitors as Germany, France, and Italy—came to an end. By the 1990s, the country was outperforming most other advanced economies in the level of unemployment and in producing a high employment to population rate. At the same time, there was a large rise in income inequality, which was the result of rapidly growing incomes for persons at the top of the income distribution rather than of falling incomes for persons at the bottom of the distribution. This meant that the United Kingdom avoided the U.S. problem of falling real earnings for lower-paid workers.

The rough concordance of economic changes with reforms provides weak or circumstantial evidence that the reforms succeeded in altering the U.K. economy. The macroeconomic evidence is weak or circumstantial because, at the level of an entire economy, it is difficult to determine what the appropriate counterfactual is for the observed patterns. Perhaps the relative economic performance of the United Kingdom would have improved even absent market-friendly changes in policies. New Zealand introduced diverse market reforms much like those in the United Kingdom, but its economic performance worsened relative to other countries. Some smaller EU countries, such as the Netherlands or Ireland, performed well without undertaking massive pro-market reforms. To determine whether reforms did in fact contribute to the United Kingdom's improved economic performance, to the United Kingdom's rise in inequality, or to both, one must examine the microeconomics of particular reforms and their impact on intended and unintended economic outcomes.

This volume presents a set of studies that assesses some of the economic reforms that the United Kingdom adopted in the 1980s and 1990s. Since it is not feasible to study the full set of reforms in detail, researchers selected some reforms for investigation—in particular, those dealing with labor and product markets that are likely to have had an impact on productivity, employment, and income inequality—while leaving analyses of other reforms to other groups, notably the changes in the national health system and in transportation.

The studies were undertaken by a team of British, Canadian, and American economists under the auspices of the NBER, the Centre for Economic Performance (CEP), and the Institute for Fiscal Studies. The researchers regularly discussed the issues with government, union, business, and academic decision makers as well as with experts in the United Kingdom as the work proceeded. The studies were conducted during 1998–2001, when the U.K. economy was performing exceptionally well and when many analysts around the world viewed the U.S. economic model as being the most effective capitalist economy and viewed the United Kingdom as the closest representative of that model in the EU.

With the exception of chapter 1, the work is almost entirely microeconomic in approach, focusing on the impacts of particular reforms on closely associated outcomes rather than on the macroeconomy. This microeconomic approach offers more readily determinable counterfactuals than do analyses of aggregate outcomes. It allows researchers to compare specific outcomes before and after reforms; to compare the outcomes for persons, firms, or sectors more or less affected by the reforms; and to make composite comparisons of outcomes before and after reforms between people or enterprises more or less affected by the reforms (differences in differences). Given the measurement error of GDP, any particular reform will probably have impacts on GDP that are hard to discern, and so the micro approach provides the only reliable way to assess the benefits and costs of particular changes. At the same time, the microeconomic approach misses the possibility that reforms cumulate to something greater than their linear sum and that they produce nonlinear synergies or externalities in the aggregate economy.

The Major Theme

The principal finding of this volume is that the bulk of the U.K. economic reforms that were studied contributed positively to the economic performance of the country but with some cost in rising inequality. Since the real wage rose, however, policy did not create poverty, although possibly some other set of policy changes might have reduced (or raised) poverty. However, some heralded reforms in social programs, such as changes in benefit schedules, had more modest positive impacts on economic performance than proponents anticipated and correspondingly less adverse impacts on income distribution than opponents feared. The reason for this is that the United Kingdom's income-linked benefit system is highly interrelated, so that the declines in the amount received or the eligibility to participate in one benefit program are often partially offset by increased participation in other benefit programs. This makes both the incentive effects and the income distribution effects of reforms much less than might first appear to be the case from an analysis of a single program. Reforms of trade union law accomplished their purpose of weakening union power in the labor market but, in conjunction with a more competitive economy, also contributed to important changes in union behavior. Underlying this broad theme is a set of specific findings pertaining to the reforms that our project analyzed.

Specific Findings

First, the U.K. reforms accomplished their main policy goal of making the economy and, in particular, the labor market more market-friendly. Diverse measures of the degree to which market forces rather than administrative rulings determine economic outcomes show that the United Kingdom became one of the most market-friendly economies in the advanced world. These measures range from the broad aggregate "indexes of economic freedom" developed by conservative think tanks to more specific indexes of labor market and product market regulations that the OECD and various independent scholars have developed. The United Kingdom deregulated product markets and privatized nationalized industries earlier and/or to a greater extent than its main EU partners. In the labor market, the absence of employment protection and other regulations meant that the United Kingdom was more market dependent than other EU countries, even while they reduced regulations and the United Kingdom did not do so (Card and Freeman, chap. 1 of this volume).

Second, in the area of product-market reforms, our studies have found that the privatization of traditionally nationalized industries was a major part of the U.K. economic reforms and reduced the publicly owned proportion of GDP from 12 percent in 1979 to 2 percent two decades later. Much of the privatization effort was undertaken so that the private sector would make the massive investments needed in the relevant sectors, rather than having the public sector make the investments, which would be counted as part of public spending. In most cases, however, because of the nature of the business, privatization was accompanied by increased regulatory activity. Privatization was associated with improved productivity, but the improvement occurred largely before the actual act of privatization as the public-sector managers restructured existing plants in order to bring the public firm to market. Whether the public-sector firms could have undertaken similar changes while remaining public is uncertain (Green and Haskel, chap. 2 in this volume).

Third, with its freedom to move capital and extensive stock market, the United Kingdom has a particularly open capital market, which makes it easy for foreign firms to enter. Establishments that are foreign owned tend to have higher and more rapidly increasing labor productivity than domestic firms. This is due primarily to higher levels of investment and a larger proportion of skilled and higher-paid workers. But establishments that change ownership nationality do not experience large changes in productivity. Thus, it appears that it is largely through greater investment in human and physical capital that foreign-owned firms make a special contribution to the U.K. economy (Griffith and Simpson, chap. 4 in this volume).

Fourth, the United Kingdom sought to increase share ownership by workers in their own firms with the hope of improving the commitment of workers to the firm and raising productivity through employee ownership. The specific policies to encourage employee ownership and involvement varied modestly over time, but the basic idea in all cases was to give tax breaks to firms that provided profit sharing, stock options, or stock ownership to workers. Unlike the United States, where employee stock ownership plans encourage collective ownership in retirement plans, the U.K. schemes encourage individual ownership. The results of this policy appear to be positive. Firms that reward workers in part on the basis of company performance have a higher incidence of information sharing and consultation with workers than do other firms. Also, while the productivity effects of programs vary with the particulars, firms that have profit sharing and employee share in ownership tend to outperform other firms in productivity and financial performance (Conyon and Freeman, chap. 3 in this volume).

In the area of social policy reforms, the United Kingdom sought to improve the incentive for working in its social welfare system, with some modest success.

The fifth finding is that the main thrust of U.K. reforms of welfare programs has been to increase the benefits that accrue to those who work compared to those who do not. In 1988, the relevant legislation was the Family Tax Credit of 1988. In 1999, this was replaced by the Working Families Tax Credit. The U.K. reforms had a much more modest effect on labor supply than comparable reforms in the United States, where the Earned Income Tax Credit and the Temporary Assistance for Needy Families (TANF) welfare policy produced a sizable drop in welfare roles and increased employment among the affected families. The prime reason for this is that in the United Kingdom income from in-work benefits counts as income in the computation of housing and other benefits, and thus policy reforms have a much-dampened impact on the incentive to work. In addition, the United Kingdom increased out-of-work benefits while the United States reduced those benefits, providing less incentive to increase labor supply (Blundell and Hoynes, chap. 10 in this volume).

Sixth, U.K. policies toward unemployed young persons were also designed to move people from dependence on the state to work. The New Deal for young people introduced in 1998 had both push and pull elements to get young unemployed persons into work. Some of the push involved toughening the work search criterion along lines originally developed in the mid-1980s. The pull involved a job subsidy for employers as well as government or volunteer work for young persons unable to find regular jobs. Despite publicity that implied that the program involved massive increases in spending and huge numbers of young people, the program had a marginal positive impact in raising youth employment at a modest additional cost. On net, the social benefits of the additional employment appear to have outweighed the costs (Van Reenan, chap. 11 in this volume).

Seventh, the basic design of the United Kingdom's pension reforms was to encourage workers and firms to contract out a portion of pensions through fully funded occupational schemes, which would reduce the pay-as-you-go costs of publicly provided pensions. The law required individuals to belong to some pension plan: an employers' scheme, a state-funded scheme, or an individually purchased scheme. Favorable tax advantages induced a large proportion of the population to purchase personal pensions in the 1980s and 1990s. At the end of the 1990s, the Labour Party government introduced further reforms with its stakeholder pensions for low-wage workers. The shift to greater reliance on private pension provision allowed the United Kingdom to have the lowest rate of future state spending on pensions among advanced countries. The development of private pensions appears to have improved job mobility, with workers who chose private pensions evincing more mobility than those with company pension plans (Disney, Emmerson, and Smith, chap. 6 in this volume).

In the area of the labor market and income distribution, the eighth finding is that the United Kingdom moved from reliance on collective bargaining in the determination of wages and working conditions to reliance on the competitive market. The decline was due in part to labor-law reforms designed to curb union power but also to the greater competition in the product market that required firms to reform their industrial-relations practices. Prior to reforms, the United Kingdom's unionized sector was marked by lower productivity and considerable strike activity. Faced with a tight macroeconomic environment, greater competition from nonunion firms, and loss of government statutory and nonstatutory support, unionized establishments adopted new work practices that brought labor productivity up to nonunion levels. Since U.K. employers do not have the same antiunion animus of U.S. firms, the Labour government's industrial-relations reforms that make it easier for unions to gain recognition from firms are likely to have only small consequences for the coverage of collective bargaining (Pencavel, chap. 5 in this volume).

Ninth, institutional changes in the labor market—such as the decline of unionization in the 1980s and 1990s and the introduction of the national minimum wage in 1999—had substantial impacts on the level of income inequality. The more rapid decline of unionization in the United Kingdom than in the United States was a major factor in the more rapid increase in inequality in the United Kingdom. By contrast, the introduction of the national minimum wage in the United Kingdom contributed to the convergence in the pattern of inequality among women. Inequality among women was higher in the United Kingdom than in the United States before the United Kingdom enacted its minimum wage and remained higher afterwards, but the minimum wage reduced the U.K. inequality toward the American level in 1999. Overall, the extent and pattern of wage inequality in the United Kingdom became increasingly similar to that in the United States as the United Kingdom adopted a more market-driven U.S.-style economy (Gosling and Lemieux, chap. 7 in this volume).

Tenth, the United Kingdom subsidizes council housing to tenants and sells the housing to tenants at attractive rates. Although home ownership can be viewed as a positive good in itself, it has been criticized as potentially immobilizing tenants and thus producing pockets of poverty and unemployment. However, the implicit rent subsidy in council housing appears to be less important in reducing mobility than the lack of skills among tenants: U.K. residential mobility is in the middle of rates in the EU, and the sale of council housing in the 1990s did not produce ghettoized neighborhoods. In contrast to the localized job market for nongraduate workers, the United Kingdom developed an integrated market for graduate workers. A principal reason for the difference is that unemployed less-educated workers rarely move to different regions without having first found a job, whereas university graduates are highly mobile upon graduation (Gregg, Machin, and Manning, chap. 9 in this volume).

In sharp contrast to the convergence of inequality between the United

Kingdom and the United States, the eleventh finding is that the rates of poverty measured in absolute terms diverged between the two countries. In the United Kingdom, expanding government benefits reduced poverty considerably, whereas in the United States the impact of benefits was almost negligible. The greatest divergence in benefits is for workless households, whose proportion has grown sharply in the United Kingdom while falling in the United States. Over the same period, relative poverty, which depends critically on the distribution of wages, rose more sharply in the United Kingdom than in the United States, bringing the overall income distribution of the two countries closer together (Dickens and Ellwood, chap. 8 in this volume).

Conclusion

Overall, the efforts of successive U.K. governments to make the economy more market oriented appear to have succeeded, particularly in the 1990s. The reforms studied in this volume improved productivity and contributed to the greater work activity of persons obtaining social benefits, while at the same time contributing to earnings and income inequality although not to absolute poverty. Since the reforms—like most other economic changes—almost surely had adverse effects on some groups in society, for which compensation is rarely paid, some may decide that those costs are not worth the improvement in economic performance, while others believe that the benefits exceed the cost. In any case, the general message of the studies in this volume is clear: The market-oriented reforms of the United Kingdom seem to have accomplished their broad goal of improving U.K. economic performance after a long period of relative decline. Still, we note that the market-oriented reforms did not bring U.K. productivity to the level of the United States or to the level of its major EU partners, leaving it a bit short of the premier-league status that the country hoped to attain. This suggests that further reforms may be necessary for the United Kingdom to catch up with the best-performing economies. What those reforms might be, as well as the potential benefits and risks of further movements toward market determination of economic outcomes or of increased public spending and administrative allocation of resources, lies beyond the scope of our study.

1

What Have Two Decades of British Economic Reform Delivered?

David Card and Richard B. Freeman

For much of the nineteenth and twentieth centuries, the British economy, which pioneered the Industrial Revolution, had a disappointing growth record, falling markedly from the top ranks in the league economic tables. In 1979, the United Kingdom was twelfth in per capita gross domestic product (GDP) among advanced Organization for Economic Cooperation and Development (OECD) member countries, well below Germany, France, and other European Union (EU) economies.[1] In response to this weak economic performance, successive U.K. governments adopted policies designed to move the economy back to "premiere league" status. Beginning with Margaret Thatcher and continuing under John Major and Tony Blair, these reforms sought to increase the efficacy of labor and product markets and limit government and institutional involvement in economic decision making.

The trend toward more markets and less government is not unique to the United Kingdom. Many other advanced economies also responded to the economic challenges of the 1980s and 1990s by granting markets more leeway in the allocation of resources and the setting of prices. All the major

David Card is the Class of 1950 Professor of Economics at the University of California–Berkeley and a research associate of the National Bureau of Economic Research (NBER). Richard B. Freeman is the Herbert Ascherman Professor of Economics at Harvard University, program director of the NBER labor studies program, and senior research fellow at the Centre for Economic Performance of the London School of Economics.

We are grateful to Till von Wachter and Rishi Madlani for research assistance and to Mary O'Mahoney for generously sharing her data.

1. This refers to GDP per capita in purchasing power parity (PPP) units, as reported in our table 1.8, which includes thirteen OECD countries. The precise position of the United Kingdom varies with the number of countries included in the analysis and particular PPP adjustments used.

economies eliminated restrictions on the flow of capital by the early 1980s. Most privatized state-run industries in the 1980s and 1990s. All lowered marginal-tax rates for high-income earners. Most also made labor contracts more flexible and moved from national wage setting to more localized collective agreements in the 1990s. For its part, the EU Commission pushed competition policies and the reduction of subsidies to declining industries while seeking a uniform social charter to regulate labor market outcomes. Outside the EU, the other English-speaking economies—the United States, Canada, Australia, and New Zealand—moved toward less state and institutional intervention in the economy.

Have two decades of economic reform significantly shifted the market orientation of the U.K. economy relative to other advanced OECD economies, or has the United Kingdom only kept pace with its peers? What have the reforms done for aggregate economic output and the average income of citizens? Have the reforms improved the position of the United Kingdom in the economic league tables?

This paper examines these questions. Section 1.1 compares the market orientation of the United Kingdom relative to other advanced economies using a diverse set of market indicators. We find that the post-1980 reforms have made the United Kingdom more market friendly than its EU competitors and that, in the 1990s, the United Kingdom ranked higher on some measures of freedom of markets than the United States. Section 1.2 contrasts macroeconomic outcomes. We show that from the 1980s through the 1990s the United Kingdom arrested the relative declines in gross domestic product (GDP) per capita and labor productivity that characterized earlier decades, and partially closed the gap in per capita income with France and Germany through relative gains in employment and hours. While the United Kingdom did not experience an American-style "New Economy" boom, it combined high employment-population rates with rising real wages for workers—an achievement that the United States was unable to match until the late 1990s. Section 1.3 examines the link between the reforms and outcomes. Since there is no ready counterfactual against which to compare the observed U.K. performance, our analysis is more judgmental. Based on macro-level analyses and the micro-level evidence available from several companion studies, we conclude that economic reforms contributed to halting the nearly century-long trend in relative economic decline of the United Kingdom relative to its historic competitors, Germany and France.

1.1 The Market Friendliness of the United Kingdom and Other Advanced Economies

> They used, when I first came in, to talk about us in terms of the British disease. Now they talk about us and say, "Look, Britain has got the cure.

Come to Britain to see how Britain has done it." That is an enormous turn-around. (Margaret Thatcher, *Financial Times,* 15 February 1988)

Government should have a role that is enabling: supporting small businesses, encouraging technological advance; investing in science; above all, promoting competition and removing the barriers to business growth . . . I call it a Third Way . . . Supporting wealth creation. Tackling vested interests. Using market mechanisms. (Tony Blair, speech at World Economic Forum, Davos, Switzerland, 18 January 2000)

For the past two decades, British economic reforms have been motivated by a desire to increase the reliance on market forces relative to the role of the state in the determination of prices and the allocation of resources. Thatcher's Conservative government privatized industries and council housing, enacted laws to weaken trade unions, created financial incentives for workers to choose private pensions, and reduced the benefits available to unemployed workers—all the while preserving national health insurance and other features of the welfare state. The subsequent Major government pursued a similar agenda, abolishing the Wages Councils and privatizing many of the remaining state-owned enterprises. In the late 1990s, Blair's New Labour government continued to introduce market-enhancing reforms. It created tax breaks for employee share-ownership programs, opposed EU directives that business interpreted as antibusiness, and enhanced the work incentives of the income support system. In the realm of monetary policy, the Labour Party went beyond the Tories by shifting interest-rate-setting authority from the Treasury to an independent Monetary Policy committee. While there are some exceptions—the Thatcher campaign to centralize public-sector decision making and limit the independence of local government, and the Blair efforts to ease the formation of unions and introduce a national minimum wage—the main goal of the U.K. policy reforms has been to reduce the economic role of the state and enhance the role of markets in determining economic outcomes.[2]

For purposes of analyzing the potential effect of these reforms on the economic performance of the United Kingdom *relative* to other advanced countries, it is important to determine whether these reforms were larger or smaller than, or similar to, those in other advanced countries. This in turn requires measures of the institutional and policy stance of advanced countries. In the absence of a single GDP-style measure of the free-market stance of economies, we use a variety of indicators that rate countries by the way different markets determine outcomes. Some of these indicators are based on objective data, while others are based on the assessments of

2. Since local governments must compete for residents and businesses (in the Tiebout sense), we suspect that market forces exert greater discipline on the local public sector than on the central government. We therefore classify reforms that decentralize political decision making as pro-market and those that centralize authority as anti-market.

expert analysts or surveys of managers. Some of the measures are produced by think tanks with conservative ideological bents, such as the Fraser Institute's and Heritage Foundation's "economic freedom" indexes. These indexes stress particular measures of economic freedom, including low taxes, that fit a more conservative agenda while excluding social-inclusion factors such as education spending. Another broad set of measures are the indexes of "competitiveness" produced by the World Economic Forum, most recently in conjunction with the Harvard Center for International Development. These indexes mix the stance of policy, institutions, and specific outcomes and give more favorable scores to social democratic regimes that perform well economically than do the economic freedom indexes. Finally, the OECD and some independent scholars have produced diverse indexes of regulations and procedures in particular markets, such as labor markets, product markets, and capital markets.

All of these measures of the market friendliness of institutions have shortcomings. Some are formed by weighting linear sums of subindexes, with the weights determined subjectively and with some potential measures excluded; some choose scalings for their measures that have little basis in theory or other empirical work; and some treat written regulations as if laws or administrative decrees were enforced, when in fact enforcement of regulations that limit markets may vary across countries. All of the measures ignore potential complementarities or substitutions among institutions. The economic freedom indexes, which are designed to measure the economic stance of entire economies, differ in several ways among themselves. The Fraser Institute index includes military conscription, top-marginal-tax rates, transfers and subsidies, and the size of government expenditure. The Heritage Foundation and Wall Street Journal (Heritage/WSJ) index includes corporate and value added taxes as well as government expenditure, but it ignores conscription and individual tax rates. Both the Fraser and Heritage measures include low inflation, which is an outcome of institutions and policies rather than a measure of freedom in markets.

Competitiveness indexes have other problems. The groups who provide these measures have changed their modes of calculating competitiveness over time, and so their indexes do not reflect the same underlying data over time. In 2001, for example, the Fraser Institute revised its historical indexes, producing generally modest adjustments as it accumulated additional data (see http://www.fraserinstitute.ca). The World Economic Forum and Harvard Center for International Development's 2000 *Competitiveness Report* reported two different indexes, one for "current competitiveness" and one for "growth competitiveness," reflecting the different weights placed on the same data for different purposes. Finally, the measures for individual markets can be criticized for focusing on some features of markets and regulatory mechanisms but not on others. For instance, measures of labor market performance concentrate on the extent of centralization of bargaining and employment protection legislation but not on the potential for court suits over discrimination or insurance of pension moneys. Comparisons of the market friendliness of product markets ignore differences in bankruptcy laws, which can greatly affect business formation and dissolution. While the subindexes necessarily cover only parts of economies, they provide checks on the more aggregate measures. If an aggregate index rates an economy as market friendly even though it has highly restrictive labor contracts or a highly regulated product market, then we will know that something is amiss. These measures also allow analysts to relate policies or institutions to the specific outcomes they are designed to affect, rather than to measures like GDP per capita, which depend on a wider set of factors.

Differences and shortcomings among the indexes notwithstanding, the principal indicators of the market stance of economies show that the policy reforms of the 1980s and 1990s made the United Kingdom one of the most market-friendly economies in the world. The high ranking of the United Kingdom in market friendliness at the turn of the twenty-first century reflects that there were more rapid market-oriented reforms in the United Kingdom than in most other advanced economies, rather than any increased regulation in other countries.

1.1.1 Measures of Economic Freedom

The indexes of economic freedom produced by the Fraser Institute and the Heritage Foundation value key features of capitalist economies: private property rights, freedom to operate a business, and freedom of capital and labor markets. Both include measures of free trade, which reflect international policies, while neither includes measures of immigration policies. Each treats cursorily the labor market institutions on which much policy discourse concentrated in the wake of the divergence of unemployment- and employment-population rates between the United States and the EU in the 1980s and 1990s. The indexes differ in their emphasis on particular dimensions of "freedom" (Hanke and Walters 1997). The Fraser Institute index rates countries with military conscription as having less economic freedom and gives countries with high top-marginal tax rates and government transfers and subsidies low scores.[3] The Heritage/WSJ index includes low corporate taxes and low value added taxes. Reflecting the view that even a democratically chosen state sector is inimical to economic freedom, the Fraser and Heritage indexes rate the size of government as an important negative indicator of freedom. The Fraser and Heritage measures

3. Comparing the higher ranking that the Heritage/WSJ gives to Israel, which has conscription, than the rank given by the Fraser Institute, Alvin Rabushka (2000) argues that the "Fraser Institute index is far superior to that of the Heritage/WSJ. It is based on far more extensive research, deliberation, and testing by far more qualified and distinguished scholars."

also count low inflation, which is an *outcome* of institutions and policies, as a measure of economic freedom.

There is a third aggregate index of economic freedom, the Freedom House indicator, which differs somewhat from both the Fraser and Heritage measures. This indicator was produced only once, however, and we exclude it from our analysis. It differs from the Fraser and Heritage/WSJ indexes by considering freedom of association in the labor market as a measure of economic freedom but ignoring tax rates. It is sufficiently well correlated with the other two indicators in the period covered by all three measures that we do no harm to the analysis by leaving it out.

While the Fraser and Heritage measures lead to somewhat different rankings of the market stance of particular countries, the high correlation between them shows that they are measuring essentially the same phenomenon. For all of the countries covered, including the less developed countries, Hanke and Walters (1997) report a rank-order correlation between the two indexes of 0.85 in 1995 to 1996. For advanced OECD countries, we obtain rank correlations of 0.83 between the Fraser and Heritage/WSJ measures. Most important, both indexes give a relatively high rank to the United Kingdom in the 1990s. In the Heritage/WSJ, the United Kingdom ranks third in 1996 among advanced OECD countries in market friendliness (after the United States and New Zealand, tied with the Netherlands) and fifth in 2001 (after Ireland, New Zealand, the United States, and Luxemburg).[4] According to the Fraser Institute index, in 1995 the United Kingdom was tied for second with the United States among the advanced OECD countries (after New Zealand), while in 1999 it ranked second after New Zealand and just ahead of the United States.[5]

The Fraser Institute Index

Because the Fraser Institute index (FII) is available from 1970 to the present, while the Heritage index covers a shorter period, we use the FII to measure the *change* in the United Kingdom's position over time. The FII measures the degree of economic freedom on a scale from 1 to 100, with higher values reflecting more freedom in market transactions.

Table 1.1 reports the FII for the United Kingdom and other major OECD countries every five years from 1970 to 1995 and for 1999. The levels and trends in the FII for various countries accord well with informal observations on the level and change in policy stances toward markets. Most analysts place the United States and other English-speaking coun-

4. In the Freedom House ranking in 1996, the United Kingdom was tied with the United States and four other countries for the top rank.

5. We have excluded Singapore, Hong Kong, and Bahrein from the rankings since they are not advanced OECD countries, but in various years they score higher than the United Kingdom.

Table 1.1 **Fraser Institute Economic Freedom Ratings: The United Kingdom and Other Advanced OECD Economies, 1970–1999**

	1970	1975	1980	1985	1990	1995	1999	Change 1980–1999
United Kingdom	64	63	66	79	84	87	88	22
Rank out of 22	19	13	15	5	2	2	2	2
Major comparisons								
Germany	80	73	77	77	81	80	80	3
France	72	60	63	63	76	79	75	12
United States	77	80	84	85	88	87	87	3
Other developed countries								
Australia	80	65	74	78	80	84	85	11
Austria	71	60	67	67	74	76	80	13
Belgium	91	75	78	79	80	82	79	1
Canada	80	73	79	81	84	80	82	3
Denmark	72	63	65	67	77	80	80	15
Finland	77	62	69	72	76	79	81	12
Greece	63	58	57	52	61	72	73	16
Ireland	68	61	66	67	73	86	85	19
Italy	68	54	56	59	72	72	78	22
Japan	73	69	75	76	81	81	79	4
Luxembourg	91	91	89	92	82	83	84	–5
The Netherlands	85	71	78	79	82	84	84	6
New Zealand	69	56	64	63	80	90	89	25
Norway	69	57	60	67	76	79	78	18
Portugal	58	33	56	56	64	79	78	22
Spain	67	59	61	63	69	80	76	14
Sweden	57	56	61	67	73	79	79	18
Switzerland	88	79	83	86	84	83	85	2

Source: Data from Fraser Institute (2001). The figures in this edition differ somewhat from those in earlier editions, as the Fraser Institute updated its estimates for earlier years as well as adding 1999 data.
Notes: A higher score denotes a more favorable ranking. In several cases, the United Kingdom is tied with one or more other countries at the particular rank.

tries at the market-friendly end of the spectrum, and Nordic countries and other social-democratic EU countries at the other end. The FII orders the countries in the same manner. Still, the index has potential errors. It does not deal with the implementation or enforcement of regulations that limit markets, so countries like Italy with a sizable underground economy are arguably given too low a score. It also ignores the use of the judicial system to regulate market transactions, which may lead to an overstatement of the market freedoms in the United States. From 1970 to 1975, the index shows a decline in economic freedom in most countries (although not in the United States) when governments struggled to control inflationary pressures. This is odd, since the United States introduced wage and price controls in this period, while many other countries relied on collective-bargaining agreements to contain wage pressures.[6] From 1980 to 1999, the trend was for increased market freedoms.

Focusing on the United Kingdom, the FII tells a clear story about trends in the market friendliness. In the 1970s, before the Thatcher reforms, the United Kingdom scored relatively low among advanced countries in the economic-freedom league table. In 1970 and 1975, when the United Kingdom had exchange controls, it ranked seventeenth and sixteenth. In 1980, it was in thirteenth position. It rose because it eliminated those controls. Thereafter, it jumped sharply in the rankings, so that by 1999 the United Kingdom stood second behind only New Zealand among the advanced OECD countries. Measured by the change in FII points, the United Kingdom was the third most reformed economy between 1980 and 1999, after New Zealand and Portugal. Thus, in an epoch of increasing market-friendly economic reforms, the United Kingdom reformed more than most other advanced countries.

The FII contains seven components, four of which—the total size of government expenditures, monetary policy and price stability, regulation of international exchange and freedom to trade with foreigners, and freedom to use alternative currencies—fall outside the purview of the micro-domestic policies that are our primary focus. Accordingly, in table 1.2 we show the three components of the FII that more closely reflect more domestic market freedoms: the structure of economy and use of markets, legal structure and property rights, and freedom of exchange in capital and financial markets.[7] As a crude summary, we also report the unweighted average of these components. They show that the United Kingdom ranked in the middle of the pack in 1980 but ranked at or near the top in 1999, considerably above most of its EU competitors.

1.1.2 World Economic Forum and Harvard Center for International Development Competitiveness Scores

Since 1980 the International Institute for Management Development (IMD) and the World Economic Forum (WEF) have developed jointly or separately a world competitiveness report of countries. From 1998 to 2000, the WEF collaborated with Harvard University's Center for International Development to give the *Global Competitiveness Report* (GCR). In contrast to the economic freedom indexes, indexes of competitiveness measure

6. Canada also adopted wage and price controls in the period between 1975 and 1980, and yet the FII shows a rise in economic freedom.

7. Freedom of exchange in capital and financial markets includes a subcategory for freedom of citizens to engage in capital transactions with foreigners, so this is not exclusively a measure of domestic market activities. Note that the vast majority of countries score 100 in the legal structure and property rights subindex in 1997, while the remainder are in the 90-plus range, except for Greece.

Table 1.2 **Indicators of Freedom in Markets in United Kingdom and Other Advanced OECD Economies, 1980–1999**

	Structure of Economy and Use of Markets		Legal Structure/ Property Rights		Freedom in Capital/ Financial Markets		Unweighted Average[a]		
	1980	1999	1980	1999	1980	1999	1980	1999	Change
United Kingdom	33	77	82	99	81	100	65	92	27
Rank out of 22	11	5	14	3	7	1	9	3	4
Major comparisons									
Germany	43	49	91	99	76	81	70	76	6
France	35	47	79	86	71	81	62	71	9
United States	53	81	100	98	92	93	82	91	9
Other developed countries									
Australia	50	66	85	98	67	93	67	86	19
Austria	24	53	96	99	55	85	58	79	21
Belgium	33	51	93	87	91	91	72	76	4
Canada	60	79	84	96	93	92	79	89	10
Denmark	33	51	84	99	83	98	67	83	16
Finland	42	57	79	100	68	87	63	81	18
Greece	21	49	62	58	35	73	39	60	21
Ireland	51	79	82	97	67	83	67	86	19
Italy	21	50	63	90	50	82	45	74	29
Japan	53	54	94	94	62	73	70	74	4
Luxembourg	n.a.	68	100	100	100	92	n.a.	n.a.	n.a.
The Netherlands	41	73	88	99	91	96	73	89	16
New Zealand	37	92	96	98	58	93	64	94	30
Norway	21	55	82	96	59	88	48	80	32
Portugal	10	55	95	81	35	80	47	72	25
Spain	25	46	72	75	67	85	55	69	14
Sweden	24	57	76	95	61	87	54	80	26
Switzerland	72	74	97	98	75	85	81	86	5

Source: Fraser Institute (2001).

Notes: n.a. = not available. A higher score denotes a more favorable ranking.

[a]The three indexes that we have selected are weighted in the Fraser Index as follows: (II) Structure of the Economy and Use of Markets (14.2%); (V) Legal Structure and Property Rights (16.6%); and (VII) Freedom of Exchange in Capital and Financial Markets (17.2%). Thus, they make up approximately half of the overall index. Their weights are sufficiently similar that our treating the three equally does not produce markedly different results than if we had used the Institute's weighting scheme.

the "set of institutions and economic policies supportive of high rates of economic growth in the medium run" (Harvard Center for International Development 2000, 14). The competitiveness scores are based on a mixture of quantitative economic measures and the responses of executives to questions about the situation in their country. Most of the questions in the 2000 GCR ask executives to rate on a scale from 1 to 4 the extent to which a country fits a particular statement; earlier reports used a scale from 0 (not at all) to 100 (to a great extent). The response rate to the survey has varied in the range of 15 percent to 20 percent, with nonrespondents having similar characteristics to respondents.

Because the competitiveness scores are heavily weighted toward actual (or prospective) economic performance, the rankings of countries differ from rankings based on the market friendliness of their institutions. Some highly regulated countries, such as Germany, Switzerland, and the Nordic countries, and others, such as Japan, that have performed better during various time periods than the United States, the United Kingdom, and other market-friendly English-speaking countries, receive higher competitiveness scores than economic freedom scores. For instance, in 1990 Japan, Switzerland, Germany, and Sweden scored higher on the world competitiveness index than the less-regulated United Kingdom, Ireland, and Australia. Across all countries, however, Hanke and Walters (1997) find that competitiveness scores are highly correlated with the Fraser Institute and Heritage/WSJ indexes of economic freedom, with rank-order correlation coefficients in the area of 0.85.

Table 1.3 shows the competitiveness-index rankings for advanced OECD countries in the 2000 GCR ranking and some of the subindexes that go into the aggregate measures. Column (1) records ranks in the GCR's "growth competitiveness" index, which is designed to measure a country's standing in the factors likely to produce economic growth. Column (2) gives its rank in "current competitiveness," which is designed to measure factors that are likely to determine the level of economic activity. Although the two indexes place some countries differently, most notably Germany (poor in growth competitiveness but good in current competitiveness), they give similar scores to the United Kingdom. By either measure, the United Kingdom ranks in the upper third or so of advanced OECD countries. This is considerably above the position of the United Kingdom in GDP per capita tables, but it falls short of the top-three rating that the United Kingdom received in the indexes of economic freedom.

Why does the United Kingdom rate lower in competitiveness than in market freedoms? The lower ranking of the United Kingdom in the competitiveness index does not reflect differences in the ranking that the GCR and Fraser or Heritage foundations give to indicators of market freedoms. For example, column (3) shows that the United Kingdom is second in one GCR indicator that fits well indexes of market freedoms—the time execu-

Table 1.3 **Rank of United Kingdom and Other Advanced Countries in Economic Competitiveness, 2000 (selected subindexes)**

			Market Freedoms		Public Capital	
	Growth (1)	Current (2)	Government Bureaucracy (3)	Property Rights (4)	Infrastructure (5)	Schools (6)
United Kingdom	7	8	2	6	17	20
France	18	14	13	7	2	8
Germany	12	3	19	14	7	11
United States	1	2	14	9	6	18
Australia	9	9	11	8	12	9
Austria	15	12	17	5	8	1
Belgium	14	11	19	11	14	6
Canada	6	10	12	15	9	12
Denmark	11	6	8	3	4	10
Finland	5	1	1	2	1	3
Greece	21	21	21	21	21	22
Ireland	4	17	16	13	22	4
Italy	22	19	22	22	20	17
Japan	17	13	5	19	13	13
Luxembourg	2	n.a.	3	1	5	2
The Netherlands	3	4	15	4	11	7
New Zealand	16	15	6	10	15	14
Norway	13	16	7	16	16	15
Portugal	19	20	20	20	19	21
Spain	20	18	18	17	18	19
Sweden	10	7	9	18	10	16
Switzerland	8	5	4	12	3	5

Source: Harvard Center for International Development (2000): Column (1), growth competitiveness ranking (table 1, 11); column (2), current competitiveness index ranking (table 2, 11); column (3), time with government bureaucracy—low number agrees (4.02, 246); column (4), protection of property rights—property rights are clearly delineated and protected by the law (3.11, 240); column (5), overall infrastructure—the quality of the infrastructure is among the best in the world (5.01, 256); column (6), public-funded schools—the public schools are of high quality (6.01, 268); and column (7), initiation of technology.

Note: n.a. = not available.

tives say that they spent dealing with government bureaucracies—which is far better than the United States, Germany, or France. Column (4) shows that the United Kingdom ranks sixth in protection of property rights, which was one of the major factors in indexes of economic freedom, ahead of the United States, Germany, and France. The area where the United Kingdom does relatively poorly is in the provision of public services. This is illustrated in columns (5) and (6) of table 1.3. The United Kingdom scores seventeenth in terms of overall infrastructure and twentieth in the quality of public schools. Although economists are uncertain about the contribution of infrastructure to national output and about the effect of school quality on productivity, both factors surely do affect economic performance.[8]

1.1.3 Indexes for Specific Markets: Product Markets

To assess the extent and intrusiveness of regulations on business in 1988, the OECD sent a detailed questionnaire to member states asking about 1,300 different regulations concerning economywide and industry-specific laws, regulations, and administration of laws.[9] The responses to this questionnaire form the basis of the OECD regulatory database, which is the most comprehensive and detailed body of information on product-market regulations across countries. The database deals with administrative regulations but does not take account of differences in the use of the judicial system to regulate product markets. Since legal challenges to business operations are a greater threat in the United States than in most other countries, indexes based on the OECD regulatory database arguably overstate the market-friendly orientation of the U.S. economy. Only in the United States do liability suits have the potential to bankrupt firms (as they have done in the cases of asbestos, interuterine birth control devices, and breast implants, for example), and only in the United States are class action and individual employment-discrimination suits a major concern for business.[10] In addition, the OECD regulatory database does not treat adequately the extent to which state regulators actually enforce regulations, which depends on state funding of government agencies, the salaries paid to civil servants, and modes of compliance.

There are various ways to summarize the information on the 1,300 regulations in the OECD database. In a companion report to the OECD report on the product market regulations, Nicoletti, Scarpetta, and Boylaud (1999) use a factor analysis procedure to derive aggregate measures of the

8. The GCR gives the United Kingdom a mixed record in use of modern technology. The United Kingdom scores among the top ten countries in terms of innovation but much lower in its ability to copy technological advances of other countries (Harvard Center for International Development 2000). The Fraser Institute gives the United Kingdom a rank of fourteen among fifteen advanced countries on measures of protection of patent rights (Fraser Institute 2001, exhibit 4-3A).

9. The OECD supplemented the questionnaire with information from other sources, so that about 10 percent of the data come from other sources. See Nicoletti, Scarpetta, and Boylaud (1999) and the overview in OECD (1999a, chap. 7).

10. There are factors that work in the other direction as well. The regulatory scale gives the United Kingdom a lower score in barriers to entrepreneurship than the United States, which is often cited as the ideal environment for aspiring entrepreneurs. The gap between the United States and the United Kingdom comes from two subindexes: one that measures the "regulatory and administrative opacity" (attributed to the high number of administrative procedures and services involved in business startups) and another that measures barriers to competition. However, the IRDB may be misleading in this respect, because it fails to account for lenient U.S. bankruptcy laws, which enable entrepreneurs who fail to start up again with less cost than in most other countries. Also, the OECD failed to collect data on land-use regulations (OECD 1999a, note 8), which may be less restrictive in most parts of the United States than in the United Kingdom or other European countries.

burden of regulation in various domains: inward-oriented regulations (covering state control of industry, barriers to entrepreneurship, and regulations of domestic markets) and outward-oriented regulations (covering barriers to trade and investment). The scaling is such that higher scores mean a thicker and more intrusive set of regulations and thus one nominally less friendly to market mechanisms. Different aggregations of the information in the database would give different measures to each country than Nicoletti, Scarpetta, and Boylaud produce, but would presumably give a similar ordering of countries by the scope and depth of regulatory practices. We use the Nicoletti, Scarpetta, and Boylaud measures in this paper.

Table 1.4 records the product market regulatory scores for the OECD countries. In all of the inward-oriented regulatory domains and in the overall score, the United Kingdom is the least regulated economy. The United States, Ireland, and Australia also show limited regulatory activity. At the other end of the spectrum, Italy, Norway, and Greece have the most highly regulated product markets. In the outward-oriented domain, the United Kingdom is tied with Ireland and Australia for the least regulated economy. Over all domains, the United Kingdom is ranked as the least regulated of the OECD economies, with Ireland in second place and the United States in third.

Nicoletti, Scarpetta, and Boylaud (1999) have used information from the OECD regulatory database to create a measure of the coverage of regulations for each country from 1990 to 1996 that allows us to measure the change in regulatory practices across countries. They find that all of the covered countries reduced regulations in the 1990s but that the United Kingdom deregulated its markets to a greater extent than did the United States, France, and Germany. In 1990, the United Kingdom was seventh in freedom from regulation, whereas in 1996 it was at the top of the table. This illustrates one of our major points: that the market reform stance of the United Kingdom continued after the Thatcher government.

The United Kingdom's development of a more market-friendly regulatory regime in product markets than that of Germany and France fits well with general views of government involvement in these economies. But this does not necessarily mean that consumers are uniformly better off in Britain. The prices of some goods, such as automobiles, have long been higher in the United Kingdom than on the continent, reflecting the structure of private product markets.[11] Still, the OECD has a clear message: The United Kingdom has gone from a regime of relatively medium regulation of business to a relatively deregulated regime in the period of economic reforms.

11. In April 2000, the U.K. Competition Commission issued a report finding that new car prices were about 10 percent higher in the United Kingdom than elsewhere in the EU (see U.K. Competition Commission 2000).

Table 1.4 **Country Regulatory Policies of the United Kingdom and Other Advanced Economies**

	Inward-Oriented Regulations						
	State Control (1)	Barriers to Entrepreneurship (2)	Administrative Regulations (3)	Economic Regulations (4)	Total (5)	Outward-Oriented Regulations: Barriers to Trade/Investment (6)	Total Product Market Regulations (7)
United Kingdom	55	48	50	60	50	43	50
Rank out of 21	1	1	1	1	1	1	1
Major competitors							
Germany	176	210	270	140	190	54	140
France	263	273	310	230	270	103	210
United States	85	126	70	100	110	87	100
Ireland	94	120	150	80	80	43	80
Other developed countries							
Australia	126	113	110	130	120	43	90
Austria	211	160	160	210	118	54	140
Belgium	278	255	300	240	270	63	190
Canada	129	80	90	110	100	215	150
Denmark	246	132	110	230	190	54	140
Finland	268	193	220	210	230	63	170
Greece	387	166	200	310	270	132	220
Italy	392	274	300	350	330	49	230
Japan	129	233	270	140	180	102	150
The Netherlands	228	141	150	210	180	54	140
Norway	319	133	140	270	220	215	220
New Zealand	166	121	150	140	140	95	130
Portugal	283	146	150	250	210	107	170
Spain	259	177	230	210	220	68	160
Sweden	151	180	200	130	170	84	140
Switzerland	208	224	260	190	220	132	180

Sources: Nicoletti, Scarpetta, and Boylaud (1999): data on state control (column 1) from table A3-1; data on barriers to entrepreneurship (column 2) from table A3-2; data on administrative regulations (column 3) from table A3-4; data on economic regulations (column 4) from table A3-5; data on total inward-oriented policies (column 5) from table A3-6; data on barriers to trade and foreign investment (column 6) from table A3-3; data on total product market regulations (column 7) from table A3-7.

Note: A higher score indicates more burdensome or complex regulations.

1.1.4 Indexes for Specific Markets: Labor Markets

The labor market is arguably the most idiosyncratic market in modern capitalist economies. The extent and nature of unionization, employer associations, and regulations vary widely across countries, leading many analysts to try to explain differences in economic performance across countries in terms of differences in labor market institutions (e.g., Bruno and Sachs 1985; Calmfors and Driffil 1988; Freeman 1998; OECD 1999a). To do this, these analysts have developed ratings of country wage-setting institutions and employment-protection legislation and have estimated union density and collective-bargaining coverage.

Table 1.5 shows how different analysts ranked countries by their degree of centralization of wage setting from the early 1980s to the mid-1990s. In this table, a high number means that the analyst regards the wage-setting system as highly centralized, while a low number means that the analyst regards the system as decentralized. Most analysts built their rankings from a limited number of "facts" (such as whether there is a central union-negotiating body, whether there is one bargaining federation or many, etc.) analogous to the way the freedom or competitiveness indexes are constructed. Several of the rankings give rise to ties between countries because the underlying facts are similar. Still, there is subjectivity in the building blocks chosen and, perhaps more importantly, in the weights that analysts accord them in aggregating to a single statistic. Although analysts generally place the same countries at the top or bottom of the table in terms of market-based wage setting, there are some notable differences (for instance, in rating Japan or France). The United Kingdom is invariably among the countries that have more market-based wage setting. Over the period of reforms, the United Kingdom moved up in the rankings as it shifted from a collectively bargained system of wage setting to a largely market-determined system. New Zealand followed a similar pattern.

But rankings can only tell us about changes in relative position. The final column in the table gives absolute changes in centralization of wage setting as reported by Elmeskov, Martin, and Scarpetta (1998). They code countries from 1 (decentralized wage setting) to 3 (coordinated or centralized) and specify periods of change. Eight countries change their wage-setting stance in the period they covered. Six moved toward less-centralized institutions while the Netherlands and Italy moved in the opposite direction. Ireland (not given in table) also moved toward a more centralized wage-setting system.

Quantitative data on the extent of unionism and collective-bargaining coverage in the United Kingdom confirm this picture of movement toward more market-oriented wage setting. In 1980, approximately 50 percent of United Kingdom workers were unionized and 70 percent were covered by collective bargaining (see table 1A.5). By contrast, in 1997, 30 percent of U.K. workers were unionized and only 44 percent were covered by

Table 1.5 **Ranking of Advanced Countries in Centralization/Decentralization in Wage Setting**

	1980s						Late 1980s	1990s			
	1979	1981	1984	1985	1986	1986	1988	1990	1991	1991	Change 1980s to 1990s
Australia	10	n.a.	9	3	3	10	8	n.a.	4	7	Less centralized
Austria	16	15	16	15	17	16	17	10	18	17	No change
Belgium	8	9	15	10	9	6	10	n.a.	10	11	No change
Canada	1	5	5	3	2	5	1	n.a.	2	3	No change
Denmark	13	12	13	10	11	12	14	n.a.	14	17	No change
Finland	12	12	14	10	10	8	13	n.a.	11	17	Less centralized
France	5	3	2	18	5	3	7	3	7	11	No change
Germany	9	8	11	10	16	15	12	6	12	14	No change
Italy	3	1	6	6	4	1	5	4	6	7	More centralized
Japan	6	n.a.	3	18	8	14	4	11	9	11	No change
The Netherlands	7	10	12	15	15	9	11	5	15	11	More centralized
New Zealand	11	n.a.	n.a.	3	7	4	9	n.a.	3	3	Less centralized
Norway	15	14	17	17	13	11	16	8	17	17	No change
Portugal	n.a.	n.a.	n.a.	n.a.	n.a.	n.a.	n.a.	n.a.	n.a.	n.a.	No change
Spain	n.a.	n.a.	1	n.a.	n.a.	n.a.	n.a.	n.a.	n.a.	7	Less centralized
Sweden	14	12	18	15	13	13	15	7	16	17	Less centralized
Switzerland	n.a.	7	7	10	12	n.a.	3	9	13	11	n.a.
United Kingdom	4	2	10	6	6	2	6	2	5	3	Less centralized
United States	2	5	4	3	1	7	2	1	1	3	No change

Source: OECD (1997, table 3.4): Column 1 (1979) from Blyth; Column 2 (1981) from Schmitter; Column 3 (1984) from Cameron; Column 4 (1984) from Lehmbruch; Column 5 (1986) from Bruno/Sachs; Column 7 (1986) from Tarantelli; Column 8 (1988) from Driffil; Column 9 (1990) from Soskice; Column 10 (1991) from Lijphart/Crepaz; Column 11 (1991) from Layart/Nickell/Jackman. The last column is from Elmeskov, Martin and Scarpetta (1998).

Note: Higher ranking = more centralized; n.a. = not available. Different authors gave rankings in the same year.

collective bargaining. Relative to its major European competitors, the United Kingdom has a smaller fraction of nonunion workers who are covered by collective bargaining. France, which has a very low rate of unionization, has a very high rate of collective-bargaining coverage because of laws that extend union contracts to nonunion workplaces. Germany lies somewhere between the United Kingdom and France. Over the 1980s and 1990s, unionization and collective-bargaining coverage remained roughly stable in Germany, compared to the declines in the United Kingdom. This reflects a more general pattern among OECD countries of divergence in the importance of unionism in the labor market.

In addition to having different institutions for wage setting, advanced countries have different rules that regulate employment adjustments. European Union countries like Spain, Portugal, and Italy make it difficult to lay off workers with permanent contracts, while Germany and Belgium make it difficult to hire temporary labor. All continental EU countries have works councils and require management to consult with those councils about plant closings, which invariably delays closures and increases their cost. Employment protection policies effectively shift the property rights of a job from management to the incumbent worker. Several analysts have stressed the role of employment protection legislation (EPL) in constraining employers' flexibility and ultimately holding down the rate of employment growth (Lazear 1990; Bertola 1990; Grubb and Wells 1993).

Comparisons of EPL across countries show that throughout the past two decades the United Kingdom was among the least restrictive countries regarding the rights of employers to alter employment at will. In the 1994 *OECD Jobs Study,* the United Kingdom placed in fourth position in terms of reliance on market forces as opposed to EPL intervention in the labor market. Table 1.6 records ratings of the strictness of the EPL regulations in the late 1980s and late 1990s by the OECD. The scores given to the regulations are scaled so that low values (minimum of 0) imply little employment protection, while high values (maximum of 6) imply considerable employment protection. The A measures are based on data for regular contracts and temporary contracts. The B measures (for the late 1990s only) add additional information on regulations covering collective dismissals. All the EPL measures show that the United Kingdom, the United States, and other English-speaking countries have the least restrictions on the rights of employers to alter employment at will. Over time, however, the difference between the United Kingdom and EU countries with more restrictive legislation declined over this period as other EU countries weakened their regulation of regular contracts and eased the rules on temporary contracts. Because the United Kingdom had relatively weak regulations to begin with, employment protection legislation is an area where most other EU countries have moved their policies closer to those of the United Kingdom, although substantial differences in employment protection remain.

Table 1.6 Employment Protection Indexes

	Late 1980s: A	Late 1990s		Change: A
		A	B	
	(1)	(2)	(3)	(4)
European Union				
Austria	2.2	2.2	2.3	0.0
Belgium	3.1	2.1	2.5	–1.0
Denmark	2.1	1.2	1.5	–0.9
Finland	2.3	2.0	2.1	–0.3
France	2.7	3.0	2.8	0.3
Germany	3.2	2.5	2.6	–0.7
Greece	3.6	3.6	3.5	0.0
Ireland	0.9	0.9	1.1	0.0
Italy	4.1	3.3	3.4	–0.8
The Netherlands	2.7	2.1	2.1	–0.6
Norway	3.0	2.6	2.6	–0.4
Portugal	4.1	3.7	3.7	–0.4
Spain	3.7	3.1	3.1	–0.6
Sweden	3.5	2.2	2.6	–1.3
Switzerland	1.0	1.0	1.5	0.0
United Kingdom	0.5	0.5	0.9	0.0
Non–European Union countries				
Australia	0.9	0.9	1.2	0.0
Canada	0.6	0.6	1.1	0.0
Japan	n.a.	2.4	2.3	n.a.
New Zealand	n.a.	2.6	0.9	n.a.
United States	0.2	0.2	0.7	0.0

Source: Columns (1)–(3): OECD (1999b, table 2.5).

Notes: Columns (1) and (2) use a measure of protection for regular and temporary contracts. Column (3) uses a more comprehensive measure that also includes collective dismissal legislation. Column (4) gives the difference between columns (1) and (2). n.a. = not available.

1.1.5 Indexes of Specific Market: Business Formation and Capital Markets

To assess the ease of starting a new business, researchers in corporate finance have gathered data on regulations covering start-ups (Djankov et al. 2000). Columns (1) through (3) of table 1.7 summarize their analysis in terms of three broad measures of the ease of business formation: the estimated number of procedures needed to start a business, the estimated time to meet those requirements, and the estimated direct and indirect cost of meeting the requirements relative to GDP per capita. Djankav et al. (2000, 1) note the wide variation in these measures: "To meet government requirements for starting to operate a business in Austria, an entrepreneur must complete 12 procedures taking at least 154 days and pay US$11,612 in government fees." This compares with four procedures that take seven

Table 1.7 **Regulation of Business Formation and Protection of Investors in Advanced OECD Countries**

	Business Formation			Protection of Investors[a]		
	Number of Procedures Required	Days to Get Approval	Cost/GDP per Capita	Rule of Law	Antidirector Rights	Creditor Rights
Australia	3	3	.0209	10.00	4	1
Austria	12	154	.4545	10.00	2	3
Belgium	8	42	.1001	10.00	0	2
Canada	2	2	.0140	10.00	4	1
Denmark	5	21	.0136	10.00	3	3
Finland	4	32	.0199	10.00	2	1
France	16	66	.1970	8.98	2	0
Germany	7	90	.0851	9.23	1	3
Greece	13	53	.4799	6.18	1	1
Ireland	4	25	.1145	7.80	3	1
Italy	11	121	.2474	8.33	0	2
Japan	11	50	.1144	8.98	3	2
The Netherlands	8	77	.3031	10.00	2	2
New Zealand	3	17	.0042	10.00	4	3
Norway	6	24	.0249	10.00	3	2
Portugal	12	99	.3129	8.68	2	1
Spain	11	83	.1269	7.80	2	2
Sweden	4	17	.0254	10.00	2	2
Switzerland	12	88	.1336	10.00	1	1
United Kingdom	7	11	.0056	8.57	4	4
United States	4	7	.0096	10.00	5	1

Sources: Djankov et al. (2000), La Porta et al. (1997, 1999).

Notes: The number of procedures required for entry is a count of the number of safety and health, environment, taxation, labor, and screening procedures needed to legally start a new business. The time entry is an estimate of the number of days before a new firm can start operation. The cost entry is an estimate of the monetary time and direct cost of meeting requirements as fraction of GDP per capita in 1997. The rule of law entry is an index from the International Country Risk Guide. The antidirector rights entry is an index that measures shareholder rights (scaled from 0 to 5), while the creditor rights entry is an index of creditor rights (scaled from 0 to 4).

[a]Higher = better.

days at a cost of $2,806 in the United States and even less in Canada (Djankov et al., table 3). The United Kingdom is number two in terms of the estimated costs of forming a business relative to GDP, right behind New Zealand and ahead of the United States.

To assess the protection given to investors to invest or loan money to firms, La Porta et al. (1999) have developed indexes of the rights of investors and creditors in the various countries. Columns (4) through (7) of table 1.7 present their summary measures of the assessment of law and order in the country (on a scale from 0 to 10), based on the International Country Risk Guide, and their indexes of shareholder rights (scale of 0 to 4) and creditor rights (scale of 0 to 5). The majority of the advanced countries obtain the highest value in the rule of law measure, while some of the lower-income countries score substantially lower than the maximum 10 score. There is greater variation in the protections given to shareholders and creditors, at least by these measures. The United States, for instance, provides considerable antidirector protection, while Italy does not; the United Kingdom provides considerable creditor rights, while France does not. La Porta et al. (1999) show that the different legal codes produce different corporate valuations, but they do not attempt to link these institutional differences to differences in aggregate national economic outcomes.

1.1.6 Summary

The evidence in this section shows that U.K. governments have made considerable progress in reforming the economy in a pro-market direction over the past two decades. In the late 1970s, the United Kingdom was ranked near the middle of all advanced countries in terms of the market friendliness of its institutions. Some indexes put the United Kingdom even further down, reflecting such factors as the relatively high rate of government ownership and high marginal tax rates. By the late 1990s, the United Kingdom stood at or near the top of the rankings—close to and, in some cases, even ahead of the United States. To the extent that orthodox economic thinking is correct and a greater market orientation of policy and institutions means better-functioning markets and superior economic outcomes, the United Kingdom should have benefitted from these reforms by an improvement in its relative economic performance. What in fact happened?

1.2 Trends in U.K. Economic Performance, 1960–1999

In this section, we analyze total output per capita and its constituent components, output per unit of labor input and labor input per capita, and compare the economic performance of the United Kingdom relative to its major EU peers, France and Germany, and to the United States from 1960 to 2000. We focus on these measures for several reasons. First, output per capita is the subject of many international comparisons, and policymakers regularly monitor league tables comparing GDP per capita. Second, internationally comparable data on GDP and labor inputs are available for a long period, facilitating an analysis of changes in the United Kingdom's relative performance in these dimensions. Third, other macroeconomic indicators, such as the unemployment rate, are highly correlated with labor input per capita. Finally, and most importantly, conventional economic reasoning says that market-oriented reforms will raise total income but stipulates that they may have adverse impacts on other outcomes, such as the distribution of income. Advocates for market-oriented reforms usually emphasize the goal of increasing income. Taken on their own terms, then, it is important to evaluate the effect of the U.K. reforms on total market income.

Table 1.8 **Real Gross Domestic Product per Capita for Various Countries, 1960–1998**

	In 1998 U.S. Dollars Using PPP Exchange Rates			Relative to U.S. = 100 Based on PPP Exchange Rates		
	1960	1979	1998	1960	1979	1998
United Kingdom	9,974	15,202	21,502	74	68	66
Major competitors						
West Germany	9,842	17,769	24,868	73	80	77
France	8,546	17,064	22,255	64	77	69
United States	13,414	22,254	32,413	100	100	100
Other countries						
Italy	7,286	15,369	22,234	54	69	69
Austria	7,666	15,817	23,930	57	71	74
Belgium	8,069	16,016	24,239	60	72	75
Denmark	9,793	16,807	26,176	73	76	81
The Netherlands	9,351	16,736	24,008	70	75	74
Norway	8,120	16,244	27,581	61	73	85
Sweden	9,894	16,765	21,218	74	75	65
Japan	4,672	14,812	24,170	35	67	75
Canada	10,503	19,099	25,496	78	86	79
U.K. rank (out of 13)				3	12	12

Source: U.S. Bureau of Labor Statistics (2000a).

As a starting point, table 1.8 presents data from the U.S. Bureau of Labor Statistics on the level and rank of GDP per capita for thirteen leading countries. Real GDP figures for each country have been converted to a common currency (1998 U.S. dollars) using PPP-adjusted exchange rates.[12] A comparison of 1960 and 1979 figures for the United Kingdom suggests that, prior to 1980, U.K. relative economic performance was declining relative to the United States (from 74 to 68 percent of the U.S. average) and relative to most other countries, including Germany and France. In 1960, U.K. output per capita was similar to the level in West Germany and 15 percent higher than in France. By 1979, GDP per capita in the United Kingdom was 15 percent lower than in West Germany, 12 percent lower than in France, and a little lower than in Italy. The United Kingdom's position in the league table fell from third to twelfth. Over the 1980s and 1990s, the United Kingdom did better. Relative to the United States, per capita GDP in the United Kingdom fell slightly, from 68 to 66 percent of the U.S. aver-

12. The PPP factors used by the U.S. Bureau of Labor Statistics are very similar to those used by the OECD. For the time periods shown in the table, the use of PPP-adjusted real GDP (versus GDP at market exchange rates) mainly affects cross-country comparisons in 1980. The PPP factors suggest that exchange rates for most European countries (except the United Kingdom and Italy) were significantly overvalued relative to the United States. Thus, 1980 PPP-adjusted real GDP figures for Germany and France are 30 percent lower than market-based figures, while PPP-adjusted GDP figures for the Nordic countries are 60 percent lower.

age. Relative to Germany and France, the United Kingdom gained slightly. Nevertheless, the United Kingdom remained twelfth among the thirteen countries in the table.

The comparisons in table 1.8 open up a series of questions about how the United Kingdom might have done absent its market reforms. Would U.K. output per capita have continued to decline relative to other countries in the 1980s and 1990s in the absence of a sustained reform effort? Or was the relative decline of the United Kingdom in the 1960s and 1970s driven by particular forces that would have come to end anyway? To help answer this question, we delve into the sources of differential growth of the United Kingdom and three key competitors: Germany, France, and the United States in the pre-1980 and post-1980 periods. We also present some limited comparisons with Italy and Ireland.

1.2.1 Trends in the Growth Rates of Gross Domestic Product per Capita and Its Components

Tables 1.9 and 1.10 summarize decompositions of the changes in the relative rate of growth of GDP per working-age adult (ages fifteen to sixty-four in most cases) between the United Kingdom and the key comparison countries. We analyze GDP per working-age adult rather than GDP per capita to remove the variation in per capita GDP that is attributable to shifts in the fraction of children or elderly in the population and that is thus independent of economic reforms.[13] The first three columns of table 1.9 present the rates of growth of GDP per working-age adult in the 1960–1979 and 1979–1999 periods for each country. The underlying data for the United Kingdom, the United States, and Germany and France, which we plot in figure 1.1,[14] show that the United Kingdom had slower growth in output per working-age adult than Germany or France in the 1960s and 1970s, but somewhat faster growth than the United States. The United Kingdom also grew more slowly than Italy or Ireland. After 1979, the United Kingdom and the United States experienced similar growth rates of around 2.0 percent per year, while Germany, France, and Italy had slower growth. Only Ireland, which achieved 3.7 percent annual growth rate in real GDP per working-age adult, outperformed the United Kingdom and United States in the 1980s and 1990s. In terms of *changes* in growth rates before and after 1979, the United Kingdom performed well relative to Germany, France, and Italy and about the same as the United States.

The growth rate in GDP per working-age adult can be decomposed into the sum of the growth rate in GDP per unit of labor input and the growth

13. The data on population are taken from U.S. Bureau of Labor Statistics (2000b). Table 1A.1 presents data on the changing shares of young and old people in the populations of the United Kingdom, Germany, France, Italy, Ireland, and the United States.

14. The series for West Germany and France track each other very closely, and we have averaged them to avoid clutter in the graphs.

Table 1.9 **Growth Rate in Real Gross Domestic Product per Capita and Its Components**

	GDP per Capita			GDP/Labor Input			Labor Input per Capita		
	Pre-1979	Post-1979	Change	Pre-1979	Post-1979	Change	Pre-1979	Post-1979	Change
Labor Input Measured as Number of Workers									
United Kingdom	2.32	2.03	–0.29	2.50	1.76	–0.74	–0.18	0.27	0.45
	(0.09)	(0.09)	(0.12)	(0.07)	(0.07)	(0.10)	(0.07)	(0.07)	(0.10)
West Germany	2.95	1.19	–1.76	3.67	1.55	–2.12	–0.72	–0.35	0.36
	(0.10)	(0.10)	(0.14)	(0.07)	(0.07)	(0.10)	(0.07)	(0.07)	(0.10)
France	3.34	1.27	–2.07	3.66	1.76	–1.90	–0.32	–0.49	–0.16
	(0.09)	(0.09)	(0.12)	(0.08)	(0.08)	(0.12)	(0.04)	(0.04)	(0.05)
Italy	3.66	1.49	–2.17	4.56	1.99	–2.56	–0.90	–0.50	0.39
	(0.10)	(0.10)	(0.14)	(0.15)	(0.15)	(0.21)	(0.07)	(0.07)	(0.10)
Ireland	3.48	3.71	0.23	4.29	3.20	–1.09	–0.81	0.51	1.32
	(0.17)	(0.17)	(0.23)	(0.09)	(0.09)	(0.12)	(0.18)	(0.18)	(0.25)
United States	1.84	1.98	0.14	1.56	1.49	–0.08	0.28	0.50	0.21
	(0.13)	(0.12)	(0.17)	(0.10)	(0.10)	(0.13)	(0.06)	(0.06)	(0.08)
Labor Input Measured as Total Annual Hours									
United Kingdom	2.32	2.03	–0.29	3.44	2.10	–1.34	–1.11	–0.07	1.04
	(0.09)	(0.09)	(0.12)	(0.06)	(0.07)	(0.09)	(0.09)	(0.09)	(0.13)
West Germany	2.95	1.19	–1.76	4.74	2.18	–2.55	–1.78	–0.99	0.79
	(0.10)	(0.10)	(0.14)	(0.07)	(0.06)	(0.09)	(0.08)	(0.08)	(0.11)
France	3.34	1.27	–2.07	4.57	2.02	–2.55	–1.24	–0.75	0.48
	(0.09)	(0.09)	(0.12)	(0.08)	(0.08)	(0.11)	(0.08)	(0.08)	(0.11)
Italy	3.66	1.49	–2.17	5.36	2.21	–3.15	–1.70	–0.72	0.98
	(0.10)	(0.10)	(0.14)	(0.13)	(0.13)	(0.19)	(0.08)	(0.08)	(0.11)
United States	1.84	1.98	0.14	2.06	1.51	–0.55	–0.22	0.47	0.69
	(0.13)	(0.12)	(0.17)	(0.09)	(0.09)	(0.12)	(0.06)	(0.06)	(0.09)

Notes: Coefficients (and standard errors, in parentheses) obtained from linear regression models fit to annual data from 1960 to 1999; GDP per capita represents real GDP divided by total civilian working-age population (ages 15 to 64 in most cases).

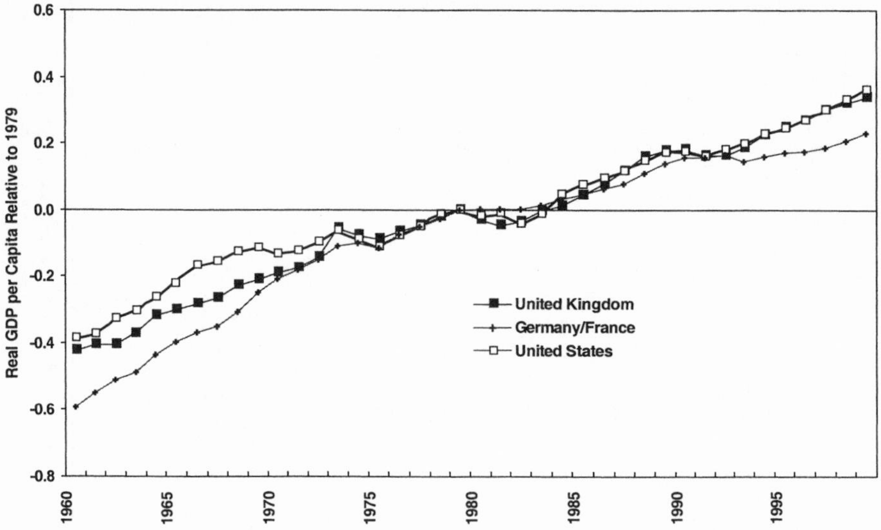

Fig. 1.1 Trends in real GDP per capita relative to 1979 for United Kingdom, West Germany and France, and the United States

in labor input per working-age adult. The upper panel of table 1.9 presents this decomposition using employment per working-age adult as a measure of labor input, while the lower panel shows a decomposition based on hours of work per working-age adult. The underlying series for the United Kingdom, Germany, France, and the United States are plotted in figures 1.2 and 1.3.[15] The figures show that all countries experienced a slowdown in the rate of growth of productivity after 1979. The slowdown was bigger in Germany, France, and Italy than in the United Kingdom, and bigger in the United Kingdom than the United States. Compared to the 1960s and 1970s, when growth rates in output per worker ranged from 1.6 percent per year in the United States to 3.6 percent per year in Germany and France, the growth rates of output per worker in the 1980s and 1990s were remarkably similar across countries. The same story characterizes the growth rates in GDP per hour. In the 1960s and 1970s, the United Kingdom lagged about 1 percent per year behind Germany and France in the growth of productivity per hour and even further behind Italy, but after 1979 productivity per hour grew at similar rates in all four countries.

Unlike the productivity trends, which converged across countries in the post-1979 period, trends in labor input show little evidence of convergence. Prior to 1979, the United Kingdom, Germany, France, Italy, and Ireland

15. For reference, table 1A.2 presents data on employment-population rates and average hours per working-age adult for the various countries.

A

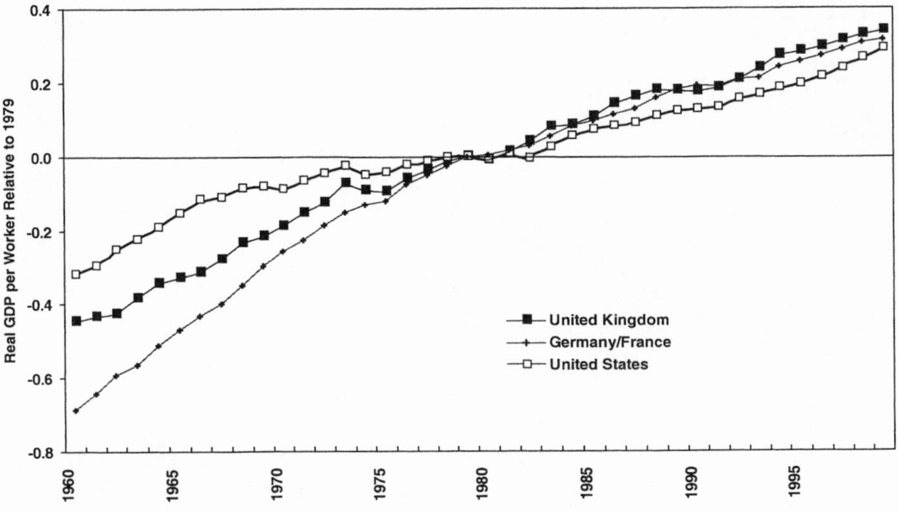

B

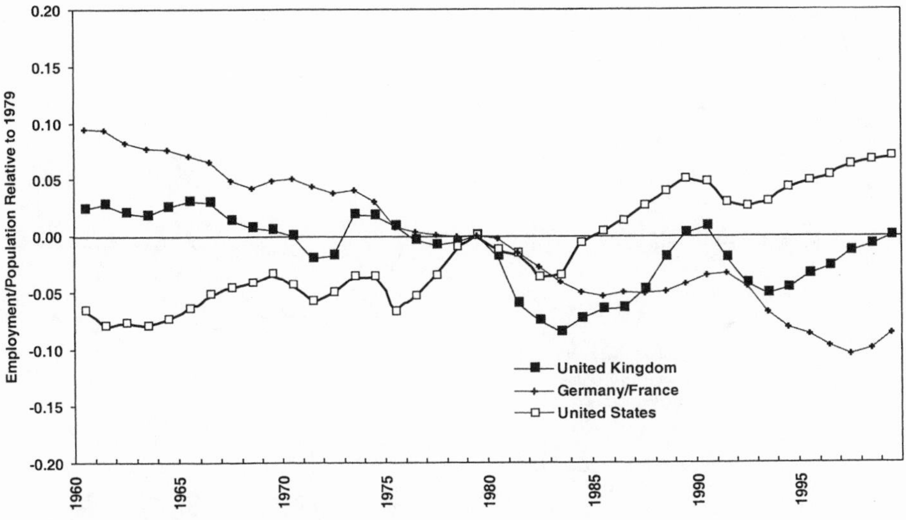

Fig. 1.2 Trends in real GDP per worker and employment per capita relative to 1979 for United Kingdom, West Germany and France, and the United States: *A*, real GDP per worker; *B*, employment per working-age person

all had declining employment-population rates, although the rate of decline was slower in the United Kingdom than elsewhere in Europe. After 1979, the United Kingdom (and Ireland) moved to a more "United States–like" pattern of *rising* employment rates, while Germany, France, and Italy continued to experience declining employment rates, albeit at a slower pace than pre-1979. Hours per working-age adult show a similar pattern of divergence after 1979. In Germany, France, and Italy, hours declined at

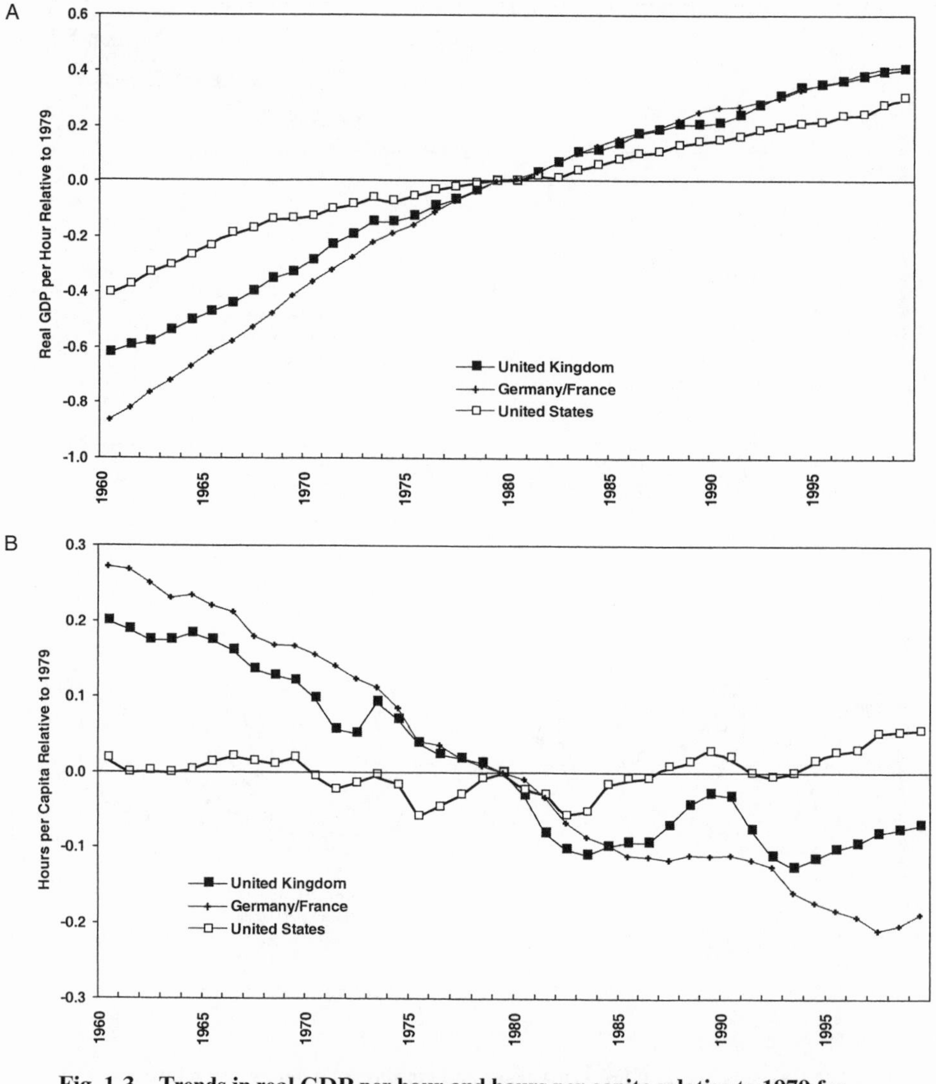

Fig. 1.3 Trends in real GDP per hour and hours per capita relative to 1979 for United Kingdom, West Germany and France, and the United States: *A*, real GDP per hour; *B*, hours per working-age person

about 0.75 to 1.00 percent per year in the 1980s and 1990s, whereas in the United Kingdom the post-1979 trend was negligible, and in the United States the trend was positive.

The implications of these shifting trends in productivity and labor input in the United Kingdom relative to other countries are summarized in table 1.10. The first column of the table shows the growth rate in GDP per working-age adult in the United Kingdom relative to a particular comparison coun-

Table 1.10 **Decomposition of Relative Growth Rates of GDP per Capita between the United Kingdom and Other Countries**

	Difference in Growth Rate of GDP per Capita (1)	Decomposition 1: GDP per Worker (2)	Decomposition 1: Employment per Capita (3)	Decomposition 2: GDP per Hour (4)	Decomposition 2: Hours per Capita (5)
		A. 1960–1979			
United Kingdom	–0.63	–1.17	0.54	–1.30	0.67
West Germany	(0.13)	(0.11)	(0.10)	(0.09)	(0.12)
United Kingdom	–1.02	–1.16	0.14	–1.13	0.12
France	(0.13)	(0.11)	(0.08)	(0.10)	(0.12)
United Kingdom	0.48	0.94	–0.46	1.38	–0.89
United States	(0.16)	(0.12)	(0.08)	(0.11)	(0.11)
		B. 1979–1999			
United Kingdom	0.84	0.21	0.62	–0.08	0.92
West Germany	(0.13)	(0.10)	(0.10)	(0.09)	(0.12)
United Kingdom	0.76	0.00	0.76	0.08	0.68
France	(0.13)	(0.11)	(0.08)	(0.11)	(0.12)
United Kingdom	0.05	0.27	–0.23	0.59	–0.54
United States	(0.15)	(0.12)	(0.09)	(0.11)	(0.11)
	C. Difference in Growth Rates: 1979–1999 Compared to 1960–1979				
United Kingdom	1.47	1.38	0.09	1.21	0.25
West Germany	(0.18)	(0.14)	(0.14)	(0.13)	(0.17)
United Kingdom	1.78	1.16	0.61	1.21	0.56
France	(0.17)	(0.16)	(0.11)	(0.14)	(0.17)
United Kingdom	–0.43	–0.66	0.24	–0.79	0.35
United States	(0.21)	(0.16)	(0.13)	(0.15)	(0.16)

Notes: Entries in column (1) represent the difference in the estimated trend growth rate in GDP per capita between the United Kingdom and the comparison country. Decomposition 1 in columns (2) and (3) divides GDP per capita into GDP per employed worker and employment per capita. Decomposition 2 in columns (4) and (5) divides GDP per capita into GDP per hour worked and hours per capita. Estimated standard errors in parentheses.

try. The second and third columns divide this difference into differences in the growth of GDP per worker and employment per working-age adult, while the fourth and fifth columns divide the difference into relative growth of GDP per hour and hours per working-age adult. Panel A decomposes relative growth rates in the "pre-reform" period (1960–1979), panel B decomposes growth rates in the "reform" period (1979–1999), and panel C shows the decomposition of the relative change in growth rates between the two periods. For example, panel A shows that in the 1960–1979 period the United Kingdom had 0.63 percent slower growth per year in GDP per working-age adult than in West Germany, and 1.02 percent slower growth per year than in France. This resulted from *slower* relative productivity growth in the United Kingdom dominating a more modest decline in the growth of labor inputs. Relative to the United States, on the other hand, the

United Kingdom had 0.48 percent faster growth in GDP per working-age adult in the 1960s and 1970s, due to relatively faster productivity growth dominating a relative decline in labor inputs.

Panel B shows that in the post-1980 reform era, U.K. productivity growth was roughly comparable to rates in Germany and France, but the United Kingdom had stable or rising labor inputs while Germany, France, and most other European nations experienced continuing declines. Thus, the 0.8 percent faster growth per year in U.K. GDP per working-age adult relative to Germany or France in the 1980s and 1990s was attributable almost entirely to the growth in labor inputs. Again, the contrast with the United States is different: Relative to the United States, the United Kingdom had somewhat faster-growing productivity but slower growth in labor inputs.

Finally, panel C shows that the United Kingdom accelerated its economic performance relative to West Germany and France in the postreform period. Relative to Germany, the differential in GDP growth per working-age adult shifted from –0.63 percent per year in the prereform era to 0.84 percent per year in the reform era, for a net relative gain of 1.47 percent per year. Regardless of whether labor inputs are measured by employment or hours, most of this relative gain is attributable to the larger drop in productivity in Germany and France than in the United Kingdom. A fairly similar story emerges in the comparison to France, although in this case a larger fraction of the United Kingdom's relative improvement is attributable to a relative gain in labor inputs in the United Kingdom. Benchmarked to the U.S. economy, however, the United Kingdom does not fare as well. In the 1960s and 1970s, the United Kingdom had faster productivity growth than the United States, but this was partially offset by relative declines in per capita labor inputs. After 1979, productivity growth slowed down everywhere, but more in the United Kingdom than in the United States, although productivity growth rates were still faster in the United Kingdom (see figures 1.3, panel A, and 1.4). This was only partially offset by the bigger turnaround in the trend toward declining work activity in the United Kingdom.

Tables 1.9 and 1.10 show that the reform era coincided with a reversal of the faster growth in GDP per working-age adult in Germany and France compared to the United Kingdom, due mainly to the slower slowdown in productivity growth in the United Kingdom. They also show that after 1979 U.K. labor productivity grew at about the same rate as in Germany and France, but the United Kingdom had stable or slightly rising labor inputs per capita, whereas Germany and France had declining labor inputs. This relative rise in work effort led to higher growth rates in U.K. GDP per capita after 1979. Finally, the tables show no apparent turnaround in U.K. performance relative to the United States. Indeed, the comparison of the United States to the United Kingdom has the same character as the comparison of the United Kingdom to Germany and France. The United States had a smaller productivity slowdown than the United Kingdom and a bigger rise in the rate of growth of labor inputs, with the net result that GDP per capita rose faster in the United States than the United Kingdom after 1979, whereas the opposite was true before 1979.

1.2.2 Explanations for Differential Trends in Labor Productivity Growth

Much of the improvement in U.K. economic performance relative to Germany and France is attributable to the closing of the gap in productivity growth rates. Similarly, the worsened performance of the United Kingdom compared to the United States in the post-1979 period, relative to earlier decades, is due mainly to the narrowing of productivity growth rate differentials. In this section, we consider three explanations for the shifting trends in labor productivity growth: relative trends in the transition out of agriculture, relative trends in the rate of growth of capital per unit of labor input, and relative trends in the quality of labor.

The Shift Out of Agriculture

One widely recognized source of economic growth is the movement of labor from low-productivity sectors such as agriculture to more highly productive sectors such as manufacturing and distribution (e.g., Feinstein 1999). By 1960, only 5 percent of U.K. workers were employed in agriculture. In West Germany and France, however, the fractions were 14 and 23 percent, respectively. The fall in agricultural employment in these countries in the 1960s and 1970s can explain some of their rapid productivity growth in this period. To the extent that the movement out of agriculture was complete by the late 1970s, the slowdown in employment reallocation can also help explain the greater slowdown in productivity growth in Germany and France than in the United Kingdom or the United States. Table 1.11 presents a share-shift analysis of the effects of declining agricultural employment on aggregate productivity growth rates in the pre-1979 and post-1979 periods.[16] To a first-order approximation, the change in aggregate productivity associated with a shift ΔS in the share of agricultural employment is $-\Delta S \times (1 - R)$, where R is relative productivity in agriculture. The entries in columns (4) and (5), drawn from sectoral productivity data reported by van Ark (1996), show that R was about 33 percent in the United Kingdom and France, 18 percent in Germany, and 60 percent in the United States in the early 1960s. In light of these differentials, the 8.7 percentage point decline in the share of agricultural employment in Germany in the 1960–1979 period contributed about 0.4 percent per year to

16. Table 1A.3 presents employment shares in three sectors: agriculture, industry, and services.

Table 1.11 Contributions of Shift Out of Agriculture to Labor Productivity Trends

	Percent of Workers in Agriculture			Relative Productivity of Agriculture		Growth Effect of Shift out of Agriculture (% per year)	
	1960 (1)	1979 (2)	1998 (3)	1960 (4)	1979 (5)	1960–1979 (6)	1979–1998 (7)
United Kingdom	4.7	2.7	1.7	32.6	56.9	0.07	0.02
West Germany	13.9	5.2	2.8	17.8	31.6	0.38	0.09
France	23.2	8.8	4.2	32.1	51.1	0.52	0.12
United States	8.5	3.6	2.6	59.3	75.3	0.11	0.01

Source: U.S. Bureau of Labor Statistics (2000a) for columns (1) through (3). Columns (4) and (5) based on data reported in van Ark (1996, appendix tables 1 and 2).

Notes: Entries in columns (1) through (3) represent the fraction of civilian employment in agriculture. The entries in columns (4) and (5) represent estimates of the value added per worker in agriculture relative to other sectors of the economy (in percent). The entries in columns (6) and (7) represent share-shift estimates of the effect of the movement out of agricultural employment on the annual growth rate of labor productivity for the economy as a whole.

the trend rate of growth of labor productivity, while the 14.4 percentage point decline in France contributed about 0.5 percent per year. By comparison, the much smaller shifts in the United Kingdom and the United States had negligible impacts on aggregate productivity (less than 0.1 percent per year). In the 1979–1998 period the contributions of the movement out of agriculture were small in all four countries, but particularly in the United Kingdom and United States. These calculations suggest that the declining share of agricultural employment can explain one-quarter to one-third of the faster productivity growth of Germany and France than of the United Kingdom in the pre-1979 period.[17] The slowdown in sectoral reallocation explains about the same fraction of the 1.2 to 1.4 percentage point faster slowdown in productivity growth in Germany and France than in the United Kingdom after 1979. As these effects are presumably independent of the reform process in the United Kingdom, we will factor them out before attempting to evaluate the contribution of the U.K. reforms.

Changes in the Capital-Labor Ratio

Standard growth-accounting exercises decompose the growth rate of labor productivity into three components: changes in the amount of capital available per unit of labor input, changes in the "quality" of labor inputs, and technological change or other efficiency improvements.[18] Specifically, assuming a constant returns to scale aggregate production function,

17. That is, the differential shift explains 0.3 to 0.4 percent per year of the 1.2 percent-per-year gap in the growth in productivity per worker.

18. See, for example, Griliches (1970). In this framework, sectoral shifts can be modeled as efficiency improvements.

$$\Delta \log\left(\frac{Y}{L}\right) \approx \alpha\, \Delta \log q + (1 - \alpha)\, \Delta \log\left(\frac{K}{L}\right) + \Delta \log A, \tag{1}$$

where $\Delta \log x$ represents the logarithmic differential (or percentage change) in the variable x, Y/L represents real output per unit of labor input, q is the relative quality of labor inputs, K/L represents real capital per unit of labor input, α represents labor's share (the cost of labor inputs divided by the value of output), and A is an index of overall efficiency. Since different institutions and policies potentially affect the accumulation of physical and human capital and the rate of growth of technological efficiency, we next decompose the shifts in the relative trends of U.K. labor productivity into these three components.

Figure 1.4 plots the trends in capital per worker for the United Kingdom, West Germany, France, and the United States from 1960 to 1999, using data on real net physical capital stocks from Mary O'Mahony (personal communication, January 2001). To maximize international comparability, O'Mahony's series use a consistent set of geometric depreciation factors. Similarly, for consistency with the practices in other countries, the underlying investment series for computer-related equipment in the United States have been deflated by a traditional cost-based index rather than by the hedonic price index developed by the U.S. Bureau of Economic Analysis (BEA; see O'Mahony 1996, 174–176). Consequently, the growth rate of the U.S. capital stock in the 1990s is somewhat slower than shown

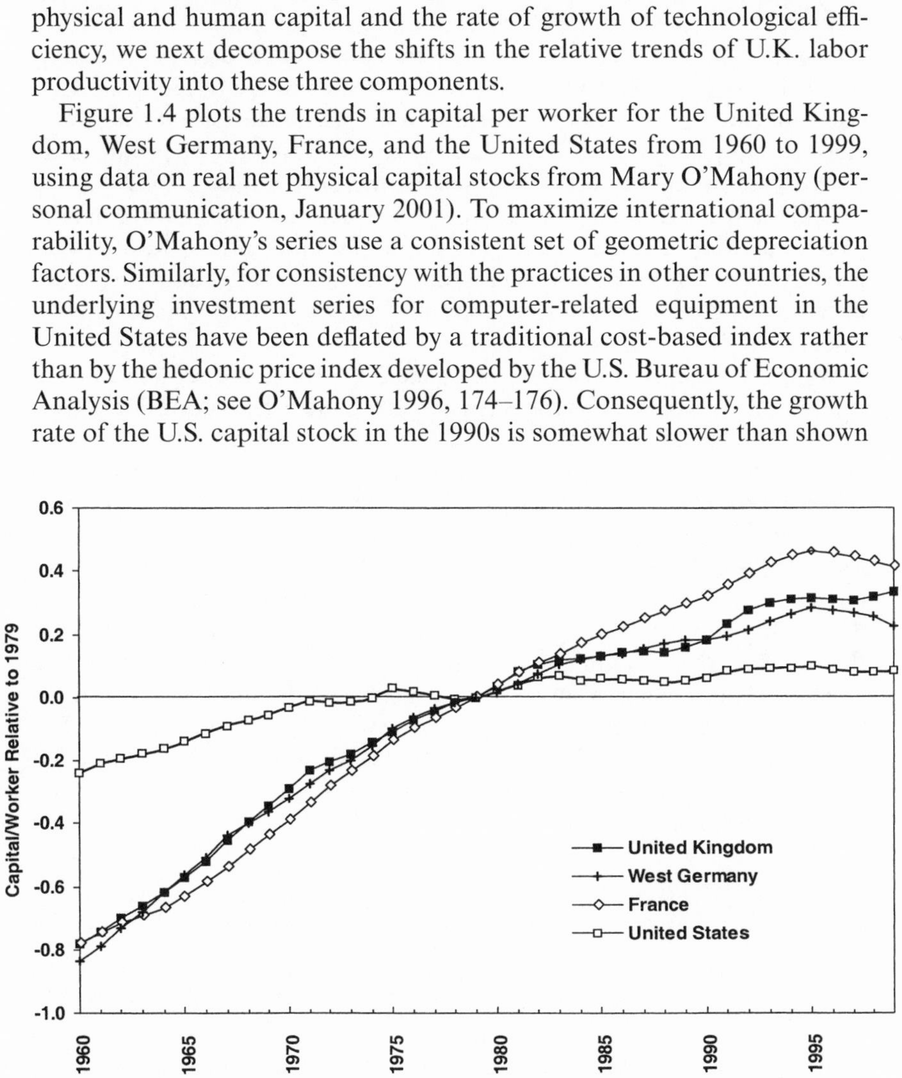

Fig. 1.4 Trends in capital per worker in the United Kingdom, West Germany, France, and the United States

by official BEA data.[19] The data in figure 1.4 show that the growth rate in capital per worker was faster in all three European countries than in the United States both before and after 1979. The U.K. growth rates in capital per worker are very similar to those in West Germany but slower than those in France in the 1980s and early 1990s.

If labor's share is constant, then equation (1) implies that we can adjust the observed growth in labor productivity for the effects of rising capital per unit of labor input by subtracting $(1 - \alpha)$ times the growth rate in capital per unit of labor. This exercise is carried out in table 1.12. As in previous tables, we consider two measures of labor input: employment and total hours. The first three columns of the table reproduce the estimated trends in GDP per unit of labor input from the middle of table 1.9. Columns (4) through (6) show the corresponding trends in capital per unit of labor. Finally, columns (7) through (9) report estimates of productivity growth rates in the prereform and postreform eras, adjusted for changing capital intensity. In these calculations we use an estimate of labor's share of 0.65 for all four countries. In view of this oversimplification, the estimates in columns (7) through (9) should be interpreted as rough guides to the adjusted productivity growth rates that would emerge from a more detailed calculation.[20]

We draw three conclusions from table 1.12. First, the growth rates in capital per unit of labor were similar in the United Kingdom, West Germany, and France in the pre-1979 period. Thus, the relatively slow rate of U.K. productivity growth in the prereform period does not reflect a shortfall in investment relative to employment growth.[21] Second, in all three countries the growth in capital per unit of labor input slowed dramatically after 1979. In the reform era, capital per unit of labor input grew at about the same pace in the United Kingdom as in West Germany (especially when labor input is measured on a basis of hours) and somewhat faster than in France. Based on these comparisons, we believe that investment is not the primary mechanism behind the gains in U.K. productivity growth relative to its European competitors in the period of market reforms. For example, using an hours-based measure of labor inputs, the United Kingdom had a 1.21 percent per year gain in the rate of productivity growth relative to West Germany after 1979 (see panel C of table 1.10). After adjusting

19. The capital series for all four countries are very highly correlated ($r > 0.99$) with the series in the *OECD International Sectoral Database* (1999 edition) and with an alternative set of series constructed by O'Mahoney (1996) using somewhat different methods.

20. Blanchard (1997) presents an interesting analysis of the sources of variation in labor's share over time. In the United Kingdom, labor's share of GDP was 65.9 percent in 1960, 69.0 percent in 1970, 68.5 percent in 1980, 65.9 percent in 1990, and 62.3 percent in 1996 (U.K. Office of National Statistics 1997, table 1.4).

21. Recall from table 1.9 that in the 1960–1979 period labor inputs per capita grew a little faster in the United Kingdom than in Germany or France. Thus, investment per capita grew slightly faster in the United Kingdom too.

Table 1.12 **Contributions of Capital Accumulation to Relative Trends in Labor Productivity**

	GDP/Labor Input			Capital/Labor Input			Productivity Growth Net of Capital Effects		
	1960–1979 (1)	1980–1999 (2)	Change (3)	1960–1979 (4)	1980–1999 (5)	Change (6)	1960–1979 (7)	1980–1999 (8)	Change (9)
			Labor Input Measured as Number of Workers						
United Kingdom	2.50	1.76	–0.74	4.39	1.59	–2.80	0.96	1.20	0.24
	(0.07)	(0.07)	(0.10)	(0.11)	(0.11)	(0.15)	(0.08)	(0.08)	(0.11)
West Germany	3.67	1.55	–2.12	4.55	1.27	–3.28	2.08	1.11	–0.97
	(0.07)	(0.07)	(0.10)	(0.11)	(0.11)	(0.15)	(0.08)	(0.08)	(0.11)
France	3.66	1.76	–1.90	4.39	2.27	–2.12	2.12	0.97	–1.16
	(0.08)	(0.08)	(0.12)	(0.12)	(0.12)	(0.17)	(0.09)	(0.09)	(0.13)
United States	1.56	1.49	–0.08	1.36	0.28	–1.08	1.08	1.39	0.30
	(0.10)	(0.10)	(0.13)	(0.08)	(0.08)	(0.12)	(0.10)	(0.10)	(0.14)
			Labor Input Measured as Total Annual Hours						
United Kingdom	3.44	2.10	–1.34	5.33	1.93	–3.40	1.57	1.42	–0.15
	(0.06)	(0.07)	(0.09)	(0.12)	(0.12)	(0.17)	(0.07)	(0.08)	(0.11)
West Germany	4.74	2.18	–2.55	5.61	1.90	–3.71	2.78	1.52	–1.25
	(0.07)	(0.06)	(0.09)	(0.11)	(0.11)	(0.16)	(0.08)	(0.07)	(0.11)
France	4.57	2.02	–2.55	5.30	2.54	–2.76	2.72	1.13	–1.58
	(0.08)	(0.08)	(0.11)	(0.15)	(0.16)	(0.22)	(0.10)	(0.10)	(0.13)
United States	2.06	1.51	–0.55	1.86	0.31	–1.56	1.41	1.40	–0.00
	(0.09)	(0.09)	(0.12)	(0.09)	(0.09)	(0.13)	(0.10)	(0.10)	(0.13)

Notes: Standard errors in parentheses. Entries in columns (1) through (6) obtained from linear regression models fit to annual data from 1960 to 1999 for real GDP per unit of labor input and real net capital per unit of labor input. Entries in columns (7) through (9) represent differences between growth rate of GDP per labor input and 0.35 times the growth rate in capital per unit of labor input. See text equation (1).

for the impact of changing trends in capital per hour, the relative gain was 1.10 (–0.15 + 1.25). Similarly, the gain relative to France in the productivity growth per hour was 1.21 percentage points per year: After adjusting for shifting trends in capital per hour, the relative gain was slightly larger (1.43 = –0.15 + 1.58).

But changing trends in capital growth per unit of labor input go a long way toward explaining the changing relative trends in productivity growth between the United Kingdom and the United States. Capital accumulation per worker slowed less in the United States than in the United Kingdom (or Germany and France), and, after adjusting for this fact, the trend rates of productivity growth are very similar in the United Kingdom and the United States. Using an hours-based measure of labor input, the trend growth rate in productivity in the U.K. net of capital was 1.57 percent per year in 1960–1979, compared to a rate of 1.41 percent per year in the United States. In 1979–1999, the trend growth in U.K. productivity net of capital was 1.42 percent per year compared to 1.40 percent per year in the United States. Thus, the changing relative trends in productivity growth between the two countries are well explained by the changing relative trends in capital per worker.

Changes in Labor Quality

A final source of growth in labor productivity is rising labor quality, which is driven by increases in educational attainment or shifts in other skill characteristics of the labor force. Available data suggest that the rise in formal-education qualifications was bigger in the United Kingdom than in Germany (e.g., Broadberry and Wagner 1996), although the disappearance of the U.K. apprenticeship system (Blanchflower and Lynch 1994) suggest that the United Kingdom has fallen behind other European countries in one area of skill formation. We evaluate the impact of changing labor quality on productivity by (1) estimating a micro-level wage equation that relates individual earnings to observed characteristics, such as education, vocational qualifications, gender, and age; and (2) by using the estimated coefficients in a base year to evaluate the changes in the relative quality of the labor force by calculating average predicted wages for workers in two different years and forming the ratio of these averages (see Griliches 1970).[22] This method weights changes in different characteristics by the same market metric (relative earnings) that underlies the construction of GDP statistics. A problem is that coefficients from different base years will give different estimates of the change in labor quality when the market returns to different skill characteristics change over time.

We use different data sets for different countries in this analysis. For the

22. In practice, we constructed weighted averages that weight each worker by his or her relative hours of work.

United Kingdom, there is no single microdata source that spans the past four decades. The best available source is the *General Household Survey* (GHS), which has sampled roughly 10,000 workers each year from 1974 onward and includes detailed information on both academic and vocational qualifications. We use GHS data to estimate changing labor quality in the United Kingdom over the period from 1975 to 1996. For the United States, the March *Current Population Survey* (CPS) provides annual data from 1967 onward. Comparable data were collected in the 1960 Census. Pooling their data sources, it is possible to construct estimates of changing labor quality in the U.S. economy over the 1959–1999 period. For Germany, there are no publicly available data sets comparable to the GHS or CPS. The German Socio-Economic Panel (GSOEP) provides microdata for a fixed panel of households starting in the early 1980s. Detailed cross-tabulations of the age, education, and gender distribution of the German labor force (based on the Mikrozensus) are available irregularly starting in 1976. We use a combination of the GSOEP microdata (to estimate the coefficients) and the Mikrozensus cross-tabulations to estimate changes in West German labor force quality over the period from 1976 to 1999. We drop France from our analysis due to the absence of publicly available microdata sets on labor skills and earnings over time:

Table 1.13 summarizes our estimates of the relative rates of change in the quality of labor in the United Kingdom, West Germany, and the United States. For the United Kingdom, our micro-level wage model includes a measure of years of total schooling, dummies for three levels of academic qualifications (university degree, A-levels, and three or more O-levels), dummies for three levels of vocational qualifications, and dummies for ten

Table 1.13 **Estimates of the Rate of Growth of Labor Quality (% per year)**

	Growth Rate of Labor Quality	
	Before 1979–1980	After 1979–1980
United Kingdom	0.23[a]	0.87
West Germany	0.49[b]	0.21
United States	0.33[c]	0.39

Sources: For the United Kingdom, General Household Survey (GHS) microdata, 1975–1996, weights from wage equation fit to 1984–1986 data; for West Germany, unpublished tabulations from Microcensus, 1976–1999, for 100 gender × education × age cells, weights from wage equation fit to GSOEP microdata in 1985; and for the United States, Current Population Survey (CPS) microdata, 1979–1999, plus 1960 Census microdata, weights from wage equation fit to 1984 CPS data hours-based index.

Notes: See text for description of method.

[a]Based on changes from 1975 to 1980.

[b]Based on changes from 1976 to 1980.

[c]Based on changes from 1959 to 1979.

five-year age categories, fully interacted with gender. The estimates in table 1.13 use coefficients from a model fit to 1984–1986 data.[23] The implied rates of growth in labor quality are about 0.2 percentage points per year in the late 1970s and 0.9 percentage points per year in the 1980s and 1990s. The relatively rapid pace of quality growth in the 1980s and 1990s reflects a substantial rise in average education among U.K. workers (+1.75 years from the mid-1970s to the mid-1990s) coupled with rises in the fractions of workers with university degrees and vocational qualifications (see table 1A.4). Offsetting these gains was a 10 percentage point rise in the fraction of women. Since women earn substantially less than men, this trend has slowed down the growth of labor force quality in the United Kingdom.

For West Germany, our wage determination model includes a full set of interactions of gender with eleven five-year age categories and five education categories. These 110 cells represent the finest level of detail available in published cross-tabulations of age, education, and gender from the Mikrozensus.[24] Compared to the United Kingdom, the rate of growth of labor quality in West Germany was relatively high in the late 1970s but much slower in the 1980s and 1990s. This is because the distribution of workers across education categories in Germany changed only modestly, whereas the fraction of female workers increased from 38 percent in 1980 to 43 percent in 1999.

For the United States, our wage determination model includes years of education, a dummy for a college degree, dummies for nonwhite race and Hispanic ethnicity, and full interactions of gender with ten age categories. Over the 1959–1979 period, we estimate that the average quality of the U.S. workforce rose by about 0.3 percent per year. The main contributors were a rise in average education (from 10.5 to 12.4 years) and a rise in the fraction of workers with a college degree (from 8.8 to 17.5 percent). Working against this trend were a rise in the fraction of young workers (from 31 percent under the age of 31 to 41 percent) and a 10 percentage point rise in the fraction of women (from 35 to 45 percent). Over the 1980s and 1990s, our model suggests that labor force quality growth was a little faster than in the 1960s and 1970s, despite a slowdown in the rate of growth of average years of education. Contributing factors were a drop in the fraction of young workers and a dramatic slowdown in the entry of women.

23. We use this for comparability with the German model, which is fit to 1985 GSOEP data. Use of estimated coefficients from earlier years gives slightly slower rates of growth, since the wage disadvantage for women is higher and the return to education is lower. Estimates from later years give higher rates of growth of quality.

24. The education categories are a regular university degree (or more); a technical college degree; a *meister* (master craftsman) qualification; a completed apprenticeship; and a residual category that includes those with only a high school education and those who started but did not finish a postsecondary program. The 1999 cross-tabulations include all of Germany. This may lead to some downward bias in the trend in education over the 1980–1999 period. Over the 1980–1989 period, the trend is similar to that observed over the longer period.

The key conclusion from table 1.13 is that labor force quality grew faster in the United Kingdom in the post-1979 reform era than in West Germany or the United States. The differential relative to Germany is 0.66 percentage points per year. Assuming that labor's share is 65 percent, this gap would be expected to lead to about 0.4 percentage points per year faster growth in labor productivity in the United Kingdom than in Germany. A similar calculation suggests that relative improvements in labor force quality contributed to a 0.3 percentage point per year difference in productivity growth relative to the United States. Since column (8) of table 1.12 shows that labor productivity adjusted for trends in capital grew at about the same rate in all three countries in the 1979–1998 period, the implication is that U.K. productivity growth net of labor quality growth was slower than expected in the reform era, relative to Germany and the United States. The absence of data on the characteristics of U.K. and German workers in the 1960s precludes any definitive assessment of whether the *shifts* in the trend growth in labor quality can account for the bigger slowdown in productivity growth in West Germany than in the United Kingdom. Extrapolating from limited data for the late 1970s, it appears that the growth rate of labor force quality accelerated in the United Kingdom and declined in Germany after 1979 to 1980. These patterns are consistent with the relative changes in productivity growth rates.

Summary of Changing Trends in Productivity Growth

Table 1.14 summarizes our attempt to decompose productivity growth in the United Kingdom, West Germany, France, and the United States into components attributable to the movement out of agriculture, the rise in capital per unit of labor input, and changing labor quality. For simplicity, we focus on trends in productivity per hour.[25] Sectoral shifts out of agriculture help explain some of the more rapid productivity growth of France and Germany relative to the United Kingdom (or to the United States) prior to 1979. After 1979, most of the adjustment was complete, leading to a bigger productivity slowdown for France and Germany than for the United Kingdom or the United States. Increasing capital per unit of labor is an important component of productivity growth in all countries. Trend rates of capital growth are quite similar in the United Kingdom, Germany, and France, however, suggesting that relative investment trends have not been a major source of differential productivity growth among these three countries. The slowdown in capital accumulation was smaller in the United States, and an adjustment for capital brings the productivity trends in the United States and the United Kingdom into close alignment.

Adjusting for sectoral shifts and capital trends, the productivity growth rate in the United Kingdom in the 1960–1979 period was 1.5 percent per

25. The calculations for trends in productivity per worker are similar.

Table 1.14 Summary of Contributions to Trends in Growth Rate of Labor Productivity per Hour Worked

		Source of Contribution			Adjusted Productivity Growth Rate	
	Productivity Growth Rate	Shift Out of Agriculture	Capital per Hour	Labor Quality	Excluding Quality	Including Quality
		A. 1960–1979				
United Kingdom	3.44	0.07	1.87	n.a.	1.50	n.a.
West Germany	4.74	0.38	1.96	n.a.	2.40	n.a.
France	4.57	0.52	1.86	n.a.	2.19	n.a.
United States	2.06	0.11	0.65	0.21	1.30	1.09
		B. 1979–1999				
United Kingdom	2.10	0.02	0.68	0.57	1.40	0.83
West Germany	2.18	0.09	0.67	0.14	1.42	1.28
France	2.02	0.12	0.89	n.a.	1.01	n.a.
United States	1.51	0.01	0.11	0.25	1.39	1.14
		C. Change from Pre- to Post-1979				
United Kingdom	–1.34	–0.05	–1.19	n.a.	–0.10	n.a.
West Germany	–2.56	–0.29	–1.29	n.a.	–0.98	n.a.
France	–2.55	–0.40	–0.97	n.a.	–1.18	n.a.
United States	–0.55	–0.10	–0.54	0.04	0.09	0.05

Sources: Productivity growth rates from table 1.9. Contributions of shift out of agriculture from table 1.11. Contributions of growth in capital per hour estimated by multiplying trends in capital per hour in columns (4) through (5) of table 1.12 by 0.35. Contributions of labor quality obtained by multiplying entries in table 1.13 by 0.65.

Note: n.a. = not available.

year—0.7 to 0.9 percent per year lower than in West Germany or France, but 0.2 percent per year higher than in the United States. Given the limitations of the available data, we are unable to estimate how much of the gap between the United Kingdom and its major European competitors was due to slower growth in labor quality: We suspect this may be a part of the story for the United Kingdom–Germany differential. After 1979, adjusted U.K. productivity growth was 1.4 percent per year—only slightly below the rate in the previous decades, and about equal to the rates in Germany, France, and the United States. We estimate that the United Kingdom had somewhat faster growth in labor quality than Germany or the United States in the 1980s and 1990s. The productivity growth rate in the United Kingdom attributable to efficiency gains, technological change, and other unobserved factors was therefore slower than in West Germany or the United States.

The bottom line is that although the various factors that we have examined explain some of the improved relative performance of the United Kingdom in the era of market reforms, there still remains an upswing in the growth of GDP per working-age adult (and per capita) in the United Kingdom compared to its major EU competitors.

1.3 Relating Reforms to Performance

Did the economic reforms adopted in the United Kingdom in the 1980s and 1990s *cause* the changes in economic performance documented in the previous section? Given the complexity and overlapping nature of the reforms, and the difficulty of specifying what would have happened in the U.K. economy in the absence of reform, this is a difficult question. Rather than attempting to answer it, we address a more modest question: Is there a plausible link between some of the major reforms and the economic changes we have identified? Our analysis highlights two key facets of the change in the economic performance of the U.K. economy after 1979.

1. Productivity: Pre-1979, U.K. productivity growth was about 1 percent per year slower than in Germany or France (net of sectoral shifts). After 1979, the gap disappeared. None of the convergence is explained by trends in capital accumulation; some may be due to rising labor quality in the United Kingdom. After adjusting for trends in capital accumulation, trends in relative productivity growth in the United Kingdom and United States were very similar before and after 1979.
2. Work effort: Pre-1979, employment rates and hours per capita were declining more slowly in the United Kingdom than in Germany and France. After 1979 this difference widened, contributing to faster growth in GDP per capita. Although work effort rose relative to Germany and France, it has not kept pace with trends in the United States.

Potential explanations for the productivity results include reforms that either lowered barriers to productivity growth in the United Kingdom or generated once-and-for-all increases in the productivity of U.K. businesses. Potential explanations for the work effort results include reforms that increased the incentives for work in the United Kingdom relative to continental Europe.

1.3.1 Productivity-Enhancing Reforms

Many U.K. policy reforms could have contributed to rising labor productivity, including laws that have weakened the coverage and power of trade unions, which led to changes in union policies; privatization of nationalized industries; and the creation of incentives for self-employment and share ownership.

Some of the most prominent early reforms introduced by Thatcher were designed to reduce trade union power. The Employment Acts of 1980, 1982, and 1984 limited secondary picketing, abolished statutory union recognition procedures, weakened the closed shop, and mandated changes to internal union governance (including compulsory prestrike balloting). In addition, other government actions, such as the privatization of highly unionized state-owned industries and the removal of contract requirements to pay union-negotiated wages, substantially weakened the government's indirect support for unionism and collective bargaining (see Pencavel, chap. 5 in this volume). Union membership rates, which had reached a peak of over 50 percent in 1980, declined steadily in the subsequent decades and by 1999 stood at under 30 percent of wage and salary workers (see table 1A.5). Strike activity plummeted in the 1980s (again, see Pencavel's chapter in this volume). The presence of multiple unions in the same workplace, which contributed to some of the worst excesses of U.K. industrial relations in the pre-1980 period, also fell. The evidence shows that the relationship between productivity and collective bargaining shifted in this period. Using data from the Workplace Industrial Relations Survey (WIRS) conducted in 1998, Pencavel concludes that by the end of the 1990s unionized establishments were no less productive on average than their nonunion counterparts. By comparison, Pencavel's analysis of similar data from the 1990 WIRS and studies by other researchers (e.g., Machin, Stewart, and van Reenan 1993) suggest that unionized establishments suffered a significant productivity disadvantage in earlier years.

These findings suggest that reforms linked to reductions in trade union power had some impact on measured U.K. productivity. For example, if the 43 percent of private-sector employees in 1979 that were working in unionized establishments had 10 percent lower productivity than other workers, then the elimination of the union productivity gap could contribute to a 4.3 percentage point gain in aggregate productivity between 1979 and 1999. Some analysts have argued that the changed industrial relations climate in the United Kingdom has led to a permanent shift in the productivity growth rate (Bean and Crafts 1996). However, the empirical analysis on this is relatively limited (see Pencavel, chap. 5 in this volume), and we regard the 4.3 percentage point gain over the entire period as a generous upper bound on the potential gains associated with elimination of the negative productivity effect of trade unions.[26]

What about the effect of privatization of industries on productivity? In 1979, 12 percent of U.K. GDP was produced in publicly owned companies;

26. One way in which unions might in theory have reduced labor productivity is by causing firms to invest less through a "hold-up" effect: A unionized firm that invests in new equipment can expect to have to pay higher wages in the future, thereby reducing the effective return on capital (Grout 1984). Our evidence gives no indication that this occurred in the United Kingdom. Despite the decline in unionization rates in the United Kingdom and the apparent shift toward more cooperative relations with employers, the rate of growth of capital per worker (or capital per hour) did not accelerate in the United Kingdom relative to West Germany or France. Either the underinvestment effect was relatively small before the reforms of the 1980s and 1990s, or deunionization and an improved industrial-relations climate have had little effect on the investment calculus of U.K. employers.

in 1997, just 2 percent of U.K. GDP was produced in publicly owned companies. While, as Green and Haskel show (chap. 2 in this volume), productivity growth was not the primary impetus for privatization in the early Thatcher years, the widespread belief that private businesses operate more efficiently than state-run businesses suggests that privatization of this magnitude could have contributed to the improvement in relative productivity in the 1970s through the 1990s. Their industry evidence shows that privatization itself had no huge effect on productivity, which improved in some industries and not in others, and that productivity increased most rapidly in the period before privatization as the government sought to improve operations in order to make the business attractive to the private sector. Labor productivity between 1980 and 1992 went up for plants that were public in 1980 and private in 1992, with the increase concentrated in the period immediately preceding privatization. Green and Haskel, as well as other analysts, have stressed that increased competition after privatization appears to be the key factor differentiating sectors where privatization was associated with improved productivity from sectors where it was associated with stagnation or declines in productivity relative to private firms or international benchmarks.

To get a rough estimate of how much this might have added to aggregate productivity growth, we assume, as they do, that the process of privatization accounts for this improvement. Appendix table 1A.7 shows that 1.4 percent of the U.K. workforce was employed in nationalized industries in 1995 compared to 7.3 percent of the U.K. workforce in 1975, which indicates that privatization shifted nearly 6 percent of the workforce from the public to private sector. While there is no single best estimate of the effect of privatization on productivity, a generous estimate based on Green and Haskel's plant data (chap. 2 in this volume, table 2.6) is that privatization induced a gain in labor productivity of nearly 20 percent more than the private-sector increase. This would imply an increase in aggregate productivity of 1.1 percent between 1979 and 1999.[27] We regard this as a generous upper bound on the potential gains associated with privatization since it gives all of the privatized sectors the 19 percent gain, whereas productivity did not in fact improve in some industries.

Another area where the United Kingdom has made major micromarket-oriented changes is in the introduction of various "shared compensation" programs that give employees a stake in the firm performance, either through profit sharing or share ownership. Evidence in Conyon and Freeman (chap. 3 in this volume) shows that productivity is higher in firms that

27. Our 1.2 percent estimate comes from taking the 0.44 rate of growth of productivity over the 1980–1992 period for plants that moved from public to private, subtracting the 0.27 rate of growth of productivity for plants that moved from private to public, and multiplying the difference (0.17 log points per year = 0.19 percent per year) by the 6 percentage point shift from the public to the private sectors.

have such programs compared to those that do not have such programs. Not all of the programs that the U.K. government has favored with tax relief have a positive impact on productivity, but the most important programs—the approved profit-sharing scheme introduced in the 1978 Finance Act, which the government replaced with an all-employee share plan in 2000—have an estimated productivity effect in the area of 10 percent (Conyon and Freeman, chap. 3 in this volume, table 3.5, based on stock market returns) to 18 percent (tables 3.4 and 3.5, based on production function estimates). Millward, Bryson, and Forth (2000, table 6.13) show that there was an increase in the proportion of industry and commerce establishments with twenty-five or more employees having profit-sharing plans, from 19 percent in 1984 to 46 percent in 1998. Inland Revenue data (U.K. Inland Revenue Service, undated, table 6.1, "Employee Share Schemes") also show a huge increase in the number of workers who received tax-advantaged payments under government-approved profit-related schemes. In 1979, approximately one-quarter as many workers were likely to have been covered by plans.[28] On the basis of the establishment surveys and Inland Revenue data, we estimate that the proportion of U.K. workers covered by these plans increased by approximately 20 percentage points. This implies a gain in productivity on the order of 2.0 percent to as high as 3.8 percent.[29]

The U.K. reforms also encouraged workers to become self-employed. Table 1A.6 shows that the proportion of the workforce in the United Kingdom that was self-employed rose from 8.4 percent in 1980 to 13.1 percent in 1990, and then stabilized. Over the entire period, the proportion of self-employed rose by 4.3 percentage points. In general, self-employed workers earn less than wage and salary workers, with about a 10 percent differential between the two. If we interpret this differential as the result of differences in productivity, the implication is that this reform reduced productivity by 0.4 percent. By contrast, the percentage of workers who were self-employed in Germany and the United States fell over this period, with the decline in German self-employment due largely to the drop in agricultural employment.

Summing up the estimated effects on productivity of the change in the relation between unionism and productivity (4.3 percent), privatization (1.1 percent), profit- and share-ownership schemes (2.0 percent), and self-employment (–0.4 percent), we estimate the microevidence of the effect of

28. The U.K. Inland Revenue Service (undated, table 6.1) gives the number of workers who actually received payments under various schemes: 225,000 received payments in 1979 under the Finance Act of that year compared to 960,000 in 1997–1998, but an additional 1,170,000 employees were granted options under the Finance Act of 1980. Since workers may be covered by plans but not receive payments in a given year, these data show a big trend but smaller magnitudes than in the establishment survey.

29. We base this estimate by multiplying the 10 percent productivity effect by the 20 point increase in the proportion of workers covered by profit-sharing-option plans.

particular reforms on productivity may have raised U.K. productivity on the order of 7 percent or approximately 0.35 percent per year, which is about one-quarter of the difference in growth rates between the 1960–1979 prereform period and the 1979–1999 reform period shown in panel C of table 1.10, and a potentially higher proportion of growth rates adjusted for the improved quality of the workforce. These estimates are crude, to be sure. They are based solely on changes in the United Kingdom rather than changes in the United Kingdom relative to other countries, although we have seen that the U.K. reforms were considerably greater than those in France, Germany, and the United States. We conclude that the estimated effects of the microreforms cumulate to an order of magnitude that suggests that they explain part of the acceleration in U.K. productivity growth compared to Germany or France.

1.3.2 Reforms in the Incentives for Work

Many important reforms have affected the economic incentives for work in the United Kingdom relative to other advanced countries, including West Germany and France. These include changes that lowered the generosity and availability of unemployment benefits; the taxation of various previously untaxed socially provided benefits; the elimination of the earnings-related supplement; the suspension of indexing of benefit levels for several years in the 1980s; the elimination of unemployment benefits for young people; the establishment of the ReStart and later New Deal programs to monitor job search efforts of benefit claimants; the lowering of marginal tax rates; the introduction of the Family Credit in 1988 and the ensuing 1999 Working Families Tax Credit (WFTC) to improve the work incentives for families with low incomes; and reforms in pensions designed to increase labor mobility. The Thatcher-era reforms sought to increase the incentive to work (Blanchflower and Freeman 1994), and ensuing reforms had a similar intent. If these reforms exceeded those in France and Germany, they might help explain the improved employment rate in the United Kingdom versus the rates of those (and other) advanced OECD countries. Consistent with the picture given by our indexes on the labor market (tables 1.5 and 1.6), it appears that, in some policies that might affect employment, the United Kingdom did indeed undertake greater market-oriented changes than other advanced countries. Table 1.15 shows that, from the 1965–1972 period to the 1988–1995 period, the United Kingdom reduced the replacement ratio on unemployment benefits (the percentage of the wage paid to the unemployed) by more than any other country, so that in the 1990s it had the lowest rate among covered countries. Because unemployed workers receive other benefits—housing subsidies, child support, and so on—the reduction in welfare state support for them was much less than indicated in the replacement rate. Still, the table captures the greater effort made by the United Kingdom than by most other countries

Table 1.15 Unemployment Benefit Replacement Ratios, 1960–1995

	1965–1972	1973–1979	1980–1987	1988–1995
Australia	0.15	0.23	0.23	0.26
Austria	0.17	0.30	0.34	0.34
Belgium	0.40	0.55	0.50	0.48
Canada	0.43	0.59	0.57	0.58
Denmark	0.35	0.55	0.67	0.64
Finland	0.18	0.29	0.38	0.53
France	0.51	0.56	0.61	0.58
West Germany	0.41	0.39	0.38	0.37
Ireland	0.24	0.44	0.50	0.40
Italy	0.06	0.04	0.02	0.26
Japan	0.38	0.31	0.29	0.30
The Netherlands	0.64	0.65	0.67	0.70
Norway	0.13	0.28	0.56	0.62
New Zealand	0.30	0.27	0.30	0.29
Portugal	n.a.	0.17	0.44	0.65
Spain	0.48	0.62	0.75	0.68
Sweden	0.16	0.57	0.70	0.72
Switzerland	0.02	0.21	0.48	0.61
United Kingdom	0.36	0.34	0.26	0.22
United States	0.23	0.28	0.30	0.26

Source: OECD Database on Unemployment Benefit Entitlements and Replacement Rates. For information on the database see OECD (1994); based on the replacement ratio in the first year of an unemployment spell averaged over three family types.

Note: n.a. = not available. Measures of replacement rates vary because some studies include some benefits but not others. The OECD changed the benefits it included in Italy after 1991, which explains the rise in the final column. But there are serious problems in inclusion of benefits among all countries. See Martin (1996).

to reduce the disincentive to work. Studies that look at the impact of changes in the replacement rate and other measures of unemployment benefit on unemployment or employment show that reforms that lessen the payoff and, in particular, the length of access to benefits tend to increase employment, although only modestly.[30]

Blundell and Hoynes (chap. 10 in this volume) have examined the shift in U.K. welfare support toward in-work benefits. By shifting support to working families, the WFTC reform should also increase employment. They show, however, that any such effects are relatively small, in large part because U.K. in-work benefits are counted as income for other benefits (notably rent rebates under the Housing Benefit) so that the effect of these reforms on incentives to work were relatively modest. In addition, the United Kingdom increased the generosity of other welfare programs at the

30. See OECD (1997, chap. 2) and Atkinson and Mickelwright (1991). The most recent work covering the United States tells a similar story: See Ashenfelter, Ashmore, and Deschenes (1999).

same time, further reducing the employment incentive in these reforms. The result is that very little of the rise in the employment rate of women can be plausibly related to these changes. Van Reenan's analysis (chap. 11 in this volume) of the New Deal program initiated by the Labour government gives a similar picture of modest impacts of reforms on employment. In this case, the combination of assistance in job search, wage subsidies to employers, and education and training coupled with time-limited benefits produced an estimated gain of 17,000 employed young persons—a modest amount in an economy with some 27 million workers in 2000.

Some might argue that the decline in union power and increase in inequality that the various labor market reforms helped bring about may have contributed to the expansion of employment. Since unionization fell rapidly in manufacturing, where employment was decimated, it is difficult to make any sectoral link between changes in union power and growth of jobs. On the wage side, the fact that real wages in the United Kingdom rose throughout the 1980s and 1990s makes it hard to tell a story in which declining wages created employment. Similarly, the fact that groups and sectors where wages increased the most had the biggest increase in employment also raises doubts about any simple microreform–job-creation story. The biggest problem in assessing the contribution of the reforms on employment from microstudies is, of course, that the macroperformance of the U.K. economy dominates overall employment patterns. In the 1980s through the early 1990s, the United Kingdom had relatively high unemployment, despite the various economic reforms, because of poor macroeconomic policy and outcomes. The adverse effects of high and rising unemployment masked any positive effects of microinstitutional changes on labor-market outcomes. From the mid-1990s to early 2000s, the employment-creating effects of an extended boom dominated any impacts of microreforms on outcomes. If the market-oriented policy reforms in the labor market contributed to the length and extent of the economic expansion, they would indeed help explain the good performance of the United Kingdom in employment in this period, but such a contribution cannot be readily determined from microeconomic data.

1.3.3 An Alternative Approach

There is another way in which we can try to assess the impact of the U.K. reforms on economic performance. This is to estimate the effect of indicators of market-oriented institutions and policies captured by the FII on economic performance across advanced OECD countries and to use the estimated coefficient on the FII to estimate how much the U.K. reforms affected U.K. outcomes. As with other cross-country analyses, this procedure has advantages and disadvantages. It provides a statistical assessment of purported effects of reforms using the data for the set of covered countries, and it specifies the counterfactual for the United Kingdom (and other reforming countries) as that of the countries that underwent less market-oriented reforms. With data from the Fraser Institute available from 1970 to 1995, it allows for fixed effects that focus on the before-and-after changes in the same country. On the negative side, however, it does not isolate the effects of reforms in the United Kingdom, per se. Rather, the estimated coefficients on the FII measure reflect the experience of all the countries that also undertook substantial free-market reforms but that may not have had good economic performances, notably New Zealand. The pro-market reforms may have been the right medicine for the United Kingdom but not for New Zealand, or they may have been the right medicine for New Zealand but were overpowered by greater adverse problems. Still, it is useful to examine what such an analysis shows about the impact of reforms similar to those adopted in the United Kingdom on advanced countries in general. Table 1.16 records the coefficients and standard errors for a set of cross-country regressions of the level and growth of macroeconomic outcome variables on the FII for the period 1970–1999. Since the FII is reported every five years, the calculations relate to five-year periods: 1970, 1975, 1980, 1985, 1990, and 1995. When the dependent variable is the ln of the level of an outcome, it refers to the same five years. When the dependent variable is the ln change in the outcome, it refers to the ensuing five-year period: That is, the FII for 1970 is related to the change from 1970 to 1975. For 1995, the change relates to 1995–1999, weighted to allow for the fact that this change covers four rather than five years.

Each line in the table comes from a separate regression. The odd-numbered regressions include a dummy variable for the year, so that they

Table 1.16 Coefficients and Standard Errors on the Fraser Index of Economic Freedom in Regressions of the Level and ln Change in Macroeconomic Variables, OECD Countries, 1970–1999

Dependent Variable		Fraser Index Coefficient	Fraser Index Standard Error	Year Dummy	Country Dummy	R^2
ln GDP/capita	(1)	0.144	–0.017	Y	n.a.	0.593
	(2)	–0.001	–0.016	Y	Y	0.929
Δ ln GDP/capita	(3)	–0.006	–0.006	Y	n.a.	0.183
	(4)	0.001	–0.011	Y	Y	0.449
ln GDP/employee	(5)	0.332	–0.149	Y	n.a.	0.053
	(6)	–0.001	–0.015	Y	Y	0.998
Δ ln GDP/employee	(7)	–0.012	–0.005	Y	n.a.	0.170
	(8)	–0.004	–0.009	Y	Y	0.425
ln employment/population	(9)	1.349	–0.759	Y	n.a.	0.044
	(10)	0.351	–0.606	Y	Y	0.876
Δ ln employment/population	(11)	0.005	–0.005	Y	n.a.	0.113
	(12)	0.020	–0.010	Y	Y	0.213

Source: Calculated using OECD (1999b) and Gwartney, Lawson, and Samida (2000).
Note: n.a. = not available.

are cross-sectional comparisons of countries with different levels of the Fraser economic freedom index. The even-numbered regressions include dummies for country as well as for the year, so that they are fixed-effects regressions that relate differences in outcomes to differences in the FII over time within countries. They show the effect of reforms within a country on outcomes. The table shows that countries with greater market freedoms had higher GDP per capita, productivity per employee, and employment per adult in the population. In part, this reflects the fact that the countries with the highest FII scores include the United States and Canada, while the countries with the lowest scores include Portugal and Greece. At the same time, growth rates of GDP per capita and productivity are negatively related to the index, indicating a convergence in output and productivity over the period. Finally, the results on employment to population give the most consistent pattern, with positive coefficients on the FII in both the level and growth equations.

Taking the even-numbered calculations, which include the country dummies so that they reflect the effect of reforms on outcomes, we find that reforms had moderate positive effects on employment but not on the other outcome variables. This is consistent with the evidence that the U.K. reforms contributed to the country's improved employment record but raises some doubt about the impact of the reforms on productivity. The case that reforms improved productivity rests on the microanalyses in this volume that are specific to the United Kingdom.

1.4 Conclusion

This chapter has examined two of the main facts that constitute the subject matter for this volume: the market reforms that the United Kingdom undertook in the 1980s and 1990s and the relative economic progress of the country compared to other advanced countries. The evidence shows that the United Kingdom made greater market reforms than most other advanced countries; arrested the nearly century-long trend of economic decline in the United Kingdom relative to its historic competitors, Germany and France; and improved the place of the United Kingdom in the economic league tables. It is difficult to link the reforms to the improved economic performance relative to these other countries, but at the minimum our analysis has shown that the change in the U.K. economy cannot be readily explained by standard macroeconomic changes in labor or capital. Ensuing chapters present some of the more micro-based evidence that we used to judge the contribution of the reforms, and they examine some of the accompanying costs, in terms of income distribution, as well. Absent an unequivocal counterfactual of what would have happened had the United Kingdom not proceeded with its reforms, we cannot definitively judge the market reforms, although, when we weigh the diverse evidence, they do seem to have played a positive role in aggregate economic growth.

Appendix

Table 1A.1 Age Structure of the Population, 1960 and 1997 (%)

	1960			1997		
	Under Age 15	Age 15+	15+ Who Are Over 64	Under Age 15	Age 15+	15+ Who Are Over 64
United Kingdom	23.3	76.7	15.2	19.3	80.7	19.5
Germany	21.3	78.7	13.7	15.9	84.1	19.3
France	26.7	73.4	15.8	19.1	80.9	19.1
Italy	23.4	76.6	11.7	15.3	84.7	18.5
Ireland	30.5	69.5	15.7	23.1	76.9	14.8
United States	31.0	69.0	13.3	22.3	77.7	15.4

Note: Based on data in OECD (1998).

Table 1A.2 Employment-Population Rates and Annual Hours per Capita, 1960–1999

	United Kingdom	West Germany	France	Italy	Ireland	United States
	Employment-Population Rate (ages 15+ or 16+)					
1960	60.6	59.2	58.6	54.0	53.1	56.1
1965	61.0	58.5	56.4	49.6	53.8	56.2
1970	59.2	56.6	56.0	47.4	52.0	57.4
1975	59.7	53.2	54.8	46.0	48.4	56.1
1980	58.1	53.1	53.8	46.1	48.3	59.2
1985	55.5	50.7	50.9	44.4	42.4	60.1
1990	59.6	52.6	50.9	43.9	44.2	62.8
1995	57.2	49.6	48.7	41.5	46.9	62.9
1999	59.1	48.8	49.6	42.3	54.1	64.3
	Annual Hours per Capita (ages 15+ or 16+)					
1960	1,250	1,260	1,184	1,132	1,137	1,096
1965	1,219	1,192	1,130	970	n.a.	1,091
1970	1,128	1,091	1,084	933	n.a.	1,071
1975	1,063	947	991	847	1,000	1,016
1980	993	916	927	824	913	1,052
1985	933	849	816	770	766	1,068
1990	992	851	815	759	764	1,100
1995	924	775	776	712	797	1,106
1999	956	755	788	724	920	1,138

Notes: n.a. = not available. Employment and population data from U.S. Bureau of Labor Statistics (2000a). Population refers to the adult population (ages 16 and older in the United States, ages 15–64 in other countries). Hours data for the United Kingdom, Germany, France, and the United States are based on estimates of annual hours per worker from Mary O'Mahoney (unpublished tables), updated using data from the OECD and the International Comparisons of Output and Productivity (ICOP) project. Hours data for Italy are based on data from OECD. Hours data for Ireland are based on data from ICOP.

Table 1A.3 **Employment Shares in Three Major Sectors, 1960–1998**

	United Kingdom			West Germany			France			United States		
	Agr.	Ind.	Srv.	Agr.	Ind.	Srv.	Agr.	Ind.	Srv.	Agr.	Ind.	Srv.
1960	4.7	46.1	49.2	13.9	46.0	40.1	23.2	37.5	39.3	8.5	33.4	58.1
1979	2.7	37.3	60.0	5.2	42.9	51.9	8.8	35.4	55.8	3.6	30.2	66.2
1998	1.7	26.1	72.2	2.8	33.6	63.6	4.2	23.9	71.9	2.6	22.2	75.2

Source: U.S. Bureau of Labor Statistics (2000a).

Note: Entries represent civilian employment shares in agriculture (agr.), industry (ind.), and services (srv.).

Table 1A.4 **Changes in Skill Characteristics of U.K. Workers, 1975–1996**

Period	Mean Years Schooling	Higher Vocational Qualifications (%)	University Degree (%)	Male (%)
1975–1977	10.8	6.5	4.6	59.5
1978–1980	11.1	7.6	5.8	57.7
1981–1983	11.2	8.5	6.6	56.8
1984–1986	11.6	11.5	9.0	54.8
1987–1989	11.8	13.1	9.9	53.0
1990–1992	12.0	13.7	10.6	51.1
1993–1996	12.4	14.8	13.3	49.8

Notes: Based on unweighted tabulations of individuals who were employed during the survey week in the 1975–1996 General Household Surveys. Mean years of schooling is calculated following Schmitt (1995). Higher qualifications include National Higher Certificate or Diploma, City and Guilds Advanced and Full Technological Certificates, qualifications obtained from polytechnical and similar institutions, and Ordinary National Certificate or Diploma.

Table 1A.5 **Union Membership Rate among Wage and Salary Employees in the United Kingdom and the United States, 1960–1999**

	United Kingdom		United States
	(1)	(2)	(3)
1960	41.3	n.a.	30.4
1965	40.5	n.a.	27.6
1970	48.2	n.a.	26.4
1975	49.4	n.a.	24.6
1980	52.9	n.a.	22.2
1985	46.6	n.a.	17.5
1990	40.0	38.1	15.3
1995	n.a.	32.1	14.0
1999	n.a.	29.5	13.5

Sources: Column (1) is taken from Metcalf (1994, table 4.1) and is estimated from union membership data. Column (2) is taken from Hicks (2000, table 2) and is based on Labor Force Survey data. Column (3) is taken from Freeman (1998), updated by Farber and Western (2000), and is based on a combination of data sources.

Note: n.a. = not available.

Table 1A.6 **Self-Employment Rates in the United Kingdom, West Germany, and the United States, 1960–1999**

	United Kingdom (1)	West Germany (2)	United States (3)
1960	7.2	n.a.	n.a.
1965	6.7	n.a.	8.9
1970	7.7	16.6	8.3
1975	8.0	14.0	8.9
1980	8.4	11.7	9.6
1985	11.3	11.4	9.9
1990	13.1	10.6	10.6
1995	13.0	11.0	10.9
1999	12.7	11.3	10.3

Sources: Column (1) is derived from data in the U.K. Office of National Statistics (1997, table 3.8), updated with data from the Labor Force Survey. Column (2) is derived from data in Federal Republic of Germany, Federal Statistical Office (1998, table 6.3); the estimated self-employment count includes family workers. Column (3) is based on authors' tabulations of the U.S. Bureau of the Census (various years); the 1965 entry for the United States is based on 1967 data.

Note: n.a. = not available.

Table 1A.7 **Fraction of Employment in Government or Public Sectors**

	United Kingdom				
	Government (1)	Nationalized Industries (2)	Germany[a] (3)	France[a] (4)	United States[b] (5)
1960	15.2	8.8	8.1	n.a.	n.a.
1965	16.3	7.5	n.a.	n.a.	15.3
1970	18.7	7.6	10.9	n.a.	15.6
1975	21.7	7.3	13.0	17.4	17.5
1980	21.9	7.1	n.a.	n.a.	16.2
1985	22.7	4.6	15.5	22.9	15.0
1990	21.3	2.5	15.1	22.8	15.0
1995	19.7	1.4	15.1	24.8	14.4
1999	n.a.	n.a.	n.a.	n.a.	14.1

Notes: Data in columns (1) and (2) are derived from data in the U.K. Office of National Statistics (1997, table 3.8). Government includes general government and National Health Service Trusts (after 1991). Nationalized industries include the post office. Data in columns (3) and (4) are taken from OECD (1995, table 2.13). Data in column (5) are based on authors' tabulations of U.S. Bureau of the Census (various years) and include employees who report that they work for the government. n.a. = not available.

[a]General government.

[b]Public sector.

References

Ashenfelter, Orley, David Ashmore, and Olivier Deschenes. 1999. Do unemployment insurance recipients actively seek work? Randomized trials in four U.S. States. NBER Working Paper no. 6982. Cambridge, Mass.: National Bureau of Economic Research, February.

Atkinson, Anthony B., and John Mickelwright. 1991. Unemployment compensation and labour market transitions: A critical review. *Journal of Economic Literature* 29 (4): 1679–727.

Bean, Charles, and Nicholas Crafts. 1996. British economic growth since 1945: Relative economic decline . . . and renaissance? In *Economic Growth in Europe since 1945,* ed. Nicholas Crafts and Gianni Toniolo, 131–172. Cambridge: Cambridge University Press.

Bertola, Giuseppi. 1990. Job security, employment and wages. *European Economic Review* 34 (4): 851–886.

Blanchard, Olivier J. 1997. The Medium Run. *Brookings Papers on Economic Activity,* Issue no. 2:89–141. Washington, D.C.: Brookings Institution.

Blanchflower, David, and Richard Freeman. 1994. Did the Thatcher reforms change British labour market performance? In *The UK labour market: Comparative aspects and institutional developments,* ed. Ray Barrell, 51–92. Cambridge, U.K.: Cambridge University Press.

Blanchflower, David G., and Lisa M. Lynch. 1994. Training at work: A comparison of U.S. and British youths. In *Training and the private sector,* ed. Lisa M. Lynch, 233–260. Chicago: University of Chicago Press.

Broadberry, Stephen N., and Karin Wagner. 1996. Human capital and productivity in manufacturing during the twentieth century: Britain, Germany, and the United States. In *Quantitative aspects of post-war European economic growth,* ed. Bart van Ark and Nicholas Crafts, 244–270. Cambridge: Cambridge University Press.

Bruno, Michael, and Jeffrey Sachs. 1985. *Economics of worldwide stagflation.* Cambridge, Mass.: Harvard University Press.

Calmfors, Lars, and John Driffil. 1988. Bargaining structure, corporatism and macroeconomic performance. *Economic Policy* 6 (1): 13–62.

Djankov, Simeon, Rafael La Porta, Florencio Lopez-de-Silanes, and Andrei Shleifer. 2000. The regulation of entry. NBER Working Paper no. 7892. Cambridge, Mass.: National Bureau of Economic Research, September.

Elmeskov, Jorgen, John Martin, and Stefano Scarpetta. 1998. Key lessons for labour market reforms: Evidence from OECD countries' experience. *Swedish Economic Policy Review* 5 (2): 205–252.

Farber, Henry S., and Bruce Western. 2000. Round up the usual suspects: The decline of unions in the private sector, 1973–1998. Princeton University Industrial Relations Section Working Paper no. 437. Princeton, N.J.: Princeton University, April.

Federal Republic of Germany, Federal Statistical Office. 1998. *Statistiches jahrbuch* (Statistical yearbook). Wiesbaden, Germany: Statistiches Bundesamt.

Feinstein, Charles H. 1999. Structural change in the developed countries during the twentieth century. *Oxford Review of Economic Policy* 15 (Winter): 35–55.

Fraser Institute. 2001. *Economic freedom of the world 2001 annual report.* http://www.fraserinstitute.ca. Retrieved January 2001.

Freeman, Richard B. 1998. Spurts in union growth: Defining moments and social processes. In *The defining moment: The Great Depression and the American econ-*

omy in the twentieth century, ed. Michael Bordo, Claudia Goldin, and Eugene White, 265–296. Chicago: University of Chicago Press.
Griliches, Zvi. 1970. Notes on the role of education in production functions and growth accounting. In *Education, income and human capital,* ed. W. Lee Hansen. New York: Columbia University Press.
Grout, Paul A. 1984. Investment and wages in the absence of binding contracts: A Nash bargaining approach. *Econometrica* 52 (March): 449–460.
Grubb, David, and William Wells. 1993. Employment regulation and patterns of work in EC countries. *OECD Economic Studies* 21 (1): 7–58.
Gwartney, James, Robert Lawson, and Dexter Samida. 2000. *Economic freedom of the world, 2000 annual report.* Vancouver, Canada: Fraser Institute.
Hanke, Steve, and Stephen Walters. 1997. Economic freedom, prosperity, and equality: A survey. *The Cato Journal* 17 (2): 1–23.
Harvard Center for International Development. 2000. *The global competitiveness report 2000.* Geneva: World Economic Forum.
Hicks, Stephen. 2000. Trade union membership 1989–99: An analysis of data from the certification officer and labour force survey. *Labour Market Trends* 108 (7): 329–340.
La Porta, Rafael, Florencio Lopez-de-Silanes, Andrei Shleifer, and Robert Vishny. 1997. Legal Determinants of External Finance. NBER Working Paper no. 5879. Cambridge, Mass.: National Bureau of Economic Research, January.
———. 1999. Investor protection and corporate valuation. NBER Working Paper no. 7403. Cambridge, Mass.: National Bureau of Economic Research, October.
Lazear, Edward P. 1990. Job security provisions and employment. *Quarterly Journal of Economics* 105 (August): 699–726.
Machin, Stephen, Mark Stewart, and John van Reenan. 1993. Multiple unionism, fragmented bargaining and economic outcomes in unionized U.K. establishments. In *New perspectives on industrial disputes,* ed. David Metcalf and Simon Milner, 55–69. London: Routledge.
Martin, John P. 1996. Measures of replacement rates for the purpose of international comparisons: A note. *OECD Economics Studies* 1(26): 99–114.
Metcalf, David. 1994. Transformation of British industrial relations? Institutions, conduct, and outcomes. In *The U.K. labour market: Comparative aspects and institutional developments,* ed. Ray Burrell, 126–157. Cambridge: Cambridge University Press.
Millward, Neil, Alex Bryson, and John Forth. 2000. *All change at work? British employment relations 1980–98.* New York: Routledge.
Nicoletti, Giuseppe, Stefano Scarpetta, and Olivier Boylaud. 1999. Summary indicators of product market regulation with an extension to employment protection legislation. OECD Economic Department Working Paper no. 226. Paris: Organization for Economic Cooperation and Development (OECD), April.
O'Mahony, Mary. 1996. Measures of fixed capital stocks in the post-war period: A five country study. In *Quantitative aspects of post-war European economic growth,* ed. Bart van Ark and Nicholas Crafts, 165–214. Cambridge: Cambridge University Press.
Organization for Economic Cooperation and Development (OECD). 1994. *OECD jobs study.* Paris: OECD.
———. 1995. *Main economic indicators: Historical statistics 1960–1994.* Paris: OECD.
———. 1997. *OECD employment outlook 1996.* Paris: OECD.
———. 1998. *Labor force statistics, 1977–1997.* Paris: OECD.

———. 1999a. Cross-country patterns of product market regulation. *OECD Economic Outlook* 66 (2): 179–189.

———. 1999b. *OECD historical statistics.* Paris: OECD.

Rabushka, Alvin. 2000. The director's column. *Institute for Advanced Strategic and Policy Studies Quarterly Report* 9 (Winter). http://www.israeleconomy.org/quarterly/winter00/rabushka.htm. Retrieved January 2001.

Schmitt, John. 1995. The changing structure of male earnings in Britain, 1974–1988. In *Differences and changes in wage structures,* ed. Richard B. Freeman and Lawrence F. Katz, 177–204. Chicago: University of Chicago Press.

U.K. Competition Commission. 2000. *New cars: A report on the supply of new motor cars within the UK.* London: U.K. Competition Commission.

U.K. Inland Revenue Service. *National statistics.* Available at http://www.inlandrevenue.gov.uk/stats/. Retrieved January 2001.

U.K. Office of National Statistics. 1997. *Economic trends. Annual supplement 1997.* London: The Stationery Office.

U.S. Bureau of the Census. Various years. *March current population survey.* Washington, D.C.: Data User Services Division.

U.S. Bureau of Labor Statistics. 2000a. *Comparative civilian labor force statistics for ten countries, 1959–1999.* Washington, D.C.: U.S. Bureau of Labor Statistics, Office of Productivity and Technology.

———. 2000b. *Comparative real gross domestic product per capita and per employed person for fourteen countries, 1960–1998.* Washington, D.C.: U.S. Bureau of Labor Statistics, Office of Productivity and Technology.

van Ark, Bart. 1996. Sectoral growth accounting and structural change in post-war Europe. In *Quantitative aspects of post-war European economic growth,* ed. Bart van Ark and Nicholas Crafts, 84–164. Cambridge: Cambridge University Press.

2

Seeking a Premier-League Economy
The Role of Privatization

Richard Green and Jonathan Haskel

> Taken together, the privatisation program in Britain probably marked the largest transfer of power and property since the dissolution of the monasteries under Henry VIII.
> —M. Pirie, *Privatisation*

2.1 Introduction and Summary

In 1979, when Margaret Thatcher came to power, publicly owned companies produced roughly 12 percent of U.K. gross domestic product (GDP). By the time of the election of the Labour government in 1997, this figure had fallen to 2 percent. At least in the United Kingdom, public ownership seems to have been discredited. The Labour Party, which had initially met the privatization program with the policy of renationalization without compensation, is now running privatizations of its own. In the meantime, the opinion and experience of U.K. privatization practitioners and regulators is sought throughout the world. In the United Kingdom, the debate has now shifted from the sales of publicly owned assets to the issues of franchise design for public services, public-private partnerships, and internal markets in state organizations.[1]

In this chapter we try to answer some of the following questions. First, what were the origins of privatization? Was the policy the natural outcome of Conservative thinking, or was it a decisive break from the past? Second, why has privatization proved so enduring? Why is renationalization off the

Richard Green is professor of economics at the University of Hull Business School. Jonathan Haskel is professor of economics at Queen Mary University of London.

We thank David Card, Richard Freeman, John Kingman, and conference participants for comments on an earlier draft. Thanks also to Jonathan Ashworth and Matt Barnes for expert research assistance. The plant-level data in this paper were prepared under the Office for National Statistics Business Data Linking Project. Errors are our own.

1. Following Kay and Thompson (1986), we think of privatization as a term covering various means of changing the relationships between government-provided economic activity and the private sector. The main areas of government activity are (or were) in (1) various industries, such as utilities, steel, and cars; (2) infrastructure, such as roads and railways; and (3) social services, such as pensions, health, and schools.

agenda? Third, and important in the context of diagnosing Britain's failure to reach the premier league of output per head over the last twenty years, did privatization raise productivity in the companies concerned? If it did not, what future steps concerning privatization or the privatized companies can be taken that might improve performance?

Our purpose in the chapter is partly to survey existing evidence and partly to bring new evidence to bear on these questions.[2] The following summarizes our argument. We start in the next section with an overview of the history of public-ownership levels in the United Kingdom and other countries. Before World War II, industries such as steel, coal, and transportation were mostly privately owned, with a few exceptions (the British Broadcasting Corporation [BBC] and British Overseas Airways Corporation). Utilities (gas, electricity, and water) were a mix of private and municipally owned, with some regulation (a position similar to the United States today). The major wave of nationalization occurred during the postwar Labour government (gas, electricity, steel, coal, and rail), aligning the United Kingdom with other European countries. Subsequent pre-Thatcher Conservative administrations privatized some industries (steel in 1953, for example) but equally nationalized some (Rolls-Royce in 1971) and attempted no major privatization of, for example, the utilities. Thus, privatization was in no sense inevitable; The Thatcher program was a decisive break from the past.

Although Thatcher came into office with a pro-market philosophy, the word "privatization" does not appear anywhere in the 1979 Conservative Party manifesto.[3] Privatization, at least on a large scale, was in fact something of an accident. During the early 1980s, it became apparent that the state-owned telephone monopoly, British Telecommunications, would have to undertake huge investment, in part because of previous unwise decisions on which technology to adopt (Galal et al. 1994). By Treasury accounting rules, such investment would count as public spending, which the government was committed to reduce, and all schemes to finance this public investment off the public balance sheet failed. The government decided to sell the company, ensuring that its investment would take place in the private sector, and they discovered that the sale was very popular with its supporters and extended the policy.

What effect is privatization likely to have? As we discuss in section 2.3,

2. This paper is predominantly a survey, but it does offer two original pieces of research. First, we look at newly assembled data on total factor productivity (TFP) for a series of previously public companies. Second, we use plant-level data for an industry that had a mix of public and private plants in 1979 (confidentiality precludes us from revealing the plants concerned), and we look at their relative productivities and at the contributions of plant closure to productivity growth.

3. There were commitments to return a few companies to the private sector, but the term "privatization" is not used.

economists have naturally focused on the possible efficiency gains from privatization, but these were not uppermost in politicians' minds at the time. Rather, as sections 2.4 and 2.5 set out, privatization was a way of meeting a number of economic and political objectives, such as reducing the power of public-sector trade unions. Management remained more or less the same, as did market structure (at least until the later privatizations of electricity and the railways). A number of steps were taken to try to make privatization irreversible, such as making shareholding widespread enough so that the opposition Labour Party's then stance of renationalization without compensation (later dropped) would potentially harm a large pool of shareholders.

Section 2.6 studies efficiency. Most studies of the major industries and utilities in the 1979 public sector start from the observation that the biggest improvements in productivity came before much of the sector was privatized. This suggests that restructuring and competition are more important in raising productivity than ownership per se. Studies of contracting out reach a similar conclusion. In refuse collection, for example, it is possible to compare costs when collection remains in the public sector without competition (i.e., the service being tendered), when it remains in the public sector with competition, and when it passes to the private sector. Evidence suggests that savings are similar whether collection is public or private as long as there is competition (i.e., tendering) for the service.

After all this, it seems appropriate to ask: Did the U.K. economy need privatization? To the extent that competition (and not ownership) matters, privatization would seem irrelevant. Thus, the imperative question is to devise appropriate regulation mechanisms and introduce competition, and these design issues are important in developing the next phase of privatization—namely, the Private Finance Initiative (PFI) and other public-private partnerships.

But to the extent that preprivatization restructuring matters, the effect of privatization is rather subtle (and would not be picked up in conventional regression analysis of company performance). Restructuring of public-sector firms needs tough decisions (e.g., deciding to close down plants). That toughness may come from a strong ministerial personality, but this is all too rare. However, it may also come from the threat (or promise) of privatization in the future. Thus, privatization is perhaps seen as a credible signal of public-sector toughness that politicians cannot otherwise give. Furthermore, the fact that privatization has been carried out confers an advantage to ministers on the left of the political spectrum: They can now credibly commit not to have to intervene in many formerly public-sector decisions. This might explain why renationalization has vanished from the U.K. Labour government's agenda, although it has intervened selectively from time to time.

2.2 Public Ownership in the United Kingdom

In 1979, government-owned firms produced approximately 12 percent of GDP. Public ownership predominated in the utilities, transport, and the "heavy industries" (i.e., coal, steel, and shipbuilding), although there were state-owned companies in other sectors. Table 2.1 shows how the pattern of public ownership in the United Kingdom developed over time. Since there is a longer history of public ownership in the utilities, we begin with these.

Utility public ownership began at the level of local, not national, government. Clean water supplies, and later gas (for lighting), were provided by local councils in some areas and by the private sector in others. Joseph Chamberlain's "gas and water socialism," which gave Birmingham improved services in the 1870s, was perhaps the most famous example, but there were many others. In the last two decades of the century, when the electricity supply industry began to emerge, some areas were served by privately owned companies and others by municipal undertakings. The 1882 Electric Lighting Act allowed the local authorities to buy out the private companies (at their written-down asset value) after twenty-one years, later extended to forty-two years. Unfortunately, this fragmented ownership structure made it almost impossible to gain economies of scale, since municipal undertakings could not expand beyond their boundaries, and the private companies, potentially larger, were in practice smaller (Hannah 1979).

Telephone services were initially also fragmented, but the post office became a near-national monopoly from 1912 onwards.[4] At that time, the post office was a government department headed by a minister, but it eventually became a conventional nationalized industry, a "public corporation," in 1969. The possibility of greater state control of the electricity industry to solve the problems caused by its fragmentation was discussed soon after the first World War, but was rejected. In 1926, however, the government set up the Central Electricity Board to construct a national transmission grid and allow the industry to gain economies of scale through better coordination of (still independent) generating stations.

Nationalization on a large scale followed the second World War and the election of the first majority Labour government. The private electricity companies were bought out, and the municipal undertakings transferred to central government ownership, in 1947. The gas industry was nationalized in a similar manner the following year. The water industry remained a mixture of local authority water boards and regulated private companies until 1973, when the local authority undertakings in England and Wales

4. Kingston-Upon-Hull City Council continued to provide its own telephone services. The first author used to assume that the civil service had simply forgotten the city when planning the reorganization. He now knows that the decision was made because the people of Hull deserve a better service than the rest of the country.

Table 2.1 **Public Ownership in the United Kingdom**

Industry	Pre-1914	1919–1939	1945–1951	1950s and 1960s	1970s	1980s	1990s
Aerospace		P			N 1977	P 1981	
Airlines		P; N 1939				P 1987	
Airports		P; M		N 1965 (some)		P 1987	
Bank of England	P		N 1946				
British Petroleum	P; stake bought 1914				Shares sold 1977–1987		
Broadcasting (BBC)		P; N 1927		P; stations added			
Cable and wireless (telecoms)	P	N 1938 (Part)	N 1946			P 1981	
Coal	P		N 1947				P 1994
Electricity	P; M	N 1933 (Grid)	N 1948				P 1990
Gas	P; M		N 1948			P 1986	
Oil (North Sea exploration)[a]				P	N 1975 (partly)	P 1982	
Ports						P 1983	
Post Office[b]	Govt. Dept.			N 1969			
Railways	P		N 1948				P 1994–1997
Road freight	P		N 1948	Mostly P		P 1982	
Rolls-Royce	P				N 1973	P 1987	
Shipbuilding	P				N 1977	P 1980s	
Steel	P		N 1949	P 1953; N 1967		P 1989	
Telecommunications	P; M; N 1912					P 1984	
Vehicles (British Leyland)	P				N 1975	P 1988	
Water[c]	P; M				N 1973; M	P 1989	

Notes: Blank cells indicate that the status of the industry in question did not change in the decade in question. M = municipal ownership; P = private ownership; N (date) = nationalization in that year; P (date) = privatization in that year (the first sale for companies privatized in tranches); and Govt. Dept. = government department.

[a]Britoil was set up alongside private-sector oil companies in 1975—no companies were taken over.

[b]The government department was transformed into a nationalized industry in 1969, but this was not a change of ownership.

[c]Only the municipal water undertakings were nationalized in 1973.

were reorganized into ten Regional Water Authorities. The private companies, which supplied about a quarter of the consumers in England and Wales with water, were not affected by this reorganization.

The postwar Labour government also nationalized a number of nonutility industries. The "commanding heights" of coal and steel were nationalized in 1946 and 1949, although the steel industry was to be sold back to the private sector by the next Conservative government. Similarly, much of the long-distance road freight industry was nationalized in 1948, and most of it privatized again in the early 1950s. The railways, losing traffic to roads and starved of investment during the war, were nationalized in 1948. The British Overseas Airways Corporation, including most of the country's fledgling airlines, had been nationalized in 1939. The steel industry was renationalized in 1967, and shipbuilding and aerospace were nationalized in 1977.

These latter nationalizations were bitterly opposed by the Conservative Party, even though the previous Conservative government had effectively nationalized Rolls-Royce (aircraft engines). Rescued from bankruptcy, the company did not become a public corporation, but it remained a limited company with the government as the major shareholder, as did the vehicle firm British Leyland, which was rescued a couple of years later. They were not the only private companies with substantial government shareholdings—the government had taken a strategic stake in British Petroleum before the first World War and later acquired Cable and Wireless, which provided telecommunications services in a number of (then) British colonies.

In 1979, therefore, Britain had a much higher degree of public ownership in industry than the United States, but it was not far out of line with the pattern in many other European countries. Public ownership of gas and electricity was common in Europe (sometimes in the charge of local government, sometimes central), while government ownership in the United States was much more limited (to municipal distribution bodies and the New Deal–era generating boards, such as the Tennessee Valley Authority). Telecommunications was usually public in Europe (as in the United Kingdom) and private in the United States. Public railways and "flag carrier" airlines (with smaller private competitors) were common in Europe but not in the United States. The United Kingdom had a mixture of public and private water suppliers. In the United States, water was (and is) predominantly municipal. In France, however, although municipalities own the water assets in their districts, operation is usually contracted out to private companies. The United Kingdom was relatively unusual in the number of industrial companies in the public sector, including coal, steel, shipbuilding, and car manufacturing; most companies in these sectors were in the private sector in Europe and the United States. However, some industrial companies in Europe were state owned, and the Mitterand government in France embarked on a large program of nationalization in the early 1980s, after privatization had started in the United Kingdom.

How, in practice, did the government control its nationalized industries? Most were organized as public corporations, a type of organization invented for the BBC, which was nationalized in 1927. A public corporation is established by an Act of Parliament and governed by a board responsible to a minister. The corporation is financially independent of government, although any borrowing had to be approved by the Treasury. The Act laid down the board's duties, and, although ministers are allowed to give the board general directions, they are meant to keep away from detailed decision making.[5] Morrison summed up the attitude sought of board members when he called upon them to regard themselves as "the high custodians of the public interest" (1933, 157).

It soon became apparent that merely requiring corporations to break even, taking one year with another, as most of the nationalization statutes did, would lead to an inadequate financial performance. The first step toward greater control was taken in a 1961 white paper that set out financial targets in terms of a target rate of return. A 1967 white paper, which was perhaps the high point of economic analysis in the control of nationalized industries, required corporations to base their prices on costs at the margin and to use a test discount rate of 8 percent (in real terms) in all investment appraisals. Financial targets were intended to be compatible with these economic rules. In the early 1970s, however, many corporations were required to hold down their prices to combat inflation, producing heavy losses. Two more white papers were produced, in 1975 and 1978, that concentrated on the financial objectives of safeguarding cash flow and restoring profitability.

The 1978 white paper also required ministers to set a range of performance targets for the nationalized industries, including measures such as productivity and service standards. This was due to the gradual recognition that the industries had not been performing well—their productivity was typically well below that of comparable foreign enterprises and was growing too slowly. Labor relations at British Leyland became a national joke during the 1970s, and other industries had similar problems. Possible reasons for these problems are discussed in the next section.

2.3 The Rationale for Privatization

To the extent that privatization is a change in ownership, the private and public sectors differ because the public sector has different *objectives* than the private (i.e., broader objectives than profit maximization) and different *incentives.* The different incentives arise because a public-sector firm is not

5. In practice, ministers almost never gave general directions of the kind envisaged in the Acts but intervened far too frequently in matters of detail, even though Morrison (1933, 171) had feared that a "mischievous and not too competent minister could easily ruin any business undertaking if that were permitted."

vulnerable to takeover or bankruptcy and has a different information relationship with its owners.[6]

The textbook argument for public ownership centers on differences in objectives between private and public firms. Profit-maximizing firms with market power will produce inefficiently low levels of output relative to welfare-maximizing firms (assuming that costs are independent of ownership). Furthermore, many utilities have increasing returns and, thus, market power. The rationale for public ownership is then clear—namely, a change in objectives to increase social welfare—although the rationale for public ownership of industries without market power is less clear.

There are at least two problems with this view. First, it is not clear that ownership is necessary to obtain a socially optimal output level, since a regulator could simply require firms to produce at that necessary level. The problem is, of course, that regulators are unlikely to know what the socially efficient output level is, but then neither will government. Second, the apparent inefficiency in public firms (Pryke 1982) suggests relaxing the assumption that public and private firms have similar costs. Both these arguments suggest examining productive efficiency in public and private firms.

There are two main approaches to this. The agency approach to privatization focuses on the principal/agent relationship between the owner and a manager (private sector) and government and manager (public sector). Assuming that the private sector is more effective at monitoring managerial activity than the public sector, privatization improves productive efficiency by ensuring that managers supply effort and keep down costs (Bos 1990; Rees 1988). This is therefore primarily an argument about the effect of incentives on productive efficiency.

The delegation approach is primarily about the effect of objectives on efficiency. It begins with the observation that worker effort is frequently bargained over between managers and workers.[7] Furthermore, private firms are assumed to maximize profits, whereas the objectives of public-sector organizations are a combination of profits, consumer surplus, and the welfare of public-sector employees.[8] Under various conditions (Haskel and Sanchis 1995), it can be shown that the effect of changing objectives

6. Owners of public firms are voters and ministers, whereas owners of private firms are shareholders and managers.

7. Millward and Stevens (1986, table 9.19) report that, in 1984, 87 percent of nationalized industries negotiated with trade unions over working conditions, and 77 percent over manning levels.

8. According to former minister John Moore, as quoted in Martin and Parker (1997, 3), "the priorities of elected politicians are different from and often in conflict with the priorities of effective business managers. Yet in state-owned industries politicians are in charge, which means that whenever politicians cannot resist getting involved in what should be management decisions, political priorities take precedence over commercial ones. Politicians may overrule commercial judgements in other to build a new factory in an area where voters need jobs, or they may refuse to close an uneconomical plant. They can become involved in policies affecting the hiring and the size of the workforce."

toward profit maximization is to raise effort. The intuition for this result is straightforward. Privatization can then be viewed as a way of committing the government not to pay high wages, to accept low effort, or both. It is a method of delegating authority over wage and effort bargaining for a government that is unable to commit itself to bargaining at arms' length with the workforce. A union bargaining with a private firm faces, at the margin, a firm unwilling to concede to demands for high wages and low effort.[9]

Both models would predict relatively high employment and low effort before privatization.[10] Similarly, any liberalization of markets raises effort. Note, too, that while privatization shifts the objectives of the public-sector firms toward profit maximization, this process may take place before private ownership is instituted. This may be important empirically in the U.K. case, since, typically in the United Kingdom, more commercially orientated managers were brought in while firms were still in the public sector.

Privatization of natural monopolies will usually require regulation. Cost of capital regulation—common in the United States, for example—is likely to lead to overcapitalization (Averch and Johnson 1962). The regulation of prices faces a fundamental trade-off: profit regulation gives firms little incentive to reduce costs but may keep prices more aligned with marginal costs, whereas price cap regulation gives ample incentives for cost reduction at the cost of a possible wedge between prices and marginal costs. Furthermore, dynamic price cap regulation faces the problem of resetting the price cap. As we document later, proponents of the first U.K. price cap scheme believed this dynamic problem to be of academic interest only since they expected that competition would arrive before the price cap had to be reset. In reality, if resetting the price cap involves looking at profits, then price cap regulation becomes de facto profit regulation (Beesley and Littlechild 1989).

It is often argued that competition is not feasible in natural monopolies. However, it is worth noting that, first, such arguments generally refer to competition within the market, but competition for the market, such as rail franchises (or more generally contracting out), is often feasible. Second, on close examination, natural monopolies often consist of parts where competition is indeed not feasible (e.g., transmission of electricity and railway lines) and others where it is feasible (e.g., generation of electricity and energy retailing), and the privatization and restructuring process can take account of this. Third, with technical change, the technology that causes

9. The complication here is that the result depends on the functional form of the utility function. If workers care a good deal about effort but not wages, they may agree to wage cuts after privatization. If such cuts are deep enough, then effort can even fall. See Haskel and Sanchis (1995) for discussion.

10. The agency model is usually cast in terms of managerial effort, and the effect on employment is seldom derived. The delegation model obtains specific predictions on overemployment and undereffort (see Haskel and Szymanski 1992; Haskel and Sanchis 1995).

natural monopoly can cease to be of such great importance (e.g., the development of mobile phones). Finally, competition can become part of regulation. Yardstick competition (Shleifer 1985) regulates a firm by making prices (e.g., in a firm with the monopoly of a particular region) dependent on other regions' costs, thus providing good incentives for cost reduction.[11]

Finally, the regulation of quality of service has become an important factor in the U.K. debate. Such an issue amply illustrates the information problems confronting the regulator. Since it is impossible for the regulator to write complete contracts specifying all dimensions of quality, firms can neglect nonregulated quality dimensions.

2.4 Privatization in the United Kingdom since 1979

In 1975, Margaret Thatcher became leader of the Conservative Party. The party had supported the corporatist consensus of the 1950s and 1960s and had expanded the state's role in industry by taking over Rolls-Royce and British Leyland. Thatcher and her advisors gradually became determined to move away from this consensus, which they saw as responsible for the country's relative decline. They planned to introduce "free-market" policies that would reduce the role of the state in the economy. Private enterprise was not only believed to be more efficient than state provision; many thought it was morally superior.

The Conservatives also sought to reduce trade union power, which was strongest in the nationalized industries. In 1974, the National Union of Mineworkers, working for the dominant state-owned mining industry, called a national strike for better pay. The resulting power cuts caused the Conservative Prime Minister at the time, Edward Heath, to call an election under the slogan "who governs Britain?" He lost the election and, later, the leadership of his party. In opposition, in 1978, the Conservatives' Ridley Report[12] argued that where industries "have the nation by the jugular vein the only feasible option is to pay up." John Moore, who later became Financial Secretary to the Treasury, was to say that "Public Sector trade unions have been extraordinarily successful in gaining advantages for themselves in the pay hierarchy by exploiting their monopoly collective bargaining position. . . . Privatisation . . . makes it possible to link pay to success and to provide appropriate rewards" (as quoted in Kay and Thompson 1986).

11. While competition might improve productive efficiency, a more difficult question is whether this by itself improves welfare. No one disputes that welfare improves if competition aligns prices closer to marginal costs, but if it simply reduces costs, then this does not necessarily raise welfare since it may just be a transfer of welfare from managers (who may have to work harder) to consumers (who get lower prices). Yardstick competition is a case in which welfare is increased, since splitting a firm into many units expands the information base upon which to write contracts. Auctions are also likely to be welfare-improving since they reveal what was private information (on all this, see Vickers 1995).

12. Nicholas Ridley, MP, chaired a Conservative study group whose unpublished report was leaked to *The Economist* ("Appomattox or civil war," 27 May 1978, pp. 21–22).

In the light of subsequent developments, it is interesting to note that the word "privatization" does not appear in the Conservative Manifesto for the 1979 election. The party pledged to sell the National Freight Corporation (the rump of the road-haulage industry that had not been denationalized in the 1950s) and some of the companies owned by the National Enterprise Board (a Labour creation designed to provide finance for industrial investment). During the election, the party also proposed the sale of British Airways. The most eye-catching commitment, however, was to allow council-house tenants to buy their own homes, with discounts reflecting the length of time they had been living there. This proved to be a very popular policy, with more than 1.5 million homes sold to date, or roughly 25 percent of the 1979 stock of 6.5 million council houses. The arguments for this policy were not primarily economic, however, and its effect on economic efficiency is likely to be limited, as discussed by Gregg, Machin, and Manning (chap. 9 in this volume).

With no plans for large-scale privatizations, in the early 1980s the government began to sell shares in the private companies that it owned. The 1980 Civil Aviation Act allowed the government to turn British Airways from a public corporation into a limited company suitable for privatization, but it started to incur huge losses due to the recession in the airline industry, and a sale was clearly inappropriate.[13] The National Freight Corporation was also suffering in the recession, but it was bought by a consortium of managers, employees, and pensioners who believed that the company was about to turn around. Helped by the sale of some of its surplus property, it did so. Nevertheless, privatization was proceeding on a small scale and was not a major political issue.[14]

All this was to change with the privatization of British Telecommunications (BT). During the 1970s, BT had built up a backlog of investment, in part due to previous misguided decisions on the right technology to adopt (Galal et al. 1994). The main reason, however, was the tight external financing limit that controlled the amount that BT could borrow from the government. In the early 1980s, macroeconomic policy was based upon the medium-term financial strategy, which depended on reductions in the Public Sector Borrowing Requirement (PSBR) to reduce the money supply and hence inflation. Under Treasury accounting rules, BT's investment would add directly to the PSBR. Various attempts were made to finance the investment outside the PSBR, and all fell foul of the "Ryrie rules" that determined whether a transaction should be counted as public spending. In

13. British Airways became profitable a few years later, but its privatization was delayed by legal action concerning the demise of Laker Airways, which went bankrupt during the recession, alleging that other airlines, BA among them, had engaged in predatory pricing. The matter was settled out of (U.S.) court, after which BA was sold.

14. The sale of Amersham International in February 1982 attracted some controversy when the shares rose by 32 percent on the first day of trading, giving large profits to some investors, but most voters probably remained blissfully unaware of this.

the end, privatizing BT seemed to be the only way to finance the investment within the government's self-imposed macroeconomic constraints.

The privatization of 51.2 percent of BT would be the largest share sale ever seen on the London Stock Exchange, however. The government's advisors doubted that the financial sector would be able to absorb the new shares. The only possibility seemed to be to offer shares to the general public in the hope that they could mop up the excess. A new kind of advertising campaign was designed,[15] and the shares were sold in November 1984. The advertising proved extremely successful: the issue was greatly oversubscribed, and when trading started on December 3 the shares closed at a premium of 33 percent to the offer price.[16]

From this time onward, a significant part of the electorate saw privatization as an easy way to make money,[17] and the policy acquired a large number of supporters. It soon seemed as if the only obstacle to privatizing a company was finding a place in the queue, since the government had to leave an interval after each major sale in order to allow investors to find money for their next purchase. As the recession of the early 1980s abated, state-owned companies that had been making huge losses became sufficiently profitable for privatization. Table 2.2 shows the major events affecting a selection of these companies, while table 2.3 records the more important sales. By May 1997, when the Conservatives lost power, very few firms remained in public ownership, and some of those became candidates for privatization under the Labour government. In most cases, privatization has meant the end of specific state involvement in the formerly nationalized firms. Some in ailing industries, such as coal and shipbuilding, have continued to receive state aid, although this is restricted by European Union rules (Besley and Seabright 2000). The Rover Group, formerly British Leyland, has changed hands twice since it was sold to British Aerospace,

15. Only an investment advisor can legally recommend that someone should buy a particular share, so the campaign could do no more than tell people that the sale was taking place—while also introducing many of them to the whole concept of share ownership.

16. Small shareholders who bought with the intention of selling their shares quickly made an even greater profit because the offer price was payable in three installments, and the rise represented 86 percent of the first installment. The phrase "stagging" soon entered the national vocabulary.

17. The shares of privatized companies generally outperformed the stock market in the period immediately after their privatization—the twenty-three companies that are still quoted on the stock market today outperformed the *Financial Times* all-share index by 43 percent (unweighted average) in the two years after their privatization. Kay (2001) has pointed out, however, that twenty-two of these twenty-three companies subsequently underperformed the market by an average of 39 percent ("More Brickbats than Bouquets," *Financial Times,* 7 February 17). The unweighted average performance from privatization to the end of 2000 is a loss of 15 percent relative to the all-share index. Individual figures range from a gain of 131 percent (Forth Ports) to a loss of 83 percent (British Steel/Corus). Kay suggests that this reflects the difficulties of truly transforming a nationalized industry into a private company, difficulties that only gradually became apparent. A gradual toughening of regulation and the very mixed record of diversifying acquisitions by privatized companies will also have affected their performance.

Table 2.2 **Events in Key Nationalized Industries**

	Nationalized	Privatization Announced	Restructured While Public	Privatized	Subject to RPI-X?	Liberalized	Postprivatization Events
British Airports Authority	1965	1985		1987	Yes		
British Airways	1939	1979	1982	1987	No		1988 merger with British Caledonian 1997 EU liberalization completed
British Coal	1946	1988	1985	1994	No		1998 contracts with ESI ended
British Gas	1948	1985		1986	Partly	1986, 1996	1988 MMC report on large users 1993 MMC report on entire industry 1997 British Gas splits itself in two
British Rail	1948		1981, 1993	1994–1997	Yes		1998 Strategic Rail Authority announced
British Steel	1967		1980	1988	No		
British Telecom	1912	1982	1981	1984	Partly	1984, 1991	1985 interconnection determination 1989 price controls reviewed 1991 duopoly review
Electricity	1948	1987	1983, 1990	1990–1991	Partly	1990–1998	1994 Generators' undertakings 1994–1995 REC price controls tightened 1995 first REC mergers
Water Authorities	1973	1986	1983, 1988	1989	Yes	Slowly	1994 price controls reviewed

Notes: British Caledonian was then the second largest U.K. carrier. The MMC is the Monopolies and Mergers Commission, REC is a regional electricity company (a local electricity distributor), EU is the European Union, and ESI is the electricity supply industry.

Table 2.3 **Major Privatizations in the United Kingdom**

Company	Float or Private Sale	Date	Proceeds (£millions; net of debt issue/cancellation) Current Prices	2000 Prices
British Petroleum	F	1977–1987	6,226	11,454
British Aerospace	F	1981–1985	413	749
Cable and Wireless	F	1981–1985	1,066	2,014
National Freight Consortium	PS	1981	54	105
Amersham International	F	1982	65	134
Britoil	F	1982–1985	1,090	2,206
Associated British Ports	F	1983–1984	18	30
Enterprise Oil	F	1984	392	728
Jaguar	F	1984	—	—
British Telecom	F	1984–1993	13,201	17,621
British Gas	F	1986	7,720	13,254
British Airways	F	1987	900	1,472
Royal Ordnance	PS	1987	186	304
Rolls-Royce	F	1987	1,080	1,766
British Airports Authority	F	1987	1,281	2,094
Rover Group	PS	1988	150	231
British Steel	F	1988	2,425	3,738
Water authorities	F	1989	3,740	5,357
Regional electricity companies	F	1990	7,907	10,504
National Power and PowerGen	F	1991–1995	6,548	7,727
Scottish electricity companies	F	1991	3,481	4,369
Northern Ireland Electricity	F	1993	362	419
Coal	PS	1994–1995	1,633	1,859
Rail stock leasing companies	PS	1996	1,800	1,901
Railtrack	F	1996	1,950	2,059
British Energy (nuclear)	F	1996	2,108	2,226

Source: Pollitt (1999).
Note: Dashes indicate that amount is negligible.

and it narrowly escaped closure in 2000, causing a major political row. The government and its agents have continued to play a major role in the development of one group of the privatized industries, however. These are the utilities, and we now turn to consider them.

2.5 The Privatized Utilities

The 1979 Conservative Manifesto had not suggested that any utilities would be privatized, but once BT's privatization had proved a political success, the government started to look upon the other utilities as possible candidates for privatization. In April 1985, the government announced that British Gas would be sold, and the company became the second privatized utility in December 1986. The water industry followed in 1989.

None of these privatizations involved significant restructuring of the firms to be sold. The government had hoped that competition would develop in gas and telecommunications, but the process was very slow in the face of dominant, unrestructured incumbents. Not until the electricity industry was reorganized in 1990 did the privatization process involve the significant restructuring of an industry in order to promote effective competition. The railways were also restructured, in a more complicated process, and were privatized between 1994 and 1997.

The government recognized that it would be inappropriate to privatize the utilities as unregulated monopolies. The telecommunications industry had been opened up to competition in 1982 when the government gave Mercury a licence to build its own network in competition with BT. The hope was that this competition would soon be sufficient protection for consumers, but in the short term some regulation was needed. Thus, the first concern was to devise an appropriate regulatory system to restrain the company's behavior until competition became effective. At the same time, the government was conscious that the opposition Labour Party was deeply opposed to privatization. Thus, the second matter was to ensure that a future Labour government could not interfere with the regulatory system in order to disadvantage the company.

To cope with the second issue, the government established an independent regulator, the Director General of Telecommunications, with statutory duties that required the regulator to ensure that the company could finance its activities. The details of the company's regulation were enshrined in its licence, a contract that could only be revoked with twenty-five years' notice. Under English law, contracts cannot be changed unilaterally. The regulator would be allowed to impose a change against the wishes of the company, however, if the matter was referred to the Monopolies and Mergers Commission (MMC; the United Kingdom's competition authority, now the Competition Commission) and the MMC supported the change. The regulator was also subject to judicial review of his or her decision making. If the company felt that the regulator had not followed the proper procedures or that the decision taken was manifestly unreasonable,[18] it could ask a court to review the matter. This system of checks and balances was designed to protect the company's interests while ensuring that the regulator could still control its behavior (Levy and Spiller 1994).

What was this independent regulator expected to regulate while waiting for effective competition? At first, the Treasury had suggested a modified version of U.S.-style rate-of-return regulation, which would set a maximum rate of return but no minimum. This was intended to give the company stronger incentives for cost efficiency than a pure rate-of-return

18. Note that judicial review does not ask whether a decision was actually right or wrong, but whether it was unreasonable, which is less of a constraint on the regulator.

scheme, under which the company could appeal for higher prices if its costs rose and depressed its rate of return. When Alan Walters, the Prime Minister's economic advisor, suggested an alternative—namely, an output-related levy on profits (which was designed to give the company an incentive to keep prices low, since the levy rate would fall as output rose)—Stephen Littlechild (then a professor of economics at the University of Birmingham and later the U.K. electricity regulator) was commissioned to decide between the two schemes. He came up with a third: a local tariff reduction scheme, under which a basket of BT's prices (in the markets with the least competition) would have to fall by a preset amount in real terms each year. In nominal terms, they could rise by (RPI-*X*) percent, where RPI was the change in the retail price index and *X* was the preset real reduction, and this soon became the nickname for the scheme. Littlechild (1983) saw the scheme as a temporary expedient until competition became effective in holding prices down, because if it was needed for a permanent control, it would be necessary to reset the level of *X* from time to time. This could not sensibly be done without looking at the company's costs and profits, which would blur the distinction between his scheme and rate-of-return regulation. In practice, RPI-*X*, or price cap, regulation was later adopted for every other utility privatization, including those in which there was little prospect of competition (table 2.2).

The RPI-*X* regulation limits price increases for a basket of goods to *X* percent below the rise in the retail price index, with *X* being set by the regulator for a period of four or five years at a time. This system does away with the nationalized industry policy of tying prices to marginal costs in favor of providing strong incentives for cost reduction, since firms can keep any profits they make as long as they do not exceed the price cap. Thus, theoretically RPI-*X* should promote productivity improvement. In practice, a number of problems have emerged with the system. The first issue relates to the rebalancing of relative prices. If the company faces competition for some regulated services, it will have an incentive to reduce their prices. Doing so will relax the constraint on its other prices and thereby weaken the regulator's control of its activities as a monopolist. In the case of BT, an explicit constraint on domestic line rentals was introduced to limit the scope for this rebalancing, but other industries have not faced such constraints. The second point relates to quality. For BT, for example, there were initially no quality controls, and it was widely perceived that quality had deteriorated. Explicit quality targets have now been introduced. Finally, Beesley and Littlechild (1989) characterize the initial choice of *X* as the outcome of a bargain between incumbent managers and government. Managers were in a position to hold up the privatization process that politicians were anxious to speed along, and they often obtained favorable values of *X* as a result. Since then, in reviews, regulation has been set more toughly, but if *X* is to be chosen in the light of observed previous profit rates, then RPI-*X* regulation is in danger of becoming like rate-of-return regulation with all the attendant incentive problems.

Some of these problems can be reduced by using yardstick regulation (Shleifer 1985). In its pure form, this suggests that the price allowed for one company is based on the average of its rivals' costs, breaking the link between the company's price and its own costs while still allowing it to offset industrywide movements in costs. The existing regional structure of the water industry and of electricity distribution allowed the adoption of yardstick competition, but in a slightly different form. In practice, the U.K. regulators use yardstick comparisons to assess the efficiency of each company in their industry and, hence, to predict the cost savings that each company might make over the next four or five years. The company's price control is based on the regulator's forecast of the company's costs (Waddams Price 1999). However, as well as predicting operating costs, in practice, regulators also have to predict the company's investment needs. Since the amount of investment needed depends on the state of each company's infrastructure, which is private information, regulators are compelled to rely on the company's own reports. This reintroduces scope for opportunistic behavior and bargaining between the regulator and the company.

The water regulator has placed the greatest stress upon yardstick techniques, asking the MMC to block mergers that would have reduced the number of water and sewerage companies to compare.[19] Despite this, a large number of the smaller water-only companies have been acquired, either by water and sewerage companies or by international groups. The electricity regulator has placed rather less stress on yardstick comparisons, in part because the fourteen companies in the industry did not allow much scope for formal statistical analysis. So far, mergers between electricity distribution networks (five to date) have not been blocked.

Figure 2.1 shows the development of prices in the main regulated utilities. In each case, the price level at privatization is taken as 100. The first company to be privatized with an RPI-*X* constraint was BT—in this case, *X* was set at 3 for five years. When he wrote the report proposing RPI-*X*, Littlechild (1983) seems to have envisaged that competition would develop so rapidly that regulation would not be needed after this initial period. That hope proved too optimistic, and the price control has been reset four times so far, with larger *X* values each time.[20] British Gas was the second company to be privatized, and the price cap for gas transportation has also

19. The MMC (1995) estimated that losing one water company through a merger would cause losses, due to the increased difficulty in making comparisons, with a present discounted value of between £50m and £250m.

20. Strictly speaking, when *X* was reset in 1996, the value chosen was lower than before, but it applied to a smaller bundle of services with prices that had been rising in relative terms. The regulator claimed that the headline cap of RPI-4.5 would have the same effect on those prices as a cap of RPI-8.5, applied to the company as a whole, and then subjected to the same degree of rebalancing.

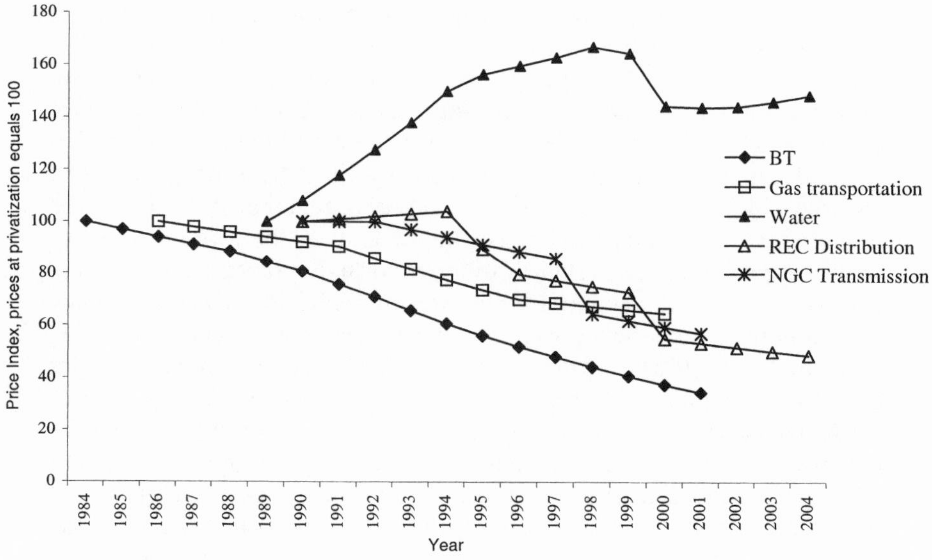

Fig. 2.1 Regulated prices in the United Kingdom

declined continuously since privatization. The cost of gas, which also fell dramatically in the years after privatization, was a separate pass-through element in the cap and is not shown in the figure. Both companies have been able to reduce their costs at least as rapidly as their price caps required, and have been highly profitable.

The first price caps implied real-price reductions, but the transmission-price cap for the National Grid Company (NGC) implied constant prices, while most of the Regional Electricity Companies (RECs) were allowed small real increases in their distribution charges for several years. NGC's cap was first reset roughly two years after privatization and was only tightened to a small extent, but by the time the RECs' price caps were reset, in 1994, the companies had reduced their costs significantly and were very profitable. When BT's profits were above the level that the regulator thought necessary, he had tightened the company's price control to reduce profits in a gradual manner, allowing the company to keep the benefits of its extra productivity for a longer period and maintaining incentives for future reductions. The electricity regulator, in contrast, believed that the RECs' profits were so exceptional that a one-off price cut could be justified without affecting their incentives for future price reductions. The regulator proposed a one-off price reduction averaging 14 percent, but had to follow it with a further 11 percent the next year amid widespread criticism of his leniency. The most recent REC price control review has imposed a further one-off cut, implying that the companies continued to cut costs by more than the regulator had expected in 1995. Over time, regulators have come to release far more information during the process of reviewing a price control—including predictions of the companies' costs (on which the control will be based)—in part to ensure that the companies and commentators do not comment adversely because they are surprised by the level chosen.

The water industry has been allowed significant real price increases since its privatization. This is largely because of the need to finance new investment in higher quality; indeed, the desire to keep this investment away from the PSBR was one of the motives for the privatization. Although the steadily rising prices might imply that there have been few efficiency gains, the regulator pointed out that efficiency improvements actually halved the price increases that would otherwise have been required between 1995 and 2000. In fact, the companies did better than the regulator expected, and so the latest price control, scheduled to start in 2000, started with a one-off cut to finance additional investment before the prices rose again. Thus, figure 2.1 is consistent with improvements in efficiency in all of these industries.

2.5.1 Competition

An alternative to regulation is competition, although it is increasingly felt to be desirable to introduce competition as part of regulation (Schmalensee 1989). Restructuring was strongly resisted by the incumbent managements, and so little restructuring occurred in the initial utility privatizations. Before electricity generation and the railways were privatized, however, they were restructured to introduce competition.

In the case of electricity generation, the Central Electricity Generating Board was split into a transmission company and three generating companies. Two of these generators were privatized in 1991, whereas nuclear power remained in state ownership until 1996, when the newer stations were privatized. The generators competed to sell power to electricity suppliers (and thence to consumers) in a wholesale market organized around the Electricity Pool, which took daily price bids from every power station and selected the cheapest ones. The two largest generators controlled 70 percent of the industry's capacity in 1990, however, and clearly had the ability to raise prices above competitive levels (Green and Newbery 1997). One response to this was entry by new stations, mostly gas fired, which hastened the decline of the coal industry. A second was pressure from the regulator to keep prices down, which eventually led the major generators to divest some of their plant. Taken together, entry and the divestitures have created a more balanced market structure, but the limited amount of competition in the initial market structure meant that prices were higher than they needed to have been for several years. By 2002, however, surplus capacity and a more competitive market structure had depressed wholesale electricity prices to the extent that several generators faced severe financial troubles, and the government organized a financial rescue package for British Energy. The privatization did introduce rules for separating the distribution of electricity from its retail sale (supply), which allowed customers to choose their supplier. The incumbents rapidly lost market share among larger customers, bringing the margins on serving them down to competitive levels.

The railways were split into even more pieces before their privatization. Railtrack, which was floated in May 1996, owned the track network and most stations but did not run any services. Instead, the services were split up into more than twenty franchises, which were let out for periods of between seven and fifteen years by the franchising director. Some franchisees required subsidies from the government (typically declining over time), while others (particularly the intercity routes) were able to pay for their franchises. It is difficult to replace a franchisee who owns a large amount of sunk capital, and so three rolling stock companies were created, which lease trains to the franchisees for the duration of their franchises. In practice, however, the rolling stock companies have been reluctant to invest without commitments from the train-operating companies. Some of the first franchises are now being renewed, and the new contracts are likely to last longer. This should allow for more investment but may reduce the competitive pressure on the franchisees.

Railtrack, however, was placed in administration by the government in October 2001 and replaced by a company limited by guarantee, Network Rail, in October 2002. Railtrack's current and predicted future costs had risen rapidly after a major accident at Hatfield in October 2000 (discussed later) and had exposed a maintenance backlog, and its predicted revenue streams were inadequate to finance these. Rather than finding additional revenues (which must, ultimately, come from either the rail traveller or the Treasury), the government decided to replace Railtrack with a new organization. Instead of shareholders, Network Rail has about 100 members (rail companies, organizations with an interest in the rail industry, and individuals) to whom its board will report at annual general meetings, but the company will not pay dividends. The structure was carefully designed to ensure that Network Rail's borrowings will not count against the PSBR, but it does represent a move away from the previous philosophy that "standard" public limited companies would normally give the best performance.[21]

It is also possible to introduce competition without restructuring an industry, although this is often less effective since it may leave the incumbent

21. A similar organization, Glas Cymru, took over in May 2001 the assets of Welsh Water public limited company, which also faced problems financing future investment.

in a position to harm entrants. Perhaps the earliest example of this type of liberalization was the deregulation of interurban coaching in 1980 (Thompson and Whitfield 1995). Until 1980, the sole licensed operator was National Express. The 1980 Transport Act allowed entry subject only to quality standards, and large-scale entry took place, with substantial price reductions (see following discussion). However, the wave of new entrants did not survive long, and by 1983 National Express was practically the sole operator on the English and Welsh routes (competition remained on the Scottish routes). The U.K. and European Union (EU) air routes have also been deregulated, following initiatives from the U.K. government and Brussels (see Abbot and Thompson 1989; McGowan and Seabright 1989). There has been some entry here, but again the incumbents appear mainly to have held their own.

Another example of the failure of competition to develop unaided was the gas industry. At privatization, rival suppliers were given permission to enter the market. However, they would need to buy gas from North Sea operators, who sold most of their output to British Gas (and were presumably reluctant to upset their major customer), and then ship it through British Gas's pipes—at charges set by British Gas—to gas consumers with individual, confidential, contracts. Practically no entry occurred, presumably because rival suppliers feared that, while they were negotiating transportation charges with British Gas, that company would make selective price reductions to their chosen customers. In 1988, the MMC ordered British Gas to provide more information on transportation charges, to sell to all its consumers on published tariffs, and to buy no more than 90 percent of any new gas field, thus allowing rivals access to gas and to the information they would need to compete with the company. Even these measures, however, only allowed a very gradual development of competition. It was not until the early 1990s, when British Gas negotiated specific (and rapidly declining) targets for its market share and took several steps to help rival suppliers, that competition really took off. Eventually, following a second reference to the MMC, the government decided to allow all gas consumers to choose their supplier. Roughly a third of domestic gas consumers now buy from another company (very often their local electricity company), in part because the regulator allowed British Gas to set prices that recover most of the costs of past gas purchases at what had become above-market prices, while new suppliers based their prices on the lower prices then in effect.[22]

The main question regarding competition is whether new firms constitute a sufficient threat to incumbents and so force price reductions and

22. The electricity regulator returned the favor and allowed entrants to undercut the incumbents in electricity as well. The largest entrant is British Gas.

quality improvements. In the industries considered here, this requires them to have access to essential facilities that were previously controlled by the incumbents, given the sunk costs of recreating these facilities. In the case of gas, the pipeline network is (literally) the sunk cost. In the U.K. coaching market, the physical facilities of the Central London coach terminal owned by the incumbent might have been recreated at moderate cost but not the network benefits of being able to change between so many routes at one place. To obtain these benefits, an entrant denied access to the terminal might have had to set up a national route network, making small-scale entry impossible (Thompson and Whitfield 1995). British Airways (BA), which has grandfathered rights to many of the choice Heathrow Airport landing and take-off slots, also gains from network externalities. Low-cost entrants operating from other airports have been able to compete for passengers who do not wish to change planes at a busy hub, and policymakers have been considering ways of reducing BA's dominance at Heathrow (such as U.S.-style slot auctions). Experience suggests, however, that the success of liberalization depends crucially on not endowing the incumbent public firm with advantages on access to essential facilities.

2.6 The Effect of Privatization

This section reviews the evidence on the effects of privatization on productive efficiency, product quality, public-sector union power, and attitudes toward privatization. Beginning with efficiency, the ideal experiment would presumably be to privatize randomly a set of firms and to observe the difference in their efficiency after privatization in comparison with a control group. In practice, one cannot do this, and so the following issues arise in trying to judge the effect of privatization on efficiency.

First, what is a good measure of efficiency? Labor productivity is one widely used measure. It has, however, a number of drawbacks. First, there have been widespread falls in labor input following privatization and hence substitution to capital (Haskel and Szymanski 1992). Second, capital investment rose after privatization in most firms. For example, in the data that we describe later, in the case of BT and British Gas, investment during the period after privatization averaged 20 percent more than the level between 1979 and privatization. In the case of British Steel, the increase after privatization was 50 percent, although even this left investment at a third of its level during the 1970s. British Airways' investment doubled soon after privatization and doubled again in the late 1990s, linked to the exponential growth of air travel. The coal industry is the only industry in our sample in which investment was lower in the 1990s than in the 1980s, and this was due to the secular decline of the industry.

Third, many companies have replaced direct labor with contractors, and so measures of output per employee will not reflect the true relationship between output and labor input.[23] Fourth, value added per worker would increase if a privatized company used market power to increase its markups. We have attempted to use physical measures of output wherever possible in our own study.

Thus, total factor productivity (TFP) would appear to be preferable, although factor shares may not reflect output elasticities if firms have market power, so that if market power changes with privatization, then measured TFP may change for reasons not related to efficiency. One solution to this problem is to regress real output changes on input changes, although sufficient time series is required to avoid imposing the same output elasticities across firms. In practice, however, most studies look at TFP.

Second, privatization is likely to be endogenous, especially since many firms were explicitly restructured in order to be privatized and could not be sold until they had become more efficient and profitable. Thus, one must at least examine preprivatization performance. Whether this restructuring is due to privatization is a difficult issue since one might argue that it was only the threat of privatization that provided a credible commitment to restructure. Third, many privatizations, like that of British Gas, are of the whole industry, and thus one has no suitable control group. International comparisons are potentially valuable here, and if, for example, regional accounts are available pre- and postprivatization, internal comparisons can be made. Unfortunately, privatization frequently tends to render regional accounts commercially sensitive and thus confidential, and so rather few publicly available studies have been undertaken in practice.

All this suggests looking at a variety of national and international evidence. Beginning with U.K. evidence, the upper panel of table 2.4 shows multicompany and single-company studies. Pryke's (1982) study, despite not being about privatization, is included since it was one of the first authoritative studies to document low efficiency and productivity in public-sector enterprises. Bishop and Kay (1989) was an early study that looked at TFP growth for a number of firms in the 1979 public sector. They did not explicitly study what happened to firms after privatization but rather compared TFP growth between 1979–1983 and 1983–1988, and they observed strong TFP growth, particularly in steel, gas, and coal, in the second period. (Note that this was before steel and coal were privatized.) Bishop and Thompson (1992) compared TFP in 1970–1980 and 1980–1989 with similar findings. In an update to the study, Bishop and Green (1995) found a

23. The most extreme example of this is Railtrack, which had 11,204 employees on 31 March 2000 but contracted out its track maintenance services. The prime contractors also used subcontractors, and there were more than 2,000 registered railway infrastructure companies with between 15,000 and 19,000 permanent staff, and a total pool of 84,000 registered workers, often recruited on a temporary basis through employment agencies (Juliette Jowitt, "Why an Accident Like Hatfield Was Waiting to Happen," *Financial Times,* 22 February 2001, p. 4). To get a more complete picture, we should look at total costs or total factor productivity, including services purchased as an input.

Table 2.4 Studies of Privatization and Regulation Effects

					Findings: Productivity Rises with . . .				
					Privatization				
Study	Measure of Productivity	Controls	Companies Studied	Years	After	Before	Regulation	Competition	Remarks
				Multicompany Studies					
Pryke (1982)	TFP	None	BAA, BCoal, BGas, BRail, BSteel, BT, Electricity, PO	1960–1979	—	—	—	—	Preprivatization study; found slow TFP growth relative to whole economy
Bishop and Kay (1989)	TFP growth	None	BAA, BCoal, BGas, BRail, BSteel, BT, Electricity, PO	1979–1983, 1983–1988	—	Yes	No	—	No specific study of pre- and postprivatization, or regulation
Haskel and Szymanski (1992)	*Y*/*L*	*K*/*L*, competition, hours, unions, privatization, restructuring, regulatory dummies	BAA, BCoal, BGas, BRail, BSteel, BT, Electricity, PO, BA, Water, LRT, STG	1972–1989	No	Yes	No	Yes	Little effect of privatization and regulation
Bishop and Thompson (1992)	TFP growth	None	BAA, BCoal, BGas, BRail, BSteel, BT, Electricity, PO	1970–1980, 1980–1990	—	Yes	No	—	No specific study of pre- and postprivatization or regulation
Bishop and Green (1995)	TFP growth	None	BAA, BCoal, BGas, BRail, BSteel, BT, Electricity, PO	1979–1983, 1983–1988, 1989–1994	—	Yes	No	—	No specific study of pre- and postprivatization or regulation

Martin and Parker (1997)	TFP	Whole-economy TFP, privatization, announcement dummies	BGas, BSteel, BT, BA		—	Yes	—	—	Postprivatization slowdown in BGas, BSteel, BT; speedup in BA
O'Mahony (1999)	*Y/L*	Other countries	Sectors: gas, electricity, water	1965–1995	Yes	—	—	—	Industry data, changes are after 1990 so no specific correlation with actual event (e.g., regulation)
				Individual Company Studies					
Waddams Price and Weyman-Jones (1996)	TFP	None	Gas	1980–1992	—	Yes	—	—	Comparison of different regions shows regions not catching up (BGas privatized as a whole)
Markou and Waddams Price (1999)	Labor productivity	None	Water	1980–1995	—	Yes	—	—	Real turnover per hour (water industry is confidential data)
Tilley and Weyman Jones (1999)	Frontier estimation	Inputs	Electricity		Yes	—	—	—	No catching up of regional firms

Notes: Findings: Productivity rises column, "Yes" indicates that the study examines the effect on efficiency of the column heading and finds a significant effect; "No" indicates investigation but no significant effect; and the dashes indicate that the column heading was not investigated. LRT = London Regional Transport; STG = Scottish Transport Group; PO = Post Office; BCoal = British Coal; BGas = British Gas; BRail = British Rail; BSteel = British Steel; *Y/L* = output-labor ratio; *K/L* = capital-labor ratio.

strong TFP growth performance in 1989–1994 in BT and the post office, with slow growth in British Airports Authority (BAA), British Gas, British Coal, and British Rail. They attribute BT's strong growth to technical innovation and the growth of the post office (which is still publicly owned) to a combination of growth-exploiting economies of scale and restructuring. All in all, both studies show productivity increases in advance of privatization.

Haskel and Szymanski (1992) attempted to control for some of the different factors that might affect productivity. Using panel data on output and inputs for twelve U.K. firms that were publicly owned in 1979, they attempted to measure factors such as demand, union and market power, and so forth. As well as identifying the date of privatization and regulation, they also attempted to look at preprivatization effects. First, they tried to identify the dates of restructuring (e.g., new teams of managers being brought in, or the company being reoriented toward more profitable goals). Second, they identified the dates when it was first announced that the company would be privatized. There were four main findings. First, privatization itself was not strongly associated with rises in TFP. Second, preprivatization restructuring was associated with rises in TFP. Third, market competition was associated with increased TFP, but, since there had been comparatively small rises in competition over the period, this did not contribute much to the actual TFP rise. Finally, most of the rise in labor productivity was due to fast labor shedding. Their study did stop, however, in 1989, which is, again, somewhat early in the privatization process and does not cover periods when regulatory targets are being tightened.

Parker and Martin (1995) also looked at a range of firms that were publicly owned in the 1970s in a study that covered up to 1995. One innovation was to look at TFP in companies relative to the whole economy (they also looked at postannouncement and postsale figures). Their figures confirm the very high TFP growth in British Steel postannouncement but preprivatization, which was also seen in BT and British Gas. Their data show a slowdown in TFP growth postprivatization for British Steel, British Gas, and BT, but an increase for BA.

Turning to international evidence, O'Mahony (1999) calculates labor productivity in gas, electricity, and water in the Group of Five (G5) countries (see figure 2.2). These data are of interest since they provide an international productivity comparison. The United Kingdom has the lowest level of productivity throughout the 1970s and 1980s, and it is hard to identify any change in trend between 1973 and 1990. (The annual average increase between 1973 and 1979 was 3.1 percent; in the following decade, it was 4.0 percent. The downward blip in 1984 is likely to be related to the miners' strike in that year.) From 1990 onward, however, labor productivity growth more than doubles to 9 percent a year, so that the United Kingdom overtakes France and closes the gap with the other countries in the

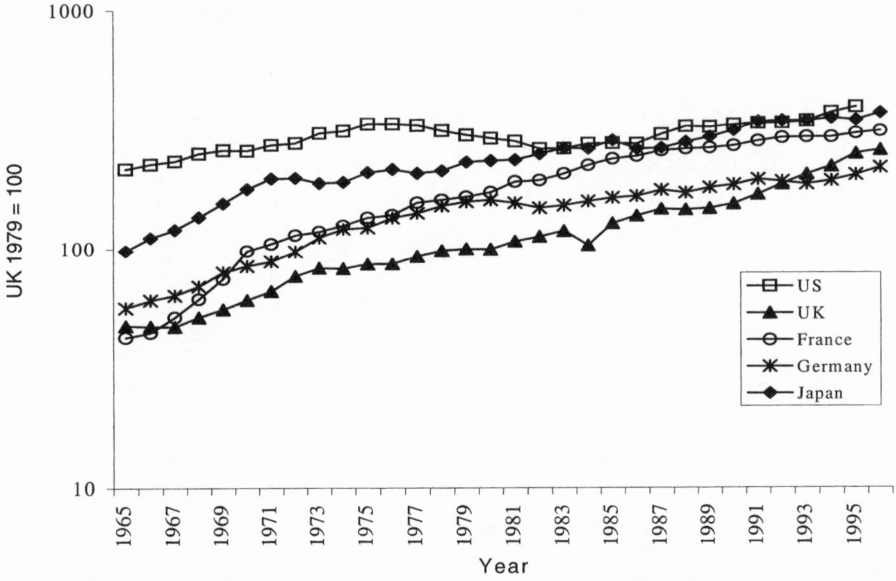

Fig. 2.2 Comparative productivity in gas, electricity, and water industries; labor productivity in gas, electricity, and water
Source: O'Mahony (1999).

sample. Productivity growth in the other countries only rose slightly—on average, from 2.4 percent in the 1980s to 3.1 percent between 1990 and 1996—and so an exogenous technical change is unlikely to be responsible for the acceleration in the United Kingdom.[24] This would appear to provide evidence of an effect from privatization and tightened regulation, but, since the dates of privatization of gas, electricity, and water vary, one cannot be conclusive whether it is due to privatization, preprivatization restructuring, or regulation.

Table 2.5 presents our own estimates for TFP growth in six formerly nationalized industries. The firms have been chosen on the basis of data availability, and so industries that underwent major restructuring as they were privatized had to be excluded. Most data are taken from company accounts. Labor inputs are represented by the "head count" total from the accounts, and gross capital inputs are derived using a perpetual-inventory method. Given the capital stock in year t, we estimate the capital stock in year $t + 1$ by adding that year's investment and subtracting the assets that

24. The United States had the largest rise, from a dismal 0.7 percent a year during the 1980s to 3.9 percent a year during the 1990s, but this is far closer to the worst performer, France (where productivity growth fell from 4.8 percent a year to 2.4 percent) than it is to the United Kingdom's figures.

Table 2.5 **Total Factor Productivity in the U.K. Public Sector (annual rate of increase; %)**

Company	1970s	1980s	1990s	Privatization Date
	1972–73 to 1978–79	1978–79 to **1987–88**	1987–88 to 1999–2000	
British Airways	4.7	2.9	3.7	1987
	1972–73 to 1978–79	1978–79 to 1986–87	1986–87 to **1993–94**	
British Coal	–2.8	0.1	9.0	1994
	1972–73 to 1978–79	1978–79 to **1986–87**	**1986–87** to 1994–95	
British Gas	8.2	2.0	1.5	1986
	1972–73 to 1978–79	1978–79 to **1988–89**	**1988–89** to 1997–98	
British Steel	–5.0	3.8	1.8	1988
	1972–73 to 1978–79	1978–79 to **1984–85**	**1984–85** to 1994–95	
British Telecom	0.6	3.2	3.0	1984
	1972–73 to 1978–79	1978–79 to 1988–89	1988–89 to 1998–99	
Post Office	1.6	1.8	1.6	Still public

Source: Authors' calculations (see text for details).
Note: Dates in bold indicate the break-points between public and private ownership.

the company disposed of.[25] All the companies published some current cost accounting information during the 1980s, including the gross replacement cost of their assets in current prices, and we based our estimates upon these figures. We estimated earlier values of the capital stock by subtracting investment and adding disposals. The user cost of capital was the sum of the industry's depreciation rate and the public-sector test discount rate. The costs of other inputs were taken from the accounts and deflated by the producer price index (PPI) for manufacturing inputs of fuel and materials or by a more appropriate index where one existed (such as the PPI for the steel industry, which was used for British Steel). In most cases, physical output data are available, but for British Steel the company's turnover was deflated by the PPI for the steel industry's output. We used these data to produce year-by-year Tornqvist indexes of the changes in TFP and took geometric averages over several years. Our first period, 1972–1973, was in the middle of a cyclical upswing, and most of the other years we compare with it were at similar points in the cycle.

We find that the performance in the 1970s was often weak, although

25. When working with historic cost accounts, we must estimate the age of the assets being retired in order to perform all the calculations with prices reflated to a single year. With current cost accounts, this reflating was done by the company.

British Gas saw high TFP growth as it completed the country's conversion to natural gas, and BA also did well. In the 1980s, most firms improved, although British Coal continued to show stagnant TFP in the few years before the miners' strike of 1984–1985.[26] After that strike, however, British Coal's productivity rose rapidly while still in the public sector. British Airways, which saw dramatic improvements in profitability and labor productivity, suffered a decline in TFP growth after 1979. Four of our firms were privatized within our sample period, and three of these saw slight declines in TFP growth after privatization. Only BA improved its performance after privatization, and the company did not regain its growth rate of the 1970s. The one industry that has not been a serious candidate for privatization, the Post Office, had the lowest TFP growth over the period, although this may reflect the limited technological opportunities facing its delivery operations. Overall, it is probably fair to characterize our results as showing that firms tended to improve their productivity significantly in the run-up to privatization (with some exceptions) but giving little evidence that the faster growth rate was sustained after privatization. In other words, there is a catch-up rather than a permanent change of pace.

Our results can be compared to the lower panel of table 2.4, which shows some studies of individual firms. Waddams Price and Weyman-Jones (1996) compared British Gas's twelve operating regions and found continuous improvements, although there was little sign that the less efficient regions were catching up with the better ones. Similarly, Tilley and Weyman-Jones (1999) found that there was no catching up among electricity-distribution companies, although there was productivity growth from an outward shift of the efficient frontier. Markou and Waddams Price (1999) looked at labor productivity growth in water and found that it rose before privatization but, owing to confidentiality, were unable to look at data by region.

Overall, then, table 2.4 and most commentators (e.g., Pollitt 1999; Waddams Price 1999) seem to agree that preprivatization restructuring was an important source of productivity gains, as is increased competition. Privatization itself does not seem to be correlated with productivity growth, and most studies stop before the effect of regulation can be estimated with any reliability. Whether the commitment to privatize is essential to getting the gains from preprivatization restructuring remains an open question that is unlikely to be econometrically testable.

2.6.1 The Sources of Productivity Growth

Even if such studies show improvements in TFP, they do not isolate the sources of such improvements. There are a number of possible sources.

26. Our break point, 1986–1987, is chosen to allow the industry to recover from the 1984–1985 strike and the preceding overtime ban.

First, there might be changes in work practices in given plants. Sanchis (1997) uses the U.K. Workplace Industrial Relations Survey, which provides detailed survey information on working practices at a representative sample of U.K. plants, some of which have been privatized. Controlling for cyclical variables and union presence, she finds that privatization is significantly linked with improvements in working practices on the shop floor.[27] These improvements might allow the elimination of "slack" and labor shedding, which would also raise the capital-labor ratio without necessarily improving the firm's capital stock.

Second, the private sector might be able to close plants that a nationalized industry would have been constrained to keep open. If these are the less-efficient plants in the firm, its average TFP will rise, whether or not there are improvements at "survivor" plants. The firm-level studies in table 2.4 are unable to shed light on this issue, and there is, to the best of our knowledge, no evidence on this for the United Kingdom.

We therefore turn to plant-level data drawn from the Annual Respondents to the Census of Production (ARD) database, which is in turn based on the U.K. Census of Production (see Disney, Haskel, and Heden 2003 for details). Here we use data on public- and private-owned plants in a U.K. manufacturing industry, where the firm concerned was privatized in the 1980s (confidentiality rules preclude us from naming the firm or industry).

Table 2.6 sets out some raw data. Consider the top row. Employment in the industry as a whole shrank from just over 200,000 in 1980 to 95,821 at privatization to 72,276 in 1992 (when our data end).[28] In 1980, 102,672 employees worked in private plants, with 112,251 in public-sector plants. At privatization, the figures were 41,246 and 54,565, respectively. By 1992, private plants employed 45,940 and formerly public plants 26,336. So, as the second panel shows, public plants went from accounting for over 50 percent of employment in 1980 to around 36 percent in 1992. As the third panel shows, there was also a considerable fall in the number of plants, with, interestingly, proportionately more closure in the private sector in the years before privatization at least.

The last few rows of table 2.6 show labor productivity levels and growth.[29] The picture is clear. The public sector had similar labor productivity to the

27. Privatization is associated with changes in working practices that reduced job demarcation and increased work flexibility, for example.

28. The fall in employment (of about 8 percent per annum) dwarfed the economywide fall (between 1980 and 1992, U.K. manufacturing employment fell by 3 percent per annum).

29. The labor productivity ($\ln Y/L$) is real gross output per person-hour, deflated by a four-digit industry output deflator. The values of Y and L are available directly from the census, and the hours variables are two-digit manual hours. We calculate TFP as $\ln \text{TFP} = \ln Y - \alpha_k \ln K - \alpha_L \ln L - \alpha_M \ln M$, where Y is real gross output, K real capital, L worker hours, and M real material use, the α is share of each factor in gross output, and i denotes establishment; M is recorded directly from the ARD. Capital stock is estimated from establishment-level investment on in-plant vehicles and buildings, using perpetual-inventory methods with the

Table 2.6 Industry Data Relevant for the Plant-Level Study

	1980	Privatization	1992
Employment	214,923	95,821	72,276
Private	102,672	41,256	45,940
Public (ex-public after privatization)	112,251	54,565	26,336
Industry employment (%)			
Private	0.48	0.43	0.64
Public (ex-public after privatization)	0.52	0.57	0.36
Number of plants			
Private	1,272	583	577
Public (ex-public after privatization)	46	31	15
Labor productivity (industry = 100)	100	139.5	139.7
Private	96.8	121.9	127.3
Public (ex-public after privatization)	102.6	156.1	158.8
Labor-productivity growth (% per annum)	—	4.9	0.04
Private	—	3.2	1.1
Public (ex-public after privatization)	—	6.5	0.43
TFP levels (industry = 100)	100	235.8	221.0
Private	162.6	250.1	224.5
Public (ex-public after privatization)	49.1	222.2	215.6
TFP growth (% per annum)	—	17.0	–1.6
Private	—	6.7	–2.6
Public (ex-public after privatization)	—	44.1	–0.7

Source: Authors' calculations from ARD.

Note: Data for "public" in 1992 refers to those plants present in 1992 but that were publicly owned before privatization. Growth rates are percent per annum from 1980 to privatization (column [2]) and privatization to 1992 (column [3]). Dashes indicate missing data.

private sector but much lower TFP, whereas productivity growth was much higher in the public sector. This suggests that public plants substantially caught up to private plants over the period. Note that in the postprivatization years there was negative TFP growth, which was during a recession. Although we have data on hours worked, we may not measure short time working and so have negative TFP.

How did the productivity gains come about? If the 1980 public-sector inefficiency was widespread throughout plants, one would expect there to be plenty of scope for productivity improvement without closure. Alternatively, it could have been that the average was brought down by some very poor plants (kept open due to soft budget constraints in the public sector,

starting values and depreciation rates taken from Oulton and O'Mahoney (1994). Labor input is person-hours, as before. Output, capital, and materials are all deflated by the appropriate four-digit industry price deflator. Following Foster, Haltiwanger, and Krizan (2001), the factor shares are calculated at the four-digit industry level to minimize the effects of measurement error. We chose to work with the Solow measure, since it is relatively transparent and the empirical implementations of superlative index numbers in unbalanced panels raise a number of significant complications (Good, Nadiri, and Sickles 1997).

for example), in which case it could have been substantially raised by closure. To measure this we therefore decompose productivity growth as follows. We write industrywide productivity in year t as $P_t = \Sigma\theta_{it}p_{it}$, where θ_i is the employment share of establishment i, and P_t and p_{it} are productivity measures (labor productivity and TFP). The decomposition proposed by Foster, Haltiwanger, and Krizan (2001) relates to the change in industrywide productivity between $t - k$ and t, ΔP_t, and is written

$$(1)\qquad \Delta P_t = \sum_{i\in S}\theta_{it-k}\Delta p_{it} + \sum_{i\in S}\Delta\theta_{it}(p_{it-k} - P_{t-k}) + \sum_{i\in S}\Delta\theta_{it}\Delta p_{it} + \sum_{i\in N}\theta_{it}(p_{it} - P_{t-k}) - \sum_{i\in X}\theta_{it-k}(p_{it-k} - P_{t-k}),$$

where S, N, and X denotes the establishments that survive, enter, and exit, respectively, between t and $t - k$. The first term in the decomposition shows the contribution to productivity growth of growth among the surviving establishments, or the "within" effect. The second term shows the contribution of changes in shares of the survivors weighted by the deviation of initial-period productivity from the average (often termed the "between" effect). This is positive when market shares increase for those survivors with above-average base-year productivity. The third term is a covariance term that is positive when market share increases for establishments with growing productivity or falls for establishments with falling productivity. The entry and exit terms are positive when there is entry (exit) of above- (below-) average productivity establishments.[30]

To get a picture of the overall period, the first panel of table 2.7 sets out the decompositions for 1980–1992. The top panel of the table shows the results for $\Delta \ln(Y/L)$ and the bottom panel for $\Delta \ln(\text{TFP})$. Each panel shows the results for the industry as a whole and then for the public and private parts of it. Each cell shows the percentage of total growth accounted for by each component of the disaggregation. Consider first the results for $\Delta \ln(Y/L)$ in the top row of the top panel. The first column shows the contribution of the within effect and suggests that productivity growth in surviving plants accounted for about 53 percent of $\Delta \ln(Y/L)$ over the whole period for the whole industry. The second and third columns show that 2 percent and 16 percent of productivity growth was due to the between and cross effects. That both effects are positive suggests that the most productive plants were gaining market share (the between effect) and that plants whose productivity was growing were also gaining market share (the cross effect). The final term shows that net entry accounts for 29 percent of productivity growth (i.e., that the opening and closure of plants accounted for 29 percent of industry productivity growth).

30. There are a number of other decompositions in the literature that have different interpretations and vary in their robustness to measurement error (see Haltiwanger 1997; Foster, Haltiwanger, and Krizan 2001; and Disney, Haskel, and Heden 2003 for discussion).

Table 2.7 **Productivity Decompositions**

	Within	Between	Cross	Net Entry
	1980–1992			
Δ ln(*Y*/*L*) (average productivity growth 3.3% per annum)				
Industry	53	2	16	29
Private	38	4	–7	65
Public	51	1	48	0
Δ lnTFP (average productivity growth 18.4% per annum)				
Industry	43	4	20	32
Private	20	8	11	61
Public	51	1	49	0
	1980 to Privatization			
Δ ln(*Y*/*L*) (average productivity growth 4.9% per annum)				
Industry	59	2	10	29
Private	61	3	1	35
Public	61	2	10	27
Δ lnTFP (average productivity growth 17.0% per annum)				
Industry	52	4	19	25
Private	27	16	20	37
Public	63	1	13	23

Source: Authors' calculations from ARD.
Note: In top panel, "public" refers to plants publicly owned in 1980.

The next two rows split the data into public and private. For both labor productivity and TFP, most growth in the public sector is accounted for by productivity growth within surviving plants, whereas most productivity growth in the private sector is accounted for by the net exit of poorly performing plants. Taking the within results for labor productivity growth and TFP growth together, the table is consistent with the idea that the public-sector plants in the 1970s were operating inefficiently and hence had plenty of scope for productivity improvements even without closure.

The second panel of table 2.7 looks at the preprivatization period.[31] The preprivatization picture is similar to that for 1980–1992, with most public-sector gains due to within-plant improvements. It seems safe to conclude that the scope for internal productivity growth within the public company was greater than that for private companies. The decompositions also offer an interesting perspective on efficiency gains, for this industry at least. Rather than keeping open inefficient plants, it would seem that much of the inefficiency is due to inefficient work practices within existing plants.

31. The postprivatization period has very small productivity growth and negative TFP growth and so is hard to interpret.

Table 2.8 **Quality Indicators in British Telecommunications**

	1979	1987	1990	1999
Average waiting time for a new phone (days)	71	15[a]		
Telephones installed within two weeks (%)	25[b]	50	64	—
Faults cleared by next working day (%)	50	72	—	—
Business orders completed in fewer than 6 working days (%)		28.4	67.9	88.5
Faults cleared in fewer than 2 working days (%)		74.3	90.1	—
Operator calls answered within 15 seconds (%)	84.2	83.5	87.7	85.8
Pay phones serviceable (%)		77	95.0	96.5
Faults per line per annum		0.25	0.25	—

Source: British Telecommunications Company accounts, data from http://www.bt.com/quality_of_service/index.htm and Rovizzi and Thompson (1991).

Note: Dashes indicate missing data.

[a]Data for 1989.

[b]Data for 1983.

2.6.2 Quality of Service

While productivity is important, service quality clearly also affects welfare. Critics of privatization have feared that it would lead to lower levels of quality. In competitive industries, this should not be a problem, but monopolies face different incentives, and a privatized firm might be able to raise its profits by reducing quality (especially if it can economize on quality in order to hit regulated target indicators). These fears were intensified in 1987, when BT's quality of service appeared to decline, hit by the effects of a strike. The word "appeared" was chosen deliberately—BT had published statistics on its quality when it was in the public sector but stopped doing so on privatization. As table 2.8 shows, at that time, almost a quarter of BT's pay phones were out of service.[32] Following pressure from the regulator, however, the company started to publish the figures again, and quality has generally risen since, helped by rapidly improving technology. To take a single example, in 1980, the average waiting time for a new phone was seventy-one days (Galal et al. 1994, tables 4 and 5). By 1989, this had fallen to fifteen days, although more than 1 million phones were installed in each year. Table 2.8 sets out these and some other relevant data and shows particular improvement in serviceable payphones.

The political fallout from BT's quality problems encouraged the government to give a quality-control role to the water and electricity regulators and to introduce competition into the electricity supply industry. At first, the regulators were limited to publishing quality statistics, but the Competition and Service (Utilities) Act of 1992 gave customers the right

32. Pollitt (1999) notes that although BT had a statutory obligation to operate a pay phone system it was not obliged to ensure that the pay phones worked.

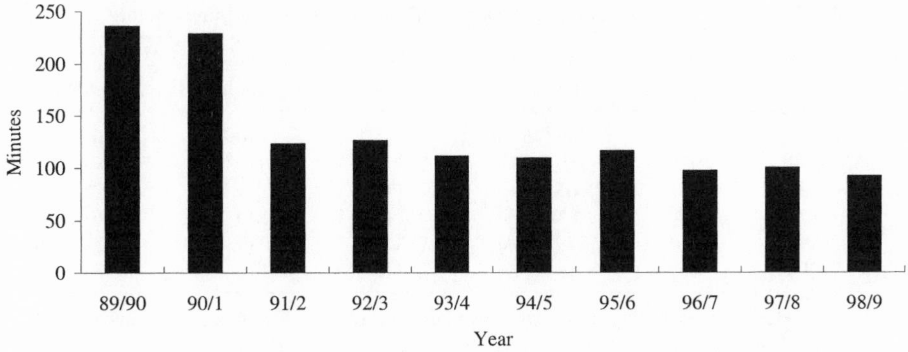

Fig. 2.3 Quality indicators in electricity—electricity distribution availability statistics: minutes lost per customer
Source: Office of Gas and Electricity Markets (2000).

to compensation for specific instances of bad service, such as power interruptions or the failure to reply to correspondence. By the time that the railways were privatized, this had been extended, so that companies were fined if they failed to meet overall performance targets. There is always a danger that companies will respond to incentives of this kind by concentrating on the aspects of quality that are being monitored while ignoring other aspects, but the data for the electricity industry imply a broad improvement since privatization. For example, figure 2.3 shows the number of minutes lost per customer in the electricity industry in Great Britain since 1989–1990, the year before privatization. The high values for the first two years are almost certainly weather related and should not be used to define a trend, but there is a clear, if slight, downward trend since 1991.

Quality is more difficult to define in the gas industry, but a good deal of political controversy was caused by the seeming rise in the number of customers disconnected by British Gas (BG) after privatization (the company cut off 0.28 percent of its credit customers in 1979, 0.31 percent in 1987, and 0.40 percent in 1998; Rovizzi and Thompson 1991). The regulator asked BG to take steps to reduce disconnections, and they did then fall, in part because the company installed prepayment meters for many customers likely to get into debt.[33]

Quality has been more controversial in the rail industry. There has been a rapid expansion in demand since privatization without a corresponding increase in network capacity. Many travellers perceived an increase in de-

33. Airports are one of the few industries where quality is not regulated; BAA have extensive quality surveys, and the regulator seemed satisfied that no quality regulation was required. Rovizzi and Thompson (1991) report 1986 data for the percent of passengers satisfied with Heathrow cleanliness, catering, trolley availability, and staff helpfulness at 97.9, 75.7, 97.0, and 96.7, with corresponding data for 1990 at 98.6, 82.5, 99.4, and 98.2.

Table 2.9 **Signals Passed at Danger on Railtrack Controlled Infrastructure**

Year	Total	Level 1 Severity	Level 2 Severity	Level 8 Severity	Other
1994–1995	771	355 (46%)	239 (31%)	1 (0.1%)	176 (23%)
1995–1996	729	299 (41%)	284 (39%)	0 (0.0%)	146 (20%)
1996–1997	688	303 (44%)	227 (33%)	1 (0.1%)	157 (23%)
1997–1998	640	282 (44%)	211 (33%)	1 (0.2%)	146 (23%)
1998–1999	664	279 (42%)	232 (35%)	0 (0.0%)	153 (23%)
1999–2000	551	215 (39%)	187 (34%)	1 (0.2%)	148 (27%)

Source: Health and Safety Executive, available at http://www.hse.gov.uk/railway/spad/spadfeba.htm#Table 3.

Notes: Minimum severity: overrun 0–25 yards, no damage; level 2 severity: overrun 26–200 yards, no damage; level 8 severity: fatalities to staff or passengers. The absolute numbers by severity level in the table are derived from the percentage breakdowns and are therefore accurate only to ±5 (apart from the figures for level 8).

lays and cancellations after privatization, and, while some companies were fined for these, some received bonus payments for other aspects of their operations that far exceeded the fines, creating political difficulties. Furthermore, three major accidents in four years (Southall, September 1997, with seven killed; Paddington, October 1998, with thirty-one killed; and Hatfield, October 2000, with four killed)[34] led to a public crisis of confidence in rail safety. Table 2.9 sets out some data on signals passed at danger (SPADs), which is a standard index of safety, along with the fraction of SPADs falling into various categories defined by their consequences. As the table shows, the number of SPADs on Railtrack's infrastructure has declined. There has been a small rise in SPADs at level 2 of seriousness. The level 8 measures reflect the Southall and Paddington crashes, and because such events are comparatively infrequent it is hard to discern a trend. Although there is a perception that the industry has been reluctant to spend money on safety improvements that would save lives, the verdict on safety and quality in the railways is, at worst, "not proven." Rail travel remains far safer than road transport, of course.[35]

2.6.3 The Wider Impact of Privatization

We now consider a number of other issues. First, having looked at the impact of privatization on the various sectors concerned, one might ask what impact it had on productivity growth in the rest of the economy. Since

34. The accident at Selby, February 2001, in which ten people were killed, was caused by a car running off a bridge onto the line, rather than a problem with the track, signalling, or rolling stock.

35. Rail death rates have been falling steadily over time: Rates per billion passenger km are 1981, 1.0; 1986, 0.9; 1991, 0.8; 1996, 0.3 (Office for National Statistics 1999, table 12.18).

privatization covered the energy sector, one possibility is that privatization lowered energy prices below what they would otherwise have been. This raises the possibility that privatization might have been a positive energy price shock and hence may have affected productivity just as the negative energy shocks may have done so (Bruno and Sachs 1985; Jorgenson 1984). Leaving aside the question of whether privatization affected energy prices relative to what they would have been, the effects of energy prices on TFP are likely to have been small. As Jorgenson (1984) points out, energy prices can affect TFP if technical progress is energy using (i.e., biased toward the use of energy), since a fall in energy prices causes substitution toward energy and hence a rise in TFP growth. Jorgenson's estimates for U.S. manufacturing, however, suggest that the biases are, in practice, very small, and hence even a halving of energy prices (which seems an overestimate of the effects of privatization) would still lead to a rise in TFP growth of around 0.05 percentage points per annum.[36]

How successful was privatization in weakening the power of the public-sector unions? As Pendleton (1997) argues, this rather depends on what one thinks the source of public-sector union power is. To the extent that it is unions having high-level consultation with ministers on strategic policy for nationalized industries, then privatization has clearly reduced this drastically. However, since in the 1970s many workers in nationalized companies were denied the money for pay raises as part of government incomes policy, this could help unions to gain advantages for their members. To the extent that it is unions having, for example, particular bargaining rights (when established nationalized industries were required to consult and negotiate with workers), the picture is very mixed. Bargaining arrangements changed, for example, in the Post Office, in which the separation into mail, parcels, and counters in the early 1980s led to the devolution of bargaining. Parry, Waddington, and Critcher (1997) argue that there has been a greater trend toward "management assertiveness" in electricity, shipbuilding, and water. On the other hand, Ogden (1990) finds that union membership and the scope of bargaining in water, telecoms, and gas did not change on privatization, and Millward et al. (1992), reviewing the Workplace Industrial Relations Survey (WIRS) evidence, "saw virtually no evidence" that trade union negotiating rights were withdrawn from unionized workplaces. Thus, it seems hard to argue that, in general, public-sector unions were weakened any more than unions were generally weakened by labor legislation and the macroeconomy. Finally, Bishop and Thompson (1994) docu-

36. With a translog cost function, TFP growth is the sum of Hicks neutral technical change (α_O) and biased technical progress times the log of the price of the particular factor (Berndt and Wood 1982)—that is, $\Delta \ln \text{TFP}_i = \alpha_O + \alpha_E \ln p_E + \alpha_Z \ln p_Z$, where E denotes energy and Z is other factors. As reported by Oulton and O'Mahony (1994), Jorgenson finds that α_E is, on average, 0.0007 for U.S. manufacturing. Hence, a halving of energy prices raises TFP growth by $0.0007 \cdot \ln 2 \cdot 100 = 0.049$ percentage points.

Table 2.10 Public Attitudes toward Privatization (% of favoring responses)

	1983	1986	1987	1989	1990	1991
"Are the nationalized industries well run?" (% agreeing)	21	31	33			
Control of wages by law	48	40	34	28	30	33
Control of prices by law	70	61	58	56	56	60
Less state ownership of industry	49	30	30	24	24	—
More state ownership of industry	11	16	16	18		
About the same level of state ownership of industry as now	33	49	48	53		
Government should own the electricity industry	—	28	26	32	28	—

Sources: Top row, Jowell, Witherspoon, and Brook (1988); other rows, Jowell et al. (1992).
Note: Blank cells indicate that question was not asked in that year. Dashes indicate missing data.

ment that performance-related pay was introduced in the period of preprivatization restructuring in all of the 1979 public sector (except BA).

Third, did privatization change people's attitudes to the public sector? Table 2.10 sets out some findings from the British Social Attitudes Survey. The first row reports the proportion agreeing that nationalized industries are well run and shows a rise in that proportion between 1983 and 1987. This could reflect the increased productivity in these industries, or it could reflect that people are referring to previously nationalized industries.

Rows (4), (5), and (6) show attitudes to state ownership (with attitudes to wage and price control added for reference). The proportion favoring wage and price control has fallen steadily. The proportion favoring less state ownership has fallen a good deal, but, since the state sector has fallen as well, this suggests decreasing support for *further* privatization. The proportion favoring more state ownership has grown, but only somewhat. The proportion favoring about the same level of state ownership has grown substantially, and, since the sector has shrunk, this is de facto approval of privatization. Finally, the proportion favoring state control of the electricity industry shows no clear trend (privatization was announced in 1987 and implemented in 1990–1991). Overall, however, the data suggest no strong support for renationalization and increasing support for the privatizations that have occurred.

2.7 Contracting Out

In the 1970s, practically all central and local government services were provided directly by government employees. In the early 1980s, however, some local councils began to contract out services, such as refuse collection, to private firms, while some hospitals obtained cleaning, catering, and laundry services from the private sector. In an influential study, Domberger, Meadowcroft, and Thompson (1986) modeled the refuse collection costs of 305 local authorities, accounting for collection method, population density, and so forth, and whether the service had been contracted out and awarded to a private contractor, awarded to the in-house organization after competition, or had not been the subject of competition. Thus, this study is of particular interest since it provides a control group to contrast with private ownership. Relative to not being contracted out at all, costs were 22 percent lower when awarded to a private contractor and 17 percent lower when contracted out but awarded in-house. These cost savings were insignificantly different from each other, suggesting that it was the injection of competition from the contracting-out process that was important for cost savings rather than whether the operator was public or private. In a study of contracting for domestic services in hospitals, Domberger, Meadowcroft, and Thompson (1987) also found savings of about 20 percent (although there was some evidence that early contract awards had involved much lower prices than this, which they argued were unsustainable and reflected "winner's curse" effects).

Domberger and Jensen (1997) report a number of other studies, including a meta-analysis by the Australian Industry Commission, which produced a "rather wide" distribution of reported savings (from a cost *increase* of more than 10 percent to a saving of more than 50 percent). The most frequently reported savings, however, were between 10 and 30 percent, which "is entirely consistent with the conclusions based on U.K. data" (73). Given these savings, and the government's desire to reduce the size of the public sector, compulsory competitive tendering was introduced in 1988. The central government also started to contract out services, and approximately £2 billion of white-collar services had been subjected to competitive tendering by 1995 (Domberger and Jensen).

There have been claims that most of these savings have come from reductions in quality or in the terms and conditions offered to staff. Domberger and Jensen (1997) conclude, however, that most of these savings have come from "better management, more flexible working practices, more efficient use of capital and greater innovation spurred by competition" (1997, 74). Cubbin, Domberger, and Meadowcroft (1987) found that the technical efficiency of private refuse operators was 17 percent higher than that of authorities that had not put their services out to tender. This would account for three-quarters of the savings identified by Domberger, Meadowcroft, and Thompson (1986). However, insofar as employees gained rents from technical inefficiency, increasing efficiency would destroy those rents and reduce the employees' welfare. (For example, refuse workers might be able to serve an area in a shorter time than was allowed in their roster and would take the difference as leisure. Preserving such rents is not necessarily a legitimate objective of public policy, however.)

Councils' direct-labor organizations were allowed to bid against private firms. In the early studies in which these organizations won contracts, they were offering cost savings that were not significantly different from those under contracts awarded to the private sector, suggesting (yet again) that competition rather than ownership is the key to efficiency. After the introduction of compulsory competitive tendering, however, Szymanski (1996) found that local authorities that awarded contracts to their in-house teams were achieving significantly lower savings—a 10 percent rather than the 20 percent reduction from private contractors. It is at least possible that some of these councils, which had resisted compulsory tendering, were favoring their in-house organizations when they awarded contracts. If the in-house teams appreciated this reduction in competition, they could rationally offer fewer cost savings when bidding. In other words, what appears to be a difference due to ownership could still be related to competition.

There were fears that quality would also be impaired when services were contracted out. In practice, however, service levels appear to have been maintained or even enhanced, perhaps because contracting out has been associated with greater monitoring and more explicit standards (Domberger and Jensen 1997). In general, therefore, we conclude that efficiency gains from privatization are not due to lower levels of quality.

2.8 The Private Finance Initiative

The last kind of privatization that we consider is sometimes presented as a form of contracting out, in that the government is buying services from a private company. The difference is that the private finance initiative (PFI) involves investment, or the purchase of existing assets, which are used to provide the services required.[37] The PFI has been used to finance roads, prisons, hospitals, and schools. The Channel Tunnel Rail Link was finally started as a PFI project, and the government is planning to finance much-needed investment for the London Underground through the PFI. So far, the PFI has funded £15 billion in investment, about 20 percent of the government's capital spending over the period.

The administration of the PFI reflects a number of the principles the government has announced for it. First, there must be transfer of risk to the private sector. When a prison is built under the PFI, this means that the private company takes on the risk of building and operating it. When a road is funded in this way, a further risk transfer is achieved by making payments to the company conditional on the number of vehicles using the road. Second, the project must deliver value for money, and, third, there must be open competition for the project.

The PFI has a number of potential advantages. Even if there are good

37. For excellent reviews of the PFI, see Grout (1997) and Pollit (2000).

reasons for the state to subsidize services, due to externalities (e.g., roads), this does not necessarily mean that the public sector should build the assets to deliver the services or, in some cases, provide the services itself. One particular advantage arises due to risk allocation. Some of the risks of building, for example, a prison arise mainly from factors under the construction company's control, such as poor management. Traditional public procurement has often passed these risks back to the state, whereas PFI contracts for services may ensure that there is no payment to the private sector until building is completed, therefore transferring risk to the private sector.[38] There would be no need for such a policy if the government and private sector could write complete contracts that could, for example, specify varying payments for late completion of an asset depending on all possible circumstances that could in turn be verified.[39] Once the prison is in service, risks are more likely to come from government policy, such as new legislation raising the prison population, and a more flexible contract may be appropriate. Another advantage claimed for the PFI is that it removes public-sector investment from the PSBR. This is not just cosmetic, as the PSBR can be a binding constraint on governments, and moving investment outside the PSBR allows increased spending. The requirement to transfer risk is, in part, a way of ensuring that a PFI project is more than just a way of borrowing money without counting it toward the PSBR.

Against this, the PFI has some potential disadvantages. First, it can only work well if outputs and inputs can be measured and contracted over clearly. Second, PFI contracts can be inflexible: the government has to carry on with a project even if it decides it does not wish to do so. Third, the PFI, just as with direct borrowing by the government, transfers costs to future generations (compared with spending out of current tax revenue), which may or may not be desirable.

Critics of the PFI point out that the cash cost of PFI projects is increased by the higher interest rates required by the private sector compared to the cost of public borrowing. Some of the value-for-money comparisons, in which the PFI nevertheless appears to be the cheaper option, assume very large efficiency gains from private-sector delivery to offset the higher interest cost. Grout (1997) points out that this additional interest cost ought to be disregarded, since the cost of public-sector borrowing should be project specific and should depend upon the risks involved. Public borrowing for a risky project appears cheaper only because it is being subsidized by the government's ability to raise taxes if things go wrong. If this hidden subsidy

38. The National Audit Office (NAO; 1992), for example, estimated that the Department of Transport was paying an average of 28 percent more for roads than the price originally agreed.

39. Such risks can be hard to predict, however. The Skye Bridge PFI project local public enquiry resulted in delays and design changes (in order to protect a local otter population) costing £3.8 million out of a total cost of £39 million (Pollitt 2000).

is made explicit, public provision appears more expensive, and the PFI seems to be a relatively better value for money. In a sample of seventeen PFI projects, the value of the risk transferred to the private sector accounted for 60 percent of the expected savings from using the PFI, and six projects depended on these savings to pass the value-for-money test (Arthur Andersen and Enterprise London School of Economics 2000, table 5.9).

The question is whether the subsidy should be made explicit in this way. If the PFI transfers some risks away from the government, does that reduce the interest rate on the national debt? If the capital markets believe that there is no chance of default by the British government—whether or not it has to bear the risks involved in PFI projects—the implication is that the interest rate on the national debt is not affected by the PFI.[40] If this is the case, it could be argued that projects within the public sector receive "insurance" against risks at no real cost to the taxpayer, while the PFI requires the taxpayer to pay the private sector for risk bearing.[41] It may well be appropriate to use a higher test discount rate when assessing the desirability of a risky project, but that does not mean that the public sector should pay that higher rate through the PFI if cheaper financing is available. The case for the PFI would come back to the private sector's ability to produce services more efficiently than the public sector, and the efficiency must be great enough to offset the higher financing cost.

A series of NAO reports point to a mixed experience of the PFI. On the positive side, the NAO reports that a number of projects have gone ahead that simply would not have been financed were they to have come out of the public-sector capital budgets (e.g., the Channel Tunnel Rail link and the Skye Bridge; NAO 1997). On the negative side, bidding costs are high—estimated at £500 million for all outstanding PFI contracts in 1998 (Kerr 1998), which are then reflected in the final price—and delays can be long (up to two years). Furthermore, some contracts have substantially overrun, with some contract terms requiring the government to withstand the costs (e.g., computerizing post office payments). Finally, in practice, private-sector firms may have been adept at convincing the government to withstand more of the risks than would be optimal.

Thus, some PFI projects seem to have been successful and some not. The NAO judges the PFI prison contracts to have been well planned, to have offered good value for money, and to have been completed in almost half the time relative to public prison projects. On the other hand, the wrong discount rate was used in the evaluation of the comparative costs of several

40. This argument applies to the current state of the British economy—it would certainly not hold true for all countries or even all periods in British economic history.

41. A public-sector union has suggested that some services are suffering because public-sector budgets have not been increased to cover the extra capital charges involved in buying services through the PFI (Unison 2000).

road projects, potentially biasing the choice of financing method (Pollitt 2000).

2.9 Conclusions

Did privatization *itself* raise productivity? No. There seems to be very little evidence that the transfer of a public undertaking to a private one raises efficiency. British Gas is perhaps the classic example: a company that was transferred to the private sector with the same structure, same management, and very light regulation. Other companies were allowed to use British Gas's pipes to carry gas but at tariffs set by British Gas. No productivity gain occurred.

Did the *process* of privatization raise productivity? The answer is a resounding yes: Preprivatization restructuring, more competition, and tighter regulation all raised efficiency. Real change in the gas industry, for example, started in the early 1990s, once the competition authorities started to force open the industry. An open question is whether the commitment to privatization was essential to obtaining these gains.

We should also ask whether the clear change in the *level* of productivity that has been associated with privatization has evolved into higher rates of productivity *growth.* The problem here is that the process of catching up to private-sector levels of productivity can easily take the best part of a decade, and it is only after that process is complete that we will be able to discern what has happened to growth rates. At the moment, all that we can say is that it is hard to see an effect of privatization on productivity growth rates. The effect of privatization on quality seems to depend on strong regulation.

Privatization in the sense of asset sales is now more or less finished in the United Kingdom for the simple reason that there is little left to sell. Thus, the key concerns for the future are developing regulation and reshaping the PFI. It is also likely that future administrations will want to use the private sector more in delivering health and education services.

References

Abbot, K., and D. Thompson. 1989. Deregulating European aviation: The impact of bilateral legislation. London Business School Centre for Business Strategy. Working Paper no. 73. London: London Business School.

Arthur Andersen and Enterprise London School of Economics (LSE). 2000. *Value for money drivers in the private finance initiative.* London: Treasury Taskforce.

Averch, H., and H. Johnson. 1962. Behavior of the firm under regulatory constraint. *American Economic Review* 52 (5): 1053–1069.

Beesley, M., and S. C. Littlechild. 1989. The regulation of privatized monopolies in the United Kingdom. *Rand Journal of Economics* 20 (3): 454–472.
Berndt, E. R., and D. O. Wood. 1982. The specification and measurement of technical change in U.S. manufacturing. In *Advances in the economics of energy and resources,* Vol. 4, ed. John R. Moroney, 199–221. Greenwich, Conn.: JAI Press.
Besley, T., and P. Seabright. 2000. State aids in the EU. *Economic Policy,* issue no. 28:13–42.
Bishop, M., and M. Green. 1995. Privatisation and recession: The miracle tested. Centre for the Study of Regulated Industries. Discussion Paper no. 10. London: Chartered Institute of Public Finance and Accountancy.
Bishop, M., and J. Kay. 1989. *Does privatisation work? Lessons from the UK.* London: London Business School, Centre for Business Strategy.
Bishop, M., and D. Thompson. 1992. Regulatory reform and productivity growth in the UK's public utilities. *Applied Economics* 24 (11): 1181–1190.
———. 1994. Privatisation, internal organisation and productive efficiency. In *Privatisation and economic performance,* ed. M. Bishop, J. Kay, and C. Mayer. Oxford, U.K.: Oxford University Press.
Bos, D. 1990. *Privatisation.* Cambridge: Cambridge University Press.
Bruno, M., and J. D. Sachs. 1985. *The economics of worldwide stagflation.* Oxford, U.K.: Blackwell.
Cubbin, J., S. Domberger, and S. Meadowcroft. 1987. Competitive tendering and refuse collection: Identifying the source of efficiency gains. *Fiscal Studies* 8 (3): 49–58.
Disney, R., J. Haskel, and Y. Heden. 2003. Restructuring and productivity growth in UK manufacturing. *Economic Journal* 113 (489): 666–694.
Domberger, S., and P. Jensen. 1997. Contracting out by the public sector: Theory, evidence, prospects. *Oxford Review of Economic Policy* 13 (4): 67–78.
Domberger, S., S. Meadowcroft, and D. Thompson. 1986. Competitive tendering and efficiency: The case of refuse collection. *Fiscal Studies* 7 (4): 69–87.
———. 1987. The impact of competitive tendering on the costs of hospital domestic services. *Fiscal Studies* 8 (4): 39–54.
Foster, J., J. Haltiwanger, and C. J. Krizan. 2001. Aggregate productivity growth: Lessons from microeconomic evidence. In *New developments in productivity analysis,* ed. Charles R. Hulten, Edwin R. Dean, and Michael J. Harper. Chicago: University of Chicago Press.
Galal, A., L. Jones, P. Tandon, and I. Vogelsang. 1994. *The welfare consequences of selling public enterprises.* New York: Oxford University Press and World Bank Publications.
Good, D., M. Nadiri, and R. Sickles. 1997. Index number and factor demand approaches to the estimation of productivity. In *Handbook of applied econometrics,* vol. 2, *Microeconometrics,* ed. M. Pesaran and P. Schmidt, 14–50. Oxford: Basil Blackwell.
Green, R., and D. Newbery. 1997. Competition in the electricity industry in England and Wales. *Oxford Review of Economic Policy* 13 (1): 27–46.
Grout, P. 1997. The economics of the private finance initiative. *Oxford Review of Economic Policy* 13 (4): 53–66.
Haltiwanger, J. 1997. Measuring and analyzing aggregate fluctuations: The importance of building from microeconomic evidence. *Review of the Federal Reserve Bank of St. Louis* (May/June): 55–78.
Hannah, L. 1979. *Electricity before nationalisation.* London: Macmillan.
Haskel, J., and A. Sanchis. 1995. Privatisation and X-inefficiency: A bargaining approach. *Journal of Industrial Economics* 43 (3): 301–321.

Haskel, J., and S. Szymanski. 1992. The effects of privatisation, competition and restructuring on productivity growth in U.K. manufacturing. Queen Mary and Westfield College, Department of Economics. Discussion Paper no. 286. London: Queen Mary and Westfield College, January.

Jorgenson, D. 1984. The role of energy in productivity growth. *American Economic Review* 74 (2): 26–30.

Jowell, Roger, Lindsay Brook, Gillian Prior, and Bridget Taylor, eds. 1992. *British social attitudes: The 9th report.* Aldershot, U.K.: Dartmouth.

Jowell, Roger, Sharon Witherspoon, and Lindsay Brook, eds. 1988. *British social attitudes: The 5th report.* Aldershot, U.K.: Gower for Social and Community Planning Research.

Kay, J., C. Mayer, and D. Thompson. 1986. *Privatisation and regulation: The U.K. experience.* Oxford, U.K.: Oxford University Press.

Kay, J., and D. Thompson. 1986. Privatisation: A policy in search of a rationale. *Economic Journal* 96 (381): 18–32.

Kerr, D. 1998. The PFI miracle. *Capital and Class* 64:17–28.

Levy, B., and P. Spiller. 1994. The institutional foundations of regulatory commitment: A comparative analysis of telecommunications regulation. *Journal of Law, Economics, and Organization* 10 (2): 201–46.

Littlechild, S. C. 1983. *The regulation of British Telecommunications profitability.* London: Her Majesty's Stationery Office.

Martin, S., and D. Parker. 1997. *Privatisation.* Cheltenham, U.K.: Edward Elgar.

Monopolies and Mergers Commission (MMC). 1995. *Lyonnaise Des Eaux SA and Northumbrian Water Group: A report on the merger situation.* Command Paper no. 2936. London: Her Majesty's Stationery Office.

McGowan, P., and P. Seabright. 1989. The de-regulation of European airlines. *Economic Policy,* issue no. 9:284–385.

Markou, E., and C. Waddams Price. 1999. UK utilities: Past reform and current proposals. *Annals of Public and Co-operative Economics* 70 (3): 371–416.

Millward, N., and M. Stevens. 1986. *British workplace industrial relations 1980–84.* Aldershot: Gower Press.

Millward, N., M. Stevens, D. Smart, and W. Hawes. 1992. *Workplace industrial relations in transition.* Aldershot, U.K.: Gower Press.

Morrison, H. 1933. *Socialism and transport.* London: Macmillan.

National Audit Office (NAO). 1992. *Department of Transport: Contracting for roads.* London: Her Majesty's Stationery Office.

———. 1997. *The Skye Bridge.* House of Commons report no. 5 of Parliamentary session 1997–1998, London: Her Majesty's Stationery Office.

Office of Gas and Electricity Markets. 2000. *Report on distribution and transmission performance 1998/99.* London: Office of Gas and Electricity Markets.

Office for National Statistics. 1999. Social trends. London: Office for National Statistics.

Ogden, S. 1990. Privatisation and industrial relations: The shock of the new? University of Leeds Business School. Discussion Paper no. 90/12. Leeds, U.K.: University of Leeds.

O'Mahony, M. 1999. *Britain's productivity performance 1950–1996: An international perspective.* London: National Institute for Economic and Social Research.

Oulton, N., and M. O'Mahony. 1994. *Productivity and growth: A study of British industry 1954–1986.* Cambridge: Cambridge University Press.

Parker, D., and S. Martin. 1995. The impact of U.K. privatisation on labour and total factor productivity. *Scottish Journal of Political Economy* 42 (2): 201–220.

Parry, D., D. Waddington, and C. Critcher. 1997. Industrial relations in the privatised mining industry. *British Journal of Industrial Relations* 35 (3): 173–196.
Pendleton, A. 1997. The evolution of industrial relations in U.K. nationalized industries. *British Journal of Industrial Relations* 35 (2): 145–172.
Pirie, M. 1988. *Privatisation.* Aldershot, U.K.: Gower.
Pollitt, M. 1999. A survey of the liberalisation of public enterprises in the U.K. since 1979. In *Privatization, deregulation and institutional framework,* ed. M. Kagami and M. Tsuji, 120–169. Tokyo: Japan External Trade Organization, Institute of Developing Economies.
———. 2000. The declining role of the state in infrastructure investments in the U.K. In *Private initiatives in infrastructure: Priorities, incentives and performance,* ed. M. Tsuji, S. V. Berg, and M. G. Pollitt. Tokyo: Japan External Trade Organization, Institute of Developing Economies.
Pryke, R. 1982. *The nationalised industries: Policies and performance since 1968.* Oxford: Oxford University Press.
Rees, R. 1988. Inefficiency, public enterprise, and privatisation. *European Economic Review* 32 (2–3): 422–431.
Rovizzi, L., and D. Thompson. 1991. Price-cap regulated public utilities and quality regulation in the UK. Centre for Business Strategy, London Business School, Working Paper no. 111. London: London Business School.
Sanchis, A. 1997. Does privatisation remove restrictive working practices? Evidence from U.K. establishments. Queen Mary and Westfield College. Discussion Paper no. 375. London: Queen Mary and Westfield College.
Schmalensee, R. 1989. Good regulatory regimes. *Rand Journal of Economics* 20 (3): 417–436.
Shleifer, A. 1985. A theory of yardstick competition. *Rand Journal of Economics* 16 (3): 319–327.
Szymanski, S. 1996. The impact of compulsory competitive tendering on refuse collection services. *Fiscal Studies* 17 (3): 1–19.
Thompson, D., and A. Whitfield. 1995. Express coaching: Privatisation, incumbent advantage and the competitive process. In *Privatization and economic performance,* ed. M. Bishop, J. Kay and C. Mayer. Oxford, U.K.: Oxford University Press.
Tilley, B., and T. Weyman-Jones. 1999. Productivity growth and efficiency change in electricity distribution. Paper presented at the British Institute of Energy Economics conference, St. John's College. 20–21 September, Oxford, U.K.
Unison. 2000. *Unison submission to the House of Commons Treasury Committee Inquiry into the Private Finance Initiative.* London: Unison.
Vickers, J. 1995. Concepts of competition. *Oxford Economic Papers* 47 (1): 1–23.
Waddams Price, C. 1999. Efficiency and productivity studies in incentive regulation of U.K. utilities. Address to the Sixth European Workshop on Efficiency and Productivity Analysis, Royal Agriculture College. 29–31 October, Copenhagen, Denmark.
Waddams Price, C., and T. Weyman-Jones. 1996. Malmquist indices of productivity change in the U.K. gas industry before and after privatisation. *Applied Economics* 28 (1): 29–39.
Weingast, B., K. Shepsle, and C. Johnsen. 1981. The political economy of benefits and costs: A neoclassical approach to distributive politics. *Journal of Political Economy* 89 (4): 642–664.

3

Shared Modes of Compensation and Firm Performance
U.K. Evidence

Martin J. Conyon and Richard B. Freeman

Share ownership offers employees a real stake in their company . . . I want, through targeted reform, to reward long term commitment by employees. I want to encourage the new enterprise culture of team work in which everyone contributes and everyone benefits from success.
—U.K. Chancellor of the Exchequer Gordon Brown (Her Majesty's Treasury 1999)

3.1 Background and Motivation

Many analysts and decision makers in industry, labor, and government believe that the traditional wage-employment relationship is not appropriate for a modern competitive economy. In place of the historic capital-labor dichotomy in which employers pay a fixed wage for the right to tell employees what to do, a new system of work arrangements has developed in which employees share in the financial fortunes of the firm and make many of the decisions that determine firm performance. This shared capitalist model of work and compensation (Freeman 1999) dominates new information technology firms in the United States, but it is found in other sectors and countries as well.

For over two decades, the United Kingdom has tried to encourage shared capitalist practices by offering tax advantages to firms that link pay to profits, provide company shares to workers, encourage workers to save through stock options, or develop approved share-option plans. In 1999,

Martin J. Conyon is assistant professor of management at the Wharton School, University of Pennsylvania. Richard B. Freeman is the Herbert Ascherman Professor of Economics at Harvard University, senior research fellow at the Centre for Economic Performance (CEP) of the London School of Economics, and program director of labor studies at NBER.

We would like to thank participants at the December 2000 London School of Economics and CEP conference for comments and suggestions, especially our discussant Sushil Wadwhani. Further suggestions from John Abowd, Peter Cappelli, Chip Hunter, Steve Nickell, and seminar participants at Wharton added to the ideas in this paper. We are very grateful to those companies that responded to our survey on employee reward strategies and involvement. Laura Read deserves special thanks for all her work in constructing the firm-level panel. Wayne Diamond provided invaluable assistance in analyzing the Workplace Employment Relations Survey (WERS). The financial support of the Economic and Social Research Council (ESRC) is gratefully acknowledged.

the U.K. government issued draft legislation introducing two new plans: the All Employee Share Plan, through which employees will be able to buy "partnership" shares in their firm out of their pretax and pre–National Insurance contribution salary, and Enterprise Management Incentives intended to help smaller companies with the potential for growth to recruit and retain high-caliber employees by giving tax advantages to options granted to a small number of employees.[1] By contrast, the government has moved to eliminate tax advantages for profit-related pay, based on the notion that many firms used this to get tax advantages without really linking pay to profits. The 1998 Workplace Employment Relations Survey shows that 86 percent of the establishments that had profit-related pay were taking advantage of the tax break.

Behind the desire to increase shared compensation in the United Kingdom is the widespread belief, expressed by the Chancellor of the Exchequer, that shared capitalist arrangements will create a better work culture with improved productivity and commitment by employees. Existing studies on profit sharing, employee ownership, and employee participation lend general support to this proposition (Weitzman and Kruse 1990; OECD 1995; Doucouliagos 1995), but these studies also show considerable variability in the effects of practices on firm performance. In addition, the economic context in which the programs operate (e.g., whether information sharing takes place) and the details of the schemes seem to affect their success rate.

Our goals address the following two questions. How far has the United Kingdom moved from standard wage-employment contracts toward a shared mode of compensation? What effect has shared compensation had on economic outcomes?

This paper examines these questions using a 1999 survey of the shared compensation strategies used by a sample of U.K. listed companies between 1995 and 1998; the 1998 Workplace Employment Relations Survey (WERS) of some 2,000 U.K. establishments or workplaces; and the 1990–1998 longitudinal WERS panel survey of nearly 900 workplaces. We use these data to describe the growth and use of shared capitalist compensation practices and to assess the effects of these practices on productivity and related economic outcomes. We have three findings:

1. Shared-compensation practices are substantial and growing in the United Kingdom largely in response to Treasury policies designed to encourage them. Upwards of half of U.K. workplaces have some form of shared-compensation program and over one-third have something beyond profit-related pay (which the government abolished as of 2000). About half

1. The government introduced further new legislation in 2001 (see http://www.inlandrevenue.gov.uk/pbr2000/ir2.htm).

of the listed firms in our firm-based data also have some form of shared compensation.

2. Firms and establishments with shared compensation, particularly those with deferred profit sharing and employee share ownership, are more likely to establish formal communication and consultation channels with workers than other establishments.

3. Firms and establishments that use shared compensation tend to outperform other firms and establishments in productivity and financial performance. Moreover, the stock price of firms with shared-compensation practices has also performed better than those of other firms. But combining shared compensation and information or communication systems does not add extra productivity impact.

Overall, our findings are quite similar across firm and establishment data sets in that they tell a favorable story about shared-compensation modes of pay, including the share ownership schemes that have become a U.K. government priority. The one area where our two data sources tell a different story is the area of profit-related pay: Our firm analysis finds that profit-related pay has no effect on productivity, while our establishment data finds an effect.

The remainder of the paper is organized as follows. Section 3.2 deals with shared-compensation policies and practices in the United Kingdom. Section 3.3 asks how shared compensation arrangements should affect firm performance. Sections 3.4 and 3.5 provide the main evidence. Section 3.4 deals with the firm-level evidence using the company survey, and section 3.5 uses the WERS data. Finally, in section 3.6 we offer some concluding remarks.

3.2 Shared Compensation Policies and Practices in the United Kingdom

As noted, the United Kingdom has experimented with a rich variety of policies to encourage shared compensation. The following subsection provides a capsule summary of policies dating from the late 1970s to 2000 and is divided between schemes designed for all employees and schemes designed for top management and other special workers.

3.2.1 U.K. Programs to Encourage Shared Capitalism; All Employee Schemes

Approved Profit-Related Pay

In 1987, the scheme was introduced for employers to pay a profit-related compensation package. Initially, tax relief was given on half of the profit-related payments up to a limit of the lower of £3,000 or 20 percent of the employee's pay. The cash limit was increased to £4,000 in 1989. In 1991, the tax relief was increased to the whole of the payment. In the Finance Act of 1997, the income tax relief was set to be phased out over a three- to four-year period. For profit periods beginning in 1998 the cash ceiling was reduced to £2,000, and for periods beginning in 1999 the ceiling was reduced to £1,000. As of January 2000, this scheme was no longer running.

Approved Profit-Sharing Scheme

The approved profit-sharing scheme is a vehicle for companies to provide free shares to employees that are free from tax liabilities. Profit-sharing schemes were introduced in the 1978 Finance Act. In 2000, there were about 950 approved profit-sharing schemes in operation with an estimated cost to the government in tax relief of £150 million. Profit-sharing schemes must be open to any employee who has been employed by the company for more than five years. There are about 1.25 million participants covered under these arrangements (data taken from http://www.proshare.org). However, the approved profit-sharing scheme is being phased out with the introduction of the new all-employee plan (see http://www.inlandrevenue.gov.uk).

New All Employee Share Plan (2000)

This plan stipulates that firms can give free shares tax free; employees buy shares out of pretax income, and firms can match employee purchases. Employees who leave the firm must withdraw shares. The firm has a flexible performance criterion for tax relief: Employees who keep shares in the employee share ownership plan trust for five years pay no income tax and pay capital gains only on an increase in value. Companies get relief for costs of providing shares for employees.

Approved Save as You Earn Scheme

The SAYE scheme, or savings-related option scheme, is an arrangement such that an employee has the right to buy shares at a future date at a prespecified purchase price. The company grants employees the option to buy the company's shares in three, five, or seven years' time. Either the price is the current market price or the option can be issued at a discount of up to 20 percent of that price. The scheme has to be open to all employees of the company with more than five years of service (see http://www.inland revenue.gov.uk). There are currently over 1,200 SAYE schemes in operation, with an estimated cost to the government in tax relief of £600 million. There are about 1.75 million participants covered under these arrangements (see http://www.proshare.org).

Management and Special-Employee Schemes;
Approved Company Share Option Plan

The approved company share option plan (CSOP) is a scheme under which an employee has the right to purchase a fixed number of shares at a predetermined price at some date in the future. Under this scheme, options may not be offered at a discount. The employee does not pay income tax on the grant of the option or any increase in the market value of shares before the option is exercised. Unlike SAYE schemes, discretion is given to the company as to which employees are eligible and are granted options. They tend to be granted to company directors. There are currently over 3,750 such approved CSOPs in operation, with an estimated cost to the government in tax relief of £130 million. There are about 450,000 participants covered under these arrangements (see http://www.proshare.org).

The most widely used system was profit-related pay, which gave income tax relief to workers for compensation related to profits. Profit-related pay schemes were widely adopted after the 1987 introduction of the tax break to the extent that by 1998 32 percent of British workplaces and 37 percent of workers were receiving part of their pay for profit-related reasons. However, the Treasury came to view the system as overly open to scam behavior because firms found ways to classify any sort of pay as profit related in order to take advantage of the tax break. It began phasing out the program in 1997. As of 2000, profit-related pay was history in the United Kingdom.

The U.K. government has programs that encourage firms to pay workers in shares or stock options or that encourage employees to invest in shares. One important U.K. plan is the Save as You Earn (SAYE) share option scheme, which gives tax relief to workers who enter a savings contract that puts money into an account to buy the shares when the period ends. The 1978 Finance Act introduced approved profit-sharing schemes as a vehicle for companies to provide free shares to employees that carry no tax liabilities. This plan is being phased out and replaced by the All Employee Share Plan, which allows firms to give free shares to workers without tax liability and also gives tax breaks to employees who buy shares that they hold for five years (with smaller tax breaks to workers who hold them for three years).

In addition to these schemes, the United Kingdom gives tax advantages to shared-compensation plans that go largely to top management. Company share option plans allow employees to purchase shares at a predetermined price at some future date, without paying income tax on the grant or on any increase in the market value of shares. In 2000, the government introduced an Enterprise Market Incentive option program to help smaller companies with potential for growth to recruit and to retain high-caliber employees.

3.2.2 Data on Shared Compensation in the United Kingdom

Our information on shared-compensation practices in the United Kingdom comes from two bodies of data: the WERS and a special survey of listed firms that Martin Conyon and Laura Read conducted in 1999 (Conyon and Read 2000). From the WERS, we use the 1998 cross-sectional survey, which contains information on compensation and employment practices at 2,191 workplaces in Britain with ten or more employees, and the 1990–1998 WERS panel survey, which contains information on 882 surviving workplaces from the 1990 survey. The WERS surveys have extremely high response rates—80 percent for the 1998 cross section and 86 percent for the 1990–1998 longitudinal survey[2]—which make them particularly valuable for obtaining an accurate picture of shared-compensation practices at British workplaces. But the WERS is not perfect for our analysis. It has only categorical measures of establishment outcomes (whether productivity and financial performance are a lot above, somewhat above, or below average in a sector) and little information about the company as a whole. To obtain better data on firm-level compensation strategy and performance, we rely on the Conyon and Read 1999 survey of U.K. firms listed on the London Stock Exchange.[3] This survey contains 299 completed usable responses from a sample of 1,518, giving a response rate of 20 percent, which is good for surveys of this type. The sample is generally representative of the sampled population.[4] Because these are listed companies, we can measure actual value added and related variables as well as track share prices, which we cannot do with the WERS data. By combining information from the two sources, we provide more robust results about the effects of shared compensation than would otherwise be the case.

Table 3.1 contains statistics on shared-compensation practices in 1998 from the WERS and WERS panel surveys. The top section gives the percentage of firms with the specified compensation practice in 1998, weighted by the sample weights.[5] It shows that the most popular form of

2. Interviews were conducted with a manager in each workplace, and 950 worker representatives were also interviewed, representing 82 percent of cases in which an eligible representative was identified. Completed questionnaires were obtained from 28,323 employees, around two-thirds of those distributed.

3. Investment trusts were excluded from the sampling frame. A potential population of 1,505 companies was effectively identified on 11 April 1999. The survey questionnaire was sent to the human resources director or company secretary at each firm. Where possible, the individual human resources director was identified by name and the survey was personally addressed to him or her. We administered the survey as follows. There were three waves to the survey: The first was a fax survey, the second was a postal survey, and the third was another fax survey. The number of firms completing the survey in each wave was 157, 80, and 62, respectively. In addition, another 52 companies in total responded but declined to take part in the survey. The reasons for not completing the survey included (1) it was company policy not to complete surveys; (2) they do not hold relevant statistics; (3) they were too busy; and (4) the survey was not applicable to that company.

4. The procedure involved estimating a standard probit model in which the outcome variable was equal to 1 if the company was in the sample and 0 otherwise. The right-hand-side variables were log of market value, log of employment, log of capital, and ten sector dummies. The null hypothesis of no differences between the sample and nonsample firms in terms of these characteristics was tested. This would be confirmed by nonsignificant coefficients on each of the right-hand-side variables. In the event, it was found that companies with a high market value were about 4 percent more likely to respond and that companies with more employees were about 4 percent less likely to respond. Other control variables (capital intensity variable and sector dummies) were not significant.

5. Weighting by the establishment weights is very important for obtaining nationwide representative figures because of the WERS sampling design. Unweighted figures show much higher proportions with shared-capitalist forms of pay because the sample has disproportionately many large firms with such practices.

Table 3.1 **Percentages of Employees with Shared Compensation in British Establishments, 1998 (%)**

	No. of Establishments	Employees Sum
Any employees eligible for variable pay scheme[a]		
Profit-related payments or bonuses	31.8	37.4
Deferred profit-sharing schemes	5.8	6.4
Employee share ownership schemes	14.6	22.0
Other cash bonus schemes	21.2	24.7
Any variable pay scheme	53.0	63.8
Nonmanagerial employees eligible for variable pay scheme[a]		
Profit-related payments or bonuses	27.9	34.5
Employee share ownership schemes	12.9	20.4
Any group performance-related schemes	11.5	17.3
All employees[b]		
Profit-related payments or bonuses	41.1	40.3
Deferred profit-sharing schemes	7.8	8.5
Nonexecutive employee share ownership	7.9	6.1
SAYE share options	30.0	28.9
Discretionary or executive share ownership schemes	20.8	25.5

Source: 1998 WERS, WERS Panel 1990–1998.
[a]WERS 1998, weighted.
[b]WERS panel, 1990–1998, unweighted.

shared compensation was profit-related pay or bonuses, the vast majority of which were part of the approved Inland Revenue scheme. The second most important form of shared compensation was "other cash bonus" schemes. This was followed by employee share ownership schemes, covering 14.6 percent of workplaces and 22 percent of employees. Deferred profit-sharing schemes were the least frequently used form of shared compensation. The second section of table 3.1 gives figures for nonmanagerial workers. For the plans on which we have data for all workers and nonmanagerial workers, the percentages covered are modestly lower for the latter, indicating that the bulk of these plans are offered to the majority of the workforce. In fact, questions in the WERS on the proportion of covered nonmanagerial workers show a bimodal distribution, with most firms offering plans to 90 percent to 100 percent of the work force or to no one at all. Finally, 11.5 percent of establishments and 17.3 percent of workers have some form of group performance-related pay.

The bottom section of table 3.1 shows the pattern of shared compensation in the longitudinal WERS file in 1998. The questions on shared compensation in the longitudinal file relate specifically to the legal schemes and thus give a more precise link to the policies in subsection 3.2.1. We report the figures here without taking account of the sample weights because our ensuing analysis focuses on each establishment as an independent observation, and the weights have less meaning given what ultimately turns out to be a relatively small sample of establishments that change their shared-compensation strategy. These data show that about 40 percent of establishments were covered by profit-related pay, about 30 percent covered by SAYE share options, 21 percent by discretionary or executive option schemes, and about 8 percent by deferred profit sharing or other share ownership schemes.

Turning to our firm-based survey, table 3.2 gives the prevalence of practices across the sample of listed firms for all employees and for managerial and nonmanagerial employees taken separately from 1995 to 1998. Consistent with the establishment results, the data show that firms in the sample increased their use of Inland Revenue–approved compensation practices over this period. For instance, 31.1 percent of firms report that use of SAYE schemes in 1995 increased to 45.8 percent in 1998; the 18.8 percent who used the (now defunct) approved profit-related pay schemes in 1995 increased to 25.1 percent in 1998; and so on. But the data also show increases in the use of nonapproved schemes. The proportion of firms with discretionary option schemes, which are directed at selected employees (such as directors), doubled over the period 1995–1998 from 22.9 percent to 42.8 percent. U.K. firms rarely use companywide bonus schemes related to improvements in productivity. Finally, conditional on having a particular scheme, the data also show that companies are more likely to use shared-compensation practices for managerial employees than for nonmanagerial employees, with one exception: the approved profit-related pay schemes (which were phased out as of the year 2000).

3.3 How Should Shared Compensation Affect Firm Performance?

3.3.1 Agency Considerations

In principle, shared compensation should motivate workers to work harder and to make decisions that are favorable to the firm, thereby improving corporate performance and ultimately the present discounted value of the enterprise. Shared compensation helps resolve the moral hazard problem between the owner of the firm and the employee when effort levels of the employee are not perfectly observed or verified. An optimal second-best shared-compensation contract motivates the employee to focus upon what the owner cares about while recognizing the trade-off between risk and incentives.

Agency theory predicts that the extent of shared compensation will depend on the characteristics of employees and the firm. The less risk-averse the employee, the higher is the optimal sharing rate between the owner and the employee, because the employee is more willing to bear the relevant

Table 3.2 **Compensation Strategies in Firm-Based Data Set (%)**

	Percent of Firms with Specified Strategy				Percent of Management Employees with Specified Strategy				Percent of Nonmanagement Employees with Specified Strategy			
Compensation Strategy	1995	1996	1997	1998	1995	1996	1997	1998	1995	1996	1997	1998
Approved profit-sharing scheme	18.9	19.0	22.0	25.1	77.0	79.5	73.8	78.5	62.8	65.1	62.7	65.1
Other share-based profit-sharing scheme	4.3	5.9	8.8	10.4	40.6	44.6	51.5	43.2	17.0	11.3	21.8	17.7
Cash-based profit-sharing scheme	13.6	14.5	15.9	17.1	72.1	69.0	69.9	65.2	49.5	49.7	47.4	45.5
Approved profit-related pay scheme	27.6	34.7	38.1	36.9	87.1	89.0	90.2	87.3	85.7	86.9	88.1	86.5
Gain-sharing scheme[a]	3.2	3.5	4.4	4.7	80.0	82.5	76.8	78.8	61.4	53.8	53.4	58.1
Approved SAYE share option scheme	31.1	35.6	43.7	45.8	63.3	63.6	61.3	61.5	47.6	49.6	47.4	49.4
Other all-employee share option scheme	6.1	9.3	11.5	12.4	62.8	71.9	65.2	68.3	59.7	48.1	50.4	50.8
Approved company share option plan	41.2	45.8	54.6	56.6	52.0	54.8	56.0	56.3	13.2	16.5	18.7	18.6
Other discretionary share option scheme	22.9	31.1	40.7	42.8	39.2	38.0	40.9	44.2	10.6	9.9	11.5	10.8

Source: Based on a sample of 299 U.K. stock market firms surveyed in 1999.

Notes: Actual numbers of firms per cell may differ. The results in Management and Nonmanagement columns are conditional upon the firm's having the particular compensation strategy.

[a]Companywide bonus scheme related to improvements in productivity.

risk. Similarly, the less effort-averse the employee, the higher is the optimal sharing rate, since that employee will be more willing to put out the requisite effort. On the firm's side, the greater the likely impact of effort on profits, the bigger is the incentive to link employee income to performance. In addition, the more accurate the firm's signal of employee effort and activity, the higher is the optimal sharing rate. The firm should share more rewards when it is more certain that output results come from employee activity rather than from some exogenous factor. At the same time, the firm should not be able to monitor perfectly the effort or activity of the worker, for if management could do that, it would not need an incentive contract in the first place to induce appropriate employee actions.

This analysis has several implications for understanding shared capitalist arrangements. First, in general we would expect that, in the absence of the free-rider problems that are discussed later, shared-compensation systems are associated with improved performance. However, the analysis also suggests that firms with shared-compensation practices are likely to draw upon workers with different characteristics than those that choose other firms—workers with less risk aversion and less disutility from work—and will also themselves have different characteristics from other firms. This creates a problem in inferring causal relations from regressions based on cross-sectional comparisons. Our response is to rely largely on fixed effects models that contrast a firm before and after introduction of shared-compensation practices. This is not perfect, since the introduction of new shared arrangements is itself endogenous, but it does give an accurate picture of performance of the same firm or workplace under different conditions.

3.3.2 Decentralization of Decision-Making Rights

Second, the analysis suggests that shared compensation should be accompanied by shared decision making. The process of transforming inputs into outputs in capitalist firms increasingly relies on the performance of multiple tasks by employees. These tasks are bundled into jobs that vary by the number of tasks performed by the employee as well as the decision-making authority assigned to the worker. The trend in the 1990s has been toward jobs that have a wider variety of tasks and that allow employees to make more decisions. The benefits to the firm of decentralizing decision-making authority will depend on factors such as worker-specific (localized) knowledge in the performance of the tasks, the conservation of management time, and more effective motivation of workers. It pays the firm to give incentives to workers only when workers have discretion to vary what they do at workplaces, and it pays management to devolve decisions to employees only when employees have incentives to make decisions that raise the value of the firm. We examine this linkage in our empirical work.

Third, there are potentially important costs to decentralizing decision-making rights. These include agency costs, coordination costs, and the inefficient use of central information by local decision makers. There are also important questions about the potential efficiency effects of all-employee stock option plans and other schemes that link worker pay to measures of aggregate company performance rather than to group or workplace performance. Chief executive officers (CEOs) and other top executives can affect share prices, so that options or share ownership can help resolve the principal-agent problem for them (see Conyon and Murphy 2000). But employees lower in the firm's hierarchy have little direct effect on the company stock price. They lack a clear "line of sight" to link their decisions to the share prices and company profit levels that would affect their pay. As a result, we would expect firms to use more narrowly defined performance targets—establishment, group, or workplace-related incentive pay systems—for these workers, and that those forms of shared compensation would be more effective in motivating workers than programs that link pay to more aggregate measures.

Core and Guay (2001), using U.S. data, show that the provision options to all employees are consistent with incentive theory. Firms with more monitoring costs, greater growth opportunities, and employees who have greater marginal products allocate greater amounts of option incentives to all employees.

3.3.3 The Free-Rider Problem

The classic problem with any group performance–related pay scheme is the free-rider problem (also known as the "$1/N$ problem," where N is the total number of employees in the team or group). In most work situations, employees perform tasks that involve productive interactions with colleagues in which total output reflects the contribution of many individuals. Team production suggests that individual contribution to output cannot be easily identified and that compensation must be based on some aggregate measure of output, such as team or division output. But in such settings there is a potentially weak connection between individual effort and reward. If rewards are shared equally on the basis of team production (and rewards cannot exceed the revenues of the group), then each individual has the incentive to shirk because he or she will gain only $1/N$ of the combined gains from increased effort (Kruse 1993; Blasi, Conte, and Kruse 1996; Kandel and Lazear 1992). Each employee hopes that his or her colleague will put forth the effort to increase output so that he or she will not have to do so and will benefit from increased productivity without bearing the costs.

A number of potential solutions have been suggested to overcome the free-rider problem. One solution is for workers to self-monitor or act as de facto monitors themselves. Another is for firms to invest in policies that promote team culture and employee participation in which group incentives provide a substitute for monitoring through peer pressure. This horizontal monitoring may help resolve the free-rider problem (Kandel and Lazear 1992; Lazear 1995). It is possible that firms that use all-employee stock options or other ownership schemes do so to help create a culture of teamwork and cooperative company spirit that overrides the free-rider problem.

3.3.4 Extant Evidence for the United Kingdom

There is considerable evidence on the relationship between employee ownership or profit sharing and corporate performance, but less on the relationship between all-employee stock options and performance or between individual ownership of shares, which U.K. legislation favors, and performance. The majority of the studies are of U.S. origin, but there have been some notable British studies and important studies in other countries as well. The first important analysis was the U.S. General Accounting Office study in 1987, which found that ESOPs had an inconclusive impact on outcomes. Since then, research findings have been more positive, so that a general summary is moderately favorable to shared compensation. The strongest results are for profit sharing (Kruse 1993; Doucouliagos 1995), whereas those for employee ownership are more problematic. Kruse and Blasi (1995) report on ten studies of U.S. ESOPs that have compared before-and-after implementation productivity effects using large databases. The majority of studies yield positive, but often insignificant, estimated effects of ESOP adoption on output.

We briefly summarize extant U.K. studies. In the 1980s, analysts looked at the impact of profit sharing and employee ownership through cooperatives on firm performance. Using the Workplace Industrial Relations Survey (WIRS), the predecessor to the WERS survey, Blanchflower and Oswald (1988) found no relationship between financial performance or the quality of industrial relations and measures of shared compensation (i.e., the existence of share ownership, a stock option plan, profit sharing, or bonus schemes). In a sample of about 100 U.K. companies between 1974 and 1982, Wadhwani and Wall (1990) found weak evidence that profit sharing boosted productivity. Cable and Wilson (1989) found a positive significant productivity effect for profit sharing in a sample of fifty-two British engineering firms; they also found that quality circles, briefing groups, or job rotation had a positive effect on productivity as well, and that having both profit sharing and employee involvement added most to productivity.

Studies in the 1990s have added to the general picture of a modest positive effect of shared compensation on outcomes. Estrin et al. (1997) report a productivity improvement of about 6 percent in cases where profit-sharing bonuses were of the order 5 percent to 10 percent of market wages. Robinson (1998) found that the SAYE scheme was associated with a productivity premium of 23 percent and that consultative and representative forms of employee participation also raised productivity. McNabb and Whitfield (1998) used establishment data from WIRS and found that financial participation is positively related to financial performance, as is profit-related pay.

In short, the extant U.K. evidence paints a picture much like that in the U.S. studies: Profit sharing has larger effects than ownership on productivity, but neither is overwhelmingly powerful across studies.

3.4 Production Function Evidence: Firm-Level Results

We begin with our firm-based production function analysis. Appendix table 3A.1 shows the main characteristics of the data in our sample in addition to the shared-compensation characteristics previously shown in table 3.2. We have information on sales, employment, and capital that allows us to estimate production functions for 284 companies between 1995 and 1998. Trade union presence is constant across time at around 23 percent. Our measure of product market competition, the number of firms reporting more than five competitors, increased from 72 percent of firms in 1995 to 77 percent in 1999. Our measure of information sharing shows a more marked increase from 43 percent in 1995 to 61 percent in 1998. However, firms are much less likely to have a joint committee of managers and employees for the purposes of consultation.

To assess the productivity effects of different Inland Revenue–approved shared-compensation systems on firm-level performance, we used a Cobb-Douglas production function of the following form:

$$\text{Log}(Q_{it}) = \alpha_i + \beta_1 \ln(L_{it}) + \beta_2 \ln(K_{it}) + \beta_3(\text{Union}_{it}) + \beta_4(\text{Competition}_{it}) + \beta_5(\text{Share Compensation}K_{it}) + \beta_t(\text{Year Dummies}) + e_{it},$$

where Q is real sales (Datastream item 104), L is total employment (Datastream item 219), K is an estimate of the current real capital stock (based on an accrual method), Union is a time-varying measure of trade union presence (available from the Conyon and Read [2000] survey data), and Competition is product market competition measure (a dummy variable = 1 if there are more than five competitors; available from the Conyon and Read [2000] survey data).

The key explanatory variables are the measures of shared compensation. They are dummy variables for (1) approved profit-sharing scheme, (2) approved profit-related pay scheme, (3) approved all-employee share scheme, and (4) approved company share option scheme.

The α_i terms are the company fixed effects. By including them we eliminate time-invariant firm factors, such as short-run managerial ability, risk, and so forth. But a fixed effects model does not resolve all problems with nonexperimental data. Issues about endogeneity and dynamics remain.

The endogeneity issue is straightforward: Employees in highly profitable firms may demand some form of their pay in the form of shared compensation. However, in the absence of suitable instruments (as in Blanchflower and Oswald 1988, 724), we estimated a single equation with fixed effects. The key dynamic issue relates to the timing of the shared-compensation practices. Ideally, we would have lagged the compensation practice variables to see whether the introduction of a scheme was subsequently associated with increased productivity or if costs of adjustment delayed its benefits, but the short time series precluded this strategy.

Table 3.3 contains our principal results on the relationship between firm-level productivity and shared modes of compensation. Columns (1) through (4) enter each of the schemes separately into the productivity equation, with year and firm dummies to control for the fixed effects of these variables. Column (5) enters each of the four schemes jointly. Finally, column (6) replaces the firm dummy variables with industry dummy variables, which changes the model from a fixed effects to a cross-sectional analysis. The estimated coefficients on the shared-compensation variables show a significant positive correlation between firm productivity and two of the Inland Revenue–approved schemes: the approved profit-sharing scheme and the company share option plan. In contrast, we find no evidence of a relationship between productivity and the approved profit-related pay scheme (no longer in operation as of 2000) or between productivity and the approved all-employee share option scheme. Column (6) shows that, absent the firm dummy variables, all the proxies for the shared capitalism and compensation variables are positive and significant. The difference between the results in columns (5) and (6) show that the cross-sectional relation between the approved profit-related pay scheme and the SAYE scheme and productivity is attributable to the unobserved characteristics of firm, whereas the relation between the approved profit-sharing scheme and the approved company share option scheme and productivity results from the actual adoption of those programs by particular firms.

The coefficient estimates imply large—seemingly implausibly large—productivity effects. For instance, from column (5), the point estimate on the approved profit-sharing scheme (0.173) implies an increase in productivity of 18.9 percent.[6] Similarly, the productivity effect associated with the approved company share option plan (coefficient estimate 0.121) is 12.2 percent.[7] Because of the $1/N$ problem, we expected the observed effects of the shared-compensation variables to have modest positive impacts on productivity, rather than such huge effects.[8] Various reasons may account

6. Calculated as $(e^{0.1733} - 1) \times 100$.
7. Calculated as $(e^{0.1213} - 1) \times 100$.
8. Lazear (2000) found large productivity effects in an econometric case study of the Safelite Glass Company. Moving from hourly wages to a piece-rate regime was associated with a 44 percent increase in productivity. This could be decomposed into an incentive effect (about 22 percent) and a sorting effect (the remainder).

Table 3.3 **Firm-Level Productivity Regressions: The Impact of Shared Modes of Compensation in Listed U.K. Firms, 1995–1998**

	(1)	(2)	(3)	(4)	(5)	(6)
log(employment)	0.6990***	0.6997***	0.7018***	0.7018***	0.6990***	0.6449***
	(0.0885)	(0.0867)	(0.0888)	(0.0866)	(0.0855)	(0.0219)
log(capital)	0.1707***	0.1690***	0.1690***	0.1833***	0.1870***	0.3311***
	(0.0400)	(0.0398)	(0.0397)	(0.0471)	(0.0479)	(0.0180)
Union	–0.0444	–0.0318	–0.0279	–0.0282	–0.0593	–0.0443
	(0.0502)	(0.0460)	(0.0456)	(0.0441)	(0.0529)	(0.0623)
Competition	–0.1244	–0.1667	–0.1624	–0.0061	0.0337	0.1012
	(0.1818)	(0.1670)	(0.1680)	(0.1103)	(0.1305)	(0.0640)
Approved profit-sharing scheme	0.1739***				0.1733***	0.1731***
	(0.0704)				(0.0728)	(0.0603)
Approved profit-related pay scheme		0.0369			0.0446	0.2091***
		(0.0605)			(0.0625)	(0.0515)
Approved all-employee share option scheme SAYE			–0.0142		–0.0292	0.1003**
			(0.0396)		(0.0409)	(0.0546)
Approved company share option scheme				0.1314***	0.1213***	0.1570***
				(0.0578)	(0.0594)	(0.0584)
No. of observations	942	938	942	936	932	932
Firms	284	283	284	283	282	282
Year dummies	Yes	Yes	Yes	Yes	Yes	Yes
Firm fixed effects	Yes	Yes	Yes	Yes	Yes	No
Industry dummies	No	No	No	No	No	Yes
Time period	1995–1998	1995–1998	1995–1998	1995–1998	1995–1998	1995–1998
Adjusted R^2	0.9826	0.9824	0.9824	0.9824	0.9825	0.8711

Notes: Dependent variable in each column is log of total output. Robust standard errors reported in parentheses. All regressions contain an unreported arbitrary constant.

***Significant at the 1 percent level.

**Significant at the 5 percent level.

for our high estimates. The firms that introduced these schemes may have simultaneously introduced other high-performance management practices that also contributed to productivity.[9] Without any measure of these other changes, our regression attributes the improvement in productivity solely to the compensation scheme rather than to the full set of changed practices.

We investigated our basic findings further by lagging the compensation scheme variables to see if there was any evidence of lagged effects in the link between having a shared capitalism arrangement and productivity. Lagging the shared-compensation variables by one period altered our results modestly. Reestimating the models in table 3.3, columns (1) through (5),

9. There is a range of estimates of the relationship between shared capitalism or profit-sharing arrangements and productivity that average around modest positive values. Our results may simply be the upper end of that range.

with the four compensation variables lagged one period produced the following estimates. The coefficient (standard error) on the approved profit-sharing scheme was 0.060 (0.083); on the approved profit-related pay scheme, it was –0.015 (0.066); and on the approved all-employee share option scheme (SAYE) it was significantly negative, –0.104 (0.058). However, on the approved company share option scheme, the estimate (standard error) was positive 0.096 (0.057) and significant at the 10 percent level. This suggests that the results in table 3.3 are sensitive to the specification of timing, which itself suggests that the firms introduced other changes as well. In sum, the firm-level results suggest that productivity is positively related to shared capitalism arrangements, but they do not conclusively establish that relation. For that, we would have to vary the compensation schemes (and other accompanying changes in labor practices) through an experimental design.

This said, we note that the differential effect of the alternative shared-compensation systems reported in table 3.3 broadly fits with our earlier discussion. Approved company share option schemes cover selected employees, typically directors, who can affect company performance in response to stock option incentives. The impact of the profit-sharing scheme is more difficult to account for: On the one hand, it is based on profits, which are more susceptible to employee effort than share prices, but the reward is shares, which are more risky than cash or profit-related bonuses would be. Since the new all-employee partnership share system is a close lineal descendent of the approved profit-sharing scheme, the results suggest that the new program will have positive effects. Finally, the negligible coefficient on the profit-related pay scheme (consistent with Blanchflower and Oswald 1988) indicates that the decision to terminate this program will have no adverse productivity effects (although it will hurt employee-owned firms that have used the program—such as John Lewis, among others—at least until they find substitute ways to reward staff).

Further experiments were carried out to test the robustness of our firm-level findings. We imposed constant returns to scale on the production function. The overall results remained unchanged. For example, the re-estimated full model contained in table 3.3, column (5), yielded labor and capital coefficients of 0.789 and 0.211, respectively. The qualitative effects of the shared-compensation indicator variables remained unaltered. The approved profit-related pay and SAYE dummies were insignificant. The point estimate (robust standard error) on the approved profit-sharing scheme was 0.176 (0.075), and for the approved company share option plan it was 0.106 (0.064). Both variables are significant, although the estimate on the company share option plan falls slightly.

Our firm-based survey also gathered data on whether or not the firm shared information with employees, consulted with employees, or communicated with them extensively. We use these data to develop an information-sharing dummy variable for firms that had at least one of the schemes, and we added this variable to the equation and interacted it with the shared-compensation variables.[10] A positive interaction term indicates that a shared-compensation system is more effective in environments where information, consultation, and communication between employees and managers are also found. The results of this analysis (given in table 3A.2) indicate that information sharing is not associated with higher productivity, conditional on shared compensation, and that the interaction effects between the shared compensation variables and forms of information sharing, communication, and consultation between managers are by and large insignificant in this data set and so appear not to contribute to higher productivity.[11]

Table 3.4 further investigates the association between productivity and shared-compensation arrangements by differentiating the effect of our four compensation schemes between the type of employee covered by each scheme: managerial employees in column (1) and nonmanagerial employees in column (2). This distinction is motivated by the notion that company share option schemes ought to have a much greater effect among managerial employees, while approved profit-sharing schemes might have a more evenhanded impact. In addition, the data tell us the percentage of managerial employees and of nonmanagerial employees covered by each compensation arrangement. This contrasts with the 0-1 dummy variable for the presence of shared-compensation arrangements used in table 3.3.[12] Presumably, the more-refined percentage of employees covered by a scheme gives us a better indicator of the potential incentive effect of the scheme than the simple measure of the presence or absence of the scheme. The evidence in table 3.4 shows a positive, although not statistically significant, relation between share options and productivity for managers but no such relation for nonmanagers. By contrast, the estimates show a larger impact of approved profit-sharing schemes on productivity for nonmanagerial workers than for managerial workers. The different proportions of managers and nonmanagers covered by the schemes make it hard to reach a sharp conclusion, however, since the results may be partly driven by those proportions rather than any differences in behavior.

3.4.1 Stock Market Evidence

A different way to examine the effect of shared compensation on the performance of listed firms is to compare the development of the stock price of firms with shared compensation to the stock prices of other firms. If

10. The equation is $\log(Q_{it}) = \alpha_i + \beta_1 \ln(L_{it}) + \beta_2 \ln(K_{it}) + \beta_3(\text{Union}_{it}) + \beta_4(\text{Competition}_{it}) + \beta_5(\text{Share Compensation}K_{it}) + \beta_6(\text{Information Sharing}) + \beta_7(\text{Information Sharing} \times \text{Share Compensation}K_{it}) + \beta_t(\text{Year Dummies}) + e_{it}$.

11. Recall that the information-sharing variable is made up of three other variables (see tables 3.3 and 3.4). These component variables were tried separately to see whether this altered the results. They did not.

12. Where a company does not have a scheme the variable is coded zero.

Table 3.4 **Firm-Level Productivity Regressions: Management and Nonmanagement Participation in Shared-Compensation Schemes**

	Only Managerial Employees Are Covered (1)	Only Nonmanagerial Employees Are Covered (2)
log(employment)	0.7015***	0.7039***
	(0.0886)	(0.0905)
log(capital)	0.1891***	0.1937***
	(0.0491)	(0.0488)
Union	–0.0333	–0.0404
	(0.0517)	(0.0564)
Competition	–0.0306	0.0310
	(0.1241)	(0.0970)
Employees participating (%)		
Approved profit-sharing scheme	0.1128***	0.1975***
	(0.0625)	(0.0693)
Approved profit-related pay scheme	–0.0464	–0.0643**
	(0.0382)	(0.0364)
Approved all employee share option scheme SAYE	–0.0066	–0.0159
	(0.0701)	(0.0833)
Approved company share option scheme	0.1065	–0.0356
	(0.0913)	(0.0931)
No. of observations	932	932
Firms	282	282
Year dummies	Yes	Yes
Firm fixed effects	Yes	Yes
Time period	1995–1998	1995–1998
Adjusted R^2	0.9823	0.9823

Notes: Shared-compensation arrangement is measured as proportion of employees of given type participating in scheme. Dependent variable is log of total output. Robust standard errors reported in parentheses. All regressions contain an unreported arbitrary constant.

***Significant at the 1 percent level.

**Significant at the 5 percent level.

firms with shared compensation make investments that raise sales in the future and thus raise the value of the firm, this could show up in the growth of their stock prices but not in current productivity figures.[13] Accordingly, we examined the association between stock prices and the extent of shared compensation. A London firm, Capital Strategies, produces an Employee Ownership Index (EOI) of the share prices of firms that have a "significant degree of employee share ownership," which it then compares to general movements in the London stock market. Figure 3.1 shows that the EOI

13. In equilibrium, the impact should be on price-earnings ratios, but in a period of increased use of shared compensation, such as the 1990s, it would be reflected in the growth of share prices.

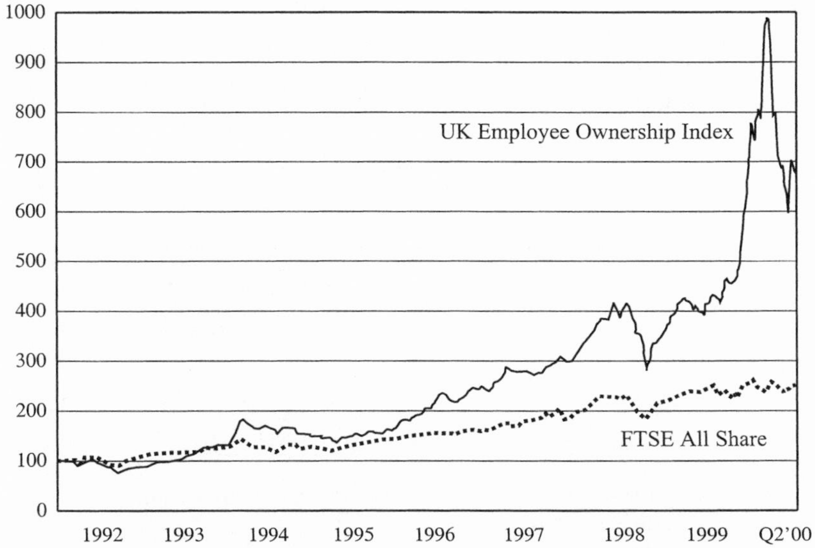

Fig. 3.1 Stock returns 1992–2000: companies with all-employee share plans versus the FTSE All-Share Index

Source: Capital Strategies ([http://www.esop.co.uk/press/210800.htm]).

outperformed the all-share index in the 1990s. An investment of £100 in the EOI in 1992 would be worth £667, while the same investment in the FTSE Group All-Share Index would be worth £244 (see http://www.esop.co.uk/press/210800.htm). Using our database of 299 listed firms, we identified companies that used approved profit sharing or all-employee share schemes and created an index of their share prices from 1991 to 1999. Figure 3.2 shows that £100 invested in the portfolio of companies that use share-based compensation plans grew to £350. However, the same £100 invested in the FTSE All-Share Index in 1990 is worth about £250 in 1999.

Since neither the Capital Strategies index nor our index controls for risk factors or for the concentration of these firms in particular sectors, it is possible that a more refined analysis might find that these (or other) factors explain the observed results. The consistency with our productivity results, however, lends weight to the overall conclusion that shared capitalism pays off for firms. To explore this issue further, we estimated stock returns equations similar to those advocated by Wadhwani and Wall (1990).[14] We regressed the estimated annual return to owning the firms' shares on a dummy variable that is equal to 1 whenever the shared-compensation

14. The stock return for a company was defined as the annual change in the company-return index to the 31 December end of the year. The return index was derived from Datastream item RI and captures capital appreciation and dividends reinvested on a continuous basis. The market return was calculated the same way for the FTSE All-Share Index.

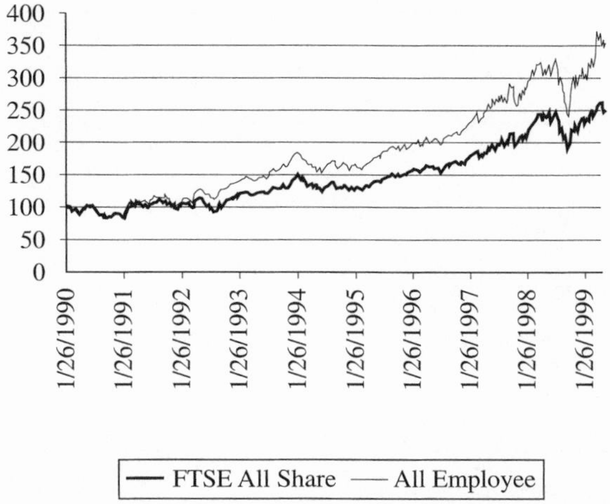

Fig. 3.2 Stock returns 1990–1999: companies with all-employee share plans versus the FTSE All-Share Index

Source: Datastream International.

Note: Stock returns calculated as the daily change in company market value.

scheme is in effect and a set of covariates to control for other factors that will affect the stock price: the return on the FTSE All-Share Index and industry dummies; year and industry dummies; year, industry, and industry × year interaction variables; and finally year and firm dummy variables. Although this analysis falls short of a typical event study,[15] because we only observe whether there is a scheme in place in a particular year, not the exact day the firm announced the adoption of the scheme, it should still cast some light onto the impact of the schemes on share prices.

Table 3.5 gives the results of our analysis. Column (1) records the regression coefficients on the four compensation variables with the aggregate market return and industry dummy variables as covariates. Column (2) records the regression coefficients on the four compensation variables, with the industry dummy variables and year dummies as covariates. Column (3) records the regression coefficients on the four compensation variables, with year dummies, industry dummies, and industry and year dummy interactions. In all of these calculations there is a statistically significant positive association between stock returns and two of the shared compensation variables: the all-employee profit-sharing scheme and the SAYE scheme. The positive effect of the all-employee profit-sharing scheme on stock returns mirrors the positive relation between all-employee profit sharing and productivity in our firm productivity regressions. But we do not find a pos-

15. In an event study, one compares the stock price immediately after an announcement of economically important information with the price immediately before the information became known.

Table 3.5 Firm-Level Stock Returns and Shared-Compensation Practices, 1995–1998

	Firms' Annual Stock Returns			
	(1)	(2)	(3)	(4)
Approved profit-sharing scheme	0.0910***	0.0935***	0.0832***	0.1598
	(0.0314)	(0.0308)	(0.0315)	(0.1106)
Approved profit-related pay scheme	0.0223	0.0157	0.0152	0.0393
	(0.0293)	(0.0287)	(0.0292)	(0.0820)
Approved all-employee share option scheme SAYE	0.0749***	0.0815***	0.0778***	0.0529
	(0.0299)	(0.0292)	(0.0291)	(0.0546)
Approved company share option scheme	0.0204	0.0308	0.0282	0.0769
	(0.0312)	(0.0301)	(0.0295)	(0.1036)
Return on FTSE All-Share Index	Yes	No	No	No
Year dummies	No	Yes	Yes	Yes
Industry dummies	Yes	Yes	Yes	No
Industry × year dummies	No	No	Yes	No
Firm fixed effects	No	No	No	Yes
No. of observations	913	913	913	913
Time period	1995–1998	1995–1998	1995–1998	1995–1998
R^2	0.043	0.103	0.155	0.248

Notes: Dependent variable is firm shareholder return (defined as the annual percentage change in the Datastream return index for each company). Robust standard errors reported in parentheses. Compensation scheme variables are dummy variables equal to 1 if a scheme is in effect, 0 otherwise. All regressions estimated by ordinary least squares (OLS).
***Significant at the 1 percent level.

itive link between the approved company share option plan and the share price, perhaps because the option plan distributes some of the benefits of better performance to workers rather than to shareholders.

Column (4) of the table provides a stronger test of the effect of the introduction of the shared-compensation schemes on share prices. Here we regress the annual stock return on dummy variables for each firm and for the year. This effectively compares share prices of the same firm when it has a particular scheme in place and when it does not. All of the shared-compensation variables obtain positive coefficients in this regression, but only the approved profit-sharing scheme has an estimated coefficient greater than its standard error. We conclude that when a firm introduces an approved profit-sharing scheme its stock performs modestly better, but that much of the positive relation between share prices and shared compensation is due to unobserved firm characteristics that yield high firm returns.

3.4.2 Shared Compensation and Information and Decision Making: Firm-Level Effects

An important prediction from the theory of shared compensation is that there should be a complementarity between shared-compensation practices and the allocation of decision-making rights and information sharing with workers. To get at this issue we used questions from our firm-level survey that relate to consultation, communication, and information sharing. In particular, the survey asked firms to indicate whether they had "a joint committee of managers and employees primarily concerned with *consultation* rather than negotiation"; "a formal structure for *information sharing* with employees (e.g., provision of data on financial status, production and labor market position, and market strategy)"; and, finally, "a formal structure for *communication* between all levels of employees and management (e.g., quality circles, newsletters, and suggestion schemes)." In addition, we created an aggregate variable that represents the presence of any of these forms of information or decision.[16]

To see whether these forms of information and decision making are more likely in firms with shared-compensation modes of pay, we regressed the dichotomous variables indicating the presence of these four forms of information and decision sharing on the presence of the shared-compensation schemes in place at listed U.K. firms. We estimated simple probit models on the pooled data over the whole sample period. In addition to the experimental shared-compensation variables, we also included two other measures of pay practices. Specifically, firms were asked to indicate the existence of "team-based performance-related pay (related to the achievement of team objectives)" and the existence of "individual performance-related pay (merit pay or bonuses determined by agreed individual objectives)."

The results contained in table 3.6 report the marginal effects from the probit estimation. They show, as expected, a generally positive correlation between information sharing and decision rights and the use by firms of shared-compensation structures.[17] The general pattern of results, therefore, seems to fit with the prediction from incentive theory. Team-based pay increases the likelihood of firms' using consultation, information sharing, and communications systems. They are always positively correlated. Moreover, the incidence of some shared-compensation systems increases the likelihood of firms' adopting particular information-sharing and decision-making environments. For instance, approved profit sharing is generally positively related to consultation and communication systems but not to information sharing. Approved SAYE schemes increase the likelihood of all forms of information sharing and decision making. However, there is generally no relation between approved company share option plans

16. These questions are based upon and hence similar to the WIRS and WERS questions. See the establishment-level results that follow. The descriptive statistics for the firm-level questions are contained in table 3A.1.

17. We experimented with other estimation methods. For instance, a random-effects logit model yielded qualitative results similar to those presented in the paper.

Table 3.6 Relationship between Shared Compensation, Communication, and Consultation: Firm-Level Estimates

	Dependent Variables			
	Joint Consultation Committees	Information Sharing	Communication Structure	Any Consultation or Communication
Approved profit sharing (YN)	0.097**	0.043	0.152**	0.186**
	(0.034)	(0.043)	(0.046)	(0.044)
Approved profit-related pay (YN)	–0.004	–0.044	0.103**	0.112**
	(0.026)	(0.037)	(0.038)	(0.038)
Approved SAYE (YN)	0.072**	0.101**	0.107**	0.138**
	(0.028)	(0.037)	(0.039)	(0.038)
Approved company share option plan (YN)	–0.086**	–0.035	0.011	–0.046
	(0.024)	(0.034)	(0.037)	(0.036)
Team-based pay (YN)	0.087	0.121	0.275	0.239
	(0.042)	(0.050)	(0.049)	(0.046)
Individual performance-related pay (YN)	0.1556	0.019	0.047	0.022
	(0.052)	(0.052)	(0.057)	(0.058)
log (real sales)	✓	✓	✓	✓
log (total employees)	✓	✓	✓	✓
Union recognized in workplace (YN)	✓	✓	✓	✓
Industry (YN)[a]	✓	✓	✓	✓
Year dummies (YN)	✓	✓	✓	✓
	✓	✓	✓	✓
Constant	✓	✓	✓	✓
No. of observations	928	965	965	969
Pseudo R^2	0.247	0.175	0.201	0.241

Source: Authors' survey.

Notes: Marginal effects reported; robust standard errors in parentheses. Y = yes; N = no. Checks indicate that variable is included.

[a]1-digit SE dummies.

**Significant at the 5 percent level.

and information sharing (except the negative impact observed for joint-consultation committees). Finally, we find little evidence of a relationship between approved profit-related pay schemes and decentralized decision making. This is consistent with the notion that many firms used this to get tax advantages without really linking pay to profits. We reconsider these issues using the establishment-level data in the following section.

3.5 Production Function Evidence: Establishment-Level Results

The WERS survey asks managers to rate the performance of their workplace relative to their industry on the basis of financial performance and labor productivity.[18] The rating is on a five-point scale, according to which many more managers rate their establishment as better than average rather than below average. We analyze these data using an ordered probit analysis, with the outcomes ordered so that positive coefficients imply better outcomes. Our cross-sectional analysis links financial performance and productivity of each establishment to measures of shared compensation that are conditional on the number of employees, age of establishment, one-digit industry, and distribution of the workforce by skill and gender, along with dummy variables for the degree of competition in the sector.

Table 3.7 presents the results for the 1998 WERS cross section. In these calculations we use two different measures of shared compensation as independent variables: a 0/1 absence/presence measure of particular types of shared compensation and, in separate calculations, a continuous measure of the percentage of nonexecutive workers covered by the schemes. We examine the effects of each program and also examine the effect of a simple aggregate measure of all the programs within an establishment. Regardless of the particular measure, the results show a positive relationship between shared compensation and economic performance.

Consider first the results for financial performance. The calculations for the separate programs show that each of the measures of shared compensation is positively related to the financial performance of the firm. The largest and most significant coefficients are for employee share ownership and profit-related pay; the smallest and least significant coefficient is for deferred profit share. We are dubious about the interpretation of the profit-related pay variable, since firms that have profits are more likely to use profit-related pay, but there is no comparable reverse causality problem in the linkage between other shared-compensation schemes and performance. In the summary columns we report results when we aggregate the four shared compensation systems into a single "summated rating" (Bartholomew 1996). The summated rating simply adds together the 0/1 variables to obtain an index from 0 to 4, depending upon how many forms of shared compensation the firm used. In the calculation the coefficient is positive and over four times its standard error, indicating that, broadly speaking, establishments with shared compensation have better performance. The next columns repeat these calculations with the proportion of workers covered by each system (or the summation thereof) as the independent variables. They give modestly stronger results to those with the presence of program measures.

The calculations for labor productivity show that employee share ownership and profit-related pay are significantly positively linked to produc-

18. We have also examined the effect of shared compensation on two other variables—quality of goods or services and changes in productivity over the previous five years—and found weaker positive effects for the impact of shared compensation on quality and stronger effects for its impact on changes in productivity than the effects shown in the exhibit.

Table 3.7 **Ordered Probit Estimates of the Link between Shared Compensation and Financial Performance and Labor Productivity**

	Financial Performance (5-point scale)				Labor Productivity (5-point scale)			
	Presence (YN)		Coverage (%)		Presence (YN)		Coverage (%)	
	Separate	Summary	Separate	Summary	Separate	Summary	Separate	Summary
Profit-related pay (YN)	0.18		0.19		0.14		0.18	
	(0.06)		(0.07)		(0.07)		(0.07)	
Deferred profit sharing (YN)	0.08		0.10		0.01		0.04	
	(0.10)		(0.10)		(0.10)		(0.10)	
Employee share ownership (YN)	0.21		0.23		0.25		0.23	
	(0.07)		(0.08)		(0.07)		(0.08)	
Any group performance-related pay (YN)	0.11		0.08		0.04		0.12	
	(0.07)		(0.10)		(0.08)		(0.10)	
Number of group variable pay schemes		0.14				0.12		
		(0.03)				(0.03)		
Sum % eligible for group variable pay				0.19				0.19
				(0.04)				(0.04)
Individual performance-related pay only (YN)	0.07	0.07	0.10	0.12	0.07	0.09	0.31	0.32
	(0.12)	(0.12)	(0.19)	(0.19)	(0.12)	(0.12)	(0.20)	(0.20)
Union recognized in workplace (YN)	–0.13	–0.12	–0.14	–0.13	–0.06	–0.05	–0.06	–0.05
	(0.06)	(0.06)	(0.06)	(0.06)	(0.06)	(0.06)	(0.06)	(0.06)

(*continued*)

Table 3.7 (continued)

	Financial Performance (5-point scale)				Labor Productivity (5-point scale)			
	Presence (YN)		Coverage (%)		Presence (YN)		Coverage (%)	
	Separate	Summary	Separate	Summary	Separate	Summary	Separate	Summary
Age of establishment (years)	✓	✓	✓	✓	✓	✓	✓	✓
Number of employees (N)	✓	✓	✓	✓	✓	✓	✓	✓
Women in the workplace (%)	✓	✓	✓	✓	✓	✓	✓	✓
Skilled—3 levels (%)	✓	✓	✓	✓	✓	✓	✓	✓
Industry—11 levels (YN)	✓	✓	✓	✓	✓	✓	✓	✓
Competition—5 levels (YN)	✓	✓	✓	✓	✓	✓	✓	✓
Cut 1	–2.35	–2.35	–2.36	–2.35	–2.26	–2.27	–2.27	–2.27
	(0.16)	(0.16)	(0.16)	(0.16)	(0.16)	(0.16)	(0.16)	(0.16)
Cut 2	–1.37	–1.38	–1.39	–1.38	–1.34	–1.34	–1.34	–1.34
	(0.13)	(0.13)	(0.13)	(0.13)	(0.13)	(0.13)	(0.13)	(0.13)
Cut 3	–0.07	–0.08	–0.09	–0.09	0.26	0.25	0.25	0.26
	(0.12)	(0.12)	(0.12)	(0.12)	(0.13)	(0.12)	(0.13)	(0.13)
Cut 4	1.13	1.11	1.10	1.11	1.52	1.50	1.52	1.52
	(0.12)	(0.12)	(0.12)	(0.12)	(0.13)	(0.13)	(0.13)	(0.13)
No. of observations	1,772	1,773	1,767	1,767	1,691	1,692	1,685	1,685
Pseudo R^2	0.01	0.01	0.01	0.01	0.01	0.01	0.01	0.014

Source: 1998 WERS cross section.

Notes: Standard errors in parentheses. Y = yes; N = no. Checks indicate that the variable is included.

tivity, while deferred profit-sharing schemes and group performance-related pay are not. Again, the summated rating measure of programs yields a positive, highly significant coefficient. In the last two columns, which use the proportion of nonmanagerial workers covered by the schemes as the independent variables, we obtain comparable results, with employee share ownership and profit-related pay most strongly related to productivity among the individual programs. The summated rating statistic has the same strong impact on labor productivity that it did on financial performance.

In addition to the shared-compensation variables, we included two other human resource–related measures: whether or not the firm has some form of individual performance-related pay and no group performance pay (i.e., piece rates or commissions), and union recognition. The individual pay measures are weakly positively related to financial performance and productivity, while unionism is negatively related to financial performance and obtains an insignificant negative coefficient in the productivity equation.[19]

Finally, table 3.8 considers two other outcome measures: the quality of product and services and changes in labor productivity. The relationship between the experimental shared-compensation variables and changes in labor productivity are qualitatively similar to those established so far—namely, a positive relationship between shared compensation and economic performance (in this case, productivity growth). On the other hand, we are unable to identify a relationship between the shared-compensation system and the quality of products and service produced.

3.5.1 Shared Compensation and Information, and Decision Making: Establishment Effects

As noted, a key prediction of the theory of shared compensation is that establishments with shared-compensation practices should also share information and decision making with workers. The 1998 WERS contains a module on consultation and communication that allows us to examine this prediction at the establishment level. Specifically, the WERS asks managers whether their workplace has "a system of briefings for any section or sections of the workforce"; "committees of managers and employees . . . primarily concerned with consultation, rather than negotiation"; "groups at this workplace that solve specific problems or discuss aspects of performance or quality . . . sometimes known as quality circles"; and "consultative committees of managers and employees in your organization that operates at a higher level than this establishment."

To see whether these forms of information and decision making are more likely in firms with shared-compensation modes of pay, we regressed

19. Metcalf finds that this effect occurs exclusively in establishments where competition is low, which suggests that unions are redistributing rents.

Table 3.8 **Ordered Probit Estimates of the Link between Shared Compensation and Quality of Product and Services and Changes in Labor Productivity**

	Quality of Product and Services (5-point scale)				Changes in Labor Productivity (5-point scale)			
	Presence (YN)		Coverage (%)		Presence (YN)		Coverage (%)	
	Separate	Summary	Separate	Summary	Separate	Summary	Separate	Summary
Profit-related pay (YN)	0.08		0.17		0.19		0.25	
	(0.06)		(0.07)		(0.07)		(0.08)	
Deferred profit sharing (YN)	–0.04		–0.03		–0.08		–0.06	
	(0.10)		(0.10)		(0.11)		(0.11)	
Employee share ownership (YN)	0.07		0.02		0.14		0.13	
	(0.07)		(0.08)		(0.08)		(0.08)	
Any group performance-related pay (YN)	0.06		0.10		0.30		0.35	
	(0.07)		(0.10)		(0.08)		(0.10)	
Number of group variable pay schemes		0.04				0.14		
		(0.03)				(0.03)		
Sum % eligible for group variable pay				0.10				0.22
				(0.04)				(0.04)
Individual performance-related pay only (YN)	–0.19	–0.19	–0.13	–0.12	0.29	0.24	0.23	0.21
	(0.11)	(0.11)	(0.17)	(0.17)	(0.12)	(0.12)	(0.19)	(0.19)
Union recognized in workplace (YN)	–0.26	–0.26	–0.26	–0.27	0.22	0.22	0.22	0.20
	(0.06)	(0.06)	(0.06)	(0.06)	(0.06)	(0.06)	(0.06)	(0.06)

Age of establishment (years)	✓	✓	✓	✓	✓	✓	✓	✓
Number of employees (N)	✓	✓	✓	✓	✓	✓	✓	✓
Women in the workplace (%)	✓	✓	✓	✓	✓	✓	✓	✓
Skilled—3 levels (%)	✓	✓	✓	✓	✓	✓	✓	✓
Industry—11 levels (YN)	✓	✓	✓	✓	✓	✓	✓	✓
Competition—5 levels (YN)	✓	✓	✓	✓	✓	✓	✓	✓
Cut 1	–3.14	–3.16	–3.13	–3.14	–2.11	–2.12	–2.12	–2.12
	(0.24)	(0.24)	(0.24)	(0.24)	(0.16)	(0.15)	(0.16)	(0.15)
Cut 2	–2.02	–2.03	–2.00	–2.01	–1.33	–1.35	–1.34	–1.35
	(0.13)	(0.13)	(0.13)	(0.13)	(0.13)	(0.13)	(0.13)	(0.13)
Cut 3	–0.60	–0.61	–0.59	–0.60	–0.49	–0.51	–0.51	–0.51
	(0.12)	(0.12)	(0.12)	(0.12)	(0.12)	(0.12)	(0.12)	(0.12)
Cut 4	0.83	0.82	0.85	0.83	0.59	0.57	0.58	0.57
	(0.12)	(0.12)	(0.12)	(0.12)	(0.12)	(0.12)	(0.12)	(0.12)
No. of observations	1,878	1,879	1,872	1,872	1,830	1,831	1,823	1,823
Pseudo R^2	0.03	0.03	0.03	0.03	0.02	0.02	0.02	0.02

Source: 1998 WERS cross section.

Notes: Standard errors in parentheses. Y = yes; N = no. Checks indicate that the variable is included.

0/1 variables for the presence of these four forms of information and decision sharing on the absence or presence of the shared-compensation schemes for nonmanagerial workers at the establishment. For simplicity, we used a linear probability regression format for these computations. The results in table 3.9 show the expected complementarity, with share ownership and (the relatively rare) deferred profit-sharing having the most substantial link to the various forms of communication and consultation. Once again, profit-related pay shows the weakest link to the various communication and consultation groups—indeed, it is negatively related to joint consultation committees and substantially related to higher-level committees. The pattern fits broadly, moreover, with what we might reasonably expect from incentive theory. Group-related pay is linked to brief-

Table 3.9 **Regression Estimates of the Relationship between Shared Compensation for Nonmanagerial Employees and Communication and Consultation**

	Dependent Variables			
	Briefings	Joint Consultation Committees	Quality Circles	High-Level Joint Consultation Committees
Profit-related pay (YN)	0.03	0.05	0.09	0.06
	(0.02)	(0.03)	(0.03)	(0.03)
Deferred profit sharing (YN)	0.06	0.15	0.15	0.14
	(0.03)	(0.04)	(0.04)	(0.04)
Employee share ownership (YN)	0.04	0.06	0.08	0.09
	(0.02)	(0.03)	(0.03)	(0.03)
Any group performance-related pay (YN)	0.06	0.06	0.07	0.02
	(0.02)	(0.03)	(0.03)	(0.03)
Individual performance-related pay only (YN)	0.05	0.08	0.04	0.04
	(0.03)	(0.05)	(0.05)	(0.05)
Union recognized in workplace (YN)	0.09	0.19	0.13	0.27
	(0.02)	(0.02)	(0.03)	(0.02)
Age of establishment (years)	✓	✓	✓	✓
Number of employees (N)	✓	✓	✓	✓
Women in the workplace (%)	✓	✓	✓	✓
Skilled—3 levels (%)	✓	✓	✓	✓
Industry—11 levels (YN)	✓	✓	✓	✓
Competition—5 levels (YN)	✓	✓	✓	✓
Constant	0.72	0.28	0.26	0.19
	(0.03)	(0.05)	(0.05)	(0.05)
No. of observations	2,075	2,075	2,074	2,031
R^2	0.08	0.15	0.09	0.18
Adjusted R^2	0.06	0.14	0.79	0.17
Standard error of the estimate	0.30	0.46	0.48	0.46

Source: WERS 1998 (available at [http://www.dti.gov.uk/er/emar/1998wers.htm]).
Notes: Standard errors in parentheses. Y = yes; N = no. Checks indicate that the variable is included.

ings, consultation committees, and quality circles, but not to higher-level committees, while employee ownership and deferred profit sharing are relatively strongly related to higher-level committees, as well as to the lower-level forms of communication and consultation. But the strongest single variable that increases the probability of communication and consultation is the recognition of a union at the workplace (see Gregg and Machin 1988).

In addition, following the same procedures that we used for analyzing our firm-based data set, we examined whether the existence of consultation and communication channels affected the link between shared compensation and outcomes. We found no evidence that it did and no evidence that the presence of both shared compensation and more communication raised productivity more than did the separate impact of each.[20]

3.5.2 Longitudinal Analyses

The cross-relation patterns in the WERS in tables 3.7, 3.8, and 3.9 are consistent with the notion that shared-compensation systems have beneficial economic effects and are associated with greater communication and consultation with employees. But they leave the door open to alternative interpretations of the positive relationships. One interpretation is that the data reflect unobserved differences among firms: "Good firms" use shared compensation systems, consult or communicate more with employees, and have higher productivity. To examine the unobservable good-firm effect, we use a fixed effects longitudinal analysis that compares the same firm before and after a given change in shared-compensation modes of pay. As noted earlier, fixed effects models do not resolve all questions about causality in nonexperimental data—in particular, there are issues relating to the endogeneity of policy—but they do take us one step closer to the ideal experimental design, particularly if changes in policies reflect factors that are themselves uncorrelated with ensuing performance.

The WERS files permit two types of before-and-after comparisons. First, the 1998 WERS "change in the workplace" module asked managers about changes in the past five years (1993–1998) in the establishment's labor practices and economic outcomes, including, which is critical to us, whether the firm increased or decreased (by a lot or a little) the proportion of nonmanual workers covered by variable pay or instead kept the proportion constant. By relating changes in the proportion of workers covered by variable pay to changes in other key economic measures—such as information provided to workers, employee decision making, and productivity—we have a fixed effects analysis, albeit one based on questions of a retrospective nature.

20. We entered the consultation and communication variables into the ordered probit calculations in table 3.6 and found they did not affect the results substantively; nor did various forms of interaction between composites of the variables and shared-compensation variables.

Table 3.10 shows the link between the change in variable pay, which is given in the rows, and changes in other variables, given in the columns. The first panel shows that firms that increased the proportion of workers receiving variable pay also increased information flows to employees, while firms that decreased variable pay disproportionately reduced the information provided. The second panel shows that changes in variable pay and changes in employees' influence over their job also moved in the same direction, while the third and fourth panels show the relation for employee

Table 3.10 Change in the Proportion of Variable Pay for Nonmanagerial Workers by Changes in Workplace Activities over a Five-Year Period, 1993–1998 (%)

Change in Proportion of Variable Pay for Nonmanagerial Employees	Up a Lot	Up a Little	No Change	Gone Down	Total
Change in Information Provided to Employees by Employers					
Up a lot	67.8	24.6	6.2	1.4	100.0
Up a little	53.1	30.7	16.0	.2	100.0
No change	41.3	37.6	19.9	1.3	100.0
Gone down	36.7	38.8	22.4	2.0	100.0
Total	47.0	34.5	17.5	1.0	100.0
Change in Employees' Influence over Job by Employers					
Up a lot	31.3	50.2	17.1	1.4	100.0
Up a little	21.3	48.8	28.1	1.7	100.0
No change	12.6	44.2	38.4	4.8	100.0
Gone down	18.4	36.7	36.7	8.2	100.0
Total	16.9	45.8	33.5	3.8	100.0
Change in How Hard People Work by Employers					
Up a lot	55.0	33.2	10.9	.9	100.0
Up a little	43.7	42.4	12.2	1.7	100.0
No change	39.8	37.3	21.3	1.6	100.0
Gone down	39.6	29.2	22.9	8.3	100.0
Total	42.4	37.9	18.0	1.7	100.0
Change in Employee Influence over Managerial Decision Making by Employers					
Up a lot	20.9	48.3	28.9	1.9	100.0
Up a little	10.2	49.7	37.7	2.3	100.0
No change	7.6	39.6	50.5	2.3	100.0
Gone down	8.0	24.0	52.0	16.0	100.0
Total	9.7	42.6	45.0	2.6	100.0
Change in Labor Productivity by Employers					
Up a lot	62.1	28.2	5.8	3.9	100.0
Up a little	47.1	39.1	9.7	4.1	100.0
No change	40.4	38.4	17.1	4.2	100.0
Gone down	37.5	31.3	18.8	12.5	100.0
Total	44.4	37.2	14.0	4.3	100.0

Source: WERS 1998 (available at [http://www.dti.gov.uk/er/emar/1998wers.htm]).

influence over managerial decision making and "how hard people work." In all of these cases, changes in variable pay are positively related to changes in employee involvement in the workplace, and this is impressive and supportive of the incentive-based model of shared-compensation systems that we sketched out earlier.

Regarding our bottom-line measure of the effect of shared compensation—labor productivity—the last panel records the link between changes in variable pay and changes in labor productivity. This can be viewed as a longitudinal test of the cross-sectional productivity calculations in tables 3.7 and 3.8. The results are striking. Sixty-two percent of managers in firms that increased variable pay a lot reported that productivity went up a lot, compared to much lower proportions of managers in firms where variable pay increased only a little, didn't change, or went down. At the other end of the spectrum, proportionately fewer managers in firms that increased variable pay a lot reported worsened productivity performance than did managers in firms with other changes in the proportion of workers covered by variable pay.

3.5.3 Workplace Employment Relations Survey 1990–1998 Panel

The WERS panel data identify establishments that changed their system of shared-compensation between 1990 and 1998. Some establishments in the panel survey added nonexecutive stock ownership plans or profit-sharing plans, while a small number withdrew such plans. If these forms of shared compensation in fact contribute to financial performance or labor productivity, we would expect to see that proportionately more managers in establishments adopting plans would see an improvement in outcomes than in other establishments and that the converse would hold for managers in establishments discarding such plans. However, given that establishments that changed their policies in any direction presumably did so in the expectation of improving outcomes, the endogeneity of the choice to change plans presumably operates against our finding such an effect. Table 3.11 compares the results for establishments that changed their profit-sharing or nonexecutive ownership schemes between the 1990 and 1998 WERS surveys. It records the number that changed their programs according to their financial performance or labor productivity in the two years. The number of firms covered is smaller than the number of changers given in the 1998 WERS panel because we deleted observations for establishments that did not respond to the 1990 survey question about profit sharing or ownership even though the 1998 WERS panel reported a change from 1990. We were not sure this was an accurate change.

As a crude summary of the direction of change in productivity and financial performance, we have coded the responses to these questions according to a simple numeric scheme. We give a 0 to establishments that reported doing about average; 1 to those that did somewhat above average; 2

Table 3.11 **Number of Establishments with Varying Levels of Financial Performance and Labor Productivity in 1990 and 1997, by Change in Shared-Compensation Systems, 1990–1997**

	Profit Sharing				Nonexecutive Share Ownership			
	Added		Removed		Added		Removed	
	1990	1997	1990	1997	1990	1997	1990	1997
Financial performance relative to average								
A lot below	4	2	2	0	0	0	2	1
Below	7	4	1	1	0	3	3	3
Average	35	26	7	12	17	15	9	11
Above average	16	32	9	6	14	9	8	9
A lot above	24	22	4	4	9	13	8	6
Total	86	86	23	23	40	40	30	30
Average score	.57	.79	.52	.57	.80	.80	.57	.53
Change, 1997–1990	.22		.05		.00		.04	
Difference in difference		.17				–.04		
Labor productivity relative to average								
A lot below	1	3	0	0	0	0	1	2
Below	12	11	0	0	2	3	2	4
Average	36	33	8	15	22	19	18	11
Above average	33	33	16	6	13	12	9	13
A lot above	12	14	5	8	5	8	5	5
Total	94	94	29	29	42	42	35	35
Average score	.46	.47	.90	.76	.50	.60	.43	.43
Change, 1997–1990	.01		–.14		.10		.00	
Difference in difference		.15				.10		

Source: Calculated from 1990–1998 WERS panel, with average scores based on assigning 0 to average, 1 to above average, 2 to a lot above average, –1 to below average, and –2 to a lot below average.

to those that did a lot above average; and –1 and –2 for the corresponding groups that did somewhat and a lot below average, respectively. We then calculated the score for each group. For instance, the number 0.57 in the 1990 column under profit sharing added means that the eighty-six establishments that added a profit-sharing system had a financial performance that was modestly above average in 1990. Because managers tend to overreport their performance, this performance is, in fact, about average. The number 0.79 in the 1997 column shows that establishments that added profit sharing had that score for their financial performance in 1997. The change from 1990 to 1997 was 0.22, so establishments that added a profit-sharing scheme improved their financial performance by that amount on our scale. Similarly, we calculated the change in performance for the twenty-three establishments that removed a profit-sharing scheme in the period. This is 0.05. The difference-in-difference calculation for the establishments is obtained by comparing the change in the summary statistic for establishments that added a program and the change in the summary statistic for establishments that removed the program. Positive differences in differences imply that the shared-compensation system improved an outcome, while negative differences imply that it made matters worse. In our case, this is 0.17, which means that firms that added profit sharing improved their performance relative to firms that reduced profit sharing.

The results in table 3.11 show that, in three of the four of the comparisons, the differences in differences are positive, implying that, with this simple scale, firms that introduced programs had improved performance relative to firms that removed programs. The small samples, however, make this at best a suggestive result.

3.6 Conclusions

The use of shared compensation arrangements by companies increased considerably in the 1990s, with the biggest growth occurring among employee ownership schemes. Our firm-level survey indicates that companies were more likely to use profit-sharing schemes, SAYE schemes, and company share option plans in 1998 than in 1995. Our establishment-level panel data showed an increase in the proportion of establishments with profit sharing and with nonexecutive ownership schemes.

In part, the growth of shared compensation can be attributed to government policies that introduced tax incentives to encourage shared-compensation systems in an attempt to enhance corporate productivity. In this respect, the policies of the United Kingdom to encourage shared compensation differ noticeably from those of the United States. The United Kingdom encourages individual ownership, while the United States encourages collective ownership through ESOPs. The market, rather than the state, has spurred the growth of options and individual share ownership in the United States.

Shared capitalist modes of pay should improve the economy in two ways. They should increase communication and consultation with workers, which spurs economic democracy. Our evidence shows that shared compensation is indeed linked to various forms of communication and consultation. They also should ideally induce employees to think and act like owners, making decisions that increase corporate value. Our evidence shows that shared-compensation systems in the United Kingdom are positively associated with productivity, although, as in other studies, we find that the effect of the systems varies across data sets and measures of outcomes.

Appendix

Table 3A.1 Descriptive Statistics on the Firm-Level Data

	Year			
Variable	1995	1996	1997	1998
log(real output)	10.84	10.66	10.65	10.75
log(employment)	6.04	5.90	5.86	5.96
log(capital)	10.47	10.29	10.31	10.41
Trade unions or staff associations recognized by management for negotiating pay and conditions	24.3%	23.5%	23.4%	23.4%
Competition (greater than five product-market competitors)	71.9%	73.6%	75.6%	76.9%
Information sharing (which is an indicator variable if the firm has any one of the following three practices)	43.1%	48.4%	56.5%	61.2%
Consultation[a]	13.6%	15.2%	18.0%	18.7%
Information sharing[b]	27.6%	32.9%	37.6%	41.5%
Communication[c]	39.6%	43.3%	48.8%	53.2%

Source: Based on a sample of 299 U.K. stock market firms surveyed in 1999.

Note: Actual numbers of firms per cell may differ.

[a]A joint committee of managers and employees primarily concerned with consultation rather than negotiation.

[b]A formal structure for information sharing with employees (e.g., position of data on financial status, production and labor-market position, and market strategy.

[c]A formal structure for communication between all levels of employees and management (e.g., quality circles, newsletters, and suggestion schemes).

Table 3A.2 Firm-Level Productivity Regressions (fixed effects): The Impact of Shared-Compensation Systems in Listed U.K. Firms, 1995–1998

	(1)	(2)	(3)	(4)	(5)
log (employment)	0.6990***	0.6995***	0.7030***	0.7028***	0.7016***
	(0.0886)	(0.0851)	(0.0890)	(0.0855)	(0.0834)
log (capital)	0.1679***	0.1625***	0.1691***	0.1785***	0.1783***
	(0.0405)	(0.0392)	(0.0402)	(0.0462)	(0.0484)
Union	–0.0520	–0.0081	–0.0244	–0.0346	–0.0378
	(0.0509)	(0.0405)	(0.0451)	(0.0454)	(0.0503)
Competition	–0.1264	–0.1688	–0.1612	–0.0059	0.0384
	(0.1784)	(0.1649)	(0.1661)	(0.1077)	(0.1277)
Information sharing	–0.0288	–0.0036	–0.0481	0.0046	0.0034
	(0.0785)	(0.0742)	(0.0809)	(0.0544)	(0.0826)
Approved profit-sharing scheme	0.2459***				0.2206***
	(0.0968)				(0.1048)
Approved profit-sharing scheme × information sharing	–0.0936				–0.0540
	(0.0988)				(0.1050)
Approved profit-related pay scheme		0.1646			0.1320
		(0.1370)			(0.1377)
Approved profit-related pay scheme × information sharing		–0.1828			–0.1221
		(0.1258)			(0.1279)
Approved all-employee share option scheme SAYE			–0.0344		–0.0764
			(0.0759)		(0.0889)
Approved all-employee share option scheme SAYE × information sharing			0.0335		0.0765
			(0.0805)		(0.0940)
Approved company share option scheme				0.2278***	0.2182***
				(0.1140)	(0.1188)
Approved company share option scheme × information sharing				–0.1512	–0.1495
				(0.1143)	(0.1214)
No. of observations	942	938	942	936	936
Firms	284	283	284	283	283
Years	Yes	Yes	Yes	Yes	Yes
Time period	1995–1998	1995–1998	1995–1998	1995–1998	1995–1998
Overall R^2	0.9826	0.9825	0.2929	0.9825	0.9826

Notes: Interaction effects between information sharing included. Dependent variable in each column is log of total output. Robust standard errors reported in parentheses.

***Significant at the 1 percent level.

References

Bartholomew, D. 1996. *Statistical approach to social measurement.* New York: Academic Press.

Blanchflower, D. G., and A. J. Oswald. 1988. Profit-related pay: Prose discovered? *The Economic Journal* 98:720–730.

Blasi, J., M. Conte, and D. Kruse. 1996. Employee stock ownership and corporate performance among public companies. *Industrial and Labor Relations Review* 50 (1): 60–79.

Cable, J. R., and N. Wilson. 1989. Profit-sharing and productivity: An analysis of U.K. engineering firms. *The Economic Journal* 99 (396): 366–75.
Conyon, M. J., and K. J. Murphy. 2000. The prince and the pauper? CEO pay in the United States and United Kingdom. *Economic Journal* 110 (467): F640–F671.
Conyon, M. J., and L. Read. 2000. Human resource practices and corporate performance. Available at [http://www.regard.ac.uk].
Core, J., and W. Guay. 2001. Why do they go so low? Option plans for non-executive employees. *Journal of Financial Economics* 61 (2): 253–87.
Datastream. [http://www.datastream.com].
Doucouliagos, C. 1995. Worker participation and productivity in labor-managed and participatory capitalist firms: A meta-analysis. *Industrial and Labor Relations Review* 49 (1): 58–77.
Estrin, S., V. Perotin, A. Robinson, and N. Wilson. 1997. Profit sharing in OECD countries: A review of some evidence. *Business Strategy Review* 8 (4): 27–32.
Freeman, R. 1999. Shared capitalism. Lionel Robbins Memorial Lecture. 1–3 March, London School of Economics.
Gregg, P. A., and S. J. Machin. 1988. Unions and the incidence of performance linked pay schemes in Britain. *International Journal of Industrial Organisation* 6 (1): 69–90.
Her Majesty's Treasury. 1999. Consultation on employee share ownership. Available at [http://www.hm-treasury.gov.uk/media/A6B49/2.pdf].
Kandel, E., and E. P. Lazear. 1992. Peer pressure and partnerships. *Journal of Political Economy* 100 (4): 801–17.
Kruse, D. L. 1993. *Profit sharing: Does it make a difference?* Kalamazoo, Mich.: W. E. Upjohn Institute for Employment Research.
Kruse, D. L., and J. Blasi. 1995. Employee ownership, employee attitudes and firm performance. NBER Working Paper no. 5277. Cambridge, Mass.: National Bureau of Economic Research, September.
Lazear, E. P. 1995. *Personnel economics.* Cambridge, Mass.: MIT Press.
———. 2000. Performance pay and productivity. *American Economic Review* 90 (5): 1346–61.
McNabb, R., and K. Whitfield. 1998. The impact of financial participation and employee involvement on financial performance. *Scottish Journal of Political Economy* 45 (2): 171–188.
Organization for Economic Cooperation and Development (OECD). 1995. *Employment outlook.* Paris: OECD.
Poole, M. J. 1988. Factors affecting the development of employee financial participation in contemporary Britain: Evidence from a national survey. *British Journal of Industrial Relations* 26 (1): 21–36.
Robinson, A. 1998. Employee participation and firm level performance: A stochastic frontier approach. Paper presented at the ninth international conference of the International Association for the Economics of Participation. 26–28 June, Bristol, England.
Wadhwani, S., and M. Wall. 1990. The effects of profit-sharing on employment, wages, stock returns and productivity: Evidence from U.K. micro-data. *The Economic Journal* 100:1–17.
Weitzman, M., and D. L. Kruse. 1990. Profit sharing and productivity. In *Paying for productivity: A look at the evidence,* ed. Alan S. Blinder, 95–140. Washington, D.C.: Brookings Institution.

4

Characteristics of Foreign-Owned Firms in British Manufacturing

Rachel Griffith and Helen Simpson

4.1 Introduction

The 1970s and 1980s saw an increase in the international openness of the British economy. By 1980 the British government had removed exchange controls and had joined the European Economic Community. By the late 1980s Britain was embarking on the European Union (EU) Single Market Program, which aimed to improve the international mobility of capital. Over the 1980s there were also large numbers of privatizations and reforms to product and factor markets. This opening up of the U.K. economy was expected to bring increased growth through a number of routes, one of which was through making the United Kingdom a more attractive location for internationally mobile investment. In this paper we focus on the impact of inward investment. From the early literature of Vernon (1966), Dunning (1977), and Caves (1974) it has been suggested that multinational firms are more productive and are concentrated in knowledge-intensive industries. The endogenous growth[1] and new trade literatures[2] focus on the role

Rachel Griffith is a deputy director of the Institute for Fiscal Studies and a reader in industrial organization at University College London. Helen Simpson is the program director of productivity and innovation research at the Institute for Fiscal Studies.

The authors would like to thank Richard Blundell, David Card, Steve Nickell, John Van Reenen, Frank Windmeijer, and an anonymous referee for helpful comments, and the Gatsby Charitable Foundation and the Economic and Social Research Council (ESRC) Centre for Microeconomic Analysis of Fiscal Policy at the Institute for Fiscal Studies for financial support. This report has been produced under contract to the Office for National Statistics (ONS). All errors and omissions remain the responsibility of the authors.

1. See, inter alia, Barro and Sala-i-Martin (1995), Aghion and Howitt (1998), and Grossman and Helpman (1991).

2. See, inter alia, Krugman (1991a,b, 1994), Venables (1994), Smith (1994), and Edwards (1998).

multinational firms play in transferring technology from the frontier to economies that lag behind technologically. Empirical work, largely at the aggregate level, has identified correlations between the openness of an economy and growth in productivity or export performance.[3]

Foreign direct investment (FDI) both into and out of the United Kingdom rose over the 1980s but fell off in the early 1990s, before recovering (strongly) in the middle to late 1990s. Here, rather than considering FDI flows, we consider real economic activity by looking at subsidiaries of foreign-owned multinationals operating in Great Britain. Like a number of other countries, the United Kingdom uses fiscal policy to attract foreign multinationals and hence potentially capitalize on technological spillovers. In the 1980s Regional Selective Assistance grants replaced Regional Development Grants as the main form of inducement. Regional Selective Assistance (RSA) grants are discretionary and are awarded to firms located in designated assisted areas. Although their primary aim is to create or safeguard employment, they are also used to attract inward investment. Over the four years from 1985 to 1988, foreign-owned firms accounted for only 8 percent of the total number of RSA offers. But grants to foreign-owned firms totaled around £325 million, representing 44 percent of the total value of offers over this period. The average grant offer was therefore higher for foreign-owned firms, as was the average grant per expected job created.[4]

Value added per worker in British manufacturing grew rapidly over the 1980s relative to the 1970s, with slower but continued growth during the 1990s (see fig. 4.1). But Britain remains at the bottom of the premier league of countries. Figure 4.2 compares labor productivity in the manufacturing sector within each of these countries. It shows that, while the position of the United Kingdom relative to the United States has improved somewhat, it still lags behind the United States and to a lesser extent behind France, Germany, and Japan. The figure shows labor productivity of manufacturing activity undertaken within these countries, by both domestic- and foreign-owned firms. Studies comparing total factor productivity show a similar picture.[5] One interesting question is whether improvements in the United Kingdom's relative position have been driven by the presence of foreign-owned multinational firms in the United Kingdom.

In this paper we investigate whether similar differences arise when we

3. These studies have generally used labor productivity; see, for example, Bernard and Jones (1996a,b) and Barrell and Pain (1997). Cameron, Proudman, and Redding (1998) look at total factor productivity. Studies using microdata include Blomstrom and Persson (1983), Davies and Lyons (1991), and Globerman (1979).

4. Source: Department of Trade and Industry (1993), section 2.4. Value of offers to foreign-owned firms is in 1990 pounds sterling.

5. See, inter alia, O'Mahony (1999), Dougherty and Jorgenson (1997), Nickell, Wadhwani, and Wall (1992), Layard and Nickell (1989), Bean and Crafts (1995), Bean and Symons (1989), Oulton and O'Mahony (1994), Mayes (1996), Cameron, Proudman, and Redding (1998), van Ark (1996), Lansbury (1995), and Oulton (1998).

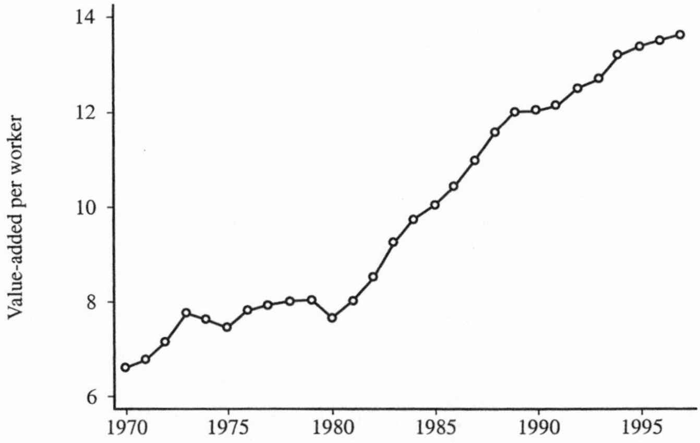

Fig. 4.1 Value added per worker (in thousands of 1980 UK£) in manufacturing
Source: Data from OECD STAN database.

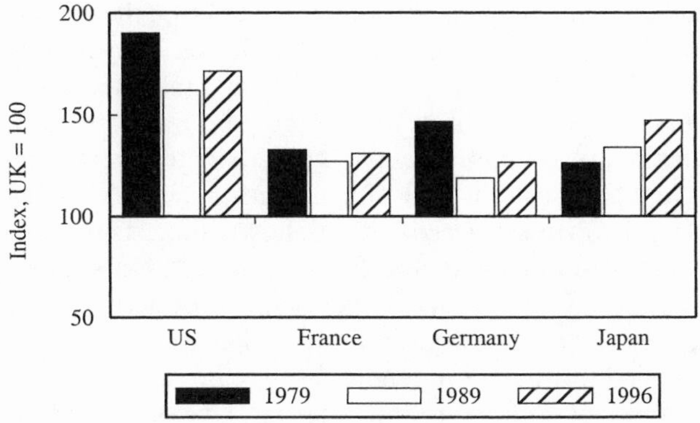

Fig. 4.2 Output per hour worked in manufacturing, by country of location
Source: O'Mahony (1999).

look across different nationalities of establishments operating within Britain. We examine differences in labor productivity and factor usage between foreign-owned and domestic-owned firms using establishment-level data. In doing so we control for industry, age, size, year of exit, and establishment-specific unobservable characteristics. This will be informative in understanding the extent to which it is physical location in Britain, as opposed to U.K. ownership, that underlies the observed international differences in labor productivity. If it is location in Britain that matters, this may point to factors such as national competition policy, employment laws, or the regulatory environment—for example, planning regulations, as highlighted in a recent report by McKinsey Global Institute (1998). However, if we find labor productivity differences between foreign- and domestic-owned establishments both operating within Britain, this may indicate differences in the organization of production and input usage, or that domestic-owned establishments differ from their foreign-owned counterparts technologically.

There are many studies of labor productivity using establishment-level data in the United States and a growing number in the United Kingdom.[6] Two studies that are particularly relevant for our purposes are Doms and Jensen (1998) and Howenstine and Zeile (1994). Using U.S. data, Doms and Jensen show that there are substantial differences between domestic- and foreign-owned establishments. They find that foreign-owned establishments have higher labor productivity than the average U.S.-owned establishment, but lower labor productivity than those owned by U.S. multinationals. This indicates that what may be important in explaining productivity differences is ownership by a multinational rather than foreign ownership per se. They also find that foreign-owned establishments are more capital intensive and pay higher wages than the average U.S.-owned establishment. Howenstine and Zeile describe the characteristics of foreign-owned establishments in the United States. They find that foreign-owned establishments are larger and more capital intensive. They have higher average wage rates, but this is largely because they are in higher-wage industries, not because they pay workers higher wages compared to other firms in the same industry. Using Canadian plant-level data, Globerman, Ries, and Vertinsky (1994) have shown that there are significant differences between domestic- and foreign-owned plants. Foreign-owned establishments are found to have higher labor productivity, but after size, capital intensity, share of nonproduction workers, and share of male workers are controlled for these differences disappear.

A further motivation for this line of research is that establishment-level studies in both the United Kingdom and the United States have found that within-industry variation in labor productivity is greater than between-industry variation.[7] Understanding sources of within-industry variation helps explain both the determinants of productivity differentials between establishments, such as differences in capital intensity, and the determinants of industry-level productivity growth—for example, the replacement of low-productivity incumbents with high-productivity entrants.

Here we look at differences in characteristics between foreign- and domestic-owned establishments located in the United Kingdom. We consider establishments that do not change ownership nationality separately from those that experience a change in ownership nationality, due to a takeover

6. See Bartelsman and Doms (2000) for a review, also Caves (1998). For the United Kingdom see, for example, Harris and Robinson (2002), Disney, Haskel, and Heden (2003), and Griffith (1999).

7. See, inter alia, Disney, Haskel, and Heden (2003) and Doms and Jensen (1998).

or merger. Both of these samples include both greenfield entrants and incumbents. The findings suggest that establishments that are always foreign owned have significantly higher labor productivity than those that are always domestic owned. In addition, labor productivity improves faster with age in foreign-owned establishments. This is matched by an equivalent difference in levels of investment per employee. Both the proportion of skilled workers employed in the workforce and wages for both skilled and operative workers are higher in foreign-owned establishments than domestic-owned ones, a finding that is in line with differences in labor productivity. For establishments that change nationality, differences in labor productivity are smaller. However, there is some evidence that labor productivity improves in domestic establishments after they are taken over by a foreign-owned firm compared to those that go from being foreign to domestic owned.

The remainder of the paper is structured as follows. The next section describes the data, and section 4.3 presents some descriptive statistics on trends in foreign ownership in Britain. Section 4.4 examines differences between domestic- and foreign-owned establishments, and a final section summarizes. A more detailed description of the data is given in an appendix.

4.2 Data Description

Our main data source is the Annual Respondents Database (ARD). This encompasses the plant- and establishment-level data that underlie the Annual Census of Production in Britain.[8] The ARD contains basic information on the population of production plants and establishments in Britain, including the industry, the number of employees, and the nationality of the ultimate owner. More detailed information, including output, intermediate inputs, and wages, is collected from a sample of establishments.[9] We do not observe capital stock in the ARD, but we do have information on purchases and sales of investment goods, and from this we construct a capital stock series using the perpetual inventory method (see the data appendix for details). We use both the basic information on the population of establishments and, for our main analysis, a cleaned-up sample of the more detailed establishment-level data, which we gross up to the population. The data appendix provides details on how we construct our sample and our grossing-up factors.

In 1980 there were around 29,000 incorporated establishments with at

8. An establishment can comprise a single plant or a group of plants under common ownership. The ARD is the British equivalent of the U.S. Census Bureau's Longitudinal Research Database. See Barnes and Martin (2002), Griffith (1999), Oulton (1997), and Perry (1995) for descriptions of the structure of the ARD.

9. The sample comprises a census of larger establishments and below a size threshold a stratified sample of smaller establishments. For most of the period considered the threshold was 100 employees.

least twenty employees in the manufacturing sector included in the ARD, as shown in the top section of table 4.1. By 1996 there were one thousand more, although total employment in British manufacturing fell during this period. Around 7 percent of these establishments were foreign-owned. These were on average larger than domestic-owned establishments, but the average size of both domestic- and foreign-owned establishments has fallen over time. Our sample contains around 12,000 annual observations on establishments, which account for around 70 percent of employment in the population. It contains a higher proportion of foreign-owned establishments than the population, and the establishments are on average larger (due mainly to the sampling procedure).

Figure 4.3 shows the distribution of the population of establishments by employment size band. Panels A and B show the distribution of foreign- and domestic-owned establishments across size bands in the population for 1980 and 1996, respectively. The largest group of domestic establishments is in the twenty-to-forty-nine-employee range, while foreign-owned establishments are fairly evenly distributed across size bands. There is a larger proportion of domestic-owned establishments in the smallest size band in 1996, due in part to efforts by the statistical authorities to improve the register of businesses, but also reflecting a trend toward downsizing. Panels C and D show the same distributions for our sample of establishments. In contrast to the population, domestic-owned establishments are more evenly distributed, and foreign-owned are concentrated in the larger size bands. In our regression analysis we gross up to population levels using grossing-up factors at the industry-size-year level (see the data appen-

Table 4.1 **Sample Statistics**

	1980	1996
Population		
Total employment (millions)	5.3	4.0
Number establishments	28,605	29,748
Foreign-owned establishments (%)	6.9	7.3
Average employment per domestic-owned establishment	167	114
Average employment per foreign-owned establishment	425	391
Sample		
Total employment (millions)	4.1	2.6
Number establishments	12,900	10,457
Foreign-owned establishments (%)	9.2	12.4
Average employment per domestic-owned establishment	295	205
Average employment per foreign-owned establishment	566	534

Notes: Establishments with less than twenty employees are excluded from both the population and the sample. Only incorporated establishments that are in production are included (sole proprietors, partnerships, government-owned, and other legal structures are excluded, as are plants that are not yet in production). See the appendix for details on the construction of the sample.

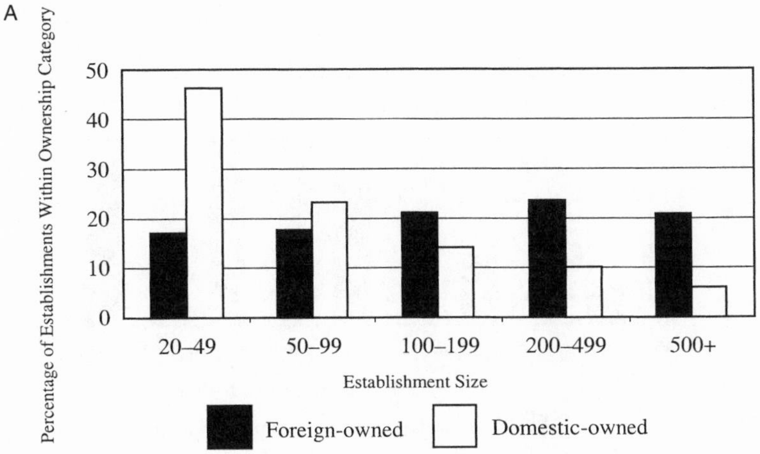

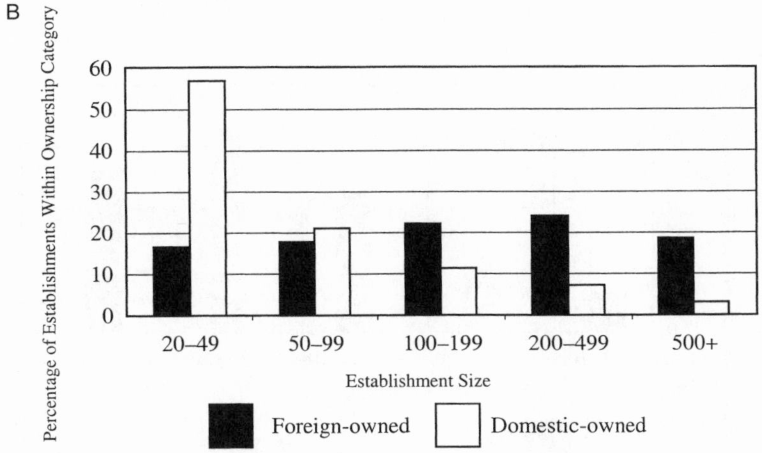

Fig. 4.3 ***A*, Employment size distribution population of establishments 1980; *B*, employment size distribution population of establishments 1996; *C*, employment size distribution sample of establishments 1980; *D*, employment size distribution sample of establishments 1996**

Source: Authors' calculations using the ARD.

dix for details). Figure 4.4 shows aggregate value added per worker calculated using our grossed-up sample. This is similar to figure 4.1, which was calculated using aggregate data from the Organization for Economic Cooperation and Development (OECD) STAN data set and gives an indication that our grossed-up sample is representative of manufacturing as a whole.

In our analysis we are interested in controlling for the age of an establishment and looking at how labor productivity changes with age. We do

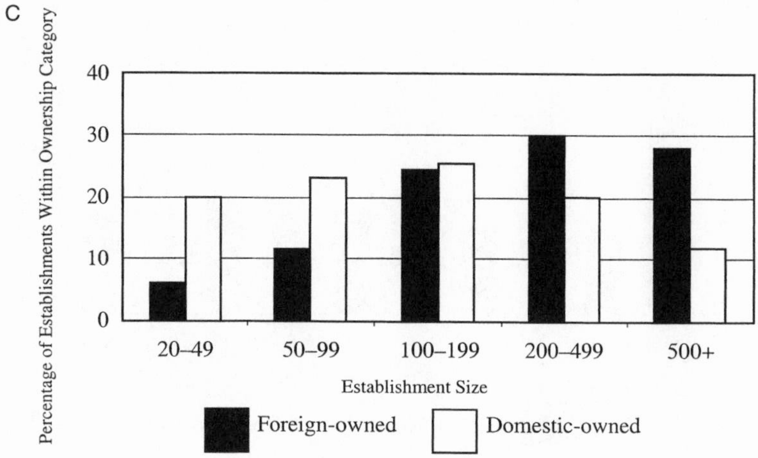

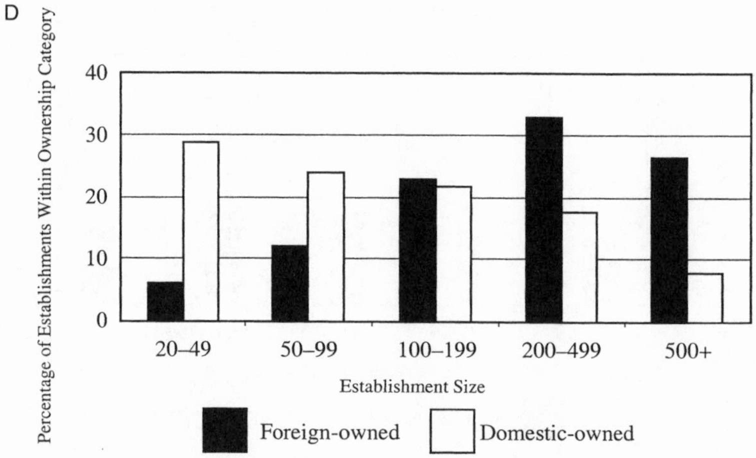

Fig. 4.3 (cont.) *A,* Employment size distribution population of establishments 1980; *B,* employment size distribution population of establishments 1996; *C,* employment size distribution sample of establishments 1980; *D,* employment size distribution sample of establishments 1996

Source: Authors' calculations using the ARD.

not observe the date that establishments were set up, but we can use information on the population of establishments back to 1973 to construct a truncated age variable. This gives us the length of time that a particular production facility has existed; that is, it is linked to the physical existence of the plant rather than to ownership.

Table 4.2 shows the age distribution of establishments in the sample in 1996 for both domestic- and foreign-owned establishments. The distribu-

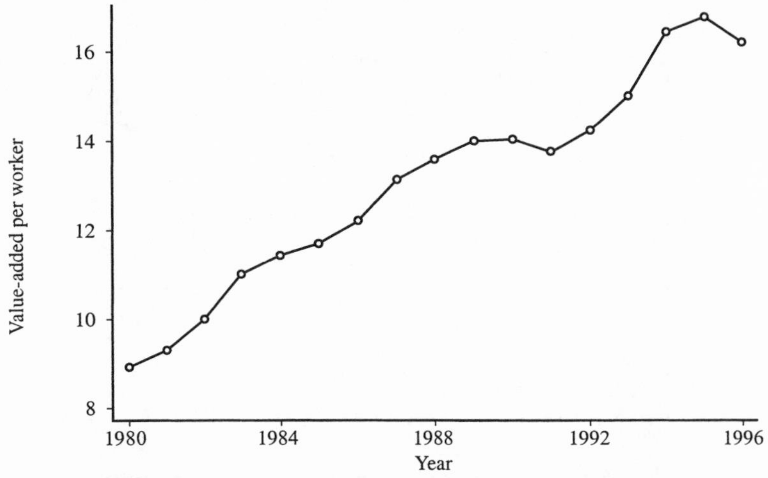

Fig. 4.4 Value added per worker (in thousands of 1980 UK£) in manufacturing
Source: Grossed-up ARD sample.

Table 4.2 Age Distribution of Establishments in 1996

Age	Domestic-Owned	Foreign-Owned
1–3	17.3	13.9
4–6	10.9	6.8
7–9	7.6	7.2
10–12	8.3	7.4
13–15	6.1	5.9
16–18	2.9	2.5
19–21	3.9	3.6
22+	42.9	52.6

Notes: See notes to table 4.1. Calculated for the sample of establishments.

tions are largely similar, although there is a larger proportion of young domestic-owned establishments.[10]

4.3 Trends in Foreign Ownership

This section describes the level of activity in foreign-owned establishments in British manufacturing over the period 1980 to 1996. We find that

10. Note that there are some problems with the continuity of the establishment-level identifier code that may affect the age calculation. In addition, age is calculated from 1973, so the largest proportion of establishments is always in the highest age category. See the appendix for details.

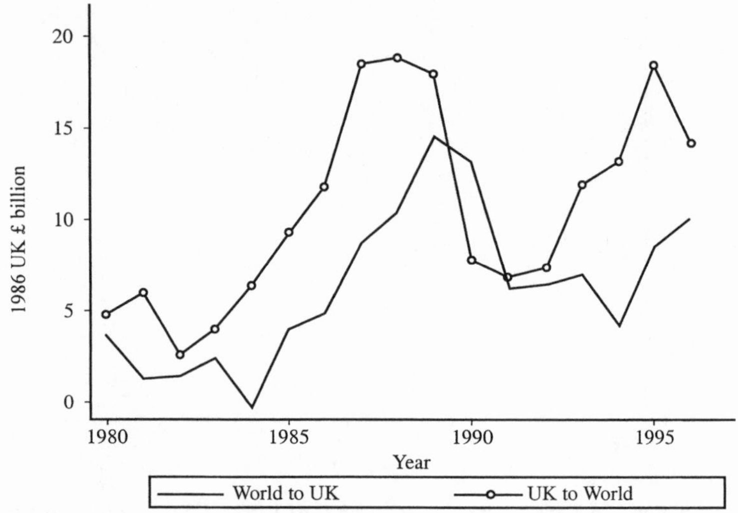

Fig. 4.5 Foreign direct investment
Source: OECD (www.sourceoecd.org).

the proportion of employment in foreign-owned establishments in the population of manufacturing establishments increased over the period from around 15 percent to 20 percent, and slightly more so in our sample. North American–owned[11] establishments represent by far the largest share, although there has been an increase in the presence of European Union– and Japanese-owned activity. We also look at the presence of foreign-owned establishments within two-digit industrial sectors and at the entry of foreign-owned establishments.

We analyze the real production activity of foreign-owned establishments located in Britain. Much empirical research addressing the issue of how multinational investment affects the local economy has used data on the flows or stocks of foreign direct investment. Figure 4.5 shows the time trend in inward and outward FDI[12] from the United Kingdom. This rose over the 1980s, fell off during the early 1990s, and recovered up to the mid-1990s (since 1996 it has grown much more rapidly). But foreign production (or even investment by foreign-owned firms) and FDI are not the same thing. The former is a measure of the amount of real activity that is undertaken by a firm that is resident in another country, while the latter is a measure of the flow of financial capital. They will differ to the extent that foreign-owned firms finance expenditure from local capital markets and repatriate profits back to the parent country. This difference is pointed out

11. U.S.- and Canadian-owned establishments.
12. Data from OECD SourceOECD database (www.sourceoecd.org).

by Auerbach and Hassett (1993). Grubert and Mutti (1991) show that the two series are unrelated using data on U.S. firms' investment in Canada.

Table 4.3 shows how employment, value added, and investment are broken down between different nationalities of ownership in our sample. The main entry rows give the totals of value added, employment, and investment. While employment declined over this period, total value added and investment have increased. In our sample the proportion of employment by foreign-owned establishments has risen by around 10 percentage points over this period, and the composition has changed. The proportion of employment in North American–owned establishments has fluctuated but increased over the whole period. There has also been an increase in the proportion of employment in European- and Japanese-owned establishments. Foreign-owned establishments account for a larger percentage of total value added and investment than they do the number of establishments (from table 4.1 we see that 12.4 percent of establishments in the sample

Table 4.3 Percentage of Sample by Nationality of Owner

	1980	1984	1988	1992	1996
Employment (millions)	4.1	3.6	5.0	3.0	2.6
U.K.-owned	83.7	83.9	90.3	78.8	73.1
North American	12.1	11.2	6.2	10.6	13.3
European Union	2.5	2.4	1.7	5.6	7.7
Other European	1.3	1.8	1.2	2.7	3.2
Japanese	0.0	0.1	0.3	1.8	2.0
Other foreign	0.4	0.6	0.3	0.6	0.7
Value added (1980 £millions)	37,924	39,991	45,229	40,991	43,363
U.K.-owned	80.5	79.1	79.8	73.5	65.6
North American	15.3	15.6	13.4	14.4	20.6
European Union	2.5	2.7	3.5	5.6	7.7
Other European	1.3	1.8	2.0	3.1	3.1
Japanese	0.0	0.1	0.5	2.3	1.9
Other foreign	0.4	0.7	0.9	1.0	1.0
Investment (1980 £millions)	4,573	4,760	6,125	5,779	6,973
U.K.-owned	79.1	79.4	77.9	68.0	60.7
North American	15.2	15.3	12.0	15.0	20.3
European Union	3.0	2.5	3.5	6.1	11.1
Other European	2.2	2.1	3.5	4.7	3.4
Japanese	0.1	0.3	2.5	5.2	3.2[a]
Other foreign	0.3	0.3	0.6	1.0	1.3

Source: Authors' calculations using ARD.

Note: Percentages are calculated from our cleaned-up sample. North American includes U.S.- and Canadian-owned. European Union countries are Belgium, Denmark, France, Germany, Greece, Ireland, Italy, Luxembourg, the Netherlands, Portugal, and Spain.

[a]In the full sample, Japanese investment accounts for over 4 percent of total investment in 1996; however, some establishments are excluded from our sample because they have negative value added (see appendix).

were foreign owned in 1996). The proportions of value added and investment accounted for by each ownership nationality follow a broadly similar pattern to the employment shares, except for Japanese-owned establishments, which consistently accounted for a larger share of investment than employment or value added.

Table 4.4 shows how activity in foreign-owned establishments is divided across two-digit industries within the population. The first column gives the proportion of total manufacturing employment in foreign-owned establishments in each industry in 1980. Column (2) shows the same figure for 1996. In 1980 nearly 20 percent of all employment in foreign-owned firms was in the mechanical engineering industry (32). By 1996, the sector that accounted for the highest proportion of employment in foreign-owned firms was motor vehicles (35), which increased from around 11 percent of total employment in foreign-owned establishments in 1980 to 16 percent in 1996.

Foreign-owned firms may enter the United Kingdom either by taking over an existing establishment or by setting up a greenfield site. The final four columns of table 4.4 show how both foreign- and domestic-owned entrants of different types were distributed across industries. The distribution of foreign-owned greenfield entrants shown in column (3) can be compared to that of domestic-owned greenfield entrants in column (4). Foreign-owned greenfield entrants were more likely to be in high-tech sectors such as chemicals (25), office machinery and data processing equipment (33), and electrical and electronic engineering (34) than their domestic-owned counterparts, but less likely to be in the food, drink, and tobacco (41/42) and clothing (45) industries.

Table 4.5 shows the extent of foreign ownership within each sector. Columns (1) and (2) show that in most industries this period saw an increase in the proportion of employment that was in foreign-owned establishments, notably in the office machinery and data processing equipment (33) and motor vehicles (35) sectors, where in 1996 over 60 percent of employment was in foreign-owned establishments. Only two industries experienced a decline in the proportion of employment in foreign-owned establishments: instrument engineering (37) and other manufacturing (49).

Columns (3) to (5) show the proportion of greenfield entrants and exiting and incumbent establishments that were foreign owned for each industry. In almost all industries the proportion of greenfield entrants is less than the proportion of incumbents, which suggests that the growth in the share of employment is due more to changes in employment patterns between surviving establishments (i.e., employment growth in foreign-owned incumbents and a decline in employment levels in domestic incumbents) than to greenfield entry. The final three columns show the proportion of foreign entrants within an industry that enter via setting up a greenfield site versus a takeover. Takeover is the dominant form of entry in all industries

Table 4.4 **Sectoral Composition of Employment and Entry in the Population of Foreign-Owned Establishments**

Two-Digit Industry (SIC80)	Total Manufacturing Employment in Foreign-Owned Establishments (%) 1980 (1)	1996 (2)	Foreign Greenfield Entrants (%) (3)	Domestic Greenfield Entrants (%) (4)	Domestic-to-Foreign Takeovers (%) (5)	Foreign-to-Domestic Takeovers (%) (6)
22 metal manufacturing	3.3	1.9	2.8	1.7	3.3	3.5
24 nonmetallic mineral products	2.0	2.2	2.7	3.7	4.5	4.1
25 chemicals	12.5	11.8	9.6	3.0	8.9	8.7
31 metal goods not elsewhere specified	3.9	3.9	6.2	9.2	7.1	6.5
32 mechanical engineering	19.7	12.3	17.5	14.9	15.6	18.4
33 office machinery and data-processing equipment	2.4	4.4	3.4	1.5	1.7	1.2
34 electrical and electronic engineering	15.9	14.3	16.3	12.0	13.7	12.0
35 motor vehicles	10.5	16.2	3.6	2.4	4.3	4.4
36 other transport	0.6	4.1	2.5	2.1	2.3	1.5
37 instrument engineering	2.9	2.3	5.9	2.6	3.8	4.3
41/42 food, drink, and tobacco	9.0	9.5	4.6	8.2	6.4	6.6
43 textiles	1.2	1.4	1.8	3.1	2.5	3.0
45 clothing	1.5	1.0	0.9	7.8	1.6	1.6
47 paper and paper products	6.9	7.1	11.0	10.1	12.5	12.8
48 rubber and plastics	5.4	5.6	5.4	5.7	8.0	6.9
49 other manufacturing	1.1	0.8	3.1	3.7	1.4	1.4
Total (%)	100.0	100.0	100.0	100.0	100.0	100.0
Total number 1980–1996			1,519	28,547	2,055	1,093

Notes: Columns (1) and (2) show the distribution of total manufacturing employment in foreign-owned establishments across industries. Columns (3) through (6) show how establishments were distributed across industries for each category of entrant. These are the annual average percent for 1980–1996. The omitted sectors (21, 23, 26, 44, and 46) each accounted for less than 1 percent of employment in foreign-owned establishments.

Table 4.5 **Within-Industry Shares of Foreign Activity, 1980–1996**

Two-Digit Industry (SIC80)	Industry Employment in Foreign-Owned Establishments (%) 1980 (1)	1996 (2)	Foreign-Owned Establishments (%) Industry Greenfield Entrants (3)	Industry Exits (4)	Industry Incumbents (5)	Industry Foreign Entrants (%) Greenfield (6)	Takeover D-F (7)	F-F (8)
22 metal manufacturing	16.2	15.7	7.8	9.4	11.5	36.8	59.75	—
24 nonmetallic mineral products	6.8	11.3	3.7	4.9	5.9	29.9	67.2	—
25 chemicals	31.2	38.0	14.5	21.1	23.5	41.2	51.4	7.4
31 metal goods not elsewhere specified	8.3	14.3	3.5	3.7	3.9	37.0	57.5	5.5
32 mechanical engineering	21.1	23.2	5.9	7.6	7.6	41.9	50.6	7.4
33 office machinery and data-processing equipment	48.3	67.4	10.7	13.4	17.9	58.4	38.2	—
34 electrical and electronic engineering	20.8	27.0	6.7	11.4	11.1	44.0	50.1	5.9
35 motor vehicles	23.1	61.9	7.3	7.4	10.0	36.0	58.7	5.3
36 other transport	3.0	18.6	6.1	6.2	6.2	41.8	51.7	6.6
37 instrument engineering	28.0	22.6	10.8	14.7	11.2	51.2	45.4	3.5
41/42 food, drink, and tobacco	11.5	16.7	2.9	4.6	5.3	33.0	62.3	4.7
43 textiles	3.3	7.5	3.0	2.9	2.6	32.1	60.7	7.1
45 clothing	3.8	4.8	0.6	1.2	1.5	28.6	67.4	—
47 paper and paper products	13.1	16.8	5.5	7.8	6.6	37.3	57.4	5.4
48 rubber and plastics	19.2	23.2	4.8	6.3	7.6	31.7	63.7	4.6
49 other manufacturing	14.9	12.0	4.3	6.2	4.5	58.8	36.3	—
Mean	18.7	24.7	7.8	9.4	7.9	41.3	51.3	7.4

Notes: D-F = domestic to foreign. F-F = foreign to foreign. Columns (1) and (2) show the annual average percentage of employment in foreign-owned establishments within each industry, 1980–1996. Columns (3) through (8) show the annual average percentage of establishments within each industry for each category, 1980–1996. The omitted sectors (21, 23, 26, 44, and 46) each account for less than 1 percent of employment in foreign-owned establishments. Dashes indicate that figures cannot be disclosed for data confidentiality reasons.

Table 4.6 **Distribution of Establishments by Nationality**

	Establishments	Observations
Always domestic	38,725	173,102
Always foreign	1,248	7,340
Domestic to foreign	2,342	21,028
Foreign to domestic	1,091	9,895

Note: Calculated from sample of establishments from 1980 to 1996.

except office machinery and data processing equipment (33) and instrument engineering (37), although in most cases it does not comprise a much higher proportion of entry than greenfield.

In the next section we compare the characteristics of domestic- and foreign-owned establishments and divide our sample into two groups: (1) establishments that are either always domestic owned or always foreign owned, and (2) establishments that change nationality between foreign and domestic ownership (at any point between 1973 and 1996). Note that the first group also includes establishments that are taken over—that is, those that go from domestic to domestic ownership or from foreign to foreign ownership. Note that all categories include both greenfield entrants and incumbents. Table 4.6 shows that the establishments that remain under U.K. ownership make up the largest proportion of establishments. The next largest category is those that are initially domestic and are taken over by a foreign-owned firm.

4.4 Characteristics of Establishments

This section compares the characteristics of foreign-owned manufacturing establishments that operate in Britain with U.K.-owned establishments. Figure 4.6 shows real value added per worker in French-, German-, Japanese-, and U.S.-owned establishments relative to U.K.-owned establishments. These were calculated by aggregating up the establishment-level data to the nationality-year level and constructing labor productivity measures in an analogous way to the aggregate measures shown in figure 4.2. Value added per worker in U.S.-owned establishments increased relative to that in U.K.-owned ones. This is in contrast to figure 4.2, where we saw that the level of labor productivity in manufacturing activity located in the United States became more similar to that located in the United Kingdom. This is interesting and suggests that one source of the convergence seen in figure 4.2 may be the increased productivity of U.S.-owned establishments located in Britain.

In this section we examine the differences between domestic- and foreign-owned establishments at the micro level. We first look at differences in labor

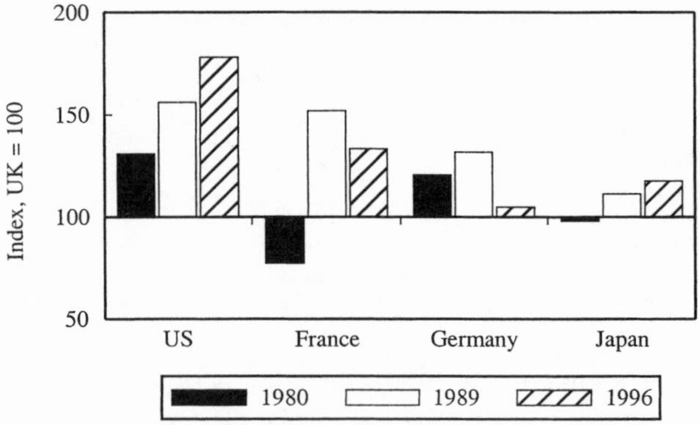

Fig. 4.6 Value added per worker in manufacturing, by nationality of ownership, establishments located in Britain

Source: Authors' calculations using the ARD.

productivity as measured by real value added per worker.[13] We also look at differences in the usage of intermediate inputs, in investment and in workforce composition. Differences in intermediates usage may reflect the fact that establishments are at different positions on the value added chain; for example, higher intermediates usage may indicate that an establishment is an assembly plant. Higher investment per worker will reflect more capital-intensive production and newer capital stock. These differences may to some extent explain differences in labor productivity. More intensive use of skilled workers may also explain labor productivity differences between establishments. We would expect labor productivity differences to be reflected in differences in wages. It may also be the case that the use of performance-related pay or efficiency wages induces higher labor productivity.[14]

4.4.1 Comparison of Firms That Are Always Foreign Owned

We first look at establishments that remain under either domestic or foreign ownership, over the entire period 1973–1996. Foreign-owned establishments are much larger than U.K.-owned, as is shown in table 4.7. They have higher output and value added per employee, invest more per employee, and use more intermediate inputs than U.K.-owned establishments. They also use a higher proportion of administrative, technical, and clerical (ATC) workers (used as a measure of skilled workers) and pay both ATC workers and operatives (OPS) higher wages.

13. We deflate reported value added by a four-digit output price deflator. Employment in the ARD is measured as the average number employed in an establishment during the year.

14. We do not present estimates of total factor productivity (TFP) because of a number of concerns we have about the appropriate methodology for measuring TFP in the presence of imperfectly competitive factor markets; see Hall (1988), Nickell (1996), and Klette (1999).

Table 4.7 **Descriptive Statistics, Constant Nationality Sample**

	1980		1996	
	Foreign	Domestic	Foreign	Domestic
Number of establishments	446	10,798	500	8,756
Gross output[a]	27,142	6,500	58,539	8,752
Value added[a]	8,982	2,312	15,798	3,013
Investment[a]	1,222	260	2,792	442
Intermediate inputs[a]	16,109	3,667	44,200	5,742
Employment	763	264	597	197
Output per employee[b]	40,541	22,891	87,570	37,461
Value added per employee[b]	13,326	8,071	25,869	13,028
Investment per employee[b]	1,948	808	3,528	1,709
Intermediate inputs per employee[b]	25,466	13,572	68,459	25,121
Employees ATC (%)	41	26	42[c]	33[c]
Average wage ATC[b]	6,797	5,874	9,984[c]	8,235[c]
Average wage OPS[b]	5,301	4,466	7,089[c]	5,414[c]

Source: Authors' calculations using the ARD data.

Notes: Price deflators for output and value added are at four-digit level and for investment are a combination of three-digit and aggregate. Wages are deflated by the Retail Prices Index. ATC = administrative, technical, and clerical; OPS = operatives.

[a]In 1980 UK£ (thousands).

[b]In 1980 UK£.

[c]Data are from 1995 (variable not available in 1996).

These findings are similar to the results seen in the U.S. work by Doms and Jensen (1998), where there were large unconditional differences in characteristics. That work found it to be important to compare domestic multinationals with their foreign-owned counterparts. It is not possible for us to differentiate U.K.-owned multinationals in our data. Instead we condition on observable and unobservable characteristics.

We concentrate on the following explanatory variables:

- nationality of parent, $f(F_i)$;
- age of the establishment, and a separate age profile for foreign-owned establishments, $g(\text{age}_{it}, F_i)$;
- size of establishment (measured by employment and normalized on mean four-digit industry employment), $h(\text{size}_{it})$;
- year of exit, exit_{it};
- time effects, and a separate time effect interacted with foreign ownership, $\delta(t_t, F_i)$,

where i indexes establishment and t time. We are concerned that there may be other unobservable differences in firms that may be correlated with age, size, or probability of exit. We allow for this by including a time-invariant firm-specific effect, η_i:

$$\ln(lp_{it}) = \beta f(F_i) + \gamma g(\text{age}_{it}, F_i) + \phi h(\text{size}_{it}) + \lambda \text{exit}_{it} + \delta t(t_t, F_i) + \eta_i + e_{it}.$$

We estimate this model in two steps (see Hsiao 1986). First we estimate

$$(1) \qquad \ln(lp_{it}) = \gamma g(\text{age}_{it}) + \phi h(\text{size}_{it}) + \lambda \text{exit}_{it} + \delta t(t_t) + \eta_i + e_{it}$$

using the within-groups estimator. Then we estimate the residual (including the fixed effect), take the time series mean, and estimate a regression of the form

$$(2) \qquad \overline{\hat{\eta}_i + \hat{e}_{it}} = \beta f(F_i) + u_i.$$

We assume a quadratic form for $g(\cdot)$ and $h(\cdot)$, while $f(\cdot)$ is represented by a series of dummies for different nationalities, and $t(\cdot)$ is a full set of time dummies (in some specifications interacted with a foreign-ownership dummy).

Table 4.8 compares differences in real value added per worker in establishments that do not change nationality (including greenfield entrants and incumbents). The top half of the table shows the first-step estimates (i.e., the coefficients from equation [1]), and the bottom half shows the second-step estimates (i.e., the coefficients from equation [2]). In column (1) labor productivity is regressed on age, size, a dummy for the year of exit, and a full set of time and industry dummies. In column (2) and subsequent columns the sample is restricted to only those establishments that we observe five or more times. Conditioning on this sample is necessary to enable us to use the within-groups estimator. This does not change the coefficients significantly. In column (3) individual establishment fixed effects are included. This changes the sign and significance of most variables.

In column (3) we see that labor productivity is increasing in age, and at an increasing rate, and is decreasing in size, although at a decreasing rate. This suggests that greenfield entrants (age equals 1) have lower value added per worker than incumbents. Establishments have lower labor productivity in their year of exit than in previous years. In column (4) we explore the idea that foreign-owned establishments may adapt to new technologies better than U.K.-owned establishments. We do this by interacting a foreign-ownership dummy with the age terms. If foreign-owned establishments improve their productivity faster with age, then this should be captured by this term. Although these interactions are not individually significant they are jointly significant (as indicated by the F-test). The domestic and foreign age effects are shown in figure 4.7 by the solid lines (the dashed lines are explained in the discussion after table 4.9). After twenty-four years the contribution of the age effect is almost twice as large in foreign-owned establishments as in domestic-owned ones. We also tried interacting the year dummies with foreign ownership. These were individually and jointly insignificant.

In the bottom half of the table we use the estimates from the top half to obtain estimates of the unexplained part of labor productivity, $\overline{\hat{\eta}_i + \hat{e}_{it}}$,

Table 4.8 **Differences in Real Value Added per Worker, Constant Nationality Sample**

	(1)	(2)	(3)	(4)
Dependent variable: $\ln(lp_{it})$				
Age	–0.005	–0.011	0.018	0.017
	(0.003)	(0.003)	(0.003)	(0.003)
Age²	–0.00001	0.0002	0.0003	0.0003
	(0.0001)	(0.0001)	(0.0001)	(0.0001)
Foreign · age	—	—	—	0.014
				(0.013)
Foreign · age²	—	—	—	0.0001
				(0.0004)
Size	0.029	0.032	–0.034	–0.034
	(0.002)	(0.003)	(0.006)	(0.006)
Size²	–0.0007	–0.0009	0.001	0.0007
	(0.0001)	(0.0001)	(0.0002)	(0.0002)
Exit	–0.079	–0.099	–0.094	–0.093
	(0.027)	(0.028)	(0.022)	(0.022)
No. of observations	180,442	131,097	131,097	131,097
F-test, foreign-age interaction				21.45
P-value				0.00
Year	yes	yes	yes	yes[a]
Industry	yes	yes		
Within groups			yes	yes
Dependent variable: $\overline{\hat{\eta}_i + \hat{e}_{it}}$				
North American	—	—	0.517	0.311
			(0.042)	(0.044)
European Union	—	—	0.424	0.202
			(0.086)	(0.076)
Other European	—	—	0.351	0.168
			(0.052)	(0.053)
Japanese	—	—	0.496	0.376
			(0.132)	(0.132)
Other foreign	—	—	0.572	0.432
			(0.146)	(0.153)
No. of observations			13,909	13,909

Notes: Numbers in parentheses are robust standard errors. All regressions are grossed up to population weights and weighted by establishments' employment. $\ln(lp)$ = log of real value added per worker. Year indicates full set of year dummies; industry indicates full set of four-digit industry dummies. Size is number of employees normalized on four-digit industry-year average employment. Columns (2) to (4) contain only establishments that we observe at least five times.

[a]Includes interaction of year dummies with foreign-ownership dummy.

and regress this on dummies for different nationalities of ownership, as described in equation (2). The results in column (3) suggest that North American–owned establishments have around 68 percent higher labor productivity than U.K.-owned, EU-owned around 53 percent higher, other European-owned 42 percent higher, Japanese-owned around 64 percent,

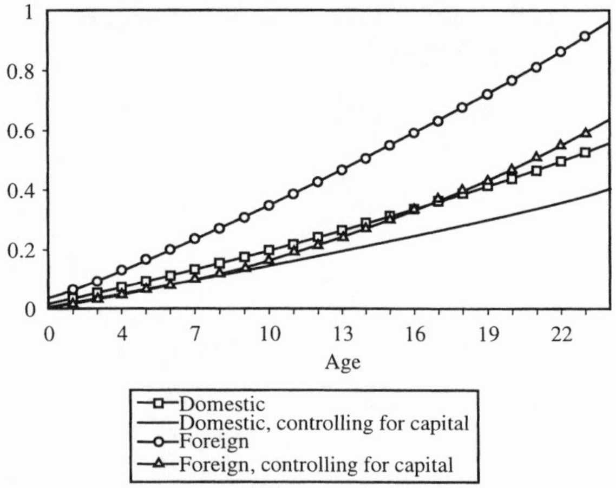

Fig. 4.7 Age effect on real value added per employee

and other foreign-owned around 77 percent higher.[15] These are all significant and quite large differences. In column (4) we repeat this exercise. Conditioning on differences in the age profile explains some of the differences in labor productivity, but large and significant differences remain. North American–owned establishments have around 36 percent higher labor productivity than U.K.-owned, EU-owned around 22 percent higher, other European-owned 18 percent higher, Japanese-owned around 46 percent, and other foreign-owned around 54 percent higher.

Differences in inputs are investigated in table 4.9. In the first column we see that investment per employee is increasing in age, at an increasing rate. The profile for foreign firms is different. While the coefficients on the interaction between the foreign dummy and age are individually insignificant, they are jointly significant. Not surprisingly, establishments invest less per employee in their final year before exit. In the bottom half of the table the unexplained part of investment per employee is regressed against the nationality of ownership dummies using the same procedure as before and as described by equation (2). The coefficients are all positive and significant. Their magnitude is larger than those for labor productivity. North American–owned establishments invest twice as much per worker as U.K.-owned, EU-owned around twice as much, other European-owned two and a half times as much, Japanese-owned around eight times as much, and other foreign-owned around twice as much. This suggests that the differences in value added per worker seen in table 4.8 are largely attributable to differences in investment levels.

15. $\exp(\beta) - 1$ is approximately the proportional difference, where β is the coefficient on a dummy variable in a log-linear regression.

Table 4.9 Differences in Inputs, Constant Nationality Sample

	Dependent Variable			
	ln(investment per employee)$_{it}$ (1)	ln(proportion skilled workers)$_{it}$ (2)	ln(average skilled wage)$_{it}$ (3)	ln(average operative wage)$_{it}$ (4)
Age	0.010	0.003	0.024	0.012
	(0.005)	(0.002)	(0.001)	(0.001)
Age^2	0.0007	0.00014	–0.00014	0.00004
	(0.0002)	(0.00007)	(0.00005)	(0.00004)
Foreign · age	–0.010	–0.0001	–0.002	0.005
	(0.018)	(0.0055)	(0.004)	(0.005)
Foreign · age^2	0.0009	–0.0001	0.0003	–0.0001
	(0.0006)	(0.0002)	(0.0001)	(0.0002)
Size	–0.031	–0.004	–0.0007	–0.010
	(0.009)	(0.003)	(0.002)	(0.003)
Size^2	0.0008	0.00003	0.0002	0.0002
	(0.0003)	(0.00013)	(0.0001)	(0.0001)
Exit	–0.106	–0.013	–0.009	–0.012
	(0.042)	(0.013)	(0.010)	(0.009)
No. of observations	122,398	125,917	125,910	124,525
F-test, foreign-age interaction	8.08	3.25	31.29	4.03
P-value	0.00	0.04	0.00	0.02
Year	yes	yes	yes	yes
Within groups	yes	yes	yes	yes
Dependent variable: $\overline{\hat{\eta}_i + \hat{e}_{it}}$				
North American	0.817	0.386	0.183	0.179
	(0.095)	(0.055)	(0.022)	(0.021)
European Union	0.713	0.418	0.197	0.108
	(0.097)	(0.074)	(0.024)	(0.027)
Other European	0.934	0.166	0.157	0.136
	(0.137)	(0.088)	(0.026)	(0.038)
Japanese	2.25	0.012	0.271	0.166
	(0.39)	(0.066)	(0.075)	(0.109)
Other foreign	1.09	0.448	0.133	0.185
	(0.31)	(0.131)	(0.092)	(0.096)
No. of observations	13,898	13,908	13,908	13,832

Notes: Numbers in parentheses are robust standard errors. All regressions are grossed up to population weights and weighted by establishments' employment. Year indicates full set of year dummies. Size is number of employees normalized on four-digit industry–year average employment.

In figure 4.7 we investigate the extent to which the steeper age profile for labor productivity in foreign-owned establishments is explained by differences in their capital stocks. We run a regression of capital stock per employee similar to that shown in column (1). We take the coefficients on the age and foreign-age profiles and subtract them, multiplied by the average share of capital in value added, from the age profiles for labor productivity from column (4) in table 4.8.[16] These capital-adjusted age profiles for labor productivity are shown by the dashed lines in figure 4.7. We see that the age profiles are now very close for the first ten years. This is because foreign-owned firms have both higher labor productivity and a correspondingly higher capital stock. After twenty-two years the adjusted profiles diverge by around 20 percentage points.

Finally we investigate differences in the type of workers employed and their average wages. In column (2) we see that the proportion of skilled workers in an establishment's workforce is increasing in age and in size. We also see that foreign-owned establishments employ more skilled (ATC) workers. This could also partly explain higher levels of labor productivity. In columns (3) and (4) we see that wages are increasing in age, decreasing in size, and lower in the year before exit. We see that foreign-owned establishments pay higher wages to both skilled workers and OPS, which is consistent with higher levels of labor productivity.

4.4.2 Comparison of Firms That Change Nationality

In this section we compare establishments that change nationality and look at how their characteristics compare before and after the ownership change. Table 4.10 describes establishments that change nationality (at some point between 1973 and 1996).[17] The first two columns consider establishments that go from being U.K. owned to foreign owned and describe their characteristics before and after the takeover. The size of establishment does not change noticeably, apart from a fall in average employment. Labor productivity, investment per employee, and wages all increase. The final two columns describe establishments that go from being foreign to U.K. owned. We observe fewer of these. Labor productivity prior to takeover is higher than for the domestic to foreign takeovers. The size of establishment is on average less after the change of ownership, while labor productivity remains fairly stable.

For this group of establishments, those that change nationality, we consider the same variables as for the constant nationality group, and we additionally consider the number of years since the establishment changed nationality (t.o.) and whether the change of ownership was from domestic to foreign or vice versa. In this case we can estimate the equation directly because the foreign-ownership dummies are now time varying:

$$(3)\quad \ln(lp_{it}) = \beta f(F_{it}) + \gamma g(\text{age}_{it}, \text{t.o.}) + \phi h(\text{size}_{it}) + \lambda \text{exit}_{it} + \delta t(t_t) + \eta_i + e_{it}.$$

16. The coefficients are age (0.015), age^2 (0.00035), age · foreign (0.0657), and age^2 · foreign (0.0015). The average share of capital in value added is 0.26.

17. We do not necessarily observe input and output data on an establishment both before and after the change in ownership nationality due to the random sampling.

Table 4.10 Descriptive Statistics, Changing Nationality Sample

	Domestic-to-Foreign Takeover		Foreign-to-Domestic Takeover	
	Before (domestic)	After (foreign)	Before (foreign)	After (domestic)
No. of observations	8,846	11,117	4,598	4,828
Gross output[a]	19,927	18,330	17,089	13,075
Value added[a]	7,104	6,014	5,541	4,439
Investment[a]	1,019	945	692	647
Intermediate inputs[a]	12,201	12,453	10,972	8,538
Employment	563	379	388	296
Output per employee[b]	35,804	45,764	39,903	39,402
Value added per employee[b]	12,385	15,098	13,428	13,580
Investment per employee[b]	1,633	2,101	1,587	1,769
Intermediate inputs per employee[b]	22,848	31,181	25,327	25,993
Employees ATC (%)	35	38	38	36
Average wage ATC[b]	7,509	7,824	7,365	8,113
Average wage OPS[b]	5,510	5,876	5,514	5,755

Source: Authors' calculations using the ARD data.

Notes: Price deflators for output and value added are at four-digit level, and for investment they are a combination of three-digit and aggregate. Wages are deflated by the RPI.

[a]In 1980 UK£ (thousands).

[b]In 1980 UK£.

The coefficient on the foreign nationality dummies, β, now picks up the difference in the level of labor productivity between when the establishment was domestic owned and when it was foreign owned.

Column (1) of table 4.11 shows estimates for the coefficients from this model including only nationality dummies and year effects (i.e., not controlling for unobservable firm-specific characteristics). This suggests that establishments have around 13 percent higher labor productivity when they are North American–owned, other European-owned around 5 percent higher, and other foreign-owned around 30 percent higher than when they were U.K.-owned.

In column (2) we condition on establishments that we observe at least five times; this makes little difference to the coefficient estimates. In column (3) we add four-digit industry dummies. This reduces the North American difference to around 6 percent. Japanese-owned establishments exhibit around 11 percent lower labor productivity, and other foreign-owned have around 9 percent higher labor productivity. In column (4) we condition on age, size, and year of exit. This drives the Japanese-owned dummy into insignificance. Labor productivity is increasing in size and is lower in the year before exit.

Table 4.11 **Differences in Real Value Added per Worker, Changing Nationality Sample**

	Dependent Variable				
	$\ln(lp_{it})$ (1)	$\ln(lp_{it})$ (2)	$\ln(lp_{it})$ (3)	$\ln(lp_{it})$ (4)	$\ln(lp_{it})$ (5)
North American	0.123	0.123	0.055	0.058	–0.018
	(0.021)	(0.021)	(0.023)	(0.021)	(0.030)
European Union	0.006	0.009	0.004	0.006	–0.041
	(0.028)	(0.029)	(0.031)	(0.029)	(0.039)
Other European	0.048	0.047	0.032	0.035	0.069
	(0.027)	(0.028)	(0.022)	(0.021)	(0.035)
Japanese	0.045	0.049	–0.113	–0.077	–0.205
	(0.083)	(0.084)	(0.060)	(0.061)	(0.089)
Other foreign	0.260	0.277	0.083	0.068	–0.012
	(0.052)	(0.054)	(0.041)	(0.040)	(0.040)
Age				0.003	0.025
				(0.007)	(0.011)
Age^2				0.00004	0.0002
				(0.00026)	(0.0003)
Size				0.036	–0.035
				(0.005)	(0.010)
$Size^2$				–0.0015	–0.00003
				(0.0003)	(0.00041)
Year of exit				–0.157	–0.118
				(0.049)	(0.046)
No. of observations	26,651	24,070	24,070	24,070	24,070
Year	yes	yes	yes	yes	yes
Industry			yes	yes	
Within groups					yes

Notes: Numbers in parentheses are robust standard errors. All regressions are grossed up to population weights and weighted by establishments' employment. Year indicates full set of year dummies; industry indicates full set of four-digit industry dummies. Size is number of employees normalized on four-digit industry-year average employment. Columns (2) to (4) include only establishments that we observe at least five times.

In column (5) we use a within-groups estimator to condition on establishment-specific unobservables. This means that the nationality coefficients are capturing the difference in productivity that arises due to different ownership. This drives the coefficient on North American ownership into insignificance. Establishments have around 7 percent higher labor productivity when they are owned by other European firms, compared to U.K.-owned. Those that are owned by Japanese firms have around 23 percent lower labor productivity compared to U.K.-owned firms.

We also experimented with allowing separate profiles for the number of years since the change in the nationality of ownership and whether it was domestic to foreign or foreign to domestic. This was intended to capture learning effects. The coefficients were not significant. However, from table 4.10 it is clear that there is an improvement in value added per worker when establishments go from being domestic to foreign owned (from 12,385 to 15,098), whereas when they go in the other direction there is no increase.[18] In all specifications establishments have lower labor productivity in the year before they exit.

In table 4.12 we compare input usage in establishments that change nationality. In column (1) we regress the log of investment per worker on nationality dummies, age, size, year of exit, and year and industry dummies. In column (2) we use a within-groups estimator to control for unobservable differences in establishments. Establishments invest more per worker when they are North American, EU, or Japanese owned than when U.K. owned. Finally we look at whether differences in labor productivity are reflected in the type of labor used and in wages. In columns (3) and (4) we see that a higher proportion of skilled workers are employed when an establishment is under North American ownership than when it is U.K. owned. In columns (5) and (6) we see that skilled workers are paid more in Japanese-owned establishments, and in columns (7) and (8) we see that operatives are paid more when establishments are EU or other European owned.

4.5 Summary and Conclusions

This paper has investigated differences in characteristics between U.K.-owned and foreign-owned manufacturing establishments in Britain over the period 1980 to 1996. At the aggregate level we see that value added per worker has grown rapidly in the United Kingdom since the early 1980s. But the United Kingdom remains behind other Group of Five (G5) countries in the league tables. We see a somewhat similar picture when we look within the United Kingdom. In aggregate, U.K.-owned firms have lower labor productivity than firms of other nationalities operating in Great Britain. There are some differences between the international picture and that within Britain. Comparing across countries, over the period 1980 to 1996, the United Kingdom caught up with the United States, but looking within Britain we see that North American–owned firms widened the gap with domestic-owned firms.

When we look at the micro level we find that establishments that are always foreign owned have significantly higher labor productivity than those that are always domestic owned. In addition, labor productivity improves faster with age in foreign-owned establishments. This is matched, however, by an almost equivalent increase in levels of investment per employee.

18. Harris and Robinson (2002) look at TFP using the same data as here. They find some evidence that performance declined after acquisition. Conyon et al. (2002), using a different U.K. data source, do find a labor productivity increase as a result of foreign acquisition.

Table 4.12 **Differences in Inputs, Changing Nationality Sample**

	Dependent Variable							
	$\ln(\text{investment per employee})_{it}$		$\ln(\text{proportion skilled workers})_{it}$		$\ln(\text{average skilled wage})_{it}$		$\ln(\text{average operative wage})_{it}$	
	(1)	(2)	(3)	(4)	(5)	(6)	(7)	(8)
North American	0.118	0.067	0.076	0.048	0.062	0.011	0.046	0.007
	(0.028)	(0.041)	(0.010)	(0.013)	(0.006)	(0.009)	(0.007)	(0.008)
European Union	0.140	0.134	0.004	0.005	0.017	0.013	0.017	0.026
	(0.034)	(0.043)	(0.016)	(0.015)	(0.008)	(0.012)	(0.008)	(0.010)
Other European	0.051	0.069	–0.055	–0.037	0.030	0.015	0.031	0.033
	(0.048)	(0.062)	(0.020)	(0.022)	(0.011)	(0.016)	(0.009)	(0.010)
Japanese	0.481	0.461	–0.057	–0.028	0.009	0.105	–0.021	0.028
	(0.092)	(0.120)	(0.045)	(0.039)	(0.027)	(0.042)	(0.023)	(0.036)
Other foreign	–0.000	–0.146	–0.093	0.028	0.060	0.022	0.005	–0.018
	(0.096)	(0.105)	(0.040)	(0.021)	(0.019)	(0.018)	(0.017)	(0.015)
Age	–0.046	–0.010	0.009	0.010	–0.010	0.021	–0.009	0.013
	(0.012)	(0.015)	(0.004)	(0.005)	(0.003)	(0.003)	(0.002)	(0.002)
Age^2	0.0013	0.0018	–0.000	–0.0002	0.0002	0.0001	0.0002	0.0001
	(0.0005)	(0.0005)	(0.000)	(0.0002)	(0.0001)	(0.0001)	(0.0001)	(0.0001)
Size	0.075	–0.034	–0.002	–0.014	0.022	–0.002	0.028	–0.006
	(0.007)	(0.016)	(0.003)	(0.005)	(0.002)	(0.003)	(0.002)	(0.003)
Size^2	–0.0023	0.0007	0.0004	0.0009	–0.0009	–0.0001	–0.0089	0.0002
	(0.0003)	(0.0005)	(0.0002)	(0.0002)	(0.0002)	(0.0001)	(0.0001)	(0.0001)
Year of exit	–0.165	–0.109	0.038	0.030	0.014	0.020	0.036	0.023
	(0.104)	(0.092)	(0.035)	(0.027)	(0.029)	(0.025)	(0.028)	(0.023)
No. of observations	22,717		23,011		23,009		22,680	
Year	yes	yes	yes	yes	yes	yes	yes	yes
Industry	yes		yes		yes		yes	
Within groups		yes		yes		yes		yes

Notes: Numbers in parentheses are robust standard errors. All regressions are grossed up to population weights and weighted by establishments' employment. Year indicates full set of year dummies; industry indicates full set of four-digit industry dummies. Size is number of employees normalized on four-digit industry-year average employment.

Once we take these differences in capital intensity into account there is little difference between firms of different nationalities. When we look at establishments that change nationality, differences in labor productivity between foreign- and domestic-owned establishments are smaller.

These findings suggest that investment patterns, and usage of other inputs such as skilled workers, may go a long way toward explaining differences in value added per worker between establishments. This raises the question of why foreign-owned establishments are investing more and using more skilled workers. Do U.K.-owned establishments face some constraint, or is there some other explanation?

Appendix

Data

Our main data source is the Annual Respondents Database (ARD). These data are collected annually by the Office for National Statistics (ONS).[19] Two types of information are contained in the ARD. First, information on employment, industry, and group structure is available for the population of local units and establishments involved in production. A local unit is the smallest entity reported in ARD—effectively a plant (a single address).[20] An establishment can comprise one or more local units, (almost) always within the same four-digit industry (five-digit after 1992). Three main identifier codes are given—at the local unit, establishment, and enterprise group level. These indicate which local units and establishments are linked through common ownership.

Second, additional detailed information on inputs and output is collected for a sample of establishments. The sample comprises a census of larger establishments and, below a size threshold, a stratified sample of smaller establishments. For most of the period we consider the threshold was 100 employees. When collecting production-sector data the ONS asks that all nonproduction activities undertaken within the production establishments be excluded. There is no information on activities located in other countries.

We use data on the population of manufacturing establishments (we construct the population from the raw data), and to look at labor productivity and input usage we use a sample of manufacturing establishments. We gross up the sample in our main analysis. Further details of how we

19. See Barnes and Martin (2002), Griffith (1999), Oulton (1997), and Perry (1995) for descriptions of the structure of the ARD.

20. There are a small number of cases where the local unit is reporting for several plants. Since 1993 the list of local units comes from the InterDepartmental Business Register.

identify entrants, exitors, and ownership changes, of the grossing-up factors and of the sample we use, are given herein.

The ARD categorizes establishments into seven types: incorporated or company, sole proprietor, partnership, public corporation, central government body, local authority, and other (including non–profit-making bodies). We only use those classified as incorporated or company.[21] We exclude establishments that are not yet in production.

The entry and exit year of an establishment is calculated by identifying the first and last years that it is present in the population of incorporated establishments that are in production. We do this using data on the population back to 1973. The ONS has made changes to the establishment identifier codes several times. Where possible we map over coding changes using postal code and industry code information. If an establishment changes from a public corporation to being incorporated it counts as an entrant, as are establishments that go from being "not yet in production" to "in production."

The ARD gives the country of residence of the ultimate owner of the local unit, or establishment. The domestic-to-foreign and foreign-to-domestic takeovers are identified using the nationality of ownership indicator. There appear to be some miscodings in this variable. Where we observe the indicator changing for one year and then reverting to its previous value we assume that this is a miscoding. We discard establishments that appear to be taken over more than twice during the period.

The foreign ownership data in the ARD are collected under a separate annual survey that is also used for the FDI statistics: Thus, the ownership data for FDI are exactly the same as for ARD. These data are augmented with information from Dun and Bradstreet. The definition of FDI into Britain used for statistical purposes in collecting the FDI data is

> investment that adds to, deducts from or acquires a lasting interest in an enterprise operating in an economy other than that of the investor, the investor's purpose being to have an effective voice in the management of the enterprise. For the purposes of the statistical inquiry, an effective voice is taken as equivalent to a holding of 20% or more in the foreign enterprise. Other investments in which the investor does not have an effective voice in the management of the enterprise are mainly portfolio investments. (Central Statistical Office [CSO] 1996)

We allocate establishments to their mode four-digit standard industrial classification (SIC) code (so it is time invariant for each establishment). From 1992 we map SIC92 codes to SIC80 codes. The mapping is constructed using data from 1992 and 1993 when both industry codes are reported in the ARD. For each SIC92 we use the SIC80 from which the

21. At the local unit level these represent 96 percent of local units on average over the period 1980–1996.

largest number of local units was recoded. We verify these mappings using *Indexes to the Standard Industrial Classification of Economic Activities 1992* (ONS 1997).

We create grossing-up factors using employment in the population of establishments. Two populations are used for this purpose. The first contains all establishments that are always under either domestic or foreign ownership, and the second contains establishments that change ownership nationality due to a takeover. Grossing-up factors are calculated at the four-digit SIC80-size-year level. Grossing-up factors are not calculated by ownership nationality, as there are too many empty cells, where no foreign-owned establishments in a particular industry and size category are observed in the sample, but they are in the population.

Our Sample

In the establishment sample, output, investment, employment, and intermediate inputs are reported in nominal terms. We use price deflators for output and intermediate inputs at the four-digit industry level obtained from the ONS directly. Price indexes for investment in plant and machinery are at the two- and three-digit level from *Price Index Numbers for Current Cost Accounting* (CSO, various years). For investment in buildings and land an annual price index from *Price Index Numbers for Current Cost Accounting* (CSO, various years) is used. For vehicles an annual price index is obtained using prices series for road motor vehicles from three series from *Price Index Numbers for Current Cost Accounting* (CSO, various years). The first series ran from 1974 to 1983 (1980 = 100) and the second from 1984 to 1993 (1985 = 100), but there was no common year to convert it. The price index for private vehicles published in *Retail Prices 1914–1990* (CSO, 1991, tables 70 and 71) is used to merge the two series. The third series runs 1994 to 1996 (1995 = 100). The retail price index (RPI) is available at the aggregate level (www.statistics.gov.uk). Price deflator series for output and inputs are interpolated using the RPI up to 1996, where there are missing data.

Capital stock data are not available in the ARD, and we construct these data using the perpetual inventory method (PIM) at the establishment level. To do this we need to approximate the first-period capital stock. We do this by allocating each establishment a share of an estimated three-digit industry-level capital stock. The industry-level capital stocks are estimated using a 1979 value from a study by Oulton and O'Mahony (1990) and then using the PIM, with three-digit industry-level investment calculated by aggregating the ARD and grossing it up. An initial capital stock for each establishment is then estimated by using that establishment's share of energy usage within its three-digit industry in that year. Where the capital stock is negative we set the capital stock to zero.

Around 1 percent of observations in the sample have negative value

Table 4A.1 Characteristics of Establishments with Wage Bill Greater Than Value Added

Characteristic	Dummy = 1 if Wage Bill Greater than Value Added
Value added per employee	–0.37
	(0.01)
Investment per employee	–0.23
	(0.02)
Wage ATC	–0.01
	(0.01)
Wage OPS	–0.02
	(0.01)

Notes: The coefficients are from weighted regressions of log characteristic on a dummy equal to 1 for observations to be dropped from the sample, industry, and time dummies. Standard errors are in parentheses.

added (expenditure on intermediate goods is greater than the value of output). We drop these observations. Around 20 percent of observations have a wage bill that is greater than value added (that is, variable costs are greater than the value of output). This occurs more often in recessions but is spread fairly evenly over years, industries, ages of establishments, and foreign and domestic establishments. These observations have lower value added per employee, have lower investment, and pay lower wages, as shown in table 4A.1.

References

Aghion, P., and P. Howitt. 1998. *Endogenous growth theory.* Cambridge: MIT Press.

Auerbach, A. J., and K. Hassett. 1993. Taxation and foreign direct investment in the United States: A reconsideration of the evidence. In *Studies in international taxation,* ed. A. Giovannini, R. G. Hubbard, and J. Slemrod, 119–147. Chicago: University of Chicago Press.

Barnes, M., and R. Martin. 2002. Business data linking: An introduction. *Economic Trends* 581 (April): 34–41.

Barrell, R., and N. Pain. 1997. Foreign direct investment, technological change, and economic growth within Europe. *Economic Journal* 107:445.

Barro, R., and X. Sala-i-Martin. 1995. *Economic growth.* New York: McGraw Hill.

Bartelsman, E., and M. Doms. 2000. Understanding productivity: Lessons from longitudinal microdata. *Journal of Economic Literature* 33 (3): 569–594.

Bean, C., and N. Crafts. 1995. British economic growth since 1945: Relative economic decline . . . and renaissance? CEPR Discussion Paper no. 1092. London: Center for Economic Policy and Research.

Bean, C., and J. Symons. 1989. Ten years of Mrs. T. In *NBER macroeconomics annual 1989,* 13–61. Cambridge: MIT Press.

Bernard, A., and C. Jones. 1996a. Comparing apples to oranges: Productivity convergence and measurement across industries and countries. *American Economic Review* 86 (4): 1216–238.

———. 1996b. Productivity across industries and countries: Time series theory and evidence. *Review of Economics and Statistics* 78 (1): 135–146.

Blomström, M., and H. Persson. 1983. Foreign investment and spillover efficiency in an underdeveloped economy: Evidence from the Mexican manufacturing industry. *World Development* 11:493–501.

Cameron, G., J. Proudman, and S. Redding. 1998. Openness and its association with productivity growth in UK manufacturing industry. In *Openness and growth,* ed. J. Proudman and S. Redding, 173–211. London: Bank of England.

Caves, R. 1974. Multinational firms, competition and productivity in host-country markets. *Economica* 41:176–193.

———. 1998. Industrial organization and new findings on the turnover and mobility of firms. *Journal of Economic Literature* 36 (5): 1947–982.

Central Statistical Office (CSO). 1991. *Retail prices 1914–1990.* London: Her Majesty's Stationery Office.

———. 1996. Foreign direct investment 1996, business monitor MA4. London: Her Majesty's Stationery Office.

———. Various years. *Price index numbers for current cost accounting MM17.* London: Her Majesty's Stationery Office.

Conyon, M., S. Girma, S. Thompson, and P. Wright. 2002. The impact of foreign acquisition on wages and productivity in the UK. *Journal of Industrial Economics* 50:85–102.

Davies, S., and B. Lyons. 1991. Characterising relative performance: The productivity advantage of foreign owned firms in the UK. *Oxford Economic Papers* 43 (October): 584–595.

Disney, R., J. Haskel, and Y. Heden. 2003. Restructuring and productivity growth in UK manufacturing. *Economic Journal* 113 (489): 666–694.

Doms, M., and B. J. Jensen. 1998. Comparing wages, skills, and productivity between domestically and foreign-owned manufacturing establishments in the United States. In *Geography and ownership as bases for economic accounting,* ed. R. E. Lipsey, R. E. Baldwin, and J. D. Richardson, 235–258. Chicago: University of Chicago.

Dougherty, C., and D. Jorgenson. 1997. There is no silver bullet: Investment and growth in the G7. *National Institute Economic Review* 162 (October): 57–74.

Department of Trade and Industry (DTI). 1993. *Regional selective assistance 1985–1988: An evaluation by PA Cambridge Economic Consultants.* London: Her Majesty's Stationery Office.

Dunning, J. 1977. Trade, location of economic activity and MNE: A search for an eclectic approach. In *The international allocation of economic activity,* ed. B. Ohlin, P. O. Hesselborn, and P. M. Wijkman, 395–418. London: McMillan.

Edwards, S. 1998. Openness, productivity and growth: What do we really know? *The Economic Journal* 108 (447): 383–398.

Globerman, S. 1979. Foreign direct investment and spillover efficiency benefits in Canadian manufacturing industries. *Canadian Journal of Economics* 12 (1): 42–56.

Globerman, S., J. Ries, and I. Vertinsky. 1994. The economic performances of foreign-owned subsidiaries in Canada. *Canadian Journal of Economics* 27 (1): 143–156.

Griffith, R. 1999. Using the ARD establishment level data to look at foreign ownership and productivity in the UK. *Economic Journal* 109 (June): F416–F442.

Grossman, G., and E. Helpman. 1991. *Innovation and growth in the global economy.* Cambridge: MIT Press.

Grubert, H., and J. Mutti. 1991. Financial flows versus capital spending: Alternative measures of US-Canadian investment and trade in the analysis of taxes. In *International economic transactions, issues in measurement and empirical research,* ed. P. Hooper and J. D. Richardson, 293–317. Chicago: University of Chicago Press.

Hall, R. E. 1988. The relationship between price and marginal cost in U.S. industry. *Journal of Political Economy* 96:921–947.

Harris, R. I. D., and C. Robinson. 2002. The impact of foreign acquisitions on total factor productivity: Plant level evidence from UK manufacturing 1987–1992. *Review of Economics and Statistics* 84 (3): 562–568.

Howenstine, N., and W. Zeile. 1994. Characteristics of foreign-owned U.S. manufacturing establishments. *Survey of Current Business* 74 (1): 34–59.

Hsiao, C. 1986. *Analysis of panel data.* Cambridge: Cambridge University Press.

Klette, T. J. 1999. Market power, scale economies and productivity: Estimates from a panel of establishment data. *Journal of Industrial Economics* 47 (4): 451–476.

Krugman, P. R. 1991a. *Geography and trade.* Cambridge: MIT Press.

———. 1991b. Increasing returns and economic geography. *Journal of Political Economy* 99:483–499.

———. 1994. *Rethinking international trade.* Cambridge: MIT Press.

Lansbury, M. 1995. UK manufacturing employment since Beveridge: The chemical and motor vehicle industries. NIESR Discussion Paper no. 83. London: National Institute of Economic and Social Research.

Layard, R., and S. Nickell. 1989. The Thatcher miracle? *American Economic Review (Papers and Proceedings)* 79:215–219.

Mayes, D., ed. 1996. *Sources of productivity growth.* Cambridge: Cambridge University Press.

McKinsey Global Institute. 1998. Driving productivity and growth in the UK economy. London: McKinsey.

———. 1996. Competition and corporate performance. *Journal of Political Economy* 104:724–746.

Nickell, S. J., S. B. Wadhwani, and M. Wall. 1992. Productivity growth in UK companies, 1975–1986. *European Economic Review* 36:1055–085.

Office for National Statistics (ONS). 1997. Indexes to the standard industrial classification of economic activities 1992. London: The Stationery Office.

O'Mahony, M. 1999. *Britain's productivity performance 1950–1996: An international perspective.* London: National Institute of Economic and Social Research.

Oulton, N. 1997. The ABI respondents database: A new resource for industrial economics research. *Economic Trends* 528 (November): 46–57.

———. 1998. Investment, capital and foreign ownership in UK manufacturing. NIESR Discussion Paper no. 141. London: National Institute of Economic and Social Research.

Oulton, N., and M. O'Mahony. 1990. Industry-level estimates of the capital stock in UK manufacturing, 1948–85. NIESR Discussion Paper no. 172. London: National Institute of Economic and Social Research.

———. 1994. *Productivity and growth: A study of British industry 1954–1986.* London: National Institute of Economic and Social Research.

Perry, J. 1995. The inter-departmental business register. *Economic Trends* 505 (November): 27–30.

Smith, A. 1994. Strategic trade policy in the European car market. In *Empirical studies of strategic trade policy,* ed. P. Krugman and A. Smith, 63–83. Chicago: University of Chicago Press.

van Ark, B. 1996. Productivity and competitiveness in manufacturing: A comparison of Europe, Japan and the United States. In *International productivity differences: Measurement and explanations,* ed. K. Wagner and B. van Ark, 23–52. Amsterdam: North-Holland.
Venables, A. 1994. Trade policy under imperfect competition: A numerical assessment. In *Empirical studies of strategic trade policy,* ed. P. Krugman and A. Smith, 41–62. Chicago: University of Chicago Press.
Vernon, R. 1966. International investment and international trade in the product cycle. *Quarterly Journal of Economics* 80:190–207.

5

The Surprising Retreat of Union Britain

John Pencavel

5.1 Introduction

An assessment of unionism in a society may be organized around three classes of questions: Do unions produce a better distribution of income in society? Do unions contribute to a more efficient society? And do unions enhance a society's "social capital"?[1] The first two questions are the familiar distributional and efficiency considerations that figure in any interesting economic question. The third class of questions is less familiar to economists. It concerns aspects of social organization, such as civic responsibility and engagement, that enhance self-government and voluntary cooperation. Associations such as labor unions are an important component of a society's network of institutions that give individuals an opportunity to shape their environments and to promote mutual assistance. Collective bargaining can be a constructive force at the workplace to resolve problems that arise from the necessary incompleteness of labor contracts and, in this way, unionism has the potential of being an effective vehicle for representing workers' concerns and for influencing their work conditions.

John Pencavel is the Pauline K. Levin, Robert and Pauline C. Levin-Abraham Levin Professor in Humanities and Sciences, Department of Economics, Stanford University.

I have benefitted from comments on previous drafts of this paper by Richard Blundell, Alison Booth, Adam Seth Litwin, David Metcalf, Andrew Oswald, Norma Virgoe, and an anonymous referee. Research assistance from Benjamin Liu is acknowledged.

1. While *physical* capital and *human* capital refer to the machines and skills that augment an organization's or an individual's productivity, *social* capital alludes to aspects of the social structure such as trust, networks, and conventions that encourage collaboration and coordination for shared advantage. Social capital is not embodied in a single organization or single individual, but in the relations among organizations and individuals. See Coleman (1988).

At the same time, unionism has the potential to be a destructive agent. It can frustrate cooperation, incite antagonisms, and create hardship. Whether, on balance, unionism is a source that adds to or detracts from a society's "social capital" is a matter for determination in any particular context.

In the context of Britain over the past forty years or so, the condition of unionism has changed remarkably. In the 1970s, the union movement in Britain appeared strong: the leadership was consulted on important matters of economic policy, union membership and density were rising, and a royal commission (the Bullock Commission) proposed putting union leaders on company boards. This strength arose not because collective bargaining was explicitly supported by a favorable statutory framework, but because various indirect ways had been devised to promote unionism. This indirect support had been nurtured by governments of different political stripe and found favor with the electorate, which habitually expressed approval of collective-bargaining as a system for determining labor contracts.

This broad consensus broke down by the close of the 1970s. There were several reasons for this. Increasingly, Britain's lackluster productivity performance was attributed to restrictive work practices enforced by unions. The system of collective bargaining was implicated in the accelerating rate of price inflation. A succession of strikes imposed a good deal of hardship on the community. For these and perhaps other reasons, the public's support for unionism reached a low point in 1979 when a new government was elected to power. Even though public support for unionism recovered quickly, the new government pursued an active policy of taming the power and reach of unions. It was as if, in the relatively brief moment of the electorate's disenchantment with unionism, the government seized the opportunity to curb collective bargaining over the subsequent fifteen years or so and to subject it to disciplines that have left it debilitated. The retreat of unionism is illustrated by the drop in the fraction of workers who are union members in figure 5.1 and by the decline in strike activity in figure 5.2. By the year 2000, unionism's role in private industry looks precarious, especially in light of its difficulty in organizing new establishments. I have found nothing in the writing in the 1970s on unions and industrial relations that forecast this change in fortunes. From the perspective of the 1970s, this retreat of union Britain is surprising.

This experience raises many important questions. What caused unionism's retreat? How has the decline in collective bargaining affected the growth and distribution of incomes? What is the prevailing link between productivity and unionism? How has the decline in unionism affected the workplace experience of employees? How have unions themselves been affected by this reduced status? Answers to these questions are offered in this paper, drawing heavily on previous research and making use especially of the detailed data derived from the four Workplace Industrial Relations

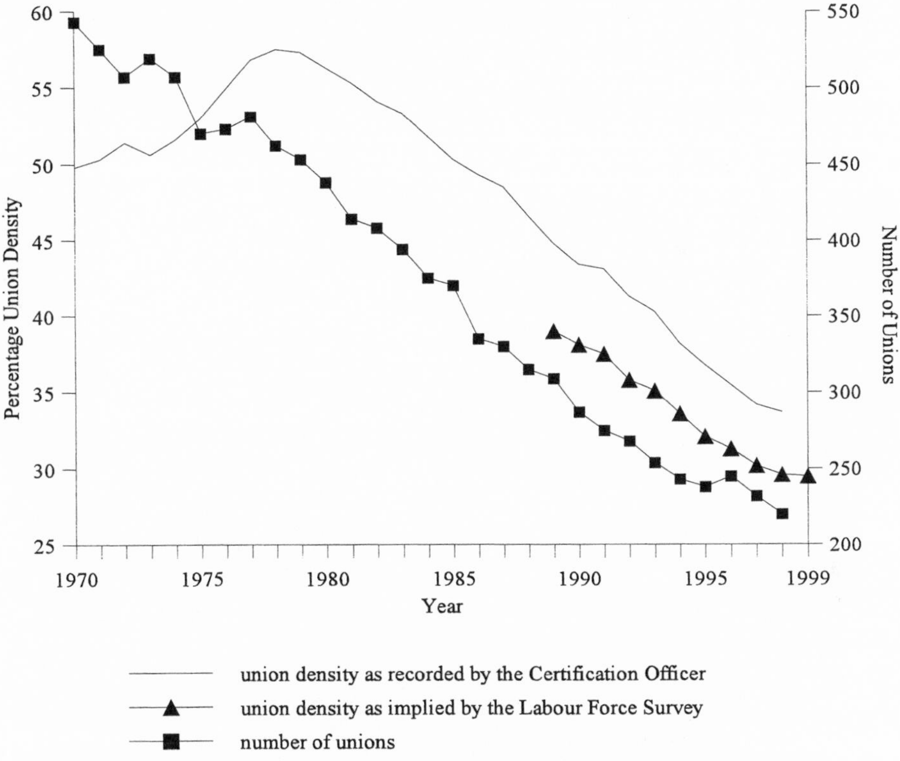

Fig. 5.1 Number of unions and union membership density, 1970–1999
Sources: Data drawn from issues of the *Employment Gazette* and *Labour Market Trends.*

surveys conducted in Britain in 1980, 1984, 1990, and 1998.[2] This and other information will be used to describe the changes that have taken place. However, while these and other data allow for a *description* of the changes, identifying causal relations requires a heavy dose of judgment. Indeed, the perennial problem with issues in labor relations is in unscrambling causal relationships where the key forcing variables are often unmeasured or poorly measured.

The paper proceeds by sketching the state of unionism in the 1960s and 1970s, arguing that, unlike in most other countries, British unionism was nurtured less by explicit statutory support and more by various indirect mechanisms. Because of the importance of these indirect mechanisms, the statutory reforms in the 1980s and 1990s were probably of less consequence

2. Though linked to the earlier surveys, the 1998 survey was renamed the Workplace Employee Relations Survey (WERS). The Workplace Industrial Relations surveys will be referenced subsequently as WIRS (year) and, in 1998, as WERS (1998).

Fig. 5.2 Disputes, 1970–1999

Sources: Data on stoppages are taken from issues of the *Employment Gazette* and *Labour Market Trends.*

in accounting for the decline of unionism than the withdrawal of the state's indirect support for collective bargaining. Perhaps the principal goal of the reforms was to break the link between unionism and low productivity, so the paper addresses what is known about unions and productivity with special emphasis on what remains of the association between productivity and unionism in the late 1990s. Some original research on this issue is presented. Section 5.5 asks how workers are benefitting from unionism today, and general conclusions complete the paper.

5.2 The Condition of Unionism in the 1960s and 1970s

5.2.1 General Overview

In the 1960s and 1970s, Britain's labor markets and industrial relations practices came under increasing scrutiny. This was manifested not only in extensive public debate of the issues and the establishment of a royal commission (the Donovan Commission) in 1965, but also in an increasingly active statutory agenda. A principal reason for this scrutiny grew out of the realization that Britain's rate of economic growth was inferior to that of almost all comparable economies and that Britain frequently scored poorly in comparisons of productivity across countries. Many explanations were offered for these chastening international comparisons, but the role of industrial relations was frequently alluded to.

For example, Pratton's (1976) comparison of the productivity of companies with operations in more than one country in the early 1970s found that those company divisions in Britain had a poor productivity record, and he ascribed an important part of this to union-enforced restrictive work practices, overmanning, and strikes. Prais's (1981) study of manufacturing industry came to similar sobering conclusions about British productivity and again identified the poor state of labor relations in Britain as partly responsible. One feature of British industrial relations that came in for frequent censure in accounting for these productivity patterns was the multiplicity of unionism. Such a union structure was said to contribute to jurisdictional disputes and to give undue emphasis to the interests of narrow occupational groups.[3]

However, by the end of the 1970s, the link established by economists between unionism and productivity was circumstantial. Though some case studies indicated that unions were defending work practices that harmed productivity, sufficient evidence had not been accumulated to justify a statement to the effect that, in general, unionism harmed productivity.[4] Nevertheless, this belief came to be widely shared and contributed to the view that unions were a drag on productivity and economic growth.

In their distributional activities, the popular view was that unions were involved in a constant effort to reallocate incomes away from dividends and interest and toward wages and salaries. In fact, economists brought forward little evidence that unionism materially affected the distribution of national income in this way.[5] More attention was directed to the association between unionism and individual earnings. The first empirical studies of union-nonunion wage gaps in Britain were appearing in the 1970s, but the available data at that time did not permit confident inferences. Subse-

3. See, for instance, Aylen's (1982) study of the steel industry in Britain, Germany, and the United States.

4. Metcalf's useful surveys (1989, 1990) list only two relevant studies prior to 1980 and one of these relates to unionism before the First World War.

5. In the classic account of movements in the share of wages in national income in Britain by Phelps Brown and Hart (1952), unions are given a role, but it is largely a secondary one: "The course of the trade cycle brought . . . changes in the effective strength of trade unions. From time to time there were some greater and in part exogenous changes in union strength. Whether these changes affected the relative size of wages and profits depended on the market environment" (274).

quent research suggests that the wage gaps were modest. For instance, Stewart (1991) estimates union-nonunion wage gaps in 1980 of almost 7 percent for semiskilled workers and 2 percent for skilled workers.[6] This suggests that unionism had modest effects on the wage structure.

However, unions' efforts to redistribute incomes toward wages contributed to chronic upward pressure on wages and prices. When a firm or industry experiences wage increases induced by collective bargaining, typically a contraction in employment and output is to be expected. The issue then becomes the policymaking authorities' response to this wage-induced employment reduction. Britain's tragic experience with unemployment between the two world wars[7] caused governments to give a very high priority to maintaining full employment, and this strong aversion to allowing unemployment to rise tended to make wages one of the fixed points in the system to which other variables adjusted.[8] In Hicks' (1955) words, no longer was the British economy on the "Gold Standard" but on a "Labour Standard."[9]

With the aim of moderating wage increases without inducing a rise in unemployment, governments invited unions into policymaking circles and encouraged them to participate in programs aimed to restrict the growth of all types of money incomes. These were largely fruitless in that, after removing the effects of the business cycle, wage inflation tended to rise inexorably and the unemployment rate seemed to rise along with it. The form of this policy in the last Labour government of the 1970s, the so-called Social Contract, fell apart amid a wave of strikes in 1978–1979. But until Keynesian demand-management policies were totally discarded in the 1980s, the dominant ideas in macroeconomic policy provided an environment that accorded unions an influential role in the management of the economy.[10]

6. In the special case of workplaces with a pre-entry closed shop, these gaps were larger: 15 percent for semiskilled and 10 percent for skilled workers.

7. From 1921 until the outbreak of the Second World War, national insurance unemployment rates were above 10 percent for every year except 1927, when the unemployment rate was 9.7 percent.

8. Another fixed point was the foreign exchange rate, although several times devaluation was the chosen option to adjust to macroeconomic disequilibrium.

9. Hicks (1955, 391) wrote, "[T]he world we now live in is one in which the monetary system has become relatively elastic, so that it can accommodate itself to changes in wages, rather than the other way about. Instead of actual wages having to adjust themselves to an equilibrium level, monetary policy adjusts to the equilibrium level of money wages so as to make it conform to the actual level. It is hardly an exaggeration to say that instead of being on a Gold Standard, we are on a Labour Standard."

10. In fact, the first signs of the rejection of Keynesianism came from elements in Callaghan's Labour government of the 1970s. In response to yet another run on the pound, in 1976, the chancellor of the exchequer, Dennis Healey, proposed radical reductions in public expenditure and the prime minister told the Labour Party Conference, "You cannot spend your way out of recession." Subsequently, an abashed government sought a loan from the International Monetary Fund (IMF) that came with further strings attached in the form of cuts in public expenditure. The contradictions of a Labour government with close ties to the trade union movement pursuing balanced budget policies that conflicted with union aspirations finally brought the government down in 1979.

Hence, by the 1970s, it is difficult to make the case that unions in Britain enhanced productivity or materially improved the distribution of income in society. However, unions were often a force for involving employees in shaping their work environments. The scope of collective bargaining had widened considerably beyond issues of wages and work hours. Unions were involved in issues of work assignment, the speed and organization of production, workplace health and safety, and procedures for the laying off of workers. Indeed, these were often the very same issues that gave rise to questions about the effects of unionism on productivity. By involving themselves in such matters, union representatives at the place of work gave employees a sense of participation. The trouble is that, in some instances, this participation was accompanied with hostile and obstructionist postures. Furthermore, in pursuing their goals, unions became increasingly tolerant of the costs imposed on the community in the form of highly disruptive strikes. In this respect, unionism in the 1970s tended to heighten antagonisms within society rather than act as a force for civic engagement and cohesion.

5.2.2 Strikes

Because each country's definition of disputes tends to differ, meaningful comparisons of strike activity across countries are notoriously difficult to make. However, taking the data at face value, by international standards, British unions in the 1970s did not appear reluctant to invoke the strike weapon. In the seventeen countries listed in table 5.1 for the 1970s, the United Kingdom ranks in the top half of strike-prone economies. The year 1979 stands out as the particular "winter of discontent" that presaged Margaret Thatcher's electoral victory. When the strikes were against monopolies, they tended to impose considerable hardship on the community. In addition, there was evidence to suggest that the nature of these strikes damaged productivity.[11]

The vast majority of strikes were unofficial in that they occurred without following specified procedures for settling disagreements. Often, the national unions did not sanction them. Indeed, in many instances, the national leadership might be quite surprised by them, although, to grant the strikes greater legitimacy and to exert some control over them, the national union would sometimes declare the strikes "official" after they had begun.

The key figures in these unofficial strikes were the union officials at the place of work, the shop stewards. To many workers, the shop steward was

11. For instance, in his research on productivity in manufacturing, Prais (1981, 262–263) emphasized the frequency of strikes in large plants: "Not only are more man-days lost per employee in Britain, but there are added costs from the greater frequency of stoppages, verging in some plants on continuous disruption; British management in large plants is not able to devote its main energies to the pursuit of more efficient production methods, since so much time is taken up in 'fire fighting' to keep the plant at work. . . . The present so-called 'voluntary approach' to industrial relations seems to have been an important factor that has made large-scale production uncompetitive in this country."

Table 5.1 **Working Days Lost through Stoppages per Thousand Employees in All Industries and Services, Annual Averages, 1971–1980**

Country	1979	1971–75	1976–80	1971–80
United Kingdom	1,291	585	566	575
Australia	795	728	596	662
Belgium	199	236	219	228
Canada	837	919	864	892
Denmark	83	436	92	264
Finland	133	753	615	684
France	207	232	186	209
West Germany	22	57	52	54
Ireland	1,757	415	1,064	739
Italy	1,659	1,367	1,174	1,271
Japan	24	188	43	115
The Netherlands	77	43	30	37
New Zealand	373	150	378	264
Norway	4	52	42	47
Spain	2,288	141	1,749	856
Sweden	7	85	241	163
United States	388	484	420	452

Source: Employment Gazette (February 1982, 69).

Notes: Stoppages cover both strikes and lock-outs. Definitions and coverage of stoppages vary across countries, so these data should not be relied upon to justify strong inferences about intercountry differences.

the human face of the union movement while the national union leadership consisted of remote figures with little understanding and knowledge of the particular issues at an employee's place of work. Unofficial strikes tended to be short and they tended to be unpredictable except to some of those people at the place of work. Some saw unofficial strikes as the assertion by workers of their control over their workplaces, a form of syndicalism. Official strikes tended to be national (rather than local), longer, and more predictable. It was often argued that it was the unpredictable nature of unofficial strikes that made them more costly to employers than the more predictable official strikes and, therefore, the sort of reforms most desirable were those that reduced the incidence of the unofficial strikes.[12]

5.2.3 A Voluntary System

According to the conventional account, British unionism flourished with little direct statutory support. Whereas many countries closely regulated and nurtured unionism by statutory legislation, such direct support

12. The Donovan Commission, for example, declared, "We have no hesitation therefore in saying that the prevalence of unofficial strikes, and their tendency (outside coalmining) to increase, have such serious economic implications that measures to deal with them are urgently necessary" (United Kingdom: Royal Commission, 1968a, 112).

of collective bargaining was remarkably absent in Britain. What distinguished Britain among industrialized countries by the 1970s was the degree to which unionism evolved largely independent of direct regulation by the state. There is nothing in Britain comparable to America's National Labor Relations Act or Australia's Conciliation and Arbitration Act, an encompassing piece of statutory legislation providing a definitive reference for the regulation of unionism and collective bargaining.

Illustrative of the prevailing attitudes toward unionism was the process by which unions became recognized by employers. Until the 1970s, there was no machinery to permit workers to select union representation nor to require an employer to recognize a union of his workers.[13] Indeed, "yellow-dog" contracts, long outlawed in the United States, were not only legal in Britain, but in some firms still invoked.[14] As a group strongly supporting collective bargaining, the Donovan Commission deplored the lack of formal procedures to handle the issue of union recognition and the disputes that sometimes resulted.[15] However, to an American audience familiar with the formal procedures enshrined in the National Labor Relations Act to deal with union recognition and representation, what is remarkable is the high union density achieved in Britain without legalistic machinery designed to force unionism on reluctant employers.

In the 1970s, the historical narrative of British unionism highlighted a relatively modest piece of legislation, the Trade Disputes Act of 1906. This established that a union could not be sued by an employer for damages resulting from a strike. This immunity had been the practice until 1901, when the House of Lords ruled otherwise in the Taff Vale case, and the 1906 act restored the unions' rights in law. Prior to the 1980s, this act giving a union

13. The 1975 Employment Protection Act gave the Advisory, Conciliation, and Arbitration Service (ACAS) the task of resolving disputes over union recognition. However, as ACAS was also given the duty of "encouraging the extension of collective bargaining," employers resistant to union recognition saw ACAS not as a neutral arbiter, but as another arm of the union movement. Because employers were not compelled by law to cooperate with ACAS, ultimately its authority was eroded and it became ineffectual. See the description of its activities and a comparison with union recognition procedures in North America in Wood and Godard (1999).

14. A "yellow-dog" contract is a document signed by a worker who, as a condition of employment, promises not to join a union. Examples of such contracts in Britain were provided by the Donovan Commission (United Kingdom: Royal Commission 1968b, 54–55).

15. In its evidence to the Donovan Commission, the Trades Union Congress wrote colorfully: "It may from some points of view be unfortunate that many employers only recognize the strength of trade unionism when this strength is exercised overtly in the form of strike action, but it is undoubtedly a fact that strike action to secure trade union recognition is by far the most successful method of dragging such employers into the twentieth century and at the same time, through its stimulus to the trade union recruitment, of exposing the oft-heard shibboleth that it is only a few troublemakers who are claiming to represent the interests of the employees. Strike action to force trade union recognition is a good example of the principle that industrial peace is not the same thing as good industrial relations. Strike action to secure recognition is often the pre-condition for improving industrial relations" (United Kingdom: Royal Commission 1968b, 171).

immunity from litigation stemming from costs imposed on an employer through a strike was often singled out as the most important statute underpinning British unionism. Though an important piece of legislation, the act is remarkable by international standards for what little it did. For instance, unlike other countries' major pieces of statutory law on collective bargaining, this act did not precisely specify rules about the formation of unions and the manner in which collective bargaining was to be conducted. On the contrary, up to the 1970s, Britain's industrial relations are distinctive among wealthy economies for the small role played by statutory legislation.

The exceptions to this statement concern the years of and immediately following the two world wars when the state played a much more intrusive role in collective bargaining and these actions had lasting effects. In addition, there was a period between 1971 and 1974 when an Industrial Relations Act specified collective-bargaining agreements to be legally enforceable contracts unless the parties specified otherwise. In fact, in these years, contracts routinely inserted disclaimer clauses of the form "this is not a legally enforceable agreement." The act was largely inconsequential because it was boycotted by most unions and it was repealed by the Labour government in 1974. With these important exceptions, private employers and unions in Britain have usually found it in their interest to reach agreements without the law's compelling them to do so or how to go about it. This is why it was often described as a "voluntary" system and it allowed Henry Phelps Brown (1959, 355) to write, "When British industrial relations are compared with those of other democracies they stand out because they are so little regulated by law."

In Britain, there was no law obliging private employers to bargain with unions nor anything making collective-bargaining agreements enforceable in a court. Unlike in many other countries, no statement in law exists that gives workers the right to strike. Collective-bargaining agreements have an "untidy" appearance in that some cover all workers over the entire country in a particular industry while others are restricted to a small group of workers within a particular plant. Some unions represent workers in a large number of different industries while other unions organize a small number of workers. The law in Britain has taken the position that these issues are best determined by the parties concerned with little need for state regulation.

5.2.4 Indirect Support of Collective Bargaining

This popular characterization of unionism in Britain before the 1980s is misleading. First, in its capacity as an employer, the state championed collective bargaining and, given the important role of the state as an employer by the 1970s, this implied that a large section of the economy was covered by legislation promoting unionism. Second, even in the private sector of the economy, the state intruded to encourage unionism, but this intrusion was largely *indirect.* Third, the Keynesian macroeconomic policies followed by successive governments in the 1960s and 1970s provided a hospitable climate for unionism.

First, consider the role of the state as an employer. The support of collective bargaining in public employment went back at least to the Whitley Committee reports of the Great War.[16] In the 1920s, while unionism was languishing in private industry, the notion that employees of the state should be represented by unions was widely accepted.[17] The Second World War saw similar pressures to those in the First World War and, immediately after the war, the nationalization of major industries resulted in the establishment of public corporations which were legally required to recognize trade unions and to set up collective-bargaining machinery. The consequence was that the employees of all public corporations were represented by unions and had their terms of employment settled through collective bargaining. By 1980, union density among full-time employees of nationalized industries was 97 percent and that in public administration (principally, local and central government) was 89 percent.[18] At that time, about 31 percent of workers were employed in public administration or employed by public corporations, so a significant fraction of all employees worked for an employer—the state—that expressly promoted collective bargaining for its workers.

Furthermore, government encouraged private employers to recognize unions. It did so not by setting up procedures by which workers may determine whether they wanted union representation. On the contrary, as noted above, British law had been largely silent on the issue of union recognition. However, the law did specify consequences if an employer refused to recognize a union. This became explicit during the Second World War when the National Arbitration Tribunal could impose on a nonunion firm wages and working conditions that the tribunal felt appropriate. When presented

16. The outbreak and furtherance of the Great War gave a boost to the role of trade union leaders in the administration of industry and government. This helped to portray unions as responsible organizations representing the legitimate interests of working people. Simultaneously, tight labor markets gave labor organizations at the factory floor the sort of muscle that was largely denied them before the war. To contain the shop stewards' movement, David Lloyd George's Coalition government appointed in 1916 a committee under the chairmanship of J. H. Whitley, a Liberal member of Parliament, to suggest ways "for securing a permanent improvement in the relations between employers and employed." The reports of the Whitley committees encouraged the recognition by employers of unions and proposed, in sectors where unions were well-established, a hierarchical structure of employer-union industrial councils designed to discuss and negotiate wages, work hours, and other aspects of employment contracts. The reports embraced public employment as well as private employment and, though the government was initially resistant to accord unions rights of negotiation and representation, soon government employees found themselves so represented.

17. The House of Commons debated in 1923 a resolution stating "that local authorities, banks, insurance and shipping companies, and other employers of professional and clerical workers should follow the example of the Government in recognizing the organizations of these workers." Receiving broad support, the resolution passed without division on a free vote.

18. See table II.1 of Daniel and Millward (1983).

with the possibility of having terms of employment imposed on them by the state, many nonunion employers felt it preferable to recognize a union and engage in collective bargaining to ensure it had some role in determining its wages. Such compulsory measures were made less draconian in peacetime. Nevertheless, by a series of Fair Wages resolutions, those private-sector employers with government contracts were obliged to pay their workers wages set by collective bargaining in neighboring or comparable firms.[19]

Another mechanism bolstering collective bargaining in Britain was provided by minimum-wage regulation. Unlike in France and the United States, where minimum-wage laws embrace almost all blue-collar workers, Britain's minimum-wage regulation had been selective. For instance, with legislation in 1917, agriculture was identified as an industry warranting wage floors and other low-wage sectors (such as retail trade and catering) were added subsequently by the establishment of sector-specific wages councils.[20] By 1980, among employers outside of collective bargaining, about one-third of managers claimed that the pay of their manual workers was set by wages councils.[21] Such wage-setting machinery was regarded as inferior to collective bargaining and the expressed hope was that, in due course, the wages councils would be supplanted by union-negotiated agreements. In practice, wages councils set wages with reference to those negotiated by unions in neighboring industries. The consequence was to extend union wage regulation to sectors beyond those where unions were explicitly organized.

There were other ways in which government lent indirect support to

19. Otto Kahn-Freund regarded the 1946 Fair Wages Resolution as "one of the cornerstones of British labour law" while Wedderburn described it as "at least a prop for the British structure of collective bargaining" (Wedderburn 1986, 347–349). (The 1946 Fair Wages Resolution was preceded by analogous resolutions in 1891 and 1909.) The extension of collectively bargained wages to workers not covered by the collective agreements was effected by arbitration by the Ministry of Labour between 1940 to 1959. The same principle was enshrined in the terms and conditions of the Employment Act of 1959 (see United Kingdom: Royal Commission 1968a, 60–61). The Employment Protection Act of 1975 set up the Central Arbitration Committee, which had the power to oblige employers of nonunion labor to observe those terms of employment obtaining in similar unionized activities or in the same district. This was rescinded in the 1980 Employment Act. In September 1983, the Fair Wages Resolution was annulled.

20. It is intriguing to note that, whereas in Britain agriculture was singled out early for statutory wage regulation, in the United States it was singled out for exclusion from the Fair Labor Standards Act in 1938. The exclusion of farm workers from various pieces of New Deal legislation was engineered in the U.S. Congress by Southern legislators who faithfully represented the interests of Southern landowners. See Alton and Ferrie (1999).

21. See Daniel and Millward (1983, 179–180). The authors maintain that these responses exaggerate the extent of wage regulation by the councils because "First, . . . some managers erroneously took negotiating bodies like Whitley Councils or joint industrial councils to be wages councils. . . . Secondly, . . . some establishments that did not recognize unions adopted the rates specified by some wages council . . . as the basis for their rates of pay, even though formally they were not bound by those rates." In either event, through error or voluntary consent, a substantial number of nonunion employers set wages in relation to those specified by regulatory bodies.

unionism. One took the form of discouraging competition in product markets. A monopolistic or oligopolistic firm normally provides a much more hospitable environment for unions to survive and flourish than a competitive firm, so government may influence the extent and strength of unionism by its posture toward product market competition.

Though its origins can be traced to the nineteenth century,[22] the view that competitive markets would produce the least objectionable outcomes for society became an increasingly unfashionable doctrine in Britain as the twentieth century evolved. Again, the Great War was a catalyst in this development because the successful conduct of the war was seen to require a sudden and extensive intrusion of the state in all kinds of activities. When peace was restored, some looked to restore a modest role for the state. However, many others had become accustomed to an interventionist state and they viewed the state as the primary vehicle for effecting change within British industry, which was diagnosed as too small and balkanized to compete effectively in international markets with larger and more efficient American and German companies. In the 1920s, the "rationalisation" of British industry was the label given to mergers and takeovers that the state expressly encouraged to create benefits of large economies of scale.[23]

In the interwar period, the monopolization and oligopolization of industry occurred with ownership remaining in private hands. In the years after the Second World War, the same process took the form of creating public monopolies covering large swathes of industry—electricity, gas, coal, railways, urban transport, airlines, telecommunications, and (for many years) steel. The dominant philosophy behind the "rationalisation" movement in the 1920s and the nationalization movement after the Second World War was one of skepticism of the virtues of competition and approval of large and monopolistic enterprises.

Labor unions firmly supported the nationalization of industry. Some unionists believed public ownership of industry would eliminate the adversarial nature of bargaining, but this tenet was soon belied by highly contested disputes whether government was in the hands of the Labour Party or the Conservative Party. Public ownership tended to politicize collective bargaining, with government ministers entangled in disputes that were resolved often with little relation to the financial performance of the industries. Being monopolies, these nationalized industries' strikes imposed heavy costs on consumers.

Hence, in summary, collective bargaining in Britain by the end of the 1970s was frequently described as a "voluntary" system because the law was largely silent on important issues such as union recognition, the re-

22. The classic statement of these trends is, of course, found in Dicey (1914).
23. On rationalization in the 1920s, see Robinson (1931, 169) who defines it as the "semi-compulsory reorganisation" of industry.

quirement to bargain, the enforcement of collective-bargaining agreements, the right to strike, and the structure of unionism. The dominant attitude up to the end of the 1970s was that these factors were best addressed by the parties concerned, with little need for state regulation.[24] However, this characterization is misleading in that, through a number of *indirect* channels, government in Britain exercised a large influence on unionism and collective bargaining. By its activities as an employer, by setting minimum wages in selected industries, by requiring government contractors often to pay union-negotiated wages, and by discouraging product market competition, the state played an important indirect role. In these activities, the state encouraged collective bargaining and helped to create the conditions in nonunion labor markets and in product markets that fostered unionism.[25] On top of this, as noted above, the macroeconomic policies followed by successive postwar British governments and especially the importance attached to the goal of full employment provided the backdrop for unions to assume a conspicuous role in the formation and execution of economic policy.

In providing this indirect support for collective bargaining and unionism, the Labour and Conservative governments from the Second World War to the 1970s were responding to the dominant views in the country. Until 1979, when asked "Generally speaking, do you think trade unions are a good thing or a bad thing?" the percentage responding "a good thing" always exceeded the percentage responding "a bad thing" (see fig. 5.3). Only once, in fact (shortly after the miners' strike in 1974), was the percentage responding "a good thing" less than 50 percent.[26] The state's indirect support of collective bargaining, therefore, appeared to be more or less what the electorate wanted. This was not an instance where a small, yet influential, pressure group hijacks government policy to further its own ends without the general public's acquiescence. On the contrary, whatever doubts economists may have had about the beneficial effects of unionism, a majority of the electorate had a benign and favorable view of unionism.[27]

24. As noted above, Edward Heath's Conservative government at the beginning of the 1970s took a very different posture, but it was not acting with a mandate to make industrial relations more legalistic. Indeed, when asked in February 1974, "Who runs the country?" the electorate did not give Heath's government the ringing endorsement it was seeking.

25. Roy Adams (1993, 295) makes a similar argument: "Despite the absence of extensive legislation, the policy of British governments in the 20th century has not been neutral, as the policy of voluntarism is sometimes interpreted to imply. In fact, British policy has been to encourage collective bargaining. It has done so by notifying all public servants that collective bargaining is the preferred means of establishing conditions of work, by requiring government suppliers to recognize the freedom of their workers to join unions and engage in collective bargaining, and by directly intervening in many disputes in order to pressure intransigent employers to recognize unions and to negotiate with them."

26. A discussion of these Gallup Opinion Poll responses from 1954 to 1985 is provided by Edwards and Bain (1988) and Marsh (1990).

27. Along with the dominant view of the electorate, some employers felt workers were entitled to the protections and representations of labor unions and, instead of fighting them, some employers readily acceded rights of union representation to their workers. This was by

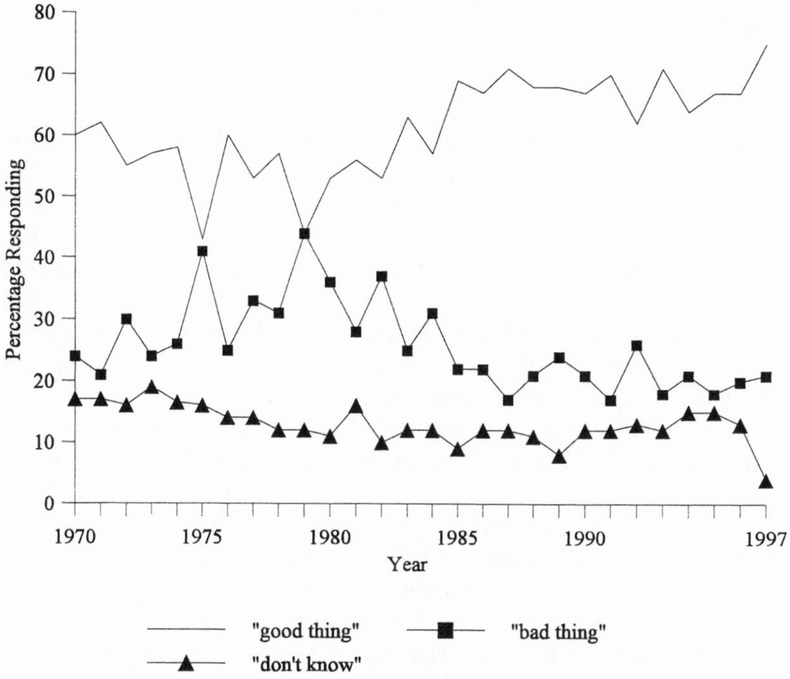

Fig. 5.3 Responses to survey question about trade unions, 1970–1997

Sources: The Gallup Political and Economic Index, the Gallup Organization, and the Daily Telegraph.

Notes: Percentage responding "a good thing," "a bad thing," and "don't know" (or who refused to respond) to the question, "Generally speaking, do you think trade unions are a good thing or a bad thing?" There were two surveys in 1974 and the entry in the graph for this year is a simple average of the two responses.

In the almost forty years from the outbreak of the Second World War to some point in the 1970s, there was broad consensus regarding the appropriate posture toward unionism: there should be a minimum of direct statutory promotion of unionism but considerable indirect support. This view was explicitly challenged by Edward Heath's Conservative Government in the early 1970s and issues concerning unionism figured prominently in the 1974 general election campaign. However, the government's attempt to convert the system into something closer to the American legalistic structure was not endorsed by the electorate. At the same time, the Labour Party's small margin of victory in February 1974 was a signal that the broad consensus on unionism was breaking down.

no means universal: some employers (especially those operating in highly competitive product markets) stoutly resisted union representation of their workers and actively opposed attempts to organize workers. Nevertheless, in other instances, employers saw unions as the rightful agents of their employees' concerns.

5.3 The New Policy toward Unionism

5.3.1 The Change in Economic Policy

After a winter of extensive strikes in 1978–1979, the general public tired of the corporatist style of the Labour government in which labor union leaders sometimes seemed to occupy a separate arm of government. For the first time in its history, the Gallup Organization's question asking, "Generally speaking, do you think trade unions are a good thing or a bad thing?" revealed in 1979 that an equal percentage of the British public replied "bad thing" as "good thing" (see fig. 5.3). Remarkably, the corresponding Gallup Opinion Poll in the United States also recorded a record low approval percentage in the same year.[28]

In 1979, an unhappy electorate voted in the most doctrinaire British government since Clement Atlee's administration elected in 1945. In contrast to Atlee's government, Thatcher's government was committed to shrinking the public sector and emasculating corporatist institutions such as labor unions. Sure enough, the subsequent Conservative governments reduced the state's indirect support of unionism and collective bargaining by denationalizing a number of industries, by eliminating minimum-wage floors in specific industries, and by suspending the rules extending union wage scales to non-union employers.

The ideas for reform came in part from the growing influence of laissez faire critics who viewed the state of Britain's labor markets as illustrative of the pervasive and suffocating role of government on the economy. Britain's sluggish economic growth and the habitual tendency for inflation to get out of control induced the search for more drastic policies. The dominance of the two-party system in Britain meant that, by the late 1970s, the electorate looked to the opposition party, the Conservative Party, for new ideas. Within the Conservative Party, the middle-of-the-road policies associated with R. A. Butler and Harold Macmillan in the 1950s and 1960s had given way to more radical ideas. The key individual funneling laissez faire ideas from the right wing into the Conservative Party in the late 1970s was Keith Joseph who, in turn, had the ear of the party's leader, Margaret Thatcher.[29]

28. The U.S. question is, "Do you approve or disapprove of labor unions?" From 1936 to 1972, the percentage responding "approve" was 60 or above. Then, in the 1970s, a decline began that reached a minimum of 55 percent in May 1979 and August 1981. Since then, the approval percentage has climbed to 65 percent in August 1999. See Cornfield (1999).

29. The arguments of Friedrich Hayek and Milton Friedman were widely disseminated. Hayek, in British Broadcasting Corporation broadcasts in 1978, argued, "These legalised powers [from the 1906 Trade Disputes Act] of the unions have become the biggest obstacle to raising the living standards of the working class as a whole. They are the chief cause of the unnecessarily big differences between the best- and worst-paid workers. They are the prime source of unemployment. They are the main reason for the decline of the British economy in general." (Reproduced in Hayek 1980, 52.)

Trade unions were one of the principal issues of the day, so what was the new government's posture on unions and collective bargaining? Two key elements can be identified, one concerning macroeconomic management of the economy and the other relating to productivity. On macroeconomic policy, incomes policies and the bargains with unions to secure their cooperation in wage restraint were to be a thing of the past. The postwar Keynesianism that accorded full employment a primacy of place in policy goals and that provided such a hospitable environment for unionism was dropped. The pursuit of price stability became the paramount goal and control over the money supply was supposed to be the principal means.

On productivity and economic growth, by supporting a culture of restrictive work practices (especially in public-sector employment) and adversarial labor relations, unions (together with unimaginative management and excessive government regulation) were blamed for Britain's poor performance. The aspects of industrial relations marked for special attention were strikes, the closed shop, and union governance. Frequent strikes were viewed not only as inconveniencing the community, but also as damaging productivity. The closed shop was seen as making "it possible for small groups to close down whole industries with which they have no direct connection."[30] On union governance, there was a belief that the union leadership tended to be more radical than the rank and file, so the Conservative government proposed making unions more accountable to their members. In general, the goal of greater labor productivity required a shake-up of industrial relations and the trimming of trade union entitlements.

Looking at subsequent events, some components of this program were certainly met: The macroeconomic environment became much less amenable to unionism although price stability proved to be elusive. Labor union entitlements were clipped, industrial relations practices changed substantially, closed shops became rare, union governance reformed, and strike activity fell sharply. Has this caused a higher growth in productivity? This is less clear. Let us consider these issues in turn. First, consider the changes in the macroeconomic environment and how legislation on strikes, the closed shop, union governance, and indirect support for unionism changed after 1979. The issue of unionism and productivity merits special attention in the section that follows.

5.3.2 The Macroeconomic Setting and Structural Changes in the Economy

The overriding goal of macroeconomic policy was to eradicate inflationary tendencies from the economy, a goal shared by macroeconomic managers in some other countries. The chosen mechanism was a gradual

30. From Margaret Thatcher's speech to the Conservative Party Conference in Blackpool on 12 October 1979. See Harris (1997).

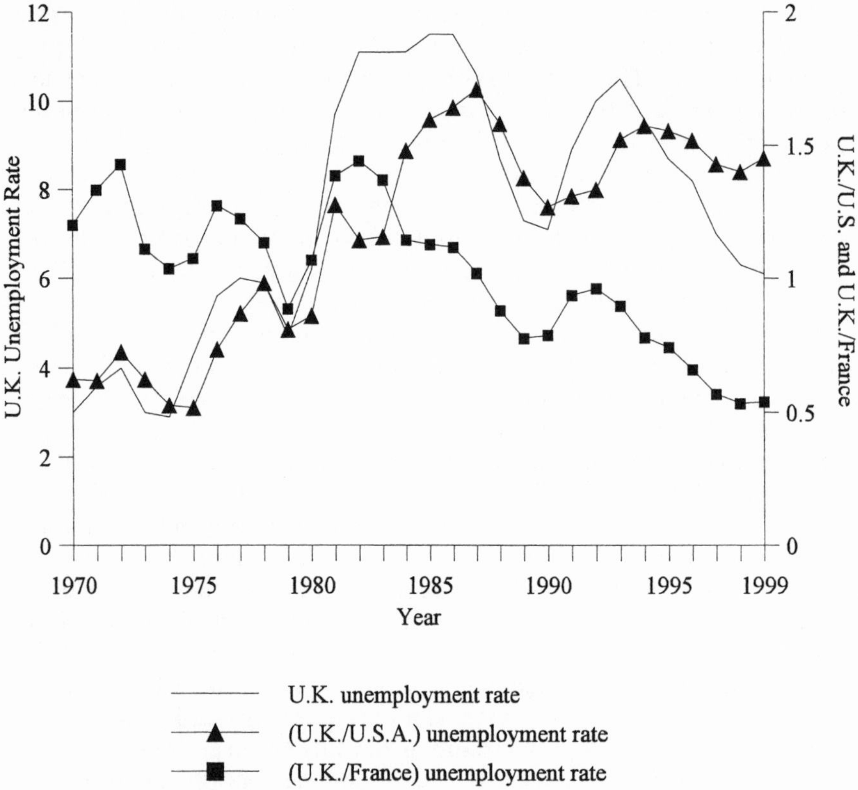

Fig. 5.4 U.K. unemployment rate, absolute and relative to unemployment rates in the United States and France, 1970–1999

Sources: The unemployment rates in this graph are "standardized" unemployment rates from the OECD, drawn from issues of OECD's *Economic Outlook.*

reduction in the rate of growth of the money supply coupled with a reduction in the public-sector borrowing requirement as a fraction of gross domestic product.[31] The consequences for unemployment were tremendous, as shown in figure 5.4. Compared with its level over the forty years since the outbreak of the Second World War, unemployment has remained high in the years after 1979 and it has only been in the late 1990s that unemployment rates have reached levels comparable with those of the 1970s.

31. To operate on expectations, a trajectory for monetary growth was declared. The minimum lending rate rose to an unprecedented 17 percent in late 1979 and 1980. In the second half of 1979, the rate of change of average earnings increased from 10.1 percent to 18.8 percent and, as this was accompanied by an appreciation in the sterling exchange rate, the impact on British competitiveness in foreign markets was severe. "The degree of overvaluation of sterling in the second half of 1980 was unprecedented in the post-war period and well in excess of the overvaluation resulting from the return to the gold standard in 1925" (Dimsdale 1991, 133).

Britain was by no means the only economy to experience a large rise in unemployment in the 1980s, but the increase in Britain was larger than in most. Figure 5.4 also shows the unemployment rate in the United Kingdom relative to unemployment rates in the United States and France. From the early 1980s, Britain's unemployment rate has been consistently above that in the United States. The U.K. unemployment rate was also higher than France's throughout the 1970s until 1987, but since that time unemployment in the United Kingdom has fallen gradually to almost half that in France.

It is customary to argue that an increase in unemployment signals a drop in alternative employment opportunities and, consequently, a fall in labor's bargaining power. If correct, the years of the 1980s until the mid-1990s are characterized by a chronic attenuation of labor union bargaining power. Indeed, this loss may well have been enhanced by the fact that some of the areas of union strength such as manufacturing and mining were especially hard hit both by the recession and by the trimming of the budgets of nationalized industries and the transfer of some of their assets to the private sector. This leads naturally to the question of whether the contraction of unionism since 1979 in Britain is simply a reflection of changes in the structure of British industry and, in particular, the consequence of the decline of employment in industries of union strength, such as manufacturing and mining, and the growth of service employment, some of whose areas have been difficult to organize. Indeed, employment in manufacturing in 1998 was less than 60 percent of its level in 1979 and coal-mining employment constituted a trivial fraction of total employment.

In fact, little of the decline in union membership density from 1979 to 1999 arises from simple industrial changes. If the industrial employment structure of 1979 is applied to the union density by industry in 1999, the difference between actual union density in 1999 and that implied by this experiment is only a few percentage points.[32] This is because many sectors of traditional union strength had already contracted substantially by 1979 (thus coal-mining employment represented only 1 percent of total employment), while employment in other areas of traditional union strength, such as health services, has expanded considerably. Changes in industrial structure are not a principal explanation for the decline in unionism over the twenty years since 1979.[33]

32. Similarly, if the broad industry structure in 1998 is applied to the union density by industry in 1979, the larger part of the decline in unionism is left unaccounted for. The data for these analyses are derived from Price and Bain (1983), the July 1980 issue of the *Employment Gazette* (for employment figures in 1979), the June 2000 issue of *Labour Market Trends* (for employment figures in 1998), and the July 2000 issue of *Labour Market Trends* (for union density in 1999). This analysis is undertaken at the broad industry level (eleven industries identified) because more-disaggregated data appear not to be available.

33. This conclusion was reached also by Disney (1990) and Freeman and Pelletier (1990) for the years of the first half of the 1980s.

Other changes in the structure of unionism are suggested by the data in table 5.2. According to all of the categories of union density listed in this table, the record is one of union decline—by gender, by broad occupation, by industry, by region, and by private-public ownership.[34] These are figures on union membership, but the message is the same if data on the coverage of collective bargaining agreements are examined: in 1973, the wages of about 73 percent of employees were covered by collective-bargaining agreements; this fell to 70 percent in 1984, to 54 percent in 1990, and to 40 percent in 1998. In the private sector, the 1998 figure is 21 percent.[35] In other words, there has been a steady erosion in the extent of unionism and in union-negotiated agreements in the economy. Though there were some highly publicized cases of derecognition of unions, the principal factor in this membership decline has been the failure of unions to gain recognition in newly formed workplaces: The greatest declines in the extent of unionism are found in plants in private manufacturing that have been established since 1980; by contrast, in the public sector, there is no decline in union recognition in newly established workplaces (see Disney, Gosling, and Machin 1996; Machin 1999; and Millward, Bryson, and Forth 2000, 84–85).

Given the critical role of management in determining whether to grant union recognition, the failure of unions to gain a foothold in newly formed establishments is, in part, a commentary on employers' attitudes toward collective bargaining. From 1979 until 1997, successive government ministers and "experts" attacked the notion that unionism enhances the performance of the economy and, indeed, they replaced this with the idea that union leaders tend to behave capriciously and without due reference to the wishes and interests of their members. Certainly, some union leaders appeared to fit this profile well.[36] This campaign against collective bargaining and the endorsement of the virtues of narrow self-interest have generated an environment in which managements are less inclined to see unions as the legitimate representatives of the interests of the workers. Compared with the decades of the 1940s, 1950s, and 1960s, the new breed of employers is less altruistic in their dealings with their own employees and this has manifested itself in the view that unions are irrelevant or, worse, damaging to the enterprise. A long and sustained campaign would be required to change these attitudes among those who will be managers in the next few decades. Legislation stipulating that, provided that a workplace vote of

34. As indicated in the footnote to table 5.2, precise comparisons of union density across these years are impossible because of differences in definitions of union membership and in employment. This table is useful, therefore, for broad trends only.

35. These figures are from Milner (1995) and Millward, Bryson, and Forth (2000, 197). According to Hicks (2000), in 1999, 17 percent of employees who were not members of unions claimed their pay and work conditions were covered by a union-negotiated agreement. This implies that, approximately, three million workers are "free riding" on union activities.

36. A conspicuous example was provided by the coal miners' leader, Arthur Scargill. He refused to hold a ballot before calling a momentous strike in 1984–1985 and he managed to have himself elected president of the union for life.

Table 5.2 Union Membership Density, by Various Characteristics, 1979 and 1999

Characteristic	1979	1999
Gender		
Male	63	31
Female	40	28
Occupation		
Manual	63	30
Nonmanual	44	31
Broad industry		
Manufacturing	70	28
Construction	37	21
Distribution	15	12
Health services	74	45
Region		
East Anglia	40	23
Southeast	43	22
Greater London	47	27
Southwest	55	26
East Midlands	61	30
Yorkshire and Humber	67	34
Northwest	71	34
Northeast	72	40
Wales	71	39
Scotland	63	35
Sector		
Private	43	19
Public	82	60

Sources: The data for 1979 are taken from Price and Bain (1983), except for the regional data, which are from Millward and Stevens (1988). The regional data are for 1984. (The Southeast excludes greater London.) The data for 1999 are from Hicks (2000). These three sources define union density differently and the delineation of the regions is not the same for the two years.

employees so determines, a union may be foisted onto a reluctant management may be the prelude to more adversarial industrial relations and, ultimately, unsuccessful unionism.

5.3.3 Strikes

The Thatcher administration's posture toward strikes belied its laissez faire proclivities. This was because statutory law regulating strikes became more, not less, extensive under her governments. Really radical legislation would have been the repeal of the Trade Disputes Act of 1906, which protected a union from being sued by an employer for damages resulting from a strike.[37] What happened under the post-1979 Conservative governments

37. After all, proponents of laissez faire sided with Dicey in describing the 1906 act as conferring "upon every trade union a privilege and protection not possessed by any other person or body of persons, whether corporate or unincorporate, throughout the United Kingdom. . . . It makes a trade union a privileged body exempted from the ordinary law of the

was that unions' legal immunity from damages became more qualified: A union became liable for damages if striking against a secondary employer; an employer could sue a union if the strike was not over industrial relations issues that the employer could address, but over, say, political issues or interunion feuds that the employer had no control over; and a union would lose its immunity if the strike had proceeded without the union's first secretly balloting its members and obtaining the support of a majority for strike action. In 1993, unions were obliged to give seven days' warning of a forthcoming strike. Regulations on picketing became more stringent, with the police granted more power to confine the influence of pickets. In those circumstances where the union lost its immunity, its financial liabilities for damage were proscribed by law. In instances where the union undertook strike action without first balloting its members and ignored court injunctions to desist, the union's funds can be sequestered.[38]

Employers were granted more discretion over the dismissal of strikers.[39] Early in the 1980s, employers had the authority to reengage strikers selectively after a certain time had passed while, in 1990, employers could dismiss striking workers selectively if the union had not authorized the strike. Given the tendency for strikes to be unofficial, these seemingly small modifications in the law sapped the shop stewards' bargaining power.[40]

The number and importance of strikes in Britain have fallen considerably (see fig. 5.2). Whereas in 1980 some 22 percent of establishments reported some sort of "industrial action" during the previous twelve months, in 1998 the corresponding figure was 2 percent.[41] To what extent can this decline in disputes be attributed to the legal changes in the 1980s and 1990s? Strike activity has fallen in most countries, though more in Britain than elsewhere. The last column of table 5.3 shows annual working days

land. No such privileged body has ever before been deliberately created by an English Parliament" (Dicey 1914, xivi). Thatcher's government could have simply repealed the 1906 act and allowed employers to take striking unions to court.

38. In some respects, the British law came closer to that in the United States where secondary boycotts and certain other types of strikes are illegal. Also, a case law has built up in the United States over what types of picketing are legal. However, the balloting of workers to secure approval for a strike is not the law in the United States even though many unions practice it. Whereas in Britain the concern was that union leaders tend to be more militant than the rank-and-file workers, in the United States the contract rejection problem seemed to suggest that the union rank and file tended to be more militant that the leadership.

39. Unfair dismissal law was introduced in 1971. Before that date, employers had the authority to dismiss any striking worker, although such discharges were uncommon. The 1974–1979 Labour government ruled that employers could dismiss striking workers and not be liable for damages for violating the law on unfair dismissals, provided all those striking were dismissed. Dismissing some workers and retaining others or rehiring some workers and not hiring others rendered the employer liable for damages.

40. Of course, the national union could declare the strike official, but if the necessary balloting had not taken place this exposed the union to damage claims.

41. See Millward and Stevens (1986, table 10.1) and Cully et al. (1999, fig. 6.4). It is revealing that, in 1986, Millward and Stevens devote an entire chapter of over thirty pages to "industrial action" while, in 1999, Cully et al. allocate a little over a page to the topic.

Table 5.3 **Working Days Lost through Stoppages per Thousand Employees in All Industries and Services, Annual Averages, 1981–1998**

Country	1981–85	1986–90	1989–93	1994–98	(1994–98)/(1976–80)
United Kingdom	442	137	72	22	0.04
Australia	386	224	179	91	0.15
Belgium		48	37	80	0.37
Canada	498	429	255	215	0.25
Denmark	306	41	34	309	3.36
Finland	326	410	174	182	0.30
France	84	111	34	39	0.21
West Germany	50	5	19	4	0.08
Ireland	474	242	143	73	0.07
Italy	774	315	250	112	0.10
Japan	10	5	3	2	0.05
The Netherlands	24	13	16	26	0.87
New Zealand	408	425	130	30	0.08
Norway	58	142	63	99	0.47
Spain	584	602	428	267	0.31
Sweden	40	134	73	43	0.26
United States	128	82	65	43	0.10
OECD average		161	86	52	

Sources: Employment Gazette (December 1991, 653), *Labour Market Trends* (April 1997, 130; April 2000, 148).

Notes: Stoppages cover both strikes and lock-outs. Definitions and coverage of stoppages vary across countries so these data should not be relied upon to justify strong inferences about intercountry differences.

lost through strikes per thousand employees in the years 1994–1998 as a fraction of those in 1976–1980. This ratio is consistently less than unity, but its lowest value is for Britain: in the period from 1994 to 1998, annual working days lost per employee in Britain constituted merely 4 percent of their level in 1976–1980!

There are many competing explanations for this change, so it is difficult to determine the particular contribution of the law. Even if the power of unions were throttled, it always takes two parties to strike, so an explanation may focus as much on the enhanced opportunity of management to wage a profitable strike as on the reduced power of unions to conduct a successful strike. Current modelling of disputes would suggest that they are the consequence of information asymmetrically shared between the union and management. Did the Conservative governments' legislation alter the allotment of information and, in this way, did it result in fewer disputes?

It is plausible that the mandatory balloting of workers before strikes provides information to both management and the union about the workers' resolve if a strike does occur—provided those voting reveal their propensities accurately. In an analysis of the impact of balloting procedures, Undy et al. (1996) argue that these procedures had a small effect on the course of strike activity. However, they did find that "balloting provided a comparatively low-cost and credible way of demonstrating the resolve of union members without calling on them to engage in strike action" (230) and, in this sense, the legislation contributed to alleviating the informational asymmetry between management and unions and helped to reduce strikes. Undy et al. also conclude that "the threat, and demonstration of the damaging financial effects, of legal actions by employers made many union negotiators more cautious and risk-averse in their dealings with employers during disputes" (230). On balance, this balloting legislation helped reduce strike activity although it is unlikely to have been a principal factor.

Of course, the vast majority of strikes occur at unionized establishments, so, insofar as the legislation clipped the reach of unionism, the government's agenda can be said to have caused a decline in strike activity.

5.3.4 Closed Shops

The Conservative governments directed several pieces of legislation to the closed shop. In 1974, the Labour government established that an employer could not legally use union membership as a criterion for firing a worker. However, it was permissible to fire an employee if he or she refused to join a closed shop. In 1988, dismissal because of either union membership or nonmembership was determined unfair and, in this respect, an equivalence between members and nonmembers was resolved. Because nonmembers could not be fired, this dealt a blow to the postentry closed shop. In 1990, the law turned from dismissal to hiring: employers could not refuse to hire workers based on their union membership status. This undercut the preentry closed shop.[42]

This legislation has contributed to the virtual elimination of the closed shop. In 1980, some workers were covered by a closed shop in 23 percent of workplaces. This number was as high as 88 percent in the nationalized industries. In 1998, according to the responses of managers, merely 2 percent of workplaces were identified where employees had to be union members to retain their jobs.[43] In some respects, the closed shop has gone underground in that sometimes employers (especially in the public sector) "strongly recommend membership." Nevertheless, the attack on the closed shop has been largely won.

There are two questions. The first is whether this victory over the closed

42. In the United States, the "closed shop" corresponds to the British "pre-entry closed shop," while the "union shop" is what in Britain goes by the name of the "postentry closed shop." The Taft-Hartley Act of 1947 made the closed shop illegal in the United States in interstate commerce, while states with "right-to-work" laws prohibit the union shop.

43. The 1980 figures are taken from Millward and Stevens (1986, table 4.3) and describe workplaces with at least twenty-five employees. The 1998 figure is from Cully et al. (1999, 89) and describes workplaces with at least ten employees. Whereas in Millward and Stevens the closed shop merits a seventeen-page chapter, in Cully et al. the closed shop receives a couple of paragraphs.

shop may be attributed to the legislation alone. This is doubtful. The pre-entry closed shop was most extensive in old craft-related activities that have been heavily affected by technological change—newspapers, printing, shipping, and docks—and it is probable that many closed shops would have been swept aside anyway by the onslaught of the new technology.

The second question is whether this victory over the closed shop is an important one. There is no doubt that the closed shop was correlated with a number of outcomes: For instance, in 1980 and 1984, the union-nonunion wage differential tended to be greater when the unionized establishment had a pre-entry closed shop.[44] However, the unresolved question is whether this was the consequence of the closed shop or the consequence of something else that also produced the closed shop. Indeed, this problem frustrates the interpretation of many correlations between variables in industrial relations where cause and effect are especially hard to disentangle. According to this alternative hypothesis, the closed shop is as much an outcome variable as wages or work hours, so the closed shop should be seen as an indicator of union influence or as a signal of managerial preferences,[45] not their cause.

5.3.5 Union Governance

Laws were introduced strengthening the rights of rank-and-file union members in dealing with their own organizations. It was stipulated that direct, secret elections of union officials must occur within every five years while, every ten years, ballots must be held to approve any political expenditures the union makes. Union members were given rights to examine their unions' accounting records. A worker was required to provide prior written consent to an employer who automatically deducts union dues from the worker's paycheck. This consent needed to be renewed every three years. This prompted the unions to wage a campaign to encourage workers to approve automatic check-off and to encourage employers to support the practice. By 1998, some two-thirds of unionized establishments practiced the check-off (Cully et al. 1999, 89). In that year, the Labour government repealed the requirement for written approval of the check-off.

The drop in union membership,[46] the penalties incurred by some unions

44. See Stewart (1987, 1995) and Metcalf and Stewart (1992).

45. It was sometimes argued that management used the closed shop to discourage the formation of more unions and to help enforce discipline in environments with a propensity toward anarchy.

46. It needs emphasizing that not only has union membership as a fraction of employment dropped, but the absolute level of union membership has fallen considerably. According to data published in the *Employment Gazette* and reported to the certification officer, union membership at the end of 1979 was 13,289 thousand whereas at the end of 1998 it was 7,807 thousand, more than a 40 percent drop. There is a large literature devoted to accounting for movements over time in union membership and density. For example, by constructing their own indicator of the legal climate of collective bargaining and by drawing inferences from the differences between union density in Britain and that in Ireland, Freeman and Pelletier (1990)

for illegal actions, and the effect of various measures (such as balloting before taking strike action) to make the union leadership more accountable to its rank and file left the finances of the unions in a more precarious state by the late-1990s than for many decades. Though many unions operate more efficiently than they have ever done and increasingly have the appearance of friendly societies (just as they did in the nineteenth century, when they provided a whole array of cash payments to cover untoward events such as accidents, illness, and retirement), their resources to support their members in lengthy strikes have been severely attenuated.

5.3.6 Indirect Effects on Collective Bargaining and Unionism

In describing the state of labor markets before the accession to power of a series of Conservative governments, I argued that, through a number of indirect measures, the state provided widespread support of unionism and collective bargaining. These indirect measures included the role of the state as an employer, the practice of setting minimum wages in certain industries, the requirement that government contractors pay union-negotiated wages, and the impediments to product market competition. The Conservative governments explicitly addressed all these indirect measures.

Public-sector finances were placed under stringent constraints and pay negotiations were governed less by notions of "comparability" with private-sector wages and more by whether pay levels were generating adequate supplies of labor. Where possible, collective bargaining was decentralized. Indeed, one of the most important changes in bargaining since 1979 has been the notable decrease in multi-employer agreements.[47] Such decentralized agreements tend to be more sensitive to the particular circumstances of the employer and the plant.

By denationalizing (or "privatizing") large parts of the public sector, the state became a less far-reaching employer. In 1978, public-sector employees represented 31 percent of all employees. Twenty years later, the number had fallen to 20 percent.[48] The policy was designed also to encourage competition in product markets. However, privatizing industries is not the same as ensuring a competitive environment and, in many cases, the issue became one of choosing between a private monopoly and a public monopoly. Strikes against private monopolies have the same opportunity for imposing costs on consumers as strikes against public monopolies. Moreover, a

ascribe most of the decline in density in Britain in the 1980s to the less supportive legal environment for collective bargaining. See Metcalf (1991) for a brief critical review of the research on union density in Britain.

47. In 1984, of all workplaces where collective bargaining was the dominant form of pay setting, 69 percent of them were multi-employer agreements. By 1998, this had fallen to 46 percent. Among all workplaces in 1998, just 13 percent had wages determined by multi-employer agreements and 6 percent in private-sector manufacturing. See Millward, Bryson, and Forth (2000, 186–188).

48. See MacGregor (1999, table C).

number of these industries are still in the state's hands, so the unions in these sectors retain considerable leverage. Yet, the public sector itself was obliged to be more sensitive to its costs: in the 1970s most local and central government services were delivered by unionized, state employees; in the 1980s and 1990s, by "contracting-out" these services to (often nonunion) private firms, competitive pressures were injected into union-supplied activities.

The practice of setting minimum wages in certain industries was attacked by eliminating wages councils while the requirement that government contractors pay union-negotiated wages was eliminated by repealing the Fair Wages Resolution in 1983. More generally, statutory rules guided wage determination much less and firm- or plant-specific factors have directed earnings changes. Performance-related pay mechanisms have gained in popularity and earnings structures simplified. The consequence has been for real wages to rise throughout the earnings distribution, but high-paid workers have seen their wages increase much faster than the low-paid (see Organization for Economic Cooperation and Development [OECD] 1996 and Schmitt 1995). More generally, notwithstanding the introduction of a new National Minimum Wage in 1999, the relatively narrow wage differentials characteristic of corporatist economies are not an appropriate description of British labor markets in 2000.

5.4 Unionism and Productivity

5.4.1 The Contribution to Changes in Productivity

The relationship between productivity (measured in different ways) and unionism has been the subject of a good deal of research. The basic reason this has been difficult to unravel is that, even if production functions were identical in unionized and nonunionized workplaces, productivity differences would emerge between the two classes of firms insofar as collective bargaining affects wages. If wages are higher in the unionized firm, if the firm may freely adjust inputs in response to these price differences, and if the firm does not throw resources away, employment will tend to fall and *labor productivity will be higher in the union firm.* Ideally, the researcher would like to present the unionized and nonunion firms with various combinations of the same inputs and then observe their outputs. In fact, the researcher does not select the inputs; the firms select the inputs and this selection is made in response to input prices.

In addition to the wage effects of collective bargaining, unionism has nonwage effects on a firm's operations, which implies that, even when management is free to make decisions about the use of labor, the unionized firm's labor productivity will differ from that of the nonunion firm. For instance, some have suggested that, with an agent—the union—to protect their interests, workers will tend to be more cooperative and forthcoming in unionized workplaces, and that unionism involves participation and participation begets higher productivity. Conversely, unionism may protect slothful working habits and defend malfeasance, which lower labor productivity. As most scholars have recognized, a priori arguments cannot settle whether, on balance, this effect works to raise or lower productivity in union workplaces.

The previous two arguments assume labor input choices are made unilaterally by management. There is a third effect of unionism on productivity insofar as unions do not grant management a free hand in labor input decisions. Through bargaining either explicitly over the level of labor input or implicitly through resisting organizational changes that raise productivity, labor input in unionized establishments may exceed the levels otherwise implied by the wages and technical efficiency of the labor force.[49] In fact, when the subject of unionism and productivity was posed in Britain in the 1970s and 1980s, it was this third class of arguments that tended to find most frequent expression.

Other routes by which unionism may affect productivity have been conjectured. For instance, the fear that a union may capture the rents from investment in physical plant and equipment may discourage management from undertaking such investments (Grout 1984). This implies lower capital stock in unionized plants. The impact on productivity is less clear. With lower capital, output will be lower and, if output per worker is a positive function of the level of physical capital, then labor productivity will be lower. But whether output per factor input (total factor productivity) will be lower is less obvious. Indeed, in the simplest of cases, in this situation, total factor productivity is likely to be greater in the unionized plant. This illustrates that the impacts of unionism on productivity and on productivity growth are far from obvious and that they are likely to depend on prosaic issues of variable definition and measurement (such as whether labor productivity or total factor productivity is being measured).[50]

Productivity in unionized establishments will compare unfavorably with that in nonunion establishments insofar as unions are effective in discouraging the introduction of new production technologies into workplaces. However, the examination of the responses to questions in the 1984 Workplace Industrial Relations surveys (WIRS) about technological change

49. This form of productivity effect of unionism accords well with the stories about the inefficient use of workers in British industry entertainingly illustrated by Fred Kite's union in "I'm All Right Jack." If the bargaining power of the union over employment is reduced, then employment will fall and output per worker will rise. This is a once-and-for-all increase in labor productivity, not a permanent increase in the rate of growth of productivity.

50. Another awkward measurement issue arises out of the fact that a number of studies use some measure of the value of output in the definition of productivity: If unionism has effects on input prices, these will normally be transmitted to output prices, ensuring, by construction, some positive correlation between this indicator of productivity and unionism.

does not support the popular view of British unions as twentieth-century Luddites.[51] Thus, Daniel (1987) finds that trade union resistance to technical change is very much the exception. Shop stewards tend to be more supportive of the introduction of advanced technology than the workers, who, in turn, are generally favorably disposed. There were exceptions to this finding. Most noticeably, the nationalized industries constituted an important pocket of resistance to technical change. However, in general, unions much more frequently supported, not opposed, such change.

The weight of the evidence seems to suggest the following assessment: Up to the early 1980s, unionism was associated with lower labor productivity, but, in the 1980s, this gap was narrowed because the highly unionized sector tended to exhibit faster productivity growth.[52] The causes of this faster growth are difficult to identify, but most frequently mentioned are the combined consequences of a more competitive product market environment and the Conservative government's labor relations legislation.[53] This raises the distinction between the effects of unionism on the level of productivity and the effects of unionism on the rate of growth of productivity. Some authors have gone so far as to suggest that a lower level of union density will result in a permanently higher growth in productivity.

This is exactly the position taken by Bean and Crafts, who argue that "the changed industrial relations scene of the recent past has not only allowed a once-and-for-all productivity gain, but also improved future growth potential" (1996, 161). What aspects of this "changed industrial relations scene" have contributed to these permanent productivity gains? The legislation against closed shops is unlikely to have been profound because closed shops are more a symptom than a source of union strength. Similarly, legislation making unions more accountable to their own members is unlikely to have enhanced workplace productivity.

Bean and Crafts (1996) suspect that the decline in multi-unionism (i.e., the presence of more than one union at a workplace) was the foremost labor market feature raising Britain's productivity growth. The key piece of evidence they offer for this is a regression fitted to a pooled data set of about 137 three-digit industries (predominantly manufacturing) and eight

51. Of course, the popular view of the Luddites is also wanting. See Hobsbawm (1964).

52. This assessment conforms to Metcalf's (1989, 1990) very informed statement of our knowledge by the end of the 1980s. Also see Booth's (1995) review.

53. An example of a study supporting this conclusion is that of Gregg, Machin, and Metcalf (1993), who show that, in a sample of 328 private companies in the late 1980s, real sales growth was greater in those firms employing workers where some union derecognition had occurred. Also included in the specification is a variable measuring increased foreign competition, although the presence of unionism in this equation implies that the coefficient on increased competition measures the effect of competition on real sales growth holding unionism constant. In fact, increased foreign competition may have been the spur to derecognize the union, in which case the full effects of competition involve consideration of the unionism variables, too. In this study, unionism and the change in union status are treated as predetermined.

subperiods from 1954–1958 to 1982–1986. The dependent variable is the annual growth in total factor productivity. However, there is no time series information on their key variable, the fraction of workplaces in which there is more than one manual union, so the 1980 cross-section variation in this variable is assumed to take on the same values over three decades. This is quite heroic: there were more than 700 unions in 1954, the beginning year of their estimating period, and about 400 in the early 1980s, the end of their period of study. The assumption that the incidence of multi-unionism is a constant also prevents them from allowing for permanent unobserved differences among these industries.[54] This specification constitutes a weak reed for any reliable inferences about the impact of multiple unionism on the growth in productivity.

Nevertheless, the issue of multi-unionism recurs in evaluations of industrial relations practices. For instance, using the 1984 WIRS, Machin, Stewart, and Van Reenan (1993) exploit information on responses by managers who assess their establishments' financial performance compared with that of other establishments in the same industry. They find that, where management bargains separately with each of the unions—a so-called "fragmented bargaining structure"—the firm's financial performance suffers. They suggest that where the union forms a single bargaining committee and management bargains with this committee "around a single table," unfavorable outcomes are not apparent. In other words, where management insists on the unions' joining together for purposes of bargaining with them, there are no untoward effects of multi-unionism on pay, financial performance, and strikes.[55]

The history of unionism in Britain abounds with instances in which groups of workers seek to preserve their identities in separate organizations and find it more effective to pursue their aspirations in their distinct associations. This evidence suggests that such multi-unionism does not damage the financial performance of firms, provided the unions band together for the purposes of collective bargaining with management. In creating an environment in which managements had greater authority to insist upon the elimination of fragmented bargaining structures, public policy in the 1980s

54. A part of their argument involves the use of what they call a "multiple union dummy" that prior to 1979 takes the value of zero and from 1979 equals the value of the fraction of workplaces with more than one union. This allows for the effect of multiple unionism to differ in the 1979–1982 and 1982–1986 subperiods from that in earlier periods. The coefficient estimated on this variable is positive, from which they infer that the damaging effects of multiple unions was less in the early 1980s. Because the extent of multiple unionism barely changed in the early 1980s (see Millward and Stevens 1986, 73), something happened in the early 1980s to ameliorate the impact of multiple unionism. This "something" would seem to be the variable we seek rather than multiple unionism itself.

55. In related work, Machin and Stewart (1990, 1996) report that in 1980, 1984, and 1990, financial performance is lower in unionized establishments although much of this takes the form of unions' capturing product market rents.

and 1990s made British industrial relations less of a drag on economic growth—or so some observers would have it.

5.4.2 Labor Productivity, Financial Performance, and Unionism in 1998

What is the most recent evidence of the effects of multi-unionism and fragmented bargaining? And, after all this remarkable retreat in unionism, what is left of the association between productivity and unionism? To address this, I turned to the 1998 Workplace Employee Relations Survey (WERS) and examined the responses concerning financial performance and labor productivity. In this survey, a representative from management was told, "I now want to ask you how your workplace is currently performing compared with other establishments in the same industry. How would you assess your workplace's financial performance/labor productivity?" The following five categories of responses were used in the subsequent analysis: "a lot below average"; "below average"; "about average for the industry"; "better than average"; and "a lot better than average."[56]

There are some obvious shortcomings in assessing an organization's financial performance and productivity on the basis of management's perceptions. How well-informed is the manager of the competitors' performance, and how much wishful thinking goes into his or her responses? However, there are also severe shortcomings in conventional measures of performance and productivity. When firms produce different goods and employ different types of labor, the configuration of output per labor input across firms must use some price indices to put diverse outputs on a common footing, and the quantity of worker-hours ought to be adjusted in some way for skill differences in labor. Most workers are now employed in the service sector where the measurement of output is fraught with special problems.

Similar concerns arise in conventional measures of financial performance. Even when available (and frequently it is not), accounting profits does not map precisely into the organization's rate of return and, when a workplace is part of a larger organization, its "profits" are not only not defined, they are also secondary to the organization's "bottom line." This does not mean that the answers of a manager to these questions provide ideal indicators of a workplace's productivity and performance. The argument is simply that they contain information that may well be useful in drawing inferences about a workplace's effectiveness.[57] Indeed, manage-

56. There are two other categories—"no comparison possible" and "relevant data not available"—but few observations are in these categories and they will not be used. Most of these workplaces are in public administration, health, and education.

57. "[A] quarter of workplaces did not operate in the trading sector, and for these notions of profit and loss simply do not apply. Similarly, the concept of labour productivity has meaning in all workplaces, but there are no standardised measures in many sectors. For example, there are no conventional measures of value-added which would allow a comparison of the labour productivity of a hospital against a school" (Cully et al. 1999, 120).

Table 5.4 Cross-Classification of Workplaces by Labor Productivity and Financial Performance, 1998

	Labor Productivity					
Financial Performance	A Lot Below Average	Below Average	Average	Better Than Average	A Lot Better Than Average	Total
A lot below average	4	2	0	3	0	9
Below average	2	25	46	14	5	92
Average	1	28	343	143	12	527
Better than average	2	13	209	337	41	602
A lot better than average	0	2	39	98	115	254
Total	9	70	637	595	173	1,484

ment's assessments may well embody qualitative considerations that conventional measures of productivity and financial performance have difficulty in recognizing. In fact, Machin and Stewart (1996) report that the less favorable the managers' assessments of their financial performance in the 1984 WIRS, the greater the probability of the workplace having closed down by 1990.

For the investigation in this paper, workplaces were discarded if they had missing values on any variables used in the analysis below, and this left 1,484 workplace observations from the 1998 WERS to investigate. The distribution of responses on labor productivity cross-classified by responses on financial performance is provided in table 5.4. Evidently, most managers like to think that their workplaces are either average or better than average. There is a clear positive correlation between the responses on labor productivity and those on financial performance: the null hypothesis of no association between the two responses is rejected on a chi-square test at a very high level of significance.[58]

Workplaces are divided into four categories based on their union and bargaining status: nonunion workplaces; workplaces with a single union; workplaces with many unions but with joint bargaining; and workplaces with many unions engaging in separate bargaining. In the 1998 WERS, of the 1,484 workplaces, 597 are nonunion, 322 are single-union workplaces, 337 are workplaces with many unions engaging in joint bargaining, and 228 are workplaces with many unions engaging in separate bargaining. The distribution of responses on labor productivity by type of workplace is given in figure 5.5 and those on financial performance in figure 5.6. The proportion of managers in nonunion workplaces who assess their workplace to be "a lot better than average" is greater in the nonunion sector, but this is offset, at least in part, by their lower frequency of assessing their

58. The calculated chi-square statistic is 622 with 16 degrees of freedom.

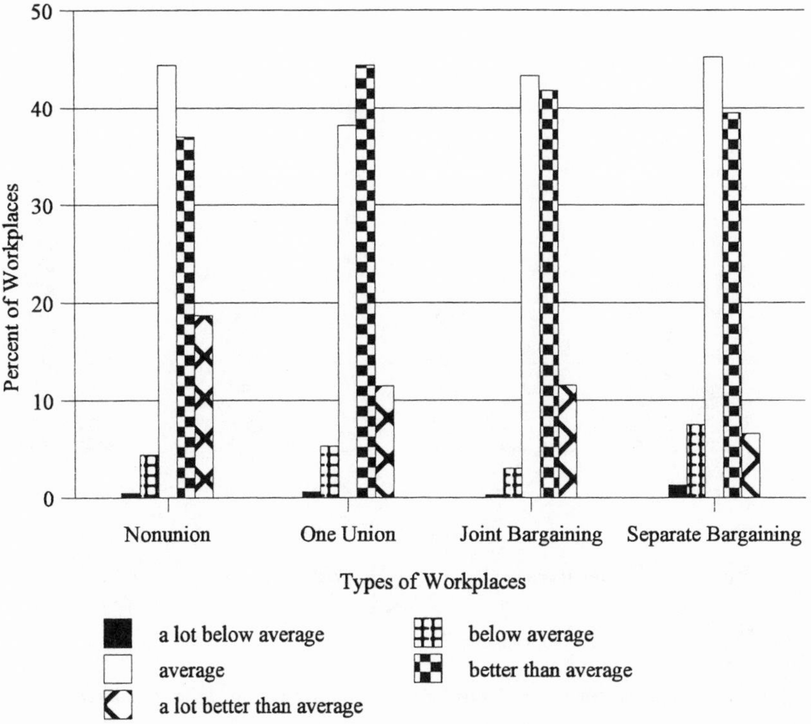

Fig. 5.5 Labor productivity by unionism and bargaining structure, 1998

workplace as simply "better than average." If the percentage of responses of "a lot better than average" and "better than average" are aggregated, the distribution of responses across the four types of workplaces is as follows:

	Nonunion	Single Union	Many Unions and Joint Bargaining	Many Unions and Separate Bargaining
Labor productivity	50.7	55.9	53.4	46.1
Financial performance	59.0	60.9	56.9	50.8

The workplaces with the least favorable aggregate responses are those where many unions operate and bargain separately with management. This general theme will recur.

To determine whether union-nonunion differences in labor productivity and financial performance are contained in these data and whether differences exist by bargaining structure, suppose π_i is a latent measure of labor productivity or of financial performance in workplace i. Initially, posit that π_i is a linear function of whether the workplace is unionized (U_i) and of

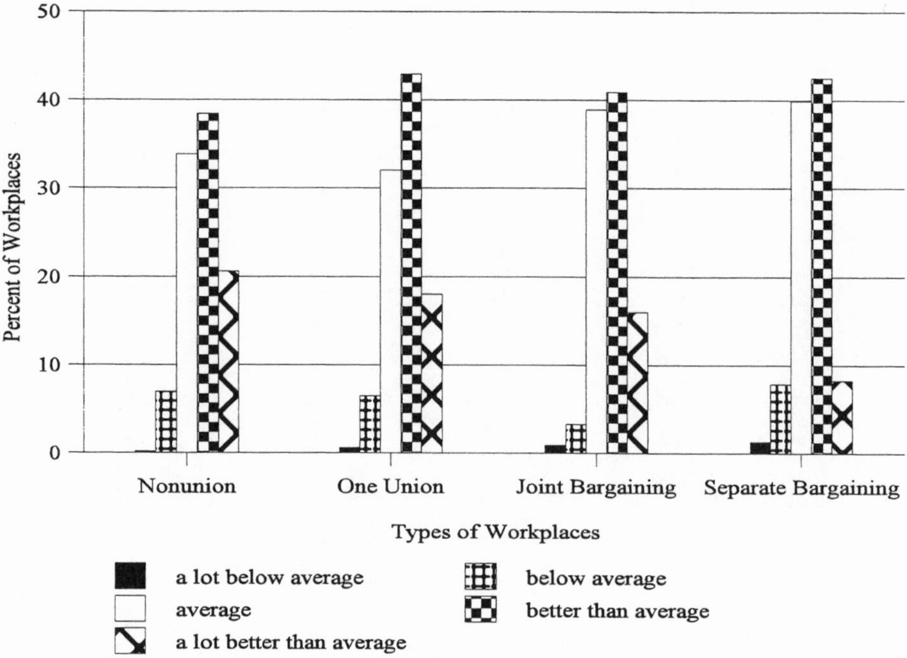

Fig. 5.6 Financial performance by unionism and bargaining structure, 1998

other variables X_i, and of unmeasured factors, e_i, that include the characteristics of the respondent:

$$\pi_i = \alpha U_i + \beta X_i + e_i, \tag{1}$$

where e_i is assumed to be distributed normally with zero mean and unit variance. This standardized normal assumption will permit the estimation of an ordered probit model. Although π_i is unobserved, the categorical responses to the questions do provide information on this latent variable. These categorical responses are denoted by p_i where we adopt the convention that $p_i = 1$ for workplaces designated to be a lot below average, $p_i = 2$ for those reported as below average, $p_i = 3$ for those described as average, $p_i = 4$ for workplaces better than average, and $p_i = 5$ for those characterized as a lot better than average. The relation between the observed variable p_i and the unobserved variable π_i is given as follows:

$$p_i = 1 \quad \text{if} \quad \pi_i \leq m_1$$

$$p_i = j \quad \text{if} \quad m_{j-1} < \pi_i \leq m_j, \quad j = 2, 3, 4$$

$$p_i = 5 \quad \text{if} \quad m_4 \leq \pi_i,$$

where the censoring parameters, the m's, are to be estimated jointly with α and β. The maximum likelihood estimation of equation (1) yields estimates

Table 5.5 **Maximum-Likelihood Estimates of the Effects of Unionism and Bargaining Structure on Labor Productivity and Financial Performance (estimated asymptotic standard errors in parentheses)**

	1998 Survey		1990 Survey	
	Labor Productivity (1)	Financial Performance (2)	Labor Productivity (3)	Financial Performance (4)
		Equation (1)		
1. U_i	–0.031	–0.134	–0.382	–0.220
	(0.063)	(0.062)	(0.157)	(0.160)
		Equation (2)		
2. U_i	–0.007	–0.052	–0.247	–0.142
	(0.077)	(0.076)	(0.168)	(0.172)
3. $U_i \cdot M_i$	0.058	–0.054	0.145	–0.085
	(0.089)	(0.088)	(0.266)	(0.267)
4. $U_i \cdot S_i$	–0.191	–0.283	–0.386	–0.187
	(0.097)	(0.096)	(0.143)	(0.143)
		Equation (3)		
5. M_i	0.054	–0.041	0.156	–0.071
	(0.091)	(0.090)	(0.268)	(0.269)
6. S_i	–0.198	–0.271	–0.388	–0.198
	(0.099)	(0.098)	(0.146)	(0.145)

of the coefficient on U_i given in columns (1) and (2) of line one in table 5.5.[59] By conventional statistical criteria, the null hypothesis of no association between these indicators of labor productivity and the incidence of unionism cannot be rejected. However, this is not the case for the measures of financial performance where the presence of unionism is associated with lower financial returns.

The implications of these estimates are provided in table 5.6, where column (1) lists union-nonunion differences in labor productivity and column (2) lists union-nonunion differences in financial performance as implied by the estimates in line one of table 5.5.[60] Union-nonunion differences in labor productivity are trivial. Those in financial performance suggest that union workplaces are 3 percent less likely to be a lot better than average and 2

59. For the estimates of the α parameters in table 5.5, the X_i variables consist of the fraction of employees who are part-time, the fraction of employees who are women, six dichotomous variables of workplace size, and six dichotomous variables indicating how long the workplace has been at the present location. Workplace size and years of operation seem necessary control variables in a study of productivity. A number of other specifications were applied with small changes in general inferences. The U_i variable takes the value of unity if any of the workplace's employees belong to a union. For all the equations whose results are reported, likelihood-ratio tests suggest a statistically significant relationship between, in turn, the productivity and performance indicators and the set of right-hand-side variables.

60. The union-nonunion differences and the separate-joint bargaining differences are evaluated at the mean values of all the other variables.

Table 5.6 **Implications of Estimates for Differences in Labor Productivity and Financial Performance, by Union and Bargaining Status**

	Equation (1): Difference between Union and Nonunion Workplaces		Equation (2): Difference between Separate and Joint Bargaining		Equation (3): Difference between Separate and Joint Bargaining	
	Labor Productivity (1)	Financial Performance (2)	Labor Productivity (3)	Financial Performance (4)	Labor Productivity (5)	Financial Performance (6)
1998 Survey						
Prob(a lot below average)	0	0	0	0	0	0.01
Prob(below average)	0	0.02	0.02	0.04	0.02	0.03
Prob(average)	0	0.04	0.06	0.07	0.06	0.07
Prob(better than average)	–0.01	–0.02	–0.04	–0.05	–0.05	–0.05
Prob(a lot better than average)	–0.01	–0.03	–0.04	–0.06	–0.03	–0.05
1990 Survey						
Prob(a lot below average)	0	0.01	0	0.02	0	0.01
Prob(below average)	0.05	0.02	0.06	0.02	0.06	0.02
Prob(average)	0.10	0.06	0.09	0.04	0.10	0.04
Prob(better than average)	–0.06	–0.01	–0.08	–0.01	–0.07	–0.01
Prob(a lot better than average)	–0.09	–0.08	–0.08	–0.06	–0.09	–0.07

percent less likely to be better than average compared with nonunion workplaces. The superior performance of nonunion workplaces in financial performance is compatible with a rent-reallocation view of unions according to which unions appropriate some of an organization's rents.

To determine whether the bargaining structure plays a role in this, consider specifying the union's impact in equation (1) in the following manner: $\alpha = \alpha_0 + \alpha_1 M_i + \alpha_2 S_i$. Here, M_i is a dichotomous variable taking the value of unity in those workplaces where more than one union operates, but where these unions collaborate as far as collective bargaining is concerned. Such workplaces are characterized by joint bargaining. S_i is a dichotomous variable taking the value of unity for those workplaces with many unions and with separate (or "fragmented") bargaining. Substituting this expression for α in equation (1) yields the following estimating equation:

$$\pi_i = \alpha_0 U_i + \alpha_1 U_i M_i + \alpha_2 U_i S_i + \beta X_i + e_i, \tag{2}$$

where α_0 denotes any effect on π_i of a single union workplace, $\alpha_0 + \alpha_1$ of a multiple-union workplace where the unions bargain jointly, and $\alpha_0 + \alpha_2$ of a multiple-union workplace where the unions bargain separately. The ordered probit estimates of the α coefficients of this equation are contained in lines two, three, and four of columns (1) and (2) of table 5.5. By conventional criteria, the estimates of the coefficients of α_0 and α_1 would not be judged as significantly different from zero. However, the estimate of α_2 would be judged as significantly less than zero both for the labor productivity equation and for the financial performance equation. The implications of these estimates of α_2 are contained in columns (3) and (4) of table 5.6, which reports the difference between two multiple-union workplaces, one where unions bargain separately and one where the unions bargain jointly. For labor productivity, workplaces with fragmented bargaining have a 4 percent lower probability of being a lot better than average and a 4 percent lower probability of being better than average compared with a workplace where the unions bargain jointly. Similarly, in terms of financial performance, when bargaining is fragmented, the workplace is 6 percent less likely to be a lot better than average and is 5 percent less likely to be better than average compared with a workplace with joint bargaining. These results are consistent with the view that, if a union-nonunion difference obtains, it is the bargaining structure that accounts for this difference, with fragmented workplaces reporting relatively lower productivity and lower financial performance than multiple-union workplaces where bargaining is joint.

Finally, consider fitting equation (2) to the 887 unionized workplaces only (so for all observations $U_i = 1$):

$$\pi_i = \alpha_1 M_i + \alpha_2 S_i + \beta X_i + e_i. \tag{3}$$

The ordered probit estimates of the α coefficients of equation (3) are given in columns (1) and (2) of lines five and six in table 5.5 and again the suggestion is that what matters for labor productivity and financial outcomes is not multi-unionism per se, but whether bargaining is joint or fragmented. The implications of these estimates are contained in columns (5) and (6) of table 5.6 where, among multi-union workplaces, those where fragmented bargaining take place are 3 percent less likely to have labor productivity a lot better than average and 5 percent less likely to have labor productivity better than average compared with those workplaces with joint bargaining. Similarly, on financial performance, workplaces with a fragmented-bargaining score 5 percent lower on the probability of being a lot better than average and 5 percent lower on the probability of being better than average compared with workplaces with joint bargaining.

These results are compatible with the following interpretation. On average, by the late 1990s, unionism per se has negligible effects on productivity; the state of labor relations is the key variable associated with productivity; and, in Britain, workplaces with fragmented bargaining are associated with poorer productivity. With respect to financial performance, unions tend to reallocate an organization's rents toward workers and, in Britain, this occurs more substantially in fragmented-bargaining workplaces.

Having arrived at these findings from the 1998 WERS, I went back to the 1990 WIRS to determine whether similar patterns are evident in this establishment survey, too. Trying to fit the very same equations to the 1990 data as already estimated to the 1998 data, the results are given in columns (3) and (4) of table 5.5 with inferences regarding the probability distributions in the bottom part of table 5.6.[61] The results are broadly similar to those for 1998, although there are a few interesting differences. According to column (3) of line one in table 5.5, in 1990 unionized workplaces have significantly lower labor productivity than nonunionized workplaces. Thus, as reported in column (1) in the lower part of table 5.6, unionized workplaces have a 6 percent lower probability of being classified as "better than average" and a 9 percent lower probability of being classified as "a lot better than average" compared with nonunionized workplaces. It appears again as if it is workplaces with fragmented bargaining where this differential is concentrated. This is suggested by the estimates in lines two, three,

61. Regrettably, by trying to fit the very same equation and dropping observations on workplaces if a missing value is encountered on any one variable, we arrive at a much smaller number of establishments: 380 workplaces. Of these, 66 consist of nonunion workplaces, 139 are single-union workplaces, 20 are workplaces with many unions but with joint bargaining, and 155 are workplaces with many unions and fragmented bargaining. (Note that, in the 1990 survey, eleven of the single-union workplaces were said to have more than one bargaining unit. For our analysis, we assumed that such multi-unit bargaining by a single union may be interpreted as joint bargaining, although, in principle, this is something that could be tested.) As in the 1998 survey, the responses on labor productivity and those on financial performance are strongly positively correlated on a conventional chi-square test. The cross-classification of workplaces by labor productivity and financial performance in 1990 is given in table 5.7.

Table 5.7 **Cross-Classification of Workplaces by Labor Productivity and Financial Performance, 1990**

Financial Performance	A Lot Below Average	Below Average	Average	Better Than Average	A Lot Better Than Average	Total
A lot below average	0	2	5	1	3	11
Below average	0	9	8	6	0	23
Average	1	11	72	38	11	133
Better than average	0	10	27	29	26	92
A lot better than average	0	5	38	68	10	121
Total	1	37	150	142	50	380

and four of table 5.5 and the probability differences in column (3) in the lower part of table 5.6.

With respect to financial performance, there is again the suggestion that workplaces with fragmented bargaining tend to report lower financial performance compared with workplaces with joint bargaining. However, this is less evident than it was in the 1998 data. The point estimates in column (4) of table 5.5 are not much greater than their estimated standard errors. The implications of these point estimates for the probability distributions (table 5.6) suggest that meaningful differences occur only for the probability of being "a lot better than average" where workplaces with fragmented bargaining have a 6 or 7 percent lower probability compared with workplaces with joint bargaining. All this is compatible with the view that such fragmented workplaces are the establishments where remnants of the industrial relations climate of the 1970s live on.

5.4.3 Conclusion on Unionism and Productivity

A maintained hypothesis throughout this section is that the association between π_i, on the one hand, and unionism and the bargaining structure, on the other hand, reflects the impact of unionism and bargaining structure on π_i. In other words, I follow the assumption (mostly tacit) in this literature that the relationships computed embody the effects of unionism on productivity and on financial performance. There is ample reason to question this maintained hypothesis: The incidence of unionism (and different bargaining structures) may well depend on an establishment's productivity or financial standing, so the associations computed reflect the effects of productivity (or financial performance) on patterns of unionism and the bargaining structure. As mentioned in the introduction to this paper, identifying causal relationships in these labor issues is hard.

Subject to this important qualification, this empirical research suggests that, by the end of the 1990s, average union-nonunion differences in labor productivity appear to be negligible. Where differences emerge, they are in those establishments with fragmented bargaining. Such bargaining is unusual—approximately only 7 percent of workplaces in 1998 were characterized by fragmented bargaining.[62] This allows the generalization that unionism may serve as an agent permitting employees to participate in shaping their work environments with little or no loss in productivity.

5.5 The Benefits of Unionism to Workers

The ultimate mission of unionism is to enhance the lot of employees in various ways. Some of these ways are through increasing the employees' monetary compensation. In addition, unions aim to increase the participation of workers in fashioning their work environments. One might expect that the decline in unionism in Britain over the past two decades would have been accompanied by a fall in employees' monetary and nonmonetary rewards from work. Is there evidence that this has happened?

5.5.1 Unions and Wage Differences

First consider the benefits from unionism as suggested by the gap between the wages paid to unionized and to nonunionized workers. Here there appears to be more disagreement than there is in the United States over each economy's patterns of union-relative wage effects. For manual workers in Britain, the central tendency of the estimates of the gap between union and nonunion wages was approximately 10 percent in the 1980s. This estimate varied by plant and worker characteristics so that, for instance, it was near to zero for a very large number of establishments, but was as much as 14 percent for semiskilled manual workers in a pre-entry closed shop condition (see Stewart 1987, 1991). The union-nonunion wage differential is higher when product markets are not competitive and is close to zero when product markets are competitive (Stewart 1990). However, there are studies where both smaller and larger wage differentials have been estimated (see, e.g., Andrews, Bell, and Upward 1998 and Hildreth 1999). Some of these variations may be attributed to differences in the workers being studied and to control variables used. There is need for a systematic explanation for the variations among these estimates.[63]

There is also not a consistent pattern regarding estimates of the change in the union-nonunion wage gap over time. Some researchers (e.g., Blanchflower 1999) infer that the union-nonunion wage gap has remained re-

62. This figure of 7 percent is arrived as follows. According to WERS, collective bargaining was the dominant form of pay setting in 1998 in 29 percent of workplaces (Millward, Bryson, and Forth 2000, 186). Among these workplaces, the proportion not using single-table bargaining fell from 60 percent in 1990 to 23 percent in 1998 (Millward, Bryson, and Forth, 203). Hence, among all workplaces, the incidence of fragmented bargaining is about 7 percent (23 percent of 29 percent).

63. An important step toward that systematic explanation is supplied by Andrews, Stewart et al. (1998), who apply different estimating procedures and specifications to a single data set.

markably constant since the early 1980s; others suggest small declines (e.g., Stewart 1991, Hildreth 1999); while still others hint at rising union-nonunion wage gaps (e.g., Andrews, Bell, and Upward 1998). In view of these mixed results, it is difficult to be confident about the movements over time in union-nonunion wages. However, I am inclined to accept the implications from the more straightforward computations (such as those of Blanchflower) that suggest small variations over time in union-nonunion wage gaps.[64] If this is true, then is this stability in the face of declining unionism a paradox? Not necessarily. Suppose union-nonunion wage gaps in 1980 varied across workplaces, and suppose workplaces where these gaps were least have dropped out of the union sector; then declining unionism will be accompanied by rising union-nonunion wage gaps. This example illustrates how the changing composition of workplaces in the union sector may yield average union-nonunion wage differentials that are rising, falling, or constant over time. But taken at face value, the typical union worker's higher pay over his or her nonunion counterpart has changed little over the past twenty years. Or, expressed differently, for those who believe that unions raise the pay of nonunion workers as well as those of union workers, the decline in unionism since the late 1970s has not hurt the average nonunion worker's pay any more than the average union worker's pay.

5.5.2 Unions and Work Life

Consider now some nonmonetary aspects of the work environment. Drawing on data from the repeated British Social Attitudes surveys, figure 5.7 graphs the percentage of employees who give unfavorable responses to questions regarding labor relations and the quality of management. For instance, the series "poor employee relations" measures the percentage of employees who believe they work at establishments where labor relations are unsatisfactory. The series "not well managed" measures the percentage of employees who have unfavorable views of the quality of management at their places of work. These two series may have drifted up slightly over the decade since 1983, but whatever changes there have been look very small by comparison with the decline of unionism.[65] Not surprisingly, the percentage of employees who believe they have no voice in workplace decisions (given by the series "no say in work decisions") has risen, although again the change is very much smaller than the drop in union representa-

64. This preference derives from what seems to be the case with the U.S. research, where ingenious, sometimes baroque, estimating methods yield much more fickle and unreliable estimates than more prosaic methods; see Lewis (1986). This does not mean necessarily that the same will be the case in Britain, but it does affect the way I place my bets.

65. The unfavorable percentage response in 1996 for "poor employee relations" is significantly greater than that for 1983 on a standard normal test while the response in 1996 for "not well managed" is not significantly different from the response in 1983. Regardless, the argument in the text is that the changes between 1983 and 1996 are very much smaller than the retreat of unionism.

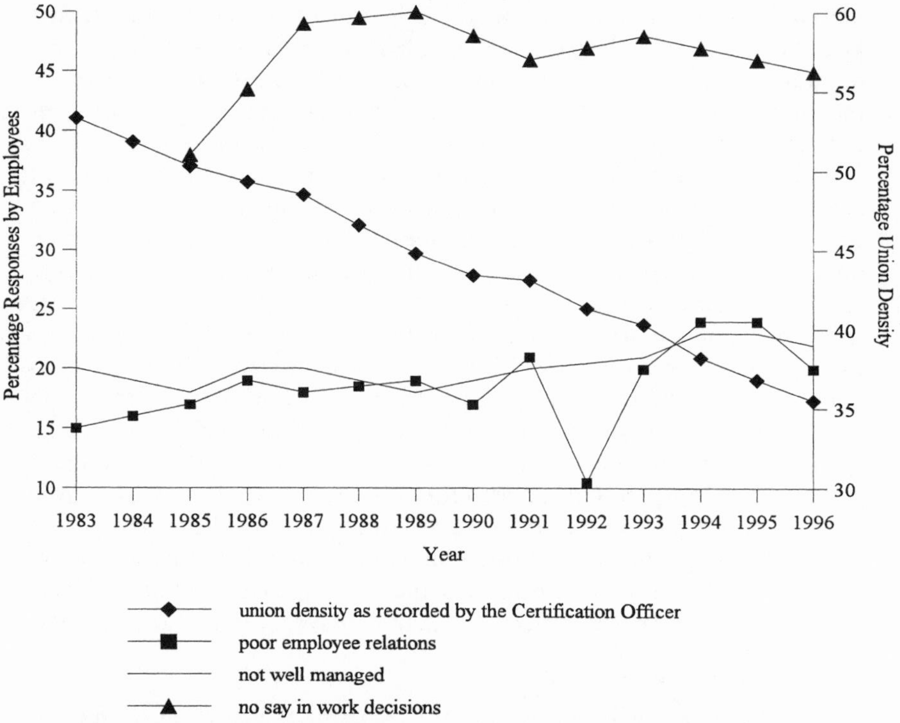

Fig. 5.7 Employees' perceptions and union membership density, 1983–1996

Notes: The series measuring employees' perceptions are drawn from Bryson and McKay (1997). Union density data are the same as those graphed in figure 5.1.

The series "poor employee relations" measures the percentage of employees who respond "not very" or "not at all" to the question, "In general, how would you describe relations between management and other employees at your workplace: very good, quite good, not very good, or not at all good?" The values for 1988 and 1992 are interpolated.

The series "not well managed" measures the percentage of employees who respond "not well managed" to the question, "In general, would you say your workplace was very well managed, quite well managed, or not well managed?" The values for 1988 and 1992 are interpolated.

The series "no say in work decisions" measures the percentage of employees who respond "no say" when asked, "Suppose there was going to be some decision made at your place of work that changed the way you do your job. Do you think that you personally would have any say in the decision about the change or not?" The values for 1986, 1988, 1990, 1992, 1994, and 1995 are interpolated.

tion and most of the change took place in the 1980s, not the 1990s as unionism continued its retreat. Given the sharp drop in union density over this same period from the 1980s to mid-1990s, the absence of a strong movement in these perceptions is noteworthy.

The 1998 WERS reported that about half of employees felt managers treated them fairly and that 65 percent agreed or strongly agreed that they felt loyalty toward the organizations they worked for (see Cully et al. 1999, table 8.3 and fig. 8.6). A suppressed resentment of management is not evident from these figures. Workers are much more likely to have unfavorable attitudes regarding labor relations at their places of work if those workplaces were unionized. Employees at establishments with no worker representation were most likely to see their industrial relations as "very good."[66]

Moreover, the belief that unions make a meaningful difference to work life is not widely maintained: 46 percent of union members and only 30 percent of nonunion members believe that unions make a difference to what it is like at work.[67] Even among union members in recognized workplaces, about the same fraction felt the union was no better than the individual at representing an employee's interests about work complaints (see tables 9.6 and 9.7 of Cully et al. 1999). In the 1999 British Social Attitudes survey, among employees in unionized workplaces, fewer than two in five (37 percent) felt the union helped in running the establishment (Bryson 1999). Though there are some exceptions, the fall in unionism within continuing workplaces in the private sector is not attributable to management's hostility to unions, but to "a withering of support for membership among the existing workforce, plus a lack of recruitment as the workforce evolved" (Millward, Bryson, and Forth 2000, 92). Management attributed the decline in the recognition of unions at the workplace to a drop in employees' interest in union representation and to a rethinking of policies toward employee relations by management (Millward, Bryson, and Forth, 105). The impression from these figures is that unions are not being successful in persuading employees that they need union representation, so there is little in these numbers to support Towers' (1997) claim that there is a serious representation gap in British workplaces.

One reason workers appear not to have grieved over the loss of union representation is that various "direct" forms of participation—workplace meetings, briefing groups, and problem-solving groups—have grown in place of "indirect" forms, such as unions and consultative committees. Asking employees for their assessment of the effectiveness of these direct mechanisms, Millward, Bryson, and Forth (2000, 128–135) find that these nonunion voice mechanisms seem to work well in informing employees of proposed workplace changes and in making management responsive to

66. It has sometimes been argued that unions are inclined to make workers more aware of shortcomings in their work environments and that this explains why union members tend to report less-favorable labor relations. However, in the 1999 British Social Attitudes survey, nonmembers working in unionized workplaces had significantly less favorable perceptions on labor relations than nonmembers in workplaces without unions. See Bryson (1999).

67. In fact, employees were divided into three groups: union members; never union members; and those who were once union members, but are no longer union members. When asked whether "unions make a difference to what it is like at work," 46 percent of current union members agreed, 30 percent of never union members agreed, and 26 percent of former union members agreed. In a separate survey, "participation through union representation was associated with a generally more negative view of the effectiveness of work arrangements" (Gallie et al. 1998, 113).

suggestions from employees. On only one dimension—whether workers feel they are being treated fairly by management—is it the case that unionized workers (when represented on a consultative committee) are more satisfied with their workplace environments than nonunion workers with these "direct" forms of representation. Though unions may derive solace from this result, what is striking is that this is the only issue on which unionism scores significantly better than these other mechanisms. Moreover, it is not unionism per se that produces this result, but the combination of union recognition and union presence on a consultative committee, a combination found in merely 4 percent of workplaces in 1998.

These findings should be of real concern to union leaders. To express the issue starkly, they raise the question of whether unions are becoming irrelevant. Instead of interacting with the agents of the union, managements (especially in the private sector) are making use of other means to communicate with their employees, many of whom have ambivalent feelings about unions. Neither workers nor employers are expressing strong preferences for the need for unionism at the workplace. While the Gallup Opinion Poll reports general sympathy (and growing approval in the 1990s—see fig. 5.3) among all adults for the activities of unions, this does not appear to translate into a great unmet need among workers for union organization. Unions have lost 5.5 million members since 1979 and yet the labor force appears not to be clamouring for much more representation.

5.6 A Summing-Up

The British experience over the past forty years or so offers an opportunity to draw some particular conclusions about unions in Britain and also to speculate on unionism in general.

First, what explains the retreat of unionism in Britain? The changed legal framework for unionism provides an obvious explanation. However, laws never operate in a vacuum but in a particular context, and the context defines their impact. It is the context that accounts for the fact that the legal changes introduced by Heath's government in the early 1970s failed to reform industrial relations. What are the principal features of the 1980s and 1990s context that explain why the changed legal environment had so much bite?

One feature is the abandonment in the 1980s of the goal of full-employment macroeconomic policies, which meant that organized labor operated in a much more inhospitable environment. The second key feature is that the rigors of considerably greater product market competition in the 1980s and 1990s were transmitted to labor markets as firms recognized the necessity of reforming their labor practices. The new legal backdrop permitted managements to take charge of industrial relations, the "harder" product market environment made the reform of labor relations practices urgent, and the increased unemployment weakened the ability of unions to resist them. Above all, the legal framework allowed *new* firms greater flexibility in choosing labor relations procedures that fitted their circumstances and, in fact, these procedures often involved no union presence. According to this argument, the new legislative framework of the 1980s and 1990s *permitted* the development of a new climate of industrial relations policies, but it was the renunciation of full employment goals and the harsher competitive environment that complemented the new legal setting and produced unionism's decline.[68]

How did the decline in unionism affect the growth and distribution of incomes? The growth in real incomes ultimately matches the growth in productivity and there is some slight evidence that the decline in unionism contributed to faster growth than would have otherwise occurred. It was argued above that, by the end of the 1990s, the association between unionism and low labor productivity appears to have been broken except in those workplaces where many unions bargain separately. Such fragmented bargaining is now unusual so that, in general, unions are no longer a factor depressing labor productivity.

With respect to the distribution of incomes, the sharp rise in wage inequality coincides with the decline in unionism and it is difficult to resist the temptation to link the two. This presents the familiar dilemma: suppose the decline of unionism contributed, first, to a faster growth in productivity and thus in income and, second, to greater inequality in incomes; is greater income inequality at a higher level of real income preferred to narrower inequality at a lower level of income?

How has the decline in unionism affected the workplace experience of employees? Given the sharp reduction in union representation, the change in indicators of the quality of work life has been surprisingly small. There does not appear to be a pervasive, unmet demand for union representation. On the contrary, the creation of new, direct forms of communication between management and employees have made many workers believe that union representation is unnecessary. Increasingly, unions are returning to

68. Other assessments of the causes of the decline in unionism have come to conclusions consistent with this. Thus, Brown and Wadhwani (1990, 68) conclude that "the driving force behind changes in industrial relations practices in the 1980s . . . has been increased product market competition, precipitated by a variety of circumstance, which has obliged employers to put their own houses in order." In the same vein, Dunn and Metcalf (1996, 93) determine that "unemployment, including two deep recessions, and stiffer product market competition remain of paramount importance in weakening unions and stimulating management . . . where we can pinpoint the law's impact, legislative intrusion does not automatically bring the expected economic changes. Notably, when management eliminated closed shops in favour of merely recommending union membership, some economic consequences of 'compulsory' unionism survived." Haskel's (1991) empirical analysis of labor productivity growth in eighty-one manufacturing industries from 1980 to 1986 suggests that the effects of greater product market competition were transferred to the labor market by shedding productivity-restraining practices.

their nineteenth-century role as "friendly societies" providing members with personal services such as group insurance policies, adult-learning opportunities, and legal advice.

Although the statutory agenda of the Conservative governments' approach to labor markets in the 1980s and 1990s was contentious at the time of its introduction, today much of it has passed into general acceptance. What has not been accepted? First, the removal of wage floors by abolishing wages councils at a time when the wage structure widened considerably has left observers disturbed by the consequences for low-paid workers of unregulated labor markets. The response has been the imposition of a National Minimum Wage in April 1999. Introduced at a time when general unemployment is not regarded as a principal policy problem, there appears remarkable agreement on the value of a National Minimum Wage. In part this is a by-product of the fact that it has been set at a level that risks only small employment consequences.[69]

The second area of policy disagreement with the deregulation of the 1980s and 1990s concerns procedures for the recognition of unions in workplaces. To address this, in situations where an employer rejects a union's request for recognition, the current Labour government proposes a version of the North American system of representational elections.[70] How this will change the climate of industrial relations and the extent of unionism is difficult to forecast. Much depends on the precise operation of the system. However, even with the cooperation and goodwill of employers, if the evidence brought forward in section 5.5 of this paper is correct, workers' attitudes toward unions need to become more favorable before the drop in union representation is reversed.

There is no general nostalgia for the 1970s brand of unionism in Britain. There is a sense that British labor markets are working more effectively than some on the European continent. The drop in unemployment in Britain compared with that in continental Europe is sometimes attributed to a delayed reaction to the deregulation of the 1980s and 1990s. Cross-country comparisons are fraught with difficulties, but among large economies there does seem to be a pattern such that those countries that have avoided increases in unemployment have done so only at the cost of greater earnings inequality. And this trade-off seems to be related to changes in collective bargaining: Unemployment has tended to increase least where collective bargaining has shrunk the most. This is suggested by the data in table 5.8, which lists changes in male unemployment rates, changes in male earnings inequality, and changes in the coverage of collective-bargaining

69. The National Minimum Wage was introduced at £3.60 for those aged twenty-one years and over and at £3.20 for those aged eighteen to twenty years. Metcalf (1999) estimates the National Minimum Wage affected 8 percent of previously employed workers.

70. If the union can show that a majority of workers in the bargaining unit are union members, no representation election is needed and the union will be granted bargaining rights.

Table 5.8 **Changes in Male Unemployment Rates, Male Earnings Inequality, and the Coverage of Collective Bargaining Contracts from the Late 1970s to 1990s: Selected Countries**

	Proportional Changes in Male Unemployment Rates (1)	Percent Changes in Male Earnings Inequality (2)	Percent Changes in Coverage of Union Contracts (3)
Australia	0.50	7.30	–9.09
Canada	0.20	8.96	–2.70
France	1.58	1.18	11.76
Germany	2.32	–5.46	1.10
Italy	0.88	15.28	–3.53
Sweden	2.95	4.46	3.49
Japan	1.27	6.95	–25.00
United Kingdom	0.24	36.78	–32.86
United States	–0.18	36.79	–30.49

Notes: Column (1): Let $U(i, t)$ be the male unemployment percentage of country i in year t. Column (1) lists $[U(i, 1999) - U(i, 1979)]/[U(i, 1979)]$. The data are drawn from the September 1983 and June 2000 issues of OECD's *Employment Outlook.*

Column (2): Let $D(i, t)$ be the ratio in year t and in country i of the earnings of male workers at the 90th percentile to the earnings of male workers at the 10th percentile. Column (2) lists $100^*[D(i, 1995) - D(i, 1979)]/[D(i, 1979)]$. The data are drawn from the July 1996 issue of OECD's *Employment Outlook.*

Column (3): Let $C(i, t)$ be the percentage of workers in country i and year t covered by collective bargaining contracts. Column (3) lists $100^*[C(i, 1994) - C(i, 1980)]/[C(i, 1980)]$. The data are drawn from the July 1997 of OECD's *Employment Outlook.*

contracts in nine major economies.[71] Figure 5.8 graphs the relationship between unemployment changes and changes in collective bargaining for these nine countries: Where the range of collective bargaining contracts has grown (in France, Sweden, and Germany), unemployment rates have increased the most; where the coverage of collective bargaining has contracted (Britain and the United States), unemployment rates have increased least.[72] It appears as if, over the past twenty years or so, competitive and

71. The unemployment rates of men are used to avoid the persistent differences among countries in the propensity of women to work. In fact, it would be better to use not merely unemployment rates to measure labor utilization rates, but also employment propensities, hours of work, and early retirement rates. Earnings inequality usually changes slowly while cyclical movements in unemployment rates are much more evident. Therefore, the association between unemployment changes and wage-inequality changes is much more sensitive to choice of the year to compute unemployment-rate changes than earnings-inequality changes. Presumably "permanent" unemployment rates and other measures of labor utilization should be used, not those in column (1) of table 5.8.

72. Some smaller economies do not conform easily to this story. Thus, New Zealand provides an example of an economy where both unemployment and earnings inequality have increased while the extent of collective bargaining has fallen considerably. In the Netherlands, unemployment has not risen while earnings inequality and the coverage of collective bargaining agreements have changed little. The trade-offs suggested in table 5.8 seem more evident in the larger than the smaller economies.

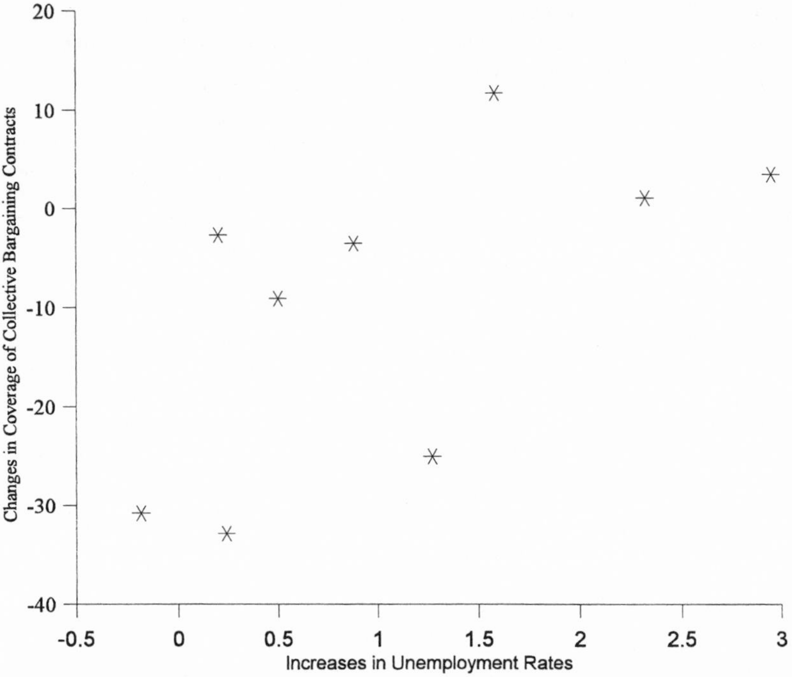

Fig. 5.8 Changes in unemployment rates and in the coverage of collective bargaining contracts: selected countries
Sources: See table 5.8.

technological pressures on labor markets have tended to manifest themselves in changes in labor utilization in economies where government and labor union wage-setting institutions are extensive, and in earnings inequality where these wage-setting institutions are less intrusive or where they have been brushed aside.

This is a sweeping simplification of a much more complex situation. Though this emphasizes the similarity of the experience of British and U.S. labor markets, there are very important differences. For instance, it appears as if flows of individuals into and out of unemployment in Britain are nothing like as large as those in the United States. Also, the increases in earnings inequality in Britain and the United States are around different trends in real wages, rising trends at the 10th earnings decile in Britain and falling trends at the 10th earnings decile in the United States. Moreover, while the case for a "representation gap" may be moot for Britain, it is far less so for the United States (see Freeman and Rogers 1999). Further, Britain's place in the European Union points to the likelihood of new regulatory initiatives in the future, including a growing role for works councils. All this cautions against simple classifications of countries that gloss over the richness of experiences.

However, it is palpable that British labor markets look far less "corporatist," far more like textbook competitive markets, than they did at the close of the 1970s. And the retreat of unionism is very much a part of this change. Indeed, because British labor markets today have a much more exacting competitive character, unions in the future will need to run much faster to stay in the same place. The relentless decline of unionism in Britain since 1979 testifies to its somewhat fragile character. The decline cannot be traced to a single event or circumstance, yet, bit by bit, through a slow yet inexorable process, British unionism has become marginalized in the private sector of the economy. Given the birth-and-death character of firms in a market economy, when the locus of unionism is at the workplace, unionism must constantly recruit new members and organize new firms simply to stay in the same place. To extend their reach, unions have to run even faster, something that has happened neither in Britain nor in the United States. The new environment that will change this is not at all evident. Yet it seems to be in the nature of unionism that its cycles of growth and decline are often unexpected. Perhaps a period of union growth in Britain (instigated by the growing influence of European Union legislation) is just around the corner. If so, it will be another surprise.

References

Adams, Roy J. 1993. Regulating unions and collective bargaining: A global, historical analysis of determinants and consequences. *Comparative Labor Law Journal* 14 (3): 272–301.

Alton, Lee J., and Joseph P. Ferrie. 1999. *Southern paternalism and the American welfare state: Economics, politics, and institutions in the South, 1865–1965.* Cambridge: Cambridge University Press.

Andrews, Martyn J., David N. F. Bell, and Richard Upward. 1998. Union coverage differentials: Some estimates for Britain using the New Earnings Survey panel data set. *Oxford Bulletin of Economics and Statistics* 60 (1): 47–77.

Andrews, Martyn J., Mark B. Stewart, Joanna K. Swaffield, and Richard Upward. 1998. The estimation of union wage differentials and the impact of methodological choices. *Labour Economics* 5:449–474.

Aylen, Jonathan. 1982. Plant size and efficiency in the steel industry: An international comparison. *National Institute Economic Review* 100 (May): 65–76.

Bean, Charles, and Nicholas Crafts. 1996. British economic growth since 1945: Relative economic decline . . . and Renaissance? In *Economic growth in Europe since 1945,* ed. Nicholas Crafts and Gianni Toniolo, 131–172. Cambridge: Cambridge University Press, Center for Economic Policy Research.

Blanchflower, David G. 1999. Changes over time in union relative wage effects in Great Britain and the United States. In *The history and practice of economics: Essays in honor of Bernard Corry and Maurice Peston,* ed. Sami Daniel, Philip Arestis, and John Grahl, 3–32. Cheltenham, U.K.: Edward Elgar.

Booth, Alison L. 1995. *The economics of the trade union.* Cambridge: Cambridge University Press.

Brown, William, Simon Deakin, and Paul Ryan. 1997. The effects of British industrial relations legislation 1979–97. *National Institute Economic Review* 161 (July): 69–83.

Brown, William, and Sushil Wadhwani. 1990. The economic effects of industrial relations legislation since 1979. *National Institute Economic Review* 131 (February): 57–70.

Bryson, Alex. 1999. Are unions good for industrial relations? In *British social attitudes: The 16th report. Who shares new labour values?,* ed. Roger Jowell et al., 65–95. Aldershot, U.K.: Ashgate. National Centre for Social Research.

Bryson, Alex, and Stephen McKay. 1997. What about the workers? In *British social attitudes: The 14th report. The end of conservative values?,* ed. Roger Jowell et al., 23–48. Ashgate, U.K.: Social and Community Planning Research.

Coleman, James S. 1998. Social capital in the creation of human capital. *American Journal of Sociology* 44 (Supplement): S95–S120.

Cornfield, Daniel B. 1999. Shifts in public approval of labor unions in the United States, 1936–1999. The Gallup Organization. Available at [http://www.gallup.com/poll/gs990902.asp].

Cully, Mark, Stephen Woodland, Andrew O'Reilly, and Gill Dix. 1999. *Britain at work: As depicted by the 1998 Workplace Employee Relations Survey.* London: Routledge.

Daniel, W. W. 1987. *Workplace industrial relations and technical change.* London: Her Majesty's Stationery Office, Economic and Social Research Council.

Daniel, W. W., and Neil Millward. 1983. *Workplace industrial relations in Britain.* London: Heinemann Educational Books.

Dicey, A. V. 1914. *Lectures on the relation between law and public opinion in England during the nineteenth century.* 2nd ed. London: Macmillan.

Dimsdale, N. H. 1991. British monetary policy since 1945. In *The British economy since 1945,* ed. N. F. R. Crafts and N. W. C. Woodwards, 89–140. Oxford, U.K.: Clarendon Press.

Disney, Richard. 1990. Explanations of the decline in trade union density in Britain: An appraisal. *British Journal of Industrial Relations* 28 (2): 165–177.

Disney, Richard, Amanda Gosling, and Stephen Machin. 1996. What has happened to union recognition in Britain? *Economica* 63 (249): 1–18.

Dunn, Stephen, and David Metcalf. 1996. Trade union law since 1979. In *Contemporary industrial relations: A critical analysis,* ed. Ian Beardwell, 66–98. Oxford: Oxford University Press.

Edwards, P. K., and George Sayers Bain. 1988. Why are trade unions becoming more popular? Unions and public opinion in Britain. *British Journal of Industrial Relations* 26 (3): 311–326.

Freeman, Richard, and Jeffrey Pelletier. 1990. The impact of industrial relations legislation on British union density. *British Journal of Industrial Relations* 28 (2): 141–164.

Freeman, Richard B., and Joel Rogers. 1999. *What workers want.* Ithaca, N.Y.: Cornell University Press.

Gallie, Duncan, Michael White, Yuan Cheng, and Mark Tomlinson. 1998. *Restructuring the employment relationship.* Oxford, U.K.: Clarendon Press.

Gregg, Paul, Stephen Machin, and David Metcalf. 1993. Signals and cycles? Productivity growth and changes in union status in British companies, 1984–89. *Economic Journal* 103 (419): 894–907.

Grout, Paul A. 1984. Investment and wages in the absence of legally binding labour contracts. *Econometrica* 52 (2): 449–460.

Harris, Robin, ed. 1997. *The collected speeches of Margaret Thatcher.* London: HarperCollins.

Haskel, Jonathan. 1991. Imperfect competition, work practices, and productivity growth. *Oxford Bulletin of Economics and Statistics* 53 (3): 265–279.
Hayek, F. A. 1980. 1980s unemployment and the unions. Hobart Paper no. 87. London: Institute of Economic Affairs.
Hicks, John R. 1955. Economic foundations of wage policy. *The Economic Journal* 259 (65): 389–404.
Hicks, Stephen. 2000. Trade union membership 1998–99: An analysis of data from the Certification Officer and the Labour Force Survey. *Labour Market Trends* 108 (7): 329–340.
Hildreth, Andrew. 1999. What has happened to the union wage differential in Britain in the 1990s? *Oxford Bulletin of Economics and Statistics* 61 (1): 5–31.
Hobsbawm, E. J. 1964. The machine breakers. In *Labouring men: Studies in the history of labour,* 5–22. New York: Basic Books.
Kahn-Freund, Otto. 1983. *Labour and the law.* 3rd ed. Edited by Paul Davies and Mark Freedland. London: Stevens & Sons.
Koedijk, Kees, and Jeroen Kremers. 1996. Market opening, regulation, and growth in Europe. *Economic Policy* 23 (October): 443–467.
Lewis, H. Gregg. 1986. *Union relative wage effects: A survey.* Chicago: University of Chicago Press.
MacGregor, Duncan. 1999. Employment in the public and private sectors. *Economic Trends* 547 (June): 25–38.
Machin, Stephen. 1999. Union decline in Britain. Unpublished paper, December.
Machin, Stephen, and Mark Stewart. 1990. Unions and the financial performance of British private-sector establishments. *Journal of Applied Econometrics* 5 (4): 327–350.
———. 1996. Trade unions and financial performance. *Oxford Economic Papers* 48 (2): 213–241.
Machin, Stephen, Mark Stewart, and John Van Reenan. 1993. Multiple unionism, fragmented bargaining and economic outcomes in unionised U.K. establishments. In *New perspectives on industrial disputes,* ed. David Metcalf and Simon Milner, 55–69. London: Routledge.
Marsh, David. 1990. Public opinion, trade unions, and Mrs. Thatcher. *British Journal of Industrial Relations* 28 (1): 57–65.
Metcalf, David. 1989. Water notes dry up: The impact of the Donovan reform proposals and Thatcherism at work on labour productivity in British manufacturing industry. *British Journal of Industrial Relations* 27 (1): 1–31.
———. 1990. Union presence and labour productivity in British manufacturing industry: A reply to Nolan and Marginson. *British Journal of Industrial Relations* 28 (2): 249–266.
———. 1991. British unions: Dissolution or resurgence? *Oxford Review of Economic Policy* 7 (1): 18–32.
———. 1999. The British national minimum wage. *British Journal of Industrial Relations* 37 (2): 171–201.
Metcalf, David, and Mark Stewart. 1992. Closed shops and relative pay: Institutional arrangements or high density? *Oxford Bulletin of Economics and Statistics* 54 (4): 503–516.
Millward, Neil, Alex Bryson, and John Forth. 2000. *All change at work? British employment relations 1980–1998, as portrayed by the Workplace Industrial Relations Survey Series.* London: Routledge.
Millward, Neil, and Mark Stevens. 1986. *British workplace industrial relations 1980–1984.* Aldershot, U.K.: Gower Publishing.
———. 1988. Union density in the regions. *Employment Gazette* 96 (5): 286–295.

Milner, Simon. 1995. The coverage of collective pay-setting institutions in Britain, 1895–1990. *British Journal of Industrial Relations* 33 (1): 69–91.

Organization for Economic Cooperation and Development (OECD). 1996. Earnings inequality, low-paid employment, and earnings mobility. *Employment Outlook* (July): 59–108.

Oulton, Nicholas. 1990. Labour productivity in U.K. manufacturing in the 1970s and in the 1980s. *National Institute Economic Review* 132 (May): 71–91.

Phelps Brown, E. H. 1959. *The growth of British industrial relations.* London: Macmillan.

Phelps Brown, E. H., and P. E. Hart. 1952. The share of wages in national income. *The Economic Journal* 246 (62): 253–277.

Prais, S. J. 1981. *Productivity and industrial structure.* Cambridge: Cambridge University Press.

Pratton, C. F. 1976. Labour productivity differentials within international companies. University of Cambridge, Department of Applied Economics. Occasional Papers no. 50. Cambridge, U.K.: University of Cambridge.

Price, Robert, and George Sayers Bain. 1983. Union growth in Britain: Retrospect and prospect. *British Journal of Industrial Relations* 21 (1): 46–68.

Robinson, E. A. G. 1931. *The structure of competitive industry.* London: Pitman Publishing.

Schmitt, John. 1995. The changing structure of male earnings in Britain, 1974–1988. In *Differences and changes in wage structures,* ed. Richard B. Freeman and Lawrence F. Katz, 177–204. Chicago: University of Chicago Press.

Stewart, Mark B. 1987. Collective bargaining arrangements, closed shops, and relative pay. *The Economic Journal* 97 (385): 140–156.

———. 1990. Union wage differentials, product market influences, and the division of rents. *The Economic Journal* 100 (403): 1122–137.

———. 1991. Union wage differentials in the face of changes in the economic and legal environment. *Economica* 58 (230): 155–172.

———. 1995. Union wage differentials in an era of declining unionization. *Oxford Bulletin of Economics and Statistics* 57 (2): 143–166.

Towers, Brian. 1997. *The representation gap: Change and reform in the British and American workplace.* Oxford: Oxford University Press.

Undy, Roger, Patricia Fosh, Huw Morris, Paul Smith, and Roderick Martin. 1996. *Managing the unions: The impact of legislation on trade unions' behavior.* Oxford: Oxford University Press.

United Kingdom: Royal Commission on Trade Unions and Employers' Associations 1965–68. 1968a. *Report* (Donovan Commission). Cmnd. 3623. June.

———. 1968b. Selected Written Evidence Submitted to the Royal Commission. London: Her Majesty's Stationery Office.

Wedderburn, K. William. 1986. *The worker and the law.* 3rd ed. London: Street & Maxwell.

Wood, Stephen, and John Godard. 1999. The statutory union recognition procedure in the Employment Relations Bill: A comparative analysis. *British Journal of Industrial Relations* 37 (2): 203–245.

6

Pension Reform and Economic Performance in Britain in the 1980s and 1990s

Richard Disney, Carl Emmerson, and Sarah Smith

6.1 Introduction

6.1.1 Overview of Reform Process

Over the last twenty years, successive governments of Great Britain have embarked on a series of reforms of the pension[1] program designed both to reduce the prospective costs of social security, and to permit more flexibility and individual choice in secondary pension provision.[2] Central to this

Richard Disney is professor of labor economics at the University of Nottingham and a research fellow of the Institute for Fiscal Studies (IFS). Carl Emmerson is director of the pensions and public-spending research sector at IFS. Sarah Smith is a lecturer at the London School of Economics and Political Science and a research associate at IFS.

We are grateful to participants at the preconference, the editors, a referee, and Alissa Goodman for comments on an earlier draft. Colleagues at IFS offered useful advice. The research was funded by the Economic and Social Research Council Centre for the Microeconomic Analysis of Public Policy at IFS. The Family Resources Survey is Crown copyright and the data archive is thanked for access to the British Household Panel Survey. The views expressed here do not necessarily represent the official view of the Financial Services Authority.

1. There are some important differences in nomenclature between the United States and Europe. In Europe, the term "pension" tends to refer to all pensions, whether provided publicly (by the state) or privately. "Social security," the term used for state-provided pensions in the United States, has a different connotation in Europe, generally referring to the whole social insurance program. "Occupational pension scheme" is a specific term in Great Britain, referring to an employer-provided (group) pension plan. The basic state retirement pension in Great Britain, which pays (broadly) the same weekly amount to all pensioners, is often referred to as a "flat rate" pension—although in the United States, "flat rate" is sometimes used as a term for a proportional tax system. Finally, the word "scheme" does not have the same negative connotation as in U.S. parlance. We have broadly tried to adopt U.S. terminology in this paper.

2. The structure of the first tier of coverage (the basic state pension) was unchanged by these reforms, though its generosity was reduced. See Dilnot et al. (1994), Disney, Emmerson, and Tanner (1999), and Banks and Emmerson (2000).

strategy has been an evolution of the mechanism of "contracting-out," introduced originally in 1978 as a means of integrating existing occupational pension plans into the new State Earnings-Related Pension Scheme (SERPS). In essence, contracting-out means that employers and employees obtain part of their social security pension through a private pension fund instead of the state. In compensation for establishing a private arrangement, employers and employees pay a lower payroll tax rate (known as the National Insurance contribution). An important consequence arises because the social security program is purely pay-as-you-go (PAYG) financed, whereas most pension plans, at least in the private sector, are fully funded. Thus, greater contracting-out implies greater prefunding of pension commitments.

Under the 1978 arrangements, individuals could opt out of part of the social security pension, SERPS, only if they worked for an employer who provided an approved defined benefit (DB) occupational pension plan. The approved employer's plan guaranteed to pay the employee a pension approximately equal to what they would have received from the state, known as the Guaranteed Minimum Pension (GMP).[3] In return, the employer would pay a lower combined rate of employee and employer National Insurance contributions to the government.[4]

However, a major innovation in pension policy occurred in 1988, as a result of the 1986 Social Security Act. The government was worried by the projected cost of SERPS once the baby boom generation began to retire in the first quarter of the twenty-first century (Hemming and Kay 1982; Department of Health and Social Security 1984), and sought to cut projected public pension expenditure. To do this, it needed ways to encourage a greater number of individuals to contract out of SERPS. The government adopted a "stick-and-carrot" strategy to this problem. The "stick" was to reduce the generosity of SERPS considerably, so giving a greater incentive to opt out. But coverage by existing DB occupational pensions was stagnating; therefore a "carrot" was needed. This took the form of giving individuals and employers new incentives to contract out, by permitting defined contribution (DC) pension plans also to opt out of SERPS, on what turned out be extremely favorable terms.[5] The government perhaps expected this extra "wave" of opting-out to occur through employer-based DC plans,

3. There were, however, some important differences—for example, indexation postretirement of the GMP was in part subsidized by the government; see Dilnot et al. (1994) for further details.

4. The difference between the "contracted-in" and "contracted-out" National Insurance rates is known as the "contracted-out rebate." Note that, in Britain, most income tax and National Insurance contributions, whether notionally levied on the employee or employer, are collected at source from the employer by the Inland Revenue.

5. See discussion below, and National Audit Office (1991). Of course, employers offering DC plans could not guarantee a target benefit, so the employer was instead required to make a guaranteed minimum *contribution* in such schemes.

but in fact the dominant new form of arrangement became the individually purchased retirement saving account known as a *personal pension.*[6]

Contracting-out works in a somewhat different manner in an individually purchased personal pension. Here the individual makes a contract with an approved private insurance company. The Department of Social Security (DSS) acts as the "clearinghouse," so that the full National Insurance contribution is paid by the employer to the Inland Revenue, and the contracted-out rebate component is then transferred and paid directly by the DSS to the individual's approved personal pension provider.[7]

Personal pensions were also encouraged by the fact that the 1988 legislation made membership of a pension plan, whether state provided or employer provided, entirely a matter of choice. This meant that an individual *had* to have an approved contracted-out pension or belong to SERPS, but could not be forced by the employer to join the employer's plan, if one was offered.[8] Roughly 25 percent of the workforce (over 6 million employees) opted to purchase personal pensions over the period 1988–1992, including some 1 million who opted to leave or not to join an existing employer's pension plan. By the middle of the 1990s, roughly three-quarters of the workforce had contracted out of SERPS into some form of private plan, whether DB or DC, or whether employer provided or individually purchased.[9]

It should be noted, finally, that individuals are also free to switch in their working lives between different types of pension plans. Crucially, and unlike some other countries that have gone down this road, contracting-out of the social security program need not be permanent.[10] Indeed, between

6. Defined benefit plans are plans that guarantee a nominal benefit, typically related to a measure of salary. Defined contribution plans simply promise to pay an (unknown) annuity based on the accumulated fund of contributions plus investment returns. A reason for the popularity of personal pensions was that they were heavily advertised and sold. They offered greater flexibility and very generous tax reliefs, but a contributing factor arose because the government had just eliminated tax relief on life insurance. Many insurance companies therefore switched their sales forces to the pension market, and this decision contributed a good deal to the subsequent controversy concerning the "mis-selling" of personal pensions.

7. Thus the contracted-out rebate can be varied across individuals, which is not possible in a group scheme, where the same percentage rebate is paid for all scheme members.

8. An individual could not contribute to a different company plan—say, that of a previous employer. Benefits from such a plan would be "preserved" (deferred) and are revalued in line with price inflation. However, some pension plans, especially in the public sector, are sector specific rather than company specific. At the same time, an employer could not refuse to let an employee join the company plan on the grounds of, say, being part-time, as this constituted a form of indirect discrimination (against women). For the same reason, differential vesting on grounds of gender is not permitted, and indeed, vesting periods in employer-provided plans are not a big issue in Britain, being very much shorter than in, say, the United States.

9. Somewhat surprisingly, it is impossible to find any official data that provide the proportions of workers contracted-in or contracted-out to different types of pension plans, over time.

10. For an analysis of opting-out arrangements in a number of countries, see Disney, Palacios, and Whitehouse (1999).

1988 and 1995, there were incentives for individuals who contracted out of SERPS to contract back in to the social security program at a later age (Disney and Whitehouse 1992b).

These reforms, augmented by further substantial measures in 1995, are far from the end of the pension reform program in Great Britain. Indeed, in 1998 and 1999 the new Labour government proposed a number of further reforms, including yet another "route" for contracted-out private provision (alongside occupational and personal pensions) known as "stakeholder pensions" (DSS 1998). These will basically be benchmarked personal pensions, which all employers employing five or more people will be required to make available to their employees at the workplace (although they will not be directly provided by employers). The idea of this reform is to provide a low-cost pension for those not covered by traditional employer plans, thereby reducing administrative charges relative to individual plans and making pension arrangements more transparent. While this is in some ways a positive step, given some of the difficulties with the other pension routes, there must be some concern as to whether further augmenting choice of individual pension arrangement assists in clarifying or simplifying Great Britain's pension system. At the same time, over a long transition period, SERPS will be replaced by a more explicitly redistributive public pension benefit known as the State Second Pension (or, in some quarters, as S2P).[11]

The main thrust of this paper, however, is not to go through the intricacies of Great Britain's pension reform process in the 1980s and 1990s, which would require a whole volume. We do indeed sketch out Britain's pension program in section 6.2, mentioning some other important facets to the reform process, such as cutbacks in the flat basic state pension, and greater targeting on poor pensioners. The primary purpose, however, is to ask what impact these reforms might have on Britain's economy.[12] The shifts to a greater share of private pension provision and to greater choice of pension provision reflect the central tenets of the Conservative administrations of the 1980s and the first half of the 1990s. However, the Labour administration that came to power in 1997 showed no inclination to reverse this process of opting out of state provision, preferring instead further to focus public resources available on poorer pensioners by increasing the generosity of the main means-tested benefit, through the Minimum Income Guarantee. While 60 percent of pensioner income is currently provided by the state, the current government has stated that it expects this to fall to 40 percent by the middle of this century (DSS 1998).

11. For further discussion of all these issues, see Disney, Emmerson, and Tanner (1999).

12. For some interesting details on the political process, see Lawson (1992) and Peacock (1992).

6.1.2 Pension Reform in Great Britain: The Issues and Summary of Our Main Findings

This chapter therefore examines some of the implications of the sequence of pension reforms for Britain's economy. Given space constraints, we focus on impacts on the *real* economy, leaving aside developments in the *financial* economy, such as the consequences of greater private pension provision for the British capital market. In particular, we examine five aspects of the economy where pension arrangements, and pension reform, might be expected to have some effects. These areas, with a summary of the main findings are as follows:

- *The effect on macroeconomic performance through its impact on household savings rates.* Contributions to occupational pension funds have significantly contributed to household saving for many years in Britain. The introduction of personal pensions in 1988 had both a positive substitution effect, increasing household saving rates, and a positive effect on wealth that will have reduced household saving rates. Our tentative conclusion is that personal pensions contributed a negligible net amount to household saving at the end of the 1980s, despite massive take-up. But a decade later, due to the fact that contributions direct from individuals and their employers had become more important than those from the DSS-paid, contracted-out rebate, personal pensions are likely to have contributed more substantially to household saving.
- *The effect on public finances, and especially the government's intertemporal budget constraint.* Permitting individuals to opt out of part of the state pension program has both intertemporal effects (current versus future tax rates) and intragenerational effects (the relative tax rates paid by opted-out [contracted-out] and contracted-in individuals). These effects arise from the PAYG nature of the financing of the state pension program. Our conclusion is that the contracting-out arrangements have raised payroll tax rates by around 2 1/2 to 3 percentage points, relative to the status quo. It will reduce payroll tax rates by somewhat less as opted-out pensioners retire later in this century. Note that it is inherent in rational voluntary switching that the government never recoups fully its initial payroll tax reductions designed to encourage opting out.
- *The impact on the distribution of incomes.* Ideally, we need a lifetime perspective to trace the impact of greater contracting-out on lifetime incomes. In static comparisons, for example of pensioner inequality, we might expect greater contracting-out to lead to greater inequality for two reasons. First, private pension incomes may be more volatile.

Second, in the 1980s and 1990s, average private pensions grew much faster than the contracting-out arrangements had assumed. This made them worth more than state pensions, and better-off earners tend to contract out. The future impact of personal pensions on income inequality will depend not just on future investment returns but also on the retirement behavior of optants.

- *Effects on labor supply (and especially retirement behavior).* Different types of pension plans have different effects on retirement behavior. There has been a trend to earlier retirement, especially among men, in Great Britain in the 1980s and 1990s. This has been encouraged by the use of existing occupational pension plans and by the relative generosity of the public disability system—since somewhat reduced (Blundell and Johnson 1999; Disney 1999). The majority of optants to personal pensions are somewhat younger than the average workforce and the effect on retirement behavior cannot yet be seen. It is clear that DB plans will discourage early retirement relative to DC plans, due to the fact that the former are back-loaded while the latter are front-loaded (Blundell, Meghir, and Smith 2001). However, contracting out of state pensions into a personal pension has both a wealth effect and a substitution effect that work in opposite directions for the labor supply of older workers. The net impact on labor supply could go either way.
- *Effects on the general operation of the labor market—in particular, how pension reforms might have affected labor market flexibility.* Here we focus on job mobility and take-up of personal pensions, the hypothesis being that individualized personal pensions encourage more mobility, or at least, are taken up by more mobile workers. Given the inherent simultaneity of this issue, it is hard to identify causation. Nevertheless, the introduction of personal pensions offers an unusual "natural experiment," arising from the ability of individuals to choose a personal pension in preference to a company pension plan, if offered. We show that individuals that chose to opt out of a *company* pension plan did indeed exhibit significantly higher subsequent job mobility. In principle, further analysis of this experiment will offer a more precise test than the existing (largely inconclusive) literature on pension plan tenure and job mobility.

6.2 Overview of Reforms in Great Britain

6.2.1 Broad Framework of Britain's Pension Provision

This section briefly outlines Britain's current pension system, and the reforms made over the last twenty years. A more detailed description can be found in, among others, Budd and Campbell (1998); Dilnot et al. (1994);

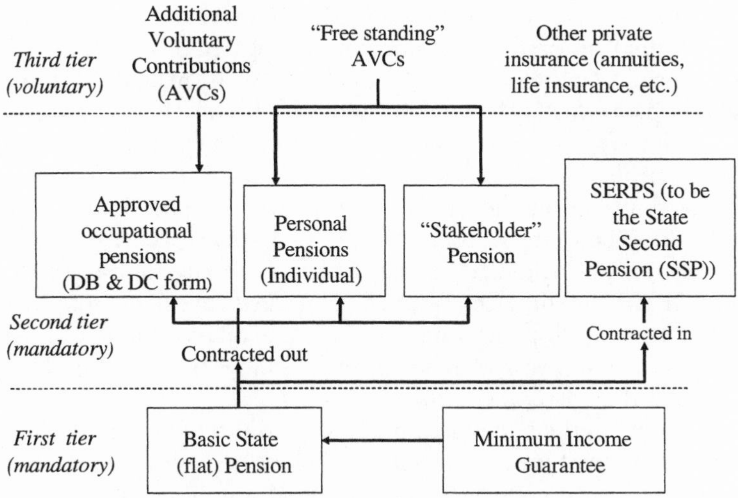

Fig. 6.1 Schema of Great Britain's pension scheme, 2001
Source: Disney, Emmerson, and Tanner (1999).

Banks and Emmerson (2000), and Emmerson and Johnson (2002). Figure 6.1 provides a diagrammatic representation of the current pension system.

Britain's pension system is split into three tiers. The first is provided by the state, and consists of the basic state pension and a significant means-tested (noncontributory) benefits sector. The basic state pension is a flat contributory benefit that is financed on a PAYG basis. The basic state pension in 2001–2002 was worth £72.50 a week for a single pensioner,[13] which is about 15 percent of average male earnings. This is down from around 20 percent of average earnings in the early 1980s, which is as a result of the basic state pension's having been increased broadly in line with price inflation since 1981 while average earnings have grown in real terms.

Those on low incomes are eligible for the Minimum Income Guarantee (MIG), which in 2001–2002 was worth £92.15 a week for a single pensioner, nearly £20 more than the basic state pension (Her Majesty's Treasury 2000c). In addition, pensioners on low incomes may be eligible for housing benefit and council tax benefit, which are means-tested benefits designed to provide assistance toward housing costs and local taxes, respectively. In 1998–1999 some 21 percent of pensioner couples and 47 percent of single pensioners were in receipt of means-tested benefits (DSS 2000c). Government policy is, in the medium term at least, to continue increasing the basic state pension in line with prices while increasing the MIG in line with average earnings. Since the MIG is withdrawn at a rate of

13. The rate for couples was £115.90 (Her Majesty's Treasury 2000b).

100 percent, those with small amounts of income are left no better off than those with small amounts of income from savings. In response, the government has proposed the introduction of a new "pension credit" from October 2003, which will also be targeted at those with relatively low incomes.[14]

The social security system is financed on a PAYG basis. There is no equivalent of the U.S. Social Security Trust Fund, although the National Insurance fund has accrued surpluses over recent years (House of Commons 2000). There are no plans to prefund social security, other than through the indirect route of contracting out. Formally, the basic state pension and SERPS are financed from an earmarked payroll tax, the National Insurance contribution, notionally levied on employees up to an earnings ceiling and on employers with no earnings ceiling. Income-tested benefits are funded out of general taxation.

As described in the introduction, the second tier of mandatory pension provision is split between both state provision, in the form of the SERPS, and private pension provision, in the form of occupational pensions and personal pensions. The original SERPS scheme was introduced in 1978. This paid an individual one-quarter of his or her earnings between a lower and an upper limit from the best twenty years of the individual's lifetime. Earnings were to be uprated to pension age by growth in average earnings, with payments in retirement then being indexed to prices. The Social Security Act of 1986 reduced the generosity of SERPS by lowering the payments to 20 percent of an individual's average earnings, with the average now to be calculated over the individual's entire lifetime, rather than his or her best twenty years.[15]

Individuals were able to contract out of SERPS into an employer's occupational pension plan as long as it guaranteed a retirement income at least as high as SERPS—hence these plans had to operate on a DB basis. In return for opting out, both they and their employers paid a lower rate of National Insurance contribution. The 1986 Social Security Act took the principle of opting-out further by allowing individuals to choose to contract out of SERPS into a DC pension. In return for opting out of SERPS in this way the government paid part of an individual's National Insurance contribution into his or her pension fund. Since this payment was relatively generous, this led to an enormous growth in personal pension take-up. More controversially the 1986 Social Security Act also allowed individuals the right to opt out of an occupational pension plan and into a personal pension. This underlay the "mis-selling" scandal of the late 1980s–early

14. For more information, see DSS (2000b) and Clark (2001, 2002).

15. For more details see, for example, Emmerson and Johnson (2002). The original SERPS scheme could also be inherited in full by a surviving spouse. The 1986 Social Security Act reduced this to 50 percent for those widowed after April 2000. However, this change is now being phased-in over a longer period as a result of government documentation failing to inform individuals of this change. See National Audit Office (2000) for more details.

1990s. This involved cases of people who were badly advised to take out personal pensions when they would have been better off staying in—or joining—their employers' occupational pension plans. A large number of people were affected. By August 1999, some 400,000 people had been offered more than £2.6 billion compensation for having been mis-sold a personal pension.[16]

Further reform is also underway. SERPS is set to be replaced by the State Second Pension—which will be a flat rate-top up to the basic state pension and hence more redistributive toward lower earners.[17] In addition, the government is introducing a "stakeholder pension," which is essentially a personal pension with a heavily regulated charging structure, including an overall cap on charges. Every employer will have to designate a pension provider (such as an insurance company) to the employees and allow individuals to make contributions direct from their wages. Employers will not, however, have to make any contribution on their employees' behalf.[18]

Finally, there is a third tier of voluntary private retirement saving. This can involve making additional voluntary contributions (AVCs) into occupational pension plans, or additional saving through personal pensions or in close substitutes among other financial assets (see Emmerson and Tanner 2000).

6.2.2 Demographic Trends and Projections of Pension Costs

As in most developed countries, the ratio of those over pension age to those in work is set to rise in Great Britain over the next thirty years. However, aging of the population is set to be less severe than in many Organization for Economic Cooperation and Development (OECD) countries (Bos et al. 1994). Moreover, due to the reforms made to Britain's pension system over the last twenty years, the cost of the current system is not projected to require higher rates of National Insurance, as shown in table 6.1. This is a result of reforms such as the change to price indexation of the basic state pension in 1981, the substantial reduction in SERPS generosity in the Social Security acts of 1986 and 1995, and the increase in the state pension age for women aged sixty to sixty-five, which is being phased in by 2020. The reforms to SERPS reduce expenditure on SERPS in 2030–2031 to around just 30 percent of the level implied by the original scheme (Banks and Emmerson 2000). While the replacement of SERPS with the State Sec-

16. See Financial Services Authority (2000) for more details.

17. Under current policies, while the State Second Pension will be a flat-rate pension, the rebates paid to those opting out of this scheme will remain related to earnings. This will provide greater incentives for lower earners to stay in, or return to, the state scheme and for middle and higher earners to opt out of the state scheme. In future the rebate structure could be changed to mitigate these effects.

18. For a more detailed description of the government's proposed pension reforms see, for example, Disney, Emmerson, and Tanner (1999), Emmerson and Tanner (1999), and Agulnik et al. (1999).

Table 6.1 Long-Term Projections for the National Insurance Fund (July 1999)

	2000–01	2010–11	2020–21	2030–31	2050–51
Demographic forecasts (millions)					
Contributors	20.2	21.6	22.2	21.5	21.3
Pensioners	11.0	12.3	12.6	15.2	15.8
Support ratio	1.8	1.7	1.8	1.4	1.4
State expenditures (£billions, 1999–2000 prices)					
Basic state pension	34.4	38.0	41.3	49.4	51.2
SERPS	5.2	9.9	12.6	14.9	15.8
Total expenditure[a]	48.6	57.7	65.9	76.2	79.0
Total expenditure as a share of GDP (%)	5.4	5.6	5.5	5.5	4.2
Joint employee and employer contribution rates[b]	19.9	18.9	18.1	18.6	15.2
GDP per pensioner spending (1999 – 2000 = 100)	99.5	93.0	87.8	75.4	56.2

Source: Government Actuary's Department (1999). These costings do not include the government announcement that the basic state pension was set to rise by more than inflation in April 2001 and April 2002. These increases do not stop National Insurance contribution rates' being able to fall in future.

Notes: See text for explanation of abbreviations.

[a]Includes incapacity benefit, jobseeker's allowance, and some other (more minor) benefits and expenses.

[b]Contribution rates exclude the 1.95 percent currently payable to the National Health Service, and are based on the rate structure introduced in the Social Security Act 1998.

ond Pension will lead to an increase in state expenditure, the required National Insurance contribution rate is still projected to fall by 2030.

6.2.3 The "Pension Burden": Comparison with Other Countries

The reforms to Britain's pension system have ensured that future liabilities will, at the very least, not require substantial rises in tax rates. This is in contrast with many other developed countries, as shown in table 6.2. Great Britain is the only country in which state pension expenditures are forecast to fall. The table also shows that only the United States, of the countries considered, spends a smaller percentage of national income on public pension benefits.

While these reforms have led Britain's pension system to sustainability in terms of costs it remains to be seen whether it is politically sustainable, with the proportion of national income given in public pensions to each pensioner falling to 75 percent of the current level by 2030 and 56 percent by 2050. It should also be remembered that these costings do not include the cost of means-tested benefits to pensioners, which in 1998–1999 was some 1.0 percent of gross domestic product (GDP; Banks and Emmerson 2000). The government's long-term aim to increase the MIG in line with average earnings, and the introduction of the pension credit in October 2003, will

Table 6.2 **Projected Future State Spending on Pensions, as a Percentage of GDP**

	2000	2010	2020	2030	2040	2050	Net Liability, 1995–2050[a]
Canada	5.0	5.3	6.9	9.0	9.1	8.7	67.8
France	9.8	9.7	11.6	13.5	14.3	14.4	113.6
Germany	11.5	11.8	12.3	16.5	18.4	17.5	110.7
Italy	12.6	13.2	15.3	20.3	21.4	20.3	75.5
Japan	7.5	9.6	12.4	13.4	14.9	16.5	106.8
New Zealand	4.8	5.2	6.7	8.3	9.4	9.8	20.4
Great Britain	4.5	5.2	5.1	5.5	4.0	4.1	4.6
United States	4.2	4.5	5.2	6.6	7.1	7.0	25.7

Sources: Roseveare et al. (1996); Chand and Jaeger (1996) for net pension liabilities.
[a]The sum of projected future deficits, each expressed as percentage of projected future GDP.

add to these future liabilities. Also, previous demographic forecasts have tended to underestimate improvements in longevity and hence underestimate pension liabilities (Disney 2000).

6.2.4 Economics of the Choice of Private Pension Provider

The decision to opt out of the social security program involves assessing the present value of the alternatives (Disney, Palacios, and Whitehouse 1999). For an individual offered the chance of joining an occupational pension plan, the decision will depend on the likely time path of salary and expected job tenure. For an individual choosing between a personal pension and some form of DB plan—whether publicly or employer provided—age and expected returns are key determinants. Simply put, contributions put into a DC plan such as a personal pension earlier in the working life compound over a longer period, while the fund will cumulate over both negative and positive investment shocks the longer the period to retirement. Moreover, predicted returns to the social security program for later cohorts are expected to decline significantly (Disney and Whitehouse 1993b).

In contrast, in any DB plan where there are penalties to early leaving and where pension benefits are in some way related to length of tenure and to final salary, later contributions "earn" a greater prospective pension (for illustrations, see Bodie, Marcus, and Merton 1988; and, in the British context, Disney and Whitehouse 1996). Consequently, we should expect optants for personal pensions to be relatively young, in contrast to, say, the age structure of purchasers of individual retirement accounts in the United States, where there is no similar choice-based structure of second-tier pension provision.

This finding is confirmed in figure 6.2: the median age of personal pension optants is the early thirties. This is important if we are to understand where personal pensions might have had an impact (e.g., on job mobility)

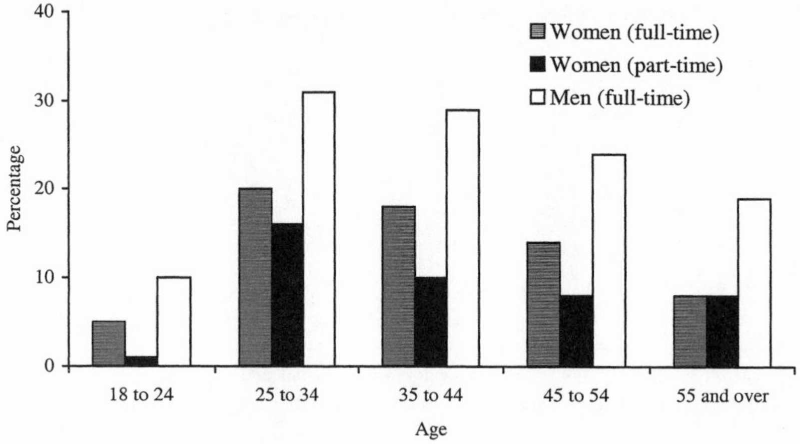

Fig. 6.2 Personal pension coverage, by age, gender, and employment status, 1998
Source: Office for National Statistics (2000).
Notes: Employees in Great Britain aged 18 and over, excluding those in youth training and employment training. Part-time male employees not shown due to small sample sizes.

and where they might not (e.g., on observed retirement behavior). Of course it is hard for people to make this type of forward-looking calculus, and Britain's program is overly complex. Nevertheless, the evidence on the age distribution of optants and on the association of pension choice with subsequent job tenure described in section 6.6 do suggest that people make some effort to understand the consequences of the pension choices that they make.[19]

Private pension coverage also varies by earnings. Those in more highly paid jobs are more likely to be members of an occupational pension plan. As shown in figure 6.3, coverage of personal pensions is distributed more widely across the earnings distribution. Only among those not in paid employment and those in the lowest 10 percent of the earnings distribution does personal pension coverage fall below 20 percent.[20]

19. We reiterate that it is important to differentiate between people choosing to buy a personal pension instead of joining SERPS, where most evidence (such as Disney and Whitehouse 1992b) suggest that optants made the "right" choice given expected returns and tax incentives in the early 1990s, and those choosing to opt out of a company plan to buy a personal pension, where there was some evidence of overenthusiastic "mis-selling" for which some optants subsequently received compensation.

20. Before April 2001, people with no earnings could not contribute to a personal pension since contributions were earnings related. The fact that personal pension coverage among non-earners is nonzero reflects the fact that the question on personal pensions asks about the previous twelve months. From April 2001 the annual contribution limit is a flat £3,600 per year or an earnings-related amount, whichever is greater (subject to a cap on pensionable earnings). This means that non-earners will be able to contribute to a personal (or stakeholder) pension for the first time. There is also no age limit, so some babies will find themselves with a pension taken out on their behalf.

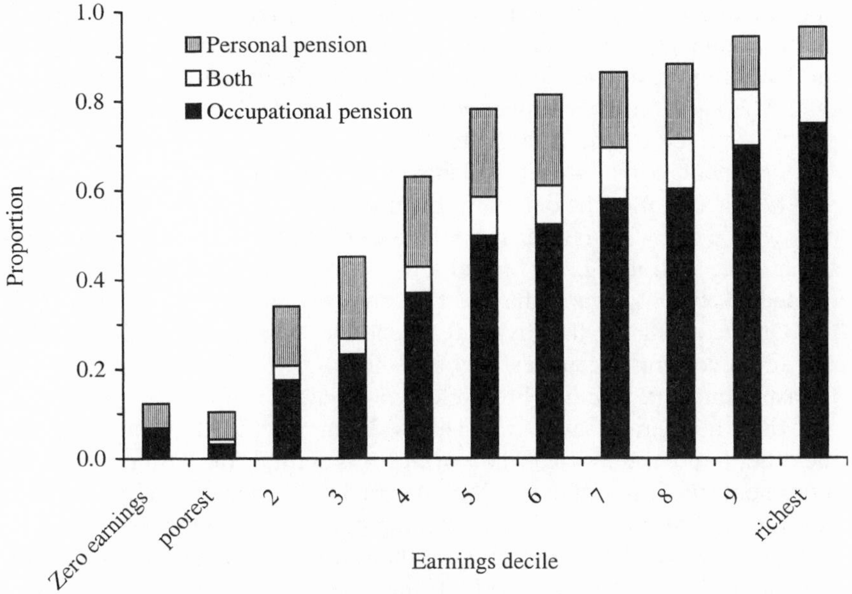

Fig. 6.3 Private pension coverage, by earnings decile, 1992

Sources: Adapted from Disney, Emmerson, and Wakefield (2001), using data from the British Household Panel Survey.

Notes: Includes only those individuals aged 20 to 59 in 1991 who are present in the first eight waves of the BHPS. Those reporting to be self-employed in any of waves 1 to 8 have been excluded from the analysis.

6.3 Pension Reform and Macroeconomic Performance

6.3.1 Impact on Saving of the Demographic Transition and Pension Reform

At the macroeconomic level, the simplest view of contracting-out sees it as shifting pension provision from a tax-financed basis to one in which pensions are increasingly funded through private saving. With greater inducements to contract out, as were put in place in the late 1980s, measured personal saving rates should therefore rise simply because of the way that national accounts data treat individual saving relative to payroll tax contributions. Leaving aside accounting conventions, however, it is still generally accepted in the literature that the national saving rate and capital stock will be higher in an economy where pension provision is funded rather than tax financed, although the rate of return on capital will be lower.[21] Whether,

21. This is in general the case so long as Ricardian equivalence does not hold—that is, individuals do not adjust their saving behavior fully to offset changes in future tax liabilities, and abstracting from international capital flows.

in turn, an economy with a funded pension program *grows* faster depends on the exact growth mechanism postulated—in the basic Swan-Solow model, for example, the long-run growth rate is independent of the saving rate, whereas in many endogenous growth "stories," the growth rate depends positively on the saving rate.

This speculation on the likely behavior of household saving rates should also take account of the demographic transition. The future British economy will be one with a lower support ratio of those of working age to pensioners (see section 6.2.2)—indeed, this was one motivation for the shift to funded provision. What is the effect on saving of this declining support ratio? On the one hand, if individuals live longer with a constant retirement age and a continued replenishment of the labor force (as seems to be the British scenario), a simple life-cycle hypothesis (LCH) model would suggest that the average saving rate should be higher (Modigliani 1986). On the other hand, if the size of the workforce is actually declining, capital requirements are less and the saving rate need no longer be so high to maintain the workforce's capital stock (Cutler et al. 1990). Hence we also need to take account of the fact that the baby boom generation is currently middle-aged, and, in a standard LCH model of saving, are strong net savers. As they retire, however, they should become net dissavers, even if the way that saving rates are measured often conceals this fact (Miles 1999). On balance, therefore, this combination of demographic trends and pension reform suggests that the underlying saving rate in Britain's economy should be increasing.

Figure 6.4 charts the annual average household saving rate against net accumulation in private pension plans over the period 1970–1996.[22] This latter series, which is the *difference* between inflows of accumulated contributions and investment returns, and outflows of pension lump sums and disbursements of annuities, is much more stable than the household saving rate, which exhibits some countercyclical volatility. Since aggregate household saving rates are *net* flows, typically calculated as residuals, it is hard exactly to measure the contribution of pension contributions in total saving. Disney (1997) suggests that of around £65 billion net saving in nonfixed assets in Great Britain in 1996, roughly £21 billion was through employer-provided pension plans and £3.7 billion through personal pensions.

There is no obvious trend in retirement saving despite the introduction of new retirement saving instruments, notably personal pensions. But as can be seen from the cited statistics, saving in personal pensions is still relatively low. An important related issue, however, is how much saving

22. As a result of Great Britain's introducing the European System of Accounts 1995, the methodology for calculating the saving rate has changed and it is no longer possible to get a consistent series for saving in private pensions. Between 1996 and 2000 the saving rate fell sharply. For more details see Disney, Emmerson, and Wakefield (2001).

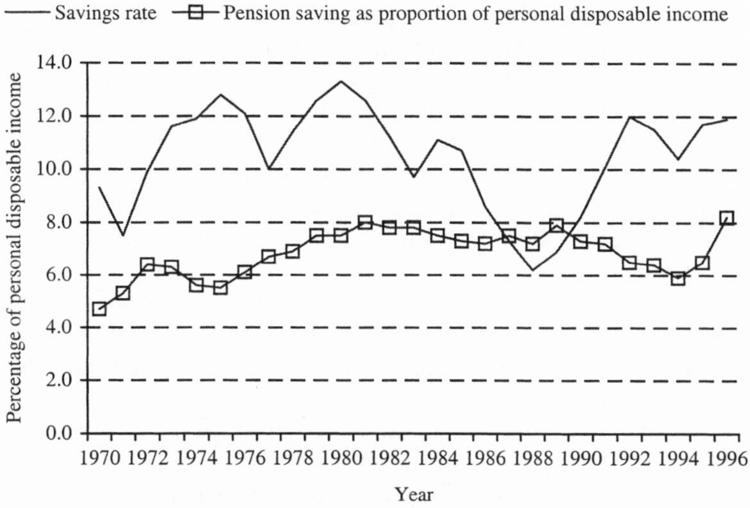

Fig. 6.4 Saving rate and rate of saving in funded pensions, 1970 to 1996
Source: Office for National Statistics (1998).
Note: Uses figures calculated before the introduction of the 1995 European System of Accounts.

through personal pensions is net *new* saving, rather than just saving that would have been held in other forms. To examine this, we have to consider some further extensions of our model. Implicit in our stylized discussion is a LCH model of a representative individual, with identical rates of return between all forms of pension "saving," no precautionary saving, and no differences in the risk attached to contributions to the social security program and to private pension plans. The pension reform process in Britain does not warrant such assumptions, and some further analysis is required.

Differential Rates of Return

When considering whether the introduction of personal pensions would be expected to have led to an increase in saving it is important to consider both wealth and substitution effects arising from the policy change. A basic issue is whether "saving" in the form of contributions to a private pension plan rather than through the social security system has a zero impact on private-sector wealth, when discounted at the risk-adjusted rate of return (Engen and Gale 1997). The answer depends on the implicit internal rate of return on social security contributions relative to the return on saving in a private pension plan. It also depends on the return on savings in new pension instruments (such as personal pensions) relative to the return on similar financial assets (if any) that were previously available. If the discounted return on net social security wealth is negative (as has clearly been the case in Britain),[23] then permitting individuals to "invest" part of their National Insurance contribution in a contracted-out scheme generates a positive retirement wealth effect. This might induce an increase in consumption and therefore a reduction in other personal saving. On the other hand, to the extent that personal pensions, for example, are "new" assets—for example, if they are able to offer higher returns (at least, in their tax-relieved treatment)—the reforms may have created new saving and as well as diverting saving.

There are two types of contributions to personal pensions. First, there are payments of contracted-out rebates (CORs) via the DSS. Assuming these would otherwise have been contributed to the social security program (SERPS) and earned low returns, these transfers induce a positive lifetime wealth effect that should increase consumption and reduce other saving. On the other hand, payments of discretionary contributions into plans, on top of CORs, should represent some new net saving, depending on how substitutable personal pensions are with existing financial assets that are not retirement-saving vehicles.[24]

Figure 6.5 charts both payments of contracted-out rebates by DSS into personal pension accounts and discretionary contributions by employees and by employers on their behalf over the period 1988–1989 to 1998–1999. Note the reversal of the relative magnitude of these inflows over the period, largely arising from effective cutbacks in the value of CORs in the 1993 and 1995 Social Security acts.[25] Given the wealth and substitution effects, one might reasonably conclude that there was little or no net saving through personal pensions at the start of the period but a more significant amount by the late 1990s.[26]

23. Disney and Whitehouse (1993a,b) found negative returns on social security contributions for men born after 1955 even *before* the cutbacks in provision in the 1990s.

24. Pinning down the magnitude of this substitution effect has proved difficult in the U.S. literature; for contrasting views see the *Journal of Economic Perspectives* (1996).

25. The 1993 legislation reduced the generous rebates given to people aged under thirty to opt into a personal pension. The 1995 legislation as a logical extension, implemented in 1997, related the size of the contracted-out rebate to age—see Disney and Whitehouse (1992a). There are falls in the aggregate contributions of CORs to personal pensions after both 1993–1994 and 1997–1998 in figure 6.5.

26. Disney, Emmerson, and Wakefield (2001) use the following benchmarks. Suppose the marginal propensity to consume out of wealth is 0.07, and 70 percent of payment of CORs into personal pensions is treated as "new" pension wealth by households. Then other saving will be reduced by 4.9 percent of contracted-out rebates paid into personal pensions—this is a pure wealth effect. The net saving effect is the total amount paid in discretionary contributions into personal pensions, less the "offset" impact on other saving and the tax subsidy. Assume this offset coefficient rose from 0.3 to 0.4 over the period as closer substitutes became available, and that the tax relief on discretionary contributions averaged 0.23. These figures are comparable with averages from other studies of saving effects, as discussed in that paper. Then simple arithmetic suggests that personal pensions contributed less than an additional £0.5 billion to household saving in 1988–1989 but close to £2 billion in 1998–1999. The latter is around 0.2 percent of gross domestic product (GDP).

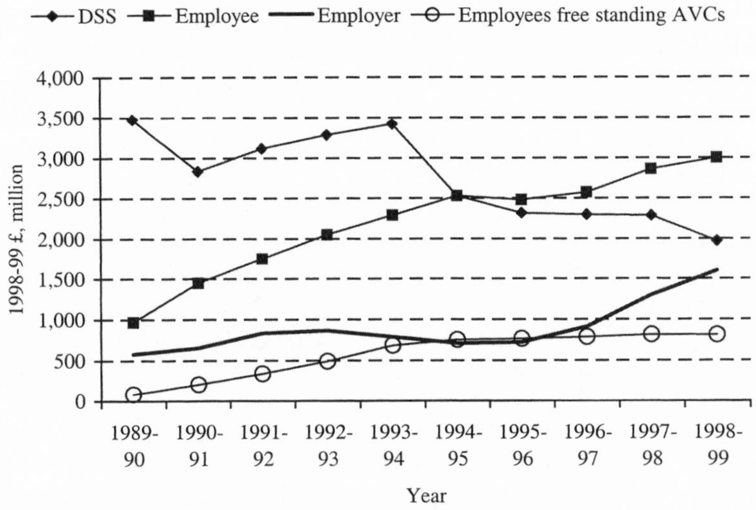

Fig. 6.5 Contributions to personal pensions, by type of contribution (1998–99 prices)

Sources: HMSO Inland Revenue Statistics (various years, tables 7.1 and 7.2), deflated by authors.

Pension Reform, Income Distribution, and Saving

Section 6.4 focuses on the distributional impact of the pension reforms. Nevertheless, some preliminary remarks are useful in the context of saving. First, social security provision is likely to be more redistributive than private provision. This factor is likely to be enhanced where contracting-out is voluntary, which permits richer households to opt out of redistribution. The fact that the majority of the workforce have contracted out of SERPS limits the potential for redistribution in both political and economic terms.

At first sight, redistribution from high- to low-income households should reduce aggregate saving when saving is disproportionately carried out by richer households.[27] But, as Gale (1998) points out, the ultimate outcome may be reduced if low- and high-income households have differing substitution elasticities between social security, private pensions, and other assets. High-income households may alter their saving patterns (e.g., by changing their asset portfolios) to offset the redistributive impact of social security; while, if low-income households do not save at all, the degree of redistribution has little impact on those households' behavior.

In addition, the redistribution inherent in pension programs is more complex than simply from "rich" to "poor" people. In the first place, we

27. For empirical evidence for Britain, see Banks and Tanner (1999).

have to look at lifetime incomes, and take differential longevity into account. Second, there are also issues to do with gender, such as how spouses are treated (Disney and Johnson 2001, Introduction). In fact, the British social security pension system, prereform, was not particularly redistributive in terms of lifetime incomes across the male income distribution (Creedy, Disney, and Whitehouse 1993). The main beneficiaries of redistribution were women, who reached state pension age earlier (sixty rather than sixty-five), lived longer, and disproportionately benefited from spouses' benefits. So how reform affects *household* saving rates is unclear a priori, depending on, for example, whether couples take account of each other's survival probabilities (or any other joint aspects, for that matter) in their individual saving decisions.

Risks Attached to Alternative Pensions

A standard argument is that DB plans involve risk sharing, whether between generations and individuals (in a public program), or between employers and employees (in occupational pension plans). If individual employees are risk averse, then contracting out into a DC account (such as a personal pension) changes the risk environment facing individuals (Bohn 1997) and should affect the amount of precautionary saving. Of course, social security is not devoid of risk (political risk)—for example, the substantial reductions in the generosity of state pensions in Great Britain that have occurred over the last twenty years. It is also true that occupational pension plans have not always been divorced from individual risk in Britain, as the Maxwell scandal indicated.[28] Nevertheless, this issue is an important one in a mandatory transition strategy, particularly where individuals perceive the change as implying a change in the risk environment. However, the voluntary nature of contracting-out in Britain presumably permits those with different risk-return trade-offs to choose alternative strategies. The issue, therefore, is one of whether people fully understand the risks involved in alternative pension choices in Britain (Banks and Emmerson 2000). But, whether they understand them or not, this risk issue should not affect the saving rate a good deal.[29]

28. There is no equivalent of the pension fund guarantee that exists in the United States to provide some insurance across plans. Instead, occupational pension funds are required to satisfy certain investment requirements that are monitored by the plan trustees. It is these arrangements that broke down in the Maxwell case when auditors discovered that the pension funds of the Robert Maxwell Group had been lent, with no collateral, to private companies within the group, leaving no funds available to satisfy the pension liabilities. For a lucid description of this event, and the aftermath, see Blake (1995). The 1995 legislation has tightened up the supervisory mechanisms. Bear in mind also that the component of the pension benefit that is supposed to substitute for the state benefit, SERPS, was guaranteed.

29. In other words, if individuals choose personal pensions because they are less risk averse, they should not engage in (greater) precautionary saving. If they do not perceive the potential change in the risk environment, it should not affect their other saving either.

6.3.2 The Public Finances and the "Transition Burden"

Our analysis of saving behavior examines the implications of the shift from tax-financed social security to funded provision. But this transition comes at a price—a price that has been a pertinent consideration for the British economy in the past two decades, and for the foreseeable future. A consequence of a transition toward a larger funded component of the pension program is a higher current average payroll tax rate than would otherwise be the case. Current social security liabilities have to be financed from a smaller tax base, given that contracting-out reduces tax receipts from National Insurance contributions.

Table 6.3 provides some official evidence on the impact of contracting-out on the average payroll tax burden. It shows that National Insurance contribution rates are some 2 1/2 to 3 percentage points higher than they would otherwise be as a result of contracting out, with around 1 percentage point arising from the introduction of personal pensions alone. Note from figure 6.5 that this percentage attributable to personal pensions was even higher in the late 1980s, at a time when the government was attempting to reduce "headline" direct tax rates.

Moreover, in two further respects, this understates the impact of private pension saving on underlying tax rates. First, private pension plans are tax relieved, relative to other saving instruments in other respects, but most notably in that they permit members to take a quarter of the accrued fund in a DC plan, or 1 1/2 times final salary in a DB plan, as a tax-free lump sum. Emmerson and Johnson (2002) estimate that, on an expenditure tax basis, this is equivalent to around £2 billion in lost revenue, in 1998–1999 prices. Second, employer contributions to pension plans are exempt from National Insurance contributions. Therefore, as policy induced greater

Table 6.3 Cost to National Insurance Fund of Contracting-Out Arrangements, 1999–2000

	Cost	
Type of Contribution	£Billions	% GDP
Occupational schemes deducted from NICs received	6.0	0.7
DC occupational schemes paid direct to scheme	0.1	0.0
Personal pensions paid direct to insurer	2.7	0.3
Total	8.8	1.0
Increase in NIC rate implied by CORs		
If employer rate increased	2½ percentage points	
If employee rate increased	3 percentage points	

Sources: Her Majesty's Treasury (2000a,d).

Notes: A larger increase in the employee rate is required to raise the £8.8 billion, since it is levied on a smaller range of earnings. See text for explanation of abbreviations.

contracting out, it also raised payroll tax rates at the time that employers and individuals chose to contract out.

Of course, the rationale for prefunding is that future tax rates will be lower because accrued social security pension rights are reduced. But note that, in a voluntary system of contracting out, so long as private agents are rational, a government can never expect to fully recoup the tax "cost" arising in the first instance, because only individuals who expect to gain from the switch should do so and this switching will be at the expense of expected government revenues in the long run. In practical terms, this implies that, in setting the CORs, the government has had to make assumptions concerning prospective future rates of return on funded contributions such as to ensure that the private funder can pay a benefit at least as high as the social security benefit forgone. If the rebate is too high, some opting agents will be compensated excessively (this is the source of the retirement wealth effect described previously). Set the rebate too low, and no agent will contract out. There is plenty of evidence that the government has systematically erred on the side of generosity in order to maximize contracting out.[30]

However, the current higher payroll tax rate is offset, and the future cost reduction enhanced, insofar as social security liabilities have been reduced over time by measures such as the decision to link pensions in payment to the growth of prices rather than the higher of prices or earnings growth, since 1981. With sustained real earnings growth over much of the period since 1981, this has reduced the value of the basic flat pension from 1981 to the present time. On current trends, the basic pension is expected to be worth less than 7 percent of earnings in 2050.[31]

The burden of the transition to greater funding of pensions in Britain is therefore shared across generations and within generations. Current pensioners bear the cost in part because state pension benefits have been cut. While current workers who remain contracted-in may well expect lower state pensions in retirement, they still bear it in part because the National Insurance contribution rate is higher than it would otherwise be, and contracted-out workers in occupational pension plans because they are generally making direct contributions to their own pension on top of their residual National Insurance contributions.[32] The only group for which incidence is unclear in principal are rebate-only optants for personal pensions—that is, individuals who make no contributions other than the contracted-out rebate to their personal pensions. Clearly their current bur-

30. See Disney and Whitehouse (1992a,b, 1993a) for details.

31. This became a political "hot potato" for the Labour government in 1999–2000, ironically as a result of the success of its anti-inflation strategy. After an increase in the basic state pension of only 75 pence per week was announced in 1999, pressure from a number of groups induced an announcement of increases in 2000 well above the rate of inflation.

32. Some public-sector occupational schemes have not levied employee contributions to cover prospective liabilities, but there is a trend toward more transparent contribution arrangements in such schemes (Cabinet Office 2000).

den within the program is zero, and whether they ultimately "pay" for the transition depends on whether their final pensions are higher or lower than they would have been had they remained contracted-in to the social security system. Since it is likely to be higher, as suggested, this retirement wealth effect may have led to a reduction in their overall saving.

6.4 Pension Reform: Distributional Outcomes in Great Britain

The presence of greater contracting-out might be expected to lead to greater inequality for two reasons. First, private pension incomes may be more volatile than state incomes. Second, because, in the 1980s and 1990s, average private pensions grew much faster than state pensions and, as we have seen, higher earners are more likely to have contracted out. Despite cutbacks in the basic pension since 1981, pensioners' incomes over the last twenty years have, on average, grown more quickly than that of the population as a whole. The net income, before housing costs, of both pensioner couples and single pensioners was some 60 percent higher in real terms in 1996–1997 than in 1979, compared to real average earnings growth over the period of 38 percent (DSS 2000c). This has been due to real increases in incomes from state pensions (as SERPS gradually matured after its introduction in 1978), means-tested benefits, occupational pensions, and investments (DSS 2000a).

This real increase in pensioner incomes has led to pensioners' now being underrepresented in the poorest 10 percent of the population, which since the start of the 1970s has tended to be occupied by other unwaged groups such as the unemployed and single parents (Goodman and Webb 1994). They are still overrepresented in the bottom half of the income distribution.[33] These real increases in incomes have not, however, been evenly spread across the pensioner distribution. Johnson and Stears (1995) show that while income inequality among pensioners fell from the early 1960s to the late 1970s, it rose sharply during the 1980s. This was caused by an increase in the inequality of income from a combination of investments and private pensions. Growing inequality alongside growing average real incomes is shown in figure 6.6, which gives gross incomes for pensioner couples in 1979 and 1998–1999, by income quintile, at July 1998 prices.

How do these levels and trends in pensioner inequality compare to those of other countries? A number of country-specific studies in Disney and Johnson (2001) yield three broad conclusions. First, as in Great Britain, pensioners are typically overrepresented in the lower half of the equivalized income distribution, but *under*represented in the lowest quintile of the

33. Of course it could be the case that, due to dissaving, consumption by the retired was actually much higher than their current incomes. However, as discussed in Banks, Blundell, and Tanner (1998), upon retirement consumption actually tends to fall faster than income.

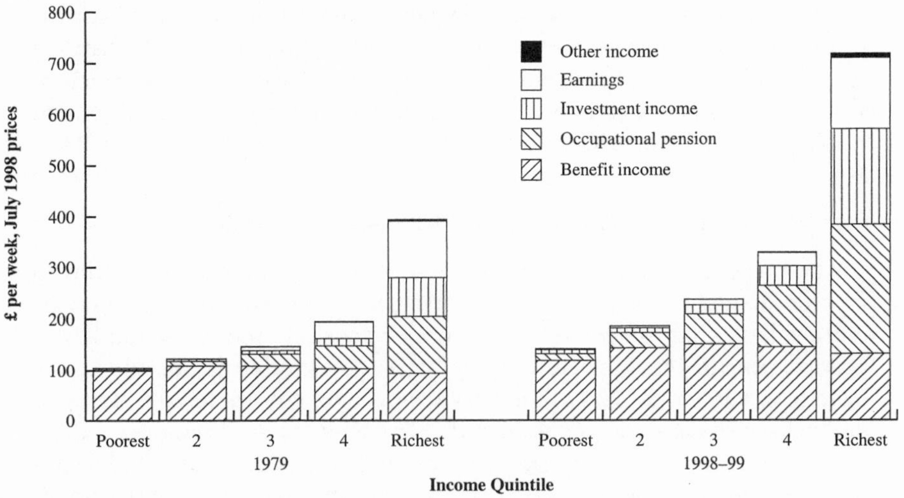

Fig. 6.6 Components of gross weekly income of each quintile of the pensioner couples income distribution, 1979 and 1998–99 (July 1998 prices)

Sources: Department of Social Security (2000c) using data from the 1998–99 Family Resources Survey and the 1979 Family Expenditure Survey. Clark and Taylor (2000) show that valid comparisons can be made between the two surveys.

income distribution. Second, income inequality among pensioners is typically greater in countries that offer comprehensive earnings replacement (the Bismarck system) than in countries where the state focuses on providing a benefit "floor" (the Beveridge system). This is true even when private sources of income are included. Third, there are no common trends in inequality of pensioner incomes across countries.

6.5 Labor Supply and Retirement: Impact of Pension Reform

Research into labor supply of the elderly, and the role of tax and pension reforms in the 1980s and 1990s, has been fairly limited in Great Britain, unlike in the United States. In any event, a number of retirement issues lie outside the scope of the present paper. A comprehensive survey of data and sources on retirement is contained in Blundell and Johnson (1999); more specific accounts of and possible explanations for the decline in labor force participation over the period of the 1980s and 1990s are contained in Dilnot et al. (1994) and Disney (1999). Again, three salient conclusions emerge from these discussions.

First, there has been a steady decline in the labor force participation of older men, punctuated by more rapid falls in the recessions that characterized the beginning and end of the 1980s. On the demand side, the massive restructuring of the economy and the lack of appropriate skills of older

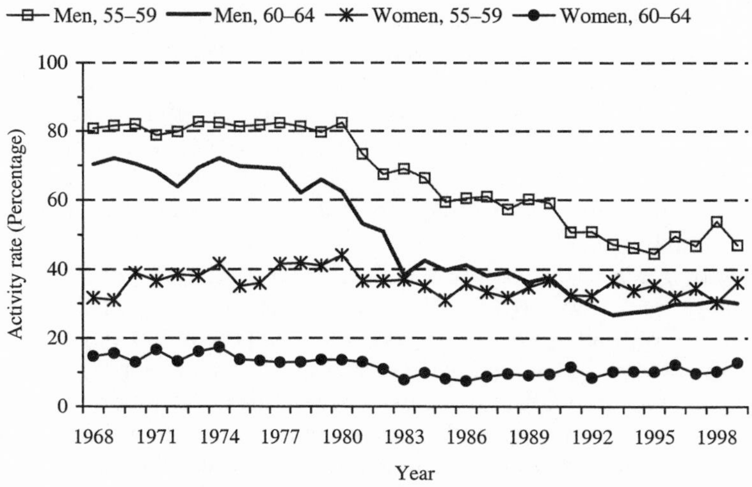

Fig. 6.7 Percentage of older men and women who are full-time employees, by age group, 1968 to 1999
Sources: Family Expenditure Survey data from 1968 to 1999.

workers probably contributed to this decline. On the supply side, the decline in participation was facilitated by the early retirement provisions of occupational pension plans and by the operation of the public program of disability benefits.[34] The decline in the percentage of older men who are full-time employees is shown in figure 6.7. As shown in Disney (1996), this is not due to individuals' reducing their hours but instead to falling employment among older age groups. Indeed, final-salary occupational pension plans encourage individuals to remain full time until they retire.[35] A fuller discussion of these issues is contained in Blundell, Meghir, and Smith (2001).

Second, there is no explicit early retirement provision within the public pension program. Nevertheless, efforts have been made to tighten other routes into retirement before state pensionable age (sixty-five for men and, from 2020, for women). Eligibility for disability benefits was tightened in the late 1990s, and the benefit made taxable, cutting its value to that of the basic state pension. Also, in an attempt to encourage employment among older workers, in 1989 the earnings-test condition for receipt of the basic state pension for earners above state pensionable age (known as the "earnings rule"), was abolished. Disney and Smith (2002) estimate that this change significantly raised the hours of working men aged sixty-five and

34. Invalidity Benefit, subsequently renamed Incapacity Benefit.
35. Although self-employment may be another route out of employment (Disney, Meghir, and Whitehouse 1994).

above, but not participation rates nor the hours of women (which is why the change does not show up clearly in fig. 6.7). Moreover, the government has become increasingly concerned as to the early retirement practices of occupational pension plans, especially those covering public-sector workers such as local and central government workers, police, fire crews, and so on.[36] It seems likely that further limits will be placed on early retirement on actuarially favorable terms and on grounds of ill health in these employer-provided plans.

Finally, however, the most pertinent issue for this paper concerns the impact on retirement behavior of the introduction of personal pensions and other new contracting-out arrangements. Since the majority of personal pension optants are young (fig. 6.2) and are still some way away from their likely retirement date, there is no evidence on the effects in practice. Basic economic principles suggest that there are both wealth and substitution effects here that rule out a definitive outcome a priori. The picture is further complicated by the fact that these incentive effects are likely to differ for someone moving from SERPS to a personal pension and someone moving from a DB plan to a personal pension (or DC-based employer plan).

To the extent that personal pensions provide a positive retirement wealth effect relative to remaining in the public scheme (SERPS), then this might induce individuals to retire earlier than they would otherwise have done (although they could not draw SERPS until reaching state pensionable age). On the other hand, the incentive of a higher return on contributions to personal pensions than the implicit return on contributions to a social security program (or, with actuarially favorable early retirement, in an occupational pension plan) might induce personal pension optants to defer retirement. Of course, contributions made to a personal pension close to retirement are not as valuable as those made at the start, but since people with personal pensions must annuitize between the ages of fifty and seventy-five, they can continue to build up their funds (through increased contributions or capital gains) past the state pensionable ages. For someone in SERPS, years worked past age sixty-five for men (and sixty for women) do not yield further pension benefits. Compared to someone in a DB occupational pension plan where the last years of work are fairly crucial in determining subsequent pension entitlement, the option value of delaying retirement and contributing to a personal pension for another year is quite a lot lower—the first years' contributions matter much more. This effect would tend to encourage people to retire earlier, but could be mitigated to the extent that people in DB plans are encouraged to leave when their salaries are at their highest points and to the extent that personal pensions allow individuals much greater flexibility.

However, as the next section will show, there is a good deal of mobility

36. See Audit Commission (1997) and Her Majesty's Treasury (2000c) for more details.

between types of pension arrangement, and it is very likely that those currently contributing to a personal pension may, later in life, be in an occupational pension plan or even revert to the social security program. Thus, no firm conclusions can yet be drawn on this important issue.

6.6 Labor Market Flexibility

6.6.1 Pensions and Labor Mobility

One of the implicit motivations for introducing more flexible contracting-out arrangements was that personal pensions, in particular, would be attractive to young, mobile workers. Greater mobility between jobs and occupations would, it was hoped, enhance the restructuring of Britain's economy that was needed after the meltdown of many traditional sectors, especially in manufacturing industry, in the early 1980s. At the same time, insofar as contributions to DB occupational pensions represented a burden on business, the relative flexibility of DC arrangements with, for example, no requirement that the employer need contribute to plans, might permit current wages more fully to reflect differences in current productivity and provide greater incentives on the margin for workers and employers to find productive "matches." Much of this reasoning was never made explicit. Nor was the more general perspective that individualized pensions, along with privatizations financed by public-share issues, would generate a culture of individual share ownership and individual risk-taking which would move Britain away from the "Eurosclerotic" model toward the entrepreneurial model associated, rightly or wrongly, with the United States and some Asian economies.

This issue of pension arrangements and labor mobility has not received so much attention in the British debate concerning personal pensions, and in this section of the paper we examine the theory and existing empirical evidence on how different *types* of pension plan affect labor mobility. Then we look at some of the empirical evidence for Britain using recent data—not so much as a test of whether pension type *affects* labor mobility (where we infer that the existing literature is fairly inconclusive), but rather as to who took out a personal pension and whether opting into a personal pension (especially where the employee was also offered membership in a DB occupational pension plan) was associated with subsequent job mobility.

6.6.2 Theory on Pension Plans and Labor Mobility

In looking at the impact of (private) pension arrangements on job mobility, it is important to differentiate between mobility in and out of pensioned jobs, in contrast to mobility between pensioned jobs that involve a change of pension plan. There are very good reasons that mobility out of jobs covered by pension plans may be a good deal lower than mobility of uncovered workers. The issue is examined in the United States by Gustman and Steinmeier (1993), who use data from the Survey of Income and Program Participation (SIPP) to show that pension mobility is much lower for people in jobs with private pensions. In a three-year period (1984–1986) they found that 6 percent of those initially in pensioned jobs moved jobs, compared to 20 percent in nonpensioned jobs. Of those who moved out of a pensioned job, 64 percent moved to a job without a pension and, furthermore, they incurred an average loss of wages of 6 percent by moving. In contrast, 14 percent of movers out of uncovered jobs gained pension coverage by moving, and all movers previously in uncovered jobs gained on average 7 percent wages by moving. This highlights the fact that there are strong deterrents to moving out of a pensioned job per se, which should be separated from the "costs" arising from moving between pensionable jobs associated with nonportability of pensions.

The fact that people in Great Britain can opt not only out of social security but also out of an existing occupational pension plan potentially allows us to separate mobility that is associated with choice of pension arrangements from mobility associated with the nature of pensioned jobs. But it also raises very clearly the more general problem with studies of pension coverage and labor mobility: that of *self-selection.* There may be large costs, as in the SIPP example above, to moving in and out of the pension-covered sector, and between pensioned jobs, so pension arrangements affect the mobility incentives of employees. But it is also likely that employers who offer pensions will select employees on the basis of their assessed propensity to move between jobs and that employees will also select jobs on the basis of job-specific costs of mobility. Indeed, nonrandom selection of employees is central to any rationalization of why employers provide pensions at all (Lazear 1979; Ippolito 1997).

This caveat applies particularly to Great Britain, where moving pension plan need not involve changing job at all. The individual opting-out strategy is likely to be followed by those most inclined to move between jobs, and who thereby require a more portable pension arrangement. So while it is possible, by comparisons across countries and over time, to ask whether more flexible pension arrangements are associated with greater labor mobility,[37] at the microeconomic level we may be observing pure selection in Britain rather than the impact of institutional arrangements on behavior.

The basic theory on pension plans and the costs of job mobility are summarized in Bodie, Marcus, and Merton (1988), Lazear and Moore (1988), and Ippolito (1997). We focus here in particular on the incentives associ-

37. And even this cross-country or temporal "experiment" may be problematic—the reforms which permitted greater flexibility in pension arrangements in Britain in the 1980s may have themselves been stimulated by the greater flexibility in the British labor market in other dimensions, such as the decline of trade unions, shift toward private services and away from manufacturing and the public sector, and so on.

ated with job mobility between pension-covered jobs (not, e.g., those incentives associated with retirement). As illustrated by Gustman and Steinmeier (1993), the costs of moving from a covered to an uncovered job are both larger and more transparent. As we shall see, in essence, portability costs in company-provided DB plans basically depend on how benefits in past plans are treated, whereas portability costs in DC plans are largely (but not exclusively) start-up costs.

For individuals moving between jobs within the sector covered by DB pension plans, the loss from job mobility arises from the loss of additional years of service and final salary in the original plan. It depends on the loss at the time of moving in the original pension plan from the lower final salary value, which depends on prospective job tenure.[38] For a person shifting to a personal pension or SERPS, the loss function is more complex. It requires comparing subsequent loss of coverage by a DB plan (although this may be reversible later), offset by the pension obtained from the contributions to the DC plan or to the public program after that time. It is often argued that the costs of leaving a DB plan are high because an employer typically contributes to a DB plan and, by leaving the plan, the employee loses these additional contributions. An individual simply leaving a DB plan to buy a personal pension or to rejoin SERPS is presumably unable to compensate for this loss of contributions but, for job movers, the absence of employer pension contributions (deferred pay) ought to be compensated by higher current pay. On the other hand, if, ceteris paribus, DB plan providers actually also pay higher wages (as suggested by Gustman and Steinmeier 1993), then the costs of leaving the covered sector—in both lost pension and wages—would be considerable.

In principle, as suggested above, DC plans such as personal pensions are fully and costlessly transferable. In practice, there may be costs where the existing personal pension plan "lapses" because the individual starts another personal pension plan, joins an occupational pension scheme, or, indeed, reverts to SERPS, the social security benefit. A cost will typically arise because personal pensions often have an up-front commission charge that is deducted from early contributions. For example, if the personal pension is held for only a short duration, then insufficient funds may have been invested in the plan, net of commission, to recoup the gross cost of contributions in the early stages. This is clearly one of the reasons the government has decided that stakeholder pensions will be able to charge only a percentage of the fund, rather than having up-front or exit charges. In addition, individuals with a personal pension who move job will lose out if the previous employer was contributing to the personal pension and the

38. Most literature overstates this loss by assuming that the individual would otherwise have remained in the DB plan until retirement. The implausibility of this assumption in valuing DB pension plan rights in Britain is demonstrated by Disney and Whitehouse (1996).

new employer is not prepared to, or to compensate in any other way.[39] Of course SERPS, the public program, is fully transferable, but appears to offer much lower returns to later cohorts than alternative, funded, plans.

Past Empirical Evidence on Labor Mobility and Pension Plans in Great Britain

McCormick and Hughes (1984) estimate *firm-specific pension capital as percentage of pension capital.* They study the loss of pension capital from moving between (DB plan) pensionable jobs. At the time that they wrote, there were three options concerning moves between covered jobs: benefits could be deferred (preserved), a cash refund of contributions could be obtained, or there could be a transfer value into the new plan. McCormick and Hughes show that the "envelope" loss-minimizing function is nonlinear with pension plan tenure.

To implement the model empirically, McCormick and Hughes (1984) use subjective data from the General Household Survey (GHS) on future job-moving intentions. The explanatory variables in their modeling strategy for the question "are you seriously considering changing job" are personal characteristics, job satisfaction, and interactions of pension status, job tenure, and age, which are supposed to capture the nonlinearity of the loss function (a simple dummy for pension plan membership is insignificant). The results all hinge on the coefficient on years of job tenure × pension status, with job tenure *not* included as an independent regressor. Since we know from other studies that search is (negatively) affected by tenure, this can be interpreted as suggesting that tenure matters only in pensionable jobs and the coefficient is indeed significant. However, while the econometric results obtain a quadratic on tenure, as predicted by the model, the curvature seems to be the "wrong way" in the results.

Henley, Disney, and Carruth (1994) argue that a better identifier of the impact of pensions on job mobility, given self-selection, is whether the particular *characteristics* of a pension plan have an impact on the propensity to move. Of course, it is still possible that individuals self-select into the type of pension arrangement according to their implicit moving probabilities, but this may require a more sophisticated calculus than a simple membership decision.[40]

The empirical strategy involves using reported job-tenure intervals to construct the hazard rather than a binary variable approach, using the 1985 GHS. The truncation of the duration intervals and the measures of housing equity (observed only for house movers) involves some standard econometric procedures for handling censored data. A key finding is that

39. There has been a certain amount of controversy on this issue: see Murthi, Orszag, and Orszag (1999) and Whitehouse (2000).

40. But since the characteristics are self-reported, a natural criticism is that these characteristics are known, even if not understood.

occupational pension plan membership significantly decreases the exit hazard from jobs, but reported transferability of pension rights increases it (on the basis of observed completed spells) relative to simple pension plan membership. Moreover, the effect on the hazard rate of membership interacted with time (duration) and time-squared is superior to a simple dummy, confirming the McCormick-Hughes proposition that the loss function is time dependent and possibly nonlinear. In fact, (for men) Henley, Disney, and Carruth (1994) get a result that approximates the curvature of the McCormick-Hughes theoretical loss function in contrast to the latter's empirical results.

Mealli and Pudney (1996) is the only published British paper that attempts to look at the endogeneity of pension status, but it does so indirectly. It uses the job histories and pension plan tenures in the Retirement Survey to model transitions. Obviously, the permutations of possible multiple state transitions are large over the lifetime, so their paper essentially uses a *competing risks model* to examine transitions between various states (e.g., a pensioned job, nonpensioned job, unemployment, etc.) conditional on treating the initial state as exogenous (but see below). Note that transitions *between* pensioned jobs but with different pension arrangements (which is the basis of the McCormick-Hughes model of job-specific pension capital) are ignored. So this is not a test of job-specific pension capital impact but of the impact of pension coverage on tenure, like Gustman and Steinmeier (1993). Their finding is that job durations are systematically longer for pensioned jobs. Using a variety of instruments for individual heterogeneity, the authors argue that the differences in duration between pensioned and nonpensioned are not wholly eliminated (see their table VIII). So there may be a "pension coverage effect" after all.

Overall, the findings of British studies are

1. that the theoretical relationship between job-specific pension capital and tenure is nonlinear;
2. that (DB) pensionable jobs have longer durations;
3. that this is not wholly due to heterogeneity (self-selection);
4. that transferable pension rights are associated with more job mobility; and
5. that there appears to be a nonlinear relationship between duration and the "pension effect" in DB plans.

6.6.3 Evidence on Personal Pensions and Job Mobility

Our aim in this section of the paper is to provide a preliminary empirical analysis of the link between individuals' pension arrangements and their subsequent labor market mobility. We will exploit the feature of the British institutional arrangements since 1988 that allows individuals who are offered an occupational pension to opt out of the plan and choose their own personal pension or SERPS. Our strategy is to compare the job mobility of people who are offered a DB employer's plan and choose not to be in it with the job mobility of people who do belong to the DB occupational pension plan offered. If the incentive effect of membership dominates, then the subsequent rates of mobility of nonjoiners will be similar to those who were not offered membership (other things being equal). If the differences between covered and uncovered workers are dominated by employer (or employee) selection, the rates of job mobility of covered workers will be similar, *whether or not they join the company's pension plan.* This does not explicitly handle the endogeneity of pension choice of employees rigorously, but provides some initial evidence as to the relative importance of the incentive and the selection effects outlined above. To examine these issues we use data from the British Household Panel Survey (BHPS). This is a panel survey that has been following the same individuals over time since 1991. We use data from waves 2 through 8 (1992–1998 inclusive). The BHPS collects detailed information on individuals' employment and their socioeconomic characteristics. It also contains a number of questions about their pension arrangements. The survey asks, "Does your present employer run a pension scheme or superannuation scheme for which you are eligible?" If the answer is yes, respondents are then asked, "Do you belong to your employer's pension scheme?"

In addition, from the second wave onward all respondents are asked questions about their personal pension arrangements: "In the past year, that is since September 1st 1991 have you paid any contributions or premiums for a private personal pension, or had such contributions paid on your behalf by the Department of Social Security?" If the answer to this is yes, respondents are asked to say whether they took out their pensions before or after June 1988 and the year they first took out their pensions. They are also asked whether they have made any additional contributions over and above the contracted-out rebate, and how much the last contribution was.

The advantage of the BHPS data is that they allow us to identify those people who were offered pension schemes by their employers but chose instead to have their own personal pensions. Also, the data allow us to identify those people who were offered pensions by their employers and chose to participate in the schemes. The main part of our analysis will focus on differences in the labor market mobility between these two groups. However, there are a number of respects in which the definition of these groups is not as clean as we would like.[41]

41. In particular, individuals are not asked whether their employers offer them occupational pension plans. Rather, they are asked about any pension schemes offered by their employers. This might include people who are offered group personal pension schemes. We should be able to identify these people since they are likely to report that they are offered pension schemes to which they belong and that they have personal pensions. We might therefore want to classify anyone who reports having a personal pension as not having an occupational

Table 6.4 **Occupational Pension Plans, by Type (%)**

	Private-Sector Schemes	Public-Sector Schemes	All Schemes
Defined-benefit plans	78	98	80
Defined-contribution plans	16	2	14
Hybrid	6	—	6

Source: National Association of Pension Funds Annual Survey of Occupational Schemes, 1997.

Note that we cannot distinguish between DB occupational pension plans and DC occupational pension plans. In total, nearly 15 percent of all occupational pension plans, and a higher percentage in the private sector, are DC plans, as shown in table 6.4. Incorrectly including people who actually belong to DC occupational pension plans with people who belong to DB occupational schemes is likely to underestimate the effect to which people opt out of occupational pension plans with a view to future labor market mobility.[42]

A final issue concerns the "mis-selling" of personal pensions that took place in the late 1980s. This suggests that a substantial number of people chose to leave their employers' plans due to bad financial advice. This will tend to reduce any observed correlation between the decision to have a personal pension instead of an occupational pension and future employment mobility.

Bearing these factors in mind, we now turn to our analysis of the data in the BHPS. Our analysis is based on the sample of individuals who are aged between twenty and fifty-nine in the first wave of the BHPS and who are present in all eight waves. Table 6.5 compares the pension status of employees in the BHPS in 1992 with that of those in the GHS, which is a larger annual cross-sectional sample containing just under 9,000 employees in 1992.

Looking first at whether an employer offers a pension scheme, around 70 percent of individuals are able to join employers' pension schemes in each of the two surveys. The BHPS has slightly larger levels of membership of these schemes with 76 percent of those eligible joining their employers' schemes, compared to 69 percent in the GHS. The table shows that pension coverage appears to be greater in the GHS than in the BHPS. This points to some potential selection caused by nonrandom attrition over the eight

pension. However, adopting this strategy might lead to our wrongly excluding some people who are in their employers' DB occupational pensions, but who also say yes to the personal pension question because they are making additional contributions in the form of Free Standing Additional Voluntary Contributions (FSAVCs).

42. But note that Gustman and Steinmeier find no evidence that mobility is affected by whether the employer's plan is of the DB or DC form.

Table 6.5 Pension Status of Employees in 1992

	BHPS	GHS
% of employees offered an employer's pension	69	72
% of those offered that joined an employer's pension	75	69
Men, full time		
% without a private pension	17	11
% in an employer's pension scheme	55	62
% in a personal pension scheme	17	27
% in both an employer's pension scheme and a personal pension	11	—
No. of observations	1,252	4,311
Women, full time		
% without a private pension	29	25
% in an employer's pension scheme	47	54
% in a personal pension scheme	16	21
% in both an employer's pension scheme and a personal pension	8	—
No. of observations	907	2,396
Women, part time		
% without a private pension	71	68
% in an employer's pension scheme	17	19
% in a personal pension scheme	9	12
% in both an employer's pension scheme and a personal pension	3	—
No. of observations	559	2,067

Sources: British Household Panel Survey, 1992–1998 inclusive; authors' calculations; Great Britain Office of Population Census and Surveys (1992).

Notes: See text for explanation of abbreviations. BHPS data include only those individuals aged 20 to 59 in 1991 who are present in all eight waves and are not self-employed in any wave; GHS data include all employees aged 16 and over apart from those in youth-training or employment-training schemes.

waves of the BHPS. Finally, individuals in the BHPS who claim to be members of both their employers' pension schemes and of personal pensions could be either individuals who have group personal pensions or those who have occupational pensions and are making additional voluntary contributions to those pensions.

Table 6.6 considers how pension coverage has changed over the last seven waves of the BHPS. Interestingly, the proportion of individuals choosing to join their employers' pension plans rose from around three-fourths in waves 2, 3, and 4 to over four-fifths of those offered schemes in the eighth wave. As a result of this, and a slight increase in the number of employers offering pension plans, there is an increase in membership of employer plans over the period.

The proportion who were able to join employers' pension plans but instead chose to join personal pensions fell from around 10 percent between

Table 6.6 **Pension Status of Employees Only, by Wave**

	Wave (1992 to 1998)						
	2	3	4	5	6	7	8
% of individuals offered an OP	69.4	66.7	66.0	69.6	71.5	72.7	72.6
% of those offered who joined an OP	75.5	75.9	75.2	78.9	80.3	81.4	83.1
All individuals							
% without a private pension	32.7	33.5	34.3	30.5	29.5	28.2	27.8
% with occupational pension	44.4	41.8	41.4	46.7	49.4	50.1	51.2
% with personal pension	14.9	16.0	16.0	14.6	13.0	12.7	11.9
% with both OP and PP	8.0	8.7	8.3	8.2	8.1	9.1	9.1
No. of observations	2,778	2,765	2,750	2,732	2,713	2,693	2,650
All individuals offered an OP							
% without a private pension	15.0	13.8	15.2	12.8	13.2	12.4	11.7
% with occupational pension	63.9	62.8	62.7	67.1	69.0	68.9	70.5
% with personal pension	9.5	10.3	9.6	8.3	6.5	6.2	5.2
% with both OP and PP	11.6	13.1	12.6	11.8	11.3	12.5	12.6
No. of observations	1,928	1,843	1,816	1,902	1,941	1,958	1,923
All individuals not offered an OP							
% without a private pension	72.8	72.8	71.4	71.0	70.6	70.2	70.3
% with occupational pension	—	—	—	—	—	—	—
% with personal pension	27.2	27.2	28.6	29.0	29.4	29.8	29.7
% with both OP and PP	—	—	—	—	—	—	—
No. of observations	850	922	934	831	772	735	727

Sources: British Household Panel Survey, 1992–1998 inclusive; authors' calculations.
Notes: Includes only those individuals aged 20 to 59 in 1991 who are present in all eight waves only and are not self-employed in any wave. OP = occupational pension; PP = personal pension.

1992 and 1994 to just over 5 percent in 1998. This is possibly evidence of individuals' learning from the "mis-selling" experience outlined above. Of those who declined to join employers' pension schemes, just over 70 percent had no private pension arrangement (and, by default, those with earnings above the lower earnings limit [LEL] would be in SERPS), with the remaining 30 percent in personal pensions. These percentages remained very stable over the eight waves of the BHPS used for this study.

Also of interest is the frequency of individual pension membership changes over the period of the study. Changes in pension status are in fact extremely common, as shown in table 6.7. This adds complexity to our study since an individual cannot be easily identified as someone who has a certain pension type. Of those with no private pension arrangement in 1992 only 60 percent were not in a private pension plan in 1998. Of those who were contributors to personal pensions in wave 2, only 42 percent were contributors in 1998. But membership of occupational pensions is relatively more stable. Some 79 percent of those in occupational pension plans in 1992 were members of occupational pension plans in 1998.

This is a striking finding for policy. Some official publications (such as

Table 6.7 Pension Transitions, by Wave (employees in wave 2 only)

	Wave (1992 to 1998)						
	2	3	4	5	6	7	8
Has no pension in wave 2							
% without a private pension	100.0	84.8	80.7	68.1	65.3	61.0	59.5
% with occupational pension		3.4	4.6	17.0	20.3	25.6	26.4
% with personal pension		11.5	13.8	12.7	12.6	11.7	10.7
% with both OP and PP		0.3	0.9	2.3	1.9	2.8	3.4
Has occupational pension in wave 2							
% without a private pension		3.5	6.3	9.2	8.5	9.3	10.8
% with occupational pension	100.0	86.2	84.0	81.7	82.6	80.1	79.4
% with personal pension		0.5	0.6	0.8	1.2	1.7	2.0
% with both OP and PP		9.8	9.2	8.4	7.7	8.9	7.9
Has personal pension in wave 2							
% without a private pension		16.4	19.5	17.4	21.9	20.0	19.5
% with occupational pension		0.7	3.6	11.8	16.9	23.4	25.8
% with personal pension	100.0	81.2	74.5	62.2	50.6	45.8	41.9
% with both OP and PP		1.7	2.4	8.7	10.6	10.8	12.8

Sources: British Household Panel Survey, 1992–1998 inclusive; authors' calculations.
Note: See table 6.6.

DSS 1998) have suggested that certain types of pension arrangement should be matched to certain types of individuals—in particular, by income level. While pension mobility may therefore also reflect income volatility and income mobility, excessive multiplicity of individual pension plan membership within the working lifetime probably results in reduced pension benefits due to start-up costs (in personal pensions prior to the introduction of stakeholder pensions in 2001) and capital losses (from moving out of DB plans). Offsetting this is the possibility that multiple pension holding may have some positive insurance characteristics if the risk properties of different pension types vary (Brugiavini and Disney 1993).

Finally, we turn to a provisional assessment of the association between pension status and subsequent job mobility. Table 6.8 shows the percentage of individuals who move jobs between each wave of the BHPS by their pension status in the previous wave. In total, just over one-third (36.6 percent) of employees in wave 2 move job at least once over the period of interest. The first part of table 6.8 shows that it is those individuals with no pension and those with personal pensions in the previous wave who are more likely to have moved employer, rather than those who are members of their employers' pension plans. However, this could simply reflect the fact that occupational pensions may be offered in the types of industries or to types of people who have lower rates of job mobility. A better indicator of whether individuals with personal pensions are more likely to move jobs is shown in the next part of table 6.8, which looks at only those individuals

Table 6.8 **Percentage of People Changing Employer, by Pension Status in Previous Wave (employees in wave 2 only)**

	Wave						
Pension Status in Previous Wave	3	4	5	6	7	8	Any Move
All individuals							
% without a private pension	12.4	15.3	15.9	17.6	16.4	17.6	46.9 (1.7)
% with occupational pension	3.6	6.7	5.8	6.6	5.7	6.1	27.4 (1.3)
% with personal pension	10.6	15.6	12.0	14.9	16.8	13.1	46.5 (2.5)
% with both OP and PP	4.9	8.1	3.9	5.3	6.7	8.0	26.5 (3.0)
All	7.6	11.0	10.2	10.9	10.3	10.3	36.6 (0.9)
Individuals offered an OP							
% without a private pension	9.3	9.0	10.1	13.6	12.8	17.9	39.4 (2.9)
% with occupational pension	3.6	6.7	5.8	6.6	5.7	6.1	27.4 (1.3)
% with personal pension	7.6	12.5	12.0	12.8	13.0	9.5	42.9 (3.7)
% with both OP and PP	4.9	8.1	3.9	5.3	6.7	8.0	26.5 (3.0)
All	5.0	7.8	6.8	7.7	7.1	7.9	30.6 (1.0)
Individuals not offered an OP							
% without a private pension	13.9	17.8	18.4	19.3	17.9	17.5	50.4 (2.0)
% with occupational pension	—	—	—	—	—	—	—
% with personal pension	13.0	17.8	15.5	16.2	18.8	15.2	49.4 (3.3)
% with both OP and PP	—	—	—	—	—	—	—
All	13.6	17.8	17.5	18.4	18.2	16.8	50.1 (1.7)

Sources: British Household Panel Survey, 1992–1998 inclusive; authors' calculations.

Notes: Includes only those individuals aged 20 to 59 in 1991 who are present in all eight waves and are not self-employed in any wave. Any move shows the proportion changing employer in any wave by pension status in wave 2. Standard errors for the proportion moving in any wave are shown in parenthesis. OP = occupational pension; PP = personal pension.

who were offered occupational pension plans. Over the period of this study, between 7.6 and 13.0 percent of those who chose to take out personal pensions rather than join their employers' occupational pensions moved job in the subsequent year. Of those who chose to "default" to SERPS, the fractions moving—ranging from 9.3 percent to 17.9 percent—are even higher. This contrasts with between 3.6 and 6.7 percent mobility for individuals who joined an occupational pension plan. Looking at those who move employer at any point over the period, 42.9 percent of those who choose not to join their employers' pension plans in favor of a personal pension moved job compared to 27.4 percent among those who did join their employers' plans. This 15.5 percentage point difference has a standard error of 3.6 and hence is highly significant. This clearly suggests that those individuals who chose to opt out of their employers' pension plans for a personal pension or SERPS were indeed more likely to move employer subsequently.

Of course, there may be other correlates with occupational pension plan take-up that are associated with lower mobility. We know, for example, that occupational pension plan members tend to be older than personal pension optants, and concentrated in certain industries and occupations (Barrientos 1998). Further multivariate analysis, conditioning out the impact of other characteristics, shows that differences in subsequent job mobility remain, and are indeed heightened (Disney and Emmerson 2002). Here we redo the analysis for more homogeneous groups of workers, selecting individuals in their thirties, who had the highest take-up rate of personal pensions (fig. 6.2). Table 6.9 therefore examines mobility rates, both year-on-year and cumulative, for this age group, in total and disaggregated by gender. We observe a similar finding to table 6.8 on average and for men:

Table 6.9 **Percentage of 30- to 39-Year-Olds Who Could Have Joined an Occupational Pension and Who Are Changing Employer, by Gender and Pension Status in Previous Wave (employees in wave 2 only)**

	Wave						
Pension Status in Previous Wave	3	4	5	6	7	8	Any Move
All individuals offered an OP							
% with OP	3.2	8.8	5.0	5.4	5.2	6.1	29.2 (2.2)
% with PP	11.1	11.9	5.2	8.5	10.5	15.9	39.7 (6.2)
Men offered an OP							
% with OP	3.5	6.8	4.8	4.5	4.3	7.8	24.8 (2.7)
% with PP	6.5	15.2	6.9	10.0	7.1	6.3	38.7 (8.9)
Women offered an OP							
% with OP	2.6	12.2	5.4	6.7	6.5	3.9	36.6 (3.9)
% with PP	15.6	8.8	3.4	7.4	12.5	21.4	40.6 (8.8)

Sources: British Household Panel Survey, 1992–1998 inclusive; authors' calculations.
Note: See table 6.8.

Subsequent mobility rates are higher for those who opted to take personal pensions although offered occupational pensions. This difference is significant at 5 percent on a one tailed t-test (10 percent on a two-tailed test). However, the difference is not significant for women.

6.7 Conclusion

This paper has examined a number of consequences of the British pension reform strategy of the 1980s and 1990s, focusing in particular on the introduction of personal pensions as an additional opting-out strategy. In particular, we examined five aspects of the economy where reform might be expected to have some effects:

1. *Household saving rates.* Our tentative conclusion is that personal pensions contributed a negligible net amount to household saving at the end of the 1980s. But a decade later, due to the fact that contributions direct from individuals and their employers had become more important than those from the contracted-out rebate, personal pensions are likely to have contributed more substantially to household saving.
2. *Public finances.* The contracting-out arrangements have raised payroll tax rates by around 2 1/2 to 3 percentage points, relative to the status quo. They will reduce payroll tax rates by somewhat less as opted-out pensioners retire later in this century. It is inherent in rational voluntary switching that the government never recoups fully its initial payroll tax reductions designed to encourage opting out.
3. *Income distribution.* In a static sense, greater contracting-out might lead to greater income inequality for two reasons. First, private pension incomes may be more volatile. Second, in the 1980s and 1990s, average private pensions grew much faster than the contracting-out arrangements had assumed. This made them worth more than state pensions and better-off earners tend to contract out. The future impact of personal pensions on income inequality will depend not just on future investment returns but also on the retirement behavior of optants.
4. *Retirement decisions.* It is too early to say whether personal pensions will affect the timing of retirement given the age structure of optants. It is clear that DB plans will discourage early retirement relative to DC plans, due to the fact that the former are back-loaded while the latter are front-loaded. But the introduction of personal pensions will have both a wealth and a substitution effect. Hence the net impact on labor supply could go either way.
5. *Labor market flexibility.* We show that individuals who chose to opt out of *company* pension plans exhibit significantly higher subsequent job mobility than those who chose to join their employers' plans. In order to condition for gender and age we show that among men in their thirties,

among whom coverage of personal pensions was highest, these differences in subsequent labor market mobility remain. In principle, further analysis of this experiment will offer a more precise test than the existing (largely inconclusive) literature on pension plan tenure and job mobility.

References

Agulnik, P., N., Barr, J. Falkingham, and J. Rake. 1999. Partnership in pensions? Responses to the Pensions Green Paper, CASEpaper no. 24. London: London School of Economics, Centre for Analysis of Social Exclusion.

Banks, J., R. Blundell, and S. Tanner. 1998. Is there a retirement-savings puzzle? *American Economic Review* 88 (4): 769–788.

Banks, J., and C. Emmerson. 2000. Public and private pension spending: Principles, practice, and the need for reform. *Fiscal Studies* 21 (1): 1–63.

Banks, J., and S. Tanner. 1999. Household saving in the U.K. Report no. 62. London: Institute for Fiscal Studies.

Barrientos, A. 1998. Supplementary pension coverage in Britain. *Fiscal Studies* 19 (November): 429–446.

Blake, D. 1995. Pension schemes and pension funds in the United Kingdom. Oxford, U.K.: Clarendon Press.

Blundell, R., and P. Johnson. 1999. Pensions and retirement in the United Kingdom. In *Social security and retirement around the world,* ed. J. Gruber and D. Wise, 403–435. Chicago: University of Chicago Press.

Blundell, R., C. Meghir, and S. Smith. 2001. Pension incentives and the pattern of early retirement. *Economic Journal* 112 (478): C153–C170.

Bodie, Z., A. J. Marcus, and R. C. Merton. 1988. Defined benefit versus defined contribution pension plans: What are the real trade-offs? In Pensions in the U.S. economy, ed. Z. Bodie, J. Shoven, and D. Wise, 139–162. Chicago: University of Chicago Press.

Bohn, H. 1997. Social security reform and financial markets. In *Social security reform: Links to saving, investment, and growth,* ed. S. Sass and R. Triest, 193–227. Boston: Federal Reserve Bank of Boston.

Bos, E., M. T. Vu, E. Massiah, and R. A. Bulatao. 1994. *World population projections: Estimates and projections with related demographic statistics.* Baltimore: Johns Hopkins University Press.

Brugiavini, A., and R. Disney. 1993. The choice of private pension plans under uncertainty in the U.K. London: Institute for Fiscal Studies. Mimeograph.

Budd, A., and N. Campbell. 1998. The roles of the public and private sectors in the U.K. pension system. In *Privatizing social security,* ed. Martin Feldstein, 99–127. Chicago: University of Chicago Press.

Chand, S., and A. Jaeger. 1996. Ageing populations and public pension schemes. Occasional Paper no. 147. Washington, D.C.: International Monetary Fund.

Clark, T. 2001. Recent pensions policy and the Pension Credit. Briefing Note no. 17. London: Institute for Fiscal Studies.

———. 2002. Rewarding saving and alleviating poverty? The final Pension Credit proposals. Briefing Note no. 22. London: Institute for Fiscal Studies.

Clark, T., and J. Taylor. 2000. Income inequality: A tale of two cycles? *Fiscal Studies* 20 (4): 387–408.

Creedy, J., R. Disney, and E. Whitehouse. 1993. The earnings-related state pension, indexation, and lifetime redistribution in the U.K. *Review of Income and Wealth* 39 (September): 257–278.

Cutler, D., M. Poterba, L. M. Sheiner, and L. Summers. 1990. An aging society: Opportunity or challenge? *Brookings Papers on Economic Activity,* Issue no. 1:1–73. Washington, D.C.: Brookings Institution.

Dilnot, A., R. Disney, P. Johnson, and E. Whitehouse. 1994. *Pensions policy in Britain: An economic analysis.* London: Institute for Fiscal Studies.

Disney, R. 1996. *Can we afford to grow older? A perspective on the economics of ageing.* Cambridge: MIT Press.

———. 1997. The United Kingdom's pension program. In *Social security reform: Links to saving, investment, and growth,* ed. S. Sass and R. Triest, 157–167. Boston: Federal Reserve Bank of Boston.

———. 1999. Why have older men stopped working in Britain? In *The state of working Britain,* ed. P. Gregg and J. Wadsworth, 24–43. Manchester: Manchester University Press.

———. 2000. Crises in OECD public pension programmes: What are the reform alternatives? *Economic Journal Features* 110 (February): F1–F23.

Disney, R., and C. Emmerson. 2002. Choice of pension scheme and job mobility in Britain. Institute for Fiscal Studies Working Paper no. 09/02. London: IFS.

Disney, R., C. Emmerson, and S. Tanner. 1999. Partnership in pensions: An assessment. IFS Commentary no. 78. London: Institute for Fiscal Studies.

Disney, R., C. Emmerson, and M. Wakefield. 2001. Pension reform and saving in Britain. *Oxford Review of Economic Policy* 17 (1): 70–94.

Disney, R., and P. Johnson, eds. 2002. *Pension systems and retirement incomes across OECD countries.* Aldershot, U.K.: Edward Elgar.

Disney, R., C. Meghir, and E. Whitehouse. 1994. Retirement behaviour in Britain. *Fiscal Studies* 15 (1): 24–43.

Disney, R., R. Palacios, and E. Whitehouse. 1999. Individual choice of pension arrangement as a pension reform strategy. Institute for Fiscal Studies Working Paper no. W99/18. London: IFS.

Disney, R., and S. Smith. 2002. The labour supply effect of the abolition of the earnings rule for older workers in the U.K. *Economic Journal* 112 (March): C136–C152.

Disney, R., and E. Whitehouse. 1992a. Personal pensions and the review of the contracting-out terms. *Fiscal Studies* 13 (February): 38–53.

———. 1992b. The personal pension stampede. London: Institute for Fiscal Studies.

———. 1993a. Contracting out and lifetime redistribution in the U.K. state pension system. *Oxford Bulletin of Economics and Statistics* 55 (February): 25–42.

———. 1993b. Will younger cohorts obtain a worse deal from the U.K. state pension scheme? In *Industrial concentration and economic inequality,* ed. M. Casson and J. Creedy, 85–106. Aldershot, U.K. Edward Elgar.

———. 1996. What are occupational pension plan entitlements worth in Britain? *Economica* 63 (May): 213–238.

Emmerson, C., and P. Johnson. 2002. Pension provision in the United Kingdom. In *Pension systems and retirement incomes across OECD countries,* ed. R. Disney and P. Johnson, 296–333. Aldershot, U.K.: Edward Elgar.

Emmerson, C., and S. Tanner. 1999. The government's proposals for stakeholder pensions. Briefing Note no. 1. London: Institute for Fiscal Studies.

———. 2000. A note on the tax treatment of private pensions and individual savings accounts. *Fiscal Studies* 21 (March): 65–74.

Engen, E. M., and W. G. Gale. 1997. Effects of social security reform on private and national saving. In *Social Security reform: Links to saving, investment, and growth,* ed. S. Sass and R. Triest, 103–142. Boston: Federal Reserve Bank of Boston.
Gale, W. G. 1998. The effects of pensions on household wealth: A re-evaluation of the theory and evidence. *Journal of Political Economy* 104 (4): 706–723.
Goodman, A., and S. Webb. 1994. For richer for poorer: The changing distribution of income in the United Kingdom, 1961–94. Commentary no. 42. London: Institute for Fiscal Studies.
Great Britain. Audit Commission. 1997. *Retiring nature: Early retirement in local government.* London: Audit Commission.
Great Britain. Cabinet Office. 2000. *Performance and innovation unit: Winning the generation game.* London: Her Majesty's Stationery Office.
Great Britain. Department of Health and Social Security. 1984. *Population, pension costs, and pensioners' incomes.* London: Her Majesty's Stationery Office.
Great Britain. Department of Social Security (DSS). 1998. A new contract for welfare: Partnership in pensions. Cm. 4179. London: Her Majesty's Stationery Office.
———. 2000a. The changing welfare state: Pensioner incomes. Department of Social Security Paper no. 2. London: DSS.
———. 2000b. The pension credit: A consultation paper. Cm 4900. London: The Stationery Office.
———. 2000c. *The pensioners' income series 1998/99.* London: DSS.
Great Britain. Financial Services Authority. 2000. *Personal pensions mis-selling: The facts.* London: FSA.
Great Britain. Government Actuary's Department. 1999. *National Insurance fund long term financial estimates.* London: The Stationery Office.
Great Britain. Her Majesty's Treasury. 2000a. Financial statement and budget report, March 2000. London: HM Treasury.
———. 2000b. Pre-budget report, November 2000. Cm4917. London: The Stationery Office.
———. 2000c. Review of ill health retirement in the public sector. London: Her Majesty's Treasury.
———. 2000d. Tax ready reckoner and tax reliefs: November 2000. London: Her Majesty's Treasury.
Great Britain. House of Commons. 2000. The contributory principle: Firth Report of the Social Security Committee, HC-56, Vol. 2, App. 25. London: Her Majesty's Stationery Office.
Great Britain. National Audit Office. 1991. The elderly: Informational requirements for supporting the elderly and implications of personal pensions for the National Insurance fund. London: Her Majesty's Stationery Office.
———. 2000. State Earnings-Related Pension Scheme: The failure to inform the public of reduced rights for widows and widowers. Hc320. London: The Stationery Office.
Great Britain. Office for National Statistics (ONS). 1998. *The United Kingdom national accounts: The blue book.* London: ONS.
———. 2000. Living in Britain: Results from the 1998 General Household Survey. London: The Stationery Office.
Great Britain. Office of Population Censuses and Surveys. 1992. *General Household Survey 1992.* London: Her Majesty's Stationery Office.
Gustman, A., and T. Steinmeier. 1993. Pension portability and labour mobility: Evidence from the Survey of Income and Program Participation. *Journal of Public Economics* 50:299–323.

HMSO Inland Revenue Statistics. Various issues.

Ippolito, R. A. 1997. Pension plans and employee performance. Chicago: University of Chicago Press.

Johnson, P., and G. Stears. 1995. Pensioner income inequality. *Fiscal Studies* 16 (4): 69–93.

Journal of Economic Perspectives. 1996. Government incentives for saving. Vol. 10 (4): 73–138.

Lawson, N. 1992. *The view from no. 11: Memoirs of a Tory radical.* London: Corgi Books.

Lazear, E., and R. Moore. 1988. Pensions and turnover. In *Pensions in the U.S. economy,* ed. Z. Bodie, J. Shoven, and D. Wise, 163–190. Chicago: University of Chicago Press.

Lazear, E. P. 1979. Why is there mandatory retirement? *Journal of Political Economy* 87 (6): 1261–284.

McCormick, B. and G. Hughes. 1984. The influence of pensions on job mobility. *Journal of Public Economics* 23:183–206.

Mealli, F, and S. Pudney. 1996. Occupational pensions and job mobility in Britain: Estimation of a random-effects competing risks model. *Journal of Applied Econometrics* 11:293–320.

Miles, D. 1999. Modeling the impact of demographic change on the economy. *Economic Journal* 109 (January): 1–36.

Modigliani, F. 1986. Life cycle, individual thrift, and the wealth of nations. *American Economic Review* 76 (June): 297–313.

Murthi, M., J. M. Orszag, and P. R. Orszag. 1999. Administration costs under a decentralized approach to individual accounts: Lessons from the United Kingdom. Discussion Paper. London: Birkbeck College.

Peacock, A. 1992. The credibility of economic advice to government. *Economic Journal* 102 (September): 1213–222.

Roseveare, D., W. Leibfritz, D. Fore, and E. Wurzel. 1996. Ageing populations, pension system, and government budgets: Simulations for twenty OECD countries. OECD Working Paper no. 168. Paris: Organization for Economic Cooperation and Development.

Whitehouse, E. 2000. Administrative charges for funded pension systems: An international comparison and assessment. Social Protection Discussion Paper no. 0016. Washington, D.C.: World Bank.

7

Labor Market Reforms and Changes in Wage Inequality in the United Kingdom and the United States

Amanda Gosling and Thomas Lemieux

7.1 Introduction

A large number of studies have shown that wage and earnings inequality increased sharply in the United Kingdom since the late 1970s.[1] With perhaps the exception of the United States, the magnitude of the increase in wage inequality was unmatched in any other industrialized countries.[2] For example, wage inequality remained relatively stable during the same period in the major continental European countries (Germany, France, and Italy) while it increased at a more moderate pace in Canada and in Japan. This increase in earnings inequality was accompanied by a decrease in the earnings gap between men and women. Again, the changes in the gender wage gap experienced by the United Kingdom and United States appear to be more dramatic than those found in other countries.

The divergent experiences of different countries in terms of wage inequality is a major challenge for explanations that focus on changes in the relative demand for labor across different skill classes. The most popular demand-side explanation for rising wage inequality is that over the last

Amanda Gosling is a lecturer in economics at the University of Essex and a research associate at the Institute for Fiscal Studies. Thomas Lemieux is professor of economics at the University of British Columbia, and a research associate of the National Bureau of Economic Research.

We would like to thank Richard Blundell, David Card, and seminar participants at University of British Columbia, University of California–Berkeley, UC–Los Angeles, and UC–Santa Barbara for comments on previous drafts of the paper, and Alan Manning for help with the data.

1. See, for example, Schmitt (1996), Machin (1996), and Gosling, Machin, and Meghir (2000).

2. See Freeman and Katz (1996) for an overview of the inequality trends in different industrialized countries.

couple of decades, technological change has been biased in favor of skilled workers. It is difficult to see, however, why this type of technical change should have been more pronounced in the United Kingdom than in countries like France and Germany.

Another possible explanation for the unique wage inequality experience of the United Kingdom is that since 1979 the institutional structures of the U.K. labor market changed dramatically. Union decline, falls in public-sector employment, contracting-out, and competitive tendering of some public-sector services resulted in changes in the way pay was formally set. Wages councils (who set minimum rates of pay in some low-paying and female-dominated industries) were weakened and finally abolished in 1993. Some women would have benefited from the increase in scope of legislation concerning sex discrimination and equal pay, however. The depth and coverage of employment protection legislation was reduced, basically making it easier for firms to sack their workers. Changes to the social security and welfare system may have affected work incentives, possibly increasing competitive pressure on wages at the bottom part of the distribution and changing the composition of the workforce.

The main question we ask in the paper is whether these reforms in the institutional structure of the labor market contributed to the increase in inequality in the United Kingdom. On the one hand, a quick comparison of the experiences of different European countries suggests that the answer to this question is yes. Countries like France and Germany experienced neither the dramatic labor market reforms nor the sharp increase in wage inequality that the United Kingdom experienced over the last two decades.[3] On the other hand, it is possible that the United Kingdom would have diverged from the experience of the rest of Europe without any policy changes, given the existing differences in the structure of collective bargaining and the educational and training systems. It is therefore difficult to identify the precise effect of these policy reforms through a broad comparison of the leading European economies.

Comparisons between the United Kingdom and the United States may be more fruitful, however, for at least three reasons. First, the U.S. and U.K. labor markets of the late 1990s are very similar. Wage setting where unions are present is decentralized and unions have little influence over pay in the private sector. In neither country is there a wide-ranging system of vocational education and training. Formal skill acquisition occurs at school or at university rather than on the job.[4] Second, given that it is possible to

3. See also Giles et al. (1998) for a comparison between the United Kingdom and West Germany over the 1980s.

4. This is not to say there is no on-the-job training in the United Kingdom and the United States, but merely that training schemes which give workers accredited transferable skills are rare.

think of the institutional changes in the United Kingdom as transforming its labor market in a more "U.S. style," the United States is a natural benchmark for assessing the impact of these reforms. Third, changes in the United Kingdom (as discussed in section 7.3) were more likely to affect men, while changes in the United States (basically the decline in the real value of the U.S. minimum wage between 1979 and 1990) were more likely to affect women. A comparison of the difference in the difference in trends between men and women across the two countries may help to disentangle the effect of these institutional changes from other country-specific trends as well as trends that are common to both countries. The primary goal of this paper is to examine this in more detail.

The plan of the paper is the following. In section 7.2, we describe the data and present descriptive statistics on the evolution of the distribution of wages in the United Kingdom and the United States during the 1980s and 1990s. In section 7.3 we look directly at the role of unionization, privatization, and the minimum wage in explaining the key differences between the evolution of wage inequality in the two countries. In section 7.4, we present some qualifications and extensions to the main results of section 7.3. We conclude in section 7.5.

7.2 Data and Descriptive Statistics

7.2.1 Data Sources

For the United Kingdom we use a multiple–data set approach as there is no one data set which is ideal for our purpose. More precisely, we compute the basic trends in wage inequality using the Family Expenditure Survey (FES) for 1978 to 1996 supplemented with the autumnal Labor Force Survey (LFS) for 1997–1999 and, in few cases, by the General Household Survey (GHS). We analyze the effect of unionization and public-sector affiliation on wage inequality by comparing the 1983 GHS and the 1998 LFS. For the United States we use data from the outgoing rotation sample of the Current Population Survey (CPS). A more detailed discussion of all the data sets we use is given in the appendix.

7.2.2 Descriptive Statistics

Throughout this paper, we focus on the evolution of overall measures of (hourly) wage inequality such as the standard deviation, interpercentiles range such as the 90-10 wage ratio, and the whole density of wages. This focus is deliberate given our interest for the role of economic reforms and labor market institutions on the wage distribution. A large number of studies have stressed the importance of supply, demand, and skilled-biased technical change in the evolution of wage differentials across education

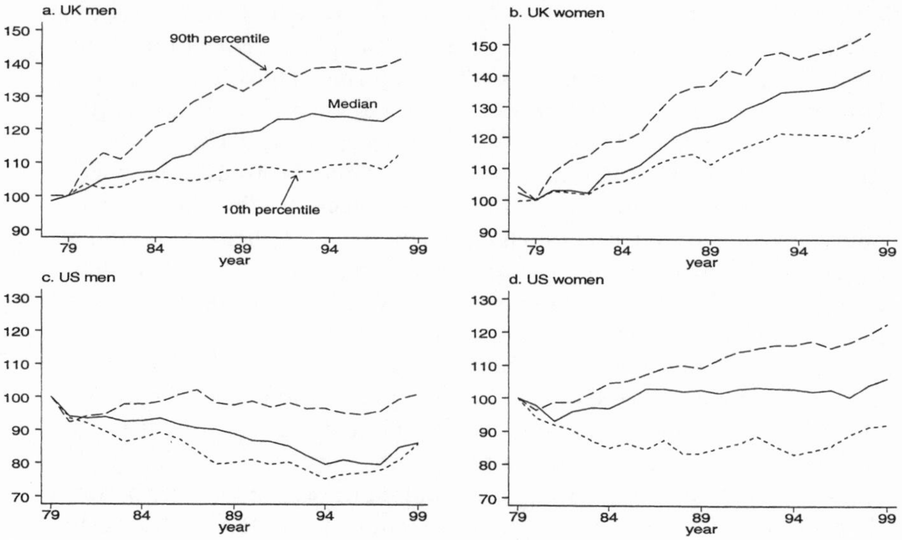

Fig. 7.1 Indexed real wages by percentile, 1978–1999 (United Kingdom and United States, 1979 = 100)

groups.[5] These wage differentials represent, however, only a small fraction of total wage variability across individuals. More importantly, previous research has shown that the effect of factors such as unions and the minimum wage are best captured by modeling the whole distribution of wages rather than focusing only on the more standard wage differentials by age or education (see DiNardo, Fortin, and Lemieux 1996). For the sake of completeness, however, we also present below a few education- and age-related wage differentials and a standard between- versus within-group variance decomposition.

Figure 7.1 plots the evolution of the median and the 10th and 90th percentiles of male and female wages in the United Kingdom and the United States between 1978 and 1999 (1978 to 1998 in the United Kingdom, 1979 to 1999 in the United States), normalized to 100 in 1979.[6] The paths of the medians indicate very different patterns of wage growth for different groups. In both the United Kingdom and the United States, median wages of women increase substantially relative to those of men. This translates into a substantial decline in the gender wage gap (at the median) as reported in figure 7.2. This finding is consistent with other U.S. and U.K.

5. See, for example, Katz and Murphy (1992) for the United States, Schmitt (1996) for Britain, and Freeman and Needels (1993) and Card and Lemieux (2001) for international comparisons among the United States, the United Kingdom, and Canada.

6. In figures 7.1 and 7.3 and table 7.1, we have adjusted the 1997 and 1998 data to ensure there is no discontinuity between the 1996 FES and the 1997 LFS due to differences in the survey instruments. See the appendix for more details.

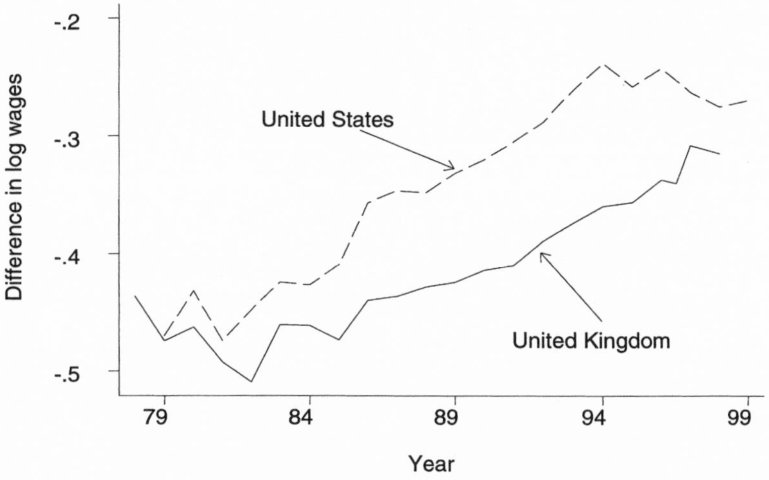

Fig. 7.2 Gender wage gap, United Kingdom and United States

studies such as Harkness (1996) and Blau (1998). Interestingly, the change in the wage gap is very similar in the two countries. Median female wages have increased from about 64 percent to 73 percent of the male median in the United Kingdom and from 64 percent to 75 percent in the United States. A second important difference is that real wages grow much faster in the United Kingdom than in the United States during this period. For instance, the median of U.S. male real wage declined between 1979 and 1998 compared to a 25 percent growth in the United Kingdom.[7]

Figure 7.1 also indicates that wage inequality increased for all four groups during this period. In all four cases, the 90th percentile grows relative to the median. A closer examination of the figure indicates, however, that most of the growth in inequality actually occurred during the 1980s, while inequality remained more stable in the 1990s. Figure 7.1 also shows that inequality increased more for some groups than others. For example, the increase in wage inequality over the whole sample period is much less pronounced for men in the United States than in the United Kingdom. These trends in wage inequality are more readily seen in figure 7.3, which reports the evolution of both the 90-10 differential and the standard deviation of log wages. Both the standard deviation and the 90-10 differential show the same steep increase in wage inequality in the 1980s, followed by more modest growth in the 1990s.

7. A similar difference has been noticed in other comparisons between the United States and France (Card, Kramarz, and Lemieux 1999) or Germany (Beaudry and Green 2003). Beaudry and Green suggest that differences in the accumulation of physical capital per capita, which grew much faster in Germany than in the United States during this period, may help explain this important gap.

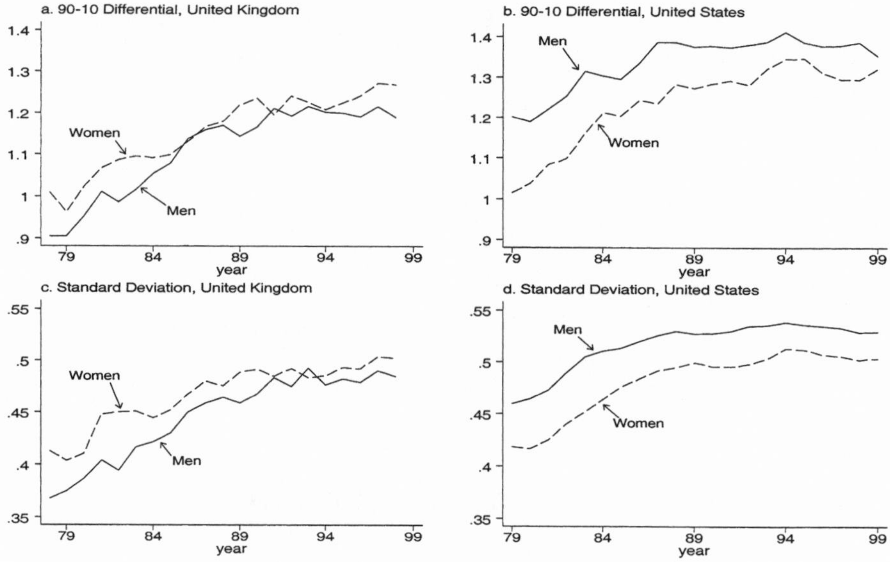

Fig. 7.3 Log wage inequality, United Kingdom and United States

Beyond these broad similarities in the pattern and growth of wage inequality in the United Kingdom and the United States, figures 7.1 and 7.3 also illustrate some important differences between the two countries. The slowdown of inequality growth in the 1990s is much more marked in the United States, particularly for women. Over the 1980s the increase in both the 90-10 differential and the standard deviation of female wages is larger in the United States than in the United Kingdom. In the 1990s the opposite is true. In addition, the level of wage inequality, as measured by the standard deviation and the 90-10 differential, is systematically *lower* for men than women in the United Kingdom, while the opposite is true in the United States. Furthermore, the figure shows that while wage inequality grows faster for men than for women in the United Kingdom, the opposite is true in the United States.

One way of summarizing the data is to say that the extent of wage inequality has converged in the two countries over the last twenty years. While there were important differences in the level and pattern of wage inequality across gender and countries in the late 1970s, much of these differences have vanished by the late 1990s. Male wage inequality in the United Kingdom has caught up to the level of female wage inequality and is moving closer to the level of male inequality in the United States.

The convergence in wage inequality in the two countries is shown more explicitly in table 7.1, which reports several measures of inequality for men

Table 7.1 **Measures of (log) Wage Inequality in the United Kingdom and the United States, 1979–1998**

	1979 (1)	1989 (2)	1998 (3)	1979–1989 Change (4)	1989–1998 Change (5)	1979–1998 Change (6)
			A. United Kingdom, Men			
50-10	0.408	0.529	0.550	0.121	0.021	0.142
90-50	0.512	0.630	0.640	0.118	0.009	0.128
90-10	0.920	1.159	1.189	0.239	0.030	0.269
Standard deviation	0.376	0.464	0.501	0.088	0.038	0.125
			B. United Kingdom, Women			
50-10	0.399	0.494	0.576	0.095	0.082	0.177
90-50	0.599	0.717	0.693	0.119	–0.025	0.094
90-10	0.998	1.211	1.269	0.213	0.058	0.271
Standard deviation	0.409	0.486	0.503	0.077	0.017	0.094
			C. United States, Men			
50-10	0.650	0.737	0.688	0.087	–0.049	0.038
90-50	0.552	0.639	0.699	0.087	0.060	0.147
90-10	1.201	1.376	1.386	0.175	0.011	0.185
Standard deviation	0.460	0.527	0.529	0.068	0.001	0.069
			D. United States, Women			
50-10	0.439	0.631	0.567	0.192	–0.064	0.128
90-50	0.575	0.642	0.728	0.067	0.086	0.153
90-10	1.015	1.273	1.295	0.258	0.022	0.281
Standard deviation	0.418	0.500	0.502	0.082	0.003	0.084

Notes: Based on hourly wages of wage and salary workers aged twenty-three to fifty-nine earning between £1 and £30 per hour (£1996) in the United Kingdom, and between $2.50 and $63.00 an hour ($1996) in the United States. United States data are from the outgoing rotation group files of the CPS. Measures of wage dispersion for the United Kingdom in 1979 and 1989 are three-year averages from the FES for 1978–1980 and 1988–1990, respectively. Measures of wage dispersion for 1998 are computed using data from the autumn LFS. Abbreviations are explained in text.

and women in 1979, 1989, and 1998.[8] For example, the 0.084 U.S.-U.K. difference in the male standard deviation in 1979 (0.460 in the United States vs. 0.376 in the United Kingdom) declines to 0.063 in 1989 and 0.028 in 1998, which is only a third of the original difference. By contrast, the U.S.-U.K. difference in the female standard deviation is relatively modest throughout the 1980s and 1990s.

As is well known, the standard deviation and the 90-10 wage differential are two standard measures of wage inequality that capture different features of the wage distribution. For example, changes in the wage distribu-

8. The statistics reported for 1979 and 1989 in the United Kingdom are averages for 1978 to 1980, and 1988 to 1990, respectively.

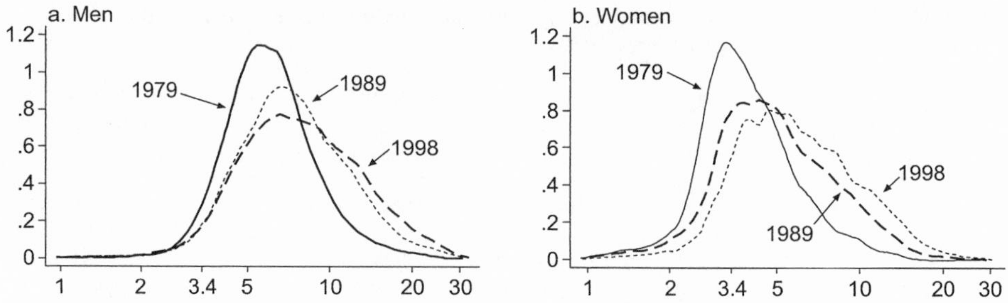

Fig. 7.4 Density of log wages in the United Kingdom in 1996 pounds

tion above the 90th percentile affect the standard deviation but not the 90-10 differential. A more general way of looking at what happens in the distribution of wages is to plot the whole distribution of wages. In this light, figure 7.4 shows kernel density estimates of the distribution of (log) wages for men and women in the United Kingdom in 1979, 1989, and 1998. For both men and women, there is clear visual evidence that the wage distribution becomes increasingly unequal over time. In both cases, the density in the middle of the distribution declines while it increases in the tails.

Figure 7.4 also shows that the female wage distribution is positively skewed in all years. The distribution of male wages is also skewed, but to a much smaller extent. This skewness in the U.K. wage distribution is also illustrated in table 7.1, which shows that the 90-50 wage differential is systematically larger than the 50-10 differential. The situation is quite different in the United States. Figure 7.5, panel A, shows that the male wage distribution in 1979 was in fact negatively skewed, though it becomes much more symmetric over time. As in the case in the United Kingdom, there is clear evidence of an overall increase in wage inequality. The density of wages declines in the middle of the distribution and increases in the tails.

These qualitative changes in the shape of the U.S. male distribution are confirmed in table 7.1, which shows that the 50-10 wage differential is substantially larger than the 90-50 differential in 1979. By 1998, however, the distribution is more or less symmetric since the 90-50 and 50-10 differentials are comparable. By contrast, the U.S. female wage distribution, shown in figure 7.5, panel B, is positively skewed, and the 90-50 wage differential is systematically larger than the 50-10 differential. The increase in overall inequality is perhaps clearer for U.S. women than for other groups because average wages are relatively stable over time. As a result, panel B of figure 7.5 clearly shows that the density declines in the middle of the distribution but increases in the tails. The same pattern is not as clearly seen for other groups because average wages shift substantially over time.

In summary, the different pieces of evidence all suggest that the U.K. wage distribution is becoming increasingly similar to the U.S. wage distri-

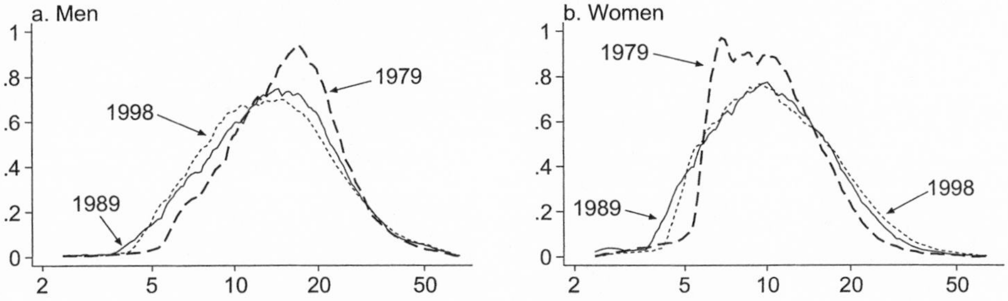

Fig. 7.5 Density of log wages in the United States in 1996 dollars

bution. This is particularly clear in the case of men, for which the shape of the wage distribution (skewness) and the extent of inequality (standard deviation and 90-10 differential) were quite different in 1979. Most of these differences had vanished by 1998. There is also a convergence between the U.K. and U.S. female wage distributions, though differences were perhaps more subtle in 1979 than in the case of men. The 1979 density in the United Kingdom has a well defined single peak while there is a relatively flat section in the middle of the U.S. distribution. By contrast, the shapes of the U.K. and U.S. distributions look much more similar in 1998.

Since real wages were initially lower but grew faster in the United Kingdom than in the United States, both the level and the distribution of wages have converged. One simple way of representing this overall wage convergence between the two countries is to show to which percentile of the U.K. real wage distribution corresponds a given percentile of the U.S. real wage distribution.[9] Panel A of figure 7.6 illustrates these "Q-Q" plots for men in 1979, 1989, and 1998.[10] The figure shows, for example, that the median wage for U.S. men is equivalent to the 90th percentile of the U.K. wage distribution in 1979. The percentile of the U.K. wage distribution corresponding to the U.S. median drops to the 70th in 1989 and to the 60th in 1998 as U.K. real wages keep catching up to U.S. levels. Overall, the relationship between U.K. and U.S. wage percentiles gets increasingly close to a 45-degree line, which illustrates dramatically the convergence between the dis-

9. We use the Organization for Economic Cooperation and Development (OECD) purchasing power parity exchange rates for 1996 (£0.65 per dollar) to convert the U.K. real wages (in 1996 pounds) into 1996 U.S. dollars.

10. To make the figure more informative, we have normalized the scales using the inverse of the cumulative normal distribution. The reason for doing so is that if the distribution of (log) wages is approximately normal in both countries, U.K. percentiles (in the normalized scale) are a linear function of U.S. percentiles and the variance of U.K. wages is lower if this slope is smaller than 1. The same interpretation of the "un-normalized" Q-Q plots applies only if the (log) wage distributions are approximately uniform. It is clear from figures 7.4 and 7.5, however, that the empirical wage distributions are much closer to a normal than to a uniform distribution.

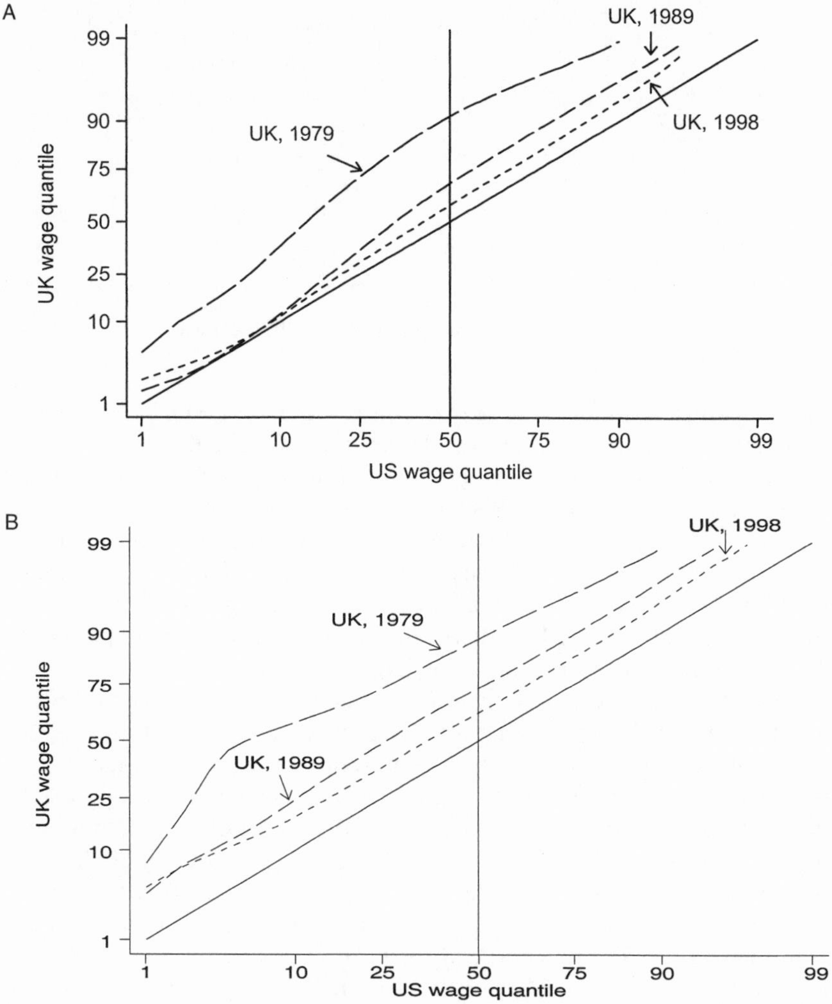

Fig. 7.6 Q-Q plots: *A*, men; *B*, women

tribution of real wages in the two countries. The same basic pattern of wage convergence is also observed for women in panel B of figure 7.6.

7.2.3 Wage Dispersion between and within Groups of Workers

Our focus on overall wage inequality is different from the bulk of the literature that has mostly focused on the evolution of wage differentials between different "skill groups" such as college and high school workers. For the sake of comparability with this literature, we present a set of standard age and education wage differentials for the United Kingdom and the United States in table 7.2. These differentials are computed by running

Table 7.2 **Standard Wage Differentials and Between- and Within-Group Variance of Wages in the United Kingdom and the United States, 1979–1998**

	1979 (1)	1989 (2)	1998 (3)	1979–1989 Change (4)	1989–1998 Change (5)	1979–1998 Change (6)
			A. United Kingdom, Men			
A-O level qualifications/no qualifications	0.248	0.288	0.246	0.040	–0.042	–0.002
University graduates/A-O level qualifications	0.231	0.242	0.375	0.011	0.133	0.144
Age 40–49/23–29	0.191	0.245	0.308	0.054	0.063	0.117
Between variance	0.0386	0.0591	0.0781	0.0205	0.0190	0.0395
Within variance	0.1000	0.1427	0.1730	0.0427	0.0303	0.0730
			B. United Kingdom, Women			
A-O level qualifications/no qualifications	0.208	0.292	0.243	0.084	–0.049	0.035
University graduates/A-O level qualifications	0.520	0.400	0.490	–0.120	0.090	–0.030
Age 40–49/23–29	0.014	0.009	0.092	–0.005	0.083	0.078
Between variance	0.0480	0.0759	0.0850	0.0279	0.0091	0.0370
Within variance	0.1119	0.1562	0.1682	0.0443	0.0120	0.0563
			C. United States, Men			
High school graduates/high school dropouts	0.221	0.247	0.285	0.026	0.038	0.064
College graduates/high school graduates	0.216	0.342	0.416	0.126	0.074	0.200
College postgraduates/college graduates	0.044	0.091	0.157	0.047	0.066	0.113
Age 40–49/23–29	0.297	0.357	0.325	0.060	–0.032	0.028
Between variance	0.0496	0.0833	0.0934	0.0337	0.0101	0.0438
Within variance	0.1617	0.1901	0.1903	0.0284	0.0002	0.0286
			D. United States, Women			
High school graduates/high school dropouts	0.175	0.251	0.274	0.076	0.023	0.099
College graduates/high school graduates	0.260	0.418	0.481	0.158	0.063	0.221
College postgraduates/college graduates	0.170	0.180	0.203	0.010	0.023	0.033
Age 40–49/23–29	0.078	0.175	0.230	0.097	0.055	0.152
Between variance	0.0323	0.0715	0.0809	0.0392	0.0094	0.0486
Within variance	0.1310	0.1827	0.1733	0.0517	–0.0094	0.0493

Notes: Based on hourly wages of wage and salary workers aged twenty-three to fifty-nine earning between £1 and £30 per hour (£1996) in the United Kingdom, and between $2.50 and $63.00 an hour ($1996) in the United States. United States data are from the outgoing rotation group files of the CPS. Measures of wage dispersion for the United Kingdom in 1979 and 1989 are three-year averages from the GHS for 1978–1980 and 1988–1990, respectively. Measures of wage dispersion for 1998 are computed using data from autumn LFS. The decomposition of the variance of log wages between and within groups is carried over by estimating log wage regressions with a set of regional dummies (ten regions and London in the United Kingdom, nine regions and SMSA status in the United States), a dummy variable for marital status, and a set of education dummies (seven in the United Kingdom, five in the United States) fully interacted with a fourth-degree polynomial in age as regressors. United States models also include dummy variables for race and veteran status. Abbreviations are explained in text.

regressions of log wages on a set of age and education dummies. We use the same set of age dummies for the age groups 23–29, 30–39, 40–49, and 50–59 in both countries. For the United States, we use a set of five education categories: high school dropouts, high school graduates, some college, college graduates, and college post-graduates.

Unfortunately, the information on educational achievement is quite limited in the FES samples. The wage differentials reported in table 7.2 for 1979 and 1989 are thus computed using the GHS, while the LFS is used for 1998.[11] To get large enough samples, we pool the 1978, 1979, and 1980 GHS to compute wage differentials for 1979, and the 1988, 1989, and 1990 GHS for 1989. We construct six education categories for the GHS and the LFS: no qualification, some vocational qualifications (low, middle, and high), A–O level qualifications, and university graduates. We also decompose the variance of wages into a between- and within-group component by running wage regressions on a rich set of individual characteristics.[12]

With few exceptions, the different measures of wage dispersion reported in table 7.2 show trends similar to those reported earlier for overall wage inequality. For instance, there is generally a more marked slowdown in inequality growth in the United States than in the United Kingdom during the 1990s. Another difference between the two countries is that the wage gap between college-educated (university) and high school–educated (A–O level) workers has expanded faster in the United States than in the United Kingdom.[13] This explains why a larger fraction of the growth in inequality comes from the between-group component in the United States.

A related point is that, in absolute terms, the growth in between-group inequality is more or less similar for men and women in the two countries. The differential evolution in inequality for men and women highlighted previously is almost entirely driven by changes in within-group inequality, which increases more for men than women in the United Kingdom, while the opposite is true in the United States. While explanations for changes in the structure of wages based on the supply and demand for different skill groups have natural implications for between-group inequality, they have few testable implications for within-group inequality. Therefore, it is unlikely that these explanations could account for the differential evolution

11. As discussed in the appendix, the GHS is not an ideal data source because weekly hours of work are not measured consistently over time. Despite this shortcoming, however, the FES and the GHS show quite similar increases in the standard deviation of log hourly wages during the 1980s. Table 7.1 indicates that between 1979 and 1989, the standard deviation computed using the FES increased by 0.088 and 0.077 for men and women, respectively. Comparable numbers from the GHS are 0.081 and 0.083, respectively.

12. The variables used in log wage regressions are a set of regional dummies (ten regions and London in the United Kingdom; nine regions and standard metropolitan statistical areas status in the United States), a dummy variable for marital status, and a set of education dummies (seven in the United Kingdom, five in the United States) fully interacted with a fourth-degree polynomial in age. The U.S. models also include dummy variables for race and veteran status.

13. Card and Lemieux (2001) report a similar finding.

of inequality among men and women in the two countries. This provides an additional motivation for focusing on the role of labor market reforms and institutional changes in the remainder of this paper.

7.3 Effect of Reforms and Institutions on the Distribution of Wages

We have just shown that the structure of wages appears to have converged for the two countries. In the introduction we highlighted the fact that institutional structures have also converged. On the one hand, U.K. men were relatively better "protected from inequality" than their U.S. counterparts in the late 1970s because of the strength of U.K. trade unions. On the other hand, U.K. women were not as well protected from inequality because of the lack of a comprehensive national minimum wage policy. These two observations may potentially explain the difference in the evolution of male and female wage inequality in the two countries between 1979 and 1998. We now examine this view in more detail.

7.3.1 Minimum Wages

The minimum wage has been closely linked to the expansion in wage inequality in the United States during the 1980s. As shown in figure 7.7, the real value of the minimum wage fell sharply between 1979 and 1989 before recovering somewhat in the 1990s.[14] DiNardo, Fortin, and Lemieux (1996) and Lee (1999) argue that the decline in real value of the U.S. minimum wage accounts for most of the increase in wage inequality in the lower end of the distribution during the 1980s. This is especially the case for women, who are more likely than men to earn wages at or close to the minimum wage.

The United Kingdom, on the other hand, had no national minimum wage until 1999. Instead, workers in some low-paying industries (e.g., clothing, retail, and catering) were covered by institutions called wage councils, which set industry-level minima. These were reformed in 1986 and abolished in 1993 (in Great Britain). In 1993 some 2.5 million workers were covered. The key distinction between the United States and the United Kingdom in 1979 was in the heterogeneity of coverage. In the United Kingdom, some low-paid workers had no protection at all, and the levels of protection varied not only across industries but also (until 1986) within industries. In terms of changes over time, the United States experienced a steady fall in the minimum wage over the 1980s affecting all workers in

14. Between 1979 and 1981, the nominal minimum wage increased from $2.9 to $3.35 but the Consumer Price Index (CPI) increased even faster. The real value of the minimum wage fell sharply as the nominal value of the minimum wage remained at $3.35 until April 1990, when it was raised to $3.80, and to $4.25 in April 1991. Inflation eroded once again the value of the real minimum wage until October 1996 and September 1997, when the minimum wage was increased successively to $4.75 and $5.15, respectively.

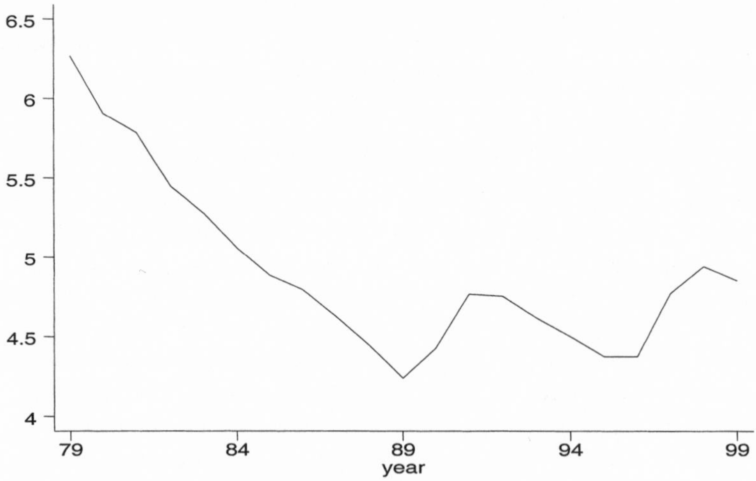

Fig. 7.7 U.S. federal minimum wage, 1996 dollars

the same way, unlike the United Kingdom, where there was no such change. In the 1990s the U.S. minimum rose in real and nominal terms and we should expect this to halt the growth in wage inequality. We should also expect to see a small increase in wage inequality for U.K. women after 1993.

The trends, reported in figure 7.1 and table 7.1, are broadly consistent with the findings of the previous literature. During the 1980s, the 50-10 wage differential expanded faster for U.S. women than for any other groups. The visual effect of the minimum wage can also be seen in Figure 7.5, panel B, where the lower end of the female wage distribution is distorted by the (relatively) high value of the minimum wage. The shape of the wage distribution evolves toward a more regular bell-shaped distribution in 1989 as the minimum wage becomes increasingly less binding. The lower end of the distribution becomes slightly more compressed in the 1990s as the minimum wage starts increasing again. By contrast, there is much less evidence of a visual effect of the minimum wage for men.[15]

Both figure 7.1 and table 7.1 also show that the 50-10 wage differential started narrowing in the United States during the 1990s as the real value of the minimum wage started increasing again. The fact that the 50-10 wage differential expands in 1980s but narrows again in the 1990s in the United States, while it keeps expanding in the United Kingdom, illustrates the im-

15. DiNardo, Fortin, and Lemieux (1996) find a clearer impact of the minimum wage for all men aged sixteen to sixty-four. We miss a substantial fraction of minimum-wage workers in this paper by focusing only on workers above the age of twenty-two.

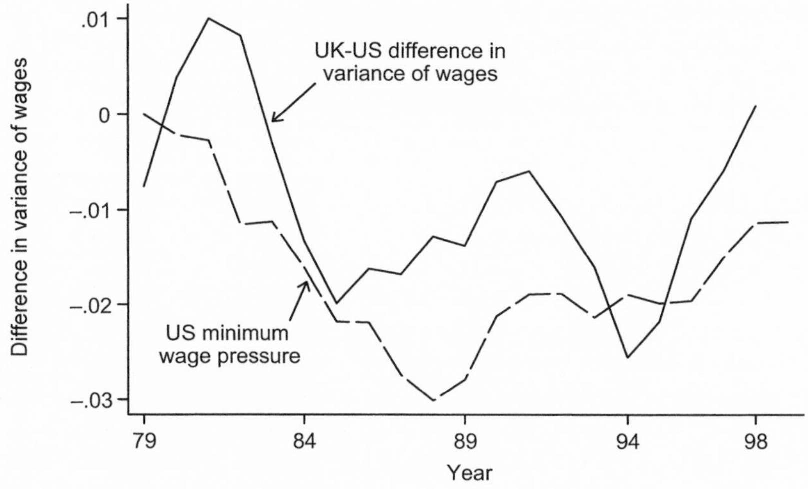

Fig. 7.8 Minimum wage and U.K.-U.S. female variance gap

portant role of the minimum wage for wage inequality. Figures 7.1 and 7.3 also show a small acceleration of the increase in female wage inequality in the United Kingdom in the mid-1990s.

Broader measures of wage inequality, such as the standard deviation and the 90-10 differential, illustrate the same qualitative story for women. Both of these measures expand faster in the United States than in the United Kingdom during the 1980s, while the opposite happens in the 1990s (table 7.1). The decline and subsequent recovery of the real value of the minimum wage in the United States is a natural explanation for this set of facts.

We explore this explanation in more detail in figure 7.8, which shows the evolution of the U.K.-U.S. difference in the variance of female wages along with a measure of the pressure that the U.S. minimum wage exerts on the U.S. variance of wages.[16] This measure of minimum-wage pressure is computed using a "tail-pasting" procedure suggested by DiNardo, Fortin, and Lemieux (1996). The procedure relies on the assumption that if the real minimum wage had remained at its highest (1979) value throughout the 1980s and 1990s, the distribution of wages at or below the 1979 minimum wage would have remained the same as in 1979. Under this assumption, a counterfactual distribution can be computed in year *t* by replacing the part of the year-*t* wage distribution at or below the 1979 minimum wage by the corresponding section of the 1979 wage distribution. Our measure of

16. Because of smaller sample sizes, we smooth the U.K. variance of wages using a three-year moving average before computing the U.K.-U.S. difference in the variance of wages.

minimum-wage pressure is the difference between this counterfactual and the actual variance of wages in each year, normalized to zero in 1979.[17]

Figure 7.8 shows that our measure of minimum wage pressure more or less follows the U-shaped pattern of the real minimum wage illustrated in figure 7.7. While the difference between the U.K. and the U.S. variances follows a more irregular pattern, the series is also U-shaped as inequality grows slower in the United Kingdom than in the United States in the 1980s, while the opposite happens in the 1990s.

Interestingly, a simple ordinary least squares (OLS) regression indicates that the minimum-wage-pressure variable has a positive and significant effect on the U.K.-U.S. gap in the variance of female wages. The estimated coefficient is 0.78 with a standard error of 0.20, which means we cannot reject the null hypothesis that a given change in the variance of U.S. wages induced by a change in the minimum wage has a one-to-one impact on the U.K.-U.S. gap in the variance of wages. This finding is robust to the inclusion of a linear time trend, which is not statistically significant. However, only about half of the variation in the variance gap can be explained by the minimum-wage-pressure variable (the *R*-squared of the regression is 0.46). The results nevertheless confirm that the U.S. minimum wage goes a long way toward explaining the relative evolution of female wage inequality in the two countries.

One interesting conjecture is that the introduction of the U.K. minimum wage in 1999 may have contributed to the U.K.-U.S. convergence in wage inequality and labor market regulations for women in the same way that U.K. de-unionization potentially did for men. Figure 7.3 shows that, though the gap has declined over time, wage inequality was still larger for U.K. women than U.K. men in 1998. This raises the obvious question of whether the introduction of the National Minimum Wage in 1999 was enough to tilt the balance in the U.S. direction by pushing U.K. female wage inequality below U.K. male wage inequality.

In table 7.3, we perform some simple simulations using the 1998 LFS to gauge the potential effect of the minimum wage on male and female inequality in the United Kingdom. In these simulations, we assume that only a fraction of workers earning less than the 1999 minimum wage of 3.6 pounds would have earned at least 3.6 pounds if this minimum wage had prevailed in 1998. As is well known, because of imperfect coverage, lack of compliance, or measurement error in self-reported wages, a substantial

17. We compute the counterfactual distribution by replacing all year-*t* observations at or below the 1979 minimum wage by corresponding 1979 observations, and reweight observations so that the total number of (weighted) observations remains unchanged. For the procedure to be valid, we need to assume that there are no employment or spillover effects due to the minimum wage. DiNardo, Fortin, and Lemieux (1996) and Lee (1999) argue that, if anything, these assumptions tend to understate the true impact of the minimum wage on the distribution of wages.

Table 7.3 **Simulated and Actual Effect of the 1999 Minimum Wage on the U.K. Wage Distribution**

	Actual 1998 (1)	Simulated 1998 with £3.60 Minimum Wage (2)	Actual 1999 (3)	Actual with New Hourly Wage Data (4)
		A. Men		
5th percentile	3.84	3.84	4.04	4.00
10th percentile	4.48	4.48	4.71	4.60
90-10 log wage	1.273	1.273	1.273	1.297
Standard deviation	0.502	0.488	0.504	0.501
		B. Women		
5th percentile	3.00	3.60	3.30	3.60
10th percentile	3.41	3.60	3.67	3.70
90-10 log wage	1.271	1.216	1.238	1.225
Standard deviation	0.502	0.472	0.497	0.480
		C. Men-Women		
90-10 log wage	0.002	0.057	0.035	0.072
Standard deviation	0.000	0.016	0.007	0.021

Notes: Statistics computed using data from the 1998 and 1999 autumn LFS for wage and salary workers aged twenty-three to fifty-nine earning between £1.06 and £31.8 per hour (between £1 and £30 in £1996). The simulated effect of the minimum wage (column [2]) is obtained by assuming that two-thirds of workers earning less than £3.6 in the autumn of 1998 would have earned exactly the 1999 National Minimum Wage of £3.6 if the 1999 National Minimum Wage had prevailed in 1998. The wage of the other third of subminimum workers are assumed to be unaffected by the minimum wage. In column (4), the (new) direct information on hourly wage rates is used instead of average hourly earnings whenever available.

fraction of workers report wages that are below the minimum wage. On the basis of recent estimates provided by the Office of National Statistics (ONS), we assume that two-thirds of workers who report wages below £3.6 in 1998 would have earned at least £3.6 if the minimum wage had prevailed in that year.[18] We carry the simulations by randomly picking two-thirds of workers earning less than £3.6 and increasing their wages to £3.6, while leaving wages of other subminimum-wage workers unchanged.[19]

The results of these simulations are reported in column (2) of table 7.3. The table shows the 5th and 10th percentiles of the wage distribution, as well as the 90-10 differential and the standard deviation of log wages. The

18. Using data from the New Earnings Survey (NES) and improved wage data from the LFS, the ONS estimates that, relative to 1998, the fraction of workers aged twenty-two and older earning less than £3.6 declined by 4.6 percentage points in 1999 and 5.7 percentage points in early 2000. The latter figure represents about two-thirds of the fraction of workers we observed below £3.6 in 1998.

19. As discussed by DiNardo, Fortin, and Lemieux (1996), we probably understate the impact of the minimum wage in these simulations by ignoring possible spillover or disemployment effects. Lee (1999) confirms that minimum-wage impacts become indeed larger when these factors are taken into account.

simulated impact of the minimum wage is the difference between the simulated value of these wage statistics in column (2) and their actual value for 1998 in column (1). The results for men in part A indicate that the minimum wage has no effect on either the 5th or the 10th percentile of the wage distribution. This simply reflects the fact that less than 5 percent of men earned less than £3.6 in 1998 (the 5th percentile is 3.84). Nevertheless, we estimate that introducing a £3.6 minimum wage would have decreased the standard deviation of log wages by 0.014.

As expected, the minimum wage has a much larger effect for women. Part B of table 7.3 shows that introducing a £3.6 minimum wage would have raised both the 5th and the 10th percentiles to 3.6. This effect is strong enough to lower the 90-10 differential by 0.054 and the standard deviation by 0.030. As a result, both the 90-10 differential and the standard deviation become lower for women than for men.

With the recent release of the 1999 LFS data, it is also possible to see how the actual distribution of wages has evolved with the introduction of the minimum wage. Column (3) shows the various wage statistics for 1999 using the same average hourly earnings measure as in 1998.[20] Since March 1999, however, the LFS has started asking directly the hourly rate of pay of hourly rated workers, just like in the U.S. CPS. In column (4), the direct information on hourly wages is used for all workers who answer this question. In both the United Kingdom and the United States, the effect of the minimum wage on direct measures of hourly wage rates is much clearer because of the measurement error in average hourly earnings measures.[21]

One difficulty with a straight comparison of the wage distribution between 1999 and 1998 is that factors other than the minimum wage may have also changed the wage distribution during this period. For instance, male wage inequality remains more or less constant during this period, suggesting that other sources of increasing wage inequality may be offsetting the impact of the new minimum wage. If these other factors have the same impact for men and women, however, a more accurate measure of minimum wage impacts is obtained by contrasting the evolution of wage inequality for men *relative* to women.

The male-female differences in wage inequality are shown in part C. In 1998, there was little difference in wage inequality between men and women (column [1]). According to the simulation reported in column (2), wage inequality should now be larger for men than women with the introduction of the National Minimum Wage. Depending on which wage mea-

20. Workers are asked to report earnings for their usual pay period (weekly, biweekly, monthly, etc.) in the LFS. Wage rates are then computed by dividing earnings by hours over the relevant period.

21. In the 1999 LFS, only 0.4 percent of workers earn exactly £3.6 per hour when average hourly earnings are used. This proportion jumps to 2.5 percent when direct measures of the hourly wage rate are used whenever available.

sure is used for 1999, the male-female difference in inequality is either slightly smaller (column [3]) or larger (column [4]) than predicted by the simulation.

Overall, these results confirm our conjecture that the introduction of the national minimum wage in 1999 was enough to pull U.K. female wage inequality below U.K. male wage inequality. The new minimum wage has, therefore, contributed to the convergence in wage distribution between the United Kingdom and the United States.

7.3.2 Unionization

The weakening of the power of U.K. unions throughout the 1980s and 1990s can be illustrated by the strong decline in the rate of union membership. Figure 7.9 shows that the rate of union membership declined by more than 20 percentage points between 1979 and 1998. Though the decline is slightly more pronounced between 1979 and 1989, the rate of union membership keeps declining up to the late 1990s. By contrast, the decline in the U.S. rate of union membership is more modest and concentrated in the 1979 to 1984 period. As a result, the difference in the rate of union membership between the two countries shrinks from about 28 percentage points in 1979 to about 16 percentage points in 1998. This change has affected men more than women. Over the 1990s, for example, male union density fell from 44 percent in 1989 to 31 percent in 1999, while female union density fell from 33 percent to 29 percent over the same period (Department of Trade and Industry).

Starting with Freeman (1980, 1982) and Metcalf (1977, 1982), several studies have clearly established that unions tend to reduce wage inequal-

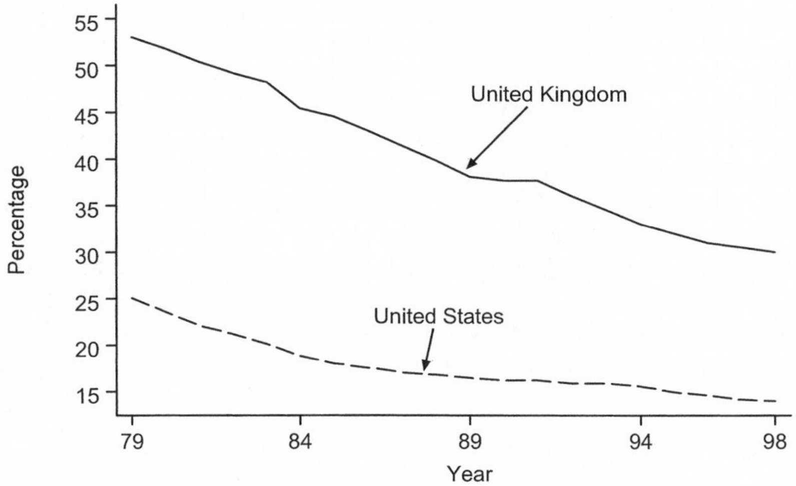

Fig. 7.9 Union membership rate, United Kingdom and United States

ity among U.S. and U.K. males. Studies have also established that de-unionization has contributed to the increase in wage inequality in both the United States and the United Kingdom during the 1980s.[22] By contrast, the existing evidence suggests that unions have relatively little effect on wage inequality among women (Lemieux 1993), and that de-unionization did not play a significant role in the increase in female wage inequality in the United States (DiNardo, Fortin, and Lemieux, 1996).

What explains this difference in the impact of unions for men and women? As is well known, unions typically have two offsetting effects on wage inequality. On the one hand, wage compression policies of unions result in lower inequality *within* the union than nonunion sector. On the other hand, since unions raise the average wage in the union relative to the nonunion sector, they may well increase the inequality *between* union and nonunion workers. Lemieux (1993) argues that this latter effect is particularly important for women, for whom unionization is concentrated in highly skilled public-sector jobs such as teaching, nursing, and so on. In other words, unions tend to increase wages for women who would have earned relatively high wages even in the absence of unions, thereby worsening this source of wage inequality. This between-group effect is not as important for union men who are not particularly skilled relative to nonunion men.

We first illustrate the effect of unions on wage inequality by performing simple variance decompositions. At this stage, we ignore altogether differences in the skill composition of the union and nonunion workforces and basically attribute to union wage policies the differences in the mean and variance of wages between the union and nonunion sectors.

We focus on the effect of unions on the wages of union members relative to nonunion members. Ideally, we would divide workers on the basis of whether their wages and working conditions are covered by a union contact. The U.K. data, however, are not available for this analysis. Though the distinction between coverage and membership is relatively minor in the United States, where a very large fraction of covered workers are union members, the distinction is more problematic in the United Kingdom. As a result, we may well understate the effect of unions on wage inequality by focusing on union members since a substantial fraction of nonmembers are covered by union agreements.

As explained in the appendix, we only have data to compute the effect of de-unionization on wage inequality for the two countries for the period starting in 1983. Given our main goal of explaining the relative evolution of U.K. and U.S. wage inequality, we do not miss any important develop-

22. See Freeman (1993), Card (1992), and DiNardo, Fortin, and Lemieux (1996) for the United States, and Gosling and Machin (1995) for the United Kingdom. Because of difference in estimation methods and data, however, it is difficult to explicitly compare the quantitative impact of de-unionization on wage inequality in the two countries.

ments by focusing on the 1983–1998 period as it is then where the time path of union membership diverges between the two countries (see fig. 7.9).

The variance of wages can be decomposed as follows:

$$\text{(1)} \qquad \text{var}(w) = \overline{U} \cdot \text{var}(w \mid U = 1) + (1 - \overline{U}) \cdot \text{var}(w \mid U = 0) + \overline{U} \cdot (1 - \overline{U}) \cdot \Delta,$$

where $\overline{U}$ is the unionization rate (actual or simulated) and Δ is the difference in mean wages between the union and nonunion sectors ($E[w \mid U = 1] - E[w \mid U = 0]$). The first two terms in equation (1) represent the within-group variance; the last term represents the between-group variance.

Table 7.4 shows the different elements of this variance decomposition. Consider first the case of men in part A. Rows one and two report the variance of (log) wages in the union and nonunion sectors, respectively. As expected, the variance of log wages is much smaller in the union than the

Table 7.4 **Variance Decomposition of Log Hourly Wages Between and Within the Union and Nonunion Sectors in the United Kingdom and the United States**

	United Kingdom			United States		
	1983 (1)	1998 (2)	Change (3)	1983 (4)	1998 (5)	Change (6)
	A. Men					
1. Variance in union sector	0.139	0.180	0.041	0.133	0.173	0.040
2. Variance in nonunion sector	0.219	0.288	0.069	0.296	0.305	0.008
3. Union wage differential	0.094	0.089	–0.004	0.150	0.138	–0.012
4. Unionization rate	0.610	0.358	–0.252	0.277	0.182	–0.095
5. Overall variance	0.172	0.251	0.079	0.256	0.284	0.028
6. Variance with 1983 unionization rate	0.172	0.224	0.052	0.256	0.272	0.016
7. "De-unionization" effect (% of total)		0.027			0.012	
		(34.4)			(41.4)	
	B. Women					
1. Variance in union sector	0.169	0.209	0.040	0.164	0.220	0.057
2. Variance in nonunion sector	0.176	0.242	0.066	0.203	0.252	0.048
3. Union wage differential	0.255	0.310	0.056	0.238	0.242	0.003
4. Unionization rate	0.456	0.330	–0.126	0.168	0.128	–0.040
5. Overall variance	0.188	0.253	0.065	0.205	0.254	0.050
6. Variance with 1983 unionization rate	0.189	0.251	0.062	0.205	0.255	0.050
7. "De-unionization" effect (% of total)		0.003			0.000	
		(4.6)			(–0.9)	

Notes: Based on hourly wages of wage and salary workers aged twenty-three to fifty-nine earning between £1 and £30 per hour (£1996) in the United Kingdom, and between \$2.50 and \$63.00 an hour (\$1996) in the United States. United States data are from the outgoing rotation group files of the CPS. United Kingdom 1983 data are from the GHS; 1998 U.K. data are from the autumn LFS. Workers are divided between the "union" and "nonunion" sectors on the basis of their self-reported membership to a trade union. The simulated variance in row six is computed using a standard variance decomposition formula (see table 7.5 note).

nonunion sector in both countries in both years. Interestingly, the variance in the union sector is almost identical in the United Kingdom and in the United States in the two years. By contrast, the variance in the nonunion is much larger in the United States (0.296) than in the United Kingdom (0.219) in 1983. By 1998, however, the variances are very similar in the two countries. Consistent with previous research, row three shows that the difference in mean wages between the union and nonunion sectors (union wage gap) is always positive but smaller in the United Kingdom than the United States.[23]

The same basic wage patterns can be seen in figure 7A.1, which shows kernel density estimates of wages among union and nonunion men. The figure shows that, in both countries, the wage distribution is more compressed and has a higher mean in the union than in the nonunion sectors. The U.K. and U.S. wage distributions look remarkably similar in 1998. In 1983, however, there is noticeably less difference between the union and nonunion distributions in the United Kingdom than the United States. The basic patterns that emerge from this figure are, therefore, consistent with patterns found for the variances in table 7.4.

Row four shows that the unionization rate among men decreased much faster (by 25 percentage points) in the United Kingdom than in the United States (10 percentage-point decline). Row five reproduces the earlier finding that wage inequality—measured by the variance of log wages in this case—increases faster in the United Kingdom than in the United States.

In row six, we compute the variance of wages that would have prevailed in 1983 and 1998 if the unionization rate had remained stable at its 1983 level using the usual variance decomposition in equation (1). Column (3) of row six shows that the variance of U.K. wages would have increased by 0.052 if the rate of unionization had remained stable, compared to an actual increase of 0.079. In other words, de-unionization contributed to a 0.027 increase in the variance of wages (row seven), which represents 34 percent of the total change. In the United States, de-unionization accounts for 0.012, or 41 percent, of the 0.028 increase in the variance of wages between 1983 and 1998.

The results reported in part B confirm the finding of the previous literature that unions have little effect on the wage inequality for women. Relative to men, there is a modest difference between the variance in the union and the nonunion sector (rows one and two). Furthermore, the raw union wage gap (row three) is much larger than for men, suggesting a much larger

23. For example, Stewart (1983) reports standard OLS estimates of the union wage gap of about 7 percent in the United Kingdom, compared to a range of 10 to 15 percent (Lewis 1986) in the United States. These estimates are not strictly comparable to those reported in table 7.2, for which differences in characteristics between the two sectors are not controlled. In table 7A.1, we report OLS estimates of the union wage gap in 1983 and 1998 for the two countries. For men, our union wage gap estimates range from 0.06 to 0.12 in the United Kingdom, and from 0.12 to 0.17 in the United States, which is similar to the estimates reported by both Stewart and Lewis.

Table 7.5 Simulated Variance of Male Log Wages in the United Kingdom and United States under Different Unionization Rates

	Simulated Unionization Rate		
	Actual	U.K. (61%)	U.S. (28%)
Simulated variance of wages in 1983			
United Kingdom	0.172	0.172	0.198
United States	0.256	0.202	0.256
Difference	0.084	0.030	0.058
% of actual difference	100	36	69
	Actual	U.K. (36%)	U.S. (18%)
Simulated variance of wages in 1998			
United Kingdom	0.251	0.251	0.270
United States	0.284	0.262	0.284
Difference	0.033	0.011	0.014
% of actual difference	100	33	42

Notes: The variances are computed using the standard variance decomposition formula $\text{var}(w) = \overline{U} \cdot \text{var}(w \mid U = 1) + (1 - \overline{U}) \cdot \text{var}(w \mid U = 0) + \overline{U} \cdot (1 - \overline{U})\Delta$, where $\overline{U}$ is the unionization rate (actual or simulated) and Δ is the difference in mean wages between the union and nonunion sectors ($E[w \mid U = 1] - E[w \mid U = 0]$).

"between-group" effect, which tends to increase inequality.[24] Finally, the decline in the rate of unionization is less than half as large for women as for men (row four). For all these reasons, de-unionization accounts for less than 5 percent of the increase in the variance of wages in either country.

In tables 7.5 and 7.6, we provide further evidence on the effect of unions on male wage inequality. In table 7.5, we use equation (1) to compute the variance of wages under various counterfactual assumptions about the rate of unionization. Column (1) reports the actual variances in the two countries. As discussed earlier, the gap in male wage inequality between the two countries shrinks between 1983 and 1998: the gap in the variance declines from 0.084 to 0.033. Columns (2) and (3) show that a large portion of this declining gap can be attributed to differences in the unionization rate between the two countries. For example, column (2) shows that the U.K.-U.S. difference in the variance would have been three times smaller if the U.S. unionization rate had been as high as that in the United Kingdom. Overall, this table provides additional evidence that the convergence in the unionization rate contributed to the convergence in male wage inequality.

24. Table 7A.1 shows that, for women, the OLS estimates of the union wage gap are systematically smaller than the unadjusted gaps reported in table 7.2, indicating that, even in the absence of unions, unionized women would have earned more than nonunionized women because of their human capital or job characteristics. This confirms the finding in the literature that unions increase the between-group variance by pushing up the wages of women who would have earned relatively high wages even in the absence of unions.

Table 7.6 **Effect of De-Unionization on Log Hourly Wage Inequality, Adjusting for Composition Effects**

	1983 (1)	1998 (2)	Predicted in 1998 with 1983 Unionization Patterns (3)	Effect of De-Unionization (4)	Effect in % (5)
			A. U.K. Men		
Unionization	61.1	35.4	58.3		
Variance	0.172	0.250	0.225	0.025	32.5
90-10	1.025	1.275	1.208	0.067	26.8
90-50	0.554	0.685	0.627	0.058	44.3
50-10	0.472	0.590	0.580	0.010	8.5
			B. U.S. Men		
Unionization	27.4	18.2	26.2		
Variance	0.255	0.279	0.271	0.008	33.9
90-10	1.314	1.386	1.375	0.011	15.8
90-50	0.602	0.699	0.693	0.005	5.6
50-10	0.712	0.688	0.682	0.006	—

Notes: The simulated measures of wage dispersion in column (3) are computed by reweighting the 1998 data by the ratio of the predicted probabilities of union membership in 1983 and 1998. The predicted probabilities are estimated using a logit model for union membership. Explanatory variables used are a set of regional dummies (ten regions and London in the United Kingdom, nine regions and SMSA status in the United States), a dummy variable for marital status, and a set of education dummies (seven in the United Kingdom, five in the United States) fully interacted with a fourth-degree polynomial in age. United States models also include dummy variables for race and veteran status.

One concern with the counterfactual exercises of tables 7.4 and 7.5 is that they may just be reflecting differences in the composition of the union and nonunion workforces, as opposed to true "causal" effects of unionization on wage inequality. For example, the variance of wages may be smaller in the union sector because the workforce is more homogeneous than in the nonunion sector, and not because unions truly compress the wage structure.

DiNardo, Fortin, and Lemieux (1996) suggest a simple "reweighting" method for controlling for differences in observable characteristics when modeling the distribution of wages. The basic idea is to estimate the probability that a worker with a given set of observed characteristics x is unionized in both 1983 and 1998. Call these probabilities $P_{83}(x)$ and $P_{98}(x)$, respectively. The counterfactual distribution of wages that would have prevailed in 1998 if the probability of unionization (as a function of x) had remained as in 1983 is obtained by reweighting observations for union and nonunion workers by $P_{83}(x)/P_{98}(x)$ and $(1 - P_{83}[x])/(1 - P_{98}[x])$, respectively.[25]

25. We estimate these probabilities using a logit model. The explanatory variables used are a quartic function of age fully interacted with education categories, and sets of dummy variables for marital status, regions (ten regions and London in the United Kingdom, nine regions and SMSA status in the United States), and dummies for race and veteran status in the United States.

Summary measures of inequality such as the variance or the 90-10 wage differential can then be computed from this counterfactual distribution. If it is the case that union workers have the same unobserved characteristics as nonunion workers conditional on observables, then these differences between the actual and counterfactual distributions can be taken as measuring the causal effect of unions on wages.[26]

Table 7.6 illustrates the effect of unions on male wage inequality obtained using this reweighting procedure. Columns (1) and (2) show the unionization rate and several measures of inequality that prevailed in 1983 and 1998, respectively. The same numbers are recomputed from the 1998 reweighted sample in column (3). Note that the counterfactual unionization rate in 1998 is lower than in 1983. This indicates that the distribution of characteristics (the *x*'s) have changed in a way that reduces the probability of being unionized.

The counterfactual measures of wage inequality in column (3) are systematically lower than in the unadjusted 1998 distribution of column (2), indicating that de-unionization could have contributed to the rise in wage inequality even when composition effects are adjusted for. In the United Kingdom, the resulting effect of de-unionization on the variance of wages shown in column (4) (0.025) is very similar to the "naïve" estimate reported in table 7.4 (0.027). The estimates reported in table 7.6 indicate that the faster decline in unionization in the United Kingdom can account for about a third of the U.K.-U.S. convergence in male wage inequality between the two countries over the 1983–1998 period.

7.3.3 Other Institutional Change: Privatization

Another reform affecting the U.K. labor market was the reduction of the role of the public sector as an employer. These changes occurred directly through the privatizations of the late 1980s and 1990s and indirectly through the contracting out of public-sector services. Public-sector employment fell from 7.45 million in 1979 to 5.23 million in 1995. In addition, competitive tendering of services forced convergence of wages between the public and private sectors for some groups of workers. By contrast, existing research indicates that the fraction of workers in the public sector has remained more or less constant in the United States during this period (see Poterba and Rueben 1994).

Wages in the public sector are more compressed in both the United Kingdom and the United States. Both the wage premia associated with observed skill and the wage distribution within skill groups are smaller in the public sector.[27] It seems plausible, therefore, that the decline in the role of

26. This assumption is discussed in more detail below.

27. For the United Kingdom see Disney and Gosling (1998) and table 7.7 in this chapter. For the United States see Poterba and Rueben (1994).

the public sector as an employer would have had an significant effect on the wage distribution in the United Kingdom, especially for men. The decline is not as steep for women, who are more heavily concentrated in such sectors as health and education that were not directly privatized, although they became more integrated into the private sector over the period.

It is important, however, to separate pure public-sector wage compression effects from union wage compression effects. Part B of table 7.7 shows that union membership and public-sector employment are two closely linked phenomena. For both men and women in 1983 and 1998, the rate of union membership in the public sector is about 40 percentage points larger than in the private sector. More importantly, coverage in the public sector is close to 90 percent. The last four rows of table 7.7 show, however, that most of the difference in the wage distributions between the public and private sectors is a consequence of the fact that unions are more present in the public than the private sector. Conditional on union status, the table shows that the standard deviation of wages is not systematically smaller in the public than private sector. It is particularly clear in the case of men that the key determinant of wage inequality is union status as opposed to public-sector affiliation. This means that the effect of privatization on the wage structure may have occurred indirectly through decreasing the likelihood that lower-paid workers would be unionized.

The other issue is that many workers affected by changes in the state's employment policy are still working in the public sector. Competitive tendering, whereby an activity stays in the public sector only if it has lower

Table 7.7 **Distribution of Workers and Wage Dispersion in the Public and Private Sectors in the United Kingdom**

	Men		Women	
	1983	1998	1983	1998
A. Percentage of workers in the public sector	37.5	21.8	42.1	36.5
B. Unionization rate				
Public sector	87.3	67.5	69.7	59.2
Private sector	45.4	26.5	28.6	17.3
C. Standard deviation of wages				
Public sector	0.416	0.456	0.387	0.463
Private sector	0.398	0.507	0.439	0.499
Union, public	0.385	0.430	0.432	0.438
Union, private	0.348	0.408	0.334	0.453
Nonunion, public	0.477	0.504	0.439	0.447
Nonunion, private	0.465	0.538	0.397	0.502

Notes: All statistics are computed from a sample of wage and salary workers aged twenty-three to fifty-nine earning between £1 and £30 per hour (£1996) from the 1983 GHS and the 1998 autumn LFS.

costs than can be found in the private sector, has meant that public- and private-sector wages have converged. Disney and Gosling (1998) find that the wage distribution of low-skilled men is basically identical in the two sectors in the 1990s. This, when taken together with the points made in the paragraph above, means that the effect of privatization is going to be hard to uncover. In fact, when we perform the same kind of counterfactual decomposition for the public sector than we did for unions in table 7.6, we find only negligible effects on wage inequality.

7.4 Effect of Reforms on Wage Inequality: Qualifications and Extensions

The empirical analysis above supports the simple story. Wage inequality increased fastest for U.S. women during the 1980s because of the decline in the minimum wage. Over the 1980s and 1990s inequality increased for men faster in the United Kingdom because of the decline in unionization. In this section we discuss some possible arguments for and against this view in more detail.

7.4.1 "Causality" of the Effect of Unions on Wage Inequality

Our findings in section 7.3.2 can be interpreted as the causal effect of the reduction of unionization on wage inequality only if the unobserved characteristics of union members are the same as for workers not in unions. If this assumption does not hold, then we cannot tell how much of the changes in wage inequality that we attribute to de-unionization are a real causal effect of de-unionization, as opposed to spurious consequences of changes in the distribution of unobservables between the union and nonunion sectors. If workers and firms respond to incentives at all, then this assumption will be violated. The real question is therefore whether *all* the changes that we attribute to unionization just reflect differences in unobservables. This is not testable, in general, but we believe it is unlikely for the following reasons.

First, the difference between the raw effects (table 7.4) and those obtained by controlling for a large set of explanatory variables (table 7.6) is small. Unless unobservables play a radically different role in the determination of the union status of workers than observables like age and education, failure to control for unobservables should not significantly affect the results. Furthermore, if selection effects are important because firms and workers respond to wage differentials, then we know that the true effects must lie somewhere greater than zero and less than the estimated effects.

Another reason to believe that our results can be interpreted as a causal effect of unionization is that existing studies that have modeled more explicitly the selection problem found that doing so did not have much impact on the estimated effect of unions on wage inequality. For example, both Freeman (1993) and Card (1992) use fixed effects methods to control for differences in the distribution of person-specific unobservables between the union and nonunion sectors. They conclude that these adjusted estimates yield a very similar impact of de-unionization on the growth in U.S. male wage inequality than simpler cross-sectional estimates like the ones considered here.

A more subtle point raised by Lewis (1986) is that these various estimators yield a causal estimate of union wage effects only under the assumption that the extent of unionization has no effect on nonunion wages. This assumption would be violated, however, in the presence of "threat" or other general equilibrium effects. If these effects are important, we may be either understating or overstating the true effect of de-unionization on wage inequality. For instance, Freeman (1996) has argued that, because of threat effects, standard estimates of the effect of de-unionization on wage inequality likely understate the full effect. The basic idea is that, as unions get weaker and the threat of unionization weakens, nonunion firms no longer feel compelled to imitate the wage structure of union firms to avoid unionization. In this light, Gosling (1998) relates wages at the workplace level to the threat of unionization when the establishment was set up, conditional on fixed industry and establishment-age/cohort effects. This paper finds the threat of unionization has a bigger effect on the dispersion of wages than actual union status.

The changes in the distribution of union and nonunion wages in the United Kingdom documented in Table 7.4 and figure 7A.1 are consistent with this view. There is much less difference between the distributions of union and nonunion wages in the United Kingdom in 1983, when unions are quite strong, than in 1998 or in the United States, where they are weaker. In other words, the fact that wage inequality in the nonunion sector expanded so fast in the United Kingdom between 1983 and 1998 is consistent with the view that the threat of unionization subsumed during this period. Attributing part of this expansion in wage inequality to de-unionization would increase substantially the estimated effect of de-unionization on wage inequality.

7.4.2 Comparison with Other Periods and Other Countries

Our original motivation for looking at the effect of unions on wage inequality was that male wage inequality expanded much faster in the United Kingdom, where the rate of unionization declined by 25 percentage points between 1983 and 1998, than in the United States, where it declined by less than 10 percentage points. This "aggregate" evidence is, in itself, inconsistent with simple selection-bias explanation. If being a union member were just a label for unobservable characteristics, then changes in wage inequality should be unrelated, on average, with changes in the rate of unionization.

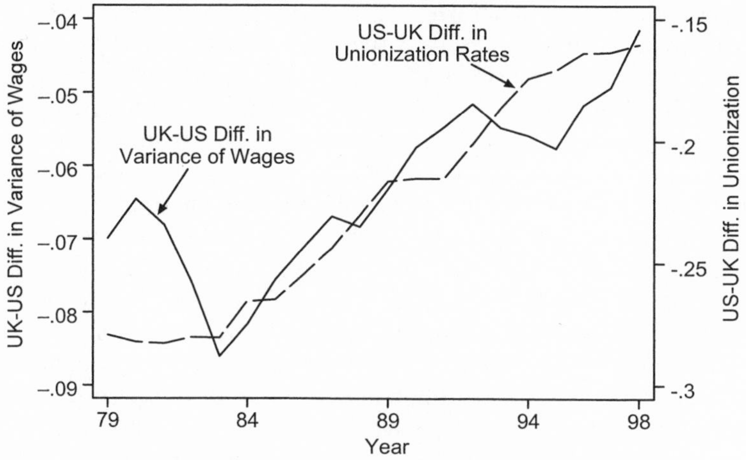

Fig. 7.10 U.K.-U.S. male variance gap and unionization

We explore this aggregate evidence in more detail in figure 7.10, which shows the evolution of the U.K.-U.S. differences in unionization and in the variance of male wages, respectively, between 1979 and 1998.[28] Interestingly, both series exhibit a break in trend around 1983. Between 1979 and 1983, the variance of male wages increases faster in the United States than in the United Kingdom, while unionization decreases at the same pace in the two countries. After 1983, however, U.K. unionization rates fall faster than in the United States while the variance of U.K. wage expands faster than in the United States. The coincidence in the trend breaks in the two series strongly supports our earlier conclusion about the role of unions in the relative evolution of male wage inequality in the two countries.

A simple OLS regression of the U.K.-U.S. difference in the variance of wages on the difference in unionization rates yields an estimated coefficient of 0.22 (with a standard error of 0.03). The R-squared from the regression is 0.74, suggesting that the differential evolution of unionization in the two countries accounts for most of the divergent trends in male wage inequality. As in the case of the minimum-wage analysis for women illustrated in figure 7.8, a linear trend is not statistically significant once differences in unionization are controlled for.

Taken at face value, the estimated aggregate effects imply that deunionization accounts for 35 percent of the 0.068 increase in the variance

28. As in the case of women in figure 7.8, we smooth the U.K. variance of wages using a three-year moving average before computing the U.K.-U.S. difference in the variance of wages. We also use the overall rate of unionization, as opposed to the rate for men only, because of data limitations.

of wages in the United States between 1979 and 1998, and for 53 percent of the corresponding 0.097 increase in the variance in the United Kingdom.[29] Another interesting observation is that, while the rate of unionization in 1998 is quite close to the U.S. rate for 1979 (see fig. 7.9), the extent of male wage inequality in the United Kingdom in 1998 is also quite similar to the U.S. one for 1979 (see fig. 7.2). A related point is that, according to the estimated regression model, the 16 percent remaining unionization rate gap in 1998 should translate into a 0.035 variance gap, which is very close to the 0.04 gap observed in figure 7.10. In other words, the regression estimates predict that the U.K.-U.S. variance gap would basically vanish if the U.K. unionization rate were to decline all the way to the U.S. level. So in addition to explaining well the *differential evolution* of male wage inequality in the two countries, U.K.-U.S. differences in unionization also seem to explain quite well the difference in the *levels* of wage inequality.

Interestingly, these findings are qualitatively similar to those of DiNardo and Lemieux (1997), who show that male wage inequality increased much less in the Canada than in the United States between 1981 and 1988. By contrast, the rate of unionization remained relatively stable in Canada while it dropped sharply in the United States during this period. Putting these pieces of aggregate evidence together reinforces our earlier conclusion that unionization is an important explanation for the U.K.-U.S. convergence in male wage inequality over the last two decades.

7.4.3 Is the Decline in Unionization Exogenous?

One possible objection against this aggregate evidence is that de-unionization is just an endogenous consequence of more fundamental labor market changes like, skill-biased technical change, that are the real underlying source of increase in wage inequality.[30] If this were true, however, then the rate of technical change (or other underlying change) must have been higher in the United Kingdom than in the United States, which is neither an appealing nor a parsimonious explanation.

The alternative explanation we implicitly have in mind here is that at least some of the U.K. changes in unionization have occurred because of changes in the legal framework rather than changes to labor market and product market conditions. Under this scenario, ascribing a causal role for the decline in unionization is more plausible.

As Pencavel (chap. 5 in this volume) shows, there is probably no single reason that unionization declined so rapidly over the 1980s and 1990s. It is, however, plausible that legislation (especially the employment acts of 1980 and 1982) did have a crucial role. These acts increased the costs of union-

29. These estimates are obtained by multiplying the estimated coefficient of 0.22 by the respective declines of unionization in the United States (0.11) and the United Kingdom (0.23).
30. See, for example, Acemoglu, Aghion, and Violante (2001).

ization by removing union immunities in a recognition dispute.[31] Previously, unions could obtain negotiating rights by threatening to go on strike.[32] The strike weapon was still available but unions were now liable for monies lost by their employers as a result of the dispute. Put simply, the threat of a strike in this instance became less credible. Disney, Gosling, and Machin (1995, 1996) show that it is conditions surrounding the workplace at set-up date rather than current conditions which determine the probability of unionization. They also find, even after controlling for industry-level conditions of the labor and product markets and macro variables at set-up date and current establishment-level characteristics (such as size), that workplaces established in the 1980s are more than 16 percent less likely to be unionized.[33] The aggregate decline carried on through the 1980s as the proportion of post-1980s workplaces in the sample increased. Again, this is consistent with the view that part of the decline in unionization was a result of the 1980s legislative changes.

Of course, it is still possible that it is not legislation which is driving the downturn but another discrete jump in the cost of unionization.[34] This could be driven by changes in the relative productivity of skilled or unskilled workers, changes in technology that reduce the beneficial effects of collective voice, and increases in competition. The issue, then, is why these caused a discrete jump in 1980. A more plausible story is that the legislative changes allowed management to respond faster to these increases in costs. The story for U.K. men is then that the change in the structure of demand increased wage inequality both directly and, because of the legislative changes, indirectly through the removal of pay-setting institutions that increased wages at the bottom end.

7.5 Conclusion

This paper compares trends in male and female hourly wage inequality in the United Kingdom and the United States between 1979 and 1998. Our main finding is that the extent and pattern of wage inequality became increasingly similar in the two countries during this period. We attribute this convergence to U.S.-style reforms in the U.K. labor market. In particular, we argue that the much steeper decline in unionization in the United Kingdom explains why inequality increased faster than in the United States. For women, we conclude that the fall and subsequent recovery in the real value of the U.S. minimum wage explains why wage inequality increased faster in

31. A union is "recognized" when it has negotiating rights with the employer for determining pay and conditions of employment.

32. Up until July 2000, employers were under no obligation to negotiate with unions even if all of their employees wanted it.

33. This 1980s "shift" effect was the only establishment-cohort variable to be significant in both statistical and quantitative terms.

34. See again Acemoglu, Aghion, and Violante (2001).

the United States than in the United Kingdom during the 1980s, while the opposite happened during the 1990s. Interestingly, the introduction of the National Minimum Wage in the United Kingdom in 1999 also contributed to the convergence in labor market institutions and wage inequality between the two countries.

Appendix

U.K. Data

The most consistent source of information on the distribution of hourly wages in the United Kingdom is the Family Expenditure Survey (FES), which has collected detailed information on weekly earnings and weekly hours of work on a consistent basis since 1966. One limitation of the FES, however, is that it contains no information on educational achievement before 1978, and only limited information from 1978 on.[35] An alternative data set that provides more detailed information on educational achievement is the General Household Survey (GHS), which has collected information on earnings and hours since 1974.[36] Unfortunately, as hours are not measured in a consistent fashion over time, it is not possible to use the GHS to construct a consistent measure of hourly wage rates over the 1980s and 1990s.

Another limitation of the FES is that it does not contain direct information on the union status of workers.[37] This information is available, however, in the 1983 GHS, which also contains information on whether individuals work in the public or private sector. More recently, the Labour Force Survey (LFS) has been collecting detailed information on wages, union status, and public-sector affiliation each year for the mid- and late 1990s. The LFS is very similar to the U.S. Current Population Survey in terms of its purpose—measuring labor market activity and unemployment in a timely fashion—and sample size. The sample sizes are also considerably larger in the LFS (around 15,000 wage and salary workers per quarter) than in the FES or the GHS (around 5,000 wage and salary workers per year).

In light of the strengths and weaknesses of the different data sets, we use a "multiple data set" approach for the United Kingdom. More precisely,

35. The FES provides limited information on school-leaving age but no information on the highest educational degree obtained. Gosling, Machin, and Meghir (2000) argue that the limited information about educational achievement available in the FES is, nevertheless, sufficient for capturing main trends in relative wages by education level.

36. See Gosling, Machin, and Meghir (2000) for more detail on the strengths and weaknesses of the GHS and FES.

37. The FES does contain a variable indicating whether the respondent has deductions from his or her earnings for the payment of union dues. Although this is highly correlated with the union status of workers at one point in time, changes in the way union members pay their fees over the 1980s and 1990s has meant that it is not a good measure of changes over time.

we compute the basic trends in wage inequality using the FES for 1978 to 1996 supplemented with the autumn LFS for 1997 and 1998. We analyze the effect of unionization and public-sector affiliation on wage inequality using the 1983 GHS and the 1998 LFS. Note that we have adjusted the 1997 and 1998 measures of wage dispersion reported in table 7.1 and figures 7.1 and 7.3 to ensure that there are no discrepancies in the series because of data differences. More precisely, we compute adjustment factors (which we apply to the 1997 and 1998 LFS) that are such that measures of wage dispersion in the 1996 LFS and 1996 FES are identical.

Following the existing literature on inequality in the United Kingdom, we also limit the analysis to workers aged twenty-three to fifty-nine. Real wages are obtained by deflating nominal wages with the Consumption Price Index (Retail Price Index). To limit the effect of outliers, we keep only those observations with an hourly wage rate between £1 and £30 (in 1996 pounds). Note that throughout the 1978 to 1998 period, there is always less than 1 percent of observations with wages that are either larger than £30 or smaller than £1. As discussed below, one additional reason for trimming the wage data above £30 is to make the U.K. data more comparable with the U.S. data, for which weekly earnings are top-coded.

U.S. Data

Since 1979, the U.S. Census Bureau has been collecting data on weekly hours, weekly earnings, and hourly earnings (for workers paid by the hour) for all workers in the "outgoing rotation group" of the Current Population Survey (CPS). Beginning in 1983, the outgoing rotation groups supplement of the CPS also asks about the union status of workers. Since the questions about wages, hours, and union status are asked at every month, the resulting merged outgoing rotation group (MORG) files of the CPS provide very large samples (around 150,000 workers per year) of wage and salary workers from 1979 to 1999. Our U.S. analysis entirely relies on this data source.

Throughout the 1979 to 1999 period, workers paid by the hour were asked their hourly rates of pay. We use this variable, which is collected in a consistent fashion over time, as our measure of the hourly wage rate for these workers. The MORG files of the CPS also provide information on usual weekly earnings for all workers. For workers not paid by the hour, we use average hourly earnings (weekly earnings divided by weekly hours) as our measure of the wage rate.

Note, however, that weekly earnings are not measured in a consistent fashion over time. From 1979 to 1993, this variable was collected by directly asking individuals about their earnings on a weekly basis. From 1994 to 1999, individuals had the option of reporting their usual earnings on the base period of their choice (weekly, biweekly, monthly, or annually). Weekly earnings are then obtained by normalizing the earnings reported

Table 7A.1 **OLS Estimates of the Union Wage Gap in the United Kingdom and the United States**

	United Kingdom			United States		
		Adjusted Gap			Adjusted Gap	
	Unadjusted Gap (1)	Adj. for Human Capital (2)	Adj. for Human Capital & Job Char. (3)	Unadjusted Gap (4)	Adj. for Human Capital (5)	Adj. for Human Capital & Job Char. (6)
Men						
1983	0.094	0.124	0.087	0.150	0.162	0.173
		(0.012)	(0.014)		(0.004)	(0.004)
1998	0.089	0.083	0.064	0.138	0.118	0.150
		(0.010)	(0.011)		(0.005)	(0.005)
Women						
1983	0.255	0.184	0.091	0.238	0.195	0.177
		(0.013)	(0.013)		(0.004)	(0.004)
1998	0.238	0.210	0.102	0.242	0.122	0.152
		(0.010)	(0.010)		(0.005)	(0.005)

Notes: Standard errors in parentheses. Dependent variable is the log of hourly wages. Sample used in the estimation includes wage and salary workers aged twenty-three to fifty-nine earning between £1 and £30 per hour (£1996) in the United Kingdom, and between $2.50 and $63.00 per hour ($1996) in the United States. United States data are from the outgoing rotation group files of the CPS. United Kingdom 1983 data are from the GHS; 1998 U.K. data are from the autumn LFS. Workers are divided between the "union" and "nonunion" sectors on the basis of their self-reported membership to a trade union. The "human capital" controls used in columns (2), (3), (5), and (6) include education-categories dummies (five in the United States, seven in the United Kingdom), region dummies (ten regions and London in the United Kingdom, nine regions and SMSA status in the United States), a quartic in age, marital status, and dummy variables for nonwhites (U.S. only) and veteran status (U.S. men only). "Job characteristics" controls in column (3) include nine industry dummies, twelve occupation dummies, a dummy variable for public-sector affiliation, and dummy variables for firm size and seniority. Job characteristics controls in column (6) include forty-six industry dummies and forty-five occupation dummies. Abbreviations are explained in text.

by workers to a weekly basis. The available evidence does not suggest, however, that this change in the way earnings are collected had a significant impact on the distribution of wages.[38]

A potentially more important problem is that weekly earnings are top-coded at different values for different periods throughout the sample period. Before 1988, weekly earnings were top-coded at $999. The top-code was later increased to $1,923 in 1988 and $2,884 in 1998. In real terms, the top-code was more than twice as small in 1988 as in 1998. Consequently, a much larger fraction of workers had their earnings top-coded in 1988 than in 1998.

We adjust for top-coding by using the 1998 distribution of weekly earnings to impute earnings in the other years where the top-code is lower. Let

38. Once the data have been trimmed for outliers and adjusted for top-coding, there is no evidence of an unusual jump in wage inequality between 1993 and 1994.

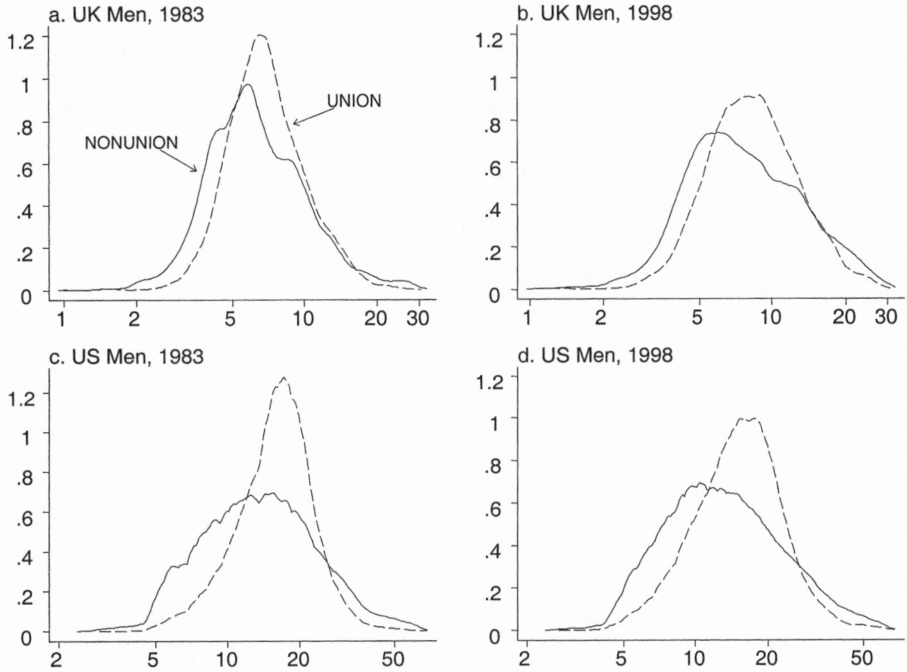

Fig. 7A.1 Union and nonunion wage densities (U.K. £1996, U.S. in $1996)

tc_t represent the earnings top-code in year t in real terms, and $f_t(y)$ represent the density of weekly earnings (not top-coded) in that year. Consider the assumption that the earnings distribution in year t between the top-code and the higher year 1998 top-code is the same as in 1998, i.e., that $f_t(y \mid tc_t < y < tc_{98}) = f_{98}(y \mid tc_t < y < tc_{98})$. Under this assumption, the empirical distribution of earnings between tc_t and tc_{98} in 1998 can be used to impute earnings in year t. While it is common to impute a fixed value of earnings to all top-coded observations, doing so removes all the earnings variability over the top-code, which in turn understates the extent of overall wage variability measured using the standard deviation or other distributional measures.[39] In practical terms, we stochastically impute earnings above the top-code by drawing at random from the empirical 1998 distribution between tc_t and tc_{98}.[40]

One final adjustment we make is to trim observations with wages above

39. In terms of between and within-group variation of earnings above and below the top-code, standard imputation amount to assuming there is no within-group variation above the top-code.

40. A similar approach is used by DiNardo, Fortin, and Lemieux (1996), who use a reweighting procedure to allocate values above the top-code. They also allow for the fact that the distribution of earnings depends on standard characteristics such as age, education, and gender.

$50 and below $2 in 1989 dollars (approximately $2.5 and $63.0 in 1996 dollars). Once top-coding has been adjusted for, less than 1 percent of observations fall outside this range in any single year. We noticed that when wage observations are not trimmed, there is an unusual jump in most measures of wage inequality between 1993 and 1994. We conjecture that the new survey instrument used to collect weekly wages since 1994 may have introduced more measurement error than before 1994.

For the sake of comparability with the United Kingdom, all wage measures presented in the paper are deflated using the CPI. Other studies have used a GDP deflator for personal consumption expenditures to deflate wages, in part because of concerns that changes in the CPI are biased upward, which understates real wage growth. Unless the bias is different in the United States and the United Kingdom, however, this should not affect comparisons of real wage growth between the two countries. All the U.S. wage statistics reported in the paper are also weighted using the CPS earnings weights.[41]

Questions about educational achievement were changed substantially in the early 1990s. Until 1991, the CPS asked about the highest grade (or years of schooling) completed. Starting in 1992, the CPS moved to questions about the highest degree. To keep a relatively consistent measure of education over time, we measure education using five categories (high school dropout, high school graduate, some postsecondary degree below a university bachelor's degree, university bachelor's degree, and postgraduate degree).

References

Acemoglu, Daron, Philippe Aghion, and G. Violante. 2001. Deunionization, technical change, and inequality. *Carnegie-Rochester Conference Series on Public Policy* 55:229–264.

Beaudry, Paul, and David Green. 2003. Wages and employment in the United States and Germany: What explains the difference? *American Economic Review* 93 (3): 573–602.

Blau, Francine. 1998. Trends in the well being of American women 1970–1995. *Journal of Economic Literature* 36 (1): 112–165.

Card, David. 1992. The effect of unions on the distribution of wages: Redistribution or relabelling? NBER Working Paper no. 4195. Cambridge, Mass.: National Bureau of Economic Research, October.

Card, David, Francis Kramarz, and Thomas Lemieux. 1999. Changes in the rela-

41. By contrast, the U.K. data are unweighted since sample weights are not available in the FES and the GHS. Sample weights are available in the LFS but since weighting make very little difference, we use unweighted data for this survey as well to be consistent with the FES and the GHS.

tive structure of wages and employment: A comparison of the United States, Canada, and France. *Canadian Journal of Economics* 32 (4): 843–877.
Card, David, and Thomas Lemieux. 2001. Can falling supply explain the rising return to college for younger men? A cohort-based analysis. *Quarterly Journal of Economics* 116 (2): 705–746.
DiNardo, John, Nicole M. Fortin, and Thomas Lemieux. 1996. Labor market institutions and the distribution of wages, 1973–1992: A semiparametric approach. *Econometrica* 64 (5): 1001–046.
DiNardo, John, and Thomas Lemieux. 1997. Changes in wage inequality in Canada and the United States: Do institutions explain the difference? *Industrial and Labor Relations Review* 50 (4): 629–651.
Disney, Richard, and Amanda Gosling. 1998. Does it pay to work in the public sector? *Fiscal Studies* 19 (4): 347–374.
Disney, Richard, Amanda Gosling, and Steve Machin. 1995. British unions in decline: Determinants of the 1980s fall in union recognition. *Industrial and Labor Relations Review* 48 (3): 403–419.
———. 1996. "What has happened to union recognition in Britain?" *Economica* 63 (249): 1–18.
Freeman, Richard. 1980. Unionism and the dispersion of wages. *Industrial and Labor Relations Review* 34 (1): 3–23.
———. 1982. Union wage practices and wage dispersion within establishments. *Industrial and Labor Relations Review* 36:3–21.
———. 1993. How much has de-unionization contributed to the rise in male earnings inequality? In *Uneven tides: Rising inequality in America,* ed. Sheldon Danziger and Peter Gottschalk, 133–163. New York: Russell Sage Foundation.
———. 1996. Labor market institutions and earnings inequality. *New England Economic Review* (May/June): 157–168.
Freeman, Richard, and Lawrence Katz. 1996. Introduction and summary. In *Differences and changes in Wage structures,* ed. Richard Freeman and Lawrence Katz, 1–22. Chicago: University of Chicago Press.
Freeman, Richard, and Karen Needels. 1993. Skill differentials in Canada in an era of rising labor market inequality. In *Small differences that matter: Labor markets and income maintenance in Canada and the United States,* ed. David Card and Richard B. Freeman, 45–67. Chicago: University of Chicago Press.
Giles Christopher, Amanda Gosling, Francois Laisney, and Thorsten Geib. 1998. The distribution of income and wages in the U.K. and West Germany, 1984–1992. London: Institute for Fiscal Studies. Mimeograph.
Gosling, Amanda. 1998. The determination of union status and wages in British establishments. Department of Economics Working Paper no. 491. Essex, U.K.: University of Essex.
Gosling, Amanda, and Steve Machin. 1995. Trade unions and the dispersion of earnings in British establishments. *Oxford Bulletin of Economics and Statistics* 56:167–184.
Gosling, Amanda, Steve Machin, and Costas Meghir. 2000. The changing distribution of male wages in the U.K. *Review of Economic Studies* 67 (4): 635–686.
Harkness, Susan. 1996. The gender earnings gap: Evidence from the U.K. *Fiscal studies* 17 (2): 1–36.
Katz, Lawrence, and Kevin Murphy. 1992. Changes in relative wages, 1963–1987: Supply and demand factors. *Quarterly Journal of Economics* 107 (1): 35–78.
Lee, David. 1999. Wage inequality in the United States during the 1980s: Rising dispersion or falling minimum wage? *Quarterly Journal of Economics* 114 (3): 977–1023.

Lemieux, Thomas. 1993. Unions and wage inequality in Canada and the United States. In *Small differences that matter: Labor markets and income maintenance in Canada and the United States,* ed. David Card and Richard B. Freeman, 69–107. Chicago: University of Chicago Press.

Lewis, H. Gregg. 1986. *Union relative wage effects: A survey.* Chicago: University of Chicago Press.

Machin, Steve. 1996. Wage inequality in the U.K. *Oxford Review of Economic Policy* 12 (1): 47–64.

Metcalf, David. 1977. Unions, incomes policies, and relative wages in Britain. *British Journal of Industrial Relations* 20 (2): 157–190.

———. 1982. Unions and the dispersion of earnings. *British Journal of Industrial Relations* 20 (2): 170–185.

Poterba, James, and Kim Rueben. 1994. The distribution of public sector wage premia: New evidence using quantile regression methods. NBER Working Paper no. 4734. Cambridge, Mass.: National Bureau of Economic Research. May.

Schmitt, John. 1996. The changing structure of male earnings in Britain, 1974–88. In *Differences and changes in wage structures,* ed. Richard B. Freeman and Lawrence F. Katz, 177–204. Chicago: University of Chicago Press.

Stewart, Mark. 1983. Relative earnings and individual union membership in the U.K. *Economica* 50 (198): 111–125.

8

Whither Poverty in Great Britain and the United States?

The Determinants of Changing Poverty and Whether Work Will Work

Richard Dickens and David T. Ellwood

Scholars in the United Kingdom emphasize that poverty in Great Britain has risen sharply since the late 1970s. According to Goodman, Johnson, and Webb (1997), after remaining steady at roughly 11 percent though the 1960s and falling to 8 or 9 percent in the 1970s, it has since doubled. Meanwhile, in the United States, both official figures and traditional poverty scholars report sharp declines in poverty. Since reaching 15 percent in the early 1980s, official poverty rates are now at 11 percent. The black poverty rate and the rate for single parents are at their lowest level in the forty years for which data are reported (U.S. Bureau of the Census 2000). What accounts for the apparent divergence? More importantly, what factors—demographic, economic, or policy—account for the changes in poverty in the two nations? And what role could policy play in reducing poverty?

Of course, a major reason for the differences in reported poverty trends is that the nations remain divided by a common language with a very uncommon set of definitions. In Britain and Europe, poverty is traditionally

Richard Dickens is senior lecturer in the department of economics, Queen Mary, University of London, and a senior research fellow of the Centre for Economic Performance, London School of Economics (LSE). David T. Ellwood is Lucius N. Littauer Professor of Political Economy at the John F. Kennedy School of Government, Harvard University, and a research associate of the National Bureau of Economic Research.

The authors gratefully acknowledge the helpful suggestions of Richard Blundell, David Card, Richard Freeman, two anonymous referees, and all conference participants. We are also grateful to seminar participants at the University of Kent; the Centre for the Analysis of Social Exclusion, LSE; the Policy Studies Institute; the Melbourne Institute of Applied Economics and Social Research; and the Research School of Social Sciences, Australian National University. We are further grateful to Jayne Taylor, Howard Reed, and Mike Brewer from the Institute for Fiscal Studies and to Steve Wilcox at the University of York for their invaluable advice. The Family Expenditure Survey is collected by the Office for National Statistics and made available by The Data Archive.

measured according to a relative scale—families are considered poor if their incomes fall below 60 percent of the (family-size-adjusted) median income. By contrast, in the United States, poverty is measured against an absolute standard that is adjusted annually only for inflation. More subtle distinctions include the fact that in Britain poverty is typically based on weekly income net of taxes, while in the United States it is based on gross annual income.

In this paper, we work to create common measures of poverty in the two nations. We develop a procedure that allows one to more fully trace out the relative impacts of altered demographics, rising wage inequality, work changes, and policy innovations in explaining changing poverty patterns than the usual aggregate models allow. And we use this procedure to determine the forces shaping poverty in the two nations. Our basic methodological idea is straightforward, if rather difficult to implement. For members of the sample in any given year, we estimate what each person's and family's work, wages, and benefits would have been if the structure of pay, employment, or aid had been equivalent to that of a base year. We can then estimate what poverty would have been if one or all of the base-year conditions still prevailed.

Using this method, we find that the forces influencing poverty differ across nations and across absolute versus relative poverty measures. A number of important findings emerge from this paper:

- Britain and the United States share some broad patterns in common—relative poverty has risen in both nations, albeit much more so in Britain, and in recent years, absolute poverty has fallen in both.
- There are very sizable differences in the magnitudes and trends. By measures used here, the United States has considerably higher relative poverty. But very importantly, relative poverty in Britain has risen far more sharply over the past twenty years, and the gap between the countries has closed considerably.
- In both nations demographic change and rising wage inequality played key roles in increasing relative poverty, but the impacts were far greater in Britain. Yet for absolute poverty, wage changes had almost no net effect in Britain, while they had a modest effect in the United States.
- Britain has experienced a dramatic rise in workless households while the United States has simultaneously had a sharp fall. In Britain this had a sizable impact on relative and absolute poverty. In the United States, increasing work has had little impact on relative poverty but resulted in a sizable reduction of absolute poverty.
- Ignoring any behavioral impacts, expanding government benefits reduced relative and absolute poverty considerably in Britain over this

period. By contrast, as compared to 1979, the impacts of U.S. benefits were almost negligible.

- Both the level and structure of government aid differ enormously across the two nations. Government benefits for workless households are higher and have grown in Britain. In the United States, government benefits for those with no earnings have been cut dramatically, while in recent years, benefits for those with low to moderate earnings have risen considerably.
- The changing patterns of benefits and work strongly suggest that, in the United States at least, policy changes have significantly influenced work behavior (particularly by single parents) and thus altered poverty. In Britain the policy changes may have had the reverse effect, reducing work among many groups, though the evidence is far from conclusive.
- The relatively modest changes in incentives currently contemplated by U.K. policymakers will still leave Britain with a vastly different structure of benefits than the United States. Based on the results of this paper, we suspect they will have a modest impact on work. Only a strategy that will dramatically increase work and significantly increase the incomes of lower-paid workers will have a really sizable impact on relative poverty, and both of these will prove hard to achieve. Any purely work-based strategy, which doesn't tackle demographics and wage dispersion, may not have a dramatic effect on relative poverty.

8.1 Measuring Poverty in Great Britain and the United States

Our first goal is to create as common a set of poverty definitions across the two countries as possible. This involves recognizing different types of poverty standards, the definitions of income, and definitions of families.

8.1.1 Relative versus Absolute Poverty Standards

Poverty is typically defined as a situation where family income falls below some standard that varies by family size. But the way the standard is determined differs by country.

There is no official poverty standard in Britain, but there is something of a conventional wisdom. Poverty has traditionally been defined as having net household income after taxes below half the mean (with appropriate adjustments for family size). However, more recently a relative measure based upon 60 percent of median income has gained prominence and has been adopted as the official poverty standard by Eurostat.[1] These relative

1. Note also that the British government's commitment to eradicate child poverty is based on a poverty definition of 60 percent of median household income.

measures are based on the assumption that poverty is best understood as depending on where a family stands in comparison to others. If the income of disadvantaged families rises slightly, but the average income of families overall rises a great deal, poverty will increase using this measure.

The United States does have an official poverty standard and it is widely used. The government defines poverty using an absolute standard that has been essentially unchanged[2] in real terms for thirty-five years. The absolute standard assumes that what matters is the absolute position of a family. If the income of disadvantaged families rises slightly, but the average income of families overall rises a great deal, poverty will decrease using this measure.

There is a large and energetic literature about the pros and cons of relative and absolute measures. Both have their virtues. The notion that a near-poor family is no worse off if the standard of living of most other families rises considerably seems implausible. What once were luxuries, such as telephones and indoor plumbing, become necessities as the society becomes more prosperous. A relative measure seems to come closer to capturing the larger notions of poverty, which might involve a sense of connection or inclusion in the overall society.

At the same time, it seems odd to assume that low-income families would be worse off if their income rose 40 percent over a decade while the income of the average family rose by 50 percent. An absolute measure captures the notion that having more food or better housing can be a benefit even if others do as well or even better.

Absolute standards pose another problem for international work—how should a common absolute standard be set? One possibility is to use a common standard adjusted for the exchange rate and differences in purchasing power. Since the United States is somewhat wealthier by this standard than Britain, there will almost inevitably be more poverty in Britain. These issues do not arise with relative standards since each country is being measured relative to its mean or median income.

For purposes of this paper, we will examine both absolute and relative measures, though we will concentrate disproportionately on relative measures since this volume is focused on the British economy. For relative poverty we use 60 percent of median income and use the family-size adjustment derived by McClements (1977), which is commonly used in Britain.

For absolute poverty standards we use slightly different procedures in each country. In Britain, we set the absolute standard for poverty equal to 60 percent of median income in 1979. Thus for 1979 in Britain, the measures of absolute and relative poverty are the same. After 1979 the relative poverty line rises or falls with median income, but the absolute measure remains unchanged (except for inflation adjustments).

2. There have been minor changes to definitions and family-size adjustments over the years.

We experimented with two different absolute poverty standards for the United States. One was to use the 60 percent of median 1979 income in the United States, just as was done for Britain. This yields a 1999 poverty standard of $32,652 for a family of four[3]—considerably above the U.S. official standard of $17,356. More importantly, this procedure also yields an absolute poverty standard that is considerably higher in purchasing power parity terms for the United States than for Britain because U.S. average incomes were higher in 1979. If the 1999 U.S.-U.K. purchasing power parity were applied to the 60 percent median 1979 income standard *for Britain,* the poverty line in the United States would instead have been $20,047—much closer to the official U.S. poverty line. Given the likely interest of U.S. readers in the official poverty line, we report in the body of the text absolute figures for the United States using the official U.S. standards. We have done all calculations using both standards. The trends for the 60 percent median 1979 U.S. income standard are virtually identical; and later in the paper, figure 8.7, which uses the official poverty line, is reproduced using the 60 percent median 1979 standard in Dickens and Ellwood (2001, fig. A1).

8.1.2 Definition of Income and Family/Household Unit

Poverty is generally measured using large cross-sectional surveys in each country, but there are important differences in what the surveys measure. Successive waves of the Family Expenditure Survey (FES), based on interviews from roughly 10,000 households annually, are typically used to determine poverty levels. Income is a weekly measure. When poverty is measured, researchers generally count as income earnings, dividends, interest, rent, pensions, and government aid, including nearly all social security benefits and housing.[4] Taxes are deducted from income to give a sense of disposable income. Often the income is calculated both before and after housing costs to control for unmeasured Imputed incomes of owner-occupiers and because housing costs often vary greatly by region.

The issue of housing is further complicated in Britain by the provision of social housing. In 1980 about 33 percent of tenants were living in government-provided housing with subsidized rents. A large proportion of the social housing stock was sold off to tenants through the "right to buy" policy of the Thatcher government. Furthermore, rents were deregulated and from 1983 housing aid was provided through Housing Benefit, which covers housing costs for eligible claimants. As rents increased, so did housing benefits. This resulted in a shift in housing aid from subsidized rents to

3. The poverty standard varies somewhat by the relationships of the four family members. This figure is the weighted average for all families with exactly four members.

4. In Britain, virtually all nonhousing aid is called social security benefits. To avoid confusion with the very different U.S. Social Security system, which is primarily for the aged and disabled, we will generally refer to British social security benefits as "government aid" broadly to include these benefits along with housing.

cash support through benefit payments. The FES does collect information on cash support from Housing Benefits, and it reports whether people resided in social housing, but it has no estimate of the value of the subsidies to these residents. If one counts the value of the cash Housing Benefit but ignores the value of these social housing subsidies, one would show a sizable increase in housing aid that is partly the result of moving such aid from the uncounted social housing subsidy to the counted Housing Benefit. Because these subsidies are administered and funded at local authority level rather than household level, there is no reliable information with which to determine the exact subsidies that different families received over time. One can, however, get a measure of the aggregate subsidy from local authority housing revenue accounts. And the FES does include a measure of the rent actually paid by housing tenants. After some experimentation, we imputed housing subsidy by applying the national percentage subsidy (expressed as a percentage of rent) to the rents reported by families and individuals in social housing.

In official U.S. statistics, the March supplement of the Current Population Survey (CPS) is used. The March CPS collects information about income and work over the previous year from respondents in 40,000–50,000 households each year. For measuring poverty, income is based on gross annual income including earnings, rent, dividends, and interest, plus cash benefits from the government. Taxes are not deducted, and so-called "in-kind benefits" are left out. This excludes some very important sources of government aid such as the Earned Income Tax Credit ("taxes") and food stamps and housing aid (in-kind benefits). Numerous scholars, including a recent panel of the National Academy of Sciences, have called for revising this standard (Citro and Michael 1995) by ensuring that income is adjusted for taxes and most in-kind aid[5] and work expenses.

We use the FES and CPS data for this study. We have no choice but to use weekly income in the FES and annual income in the CPS. Since weekly income is more volatile than annual income, we would expect British poverty would be lower if it were based on an annual measure.[6] In the U.S. data, we add the value of the Earned Income Tax Credit (EITC), food stamps, and housing benefits to other income for purposes of determining poverty. This correction should provide a more accurate picture of U.S. gross income.

We cannot create after-housing poverty measures for the United States because information on housing expenditures is not collected in the CPS.

5. The question of whether medical benefits should be included in income remains controversial.

6. Böheim and Jenkins (2000) show that income analysis based upon current monthly and annual incomes provides remarkably similar results, although there is some question over reliability of the annual income measure which is largely imputed from monthly data.

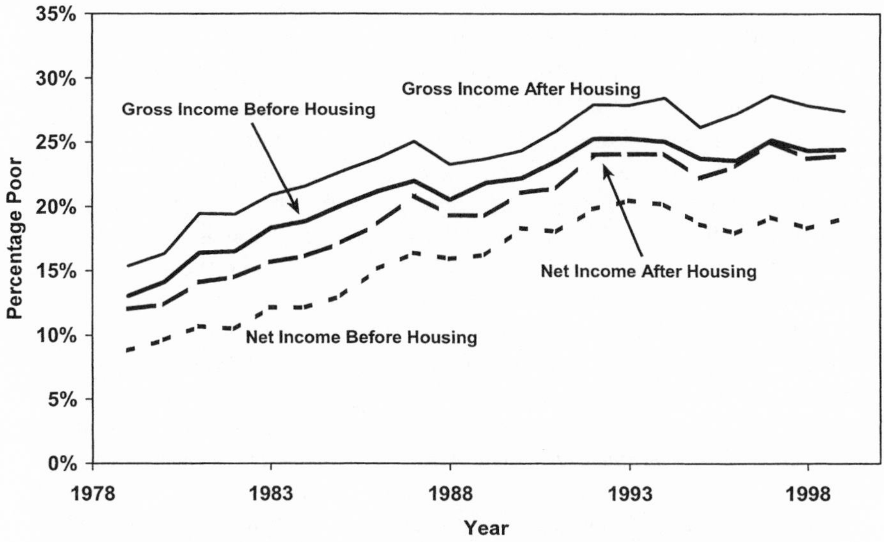

Fig. 8.1 Alternative measures of relative poverty in Britain, households headed by someone under age 60

Gross versus net income poses a different problem. Our methodology calls for estimating what each person and family would earn under different conditions in different years. As their income changes so too would their taxes owed. The structure of taxes is sufficiently complex, especially in the United States, that it is far beyond the scope of this paper to estimate the new taxes for families under a variety of changed conditions.[7]

Figure 8.1 illustrates for Britain what difference the definition makes. It tracks relative poverty in Britain using gross and net income, with and without housing. Although the measures differ in their levels, they track each other almost perfectly over time. To facilitate comparisons and calculations, we will use poverty based on gross income before housing. It is intriguing that this measure is very close to one based on *net* income *after* housing. In the 1980s, gross income before housing poverty is between 1.5 and 2.0 percentage points higher. This difference narrows somewhat in the 1990s. Since our goal is to understand the key trends, we are convinced that our measure will perform quite well.

7. In Britain, we have more hope. We have access to the Institute for Fiscal Studies Taxben model, which can calculate taxes and transfers for any family under any conditions. In later versions, we may use this model to estimate net income for Britain. We have no such model for the United States. Though such models do exist for the United States, of course, they are often quite massive and would be quite difficult to implement here.

Households, Families, and Filing Units

Unfortunately, the definitions of families and households differ slightly between countries as well. In Britain, the economic unit is based on definitions comparable to benefit units for purposes of determining social security. This comes close to a household definition of an income unit. In particular, cohabiting couples are treated equivalently to married couples. Incomes are measured at the household level since this is how some benefits are determined. The United States is based on families—defined as persons who are related by birth or marriage who are living together in the same household. Unrelated adults in the same household are usually considered separate units. Thus cohabiting couples would appear as two separate units. In the past several years the CPS has refined its procedure to allow easier identification of cohabiting couples. Moreover, it is possible to infer cohabiting couples in earlier years.[8] But we are also seeking to create units that are logically joined for benefit purposes since we estimate changes in benefits. Cohabiters are generally not included in the filing unit for benefits. Thus we choose to maintain the standard census definition of family whereby cohabiters are not included in the unit. There has been growth in cohabitation in recent years, but based on our previous work, we do not think treating cohabiters separately would change poverty trends much, though poverty would likely be slightly lower with a more inclusive definition of the unit.

Young versus Old

In this study we have also chosen to limit our attention to families with household heads who are under sixty years of age. The work, retirement activity, and benefit structures are very different for older persons. Retirement patterns have changed over time in both countries. Britain has experienced a large growth in occupational pension schemes that have raised the incomes of pensioners. In both countries, pension benefits will be linked at least partly to past earnings, which we cannot model or observe in this cross-sectional data. Thus we have chosen to limit our sample to households where the worker is unlikely to be retired or a pensioner.

8.2 The Trends in Relative and Absolute Poverty in the United States and Great Britain

Figure 8.2 shows the trends in relative poverty in Britain and the United States between 1979 and 1999 using our gross income before housing, 60 percent median income standard for households with a head under age sixty.

8. See Ellwood (2000) for a detailed description of how this can be done.

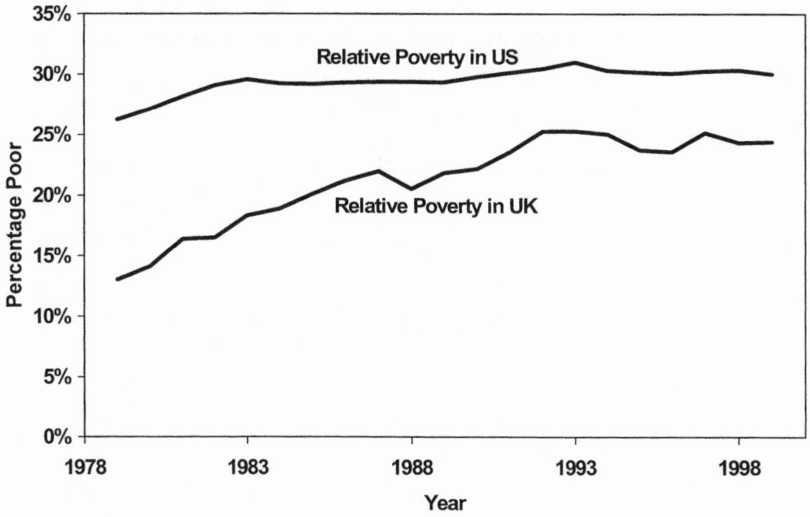

Fig. 8.2 Relative poverty in Britain and the U.S., households headed by someone under age 60

Sources: Authors' tabulations of annual FES surveys and March CPS surveys.

Note: Poverty is based on gross income, including benefits before housing.

- In 1979, the countries were far apart in relative poverty. Poverty in Britain was 13 percent; in the United States it was over 26 percent. In the following twenty years poverty grew in both countries, but poverty growth was much greater in Britain than the United States. Between 1979 and 1999, poverty rose 11 percentage points in Britain, while rising "just" 4 points in the United States.

The British trends are quite consistent with those reported by Goodman, Johnson, and Webb (1997) and Department of Social Security (1999), as well as those reported for Britain and the United States in Gottschalk and Smeeding (1997).[9]

Figure 8.3 shows the measures of absolute poverty. It illustrates absolute poverty in both countries using the 60 percent median 1979 income absolute standard, and it shows poverty in the United States using the official U.S. measure.

- In contrast to the relative measures, absolute poverty in both countries mostly follows a rather clear cyclical path, rising during the recessions

9. Note that since 1993 poverty rates have fallen slightly in the United States and there are some signs that poverty is beginning to fall in Britain. Dickens and Ellwood (2003) analyze more recent changes in child poverty (up to 2001) and show that since the advent of the Clinton and Blair administrations relative child poverty has fallen by about 3 percentage points.

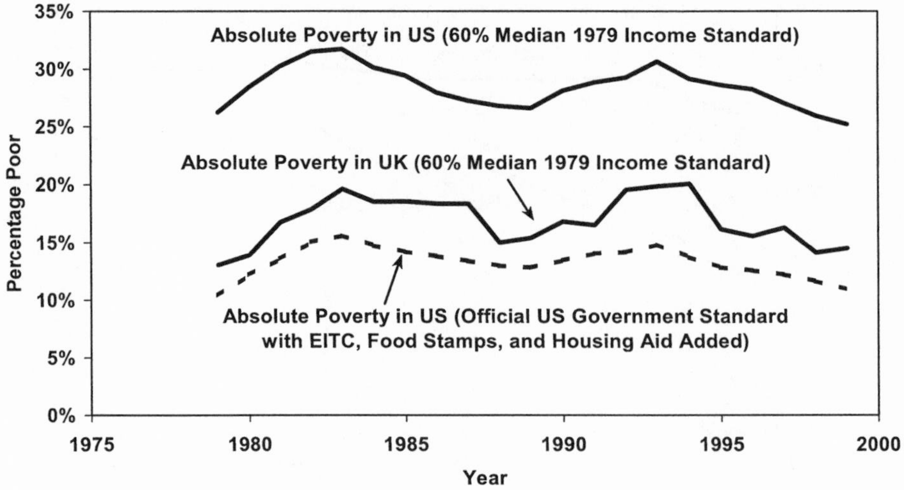

Fig. 8.3 Absolute poverty in Britain and the U.S., households headed by someone under age 60

Sources: Authors' tabulations of annual FES surveys and March CPS surveys.

Note: Poverty is based on gross income, including benefits before housing.

of 1982–1983, falling in the mid-1980s, rising again in 1992–1993, and falling back sharply in recent years.

Not surprisingly, the choice of poverty standard for the United States makes a big difference in the level of absolute poverty. The vastly lower official standard leads to half the poverty rate that one might have projected otherwise.

- When one compares absolute U.S. poverty using the official standard and absolute poverty in Britain using a 60 percent median 1979 income standard, the poverty rates are much closer. The U.S. standard is somewhat lower ($17,356 in 1999 vs. the purchasing power equivalent of $20,047 for the absolute standard in Britain) and so poverty is somewhat lower in the United States, but the trends remain similar.

Figures 8.2 and 8.3 reveal why it is important to be clear about whether one is comparing relative or absolute poverty. Using either measure, the United States does not perform very well, but relative poverty makes Britain's performance seem far worse than that of the United States: poverty grew vastly more in Britain. Using absolute poverty, Britain has done as well or better than the United States in recent years. As noted earlier, we will exclusively use the U.S. official poverty standard in exploring absolute poverty for the United States in the remainder of the paper.

What, then, explains the trends over time and, in particular, the differential performance in relative poverty? There are many possible explanations for these changes—a rise in single-parent families, rising wage inequality, changing work patterns, or altered government aid. The challenge for this paper is to understand these trends.

8.3 Possible Explanations for the Changing Patterns of Poverty

The trends for Britain described above are relatively well known. A variety of important work has already been done exploring the role of demographic and economic factors. We summarize several explanations in the following subsections.

8.3.1 Changing Demographic Patterns

Goodman, Johnson, and Webb (1997), Davies and Joshi (1998), and many others document the changing mix of demographic characteristics among the poor. In both the United States and Britain, a rising share of families are headed by women, and these families have far higher poverty rates than husband-wife families. Thus, in Britain, for example, lone parents with children have risen from 5 percent of those in the bottom income quintile in the early 1960s to 15 percent by the early 1990s.

8.3.2 Changing Wage Patterns

Real wages have risen in Britain over much of this period, but so too has wage dispersion. Machin (1999) reports that median male wages rose from £6.13 in 1980 to £7.57 in 1996. Yet during the same period the ratio of wages of men at the 90th percentile of the hourly wage distribution to those at the 10th percentile rose from 3.10 in 1975 to 3.96 in 1996. Similar changes occurred for women. Uniformly rising wages would have relatively little impact on relative poverty, but the widening dispersion would push such poverty up. (Of course, if incomes in work are rising faster than incomes out of work then relative poverty will rise with growing earnings, even if wage dispersion did not grow, because median incomes would rise and more people without earnings would fall below the poverty standard.) By contrast, a uniform rise in wages would reduce absolute poverty (as more people are pulled above the fixed standard) but growing dispersion would work in the opposite direction. Since average wages grew in Britain and the dispersion widened, wage patterns seem likely to have pushed up relative poverty and had ambiguous impacts on absolute deprivation.

In sharp contrast to Britain, Mishel, Bernstein, and Schmitt (1999) report that median wages of men in the United States fell from $14.37 to $12.80 between 1980 and 1998. But like Britain the 90-10 ratio rose over the period, from 3.62 to 4.51. For women, median wages actually rose from $9.13 to $10.00, but the 90-10 ratio grew even more than it did for men, from 2.85 to 3.89. Thus it would seem that wage changes for men in the

United States would increase both absolute and relative poverty, while patterns for women would increase relative poverty at least.

8.3.3 Changing Employment and the Pattern of "Worklessness"

Unemployment in Britain rose sharply over a large stretch of the recent period but has since fallen to a twenty-year low of around 5 percent. Nevertheless, the nonemployment rate of men has remained high due to a large increase in inactivity, particularly among older, less skilled men. Furthermore, since the mid 1970s there has been a significant polarization of work across households, so that by the late 1990s 17 percent of all households were without work as described in Gregg, Hansen, and Wadsworth (1999) and Gregg and Wadsworth (2000). These households contain 4 million adults (13 percent) and 2.6 million children (18 percent). Some 70 percent of these workless households are poor, and this rises to 90 percent where children are present. Ercolani and Jenkins (1998) use shift-share analysis to show that the small increases in income inequality in the first half of the 1990s occur within and not between *work-rich* and *work-poor* households. We suspect that such polarization may have been more important in influencing poverty in earlier periods and perhaps later periods as well.

By contrast, in the United States, employment levels seem to be high and growing in recent years. Unemployment rates are extremely low by U.S. standards. A number of authors, including Blank, Card, and Robbins (2000), Ellwood (2000), and Meyer and Rosenbaum (2000), have emphasized the sharp rise in work among single mothers in the United States in recent years. There has been some decline in work among men over this period, a trend that some authors attribute to expanded disability benefits, though this conclusion remains quite controversial.[10]

8.3.4 Social Policy Structures and "Reforms"

Social policies are generally designed to mitigate hardships caused by low incomes that result from limited work, low pay, or single parenthood. Thus one would expect them to dampen the impact of the other factors cited above. In addition, social policies in Britain and the United States have undergone repeated "reforms" over the past quarter-century. Benefits have risen and fallen. New programs have been added. Some have been eliminated and most recently in both countries, governments have moved toward a more work-oriented strategy, including expanded tax credits for workers, and at least some increase in work expectations. Policy changes obviously influence poverty both directly, by affecting the total income that individuals and families in a particular situation receive, and by altering behavior. There is a sizeable body of work in both countries examining the

10. See, for example, Bound and Waidmann (1992), DeLeire (2000), Gruber and Kubik (1994), and Haveman (1991).

role that social policies and incentives can have on work behavior and poverty.[11]

All of these factors—demography, work, wages, and benefits—may have influenced policy in complex ways. We propose to extend the work of others on each of these individual topics by decomposing the altered patterns of poverty over time into the relative roles that each of these factors may have played. The work of Goodman, Johnson, and Webb (1997) offer the closest analogy, but their focus is primarily on inequality and they seek to decompose the aggregate level of inequality into various components, whereas we are more narrowly focused on poverty and will do the decomposition on a more micro level.[12]

8.4 Decomposing the Trends in Poverty among Families and Working Age Adults: Aggregate Methods and Micromethods

There are two different strategies one might pursue in seeking to parse the changing patterns of poverty—one using aggregate data at its heart and the other using microdata. While we always intended to rely primarily on the use of a time series of cross-sectional microdata for our work, we initially tried estimating some aggregate models because their simplicity makes them relatively easy to perform and common in the literature.

8.4.1 Aggregate Analyses

Blank and Blinder (1986), Blank and Card (1993), and Cutler and Katz (1991) are among the chief contributors to the literature that seeks to explain variations in poverty using aggregate data in the United States, while Gregg and Machin (1995) and Nolan (1986) have done key work for Britain. The basic strategy has typically been to regress aggregate poverty rates on factors such as unemployment rates, mean wages, inflation rates, gross domestic product (GDP), demographic measures, government benefit levels, and so on.

Unfortunately, when we estimated such models we found them to be unstable and quite sensitive to specification. This should presumably come as no surprise given the time series nature of the data. Especially when we tried to separately identify wage levels, wage dispersion, unemployment, worklessness, and government benefits, we found that the results had no power at all. Aggregate methods by their very nature cannot do a very good job of distinguishing spurious from real effects. Thus we turned to micromethods for our analysis.

11. See, for example, Blundell (2000), Blundell et al. (2000), Gregg, Johnson, and Reed (1999), Meyer and Rosenbaum (2000), and Moffitt (1992).

12. Goodman, Johnson, and Webb (1997) do have a chapter on poverty, but they do not offer much decomposition of the trends in that segment.

8.4.2 Micromethodology

The overall aim of this paper can probably best be represented with the question, "What would the poverty rate have been today if the structure of wages, work, or benefits had remained at some base-year level?" For example, since 1979 the distribution of wages has widened considerably, but employment, family structures, and benefit structures have changed as well. Thus a natural first question would be to ask how different the poverty rate would have been in 1999 had the distribution of wages been the same as in 1979 while everything else was at the actual 1999 level. This kind of experiment essentially requires that we assign each person who was working in 1999 a wage that an equivalent person would have earned in 1979, and then recalculate the poverty rate. A similar methodology can also be applied to work and benefit structures.

For all members of the sample in any given year, we estimate each person's and family's work, wages, and benefits given the structures of pay, employment, or benefits in a chosen base year. We can then estimate what poverty would have been if the base-year conditions still prevailed. For this work we need to look at individual family income. A family is poor if their equivalized family income is below the poverty threshold.

$$\text{Total Income}_t = \sum_{i=1}^{\text{nadults}} (\text{wage}_{it} \cdot \text{hours}_{it}) + \text{govtben}_t + \text{othinc}_t$$

where

Total Income_t = total family income for the family at time t,
nadults_j = number of adults in the family,
wage_{it} = wage of adult i at time t,
hours_{it} = hours worked by adult i at time t,
govtben_t = government benefits received by family at time t, and
othinc_t = other income of the family at time t.

We would like to have a model of each of the key variables above—wages, hours, and government benefits—that would allow us to explore what might have happened had wage or work or government benefit patterns been different.

8.4.3 Wages

For each year we estimate the following wage equation:

$$\text{wage}_{it} = W_t(X_{it}) + \varepsilon_{it}$$

where X_{it} = measured characteristics of the person at time t.

In practice, we estimate separate wage equations for men and women in each year. The characteristics included vary somewhat across Britain and the United States. Both include age and education dummies and number of children. In the United States we also include race dummies.

We will need a wage prediction for everyone (aged over sixteen) in the sample in each year t because under some assumptions more people will be working. This is relatively straightforward. We predict an individual's wage in year t based on their characteristics X_{it}. For those with an observed wage we assign them their actual residual from the wage equation (the predicted wage in year t is therefore the observed wage in that year for people who already work). For those who are not working we do not observe a residual and so randomly assign them a residual from the year-t residual distribution. This gives us predicted wages in year t for all individuals in the sample without changing the distribution. Of course, if more people worked the distribution might change even beyond that predicted by the model. Those who did not initially work might be drawn from the lower tail of the wage distribution. Much of this is already accounted for in the base prediction, which does depend on measured characteristics. We experimented with Heckman-type selection models in this work. In principle, nothing prevents their use, but we lacked a good selection instrument and found that including these selection equations did little to change our results. Thus we have chosen instead to maintain the original distribution.

We then want to predict an individual's wage in year t given the wage structure of some base year s. To do this we need to account for the impact of the implicitly different returns to measured characteristics X_{it} in the base year s, but we also need to take account of the changed distribution of the error term between year s and year t. We predict wages using the following methodology:

$$\overline{\overline{\text{wage}}}_{it}^{s} = W_s(X_{it}) + \varepsilon_s(\text{errorptile}_{it})$$

where

$\overline{\overline{\text{wage}}}_{it}^{s}$ = predicted wage for person i in year t using the wage distribution of year s,

X_{it} = measured characteristics of the person at time t,

ε_s = the observed residual distribution function in the wage equation for year s, and

errorptile_{it} = the observed percentile of the residual of person i in the year-t wage equation.

We use each person's characteristics in year t in the base-year s wage equation. To determine what the predicted error would be in the base-year equation, we assume that the person's percentile ranking in the *unexplained* variance of wages remains unchanged in the two time periods. Thus if the residual ε_{it} for the person i in the year-t wage equation placed the person in the 37th percentile of the residual distribution, he or she would be assigned the residual of the 37th percentile of the distribution in year s. This method thus preserves both the ranking of the individual's unobserved components of earnings over time while adjusting for altered levels of unexplained variance in pay over time.

A problem arises with those individuals for whom we do not observe a wage in year t. We chose to randomly assign a residual for these individuals from the year-s residual distribution. This methodology allows us to predict wages for all individuals in each year, whether they work or not, given the current-year or base-year wage equation.

8.4.4 Work

There are two components to our work specification: the participation decision and the choice of hours of work. We treat these separately. First, we estimate an equation each year that describes whether an individual works:

$$\text{work}_{it} = L_t(X_{it}, Z_{it}) + v_{it}$$

where

$\text{work}_{it} = 1$ if person i is working in year t and 0 if person i is not working in year t,
X_{it} = measured characteristics of person i at time t as in the wage equation, and
Z_{it} = measured household characteristics of person i at time t.

X_{it} is the same as specified above. Z_{it} includes the number of children, spouse's education, and other nonlabor, nonbenefit income. And, for women in couples, we also include the partner's work status to account for covariance in work decisions of couples. We estimate this equation separately for men and women and for individuals in different household types (husbands or wives, single household heads with other household members, single heads with no other members, and other household members).

We now want a prediction of the work status of person i in year t given the work specification of some base year s. Our aim here in predicting work status in year t given the work equation of year s is to change the status of as few people as possible from their actual status observed in year t. Clearly, to the extent there are aggregate changes in work we need to adjust the work status of at least some individuals. Hence we predict work status in the following way:

$$\text{If work}_{it} = 0 \text{ and } P(\text{work})^s_{it} - P(\text{work})^t_{it} > 0 \text{ and } U_i < \frac{P(\text{work})^s_{it} - P(\text{work})^t_{it}}{1 - P(\text{work})^t_{it}}$$

$$\text{then } \overline{\overline{\text{work}}}^s_{it} = 1.$$

$$\text{If work}_{it} = 1 \text{ and } P(\text{work})^s_{it} - P(\text{work})^t_{it} < 0 \text{ and } U_i < \frac{P(\text{work})^t_{it} - P(\text{work})^s_{it}}{P(\text{work})^t_{it}}$$

$$\text{then } \overline{\overline{\text{work}}}^s_{it} = 0,$$

$$\text{otherwise } \overline{\overline{\text{work}}}^s_{it} = \text{work}_{it}.$$

$\overline{\overline{\text{work}}}^s_{it}$ = predicted work status of person i in year t given year-s work specification,
work_{it} = observed work status of person i in year t,
$P(\text{work})^s_{it} = L_s(X_{it}, Z_{it})$ is the predicted work probability of person i in year t using the year-s work equation,
$P(\text{work})^t_{it} = L_t(X_{it}, Z_{it})$ is the predicted work probability of person i in year t usign the year-t work equation, and
U_i is a uniformly distributed random number for person i.

Thus, to construct the predicted work status of person i in year t under the year-s specification $\overline{\overline{\text{work}}}^s_{it}$, we apply the following procedure. Initially we assign the person a predicted work status that is equal to his or her observed work status. We then compare the person's predicted probability of work in year t under the year-t equation, $P(\text{work})^t_{it}$, with that predicted by the year-s equation, $P(\text{work})^s_{it}$. If an individual's $P(\text{work})^s_{it} > P(\text{work})^t_{it}$ and the person is already working, we do nothing; as predicted, the odds of working have increased. If the person is not now working (and $1 - P(\text{work})^t_{it}$ of such individuals will not be working), then there is some chance the person would in fact have gone to work. To assure that the fraction working matches the predicted probabilities, we need to randomly assign some of the individuals who are not working into work based on the difference in their predicted work probabilities and the odds that the person is not now working. This can be done on an individual basis using the equations above. However, if $P(\text{work})^s_{it} < P(\text{work})^t_{it}$ then we need to assign some individuals who are working out of work. Again, we randomly assign a proportion of these workers out of work. These proportions are specified such that the overall proportion in work in year t under the year-s specification corresponds to that predicted by the year-s work equation given year-t characteristics.

8.4.5 Hours

Second, we estimate an hours equation for each year for those individuals with positive hours of work:

$$\text{hours}_{it} = H_t(X_{it}, Z_{it}) + \eta_{it}$$

where

hours_{it} = hours worked by person i in year t (for those with positive hours),
X_{it} = measured characteristics of the person at time t, and
Z_{it} = measured household characteristics of person i at time t.

Again we estimate this equation separately for men and women and for different household types (as discussed above). In order to obtain a prediction of the work hours of person i in year t under the base-year s equation we apply the same method as employed with wages.

$$\overline{\text{hours}}^{s}_{it} = H_s(X_{it}) + \eta_s(\text{errorptile}_{it})$$

where

$\overline{\text{hours}}^{s}_{it}$ = predicted hours for person i in year t using the hours distribution of year s,
X_{it} = measured characteristics of the person at time t,
Z_{it} = measured household characteristics of person i at time t,
η_s = the observed residual distribution function in the hours equation for year s, and
errorptile_{it} = the observed percentile of the residual of person i in the year-t hours equation.

We use each person's individual and household characteristics in year t in the base-year s hours equation. To determine what the predicted error would be in the base-year equation, we assume that the person's percentile ranking in the *unexplained* variance of hours remains unchanged in the two time periods. For those who are not working in year t we randomly assign a residual from the year-s residual distribution.

8.4.6 Benefits

In our benefit specification we need to predict both whether a household is in receipt of benefits and the amount received. Ideally we would like to have access to a benefit model that uses observed household characteristics to predict the amount of benefit entitlement. In the absence of such a model we employ a regression-based approach, using observed individual and household characteristics to predict benefit receipt. As with work, there are two components to our benefit specification: First, we need to model whether the household is in receipt of benefits, and then the benefit amount.

We estimate a benefit receipt equation for each household head i as follows:

$$\text{benp}_{it} = R_t(X_{it}, Y_{it}) + \xi_{it}$$

where

benp_{it} = 1 if household i is receiving benefits in year t, and 0 if household i is not receiving benefits in year t,
X_{it} = measured characteristics of household head i at time t, and
Y_{it} = measured characteristics of household i at time t.

We estimate this equation separately for our different household types (see above). Y_{it} includes own education dummies, spouse's education dummies, own hours of work, spouse's hours of work, number of adults, number of children, household earnings dummies, and nonwage income dummies.

For the United States we also include the state maximum Aid to Families with Dependent Children (AFDC) level, whether the head has a disability, and whether the head was a widow.

We wish to predict the benefit participation of households in year t given a base-year s benefit participation equation. We employ an analogous methodology to that described above in terms of work participation.

$$\text{If benp}_{it} = 0 \text{ and } P(\text{benp})^s_{it} - P(\text{benp})^t_{it} > 0 \text{ and } U_i < \frac{P(\text{benp})^s_{it} - P(\text{benp})^t_{it}}{1 - P(\text{benp})^t_{it}}$$

$$\text{then } \overline{\overline{\text{benp}}}^s_{it} = 1.$$

$$\text{If benp}_{it} = 1 \text{ and } P(\text{benp})^s_{it} - P(\text{benp})^t_{it} < 0 \text{ and } U_i < \frac{P(\text{benp})^t_{it} - P(\text{benp})^s_{it}}{P(\text{benp})^t_{it}}$$

$$\text{then } \overline{\overline{\text{benp}}}^s_{it} = 0,$$

$$\text{otherwise } \overline{\overline{\text{benp}}}^s_{it} = \text{benp}_{it}$$

$\overline{\overline{\text{benp}}}^s_{it}$ = predicted benefit status of household head i in year t given year-s benefit specification,
benp_{it} = observed benefit status of household head i in year t,
$P(\text{benp})^s_{it} = R_s(X_{it}, Z_{it})$ is the benefit participation probability of household head i in year t, using the year-s benefit equation,
$P(\text{benp})^t_{it} = R_t(X_{it}, Z_{it})$ is the benefit participation probability of household head i in year t, using the year-t benefit equation, and
U_i is a uniformly distributed random number for household head i.

8.4.7 Benefit Amounts

Finally, we require a prediction of the monetary amount of benefit receipt for each year. Our goal is to model as nearly as possible the mechanical relationship between a family's earnings and other characteristics and the amount of benefits they receive. Clearly the decision to work and the level of earnings that people have will be endogenous. But *conditional on work and earnings* benefits are not endogenous, they are a function of the rules of the benefit regime. In later work for Britain, we may use the Institute for Fiscal Studies Taxben model to get more accurate estimates of benefit entitlement. But we do not have such a model for the United States, and we seek to have as comparable a model as possible between the two countries. We run the following regression for each household head separately for our different household types and also separately for households with and without children:

$$\text{benefits}_{it} = B_t(X_{it}, Y_{it}) + \psi_{it}$$

where

benefits_{it} = benefit receipt of household head i at time t,
X_{it} = measured characteristics of head of household i at time t, and
Y_{it} = measured characteristics of household i at time t.

In order to obtain a prediction of benefit receipts of household head i in year t under the base-year s equation we apply the same method as employed with wages and hours above.

$$\overline{\overline{\text{benefits}}}{}^{s}_{it} = B_s(X_{it}, Y_{it}) + \psi_s(\text{errorptile}_{it})$$

where

$\overline{\overline{\text{benefits}}}{}^{s}_{it}$ = predicted benefits for household head i in year t using the benefits distribution of year s,
X_{it} = measured characteristics of household head i at time t,
Z_{it} = measured household characteristics at time t,
ψ_s = the observed residual distribution function in the benefits equation for year s, and
errorptile_{it} = the observed percentile of the residual of household head i in the year-t benefits equation.

We use each household head's individual and household characteristics in year t in the base-year s benefits equation. To determine what the predicted error would be in the base-year equation, we assume that the household's percentile ranking in the *unexplained* variance of benefits remains unchanged in the two time periods. For those who are not in benefit receipt in year t we randomly assign a residual from the year-s distribution.

We now have a predicted wage, work status, hours, and benefit status and receipt for every person in our sample in each year t. In addition, we have a prediction in each year t given the wage, work, and benefits specification of the base year s. This allows us to answer questions such as "What would household income, and hence poverty, be in year t given the wage, work, or benefit specification and residuals from year s?"

8.5 Results: The Forces Shaping Poverty in Great Britain and the United States

With this methodology we can pose a blistering array of hypothetical "what-if" scenarios. What would happen to poverty if wages had remained as they were in 1979 (or in 1984 or any other year) but demographic, work, and benefit patterns had all evolved as they did in actuality? What if the demographics only had changed? We have chosen 1979 as our base year partly because it just precedes most of the burst of inequality and policy change in both countries. We could have selected any year. Our basic question is straightforward: what factors caused the sharp changes in poverty?

We settled on an additive approach to understanding the changes. We start with everything as it was in 1979, and add in one change at a time. We begin by projecting what poverty would have been had demographic changes alone occurred. Methodologically, this involves estimating what work, wages, and benefits would have been in every year applying 1979 models (with their residuals) to the actual characteristics of the population in each year. Because family structures, education, and ages would have changed over time, work, wages, and benefits would have changed somewhat and poverty would have been changed as well. The change in poverty created by this model is the estimated impact of demographics. Next, we projected poverty with wages and demographics set to their actual levels while work and benefits were kept at their 1979 level.[13] The change in poverty from the previously measured impact of demographics alone indicates the impact of altered wage patterns. Then, we calculated poverty allowing demographics, wages, and work to change, but still keeping government benefits at their 1979 base level.[14] The net change in poverty now is the work effect. Finally, the change from this to actual poverty is the impact of changes in benefits.

This type of decomposition involves several critical assumptions. The most obvious is that each change is being treated as though it were exogenous. But, of course, demographic changes may, in part, be the result of wage or benefit changes. Wage changes may be influenced by the fraction of people working. Work patterns will surely be influenced by wage and benefit patterns. These results thus must be seen as partial effects—not capturing any behavioral impacts. The place where this is most at issue is the potential impact of government benefits on work and worklessness. In the later sections of this paper, we shall confront this issue directly. Here we do adjust benefits for altered earnings, but not vice versa.

The other obvious feature of using this additive approach is that the decomposition it yields is somewhat path dependent. Depending on the order we added changes, the fraction attributed to various factors could differ. In our experiments, the order makes surprisingly little difference,

13. For most persons we use their actual wage multiplied by their predicted work hours if conditions had remained as in 1979. If some people were projected to work in a particular year who were not projected to work in 1979, we use an imputed wage for them.

14. We actually estimated two effects: first, the projected poverty if benefits remained exactly at the level we predicted each family would have received in 1979 had their work and wages been as predicted using models for 1979. Then we projected poverty after allowing for the fact that under 1979 rules, benefits would have adjusted to the changed economic situation. This is the income stabilization effect of the benefit systems. In these charts, the lines are shown assuming benefits were set at the 1979 levels when work and wages were also set in 1979. Thus when we change wages or work we get the pure impact on poverty, not net of a stabilization effect.

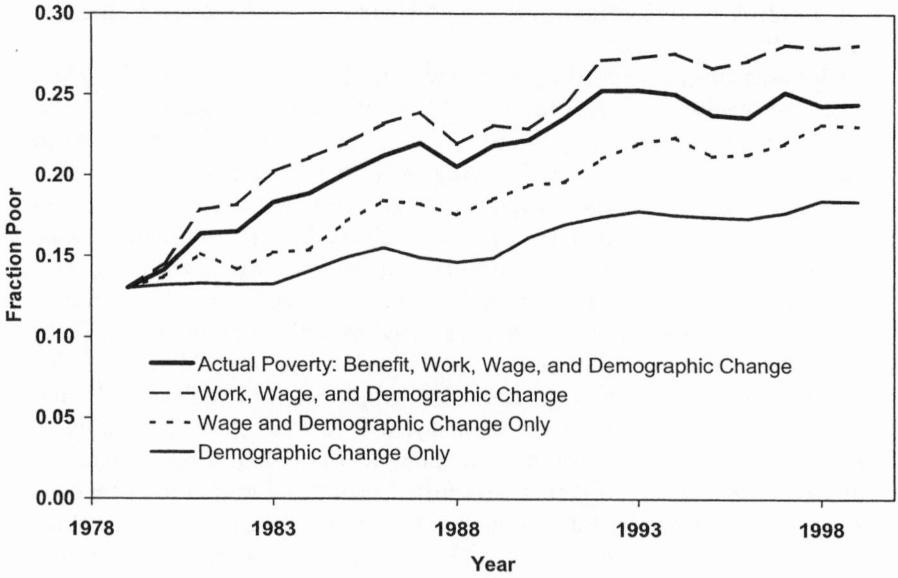

Fig. 8.4 Components of change in relative poverty in Britain since 1979

though the order in which work or wage changes are added makes some difference in the United Kingdom because slightly more people are affected by wage changes when work levels are kept at 1979 levels.

Because we estimate changed outcomes for every member of our sample, we can report on a very wide range of impacts. In each nation, we can look at effects on any possible measure of poverty for any demographic or family group. Here, we have chosen to report on relative and absolute poverty overall, and for four family subgroups: couples with children, couples without children, singles with children, and singles without children. Note that "singles without children" is not necessarily a household with only one member (e.g., in a small number of cases it includes grown children or other adults). With two nations, two poverty measures, and four family groupings, we have sixteen different combinations to report about—and for each there is a different impact of demographics, wages, work, and public aid. Obviously we will not be able to comment fully on each of these, and many detailed results can be found in Dickens and Ellwood (2001).

Figure 8.4 illustrates the various impacts on relative poverty in Britain. It shows how each change would have altered poverty. The impacts are also summarized in the first column of the top part of table 8.1. The figure and table reveal a very straightforward and reasonable story.

- Demographics, wage change, and increased worklessness all contributed considerably to growing relative poverty in Britain through-

Table 8.1 **Decomposition of Changes in Poverty between 1979 and 1999, by Family Type (%)**

	Great Britain		United States	
	Relative Poverty (%)	Absolute Poverty (%)	Relative Poverty (%)	Absolute Poverty (%)
	All Persons			
Poverty in 1979	**13.0**	**13.0**	**26.2**	**10.4**
+ Demographics	+5.4	+1.2	+3.3	+1.2
+ Wages	+4.6	+0.7	+1.3	+1.2
+ Work patterns	+5.1	+6.3	−0.8	−2.3
+ Government benefits	−3.7	−6.8	+0.0	+0.3
= Poverty in 1999	**24.4**	**14.5**	**30.0**	**10.9**
	Couples with Children			
Poverty in 1979	**13.1**	**13.1**	**23.4**	**6.4**
+ Demographics	+2.7	−2.2	+2.7	+0.8
+ Wages	+5.3	+0.8	+2.2	+1.4
+ Work patterns	+3.8	+5.4	−1.7	−2.4
+ Government benefits	−2.3	−3.4	+0.1	+0.0
= Poverty in 1999	**22.6**	**13.7**	**26.8**	**6.4**
	Couples without Children			
Poverty in 1979	**3.5**	**3.5**	**9.5**	**2.5**
+ Demographics	+0.9	+0.3	+2.3	+0.4
+ Wages	+2.8	+0.4	+0.7	+0.3
+ Work patterns	+3.7	+3.7	−0.5	−0.3
+ Government benefits	−1.9	−3.1	−0.3	−0.0
= Poverty in 1999	**9.0**	**4.9**	**11.7**	**2.8**
	Singles with Children			
Poverty in 1979	**48.3**	**48.3**	**63.9**	**36.9**
+ Demographics	+11.9	+2.5	−2.3	−5.1
+ Wages	+6.9	+0.8	−0.6	+2.3
+ Work patterns	+8.4	+12.0	−0.2	−6.5
+ Government benefits	−10.9	−26.5	+0.3	+1.4
= Poverty in 1999	**64.7**	**37.2**	**61.1**	**29.0**
	Singles without Children			
Poverty in 1979	**13.3**	**13.3**	**26.6**	**15.0**
+ Demographics	+3.8	+1.0	+2.6	+0.3
+ Wages	+2.7	+0.2	+0.9	+0.9
+ Work patterns	+10.5	+10.6	+0.7	−0.5
+ Government benefits	−6.5	−10.2	−0.1	+0.4
= Poverty in 1999	**23.9**	**15.0**	**30.8**	**16.0**

out the 1979–1999 period. Demographic changes alone pushed poverty from roughly 13.0 percent up to 18.4 percent. Wages moved the rate up another 4.6 points to 23.0 percent. Worklessness raised poverty another 5.1 points to 28.1 percent. On the other hand, government benefits expanded over the period and, ignoring any behavioral impacts,

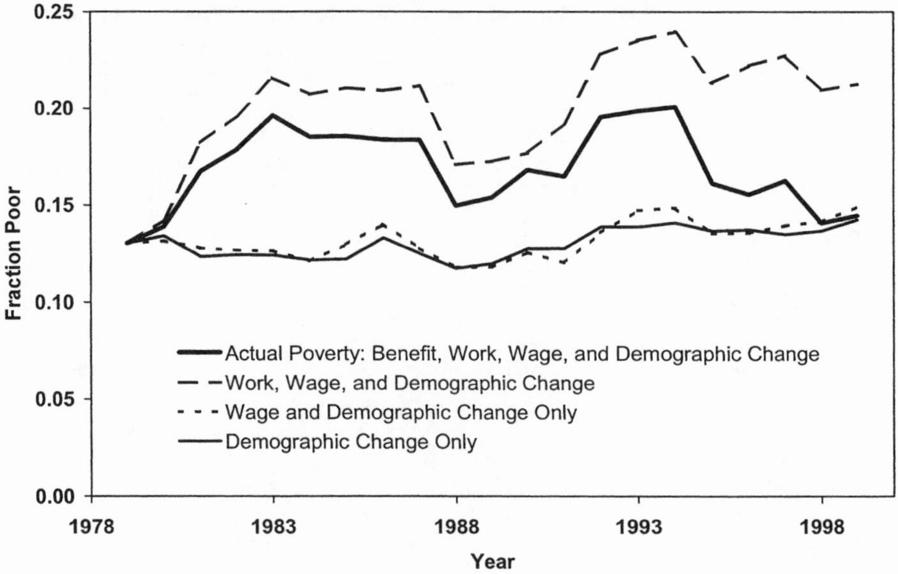

Fig. 8.5 Components of change in absolute poverty in Britain since 1979

reduced poverty to 24.4 percent—3.7 points lower than it would have been in the absence of expansion.

We should point out that much of the increase in benefits was in the form of increased housing benefit arising from increased rents. This is subject to interpretation and we will return to this below. Also, it is worth noting that the role of worklessness was larger during the mid-1980s and mid-1990s, when overall levels of unemployment were much higher.[15]

Figure 8.5 and the second column of table 8.1 shows the same information for absolute poverty, and a rather different picture emerges.

- In sharp contrast to relative poverty, neither demographic nor wage changes had a large net impact on absolute poverty. Demographic changes alone would have pushed up absolute poverty from 13.0 percent to 14.2 percent. Wage changes had a small impact of 0.7 points. On the other hand, work changes had a very large impact on absolute poverty, pushing it up from 15 percent to over 21 percent. Indeed, the only reason absolute poverty did not rise much over this period was a large increase in government aid, which pushed absolute poverty down by almost 7 points below what it would have been.

15. When we use the more standard definition of relative poverty based upon half *mean* contemporary income in Britain we find the role of work diminished and a larger impact from wages and demographic change. Since mean wages have risen faster than median wages this will raise this alternative poverty threshold by more.

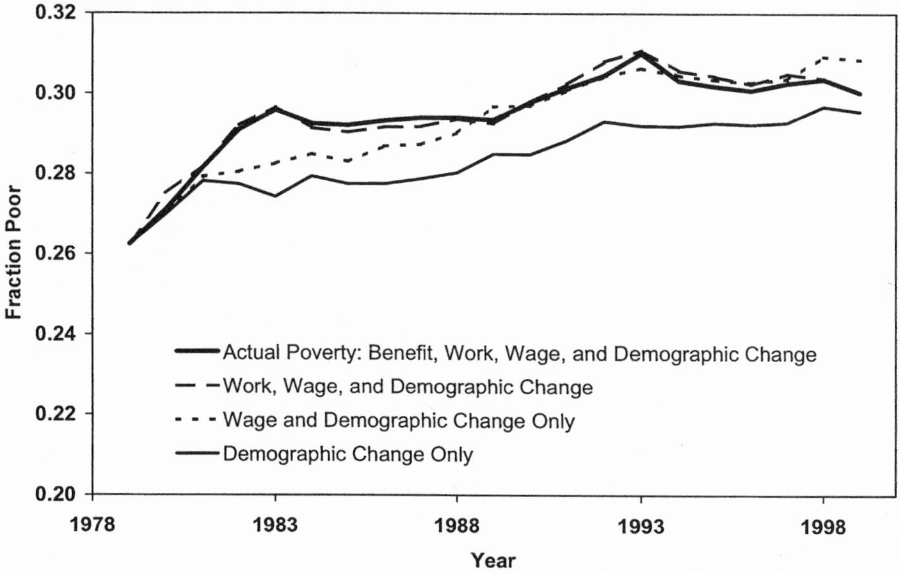

Fig. 8.6 Components of change in relative poverty in the U.S. since 1979

Figures 8.6 and 8.7 and the last two columns of table 8.1 show similar decompositions of poverty for the United States. A very different pattern emerges:

- Demographic and wage changes in the United States had smaller impacts on relative poverty as in Great Britain. On the other hand, wages played a slightly larger role in raising absolute poverty in the United States than in Britain.
- Moreover, in very sharp contrast to Britain, work changes significantly reduced absolute poverty and slightly reduced relative poverty in the United States, and the direct effects of changes in government aid were almost negligible by 1999. (Figure 8.7 actually shows that in the mid-1980s policies increased poverty slightly, in the early 1990s they reduced it, and by 1999, the impact was roughly zero.)

In interpreting these results, one must again remember that what is being measured is the effect of benefit (or wage or work) changes on poverty changes. The zero impacts for government benefits in table 8.1 for the United States does not mean that the level of government aid did not reduce poverty below what it would have been, only that *changes* in aid relative to 1979 did not affect *changes* in poverty. And indirect effects through behavioral changes remain to be considered.

The bottom four parts of table 8.1 display a plethora of results showing the impact of various types of changes on poverty among subgroups. More

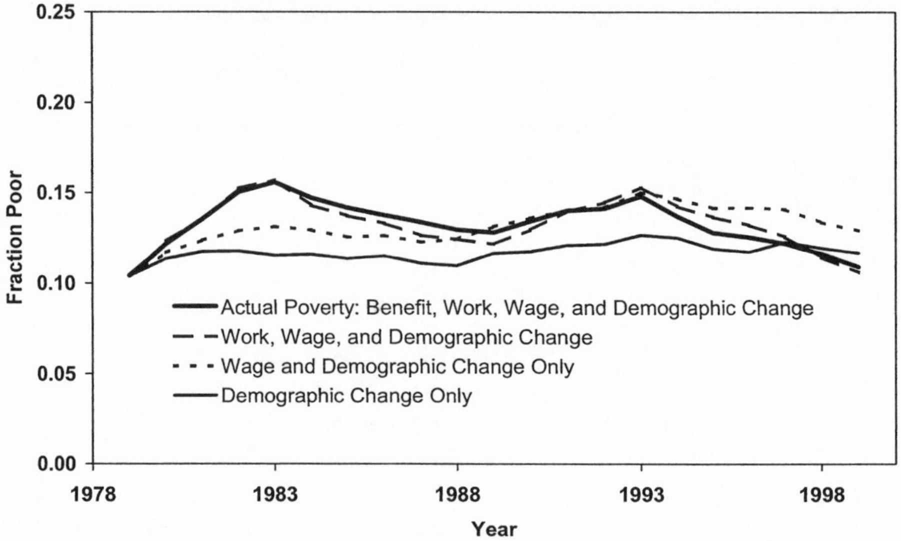

Fig. 8.7 Components of change in absolute poverty in the U.S. since 1979, using official standard

detail is available in Dickens and Ellwood (2001, tables A1–A4). In reading these results, it is important to remember that the experiment being contemplated is changing demographics or wages for *everyone,* not just the subgroup. A factor can have an effect on the relative poverty of a group even if it does not affect the income of the group, provided it changes mean incomes overall and hence the poverty line. Thus the change in wages has large effects on relative poverty of single mothers (who do not work a great deal) because the higher overall mean wages result in a higher relative poverty standard, which in turn leads more single mothers to be counted as poor.

The many results in table 8.1 are too numerous to summarize, but a few key points do stand out:

- Among couples in Britain, work and pay changes are the big story: Wage changes pushed up relative poverty significantly, work declines pushed up relative poverty somewhat and absolute poverty quite considerably.
- Among couples in the United States, work and wages are the story also, but in a different way. Wage changes did push up relative and absolute poverty somewhat, but work changes diminished both relative and absolute poverty.
- For single parents, the most striking findings involve work and benefits. In Britain, falling work pushes up poverty, especially absolute

poverty, while rising aid dramatically cuts poverty—reducing absolute poverty by an astonishing 27 percentage points. In the United States, rising work of single parents apparently reduced absolute poverty a great deal, though this was partly offset by government benefit cuts. But, intriguingly, the changes in work have virtually no impact on relative poverty.

- For singles without children, in Britain, the story is again one of reduced work being offset by higher benefits. In the United States, neither of these factors appears to be important.

What seems to emerge overall, then, is a story in which

- Demographic change pushed up poverty in both nations, but far more for relative than absolute poverty.
- Changing wages pushed up relative poverty in both nations, but had a small impact on absolute poverty in Britain and only a modest negative impact on absolute poverty in the United States.
- Changing work patterns increased poverty in Britain and reduced it in the United States, but in both countries the impacts are larger on absolute than relative poverty.
- The direct effect of changing government benefits since 1979 was to reduce poverty considerably in Britain while having essentially no impact in the United States.

8.6 Understanding How Demographic, Wage, and Work Changes Influenced Poverty

These somewhat divergent results are actually quite plausible and fairly easy to understand. We briefly examine each factor in turn.

8.6.1 Demographics

There were two major types of demographic change in both countries. On the one hand, two-parent families diminished in proportion, being replaced by lone parents and singles without children. The number of single-parent households increased from about 5 percent to 12 percent in Britain and from about 12 percent to 15 percent in the United States between 1979 and 1999. As poverty rates are much higher in these settings, both absolute and relative poverty would be expected to rise as the mix shifted.

At the same time, education levels rose significantly over the period. The increased education would have been expected to push up wages and work (and our models do project modest rises if 1979 work models had remained in place). This improvement in earnings would tend to reduce absolute poverty as more people moved above a fixed threshold. But its impact on relative poverty is ambiguous at best, since it raises incomes across the board. Indeed, educational change could act to increase relative poverty both because education rises could have been greater in the upper percentiles and because low-percentile families are far less likely to be working and thus would not see the impact of any wage rise associated with higher education.

- Changing demographics pushed up relative poverty due to altered family structures and rising education. But demographic effects on absolute poverty reflect the partially offsetting forces of changing family structures and rising education.

8.6.2 Wages

The picture for wages in Britain has much the same flavor: unambiguous increases in relative poverty, offsetting forces for absolute deprivation. Figures 8.8 and 8.9 show the well-known trends in wages for men and women in Great Britain using the FES. Mean and median hourly wages rose sharply, but the distribution also spread considerably. The striking fact on these figures is that wages for men and women in the 10th percentile rose only slightly over this period, particularly for men. Relative poverty essentially measures inequality, so the widening distribution increased poverty regardless of the growth of the mean. And since absolute poverty captures what is happening to incomes of people at the bottom, the fact that wages were essentially unchanged at the lower tail left absolute poverty essentially untouched. In effect, the beneficial effects of rising mean pay were offset by the negative impacts of a widening pay distribution.

As shown on figures 8.10 and 8.11, in the United States, pay distribu-

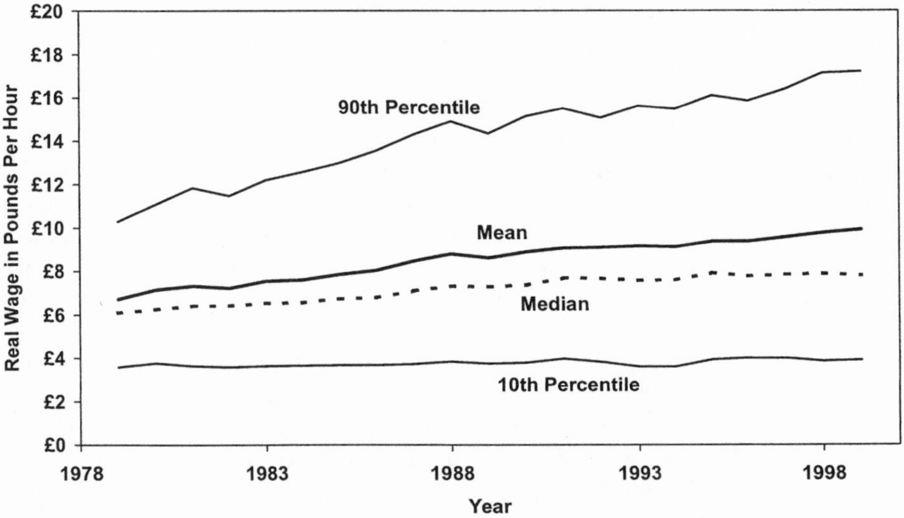

Fig. 8.8 Real wages in Britain for males working at least half time

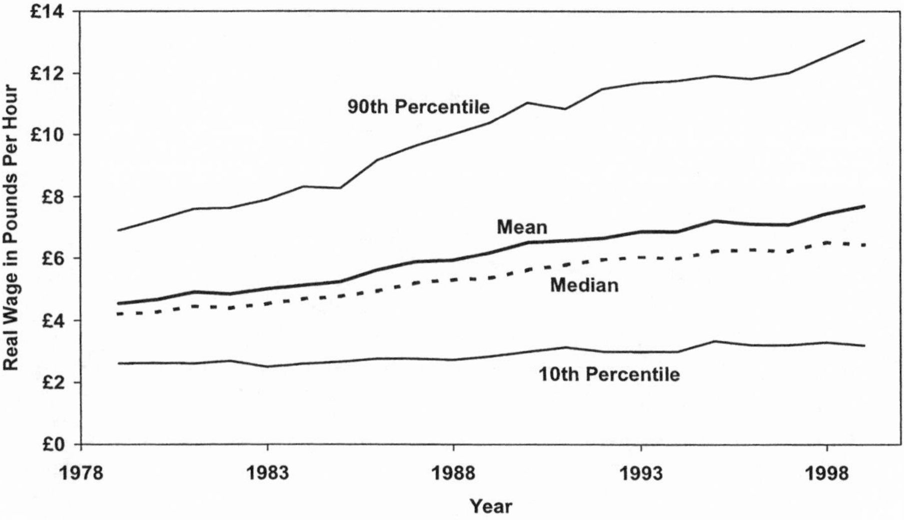

Fig. 8.9 Real wages in Britain for females working at least half time

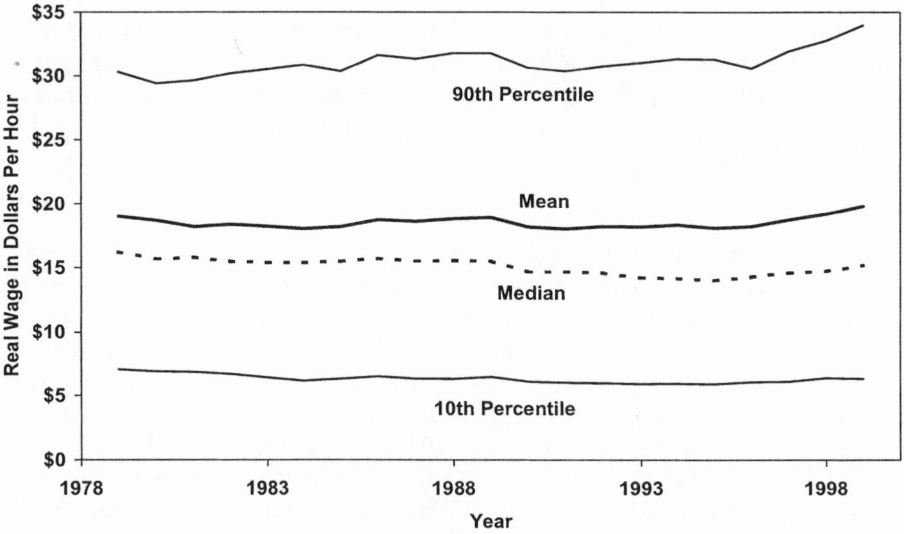

Fig. 8.10 Real wages in the U.S. for males working at least half time

tions also widened, but for men at least, there was no concomitant rise in mean pay. Indeed, the pay of men in the 10th percentile fell from $7.06 to $5.91 in 1993, before recovering somewhat to $6.36 by 1999. Such a change inevitably pushed up absolute poverty. Women's pay rose somewhat, but not enough at the bottom to offset the negative impacts of male earnings.

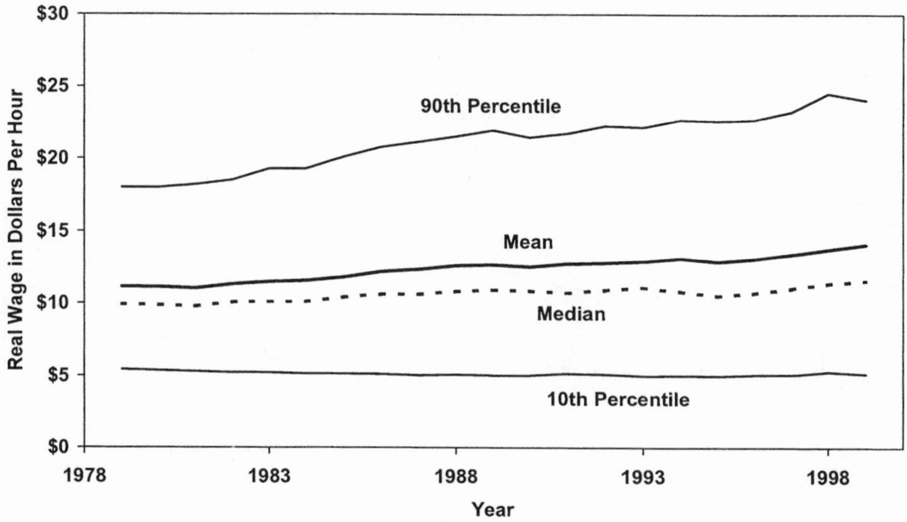

Fig. 8.11 Real wages in the U.S. for females working at least half time

- Rising wage inequality in both countries played a leading role in raising relative poverty. But at the bottom of the distribution, stagnant pay in Britain and falling pay in the United States meant that the absolute level of deprivation was unaffected in the former nation and worsened in the latter.

8.6.3 Work

Figure 8.12 plots the oft-cited rise in worklessness[16] in Britain—reproducing the results of Gregg, Hansen, and Wadsworth (1999) and others. For every family type, worklessness has risen rather considerably since 1979. This rise is quite remarkable since the unemployment rate is back down to where it had been in 1979 (as are overall employment rates) and wages are, on average, considerably higher. Worklessness rose from 35 percent of single-parent households in 1979 to 56 percent in 1999. Among couples with children, the rise was from 4.5 percent to 7.3 percent, down from its peak of nearly 12 percent in 1992 but still considerably higher than previously. In absolute terms the rises were greatest for single parents, but in percentage terms the rises were especially high for couples.

The story for couples is somewhat more complex than it first appears. On the one hand, men in couples are working considerably less than they did in 1979—nonwork has risen from 7 to 13 percent, even among men

16. For comparability with the United States, where young adults often live at home and work, we define worklessness as being where neither the household head nor the partner (if present) works.

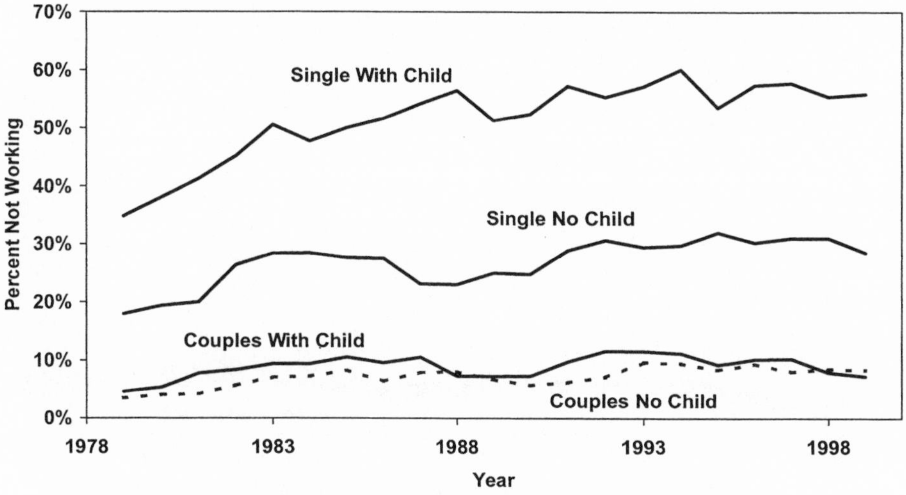

Fig. 8.12 Percent workless households in Britain, by type of household

with children. Simultaneously, work among women has grown even more dramatically. The fraction of mothers working outside the home has jumped from 59 percent to 71 percent. Figure 8.13 shows that while worklessness has risen, so too has the frequency of both men and women working within couples. Gregg, Hansen, and Wadsworth (1999) report this redistribution of work into work-rich and work-poor households. Bifurcation of work within couples almost certainly contributed to a widening family income distribution.

In many respects it is a puzzle that work changes did not increase poverty more, especially relative poverty. Altered work did have large effects on absolute poverty. It appears that a large share of the newly workless poor would have previously been the working poor when one uses the higher relative poverty standard.

Nothing like this occurred in the United States. Figure 8.14 shows that worklessness[17] is on the decline, particularly among single mothers. Less than 5 percent of husband-wife families with children are workless. Among single parents, worklessness has fallen from a peak of 44 percent in 1982 to its current level of 27 percent. Naturally, these patterns are relevant in explaining poverty patterns.

Note, however, one very important fact—the impact of rising work in the United States is felt mainly in absolute, not relative, poverty. Increasing

17. In all calculations relating to work and worklessness, we use whether the person was working at the March survey date. If we defined work based on annual work hours (which drives our model for the United States) it would not be comparable to FES data, which are for a survey week.

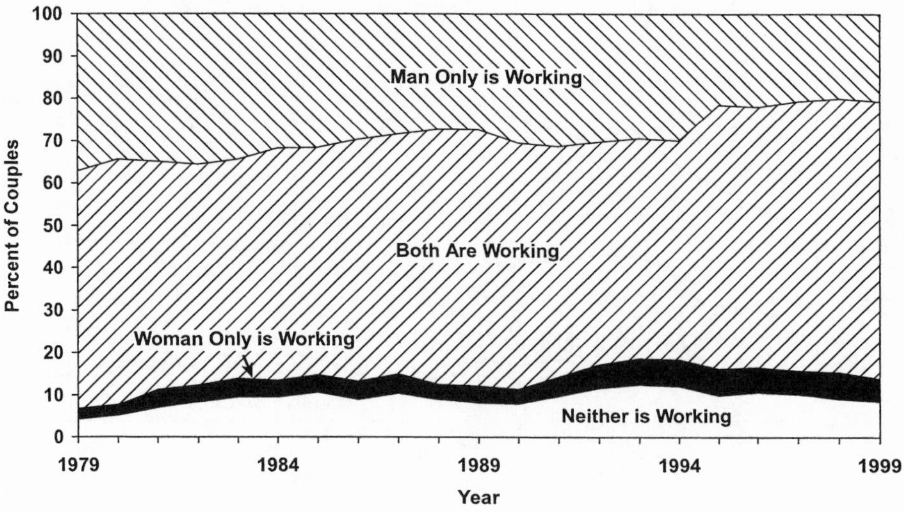

Fig. 8.13 Work patterns of men and women in couples in Britain

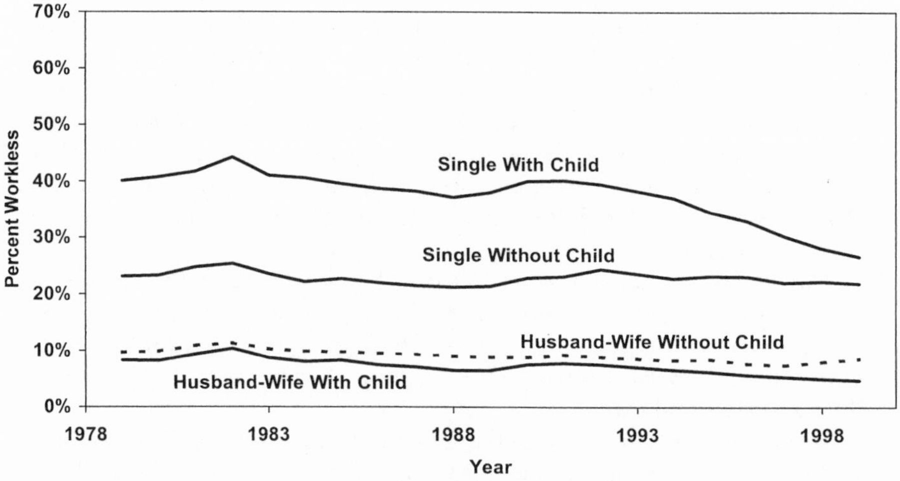

Fig. 8.14 Percent workless households in the United States by type of household
Note: Workless is defined as neither the head nor the spouse working.

work by single parents sharply reduced absolute poverty, but had no impact on relative poverty. The obvious reason must be that the move to work pushed single-parent incomes up somewhat, but not high enough to get above the much higher relative poverty line. From the vantage point of relative poverty, in the United States large numbers of single parents have gone from the nonworking poor to the working poor.

- Work patterns were radically different in Britain and the United States. Worklessness is on the rise in all types of households in Britain, while it is falling sharply in the United States, especially among single parents. Interestingly, changes in work have large effects on absolute poverty in both countries, but much smaller impacts on relative poverty. Moving people to work apparently moves their incomes up somewhat, but often not enough to avoid relative poverty.

8.7 The Role of Social Policies

It is evident that in Britain and the United States benefits changed over time. These clearly influenced poverty, and they may be linked to changes in behavior. One would like to compare the benefit structures, but past efforts at comparison have illustrated just how difficult that can be. The United States has a set of overlapping programs often targeted to only a select group of beneficiaries, such as single parents (AFDC-Temporary Assistance to Needy Families), the unemployed (unemployment insurance), the disabled (Supplemental Security Income), working parents (EITC), widows (Social Security Administration–Survivors), as well as one fairly general support program called "food stamps." In Britain, although there are important distinctions between aid for the unemployed or disabled or for housing, the variations among these are quite small in comparison to that in the United States.

Comparison is further complicated by the fact that much of what influences benefit receipt and participation, especially in the United States, has to do with administrative procedures and the treatment of clients. Statutory benefit levels have not been cut dramatically in the United States in recent years, but by all accounts the attempt to deter potential recipients from getting some forms of aid (in hopes of keeping them working) and the stigma of getting aid have increased significantly. Sanctions have grown and other administrative tightening seems omnipresent. The effect of this is to reduce the effective benefits people actually receive.

How then are we to compare the nature of support in the two nations over time? Our benefit model provides a rather straightforward conceptual way of comparison. For each country and for each family type, we can observe over time the amount of aid a family or household actually receives conditional on their earnings. Thus one can see how much aid a couple with zero earnings receives in 1979, in 1989, in 1999 and compare the levels and trends across countries. Similarly, one can compare the aid of couples with earnings of £1–150, or earnings of £151–300, and so on. Of course, this is not perfect, because the households in each category are in part a selected group, so there is an element of endogeneity. It is important to remember that we are conditioning on earnings, and asking whether someone of a given earnings gets more benefits across countries and over time—certainly a well-defined question. Still, persons who have some condition we do not capture in the model or observe in the data that allows them to qualify for added aid may be more likely to be workless, and thus the method could not fully reflect the true potential benefit that another worker without this unobserved condition would get.[18] Nonetheless, country differences and trends over time should be quite revealing.

Let us begin by comparing the patterns for single parents because the differences are so striking. Figure 8.15 shows the amount of benefits a single parent in Britain received on average by weekly earnings category. For someone with zero earnings, benefits were roughly flat at £130 during most of the 1980s, then rose significantly during the 1990s to nearly £170 in 1999. As noted before, about 65 percent of this increase was due to rising housing aid. For someone earning from £1 to £150 per week, benefits averaged £95 and rose to £120 by 1999.

Compare this to the benefits in the United States, as shown in figure 8.16. In deriving these and the other charts for the United States, we have excluded the disabled and widows who have quite generous programs of support, and who would distort the comparisons. Comparison between weekly benefits in pounds in Britain and annual benefits in dollars in the United States can be tricky. In purchasing power parity terms, if one multiplies weekly benefits in pounds by roughly 80, one gets annual dollars. Figure 8.16 is scaled so that the range is roughly equivalent in annual dollars of purchasing power parity to that of the British benefits. Thus visual comparisons between them give a sense of generosity.

Several facts stand out immediately in the United States. First, benefits for zero earners have fallen throughout this period, and the fall has been particularly dramatic in the past five years. This trend can be traced first to the fact that AFDC benefits were not indexed to inflation, and then to the effects of welfare reforms at both the state and national levels in the early to mid-1990s.

Second, benefits for those with moderate earnings—$7,500 to $15,000—dipped considerably in the early 1980s, were flat until the early 1990s, and then rose sharply in recent years. These former changes are the result of Reagan-era cutbacks in aid to working poor families on AFDC, the latter the effects of the dramatic expansions in the EITC. There is one mild puzzle here. Benefits have begun to drift down again. This appears to be the result

18. The extreme example of this situation would be a disability program that paid vastly higher benefits to the disabled, but that others could not qualify for. Failing to control for disability might lead one to inappropriately predict that all persons with zero earnings would get high benefits, when in reality, only those with disabilities would. Such a disability program does exist in the United States. However, we control for disability status in our model. And there is a bias in the other direction. Some people with zero earnings actually do not qualify for aid, either because they do not meet asset tests or because their zero earnings represent measurement error in the data. These persons would get zero benefits, which would tend to pull the projected benefits for zero earners downward.

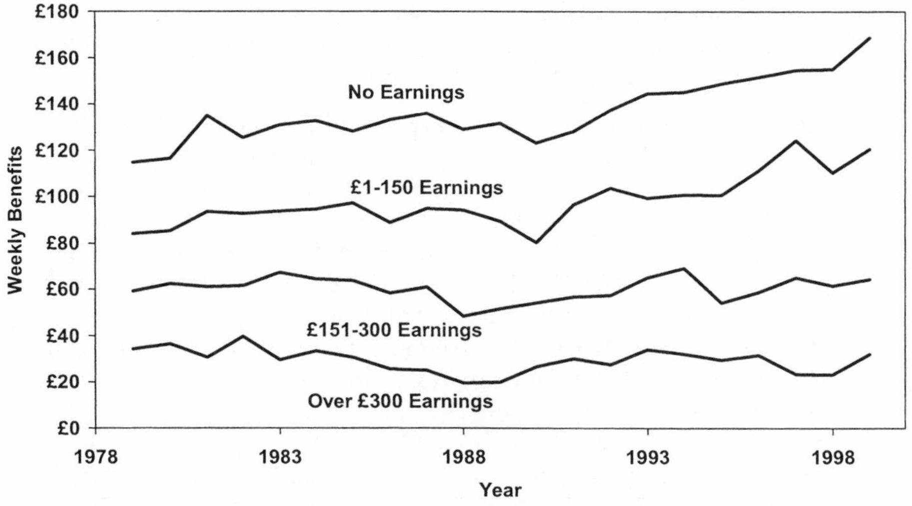

Fig. 8.15 Benefits for singles with children in Britain, by weekly earnings category

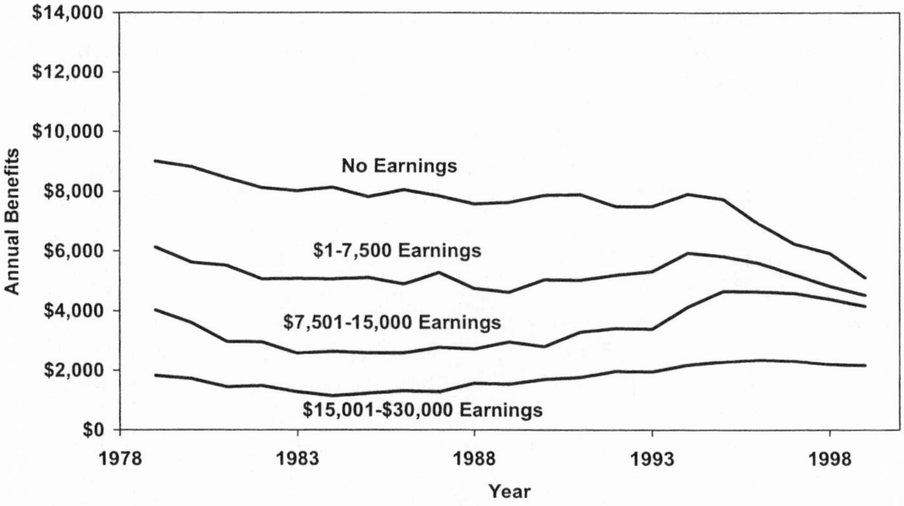

Fig. 8.16 Benefits for single-adult-headed households in the United States (nondisabled, nonwidowed), by annual earnings category

of reductions in food stamp and other benefits, for there have not been any statutory cuts at the national level. In any case, by 1999, the difference in benefits for someone with zero earnings and someone earning up to $15,000 were small.

Of particular relevance to the factors influencing poverty, the benefits for zero earnings are now considerably lower than in Britain, even though wages are often much higher in the United States. In purchasing power weekly equivalents, the U.S. benefit for a zero earner is only £65 per week.[19] Even the benefits of the 1980s were only the equivalent of £100. Thus,

- The benefit structures for single parents and the trends over time look dramatically different in the United States and Britain. In the United States, benefits received by zero-earning single parents have fallen dramatically in recent years and benefits to those with low to moderate incomes have risen sharply. By contrast, in Britain, benefits (largely due to rises in housing aid) have risen sharply for zero-earning single parents and incentives for work have, if anything, worsened.
- The average benefit for a zero-earning single parent as a fraction of the current relative poverty standard for a family of three in Britain was 62 percent in 1999 and 92 percent as a fraction of the absolute standard. In the United States, this observed benefit for a zero-earning single parents is now just 19 percent of the relative poverty line and only 36 percent of the U.S. absolute poverty line. With British benefits far closer to the poverty lines, especially for absolute poverty, it should come as no surprise that benefit expansions had a relatively large impact on single-parent poverty, particularly absolute poverty, in Britain, while benefit changes had much smaller impacts on poverty rates in the United States.

Given the sharp difference in the trends in benefits and incentives between the two nations, it is at least plausible that benefit structures are influencing the divergent patterns of work, and we consider that issue in the next section.

But before looking at the question of behavioral impacts, we examine benefit patterns for other groups. Figures 8.17 and 8.18 show benefits for couples with children in Great Britain and the United States. The British patterns show a rise in benefits for those with zero and low earnings in the early 1980s, then a flattening in the mid-1980s, perhaps because the indexing system was changed. Whereas previously benefit increases were indexed to wage increases or price rises they were now tied only to price increases—and thus just kept pace with inflation. In the late 1980s a variety of housing-benefit changes were implemented that reduced such aid. In particular, a capital limit of £6,000 was introduced before an individual could qualify (see Evans (1996) for an excellent review). These probably ac-

19. The sharp decline in the number of persons with zero earnings in the United States probably causes this figure to be exaggeratedly low. Some of the zero earners are probably data errors, or people with sizable assets who qualify for no aid. In the extreme case where one ignores all those getting zero benefits, the average benefit for a zero earner is $7,200, down from $9,000 in the 1980s, still vastly lower than the British benefit. Moreover, one would generally expect a strong potential bias in the other direction among those getting aid. Persons who could get the highest benefits should be more likely to have zero earnings.

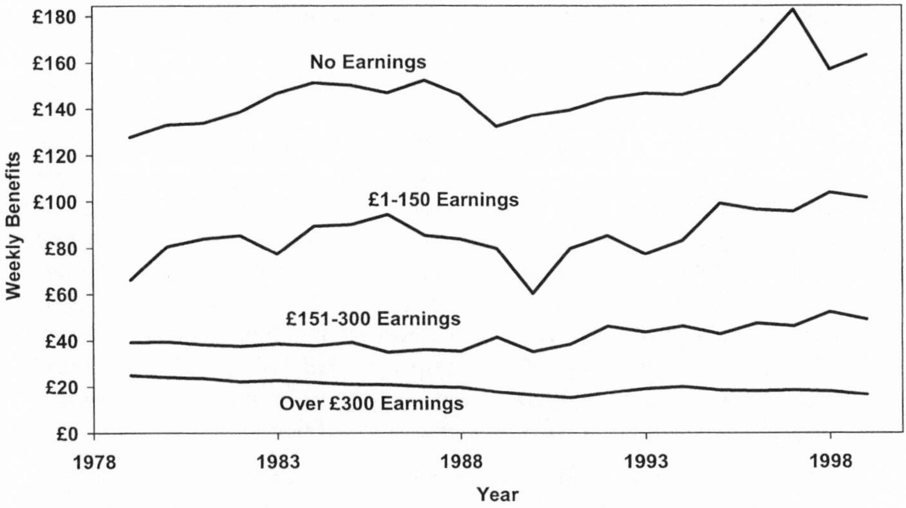

Fig. 8.17 Benefits for couples with and without children in Britain, by earnings category

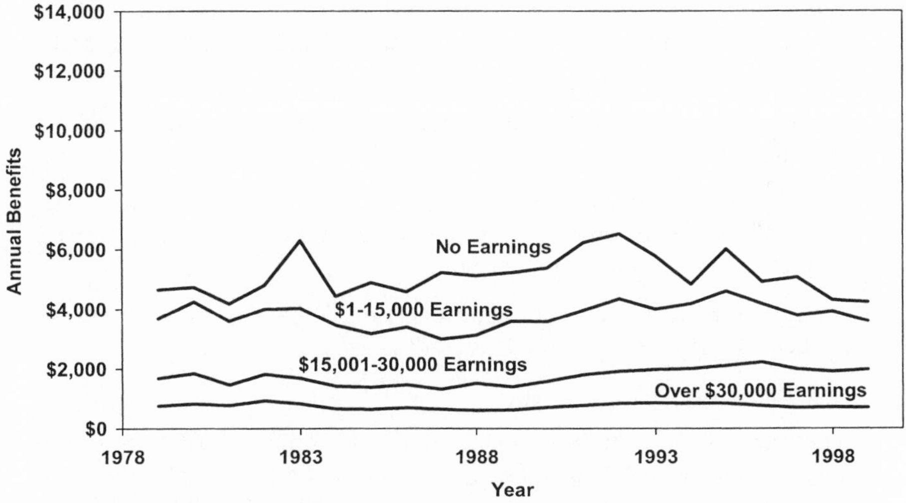

Fig. 8.18 Benefits for husband-wife households in the United States (nondisabled, nonwidowed) by annual earnings category

count for the benefit falls of the mid- to late 1980s. Finally, in 1986 the Social Security Act introduced wide-ranging reforms to the benefit system. The aim was to simplify the benefit system and to provide greater rewards to work. Supplementary Benefit was replaced by the simpler Income Support, which varied just by age and family structure. Family Credit replaced

Family Income Supplement in providing a supplement for low-income working families with children and was more generous than its predecessor. During this period benefits begin to rise again—about half due to housing-aid expansion as rents rose and capital limits were increased.

In the United States, benefits for couples are far lower and show far less change over time, though the changes vaguely mimic the patterns for single parents in that less and less aid is available for those with zero earnings and more is being offered for those with low to moderate earnings. Still, the striking feature of this figure is just how much lower benefits are for couples in the United States. One seeming peculiarity in the U.S. data can be readily explained. In years of recession the average benefits received by zero- and low-earning couples tends to jump up. That is because a group of former workers becomes unemployed and then qualifies for short-term (twenty-six to thirty-eight weeks) unemployment benefits.

- Benefits for couples differ considerably between the United States and Britain as well. British aid for low- and zero-earning families is considerably more generous and has become more so over time. In the United States, even couples with zero earnings average just $4,000–5,000 in aid, or the purchasing power equivalent of £50–65 per week. In Britain, couples with zero earnings now average £160 per week. It seems no wonder that in Britain, expanding aid has had a far larger role in reducing poverty.

The patterns of U.S./British differences persist when we examine aid for single adults (not shown):

- In Britain, benefits for single adults with zero earnings have also risen significantly over time. And in the United States, aid to nondisabled single adults is almost nonexistent.

We now turn to the most difficult question: What, if any, effects have these benefit structures had on behavior?

8.7.1 Behavioral Effects of Aid

There are several strategies that are commonly followed to determine the impact of benefits and benefit changes on work. The first is to attempt to calculate the actual level of benefits for which each family could qualify using measures of benefit levels, eligibility rules, effective tax rates, and the like and to treat these parameters as exogenous. One would then use these in a structural model of labor-supply behavior. There is a long history of such modeling in work in both Britain and United States.[20]

The difficulty of such methods when examining overall poverty patterns

20. See, for example, Bingley and Walker (1997), Blundell, Duncan, and Meghir (2000), Attanasio and MaCurdy (1997), and Moffitt (1986).

is that the wide range of often interacting benefits is difficult to model. Moreover, elements such as stigma, administrative complexity, and hostility/supportiveness of providers that sharply influence take-up rates severely complicate structural models. In the United States the recent changes have proven particularly hard to model (Ellwood 2000).

A second strategy is to include a variety of measures of the structure of benefits, such as maximum benefit amounts, tax rates, indicators of sanction regimes or time limits, and the scope of the EITC in a reduced-form labor-supply equation along with wages. Meyer and Rosenbaum (1999), Eissa and Hoynes (1999), and Meyer and Rosenbaum (2000) all offer good recent examples in the United States.

A final strategy is to compare behavior, over time, of groups of people whose incentives have been differentially affected by altered policy. Typically this work uses difference-in-difference techniques to look for evidence that the policy had an impact. This strategy or variations on it have been used by Eissa and Liebman (1996) and many others. One variation on this technique, used by Ellwood (2000), is to examine the changed incentives and track the work behavior of people at different parts of a predicted wage distribution. Often, policies affect only low-potential earners, and thus differential work behavior can be tied to changes in policy.

Our imprecise methods for estimating benefits and the enormous differences across countries largely preclude our use of the first two strategies. But we can at least use the models to gain a rough sense of how work incentives have changed over time in each country for people in different family settings who have differing potential wages, and to compare these to changes in work.

This methodology is discussed in detail in Ellwood (2000), so we will only briefly describe it here. We begin by predicting wages—this time without residuals—for everyone in our sample according to the 1979 wage model. We then use these predicted wages to break people into thirds in each year, separately for men and women. Thus, regardless of whether people worked, we have a predicted wage third. We can then track incentives and work for people in those thirds. Wage thirds make more sense than, say, educational levels, because the fraction with a given educational level changes considerably over time. We use the 1979 model for creating the wage thirds in each year to ensure that we really are tracking a comparable group over time, not following different people as returns to education and other variables shift.

Simple economic theory suggests that two factors ought to influence work decisions: first, the level of income/benefits the person would get in the absence of work (a pure income effect), and then the gain they would get by working (a substitution effect). We have already observed what happens to the benefits of persons and families with zero earnings: They rose over time in Britain for all family types, and benefits were considerably higher than in the United States. In the United States, benefits for non-workers fell over time, particularly for single parents. Thus, based on the income effect alone, one would expect work to fall in Britain and rise in the United States. But the substitution effect—the gain to working—also matters. Wages have risen in Britain (although less so in entry jobs) and benefit structures changed. It is possible that the gains to working have increased considerably as wages have gone up.

We used our model to get a rough sense of how the gains to work may have changed over time and across countries. For each person in the sample, we first predicted that person's potential wage if he or she worked using the wage equation of their sample year. Once again, we do not project residuals to avoid some forms of selection bias. We then use our benefits models to predict what benefits the household would get if the person did not work, and what would be received if the person worked full time at the predicted wage.[21] To simplify this analysis, we looked only at work behavior of the heads and partners for this work—the income of others was taken as given. For couples, we estimated benefits under a variety of joint work assumptions.[22]

Finally, we calculated a very simple predicted gain to work from earnings less benefit changes. We did so by adding the gain in earnings to the predicted benefits given this level of earnings and then subtracting the benefits the individual would have gotten had he or she not worked. This gain to work is decidedly *not* a full measure of the returns to working. We take no account of childcare costs, work expenses, or income or payroll taxes in the two countries. But we do at least have a sense of how the gains from work due to earnings plus benefit offsets have changed over time.

Single Parents

We again start by looking at single parents. We have already seen that benefits for those with zero earnings rose quite significantly over time in Britain and fell precipitously in the United States. What happened to the gains to work from earnings less benefit changes? Figures 8.19 and 8.20 show the results for Britain and the United States by predicted wage third. Once again we see large differences:

21. Note that the predicted wage used to determine benefits is based on the equation for that year. The predicted wage used to classify people into potential wage thirds is based on the 1979 model.

22. Note that this methodology could overpredict the potential wage for those who do not actually work, since those not working are more likely to have a negative wage residual. Gregg, Johnson, and Reed 1999 use "entry wages" for different groups of workers to model the expected wage. But since we are looking at potential gains to work for workers at different levels of education and age, the entry-level wage is not appropriate for use here. Additionally, entry jobs have increasingly become part time, and many of these would not be entry-level workers if they worked.

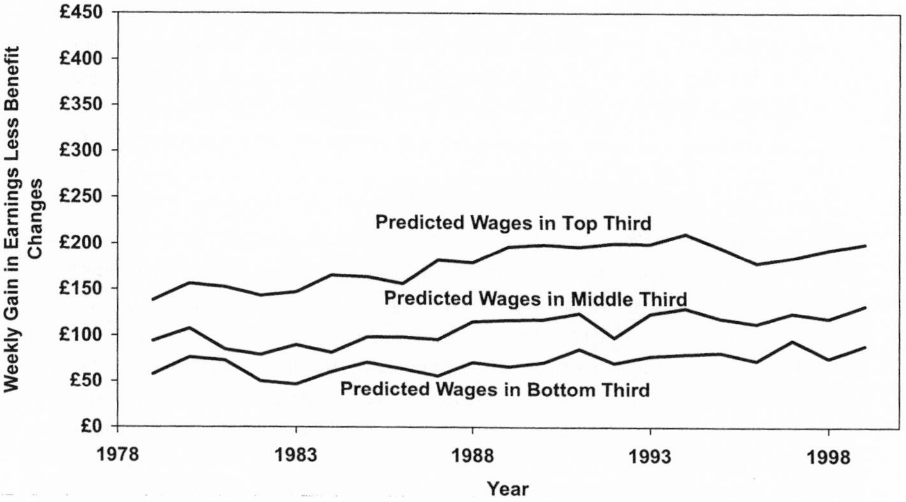

Fig. 8.19 Predicted gain in earnings less benefit changes for full-time work: single parents in Britain, by predicted wage class

Note: Predicted wage class: terciles of all men or of all women based on predicted wages (1979 models) in each year.

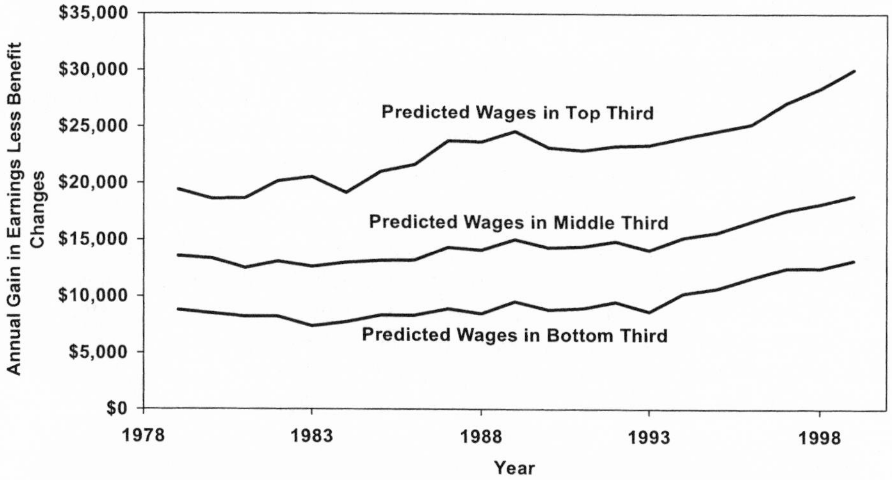

Fig. 8.20 Predicted gain in earnings less benefit changes for full-time work: single parents in the United States, by predicted wage class

Note: Predicted wage class: terciles of all men or of all women based on predicted wages (1979 models) in each year.

- For British single mothers, the predicted gain in earnings less benefit changes from entering work has risen over time somewhat, primarily because of rising wages. But the gain from work for women in the bottom third of predicted wages has risen from just £57 to £89 per week. And this ignores the costs of childcare, work expenses, and taxes. Even for single mothers in the top third, the gains from work average £200 per week—or the U.S. equivalent of less than $16,000 per year.
- For single mothers in the United States, the gains in earnings less benefit changes from working are significantly higher and they have risen dramatically. In percentage terms, gains were particularly great for single mothers in the lowest third, although in absolute terms they were greater for women in the top third. The gain (from earnings and benefits alone) for single mothers in the bottom third rose roughly $4,500 since 1993 (British equivalent of £60 per week). Single mothers in the top third stand to gain nearly $30,000.

Again, we emphasize that these gains are not the whole story. But adding other elements would, if anything, make things more dramatic. In the United States, Ellwood (2000) calculates that the returns to working, after taking out childcare costs and taxes and adding in other benefits such as aid for childcare, have risen from under $2,000 to over $7,000. The change in returns is quite close to what is predicted here, but the starting levels are lower due to accounting for other expenses.

Combining the effects of vastly higher benefits when not working and continuing low returns to work, one would presumably expect work to decline among single mothers in Britain, especially at the bottom. In the United States one would expect to see the reverse. Figures 8.21 and 8.22 show that the predictions are borne out, though not perfectly.

- consistent with changed work incentives, single parents in Britain are working less and those in the United States working more. Consistent with theory, gains in work are particularly great among low-wage single parents in the United States. One puzzle, however, is that in Britain, work declines were about as large for people in all three wage thirds. One would generally expect social policies to have their greatest impact for those with the least earning potential.

Couples

The work incentives for couples are a bit more complicated because there are four different combinations of work and nonwork for the partners—more if one allows for part-time work. Rather than focus on all of these, we shall present only two: the gains in earnings plus benefit changes if the man goes to work full time and the woman is not working, and the gains from work if the woman works full time when the husband is already working full time. Obviously, the other combinations are plausible, too,

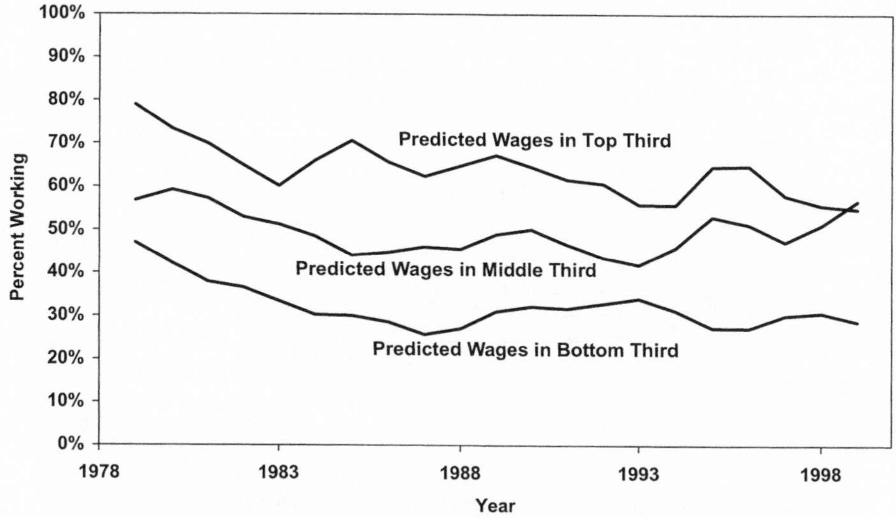

Fig. 8.21 Percentage working among singles with children in Britain, by predicted wage third (three-year centered moving averages)

Note: Predicted wage third: terciles of all women based on predicted wages (1979 models) in each year.

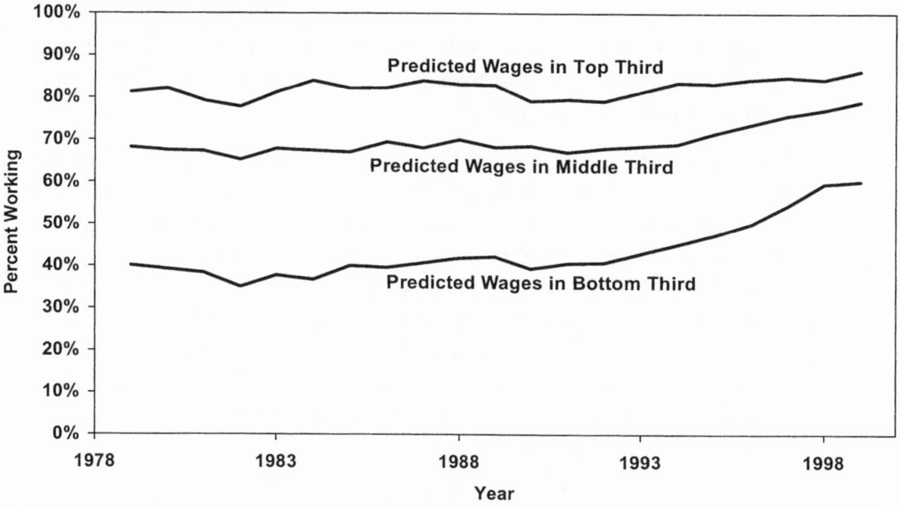

Fig. 8.22 Percentage working among singles with children in the United States, by predicted wage third

Note: Predicted wage third: terciles of all women based on the 1979 wage equation.

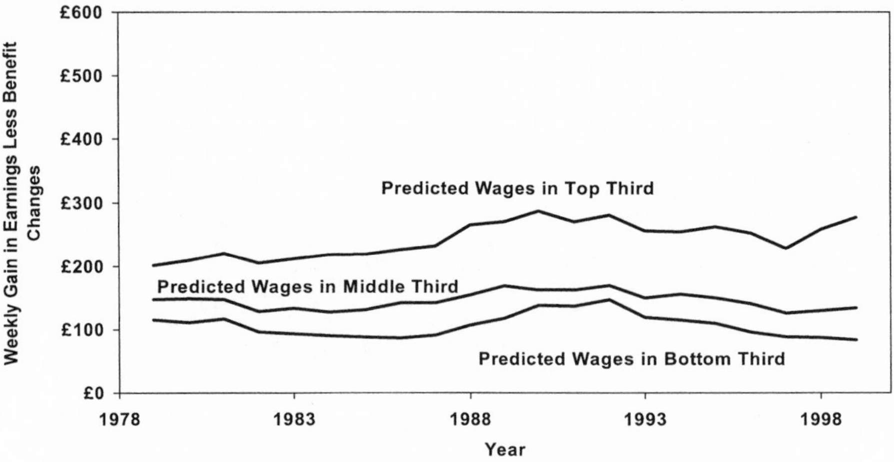

Fig. 8.23 Predicted gain in earnings less benefit changes for full-time work: men in couples with children in Britain, by predicted wage class (assuming the partner is not working)

Note: Predicted wage third: terciles of all men based on the 1979 wage equation.

but this gives the rough incentives for families considering sending one or two people into the labor market.

Figures 8.23 and 8.24 show the gains to sending the man into full-time work in an otherwise workless household in Britain and the United States. Once again we find striking differences. As always, scales are roughly equilibrated to purchasing power equity.

- There are very large differences by country in the gains to working for a man if he is to be the only worker in a joint household. In the United States, even someone in the bottom wage third can expect to see gains in earnings and benefits of close to $17,000 per year (£217 per week), and this has risen somewhat in recent years. In Britain the gain is just £82 per week, and this amount has fallen sharply since the early 1990s. Even those in the middle third stand to gain just £130 (U.S. $10,200) from a full-time job. In the United States, with lower benefits and higher median wages, workers in the middle stand to gain nearly $25,000 in earnings less any benefit changes.

Given the rising aid for those not working and low and declining returns for those in the bottom third, one would anticipate declines in work by men in Britain and, if anything, increases in work in the United States. Figures 8.25 and 8.26 show the actual patterns.

- Work by men in couples is clearly cyclical; consistent with altered incentives, however, work declined overall among men in Britain,

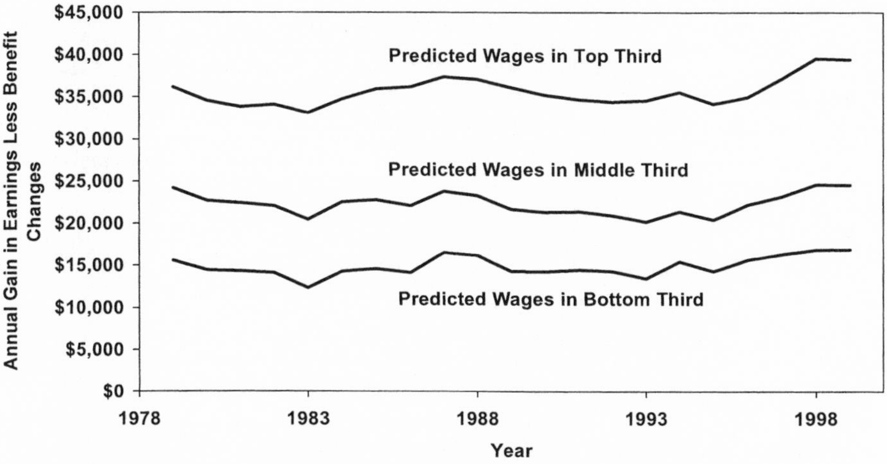

Fig. 8.24 Predicted gain in earnings less benefits changes for full-time work: husbands with children in the United States, by predicted wage class (assuming the wife is not working)

Note: Predicted wage third: terciles of all men based on the 1979 wage equation.

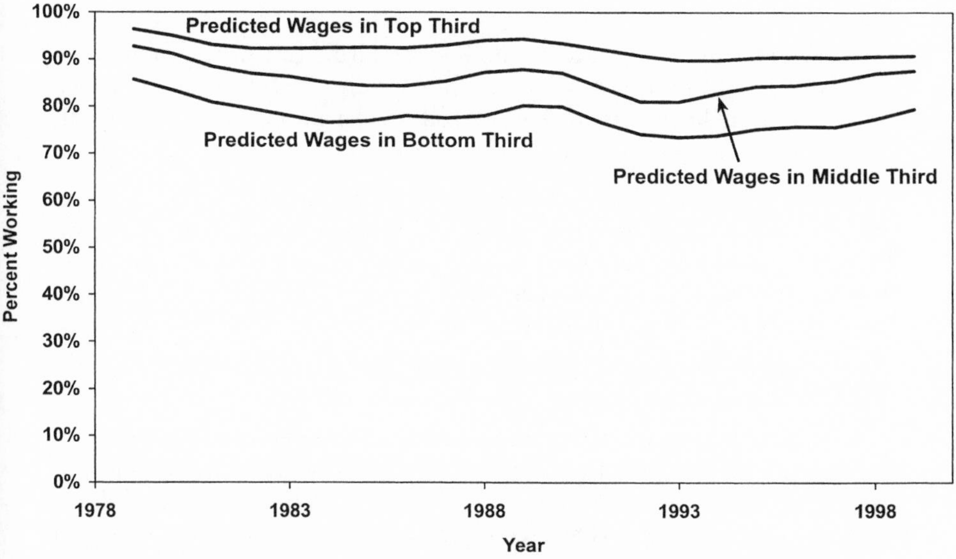

Fig. 8.25 Percentage working among males in couples with children in Britain, by predicted wage third (three-year centered moving averages)

Note: Predicted wage third: terciles of all men based on the 1979 wage equation.

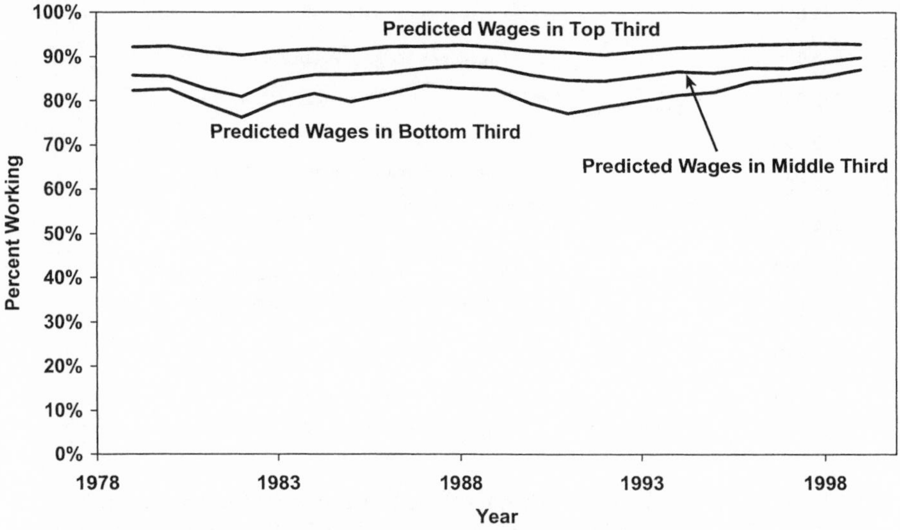

Fig. 8.26 Percentage working among husbands with children in the United States, by predicted wage third

Note: Predicted wage third: terciles of all men based on the 1979 wage equation.

particularly among men in the lowest third. And work among husbands with children rose in the United States.[23] Still, we again see the result that declines in work were sizable even among those in the highest wage categories in Britain.

One puzzle in the British data is why work by female partners is rising rapidly while work by male partners is declining. Figures 8.27 and 8.28 give some hint as to why that might be occurring. If most of the women entering the labor market are in homes where the man is already working, these are families already getting relatively low benefits, so the decision to work is primarily a question of what can be earned net of child care and work expenses.

- In Britain, the gains from sending a second worker into the labor market are much higher than for sending the first worker. Whereas a man in the bottom tercile who is the first earner in a household gained just £82, a woman who is the second earner in such settings would gain over £150 per week even though her gross pay is lower. In the United States, a comparable woman in the bottom third would gain perhaps

23. The rise in work in the United States is all the more remarkable since disability programs expanded and work by men overall did diminish somewhat.

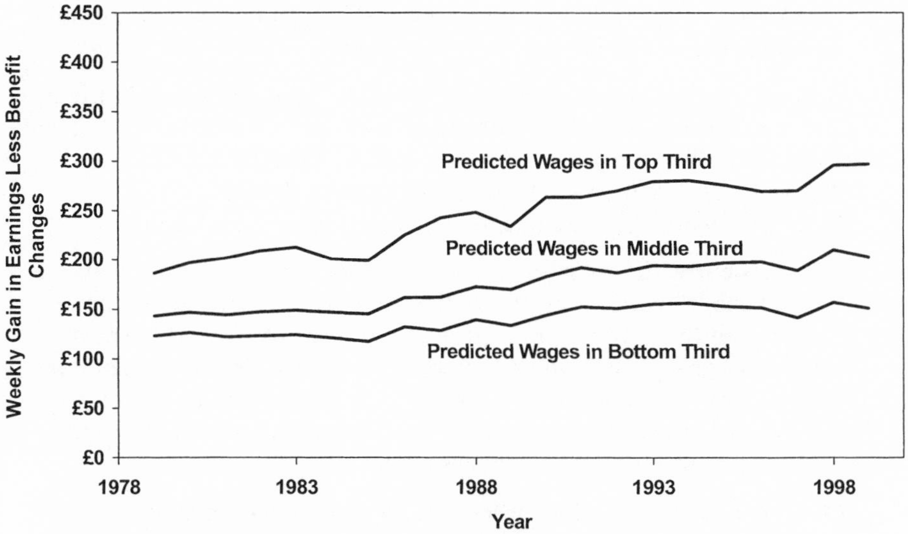

Fig. 8.27 Predicted gain in earnings less benefit changes for full-time work: women in couples with children in Britain, by predicted wage class (assuming partner already works full time)

Note: Predicted wage third: terciles of all women based on the 1979 wage equation.

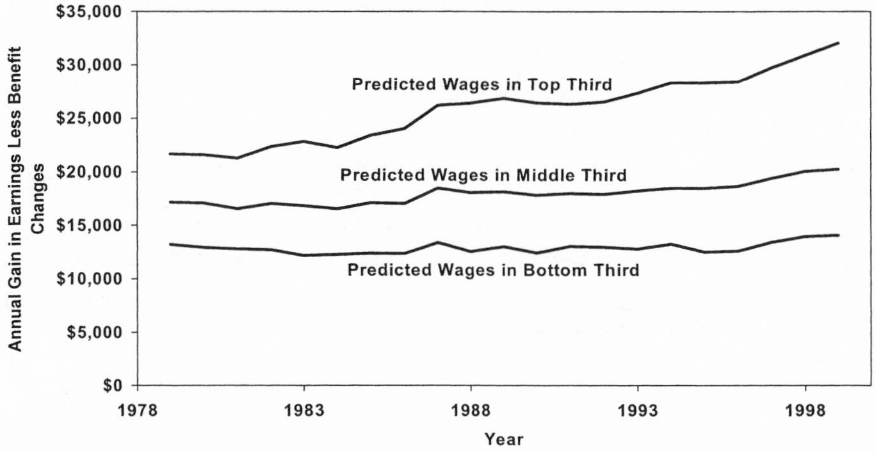

Fig. 8.28 Predicted gain in earnings less benefit changes for full-time work: wives with children in the United States, by predicted wage class (assuming husband already works full time)

Note: Predicted wage third: terciles of all women based on the 1979 wage equation.

$14,000 (£180). Women in higher wage thirds gain considerably more and the gains have been growing over time.

Actually, this example does illustrate some limits to our admittedly rather imprecise methodology. Others have shown that returns to work for women at the bottom have fallen somewhat in recent years due to the EITC, whereas this analysis shows things to be unchanged.

Figures 8.29 and 8.30 indicate work patterns of women in couples.

- Consistent with observed incentives, women in couples are working more in both nations. In Britain the rise is particularly notable among women at the bottom—in contrast to the increasing worklessness for all other groups. By contrast, work by U.S. wives in the bottom third leveled off in the late 1980s and early 1990s, unlike the pattern for wives in higher wage categories. Both of these patterns are roughly consistent with observed changes in incentives.

Of course, there are many other reasons that women may be working more, including changing attitudes and expectations. Still, what is striking is that trends among women in couples in Britain and the United States are broadly similar, but differ in specifics in ways consistent with incentives. In Britain, the lowest-wage women increased work the most. In the United States, they increased it the least. And in both cases, their behavior defies the patterns of all other low-wage groups in the country. In Britain, where all other low-skill workers are working less, low-skill wives are working

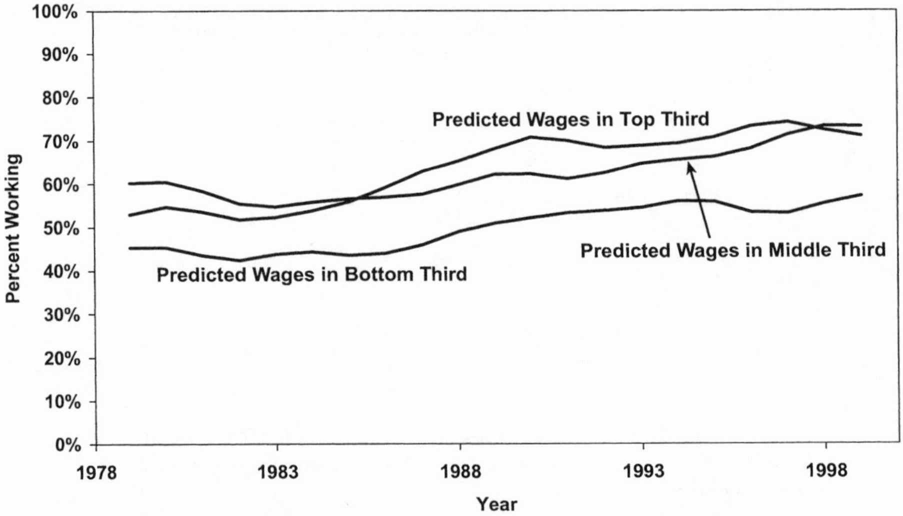

Fig. 8.29 Percentage working among women in couples with children in Britain, by predicted wage third (three-year centered moving averages)

Note: Predicted wage third: terciles of all women based on the 1979 wage equation.

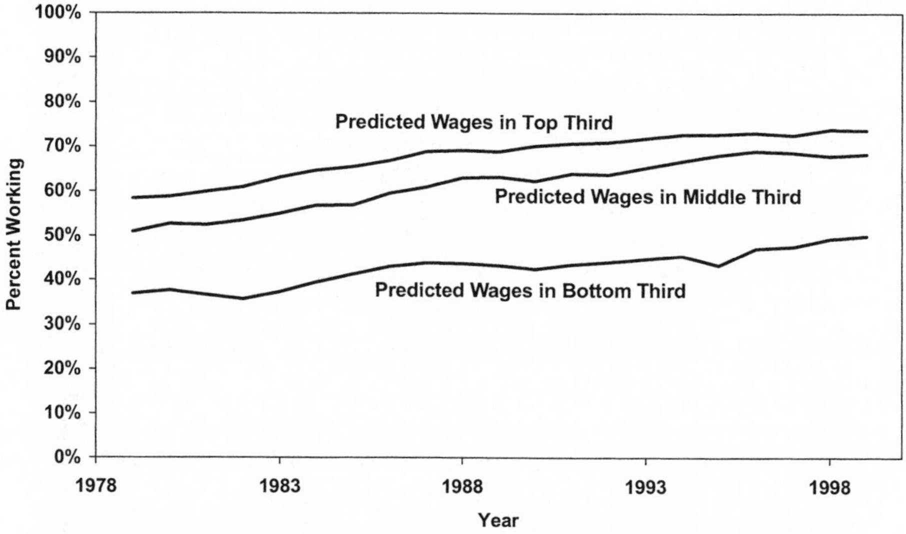

Fig. 8.30 Percentage working among wives with children in the United States, by predicted wage third

Note: Predicted wage third: terciles of all women based on the 1979 wage equation.

more. In the United States, where others are working more, low-skill wives have not increased their work. The results reinforce findings from Gregg, Hansen, and Wadsworth (1999), which suggest that the increasing polarization of work within couples in Britain may be related to features of the social benefit system that create weak work incentives among families with no workers, and relatively strong incentives for a second earner when one person is already working.

Singles without Children

Finally, we examined work incentives and work behavior in the two nations (not shown).

- In general, the returns to working seem to have changed little for single adults in the two nations. But the sharp rise in benefits for those with no earnings (the income effect) in Britain coupled with no change in the gains to working would be expected to reduce work by singles in the bottom third. That is precisely the pattern on finds in the British data.

Conclusions Regarding Behavioral Results

Our examination of the broad trends in work incentives suggest that they may explain an important part of the divergent trends in the United States and Britain.

- In general, incentives to work were always stronger in the United States and particularly for single parents they have recently become much stronger. By contrast, incentives for work in Britain have generally weakened over time—benefits for nonworkers have risen, and gains to work have fallen in some cases and been stable in others. There is one exception: gains to work by second earners have increased somewhat. And wives are the only group working more in Britain. Still, declining work even among the highest potential wage group suggests that more than just work incentives is operating here.

8.8 Reducing Poverty: Potential and Limits of Work-Based Strategies

Prime Minister Tony Blair's government committed itself to reducing child poverty by half over the next ten years and to its abolition within twenty years. A central element of this effort has included a series of policy initiatives designed to encourage work and to "make work pay." The main changes in Britain are the introduction of the Working Families Tax Credit (WFTC), which provides generous support for low-income working families and includes a (potentially very generous) childcare element; the National Minimum Wage; reform of the National Insurance system; the introduction of a 10 percent starting rate of income tax; and the National Childcare Strategy. These policies have been combined with various New Deal policies, most of which impose participation in work or training as a condition of benefit receipt. Furthermore, benefits to all families with children, regardless of work status, have become more generous with real increases in child benefit and income support and the introduction of the Child Tax Credit.

Table 8.2 helps to illustrate the larger themes of this paper, and points to the potential and the limits of work-based policies as a central element in reducing child poverty. The table shows the distribution of poor children by total work hours of everyone in the household. The first column shows that currently over half of poor children are in homes where no one is working, and only a third are in homes where people are working thirty hours or more.

- Unless demographic, economic, or policy change induces more parents of children to work, the only way to reduce poverty by 50 percent would be to reduce poverty among nonworking families. *Absent behavioral change,* added support for working families will still leave the majority of poor children poor.

The table also shows what would happen to child poverty if one could magically return to the work levels of 1979, but retain the wage and demographic patterns of 1999. The percentage of children in poverty in the current setting and under this scenario can be seen in the second and fourth

Table 8.2 **Distribution of Poor Children by Work Hours of Family: Actual 1999 and Projected If Work Patterns Were Comparable to 1979**

	Actual Patterns in 1999		Projections If Work Patterns in 1999 Had Been Comparable to Those of 1979	
Total Hours Worked by All Persons in the Household	% Distribution of Poor Children by Work Hours of the Family	Children Who Are Poor and Living in Families with Given Work Hours (as percentage of all children)	% Distribution of Poor Children by Work Hours of the Family	Children Who Are Poor and Living in Families with Given Work Hours (as percentage of all children)
No work hours	51.1	17.6	37.7	11.0
1–29 hours	16.1	5.5	12.4	3.6
30 hours and over	32.8	11.3	49.9	14.5
All work levels	100.0	34.5	100.0	29.1

columns. The overall poverty rate would fall from 34.5 percent to 29.1 percent. Impressively, the share of all children who are poor and in homes where no one is working would fall from 17.6 percent to 11.0 percent. But overall poverty would not fall as much because the number of children in working poor families would rise. One can see that the percentage of all children who are poor and living in families with more than thirty work hours would rise from 11.3 percent to 14.5 percent.

- Work changes alone are unlikely to dramatically reduce poverty of children. Even if work levels could be restored to those of 1979, continuing low pay would leave many children poor. Many families would move from being the workless poor to the working poor. Poverty would fall by only 5 percentage points (out of 35 percent).[24]

But if many more people were induced to work *and* work were made to pay, the goal of reducing child poverty by half might be achieved. In the fourth column of table 8.2, one can infer that if work were at the 1979 levels and if those who would otherwise be poor in families with thirty or more hours of work were removed from poverty, only 14.6 percent of all children would remain poor (the 11.0 percent in families that would still not be working and the 3.6 percent in families with 1–29 work hours).

- If work could be increased back to the 1979 levels, and if work were made to pay sufficiently so that no family with thirty hours of work was left poor, then poverty among children could fall from its current level of roughly 35 percent to approximately 15 percent, achieving the

24. Other evidence in support of this conclusion comes from the U.S. experience where rising work had very small effects on relative poverty. It did have large effects on absolute poverty, because the absolute poverty standard is so much lower in the United States.

goal of a 50 percent reduction in poverty. If the make-work-pay policies reduced poverty among those who were working part time as well, poverty could fall still further.

Thus, at least theoretically, a work-based strategy could significantly reduce poverty among children. Still, this table assumed that work levels that prevailed in the late 1970s could somehow be restored and that work really could be made to pay enough to keep families out of poverty. Is that level of change really feasible?

Clearly the United States has successfully raised work among low-income families, notably single parents. But the differences in the U.S. and British benefit systems are enormous. Single parents in Britain with zero earnings get benefits equivalent to just 62 percent of the relative poverty standard. The United States pays just 19 percent! Two-parent families and single adults without children get even less. To mimic the financial work incentives in the United States, benefits for nonworking families would have to be cut enormously for all families while maintaining aid for working ones. And, of course, cuts in benefits for nonworkers will surely raise poverty or increase hardship among those with little or no earnings.

Alternatively, aid for working families could be expanded dramatically, while maintaining support for nonworking families. This would also help in ensuring that working families avoid poverty. Dilnot and McCrae (1999) show that WFTC is well targeted as a redistributive tool, with most gains going to households in the 2nd decile of the income distribution. Unfortunately, increases in in-work benefits of the sort enacted to date with the WFTC seem unlikely to change work incentives to the extent seen in the United States, especially if the change in policy is largely offset by housing benefit changes, as Blundell and Hoynes (chap. 10 in this volume) seem to suggest. The gap in income for workers and nonworkers is simply too limited, and the recent increases in benefits to all families with children may induce adverse income effects on labor supply. If the WFTC were greatly expanded, costs could rise sharply or benefits would need to be phased out so rapidly for working families above the poverty line that this would create another set of adverse incentives. Still, that may be a promising domain for further reforms.

The U.S. example may again be instructive. The United States spends more now on in-work benefits than it ever did on cash-based benefits for the nonworking poor. The gain from going to work has increased considerably. Benefits paid are large enough to pull families with four or fewer members and a full-time minimum-wage worker over the U.S. absolute poverty line of $17,356. But benefits are nowhere near enough to push people above a relative poverty line that exceeds $30,000. In table 8.1 we saw that increased work led to reduced absolute poverty but little change in relative poverty. Some observers believe it will be difficult fiscally and politically to increase in-work benefits a great deal more in the United States, and economists are increasingly worried about the adverse incentives created as benefits phase out when people move toward the middle class.

Of course, if the underlying pattern of wages could be made more equal, work might increase and poverty would fall. Altering the underlying distribution of wages would require rapid and effective intervention to narrow differences in skills and opportunity—and even that may not narrow wages too much (see Devroye and Freeman 2000).

One might hope that moving people into the labor market would lead to rising experience and, with that, higher wages and ultimately less relative poverty. Keeping people working steadily rather than episodically might narrow the wage distribution somewhat. But recent work by Burtless (forthcoming), Gottschalk (2000), and others suggests that wages rise even less with experience for low-skill workers than for others. Dickens's (2000) work on mobility and Stewart's (1999) on the low pay–no pay cycle offer a similar caution. Indeed, individuals are likely to require some form of in-work support or training that enables them to progress into better jobs.

The final strategy would be to find some way to reverse some of the demographic changes, particularly in family structure. Here the United States has virtually no lessons to offer. There are few clear policy strategies that successfully reduce the incidence of single-parent families—although there are some signs that recent increases in work among single parents in Britain may be partly due to a changing composition of this group.

Difficult as it might be to halve poverty through work-based strategies, it will be even harder to move toward complete elimination. Under almost any plausible scenario, a great many workless households will still remain, so even dramatic expansions of in-work benefits will probably not pull down poverty rates enough to meet the government's goal of halving poverty. One could also seek to raise benefits for all low-income families with children with larger child credits and similar schemes. Piachaud and Sutherland (2000) argue that measures of this type introduced by the Blair government are likely to have a significant impact on nonworking poor families. The difficulty with this strategy is that one is likely to dampen down the increased work incentives. Such a policy of increasing support to nonworking families while creating strong incentives may prove to be very costly, since it inevitably runs into the basic dilemma of reform—a high guarantee and strong work incentives imply a very high break-even point, so that benefits are collected by a very large portion of the population.

There are other ways to increase work beyond the use of financial incentives. In the United States and to a lesser degree in the United Kingdom, there is a move toward requiring work (in government subsidized jobs if necessary) as a condition of aid for some persons while providing more generous aid to those not expected to work, in an attempt to deal with this dilemma. But such policies raise difficult, value-laden issues of determining who is expected to work and determining penalties when they do not do so. We suspect that the changed attitudes and expectations of welfare workers and the public at large has had every bit as much to do with the rise in work among single parents as financial incentives have in the United States. British policymakers may need to pursue both sharp improvements in incentives and various administrative policies if they are really determined to increase work and reduce poverty.

This discussion should not be seen as pessimistic about the potential for work-based strategies to reduce poverty. But only a combination of strategies that dramatically increase work and increase the pay of low-wage parents seems likely to change things dramatically. And absent ways to narrow wage differentials or change family structures, sharply reducing poverty will prove a formidable and expensive challenge.

8.9 Concluding Thoughts

This paper has provided a strategy for decomposing the factors influencing poverty in Britain and the United States. Striking similarities and differences are at work in the two nations. Demographic and wage change is a dominant force in both nations. Work is falling among many low-wage groups in Britain but rising on the other side of the Atlantic. Social policies have increased incomes but may have reduced work in Britain, and they may have done the opposite in the United States.

The paper also suggests the potential for detailed cross-national examinations. The notion that the economic incentives built into policy are influencing outcomes within a nation are reinforced in this paper by the fact that when incentives differ in the two countries, so too do work patterns. And one can see far more clearly than most casual observers realize that social policies are often profoundly different. Ultimately, the hard work of policy analysis will probably remain a within-borders affair. But understanding the larger forces shaping poverty in several nations helps to illustrate both the potential and the limits of policies to reduce it.

References

Attanasio, Orazio, and Thomas MaCurdy. 1997. Interactions in family supply and their implications for the impact of the EITC. Stanford University. Department of Economics. Mimeograph.

Bingley, P., and Ian Walker. 1997. The labour supply, unemployment, and participation of lone mothers in in-work transfer programs. *Economic Journal* 107: 1375–390.

Blank, Rebecca, and Alan Blinder. 1986. Macroeconomics, income distribution, and poverty. In *Fighting poverty: What works and what doesn't,* ed. Sheldon H.

Danziger and Daniel H. Weinberg, 180–208. Cambridge: Harvard University Press.
Blank, Rebecca, and David Card. 1993. Poverty, income distribution, and growth: Are they still connected? *Brookings Papers on Economic Activity,* Issue no. 2: 285–325.
Blank, Rebecca, David Card, and Philip Robbins. 2000. Financial incentives for increasing work and income among low-income families. In *Finding jobs: Work and welfare reform,* ed. Rebecca Blank and David Card, 373–419. New York: Russell Sage.
Blundell, Richard. 2000. Work incentives and in-work benefit reforms: A review. *Oxford Review of Economic Policy* 16 (1): 27–44.
Blundell, Richard, Alan Duncan, Julian McCrae, and Costas Meghir. 2000. The labour market impact of the Working Families Tax Credit. *Fiscal Studies* 21 (1): 75–103.
Blundell, Richard, Alan Duncan, and Costas Meghir. 2000. Work incentives and in-work benefit reforms: A review. *Oxford Review of Economic Policy* 16(1): 27–44.
Böheim, René, and Stephen P. Jenkins. 2000. Do current income and annual income measures provide different pictures of Britain's income distribution? IESR Working Paper no. 16. London: Institute for Economic and Social Research.
Bound, John, and Timothy Waidmann. 1992. Disability transfers, self-reported health, and the labor force attachment of older men: Evidence from the historical record. *Quarterly Journal of Economics* 107 (4): 1393–419.
Burtless, Gary. Forthcoming. The employment experiences and potential earnings of welfare recipients. In *Welfare reform: 1996–2000. Is there a safety net?* ed. Robert Morris and John E. Hansan. Westport, Conn.: Greenwood.
Citro, Constance F., and Robert T. Michael, eds. 1995. *Measuring poverty: A new approach.* Washington, D.C.: National Academy Press.
Cutler, David M., and Lawrence F. Katz. 1991. Macroeconomic performance and the disadvantaged. *Brookings Papers on Economic Activity,* Issue no. 2:1–74.
Davies, Hugh, and Heather Joshi. 1998. Gender and income inequality in the U.K., 1968–1990: The feminization of earnings or of poverty? *Journal of the Royal Statistical Society* 161 (1): 33–61.
DeLeire, Thomas. 2000. The wage and employment effects of the Americans with Disabilities Act. *Journal of Human Resources* 35 (4): 693–715.
Devroye, Dan, and Richard Freeman. 2000. Does inequality in skills explain inequality in earnings across countries? Harvard University, Department of Economics. Mimeograph.
Dickens, Richard. 2000. Caught in a trap? Wage mobility in Great Britain: 1975–95. *Economica* 67 (268): 477–497.
Dickens, Richard, and David T. Ellwood. 2003. Child poverty in Britain and the United States. *Economic Journal* 113 (488): F219–F239.
Dilnot, Andrew, and Julian McCrae. 1999. Family credit and the Working Families Tax Credit. IFS Briefing Note no. 3. London: Institute for Fiscal Studies.
Eissa, Nada, and Hilary Hoynes. 1998. The Earned Income Tax Credit and the labor supply of married couples. NBER Working Paper no. 6856. Cambridge, Mass.: National Bureau of Economic Research, December.
Eissa, Nada, and Jeffrey B. Liebman. 1996. Labor supply response to the Earned Income Tax Credit. *Quarterly Journal of Economics* 112 (2): 605–637.
Ellwood, David T. 2000. The impact of the Earned Income Tax Credit and social policy reforms on work, marriage, and living arrangements. *National Tax Journal* 53 (4, Part 2): 1063–106.
Ercolani, Marco, and Steven Jenkins. 1998. The polarisation of work and the dis-

tribution of income in Britain. Discussion Paper. Institute for Labour Research. Essex, U.K.: University of Essex.
Evans, Martin. 1996. Fairer or Fowler? The effects of the 1986 Social Security Act on family incomes. In *New inequalities: The changing distribution of income and wealth in the United Kingdom*, ed. John Hills, 236–264. Cambridge: Cambridge University Press.
Goodman, Alissa, Paul Johnson, and Steven Webb. 1997. *Inequality in the U.K.* Oxford: Oxford University Press.
Gottschalk, Peter. 2000. Early labor market experience: Dead-end jobs or stepping-stones for less-skilled workers? Boston College, Department of Economics. Mimeograph.
Gottschalk, Peter, and Timothy Smeeding. 1997. Cross-national comparisons of earnings and income inequality. *Journal of Economic Literature* 35 (June): 633–687.
Gregg, Paul, Kristine Hansen, and Jonathan Wadsworth. 1999. The rise of workless households. In *The state of working Britain,* ed. Paul Gregg and Jonathan Wadsworth, 75–89. Manchester, U.K.: Manchester University Press.
Gregg, Paul, Paul Johnson, and Howard Reed. 1999. *Entering work and the British tax and benefit system.* London: Institute for Fiscal Studies.
Gregg, Paul, and Steven Machin. 1995. Is the U.K. rise in inequality different? In *The U.K. labour market,* ed. R. Barrell, 93–125. Cambridge: Cambridge University Press.
Gregg, Paul, and Jonathan Wadsworth. 2000. Two sides to every story: Measuring worklessness and polarisation at the household level. CEP Discussion Paper no. 1099. London: Centre for Economic Performance.
Gruber, Jonathan, and Jeffrey D. Kubik. 1994. Disability insurance rejection rates and the labor supply of older workers. *Journal of Public Economics* 64 (1): 1–23.
Haveman, Robert, Philip de Jong, and Barbara Wolfe. 1991. Disability transfers and the work decision of older men. *Quarterly Journal of Economics* 106 (3): 939–949.
Machin, Steven. 1999. Wage inequality in the 70s, 80s, and 90s. In *The state of working Britain,* ed. P. Gregg and J. Wadsworth, 185–205. Manchester, U.K.: Manchester University Press.
McClements, L. D. 1977. Equivalence scales for children. *Journal of Public Economics* 8:191–210.
Meyer, Bruce D., and Dan T. Rosenbaum. 1999. Welfare, the Earned Income Tax Credit, and the labor supply of single mothers. NBER Working Paper no. W7363. Cambridge, Mass.: National Bureau of Economic Research.
———. 2000. Making single mothers work: Recent tax and welfare policy and its effects. *National Tax Journal* 53 (4, Part 2): 1027–062.
Mishel, Lawrence, Jared Bernstein, and John Schmitt. 1999. *The state of working America 1998–1999.* Armonk, N.Y.: M. E. Sharpe.
Moffitt, Robert. 1986. The econometrics of piecewise-linear budget constraints: A survey and exposition of the maximum likelihood method. *Journal of Business and Economic Statistics* 4:317–327.
———. 1992. Incentive effects of the U.S. welfare system: A Review. *Journal of Economic Literature* 30 (March): 1–61.
Nolan, Brian. 1986. Unemployment and the size distribution of income. *Economica* 53:421–446.
Piachaud, David, and Holly Sutherland. 2000. How effective is the British government's attempt to reduce child poverty? CASE Working Paper no. 38. London: Centre for the Analysis of Social Exclusion.

Stewart, Mark B. 1999. Low pay in Britain. In *The state of working Britain,* ed. P. Gregg and J. Wadsworth, 225–248. Manchester, U.K.: Manchester University Press.
U.S. Bureau of the Census. 2000. Poverty in the United States: 1999. Current Population Reports, P-60, No. 210. Washington, D.C.: GPO.
United Kingdom. Department of Social Security. 1999. Households below average income: 1994/5–1997/8. London: Her Majesty's Stationery Office.

9 Mobility and Joblessness

Paul Gregg, Stephen Machin, and Alan Manning

Introduction

The perceived impact of location on economic opportunity has been a constant refrain in discussions of the economic performance of the United Kingdom for as long as anyone can remember and the source of much feeling that the British economy is not as flexible as it should be. In the 1980s the preoccupation was with the so-called "North-South divide," the contrast between the booming southern part of England with its economy based on the service sector and the depressed Northern regions whose economies were struggling to deal with the decimation of the heavy manufacturing on which they had previously depended in the Thatcher recession of the early 1980s. The North-South divide appeared to diminish in the recession of the early 1990s, but there have been concerns in some quarters that it is reemerging in recent years.

More recently attention has moved away from differences in economic opportunity at the level of very aggregated regions and toward differences at a much more local level (e.g., see Noble et al. 2000). A Cabinet Office report to the Prime Minister (Cabinet Office 1999, 11) noted that "the disparity within regions is at least as great as that between them." For example,

Paul Gregg is a reader in economics at the University of Bristol. Stephen Machin is professor of economics at University College London and the Centre for Economic Performance at the London School of Economics. Alan Manning is professor of economics in the department of economics and the Centre for Economic Performance at the London School of Economics.

We would like to thank Jordi Blanes-i-Vidal and Steve Gibbons for research assistance on this project, Savvas Savouri for providing some of the migration data, Abigail McKnight for providing the data on the origins and destinations of university graduates, and David Card, Steve Pischke, and other conference participants for their comments.

inner London has some of the highest unemployment rates in the whole country at the same time that the shops of Oxford Street have the highest level of vacancies in the country. After his victory in the 1997 election, Tony Blair set up the Social Exclusion Unit, which cuts across traditional ministerial boundaries to deal with the consequences of when people or areas suffer from a combination of linked problems such as unemployment, poor skills, low incomes, poor housing, high crime environments, bad health and family breakdown. Its existence is based on the idea that there is a need for joined up solutions to joined up problems. While there have always been rich and poor neighborhoods, there is also a feeling that the poorest areas have not shared in the growing prosperity of the country. At its most melodramatic, one might argue that Britain is ghettoizing.

Many commentators have felt that the structure of the U.K. housing market contributes to some of the spatial problems that the United Kingdom faces. In the early 1980s Hughes and McCormick (1981) argued that the level of subsidy and the allocation of housing within the council sector made council tenants very immobile and made the emergence of regions or pockets of unemployment more likely. In the 1990s Muellbauer and his coauthors (e.g., Muellbauer and Murphy 1997; Cameron and Muellbauer 1998) argued that the cult of owner-occupation together with financial market deregulation makes housing prices in the United Kingdom follow speculative bubbles that interfere with the workings of the real economy. And, more recently, Oswald (1996, 1997) has suggested that home ownership is bad (or sometimes it is private renting that is good) for unemployment.[1]

The plan of this paper is as follows. In the next section, we present evidence on the extent of regional inequalities in the United Kingdom and whether they have worsened over time. Regional inequalities in Britain are substantial, but they have always been so, and there is no strong evidence of a dramatic change over time. However, we also emphasize how successful the United Kingdom has been in creating an integrated national labor market for graduates and argue that the key to understanding how we can reduce regional inequalities lies, in part, in understanding the differences between the graduate and nongraduate labor markets. A number of possible reasons for the successful creation of an integrated graduate labor market are considered.

First, we show that regional migration rates are much higher for graduates than the less educated and that this is likely to be the main reason why the graduate labor market is more integrated. But why should migration rates be so much higher for graduates? It is argued that the returns to migration may well be smaller for graduates than others so that any explana-

1. An earlier version of this paper did contain a section evaluating this hypothesis, but the evidence for it in the United Kingdom was so weak that this has been dropped from the final version.

tion must be based on differing costs of migration. We consider a number of hypotheses.

First, it may be that the process of leaving home to go to college provides a psychological break with the region of one's childhood, and we do present evidence that graduates are less likely to take a first job in their parental region if they moved away to college.

Second, we go on to consider the determinants of residential mobility. Most existing studies have emphasized that residential and regional mobility in the United Kingdom is much lower than in the United States but that the unemployed are more likely to move than the employed. We argue that it is extremely rare for the unemployed to move regions without first having found a job. As vacancies for the less skilled tend to be advertised only locally, it is then very hard for the less skilled to move regions, and this is a major reason for the lower migration rates of the less skilled. When the labor market is booming, employers in the most prosperous regions may be forced to advertise more widely to recruit even unskilled workers. We then get the pattern (seen in the data) that it is easier to move to a high-employment region when times are good, although, ironically, it tends to be only when times are bad that anyone starts worrying about the low levels of regional mobility.

We also consider the impact of housing tenure on mobility. We argue that the apparent negative impact of being in council housing on regional mobility may have less to do with the rent subsidy associated with council housing and more to do with the demographic profile of tenants.

The paper then moves on to consider inequalities between neighborhoods. Using census data from 1981 and 1991 we show that there was little change in the of distribution of unemployment and nonemployment rates across neighborhoods. While there are big differences between rich and poor areas, there seems to be little evidence that these have worsened over time. We also consider one of the biggest changes to affect neighborhoods in this period, the sale of council houses. We show that, even in the neighborhoods with the highest rates of council housing, something like 20 percent of the stock was sold. Those likely to buy were much more likely to be better off (e.g., older households, those with dual earners, the more educated, and those from higher social classes). But we could find no evidence that sales of council houses resulted in a change in the social composition of a neighborhood other than the obvious impact of the change in housing tenure.

9.1 Regional Inequalities

Regional differences in economic performance are well known (see Blackaby and Manning 1990; Hughes and McCormick 1994; Evans and McCormick 1994) and will only briefly be summarized here. Panel A of

A

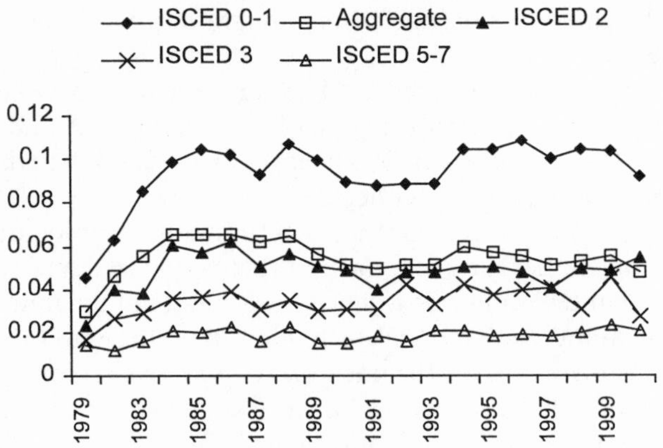

B

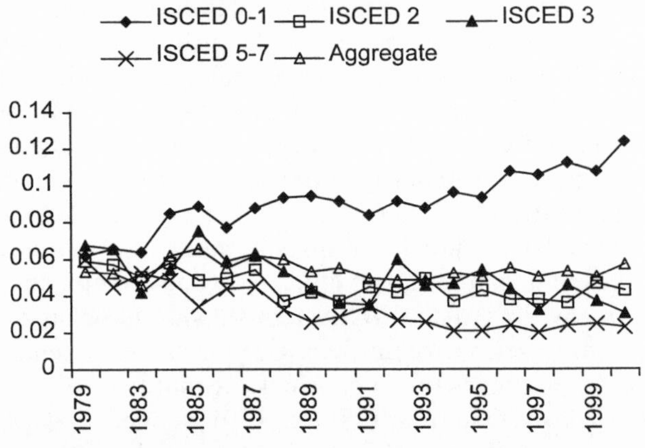

Fig. 9.1 *A,* The standard deviation of regional relative male employment-population ratios; *B,* the standard deviation of regional relative female employment-population ratios; *C,* the standard deviation of regional male unemployment rates; *D,* the standard deviation of regional female unemployment rates

Notes: A, This graph plots the population-weighted standard deviation of the employment-population ratio relative to the aggregate employment-population ratio across regions; *C,* these are the labor-force weighted standard deviations in the regional unemployment rates.

figure 9.1 presents the evolution of the standard deviation of the male employment-population ratio across regions. Several points stand out. First, there was a large rise in the standard deviation in the early 1980s, and although there has been a decline since, the gap is still wider than it was in the late 1970s. Second (as has been pointed out by McCormick, 1997, among others), regional differences are entirely the result of differences in employment-population ratios among less-skilled workers.[2] Panel B of

2. One should remember that the increase in educational attainment over time means that the low-skilled group is decreasing in importance.

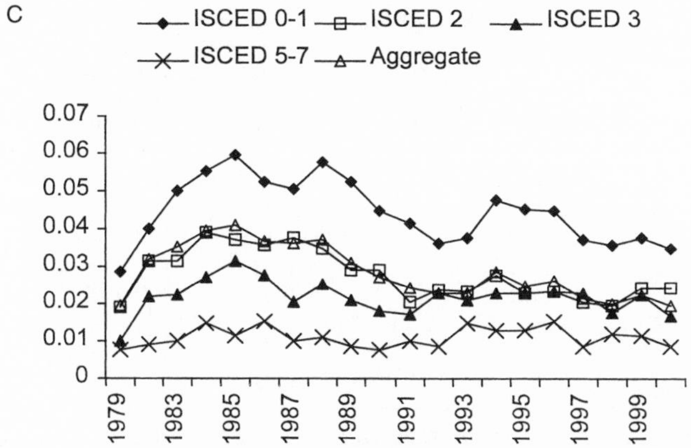

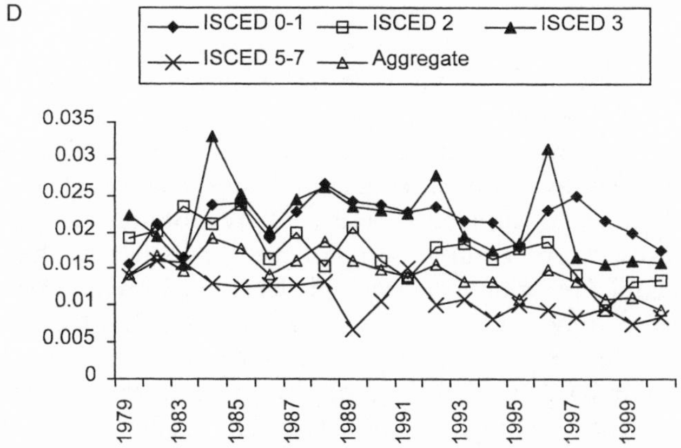

Fig. 9.1 (cont.)

figure 9.1 presents the standard deviation of relative regional female employment-population ratios, and panels C and D of figure 9.1 do the same for regional male and female unemployment rates. In all cases, the limited extent of regional inequalities among the educated is very clear.[3] For example, in 1999 the male employment-population ratio for university graduates (International Standard Classification of Education [ISCED] 5–7) ranged from 86 percent in South Yorkshire to 95 percent in the Southeast (excluding London), while that for those without educational qualifica-

3. In this paper we classify education using the ISCED measure: In the British education system ISCED 0–1 corresponds to those without any formal qualifications, ISCED 2 corresponds to those who left school at age sixteen but with some qualifications ("O" levels or General Certificate of Secondary Education [GCSEs]), ISCED 3 corresponds to those who left school at age eighteen with "A" levels, and ISCED 5–7 corresponds to those with some tertiary education (mostly college graduates).

Table 9.1 Persistence in Regional Unemployment Rates

Country/Education	Correlation Coefficient 79–99	89–99
United Kingdom		
All	0.77	0.86
ISCED 0-1	0.77	0.86
ISCED 2	0.58	0.69
ISCED 3	0.56	0.46
ISCED 5-7	0.28	–0.13
United States		
All	0.38	0.55

Note: These are the correlation coefficients for the unemployment rates across eighteen U.K. regions and fifty U.S. states.

tions ranged from 56 percent in Tyne and Wear to 82 percent in the Southeast (excluding London).

There are other ways of seeing that the United Kingdom has successfully created an integrated labor market for graduates. The previous figure shows us the variation in unemployment rates but says nothing about persistence. Table 9.1 presents some simple correlations to shed light on this issue.[4] Regional unemployment rates show a high degree of correlation over this period, but this is almost entirely the consequence of high correlations among the less educated. As a reference point (though differences in geographical size makes comparisons problematic) we also report the correlation in unemployment rates across U.S. states. The U.K. graduate labor market appears to be more integrated than the aggregate U.S. labor market. There is nothing intrinsic to the British character that makes an integrated national labor market an impossibility: One should look for more mundane explanations.

So far we have documented the extent of regional inequalities but without identifying their nature. Most popular discussion thinks of regional inequalities in terms of the North-South divide, but it is not obvious that this is the most striking geographical distinction one could make. Figure 9.2 presents the evolution in the unemployment rates and employment-population ratios for the North and the South and also for the metropolitan and nonmetropolitan areas. In many ways the gap between the metropolitan and nonmetropolitan areas is as striking as that of the North-South divide.

4. It might be better to estimate dynamic responses to regional shocks along the lines of Blanchard and Katz (1992) or Decressin and Fatas (1995). However, lack of data makes it impossible to do this disaggregated by education, and the correlations presented in table 9.1 should be thought of as a poor substitute.

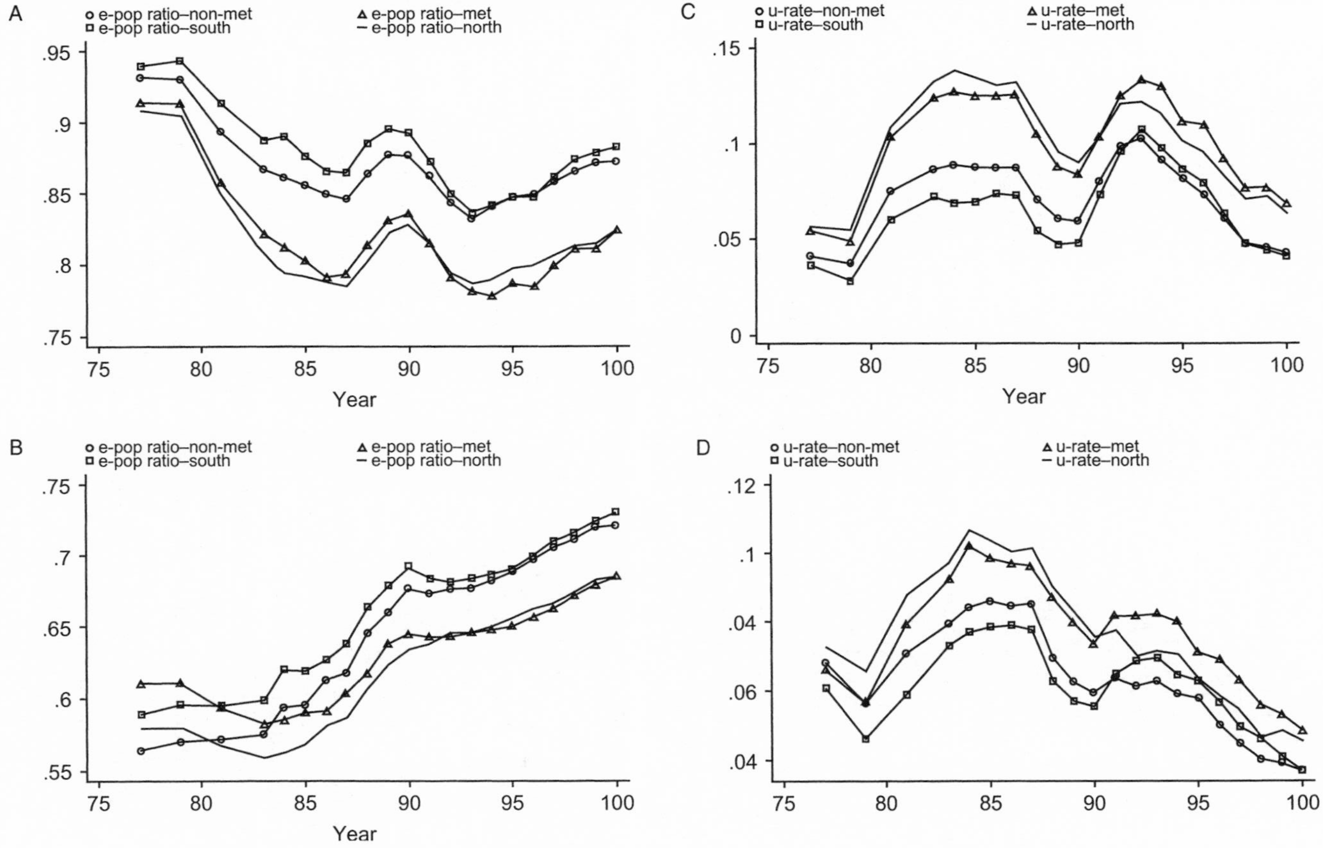

Fig. 9.2 The North-South divide and the met-non-met gap: *A,* male employment-population ratios; *B,* female employment-population ratios; *C,* male unemployment rates; *D,* female unemployment rates

We might also be interested in regional differences in wages. Comparison of the extent and evolution of regional wage inequality is complicated by the fact that it is obviously important to consider differences in real living standards, yet there are no official regional price indices for the United Kingdom. The main (and possibly the only) source of difference in regional prices is differences in housing costs. Duranton and Monastiriotis (2000) show that, although the aggregate figures appear to show an increase in regional inequality, this becomes a decline once one controls for differences in worker characteristics across regions and differences in regional living standards (see also Cameron and Muellbauer, 2000, for a discussion of the problems associated with the use of U.K. regional wage statistics).

There are a number of reasons why there might be more regional variation in employment and unemployment for the less educated. First, it may be that the shocks that affect regional labor markets are more substantial for the less educated. Second, it may be that the responsiveness to shocks is greater for the less educated (Hoynes, 1999, has presented some evidence for this in the United States). Third, it may be that regional migration acts as a "shock absorber" for regional shocks. It is difficult to distinguish between these hypotheses, although the fact that there is much more persistence in regional unemployment rates for the less educated suggests that migration might be the place to look for an explanation. This is the subject of the next section.

9.2 "On yer bike": Lack of Work and Residential Mobility

One way to escape any economic disadvantage associated with location is to move to a better area. In the 1980s the then Conservative minister for employment, Norman Tebbitt, observed that his father had not sat around on his backside in the Great Depression moaning about the lack of jobs: He had gotten on his bike and had looked for work. He is not the only person to have had similar thoughts. Over the years economists have worried about the lack of willingness of the British to move location to find work.

It is interesting to know whether overall residential and regional mobility rates have changed in the past twenty years. Figure 9.3 presents a time series on residential mobility rates over the past twenty years using Labour Force Survey (LFS) data. Residential mobility rates have varied between 10 and 13 percent, reaching a peak in the housing market frenzy of the late 1980s and then a trough in the subsequent crash (when house prices fell substantially). Figure 9.4 shows the evolution of regional mobility over the same period. The fraction of working-age individuals who have moved regions has only varied between 2 and 3 percent per annum in the last twenty-five years. The fraction coming from outside the United Kingdom has been very constant at about 0.7 percent, and the only variation has

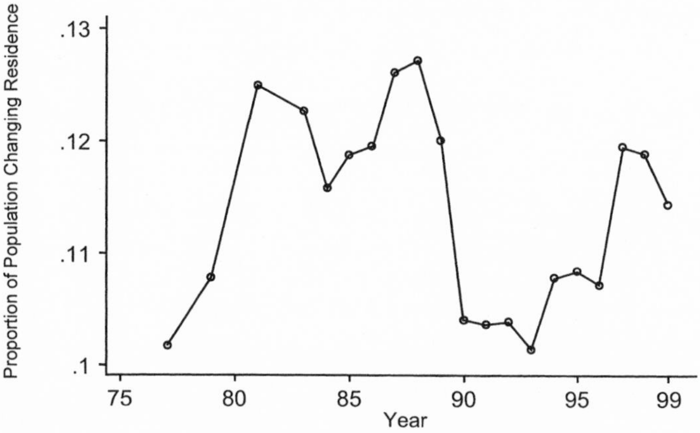

Fig. 9.3 Residential mobility in the United Kingdom, 1977–1999

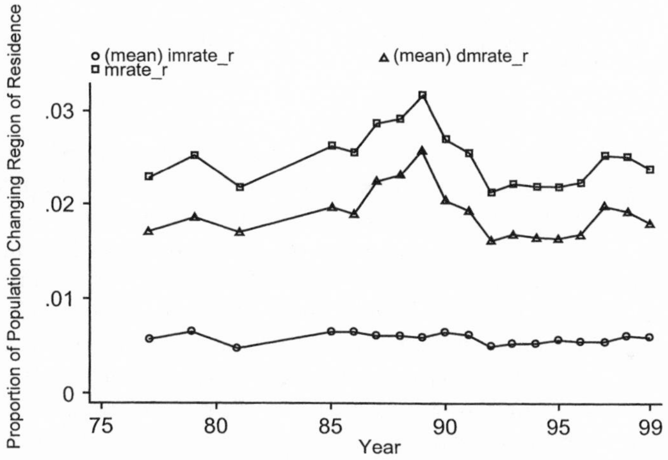

Fig. 9.4 Regional mobility in the United Kingdom: LFS data

Notes: The top line is the fraction of the population aged eighteen–sixty who have moved regions in the past year. The bottom line is the percentage who were outside the United Kingdom a year ago, and the middle line is the fraction who have moved regions within the United Kingdom.

been in regional mobility within the United Kingdom. As for residential mobility, there was a peak in the late 1980s and then a very marked decline, since which time there has only been a weak recovery. Figure 9.5 presents data on internal migration rates (for those of all ages) from a different data source: the National Health Service Central Register (NHSCR), which is based on people's changing doctors. Two series are presented with an over-

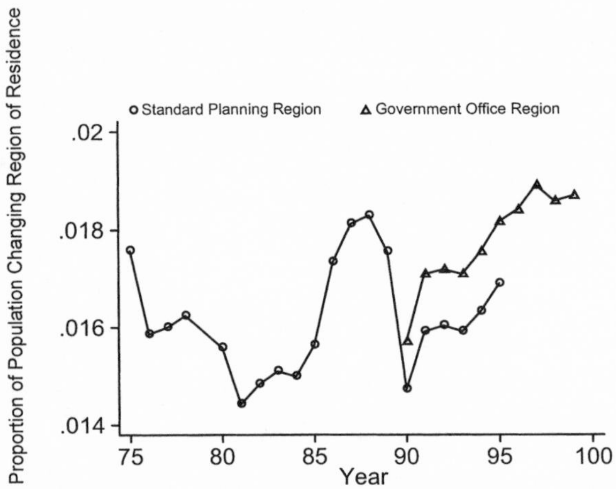

Fig. 9.5 Regional mobility in Britain: NHSCR data

Notes: This data comes from the NHSCR and is based on individuals changing doctors. It applies to all individuals.

lap, the first based on the old standard planning regions and the second based on the new government office regions.[5] Internal migration appears higher on the new regional definition and seems to now be at levels last seen in the late 1980s. Neither the LFS nor the NHSCR seems to support the second part of the claim by Hughes and McCormick (2000, 16) that there is "a striking increase in overall migration in the mid to late 1990s to rates in excess of those seen during any time in the last quarter century,"[6] but it does seem to be the case that regional migration is currently at levels similar to those seen at similar cyclical peaks in the past twenty-five years.

The U.K. mobility rates do not seem to be out of line with those found in other European countries. Table 9.2 uses data from the 1996–1997 wave of the European Community Household Panel (ECHPS) to calculate that around 8 percent of U.K. households moved in the year preceding the survey, which is in the middle of the range of mobility rates for the countries in the table. However, these numbers are considerably below those found in the "New World" countries (see Greenwood, 1997, table 1).

We saw earlier that there is much less regional variation in labor market outcomes for the more educated. Figure 9.6 shows that there is more regional mobility among the more educated with the regional mobility rate

5. The difference between the two is that Cumbria has been moved from the North to the Northwest region, and Bedfordshire, Essex, and Hertfordshire from the Southeast to the Eastern region. The latter change is by far the most substantive.

6. They use LFS data for the 1980s, but data from the Survey of English Housing for the 1990s. It is possible that the measures from the two data sets are not comparable.

Table 9.2 Residential Mobility Rates in European Countries, 1996–1997

Country	Moved in Last Year (%)
Austria	2.8
Belgium	6.9
Denmark	11.4
Finland	13.3
France	8.7
Greece	3.7
Ireland	4.5
Italy	3.9
The Netherlands	8.1
Portugal	3.4
Spain	4.3
United Kingdom	8.4

Note: Calculated from the 1996–1997 wave of the ECHPS.

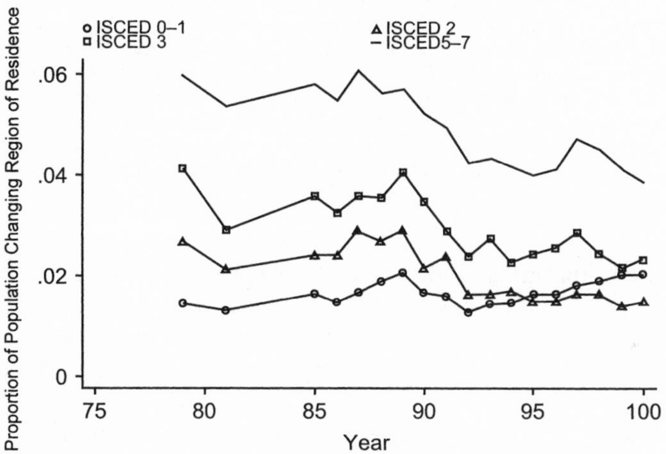

Fig. 9.6 Regional mobility in the United Kingdom, by level of education
Note: This data comes from the LFS.

for graduates currently being more than twice the level of that for those without any educational qualifications. But, interestingly, the gap appears to be narrowing: In 1979 the regional mobility rate for graduates was four times that of nongraduates.

Migration does not inevitably act to reduce differentials in unemployment: For it to have this effect it needs to be predominantly from high-unemployment regions to low-unemployment regions. A crude way of considering the extent to which migrants do tend to move in this direction is presented in figure 9.7, which presents the average regional male employ-

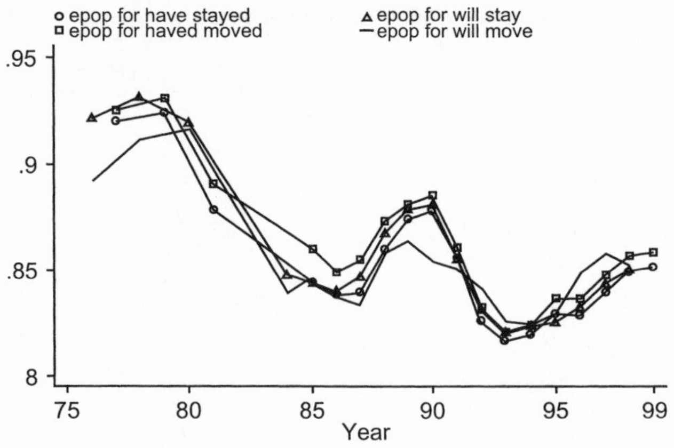

Fig. 9.7 Regional male employment-population ratios for movers and stayers

Notes: The employment-population ratio for those who will stay in their region is the employment-population ratio in the current region for those who do not move in the following year. The employment-population ratio for those who will move in their region is the employment-population ratio in the current region for those who do move in the following year (i.e., it is the employment-population ratio in the source region). The employment-population ratio for those who have stayed in their region is the employment-population ratio in the current region for those who have not moved in the past year. The employment-population ratio for those who have moved regions is the employment-population ratio in the current region for those who have moved in the past year (i.e., it is the employment-population ratio in the destination region).

ment-population ratios for those who have stayed in the same region in the past year, for those who have moved, for those who will stay in the coming year, and for those who will move. If those in high-unemployment regions are more likely to move we would expect to see a higher employment-population ratio for stayers compared to those who will move. And, if movers tend to go to areas of lower unemployment, we would expect to see a higher employment-population ratio for those who have moved compared to those who have stayed. The lines are very close, although there is some tendency for the movers to be in high-employment regions, particularly in the early 1980s recovery. This indicates that migration is only weakly related to unemployment differentials.

A somewhat clearer way of presenting the same information is in figure 9.8 where we compare the change in the regional employment-population ratios for those who stay in the same region and for those who move. If the movers are motivated by improved labor market conditions then we would expect the change in the employment-population ratio to be consistently above that for the stayers. On average, the gap is positive though small, a fact that, combined with the very small fraction of regional movers, suggests that regional migration does little to offset regional differences in labor market performance. There is also a marked tendency for the gap to be

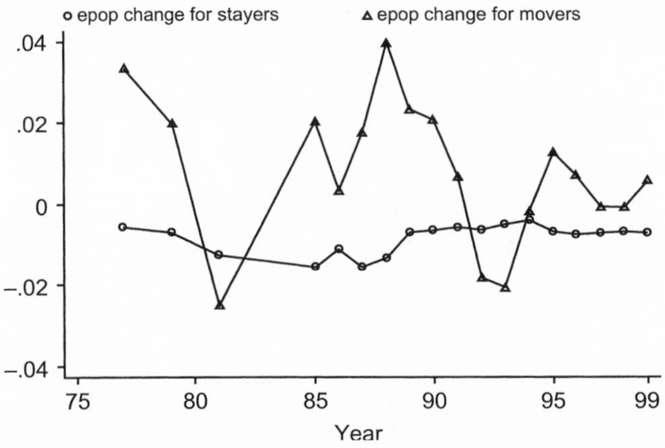

Fig. 9.8 Change in regional male employment-population ratios for movers and stayers

Notes: The employment-population change for stayers is the year-on-year change in the regional employment-population ratio for those who stay in their region. The employment-population change for movers is the year-on-year change in the regional employment-population ratio for those who move regions.

positive when the labor market is doing well (the late 1970s, the late 1980s, and the late 1990s). In recessions the gap is small, even negative. It seems to be easier to move regions for economic reasons when the economy is booming than when it is in recession.

Figure 9.9 examines whether there is any difference in this pattern for different education groups. It plots the difference in the change in the employment-population ratio for movers and stayers by education. There seems to be a tendency for the more educated movers to have bigger "gains," on average, than the less educated, but the gains for the less educated seem more cyclical. It is striking that through much of the 1990s less-educated regional movers actually seem to be moving into low-employment regions.

It is natural to see the difference in regional mobility rates by education as the main reason for why the graduate labor market is more integrated than that for less-educated workers. And an understanding of this difference might help us to think about how mobility for less-educated workers might be improved. There are a number of hypotheses:

1. The incentives for migration are highest for better-educated workers.
2. A major factor in determining choice of college among British students often seems to be the desire to escape from the parental home. This act of breaking away from the region in which one was brought up may make mobility easier later in life.
3. Recruitment for graduate jobs is often done at the national level with advertisements in the national press and magazines, whereas vacan-

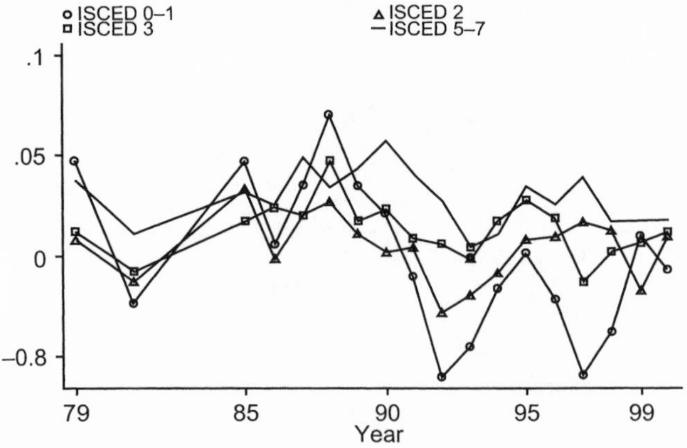

Fig. 9.9 Differences in the change in regional male employment-population ratios for movers and stayers, by education

cies in low-level jobs are typically placed in local job centers or the local press. This makes it hard to search for low-skilled jobs in regions where one is not living.

4. A higher fraction of less-educated individuals live in social housing, which has often been argued to discourage mobility (see Hughes and McCormick 1981).

9.3 The Economic Returns to Migration

It may be that the economic incentives for migration are higher for better-educated workers. Consider the following simple model for determining the economic incentives for migration. In any region, r, there will be a probability of employment, e_r; a real wage if in employment W_r; and a level of real benefits, B_r, if unemployed. Expected utility in region r, Y_r, will then be given by

$$Y_r = U(B_r) + e_r[U(W_r) - U(B_r)], \quad (1)$$

if the utility function is given by $U(\cdot)$. Given that housing benefit largely insulates the unemployed from variations in the cost of housing, it is probably not a bad approximation to assume that B_r does not vary across regions. Suppose we compare expected income in a potential region for migration with the home region (denoted by subscript h). We will have

$$Y_r - Y_h = e_r[U(W_r) - U(W_h)] + (e_r - e_h)U[(W_h) - U(B)]. \quad (2)$$

The economic incentives for migration will be higher, the higher the right-hand side of equation (2). There may be a return to migration because of regional differences in real wages or regional differences in employment rates. The importance of the latter depends on the gap between living standards when in and out of employment. The earlier discussion on regional wage inequalities suggested that, to a first approximation, there are only small differences in real regional wages so that it is the difference in employment prospects that provides the main motivation for migration in the United Kingdom. As we saw in figure 9.1, there are larger regional differences in employment rates among the less-skilled that, other things being equal, should mean that the incentive to migrate is higher for these workers. However, it is also true that the return to being in work $[U(W) - U(B)]$ is smaller for this group, and this tends to reduce the incentives to migrate.

Evaluating which effect is larger is a bit tricky as assumptions about the different employment prospects and about the marginal utility of income in different regions are needed. But let us make some back-of-the-envelope calculations using the average employment rate in different regions and assuming utility is given by the log of income. The gap in employment rates between the best and worst regions is about 0.10 for graduates and 0.25 for those without qualifications. The earnings gap between these two groups is approximately 50 log points. Using these numbers we will have that the return to migration for graduates is larger if

$$(3)\quad 0.10x[0.5 - \ln(R)] > -0.25x\ln(R) \Rightarrow \ln(R) > -0.33 \Rightarrow R > 0.72,$$

where R is the replacement ratio (B/W) for those without qualifications. The replacement ratio in the United Kingdom is normally thought to be below this level although it is sensitive to the treatment of housing costs. But this suggests that it is certainly not obvious that the economic returns to migration are highest for the more educated, and it is quite possible that the opposite is true. An explanation for the low rates of regional migration for the less educated should probably focus on the costs of migration rather than the returns.

9.4 Graduates and the Move Away from Home

In the United Kingdom, young people often move away from home when they go to college. For students studying full-time for a first degree in 1998–1999, just over half of the students were studying in a region that is not in the region where their parents live. The regional mobility among students going to college far exceeds levels of regional mobility found for any other group in the U.K. economy at any other point in the life cycle. One hypothesis for why the graduate labor market is more integrated is that the break with the parental region at age eighteen makes it easier to move regions later in life: If the individual has broken the ties of family and friends once, it may be easier to do it again.

There is some evidence for this if we look at the region in which under-

Table 9.3 **The Regional Destination of the First Jobs of Graduates**

			Study in Parental Region (%)		Do Not Study in Parental Region (%)		
Parental	Percent of Students	Percent Who Study in Parental Region	First Job in Parental Region	First Job in Other Region	First Job in Parental Region	First Job in Study Region	First Job in Other Region
East Anglia	3.3	23	75	25	43	25	32
East Midlands	7.2	26	72	28	39	27	34
Greater London	11.7	52	87	13	66	18	16
North	4.9	44	80	20	37	31	32
Northwest	10.7	45	85	15	47	25	28
Northern Ireland	4.0	99	88	12	36	35	29
Scotland	8.9	80	87	13	35	28	37
Southeast	20.0	50	74	26	46	25	29
Southwest	8.2	42	77	23	39	31	30
Wales	5.3	49	84	16	34	31	35
West Midlands	8.2	36	84	16	45	25	30
Yorkshire and Humberside	7.8	29	78	22	41	28	31

Note: These data come from HEFCE and relate to full-time first-degree students registered in 1998–1999.

graduates get their first job. Table 9.3 presents some statistics by parental region on the percentage of students who move away to college, on the percentage of first jobs in the parental region for those who studied in the parental region, and on the percentage of first jobs in the parental region and region of study for those who went away to college.[7] A number of points are worth noting. First, a much higher fraction of students who study in the parental region also get their first job in that region. Second, for those students who moved regions to go to college, the parental region still has some pulling power when it comes to getting jobs and so does the region in which they studied. But a higher fraction take their third job in a region other than the one in which they studied or lived as a child than do those who studied in the parental region. In the absence of further information, the interpretation of these statistics is problematic as it is likely that it is those children with an outward-looking mentality who go away to college and are then prepared to consider jobs in a wider range of regions. But they are consistent with the idea that breaking away from the parental home to go to college also makes it easier to move regions later in life. Figures from the British Household Panel Study (BHPS) suggest that this is not a recent phenomenon: In the adult population as a whole, only 12 per-

7. We are grateful to Abigail McKnight for providing us with these figures from the Higher Education Funding Council for England (HEFCE).

cent of graduates live in the local authority where they were born, compared to 44 percent among the rest of the population. It is perhaps worth noting that more college students are likely to live at home in the future as they now have to bear a higher fraction of their costs of tuition, and this may act to reduce regional mobility among graduates in the future.

9.5 Unemployment, Housing Tenure, and Residential Mobility

We have already seen evidence that, on average, the better educated are more likely to move regions. But figure 9.6 does not control for any other relevant factors, and we might want to know whether this remains the case even once one controls for other factors. Two of the most relevant factors are probably labor market status and housing tenure.

There is considerable research on the factors associated with residential and regional mobility in the United Kingdom (e.g., Hughes and McCormick 1981, 1985, 1987; Pissarides and Wadsworth 1989; Jackman and Savouri 1992; Henley 1998; Boheim and Taylor 2000), much of which focuses on questions like "are the unemployed more likely to move?" The research on the relationship between residence and economic fortunes is plagued by an inability to separate causality. For example, it is almost certainly true that residence is likely to change when there are changes in circumstances: changes in household structure (leaving the parental home, marriage, divorce, birth of a child, etc.) or changes in labor market outcomes (getting a job, losing a job, getting a promotion, etc.). We might expect that both "good" and "bad" shocks are related to changes in residence. On the other hand there is the feeling that residence (primarily location) determines economic opportunity and hence that changes in residence affect changes in economic opportunity.

Existing research is very poor at disentangling the direction of causality. To do it properly, researchers would seem to need some good instruments, but those are hard to find. In the absence of good instruments, we are going to describe the correlations in the data and offer an interpretation.

We use two data sets to investigate the determinants of mobility: the BHPS and the LFS. Boheim and Taylor (2000) have recently presented an analysis of residential mobility using the BHPS, and we will follow on from their research. Unlike them, we split the sample into those who are in couples for whom household mobility is likely to be most important (see Mincer 1978) and those who are not in couples for whom individual characteristics are likely to be most important.

In table 9.4 and table 9.5 we report basic residential and regional mobility equations for the BHPS for individuals and couples, respectively.[8]

8. The BHPS also asks questions about mobility across local authority district, but these are not shown here as the results were very similar.

Table 9.4 **Mobility Equations for Individuals: BHPS**

	Residential (entire sample)		Regional (entire sample)		Regional		
					New Job = 1	Social Housing	Resp = 0
	(1)	(2)	(3)	(4)	(5)	(6)	(7)
Housing Characteristics (base category: owner occupier with mortgage)							
Own house outright	.004	.004	–.004	–.004	.021		–.009
	(.012)	(.012)	(.004)	(.004)	(.023)		(.006)
Social housing tenant	.030	.028	–.013	–.013	–.012		–.030
	(.012)	(.012)	(.004)	(.003)	(.016)		(0.005)
Private unfurnished tenant	.152	.149	.007	.505	–.020		–.0115
	(.021)	(.022)	(.006)	(.006)	(.019)		(.008)
Private furnished tenant	.297	.296	.028	.024	.048		–.0097
	(.021)	(.021)	(.007)	(.007)	(.024)		(.008)
Responsible for housing	–.066	–.064	–.004	–.503	.018	.003	
	(.016)	(.016)	(.005)	(.004)	(.019)	(.008)	
Rent subsidy						.0025	
						(.0030)	
Labor Force Status (base category: employed)							
Unemployed	.019	.012	.012	.007	–.013	.0096	.0328
	(.014)	(.014)	(.006)	(.006)	(.014)	(.011)	(.0132)
Retired	.067	.073	.038	.046			
	(.057)	(.059)	(.037)	(.040)			
Family care	.020	.026	.013	.018	.015	.005	.036
	(.017)	(.018)	(.008)	(.009)	(.033)	(.009)	(.023)
Full-time student	.051	.055	.043	.048	.030	.021	.074
	(.017)	(.015)	(.008)	(.009)	(.018)	(.020)	(.013)
Long-term sick	.016	.022	.009	.014	.039		.065
	(.025)	(.026)	(.014)	(.015)	(.078)		(.050)
New job		.051		.031		.0128	.011
		(.011)		(.005)		(.0086)	(.007)
Lost job		.061		.057		.0269	.054
		(.020)		(.013)		(.0168)	(.019)
Education (base category: ISCED 3)							
ISCED 0-1	–.0245	–.0227	–.0148	–.0133	–.0390	–.0098	–.0230
	(.0136)	(.0135)	(.0042)	(.0038)	(.0173)	(.0042)	(.0065)
ISCED 2	–.0254	–.0239	–.0125	–.0110	–.0322	–.0060	–.0217
	(.0093)	(.0093)	(.0032)	(.0030)	(.0125)	(.0043)	(.0053)
ISCED 5-7	.0139	.0129	.0114	.0103	.0124	–.0043	.0128
	(.0127)	(.0126)	(.0050)	(.0047)	(.0176)	(.0031)	(.0099)
No. of observations	11,063	11,063	11,063	11,063	1,783	981	4,669
Pseudo-R^2	.150	0.153	.0169	0.190	0.186	0.268	0.133
Mean of the dependent variable	.192	.192	.046	.046	.098	0.030	0.053

Notes: Coefficients are marginal effects. Standard errors (in parentheses) are robust and corrected for clustering on the individual. Other controls are age, education, nonwhite, child of household head, lone parent, region, and wave.

Table 9.5 **Mobility Equations for Couples: BHPS**

	Residential (entire sample)		Regional (entire sample)		Regional	
					New Jobs > 0	Social Housing
	(1)	(2)	(3)	(4)	(5)	(6)
Housing Characteristics (base category: owner occupier with mortgage)						
Own house outright	.010	.009	–.001	–.002	–0.000	
	(.008)	(.008)	(.002)	(.002)	(0.010)	
Social housing tenant	.038	.033	–.000	–.001	.002	
	(.008)	(.008)	(.003)	(.002)	(.010)	
Private unfurnished tenant	.146	.141	.016	.012	.002	
	(.018)	(.017)	(.506)	(.005)	.010)	
Private furnished tenant	.328	.323	.032	.026	.063	
	(.032)	(0.31)	(.011)	(.010)	(.027)	
Rent subsidy						–.0057
						(.0068)
Labour Force Status (base category: employed)						
Workless	.018	.024	.001	.003	–.001	–.0047
	(.009)	(.009)	(.003)	(.003)	(.008)	(.0048)
Dual	.001	.001	–.000	–.000	.008	–.0006
	(.005)	(.004)	(.002)	(.001)	(.005)	(.0052)
No. of new jobs		.018		.007		.0101
		(.004)		(.001)		(.0078)
No. of lost jobs		.032		.012		.0098
		(.005)		(.001)		(.0082)
Education (base category: ISCED 3)						
ISCED 0-1	–.0189	–.0191	–.0064	–.0057	–.0065	–.0030
	(.0058)	(.0056)	(.0018)	(.0014)	(.0060)	(.0050)
ISCED 2	–.0088	–.0085	–.0046	–.0040	–.0063	–.0281
	(.0047)	(.0046)	(.0017)	(.0014)	(.0053)	(.0192)
ISCED 5-7	.0039	.0031	.0064	.0047	.0131	–.0046
	(.0057)	(.0056)	(.0026)	(.0022)	(.0077)	(.0043)
No. of observations	14,090	14,090	14,090	14,090	2,972	377
Pseudo-R^2	0.126	0.132	0.102	0.151	0.128	0.229
Mean of the dependent variable	.076	.076	.013	.013	.026	.032

Note: See table 9.4.

Tables 9.6 and 9.7 report similar equations for the LFS where we can look at changes over longer periods and have larger sample sizes but with the disadvantage that we have a narrower range of covariates (notably, we do not have initial housing tenure except in a few years). We report only the coefficients on the variables in which we are interested, namely initial labor market status, housing tenure, and education: The other controls are listed. Younger workers are more likely to move, and ethnic minorities and households with school-age children are less likely to move.

Table 9.6 **Mobility Equations for Individuals: LFS**

	Residential (entire sample)				Regional				
					ISCED 0-1	ISCED 2	ISCED 3	ISCED 4	New Job = 1
	(1)	(2)	(3)	(4)	(5)	(6)	(7)	(8)	(9)
	Labor Force Status (base category: employed)								
Unemployed	.0326	.0302	.0061	.0035	.0037	.0013	.0063	.0039	–.0158
	(.0016)	(.0016)	(.0007)	(.0006)	(.0006)	(.0009)	(.0022)	(.0028)	(.0017)
Retired	.0055	.0132	.0058	.0097	.0096	.0017	.0178	.0176	–.0289
	(.0052)	(.0055)	(.0025)	(.0028)	(.0031)	(.0049)	(.0166)	(.0110)	(.0080)
Family care	.0063	.0154	.0019	.0056	.0037	.0048	.0052	.0078	–.0160
	(.0014)	(.0015)	(.0006)	(.0007)	(.0006)	(.0013)	(.0035)	(.0045)	(.0028)
Full-time student	.0786	.0785	.0296	.0262	.0091	.0038	.0234	.0595	.0291
	(.0022)	(.0022)	(.0011)	(.0010)	(.0023)	(.0013)	(.0018)	(.0036)	(.0027)
Other inactive	.0485	.0579	.0078	.0111	.0066	.0070	.0192	.0271	–.0102
	(.0022)	(.0024)	(.0010)	(.0011)	(.0009)	(.0020)	(.0052)	(.0065)	(.0041)
New job		.0420		.0228	.0137	.0190	.0259	.0633	
		(.0013)		(.0007)	(.0009)	(.0012)	(.0016)	(.0027)	
Lost job		.0855		.0369	.0228	.0283	.0625	.0834	
		(.0024)		(.0014)	(.0016)	(.0023)	(.0044)	(.0064)	
	Education (base category: ISCED 3)								
ISCED 0-1	–.0075	–.0087	–.0066	–.0065					–.0182
	(.0011)	(.0011)	(.0004)	(.0003)					(.0019)
ISCED 2	–.0094	–.0098	–.0043	–.0042					–.0118
	(.0011)	(.0010)	(.0003)	(.0003)					(.0019)
ISCED 5-7	.0138	.0129	.0101	.0078					.0459
	(.0013)	(.0013)	(.0006)	(.0005)					(.0033)
No. of observations	555,450	555,450	555,450	555,450	245,643	140,430	88,950	80,427	69,724
Pseudo-R^2	.184	.192	.172	.202	.100	.134	.220	.231	0.194
Mean of the dependent variable	.107	.107	.0235	.0235	.0109	.0169	.0410	.0544	.0664

Note: Other controls are gender, age dummies, nonwhite, foreign-born, lone parent, number of kids, child of head of household, other relative of head of household, region, and year dummies.

Table 9.7 **Mobility Equations for Couples: LFS**

	Residential (entire sample)		Regional (entire sample)		Regional				
					ISCED 0-1	ISCED 2	ISCED 3	ISCED 4	New Jobs > 0
	(1)	(2)	(3)	(4)	(5)	(6)	(7)	(8)	(9)
			Labor Force Status (base category: single earner)						
Workless	.027	.033	.0022	.0031	.0032	.0026	.0030	.0037	.0052
	(.002)	(.002)	(.0009)	(.0009)	(.0010)	(.0016)	(.0026)	(.0031)	(.0031)
Dual	–.015	–.013	–.0067	–.0054	–.0019	–.0045	–.0067	–.0120	.0028
	(.001)	(.001)	(.0005)	(.0004)	(.0006)	(.0006)	(.0012)	(.0013)	(.0016)
No. of new jobs		.035		.0125	.0084	.0011	.0137	.0224	
		(.001)		(.0003)	(.0004)	(.0004)	(.0008)	(.0009)	
No. of lost jobs		.045		.0148	.0102	.0128	.0146	.0297	
		(.001)		(.0004)	(.0006)	(.0006)	(.0013)	(.0014)	
			Education (base category: ISCED 3)						
ISCED 0-1	.0018	.0009	–.0051	–.0048					–.0115
	(.0014)	(.0014)	(.0005)	(.0004)				(.0019)	
ISCED 2	–.0005	–.0009	–.0021	–.0021					–.0047
	(.0015)	(.0015)	(.0012)	(.0005)					(.0020)
ISCED 5-7	.0173	.0171	.0095	.0081					.0305
	(.0017)	(.0017)	(.0008)	(.0007)					(.0029)
No. of observations	294,938	294,938	294,938	294,938	95,750	77,754	57,541	63,893	58,728
Pseudo-R^2	.097	.107	.065	.110	.095	.097	.083	.136	.057
Mean of the dependent variable	.101	.101	.0179	.0179	.0123	.0142	.0195	.0291	.0391

Notes: Coefficients are marginal effects. Other controls are age and age squared of man and woman, nonwhite, foreign-born, number and age of dependent children, child of household head, region, and year dummies.

9.6 Unemployment and Residential Mobility

One of the main methods of adjustment to regional shocks envisaged by economists is that workers without work in depressed regions are motivated to move to look for work in other regions where the employment possibilities are better. It might be necessary to physically move to the new location to look for work there, or it might be possible to search for work in one part of the country from another part and only move when work is obtained. In this section, we will argue that speculative moves to find work are very rare in the United Kingdom and that the most common pattern of mobility is that first a job is obtained and then a residential move follows.

For individuals the unemployed are more likely to move both regions and residence, although the coefficient in the residential mobility equation is not significantly different from zero for the BHPS. This is in line with other studies: As McCormick (1997, 587) summarizes it, "all UK studies which examine the effect of individual unemployment . . . find this has a strong positive effect on out-migration." The implication often drawn is that those who lack work are spurred by this to change location in search of better economic opportunities. But these regressions do not justify such a conclusion as they do not identify the reason for the move. It is worth noting that other labor force states are also associated with effects on moving that are often as large as the impact of unemployment: for example, retirement. Yet such moves are unlikely to be motivated by the search for work. Being a full-time student is associated with a very high marginal effect on mobility, presumably because of the impact that being a college student has on leaving the parental home and moving regions.

One can also see very clearly the link between changes in employment status and residential moves by including in a residential mobility equation a dummy variable for whether an individual has a new job or has lost a job.[9] For an individual who was initially unemployed the variable "new job" takes the value 1 if they now have a job, while for those who were initially employed it takes the value 1 if they have changed jobs. Unsurprisingly, both these variables are incredibly significant when included in residential mobility equations. The importance of the "lost job" variable also indicates that residential mobility may be associated with bad as well as good shocks to the individual's labor market fortunes. The inclusion of the "got job" and "lost job" variables reduces the marginal effect of unemployment for individuals in both the BHPS and the LFS, although it raises the marginal effect of the workless household variable for couples. However, if we

9. Boheim and Taylor (2000) do examine the relationship between job changes and residential moves but use a bivariate probit model to do so. It is not clear that this is the best way of modeling the interactions, as it is best suited to the situation where unobserved characteristics are correlated with both outcomes rather than a case where the two outcomes themselves are linked.

restrict the sample to those who have gotten a job, the unemployed (or workless) are less likely to have moved regions than those in work (column [5] of tables 9.4 and 9.5 and column [9] of tables 9.6 and 9.7).

Of the 2.4 percent of those unemployed a year ago who move, 47 percent are now in employment, 41 percent are unemployed, and 12 percent are inactive. This compares to 31 percent, 55 percent, and 14 percent for those who do not move. This could be interpreted as showing that regional mobility is very successful in getting the unemployed jobs. But one can interpret the data in two ways. Either the unemployed move house first and then find a job, or they find a job first and then seek to move house if the commute is too inconvenient given their present location. The policy implications of the two views are rather different, as it may not be policies that make residential mobility easier that are needed but policies to make it easier for workers in one area to find work elsewhere.

Ideally, one would like data on when jobs were obtained to compare with the date of residential mobility, but we typically only have data on when jobs were started that is more likely to postdate residential mobility. There are a number of ways in which we can try to get some idea of the likely sequence of events.

Since 1996 the LFS asks specific information about the month of a residential move and the month in which the job started. If the unemployed move regions and then find work, we would expect to see a time lag between the change in residence and getting a job. In fact, the average time lag is 0.9 months. If the unemployed engage in speculative moves to look for work, this implies implausibly short durations of unemployment in the destination region. And the time lag is actually shorter than for those who have had a job-to-job move (so have no intervening period of unemployment) and moved regions (their time lag is one month). It is possible that the unemployed first move to a new region, stay with friends or family, and only move residence when they got a job. But average residential tenure among regional movers is identical for the previously unemployed and job-to-job movers (5.8 months). So this does not seem very persuasive. All of this evidence is very circumstantial, but it does suggest a picture in which it is rare for the unemployed to move regions without first having found themselves a job.

This evidence does not answer the question about the motivation for unemployed regional movers who do not make the transition into employment. The BHPS does contain information on the motivation for residential moves. In particular it asks whether the reason for a move was job-related, and, if so, the respondent is asked to elaborate. Table 9.8 tabulates the responses. Only 12 percent of residential moves are reported to be motivated by employment reasons, although this rises to 31 percent among regional movers. Employment-related reasons are less often given by those who are currently not in employment. And even where employment-

Table 9.8 Reasons for Residential Mobility: BHPS

	Residential Movers	Regional Movers	Nonemployed Movers	Nonemployed Regional Movers
Moved for employment reasons	12.3	31.0	10.4	24.6
	(5,847)	(1,194)	(2,317)	(552)
Employer relocated	4.4	5.1	0	0
	(675)	(352)	(205)	(120)
New job, same employer	11.4	13.6	3.4	2.5
	(675)	(352)	(205)	(120)
New job, new employer	36.0	42.0	41.5	43.3
	(675)	(352)	(205)	(120)
Closer to same job	17.2	9.4	5.5	2.5
	(675)	(352)	(205)	(120)
Start/relocate own business	6.8	5.9	2.9	1.6
	(675)	(352)	(205)	(120)
Salary increase—new home	3.5	0.3	0	0
	(675)	(352)	(205)	(120)
To seek work	8.7	11.6	20.5	25.0
	(675)	(352)	(205)	(120)
Other	19.2	16.8	31.5	29.4
	(675)	(352)	(205)	(120)

Notes: Sample sizes are reported in parentheses. The second and subsequent rows give the percentages of those who said they had moved for employment reasons who gave more specific answers when requested to elaborate on this.

related reasons are given, a very small fraction report that they were motivated by seeking work: Reasons that imply that the job came first and mobility subsequently are much more important. The bottom line would be that of the 2 percent of the nonemployed who move regions, 25 percent are motivated by job-related reasons, and, of those, 25 percent are motivated by the desire to seek work. It is hard to escape the conclusion that speculative regional mobility by the unemployed is very rare.

This evidence is not perfect, but it does suggest that it is important to obtain a job before moving and that it is very unlikely for the unemployed to move location without having a job.[10] This is not that surprising. It is not very easy to change location if there is no source of income. Banks and building societies are likely to be reluctant to give mortgages to those without work, even if one already has one. And private landlords are also likely to regard these people as bad risks as prospective tenants. This problem does not seem to be unique to the United Kingdom: The ethnographic account of Ehrenreich (2001) about life as a low-wage worker in the United

10. It is quite likely that the unemployed who move regions initially stay with friends and family in the destination region. The finding that immigrants in the United States tend to go where immigrants from their home country already are is consistent with this. It suggests that high levels of past migration may make current migration easier.

States is full of the difficulties caused by finding accommodation when moving to a new city.

This also suggests that one of the problems faced by the less educated in moving regions is the difficulty they have in searching for work in another region as a result of the lack of regional integration of the vacancy system. Tables 9.6 and 9.7 estimate separate mobility equations by education for LFS individuals and couples. The marginal effects of the "got job" and "lost job" variables are much larger for the more educated.

But why are vacancies for less-skilled jobs predominantly advertised at local level? It could be that there is no point in advertising in Scotland for an unskilled job in the Southeast because none of the unskilled in Scotland will be interested in taking that job. However, our earlier analysis suggests that the economic returns to job mobility may be higher for the less skilled. Perhaps more plausible is the argument that, when unemployment is high, there is a ready supply of less-skilled workers in all localities. There is no point in advertising for workers in distant regions if there is an excess supply locally. But the consequence of this policy for each individual employer is to trap some workers in high-unemployment regions and to shut off the route by which less-skilled workers can migrate from high- to low-unemployment regions.

If this hypothesis is correct, we might expect to see more attempts by employers to recruit less-skilled workers from further afield as labor markets tighten. This can then explain why the migration from high- to low-unemployment regions seems greater in booms than recessions as we saw in figure 9.8. Perhaps the most celebrated and extreme example of this was the process of recruitment of workers in the West Indies by London Transport when faced with a recruitment crisis in the 1950s and 1960s. Booms increase the supply of vacancies overall and the fraction of vacancies for jobs in other regions, so booms grease the wheels of migration.

One other possible explanation for the lack of speculative moves by the unemployed is that the structure of the housing market makes this difficult. There is some evidence for such frustrated residential mobility. Using data from the BHPS, those in social and private rented housing are more likely to want to move and particularly likely to continue to want to move, even if they have just done so. Let us move on to consider the role of the housing market in more detail.

9.7 Housing Tenure and Residential Mobility

The housing market plays a very important part in determining where people live and hence has a potentially large impact on both regional and neighborhood inequalities. And the housing market has also seen some of the most dramatic changes in the United Kingdom in the last twenty years. In 1979, something like 57 percent of the working-age population were owner-occupiers, 32 percent were in social housing (provided by local councils or nonprofit housing associations), and 10 percent were private rented tenants. By 1999, 75 percent were owner-occupiers, 16 percent were in social housing, and 9 percent were private rented tenants. The main reason for this transformation was the "right-to-buy" policy introduced by Margaret Thatcher in the 1980 Housing Act that gave council tenants subsidies to buy their houses. To date, 1.7 million tenants have taken advantage of this. At the same time, local councils were prevented from using the proceeds to build new houses: Whereas councils had completed 145,000 new homes in 1977 (46 percent of the total), by 1995 this had fallen to 2,000 (1 percent of the total).

Those who remained in social housing had their rents raised in the early 1980s, although they remain well below market rents (30–40 percent below, according to most estimates). The impact of this was mitigated in part by the system of welfare support for tenants (called Housing Benefit after 1982), which paid 100 percent of rents subject to a means-test and a number of restrictions on the maximum allowable rent. In theory the U.K. system of housing benefit should make regional mobility easier as it may pay all the housing costs of those who are unemployed. However, the system is notorious for the inefficiency of its administration, and a recent survey (United Kingdom, Department of the Environment, Transport, and Regions 1999) found that only 1 percent of landlords had a positive preference for tenants on housing benefit, while 18 percent had an aversion to tenants on housing benefit. The two most common problems with tenants on housing benefit cited were problems with administration of housing benefit and rent arrears (which are also likely to be related to administrative problems).

For private tenants in receipt of housing benefit, the deregulation of rents meant, in theory, that any rent could be charged by the landlord and paid for in full by the state.[11] Expenditure on housing benefit for private tenants rose dramatically, and steps were introduced in the mid-1990s to limit the payment of housing benefit to individuals, first to the under-twenty-five-year-olds (who are restricted to an amount that is paid for a room in a shared house) and then to others. Reform of housing benefit remains on the agenda, and a number of options for reform are discussed in the April 2000 green paper "Quality and Choice: A Decent Home for All" (United Kingdom, Department of the Environment, Transport, and Regions 2000).

For owner-occupiers, the main government policy has been the steady

11. One still sees the statement "no DSS [Department for Social Security]" in many ads for rental properties, even ones that are quite expensive, for example, £1000 per month. What is surprising is that anyone on welfare benefits could even consider living in such accommodation.

restriction and eventual withdrawal of the mortgage interest relief at source (MIRAS) scheme by which interest payments were tax-deductible. For those owner-occupiers out of work, mortgage interest payments could be covered by welfare benefits. In the mid-1990s these were restricted in the amount and a nine-month waiting period was introduced before owner-occupiers would have their mortgage covered by a welfare payment. Perhaps more important than changing government policy was financial market liberalization in the 1980s, which made it easier to get a mortgage.

Let us consider the impact of housing tenure on residential mobility. Relative to the base category of owner-occupiers with a mortgage, those in social housing are more likely to move residence but less likely to move regions, and those in private rented housing are much more likely to move both residence and regions, with those in furnished rental properties the most mobile by a large factor.

There are a number of possible reasons for why those in social housing might be less likely to move regions. One is that such housing remains heavily subsidized, and it is very difficult to move into equivalent subsidized housing in another local authority because the properties are generally allocated using a procedure that gives a very high weight to residence in the local authority. One can see this in the data—only 14 percent of new lettings in social housing are movers from another region, compared to 37 percent of new private-sector lettings.

There are a number of ways to test this hypothesis. One is to try to estimate the size of the subsidy (which differs across local authorities) and then see whether this is related to mobility. Column (6) of tables 9.4 and 9.5 does this without much success.

Another hypothesis is that it is simply the characteristics of those in social housing that make the difference. One way of looking at this is to consider those who are not responsible for the housing costs in their residence (mostly children of the head of household). For this group we still see the same pattern of housing tenure effects (see column [7] of table 9.4) as in the full sample, suggesting that housing costs may have little to do with the housing tenure effects.

9.8 Neighborhood Inequalities: Is Britain Ghettoizing?

The previous discussion has all been about interregional dispersion. But the regions are very aggregated and hide enormous differences within regions. In this section we examine the distribution of employment and unemployment at the most disaggregated level available for the United Kingdom: enumeration districts (which average about 375 residents). Data at this level of disaggregation are only available from the decennial censuses, so we only have 1981 and 1991 to work with. Although this is rather dated, this does cover a period of considerable change and turbulence in the U.K. labor market in which overall wage inequality rose substantially (see Gosling and Lemieux 2001). Unfortunately, the U.K. census contains no income information, so this discussion will focus on employment-related outcomes only.

The male unemployment rate was 11.7 percent in 1981 and 11.3 percent in 1991. The absence of any dramatic change in the level of unemployment makes it easier to consider changes in the distribution of unemployment across neighborhoods, although it should be borne in mind that the regional distribution of unemployment was rather different in the two years, with unemployment being relatively higher in the south in 1991.

Panel A of figure 9.10 shows the male unemployment rates by neighbourhood from the lowest to the highest in 1981 and 1991 (this is just the cumulative density function for the unemployment rate). As can be seen, the two lines are extremely similar, indicating that there is rather little change: The unemployment rate at the 10th percentile is about 4.5 percent, while it is 20 percent at the 90th percentile. As the lines are so similar, panel B of figure 9.10 presents the change in the unemployment rate at each percentile. The magnitudes of the changes are very small, although there seems to be some tendency for the best and worst areas to worsen, while those in the middle do slightly better.

Given the rise in male inactivity rates in this period, it is also worth considering changes in male employment-population ratios. Panels C and D of figure 9.10 do a similar exercise as the previous one for nonemployment rates. Unfortunately, it does not seem possible to compute the nonemployment rate for working-age men in 1981, so this is based on all men aged sixteen or over.[12] There is a rise in the male nonemployment rate over this period (see panel C of figure 9.10), and this is largest in absolute terms in the worst enumeration districts (see panel D of figure 9.10). However, in proportional terms there is no very dramatic change in the nonemployment rate at different percentiles.

It is also worth considering women as their employment trends were rather different over this period. Panels E–H of figure 9.10 show similar pictures for the unemployment and nonemployment rates for women. Both their unemployment and nonemployment rates were lower in 1991 than 1981. The fall in unemployment rates is larger in the worst areas, but the fall in nonemployment rates was less.

The analysis so far has made no attempt to match enumeration districts in 1981 and 1991 so that it cannot answer questions about the types of areas that had big changes in employment. Because of boundary changes, it is not always possible to match enumeration districts across the two censuses,

12. For 1991 the correlation across enumeration districts of the employment-population ratio for all men and for working-age men is 0.88.

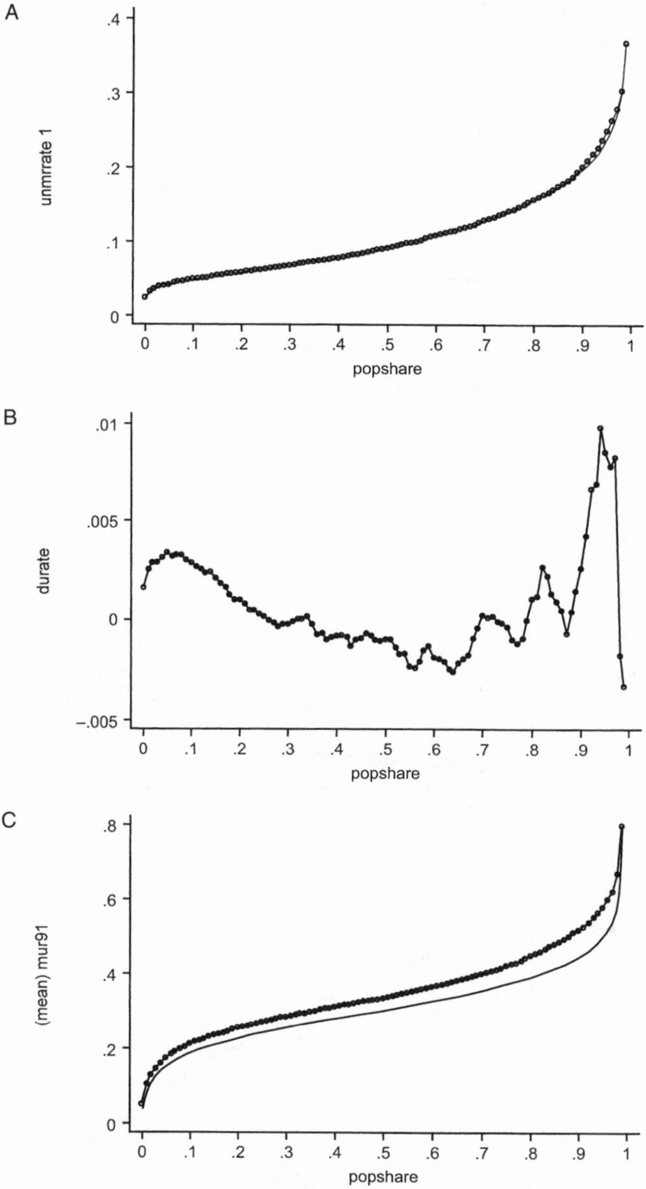

Fig. 9.10 *A,* **The distribution of male unemployment rates, 1981 and 1991;** *B,* **the change in male unemployment rates at different percentiles, 1981–1991;** *C,* **the distribution of male nonemployment rates, 1981 and 1991;** *D,* **the change in male nonemployment rates at different percentiles, 1981–1991;** *E,* **the distribution of female unemployment rates, 1981 and 1991;** *F,* **the change in female unemployment rates at different percentiles, 1981–1991;** *G,* **the distribution of female nonemployment rates, 1981 and 1991;** *H,* **the change in female nonemployment rates at different percentiles, 1981–1991**

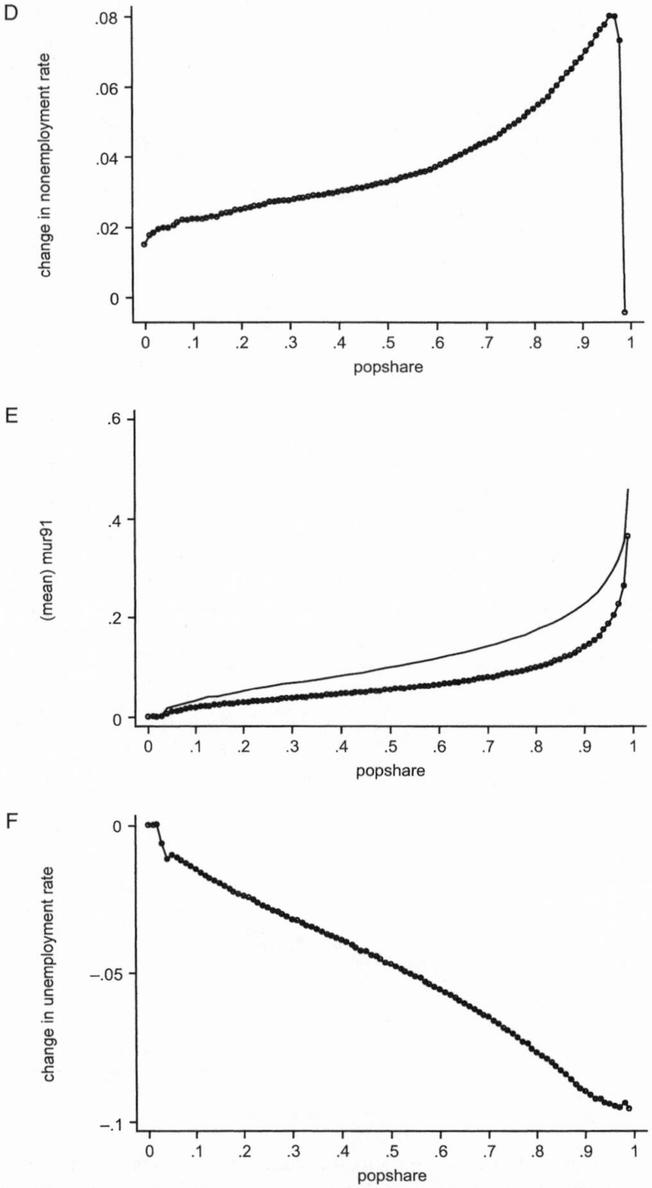

Fig. 9.10 (cont.) ***A,*** **The distribution of male unemployment rates, 1981 and 1991;** ***B,*** **the change in male unemployment rates at different percentiles, 1981–1991;** ***C,*** **the distribution of male nonemployment rates, 1981 and 1991;** ***D,*** **the change in male nonemployment rates at different percentiles, 1981–1991;** ***E,*** **the distribution of female unemployment rates, 1981 and 1991;** ***F,*** **the change in female unemployment rates at different percentiles, 1981–1991;** ***G,*** **the distribution of female nonemployment rates, 1981 and 1991;** ***H,*** **the change in female nonemployment rates at different percentiles, 1981–1991**

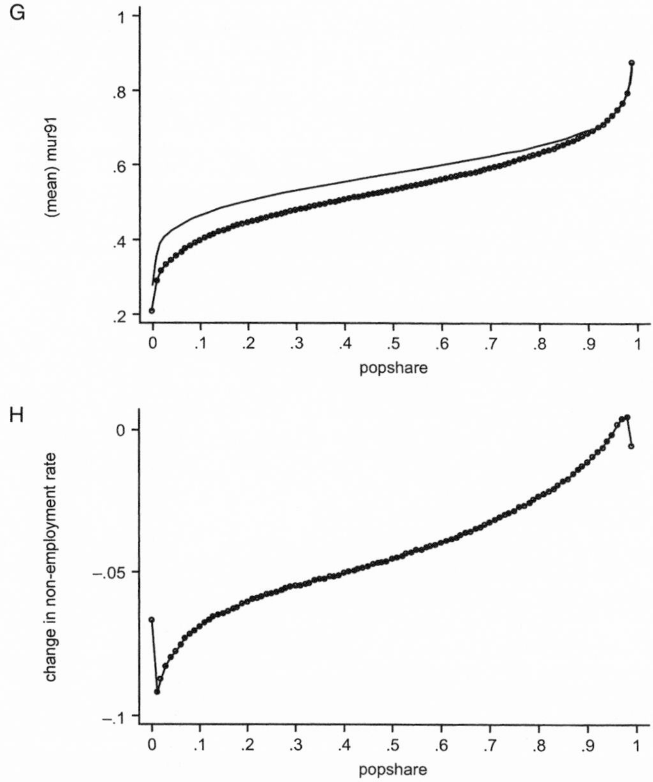

Fig. 9.10 (cont.) *G,* the distribution of female nonemployment rates, 1981 and 1991; *H,* the change in female nonemployment rates at different percentiles, 1981–1991

but this can be done for about 7,400 of them. Table 9.9 investigates the determinants of the change in unemployment and nonemployment rates on a variety of initial characteristics about its inhabitants in 1981. The variables included are limited by data availability but include the tenure distribution of the housing stock and the social class of heads of households. As can be seen, once geographical controls (here, parliamentary constituencies) are introduced, there is no evidence that those areas with more households from the lower social classes in 1981 fared less well over the ten-year period 1981–1991.

Figure 9.11 looks at whether there has been any increased polarization in area crime rates. This is based on data from the British Crime Surveys (BCS) of 1984 and 1996, which contain data on crime victimization at the household level in the year preceding the survey. The figure plots 1983 to 1995 changes in area crime rates at different percentiles for around 600 areas in the 1984 survey and 800 areas in the 1996 survey. It shows some

Table 9.9 **Changes in Unemployment and Nonemployment Rates by Wards, 1981–1991**

1981 Area Characteristics	Males				Females			
	Unemployment Rate		Nonemployment Rate		Unemployment Rate		Nonemployment Rate	
Proportion in:								
LA	.036	.014	.063	.055	.017	–.016	.100	.099
	(.002)	(.002)	(.003)	(.003)	(.002)	(.003)	(.003)	(.003)
Private rented	.087	–.006	–.048	–.110	.090	.002	.034	–.019
	(.006)	(.006)	(.007)	(.008)	(.006)	(.007)	(.007)	(.008)
HA	.084	.035	.102	.064	.059	–.009	.120	.079
	(.011)	(.009)	(.013)	(.012)	(.011)	(.010)	(.013)	(.013)
Job-related rent	–.028	.024	–.005	.058	–.142	–.083	–.260	–.115
	(.010)	(.009)	(.012)	(.012)	(.011)	(.010)	(.013)	(.013)
Nonpermanent	–.043	–.047	–.008	.022	–.056	–.044	–.039	.036
	(.020)	(.015)	(.023)	(.020)	(.022)	(.018)	(.023)	(.022)
Social class I	.049	–.001	.063	.079	.139	.046	.048	.053
	(.014)	(.011)	(.016)	(.015)	(.015)	(.013)	(.016)	(.016)
Social class II	.038	–.006	.025	.047	.123	.045	–.051	–.014
	(.011)	(.009)	(.013)	(.012)	(.012)	(.010)	(.013)	(.013)
Social class III	.047	–.004	.044	.038	.083	.024	–.070	–.005
	(.011)	(.009)	(.014)	(.013)	(.012)	(.011)	(.014)	(.013)
Social class IV	.017	.004	.029	.035	.038	.022	.001	.007
	(.013)	(.010)	(.016)	(.014)	(.014)	(.012)	(.016)	(.015)
Constituency controls	No	Yes	No	Yes	No	No	No	No
No. of observations	7,417	7,417	7,417	7,417	7,417	7,417	7,417	7,417
R^2	0.06	0.53	0.14	0.45	0.10	0.47	0.34	0.54

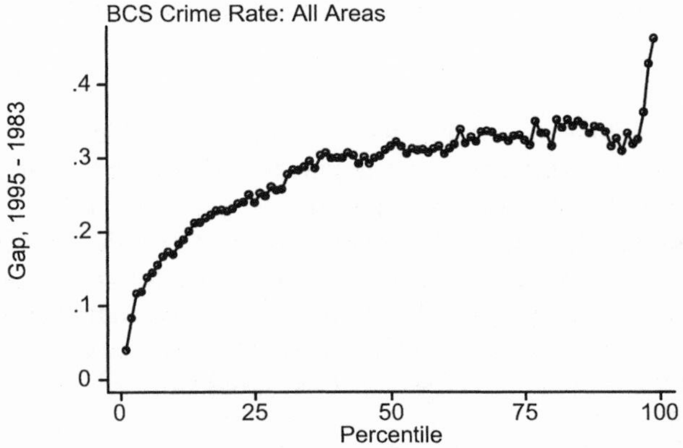

Fig. 9.11 The change in area crime rates at different percentiles, 1983–1995
Source: Calculated from the 1984 and 1996 BCSs.

evidence of increased crime at the higher percentiles, although most of the profile after the median is fairly flat (with crime rates about 0.3 higher in 1995 as compared to 1983), except right at the top of the distribution.

This section has shown that the United Kingdom does have big inequalities between neighborhoods but that it has always had them, and there do not seem to be any very clear trends in the period 1981–1991.

9.9 Council House Sales

The most dramatic change in the U.K. housing market in the last twenty years has been the sale of council houses to private individuals following on from the 1980 Housing Act. Something like one-third of council houses were sold in the following ten years. The April 2000 green paper "Quality and Choice: A Decent Home for All" claimed that "right to buy sales have helped foster mixed-income communities by keeping more affluent households in the same areas" (United Kingdom, Department of the Environment, Transport, and Regions 2000, 55). But it is not immediately obvious that this is the case. If council houses had been sold at random, then mixed communities would have been likely to result. But if, as is sometimes claimed, council houses were only sold in the "nicer" areas and virtually none were sold on the worst estates, then the mixed communities would disappear, and we would end up with a situation in which neighborhoods were either all council or all owner-occupied. The best data set for looking at these effects is the census, as the bulk of council house sales were concentrated in the period 1981–1991.

Figure 9.12 plots the change in the proportion of council house tenants

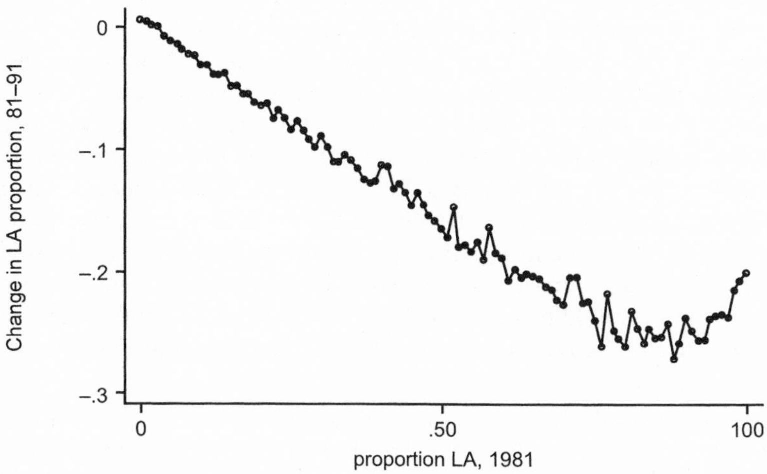

Fig. 9.12 How council house sales varied by neighborhoods, 1981–1995

in an enumeration district against the proportion council house tenants in 1981. There is some evidence that the sales in council housing were smaller in the neighborhoods with the highest initial concentrations of council housing. But the effect is very modest, and 20 percent of council houses are still being sold in the most concentrated estates. The consequence is that, whereas in 1981, 1.1 percent of neighborhoods were 100 percent council and 8.3 percent were more than 95 percent, this had fallen to 0.2 percent and 1.2 percent, respectively, by 1991.

However, these statistics do not tell us anything about the people living in the houses that had been council. Obviously, when a council house is first sold, there is no immediate change in the composition of the neighborhood. But some types of council tenants were more likely to buy than others, and, when these move on, it is the characteristics of the households who replace them that are of interest. Some anecdotal accounts suggest that excouncil houses have been sold to private landlords who then allow the properties to decay, leading to rapid worsening in neighborhoods (see, for example, Davies 1998).

Table 9.10 draws on data from the 1984 LFS, which had an extra supplement on housing, and on the Survey of English Housing in the 1990s. It presents marginal effects derived from probit models of council house purchased by people who were previously living in council accommodation (i.e., those council tenants who bought the property they lived in). Two specifications are reported for each data source, one which includes social class measures and one which does not. The pattern of purchase is clear in both time periods considered. It is very much the people with access to resources who were more likely to have bought their council property. For example, the probability of purchase is higher for older heads of household and is considerably lower in workless households. Furthermore, it is higher for people with from higher–social class backgrounds.[13]

However, this evidence cannot tell us anything about how council house sales have influenced the social composition of neighborhoods. For that, we need to know how the characteristics of those who exercised the right to buy their council house differ from those that they subsequently sold to. It is hard to get information on this. But we can see whether there is any evidence that neighborhoods in which a lot of council houses were sold between 1981 and 1991 had any dramatic change in their social composition. Table 9.11 presents some evidence on this. It regresses the change in the proportion of household heads in different social classes on differences in the proportions in different housing tenures. Social class I represents the high-

13. We do not have education data in the Survey of English Housing, but based on the 1984 LFS it is also clear that council house purchase was higher for more educated council tenants. Adding education variables to the first estimates column of table 9.10 using the ISCED classifications considered earlier produced probit marginals (standard errors) of .094 (.026) for household heads with ISCED 5–7, .061 (.013) for household heads with ISCED 3, and .026 (.008) for household heads with ISCED 2, relative to the low-education group ISCED 0–1.

Table 9.10 Who Bought Their Council House? (probit models, marginal effects, and associated standard errors)

	Excluding Social Class		Including Social Class	
	Labour Force Survey: Buying 1983–1984	Survey of English Housing: Buying since 1990	Labour Force Survey: Buying 1983–1984	Survey of English Housing: Buying since 1990
Age of HoH 18–25	–.069 (.003)	–.043 (.003)	–.068 (.003)	–.042 (.003)
Age of HoH 26–30	–.035 (.005)	–.020 (.005)	–.037 (.005)	–.020 (.004)
Age of HoH 41–50	.113 (.006)	.157 (.005)	.011 (.006)	.015 (.005)
Age of HoH 51–60	.116 (.006)	.113 (.006)	.010 (.006)	.013 (.006)
Retired HoH	.019 (.008)	.044 (.006)	.019 (.008)	.041 (.006)
Workless household	–.078 (.006)	–.075 (.006)	–.071 (.010)	–.069 (.006)
Dual earner household	.069 (.008)	.053 (.007)	.064 (.008)	.051 (.007)
Male HoH	–.009 (.007)	–.006 (.005)	–.007 (.007)	–.003 (.005)
Nonwhite HoH	–.018 (.009)	–.007 (.006)	–.017 (.010)	–.007 (.006)
Married, no kids	.049 (.011)	.022 (.006)	.052 (.011)	.021 (.006)
Married, kids	.085 (.012)	.046 (.008)	.087 (.012)	.045 (.008)
Lone parent	.051 (.012)	.025 (.007)	.052 (.013)	.024 (.007)
Multiple family	.071 (.020)	.057 (.014)	.074 (.020)	.057 (.014)
No. of kids	–.005 (.002)	–.006 (.002)	–.005 (.002)	–.006 (.002)
Professional HoH			.114 (.049)	.058 (.028)
Intermediate HoH			.114 (.022)	.055 (.011)
Skilled nonmanual HoH			.059 (.018)	.029 (.009)
Skilled manual HoH			.051 (.013)	.028 (.007)
Partly skilled HoH			.017 (.011)	.013 (.007)
No. of households	14,799	19,627	14,730	19,557

Note: HoH = head of household.

est social class and social class V the lowest. Because all household heads are allocated to one of the social classes, the coefficients in a given row sum to zero. Areas with the largest falls in council housing seem to have a larger fall in households in the highest social classes. This may be because those in the higher social classes were more likely to buy their council houses but that they then sold them on to people from lower social classes. However, the coefficients are small compared to those on the private rental proportion where neighborhoods with an increase in the proportion in private rental seem to have big increases in the fraction of households from the higher social classes. This evidence does not suggest that council house sales have transformed the social composition of neighborhoods.

9.10 Conclusions

There is little evidence of any dramatic trend in regional inequalities or regional mobility in the United Kingdom in the last twenty-five years. This is true whether one looks at aggregate regions or very small areas. It is im-

Table 9.11 The Effect of Council House Sales on the Social Composition of Neighborhoods

Change in Proportion of Households	Change in Proportion in Social Class I	II	III	IV	V
In LA	.0149	.0298	.0023	–.0560	.0089
	(.0086)	(.0160)	(.0175)	(.0130)	(.0077)
In private rented	.0660	.2516	–.1863	–.0977	–.0335
	(.0217)	(.0406)	(.0443)	(.0329)	(.0196)
In HA	.0316	–.0538	.0195	.0745	.0772
	(.0268)	(.0502)	(.0547)	(.0407)	(.0242)
In job-related rent	.0185	.0278	.1850	–.2961	.0647
	(.0320)	(.0598)	(.0652)	(.0484)	(.0289)
In nonpermanent	.0274	.0402	–.0924	.1030	–.0782
	(.0734)	(.1373)	(.1450)	(.1113)	(.0663)
No. of observations	7,415	7,415	7,415	7,415	7,415
R^2	0.11	0.11	0.10	0.10	0.11

Notes: The dependent variable is the change in the proportion of household heads in each social class from 1981–1991, and the right hand side is the change in the proportion of households in different housing tenures. The sample are the wards that can be matched in 1981 and 1991.

portant to realize how stable the United Kingdom has been over a long period: Table 9.12 presents population shares for the period 1911–1991 and the overriding impression (certainly compared to the United States) is how little has changed. There has been variation in mobility rates in the past twenty years, but it has been more connected with the cycle. Perhaps this is not surprising: There are no very dramatic policy changes in this area that might have been expected to transform mobility in the United Kingdom. The largest change is the sale of council houses, but a realistic assessment would suggest that the impact of this change is likely to be very small.

One of the most striking features of the United Kingdom is that the graduate labor market appears to be, to a first approximation, well integrated (using the United States as a benchmark). Any spatial problems occur in the labor market for the less educated. We have suggested a number of reasons for why this might be the case. First, the act of going away to college might act to sever connections with the region in which one grew up and make one more open to the possibility of residential moves.

Second, we have suggested that speculative moves in search of work by the unemployed are extremely rare in the United Kingdom. Furthermore, they are likely to remain so, given the costs of moving and the difficulty of obtaining accommodation if one is without work. The fact that vacancies for low-skilled work tend to be concentrated on local labor markets, whereas those for graduates tends to be more national, makes it difficult for the less skilled to seek work in other regions. High unemployment through-

Table 9.12 Population Shares, 1911–1991 (%)

	1911	1961	1998
North	6.5	6.1	5.2
Yorkshire and Humberside	9.2	8.8	8.5
East Midlands	5.8	5.9	7.0
East Anglia	2.8	2.8	3.7
Southeast	27.5	30.9	31.0
Southwest	6.7	6.5	8.3
West Midlands	7.8	9.0	9.0
Northwest	13.4	12.4	10.8
Wales	5.7	5.0	4.9
Scotland	11.3	9.8	8.6
Northern Ireland	3.0	2.7	2.8
Greater London	17.0	15.1	12.1
Inner London	11.8	6.6	4.7
Metropolitan areas (excl. London)	16.5	22.1	18.8
Principal metropolitan cities (excl. London)	7.5	8.0	5.8
Total population (thousands)	42,190	52,807	59,237

out much of this period has also made it unnecessary for employers to seek low-skilled workers outside the local labor market. The strong cyclicality in regional mobility suggests the overall state of the labor market may also be important in easing flows, although, ironically, it is in times of recession that commentators get most agitated about regional inequalities. Thus, regional mobility may improve as labor markets tighten, and there is some evidence of increased regional mobility among the less skilled in recent years. This process could be helped if technology allowed the creation of a national list of vacancies.

Finally, the housing market may act as a deterrent to moves. Low-skilled workers tend to be concentrated in social housing, and tenants in that sector have very low rates of regional mobility. However, we have suggested that this may be as much to do with the characteristics of workers in this sector as the intrinsic effect of the sector itself. The removal of controls on private-rental housing has led to a rapid rise in rents but only a very small change in the use of it, so it does not seem likely that dramatic changes to the structure of the housing market will be able to transform the system. It is not clear that the obstacles to migration at the moment are substantial. The costs of moving house (estate agent fees and transaction taxes—stamp duty) are low by international standards. It may be that there is an incentive in the U.K. system to put a large fraction of one's wealth into one's own housing (MIRAS, the absence of capital gains taxation on the primary residence and the lack of taxation of imputed rental income from owner-occupation), and this does expose one to the risk of a bad shock in one's locality, making it difficult to move from a region in recession to one that is booming. But it is the most educated who are most affected by this, and it is for this group that there seems to be a national labor market and for whom the U.K. labor market seems to work well.

In terms of policy for reducing regional inequalities, there are a number of possible strategies. One would be to move people to the jobs. The most important step in doing this is to make it easier for the less skilled to search for and accept jobs in other regions. Providing a national database on Job Centre vacancies should help in this regard, and moves are being made in this direction.

The other approach is to try to move jobs to the people. There are two ways in which this might be done. The first, which has been the basis for much of British regional policy, has been to provide direct employment for low-skilled workers in depressed areas by building factories (in the past) or call centers (the current reality). One can think of this employment as being in the "traded goods sector," as the demand for a region's labor does not have to come from expenditure of people living in that region.

However, many of the low skilled are employed in sectors that are not traded across regions—for example, retail or restaurants or personal services. Demand for this type of labor has to come from expenditure within the region. The strategy proposed by Rogers and Power (2000) is to try to lure the highly educated back to depressed regions and then hope that the expenditure of these individuals is the demand for the labor of the unskilled. An area with depressed demand sees the best educated leave, resulting in a further reduction in the demand for low-skilled labor.[14] The appropriateness of these two strategies does depend on the extent to which the low skilled are employed in traded goods sectors and the fraction of the expenditure of the highly skilled that is within the region where they live. These are interesting questions for further research.

References

Blackaby, D., and D. N. Manning. 1990. North-South divide: Questions of existence and stability. *Economic Journal* 100:510–527.

Blanchard, O., and L. Katz. 1992. Regional evolutions. *Brookings Papers on Economic Activity,* Issue no. 1:1–75. Washington, D.C.: Brookings Institution.

Boheim, R., and M. Taylor. 2000. Residential mobility, housing tenure, and the labour market in Britain. University of Essex, Institute for Social and Economic Research. Unpublished Manuscript.

14. The metropolitan areas (excluding London) do have lower than average shares of the well educated in the population, suggesting there may be something in this, although London has the highest proportion of graduates and some of the lowest employment rates among the less educated.

Cabinet Office. 1999. *Sharing the nation's prosperity: Variation in economic and social conditions across the UK.* London: Cabinet Office.
Cameron, G., and J. Muellbauer. 1998. The housing market and regional commuting and migration choices. *Scottish Journal of Political Economy* 45:420–446.
———. 2000. Earnings biases in the United Kingdom Regional Accounts: Some economic policy and research implications. *Economic Journal* 110: F412–419.
Davies, N. 1998. *Dark heart: The shocking truth about modern Britain.* London: Vintage Press.
Decressin, J., and A. Fatas. 1995. Regional labor market dynamics in Europe. *European Economic Review* 39:1627–655.
Duranton, G., and V. Monastiriotis. 2000. Mind the gaps: The evolution of regional inequalities in the UK. The London School of Economics and Political Science, Department of Geography and Environment. Mimeograph.
Ehrenreich, B. 2001. *Nickel and dimed: Undercover in low-wage USA.* New York: Henry Holt.
Evans, P., and B. McCormick. 1994. The new pattern of regional unemployment: Causes and policy significance. *Economic Journal* 104:633–647.
Greenwood, M. J. 1997. Internal Migration in developed countries. In *Handbook of population economics and family economics*, ed. M. R. Rosenzweig and O. Stark, 647–720. Amsterdam: North-Holland.
Henley, A. 1998. Residential mobility, housing equity and the labour market. *Economic Journal* 108:414–427.
Hoynes, H. 1999. The employment, earnings and income of less skilled workers over the business cycle. In *Finding jobs,* ed. R. Blank and D. Card, 23–71. Chicago: University of Chicago Press.
Hughes, G., and B. McCormick. 1981. Do council housing policies reduce migration between regions? *Economic Journal* 91:919–937.
———. 1985. Migration intentions in the UK: Which households want to migrate and which succeed? *Economic Journal* 95:113–123.
———. 1987. Housing markets, unemployment and labour market flexibility in the UK. *European Economic Review* 31:615–645.
———. 1994. Is migration narrowing the North-South divide? *Economica* 61:509–527.
———. 2000. Housing policy and labour market performance. University of Southampton, report for the U.K. Department of the Environment, Transport, and Regions.
Jackman, R., and S. Savouri. 1992. Regional migration in Britain: An analysis of gross flows using NHS central register data. *Economic Journal* 102:1433–450.
McCormick, B. 1997. Regional unemployment and labour mobility in the UK. *European Economic Review* 41:581–589.
Mincer, J. 1978. Family migration decisions. *Journal of Political Economy* 86:749–773.
Muellbauer, J., and A. Murphy. 1997. Booms and busts in the UK housing market. *Economic Journal* 107:1701–727.
Noble, M., C. Dibben, G. Smith, and M. Evans. 2000. How have poor areas changed in the 1990s? Oxford University, Social Disadvantage Research Group. Unpublished Manuscript.
Oswald, A. 1996. A conjecture on the explanation for high unemployment in the industrialized nations: Part I. University of Warwick, Department of Economics. Unpublished Manuscript.
———. 1997. Theory of homes and jobs. University of Warwick, Department of Economics. Unpublished Manuscript.

Pissarides, C., and J. Wadsworth. 1989. Unemployment and the inter-regional mobility of labour. *Economic Journal* 99:739–755.

Rogers, R., and A. Power. 2000. *Cities for a small country.* London: Faber and Faber.

United Kingdom, Department of the Environment, Transport, and Regions. 1999. *Housing benefit and the private landlords.* London: Department of the Environment, Transport, and Regions.

———. 2000. *Quality and choice: A decent home for all: A green paper.* London: Department of the Environment, Transport, and Regions, April.

10

Has "In-Work" Benefit Reform Helped the Labor Market?

Richard Blundell and Hilary Hoynes

10.1 Introduction

Welfare policy toward low-income families in the United Kingdom experienced a significant shift toward "in-work" benefits in the late 1980s and 1990s. Although a work requirement for some forms of benefit receipt has existed in the United Kingdom since the late 1970s, the shift in policy began in earnest with the introduction of the Family Credit (FC) in 1988—a minimum-working-hours-based credit for families with children. After a number of reforms during the early 1990s, FC was replaced by the Working Families Tax Credit (WFTC) in 1999. Over this period the generosity of these "in-work" benefit schemes also increased, enhancing the emphasis that has been placed in welfare reform on supplementing low incomes in work for adults with dependent children (see Blundell 2002). As of 2000, there are over 1 million recipients, contrasting with less than 250,000 when FC was introduced. Expenditure per recipient has also increased dramatically over this period, rising fourfold in real terms.

But what of the impact on the labor market? There have been two main target groups for in-work benefit policy reform in the United Kingdom.

Richard Blundell is the Leverhulme Research Professor at University College London, director of the Economic and Social Research Council (ESRC) Centre for the Microeconomic Analysis of Public Policy and research director, both at the Institute for Fiscal Studies (IFS). Hilary Hoynes is associate professor of economics at the University of California, Davis, and a research associate of the National Bureau of Economic Research.

We have benefited from the comments and advice of participants at the conference meetings, two anonymous referees, and especially Mike Brewer, David Card, Alan Duncan, Costas Meghir, and Michal Myck. We are also very grateful to Mike Brewer, Darren Lubotsky, and Zoe Smith for generous help in preparing and interpreting the figures and tables. The research is part of the program of the ESRC Centre for the Microeconomic Analysis of Fiscal Policy at IFS.

These target groups reflect a rise in the proportion of families with no parent working in the 1980s and early 1990s. For single parents and low-skilled couples with children, labor market attachment steadfastly refused to rise after the sharp fall in the early 1980s recession—quite against the overall trend. Single parent employment rates fell by 20 percentage points in the early 1980s and have remained well below that experienced by many of the United Kingdom's European neighbors. For women with unemployed husbands, the fall in employment was even more marked, remaining at little over 20 percent. Over the same period the overall trend for married mothers saw a continuing growth, and employment among single women without children remained around the 80 percent level. For the United States the picture is quite different. The early 1980s decline in employment was short lived and was followed by a 14 percentage point increase in the 1990s. For couples with children in the United States, there was a steady increase in employment for both parents. The behavior of these different groups in the United Kingdom and the differences in employment trends with similar groups in the United States presents us with a puzzle. This is the focus of this study.

The comparison with the U.S. system of in-work benefits is particularly useful. Like the system in the United Kingdom, the Earned Income Tax Credit (EITC) in the United States has grown significantly in terms of coverage and generosity over the past two decades. As of 1999, it has seen a fourfold increase in caseload, and expenditure per recipient has tripled in real terms. It is now the largest cash program directed toward working families in the United States, with nearly 20 million recipients. Not only are the United States and the United Kingdom similar in being at the forefront of the use of in-work benefits, but the two nations' other socioeconomic profiles also bear interesting similarities. The proportion of single parents in the United States and the United Kingdom more than doubled over the past two decades—one reason why this group featured so centrally in the policy agenda. Moreover, single parents in both countries began the period, the late 1970s, with very similar employment rates, close to those of married women with children. Both countries experienced a similar rise in employment rates of married women with children. The real contrast is the gain in employment for single parents in the United States and the higher employment rates among low-skilled couples with children.

Although the administration of the system in the United States is somewhat different from that in the United Kingdom, we do not attribute the apparent differences in impact on labor supply to this. Instead, we highlight certain distinct features of the U.K. system. First, unlike the EITC, income from in-work benefits is counted as income in the computation of other benefits—in particular, housing benefits. This is shown to significantly dampen the labor supply incentives created by the in-work benefit system. The importance of housing benefits has increased strongly since the early 1980s in the United Kingdom. Second, over the same period much of the increase in the generosity of in-work benefits has been matched by increases in the generosity of income support—available to low-income *nonworking* families with children. In particular, increases in child credits in the in-work benefit system have been matched by similar increases in the generosity in the child component of income support. There has also been a substantive increase in the real value of the universal child benefit. If anything, these increases act as an income effect and against increased employment in the target groups. Again this contrasts importantly with the United States, where there has been a relative decline in the value of out-of-work income supports.

The remainder of the paper is organized as follows. In the next section, the underlying labor market trends are presented. Section 10.3 describes the reforms in the United Kingdom and their impact on work incentives. Section 10.4 draws a direct comparison with the impact of EITC reforms in the United States. In section 10.5 we evaluate the recent WFTC reform in the United Kingdom. Section 10.6 concludes.

10.2 Trends in Labor Supply over the 1980s and 1990s

Although differences in the pattern of working behavior across different groups at any point in time can be suggestive of important impacts of financial incentives, it is the time series behavior of labor supply for groups of individuals who have been subject to changing incentives that is of direct policy interest. This is precisely the way the puzzle in the introduction was posed between the employment behavior of single mothers in the United Kingdom and the United States.

In this section we focus on trends in the United Kingdom over the last two decades but also draw on evidence from the United States where comparisons are particularly informative. One well-documented trend that occurred in both countries over this period is the shift in returns to education and skill. We do not reproduce them here, but they have certainly reinforced the arguments for increasing the generosity of in-work benefits for low-income workers' families.

Macroeconomic conditions over the past two decades differed somewhat in the United States and United Kingdom. There are two large recessions in the United Kingdom, one in 1980–1981 and one in 1991–1993. The recession in the United States in the early 1990s was shorter and less severe. For the remainder of the 1990s the United States experienced an unprecedented expansion, with unemployment rates lower than they had been in three decades. The expansion in the United Kingdom occurred much later and at a slower pace. It is likely that the differences in the strength of the labor markets across the two countries explain some of the difference in the employment trends discussed here. This may be especially important for low-education groups, who are typically found to be more sensitive to business cycles (Hoynes 2000).

10.2.1 Overall Employment Trends for Women

To describe these trends we draw on a number of data sets from the United Kingdom and the United States. These are briefly described in the data appendix. Figure 10.1 shows the fraction of women working in the United Kingdom by marital status and presence of children from 1978 to 1999. Figure 10.2 shows a similar contrast for the United States. We have selected women aged between twenty and fifty-five for this comparison.

There are many similarities in employment for women in the United Kingdom and the United States over this time period. First, single parents have very similar employment rates at the beginning of the period, at about 55 to 60 percent. These are close to those for married women with children. Second, the labor market attachment for married women, especially those with children, saw a steady rise over the period in both countries. For example, in the United States, somewhat less than one-half of married women with children worked at all in 1979, compared to almost 70 percent in 2000. Third, single women without children experienced a rather more stable and higher level of employment, at around 80 percent, over these two decades in both countries.

The differences between the United Kingdom and United States, however, are striking. First, the employment for all groups was more severely

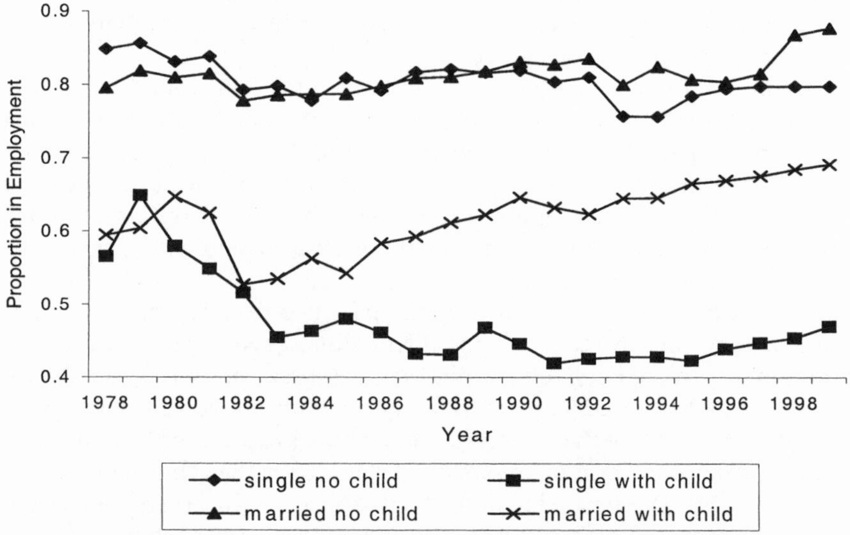

Fig. 10.1 Employment trends for women in the United Kingdom
Source: U.K. FES data.

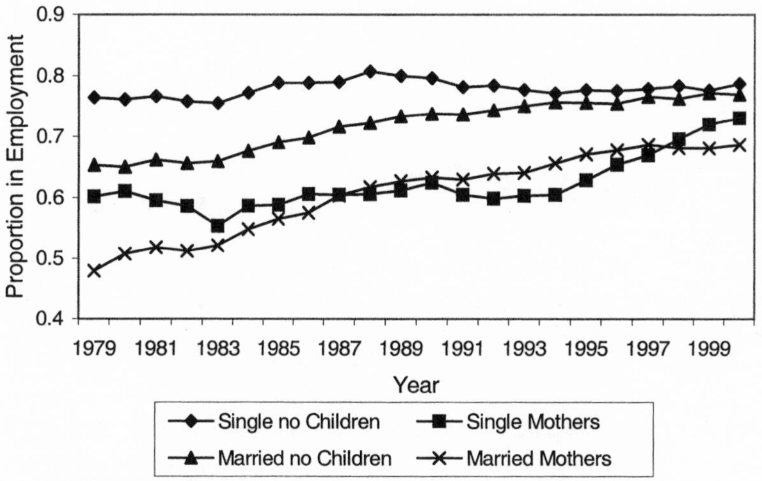

Fig. 10.2 Employment trends for women in the United States
Source: U.S. March CPS data.

reduced in the United Kingdom during the recession in the early 1980s. Second, single mothers in the United Kingdom saw little recovery from the initial decline in employment in the early 1980s. In the United States, beginning in the early 1990s, employment in this group increased dramatically, from 60 to 73 percent.[1] Married women saw steady increases in work over this period. The increase in employment among single women with children in the United States is not due to a cohort effect. When the employment trends are presented by cohort, the increase in employment is shared by all but the oldest age groups. In fact, among less-educated women the gains are largest for the youngest cohort.

10.2.2 A Focus on Single Mothers

In-work benefit reform will provide the greatest incentives for those individuals who can only attract a low market wage. One way to focus on this "incentivized" group is to consider those with lower levels of schooling. Figures 10.3 and 10.4 consider the pattern of employment by education for single mothers in the United Kingdom and United States, respectively. In both the United Kingdom and the United States, single women were an increasing share of all women over this period. In contrast, the fraction of women who are married with children is declining steadily over this period.

1. The U.S. definition of work is "working at all last week," which is chosen to be comparable to the U.K. definition of "employment in the past two weeks." An additional measure that may capture better the intensity of work is the average number of weeks worked last year. In figures not shown here, the trends for the average weeks worked show much the same pattern as those for "worked at all last week."

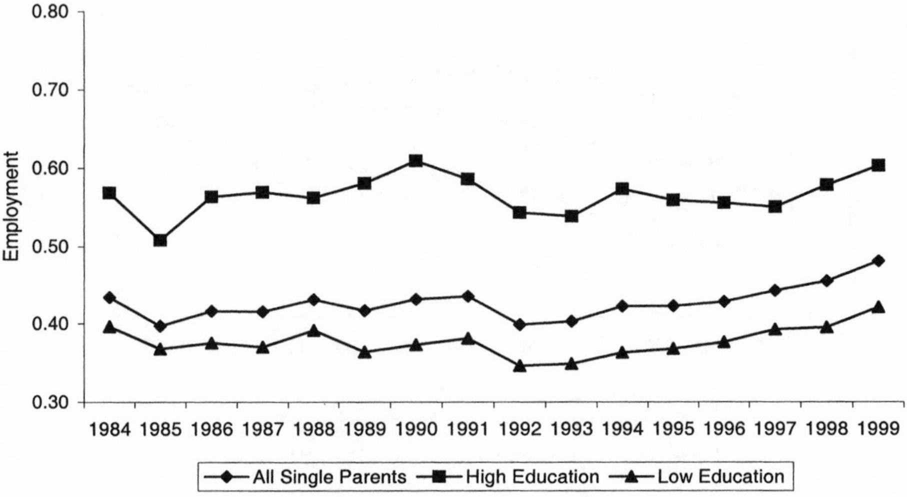

Fig. 10.3 Employment trends for single mothers by education in the United Kingdom

Source: U.K. LFS data.

Note: Low education "left school at age 16 or below."

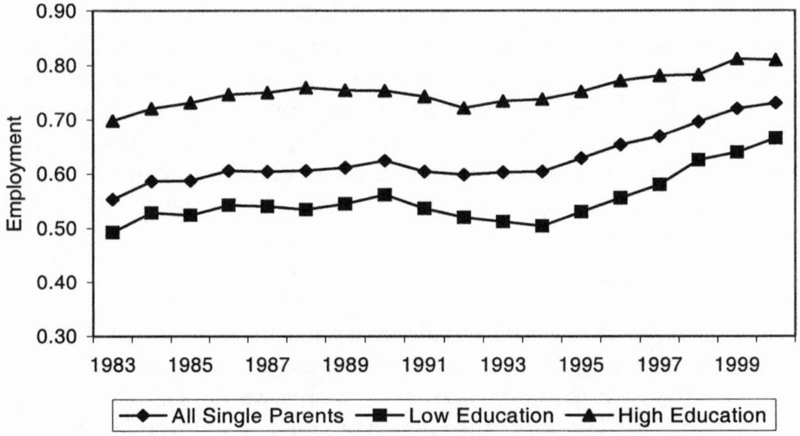

Fig. 10.4 Employment trends for single mothers by education in the United States

Source: U.S. March CPS data.

Note: Low education "left school at twelfth grade or below."

Single women with children represent an increasing fraction of all women, especially among less-educated women. By the end of the 1990s this group represented nearly one-fifth of all low-educated working-age women in the United Kingdom, up from around 6 percent at the turn of the 1980s.

These trends for low-educated single parents are presented for the period since 1984. This period is primarily chosen so that the larger Labour Force Survey can be utilized for the United Kingdom, but it also coincides with the period over which most of the action on in-work benefit reforms has taken place.

The differences between the employment patterns for women in the United Kingdom versus the United States presented previously are also evident here. In the United Kingdom the employment pattern for the lower-educated single mothers, those who left school at age sixteen (the minimum school-leaving age), is very similar to the picture for all single mothers. The employment rate for lower-education single mothers remained quite low throughout the period. In contrast, in the United States the employment rate of lower-educated single women with children increased from 50 percent in 1994 to almost 67 percent in 2000, a gain of more than 16 percentage points. Indeed, in the United States, by the end of the period, low-educated single women with children were working more than married women with children, and almost as much as single women without children. This increase has received tremendous attention in the United States and is the subject of some debate as to how much of this can be attributed to policy versus the strong economy.

One additional feature of the U.K. data for single women that will be important for the discussion of in-work benefit reform is the distribution of hours of work. As will be discussed, since 1992 the U.K. system has provided a strong incentive for single mothers to work at least sixteen hours per week. The frequency histogram for low-education single women with and without children in the United Kingdom over three recent years is presented in figure 10.5. The peak at sixteen hours for single mothers is clear.

10.2.3 Workless Couples with Children

The in-work benefit reforms in the United Kingdom have targeted both single parents and workless couples. Figure 10.6 shows the growing importance of this latter group in the United Kingdom toward the end of the 1980s and the early 1990s. In the 1980s recession, the percentage of married couples with children without an earner increased substantially.

Figure 10.6 shows that, similar to the pattern for single mothers, this rate has not declined much in the subsequent period. This pattern is not found in the United States, however. Like the increase in employment among single women with children, the fraction of married couples without any work has been in decline. In fact, even among low-educated couples, the

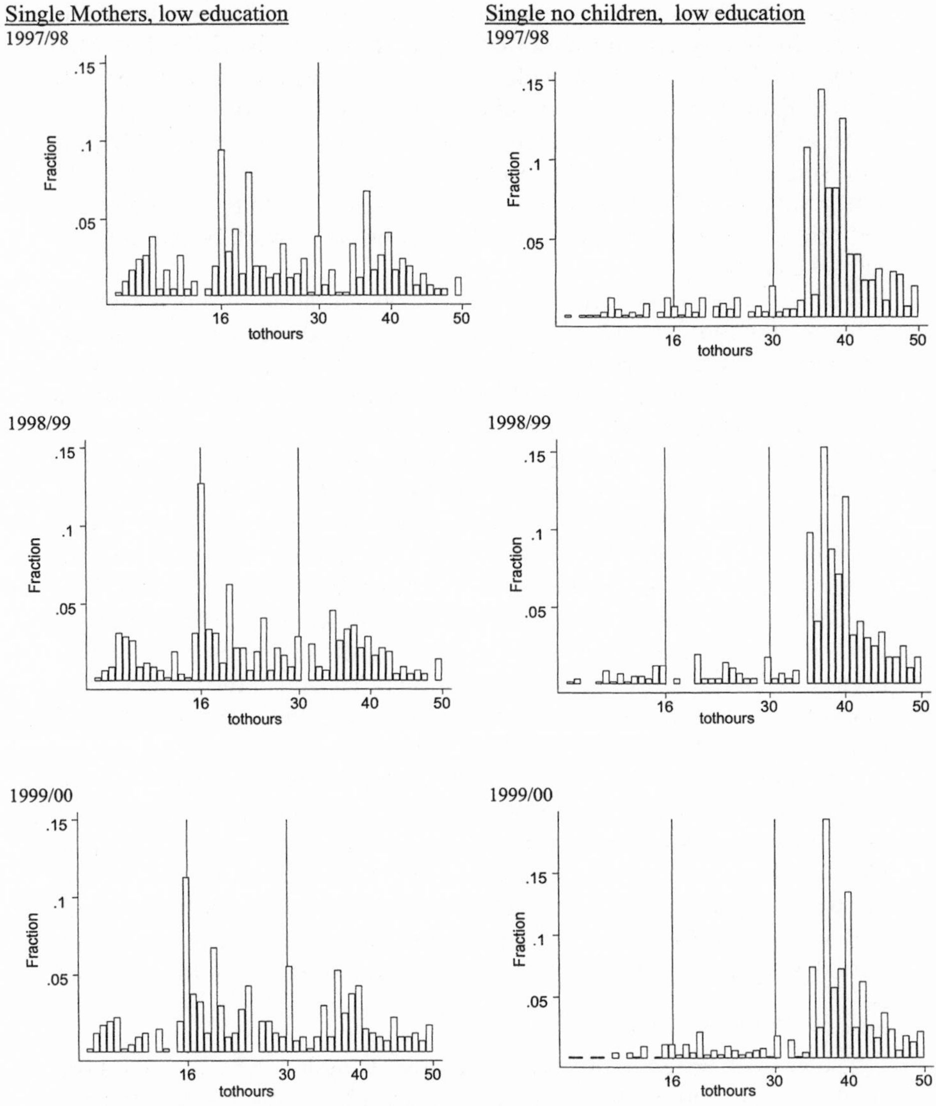

Fig. 10.5 Weekly hours of work, single low-education women with and without children

Source: U.K. FRS data.

Note: Low education is "left school at age sixteen or before."

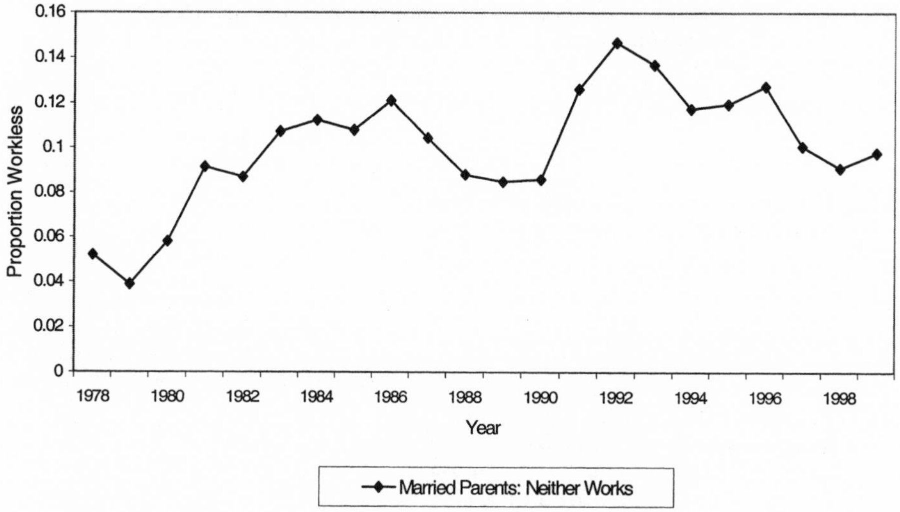

Fig. 10.6 Workless couples with children: U.K. FES low education
Source: U.K. FES data.
Note: Low education is head "left school at age sixteen or before."

later period shows declines in the workless rate, down to less than 5 percent by 2000.

10.3 History and Reforms to In-Work Benefits

In the United Kingdom, in-work benefit reform has been motivated as a method of poverty relief that does not create adverse work incentives. This is achieved by targeting low-income families with an income supplement that is contingent on work. Eligibility typically has been based on family income and requires the presence of children, reflecting in part the higher welfare benefits for families with children, partly a desire to help low-income working families, and partly the costs of child care and the like. Consequently, these benefits are most heavily targeted toward single parents and low-income couples with children. Increasingly, they are also being extended to low-income workers without children.[2] The family income–based eligibility rules and the interaction with other aspects of the tax and benefit system make the analysis of incentives for in-work benefits more complex than they may first appear.

Table 10.1 provides a timeline of the evolution of in-work benefits in the United Kingdom and the United States since their introduction in the 1970s. In the United Kingdom, Family Income Supplement (FIS), which

2. See the proposed Working Tax Credit (Her Majesty's Treasury 2000).

Table 10.1 Timeline of Developments in In-Work Benefits in the United Kingdom and the United States

	United States	United Kingdom
1971		Family Income Supplement (FIS) introduced as a means-tested in-work benefit
1975	Earned Income Tax Credit (EITC)introduced with maximum credit of $400	
1987	Increase in EITC generosity and credit rate	
1988		FIS replaced by Family Credit (FC) with increased generosity and lower MWRs (most instances of MWRs > 100% were removed); 24 hours work per week needed to qualify
1991	Increase in EITC generosity; separate rate for two or more children; requirement for applicants to earn more than received in welfare removed; EITC no longer counted in means-tested programs' income calculations	
1992		Qualifying conditions reduced to 16 hours per week
1994	Substantial increase in EITC generosity, particularly for families with 2 or more children (phased in over 1994–1996); EITC for workers without children introduced	
1995		Extra credit introduced for working more than 30 hours per week
1996	PRWORA reformed AFDC/TANF	
1999		Working Families' Tax Credit replaces FC with increased generosity, longer phase-out portion, and more generous support for child care
2000		Increase in generosity; credit paid through the wage packet

Source: Brewer (2000).

provided an earnings supplement for those families with at least one full-time worker, was introduced in 1971. Like FIS in the United Kingdom, the EITC in the United States was also introduced in the 1970s as a way of offsetting the payroll tax for low-income U.S. working families. The change in the composition of low-income households and the fall in labor market attachment in certain family types further refocused the policy debate in both countries and highlighted the implicit tax on income faced by such low-income families in the tax and benefit system. In the United Kingdom FIS was reformed and renamed Family Credit (FC) in 1988, which finally mutated into the current Working Families Tax Credit (WFTC) in 1999. Each step increased the generosity of the credit and mirrored, to some extent, the increase in generosity that occurred in the reforms to EITC in the United States.

10.3.1 The U.K. System of In-Work Benefits and Comparison to U.S. In-Work Benefits

The current system of in-work benefits in the United Kingdom is the WFTC. Introduced in October 1999, it increased the generosity of in-work support relative to the previous FC system through a larger adult and child credit, a less severe benefit reduction rate, and a new child care credit. The main provisions of the WFTC are outlined in Table 10.2. Eligibility for the WFTC requires having dependent children, working at least sixteen hours per week, and having income and assets below the limit. The basic weekly credit is £53.15, and it is phased out at a rate of 55 percent. Both single and married couples are eligible. A useful way of viewing the characteristics of the British system is in comparison with the U.S. EITC. Eligibility for the EITC, also outlined in table 10.2, requires dependent children, positive earned income, and having income below the limit. The credit is phased in at a 34 (40) percent rate and phased out at a rate of 15.98 (21.06) percent for families with one child (two or more children).

A picture of the two systems in terms of their gross transfers is given in figure 10.7. These are evaluated for a minimum-wage single parent with one and with two eligible children in both systems, assuming that eligibility and receipt continued for a complete year. The broad similarities in the programs include larger credits for two-child families and the phasing out of the benefits. The differences are also clear from the figure. The vertical rise in eligibility in the U.K. system corresponds to the minimum hours eligibility at sixteen hours. At sixteen hours the U.K. recipient receives the maximum she is eligible for. This contrasts with the U.S. proportionate tax credit up to the maximum amount. The U.K. system also displays a much steeper withdrawal, reflecting a higher benefit reduction rate. This provides for a greater degree of targeting in the U.K. system but the potential for higher implicit tax rates. There are many additional specific idiosyncrasies to each of these systems (see Brewer [2000] for an in-depth recent comparison).

Overall, for low-earning families the U.K. system can be quite generous, significantly more so than the U.S. system. This is also clear from figure 10.8, which presents per-recipient expenditures in both countries since the 1970s. Notice also the fourfold increase in spending per recipient in the United Kingdom between 1970 and 2000. However, as figure 10.9 documents, the caseloads for these two systems are quite different. By 2000, in the United States there are nearly 20 million recipients, whereas in the United Kingdom there are approaching 1 million recipients, even though

Table 10.2 Details of WFTC and EITC Operation

	Working Families Tax Credit (from June 2000)	Earned Income Tax Credit (2000)
Eligibility	Must work more than 16 hours a week, have dependent children (under 16 or under 19 and in full-time education), have less than £8,000 capital. Couples need to claim jointly; need not be married. Extension to those without dependent children proposed alongside an integrated child credit.	Must have positive earnings in past year and annual investment income under $2,350. Married couples need to file a joint tax return; unmarried couples file separately. Parents need to have a "qualifying" child (either theirs or their spouse's, or any other child that was cared for all year). "Children" are under 19, under 24 and a student, or permanently and totally dis abled. Where a child potentially qualifies two unmarried adults for EITC, only the adult with the higher income can apply (this includes multiple tax unit–households).
	Structure	
Value of basic credit	Credit is weekly. Basic credit of £53.15 plus possible 30 hour credit of £11.25 plus credits for each child at £25.60 or £26.35 for 16–18s. Child care tax credit is supplementary to this.	Credit is annual and is a fraction of annual income up to a maximum level of $353/$2,353/$3,888 for families with no, 1, or more than 1 children
Tapering	Beyond threshold of £91.45, tapered at 55%.	Phase-in threshold applies a 7.65%/34%/40% credit (for no, 1, more than 1 children) to income until maximum credit reached. Beyond threshold of $12,690 ($5,770 for no children), tapered at 7.65%/15.98%/21.06% so that runs out at $10,380/$27,413/$31,152 (for no, 1 child, more than 1 children).
	Interaction with Other Parts of Tax and Benefit System	
Definition of income	Net income (i.e., income after income tax and national insurance). Self-employed: same definition of income as for other tax liabilities.	Gross earnings or "modified adjusted gross income" if modified adjusted gross income is higher and claimant is on the taper (modified adjusted gross income is income minus standard deductions for tax purposes). Self-employed: same definition of income as for other tax liabilities.
Exclusions from the definition of income	Child benefit, Statutory Maternity Pay, attendance allowance, maintenance payments, Housing Benefit, and Council Tax Benefit awards	TANF and food stamps are not taxable.

Table 10.2 (continued)

	Working Families Tax Credit (from June 2000)	Earned Income Tax Credit (2000)
Programs for which awards count as income	Housing Benefit and Council Tax Benefit awards	Federal law prohibits EITC from being treated as income for purpose of Medicaid, SSI, food stamps, and low-income housing. Since 1991, EITC did not count for AFDC assessment; states can now count EITC when determining TANF awards.
	Assessment and Payment Mechanism	
Assessment	Assessed on average weekly income in "assessment period" prior to claim. Length of assessment period depends on frequency of claimant's earnings: 7 weeks for weekly payments, 8 weeks for fortnightly, 16 weeks for four-weekly, 4 months for monthly payments. Estimated earnings used for new workers.	Assessed at year end on past year's income.
Payable	Weekly award fixed for 26 weeks (unless family status changes). Paid through wage packet unless nonearner in couple elects to receive it or if self-employed. Timing of payments aligned with timing of wages, so if worker paid monthly in arrears, credit will be paid monthly in arrears. Nonearners paid fortnightly.	Annual award is a refund on annual tax liability with any excess paid as a lump sum. Families have to file by April 15 each year. Up to $1,418 can be paid in advance through the wage packet for claimants who have federal income tax withheld from wages. Few elect for this option.
To whom paid	Couples decide who receives it. If couple cannot agree, then Inland Revenue will probably pay to the main carer.	Married couples who claim the EITC have to file a joint tax return. Their EITC credit reduces the joint tax liability. They nominate who receives the payable part of the credit. See "Eligibility" for other rules on who can claim in nonmarried couples.

Source: Brewer (2000).

the working-age population is around one-fifth of that in the United States. The rapid growth of the caseload in the United Kingdom is also significant, especially given the slower population growth in the United Kingdom: In the United States growth was from 216 million to 273 million from 1975 to 1999, representing 26.4 percent growth, in contrast to U.K. growth of 56.2 million to 59.5 million, representing just 5.3 percent growth in the United Kingdom over the same period.

So on the face of it, the U.K. system looks generous and well targeted, with a caseload that is growing rapidly. So why does it appear to have had

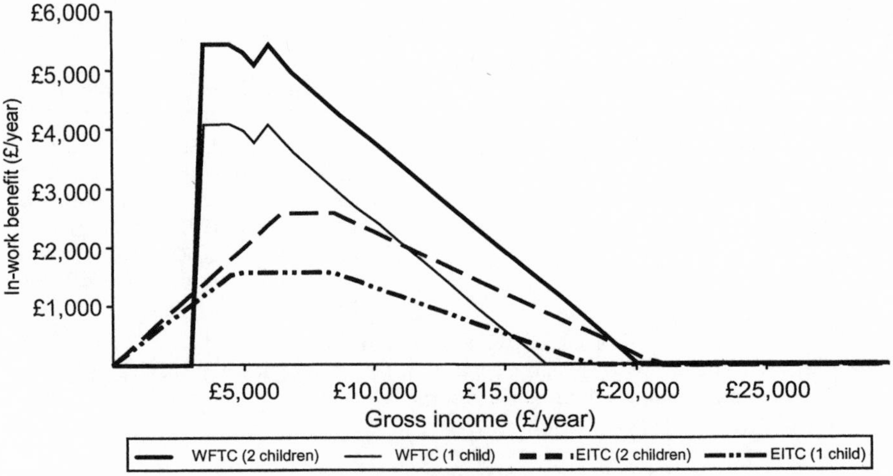

Fig. 10.7 EITC schedule and WFTC schedule, 2000
Source: Brewer (2000).
Notes: £1 = $1.50. Assumes 2000 tax system in United States, and 2000 tax system in United Kingdom.

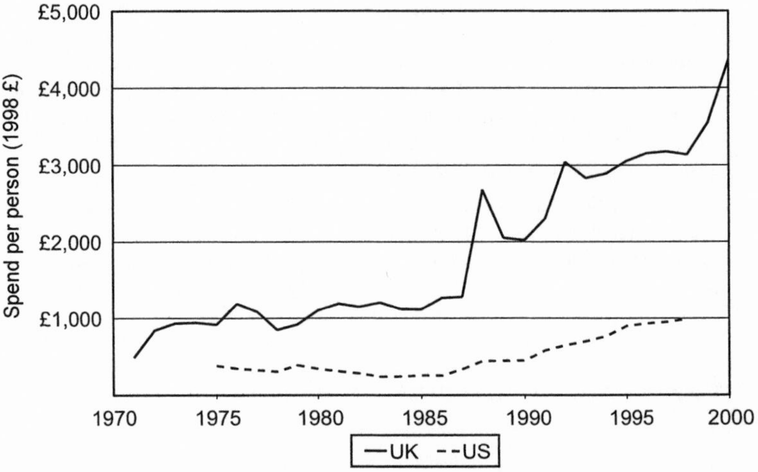

Fig. 10.8 Expenditure per claimant on in-work benefits in United Kingdom and United States
Source: Brewer (2000).

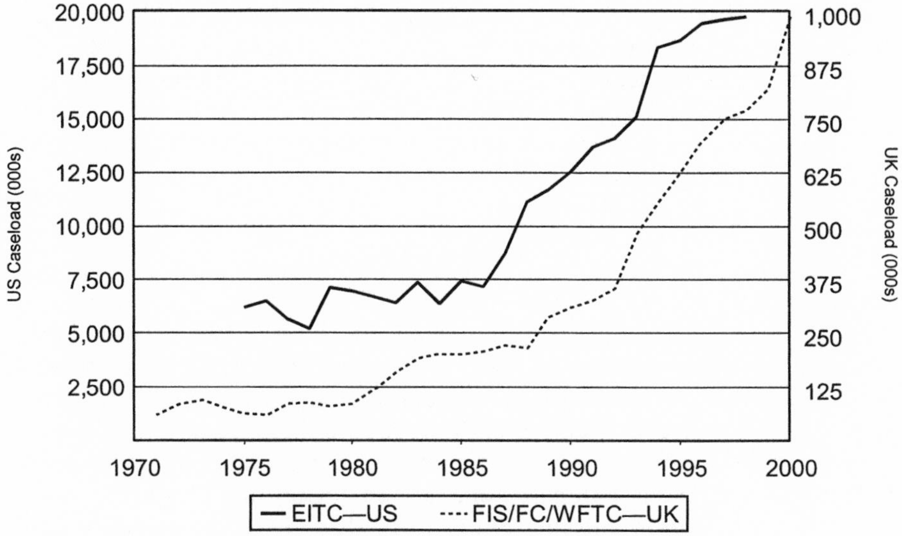

Fig. 10.9 In-work benefit caseloads

less impact on labor supply? To answer this we take a look back over the last two decades at the whole tax and benefit system in the United Kingdom as it affects work incentives.

10.3.2 The Earlier In-Work Benefits in the United Kingdom

In-work benefits have a long history in the United Kingdom. The first, the FIS, was introduced in 1971. This was a noncontributory benefit payable to low-income families with children, provided the head of the family was in full-time paid work (defined as thirty hours per week, or twenty-four if the individual concerned was a single parent). Entitlement depended on the family income's falling below a certain limit. The amount payable was half the difference between the family's income and the relevant limit.[3] In addition to receipt of FIS, entitlement to FIS automatically conferred a number of "passport" benefits available to those on supplementary benefit—the income assistance program for those not in full-time work, including free school milk and meals, prescriptions, and dental treatment (see Dilnot, Kay, and Morris [1984] for further detail).

Although FIS clearly provided some financial incentive to work, the combined effect of the 50 percent FIS benefit reduction rate, together with the impact of housing benefit, tax, and national insurance contributions, often resulted in implicit tax rates in excess of 100 percent. For example,

3. The limits in 1983 were £85.50 per week for a one-child family, with £9.50 for each subsequent child, with a maximum payment of £22 per week.

under the FIS system an eligible worker with housing costs would pay a 25 percent basic tax rate, a national insurance contribution of 7 percent, a 50 percent benefit reduction rate on FIS, and an effective Housing Benefit reduction rate of 23 percent, resulting in an implicit tax rate of 105 percent. After the FC reform this would reduce to 97 percent—still high, but below 100 percent (see Dilnot and Walker 1992).

Family Credit (FC)

Introduced in 1988, FC was an extension of FIS and was designed to increase generosity and remove tax rates in excess of 100 percent. It achieved the later objective by fully integrating the in-work credit with the rest of the tax and benefit system. An unusual feature of the FC system, retained from the FIS, was the minimum weekly hours eligibility criterion. At its introduction this was set at twenty-four hours but then reduced to sixteen hours in April 1992 to encourage part-time work by lone parents with young children. The FIS had a minimum hours criteria set at thirty hours for workers in couples and twenty-four hours for single parents. To partially offset any adverse incentive effects for full-time work from the later lower hours eligibility level, a further supplementary credit at thirty hours per week was introduced in April 1995.

In the FC system each eligible family was paid a credit up to a maximum amount that depended on the number of children. Eligibility depended on family net income's being lower than some threshold (£79.00 per week in 1998–1999). As incomes rose, the credit was withdrawn at a rate of 70 percent. In 1996 average payments were around £57 a week, and take-up rates stood at 69 percent of eligible individuals and 82 percent of the potential expenditure.

The sixteen-hour reform, proposed in the 1988 review of the U.K. benefit system, only became effective in April 1992 and moved the hours eligibility rule from twenty-four hours per week to sixteen hours per week (see Blundell and Meghir [2002] for a detailed description of this reform). Figure 10.10 shows the impact on the budget constraint of a typical single parent.[4]

Family Credit is treated as income in calculating other benefits incomes—this is not the case for the U.S. system. In the United Kingdom, this has the effect of dampening down the incentives in the underlying in-work benefit system. The impact of Housing Benefit (rent rebate), which is withdrawn at 65 percent, is particularly notable. In the United Kingdom once family income falls below a specific level all rental payments are covered through the benefit system. For example, in panel B of figure 10.10,

4. These are constructed using the IFS tax and benefit simulation model TAXBEN (see www.ifs.org.uk) designed to utilize the Family Expenditure Survey (FES) and the FRS used in this paper (see the data appendix).

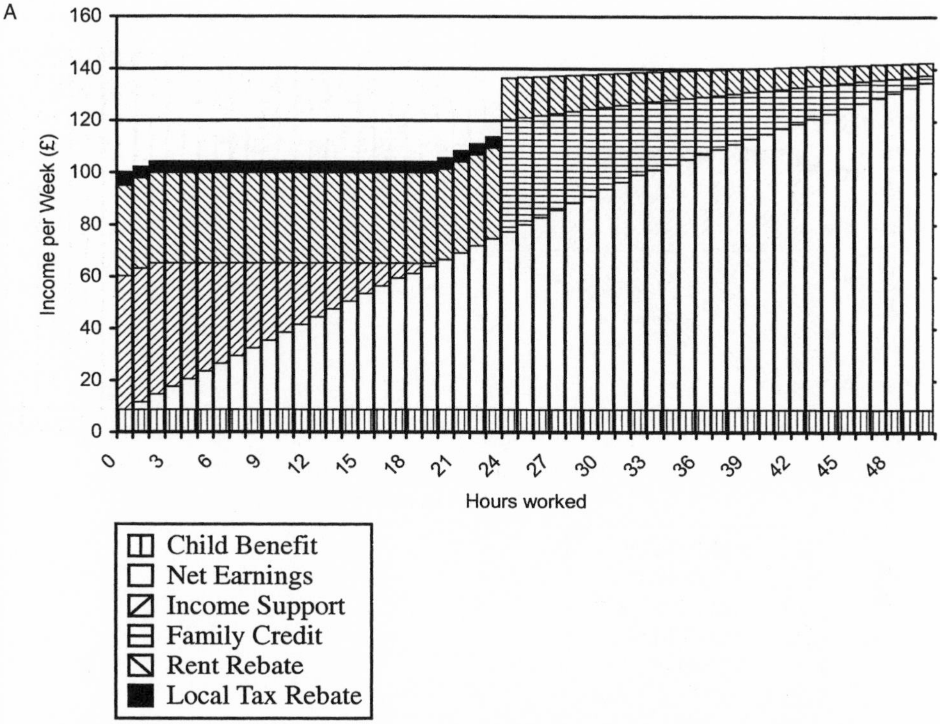

Fig. 10.10 The 1992 hours reform to FC and other taxes and benefits: *A,* single parent in 1991; *B,* single parent in 1992

Notes: A, Single parent, April 1991, earning £3.00 per hour; *B,* single parent, April 1992, earning £3.00 per hour.

when the FC becomes available at sixteen hours, the housing benefit decreases substantially, leading to a minimal increase in income.

Similar budget constraints with very similar effects can be drawn for a low-wage couple with children (see Blundell 2001). These figures show our first central point—the importance of allowing for the interaction with other benefits and taxes, especially where means-tested programs, such as Housing Benefit in the United Kingdom, extend up the income distribution to such an extent that they overlap extensively with in-work benefits.

Although these budget constraint pictures show a high replacement rate, they do nevertheless suggest some financial incentive to take a sixteen-hour job after the 1992 reform. Do the data confirm this? Recall the picture of hours of work for low-education single parents in the United Kingdom in section 10.2. This showed a strong peak at the sixteen-hour point. Blundell (2000) presents a picture of the hours changes before and after the 1992 reform. It is notable that for single mothers a spike at twenty-four hours

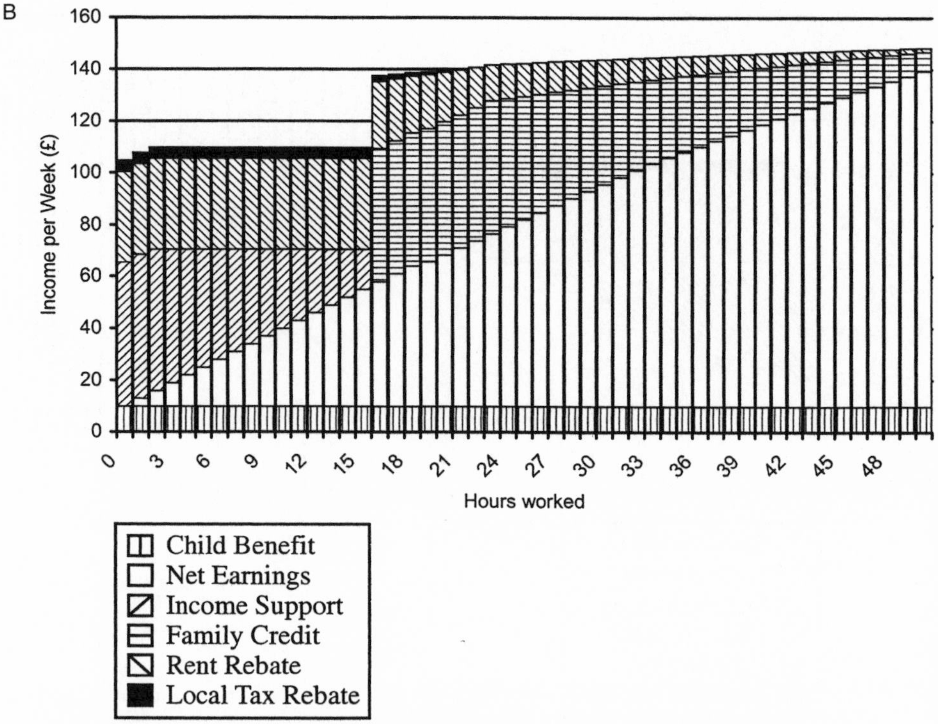

Fig. 10.10 (cont.) The 1992 hours reform to FC and other taxes and benefits: *A*, single parent in 1991; *B*, single parent in 1992

Notes: A, Single parent, April 1991, earning £3.00 per hour; *B,* single parent, April 1992, earning £3.00 per hour.

tends to disappear in 1992 as a spike at sixteen hours becomes more pronounced. This 16-hour eligibility rule has been maintained throughout all the subsequent changes to in-work benefits in the United Kingdom. Interestingly, as we saw in figure 10.5, the spike at this point in the hours distribution has also remained a predominant feature of the data for those most likely to be eligible for in-work benefits in the United Kingdom.[5]

Figure 10.10 also highlights our second central point—the out-of-work benefit system over this period was relatively generous and implied a fairly high replacement rate for a low-wage working parent. For example, income support and housing benefits amount to about £100 per week, compared to a minimum wage in 1999 of £3.60 per hour.

In the following discussion we will show that increases in the value of in-

5. As mentioned previously, a further thirty-hour supplement to FC in the United Kingdom was introduced in 1995 (see Duncan and Giles [1996] for a detailed description). This has also been maintained throughout all subsequent reforms and is what gives rise to the second peak in the in-work benefit payments in figure 10.7.

work benefits in the United Kingdom typically have been matched by similar increases in the value of out-of-work benefits. Consequently, replacement rates have remained quite high, contrasting quite dramatically with the recent experience in the United States. We return to this theme in the following discussion but first complete our brief discussion of the history of U.K. in-work benefit reforms.

The Working Families Tax Credit (WFTC)

The replacement of FC—the WFTC—was substantially more generous and was fully phased in from April 2000. It increased the level of in-work support relative to the FC system in four ways: (1) by enhancing the credit for families with younger children; (2) by increasing the threshold; (3) by reducing the benefit reduction rate from 70 percent to 55 percent; and (4) by incorporating a new childcare credit of 70 percent of actual child care costs up to a quite generous limit. The effects of these changes relative to FC are shown in figure 10.11.

The largest cash gains go to those people who are just at the end of the FC benefit reduction taper. The impact on the budget constraint of a single parent is presented in figure 10.12. Again, a similar constraint can be calculated for couples with children (see Blundell 2001). Indeed, because couples typically have higher housing costs and are eligible for higher levels of in-work credit, the replacement rate for lower hours is even higher. If anything, this reform increases the incentives for full-time jobs. As we find in section 10.5, this is borne out in the simulation model.

This discussion once again highlights the importance of interactions between benefits. The WFTC payments are counted as income in computing the entitlement to other benefits, such as Housing Benefit (Rent Rebate). The budget constraints show the importance of these interactions in reducing the impact of the increased generosity in the WFTC.

Child care credit increases the maximum amount of WFTC by 70 per-

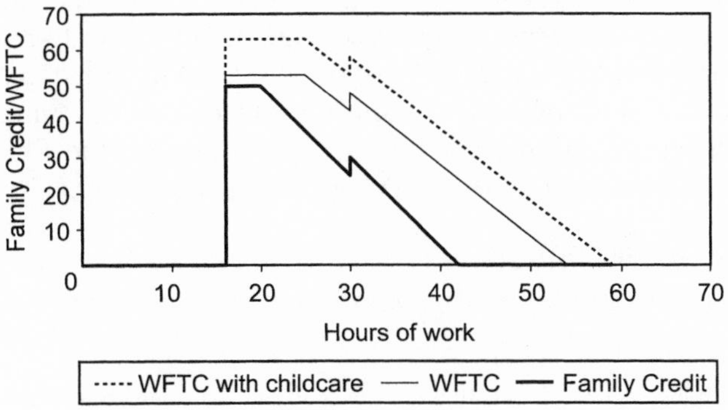

Fig. 10.11 WFTC and FC

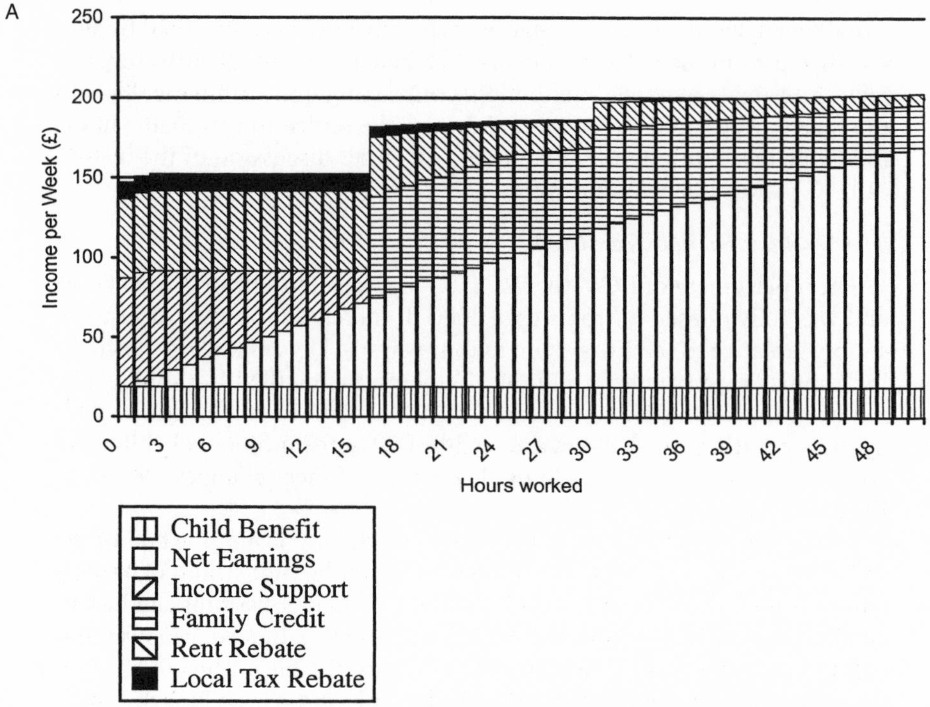

Fig. 10.12 *A*, Single mother before WFTC; *B*, single mother after WFTC
Notes: A, Single parent, April 1997, earning £3.50 per hour (2000 prices); *B,* single parent, April 2000, earning £3.50 per hour (2000 prices).

cent of child care costs up to a maximum of £100 per week for those with one child or £150 per week for those with two or more children. The child care credit component is available to all working lone parents and to couples in which both partners work more than sixteen hours per week.[6] The requirement that both parents work helps to offset the negative incentive to work on the second worker in a couple implicit in the family-based calculation of the level of the credit in both the WFTC. We return to the importance of this adverse effect on couples in our detailed discussion of the WFTC reform in section 10.5. It is also important for the EITC and reoccurs in our discussion of the EITC reforms in section 10.4.

10.3.3 The Impact on Work Incentives

In the previous discussion the importance of interactions of in-work be-

6. This is not included in the calculation of the budget constraint figures because the take-up of child care credits has been rather low. As we point out in section 10.5, recent figures of take-up under WFTC show it to have remained low but increasing quite rapidly.

B

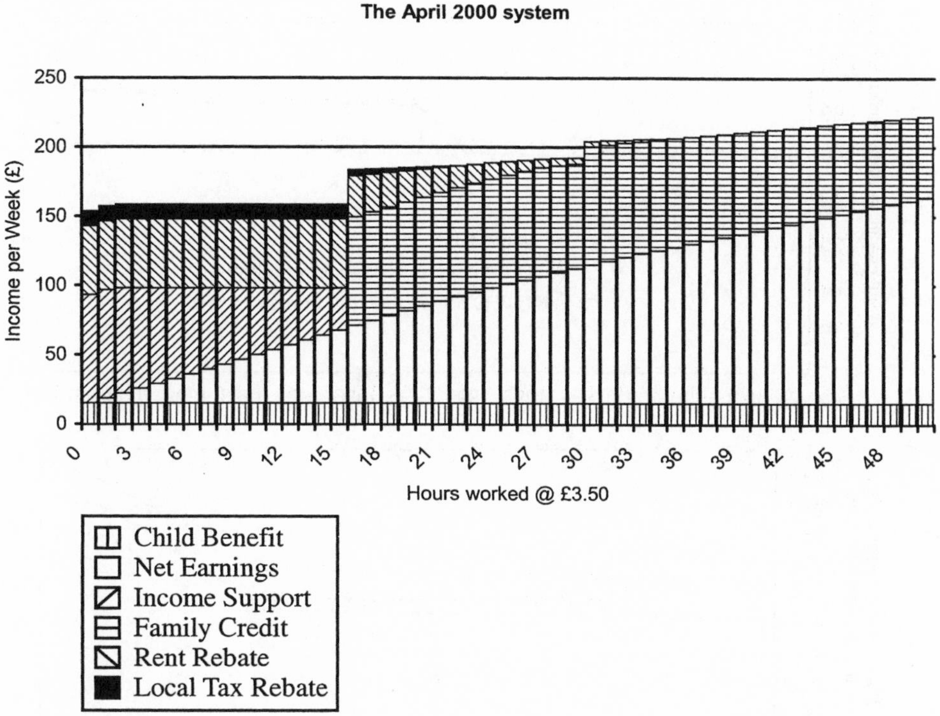

Fig. 10.12 (cont.)

nefits with other benefits in the United Kingdom and the level of those other benefits has been highlighted. It is central to our understanding of the financial incentives to work for low-wage parents in the United Kingdom. We have seen that the impact of these interactions is to dampen, often quite dramatically, the financial incentives to work. To evaluate the likely effect of these reforms to the financial incentives to work facing the target groups in the U.K. population over the 1980s and 1990s, we consider an overall view of changes to the U.K. income support and benefit system.

We first consider the impact of all reforms on the maximum amount of out-of-work income support and the maximum amount of in-work benefit over this period since the late 1970s. These figures are presented in figure 10.13 for a single mother in the United Kingdom. These maximum amounts simply depend on the hours worked and the number of children. They underscore the second important feature of the U.K. system that is in direct contrast to the U.S. experience. The real value of the maximum amount of income support in and out of work has remained almost constant over these two decades. Where in-work credits have increased, especially with regard to the recent very large increases in the real value of child

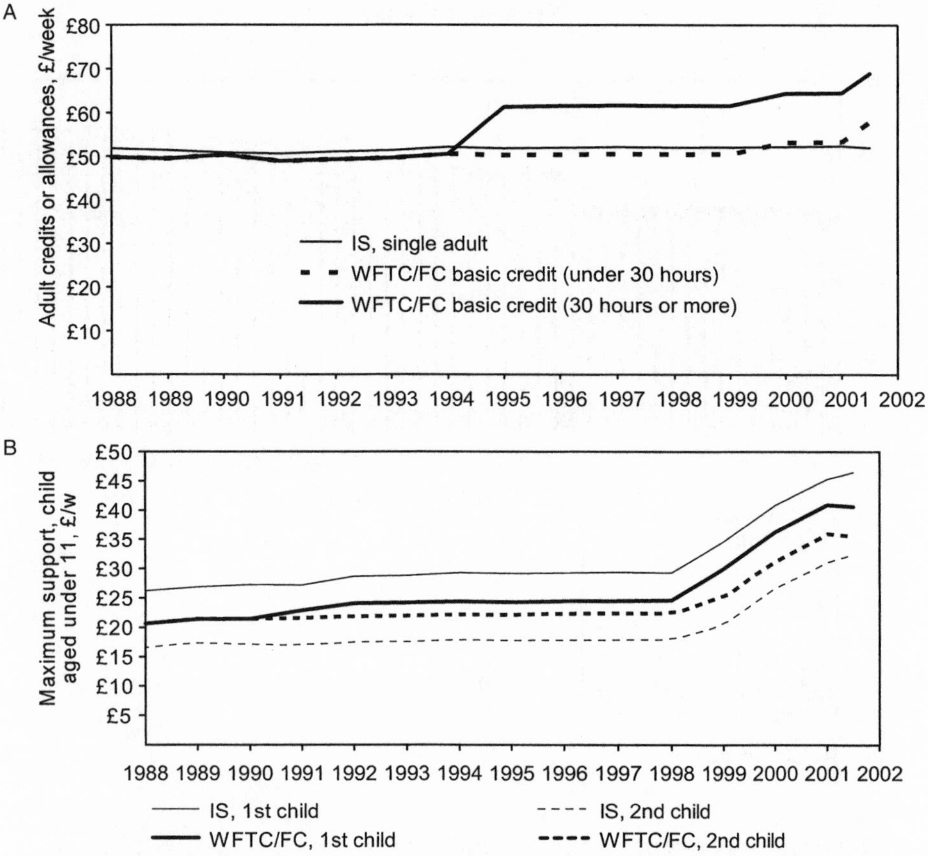

Fig. 10.13 ***A,* Adult credit and Income Support: single mother in United Kingdom; *B,* child credit and Income Support: single mother in United Kingdom**
Source: A, Brewer, Myck, and Reed (2001).

credits (see panel B of figure 10.13), they have been matched by very similar rises in the child component of out-of-work income support for low-income families. The only slight divergence from this rule came in the 1995 introduction of a supplementary adult credit at thirty hours of work.

Interesting as these figures are, they clearly miss the differences that have occurred due to changes in the minimum hours requirement and to interactions with taxes and other benefits in calculating actual receipts rather than maximum eligible amounts. Figure 10.14 attempts to capture this. We first ignore Housing Benefit and consider the financial incentives for a single parent with two children (one aged less than five and one aged between five and ten). They assume that if she works she is paid at the real value of the minimum wage in 1999 (£3.60 per hour). Three possible weekly

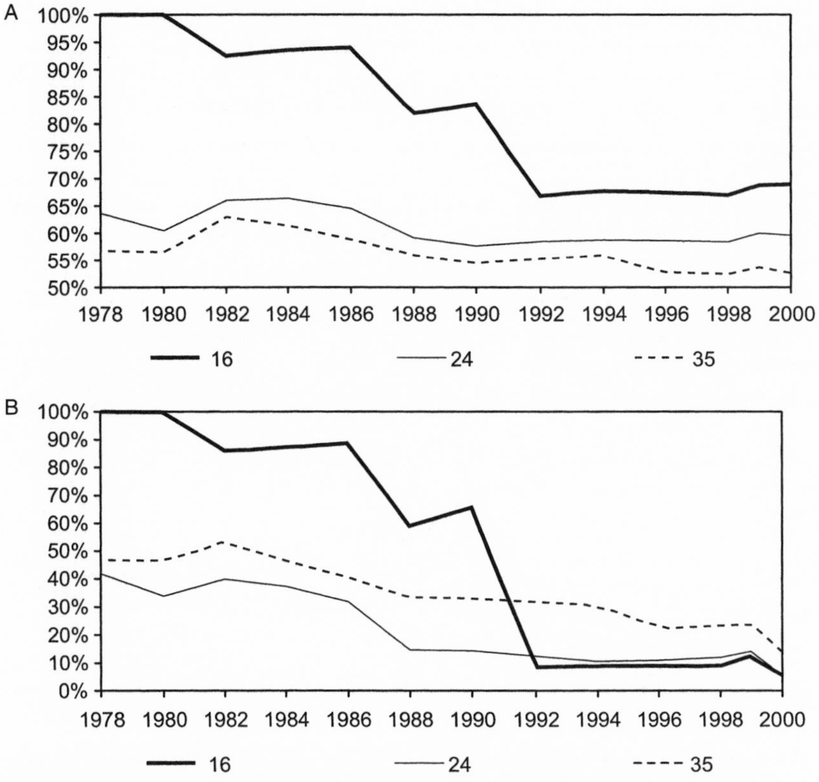

Fig. 10.14 ***A,* Replacement rate by hours of work for single mother in United Kingdom: without housing costs; *B,* average tax rate for single mother in United Kingdom: without housing costs**

hours of work are considered: sixteen, twenty-four, and thirty-five. Panel A of figure 10.14 presents the replacement rate computed as the ratio of total benefit income if out of work and total disposable income if in work. Panel B of figure 10.14 shows the corresponding average tax rate calculated as the proportionate loss in earnings in taking a minimum-wage job at these hours of work.

At the beginning of the period the replacement rates for twenty-four- and thirty-five-hour jobs were around 60 percent and relatively stable over the early and mid-1980s, falling with the introduction of FIS in 1988, especially for twenty-four-hour jobs. The replacement rate fell back a little in 1995 for higher-hour workers after the thirty-hour supplement in 1995.[7] For sixteen-hour jobs the replacement rate is very high indeed. The biggest

7. The rise in the replacement rate in 1999 reflects the removal of one parent benefit. This is reversed by the introduction of WTFC in the final year of figure 10.14.

changes in these figures come from the reform in the late 1980s that reduced eligibility for in-work benefits to sixteen hours from twenty-four hours.

Figure 10.15 presents the replacement rate and the average tax rates, including Housing Benefit. The overall pattern is very similar, but the dampening effect of Housing Benefit is clearly visible. For example, the replacement rates are, in general, higher for the twenty-four- and thirty-five-hour jobs than in panel A of figure 10.14. The drop in the rates for sixteen-hour jobs with the 1992 reform is still important but less dramatic.

These figures serve to underscore our two key points with regard to the benefit and tax credit system in the United Kingdom. First, the interaction of work-based credits with the tax and benefit system has the effect of dampening the financial incentives. This is not a feature of the U.S. EITC. Second, where generosity in the work-based credits has increased, it has

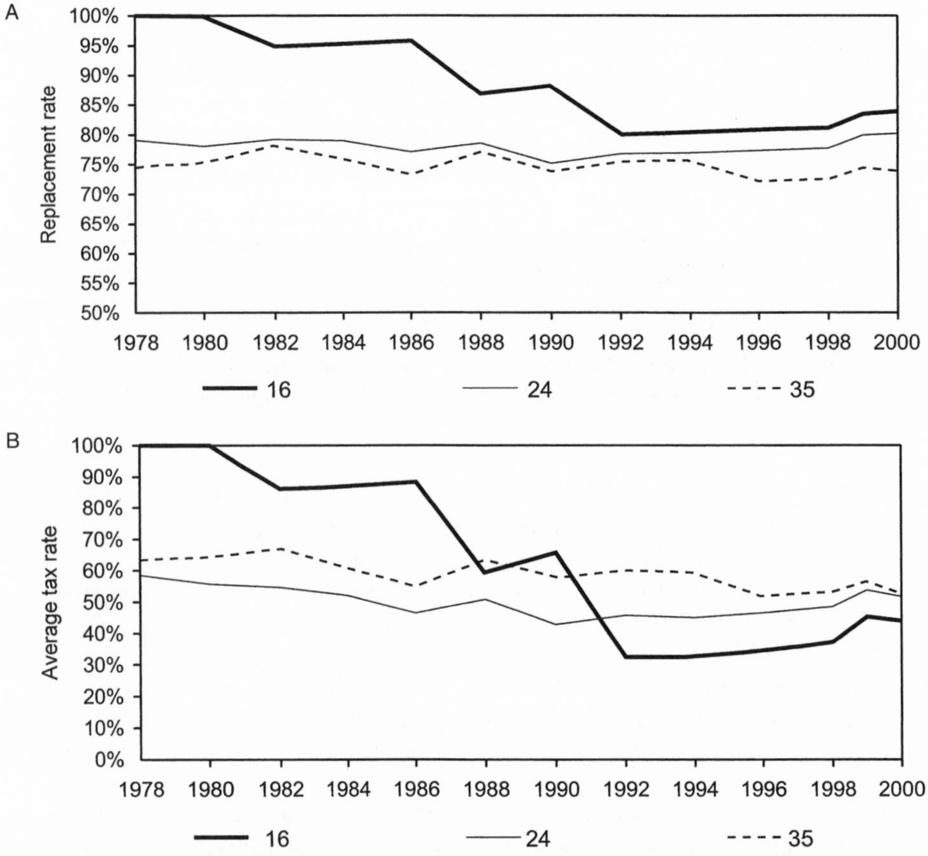

Fig. 10.15 ***A,*** **Replacement rate by hours of work for single mother in United Kingdom: with housing costs and housing benefit;** ***B,*** **average tax rate for single mother in United Kingdom: with housing costs**

been typically matched by increases in out-of-work income support for families with children. This has left the replacement rate and effect tax rates rather stable over time. Again, this contrasts importantly with the U.S. system, where there has been a relative decline in the value of out-of-work income support. The generosity of Housing Benefit and child additions to income support in the United Kingdom has left the level of out-of-work income for families with children at an increasingly higher rate than that in the United States. Four-fifths of all single parents on Income Support in 1999 were also in receipt of Housing Benefit.

Two other features of the U.K. experience are probably worth highlighting at this juncture. First, the U.K. welfare system provides benefits not only to lone parents but also to couples with children. This is in contrast to the United States, where couples with children are provided substantially more limited benefits. In fact, in the United Kingdom, Housing Benefit and Income Support are generally higher for couples due to higher housing costs and larger families. The upshot of this is that the budget constraint and replacement rate figures for couples on low incomes look very similar to those for single parents; indeed, the replacement rates can be quite a bit higher. This certainly has some bearing on the much larger incidence of workless couples with children in the United Kingdom.

The second factor, which adds to the findings so far, is the growing importance of housing costs for low-income families over the last two decades. This reflected a strong increase in the real level of rents paid in both private and public housing over the 1980s. Even though the rules of the housing benefit system were left relatively unchanged, the eligible amounts and receipts increased dramatically over this period. This was one of the main factors behind the rise in out-of-work incomes received by low-income families in rented accommodation over the 1980s (see Giles, Johnson, and McCrae [1997] and Dickens and Ellwood [chap. 8 in this volume], for example). In figure 10.15 the housing benefit is kept at the same 2000 real value throughout so that the true picture for someone in the rented sector would have an increasing financial disincentive to work, counteracting increases in in-work benefits.

10.4 Evidence from the U.S. Reforms

10.4.1 Programs for the Low-Income Population in the United States

Out-of-work benefit programs through the welfare system have been the backbone of assistance to low-income persons in the United States. Since 1935, the Aid to Families with Dependent Children (AFDC) has provided cash transfers to needy single parents with children. Since the 1960s and 1970s, the social safety net expanded to provide in-kind benefits to needy individuals. The primary in-kind benefit programs include Food Stamps,

Medicaid (health insurance), and housing subsidies. Eligibility for these welfare programs requires satisfying resource restrictions in the form of limits on current income and assets. In general, these welfare programs have primarily been limited to single parents with children, largely excluding married couples and nonelderly persons without children. Although some working families receive welfare benefits, they are not in-work programs. As with most welfare programs, families receive the maximum benefit if they are not working and face high benefit reduction rates with increases in family earnings. As is well recognized, the programs provide adverse work incentives.

The Earned Income Tax Credit began in 1975 as a modest program aimed at offsetting the Social Security payroll tax for low-income families with children. As we will discuss more, the generosity of the EITC increased in the tax acts of 1986, 1990, and 1993. The contrasts between the EITC and traditional welfare benefits are many. First, the EITC is provided through the tax system rather than the welfare system. Second, eligibility for the EITC is available to all low-income families with children, independent of marital status. Third, receipt of the credit requires positive family earnings. Consequently, the EITC creates positive incentives to work for single parent families. Because the credit is based on family earnings, however, the credit can create adverse incentives to work among married couples (Eissa and Hoynes 2004).

Reforms to the Earned Income Tax Credit (EITC)

The basic structure of the EITC has not changed substantially in the twenty-five years since its introduction. Eligibility for the EITC depends on the taxpayer's earned income (or in some cases adjusted gross income) and the number of qualifying children who meet certain age, relationship, and residency tests. Several features of the credit are different from the U.K. in-work programs. First, the credit is within the tax system and is a refundable credit, so a taxpayer with no federal tax liability, for example, would receive a tax refund from the government for the full amount of the credit. Second, the credit amount depends on annual income and earnings, and virtually all recipients receive the credit in one lump sum at the end of the year. Last, the EITC does not count as income in welfare benefit formulas. As we will see, this difference turns out to be very important.

The amount of the credit to which a taxpayer is entitled depends on the taxpayer's earned income, adjusted gross income, and, since 1991, the number of EITC-eligible children in the household. There are three regions in the credit schedule. The initial phase-in region transfers an amount equal to the subsidy rate times their earnings. In the flat region, the family receives the maximum credit. In the phase-out region, the credit is phased out at some phase-out rate.

Table 10.3 summarizes the parameters of the EITC over the history of the program. The real value of the credit increased only modestly in the

Table 10.3 **U.S. Earned Income Tax Credit Parameters**

Year	Group	Phase-In Rate (%)	Phase-In Range	Maximum Credit	Phase-Out Rate (%)	Phase-Out Range
1975–1978	1+ children	10.0	$0–4,000	$400	10.0	$4,000–8,000
1979–1984	1+ children	10.0	$0–5,000	$500	12.5	$6,000–10,000
1985–1986	1+ children	11.0	$0–5,000	$550	12.22	$6,500–11,000
TRA86						
1987	1+ children	14.0	$0–6,080	$851	10.0	$6,920–15,432
1988	1+ children	14.0	$0–6,240	$874	10.0	$9,840–18,576
1989	1+ children	14.0	$0–6,500	$910	10.0	$10,240–19,340
1990	1+ children	14.0	$0–6,810	$953	10.0	$10,730–20,264
OBRA90						
1991	1 child	16.7	$0–7,140	$1,192	11.93	$11,250–21,250
	2+ children	17.3		$1,235	12.36	
1992	1 child	17.6	$0–7,520	$1,324	12.57	$11,840–22,370
	2+ children	18.4		$1,384	13.14	
1993	1 child	18.5	$0–7,750	$1,434	13.21	$12,200–23,050
	2+ children	19.5		$1,511	13.93	
OBRA93						
1994	1 child	26.3	$0–7,750	$2,038	15.98	$11,000–23,755
	2+ children	30.0	$0–8,425	$2,528	17.68	$11,000–25,296
	No children	7.65	$0–4,000	$306	7.65	$5,000–9,000
1995	1 child	34.0	$0–6,160	$2,094	15.98	$11,290–24,396
	2+ children	36.0	$0–8,640	$3,110	20.22	$11,290–26,673
	No children	7.65	$0–4,100	$314	7.65	$5,130–9,230
1996	1 child	34.0	$0–6,330	$2,152	15.98	$11,650–25,078
	2+ children	40.0	$0–8,890	$3,556	21.06	$11,650–28,495
	No children	7.65	$0–4,220	$323	7.65	$5,280–9,500
2000	1 child	34.0	$0–6,900	$2,353	15.98	$12,700–27,413
	2+ children	40.0	$0–9,700	$3,888	21.06	$12,700–31,152
	No children	7.65	$0–4,600	$353	7.65	$5,800–10,380

Sources: U.S. House of Representatives (2000) and authors' calculations from OBRA93.

early years and was due mostly to inflation.[8] The 1987 expansion of the EITC, passed as part of the Tax Reform Act of 1986 (TRA86), represents the first major expansion of the EITC. The TRA86 increased the subsidy rate for the phase-in of the credit from 11 percent to 14 percent and increased the maximum credit from $550 to $851 ($788 in 1986 dollars). The phase-out rate was reduced from 12.22 percent to 10 percent.

The 1991 expansion, contained in the Omnibus Reconciliation Act of 1990 (OBRA90), increased the maximum credit and introduced separate credit rates for families with two or more children. By 1993, a family with two or more children could receive a maximum credit of $1,511, $77 more than a family with one child.

The largest single expansion over this period was contained in the Om-

8. The EITC was first indexed to inflation in 1987.

nibus Reconciliation Act of 1993 (OBRA93) legislation. The 1993 expansion of the EITC, phased in between 1994 and 1996, led to an increase in the subsidy rate from 19.5 percent to 40 percent (18.5 to 34 percent) and an increase in the maximum credit from $1,511 to $3,556 ($1,434 to $2,152) for taxpayers with two or more children (taxpayers with one child). This expansion was substantially larger for those with two or more children. The phase-out rate was also raised, from 14 percent to 21 percent (13 to 16 percent) for taxpayers with two or more children (taxpayers with one child). Overall, the range of the phase-out was expanded dramatically, such that by 1996 a couple with two children would still be eligible with income levels of almost $30,000.

To summarize the changes in the EITC, figure 10.16 presents the credit schedule in 1984, 1990, 1993, and 1996. This shows that 1986 and 1993 expansions were the most substantial.

Reforms to the AFDC Program

This period saw not only expansions in the EITC but also important changes in AFDC, changes that are important for analyzing the financial incentives to work. These changes generally take the form of making the out-of-work benefits less generous and creating greater work incentives. This is the opposite of the trend in the United Kingdom. This difference is critical to understanding the "puzzle" here. From the late 1970s to the early 1990s the only substantial change in the AFDC program was a gradual erosion in the real value of benefits. For example, between 1979 and 1993 real benefits for welfare recipients fell by over 30 percent. Even taking into account falling real wages for the low-skilled population in this period, benefits relative to wages still fell by over 15 percent (Hoynes and MaCurdy 1994). Beginning in the early to mid-1990s, some states made significant changes to their AFDC programs through the provision of federal waivers. These waivers, as discussed recently by Meyer and Rosenbaum (2001) and Schoeni and Blank (2000), increased work incentives by reducing the implicit tax rate on earned income and expanding work requirements. This led up to major federal welfare reform legislation passed in 1996 (the Personal Responsibility and Work Opportunity Reconciliation Act or PRWORA) that ended the entitlement nature of the AFDC program. The AFDC program was abolished and replaced by Temporary Assistance for Needy Families (TANF).

The major provision of this act is the addition of lifetime time limits on welfare receipt, typically five years in length. In addition, states are required to increase the work effort of welfare recipients and have been given much more flexibility to redesign programs to achieve this goal. Overall, these changes have unambiguously led to an increase in the financial incentive to work.

As we discussed previously, it is important whether the income from in-

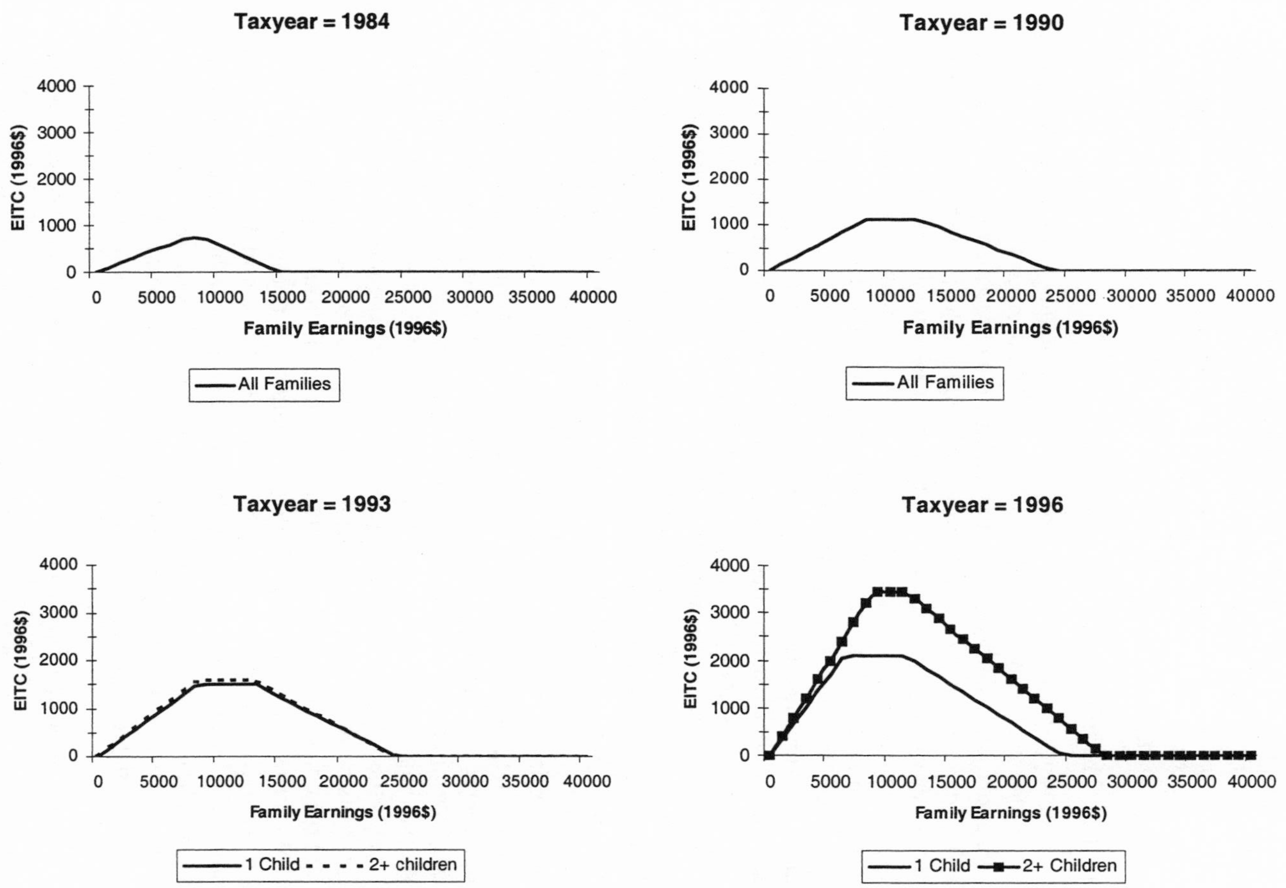

Fig. 10.16 The EITC reforms (1996 dollars)

work programs is taken into account in the calculation of welfare benefits. Over time, the rules surrounding the treatment of income from the EITC have changed (U.S. House of Representatives 2000). Between 1975 and 1978, the EITC did not count as income for the calculation of welfare benefits.[9] However, between 1979 and 1987, the credit was treated as income. Since 1988 (the main period of importance), the EITC once again is not counted as income.

10.4.2 The EITC Reforms

The trends presented in section 10.2 show the quite dramatic increases in employment among single women with children in the United States. The explanations advanced in the literature include the expansion of the EITC, increases in the minimum wage, welfare reform, and the sustained economic expansion. Of particular interest here is the role played by the EITC. An expansion in the EITC leads unambiguously to increases in employment rates for single women with children. The EITC policy reforms in 1986, 1990, and 1993 are useful in providing a before-and-after assessment of their effectiveness in changing labor market behavior. Eissa and Liebman (1996) use repeated cross sections of the Current Population Survey (CPS) to examine the effect of the 1986 reform on single mothers. They consider two comparisons: either the whole group of single women with children is used, with single women without children as controls, or the group of low-education single women with children is used, with the low-education single women without children as controls. The former control group can be criticized for not capturing the common macro effects. In particular, this control group is already working at a very high level of participation in the U.S. labor market (around 95 percent) and therefore cannot be expected to increase its level of participation in response to the economy's coming out of a recession. In this case all the expansion in labor market participation in the group of single women with children will be attributed to the reform itself. The latter group is therefore more appropriate as it targets better those single parents who are likely to be eligible for EITC, and the control group has a participation rate of about 70 percent.

With these caveats in mind, there remain some relatively strong results on participation effects that come from the Eissa and Liebman (1996) study. For single parents there is evidence of a reasonable movement in to work. The expansion of the EITC and other tax changes led to a reduction in the relative tax liability of single mothers of $1,331 (1996 dollars), and their estimated impact of the expansion was to increase employment from

9. Although the EITC was counted as income for 1979–1987, *when* it counted as income changed somewhat. For part of the period, the credit only counted as income in the month that it was received (remember that the vast majority of recipients receive it as a tax refund in one annual payment), whereas in another part of this period, the imputed value of the credit was spread out over the year.

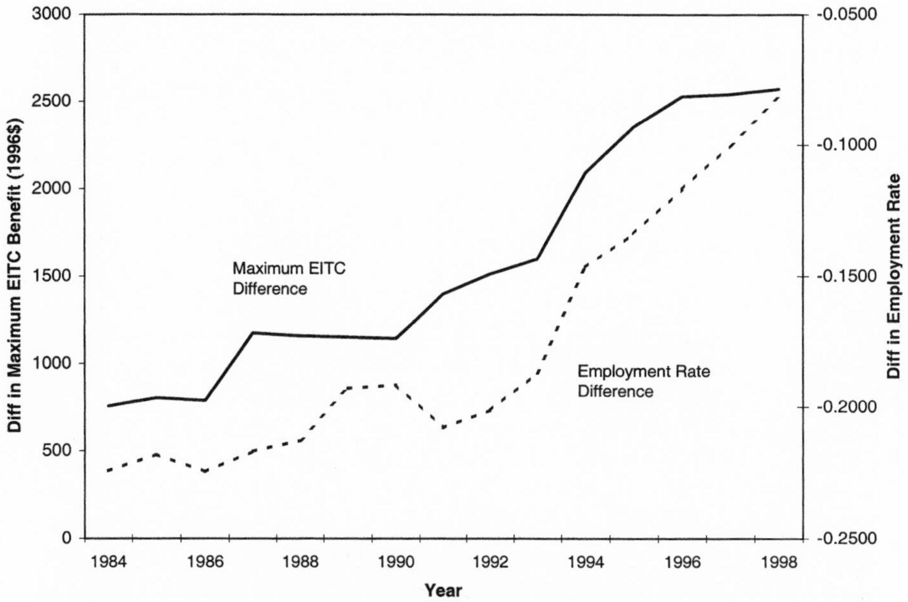

Fig. 10.17 Maximum EITC and difference in annual employment rates (comparison: single women with children to single women without children)

Source: Liebman (1998) figure 6.

Notes: Updated through 1998 using unpublished data from Liebman. The employment rate figure is based on a CPS sample of single women aged sixteen–forty-five who are not disabled or in school. Employment rate difference is the difference between the annual employment rate of single women with children and the annual employment rate of single women without children.

73.0 to 75.8 percent. There is also some evidence of negative effect on hours for those in work, but this is rather small.

Liebman (1998) and Meyer and Rosenbaum (2000) use a similar approach to examine the impact of all three of the EITC reforms. The estimated behavioral responses are very similar in magnitude to those found by Eissa and Liebman (1996). The Liebman results are summarized in figure 10.17. The figure plots the difference in employment rates of single women with and without children against the difference in the maximum EITC credit in 1996 dollars.[10] The figure shows that the relative increase in employment rates among single mothers tracks quite closely the expansion of the EITC. Meyer and Rosenbaum (2000) present similar calculations for several other comparison groups, including comparing single women with

10. In the early period, the difference in maximum credit is equal to the credit for families with children. Figure 10.17 takes into account that there was a small EITC for childless families starting in 1994. It is not clear whether Liebman (1998) took this into account in his calculation.

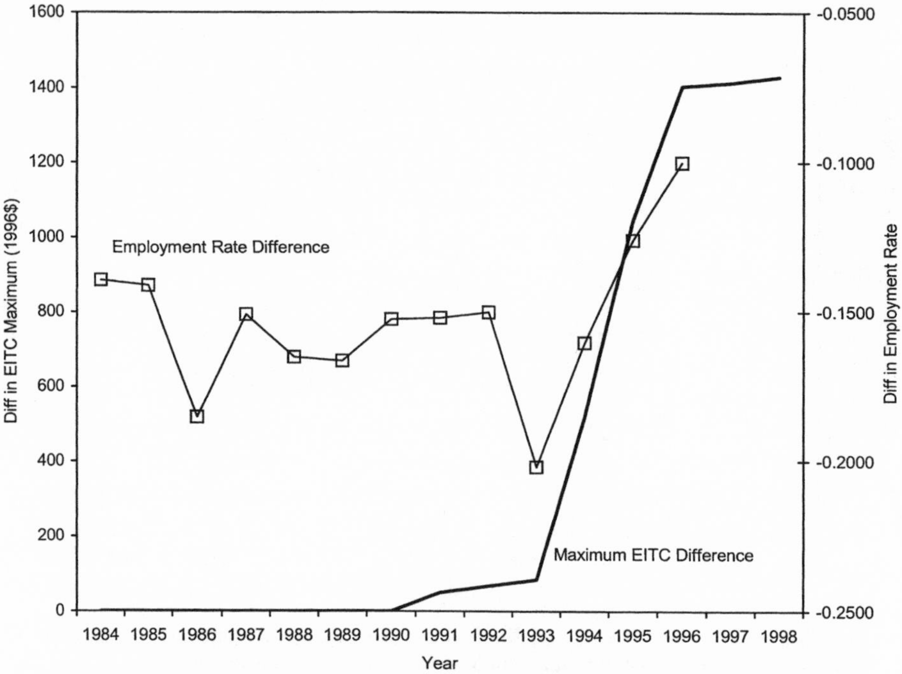

Fig. 10.18 Maximum EITC and difference in annual employment rates (comparison: single women with one child to single women with two-plus children)

Source: Employment rate differences come from table 6 in Meyer and Rosenbaum (2000).

Notes: Employment rate differences use a CPS sample of single women aged nineteen–forty-four who are not disabled or in school. Employment rate difference is the difference between the annual employment rate of single women with two or more children and the annual employment rate of single women with one child.

one child to those with two or more children, single mothers to married mothers, and single mothers to black men. Figure 10.18 summarizes the results comparing single women with one child to those with two or more children. The "treatment" here is that the 1993 EITC expansion was much more generous for families with two or more children. These results are somewhat less clear than those discussed previously but show an increase in employment of single women with two or more children relative to those with only one child at the same time that the EITC is becoming more generous for larger families.[11]

Of course, the EITC reforms were not the only changes affecting the returns to work during this period. As recently discussed by Blank (2001),

11. The employment figures in Liebman (1998) and Meyer and Rosenbaum (2000) are unconditional. The authors state that the general conclusions do not change when adding controls.

the mid-1990s simultaneously brought EITC expansions, minimum-wage increases, welfare reform, and the very strong labor market.[12] Blank argues that our ability to determine the relative importance of these factors is limited by the fact that the changes were coincident. Despite these difficulties, Meyer and Rosenbaum (2001) examine the determinants of employment of single mothers between 1984 and 1996. This period ends before federal welfare reform but includes the period when states were experimenting with welfare waivers. They use a sample of single mothers with and without children and model the gains to entering work for the two groups, taking into account a rich set of tax and transfer programs. They find that expansions in the EITC account for 60 percent of the sizeable increase in employment rates, with smaller impacts due to welfare waivers and declining real welfare benefits. Ellwood (2000), comparing employment across skill groups, also finds changes to welfare and the EITC to have stimulated the labor supply of single mothers with children. However, in contrast to Meyer and Rosenbaum (2001), his work finds that welfare program changes were slightly more important than the EITC expansions.

Overall, the literature suggests that the EITC has played an important role in the large increases in employment among single women with children. Eissa and Hoynes (2004) is one of the few papers that have considered the impact of the EITC on married couples. They use two estimation approaches. In the first, they compare the labor market outcomes of married couples with children to married couples without children. In the second, they limit the sample of married couples with children and model changes in the returns to work, including tax and transfer policy changes. Using both methods, they find that an expansion in the EITC leads to modest increases in labor force participation for married men and somewhat larger decreases in labor supply for married women. That is, they find evidence of a negative "income" effect reducing the labor supply of married women. This is precisely the adverse effect that can be expected when a work-contingent tax credit is based on a family income and will also be found in our evaluation of the likely impact of the WFTC in the United Kingdom.[13]

10.5 Evaluating the WFTC Reform

As was described in section 10.3, the WFTC introduced in October 1999 is substantially more generous than the prior in-work benefit in the United Kingdom—FC. It increases the generosity of in-work support relative to the FC system in four ways: (1) by enhancing the credit for younger chil-

12. The federal minimum wage increased in nominal terms from $3.35 in 1990 to $5.15 in 1997.

13. This negative labor supply result for married couples can also be found in Dickert, Houser, and Scholz (1995) and Neumark and Wascher (2000).

dren; (2) by increasing the threshold; (3) by reducing the benefit reduction rate from 70 percent to 55 percent; and (4) by incorporating a new child care credit of 70 percent of actual child care costs up to a quite generous limit. As we have argued, there are two important aspects of the U.K. benefit and credit system that have to be accounted for when assessing any in-work benefit reform. First, any increase in generosity will be dampened by interactions with means-tested income maintenance schemes, in particular, the Housing Benefit scheme. As we noted previously, four-fifths of single parents who do not work and who claim Income Support are in receipt of Housing Benefit. Second, increases in the credit for children and in the threshold level have been typically matched by increases to income support for nonworking parents. As our discussion in section 10.3 stressed, this has also been a feature of the WFTC reform.

10.5.1 Simulating the Reform

To provide an ex ante simulation of the impact of new reforms like the WFTC, a model is required that separates preferences from constraints. Such a model is developed in Blundell et al. (2000). This work develops earlier structural labor supply simulation models[14] by Hoynes (1996), for example, and provides a similar framework to Bingley and Walker (1997) who considered earlier reforms to the U.K. benefit system. In particular, it allows for child care demands to vary with hours worked, and it allows for fixed costs of work. It also accounts for take-up by incorporating welfare stigma, following on from Keane and Moffitt (1998).[15] This model was estimated and the simulations reported here computed before the WFTC was fully implemented.

The simulations focus on the two target groups for the WFTC reform: single parents and married couples with children. Two samples from the 1994–1995 and 1995–1996 British Family Resources Surveys (FRS) are selected: single-parent households and married or de facto married couples. Excluding self-employed and retired households, together with students and those in Her Majesty's forces, leaves samples of 1,807 single parents and 4,694 two-person households for use in estimation. Nearly 50 percent of currently working single parents were found to be in receipt of some FC. For married couples with children this proportion is smaller, at around 16 percent. However, the latter group is more than two and one-half times the size of the former.

14. Blundell and MaCurdy (1999) provide a detailed overview of such models.

15. Introducing a stigma cost to participation in WFTC allows the simulation model to predict a low probability of take-up among those with low eligibility—something found in earlier studies of welfare program take-up in the United Kingdom (Blundell and Fry 1986). Moreover, it suggests a higher take-up of WFTC (in contrast to FC) for those whose eligible amount of credit has increased as a result of the WFTC reform.

As we have seen, the WFTC reform is designed to influence the work incentives of those with low potential returns in the labor market. It does this via the increased generosity of in-work means-tested benefits. For single parents, the WFTC does unambiguously increase the incentive to work. For couples, however, the incentives created by the WFTC can lead to lower participation in the labor market. This offsetting effect on employment for secondary workers in couples has also been highlighted in the context of the EITC reforms; see Eissa and Hoynes (2004) and the previous discussion.

Panel A of figure 10.19 shows the effect of the WFTC reform on the net income and hours schedule for a typical eligible single parent. This accounts for all the interactions in the tax and benefit system and concurrent reforms to the income support system. Provided that the fixed costs of work are not too high, the financial incentive to move into work for a nonparticipant is clear. There is also an incentive to reduce hours of work among those single parents working full time. The balance between these is purely an empirical matter, although the EITC analysis, discussed in the previous section, suggested that the adverse hours effect would not dominate the positive participation effect.

Panel C of figure 10.19 presents a similar example of the financial incentives facing a male in a married couple where the partner does not work. For such couples, where neither parent is working, the incentives are unambiguously to move into work. Indeed, the gains are far larger than for our lone parent example, as the largest cash gains from the WFTC reform accrue to those at the end of the current taper. The incentives to change hours of work are ambiguous. But one interesting point is the marked increase in the effective marginal tax rate for those who become eligible for WFTC as a result of the reform. This group faces an increase in the marginal tax rates, from 33 percent, produced by income tax and National Insurance, to just under 70 percent, produced by the interaction of the 55 percent WFTC taper on posttax income. In the example, the marginal tax rate rises from 33 percent to just under 70 percent above forty hours of work.

One final point, highlighted in our discussion of the EITC reforms in the United States, is the likely incentive for some workers in married couples to move out of work altogether. Panel D of figure 10.19 shows the budget constraint for the partner of the man in panel C of figure 10.19. The panel is conditional on the man working forty hours a week. Thus the family income of the woman when she does not work is that shown at the forty-hour point. This means that the income at zero hours has increased through the WFTC reform. In the example, anyone working more than ten hours has an increased incentive to reduce their hours or move out of work altogether. The situation changes slightly when we allow for child care costs at sixteen hours as shown in panel E of figure 10.19. Here there is an additional

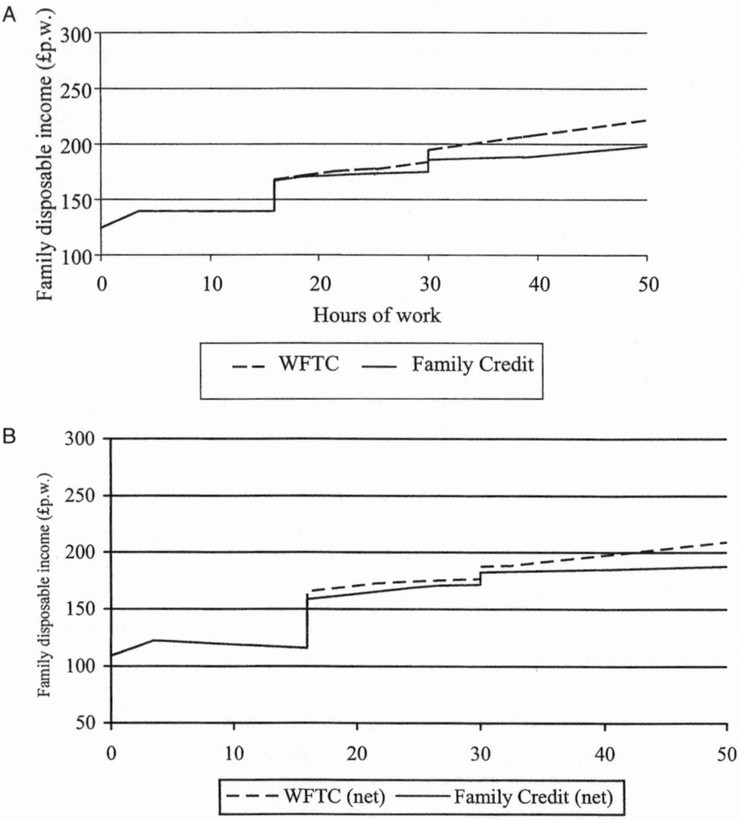

Fig. 10.19 WFTC reform budget constraints: *A*, lone parent without child care; *B*, lone parent with child care; *C*, man in couple without child care; *D*, woman in couple without child care; *E*, woman in couple with child care

Notes: A, One child aged under eleven; hourly wage £4.39 (median for lone parents); rent £41.10 per week (median for social renters with children); no child care costs; *B,* one child aged under eleven; hourly wage £4.39 (median for lone parents); rent £41.10 per week (median for social renters with children); child care at £1.96 per hour; *C,* spouse not working; one child aged under eleven; hourly wage £5.87 (25th percentile for men in couples with children); rent £41.10 per week (median for social renters with children); *D,* spouse working forty hours at £5.87 per hour; one child aged under eleven; hourly wage £3.72 (25th percentile for women in couples with children); rent £41.10 per week (median for social renters with children); no child care costs; *E,* spouse working forty hours at £5.87 per hour; one child aged under eleven; hourly wage £3.72 (25th percentile for women in couples with children); rent £41.10 per week (median for social renters with children).

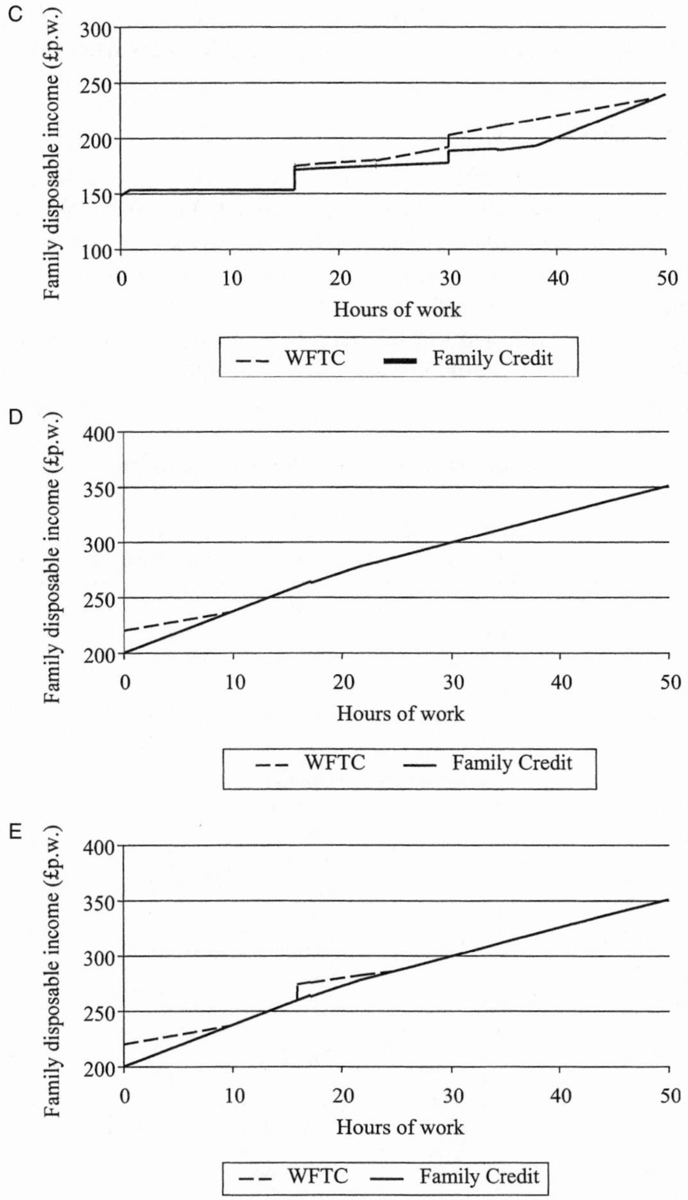

Fig. 10.19 (cont.)

incentive to work just over sixteen hours to take advantage of the child care credit. Thus, the impact on partners in eligible families where there is already one worker is again ambiguous.

WFTC Simulations: Lone Parents

In the first section of table 10.4 the simulated work responses to the WFTC among the sample of single parents are reported. The simulated transition takes around 2.2 percent of the sample from no work to either part-time or full-time work, with no offsetting movements out of the labor market. This represents nearly a 5 percent impact on employment for this group, which has employment rates around 40 percent. To take account of sampling variability, a standard error of 0.42 percent is placed around the 2.2 percent figure.

Table 10.4 **Working Families Tax Credit Reforms, Simulations**

	Postreform			
Prereform	Out of Work	Part-Time	Full-Time	Prereform (%)
		Single Parents		
Out of work	58.0	0.7	1.5	60.2
Part-time	0.0	18.6	0.5	19.1
Full-time	0.0	0.2	20.6	20.7
Postreform (%)	58.0	19.4	22.6	100
Change (%)	–2.2	0.3	1.9	
		Married Women with Employed Partners		
Out of work	32.2	0.1	0.1	32.4
Part-time	0.3	31.6	0.0	32.0
Full-time	0.4	0.1	35.0	35.6
Postreform (%)	33.0	31.8	35.2	100
Change (%)	0.6	–0.1	–0.4	
		Married Women with Partners Out of Work		
Out of work	56.8	0.4	0.9	58.1
Part-time	0.0	22.2	0.4	22.6
Full-time	0.0	0.1	19.2	19.3
Postreform (%)	56.8	22.8	20.5	100
Change (%)	–1.3	0.2	1.1	

Group	Number	Percentage
Single parents	34,000	2.20
Married women (partner not working)	11,000	1.32
Married women (partner working)	–20,000	–0.57
Married men, partner not working	13,000	0.37
Married men, partner working	–10,500	0.30
Total effect	27,500	
Decrease in workerless families	57,000	

Source: Blundell, Duncan, McCrae, and Meghir (2000) and Blundell and Reed (2000).

Table 10.5 **Numbers of Families with Children**

Group	Number in Population (thousands)
Lone parents	
Total population	1,600
Modeled population	1,550
Couples: man working	
Total population	4,550
Modeled population	3,500
Couples: man not working	
Total population	850
Modeled population	820

Source: Department of Work and Pensions (1996).

To provide the population counterparts to these changes, table 10.5 provides the total size of the population and the grossed-up equivalent from the FRS sample. One can clearly see the reason for this shift in the earlier graphs of the potential impact of the WFTC on single parents' budget constraints. At or above sixteen hours per week, the single parent becomes eligible for WFTC (with any child care credit addition to which she may be entitled). For some women this extra income makes a transition to part-time employment attractive.

We see a minor offsetting reduction in labor supply through a simulated shift from full-time to part-time employment among 0.2 percent of the sample. This is consistent with a small (negative) income effect among some full-time single women, for whom the increase in income through the WFTC encourages a reduction in labor supply. Nevertheless, the predominant incentive effect among single parents is a positive effect on participation.

WFTC Simulations: Women with Employed Partners

For married women the simulated incentive effect is quite different. The second section of table 10.4 reports estimates of the transitions following WFTC among a subsample of women with employed partners. There is a significant overall reduction in the number of women in work of around 0.57 percent. This overall reduction comprises around 0.2 percent who move into the labor market following the reform, and 0.8 percent who move from work to nonparticipation. The number of hours worked by women with employed partners is predicted to fall slightly.

The predominant negative response is clearly not one that is intended, but from the earlier budget constraint analysis one can easily see why. There will be a proportion of nonworking women whose low-earning partners will be eligible for the WFTC. The greater generosity of the tax credit relative to the current system of FC increases household income. This increase in income would be lost if the woman in the household were to work. And for those women currently in the labor market, the WFTC increases the income available to the household if she were to stop working.

WFTC Simulations: Women with Unemployed Partners

In the third section of table 10.4 the incentives for a subsample of women whose partners do not work are presented. For this group there is a significant overall increase of 1.32 percent in the number of women who work. The reason for this shift is more straightforward and stems from the increased generosity of the basic WFTC relative to the current FC system for those women who choose to move into work. Note that for this group the generosity of the child care credit component of the WFTC is not an issue, because households only qualify for the child care credit if both household members work sixteen hours or more. There is, of course, potential for both members of an unemployed household to move into work in order to qualify for the WFTC that includes the child care credit, but a joint simulation (not reported here) shows that such an outcome is virtually nonexistent.

WFTC Simulations: A Summary

The fourth section of table 10.4 provides an overall summary of the employment effects that could be expected from this reform. This table also provides the impact on male employment. The impact on single parents is quite significant. This is also the case for workless couples with children. These are the two target groups we mentioned at the outset. However, "adverse" effects on couples in which one spouse is working somewhat offset these effects. Overall the effects on participation across the two groups of men roughly cancel out, leaving the major impact operating through the effects on women, mainly single parents. However, if we consider the impact on workless households alone, then the overall impact of the WFTC is predicted to be much more substantial.

10.5.2 The WFTC Reform—Some Ex Post Evidence

The WFTC was introduced for all new recipients in October 1999 and fully phased in by April 2000. From recent administrative caseload data (Department of Social Security [various years]), the introduction of the WFTC and the substantial increase in generosity appear to have had a marked effect on the number of people claiming in-work benefits. Figure 10.20 shows that caseload has risen by 30 percent in the twelve months since May 1999. Table 10.4 shows that the average award has risen from £63 to £76 a week over the same period. Average gross weekly income of claimants is now £153, and average weekly hours worked are 30.5. Fifty-two percent of recipients are lone parents.

There has also been a large increase in take-up of the Childcare Tax

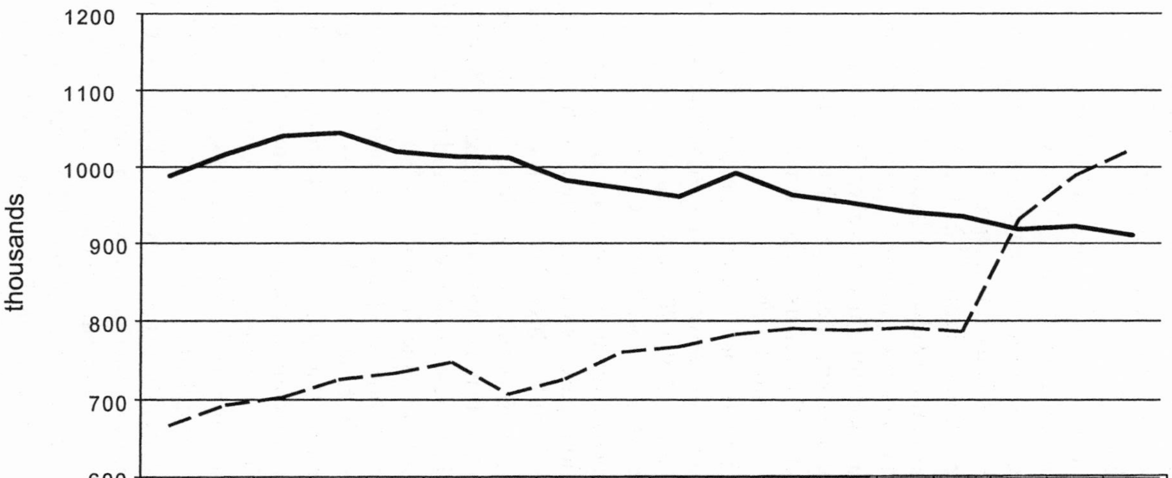

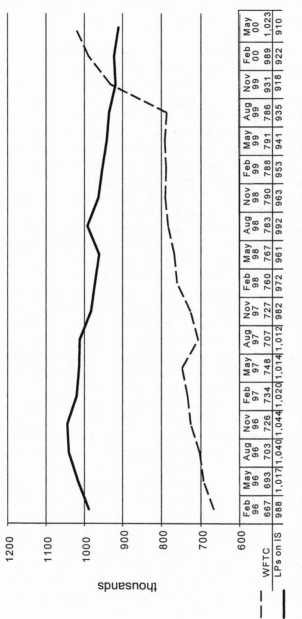

	Feb 96	May 96	Aug 96	Nov 96	Feb 97	May 97	Aug 97	Nov 97	Feb 98	May 98	Aug 98	Nov 98	Feb 99	May 99	Aug 99	Nov 99	Feb 00	May 00
WFTC	667	693	703	726	734	748	707	727	760	767	783	790	788	791	786	931	989	1,023
LPs on IS	988	1,017	1,040	1,044	1,020	1,014	1,012	982	972	961	992	963	953	941	935	918	922	910

Fig. 10.20 Caseload of lone parents on Income Support and all families on FC and WFTC, 1996–2000

Source: Blundell (2002).

Note: Great Britain only.

Credit compared to the child care disregard under FC. In May 2000 111,000 families were receiving help with child care costs, a 156 percent increase over twelve months. The average amount of costs claimed was £32 a week. Although this is a large increase, however, this is still only 10 percent of the total WFTC caseload (table 10.5).

Obviously some of the change in WFTC caseload is due to the increased numbers of already working parents who qualify for WFTC due to its increased generosity. This alone cannot be taken as a measure of success in increasing employment. We can learn a little more by looking at administrative data on cross-benefit flows. Figure 10.21 breaks down the WFTC and FC caseload by their situation twelve months ago. It shows that a large component of the caseload increase (around 75 percent, taking the last four quarters of FC as a baseline) since October 1999 has come from people who were not claiming any means-tested benefits or tax credits twelve months before. Both of these facts are consistent with the increased entitlement of the WFTC compared with FC.

It is informative to compare the predicted labor supply effects discussed earlier with the available administrative data. The simulations reported in table 10.4[16] estimate that around 30,000 currently workless lone parents with children will enter work as a result of WFTC.[17] The government's equivalent (and unpublished) estimate for the package of tax and benefit reforms is around 40,000 lone parents with children. Although we cannot make accurate inferences from this high-level analysis of administrative data, we cannot yet see a change of this magnitude in the behavior of lone parents. When we compare February 2000 with August 1999, only 5 percent (10,000 families) of the increase in the WFTC and FC caseload is due to lone parents' moving from Income Support to WFTC.

There are several important reasons that could explain the discrepancy. First, responses to reforms take time. It took two years for the strong peak at sixteen hours to appear after the 1992 reform to FC in the United Kingdom. Second, we have presented an extremely crude analysis that does not, for example, control for any underlying changes in the number of lone parents moving from Income Support to WFTC and FC (for example, the number of lone parents moving from Income Support to WFTC and FC fell by 7,000 in the twelve months prior to August 1999). Third, we also cannot identify lone parents on other out-of-work benefits.

Nonetheless, taken together with our simulation results, these administrative statistics suggest that the impact of the WFTC reform on employment among low-income families in the United Kingdom is positive but modest. This supports our overall view that the workings of the tax and

16. Similar percentage effects on single parents can be found in the Gregg, Johnson, and Reed (1999) study.

17. We cannot analyze couples who move into work because of the difficulties in classifying couples who change claimants when they change benefits and tax credits.

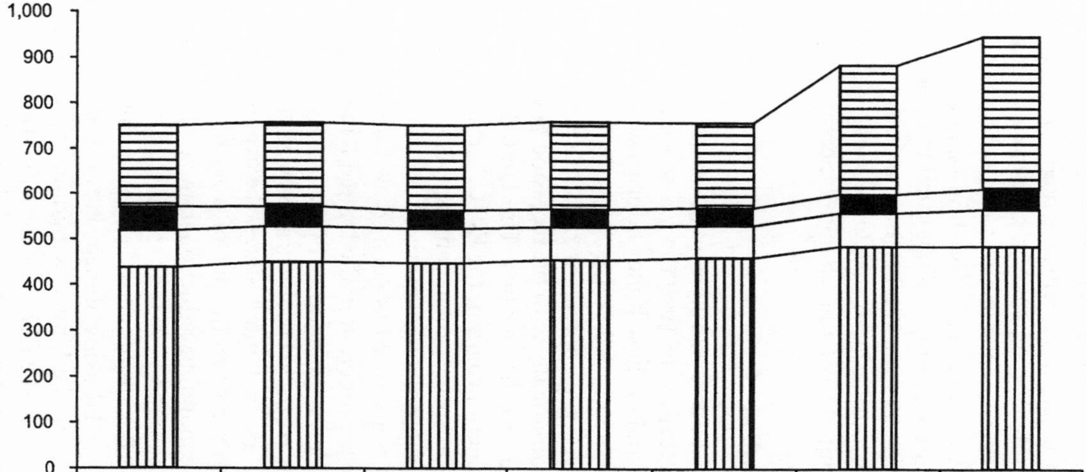

	Aug 98	Nov 98	Feb 99	May 99	Aug 99	Nov 99	Feb 00
New claimer (in own right)	180	186	189	193	188	285	334
From other MTBs	52	44	40	39	39	41	45
Lone parents from IS	81	78	76	73	71	74	81
On WFTC already	437	449	447	454	460	485	486

Fig. 10.21 Families on WFTC: Where were they twelve months ago?
Source: Blundell (2002).

benefit system in the United Kingdom, together with the increased generosity to workless families with children, mean that changes to financial work incentives from in-work benefit reforms are relatively small.

One caveat to this is the possible impact of the child care credit. Under WFTC this is a generous scheme available only to those in work (requiring both parents in a couple to work at least sixteen hours), but, as we have indicated, it is currently taken up by only a small fraction of WFTC recipients. If participation in this part of the WFTC program was to expand significantly, it could further encourage labor supply among those low-income parents who are currently out of work and claiming Income Support.

10.6 Summary and Conclusions

The late 1980s and 1990s saw substantial expansions to the U.K. system of in-work benefits. Most recently, in 1999 the FC was expanded and replaced by the WFTC. The goal of these policy reforms was clear: to significantly increase the employment of the targeted groups of lone parents and workless couples. However, employment rates of single women with children, which declined dramatically with the recession of the early 1980s, have remained low relative to other groups. The United States also expanded its main in-work benefit program, the EITC, during the late 1980s and 1990s. But the U.S. expansions were accompanied by much larger increases in the employment rates of single mothers and heralded as a great policy success. The goal of our paper has been to explore this puzzle and determine why the results were different in the United Kingdom.

Our analysis leads to two key explanations. First, in-work benefits incentives in the United Kingdom are dulled by integration with the rest of the tax and benefit system. Second, in the United States, the expansions to the in-work benefits occurred at a time when the out-of-work benefits were being reduced. There was no corresponding reduction in the United Kingdom.

In relation to the first explanation, we point to the significant benefit reduction rate in the Housing Benefit program, inducing only small gains to working for those with large Housing Benefit entitlements. Many nonworking low-income families in the United Kingdom are in this position. In the United States, by contrast, the EITC is not counted as income for the calculation of any other transfer program, so the household sees the full gain of the in-work benefit. The interaction between in-work benefits and other means-tested benefits is of central importance in understanding the precise change in incentives that reforms to the in-work benefit system have delivered.

In terms of the second explanation, welfare programs in the United States underwent major reforms, leading to a decline in the value of staying out of the labor force for single mothers. Thus the increase in incentives to work through the EITC was strengthened by the decline in the generosity of out-of-work benefits. In the United Kingdom, by contrast, the out-of-work programs either maintained levels of generosity or, in some cases, actually increased generosity in step with the increases in the in-work programs. The combination of these two forces meant that the expansions of the U.K. in-work programs generated rather modest increases in the incentives to work.

It is not that we find no positive employment responses to the reforms in the United Kingdom. Indeed, there is strong evidence that certain targeted groups responded to the incentives in their labor supply behavior. For example, our simulations point to an important impact on single parents, drawing more than 30,000 into work and off income support from the recent WFTC reform. Also, we find a significant percentage of men and women in workless couples move into employment. However, these positive increases in employment for workless couples with children are offset somewhat by a decrease in the level of employment in couples with children where both spouses are working, reflecting the income effect. The reduction in workless families is therefore much more substantial than the increase in employment.

This can only be a partial assessment of the recent reforms to the structure of in-work benefits in the United Kingdom. There are several additional issues that have been raised. The first relates to child care. The recent reform in the United Kingdom contains a generous child care component. If taken up it could significantly improve the labor supply of the target groups. Also, it mitigates the offsetting effect on working married couples because there is a requirement that both parents work in a couple for eligibility. On face value, child care should be important. The data show that the low attachment rates are concentrated among women whose youngest child is below formal school age. Indeed, one interpretation of the experimental findings in Card and Robins (1998) is that in-work benefits speed up the entry into work of mothers with young children. However, to date, the take-up among couples is less than 2 percent, and among single parents it is less than 12 percent. These low take-up rates are something of a puzzle and may reflect the time taken for the child care market to adapt.

Finally, there is the issue of earnings progression. Will the earnings of the recipients who are brought into work due to the increased generosity of in-work benefit programs see any significant growth in real wages? Will they eventually be able to earn their way out of the in-work benefit system? How does a tax credit affect incentives for wage progression? Unlike the Canadian Self Sufficiency Project (SSP) experiment, the U.K. and U.S. systems are not time limited. At first sight, this looks to set up the wrong incentives for wage progression. Certainly the incentives for individuals to seek out wage progression are probably reduced. But, as pointed out by Heckman, Lochner, and Cossa (2002), distinguishing between the method of skill formation is key. Evidence on wage progression for these types of workers is sparse, but there are three important and relevant studies—the Card and Robins (1999) study of the wages of the control and treatment groups in the

Canadian experiment, the Heckman, Lochner, and Cossa (2002) study of the impact of EITC on skill formation, and the Gladden and Taber (2000) study of true experience effects across education and gender groups in the United States. All of these studies point to modest wage growth. The first study suggests those drawn into the program do not experience significantly lower wage growth, although the level of wage growth is low. The second study highlights the importance of distinguishing between the method of skill formation—that is, whether it is dominated by on-the-job learning or learning by doing. The third study shows that, although growth is slow, it is rather similar across skill and gender groups. Positive news? Yes, but the rates of wage progression are small, and the wage levels of these individuals in the United Kingdom are very low. In Blundell (2002) it is argued that given the large impact on incomes—and implicitly on hourly wages—that is brought about through in-work benefits, it is doubtful that wage progression alone will lead to any significant movement out of in-work benefit receipt.

Appendix

Data

U.K. Labor Market Sources and Definitions

Family Expenditure Survey (FES)

The FES is a repeated continuous cross-sectional survey of households that provides consistent data on wages, hours of work, employment status in last two weeks, and education for each year since 1978. Family Expenditure Survey years correspond to the financial year. Consequently, 1998, for example, covers the twelve months up to April 1999. It therefore corresponds to 1999 in the March CPS data used in the U.S. comparisons. Prior to 1978 the FES contains no information on educational attainment. In particular, the survey contains information on usual labor market status.

Low Education

We show trends for all women and trends in a low-education sample classified as those who left full-time education at age sixteen or lower. An alternative to our method for constructing the education dummy would use those who left education at the statutory minimum age as the base group. This method is equivalent to ours from 1973 onward in the United Kingdom; before this date the minimum school-leaving age was a year lower, at fifteen. Nonetheless, interactions between date-of-birth cohort effects and the education dummy will capture any effects of the change in minimum leaving age on the relative returns to education enjoyed by the seventeen-plus group. See Gosling, Machin, and Meghir (2000). We use this criterion to better select women affected by the in-work benefit reforms under consideration.

Labour Force Survey (LFS)

The LFS is a quarterly survey of some 60,000 working-age individuals in the United Kingdom.

Family Resources Survey (FRS)

The FRS is a continuous survey with an annual sample size of around 25,000 private households. It provides detailed income and benefit data for individuals in households and is representative of the whole population.

U.S. Labor Market Sources and Definitions

The March Current Population Surveys (CPS)

The March CPS is an annual demographic file of between 50,000 and 62,000 households. For each individual in the household the survey provides detailed information on labor market, income, and demographic characteristics. In particular, the survey contains information on labor market status of the last week as well as detailed labor market information for the previous calendar year. Our main labor market measure from the CPS is work status of the last week, but as an alternative measure we consider weeks worked in the last year. As for the United Kingdom, we calculate trends in these labor market variables using women between the ages of twenty and fifty-four. We also restrict the sample in this way because we do not want to address issues of early retirement and exit from the labor market. We present trends in labor market variables by marital status and presence of children.

Low Education

The low education sample consists of women with no more than a high school education (less than or equal to twelve years of education). Again, we use this criterion to better select women affected by the EITC.

References

Bingley, P., and I. Walker. 1997. The labour supply, unemployment and participation of lone mothers in in-work transfer programs. *Economic Journal* 107:1375–390.

Blank, R. M. 2001. Declining caseloads/increased work: What can we conclude about the effects of welfare reform. *Economic Policy Review* 7:25–36.
Blundell, R. W. 2000. Work incentives and in-work benefit reforms: A review. *Oxford Review of Economic Policy* 16 (1): 27–44.
Blundell, R. W. 2001. Welfare reform for low income workers. *Oxford Economic Papers* 53:189–214.
Blundell, R. W. 2002. Welfare to work: Which policies work and why? Keynes Lecture in Economics 2001. In *Proceedings of the British Academy* 117 (November): 477–524. London: The British Academy.
Blundell, R. W., A. S. Duncan, J. McCrae, and C. Meghir. 2000. The labour market impact of the Working Families Tax Credit. *Fiscal Studies* 21:65–74.
Blundell, R. W., and V. Fry. 1986. Modeling the take-up of means tested benefits: The case of housing benefits in the UK. *Economic Journal* 83:18–34.
Blundell, R. W., and T. MaCurdy. 1999. Labor supply: A review of alternative approaches. In *Handbook of labor economics,* vol. 3, ed. O. Ashenfelter and D. Card, 1559–695. Amsterdam: Elsevier/North-Holland.
Blundell, R. W., and C. Meghir. 2002. Active labour market policy vs. employment tax credits: Lessons from recent UK reforms. *Swedish Economic Policy Review* 8 (January): 13–37.
Blundell, R. W., and H. Reed. 2000. The employment effects of the Working Families Tax Credit. IFS Briefing Note no. 6. London: Institute for Fiscal Studies, April.
Brewer, M. 2000. Comparing in-work benefits and financial work incentives for low-income families in the US and the UK. Institute for Fiscal Studies Working Paper no. W00/16, *Fiscal Studies,* forthcoming.
Brewer, M., M. Myck, and H. Reed. 2001. Financial support for families with children. IFS Commentary no. 82. London: Institute for Fiscal Studies, January.
Card, D., and K. Robins. 1998. Do financial incentives encourage welfare recipients to work? *Research in Labor Economics* 17:1–56.
———. 1999. Measuring "wage progression" among former welfare recipients. Center for Labor Economics Discussion Paper no. 20. Berkeley: University of California.
Department of Social Security. Various years. Client group analysis—Working age. London: Government Statistical Service.
Department of Work and Pensions. 1996. *Family Resources Survey, 1994–1995.* London: Her Majesty's Stationery Office.
Dickert, S., S. Houser, and J. K. Scholz. 1995. The Earned Income Tax Credit and transfer program: A study of labor market and program participation. In *Tax policy and the economy,* vol. 9, ed. J. M. Poterba, 1–50. Cambridge: MIT Press.
Dilnot, A., J. Kay, and C. Morris. 1984. *The reform of Social Security.* Oxford: Oxford University Press.
Dilnot, A., and I. Walker, eds. (1992). *The economics of Social Security.* Oxford: Oxford University Press.
Duncan, A., and C. Giles. 1996. Labour supply incentives and recent family credit reforms. *Economic Journal* 106:142–155.
Eissa, N., and H. W. Hoynes. 2004. Taxes and the labor market participation of married couples: The Earned Income Tax Credit. *Journal of Public Economics* forthcoming.
Eissa, N., and J. B. Liebman. 1996. Labor supply response to the Earned Income Tax Credit. *Quarterly Journal of Economics* 111:605–637.
Ellwood, D. T. 2000. The impact of EITC and other social programs on work and marriage in the United States. *National Tax Journal* 53 (4): 1063–106.

Giles, C., P. Johnson, and J. McCrae. 1997. Housing benefit and the financial returns to employment for tenants in the social sector. *Fiscal Studies* 18:49–72.
Gladden, T., and C. Taber. 2000. Wage progression among less skilled workers. In *Finding jobs: Work and welfare reform,* ed. D. Card and R. M. Blank, 160–192. New York: Russell Sage Foundation.
Gosling, A., S. Machin, and C. Meghir. 2000. The changing distribution of male wages in the U.K. *Review of Economic Studies* 67 (4): 635–666.
Gregg, P., P. Johnson, and H. Reed. 1999. Entering work and the British tax and benefit system. IFS Monograph. London: Institute for Fiscal Studies, March.
Heckman, J. J., L. Lochner, and R. Cossa. 2002. Learning-by-doing vs on-the-job training: Using variation induced by the Earned Income Tax Credit to distinguish between models of skill formation. University of Chicago. Working Paper.
Her Majesty's Treasury. 2000. Tackling poverty and making work pay: Tax credits for the 21st century, The Modernisation of Britain's Tax and Benefit System Treasury Monograph no. 6. London: Her Majesty's Stationery Office.
Hoynes, H. W. 1996. Welfare transfers in two-parent families: Labor supply and welfare participation under the AFDC-UP Program. *Econometrica* 64 (2): 295–332.
Hoynes, H. W. 2000. The employment and earnings of less skilled workers over the business cycle. In *Finding jobs: Work and welfare reform,* ed. R. M. Blank and D. Card, 23–71. New York: Russell Sage Foundation.
Hoynes, H. W., and T. MaCurdy. 1994. Has the decline in benefits shortened welfare spells? *American Economic Review* 84 (2): 43–48.
Keane, M. P., and R. Moffitt. 1998. A structural model of multiple welfare program participation and labor supply. *International Economic Review* 39:553–589.
Liebman, J. B. 1998. The impact of the Earned Income Tax Credit on incentives and income distribution. In *Tax policy and the economy,* vol. 12, ed. J. M. Poterba, 83–119. Cambridge: MIT Press.
Meyer, B., and D. T. Rosenbaum. 2000. Making single mothers work: Recent tax and welfare policy and its effects. *National Tax Journal* 53 (4): 1027–062.
———. 2001. Welfare, the Earned Income Tax Credit, and the labor supply of single mothers. *Quarterly Journal of Economics* 116 (3): 1063–114.
Neumark, D., and W. Wascher. 2000. Using the EITC to help poor families: New evidence and a comparison with the minimum wage. NBER Working Paper no. 7599. Cambridge, Mass.: National Bureau of Economic Research, March.
Schoeni, R., and R. M. Blank. 2000. What has welfare reform accomplished? Impacts on welfare participation, employment, income, poverty, and family structure. NBER Working Paper no. 7627. Cambridge, Mass.: National Bureau of Economic Research, March.
U.S. House of Representatives. 2000. Background materials and data on programs within the jurisdiction of the Committee on Ways and Means. Washington, D.C.: GPO.

11

Active Labor Market Policies and the British New Deal for the Young Unemployed in Context

John Van Reenen

11.1 Introduction

On March 14, 2001 the number of British people claiming unemployment benefits fell below 1 million for the first time in twenty-five years. To celebrate the event, the prime minister gave a speech on the New Deal. The March 15, 2001 edition of the *Evening Standard* quoted the prime minister as saying "Nobody says to me they're on a skivvy[1] scheme. The sort of language used about employment programs in the 1980s is not used about the New Deal."

This paper addresses two questions. Does New Labour's flagship employment policy represent a significant break from the past—and has it worked? In the 1980s and 1990s U.K. governments introduced major changes in the levels and conditions for receipt of unemployment benefits. I examine the effects of a large labor market program that was introduced (initially in pilot form) in January 1998, the year after the election of the new government. The New Deal involves a cluster of different policies designed to getting the jobless (especially the young unemployed) back to work.

Since April 1998 *all* individuals aged between eighteen and twenty-four

John Van Reenen is professor of economics at the London School of Economics and the Centre for Economic Performance.

This paper draws extensively on joint work with Richard Blundell, Costas Meghir, and Monica Costa Dias. Michal Myck and Tom Clark have both helped with the calculations. Finance came from Leverhulme Trust. The author is very grateful to comments by all participants, especially David Card, David Grubb, Paul Gregg, Marty Feldstein, Richard Freeman, Richard Layard, Howard Reed, and two anonymous referees. The usual disclaimer applies. On-line information about the New Deal is available at www.newdeal.gov.uk.

1. A "skivvy" is a low status, low quality occupation. *Oxford English Dictionary* gives the following example of its usage: "I never thought myself capable of such strenuosities as to do a skivvy's drudgery."

who have claimed unemployment benefits (called *Job Seekers Allowance* or *JSA*) enter the New Deal program. There are two stages. First, there is a "Gateway" period, where the claimant is given intensive help with job search. Those who do not secure an unsubsidized job during this stage go on to the second stage of New Deal options that include subsidized full-time training or education, a wage subsidy paid to the employer, voluntary work, or placement with the Environmental Task Force (government-provided employment). It is a mandatory program—there is no fifth option for remaining on benefits.

In this paper I focus on evaluating the success of the New Deal program in moving people into jobs. In the short run this occurs in two main ways. First, there is an enhanced job search monitored by a meeting every two weeks with a personal advisor. The job search could be increased by (1) the more credible threat of benefit sanctions, (2) the provision of a greater quality and quantity of information on vacancies, or (3) the psychological effect of being connected again with the labor market. Second, the wage subsidy reduces the cost to the employer of taking on an unemployed person (by about 40–50 percent).

The job search aspect has many antecedents in benefit reforms initiated under the previous Conservative administration. In particular, the Restart initiative in 1986 began a new era of increased monitoring of the unemployed (see section 11.3). The New Deal has continued this tightening up of the work-search rules, but has combined it with much more generous funding of job search assistance and subsidized options. For young people there is now effectively a time limit on benefit receipt. The wage-subsidy element also has antecedents in Britain (and elsewhere) that I discuss briefly in section 11.3.

I draw on results using a simple difference-in-differences approach exploiting two sources of identification. The eligibility for the New Deal is age related, so we can compare outflows by different age groups before and after the New Deal was introduced. Additionally, the New Deal was introduced earlier in some areas, so we can compare young people in these pilot areas to young people in nonpilot areas. There are numerous factors that may bias these estimates that are discussed, including selectivity, differential macro trends, job quality, substitution, and general equilibrium effects.

I have some things to say about the other parts of the New Deal program (such as training), but the truth is that it is still in its early days. The long-run success of the program will in large part depend on its ability to enhance the productivity and employability of people going through the options. Publicly available data at the time of writing ends in 1999, so we are only just starting to observe the labor market performance of those leaving the twelve-month education and training options.

The results suggest that the reforms have successfully increased net employment for the target group. Young unemployed men are about 20 percent more likely per period to gain jobs as a result of the New Deal (i.e., the probability of a young man unemployed for six months or more obtaining a job rose from about 5 percent a month to 6 percent a month). A substantial part of this effect is attributed to the wage subsidy option, but there is also some job assistance effect. An initial cost benefit analysis suggests that the program is worth continuing on efficiency grounds alone.

The plan of the paper is as follows. Section 11.2 gives some background, placing the U.K.'s labor market in historical and comparative perspective. Section 11.3 gives the history and details of the reforms. Section 11.4 offers some results on the evaluation of the New Deal. Section 11.5 gives the cost-benefit calculations, and section 11.6 offers some concluding remarks.

11.2 General U.K. Labor Market Background

In this section I sketch out some features of the labor market of the United Kingdom in historical and comparative perspective.

Figure 11.1 displays the total unemployed claimant count since 1960, and figure 11.2 shows the standard International Labour Organization (ILO) unemployment rates from 1978 onward. In many respects the United Kingdom is similar to other European countries. There has been a steady upward drift of unemployment since 1960, with a very large increase post-1979. Until the 1990s, the trough of each recession was associated with higher unemployment than the previous downturn. The expansion since 1993 has pushed the number of unemployed below that of the previous cycle to levels not seen since the last Labour government (1974–1979).

Another feature of U.K. unemployment is its volatility. The United Kingdom has experienced sharp boom-bust cycles. There were deep recessions in the early 1980s and early 1990s and a fast boom in the mid- to late 1980s. There was a similar boom in the late 1990s and early 2000s, although with lower levels of wage and price inflation.

Currently U.K. unemployment is relatively low by Organization for Economic Cooperation and Development (OECD) standards (see column [1], table 11.1). This has been a relatively recent phenomenon, however. Between 1983 and 1996, U.K. unemployment rates have been above the OECD average, certainly higher than Germany's (which has never fully recovered from the shock of reunification in 1989), although lower than France's.[2] Furthermore, in terms of its long-term unemployment rates, the United Kingdom appears much closer to a European country than to the United States.

Across almost all OECD countries youth unemployment is higher than

2. Between 1983 and 1996 OECD average unemployment was 8.2 percent—9.7 percent in the United Kingdom, 6.2 percent in West Germany, and 10.4 percent in France (Nickell 1997).

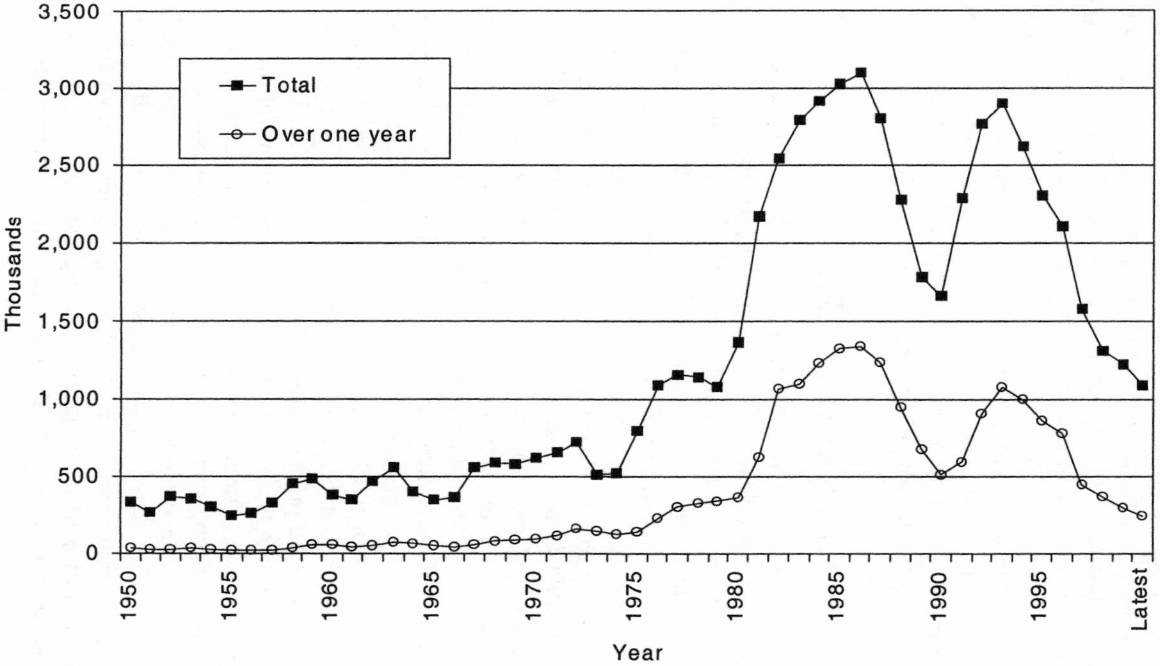

Fig. 11.1 Claimant unemployment—total and long-term

Sources: Data underlying the figure is available at http://www.statistics.gov.uk and Wells (2000).

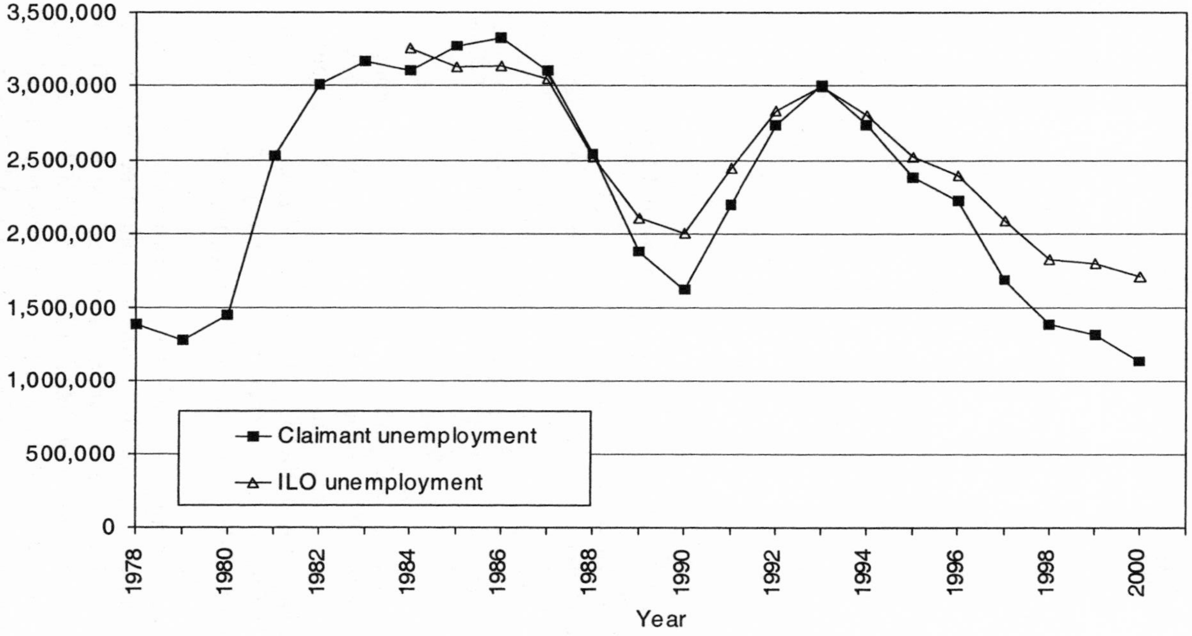

Fig. 11.2 Unemployment—claimant and ILO measures

Sources: Data on ILO defined unemployment were taken from the LFS. Data underlying the figure is available at http://www.statistics.gov.uk and Wells (2000).

Notes: The ILO definition is based on asking out of work individuals whether they would be available and prepared to accept a job within two weeks. The claimant count is the number of people who are receiving unemployment benefits (called *Job Seekers Allowance* since 1994). Although the series track each other relatively well, there will be some people who are ILO unemployed who will not be in the claimant count (e.g., if they left their job voluntarily, this will disqualify them from benefits receipt for a period of time). Similarly, some individuals could be claiming unemployment benefits without genuinely searching for a job.

Table 11.1 Benefits, Sanctions, and Unemployment: International Comparisons (%)

Country	ILO Unemployment Rate (c. 1999) (1)	Replacement Rate (c. 1997–1998) (2)	Sanction Rate (1994–1995) (3)
Australia	7.5	71	14.7
Belgium	9.1	61	4.2
Canada	8.1	66	6.1
Denmark	4.8	80	4.3
France	11.2	n.a.	n.a.
Finland	10.7	81	10.2
West Germany	7.4	79	1.1
Italy	10.0	n.a.	n.a.
Japan	4.7	59	0.02
The Netherlands	3.4	82	36
Norway	2.9	73	10.8
Sweden	7.3	85	0.8
Switzerland	1.8	84	40.3
United Kingdom	6.2	67	10.3
United States	4.3	60	25.7

Sources: International Labor Organization (ILO) unemployment rate 1999 from Nickell and van Ours (2000). Replacement rate from Martin (1998, table 4). Sanction rate from Grubb (2000), except for the Netherlands (Boone and van Ours 2000) and Sweden.

Notes: Replacement rate calculated as benefit entitlements before tax as a percentage of previous earnings before tax; first month of unemployment for a person on average earnings, assuming that person is forty years old, has a dependent spouse, has two children, and started work at eighteen. These are all 1994–1995 (except for Japan, 1996). Sanctions rate is defined as total sanctions during benefit periods as a proportion of the average stock of claims 1997–1998. n.a. = not available.

unemployment for prime-age individuals. There is a relatively high proportion of young Britons in jobs and a low proportion of young people in school. There is also a large proportion of British youth that are neither in school nor in the labor force (the "idle"). The United Kingdom has the highest numbers of eighteen-year-old men in this category.[3] Moreover, the United Kingdom has had the largest increase in the proportion of "idle" youth since 1984.

Another feature of the youth labor market is its sensitivity to the business cycle. The unemployment rates of the younger group (see figure 11.3) broadly mirror the overall picture, but are more cyclically sensitive. This is also true for the employment rates (see Bell, Blundell, and Van Reenen 1999).

Turning to wage rates, it is well known that there has been a large increase in earnings inequality in the United Kingdom since 1979 (Schmitt,

3. The proportion idle was 8.4 percent in the United Kingdom in 1997, compared to 2.3 percent in 1984. In 1997 the OECD average was 1.8 percent—5.6 percent in the United States, 4.2 percent in Germany, 3.3 percent in France, and 9.1 percent in Italy (see Blanchflower and Freeman 2000).

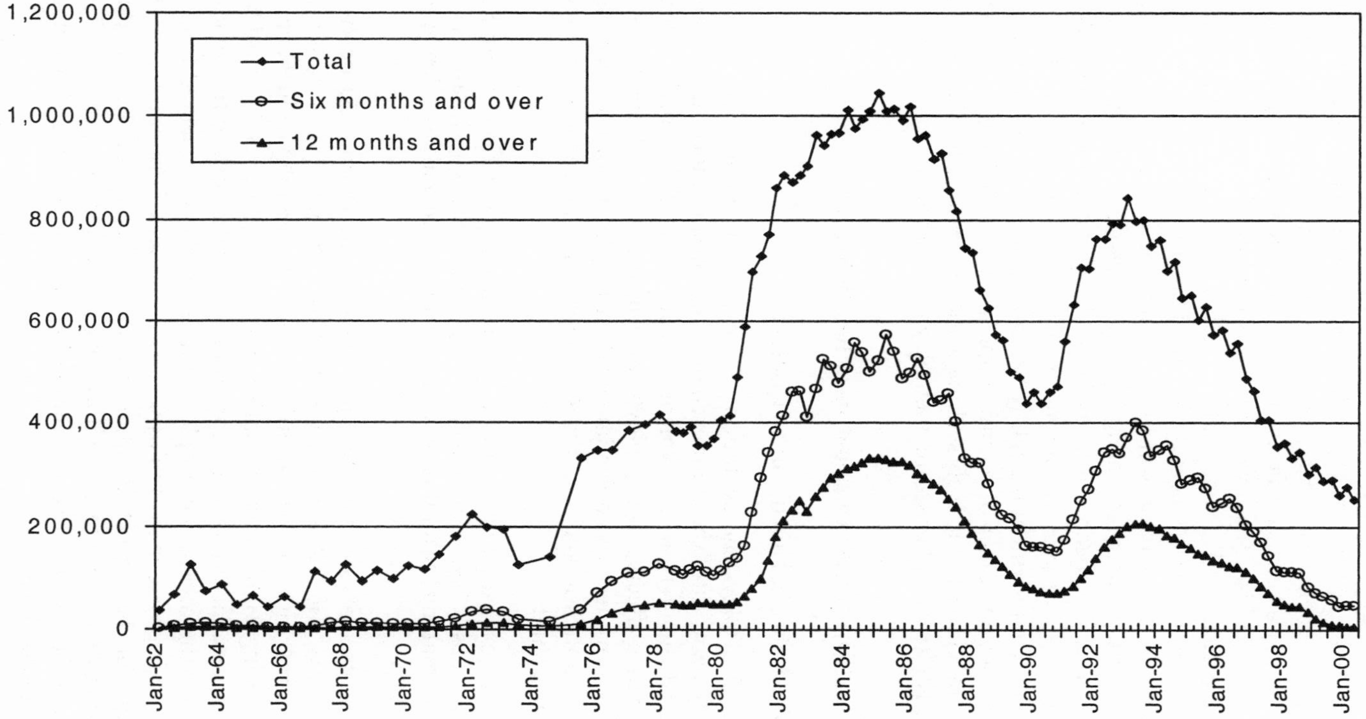

Fig. 11.3 Claimant unemployment amongst eighteen–twenty-four-year-olds

Source: Data underlying the figure is available at http://www.statistics.gov.uk and Wells (2000).

1995; Gosling, Machin, and Meghir 2000). This has occurred between the younger and older age groups, even within gender and skill classes. The uprating of many benefit levels (e.g., the state pension and unemployment benefit) in Britain was pegged to price inflation instead of earnings inflation from 1979–1980. Also, there were real cuts of about 10 percent in most means-tested benefits. This has lead to a fall in the replacement rate relative to other countries (the second column of table 11.1).

To summarize this section somewhat boldly, the United Kingdom has enjoyed lower than average unemployment rates since the mid- to late 1990s than other European countries. Over a longer time frame unemployment has been about average and more volatile than other OECD countries. Youth unemployment is slightly better than average, but there are a surprisingly large number of young people in the United Kingdom who are neither in school nor actively seeking work. Wages are relatively low for young British workers, but so are unemployment benefits.

11.3 Institutions of U.K. Unemployment Benefit Regime

11.3.1 The New Deal in Historical Context

Table 11.2 displays the evolution of the U.K. unemployment benefit regime. The network of the labor exchanges was first founded in 1910 and administered the first unemployment benefits from 1912. Worries about the disincentive effects of unemployment benefit persisted from its foundation. The work test was a fundamental part of the labor exchange but was seen as more humane than the workhouses that preceded it. As Beveridge (1909) put it

> The labour exchange opens the way for "depauperisation" more humane, less costly and more effective than that of the workhouse test—the way of making the finding of work easy instead of making relief hard. (215–216)

The work-test requirement became less pressing during the postwar "Golden Years" of low unemployment. From the late 1960s, however, there appeared to be a shift in attitude toward unemployment benefits away from being a temporary palliative of social insurance and toward being a more permanent redistribution from those with work to the jobless. Additionally, the role of the Employment Service was reoriented toward being a service provider to employers and employees. It attempted to regain a share in the market for filling vacancies because of the fear that employers were losing interest in notifying job centers of vacancies. The Employment Service focused less on finding jobs for the difficult to place long-term unemployed.

The most important consequence of these changes was that the

Table 11.2 **Timeline of U.K. Unemployment Benefit Reforms**

Year	Reform
1910, February	Labor exchange network founded by Winston Churchill
1912	Unemployment benefit introduced and administered by labor exchanges
1919	All claimants had to prove "normally in employment, genuinely seeking employment and unable to obtain it"
1946	National Insurance Act
1961	Visit Job Center once a week (twice a week before)
1974	Benefit Office and Job Center split
1979	13% cut in Employment Service staff
1980	Visit Job Center only once every two weeks
1982	Visiting Job Center voluntary
1982–1985	50% cutback in numbers of staff to enforce work search (fall of 940 to 550 in Unemployment Registration Office)
1986 Restart	Restart mandatory job-related interview; increases in staff (especially for checking fraud); vacancies displayed in benefit office; verification letters sent to unemployed; maximum period of benefit disqualification extended to 13 weeks (was 6 weeks 1913–1986) January—pilots; July—nationwide for those with 1+ year unemployment; October—extended to all with 6 months unemployment
1988	Maximum period of benefit disqualification extended to 26 weeks
1989 Social Security Act	Eligibility requirements increased over "actively seeking work" (must look every week); cannot refuse "unsuitable" jobs paying less than going rate
1990	Employment Service given more independence by being made into an "arm's-length agency"; performance targets (e.g., on referrals)
1991	Mandatory one-week job course for unemployed >2 years
1994/1995	"Stricter benefit regime" doubles number of sanctions/referrals
1996 Job Seekers Allowance	Job Seekers' Allowance (JSA) is the new legal framework based around Job Seekers Agreement: Visit Job Center once every two weeks; more random checking over search; after 3 months unemployment have to search for other occupations
1997	Various compulsory programs (1-2-1, Workwise, Project Work)
1998 New Deal	New Deal for Young People (pilots in January, nation rollout in April)
1998	New Deal for long-term unemployed—all those unemployed for over 2 years (July)
1999, April	National Minimum Wage introduced at £3.60 for adults and at £3 for youths
1999, August	New Deal for over-50s piloted
2000	New Deal for over-50s national rollout
2001	New Deal made a permanent feature of U.K. unemployment benefit regime

Sources: Wells (2000), Price (2000).
Note: Important reforms are italicized.

work-search requirements were less strictly enforced. The function of job centers (job search) and benefit offices (paying benefits) were split in 1974, and they were increasingly located on different premises. An indicator of the relaxation in work search is the number of referrals of unemployed people suspected of not searching for work—this stood at 28,270 in 1968, and, despite a big increase in unemployment, fell to 5,603 by 1976 (Price 2000).

Surprisingly, the advent of Mrs. Thatcher's administration actually reinforced this trend. In 1982 the compulsion to visit a Job Centre if someone claimed unemployment benefit was withdrawn. Cutbacks in public expenditure reduced the numbers of staff to monitor the work-search requirements and help match the unemployed with jobs.[4] These administrative changes, combined with the huge increase in unemployment in the early 1980s (see figure 11.1), swamped the ability of the Employment Service to enforce work search. In terms of gross domestic product (GDP) the U.K. recession troughed in 1981, but despite 5 years of recovery, claimant unemployment only peaked in 1986.

A major period of benefit reform began in 1986. The introduction of the Restart program made interviews with the Employment Service a condition of benefit receipt for all those whose unemployment claims had reached a duration of twelve months or more. These were piloted in January and rolled out nationally in July. Also, in 1986 the government extended the unemployment insurance disqualification period for those deemed to have left their jobs voluntarily from six to thirteen weeks (this was further increased to twenty-six weeks in 1988 and is currently six months).[5]

Since this point, there has been a successive tightening of the work-search requirement. In October 1986 Restart interviews were extended to all those unemployed in excess of six months, with repeated interviews after every subsequent six months. In 1991 mandatory job courses for the very long-term unemployed were introduced. In 1994 the number of sanctions doubled under the "stricter benefit regime."

These changes were consolidated in a new legal framework under JSA, introduced in 1996. A range of measures was introduced to improve job search,[6] and there were more checks over eligibility.

One indicator of the effect of these cumulative changes has been to reduce

4. In the early 1980s large numbers were encouraged to leave the unemployment rolls and draw other forms of benefits (and therefore exit the labor market). This gave the appearance of reducing unemployment. For example, the 1983 budget allowed men over sixty to move on to a higher benefit rate if they signed off of unemployment benefits and on to long-term supplementary benefits. Supplementary benefits *required* that the recipients did *not* look for work (Wells 2000)! The numbers of invalidity benefits rose by 300,000 between 1984 and 1988.

5. Restart also gave menu of options to help get people into work—short courses, training, job clubs, and a Jobstart subsidy (a £20 bonus to the unemployed person if they took a low-paying job).

6. Examples are the Jobseekers' agreements, the enhanced advisory interventions, and that the unemployed could not refuse jobs outside their own occupation after three months, and so on.

the proportion of people seeking work who actually claim benefits. Schmitt and Wadsworth (1999) show that in 1983 90 percent of ILO unemployed men (i.e., those who had actively sought work within the last two weeks) received unemployment benefits, compared to only 80 percent in 1993.

Previous U.K. governments had experimented with wage subsidies. The common feature of these schemes was the payment of a fixed weekly subsidy, typically of around £50 or £60 for the initial months of employment of a long-term unemployed individual. This was sometimes payable to the individual (Jobstart allowance and Jobmatch) and sometimes to the employer (Workstart). In addition, an employer's National Insurance (the main U.K. payroll tax) contributions holiday for the long-term unemployed was introduced in April 1996. Prior to the New Deal none of these schemes were very well funded, and all have suffered from low take-up. For example, in 1996 only 1 percent of all U.K. active labor market funds were spent on wage subsidies, compared to an European Union (EU) average of 10 percent (Martin 1998).

11.3.2 The Elements of the New Deal

The New Deal program has been targeted at specific groups of the unemployed, with an emphasis on the young (eighteen- to twenty-four-year-olds), long-term unemployed (eighteen months or more), lone parents, and disabled people. Pilots for the New Deal for Young People began in January 1998, and the program took effect at the national level beginning in April 1998. The number of young people on the New Deal peaked at just fewer than 150,000 in July 1999 and stood at 86,200 in September 2002.

The windfall tax on the privatized utilities raised £5.2 billion between 1997 and 1999, and all of these funds were hypothecated to financing New Deals of some variety. Table 11.3 shows the government's estimates of the allocation of windfall tax receipts to different elements of the program. The New Deal for Young People received about £1.5 billion by the end of March 2002.

It is tempting to simply divide the cost of the New Deal by the estimate number of new jobs in section 11.4 (about 17,250) to find a "cost per job created." This would imply that the scheme was expensive (e.g., using the estimates in section 11.4 of about £18,550 per job in 1999–2000). Such a calculation is misleading, however, as participants of the New Deal options would have been claiming JSA, and these costs (and others) must be deducted from the gross costs in table 11.4 to get an estimate of the net exchequer cost. We perform an explicit cost-benefit calculation in section 11.5 to address this issue. This suggests that the actual social cost per additional employee is under £4,000 (£68.1 million/17,250) and, more importantly, that social benefits exceeded social costs.

The program is composed of several parts, with different options offered to different groups of the unemployed. The New Deal for Young People is

Table 11.3 **Allocation of the Windfall Tax, 1997–1998 to 2001–2002 (spending by program in £millions)**

Program	1997–1998	1998–1999	1999–2000	2000–2001	2001–2002	1997–2002
New Deal for 18- to 24-year-olds	50	210	320	440	460	1,480
New Deal for those 25 and over	0	10	110	160	320	600
New Deal for those 50 and over	0	0	0	20	20	40
New Deal for single parents	0	20	50	60	90	220
New Deal for disabled people	0	10	30	90	80	210
New Deal for partners of unemployed people	0	0	10	20	20	50
New Deal for schools	90	270	330	580	310	1,590
Child care	0	20	10	0	0	40
University for Industry	0	5	0	0	0	5
ONE pilots	0	0	0	5	5	10
Action teams				20	20	40
Enterprise development	0	0	0	20	10	30
Total expenditure	140	550	850	1,420	1,340	4,300
Unallocated						900
Windfall tax receipts	2,600	2,600				5,200

Note: ONE indicates "ONE stop gateway."

compulsory for all those aged eighteen–twenty-four who have been receiving the JSA for more than six months. Figure 11.4 summarizes the treatment in a flow diagram. Initially, individuals enter a Gateway period, where they are assigned a personal adviser who gives them extensive assistance with the job search. If the unemployed person is still on JSA at the end of the Gateway period (formally, a *maximum* of four months),[7] they are offered up to four options:

1. Entry into full-time education or training for up to twelve months for those without basic qualifications (without loss of benefits);
2. A job for six months with a voluntary sector employer (paid a wage or allowance at least equal to JSA plus £400 spread over the six months);
3. A job with the Environmental Task Force (paid a wage or allowance at least equal to JSA plus £400 spread over the six months); or
4. A subsidy to a prospective employer for six months, with training for at least one day per week (£60 per week plus an additional £750 training subsidy spread over the six months).

7. In practice the Gateway period can last for longer than the official maximum of four months.

Table 11.4 **Level and Composition of Active Labour Market Policies (ALMPs) in the Group of Seven between 1985 and 1996**

	Spending on ALMP as a % of GDP (1)		Spending on ALMP per Person Unemployed[a] (2)		Spending on Public Employment Service as a % of All ALMP (3)		Spending on Youth Measures as a % of All ALMP (4)		Spending on Direct Job Creation in the Public Sector as a % of All ALMP (5)	
Country	1985	1996	1985	1996	1985	1996	1985	1996	1985	1996
Canada	0.6	0.5	6.2	5.6	37	36	5	5	3	6
France	0.7	1.3	6.6	10.7	20	12	25	19	n.a.	17
Germany	0.8	1.4	10	16.1	26	17	6	5	15	21
Italy	n.a.	1.1	n.a.	9	n.a.	n.a.	n.a.	n.a.	n.a.	n.a.
Japan	0.2[b]	0.1	5.8[b]	3	17[b]	26	0[b]	0	6[b]	2
United Kingdom	0.7	0.4	6.4	5	22	43	35	26	25	2
United States	0.3	0.2	3.8	3.2	25	39	12	15	3	3
European Union[c]	0.9	0.9	13.3	11.3	19	19	14	15	16	15
OECD[d]	0.7	0.7	13	11.4	21	21	11	12	17	14

Source: Martin (1998), tables 1, 2, and 5.

Notes: n.a. = not available. ALMPs include public employment service, youth measures, public-sector job creation, labor market training (for employed and unemployed adults), wage subsidies to private-sector employment, and measures for the disabled (last three items not shown in table).

[a]ALMP per person unemployed is normalized on output per head. Normalizing on productivity is in order to control for the fact that more productive countries will have higher wages, so the figure is comparable to a "replacement rate." This indicator is commonly used by the OECD and in the cross-country analysis of Layard, Nickell, and Jackman (1991) and others.

[b]1987.

[c]Unweighted average.

[d]Unweighted average excluding Czech Republic, Hungary, and Poland.

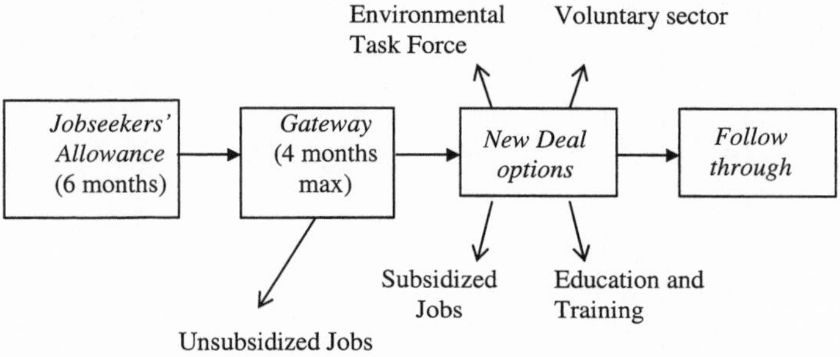

Fig. 11.4 A simplified flow diagram of the New Deal program

Notes: The New Deal for Young People is a mandatory Welfare to Work program. All young people (between the ages of eighteen and twenty-four) who had claimed unemployment insurance (JSA) for six months enter the program. During a Gateway period of at most four months participants are given extensive job-search assistance. Those failing to find an unsubsidized job have four different options: entering employment with a six-month wage subsidy to the employer, twelve-months full-time education or training, working in the Environmental Taskforce (a public-sector job), or working in the voluntary sector. The individual faces the withdrawal of unemployment benefits if they do not cooperate. After the end of the options, participants who rejoin the unemployed enter the "Follow Through," which is essentially the same as the Gateway. For more details, see DFEE (1997).

If an option is refused, the claimant is liable to suffer a benefits sanction. Initially, sanctions take the form of withdrawal of benefits for two weeks, and further refusals may result in repeated benefit sanctions. Individuals returning to unemployment within thirteen weeks after leaving an option go onto the "follow-through" program of job assistance, which is essentially the same as the Gateway.

Individuals can enter options at any time after the sixth month of JSA. The official guidance was that the first month of the Gateway was confined to unsubsidized employment. The second month would then focus on education and training and the third month on the subsidized job option. The public-employment option was only to be used as a last resort in the fourth month. In practice this schema was not rigidly adhered to.

Out of the four options, education and training has been the most popular (about 40 percent of all those who had joined the New Deal options by the end of April 1999 chose education and training). The employer's option had a much lower take-up than anticipated (only 20 percent of all those in options). The reasons for this low take-up is uncertain, but it is worth noting that low take-up has often been a problem for wage-subsidy schemes in other countries. Possible reasons include the following: (1) The U.K. economy was in a prolonged expansion. The crop of unemployed who fail to get unsubsidized jobs even after the Gateway period may have very poor basic skills, making them very unattractive to employers; (2) the requirement to have formal training may impose high costs on employers;

(3) the Employment Service has had little experience in handling job-subsidy schemes; and (4) the failure to secure a job during the Gateway period might generate a stigma effect on the individuals.

11.3.3 The Effectiveness of Previous U.K. Reforms

In general there has been a paucity of high quality evaluations of U.K. labor market reforms, compared with the United States. Random assignment has encountered serious opposition due to a mixture of political and ethical objections. In this respect the United Kingdom is more typical of other European countries.[8] "Evaluations" usually take the form of surveys of participants. Obviously, there is no obvious comparison group, so any counterfactual is purely speculative.

There are several macroeconometric evaluations where the policy is essentially indicated by a set of time dummies. For example, using a time series model the Employment Service (Sweeney and McMahon 1998) claimed that the rule changes in JSA reduced claimant unemployment by about 15,000 to 20,000. Large positive effects of Restart were found by Dicks and Hatch (1989) and Disney et al. (1991). More recently Riley and Young (2001a,b) found moderate effects of the New Deal for Young People when they used a macro approach (about 28,000 extra jobs).[9]

The major problem with these macro approaches is that (aside from conventional aggregation biases) there are many other macroeconomic events occurring simultaneously with the introduction of labor market programs. It is extremely difficult to disentangle the program effect from these macro shocks. For example, the U.K. economy experienced a very sharp upturn in the late 1980s (see figure 11.2) that would have raised employment in the absence of the Restart program.

Fortunately, however, there have been useful microeconometric evaluations of the Restart initiative using microdata. In 1989 a sample of just under 9,000 individuals were identified who were approaching their sixth month of unemployment. A random control group of 582 were selected who were not obliged to take part in the Restart interview. These individuals were followed up in surveys three months and nine months after their first Restart interview (or nine months and thirteen months after the start

8. Martin (1998, 14) recounts one leading European policy maker's frank explanation for this absence of good evaluations: "Most of our programs are lousy! They were dreamed up quickly to give the Minister some good news to announce at a time when unemployment is rising. We do not want evaluations revealing to the general public how bad our programs are; we know this already."

9. Disney et al. (1991) used the ratio of Restart interviews to eligible participants; Anderton, Riley, and Young (1999) and Riley and Young (2001b) use the number of New Deal participants as a share of the claimant count. Riley and Young (2001a) multiply the latter variable by the average number of days that individuals receive personal advisor interviews as their indicator of "New Deal intensity."

of their benefit claim, in the case of the control group). This information was matched to administrative records using their unique National Insurance (U.K. Social Security) numbers.

Dolton and O'Neill (1995, 1996)[10] analyze this data and find that the group who were randomized out of Restart had median unemployment duration one month longer than those who did receive Restart. They also examined the destinations of those leaving the claimant count using a competing risks model. They found that the strongest effects of Restart came from exits into jobs rather than exits to training or nonparticipation. This Restart effect appeared to work through both increasing the arrival rate of job offers and by making the treated group more likely to accept a job if they received an offer.

Some of the job-subsidy schemes have been evaluated, but usually through surveys without a good comparison group. One analysis of the Workstart pilots (where firms received a wage subsidy for employing the long-term unemployed) concluded that only 17 percent of the Workstart vacancies represented new employment that would not have existed without the subsidy and that much of the employment of the long-term unemployed occurred at the expense of the shorter-term unemployed (Atkinson and Meager 1994).

11.3.4 The United Kingdom in International Context

The OECD estimates of spending on active labor market policies (ALMP) across countries between 1985 and 1996 are given in table 11.4. These include administration of the public employment service (a rough proxy for resources in job assistance and job search monitoring), youth measures, training, public-sector job creation, subsidized private-sector jobs, and job help for the disabled. The first column simply gives ALMP as a proportion of GDP. This might be seen as misleading as some countries will have different unemployment and wage levels than others. To partially deal with this, column (2) presents the standard OECD measure of ALMP per person unemployed normalized on output per head. The figure can be regarded as analogous to a replacement rate with the generosity of spending on ALMP per client compared to the outside wage (as proxied by output per head).[11]

Despite the rhetoric, there has not been a rise in this measure of ALMP and GDP in the OECD as a whole over this period on either measure. If

10. White and Leakey (1992), using the same data, also found that Restart significantly reduced unemployment duration, increased the probability of finding a job, and increased the probability of moving into employment training. They could find no evidence that Restart reduced the average quality of a job match either through lower wages or deteriorating job length. Surprisingly, however, there was no evidence that this effect was driven by increased job search (as measured by number of job applications, etc.).

11. This variable is used in the cross-country comparisons of Layard, Nickell, and Jackman (1991) among others.

anything, there has been a slight decline. There is a clear difference between the main continental European countries and the United Kingdom. France and Germany both have higher spending per unemployed person, and both have increased their ALMP intensity. The United Kingdom not only spent less but also saw a decline over this period. Britain appears closer to the United States, Japan, and Canada in this respect.

The next three columns of table 11.4 decompose the spending of ALMP into its three main components—public employment service, youth programs, and government jobs. The toughening of work search requirements in the United Kingdom is indicated by column [3]—there has been a large increase in the proportion of resources devoted to the public employment service, from 22 percent in 1985 to 43 percent in 1996. In contrast there have been large falls in the proportionate spending on job creation in the public sector (from 25 percent to 2 percent) and to a lesser extent in youth programs (from 35 percent to 26 percent).

The picture is different in continental Europe. Both France and Germany spend a larger proportion of resources on state job creation, and their proportionate spending on the public employment service has fallen between 1985 and 1996. The trends are also in the opposite direction of the United Kingdom. Again, the United Kingdom is closer to the United States, who has also increased the resources going to public employment services (25 percent to 39 percent). Unfortunately, comparative data for those leaving the New Deal options are not yet available. Overall spending on ALMP in the United Kingdom has almost certainly increased after 1997 and is weighted more toward the youth component today than in 1996.

The level of U.K. unemployment benefits is low compared to most other European countries (table 11.1). Offsetting this is the fact that the sanctions regime in the United Kingdom is only about average by international standards. The Netherlands, for example, has also managed to lower unemployment in the 1990s but, unlike the United Kingdom, has maintained a high replacement rate. The Dutch introduced a very tough sanctions regime, however, to offset the disincentive effects of high replacement rates (see Nickell and van Ours, 2000, for a discussion).

11.3.5 What Elements of the New Deal Might Work? Evidence from U.S. Research

The New Deal Gateway provides both job-search assistance and job-search monitoring (with accompanying sanctions for noncompliance). The study reported in section 11.4 identifies a treatment effect over and above the impact of employment subsidy, but is this effect due to the "carrot" of mentoring from the personal adviser or the "stick" of a harsher benefit regime?

There is a large literature on the evaluation of the U.S. unemployment insurance (UI) system. The Social Security Act of 1935 created the UI system.

Each state administers and implements its own system subject to federal guidelines. In particular, there is a requirement for work-search monitoring, although the precise way this is implemented varies by state. There have been several demonstration projects (randomized trials) investigating the impact of variation in the way job-search monitoring and assistance impacts on the duration of claims and recipients' employment and earnings.

Meyer (1995) offers an excellent survey of five experiments.[12] He finds evidence that job-search monitoring and assistance together significantly reduce the duration of claims. There were less clear-cut effects on overall earnings. Unfortunately "[t]his combination of additional services and tightened eligibility checks makes it difficult to determine what aspects of the experiments induced the changes in outcomes . . ." (Meyer 1995, 114). Ashenfelter, Ashmore, and Deschenes (1999) attempt to tackle this problem by analyzing four experiments where the treatment of stricter enforcement and verification of work-search behavior can be separated from job assistance.[13] They find no significant effects on claim duration from tighter monitoring.

Anderson (2000) reports three further recent experiments.[14] Like Ashenfelter, Ashmore, and Deschenes (1999), the Maryland study allows a distinction between job assistance and monitoring. The most stringent monitoring method, wherein each of the normal two contacts per week were verified, resulted in a fall in duration of 10 percent (about 1.5 weeks), compared to dropping of all job-search monitoring. The reason for the differences between the two studies appears to be because the treatments in Ashenfelter, Ashmore, and Deschenes (1999) were relatively weak. The tougher monitoring of the job search was only in the first week after submitting a claim for UI but *before* the claim was accepted.

There have been several recent studies of the impact of reforms to the benefit regime in the Dutch labor market. Abbring, van den Berg, and van Ours (1997) and Van den Berg, van der Klaauw, and van Ours (1998) estimate that job-finding rates double after the imposition of a sanction. Van den Berg and van der Klaauw (2001) could find no effect of counseling and monitoring, but they argue that these interventions provided little significant job-search assistance to the unemployed and were targeted mainly at groups who had relatively good labor market prospects. Gorter and Kalb (1996) found that more intensive counseling to an eligible group with worse prospects had a significant impact on exits to employment.

12. The experiments include the Nevada Claimant Placement Program, the Charleston Claimant Placement and Work Test Demonstration, the Wisconsin Eligibility Review Pilot Project, the New Jersey UI Reemployment Demonstration, and the Washington Alternative Work Search Experimentation.

13. These sites were in Connecticut, Massachusetts, Virginia, and Tennessee.

14. The experiments include the Utah Quality Control Program Improvement Study, the Maryland UI Work Search Demonstration, and the Job Search Assistance Demonstration in Florida and Washington, D.C.

In our U.K. results (section 11.4), we do not find evidence that individuals were dropping off the rolls as they approached the start of the New Deal Gateway (between the fifth and sixth months of an unemployment spell—as we will see in table 11.7). If monitoring were extremely unpleasant, we would have expected more claimants to stop claiming prior to entering the New Deal (as appeared to happen with Restart). There is no significant change in outflows as the New Deal approaches; thus, we are inclined to believe that it is the carrot rather than the stick that has been most effective in delivering employment increases, a view shared by the qualitative evaluations of New Deal participants (e.g., Hasluck, 2000).[15]

There is also a more extensive U.S. literature on the use of wage subsidies. Both Katz (1998) and Dickert-Conlin and Holtz-Eakin (2000) conclude that employer-based subsidies have not proven successful. Katz argues that part of this is due to stigma effects as only the most disadvantaged are typically able to get such subsidies, and this acts as a bad signal to potential employers. This may also explain why take-up rates are usually very low. Katz does find some evidence of an effect of the targeted job tax credit (TJTC) for disadvantaged youth in his own work. In section 11.4 I report results of using a similar methodology to Katz, exploiting the age-eligibility criterion to estimate the effect of the New Deal.

Perhaps the closest experimental evidence for the New Deal is the U.S. Welfare to Work programs. Bloom and Michalopoulos (2001) survey twenty-nine different initiatives that had demonstration projects (random assignments). Eight of these schemes were job-focused (rather than education or training focused) and mandatory for welfare recipients. Although the precise impact effect differed from program to program, a statistically significant effect of the program on employment probabilities was found in all eight cases.

In this paper I do not examine the impact of the training and public-sector job element of the New Deal program due to lack of postoption data.[16] There is a large U.S. literature on the impact of training programs for the unemployed and a rather smaller literature on the impact of public work programs.[17] Generally, the outcomes of evaluations of training programs for young men have been disappointing.[18] It is worth remembering

15. Only 2 percent of participants in the New Deal have suffered sanctions.

16. Bonjour (2001) look at the relative success of different New Deal options using a special survey. They find that eighteen months after entering the New Deal, the employer option had the best outcomes in terms of getting people into work.

17. For a survey of public service employment and mandatory work, see Ellwood and Welty (2000).

18. See the survey in Heckman, Lalonde, and Smith (1999). The main argument is that most of these schemes fail to significantly raise the human capital of participants. A similar conclusion is reached about U.K. public training schemes by Dolton (1992). Previous U.K. training schemes have included Training Opportunities Programs (TOPS), the Youth Training Scheme, Employment Training, and Training for Work.

that the pool of young unemployed men in the United Kingdom is proportionately much larger than in the United States, so there may be greater scope for positive program effects. The U.S. target group of disadvantaged are more likely to be "hardcore" jobless whose human capital is very difficult to raise.

11.4 An Empirical Evaluation of the New Deal for Young People

It is possible to examine the performance of the Gateway period of job assistance using publicly available microdata (for a full analysis, see Blundell, Costa Dias, Meghir, and Van Reenen 2001).[19]

We consider the treatment group to be young people unemployed for six months (continuous claims of JSA). The outcome of greatest interest is the flow of this group into employment over the four months of the Gateway period (months six through ten of JSA). We also examine all outflows from unemployment over the same period (e.g., to training).

The New Deal treatment effect considered (the job outflow by month ten of unemployment) comprises the effects of both the job-assistance and monitoring element of the New Deal *and* the wage-subsidy element.[20] It is possible to estimate a lower bound to the job assistance and subsidy element (unsubsidized jobs) as we know from administrative sources the actual proportion of the unemployed who obtained subsidized jobs (these numbers are presented in the empirical results). By deducting the proportion that flow into the subsidized jobs from the overall treatment effect, one can obtain a lower bound of the pure Gateway effect. The "true" effect of job assistance is likely to be higher as some of those obtaining subsidized jobs would have obtained them even in the absence of a subsidy, despite the best efforts of the Employment Service to minimize this "deadweight."

In the absence of random assignment there are two possible ways to construct the comparison group. The first method is to exploit the fact that the New Deal was piloted in some areas ahead of the National rollout. We compare nineteen–twenty-four-year-olds[21] in the pilot areas (Pathfinders) to similar nineteen–twenty-four-year-olds in nonpilot areas over the same period of time before and after the introduction of the program. The second method is to examine an older age group who are ineligible for the New Deal. We choose to focus on twenty-five–thirty-year-olds who have been

19. This section is based on an analysis of the Joint Unemployment and Vacancies Operating System (JUVOS) data, which contain information over time for a sample of 5 percent of those claiming unemployment-related benefits in the United Kingdom.

20. Originally, I had hoped to deal with this problem by focusing only on the first two months of the New Deal Gateway when no one was supposed to go on the wage-subsidy option. Unfortunately, the New Deal Evaluation Database showed that some people went on the employer option even in the first month of the Gateway.

21. We drop eighteen-year-olds because there has been a large increase in the participation rate in full-time education for this group in recent years.

unemployed for six months as the comparison group. After the national rollout, only the comparison across age groups is possible.

There are many potential biases in using either of these comparison groups. Most pressing is the issue of substitution, that the older unemployed will be less likely to gain employment because firms will prefer New Deal participants (for example, firms receive a subsidy for employing a twenty-four-year-old but not a twenty-five-year-old). Consequently, using the older age group may lead us to *overestimate* the positive effects of the New Deal. The Pathfinder pilots versus the non-Pathfinder pilot comparison should be informative in this regard. Substitution effects imply that we should estimate *smaller* effects when comparing young people in pilot versus nonpilot areas than when we estimate using younger versus older individuals *within* the pilot areas. Unlike the older group, young people within nonpilot areas are unlikely to be adversely affected by the New Deal. Substitution also implies that we should, ceteris paribus, expect to see the outflow rates of the older group decline in the pilot areas (where they are losing out to the younger group) compared to the nonpilot areas.

This discussion illustrates that there is no one obviously "correct" age comparison to consider. Using the regression discontinuity design approach of comparing eligible twenty-four-year-olds with noneligible twenty-five-year-olds has some appeal as we would expect these groups to be very similar in productivity characteristics. Unfortunately, substitution would be most severe for this age comparison because the twenty-five-year-olds would be the closest substitutes for the twenty-four-year-olds. Furthermore, the precision of the estimates falls as we focus on smaller and smaller slices of the data. As a consequence, we believe the five-year age groupings for treatment and control are the best balance, but we were also careful to investigate alternative age cutoffs in the empirical work.

A second issue is that of equilibrium wage effects. If the New Deal reduces equilibrium wage pressure (for example, through increased search) then we will be *underestimating* the effects of the New Deal in increasing employment. The use of different comparison groups may again be informative in this context. Consider the scenario where there are no substitution effects and only equilibrium wage effects in the local labor market. In this case, comparing young people in the pilot versus nonpilot areas will reflect some of the positive job effects associated with reduced wage pressure. Comparing younger versus older people within the Pathfinder areas will not capture the equilibrium wage effects as the job chances of both groups are improved. Thus, equilibrium wage effects imply that we should estimate *larger* effects when comparing young people in pilot versus nonpilot areas than when we estimate using younger versus older individuals *within* the pilot areas. The bias is in the opposite direction of that of the substitution effect.

Whichever comparison group is chosen, the method is to compare the difference in the outflow rates between these two groups after the New Deal began, compared to the difference in the outflow rates before the New Deal started.

Table 11.5 contains the raw data on the outflow rates to jobs for the different groups. The data is taken from the Joint Unemployment and Vacancies Operating System (JUVOS), an administrative longitudinal database. This follows a random 5 percent of all individuals who have ever claimed unemployment benefits. The upper panel contains data from the pilot period and the lower panel from the national rollout. The pilot period considers those who reached six months on unemployment benefits (JSA) between January 1, 1998 and the end of March 1998 ("after the program"). I follow them four months later (i.e., ten months after they become unem-

Table 11.5 **Flows from the Claimant Count into Employment: Men (conditional on being on Job Seekers Allowance (JSA) for six months)**

	Flows by the End of the 8th Month on JSA			Flows by the End of the 10th Month on JSA		
	Before the Program (1)	After the Program (2)	Difference (3)	Before the Program (4)	After the Program (5)	Difference (6)
Pilot period						
1. Treatment group: 19–24-year olds in Pathfinder areas	0.141	0.180	+0.039	0.241	0.330	+0.089
2. Comparison group: 19–24-year-olds in all other areas	0.165	0.146	–0.019	0.271	0.250	–0.021
3. Difference in differences			+0.058			+0.110
4. Comparison group: 19–24-year-olds in matched non-Pathfinder areas	0.149	0.133	–0.016	0.228	0.233	+0.005
5. Comparison group: 25–30-year-olds in Pathfinder areas	0.150	0.153	+0.003	0.276	0.260	–0.016
National rollout						
6. Treatment group: 19–24-year-olds	0.158	0.170	+0.012	0.258	0.281	+0.023
7. Comparison group: 25–30-year-olds	0.138	0.124	–0.014	0.230	0.199	–0.031
8. Difference in differences			+.026			+0.054

Notes: Estimates used the Joint Unemployment and Vacancies Operating System (JUVOS) 5 percent longitudinal sample of JSA claimants. Selected observations are all unemployed individuals completing a six-month spell on JSA over a predefined time interval. The present table considers those obtaining six months of JSA between the second and fourth quarters of 1997 and 1998 for the national rollout estimates, and the first quarters of 1997 and 1998 for the pilot period estimates. Individuals verifying this criterion are then followed up to the end of the eighth and tenth months on JSA to check whether they have found a job. The eligible group (defined by the age or pilot area criterion) is compared with the selected control group.

ployed). This group is compared with the same age group who reached six months on unemployment benefits between January and March 1997 ("before the program"). The national rollout considers individuals who reached six months on unemployment benefits between April 1, 1998 and December 31, 1998 ("after the program"). They are compared with the same age group between April and December 1997 ("before the program").[22]

Focusing on the flows between six and ten months in the pilot period (row 1 column [6] in table 11.5), we can see that nineteen–twenty-four-year-olds were 8.9 percentage points more likely to obtain jobs in the post-New Deal period. In the nonpilot areas (row 2) nineteen–twenty-four-year-olds were actually less likely to get jobs (a fall of 2.1 percentage points). So the difference-in-differences effect is a full 11 percentage points (row 3)—an extremely large increase on a pretreatment base of 24.1 percent. The next two rows compare different possible comparison groups: "matched Pathfinder areas" (where we select areas with similar characteristics to the Pathfinder areas) and twenty-five–thirty-year-olds in the Pathfinder areas. The implied difference-in-differences effects are similar to the first comparison group. The lower panel of table 11.5 examines data from the National rollout (post-April 1998). The magnitude of the New Deal effect is still positive but about half the size of that estimated for Pathfinder areas. There is an increase of 5.4 percentage points compared to the preprogram base of 25.8 percentage points (a 5.4/25.8 = 20 percent increase in the outflow rate). We show in the following that this is due to the return to a big "impact" effect in the first quarter that the New Deal is introduced.

The raw difference-in-differences estimates in table 11.5 do not correct for compositional changes. These may be important if the composition of the groups changes systematically over time. In table 11.6 we include a set of extra controls—marital status, sought occupation, region, the number of past unemployment spells, and the proportion of time spent unemployed in the previous two years. The final column contains our main results. In row one we compare young people in pilot and nonpilot areas. In row two we compare younger people to older people within the pilot areas. The results are almost identical to the raw difference-in-differences estimates in table 11.5. The fact that the point estimates are both about 10–11 percentage points regardless of whether we use area or age as the comparison group is interesting. It implies that we cannot reject a simple model where there are no substitution or equilibrium wage effects of the program.[23] It is reassuring that row three shows that the trends for the older

22. An advantage of ceasing to examine any outflows after April 1999 is that the National Minimum Wage was first introduced in April 1999. Minimum-wage effects in analyses that cover this later period may confound the New Deal effects.

23. It is also consistent with a more complex model where both of these effects cancel each other out. It may be, of course, that these effects take longer to play out due to lags of adjustment.

Table 11.6 **Regression Results for Gateway Employment Effects by the End of the 10th Month: Men (conditional on being on Job Seekers Allowance [JSA] for six months; percentage point increase in the probability of leaving unemployment)**

Treatment Group	Comparison Group	No. of Observations	Estimates Based on Difference-in-Difference Method
	Pilot Period		
1. 19–24-year-olds living in Pathfinder areas	19–24-year-olds living in all non-Pathfinder areas	3,716	0.110** (0.039)
2. 19–24-year-olds living in Pathfinder areas	25–30-year-olds living in Pathfinder areas	1,096	0.104* (0.055)
3. 25–30-year-olds living in Pathfinder areas	25–30-year-olds living in all other areas	3,180	0.016 (0.042)
4. 19–24-year-olds living in Pathfinder areas	31–40-year-olds living in Pathfinder areas	1,169	0.159** (0.050)
5. 19–24-year-olds living in Pathfinder areas	19–24-year-olds living in matched non-Pathfinder areas	1,193	0.134** (0.053)
6. Outflow into the employment option (affecting 19–24-year-olds living in Pathfinder areas)[a]		4,486	0.057
	Overall Effect for the Sample including the Pilot Period and the National Rollout[b]		
7. 19–24-year-olds	25–30-year-olds	17,433	0.053** (0.013)
8. Outflows to subsidized jobs[a]		55,051	0.039
	Decomposition of New Deal into First Quarter and Second/Third Quarter Effects		
9. Effect for the pilot period—1st quarter the program operates in Pathfinder areas		1,096	0.104* (0.055)
10. Effect for the 1st quarter the program operates in non-Pathfinder areas		5,169	0.088** (0.025)
11. Effect for the 2nd and 3rd quarters the program operates in all areas		11,161	0.031* (0.016)

Source: Blundell, Costa Dias, Meghir, and Van Reenen (2001).

Notes: Standard errors are in parentheses. Estimates use the Joint Unemployment and Vacancies Operating System (JUVOS) 5 percent longitudinal sample of JSA claimants. Selected observations are all unemployed individuals completing a 6-month spell on JSA over a predefined time interval. This table considers those obtaining six months of JSA between the second and fourth quarters of 1997 and 1998 for the national rollout estimates. The first quarters of 1997 and 1998 are used for the pilot period estimates. Individuals verifying this criterion are then followed up to the end of the tenth month on JSA to check whether they have found a job. The eligible group (defined by the age or pilot area criterion) is compared with the selected control group.

Table 11.6 (continued)

All estimates from regressions include a set of other controls, namely marital status, sought occupation, region, and some information on the labor market history (comprising the number of JSA spells since 1982 and the proportion of time on JSA over the two years that precede the start of the present unemployment spell).

[a]Estimates of the outflows to options are obtained from the New Deal Evaluation Database (NDED).

[b]For the first three quarters, the New Deal is operating in each region.

[c]The decompositions are based on allowing the New Deal effect to differ in the first quarter it was introduced (January through March 1998 for the pilot period and March through May for the national rollout) from subsequent quarters.

**Significant at the 0.05 level.

*Significant at the 0.10 level.

groups were statistically identical in Pathfinder areas to non-Pathfinder areas. If young people were being substituted for older age groups in the pilot areas, one would have expected worse outcomes for the twenty-five–thirty-year-olds in the pilot areas. This does not appear to be the case. We compare the young unemployed to a slightly older age group (thirty-one–forty) in row four and to matched non-Pathfinder areas in row five. These results show (if anything) a slightly larger New Deal effect.[24]

Note that 5.7 percent of the sample joined the subsidized job option during the program (row 6). This enables us to put a lower bound on the effect of the job-assistance element of the program of about 5.3 percentage points (i.e., 11 percent–5.7 percent). Even if none of those who were given subsidized jobs would have obtained them in the absence of the program, there remains a 5.3 percentage point outflow into unsubsidized jobs attributable to the New Deal.[25] If half of all subsidized jobs are deadweight, then the effect of job assistance and monitoring rises to 8.15 percentage points (11 percent–2.85 percent).

The final three rows of table 11.5 examine the "program introduction" effect. It is noticeable that the employment impact of the New Deal was greater in the first quarter that it was introduced (both in the pilot areas and the nonpilot areas after the national rollout) than in the subsequent two quarters. Comparing rows eight and nine (first quarter) with row ten (second and third quarter) illustrates that the program introduction effect appears twice as large as the subsequent impact. Other U.K. labor market programs have also experienced "cleaning out the register" impact effects. But these are usually thought to stem from improved administrative pro-

24. Other studies have also failed to uncover significant substitution effects in the New Deal program (e.g., Anderton, Riley, and Young 1999; Riley and Young 2001a).

25. The design of the program emphasized finding unsubsidized employment when participants first entered the New Deal. So the true effect of job assistance may be close to this lower bound. The greater impact of some U.S. and Dutch assistance schemes may have been because the target group had been employed for shorter periods of time.

cedures and reductions in fraud. It is more likely that the impact effect of the New Deal came from the energizing of personal advisers in the Employment Service who greeted the New Deal with a lot of enthusiasm. This naturally diminishes over time. It would be unwise, however, to consider the post–first quarter lower figure as the "steady state" effect as it is still based on only six months of data.

There are many criticisms of these results that are partially taken up in table 11.7. First, we examined whether the quality of job matches had deteriorated by using the outflow to jobs that lasted at least thirteen weeks as the outcome variable.[26] The treatment effect is very close to that for all jobs, so there is no evidence that New Deal jobs are of significantly lower quality, on this measure at least. Second, it may be that individuals are delaying their exits from unemployment prior to the New Deal in order to take advantage of the generosity of the program. If this was the case, one would expect to see a decline in outflows in the month before the program starts. The third row of table 11.7 shows that there are no selectivity effects between month five and six of JSA (we could also find no New Deal effects on earlier months of JSA).

The third experiment we consider uses outflows to all destinations as the outcome variable (row 4). The New Deal effect is much larger—double the effect on employment. But this is to be expected as a much larger proportion of individuals flow onto some kind of option (13.7 percent of the sample in row 5). Also, the baseline proportion exiting to all destinations is much higher than to jobs alone.

The analysis focuses on men because three-quarters of all New Deal participants are male. We also found that the pre-New Deal outflow behavior of twenty-five–thirty-year-old women was trending in a very different way from that of nineteen–twenty-four-year-old women, whereas it was similar for men. These differential trends relate to changing patterns of participation due to children. Nevertheless we can still examine the pilot versus nonpilot experiments, as the outflow trends for young women were similar in pilot and nonpilot areas. The results are shown in row six of table 11.7. The point estimates are smaller than those of men (6 percent compared to 10 percent), although the smaller sample size means that the coefficients are very imprecisely estimated.

Finally, one could consider using other age cutoffs than the ones that we chose to focus on. For example, in the spirit of regression discontinuity design (see Hahn and Van der Klaauw 1999), one could simply compare twenty-four-year-olds with twenty-five-year-olds (rather than nineteen–twenty-four-year-olds with twenty-five–twenty-nine-year-olds). As discussed previously, this has the advantage that the two groups will be sub-

26. There is, unfortunately, no information on earnings in JUVOS. The survey information in Hales et al. (2000) suggests that the New Deal participants are earning only slightly above the minimum wage.

Table 11.7 **Regression Results of Further Investigations of the New Deal Effect (percentage point increase in the probability of leaving unemployment)**

Experiment	No. of Observations	Estimates Based on Difference-in-Difference Method
Pilot Period		
Men		
1. Outflows to sustained jobs (13 weeks or more in job)	17,433	0.045** (0.011)
2. Outflows to sustained subsidized jobs (affecting 19–24-year-olds)[a]	55,051	0.031
3. Outflows to employment between 5th and 6th months of JSA	20,957	0.004 (0.008)
4. Outflows to all destinations (19–24-year-olds vs. 25–30-year-olds from the national rollout areas and Pathfinder areas	17,433	0.108** (0.015)
5. Outflows to all New Deal options (affecting 19–24-year-olds)	55,051	0.137
Women		
6. Outflows to employment (using 19–24-year-olds in Pathfinder vs. 19–24-year-olds in non-Pathfinder areas)	1,169	0.061 (0.058)
Pilot Period with National Rollout		
7. Women: Outflow into the employment option (affecting 19–24-year-olds in the Pathfinder areas)	1,693	0.048
8. Men: Using 24- vs. 25-year-olds (instead of 19–24- vs. 25–29-year-olds)	2,767	0.068** (0.033)

Source: Blundell, Costa Dias, Meghir, and Van Reenen (2001).

Notes: Standard errors are in parentheses. Estimates of the effects of the New Deal used the Joint Unemployment and Vacancies Operating System (JUVOS) 5 percent longitudinal sample of Job Seekers Allowance (JSA) claimants. The table considers those obtaining six months of JSA between the second to fourth quarters of 1997 and 1998 for the national rollout estimates. The first quarters of 1997 and 1998 are used for the pilot period estimates. Individuals verifying this criterion are then followed up to the end of the tenth month on JSA to check whether they have found a job. The eligible group (defined by the age or pilot area criterion) is compared with the selected control group.

All estimates are from regressions include a set of other controls, namely marital status, sought occupation, region, and some information on the labor market history (comprising the number of JSA spells since 1982 and the proportion of time on JSA over the 2 years that precede the start of the present unemployment spell).

[a]Estimates of the outflows to options are obtained from the New Deal Evaluation Database (NDED).

**Significant at the 0.05 level.

*Significant at the 0.10 level.

ject to the same trends, but the disadvantage that substitution effects (if they exist) will be strongest for these age groups. The results of this experiment are contained in row eight. The treatment effect is larger in magnitude (0.068), although not significantly different from the baseline effect (0.053), which is unsurprising given the much smaller sample size.

In conclusion, the range of experiments contained in table 11.7 suggests that the results are quite robust.

11.5 Cost-Benefit Calculation

Any cost-benefit analysis must proceed with a large degree of caution due to the uncertainty surrounding key parameters. Nevertheless, it is important to try and put the numbers into perspective, no matter how crudely (see table 11.8 for a summary and appendix for more details). The analysis is forward looking—I seek to investigate whether the New Deal would be a program that would be worth making a permanent feature of the U.K. labor market.

One of the main benefits of the New Deal is the number of jobs (and therefore extra output) created. To estimate the number of jobs, a number of assumptions have to be made regarding the counterfactual. I simulate the change in steady state for an economy that broadly matched the U.K. economy in 1998 when the New Deal was introduced.

Table 11.8 **Preliminary Cost Benefit Analysis of New Deal (in £millions)**

Item	Description	Baseline (1)	Optimistic (2)	Pessimistic (3)
Key assumptions		Employment up by 17,250 (average wage £7,272)	Employment up by 17,250 (average wage £8,500)	Employment up by 15,000 (average wage £7,272)
1. Increased output from jobs	No. of new jobs × average earnings	125.4	146.6	98.8
2. Gross Exchequer cost	Transfers to participants in New Deal, direct cost of Gateway, etc.	250.3	250.3	254.2
3. Benefit and tax savings	JSA, Housing Benefit, income tax and NI, etc.	148.8	156.1	133.6
4. Direct cost of Gateway	Personal advisers, etc.	52.9	52.9	55.0
5. Net Exchequer cost	(Item 2) – (Item 3)	101.5	94.2	120.6
6. Excess burden of taxation	(Item 5) × excess burden (15%)	15.2	14.1	18.1
7. Total social costs	(Item 4) + (Item 6)	68.1	67.0	73.1
8. Net Social Benefit	(Item 1) – (Item 7)	57.3	79.6	25.7

Notes: See appendix and section 11.5 for details of the calculations.

The estimates from the previous section showed that the effect of the New Deal was to raise the employment outflows (see table 11.5) of young men by 5.3 percentage points—an elasticity of about 0.2 (i.e., 5 percentage points over a presample base of 25.8 percent). I consider three main labor market states only (employment, short-term or under six months of unemployment, and long-term or over six months of unemployment). I then simulate a permanent increase in monthly outflow rates from long-term unemployment to employment using this elasticity of 0.2 (keeping all the other outflow rates constant) and solve for the new steady states stocks. The stock of long-term unemployment (including those in the Gateway and on nonjob options) falls by about 20,000 per year, and the employment level rises by 17,250.[27] The number of short-term unemployed rises by 2,850 because employment is higher and the outflow rate from employment to short-term unemployment is unchanged (by assumption).

I use the estimates of the mean starting wages of workers on the New Deal subsidized job option from the survey in Hales et al. (2000) of £3.78 per hour,[28] average annual earnings are just under £7300. Using this as our measure of output leads to a social benefit of £125 million (row one).

On the costs side, we have a gross exchequer cost in row two of £250 million[29] (about £100 million in allowances for the various New Deal options, £50 million for the Gateway and £100 million for the resource inputs into the options). We have to deduct off (1) the fact that unemployment and other benefits were already being paid to these individuals, and (2) those individuals that gain jobs and enjoy higher allowances will be paying some more tax. These items total £149 million (row three). In addition, some of these costs are transfers, so these will contribute only to social costs due to the excess burden of taxation (the deadweight loss involved in a higher level of taxation). Using an excess burden rate of 15 percent, this is about £15 million (row six). On the other hand, the cost of maintaining the Gateway is a real productive cost due to the diversion of resources from other parts of the economy. There are also real resource costs involved in supplying the options, but (following Layard 2000) I assume the benefits of taking an option (e.g., the increased human capital associated with training) perfectly offset these costs. Summing the excess burden and Gateway gives a total social cost of just over £68 million.

27. This is consistent with the more macro-based approaches. Anderton, Riley, and Young (1999) estimate an employment impact of the New Deal for Young People of 18,000 between January 1998 and October 1999. Riley and Young (2001b) estimate that the New Deal for Young people has increased youth employment by 15,000 per year between March 1998 and March 2000.

28. This may be an underestimate as it does not take into account wage growth over the year and the fact that those on the New Deal subsidy may be less productive than those who left the Gateway for an unsubsidized job.

29. This is lower than the numbers in table 11.3 because our analysis is in long run. In steady state the New Deal has reduced the equilibrium numbers of the long-term unemployed, so total costs are lower.

The social cost is much less than social benefits of the extra output generated, so there ends up being an annual net social benefit of the program of just over £57 million. The figure is lower than that of the £100 million net benefit in Layard (2000), mainly because I empirically estimate slightly smaller effects of the New Deal on unemployment and employment than those on which Layard bases his calculations. Furthermore, I use actual rather than assumed wage gains. Nevertheless, I concur with his conclusion that the social benefits of the New Deal are likely to outweigh its social costs.

The other two columns of table 11.8 show the sensitivity of these calculations to changes in key assumptions. Column (2) assumes optimistically that average annual earnings of those getting jobs from the New Deal are £8500. This increases the net benefits to about £80 million. The final column makes one change from the first column by pessimistically assuming that the employment effect is only 15,800, (1 standard error below the estimated effect in table 11.6). The net benefit falls to £26 million, half of that in column (1). This illustrates the importance of the magnitude of the employment effect in determining overall benefits. If the employment effect fell to 14,000, then the social costs and benefits are broadly equal.

This analysis probably underestimates the value of the program for three reasons. First, it does not take into account the social benefits of reduced crime, teenage pregnancy, and so on. Second, it does not factor in the redistributive effects from relatively wealthy older taxpayers to the less wealthy young unemployed. Finally, we do not estimate the extent to which the New Deal program enhances the employability and productivity of individuals who participate in the options. We merely assume that the resource input per New Dealer is not more than the present value of the benefit received. On the other hand, the welfare benefits may be overstated as we have not given any weight to the value of leisure for the unemployed.

The job assistance element of the New Deal is more cost effective than the New Deal options as there is no subsidy involved. The lower bound of the job-assistance and monitoring effect works out to increase steady state employment by about 8,000.

Existing U.S. evaluations are rather pessimistic about the ability of temporary government jobs and training schemes to raise the long-term prospects of the young unemployed, especially young men.[30] It is worth remembering, however, that the U.S. schemes focus on extremely disadvantaged youth who may be from a comparatively lower part of the ability distribution than the New Deal participants considered here (especially for men). The success of the employment subsidy option will also hinge on the extent to which the experience of work and training will raise productivity, thereby enabling workers to keep their jobs when the subsidy runs out (Bell, Blundell, and Van Reenen 1999).

30. For a recent survey, see White, Auspos, and Richhio (1999).

11.6 Conclusions

In this chapter I have examined the British New Deal for the Young Unemployed. This is a major program to enhance the employment rates of eighteen–twenty-four-year-olds. The youth labor market is an important issue in most countries, especially in Europe where the unemployment rates of the young are well above the OECD average.

The main finding is from the analysis of outflow rates to jobs before and after the introduction of the New Deal. The program appears to have had a significant effect in moving more young people into jobs. According to our estimates, young unemployed men are about 20 percent more likely to find jobs each month because of the New Deal. I estimate that the New Deal has lead to an increase in "steady state" youth employment of over 17,000.

The New Deal should be seen as the latest step in the progressive moves in Britain to tighten the obligation to search for work while claiming unemployment benefits. This process began with the Restart reform of 1986 that made work-focused interviews compulsory for those on longer unemployment durations. One important difference, however, is that the New Deal is much more generous in providing advice and hard cash (e.g., for wage subsidies and training) than previous reforms.

A "reengineered" New Deal has continued since the Labour Party's reelection in 2001. The government has put greater emphasis on intensifying the job search and extending mandatory options for an ever-larger proportion of benefit recipients. The employers' wage subsidy is the element that is most vulnerable to being cut, due to its low take-up. Such a cut could be premature. As this paper has shown, the wage subsidy appears to have had a significant impact on increasing jobs (at least in the first few months on the program). The long-term success of the New Deal hinges critically upon improving employment prospects through the acquisition of better job skills, either in the Gateway period or, more likely, during one of the options. It will take some time to monitor the extent to which these dynamic gains in worker productivity really have been boosted by the New Deal.

Taken as a whole, though, the program is judged to be a modest success at a modest cost. Its social benefits appear to outweigh its social costs.

Appendix

Cost-Benefit Analysis

I perform a forward-looking analysis of the effects of the New Deal for Young People. Assuming the stock of people unemployed for more than six months has been eliminated, the New Deal for Young People will have its effect on the flow of eighteen–twenty-four-year-olds unemployed for six months.

I begin with our estimates of the effects of the New Deal on increasing outflows. The baseline estimate (table 11.6, row seven) is that New Deal has increased the probability of leaving unemployment for a job by 0.205 (=0.053/0.258). We assume that this elasticity is true for all groups (men and women, whatever duration of unemployment over six months, etc.).

I perform a simulation exercise for a counterfactual economy matched to the features of the U.K. economy in 1998. There are three states: employment, short-term unemployment (under six months), and long-term unemployment (over six months). Individuals on the nonemployer options are treated as long-term unemployed for the purpose of calculating the stocks. I assume that the labor force for young people is fixed at 1.875 million. Initially there are 125,000 long-term unemployed; 250,000 short-term unemployed; and 1.5 million employed. With an outflow rate of 10 percent, this implies an impact effect of an additional monthly outflow of 2,562 (= 0.1*0.205*125), or 31,000 per year. In steady state, however, the stocks will adjust to the new outflow *rates* so the equilibrium flows and stocks will be different. Under the assumption that the New Deal only impacts on the flow rate between long-term unemployment and employment, we can solve for the new steady-state levels of the three labor market states. Long-term unemployment falls by 20,088. Of these individuals, 17,250 enter the stock of employment, and 2,840 become short-term unemployed.

To compute the benefits we assume that young people who get jobs as a result of the New Deal produce an amount equal to the corresponding wage. Hales et al. (2000) report on a survey of people on the employer option that suggests an average hourly wage of £3.78. Assuming a thirty-seven-hour week, this implies annual earnings of £7,272. So one clear benefit is the increase in employment, multiplied by annual earnings (17,250 × £7,272 = £125.4 million).

Other benefits include the gross output of the voluntary and environmental options and the value of training.

On the cost side we have to include

- The resource cost of the Gateway period (although there was already something like this under the previous JSA regime). These are mainly administrative costs, such as the salaries of personal advisers.
- The transfers to individuals and firms involved with New Deal options. These only matter from a social point of view because of the excess burden of taxation. This has to be calculated from the increased additional taxation necessary to finance the New Deal. There are transfer payments to employers through subsidized jobs and to participants through the other options. I assume that in steady state there are 12,000 participants on the subsidized job option. Of the long-term

unemployed 72 percent are in the Gateway or Follow-Through, 14 percent are in the full-time education and training option, and 14 percent are in the Environmental Task Force or voluntary-sector option. These proportions approximate those in 1999. The subsidies given to each of these groups is defined by the program (see section 11.3.2). The sum of these is the gross exchequer cost. We must deduct from this the benefit payments that would have been received by young unemployed people if the New Deal did not exist. Also, we include the additional taxes received by the Revenue. This net exchequer cost is the additional tax that needs to be raised, and this will have a deadweight cost associated with it. Note that the transfers themselves are not included in the social costs.

- The annual cost of JSA (£2,080) for all those on New Deal options (to calculate the benefit savings). For those who are employed as a result of the New Deal, there are also potential savings in housing benefits (£2,080 on a rent of £40 per week) and council tax benefits (about £468), but not all participants on the New Deal can claim these (e.g., if they live with their parents). I extracted data on eighteen–twenty-four-year-olds on JSA using the FES. About 40 percent of the relevant group claimed these benefits, so I weighted the value by this proportion. For the employed group I used the wage (£7,200) to calculate income tax and national insurance (about £472 and £361, respectively, for those on £7,300 per year). Finally, as net disposable income has risen, consumption will rise and there will be a further tax take through value added taxes (VAT) and excise duties. Taking all these elements into account implies an average tax and benefits saving of around £3,600 for each person who moves off unemployment as a result of the New Deal.
- The resource costs of the New Deal options. We make the simplifying assumption that the output of the voluntary and environmental options is equal to the resource costs. One would expect that the output is rather higher. We also assume that the value of training is equal to the resource input. This is controversial as most U.S. studies find little effect of training on unemployed youth. The New Deal courses are, however, typically much longer than those in U.S. programs (up to twelve months in full-time education), so the assumption is not unreasonable.

I have not put any value on the lost leisure time of those who were unemployed but are now productively engaged in different activities.

These calculations ignore many of the potential benefits of the New Deal. First, it does not take into account the social benefits of reduced crime, teenage pregnancy, and so on. Second, it does not factor in the redistributive effects from relatively wealthy older taxpayers to the less wealthy young unemployed. Finally, we do not estimate the extent to which the New Deal program enhances the employability and productivity of individuals who participate in the options. We merely assume that the resource input per New Dealer is not more than the present value of the benefit received.

The calculations also assume that there are no substitution effects or general equilibrium effects. The former would increase the costs, and the latter would increase the benefits. Strong evidence of large substitution or major general equilibrium effects was not uncovered in section 11.4.

References

Abbring, J. H., G. van den Berg, and J. van Ours. 1997. The effect of unemployment insurance sanctions on the transition rate from unemployment to employment. Tinbergen Institute. Working Paper. Amsterdam: Tinbergen Institute.

Ashenfelter, O., D. Ashmore, and O. Deschenes. 1999. Do unemployment insurance recipients actively seek work? Randomized trials in four U.S. States. NBER Working Paper no. 6982. Cambridge, Mass.: National Bureau of Economic Research, February.

Anderson, P. 2000. Monitoring and assisting active job search. In *OECD proceedings: Labour market policies and the public employment service,* 217–238. Paris: Organization for Economic Cooperation and Development.

Anderton, B., R. Riley, and G. Young. 1999. The New Deal for Young People: Early findings from the pathfinder areas. Employment Service Research and Development Paper no. 34. London: Department for Education and Skills.

Atkinson, J., and N. Meager. 1994. Evaluation of Workstart pilots. IES Report no. 279. Brighton, U.K.: Institute for Employment Studies.

Bell, B., R. Blundell, and J. Van Reenen. 1999. Getting the unemployed back to work: The role of targeted wage subsidies. *International Tax and Public Finance* 6:339–360.

Beveridge, W. 1909. *Unemployment: A problem of industry.* London: Longman.

Blanchflower, D., and R. Freeman. 2000. The declining economic status of young workers in OECD countries. In *Youth unemployment and joblessness in advanced countries,* ed. D. Blanchflower and R. Freeman, 80–95. Chicago: University of Chicago Press.

Bloom, D., and C. Michalopoulos. 2001. *How welfare and work policies affect employment and income: A synthesis of research.* New York: Manpower Demonstration Research Corporation.

Blundell, R., M. Costa Dias, C. Meghir, and J. Van Reenan. 2001. Evaluating the impact of a mandatory job search program. Institute for Fiscal Studies Working Paper no. W01/20. London: Institute for Fiscal Studies.

Bonjour, D. 2001. The New Deal for young people: National survey of participants stage 2. Employment Service Research and Development Paper no. 67. London: U.K. Department of Employment.

Boone, J., and J. van Ours. 2000. Modeling financial incentives to get unemployed back to work. CEPR Discussion Paper no. 2361. London: Center for Economic and Policy Research.

Department for Education and Employment (DFEE). 1997. Design of the New Deal for 18–24 year olds. London: Department for Education and Employment.

Dickert-Conlin, S., and D. Holtz-Eakin. 2000. Employee-based versus employer-based subsidies to low wage workers: A public finance perspective? In *Finding jobs: Work and welfare reform,* ed. D. Card and R. Blank, 105–166. New York: Russell Sage Foundation.

Dicks, M. J., and N. Hatch. 1989. The relationship between employment and unemployment. Bank of England Discussion Paper no. 39. London: Bank of England.

Disney, R., L. Bellmann, A. Carruth, W. Franz, R. Jackman, R. Layard, H. Lehmann, and J. Philpott. 1991. *Helping the unemployed: Active labour market policies in Britain and Germany.* London: Anglo-German Foundation.

Dolton, P. 1992. Youth training in the UK. In *Training in the private sector,* ed. L. Lynch, 67–100. Cambridge: Cambridge University Press.

Dolton, P., and D. O'Neill. 1995. The impact of Restart on reservation wages and long-term unemployment. *Oxford Bulletin of Economics and Statistics* 57 (4): 451–470.

Dolton, P., and D. O'Neill. 1996. Unemployment duration and the Restart effect: Some experimental evidence. *Economic Journal* 106:387–400.

Ellwood, D., and E. Welty. 2000. Public service employment and mandatory work: A policy whose time has come and gone and come again? In *Finding jobs: Work and welfare reform,* ed. D. Card and R. Blank, 267–301. New York: Russell Sage Foundation.

Gorter, R., and P. Kalb. 1996. Estimating the effects of counselling and monitoring the unemployed using a job search model. *Journal of Human Resources* 31:590–610.

Gosling, A., S. Machin, and C. Meghir. 2000. The evolution of male earnings in Britain 1984–94. *Review of Economic Studies* 67 (4): 635–666.

Grubb, D. 2000. Eligibility criteria for unemployment benefits. *OECD Economic Studies* 31 (2): 147–184.

Hahn, J., P. Todd, and W. van der Klaauw. 1999. Identification and estimation of treatment effects with regression discontinuity design. UNC. Working Paper.

Hales, J., D. Collins, C. Hasluck, and S. Woodland. 2000. New Deals for Young People and for long term unemployed: Survey of employers. Employment Service Research and Development Paper no. 58. London: U.K. Department of Employment.

Hasluck, C. 2000. Early lessons form the evaluations of New Deal programmes. Employment Service Research and Development Report no. ESR49. London: U.K.: Department of Employment.

Heckman, J., R. Lalonde, and J. Smith. 1999. The economics and econometrics of active labour market policies. In *Handbook of labor economics,* vol. 2, ed. O. Ashenfelter and D. Card, 1865–2097. Amsterdam: Kluwer.

Her Majesty's Treasury. 1999. *Stability and steady growth for Britain: Pre-budget report.* London: Her Majesty's Treasury.

Katz, L. 1998. Wage subsidies for the disadvantaged. *Generating jobs: How to increase demand for less-skilled workers*, ed. R. Freeman and P. Gottschalk, 21–53. New York: Russell Sage Foundation.

Layard, R. 2000. Welfare to work and the New Deal. *The Business Economist* 31 (3): 28–40.

Layard, R., S. Nickell, and R. Jackman. 1991. *Unemployment: Macroeconomic performance and the labour market.* Oxford: Oxford University Press.

Martin, J. 1998. What works among active labour market policies: Evidence from

OECD countries' experience. Organization for Economic Cooperation and Development. Mimeograph.
Meyer, B. 1995. Lessons from US unemployment insurance experiments. *Journal of Economic Literature* 33 (1): 91–131.
Nickell, S. J. 1997. Unemployment and labour market rigidities: Europe vs. North America. *Journal of Economic Perspectives,* 10:48–76.
Nickell, S. J., and J. van Ours. 2000. The Netherlands and the United Kingdom: A European unemployment miracle? *Economic Policy* 30:137–180.
Price, D. 2000. *Office of hope: A history of the employment service.* London: Policy Studies Institute.
Riley, R., and G. Young. 2001a. Does welfare-to-work policy increase employment?: Evidence from the UK New Deal for young unemployed. National Institute for Economic and Social Research Working Paper no. 183. London: National Institute of Economic and Social Research.
Riley, R., and G. Young. 2001b. The macroeconomic impact of the New Deal for young people. National Institute for Economic and Social Research Working Paper no. 185. London: National Institute of Economic and Social Research.
Schmitt, J. 1995. The changing distribution of male earnings in Britain 1974–88. In *Differences and changes in wage structures,* ed. R. Freeman and L. Katz, 28–42. Chicago: University of Chicago Press.
Schmitt, J., and J. Wadsworth. 1999. You won't feel the benefit: Changing unemployment benefit entitlements and labour market activity in Britain. Leverhulme Trust Discussion Paper Series no. 39. Oxford: Oxford University.
Sweeney, K., and D. McMahon. 1998. The effects of job seekers' allowance on the claimant count. *Labour Market Trends* 3:195–202.
van den Berg, G., and B. van der Klaauw. 2001. Counselling and monitoring of unemployed workers: Theory and evidence from a controlled social experiment. CEPR Working Paper no. 2986. London: Center for Economic and Policy Research.
van den Berg, G., B. van der Klaauw, and J. van Ours. 1998. Punitive sanctions and the transition rate from welfare to work. Tinbergen Institute. Mimeograph.
Wells, W. 2000. From Restart to the New Deal in the United Kingdom. In *OECD proceedings: Labour market policies and the public employment service,* 35–68. Paris: Organization for Economic Cooperation and Development.
White, M., and P. Leakey. 1992. *The Restart effect.* London: Policy Studies Institute.
White, M., P. Auspos, and J. Richhio. 1999. A review of US and European literature on the micro-economic effects of labour market programmes for young people. Employment Service Report no. 20. London: U.K. Department of Employment.

Contributors

Richard Blundell
Department of Economics
University College London
Gower Street
London WC1E 6BT, England

David Card
Industrial Relations Section
Firestone Library
Princeton University
Princeton, NJ 08544

Martin J. Conyon
The Wharton School
University of Pennsylvania
2013 Steinberg-Dietrich Hall
Philadelphia, PA 19104

Richard Dickens
Department of Economics
Queen Mary, University of London
Mile End Road
London E1 4NS, England

Richard Disney
School of Economics
University of Nottingham
Room B36, Economics & Geography Building
University Park
Nottingham NG7 2RD, England

David T. Ellwood
John F. Kennedy School of Government
Harvard University
79 JFK Street
Cambridge, MA 02138

Carl Emmerson
The Institute for Fiscal Studies
7 Ridgmount Street
London WC1E 7AE, England

Richard B. Freeman
Department of Economics
Harvard University
Cambridge, MA 02138

Amanda Gosling
Department of Economics
University of Essex
Wivenhoe Park
Colchester CO4 3SQ, England

Richard Green
Department of Economics
University of Hull
Cottingham Road
Hull HU6 7RX, England

Paul Gregg
Department of Economics
University of Bristol
12 Priory Road
Bristol BS8 1TN, England

Rachel Griffith
The Institute for Fiscal Studies
7 Ridgmount Street
London WC1E 7AE, England

Jonathan Haskel
Department of Economics
Queen Mary, University of London
Mile End Road
London E1 4NS, England

Hilary Hoynes
Department of Economics
University of California, Davis
One Shields Avenue
Davis, CA 95616-8578

Thomas Lemieux
Department of Economics
University of British Columbia
997-1873 East Mall
Vancouver, BC V6T 1Z1, Canada

Stephen Machin
Department of Economics
University College London
Gower Street
London WC1E 6BT, England

Alan Manning
Department of Economics
London School of Economics
Houghton Street
London WC2A 2AE, England

John Pencavel
Stanford University
Landau Economics Building
579 Serra Mall
Stanford, CA 94305-6072

Helen Simpson
The Institute for Fiscal Studies
7 Ridgmount Street
London WC1E 7AE, England

Sarah Smith
The Financial Services Authority
25 The North Colonnade
Canary Wharf
London E14 5HS, England

John Van Reenen
Center for Economic Performance
London School of Economics
Houghton Street
London WC2A 2AE, England

Author Index

Abbot, K., 83
Abbring, J. H., 478
Adams, Roy, 194n25
Aghion, P., 147n1
Agulnik, P., 241n18
Alton, Lee J., 192n20
Anderton, B., 475n9, 485n24, 489n27
Andrews, Martyn J., 220, 220n63, 221
Ashenfelter, O., 478
Ashmore, D., 478
Atkinson, Anthony B., 52n30
Atkinson, J., 476
Attanasio, Orazio, 350n20
Averch, H., 71
Aylen, Jonathan, 185n3

Bain, George Sayers, 194n26, 199n32
Banks, J., 239, 249n27, 250
Barnes, M., 151n8, 173n19
Barrell, R., 148n3
Barrientos, A., 268
Barro, R., 147n1
Bartlesman, E., 150n6
Bean, C., 148n5, 209
Beesley, T., 71
Bell, B., 466
Bell, David N. F., 220, 221
Bernard, A., 148n3
Berndt, E. R., 99n36
Bernstein, Jared, 323
Bertola, Giuseppi, 25
Beveridge, W., 468
Bingley, P., 350n20, 444
Bishop, M., 85, 99
Blackaby, D., 373
Blake, D., 250n28
Blanchflower, David G., 42, 51, 120, 220, 221
Blank, R. M., 438, 442, 443
Blank, Rebecca, 324, 325
Blasi, J., 119
Blau, Francine, 279
Blinder, Alan, 325
Blomstrom, M., 148n3
Blundell, Richard, 52, 238, 254, 255, 325n11, 350n20, 411, 427, 444, 444n14, 444n15, 466
Bodie, Z., 243, 258
Böheim, René, 318n6, 387, 392n9
Booth, Alison L., 209n52
Bos, D., 70, 241
Bound, John, 324n10
Boylaud, Olivier, 20, 21
Broadberry, Stephen N., 42
Brown, William, 225n68
Brugiavini, A., 266
Bruno, Michael, 23, 99
Bryson, Alex, 50, 200, 200n35, 220n62, 223, 223n66
Budd, A., 238

Cable, J. R., 120
Calmfors, Lars, 23
Cameron, G., 148n3, 148n5, 372
Campbell, N., 238

Card, David, 278n5, 279, 286n13, 294n22, 324, 325
Caves, R., 147, 150n6
Clark, T., 240n14
Conte, M., 119
Conyon, Martin, 49, 113, 114, 119
Core, J., 119
Cornfield, Daniel B., 196n28
Crafts, N., 148n5, 209
Creedy, J., 250
Critcher, C., 99
Cubbin, J., 101
Cully, Mark, 202n41, 204n43, 205, 211n57, 222, 223
Cutler, D., 246
Cutler, David, 325

Daniel, W. W., 191n18, 192n21, 208
Davies, S., 148n3
DeLeire, Thomas, 324n10
Deschenes, O., 478
Dicey, A. V., 201n37
Dickens, Richard, 317, 321n9, 334, 338, 365, 435
Dickert, S., 443n13
Dickert-Conlin, S., 479
Dicks, M. J., 475
Dilnot, A., 238, 254, 364, 425, 426
Dimsdale, N. H., 198n31
DiNardo, John, 278, 288n15, 289, 290n17, 291n19, 294, 294n22, 298
Disney, Richard, 150n6, 150n7, 200, 235n10, 236, 238, 241n18, 243, 244n19, 246, 246n22, 248n23, 248n25, 248n26, 250, 252n30, 253, 254, 255, 255n35, 259n38, 266, 268, 299n27, 475
Djankov, Simeon, 26, 27
Dolton, P., 479n18
Domberger, S., 101
Doms, M., 150, 150n6, 150n7, 163
Doucouliagos, C., 110, 120
Dougherty, C., 148n5
Driffil, John, 23
Duncan, Alan, 350n20
Dunn, Stephen, 225n68
Dunning, J., 147
Duranton, G., 378

Edwards, P. K., 194n26
Edwards, S., 147n2
Eissa, Nada, 351, 436, 440, 443
Ellwood, David T., 317, 320n8, 321n9, 324, 334, 338, 351, 354, 435, 443, 479
Emmerson, C., 239, 240n15, 241n18, 246n22, 248n26, 250, 251, 268
Engen, E. M., 247
Ercolani, Marco, 324
Evans, P., 373

Ferrie, Joseph P., 192n20
Forth, John, 50, 200, 200n35, 220n62, 223
Fortin, Nicole M., 278, 288n15, 289, 290n17, 291n19, 294, 294n22, 298
Freeman, Richard, 49, 51, 109, 205n46, 228, 275n2, 278n5, 293, 294n22
Fry, V., 444n15

Galal, A., 64, 73, 96
Gale, W. G., 247, 249
Gallie, Duncan, 223
Giles, Christopher, 275n3, 435
Globerman, S., 148n3, 150
Goodman, Alissa, 253, 313, 321, 323, 325, 325n11
Gorter, R., 478
Gosling, Amanda, 200, 275n1, 294n22, 299n27, 398, 468
Gottschalk, Peter, 321, 365
Green, M., 85, 343
Green, Richard, 49, 81
Greenwood, M. J., 380
Gregg, Paul, 209n53, 324, 325, 325n11, 342, 352n22
Griffith, R., 150n6, 151n8, 173n19
Griliches, Zvi, 38n18, 42
Grossman, G., 147
Grout, Paul A., 48, 102n37, 103, 208
Grubb, David, 25
Gruber, Jonathan, 324n10
Guay, W., 119
Gustman, A., 258, 259, 261, 263n42

Hahn, J., 486
Hales, J., 486n26
Hall, R. E., 162n14
Hanke, Steve, 13, 14, 18
Hansen, Kristine, 324, 342, 343
Harkness, Susan, 279
Harris, R. I. D., 150n6
Hart, P. E., 185n5
Harvard Center for International Development, 18

Haskel, Jonathan, 49, 70, 84, 88, 150n6, 150n7, 225n68
Hasluck, C., 479
Hatch, N., 475
Haveman, Robert, 324n10
Hayek, Friedrich, 196n29
Heckman, J., 479n18
Heden, Y., 150n6, 150n7
Helpman, E., 147
Henley, A., 387
Hicks, Stephen, 186, 186n9
Hildreth, Andrew, 220, 221
Hobsbawn, E. J., 209n51
Hohnson, H., 71
Holtz-Eakin, D., 479
Houser, S., 443n13
Howenstine, N., 150
Howitt, P., 147n1
Hoynes, Hilary, 52, 351, 436, 443, 444
Hughes, G., 260, 261, 372, 373, 380, 387

Ippolito, R. A., 258

Jackman, R., 387, 476n11
Jenkins, Stephen P., 318n6, 324
Jensen, B. J., 150, 150n7, 163
Jensen, P., 101
Johnson, Paul, 238, 239, 240n15, 250, 251, 253, 254, 313, 321, 323, 325, 325n11, 352n22, 435
Jones, C., 148n3
Jorgenson, D., 99, 148n5

Kahn-Freund, Otto, 192n19
Kalb, P., 478
Kandel, E., 119, 120
Katz, Lawrence, 275n2, 278n5, 325, 479
Kay, J., 72, 85, 425
Keane, M. P., 444
Klette, T. J., 162n14
Kramarz, Francis, 279n7
Krugman, P. R., 147n2
Kruse, D. L., 110, 119, 120
Kubik, Jeffrey D., 324n10

Lalonde, R., 479n18
Lansbury, M., 148n5
La Porta, Rafael, 27, 28
Layard, R., 148n5, 476n11
Lazear, Edward P., 25, 119, 120, 258
Leakey, P., 476n10
Lee, David, 290n17
Lemieux, Thomas, 278, 278n5, 279n7, 286n13, 288n15, 289, 290n17, 291n19, 294, 294n22, 298, 398
Lewis, H. Greg, 221n64
Liebman, Jeffrey B., 351, 440, 441n10, 442n11
Littlechild, S. C., 71, 78, 79
Lynch, Lisa M., 24
Lyons, B., 148n3

Machin, Stephen, 48, 200, 209n53, 210, 275n1, 294n22, 323, 325, 468
MaCurdy, Thomas, 350n20, 444n14
Manning, D. N., 373
Marcus, A. J., 243, 258
Markou, E., 91
Marsh, David, 194n26
Martin, J., 471, 475n8
Martin, R., 151n8, 173n19
Martin, S., 70n8, 88
Mayes, D., 148n5
McClements, L. D., 316
McCormick, B., 260, 261, 372, 373, 374, 380, 387, 392
McCrae, Julian, 364, 435
McGowan, P., 83
McKnight, Abigal, 386n87
McMahon, D., 475
McNabb, R., 121
Meadowcroft, S., 101
Meager, N., 476
Mealli, F., 261
Meghir, C., 238, 255, 255n35, 275n1, 350n20, 468
Merton, R. C., 243, 258
Metcalf, David, 185n4, 204n44, 209n52, 209n53, 225n68, 226n69, 293
Meyer, Bruce D., 324, 325n11, 351, 438, 441, 442n11, 443, 478
Micklewright, John, 52n30
Miles, D., 246
Millward, Neil, 50, 70n7, 99, 191n18, 192n21, 200, 200n35, 202n41, 204n43, 210n54, 210n55, 220n62, 223
Milner, Simon, 200n35
Mishel, Lawrence, 323
Modigliani, F., 246
Moffitt, Robert, 325n11, 350n20, 444
Monastiriotis, V., 378
Moore, John, 70n8, 258

Morrison, H., 69n5, 425
Muellbauer, J., 372
Murphy, A., 372
Murphy, K. J., 119
Murphy, Kevin, 278n5
Murthi, M., 260n39

Needels, Karen, 278n5
Neumark, D., 443n13
Newbery, D., 81
Niccoletti, Giuseppe, 20, 21
Nickell, S., 148n5, 162n14, 476n11, 477
Noble, M., 371
Nolan, Brian, 325

Ogden, S., 99
O'Mahony, Mary, 39, 88, 99n36, 148n5
Organization for Economic Cooperation and Development (OECD), 207
Orszag, J. M., 260n39
Oswald, A. J., 120, 372
Oulton, N., 99n36, 148n5, 151n8, 173n19

Pain, N., 148n3
Palacios, R., 235n10
Parker, D., 70n8, 88
Parry, D., 99
Perry, J., 151, 173n19
Persson, H., 148n3
Phelps Brown, E. H., 185n5, 190
Pissarides, C., 387
Pollit, M., 102n37
Poterba, James, 299, 299n27
Prais, S. J., 185, 187n11
Pratton, C. F., 185
Price, Robert, 199n32
Proudman, J., 148n3, 148n5
Pryke, R., 70, 85
Pudney, S., 261

Read, Laura, 113, 114
Redding, S., 148n3, 148n5
Reed, Howard, 325n11, 352n22
Rees, R., 70
Ries, J., 150
Riley, R., 475, 475n9, 485n24, 489n27
Robbins, Philip, 324
Robinson, A., 120
Robinson, C., 150n6
Robinson, E. A. G., 193n23
Rogers, Joel, 228
Rosenbaum, Dan T., 324, 325n11, 351, 438, 441, 442n11, 443
Rovizzi, L., 97, 97n33
Rueben, Kim, 299, 299n27

Sachs, Jeffrey, 23, 99
Sala-i-Martin, *x,* 147n1
Sanchis, A., 70, 92
Savouri, S., 387
Scarpetta, Stefano, 20, 21
Schmalensee, R., 81
Schmitt, John, 207, 275n1, 323, 466, 471
Schoeni, R., 438
Scholtz, J. K., 443n13
Seabright, P., 83
Sears, G., 253
Seeney, K., 475
Shleifer, A., 78
Smeeding, Timothy, 321
Smith, A., 147n2
Smith, J., 479n18
Smith, S., 238, 255
Steinmeier, T., 258, 259, 261, 263n42
Stevens, Mark, 70n7, 202n41, 204n43, 210n54, 210n55
Stewart, Mark, 48, 186, 204n44, 210, 220, 220n63, 295n23
Stewart, Mark B., 221
Symons, J., 148n5
Szymanski, S., 84, 88, 102

Tanner, S., 241n18, 249n27
Taylor, M., 387, 392n9
Thompson, D., 72, 83, 84, 97, 97n33, 99, 101
Towers, Brian, 223

Undy, Roger, 203
Upward, Richard, 220, 221

van Ark, Bart, 38, 148n5
van den Berg, G., 478
van der Klaauw, B., 478, 486
van Ours, J., 477, 478
Van Reenan, John, 48, 52–53, 210, 466
Venables, A., 147n2
Vernon, R., 147
Vertinsky, I., 150
Vickers, J., 72n11

Waddams Price, C., 79, 91
Waddington, D., 99

Wadhwani, S., 120, 148n5
Wadhwani, Sushil, 225n68
Wadsworth, Jonathan, 324, 343, 387, 471
Wagner, Karin, 42
Waidman, Timothy, 324n10
Wakefield, M., 246n22, 248n26
Walker, Ian, 350n20, 426, 444
Wall, M., 120, 148n5
Walters, Stephen, 13, 14, 18
Wascher, W., 443n13
Webb, Steven, 253, 313, 321, 323, 325, 325n11
Wedderburn, K., 192n19
Weitzman, M., 110
Wells, William, 25, 470n4
Welty, E., 479n17
Weyman-Jones, T., 91
White, M., 476n10
Whitehouse, E., 235n10, 236, 243, 244n19, 248n25, 248n23, 250, 252n30, 255n35, 259n38, 260n39
Whitfield, A., 83, 84
Whitfield, K., 121
Wilson, N., 120
Wood, D. O., 99n36

Young, G., 475, 475n9, 485n24, 489n27

Zeile, W., 150

Subject Index

Absolute poverty, trends in, U.K. vs. U.S., 320–23
Active labor market policies (ALMPs), 473t; across OCED countries, 476–77
Agricultural employment, U.K. vs. France and Germany, 37–38, 38t
Aid to Families with Dependent Children (AFDC), 435; reforms to, 438–40
All Employee Share Plan, 110
Annual Respondent Database (ARD), 151–52, 173–76
Approved company share option plan (CSOP), 112–13
Approved profit-related pay scheme, 111–12
Approved profit-sharing scheme, 112
Approved save as you earn (SAYE) scheme, 112

Blair, Tony, 9, 11, 372
Britain. *See* United Kingdom (U.K.)
British Airways (BA), 73, 73n13, 84. *See also* British Overseas Airways Corporation (BOAC)
British Broadcasting Corporation (BBC), 64, 69
British Energy, 82
British Gas, 83, 83n22, 91; quality of service and, 97
British Household Panel Survey (BHPS), 262–68
British Leyland (Rover Group), 68, 72, 74–75
British Overseas Airways Corporation (BOAC), 64, 68. *See also* British Airways (BA)
British Steel, 90
British Telecommunications (BT), 64, 73–74, 80; quality indicators in, 96t
Bullock Commission, 182
Business formation, indexes of, 26–28
Butler, R. A., 196

Capital per worker, trends in, U.K., U.S., France and Germany, 39–42, 39f
Chamberlain, Joseph, 66
Channel Tunnel Rail Link, 102
Closed shops, 197, 204–5
Collective bargaining, 23–25; at end of 1970s, 193–94; government support of, 190–95; indirect effects on, 206–7; minimum wage regulation and, 192; unemployment and, 226–28. *See also* Unionism, British
Compensation. *See* Shared compensation
Competition: in natural monopolies, 71–72; utilities and, 81–84
Competitiveness: indexes of, 12–13, 16–18; rankings for advanced OECD countries for, 18–20, 19t
Contracted-out rebates (CORS), 248, 252
Contracting-out, 100–102; for pensions, 234, 235
Council house sales, 403–5

Data sources: for American wage inequality study, 307–10; Annual Respondent Database (ARD), 151–52, 173–76; British Household Panel Survey, 262; for British wage inequality study, 306–7; for in-work benefit schemes, 456–57; for studying U.K. foreign-owned establishments, 151–55; for studying wage inequality, 277; for U.K. shared compensation practices, 113–16
DB pension plans. *See* Defined benefit (DB) occupational pension plans
DC pension plans. *See* Defined contribution (DC) pension plans
Defined benefit (DB) occupational pension plans, 234, 263
Defined contribution (DC) pension plans, 234–35, 263
Demographics: changing patterns of poverty and, 323; influence of, on poverty, 339–40
Dismissal law, unfair, 202, 202n39
Donovan Commission, 185, 188n12, 189, 189n15

Earned Income Tax Credit (EITC), 412, 421–25, 422–23t, 436; impact of reforms to, 440–43; reforms to, 436–38, 439f
Economic freedom: indexes of, 12; indicators of, in U.K. and OECD markets, 17t; measures of, 13–16
Efficiency, productive, effects of privatization on, 84–91
Electric industry, quality of service and, 97, 97f
Employment adjustments, regulation of, 25
Employment protection legislation (EPL), 25, 26t
Enterprise Management Incentives, 110
Enumeration districts, inequalities in, 397–403

Family Credit (FC), 411, 420–21, 426–29. *See also* Working Families Tax Credit (WFTC)
Family Income Supplement (FIS), 419–20. *See also* Family Credit (FC)
Food Stamps, 435
Foreign direct investment (FDI), 148
Foreign-owned establishments, in U.K.: characteristics of, 161–71; data source for studying, 151–55; trends for, 155–61
France: agricultural employment in, vs. Germany and U.K., 37–38, 38t; capital per worker in, vs. Germany, U.K., and U.S., 39–42, 39f; summary of changing trends in productivity growth in, 45–47; unemployment in, vs. U.K. and U.S., 198–99, 198f
Fraser Institute, 12; index of, 14–16
Freedom House index, 14
Free-rider problem, shared compensation and, 119–20
Friedman, Milton, 196n29

Gas industry, competition and, 83–84
Germany: agricultural employment in, vs. France and U.K., 37–38, 38t; capital per worker in, vs. France, U.K., and U.S., 39–42, 39f; changes in labor quality in, 42–45; summary of changing trends in productivity growth in, 45–47
Glas Cymru, 82n21
Great Britain. *See* United Kingdom (U.K.)
Gross domestic product (GDP): trends in, U.K. vs. various countries, 28–30, 29t; trends in growth rate of, U.K. vs. various countries, 30–37
Guaranteed Minimum Pension (GMP), 234

Harvard Center for International Development, 12
Heath, Edward, 72, 194n24, 195
Heritage Foundation, 12
Housing market, residential mobility and, 395–97

Income distribution, 269; effect of income distribution on, 253–54. *See also* Wage inequality
Incomes: effect of pension reform on distribution of, 253–54; growth and distribution of, and British unionism, 225
Indexes: of business formation, 26–28; of competitiveness, 12–13, 16–18; of economic freedom, 12; Fraser Institute, 14–16; Freedom House, 14; of labor markets, 23–26; of product markets, 20–21, 22t
International Institute for Management Development (IMD), 16

In-work benefit schemes: conclusions about, 454–56; early U.K. programs for, 425–30; impact of, 430–35; impact of, on labor markets, 411–12; U.K. vs. U.S., 421–25; in U.K., 419–21, 420t; in U.S., 419–21, 420t. *See also* Unemployment

Job mobility. *See* Labor mobility
Jobs. *See* Employment adjustments; Employment protection legislation (EPL)
Job Seekers Allowance (JSA), 461–62, 471, 472
Joseph, Keith, 196

Labor markets: Dutch reforms for, 478; evaluations on reforms of, 475–76; features of U.K., 463–68; impact of "in-work" benefit schemes and, 411–12; indexes of, 23–26. *See also* Youth unemployment
Labor mobility, 269–70; pension reform and, 257–69; personal pensions and, 261–69
Labor productivity: in Britain, vs. other major countries, 148, 149t; contributions of capital accumulation to relative trends in, 40–42, 41t; explanations for growth rates for, 37–47; labor quality and, 42–45; review of studies of, 150; unionism and, 211–19. *See also* Productivity
Labor quality, labor productivity and, 42–45
Labor supply: impact of pension reform on, 254–57; trends in, over 1980s and 1990s, 413–19
Labor unions. *See* Unions

MacMillan, Harold, 196
Major, John, 9
Markets, indicators of freedom in, 17t
Maxwell scandal, 250, 250n28
Medicaid, 435
Migration. *See* Residential mobility
Minimum Income Guarantee, 236, 239
Minimum-wage regulation, 192
Minimum wages, wage inequality and, 287–93
Mobility, U.K. vs. other European countries, 380, 380t. *See also* Regional mobility; Residential mobility
Monopolies and Mergers Commission (MMC), 77, 79, 79n19
Moore, John, 72

National Express, 83
National Freight Corporation, 73
National Grid Company (NGC), 80
Nationalization, 66–68; dates in key industries for privatization, 75t; union support of, 193. *See also* Privatization; Public ownership
National Minimum Wage (U.K), 226, 226n69
National Union of Mineworkers, 72
Natural monopolies: competition in, 71–72; nationalization of, 71
Neighborhood, inequalities in, 397–403
Netherlands, impact of reforms to unemployment benefits, 478
Network Rail, 82
New all employee share plan, 112
New Deal for Young People program (U.K.), 471–74; cost-benefit analysis for, 491–94; empirical evaluation of, 480–88; flow diagram for, 474f; stages of, 461–62
New Deal program (U.K.), 461–63; cost-benefit calculations for, 488–90; elements of, 471–75; eligibility for, 462; Gateway period in, 462; historical context of, 468–71, 469t; U.S. research and, 477–80
New Zealand, 54

Organization for Economic Cooperation and Development (OECD), 1, 12; indicators of freedom in markets in, 17t
Organized labor. *See* Unions

Pelletier, Jeffrey, 205n46
Pension plans: defined benefit, 234, 263; defined contribution, 234–35, 263
Pension reform: burden of transition period and, 251–53; contracting-out and, 234, 235; effect of, on income distribution, 253–54; effect of, on tax rates, 251–53; impact of, on labor supply, 254–57; impact of, on retirement ages, 254–57; impact on saving of, 245–50; labor mobility and, 257–69; overview of, 233–36; summary of findings for, 237–38. *See also* Personal pensions

Pension system: decision considerations for selecting pension provider, 243–45; demographic trends for, 241–42, 242t; overview of, 238–41; projected costs for, 241–42, 242t; projected future spending for, vs. other countries, 242–43, 243t
Personal pensions, 235; labor mobility and, 261–69; saving and, 247–49; types of contributions to, 248–49, 250f. *See also* Pension reform
Poverty: aggregate analyses of, 325; couples and, in U.K. and U.S., 354–61; defining family/household units and, 320; defining income and, 317–19; explanations for changing patterns of, 323–25; findings about, 314–15; forces shaping, in U.K. and U.S., 332–39; influence of demographics on, 339–40; influence of wages on, 340–42; measuring, 313–14; measuring, in U. K. vs. U.S., 315–20; micromethods of analysis for, 326–32; rates of, in U.K. vs. U.S., 313; relative vs. absolute standards of, 315–17; role of social polices for reducing, in U.K. and U.S., 345–62; single parents and, in U.K. and U.S., 352–54; trends in relative and absolute, in U.K. vs. U.S., 320–23; unemployment and, 342–43; work and, 342–45; work-based strategies for reducing, 362–66
Private Finance Initiative (PFI), 102–5; advantages of, 102–3; disadvantages of, 103–4
Privatization, 63–65; contracting out and, 100–102; dates in key industries, 75t; effect of, on public-sector unions, 99; effects of, on productive efficiency, 84–91; energy prices and, 99; major U.K. companies undergoing, 76; public attitudes toward public sector and, 100, 100t; quality of service and, 96–98; rationale for, 69–72; since 1979 in U.K., 72–76; studies of, 85–89, 86–87t; Thatcher Revolution and, 64; of utilities, 76–84; wage inequality and, 299–301. *See also* Public ownership
Productive efficiency, effects of privatization on, 84–91
Productivity, unionism and, 207–11. *See also* Labor productivity
Productivity growth, summary of changing trends in, 45–47
Product markets, indexes of, 20–21, 22t
Public ownership, 63; textbook argument for, 70; in U.K., 66–69, 67t. *See also* Privatization
Public Sector Borrowing Requirement (PSBR), 73, 81
Public sector unions, effect of privatization on, 99
Public services: in U.K., 19; in U.S., 19

Quality of service: British Gas and, 97; British Telecommunications and, 96; electric industry and, 97, 97f; privatization and, 96–98; rail industry and, 97–98; utilities and, 96–97

Rail industry, quality of service and, 97–98
Railtrack, 82, 85n23
Regional Electricity Companies (RECs), 80
Regional inequalities, 373–78
Regional mobility, 378–80, 379f, 380f; conclusions about, 405–8; by education level, 380–81, 381f. *See also* Residential mobility
Regulations: for employment adjustments, 25; extent of, on business, 20–21; in OECD countries, 21, 22t; studies of effects of, 86–87t
Relative poverty, trends in, U.K. vs. U.S., 320–23
Residential mobility: determinants of, 387–92; economic returns to, 384–85; equations for, 388t, 389t, 390t, 391; housing market and, 395–97; literature on, 387; reasons for, 393–95, 394t; among students, 385–87; unemployment and, 378–84, 392–95. *See also* Regional mobility
Restart program, 470; evaluations of, 475–76
Retirement ages, effect of pension reform on, 254–57
Ridley, Nicholas, 72
Rolls Royce, 64, 68, 72
Rover Group (British Leyland), 68, 72, 74–75

Saving, 269; impact of pension reform on, 245–50

Scargill, Arthur, 200n36
Shared compensation, 109–10; establishment effects of, on information and decision making, 135–39; findings for, 110–11; firm level effects of, on information and decision making, 129–31; firm performance and, 116–21; free-rider problem and, 119–20; longitudinal analysis of, 139–41; production function evidence and, 131–35; production function evidence for, 121–25; stock market evidence for, 125–29; in U.K., 111–16; WERS surveys on, 141–43
Signals passed at danger (SPADs), 98, 98t
Single parents, poverty and, in U.K. and U.S., 352–54
Social Exclusion Unit, 372
Social policies: effects, and poverty, 324–25; role of, for reducing poverty, 345–62
Social security system, 240; decision considerations for opting out of, 243. *See also* Pension reform; Pension system
Start-ups, regulation of, 26–28
State Earnings-Related Pension Scheme (SERPS), 234, 236, 240–41
State Second Pension (S2P), 236
Strikes, unionism and, 187–88, 201–4

Taft-Hartley Act of 1947, 204n42
Tax rates, 269; effect of pension reform on, 251–53
Tebbit, Norman, 378
Temporary Assistance for Needy Families (TANF), 438
Thatcher, Margaret, 9, 11, 63, 72, 187, 196, 396, 470
Thatcher Revolution, 2; privatization and, 64
Total factor productivity (TFP), 85–88; energy prices and, 99; growth of, in U.K. public sector, 89–91; sources of growth of, 91–95
Trade Disputes Act of 1906, 189–90, 201
Trade unions. *See* Unions
Transport Act of 1980, 83

Unemployment: changing patterns of poverty and, 324; collective bargaining and, 226–28; current, in U.K., 463–68; influence of, on poverty, 342–45; residential mobility and, 378–84, 392–95; timeline for benefit regime, 468, 469t; in U.K. vs. France and U.S., 198f, 199. *See also* In-work benefit schemes; New Deal program (U.K.); Youth unemployment
Unemployment benefits, 52t; replacement ratios on, 51–52; in U.K., 476–77
Unemployment insurance (UI) system (U.S.), 477–78; literature on, 477–78
Unfair dismissal law, 202, 202n39
Unionism, British, 23–25; benefits of, to workers, 220–24; changes in characteristics of, 200–201, 201f; changing economic policies and, 196–97; changing macroeconomic settings and, 197–201; condition of, in 1960s and 1970s, 184–87; decline in, worklife and, 225–26; explanations for retreat of, 224–25; future of, 229; governance and, 205–6; growth and distribution of incomes and, 225; indirect effects on, 206–7; labor productivity and, 211–19; lack of nostalgia for, 226–27; lack of regulation and, 188–90; minimum wage floors and, 227; overview of, 181–84; procedures for recognition of unions and, 226; productivity and, 207–11; public support for, 194–95; strikes and, 187–88; wage inequality and, in U.K. vs. U.S., 293–99. *See also* Collective bargaining
Unions: procedures for recognition of, 226; public-sector, effect of privatization on, 99; support for nationalization of industry by, 193; work life and, 221–24, 225–26
United Kingdom (U.K.): absolute and relative poverty trends in, 320–23; changes in labor quality in, 42–45; collective-bargaining in, 23–25; competitiveness in, 18–19; council house sales in, 403–5; economic reforms in, 1–2, 9–10; effect of market-oriented institution and policy indicators on economic performance in, 53–55; forces shaping poverty in, 332–39; indicators of freedom in markets in, 17t; in-work benefit schemes in, 421–25; measuring poverty in, 315–20; minimum wage and wage inequality in, vs. U.S., 287–93;

United Kingdom (U.K.) (*cont.*)
neighborhood inequalities in, 397–403; North-South divide in, 371–72; privatization since 1979 in, 72–76; productivity-enhancing reforms and economic performance in, 47–51; public ownership in, 66–69, 67t; public services in, 19; regional inequalities in, 373–78; regulations in, 21; replacement ratio on unemployment benefits in, 51–52, 52t; role of social policies for reducing poverty in, 345–62; shared compensation policies and practices in, 111–16; single parents and poverty in, 352–54; strikes, 203t; strikes in, 202–3; summary of changing trends in productivity growth in, 45–47; trends in GDP per capita for, 28–30, 29t; trends in growth rates of GDP per capita for, 30–37; unemployment in, 198–99, 198f; unionism in, 23–25; wage setting in, 23; work and poverty patterns in, 342–45; work incentive reforms in, 51–53; Working Families Tax Credit (WFTC) reform in, 52–53
United States (U.S.): absolute and relative poverty trends in, 320–23; changes in labor quality in, 43–45; forces shaping poverty in, 332–39; in-work benefit schemes in, 421–25; measuring poverty in, 320; minimum wage and wage inequality in, vs. U.K., 287–93; programs for low-income persons in, 435–40; public services in, 19; regulations in, 21; role of social policies for reducing poverty in, 345–62; single parents and poverty in, 352–54; summary of changing trends in productivity growth in, 45–47; unemployment in, vs. France and U.K., 198–99, 198f; work and poverty patterns in, 342–45
Utilities: ownership of, 66; privatization of, 76–84; quality of service and, 96–97

Wage inequality, 275–77, 466–68; data sources for studying, 277; descriptive statistics for, 277–84; effects of reforms on, 301–5; between and within groups of workers, 284–87, 285t; minimum wages and, 287–93; privatization and, 299–301; unionization and, 293–99. *See also* Income distribution
Wages: changing patterns of poverty and, 323–24; influence of, on poverty, 340–42; regulation of minimum, 192; setting of, 23–25, 24t; unions and, 220–21
Wage subsidies, U.S., literature on, 479
Wards, inequalities in, 397–403
Welfare to Work programs (U.S.), 479
Work-based strategies, for reducing poverty, 362–66
Work incentives. *See* In-work benefit schemes
Working Families Tax Credit (WFTC), 411, 421–25, 422–23t, 429–30; evaluating reforms to, 443–54
Worklessness. *See* Unemployment
Workplace Employment Relations Survey (WERS), on shared compensation, 141–43
World Economic Forum (WEF), 12, 16; competitiveness scores of, 16–20

Yellow dog contracts, 189, 189n14
Youth unemployment, 461–63, 467f; features of, in U.K., 463–66; in OCED countries, 463–66. *See also* New Deal for Young People program (U.K.); Unemployment